May 6–11, 2017
Denver, CO, USA

Association for Computing Machinery

Advancing Computing as a Science & Profession

CHI'17

Proceedings of the 2017 ACM SIGCHI Conference on Human Factors in Computing Systems

Sponsored by:

ACM SIGCHI

Supported by:

Bloomberg, Facebook, Google, IBM Research, Microsoft, & NSF

Association for
Computing Machinery

Advancing Computing as a Science & Profession

The Association for Computing Machinery
2 Penn Plaza, Suite 701
New York, New York 10121-0701

Notice to Past Authors of ACM-Published Articles
ACM intends to create a complete electronic archive of all articles and/or other material previously published by ACM. If you have written a work that has been previously published by ACM in any journal or conference proceedings prior to 1978, or any SIG Newsletter at any time, and you do NOT want this work to appear in the ACM Digital Library, please inform permissions@acm.org, stating the title of the work, the author(s), and where and when published.

ISBN: 978-1-4503-4655-9 (Digital)

ISBN: 978-1-4503-5460-8 (Print)

Additional copies may be ordered prepaid from:

ACM Order Department
PO Box 30777
New York, NY 10087-0777, USA

Phone: 1-800-342-6626 (USA and Canada)
+1-212-626-0500 (Global)
Fax: +1-212-944-1318
E-mail: acmhelp@acm.org
Hours of Operation: 8:30 am – 4:30 pm ET

Printed in the USA

CHI 2017 is the premier international conference for the field of Human-Computer Interaction (HCI). This year it was held in Denver, bordering the beautiful Rocky Mountain region in the U.S., and reflected in our logo. The CHI 2017 conference began with two days of workshops and symposia, followed by four days of a technical program with 17 parallel sessions of provocative papers, panels, case studies, SIGs (Special Interest Groups), courses, and the popular student research, design, and game competitions. The growing alt.chi forum, now in its twelfth year, presented stimulating new ideas in HCI. The Interactivity forum showcased cutting-edge technology. For its second year, the CHI Art Exhibit merged art and technology in fascinating ways.

This innovative work can be found in the Proceedings and Extended Abstracts, archived in the ACM Digital Library. For papers, the conference received 2400 submissions which were rigorously reviewed, resulting in 600 accepted papers. To ensure a better fit with reviewers, new subcommittees were created. Across all tracks, CHI received nearly 5000 submissions and accepted over 1000.

Our conference theme this year, *Explore, Innovate, Inspire*, informed our planning process. A new venue held this year was CHI Stories. We generally know little of the personalities that drive the research presented at CHI. CHI Stories is a chance for CHI community members to share personal stories of inspiration, challenge, successes and failures, and grit. We also focused on inclusion this year. Hundreds of CHI attendees volunteered their skills in a Day of Service partnering with non-profit organizations. Inclusion was also manifest throughout the conference, for example, in the Diversity and Inclusion Lunch and by using telepresence robots to enable people with disabilities to participate remotely in the conference. Our keynote speakers were chosen to reflect our conference theme. The speakers were Neri Oxman, who combines computational design, digital fabrication, materials science and synthetic biology; Ben Shneiderman a founder of the CHI conference who, along with some key CHI personalities, gave a perspective on CHI's history and future; Wael Ghonim, credited with starting the Arab Spring and nominated for the Nobel Peace Prize; and best-selling author Nicholas Carr who challenges us to examine the unforeseen impacts of technology, particularly with automation.

The world has experienced a dramatic change this past year. We live in extraordinary times and this calls for extraordinary thinking, something that the CHI community excels at. One of the challenges the community faced this year was responding to a U.S. executive order to ban citizens of certain countries from entering the country to attend CHI. As CHI is committed to inclusion, we decided to hold events at the conference to discuss and plan how we can continue our commitment to inclusion. The conference held a panel to discuss impacts of current political events on science, and hastily organized a panel to promote a conversation of civil liberties in science and a SIG on how the CHI community can participate in change. We are proud to have expanded telepresence options through the use of robots to enable people to participate in the conference remotely if they were physically unable to enter the country. We had a keynote speaker who inspired us on the topic of Internet activism. Our art exhibit, *I'll Be Watching You,* examined the contemporary issue of surveillance.

We are extremely grateful to a legion of volunteers who made CHI 2017 possible, including over 7000 reviewers across all areas of the technical program, 254 senior members of the papers program committee, over 100 members of the CHI 2017 conference organization committee and importantly, the more than 175 student volunteers. We also thank SIGCHI (the Special Interest Group on Computer-Human Interaction of ACM) as well as the ACM itself for its continued support.

Gloria Mark, University of California Irvine, CHI 2017 General Conference Co-Chair

Susan Fussell, Cornell University, CHI 2017 General Conference Co-Chair

Cliff Lampe, University of Michigan, CHI 2017 Technical Program Chair

m.c. schraefel, University of Southampton, CHI 2017 Technical Program Chair

Juan Pablo Hourcade, University of Iowa, CHI 2017 Papers Co-Chair

Caroline Appert, Université Paris-Sud, CHI 2017 Papers Co-Chair

Daniel Wigdor, University of Toronto, CHI 2017 Papers Co-Chair

Loren Terveen, University of Minnesota, President, ACM SIGCHI Executive Committee

Scooter Morris, University of San Francisco, ACM SIGCHI Liaison

Table of Contents

Table of Contents

Table of Contents

Table of Contents

Table of Contents

Table of Contents

Table of Contents

Table of Contents

Table of Contents

Table of Contents

Table of Contents

Table of Contents

Table of Contents

Table of Contents

Table of Contents

Table of Contents

Table of Contents

Table of Contents

Table of Contents

Table of Contents

Table of Contents

Table of Contents

Table of Contents

Table of Contents

Table of Contents

Table of Contents

Table of Contents

Table of Contents

Table of Contents

Table of Contents

Table of Contents

Table of Contents

Table of Contents

CHI 2017 Organization

Conference Chairs
Gloria Mark, University of California, Irvine
Susan Fussell, Cornell University

Assistants to General Chairs
Yiran Wang, University of California, Irvine
Ge Gao, Cornell University

Senior Technical Program Chair
Cliff Lampe, University of Michigan

Technical Program Chair
m.c. schraefel, University of Southampton

Assistant to the Technical Program Chairs
Lindsay Blackwell, University of Michigan

Papers Chairs
Caroline Appert, Univ. Paris-Sud & CNRS
Juan Pablo Hourcade, University of Iowa
Daniel Wigdor, University of Toronto

Assistant to Papers Chairs
Michael Glueck, University of Toronto

alt.chi Chairs
Karrie Karahalios, University of Illinois at Urbana – Champaign
Jessa Lingel, University of Pennsylvania
Janet Vertesi, Princeton University

Case Studies Chairs
Stephen Snow, University of Southampton
Jessica Tsimeris, Google

Courses Chairs
Erik Andersen, Cornell University
Hilary Hutchinson, Google
Max Wilson, University of Nottingham

Demos Chairs
Ido Guy, Yahoo
Stephen Voida, University of Colorado Boulder

Doctoral Consortium Chairs
Anna Cox, University College London
Jeff Bigham, Carnegie Mellon University
Kenton O'Hara, Microsoft Research, UK

Interactive Installations Chairs
Adrian Friday, Lancaster University
Shengdong Zhao, National University of Singapore

Late Breaking Work Chairs
Sharon Ding, Fudan University
Ingrid Erikson, Rutgers University
Bryan Semaan, Syracuse University
Fanis Tsandilas, INRIA

Panels Chairs
Sarita Schoenebeck, University of Michigan
Jude Yew, National University of Singapore

Student Design Competition Chairs
Joonhwan Lee, Seoul National University
Scott Minneman, California College of Arts

Student Game Competition Chairs
Floyd Mueller, RMIT University
Josh Tanenbaum, University of California, Irvine

Student Research Competition Chairs
Jeremy Birnholtz, Northwestern University
Jenn Thom, Spotify

Special Interest Groups Chairs
Lindsay Reynolds, Facebook
Bert Scerbo, Disney

Systems Chairs
Michael Stewart, Virginia Tech
Dorota Filipczuk, University of Southampton

Symposia Chair
Lana Yarosh, University of Minnesota

Video Showcase Chairs
Danyel Fisher, Microsoft Research
Catherine Letondal, ENAC

Workshops Chairs
Duncan Brumby, University College London
Christopher Frauenberger, Vienna University of Technology, Austria
Shamsi Iqbal, Microsoft Research

Art Chairs
Jiffer Harriman, University of Colorado
Andruid Kerne, Texas A&M University
HyunJoo Oh, University of Colorado Boulder
Thecla Schiphorst, Simon Fraser University

CHI Stories Chairs
Nazanin Andalibi, Drexel University
Nick Diakopoulos, University of Maryland, College Park
Andrea Forte, Drexel University
Misa Maruyama, University of Hawaii at Manoa
Scott Robertson, University of Hawaii at Manoa

Career Development Workshop Chairs
Luigina Ciolfi, Sheffield Hallam University
Michael Muller, IBM Research

Journals Chair
Hrvoje Benko, Microsoft Research

Remix Chairs
Susan Dray, Dray & Associates
Amy Voida, University of Colorado Boulder

Student Volunteer Chairs
Patrick Carrington, University of Maryland, Baltimore County (UMBC)
Anna Kötteritzsch, Universität der Bundeswehr München

Video Previews Chair
Carla Griggio, Inria

Awards Chair
Steven Drucker, Microsoft

Accessibility Chairs
Erin Brady, Indiana University – Purdue University Indianapolis
Sean Goggins, Missouri University
Shaun Kane, University of Colorado Boulder

Data Chair
Boyu Gao, Konkuk University
Toni-Jan Keith Monserrat, University of the Philippines Los Baños

Diversity and Inclusivity Lunch Chairs
Anke Brock, Inria Bordeaux
Allison Druin, University of Maryland
Gopinaath Kannabiran, Indiana University, Bloomington

Language Inclusion Chair
Tilman Dingler, University of Stuttgart

Local Arrangements Chairs
Jed Brubaker, University of Colorado Boulder
Tom Yeh, University of Colorado Boulder

Social Impact Chairs
Kathy Baxter, Salesforce
Elizabeth Gerber, Northwestern University
Jill Woelfer, Google

Social Media Chairs
Dan Afergan, Google
Bart Knijnenburg, Clemson University
Vicky McArthur, University of Toronto Mississauga

Telepresence Chairs
Min Kyung Lee, Carnegie Mellon University
Carman Neustaedter, Simon Fraser University

Translations Chairs
Hao-Chuan Wang, National Tsing Hua University
Naomi Yamashita, Nippon Telegraph and Telephone

Design Director
Donghee Yvette Wohn, New Jersey Institute of Technology

Logo Design/Artwork
Jia Zhang, MIT Media Lab

Web Designer
Xiying Wang, Cornell University

Webmaster
Xiying Wang, Cornell University

ACM Liaison
Farrah Khan, ACM

SIGCHI Liaison
Scooter Morris, University of California, San Francisco

Conference Management
Paul Henning, Conference & Logistics Consultants, Inc.
Stacey Ogren, Conference & Logistics Consultants, Inc.
Lois Sarfo-Mensah, Conference & Logistics Consultants, Inc.
Michael O'Connell, Conference & Logistics Consultants, Inc.

Registration
Taylor Vick, Executive Events, Inc.

Sponsorship and Exhibits
Carol Klyver, Foundations of Excellence

Technical Liaison
Sara Drenner, BI WORLDWIDE

Electrick: Low-Cost Touch Sensing Using Electric Field Tomography

Yang Zhang **Gierad Laput** **Chris Harrison**
Human-Computer Interaction Institute, Carnegie Mellon University
5000 Forbes Avenue, Pittsburgh, PA 15213
{yang.zhang, gierad.laput, chris.harrison}@cs.cmu.edu

ABSTRACT
Current touch input technologies are best suited for small and flat applications, such as smartphones, tablets and kiosks. In general, they are too expensive to scale to large surfaces, such as walls and furniture, and cannot provide input on objects having irregular and complex geometries, such as tools and toys. We introduce Electrick, a low-cost and versatile sensing technique that enables touch input on a wide variety of objects and surfaces, whether small or large, flat or irregular. This is achieved by using electric field tomography in concert with an electrically conductive material, which can be easily and cheaply added to objects and surfaces. We show that our technique is compatible with commonplace manufacturing methods, such as spray/brush coating, vacuum forming, and casting/molding – enabling a wide range of possible uses and outputs. Our technique can also bring touch interactivity to rapidly fabricated objects, including those that are laser cut or 3D printed. Through a series of studies and illustrative example uses, we show that Electrick can enable new interactive opportunities on a diverse set of objects and surfaces that were previously static.

Author Keywords
Touch sensing; Finger tracking; Electric Field Sensing; Tomography; Rapid prototyping; Interactivity tools.

ACM Classification Keywords
H.5.2. [User interfaces] – Input devices and strategies.

INTRODUCTION
Today's touchscreen technologies are generally manufactured on a rigid substrate. For example, projective capacitive sensing, like that used in contemporary smartphones, uses a multi-layered, row-column matrix most often deposited onto glass. This means that most touch panels are relatively small and flat. In cases where irregular shapes or large areas have been made touch sensitive, the price tag is often substantial – touchscreens above 75" typically cost thousands of dollars [2, 30], and irregular or flexible objects with touch-sensing capabilities are mostly research prototypes unavailable to consumers [22, 27, 40, 57]. This high cost and inflexibility has limited touch interaction from being adopted by a wider array of everyday objects, despite touch being an intuitive and popular input modality. In response, researchers have long investigated ways to enable touch sensing on new classes of objects [22, 35, 55], including everyday surfaces [10, 39, 40, 58] and rapidly prototyped artifacts [24, 44, 48, 56].

In this paper, we present our work on Electrick, an inexpensive and versatile touch sensing approach, which is applicable to a wide range of objects and surfaces – including those with large, irregular, and even flexible geometries. To enable Electrick, objects must either be made from an electrically conductive material, or have a conductive coating. The latter can be easily and cheaply applied through e.g., painting, allowing for large touch surfaces (e.g., walls, furniture) at under $1 per square foot of interactive area. In total, we identified six commercially available materials that are applicable to a variety of manufacturing processes, including CNC milling, stamping/forming and molding/casting, as well as additive methods, such as FDM 3D printing.

To track a finger's touch location, electrodes are attached to the periphery of the desired interactive area. A sensor board connected to these electrodes injects an electric field into the conductive substrate, and senses changes in the field's distribution resulting from a user's touch. Sensor data can be transmitted wirelessly, allowing the electronics to be fully contained within an object, eliminating the need for external sensing infrastructure (e.g., depth cameras).

Our technique is readily accessible to hobbyists, requiring no special chemicals, equipment or facilities; everything required can be readily purchased online. This allows Electrick to be applied to existing objects and surfaces, augmenting them with new touch sensing capabilities. Of course, such coatings could also be applied during the initial manufacturing process to create new interactive goods at costs compatible with mass production. Finally, as we will show, Electrick can also bring touch interactivity to rapidly prototyped objects (e.g., 3D printed), enabling rapid iteration of both form and function.

CHI 2017, May 06-11, 2017, Denver, CO, USA
© 2017 ACM. ISBN 978-1-4503-4655-9/17/05...$15.00
DOI: http://dx.doi.org/10.1145/3025453.3025842

RELATED WORK

Electrick intersects with three key literatures. First we review prior work that relates to our core technical approach. We then discuss a broader set of work that overlaps with our application domain: infusing objects and surfaces with touch interactivity. As our technique is also applicable to rapidly prototyped artifacts, we conclude with a more specialized review of literature in this area.

Technical Approach

Our sensing principle is based on the shunting effect, where a human body proximate to an electric field draws a small amount of current to ground. This phenomenon, also called "shunt mode", has been widely utilized in Electric Field (EF) sensing systems [42, 43, 61]. EF sensing generally uses the air as a medium, enabling free-space interactions such as finger tracking [18], motion sensing [13] and activity recognition [33]. By using measurements from peripheral electrodes, it is possible to deduce the position of the shunting object. The combination of EF sensing and tomography was demonstrated in seminal work by Smith [42, 43]. We also employ Electric Field Tomography (EFT), though constrained to a conductive medium.

This shunting effect has also been utilized for many single-touch touchscreens [15, 26]. In this case, the electric field is constrained to a conductive substrate, which requires electrodes attached to the periphery. Though this setup is physically similar to Electrick, these touchscreen techniques use low-conductivity materials (e.g., ITO, PEDOT) and rectilinear sensing areas. This limits these techniques from being used in ad hoc existing objects, as well as fabricated ones. In contrast, Electrick works with a wide range of material resistances (500Ω-50MΩ/sq), and can work on irregular and non-rectangular surfaces, allowing us to use methods and materials compatible across many fabrication processes.

Finally, our measuring scheme is closely related to Electrical Impedance Tomography (EIT). This technique is widely used to reconstruct the interior structure of an object by sensing non-invasively from the exterior surface. Classic EIT applications include respiratory monitoring [49], underground detection [11] and biological inspection [50]. In the HCI domain, we recently adapted the technology for use in a hand-gesture-sensing smartwatch [62, 63].

EIT has been used in conjunction with materials that alter their local impedance when pressure is applied by a finger, such as piezo-resistive films [38], multilayer meshes [9, 51], and tactile sensor arrays [22]. This has been used, most notably, to create touch sensitive skins for robots [9, 22, 51, 52]. Like Electrick, irregular geometries are supported, though no prior work has demonstrated scalability beyond roughly 0.5 m^2. Further, although Electrick also uses tomography, the sensing principles are very different – our method does not sense changes in a material substrate (impedance in the case of EIT), but is rather based on a user's finger shunting current. This different sensing mechanism allows us to leverage different (and low cost) materials for our conductive domain, which in turn enables different fabrication methods and use cases.

Touch Sensing on Everyday Objects and Surfaces

Researchers have developed a myriad of approaches to enable touch-screen-like interactions on ad hoc objects and surfaces, ideally with minimal instrumentation of either the object itself or the environment.

The most prevalent way to achieve this level of fidelity (at scale) is through computer vision. Early systems, such as Light Widgets [17] and PlayAnywhere [55], used conventional cameras segmenting e.g., skin color, motion or shadows. Depth cameras have been a notable boon, easing the previously complex task of segmenting user inputs from a background scene; notable systems include Light Space [54] and WorldKit [58]. It is also possible to super-size touchscreen technologies to room scale; for example, Multitoe [10] uses an augmented floor with FTIR sensing.

Next most popular are acoustic methods. Multi-sensor approaches, chiefly based on time difference of arrival techniques, can enable touch sensing on large surfaces, including windows, wall and desks [37, 41, 59]. Passive acoustics can also be used to capture and recognize non-spatial gestures [20]. Several of these approaches can be applied to discrete objects. For example, Touch and Activate [35] used an emitter-receiver pair of Piezo-electric elements to recognize touches to discrete locations on ad hoc objects.

Least common are electrical methods. One option, as demonstrated by Cohn et al. [14], is to detect touch locations in an environment by passively capturing ambient electromagnetic noise that couples to users when they are near to a noise source (e.g., a power line behind a wall). Active approaches are also possible. For example, TactileTape [21] is a 1D, capacitive, flexible, touch-sensing tape that can be easily affixed to objects. MaKey MaKey [12] allows users to appropriate conductive objects (e.g., fruits, Play-doh, toys) as capacitive buttons. Touché [39] uses a more advanced swept frequency capacitive sensing approach to enable discrete touch location sensing, continuous 1D tracking and hand-gesture controls.

Finally, it is also possible to create materials with special, integrated features that enable touch capabilities. These are not ad hoc objects *per se*, but rather augmented versions of everyday materials. The most common target for these efforts has been textiles. Through silk-screening or weaving of conductive materials, sensing of discrete touch locations [34] and even multi-touch inputs is possible [40]. Most projects utilize capacitive sensing, though other techniques, such as Time Domain Reflectometry [57], have also been applied with success.

Adding Interactivity to Rapidly Prototyped Objects

The last decade has seen tremendous growth in digitally-augmented, rapid fabrication tools, especially for HCI uses such as prototyping enclosures, controllers, and new computing form factors. However, the outputs from these tools, such as CNC milling machines, laser cutters, vacuum formers and 3D printers are *static* – output embodies the desired 3D form, but rarely the interactivity of the end product. Ideally, designers should be able to prototype both in the same medium, as eloquently motivated in [24].

A variety of approaches have been considered that aim to alleviate this interactive divide. For example, DisplayObjects [8] detects touch input on passive prototyped objects by tracking fingers using an external camera array. Also using computer vision, Makers' Marks [47] allows users to annotate objects they have created with stickers, which denotes locations of desired functionality (e.g., "joystick here"); after 3D scanning and processing, the final functional object can be 3D printed and assembled by non-experts.

Due to its non-mechanical nature, capacitive sensing is a powerful and popular technique for prototyping or retrofitting touch input. Hudson and Mankoff [24] demonstrate rapid construction of functional physical interfaces using just "cardboard, thumbtacks, tin foil and masking tape". Midas [48] provides an entire workflow for authoring and fabricating complex capacitive layouts (using a CNC vinyl cutter), which can then be adhered to complex objects. The aforementioned capacitive TactileTape [21] can also be used in a prototyping context.

Owing to 3D printing's versatility, a variety of methods have been explored to enable interactive printed output. For example, by 3D printing integrated cavities, tubes, tines and other mechanical structures, active [28] and passive [45] acoustics can be used to capture user input. Sauron [46] uses an internal camera and computer vision, along with accessory mirrors and markers, to digitize user manipulated mechanical controls. It is also possible to 3D print light pipes, which can route optically driven touch input to e.g., a photodiode [56]. Similarly, it is possible to 3D print conductive material to directly integrate capacitive sensing electrodes into a model [44].

Although we did not initially set out to enable touch sensing for fabricated objects, the versatility of our technique naturally lends itself to this problem domain. Electrick can be easily applied to laser cut and 3D printed objects, as well as prototypes made from plastic, wood, ceramic, and other common non-conductive materials. As we will discuss, we can also directly 3D print and mold Electrick-capable objects using a low-cost conductive ABS.

SENSING PRINCIPLE

Electrick requires objects to have a conductive medium, either as its principle structural material, or as a surface coating. The object is further augmented with electrodes placed around the periphery of the desired interactive area. With this configuration, Electrick inserts a small AC current between a pair of adjacent electrodes (the *current-projecting* pair), creating an electric field in the conductive medium (Figure 1, left). The voltage difference is then measured at all other adjacent electrodes pairings (*voltage-measuring* pairs). This process repeats for all combinations of *current-projecting* and *voltage-measuring* pairs, resulting in a mesh of cross-sectional measurements (Figure 1, center). This sensing scheme is similar to four-pole sensing in EIT systems (see e.g., [63] for more details).

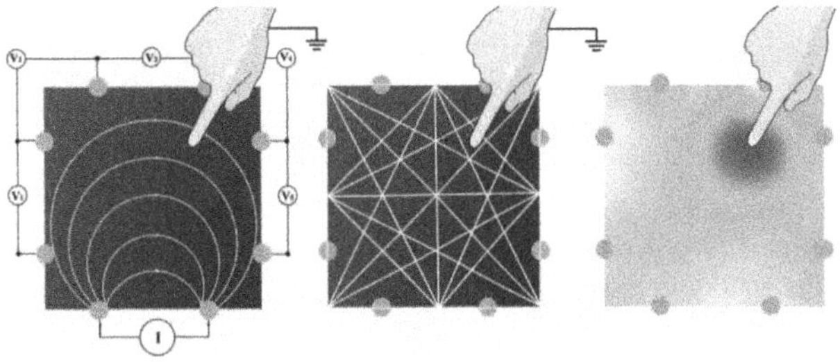

Figure 1. Left: we insert current from one pair of electrodes and measure voltage from other pairs. Center: A mesh of cross-sectional measurements. Right: A reconstructed 2D touch-sensing image. Blue indicates low current density.

As previously mentioned, our approach relies on the fact that a grounded object, such as a user's finger, will shunt some current to ground when it encounters an electric field through capacitive coupling (similar to surface capacitive screens [15] and in-air electric field sensing [61]). This current is very small, comparable to that induced by capacitive touch-screens found in smartphones. However, this shunting distorts the electric field, characteristically altering the voltages measured at receiver pairs. We can then use our cross-sectional measurements to recover the location of the shunt point (Figure 1, right).

Electrick can only be used with materials with compatible resistivity. If the resistivity is too high, the electric field will be very weak, making it hard to sense the field signal. However, if the surface resistivity is too low, the current shunted by the finger (a fairly high-impedance pathway) will be negligible, making touches hard to detect. In testing, we found that surface resistivity in the range of 500 Ω to 50 MΩ per square worked best for surface coat materials. The surface resistivity should be higher (10 kΩ to 50 MΩ) for structural materials, out of which objects can be directly 3D printed, milled or molded.

APPLICABLE MATERIALS & FABRICATION PROCESSES

We identified three classes of material of particular utility and interest: *solid*, *pliable*, and *paintable*. These basic material forms are used in a wide variety of fabrication and finishing processes, including subtractive methods (e.g., milling, laser cutting), additive methods (e.g., 3D printing), molding methods (e.g., stamping, casting, vacuum forming, blow molding, injection molding), and coating methods (e.g., brush painting, spray painting, powder coating).

Among many compatible materials, we sought low-cost examples with four key properties: 1) compatible electrical resistivity 2) non-toxicity 3) applied without exotic equipment or facilities, and 4) readily accessible. We now briefly discuss example materials we identified that fit our four criteria, and how they can be used with Electrick.

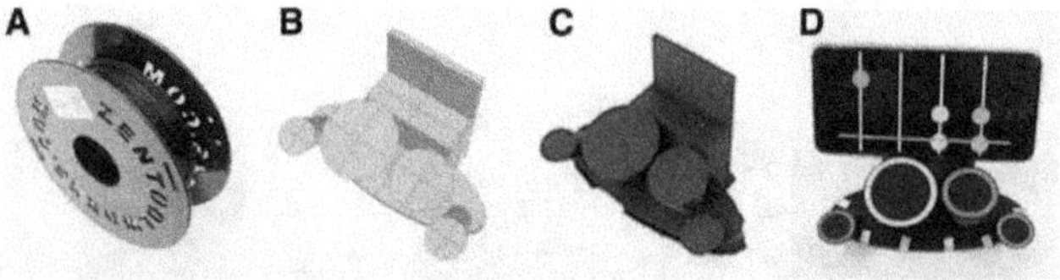

Figure 2. We used a carbon-loaded ABS filament (A) to 3D-print a custom phone accessory (B,C) for a phone game (D).

Example Solid Materials

Bulk plastics, such as ABS and Polycarbonate, are widely available in mildly conductive formulations (most often by adding carbon or metallic particles). These plastics come in many forms, including blocks (for e.g., milling), sheets (for e.g., forming/stamping), pellets (for e.g., molding/extrusion processes) and filament (for e.g., 3D printing).

As one example material, we use a static dissipating ABS, sold by Zen Toolworks as a filament (Figure 2A; $46 for a 1kg spool) [60]. At 45MΩ/sq, this black, carbon-loaded ABS is not sufficiently conductive for e.g., 3D printed circuits. However, it is perfect for 3D printing Electrick-capable objects (Figure 2C). We can also use the pellet form of this material to create molded objects (such as the mummy figurine seen in Figure 3A).

Another compatible material is Velostat, a carbon-loaded polyolefin sheet/film made by 3M [1]. It is primarily used for packaging of electronic components to mitigate electrostatic buildup. We ordered a 4mil thick, 3'×150' roll online for $200 (i.e., under 50 cents per square foot) [31], which has a surface resistivity of 72 kΩ/sq. This can be attached to surfaces directly (e.g., to walls), or laminated onto a thermal-formable sheet (e.g., polyethylene) and vacuum formed into a low-cost, durable shell of almost shape (Figure 4).

Example Pliable Materials

There are also conductive materials that are soft and pliable. As one example of an easy-to-use, off-the-shelf material, we selected Jell-O, which has a surface resistivity of roughly 12 kΩ/sq (Figure 22 offers an example application). Play-doh is also compatible with Electrick. We created our own using flour, water, salt, and food coloring to control the surface resistivity (roughly 23 kΩ/sq). Using Play-doh, users can shape objects with their bare hands and then make them interactive (example use shown in Figure 18).

Another pliable material is silicone, which is widely used in commercial molding/casting applications. We made our own conductive silicone by mixing bulk carbon fiber with standard silicone (1:18 ratio by weight). The outcome has a surface resistivity of ~16 MΩ/sq. From this material, we made a squishable, interactive Yoda toy (Figure 3B).

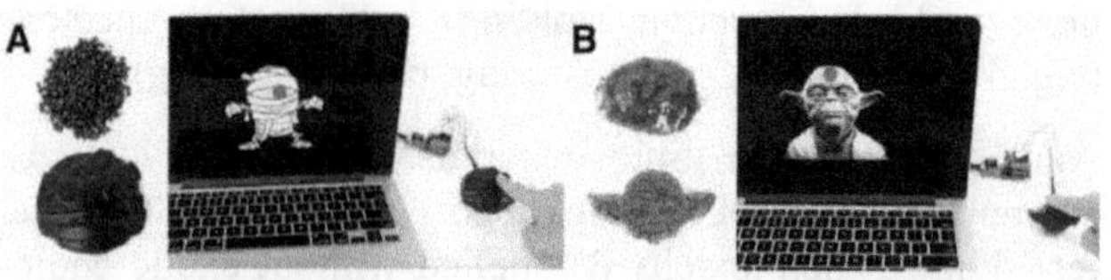

Figure 3. Conductive ABS (A) and silicone (B) can be cast, as seen in these toy examples. Touching different areas of these toys triggers different sounds and effects.

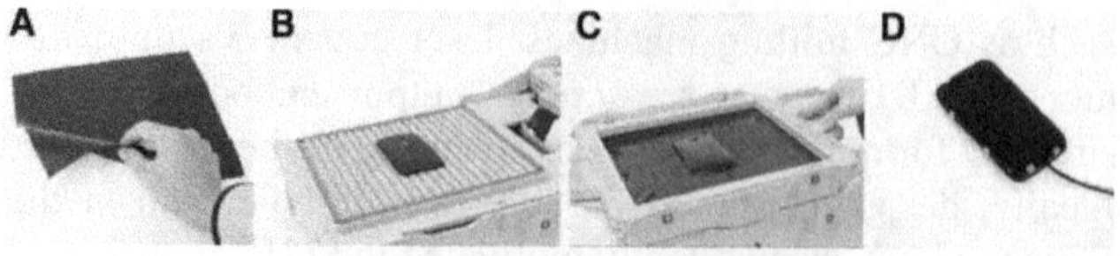

Figure 4. Velostat can be vacuum-formed, as seen in this phone enclosure example.

Example Paints

Liquid paint and spray coatings are particularly versatile, as they can be added as a postproduction step to almost *any* object or surface – small or large, flat or irregular, regardless of how the underlying object was manufactured. In addition to total paint coverage, paints can also be masked (e.g., stenciled, silk-screened) to define interactive areas.

As an example paint, we use a carbon conductive paint made by MG Chemicals [29], which is intended for electrostatic discharge and RF shielding uses. This paint can be purchased online as a 340g aerosol can for $16 [3] (Figure 5A), or as a liquid paint in quarts or gallons [32]. A single coat has resistivity of roughly 1kΩ/sq, and dries to a durable, matte black finish (Figure 5C).

Coatings

As previously discussed, the shunting effect of a user's finger occurs through capacitive coupling; direct contact is not required. This permits the use of an optional (thin) topcoat, which can be used to add color or alternate finish to an object. Although our search for compatible coatings was not exhaustive, we did experiment with spray (Figures 14 and 23), acrylic (Figure 5D), and latex paints (Figure 17), as well as paper (Figure 14).

IMPLEMENTATION

Our Electrick implementation required the development of custom hardware and software, which we now describe.

Electrodes

Once an object has been created or coated with a compatible conductive material, it must then be instrumented with electrodes around the periphery of the intended interactive region. In line with Electrick's low-cost DIY spirit, we used copper tape, to which we solder a wire that runs to our sensing board. It is also possible to reverse these fabrication steps, attaching the electrodes first, and then covering the electrodes with e.g., over-molded materials or paint.

Figure 5. We carbon sprayed (A) an off-the-shelf toy (B) to make it interactive. A new topcoat was applied (C to D).

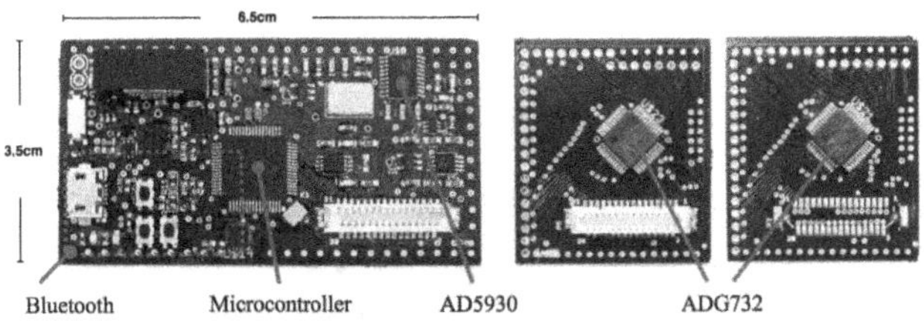

Figure 6. Left: Sensor motherboard. Right: two daughter boards with multiplexing functionality.

Sensing Board
Our custom sensing board is built around a Cortex M4 microcontroller running at 96 MHz (MK20DX256VLH7 [16]), powered by the Teensy 3.2 firmware [36] (Figure 6). The board has a voltage controlled current source (VCCS), direct digital synthesis (DDS) IC, and ADC preamp. The board also features multiplexers that allow for the cross-sectional measurements as well as a Bluetooth module to transmit data for wireless applications. The total cost of our hardware is $70, which could be made both smaller and less expensive in a high volume commercial application. A schematic view of our system is shown in Figure 7. Our current sensing board draws 120 mA during normal operation (including Bluetooth communication).

Excitation Signal
We use an AD5930 [5] DDS and an AD8220-based Voltage-controlled current source (VCCS) [6] to generate an electric field. The DDS is configured to output 200 kHz sinusoidal waves. The signal is then fed into the VCCS to output a constant AC current. Our sensor can drive up to 6 Vpp to maintain a constant AC current excitation. To improve SNR, we increased the current for low-resistance materials, and decreased it for high-resistance ones. As a result, input current levels varied across test cases (maximally 0.42 mA in the lowest-resistance, carbon-sprayed panel).

Multiplexing
A pair of 32-to-1 multiplexers [4] connect the VCCS terminals to two electrodes, forming the *current-projecting* electrode pair. Another pair of multiplexers connects two other electrodes (the *voltage-measuring* pair) to the preamp buffer terminals. This electrode selection flexibility also affords us the flexibility to vary the number of electrodes used (i.e., 8, 16, or 32).

Analog Sampling
The measured signal is amplified with a preamp to maximize the dynamic range of our ADC. We also implemented a 79.6 kHz high pass filter to dampen ambient EM noise, chiefly fluorescent light ballasts (i.e. 50 kHz) and power-line noise (i.e. 60 Hz). The input signal is then biased by AVDD/2 (1.65 V) and sampled by our microcontroller's ADCs at 4 MHz with 12-bit resolution. We used our microcontroller's two ADCs in an interleaved DMA mode to achieve this high sampling rate.

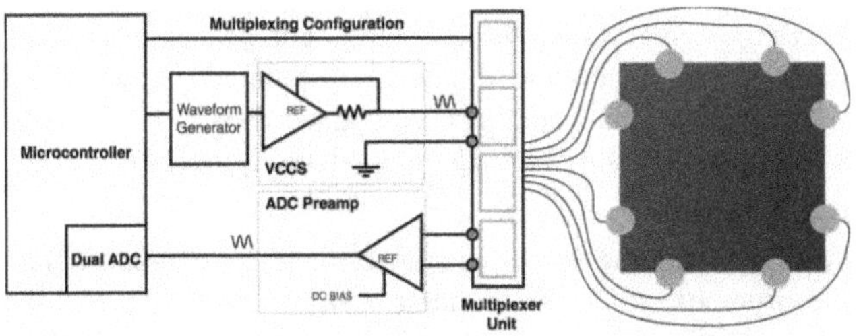

Figure 7. A schematic view of our system with e.g., 8 electrodes.

Data Acquisition
After our board selects the appropriate electrodes using its multiplexers, it waits 100 μs for the DC bias on the AC coupling capacitors to stabilize. The board then collects 200 samples (roughly 10 periods of our 200 kHz excitation signal) for a root-mean-square (RMS) computation. This constitutes a single measurement (taking ~137 μs in total).

The board then moves to the next voltage-measuring electrode pair, reconfiguring its multiplexers accordingly. After collecting all measurements for the current-projecting configuration, the board then moves to the next current-projecting pair and repeats the above procedure. Once it completes one full frame of measurements (all current-projecting pairs), the board sends the values over Bluetooth or USB to a laptop for further processing. Table 1 provides the number of measurements required when using different electrode counts, which also defines the system frame rate (as each measurement takes ~137 μs).

Number of Electrodes	8	16	32
Number of Measurements req. per Frame	40	208	928
Sensing Frame Rate (Hz)	181	35	8

Table 1. The number of measurements required per frame and the resulting sensing FPS for different electrode counts.

Touch Tracking
We initially developed our finger-tracking pipeline using a fully realized tomographic reconstruction, to which we applied standard computer vision "blob" tracking techniques (Figure 8). Specifically, we used a single step Gauss-Newton method using a maximum a posteriori estimator [7] to produce our tomographic reconstruction (provided by the EIDORS EIT toolkit [53]). On a MacBook Pro with a 2.7 GHz Intel Core i5 processor, the solver takes 1.98, 2.56 and 3.01 ms for 8, 16 and 32 electrode inputs respectively.

This approach is capable of high accuracy and even multi-touch segmentation (Figure 8, right). However, it requires construction of a finite element model (FEM) for each object before use [25]. This is relatively straightforward for planar circular or rectilinear surfaces, but is a significant obstacle for ad hoc uses and complex geometries (which would require 3D scanning equipment). We also found this method to be sensitive to small fabrication/manufacturing variances, such as electrode size, adhesion, and conductive coating thickness.

Fortunately, machine learning offers a robust and practical alternative, one that offloads much of this variability and complexity from users to computers. Instead of having to

Figure 8. From left to right: Finite Element Model, 60×60 cm touch panel, reconstructed touch image, two fingers touching, and reconstructed touch image.

model an object's geometry, users can perform a simple one-time calibration on the object itself, from which machine learning models can be initialized. In addition to permitting arbitrary geometries, this process also innately captures and accounts for variances in fabrication. For input features, we simply use our raw cross-sectional measurements with no additional featurization. Thus the lengths of the feature sets can be found in Table 1 ("Number of Measurements required per Frame" row).

Two classification approaches are possible. For sensing *discrete* touch positions (e.g., buttons), we used a classification model (built using Weka [23], SMO, RBF kernel with γ=0.07). The same parameters are used for models that distinguish between touch and no-touch states. To support *continuous* 2D touch tracking, we used two independent regression models (SMOReg, RBF kernel with γ=0.01) operating in parallel – one for X and another for Y position.

Multitouch

Tomographic techniques output a 2D reconstruction of the sensed medium. As such, localizing multiple finger touches is immediately possible, as can be seen in Figure 8 (right). Standard computer vision techniques, most notably blob detection, can be applied. However, due to the low resolution of the reconstruction, there must be substantial separation between finger contacts for robust tracking. Anecdotally, with Electrick, this has to be at least 10 cm, irrespective of material and electrode configuration. Our preliminary investigations are promising, but we leave a full exploration of multitouch capabilities for future work.

EVALUATION

The versatility of Electrick meant there was a range of factors we wished to investigate: the performance across different electrode counts (*8, 16, 32*), materials (*Velostat, carbon spray, carbon ABS*), surface sizes (*15×15, 30×30, 60×60 cm*), surface geometries (*flat, curved, angular*), and coatings (*bare, paper, spray paint*). Within each evaluation, we tested the performance of our discrete touch sensing and continuous tracking approaches. It was not feasible to run a full 3×3×3×3×3 factors design, so we instead structured our evaluation as a series of focused experiments, taking a total of 70 minutes to complete. We recruited 14 participants (8 female, mean age 26), who were compensated $20.

Apparatus

To best capture our system's performance and not user inaccuracies, we employed a template to guide user touches. This was a 15×15 cm laser-cut sheet of (non-conductive) acrylic with a 4×4 grid of 1.5 cm holes (Figure 9, left). This

Figure 9. Evaluation template next to 30×30 cm panel with 32 electrodes.

was overlaid onto the experimental surface. Our test apparatus varied slightly across our five experiments. For factors within our control, we selected values with intermediate performances, for example, all of our experiments used 16-electrode sensing (except, of course, for the electrode count experiment). We now describe the particular conditions and apparatus of our five experiments:

Electrode Count – To ensure adequate space for electrodes, we used a 30×30 cm Velostat sheet augmented with 32 electrodes (Figure 9, right). Our board configured itself for 8, 16 or 32 electrode modes in software.

Material – We selected three very different materials: Velostat, conductive ABS, and carbon paint. Due to the limited bed size on our 3D printer, we made all three of our material conditions 15×15 cm in size. Carbon Spray and Velostat were applied to 1/8" thick acrylic sheets, while the ABS condition was printed monolithically with 1 mm thickness (Figure 11).

Surface Size – We tested three surface sizes: 15×15, 30×30 and 60×60 cm (Figure 12). These were all flat, Velostat-laminated acrylic sheets. We randomized the touch template location on the 30×30 and 60×60 cm touch panels per user.

Surface Geometry – In order to test surface geometry in a controlled way, we 3D printed (using conventional filament) three 15×15 cm panels with varying surface features: flat, curved and angular (Figure 13). The latter two 3D conditions had a Z-variance of 1 cm, making them more "2.5D". However, as we will show in our Example Applications, more extreme 3D geometries are possible. To conform to the irregular surface, we used carbon spray as our conductive material. The irregular geometry also prevented us from using our flat acrylic touch template, and so touch points were denoted by painted white circles.

Coating – We tested three coating conditions: bare (i.e., unmodified), paper-coated, and spray-painted (conventional white paint). These coatings were applied to a flat, carbon-sprayed, acrylic sheet 15×15 cm in size (Figure 14).

Procedure

We employed the same procedure for all five experiments, the order of which was randomized. When first presented with a surface condition, we asked participants to hold their finger roughly 5 cm away from the surface. Over a period of roughly one second, 30 data points were recorded and labeled as "no touch". Participants were then instructed to touch each of the 16 points denoted by the touch template. This was done one at a time, in a random order, as requested by a simple visualization on a laptop screen. Each time a user touched a point, 30 data points were recorded. The laptop emitted a beep when the user could proceed to the next point. This concluded one round of data collection, the *only* training data we collected.

This data was then used to train our touch-sensing machine learning models. For discrete touch location sensing, data was used to train a touch/no-touch classifier and an independent, 16-class classifier – one class for each touch location. For our regression-based, continuous touch-tracking model, only data from the four corners was used for training. This mitigates overfitting and offers a more realistic evaluation of accuracies (vs. training on all 16 points).

We then tested our system's accuracy *live* (i.e., no post hoc calibration, algorithm tweaks, data cleaning, etc.). We followed the same procedure as above, where users moved sequentially through all touch points in a random order. This time, the system's live classification/regression result was recorded along with the requested touch location for later analysis. This testing procedure was repeated twice more, for three testing rounds in total. This four-round procedure (1 training round followed by 3 testing rounds) was repeated for every condition in all five experiments.

RESULTS

We now discuss the results of our five experiments, as well as a post hoc study investigating sensing stability across users. All figures use standard error for their error bars.

Touch Segmentation

Touch/no-touch classification accuracy averaged 99.5% (SD=0.5) across all conditions and factors. The one significant outlier ($p<0.05$) from this average was our paper-coated condition (93.2% accuracy).

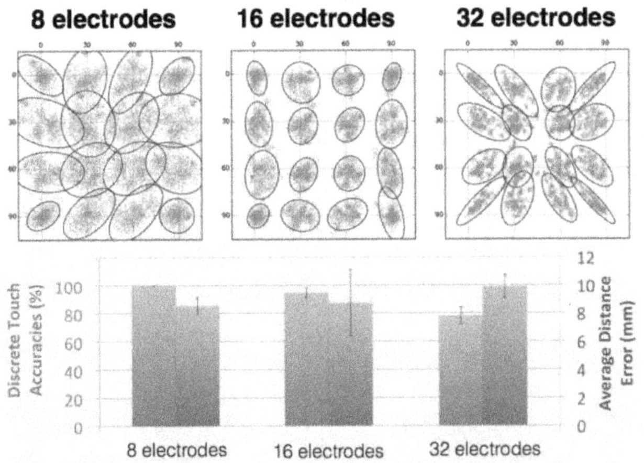

Figure 10. Evaluation results for electrode count experiment. Top: touch point distributions with 2σ ellipses. Bottom: Discrete touch and continuous tracking accuracies.

Number of Electrodes

The touch tracking accuracy across our three electrode count conditions is shown in Figure 10. Our discrete touch location classifier achieved 90.7% (SD=12.0%) mean accuracy. Of note, 57.0% of the error trials were in adjacent positions (i.e., off by one cell in our 4×4 touch grid). Our regression-based, continuous tracking method had a mean distance error of 9.1 mm (SD=4.7).

Intuitively, we expected higher electrode counts to produce a finer mesh of cross-sectional measurements, and thus offer more accurate touch tracking. However, we found the opposite effect: a paired t-test showed that the 32-electrode condition was significantly worse than the 8-electrode condition ($p<0.05$) in the case of discrete tracking. As an additional visualization, we also plot touch trials from all participants (raw; no post hoc per-user offsets, etc.) along with 2σ ellipses drawn to scale (Figure 10).

We suspect this reduction in accuracy is chiefly due to the reduced distance between projecting/measuring electrode pairs. A shorter electrode separation means that the electric field does not project as far into the conductive medium, which reduces the signal-to-noise ratio (SNR). Furthermore, the reduced distance between measuring electrode pairs similarly decreases terminal resistance, resulting in smaller voltage measurements, again reducing SNR. This result suggests that electrode count should be tuned according to surface size; e.g., for smaller interactive areas, lower electrode counts are likely to work better.

Material

Our material experiment results, seen in Figure 11, show an average discrete touch accuracy of 91.4% (SD=9.6), with

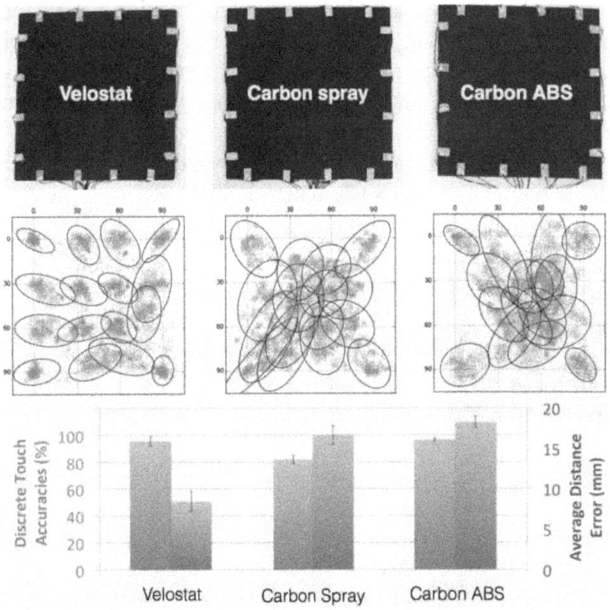

Figure 11. Evaluation results for material experiment. Top: 15×15 cm touch panels coated using the three materials. Middle: touch point distributions with 2σ ellipses. Bottom: Discrete touch and continuous tracking accuracies.

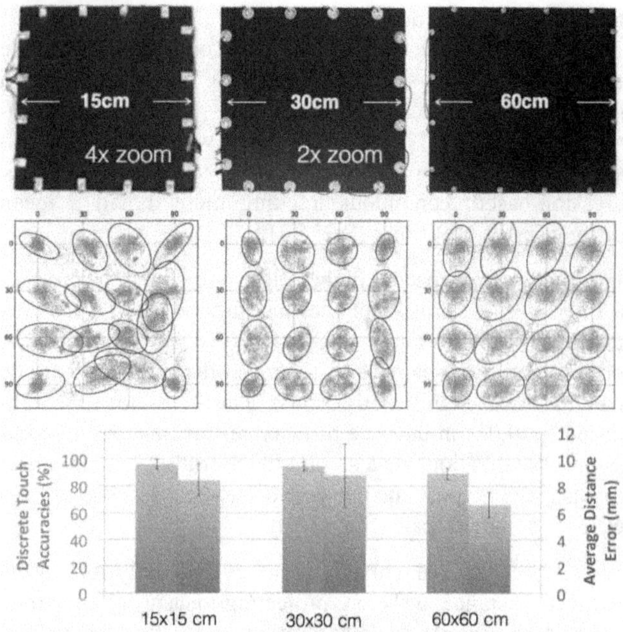

Figure 12. Evaluation results for surface size experiment. Top: touch panels of different sizes. Middle: touch point distributions with 2σ ellipses. Bottom: Discrete touch and continuous tracking accuracies.

84.8% of errors in adjacent positions. Continuous touch tracking had a mean distance error of 14.4 mm (SD=3.8); a paired t-test shows a significant difference between Velostat and our other two test materials ($p<0.05$). We suspect this is a result of Velostat's superior homogeneity (compared to our other two conditions), as it is an industrially manufactured material. This makes the electric field projection more linear, whereas small non-linearities in our Carbon Spray and Carbon ABS conditions meant our tracking regressions could not accurately interpolate interior touches. A more controlled coating process would likely yield improve accuracy. In addition, note in Figure 11 that positional accuracy improves towards the corners. This suggests that a denser calibration pattern (as opposed to a sparse, four-corner one) could compensate for such material variances.

Figure 14. Evaluation results for coating experiment. Top: touch panels of different coating materials. Bottom: Discrete touch and continuous tracking accuracies.

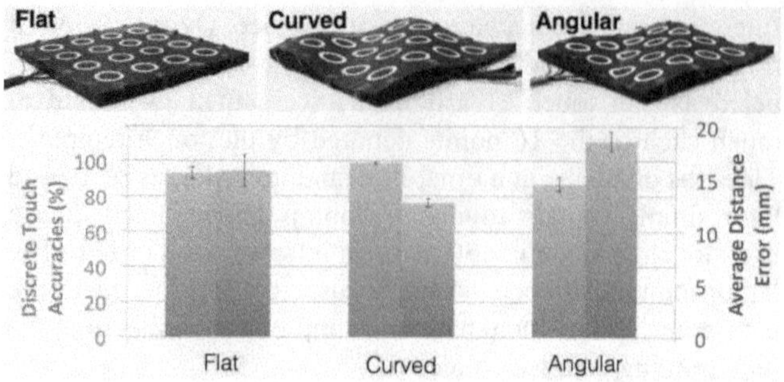

Figure 13. Evaluation results for geometry experiment. Top: touch panels of different geometries. Bottom: Discrete touch and continuous tracking accuracies.

Surface Size

Figure 12 shows the results of our surface size experiment. The average classification accuracy for discrete touch locations was 93.0% (SD=14.3), with 95.7% of errors in adjacent locations. Mean continuous finger tracking distance error was 7.9 mm (SD=5.6). Interestingly, we found that larger surfaces tend to have more linear regression results, though there was no significant difference between our three conditions. This is probably not directly related to size *per se*, but rather tied to our earlier observation about electrode separation (i.e., as surface size increases, so does electrodes electrode separation, improving accuracy).

Surface Geometry

There was no statistically significant differences between our three surface geometries (Figure 13). The average discrete touch accuracy was 92.9% (SD=9.8), with 80.3% of the errors in adjacent locations. Meanwhile, continuous touch tracking mean distance error was 15.7 mm (SD=3.5).

Coatings

Figure 14 shows the results from our coating experiment. Encouragingly, *spray paint* and *bare* performed equally well, suggesting some coatings are immediately compatible with Electrick, opening a range of finish and color options. However, the *paper* covering resulted in significantly worse performance ($p<0.05$) than both other methods, likely because paper is thicker than a spray coat, and thus impacts capacitive coupling more substantially.

Stability Across Users

We employed a train-test experimental procedure in our main evaluation in order to test our system *live*, which offers an honest appraisal of real world accuracies. However, we recorded all data, including raw sensor values, permitting us to run a post hoc study utilizing all collected data.

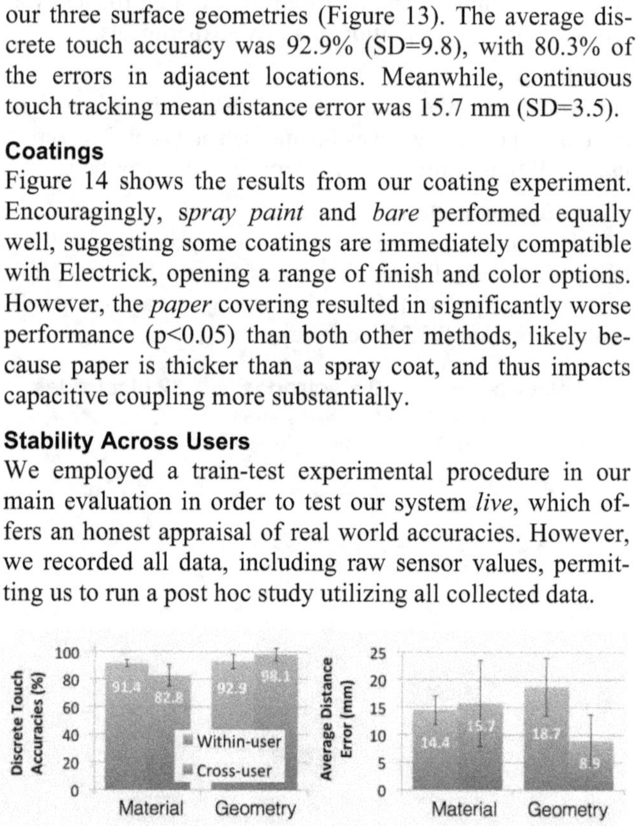

Figure 15. Within-user accuracies and cross-user accuracies for the material and geometry experiments.

Figure 16. Stickers can be placed (A) and bound (B) to laptop functions (C), creating press-able shortcuts (D).

Figure 17. A user can turn on/off a light by tapping the wall. Brightness can be adjusted by sliding up and down.

In particular, we were curious if Electrick's sensing was *user-dependent*, or if the touch sensing was *universal* across users. To explore this, we ran a leave-one-user-out crossfold validation experiment. In each fold, Electrick was allowed to train on 13 users' data, and then tested on a data from a 14th user. We repeated this process for all user combinations. This effectively simulates "walk up" accuracy, wherein the system has never previously seen the user.

We ran this post hoc test using data from our material and geometry studies, the results of which are shown in Figure 15. Overall, discrete touch location classification accuracy decreases by a mean of 3.3%, while continuous touch tracking improves by 2.5 mm. These modest fluctuations, neither of which is statistically significant, suggest that Electrick can be trained (e.g., factory calibrated) on a small subset of users and then work for all.

EXAMPLE APPLICATIONS

To demonstrate the expressivity and versatility of Electrick, we built a variety of fully functional, interactive, example applications. These were selected to include a range of sizes, geometries, materials, fabrication processes and use domains. They are best understood by viewing our Video Figure, but we include brief descriptions below.

Desk: Using a roller, we carbon painted a desk and attached eight electrodes to the sides of the desktop, allowing the whole surface to become touch sensitive. As an example application, users can place paper stickers anywhere on the table, register them to an application (e.g., browser) or function (e.g., mute), after which the stickers can be pressed to quick launch items (Figure 16).

Figure 20. This Electrick-augmented steering wheel can track hand location and gestures.

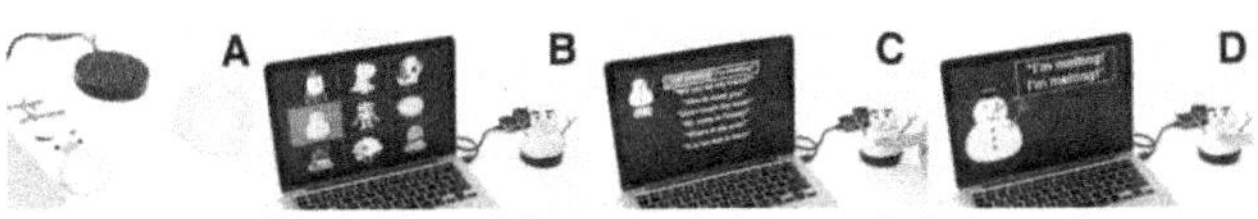

Figure 18. A Play-doh snowman is made interactive.

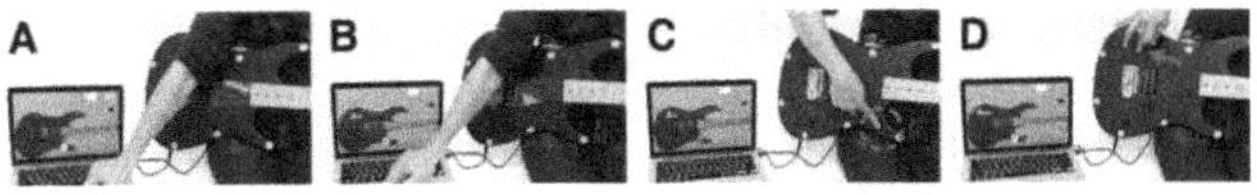

Figure 19. A guitar with dynamically configurable controls.

Wall: We also carbon painted a 4x8' sheet of drywall (Figure 17). By using 16 electrodes, we created a 107" diagonal touch surface. We then applied an off-white latex wall paint. Pervasive touch-sensitive walls could enable innumerable applications. As one example, we created a light control application; tapping the wall anywhere near a sconce light toggles it on/off; dragging up or down allows the user to control the brightness.

Toys: The low-cost nature of toys has largely precluded the integration of touch surfaces. As an example of how Electrick can be used in this domain, we carbon sprayed a dog toy and then hand painted it in colored acrylic paints (Figure 5). With this setup, touches to different locations trigger different audio effects. We made similar apps for toys molded from conductive ABS and silicone (Figure 3).

Play-doh: Play-doh can also be made interactive with Electrick, allowing a user to sculpt a figure or object, and then bind interactive functionally to different touch locations. To achieve this, the finished object is placed onto an 8-electrode base, with small pins that penetrate the play-doh. Figure 18 offers a snowman example, where different phrases are spoken when touching the nose or belly.

Guitar: In this demo, a user can add virtual controls (e.g. volume, filters and effects) to the surface of a guitar through a drag-and-drop design application on a computer (Figure 19). To achieve touch tracking, we carbon sprayed an electric guitar and used eight electrodes running along the edge of the instrument.

Car Steering Wheel: This is a perfect example of a large, irregular object that has yet to be instrumented with rich touch functionality, despite offering an immediately useful surface for user input. As an example, we added 8 electrodes to a carbon-sprayed Chevy Aveo steering wheel; Electrick can track the position of both hands, as well as detect gestures, such as swipes (Figure 20).

Phone Case: We vacuum-formed a rear cover for a Moto E smartphone (Figure 4). With Electrick, phone enclosures

Figure 21. This Electrick-augmented phone enclosure allows different grips to launch apps.

Figure 22. Students can touch different parts of this Jell-O cast to learn about the different regions of the human brain.

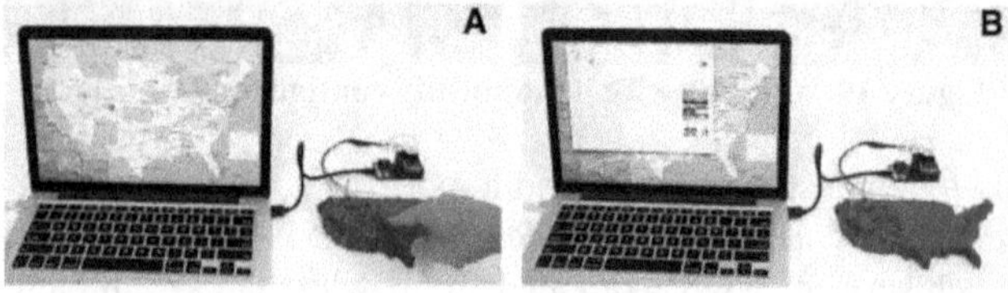

Figure 23. In this interactive topographical map, touching different regions launches local information.

could not only provide protection, but also be used to detect various grips, to e.g., quickly launch apps, such as the camera or messaging (Figure 21)

Instructional Aids: Physical props are often useful in learning visual-spatial subject matter. As an example, we cast a model of a brain using Jell-O, simulating the organic feel. By placing the model onto an 8-electode acrylic base, students can touch different regions of the brain to summon information (Figure 22). Such a base could be reused for any number of low-cost instructional objects. Similarly, we coated a US topographical map with carbon spray, instrumented it with eight electrodes, and applied a green topcoat with spray paint (Figure 23). Information about different geographical regions is retrieved upon a user's touch.

Bongo Hero: We designed a "pluggable" phone accessory featuring four miniature bongos (Figure 2). This was 3D printed using carbon ABS on an off-the-shelf MakerBot Replicator 2X (standard ABS settings, 10% infill). To this, we attached eight electrodes around the base, allowing this otherwise static 3D print to become touch interactive. In this example, we enable a "bongo hero" game (Figure 2D).

Game Controller: Finally, we laser cut a basic game controller, to which we added a Velostat layer and eight electrodes (Figure 24, left). With the surface now made touch sensitive, players or developers can pick (or customize) different interface layouts by overlaying different templates (Figure 24, bottom row). Not only are buttons supported, but also analog inputs, like sliders and joysticks. Obviously, this design flexibility has immediate implications and applications in rapid prototyping of physical interfaces.

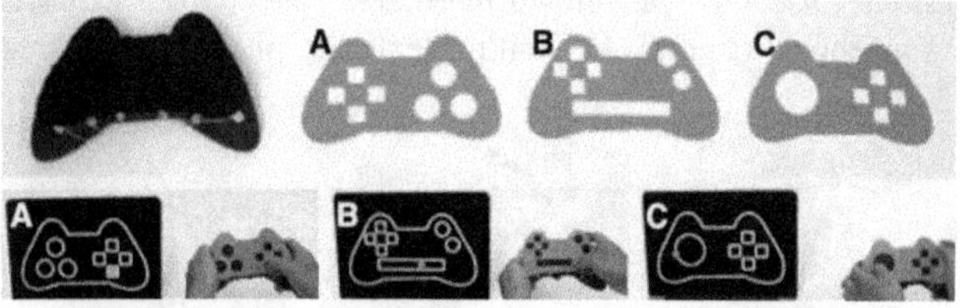

Figure 24. This Electrick-powered game controller allows different layouts to be easy swapped in.

DISCUSSION

One potential concern with Electrick is durability, especially of coatings. We did not detect wear in any of the objects we created (all pictures in the evaluation section were taken after the user study, during which each touch surface was touched 896 times by participants). Of course, this is not a long duration and there was no exposure to the elements. Also, no doubt, there are many more materials that are compatible with Electrick – such as conductive rubbers, foams and fabrics – which we did not have a chance to explore. Transparent coatings may even be possible (e.g., ITO or PEDOT). And of course, conductive material composites can often be made in the home or lab by mixing conventional and conductive materials (e.g., carbon powder), as we did with silicone.

We did find that environmental electromagnetic noise, from e.g., fluorescent lights, running appliances and power lines, can affect tracking accuracy. Not only does the conductive object act like an antenna, but so does the human body, which upon touch, introduces more noise. As discussed previously, we used a high pass filter to combat this interference, though we still found being proximate to (e.g., standing underneath) a florescent light reduced performance. We hope to explore ways to mitigate this in future work.

Finally, perhaps the biggest limitation stems from the grounding condition, which is a universal issue for Electric Field Sensing systems [19]. In Electrick, both the sensor and the user's body capacitively couples to common ground (the Earth) to complete the circuit. Bigger sensor ground planes have stronger capacitive coupling, and thus bigger shunting current and SNR. In our user study, the sensor was connected to and powered by a laptop (under both plugged-in and unplugged conditions; no statistically significant difference in performance), which offered a fairly substantial ground. When a smaller sensor ground is used (e.g., running from a small LiPo battery), the shunting current will be reduced. Although our sensor has a high input impedance, this decrease in shunting current will inevitably lower the SNR. This may preclude the ability to use Electrick in small form factors, such as wearables, though we do believe Electrick can be made to work in devices as small as smartphones.

CONCLUSION

We have presented Electrick, a low-cost and versatile touch sensing technique that can be scaled to large surfaces and irregular geometries. We further show that our technique can be used to bring touch interactivity to rapidly prototyped objects, including those that are 3D printed. Through a series of user studies, we characterized the performance characteristics of our system. Our results show that Electrick can accurately track both discrete and continuous touch input under various test conditions, materials, shapes and sizes. It is also is robust over time and across users. We believe this work can bring touch interactivity to new classes of objects, as well as enable designers to rapidly prototype objects with innate interactive capabilities.

ACKNOWLEDGEMENTS
This research was generously supported by the David and Lucile Packard Foundation. We also thank Scott Hudson for lending us his vacuum former and Robert Xiao for his help in paper revisions.

REFERENCES
1. 3M Material Safety Data Sheet. Retrieved January 5, 2017 from http://multimedia.3m.com/mws/mediawebserver?66666UtN&ZUxL99XlX&ynxM_4Vu9KcuZgVU_LXT1u666666--
2. 3M Multi-Touch Display C5567PW. Datasheet. Retrieved December 26, 2016 from http://multimedia.3m.com/mws/media/1082683O/3m-multi-touch-display-c5567pw.pdf
3. Amazon Product Details. Retrieved January 5, 2017 from https://amzn.com/B008OA931A
4. Analog Devices. 32-Channel Analog Multiplexer. ADG732. Retrieved January 5, 2017 from http://www.analog.com/media/en/technical-documentation/data-sheets/ADG726_732.pdf
5. Analog Devices. Programmable Frequency Sweep and Output Burst Waveform Generator. AD5930. Retrieved January 5, 2017 from http://www.analog.com/media/en/technical-documentation/data-sheets/AD5930.pdf
6. Analog Devices. JFET Input Instrumentation Amplifier with Rail-to-Rail Output in MSOP Package. Retrieved January 5, 2017 from http://www.analog.com/media/en/technical-documentation/data-sheets/AD8220.pdf
7. Andy Adler and Robert Guardo. 1996. Electrical impedance tomography: regularized imaging and contrast detection. IEEE transactions on medical imaging 15, 2. 170–179. http://doi.org/10.1109/42.491418
8. Eric Akaoka, Tim Ginn, and Roel Vertegaal. 2010. DisplayObjects: prototyping functional physical interfaces on 3d styrofoam, paper or cardboard models. In Proceedings of the fourth international conference on Tangible, embedded, and embodied interaction (TEI '10). ACM, New York, NY, USA, 49-56. http://doi.org/10.1145/1709886.1709897
9. Hassan Alirezaei, Akihiko Nagakubo, and Yashuo Kuniyoshi. 2009. A tactile distribution sensor which enables stable measurement under high and dynamic stretch. In Proceedings of the IEEE Symposium 3D User Interfaces. 87–93. http://doi.org/10.1109/3DUI.2009.4811210
10. Thomas Augsten, Konstantin Kaefer, René Meusel, Caroline Fetzer, Dorian Kanitz, Thomas Stoff, Torsten Becker, Christian Holz, and Patrick Baudisch. 2010. Multitoe: high-precision interaction with back-projected floors based on high-resolution multi-touch input. In Proceedings of the 23nd annual ACM symposium on User interface software and technology (UIST '10). ACM, New York, NY, USA, 209-218. http://doi.org/10.1145/1866029.1866064
11. D'Antona, G., Ferrero, A., Lazzaroni, M., Ottoboni, R. and Samarani, E. 2002. Active monitoring apparatus for underground pollutant detection based on electrical impedance tomography. In Proceedings of the IEEE Instrumentation and Measurement Technology Conference. 577–579. http://doi.org/10.1109/IMTC.2002.1006906
12. Beginner's Mind Collective and David Shaw. 2012. Makey Makey: improvising tangible and nature-based user interfaces. In Proceedings of the 6th International Conference on Tangible, Embedded and Embodied Interaction (TEI '12). ACM, New York, NY, USA, 367-370. http://doi.org/10.1145/2148131.2148219
13. Gabe Cohn, Sidhant Gupta, Tien-Jui Lee, Dan Morris, Joshua R. Smith, Matthew S. Reynolds, Desney S. Tan, and Shwetak N. Patel. 2012. An ultra-low-power human body motion sensor using static electric field sensing. In Proceedings of the 2012 ACM Conference on Ubiquitous Computing (UbiComp '12). ACM, New York, NY, USA, 99-102. http://doi.org/10.1145/2370216.2370233
14. Gabe Cohn, Daniel Morris, Shwetak N. Patel, and Desney S. Tan. 2011. Your noise is my command: sensing gestures using the body as an antenna. In Proceedings of the SIGCHI Conference on Human Factors in Computing Systems (CHI '11). ACM, New York, NY, USA, 791-800. http://doi.org/10.1145/1978942.1979058
15. Blair Evans. 1989. Method of and apparatus for sensing the location, such as coordinates, of designated points on an electrically sensitive touch-screen surface, Google Patents.
16. Freescale Microcontroller Datasheet. Retrieved January 5, 2017 from http://cache.freescale.com/files/32bit/doc/data_sheet/K20P64M72SF1.pdf
17. Jerry Alan Fails and Dan Olsen Jr. 2002. Light widgets: interacting in every-day spaces. In Proceedings of the 7th international conference on Intelligent user interfaces (IUI '02). ACM, New York, NY, USA, 63-69. http://doi.org/10.1145/502716.502729
18. Mathieu Le Goc, Stuart Taylor, Shahram Izadi, and Cem Keskin. 2014. A low-cost transparent electric field sensor for 3d interaction on mobile devices. In Proceedings of the SIGCHI Conference on Human Factors in Computing Systems (CHI '14). ACM, New York, NY, USA, 3167-3170. http://doi.org/10.1145/2556288.2557331
19. Tobias Grosse-Puppendahl, Christian Holz, Gabe Cohn, Raphael Wimmer, Oskar Bechtold, Steve Hodges, Matthew Reynolds, and Joshua R. Smith. 2017.

Finding Common Ground: A Survey of Capacitive Sensing in Human-Computer Interaction. In Proceedings of the 35th Annual ACM Conference on Human Factors in Computing Systems (CHI '17). ACM, New York, NY, USA. http://doi.org/10.1145/3025453.3025808

20. Chris Harrison and Scott E. Hudson. 2008. Scratch input: creating large, inexpensive, unpowered and mobile finger input surfaces. In Proceedings of the 21st annual ACM symposium on User interface software and technology (UIST '08). ACM, New York, NY, USA, 205-208. http://doi.org/10.1145/1449715.1449747
21. David Holman and Roel Vertegaal. 2011. TactileTape: low-cost touch sensing on curved surfaces. In Proceedings of the 24th annual ACM symposium adjunct on User interface software and technology (UIST '11 Adjunct). ACM, New York, NY, USA, 17-18. http://doi.org/10.1145/2046396.2046406
22. Eun-Soo Hwang, Jung-hoon Seo, and Yong-Jun Kim. 2007. A Polymer-Based Flexible Tactile Sensor for Both Normal and Shear Load Detections and Its Application for Robotics. Journal of Micromechanical Systems Vol. 16, No. 3, 556-563. http://doi.org/10.1109/JMEMS.2007.896716
23. Mark Hall, Eibe Frank, Geoffrey Holmes, Bernhard Pfahringer, Peter Reutemann, and Ian H. Witten. 2009. The WEKA data mining software: an update. SIGKDD Explor. Newsl. 11, 1. 10-18. http://doi.org/10.1145/1656274.1656278
24. Scott E. Hudson and Jennifer Mankoff. 2006. Rapid construction of functioning physical interfaces from cardboard, thumbtacks, tin foil and masking tape. In Proceedings of the 19th annual ACM symposium on User interface software and technology (UIST '06). ACM, New York, NY, USA, 289-298. http://doi.org/10.1145/1166253.1166299
25. Hemant Jain, David Isaacson, Peter M Edic, and Jonathan C Newell. 1997. Electrical Impedance Tomography of Complex Conductivity Distributions with Noncircular Boundary. 44, 11: 1051–1060. http://doi.org/10.1109/10.641332
26. Philip T. Krein and R. David Meadows. 1990. The electroquasistatics of the capacitive touch panel. IEEE Transactions on Industry Applications Volume: 26, Issue: 3, 529 – 534. http://doi.org/10.1109/28.55954
27. LG Inc. Media cover. Retrieved January 5, 2017 from http://www.theverge.com/2016/1/3/10706180/lg-rollable-display-flexible-screen-announced-ces-2016
28. Gierad Laput, Eric Brockmeyer, Scott E. Hudson, and Chris Harrison. 2015. Acoustruments: Passive, Acoustically-Driven, Interactive Controls for Handheld Devices. In Proceedings of the 33rd Annual ACM Conference on Human Factors in Computing Systems (CHI '15). ACM, New York, NY, USA, 2161-2170. http://doi.org/10.1145/2702123.2702414
29. MG Chemicals Inc: http://www.mgchemicals.com
30. Microsoft Surface Hub. User Guide. Retrieved January 5, 2017 from https://microsoft.com/microsoft-surface-hub/en-us
31. Mouser product page. Retrieved January 5, 2017 from http://www.mouser.com/ProductDetail/SCS/1704-36
32. MTE Solutions Product Details. Retrieved January 5, 2017 from http://shop.mtesolutionsinc.com/new-from-mg-chemicals/mg-chemicals-838ar-3-781-carbon-conductive-coating/
33. Adiyan Mujibiya and Jun Rekimoto. 2013. Mirage: exploring interaction modalities using off-body static electric field sensing. In Proceedings of the 26th annual ACM symposium on User interface software and technology (UIST '13). ACM, New York, NY, USA, 211-220. http://doi.org/10.1145/2501988.2502031
34. Maggie Orth, Rehmi Post, and Emily Cooper. 1998. Fabric computing interfaces. In Proceedings of the SIGCHI Conference on Human Factors in Computing Systems (CHI '98). ACM, New York, NY, USA, 331-332. http://doi.org/10.1145/286498.286800
35. Makoto Ono, Buntarou Shizuki, and Jiro Tanaka. 2013. Touch & activate: adding interactivity to existing objects using active acoustic sensing. In Proceedings of the 26th annual ACM symposium on User interface software and technology (UIST '13). ACM, New York, NY, USA, 31-40. http://doi.org/10.1145/2501988.2501989
36. PJRC Inc Product Detail. Retrieved January 5, 2017 from https://www.pjrc.com/teensy/teensy31.html
37. Pham, D.T., Ji, Z., Peyroutet, O., Yang, M., Wang, Z. and Al-Kutubi, M. 2006. Localization of impacts on solid objects using the wavelet transform and maximum likelihood estimation. In Proceedings of IPROMS '06. 541–547. http://doi.org/10.1016/B978-008045157-2/50095-X
38. Ganna Pugach, Alexandre Pitti, and Philippe Gaussier. 2015. Neural learning of the topographic tactile sensory information of an artificial skin through a self-organizing map. Advanced Robotics, Volume 29 Issue 21: Robotic Sensor Skins. 1393-1409. http://doi.org/10.1371/journal.pone.0026561
39. Ivan Poupyrev, Chris Harrison, and Munehiko Sato. 2012. Touché: touch and gesture sensing for the real world. In Proceedings of the 2012 ACM Conference on Ubiquitous Computing (UbiComp '12). ACM, New York, NY, USA, 536-536. http://doi.org/10.1145/2370216.2370296
40. Ivan Poupyrev, Nan-Wei Gong, Shiho Fukuhara, Mustafa Emre Karagozler, Carsten Schwesig, and Karen E. Robinson. 2016. Project Jacquard: Interactive Digital

Textiles at Scale. In Proceedings of the 2016 CHI Conference on Human Factors in Computing Systems (CHI '16). ACM, New York, NY, USA, 4216-4227. http://doi.org/10.1145/2858036.2858176

41. Joseph A. Paradiso, Che King Leo, Nisha Checka, and Kaijen Hsiao. 2002. Passive acoustic knock tracking for interactive windows. In CHI '02 Extended Abstracts on Human Factors in Computing Systems (CHI EA '02). ACM, New York, NY, USA, 732-733. http://doi.org/10.1145/506443.506570
42. Joshua R. Smith. 1995. Toward Electric Field Tomography. M.S. Thesis. Massachusetts Institute of Technology, Cambridge, MA.
43. Joshua R. Smith. 1999. Electric field imaging. Ph.D. Dissertation. Massachusetts Institute of Technology, Cambridge, MA.
44. Martin Schmitz, Mohammadreza Khalilbeigi, Matthias Balwierz, Roman Lissermann, Max Mühlhäuser, and Jürgen Steimle. 2015. Capricate: A Fabrication Pipeline to Design and 3D Print Capacitive Touch Sensors for Interactive Objects. In Proceedings of the 28th Annual ACM Symposium on User Interface Software & Technology (UIST '15). ACM, New York, NY, USA, 253-258. http://doi.org/10.1145/2807442.2807503
45. Valkyrie Savage, Andrew Head, Björn Hartmann, Dan B. Goldman, Gautham Mysore, and Wilmot Li. 2015. Lamello: Passive Acoustic Sensing for Tangible Input Components. In Proceedings of the 33rd Annual ACM Conference on Human Factors in Computing Systems (CHI '15). ACM, New York, NY, USA, 1277-1280. http://doi.org/10.1145/2702123.2702207
46. Valkyrie Savage, Colin Chang, and Björn Hartmann. 2013. Sauron: embedded single-camera sensing of printed physical user interfaces. In Proceedings of the 26th annual ACM symposium on User interface software and technology (UIST '13). ACM, New York, NY, USA, 447-456. http://doi.org/10.1145/2501988.2501992
47. Valkyrie Savage, Sean Follmer, Jingyi Li, and Björn Hartmann. 2015. Makers' Marks: Physical Markup for Designing and Fabricating Functional Objects. In Proceedings of the 28th Annual ACM Symposium on User Interface Software & Technology (UIST '15). ACM, New York, NY, USA, 103-108. http://doi.org/10.1145/2807442.2807508
48. Valkyrie Savage, Xiaohan Zhang, and Björn Hartmann. 2012. Midas: fabricating custom capacitive touch sensors to prototype interactive objects. In Proceedings of the 25th annual ACM symposium on User interface software and technology (UIST '12). ACM, New York, NY, USA, 579-588. http://doi.org/10.1145/2380116.2380189
49. Eckhard Teschner, Michael Imhoff, and Steffen Leonhardt. 2015. Electrical Impedance Tomography: The realization of regional ventilation monitoring, 2nd Edition. Dräger Medical GmbH, Germany.
50. Treetronic. 2015. PiCUS: Treetronic, Electric Resistance Tomography. Retrieved January 5, 2017 from http://www.argus-electronic.de/en/content/download/431/4060/.../ TreeTronic+3+manual.pdf
51. David Silvera Tawil, David Rye, and Mari Velonaki. 2011. Touch Modality Interpretation for an EIT-Based Sensitive Skin. In Proceedings of the IEEE Conference on Robotics and Automation (ICRA). 3770–3776. http://doi.org/10.1109/ICRA.2011.5979697
52. David Silvera Tawil, David Rye, Manuchehr Soleimani, and Mari Velonaki. 2015. Electrical Impedance Tomography for Artificial Sensitive Robotic Skin : A Review. IEEE Sensors Journal, vol. 15, no. 4, 2001-2016 http://doi.org/10.1109/JSEN.2014.2375346
53. Marko Vauhkonen, W.R.B. Lionheart, Lasse M Heikkinen, P.J. Vauhkonen and Jari P Kaipio. A MATLAB package for the EIDORS project to reconstruct two-dimensional EIT images. Physiological Measurement 22.1 107–111 http://doi.org/10.1088/0967-3334/22/1/314
54. Andrew D. Wilson and Hrvoje Benko. 2010. Combining multiple depth cameras and projectors for interactions on, above and between surfaces. In Proceedings of the 23nd annual ACM symposium on User interface software and technology (UIST '10). ACM, New York, NY, USA, 273-282. http://doi.org/10.1145/1866029.1866073
55. Andrew D. Wilson. 2005. PlayAnywhere: a compact interactive tabletop projection-vision system. In Proceedings of the 18th annual ACM symposium on User interface software and technology (UIST '05). ACM, New York, NY, USA, 83-92. http://doi.org/10.1145/1095034.1095047
56. Karl Willis, Eric Brockmeyer, Scott Hudson, and Ivan Poupyrev. 2012. Printed optics: 3D printing of embedded optical elements for interactive devices. In Proceedings of the 25th annual ACM symposium on User interface software and technology (UIST '12). ACM, New York, NY, USA, 589-598. http://doi.org/10.1145/2380116.2380190
57. Raphael Wimmer and Patrick Baudisch. 2011. Modular and deformable touch-sensitive surfaces based on time domain reflectometry. In Proceedings of the 24th annual ACM symposium on User interface software and technology (UIST '11). ACM, New York, NY, USA, 517-526. http://doi.org/10.1145/2047196.2047264
58. Robert Xiao, Chris Harrison, and Scott E. Hudson. 2013. WorldKit: rapid and easy creation of ad-hoc interactive applications on everyday surfaces. In CHI '13 Extended Abstracts on Human Factors in Computing

Systems (CHI EA '13). ACM, New York, NY, USA, 2889-2890. http://doi.org/10.1145/2468356.2479563

59. Robert Xiao, Greg Lew, James Marsanico, Divya Hariharan, Scott Hudson, and Chris Harrison. 2014. Toffee: enabling ad hoc, around-device interaction with acoustic time-of-arrival correlation. In Proceedings of the 16th international conference on Human-computer interaction with mobile devices & services (MobileHCI '14). ACM, New York, NY, USA, 67-76. http://doi.org/10.1145/2628363.2628383
60. Zen ToolWorks Inc: http://www.zentoolworks.com
61. Thomas G. Zimmerman, Joshua R. Smith, Joseph A. Paradiso, David Allport, and Neil Gershenfeld. 1995. Applying electric field sensing to human-computer interfaces. In Proceedings of the SIGCHI Conference on Human Factors in Computing Systems (CHI '95). ACM, New York, NY, USA, 280-287. http://doi.org/10.1145/223904.223940
62. Yang Zhang and Chris Harrison. 2015. Tomo: Wearable, Low-Cost Electrical Impedance Tomography for Hand Gesture Recognition. In Proceedings of the 28th Annual ACM Symposium on User Interface Software & Technology (UIST '15). ACM, New York, NY, USA, 167-173. http://doi.org/10.1145/2807442.2807480
63. Yang Zhang, Robert Xiao, and Chris Harrison. 2016. Advancing Hand Gesture Recognition with High Resolution Electrical Impedance Tomography. In Proceedings of the 29th Annual Symposium on User Interface Software and Technology (UIST '16). ACM, New York, NY, USA, 843-850. http://doi.org/10.1145/2984511.2984574

GhostID: Enabling Non-Persistent User Differentiation in Frequency-Division Capacitive Multi-Touch Sensors

Sidharth Sahdev [3,1] Clifton Forlines [2] Ricardo Jota [1] Bruno De Araujo [3,1]
Braon Moseley [2] Jonathan Deber [1] Steven Sanders [2] Darren Leigh [2] Daniel Wigdor [3]

[1] Tactual Labs
Toronto, ON, Canada
{first.last}@tactuallabs.com

[2] Tactual Labs
New York, NY, USA
{first.last}@tactuallabs.com

[3] University of Toronto
Toronto, ON, Canada
daniel@dgp.toronto.edu

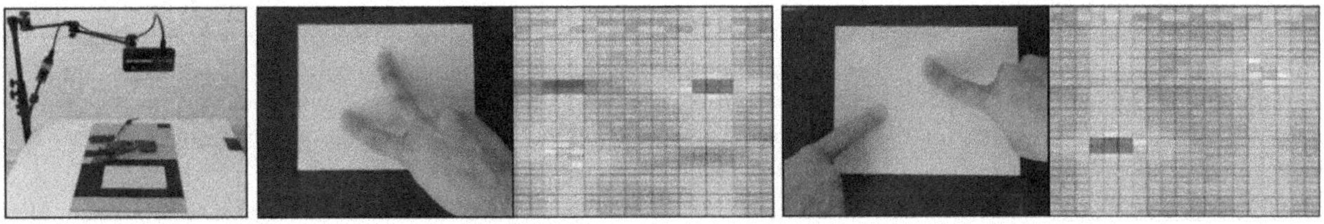

Figure 1. (a) *GhostID* prototype with a 10-inch capacitive sensor; (b) two touches from the same hand produce touch points (red and yellow) and ghost signals (dark blue); (c) two touches from two different users produce touch points but no ghosting.

ABSTRACT

Current touch devices are adept at tracking finger touches, but cannot distinguish if multiple touches are caused by different fingers on a single hand, by fingers from both hands of a single user, or by different users. This limitation significantly reduces the possibilities for interaction techniques in touch interfaces. We present *GhostID*, a capacitive sensor that can differentiate the origins of multiple simultaneous touches. Our approach analyzes the signal ghosting, already present as an artifact in a frequency-division touch controller, to differentiate touches from the same hand or different hands of a single user (77% reliability at 60 fps) or from two different users (95% reliability at 60 fps). In addition to *GhostID*, we also develop a framework of user-differentiation capabilities for touch input devices, and illustrate a set of interaction techniques enabled by *GhostID*.

Author Keywords

User Differentiation; Capacitive Touch Sensor; Signal Processing; Mobility

ACM Classification Keywords

H.5.m. Information interfaces and presentation (e.g., HCI): Interactions

CHI 2017, May 6–11, 2017, Denver, CO, USA.

ACM ISBN 978-1-4503-4655-9/17/05...$15.00.
DOI: http://dx.doi.org/10.1145/3025453.3025719

INTRODUCTION

The commoditization of multi-touch input has enabled device form factors ranging in size from 1″ smart watches to 25′ public displays. While a number of technologies have been used to detect touch input (e.g., resistive, optical, acoustic, etc.), capacitive touch sensing has come to dominate the commercial sphere.

As devices increase in scale, the likelihood and utility of multiple simultaneous users also increases. For example, the research community has repeatedly demonstrated the advantages of single-display groupware in tabletop and large display contexts [3, 10, 26, 27, 38]. Despite the benefits, there remains an important obstacle to commercial deployment in many contexts—the inability, without external hardware, to consistently differentiate between touches belonging to different users [19, 23, 30, 34, 40]. A lack of user differentiation can break well-understood user interface metaphors, such as finger painting [44]: when a single user selects a paint color, that color is then applied to all current users. In addition, further differentiation at the hand level (i.e., do a pair of touches come from two fingers on a single hand, or from one finger on each of a user's hands?) has also been shown to be beneficial [9, 16, 28]. To the authors' knowledge, no commercial devices are able to consistently differentiate multiple simultaneous touches at any level of precision.

To address this limitation, researchers have attempted to design systems that can differentiate touches from multiple users. Some systems augment touch sensing with other sensors, such as cameras [16, 36], fiber optics [12], or proximity sensors [2]. Others augment touch sensors with user-specific signal emitters [7, 18, 19, 34]. While each of these techniques can identify touch origins, the need for additional sensors or external augmentation limits their use cases. An ideal solution for user differentiation would be to enable the capacitive sensor itself to differentiate touches, without the reliance on external hardware.

In this paper, we propose a novel method to differentiate the touches from different hands of a single user, as well as touches from multiple users. The technique is based on the frequency-division multiplexing (FDM) capacitive sensing demonstrated in Leigh et al.'s Fast Multi-Touch (FMT) device [20]. While the primary purpose of FMT was to enable higher frame rates to achieve low-latency sensing, we have found that its unique approach is also well suited to touch differentiation.

A bare capacitive sensor is composed of rows and columns of conductive material. To sense multi-touch input, an FMT system injects orthogonal signals into each row. When a user touches the sensor, their finger will capacitively couple one (or more) rows to one (or more) columns. If a single user touches the sensor in multiple locations, each touch point produces its own coupling of rows and columns. However, because humans are conductive, some of the signals will travel through the hand and into the body of the user. If the user places a second finger on the sensor, these conducted signals will be received alongside the intended signals. The weaker, conducted signals produce faint "ghost" points on the sensor that do not correspond to actual touches.

Leigh et al. view these ghosts as noise, because they do not correspond to actual touches, and therefore filter them out to produce a reliable sensor. However, rather than minimizing and/or simply discarding them, we explicitly use them to differentiate touch origin. If a ghost is present, we know the touch must come from the same user who is already touching the sensor at the position where the ghost signal originated. Moreover, we can use the strength of the ghost signals to detect whether two touches are from the same or different hands of the same user.

The *GhostID* prototype, shown in Figure 1(a), consists of a touch controller implemented on a field-programmable gate array (FPGA) that drives an opaque copper-mesh touch sensor. The controller utilizes FMT principles, except ghosting is not filtered out as noise by the controller.

Our post-processing algorithms can discriminate two touches as coming from the same or different users with 95% precision. Similarly, they can discriminate two touches as coming from one or two hands of a single user with 77% precision. In this paper, we describe our processing pipeline in detail, as well as the results of a study designed to validate the system.

Following the development of our prototype, we designed and implemented a set of interaction techniques that are enabled by *GhostID*. Some of these techniques illustrate the benefits of *GhostID* in a single-user context, while others make use of the ghosting information to support multi-user systems with touch input discrimination.

The primary contributions of this paper are: (1) a framework that defines the space of touch input differentiation; (2) the *GhostID* concept and a prototype that differentiates users and hands on capacitive touch devices without additional hardware; and (3) a set of interaction techniques that are enabled by *GhostID's* capabilities.

A FRAMEWORK FOR TOUCH INPUT DIFFERENTIATION

In conducting a review of the literature on touch differentiation, we found it helpful to classify existing techniques using a three-dimensional space representing precision, persistence, and mobility. In this section, we explain these parameters and classify existing methods within the space. We hope that this framework will aid future researchers in describing their contributions. An overview of the framework is illustrated in Figure 2, and each variable is described in detail below.

Precision

In our framework, we define precision as one of four levels of detail at which a technology is able to differentiate or group touch inputs. The levels of precision are: *tracking*, *user*, *hand,* and *finger*. Each level is cumulative, so a *hand* level technique is also classified as being both *user* level and *tracking* level.

Tracking level precision is the ability to track multi-touch points in real time. The seminal work for tracking multi-touch is by Han [12], who proposed the use of frustrated total internal reflection (FTIR) as the basis of multi-touch sensing. Recent work by Leigh et al. [20] uses frequency-division multiplexing (FDM) to detect multi-touch with extremely low latency.

User level precision is the ability to differentiate between multiple users who are simultaneously using the same touch system. An example is DiamondTouch [7], a tabletop system where users are individually capacitively coupled to the table, providing each with a uniquely identifiable capacitive signature. Other examples include CapAuth [11], Collaid [5], See Me See You [46], Capacitive Touch Communication [40], and HandsDown [36].

Hand level precision is the ability to determine that multiple touches are coming from the same hand. An example is Annett et al.'s Medusa [2], a proximity aware multi-touch tabletop that uses arrays of sensors to track users and hands. Medusa's hand and user tracking technique is fairly precise, but the IR sensors sometimes yield false positives due to reflections from surrounding materials in the room (e.g., pipes, ceiling, etc.).

TouchID [21] uses a wearable glove to track the fingers and hands of users for tabletop interactions. Dhose et al. [8] track users' hands based on skin color and spatial regions around touch points, although their technique suffers from occlusion problems. *GhostID* has *hand* level precision since it can differentiate touches coming from one or two hands from a single user, or the hands of multiple users.

Finger level precision is the ability to differentiate exactly how many fingers are touching a surface, and which hands they belong to. Holz et al.'s Fiberio [16] uses an arrangement of high resolution cameras, fiber optics, and projector-based methods for sensing and identifying multiple users on tabletops. It recognizes an individual user's fingerprints with sophisticated image-processing algorithms. Extended Multitouch [28] uses hand poses to differentiate fingers from different users with a combination of a depth camera and surface touch sensor.

Ewerling et al. [9] use hand and arm images on an optical multi-touch device along with touch information to detect fingers and hands of multiple users. Most biometric fingerprint sensors (like those used to unlock smartphones) have *finger* level precision, but they are not used as general purpose input devices since they are constrained to small patches of specialized capacitive sensing, such as home buttons.

Persistence

We define persistence as the ability of a technology to retain a differentiated touch input. As shown in Figure 2, our framework describes persistence at five levels: *input frame, touch point, touch grouping, session*, and *lifetime*. As with the precision levels, persistence levels are also cumulative.

Input frame persistence is the minimum persistence required to sense touch. It is the ability to register a touch during a single sensor sampling frame without any continuity or relationship between successive frames. All of today's touch technologies have at least *input frame* persistence.

Touch point persistence is the ability to understand the continuity of a moving touch point between frames as long as the finger remains in contact with the sensor. However, there is no relationship between multiple touch points. Examples include Westerman's [42] methods of tracking multiple fingers and palms on multi-touch surfaces, and McAvinney's Sensor Frame [22] that recognizes gestures in three dimensions. Other examples of *touch point* persistence include Leigh et al. [20] and Han [12].

Touch grouping persistence is the ability to detect that multiple simultaneous touches are caused by the same user. However, this persistence only lasts as long as the user continues to touch the sensor. As one example, Zhang et al. [47] grouped touches as coming from the left or right hands for a single user on a Laser Light Plane (LLP) table. *GhostID* has *touch grouping* persistence.

Session persistence allows *touch grouping* to continue throughout a single usage session even if the user briefly stops touching the sensor. However, if the user stops interacting with the system, leaves, and later returns, the technology cannot identify that the same user has returned. DiamondTouch [7] and Medusa [2] are good examples of *session* persistence. DiamondTouch is persistent as long as the users remain seated in their capacitively coupled chairs. *Session* based differentiation has been extensively studied in the interaction techniques space due in large part to the popularity of the DiamondTouch table as a research tool [26, 37]. Another example is Harrison et al.'s research on Capacitive Fingerprinting [13] that uses Swept Frequency Capacitive Sensing (SFCS), introduced by Santo et al.'s Touché [34]. It detects different users by sensing the electrical properties of the human body and identifying impedance profiles based on variations in bone density, muscle mass, and footwear across individuals. Using a prototype built around the Touché sensor board and integrated with a small touch screen, Harrison et al. also performed a user study involving three demo applications to show the potential of user-aware interaction. More examples of *session* persistent touch input discrimination include See Me See You [46] and Clayphan et al. [5].

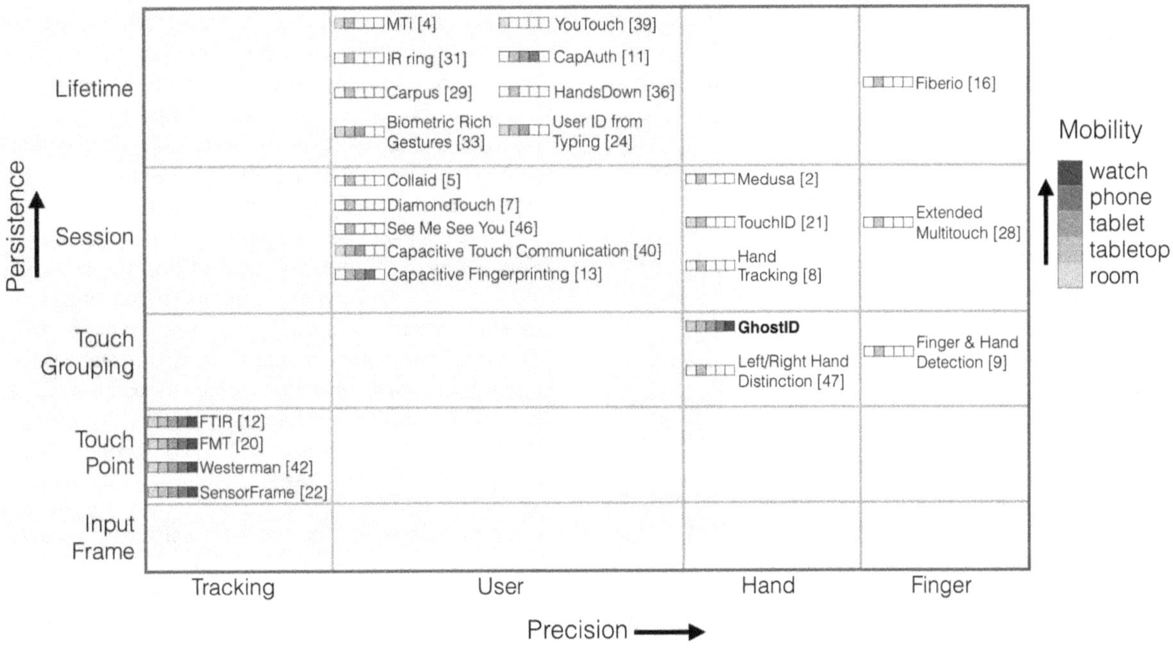

Figure 2. A framework to categorize differentiation techniques. It is parameterized by precision, persistence, and mobility.

Lifetime persistence can indefinitely and uniquely identify a user across all sessions, and can associate all of their touches with them. *Lifetime* persistence is often called *user identification*. In most cases users must perform an initial (implicit or explicit) registration operation when they first interact with the system. Guo et al.'s CapAuth [11] senses changes in the electric fields of the capacitive screen caused by a finger, and can identify users within a smaller group (up to 10 users) at 98.2% accuracy. Although they conclude that their technique is not well suited for high-security applications due to the non-scalability of the technique, the accuracy obtained gives sufficient evidence of the capabilities of capacitance based user-identification.

YouTouch [39] is a recent technique for identifying users on wall-sized displays using a depth camera. There are several other examples of user identification that use external wearable hardware [31], gesture style [33], touch typing style [24], skin texture [29], or hand geometry [4].

Mobility

We define mobility as the scalability and portability of a touch input differentiation technology. These factors fall on a continuous spectrum, but can be roughly divided into five categories in order of decreasing mobility: *smart watches*, *phones*, *tablet*, *tabletops*, and *room*.

The majority of touch input differentiation techniques are low on the mobility scale due to the external support and/or augmentation that they require. For example, Medusa [2] only works indoors since the proximity sensors do not perform well in the presence of sunlight. Likewise, Fiberio [16] is highly precise and persistent, but its integration into smaller form factors is not practical due to the bulky high precision camera that is required. Because it uses a standard capacitive sensor, *GhostID* is highly scalable and can be used across the entire mobility spectrum, ranging from 1″ smart watches to room-sized interactive wall displays.

Other user differentiation technologies

There are also techniques based on external hardware that are capable of differentiating users. These either use wearable hardware or employ user differentiation that does not use finger or palm touches, and therefore they do not fit into our framework [1, 15, 17, 18, 19, 23, 30, 34, 35, 45].

Holz and Knaust's Biometric Touch Sensing [18] seamlessly augments each touch with continuous identification. They rely heavily on a wrist-worn prototype sensor that captures user-unique features and transmits them through the body to a touch screen. Touché [34] is another capacitive touch-sensing technique that uses a small wearable hardware sensor to sense touch. However, the user identification is fragile due to changes in the biometric response to capacitive signals, and returning users are often not identified correctly.

Overall, despite the development of many such approaches, a self-contained (i.e., completely integrated into the capacitive sensor) and accurate multi-user identification system has not been developed.

In summary, *GhostID* is *hand* level precise, has *touch grouping* persistence, and offers a high range of mobility covering smart watches to wall-sized displays. It is capable of differentiating user touches on a large spectrum of capacitive sensors, and is fully integrated into the touch sensor itself.

GHOSTID: USING GHOSTING SIGNALS TO DIFFERENTIATE USERS

GhostID is based on FMT technology [20], and uses frequency-division multiplexing to sense capacitive touch. As noted in the introduction, the touch sensor is comprised of an array of conductive rows and columns. A signal transmitter is attached to each row, and a receiver is attached to each column. The top of the sensor was covered by a 0.8 mm thick sheet of white vellum (used as a top-projection surface), and a glass substrate provided structural support. A photograph of the system is shown in Figure 5a. The dimensions of this stack are 22 cm by 16 cm by 0.1 cm thick, yielding a form factor similar to a 10″ tablet. The sensor contains 40 transmitter rows, and 30 receiver columns. The entire system is powered by a 12V grounded wall adapter. Although we chose to build the prototype using a tablet form factor, the technology can be extended to much larger capacitive touch displays.

FMT transmits a unique, orthogonal sinusoidal signal (3.3 V, 80 – 120 kHz) into each row of the sensor. The rows are capacitively coupled with the receiver columns at every intersection point, and each column receives a baseline level of signal when there are no touches on the sensor. A touch changes the coupling at one or more intersection points, which can be detected by the change in signal intensity. Because the frequencies are orthogonal, multiple frequencies received on a column can be decomposed into their components with a Fourier transform, thereby allowing for a complete snapshot of every row/column intersection during every sampling frame. We refer to this signal snapshot as a *heatmap*. Our prototype is capable of sensing at about 350 Hz. (In comparison, a traditional time-division multiplexing (TDM) touch controller scans the sensor one row at a time, and requires many sampling frames to read the entire sensor; this yields a slower sampling rate. While a ghost-based classification is possible on a TDM controller, the "one-shot" sampling provided by FMT provides a more robust signal.)

A heatmap is computed by the touchscreen controller, and this data is transmitted to a host PC via UDP over Ethernet. Software on the host PC receives these packets, visualizes the heatmap, and performs processing to locate touches and perform the hand and user discrimination.

GhostID gets its name from a signal artifact that occurs when a single user touches the sensor in multiple places. Figure 5c illustrates a heatmap with this artifact. Recall that touching the sensor changes the coupling between a row and a column. With our sensor, we see a decrease in signal intensity since some of the signal is dissipated by the user's body rather than being fed into the receiver. If a single user touches the sensor in multiple places, a signal travels from the first touched row, through the user's body, and is then re-injected into the second touched column. We therefore detect a small increase in intensity of the first row's signal in the second column's receiver, and vice versa. This *crosstalk* does not occur if multiple touches are made by separate people since there is no path for the signal to travel from one person to another.

In Figure 3 (left), we see a single user touching the sensor in two locations. These fingers strongly couple row 1 to column G and row 3 to column D, resulting in two strong touch points at 1-G and 3-D. In addition to these strong pathways, the signal from row 1 passes into the user's right hand, through their body, and into their left hand, which is touching column D. Similarly, some signal from row 3 passes in the opposite direction through to column G. 1-D and 3-G therefore report weaker "ghost" touches that would traditionally be filtered out and discarded as they do not represent actual touch locations.

The strength of these ghost signals depends on the distance the signal must travel between the two touch points. Signals attenuate as they travel through the body, so shorter distances will result in stronger ghosting. If the signal cannot travel between the two points, as is the case in Figure 3 (right) when two different users touch the sensor, there is no ghosting.

Figure 4 shows how this attenuation is used to determine if two touches come from the same hand, from two hands of the same user, or from multiple users. In Path A, the finger directly couples a row to a column with very little attenuation. Path B shows the short distance between two fingers on the same hand. Path C spans from one arm, through the torso to the other arm. Finally, Path D is effectively infinite as there is no electrical connection between start and end points that reside on different users. Through this understanding of attenuation and ghosting, our technique can use the strength of the ghost signals to classify it as coming from one of these paths.

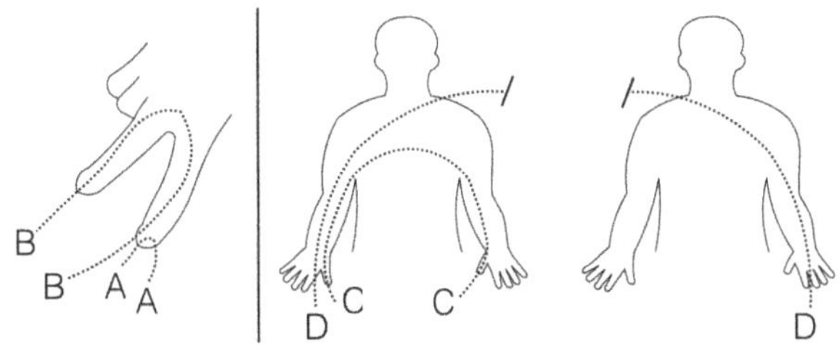

Figure 4. Differing lengths of signal paths (A, B, C, and D) allow user and hand differentiation.

Because our current prototype broadcasts signals on rows and receives signals on columns, it is not able to identify ghosts when two actual touches occur on the same row or column. The strong signals from the actual touch locations will be in the same place as the ghosts, and will therefore mask the weaker ghost crosstalk. This limitation could be overcome with changes to the sensor, as discussed in the Future Work section of the paper.

Signal Processing

This section describes the signal processing pipeline (shown in Figure 6) that enables touch differentiation. The incoming signals are passed through a Python-based software pipeline that consists of: pre-processing, touch detection, ghost detection, feature extraction, per-frame classification, multi-frame analysis, and output of *GhostID* attributes (i.e., touch origin). The *GhostID* attributes are metadata that are associated with each touch point, and are separate from the touch tracking itself; this allows normal touch processing to occur independently of the *GhostID* analysis.

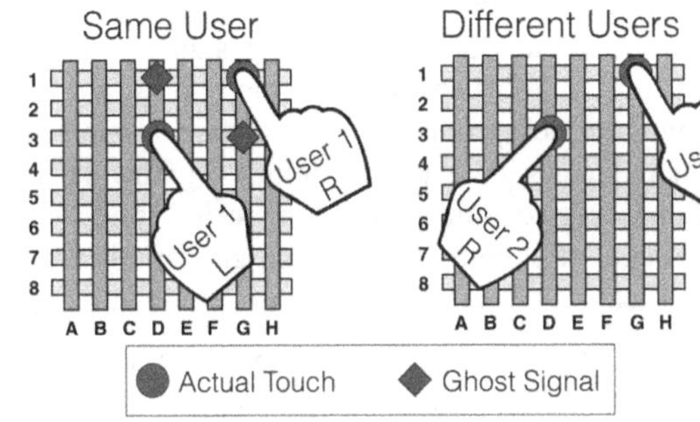

Figure 3. Two touches from the same user produce ghost signals (blue) in addition to real touch signals (red). Two touches from different users do not produce ghosts.

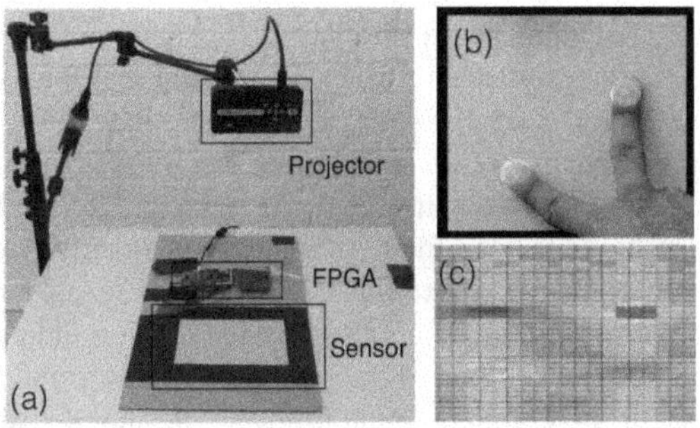

Figure 5. (a) *GhostID* prototype consisting of a 10-inch sensor, FPGA controller, and projector; (b) the sensor surface, with projected feedback; (c) a heatmap visualizing two touch points (red and yellow) from the same hand, and the two resulting ghost signals (dark blue).

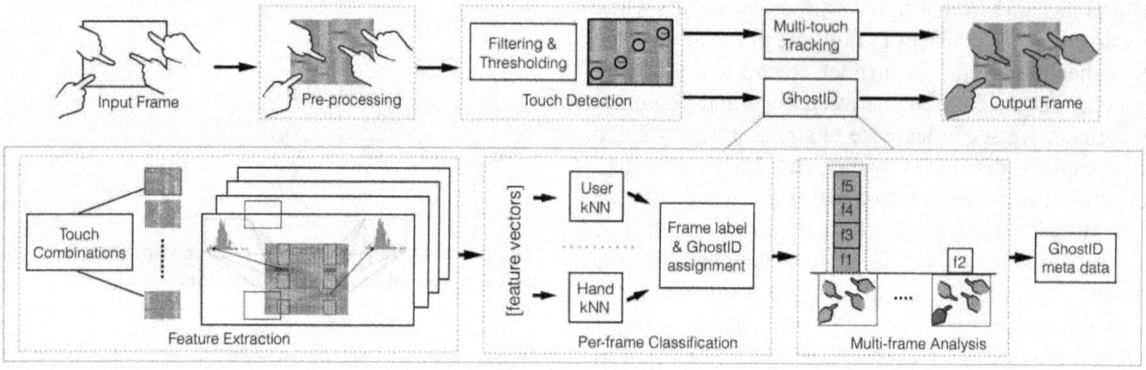

Figure 6. Signal processing pipeline.

Pre-processing. First, each heatmap from the touch controller is checked for validity and completeness. Next, we level the data. Due to several factors, including attenuation of signals across the rows of the sensor, minute variations in adhesive and material thickness and properties, and variations in connections between signal generators and rows, the baseline signal is not uniform across the entire area of the sensor. As such, each pixel (i.e., a row/column intersection in the heatmap) needs to be calibrated to produce a uniform leveling of the sensor data. We record a set of 1000 frames without any touches, and compute an average for each pixel. This average is then subtracted from the incoming raw sensor data to yield a leveled heatmap.

Touch detection. A touch is detected by thresholding the heatmap by signal strength, creating connected components with similar signal intensities, and then finding the location of the local maximum signal strength within each connected component. The threshold level is chosen to remove all ghost signals and leave us with a set of real touches, and is essentially equivalent to the touch detection and ghost removal normally performed by the touch controller. Two outputs are generated from this processing step: touch data is passed out of the pipeline up to the application level, and the heatmap is passed to the remainder of the pipeline to process the ghosts.

Ghost detection and feature extraction. If there are ghost signals, they must by definition appear somewhere along the rows and columns where we have detected real touches (see Figure 3). To search for the ghosts, we generate a list of candidate locations (i.e., a bounding box on the heatmap) by taking each possible pair of real touches and determining the two locations where their ghosts would occur. Next, we examine each ghost candidate by computing a histogram profile of its column, excluding the real touch region and the candidate ghost region. This generates a background noise profile for the column, which follows a normal distribution. We then find the lowest signal strengths within the candidate ghost region, and compute z-scores to compare them to the background noise. All of these features (the signal strength for each touch, and the signal strength and z-score for each ghost candidate) are then fed into classifiers in the next step.

Per-frame classification. We construct feature vectors, and feed them into a pair of binary classifiers (one vs. two users, and one vs. two hands of the same user). We evaluated a variety of classifiers, including k-Nearest Neighbors (kNN), Support Vector Machines (SVM), Decision Trees (iD3), and Logistic Regression. We found that a kNN classifier [6] had the best performance, and made use of a pair of binary classifiers (rather than a multiclass classifier to determine both user and hand classifications) in order to be able to independently tune the features used by each classifier. Our classifiers were trained on a dataset collected with known ground truths; details are provided in the Evaluation section of the paper.

To correctly classify more than two touches, we first classify all possible pairs of two touches using the binary classifiers. Because touch origin is transitive (i.e., if touches A and B are from the same user, and touches B and C are from the same user, we know all three are from the same user), we can assign origins to all touches. This technique scales well with increasing numbers of touch points, and we have tested it for up to four touch points (one touch per user from four users).

Multi-frame analysis. We can further improve the accuracy of the classifiers by performing a classification across multiple frames. Our sensor is capable of producing data at a frame rate of about 350 Hz, and the standard for most displays is 60 Hz. As such, we can group up to five frames together without compromising the standard frame rate for most touch devices. We use a rolling window to group multiple consecutive frames, and a majority voting system tracks the label allotments within each group; this prevents brief classification errors from impacting the final result.

Output of GhostID attributes. We output a set of attributes for each touch point, which allows the application layer to make use of our classifications. Once we output this information, *GhostID* processing can be discontinued until there is a change in the set of touch points (e.g., a new touch point appears), and thereby provide a *touch grouping* level of persistence.

EVALUATION

In order to validate the performance of our prototype and software pipeline, we conducted a study to measure the accuracy of the classifications against known ground truths (i.e., sensor signals captured with known touch origins). We collected a smaller set of initial training data, followed by a larger dataset used for our accuracy evaluation.

Training Data Collection

Our training datasets consists of two parts. The first dataset contained single user data: two touches from two fingers on the same hand vs. two touches from fingers on different hands. The second dataset consisted of data for two users, and contained single touches from pairs of users. We collected both sets of data using 6 participants. All 15 possible combinations of participants were tested in a round-robin design. The data from these experiments was used to build the models used by both classifiers.

Accuracy Study

This study evaluated the accuracy of *GhostID* differentiating touches from one, two, and three simultaneous users, as well as distinguishing one vs. two hands from a single user. Our study consisted of 21 participants (16 males and 5 females) with a mean age of 25 (sd=4) recruited from the local community. Participants were compensated \$20. All participants had previous experience with capacitive touch devices.

Apparatus

We used the 10-inch *GhostID* prototype shown in Figure 5a, which is based on an opaque touch sensor with an overhead projector. A desktop workstation with a 3.6 GHz Intel i7 CPU and 16 GB of RAM running Microsoft Windows 10 was used to log the data using a custom Java application.

Trials

The participants were randomly divided into seven groups of three. Each experimental session consisted of a single group of three, and each group performed one session. Participants were seated around the *GhostID* prototype, and each was assigned a color to serve as an identifier. A trial consisted of a standard multi-touch gesture. Each trial lasted for ten seconds, during which time all heatmap data was logged. A color-coded prompt indicated which participant(s) should make what type of gesture. Gestures were illustrated using arrows, and participants moved their fingers along the specified paths, thereby providing consistent gesture sizes.

The selected gestures were traditional multi-touch gestures: a straight swipe gesture with the index finger; a curved swipe gesture with the index finger; a pinch gesture with the index finger and thumb; two finger (index and middle) scroll; and three finger (index, middle, and ring) tap-and-hold. All gestures were performed with the right hand, unless indicated otherwise.

Design

A group session consisted of three parts. The first part involved participants interacting with the sensor individually. The second part involved all three possible pairs of participants interacting with the sensor. The third part involved all three participants interacting with the sensor simultaneously.

Part 1: Single user hand differentiation

Two types of single user gestures were performed: pinch, and two finger scroll. A total of 12 trials were run, which were performed across the entire sensor area.

Pinch. The participants were asked to perform a pinch (back and forth in both directions) using their right index finger and thumb. Participants were then asked to do the same pinch gesture using their right index finger and left thumb. A right index finger and left thumb pinch is not a common gesture; most users would be more likely to use their left index finger for a two-handed pinch. However, we elected to use the left thumb to avoid introducing an additional variable into our comparison, since an index finger would have had a very different touch footprint than the thumb used for the one-handed pinch.

Swipe. The participants were asked to do a two finger swipe back and forth using their right index and middle fingers, and then using their index fingers from their left and right hands.

Part 2: Two-user differentiation

Participants were asked to sit facing each other and perform simultaneous gestures. The positions of the participants were switched half-way through the session to remove any positional bias, and every participant performed gestures across the entire sensor surface. The gestures performed by each participant were: one finger swipe, one finger curved swipe, two finger pinch, and two finger swipe. Because our current prototype cannot perform touch discrimination on touches that are aligned in the same column of the sensor (see Limitations section for a discussion of this issue), we positioned the gestures to avoid this configuration.

Part 3: Three-user differentiation

All three participants were asked to sit around three sides of the sensor and perform simultaneous gestures. Limited physical space on the sensor precluded gestures with a large surface area, so participants performed a one finger swipe. Positions were rotated so that each participant performed the gesture in all four corners of the sensor.

Summary

In total, our dataset contained:

4 gestures × 3 individuals	*(Part 1)*
+ 4 gestures × 2 locations × 3 pairs	*(Part 2)*
+ 1 gestures × 4 locations × 1 triplet	*(Part 3)*
= 40 trials/session	

× 7 sessions (21 participants total)
= 280 trials

× ~2,174 frames/trial
= 608,720 frames

Results

Because each trial has a known ground truth, we can benchmark our classifiers.

When examining a single frame, our hand classifier (one hand vs. two hands) was able to correctly identify the origin of two touch points with a precision of 0.77 (recall = 0.76).

Table 1 shows the performance of our multi-user classifier for two and three touch points. Each column shows the results for one experimental group (each with 3 participants) and each row shows the results for a category of touch points. Averaging across all groups, we were able to differentiate touches from two users 94.9% of the time (sd=10.7%) and three users 98.5% of the time (sd=2.4%); overall precision and recall are shown in the rightmost columns of Table 1. The performance across the groups was observed to be consistent, except for groups 2 and 4. This change in performance is due to perspiration in the hands of one participant in each of those groups (P4 and P10). This moisture was absorbed by the vellum sheet used in the current *GhostID* prototype, and generated spurious signals from the sensor that swamped the relatively weak ghost signals.

If we exclude trials from P4 and P10, we achieve an overall performance of 99.45% (sd=0.6%) for differentiating two touches from two users, and 99.41% (sd=0.5%) performance for differentiating three touches from three different users. Despite the impact of the perspiration on the two participants, we do not consider it a problem moving forward, since the vellum is not a required component of the system. Future iterations will use a glass top layer, and therefore will not be subject to the same effects. Moreover, perspiration is not unique to our techniques. As an example, FTIR [12] is also susceptible to erroneous finger classification due to finger residues if not properly constructed (e.g., a malleable glue overlay of the FTIR surface to evenly distribute the finger pressure and keep finger residues away from the sensing surface).

Our 350 Hz sensor could use a window size (i.e., the number of frames used by the voting system) as large as 5 while maintaining 60 Hz output. In order to select our window size, we performed an analysis using window sizes between 1 and 100. As expected, we see an improvement in performance when using multiple frames, but we do not see significant improvements using more than 4 frames. All of the reported measurers in this paper are therefore based on a 4 frame window. Finally, although we tested our system with three users simultaneously interacting with the sensor, the *GhostID* technology is scalable to many users and is only limited by the device form factor.

	G1	*G2*	*G3*	*G4*	*G5*	*G6*	*G7*	*Precision*	*Recall*
1 user 2 fingers	0.98	0.99	0.92	0.82	0.95	0.88	0.94	0.92	0.94
2 users 2 fingers	0.99	0.71	0.99	0.96	0.99	1.00	1.00	0.95	0.92
2 users 3 fingers	0.86	0.88	0.88	0.64	0.84	0.89	0.97	0.85	0.98
3 users 3 fingers	1.00	1.00	0.99	0.93	1.00	0.99	1.00	0.99	0.86

Table 1. Precision rates for user differentiation for each of our seven session groups. The overall precision and recall across all groups are shown in the rightmost columns.

Techniques to improve differentiation

The accuracy can be further increased with simple heuristics. For example, there are location constraints associated with human anatomy; if touch points are at a sufficient distance from each other, they cannot belong to the same hand. These techniques were not used in the classifier, but future work will leverage this information to improve recognition.

In addition, the accuracy of our single user classifier could be improved with individualized per-user classifier training, since individuals tend to touch with different amounts of pressure and surface area. While this tailoring could not be used in a generic "walk up" situation, it could be useful for personal devices.

ENABLED TECHNIQUES AND SCENARIOS

In this section we discuss some of the interaction techniques we have prototyped using *GhostID*. *GhostID* can extend and enhance some existing techniques that already exist on a variety of sizes of traditional capacitive touchscreens, and can also enable new interaction techniques for mobile devices that are not possible on traditional touch devices, including techniques previously limited to specialized multi-user systems such as the DiamondTouch.

Handling Another Hand

These techniques leverage *GhostID*'s ability to differentiate between single-handed and bimanual interaction by one user.

Single handed mode. The ability to differentiate hands can be used to ignore undesired touches from the non-dominant hand that is holding the device. Accidental activation with the non-dominant hand is very common on most touch devices [43], and can interfere with the user experience. For instance, it can be difficult to hold a larger touchscreen device (e.g., a tablet) by its edges without inadvertently activating UI elements near the sides of the screen. With *GhostID* the user can hold the device without having to adjust their grip to avoid touching the screen. This is particularly useful for edge-to-edge touch screens where fringe contacts cannot be avoided.

Bimanual interactions. In use cases where a single user explicitly intends to interact using both hands, *GhostID* can provide each hand with a different functionality. For instance, the index finger on the dominant hand could be used as a drawing pen while fingers on the non-dominant hand could be used as an eraser or as a mechanism to open a contextual menu [2, 21].

Handling Another User's Hands

GhostID also enables a rich set of multi-user scenarios as depicted in Figure 7.

Ignoring secondary users. People frequently share content on a touchscreen by showing their device to someone else. However, it is quite easy for the second person to unintentionally generate touch input in the process (e.g., by pointing at something) and negatively impact the application (e.g., dismissing a full-screen image, deleting an email message, etc.) [2, 27]. With *GhostID's* ability to distinguish between users, it is possible to ignore the errant touches from the second user. The primary user must still touch the surface with their non-dominant hand to provide continuous *session* level persistence for the duration of the touch, but any additional touch input from other users can now be muted. This allows the secondary user to touch the screen freely without disturbing the contents of the UI.

Handoff. GhostID enables a specific interaction technique when handing off a mobile device to another person [14]. If a user passes a mobile device to someone else, as long as both users are in contact with the device for some moment in time (a natural result of handing something to someone else), *GhostID* will be able to tell that a new person is gripping the device. This information can be used to enable collaborative features or provide privacy protection by switching to a guest mode with restricted access. In order to return to unrestricted access, the primary user would need to re-identify themselves, which is not directly supported by *GhostID*.

Collaboration. GhostID provides explicit support for collaboration scenarios. In large displays, where multiple people can interact at the same time, the notion that two hands belong to the same user can help maintain collaboration by specifically supporting actions that only affect one user. As one example, a drawing application can support multiple users painting collaboratively, but any brush or color changes are only applied to the ink stroke that belongs to the user who changed the settings [13].

In addition, *GhostID* enables a wide range of multi-user tabletop techniques at the *touch-user* level of persistence. Many techniques have previously been explored by researchers using the DiamondTouch. Examples include Morris et al. [26] and Shen et al. [37]. We refer the reader to Benko et al. [3], Morris et al. [25], and Ryall et al. [32] for an extensive list of interaction techniques enabled by DiamondTouch and other multi-touch tabletops.

Handling Gestures

Finally, *GhostID* enables extensions and disambiguations of traditional multi-touch gestures.

Disambiguating gestures. We can support a richer set of gestures by leveraging *GhostID's* ability to determine if two points originate from the same hand, different hands of the same user, or different users. From the point of view of a person interacting with a device, the distinction between these three sets of inputs is obvious. However, from the point of view of a traditional touch sensor, those inputs can often appear to be identical. *GhostID* allows the sensor to disambiguate them, and therefore enables richer gestures. For example, two touch points from a single hand can be mapped to the 'resize' command (i.e., a familiar 'pinch' gesture), while two touch points from a user's left and right hands can be mapped to a 'duplicate command' (Figures 8a and 8b). Furthering this example, two touch points from two different users could tear that object in half (Figure 8c) [21, 26]. Traditional touch technologies would have difficulty distinguishing these scenarios.

Gesture granularity. There are also scenarios in which different gestures can be mapped to related actions [21]. For example, consider navigating a map on a large touch surface. With *GhostID*, different granularities can be encoded in the different variations of the same gesture: zooming by pinching with two fingers from the same hand could provide a fine-grain zoom, while pinching using two hands could provide a coarse zoom.

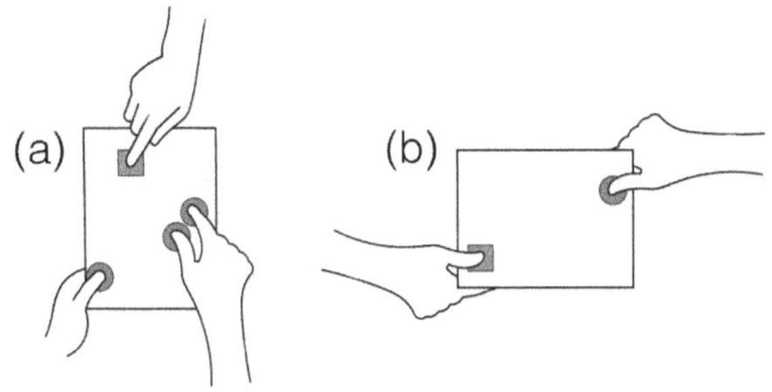

Figure 7. (a) When the primary user interacts using their dominant hand (purple circle), accidental touches from their non-dominant thumb (green circle) or from a second user (orange square) can be ignored. (b) Handing the tablet to someone else triggers a handoff mode with restricted access.

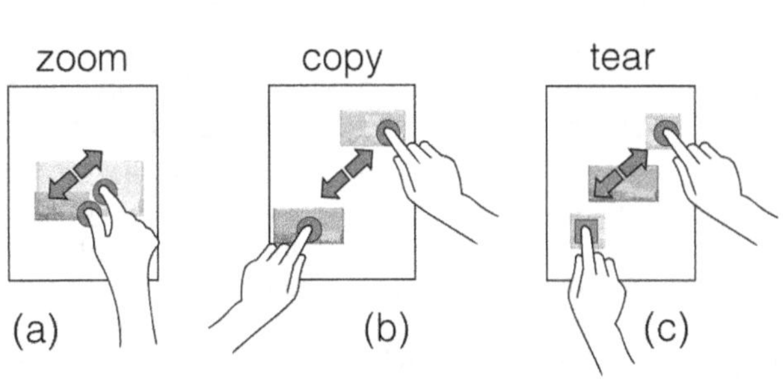

Figure 8. *GhostID* enables disambiguation of otherwise similar touch point paths. (a) A pinch with one hand zooms an image, while (b) two fingers on different hands of one user copies the image, and (c) touches from two different users tears the image.

LIMITATIONS

The current setup is not without limitations. The current implementation only supports a *touch grouping* level of persistence. As we have described in the previous section, this persistence level does enable novel interactions; however, it is not enough for security-based interactions such user identification. From our experience, the ghosting information is not unique to an individual user and, without external hardware that identifies the user, ghosting information alone cannot be used as an identification method.

In order to provide a ghost-free signal for touches originating from two different people, they must be capacitively isolated from each other. While this is the case in most situations, a couple of people can be capacitively coupled by simply holding hands. Once they are in direct contact with each other, signals will travel through both bodies. While in principle we could examine the additional signal attenuation due to the extended signal path and attempt to classify this situation, we have not yet done so. This limitation is most likely to arise in social use cases (e.g., a couple sitting together on a couch), and might actually open an interesting set of collaborative gaming applications [41]. Although we have yet to formally quantify capacitive coupling between individuals, our experience is that indirect contact (e.g., two people leaning on the same wooden table) does not have any impact on *GhostID*. Similarly, grounding a user will create a lower amount of ghosting since some of the signals will be dissipated before they can be re-injected. While we have found that the reduction in signal associated with typical activities (e.g., standing with bare feet on carpet) does not have any impact on our classification, a user who is thoroughly grounded (e.g., touching a grounded metal table frame) will not produce sufficient ghosts.

The current prototype cannot run the *GhostID* classification on touches if more than one of those touches occur in the same row or column because any potential ghosting information is swamped by the signal from the actual touch. We can still register a traditional touch event; we are simply unable to detect if it has a ghost. In practice, this is not a significant limitation, since the lack of ghosting is transient. The ghosting only disappears during individual frames when the fingers are precisely aligned; as soon as they diverge, the ghosts reappear. A brief disappearance of ghosting during a gesture can therefore be mitigated by using a larger rolling window or other heuristics (e.g., positional information). In addition, this issue will be eliminated by forthcoming hardware improvements described below.

Finally, our current prototype sensor suffers reduced accuracy if a user has particularly sweaty hands due to moisture effects on the topmost layer of the sensor. This limitation is unique to the current prototype, and will not be present on future iterations using impermeable top layers.

FUTURE WORK

As future work, we identify two paths of hardware development. First, our sensor needs to be integrated with improved top layer materials, such as glass, or integrated solutions such as ITO. This will strongly reduce the effects of perspiration, and is a necessary step for technology adoption. An ITO-based version of our prototype has been stood up in our lab and, while not ready as of the time of this writing, is showing great promise. Second, our current sensor broadcasts signals on rows and receives signals on columns. This arrangement generally works well, but as discussed above, it cannot detect ghosting information if multiple touches are aligned in the same row or column. A more sophisticated design would eliminate this issue by making several changes. First, each row and column would be connected to a high-speed switch, which would allow the row or column to flip between transmitter or receiver. We then configure the switches so that transmitters and receivers are alternated on both the rows and columns. Finally, we use the switches to flip the transmitter/receiver status of every row and column several times during each frame. This sensor configuration will produce richer ghosting information (helpful information that would allow us to simplify the complexity of the classification algorithms), but also would be able to work around many touch conformations in which touches mask ghosts.

From a software perspective, we intend to explore additional classifiers to further improve our accuracy rates. We also intend to explore additional heuristics to improve both our classification accuracy (e.g., distance between touches), as well as *GhostID's* level of persistence (e.g., time-based heuristics for brief touch removals).

CONCLUSION

We present *GhostID*, a capacitive sensing technique that can distinguish touches from multiple users and even touches from different hands of the same user. Our approach leverages the existing signals from an FDM touch controller, and does not require additional hardware or changes to the sensor itself, making it a potential drop-in replacement for sensing techniques available in the current generation of commercial devices. *GhostID* is presented in the context of a new framework that categorized touch input differentiation. In addition, the value of *GhostID* is illustrated through a description of interaction techniques that are enabled by touch origin differentiation.

Finally, we have just scratched the surface of potential applications for user and hand discrimination. We envision single-user interfaces using hand-discrimination that greatly expand the communication between user and machine, as well as multi-user interfaces that enable simultaneous multi-user interactions that "just work" as expected.

ACKNOWLEDGMENTS

We would like to thank Kate Dowd, and all of our colleagues at Tactual Labs and at the Dynamic Graphics Project lab at the University of Toronto.

REFERENCES

1. Christopher Ackad, Andrew Clayphan, Roberto Martinez Maldonado, and Judy Kay. 2012. Seamless and Continuous User Identification for Interactive Tabletops Using Personal Device Handshaking and Body Tracking. In *CHI '12 Extended Abstracts on Human Factors in Computing Systems (CHI EA '12)*. ACM, New York, NY, USA, 1775–1780. http://dx.doi.org/10.1145/2212776.2223708
2. Michelle Annett, Tovi Grossman, Daniel Wigdor, and George Fitzmaurice. 2011. Medusa: A Proximity-aware Multi-touch Tabletop. In *Proceedings of the 24th Annual ACM Symposium on User Interface Software and Technology (UIST '11)*. ACM, New York, NY, USA, 337–346. http://dx.doi.org/10.1145/2047196.2047240
3. Hrvoje Benko, Meredith Ringel Morris, A. J. Brush, and Andy Wilson. 2009. *Insights on Interactive Tabletops: A Survey of Researchers and Developers*. Technical Report. Microsoft Research.
4. Bojan Blažicaa, Daniel Vladušiča, and Dunja Mladenić. 2013. MTi: A Method for User Identification for Multitouch Displays. *International Journal of Human-Computer Studies* 71, 6 (2013), 691–702. http://dx.doi.org/10.1016/j.ijhcs.2013.03.002
5. Andrew Clayphan, Roberto Martinez-Maldonado, Christopher Ackad, and Judy Kay. 2013. An Approach for Designing and Evaluating a Plug-in Vision-based Tabletop Touch Identification System. In *Proceedings of the 25th Australian Computer-Human Interaction Conference: Augmentation, Application, Innovation, Collaboration (OzCHI '13)*. ACM, New York, NY, USA, 373–382. http://dx.doi.org/10.1145/2541016.2541019
6. Padraig Cunningham and Sarah Jane Delany. 2007. *k-Nearest Neighbour Classifiers*. Technical Report UCD-CSI-2007-4. University College Dublin.
7. Paul Dietz and Darren Leigh. 2001. DiamondTouch: A Multi-user Touch Technology. In *Proceedings of the 14th Annual ACM Symposium on User Interface Software and Technology (UIST '01)*. ACM, New York, NY, USA, 219–226. http://dx.doi.org/10.1145/502348.502389
8. K. C. Dohse, Thomas Dohse, Jeremiah D. Still, and Derrick J. Parkhurst. 2008. Enhancing Multi-user Interaction with Multi-touch Tabletop Displays Using Hand Tracking. In *Proceedings of the First International Conference on Advances in Computer-Human Interaction (ACHI 2008)*. IEEE Computer Society, Washington, DC, USA, 297–302. http://dx.doi.org/10.1109/ACHI.2008.11
9. Philipp Ewerling, Alexander Kulik, and Bernd Froehlich. 2012. Finger and Hand Detection for Multi-touch Interfaces Based on Maximally Stable Extremal Regions. In *Proceedings of the 2012 ACM International Conference on Interactive Tabletops and Surfaces (ITS '12)*. ACM, New York, NY, USA, 173–182. http://dx.doi.org/10.1145/2396636.2396663
10. Clifton Forlines and Chia Shen. 2005. DTLens: Multi-user Tabletop Spatial Data Exploration. In *Proceedings of the 18th Annual ACM Symposium on User Interface Software and Technology (UIST '05)*. ACM, New York, NY, USA, 119–122. http://dx.doi.org/10.1145/1095034.1095055
11. Anhong Guo, Robert Xiao, and Chris Harrison. 2015. CapAuth: Identifying and Differentiating User Handprints on Commodity Capacitive Touchscreens. In *Proceedings of the 2015 International Conference on Interactive Tabletops & Surfaces (ITS '15)*. ACM, New York, NY, USA, 59–62. http://dx.doi.org/10.1145/2817721.2817722
12. Jefferson Y. Han. 2005. Low-cost Multi-touch Sensing Through Frustrated Total Internal Reflection. In *Proceedings of the 18th Annual ACM Symposium on User Interface Software and Technology (UIST '05)*. ACM, New York, NY, USA, 115–118. http://dx.doi.org/10.1145/1095034.1095054
13. Chris Harrison, Munehiko Sato, and Ivan Poupyrev. 2012. Capacitive Fingerprinting: Exploring User Differentiation by Sensing Electrical Properties of the Human Body. In *Proceedings of the 25th Annual ACM Symposium on User Interface Software and Technology (UIST '12)*. ACM, New York, NY, USA, 537–544. http://dx.doi.org/10.1145/2380116.2380183
14. Ken Hinckley, Michel Pahud, Hrvoje Benko, Pourang Irani, François Guimbretière, Marcel Gavriliu, Xiang 'Anthony' Chen, Fabrice Matulic, William Buxton, and Andrew Wilson. 2014. Sensing Techniques for Tablet+Stylus Interaction. In *Proceedings of the 27th Annual ACM Symposium on User Interface Software and Technology (UIST '14)*. ACM, New York, NY, USA, 605–614. http://dx.doi.org/10.1145/2642918.2647379
15. Ken Hinckley, Seongkook Heo, Michel Pahud, Christian Holz, Hrvoje Benko, Abigail Sellen, Richard Banks, Kenton O'Hara, Gavin Smyth, and William Buxton. 2016. Pre-Touch Sensing for Mobile Interaction. In *Proceedings of the 2016 CHI Conference on Human Factors in Computing Systems (CHI '16)*. ACM, New York, NY, USA, 2869–2881. http://dx.doi.org/10.1145/2858036.2858095
16. Christian Holz and Patrick Baudisch. 2013. Fiberio: A Touchscreen That Senses Fingerprints. In *Proceedings of the 26th Annual ACM Symposium on User Interface Software and Technology (UIST '13)*. ACM, New York, NY, USA, 41–50. http://dx.doi.org/10.1145/2501988.2502021

17. Christian Holz, Senaka Buthpitiya, and Marius Knaust. 2015. Bodyprint: Biometric User Identification on Mobile Devices Using the Capacitive Touchscreen to Scan Body Parts. In *Proceedings of the 33rd Annual ACM Conference on Human Factors in Computing Systems (CHI '15)*. ACM, New York, NY, USA, 3011–3014. http://dx.doi.org/10.1145/2702123.2702518

18. Christian Holz and Marius Knaust. 2015. Biometric Touch Sensing: Seamlessly Augmenting Each Touch with Continuous Authentication. In *Proceedings of the 28th Annual ACM Symposium on User Interface Software & Technology (UIST '15)*. ACM, New York, NY, USA, 303–312. http://dx.doi.org/10.1145/2807442.2807458

19. Gierad Laput, Chouchang Yang, Robert Xiao, Alanson Sample, and Chris Harrison. 2015. EM-Sense: Touch Recognition of Uninstrumented, Electrical and Electromechanical Objects. In *Proceedings of the 28th Annual ACM Symposium on User Interface Software & Technology (UIST '15)*. ACM, New York, NY, USA, 157–166. http://dx.doi.org/10.1145/2807442.2807481

20. Darren Leigh, Clifton Forlines, Ricardo Jota, Steven Sanders, and Daniel Wigdor. 2014. High Rate, Low-latency Multi-touch Sensing with Simultaneous Orthogonal Multiplexing. In *Proceedings of the 27th Annual ACM Symposium on User Interface Software and Technology (UIST '14)*. ACM, New York, NY, USA, 355–364. http://dx.doi.org/10.1145/2642918.2647353

21. Nicolai Marquardt, Johannes Kiemer, David Ledo, Sebastian Boring, and Saul Greenberg. 2011. Designing User-, Hand-, and Handpart-aware Tabletop Interactions with the TouchID Toolkit. In *Proceedings of the ACM International Conference on Interactive Tabletops and Surfaces (ITS '11)*. ACM, New York, NY, USA, 21–30. http://dx.doi.org/10.1145/2076354.2076358

22. Paul McAvinney. 1986. *The Sensor Frame – A Gesture-Based Device for the Manipulation of Graphic Objects*. Carnegie-Mellon University.

23. Tobias Meyer and Dominik Schmidt. 2010. IdWristbands: IR-based User Identification on Multi-touch Surfaces. In *Proceedings of the ACM International Conference on Interactive Tabletops and Surfaces (ITS '10)*. ACM, New York, NY, USA, 277–278. http://dx.doi.org/10.1145/1936652.1936714

24. Philipp Mock, Jörg Edelmann, Andreas Schilling, and Wolfgang Rosenstiel. 2014. User Identification Using Raw Sensor Data from Typing on Interactive Displays. In *Proceedings of the 19th International Conference on Intelligent User Interfaces (IUI '14)*. ACM, New York, NY, USA, 67–72. http://dx.doi.org/10.1145/2557500.2557503

25. Meredith Ringel Morris. 2006. *Supporting Effective Interaction with Tabletop Groupware*. Ph.D. Dissertation. Stanford University.

26. Meredith Ringel Morris, Anthony Cassanego, Andreas Paepcke, Terry Winograd, Ann Marie Piper, and Anqi Huang. 2006. Mediating Group Dynamics through Tabletop Interface Design. *IEEE Computer Graphics and Applications* 26, 5 (Sept 2006), 65–73. http://dx.doi.org/10.1109/MCG.2006.114

27. Meredith Ringel Morris, Anqi Huang, Andreas Paepcke, and Terry Winograd. 2006. Cooperative Gestures: Multi-user Gestural Interactions for Co-located Groupware. In *Proceedings of the SIGCHI Conference on Human Factors in Computing Systems (CHI '06)*. ACM, New York, NY, USA, 1201–1210. http://dx.doi.org/10.1145/1124772.1124952

28. Sundar Murugappan, Vinayak, Niklas Elmqvist, and Karthik Ramani. 2012. Extended Multitouch: Recovering Touch Posture and Differentiating Users Using a Depth Camera. In *Proceedings of the 25th Annual ACM Symposium on User Interface Software and Technology (UIST '12)*. ACM, New York, NY, USA, 487–496. http://dx.doi.org/10.1145/2380116.2380177

29. Raf Ramakers, Davy Vanacken, Kris Luyten, Karin Coninx, and Johannes Schöning. 2012. Carpus: A Non-intrusive User Identification Technique for Interactive Surfaces. In *Proceedings of the 25th Annual ACM Symposium on User Interface Software and Technology (UIST '12)*. ACM, New York, NY, USA, 35–44. http://dx.doi.org/10.1145/2380116.2380123

30. Stephan Richter, Christian Holz, and Patrick Baudisch. 2012. Bootstrapper: Recognizing Tabletop Users by Their Shoes. In *Proceedings of the SIGCHI Conference on Human Factors in Computing Systems (CHI '12)*. ACM, New York, NY, USA, 1249–1252. http://dx.doi.org/10.1145/2207676.2208577

31. Volker Roth, Philipp Schmidt, and Benjamin Güldenring. 2010. The IR Ring: Authenticating Users' Touches on a Multi-touch Display. In *Proceedings of the 23Nd Annual ACM Symposium on User Interface Software and Technology (UIST '10)*. ACM, New York, NY, USA, 259–262. http://dx.doi.org/10.1145/1866029.1866071

32. Kathy Ryall, Clifton Forlines, Chia Shen, Meredith Ringel Morris, and Katherine Everitt. 2006. Experiences with and Observations of Direct-Touch Tabletops. In *Proceedings of the First IEEE International Workshop on Horizontal Interactive Human-Computer Systems (TABLETOP '06)*. IEEE Computer Society, Washington, DC, USA, 89–96. http://dx.doi.org/10.1109/TABLETOP.2006.12

33. Napa Sae-Bae, Kowsar Ahmed, Katherine Isbister, and Nasir Memon. 2012. Biometric-rich Gestures: A Novel Approach to Authentication on Multi-touch Devices. In *Proceedings of the SIGCHI Conference on Human Factors in Computing Systems (CHI '12)*. ACM, New York, NY, USA, 977–986. http://dx.doi.org/10.1145/2207676.2208543

34. Munehiko Sato, Ivan Poupyrev, and Chris Harrison. 2012. Touché: Enhancing Touch Interaction on Humans, Screens, Liquids, and Everyday Objects. In *Proceedings of the SIGCHI Conference on Human Factors in Computing Systems (CHI '12)*. ACM, New York, NY, USA, 483–492. http://dx.doi.org/10.1145/2207676.2207743

35. Dominik Schmidt, Fadi Chehimi, Enrico Rukzio, and Hans Gellersen. 2010. PhoneTouch: A Technique for Direct Phone Interaction on Surfaces. In *Proceedings of the 23nd Annual ACM Symposium on User Interface Software and Technology (UIST '10)*. ACM, New York, NY, USA, 13–16. http://dx.doi.org/10.1145/1866029.1866034

36. Dominik Schmidt, Ming Ki Chong, and Hans Gellersen. 2010. HandsDown: Hand-contour-based User Identification for Interactive Surfaces. In *Proceedings of the 6th Nordic Conference on Human-Computer Interaction: Extending Boundaries (NordiCHI '10)*. ACM, New York, NY, USA, 432–441. http://dx.doi.org/10.1145/1868914.1868964

37. Chia Shen, Katherine Everitt, and Kathleen Ryall. 2003. UbiTable: Impromptu Face-to-Face Collaboration on Horizontal Interactive Surfaces. In *Proceedings of Ubiquitous Computing: 5th International Conference (UbiComp 2003)*. Springer Berlin Heidelberg, Berlin, Germany, 281–288. http://dx.doi.org/10.1007/978-3-540-39653-6_22

38. Daniel Vogel and Ravin Balakrishnan. 2004. Interactive Public Ambient Displays: Transitioning from Implicit to Explicit, Public to Personal, Interaction with Multiple Users. In *Proceedings of the 17th Annual ACM Symposium on User Interface Software and Technology (UIST '04)*. ACM, New York, NY, USA, 137–146. http://dx.doi.org/10.1145/1029632.1029656

39. Ulrich von Zadow, Patrick Reipschläger, Daniel Bösel, Anita Sellent, and Raimund Dachselt. 2016. YouTouch! Low-Cost User Identification at an Interactive Display Wall. In *Proceedings of the International Working Conference on Advanced Visual Interfaces (AVI '16)*. ACM, New York, NY, USA, 144–151. http://dx.doi.org/10.1145/2909132.2909258

40. Tam Vu, Akash Baid, Simon Gao, Marco Gruteser, Richard Howard, Janne Lindqvist, Predrag Spasojevic, and Jeffrey Walling. 2012. Distinguishing Users with Capacitive Touch Communication. In *Proceedings of the 18th Annual International Conference on Mobile Computing and Networking (MobiCom '12)*. ACM, New York, NY, USA, 197–208. http://dx.doi.org/10.1145/2348543.2348569

41. Cody Watts, Ehud Sharlin, and Peter Woytiuk. 2009. Matchmaker: Interpersonal Touch in Gaming. In *Proceedings of the 4th International Conference on E-Learning and Games (Edutainment 2009)*. Springer Berlin Heidelberg, Berlin, Germany, 13–24. http://dx.doi.org/10.1007/978-3-642-03364-3_2

42. Wayne Westerman. 1999. *Hand Tracking, Finger Identification, and Chordic Manipulation on a Multi-touch Surface*. Ph.D. Dissertation. University of Delaware.

43. Daniel Wigdor, Sarah Williams, Michael Cronin, Robert Levy, Katie White, Maxim Mazeev, and Hrvoje Benko. 2009. Ripples: Utilizing Per-contact Visualizations to Improve User Interaction with Touch Displays. In *Proceedings of the 22nd Annual ACM Symposium on User Interface Software and Technology (UIST '09)*. ACM, New York, NY, USA, 3–12. http://dx.doi.org/10.1145/1622176.1622180

44. Daniel Wigdor and Dennis Wixon. 2011. *Brave NUI World: Designing Natural User Interfaces for Touch and Gesture*. Elsevier, New York, NY, USA.

45. Andrew D. Wilson. 2010. Using a Depth Camera as a Touch Sensor. In *Proceedings of the ACM International Conference on Interactive Tabletops and Surfaces (ITS '10)*. ACM, New York, NY, USA, 69–72. http://dx.doi.org/10.1145/1936652.1936665

46. Hong Zhang, Xing-Dong Yang, Barrett Ens, Hai-Ning Liang, Pierre Boulanger, and Pourang Irani. 2012. See Me, See You: A Lightweight Method for Discriminating User Touches on Tabletop Displays. In *Proceedings of the SIGCHI Conference on Human Factors in Computing Systems (CHI '12)*. ACM, New York, NY, USA, 2327–2336. http://dx.doi.org/10.1145/2207676.2208392

47. Zhensong Zhang, Fengjun Zhang, Hui Chen, Jiasheng Liu, Hongan Wang, and Guozhong Dai. 2014. Left and Right Hand Distinction for Multi-touch Tabletop Interactions. In *Proceedings of the 19th International Conference on Intelligent User Interfaces (IUI '14)*. ACM, New York, NY, USA, 47–56. http://dx.doi.org/10.1145/2557500.2557525

Essence: Olfactory Interfaces for Unconscious Influence of Mood and Cognitive Performance

Judith Amores
MIT Medialab,
Cambridge, MA, USA
amores@mit.edu

Pattie Maes
MIT Medialab,
Cambridge, MA, USA
pattie@mit.edu

ABSTRACT
The sense of smell is perhaps the most pervasive of all senses, but it is also one of the least understood and least exploited in HCI. We present Essence, the first olfactory computational necklace that can be remotely controlled through a smartphone and can vary the intensity and frequency of the released scent based on biometric or contextual data. This paper discusses the role of smell in designing pervasive systems that affect one's mood and cognitive performance while being asleep or awake. We present a set of applications for this type of technology as well as the implementation of the olfactory display and the supporting software. We also discuss the results of an initial test of the prototype that show the robustness and usability of Essence while wearing it for long periods of time in multiple environments.

ACM Classification Keywords
H.5.m. Information Interfaces and Presentation: Miscellaneous

Author Keywords
Olfactory Interfaces; Wearable Computers; Behavior Change; Unconscious; Pervasive; Prototyping/Implementation; Fabrication; Fashion/Clothing; Health - Wellbeing; Smell.

INTRODUCTION
A considerable amount of effort in HCI has been directed to make the user experience more seamless, natural and integrated in our physical lives. When designing user interfaces, we aim to create tools that will enable the user to accomplish certain tasks with a minimum effort, time and difficulty. When evaluating these tools, we take into account individuals perception of the system such as utility, easy of use and efficiency. However, we tend to consider the user as a conscious thinking mind. In reality, a lot of our perception of the environment and our behavior is unconscious and does not involve deliberate rational thinking.

CHI 2017, May 06-11, 2017, Denver, CO, USA.
 ISBN 978-1-4503-4655-9/17/05 ...$15.00.
DOI: http://dx.doi.org/10.1145/3025453.3026004

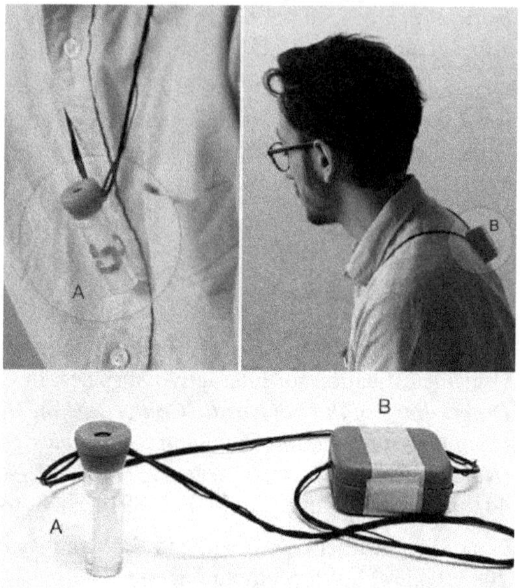

Figure 1. The Essence necklace. (A) A 3D printed cover holds the piezoelectric on top of the cotton stick filter, soaking up the fragrance from the container. Once the fragrance is depleted, the user can easily unscrew the cap and refill the container. (B) Back part of the necklace that contains the micro-controller and the rest of electronics to control the release of scent.

We perceive the world indirectly by processing and interpreting the raw data from our senses and our thoughts and behavior are frequently biased by our senses [21, 26, 25].

Among the so-called "five senses", olfactory perception takes an exceptional position in the neurological processing of sensory stimuli. The olfactory bulb has direct connections to the two brain areas that control emotions and memories: the amygdala and hippocampus [37]. Interestingly the sense of sound, sight and touch do not pass through these brain areas, they are routed through the thalamus which is the reason why sound, sight and touch interrupt sleep [27]. This makes smell an especially interesting modality to use in human-machine interaction during sleep as well as wake states because it is processed by the brain but does not disrupt the ongoing brain processes as easily.

Scent has a hidden power in our behavior and the unconscious. Positive and negative emotions not only transfer between individuals through mimicry of vision and hearing but also through smell [11, 32, 12]. Other studies show that stress and anxiety can be reduced with the use of essential oils [36, 29]. Recent findings found that a single night of olfactory aversive conditioning during sleep, significantly reduced cigarette-smoking behavior in the wakefulness state and persisted for several days [5]. Such functional studies continue to remain in the realms of research laboratories. The main aim of Essence was to fabricate a technology that people could use in their daily life, without the need for medical assistance nor burdensome devices. In this paper we describe the design and implementation of the prototype and describe potential applications for HCI.

RELATED WORK

While scent has been widely explored in Psychology, Neuroscience, Chemistry and Art, the olfactory system has been less appreciated in the world of personal technologies. Current personal, wearable devices that promote wellbeing, such as fitness and sleep trackers, mostly make use of visual, auditory and the haptic stimuli. The HCI research community has formerly looked into some of the challenges and possibilities for smell-based technology [33, 24, 23]. Most recent HCI research and product development efforts have focused on enabling scent to become part of digital communications [4, 38, 34, 42, 9, 10]. Most systems use off the shelf aromas in their prototypes, focusing research efforts on the device itself. Ranasinghe et al. [35] explored the use of smell for digital communication, enabling the sharing of smell over the Internet. By recreating smell though form, Clayodor [22] explores the possibility of form as a user-controlled navigator for smell.

The state of the art in smell-enhanced technologies is mostly limited to non-portable and non-fashionable devices that cannot be comfortably used in everyday life situations. Some artists have explored the use of scent in fashion or using the body as an atomizer [41, 28]. ICT Scent Collar [20] it is a scent delivery device in the form factor of a collar or bib that is meant to be used in a virtual environment. The "Smoke Dress" by artist Anouk Wipprecht [44] releases a cloud of smoke when it detects a person approaching. "Climate Dress" has an array of LEDs that light up depending on the CO2 levels in the air [13].

We propose Essence, a wearable olfactory display that was designed to be lightweight, fashionable and comfortable enough for people to be used in daily life. The main contributions that are distinct from previous work are the design of a fashionable olfactory necklace that is wirelessly-controlled and can be used in every-day life situations as well as the automated control of that device based on contextual and physiological data of the user. We also propose a set of novel applications for this type of technology that make use of biometric and contextual information in order to intervene with scent in particular instances.

SYSTEM DESCRIPTION

In order to make the prototype aesthetically appealing and as light as possible, most of the electronic components and the battery of the necklace are placed at the back of the neck so as to be hidden (see Figure 1).

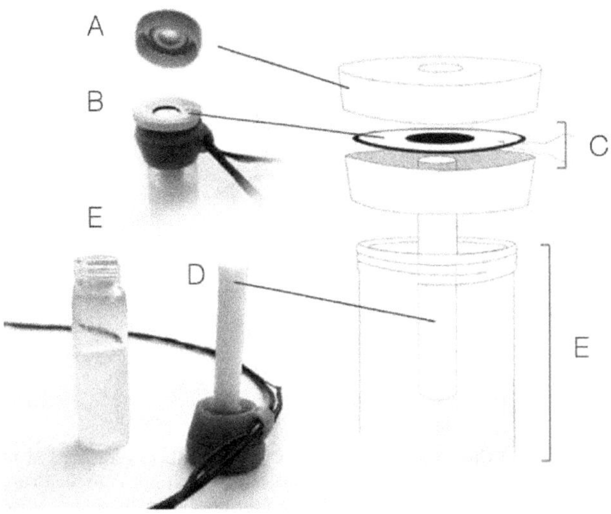

Figure 2. (A) 3D printed cover that protects and holds (B) a piezoelectric transducer with a small metal plate that vibrates at high frequency to release the fragrance. The piezo is connected to the rest of the electronics through the thread. (C) are the GND and Vcc cables. (D) is the cotton stick filter that soaks the liquid from the container (E).

A variety of form factors and materials were considered to make the prototype pretty, functional and comfortable (see Figure 3). One of our goals was to make the necklace as small and lightweight as possible so as to be comfortable enough to be worn on the neck all day and potentially all night, so that ideally the back part of the necklace would be flexible and neck-adaptable (see Figure 3 C).

Scent Release

The front part of the necklace holds a container with an encapsulated piezoelectric transducer that controls the release of the scent (see Figure 2). In order to make the piezoelectric vibrate, it needs a frequency of 100KHz, 10VAC (20Vpp). Alternating current (AC) voltage makes the plate oscillate at the same frequency and produce ultrasonic sound. These ultrasonic sounds are inaudible to the user, but they are capable of breaking the water into small particles that look like vapor. Therefore, the device transforms the fragrance/essential oil from the container into a fine mist, instantaneously distributing the scent all around the necklace. Essence has 7ml capacity that can operate for 27-28 hours with continuous 1-20-sec release. The default duty cycle frequency of 1 second of scent every 20 seconds was chosen to assure there was enough time in between burst for the smell to fade, while being enough noticeable for the average user (avoiding habituation and desensitization [8]).

Scent Selection

We used 3 different types of scents. One is natural essential oil commonly used in Aromatherapy (like lavender, peppermint, eucalyptus, etc.), the second type are fragrances, perfumes and diluted oils. Finally, we tried some experimental odor-less scents and pheromone perfumes that claim to use a patented blend of "human pheromones" including Androstadienone,

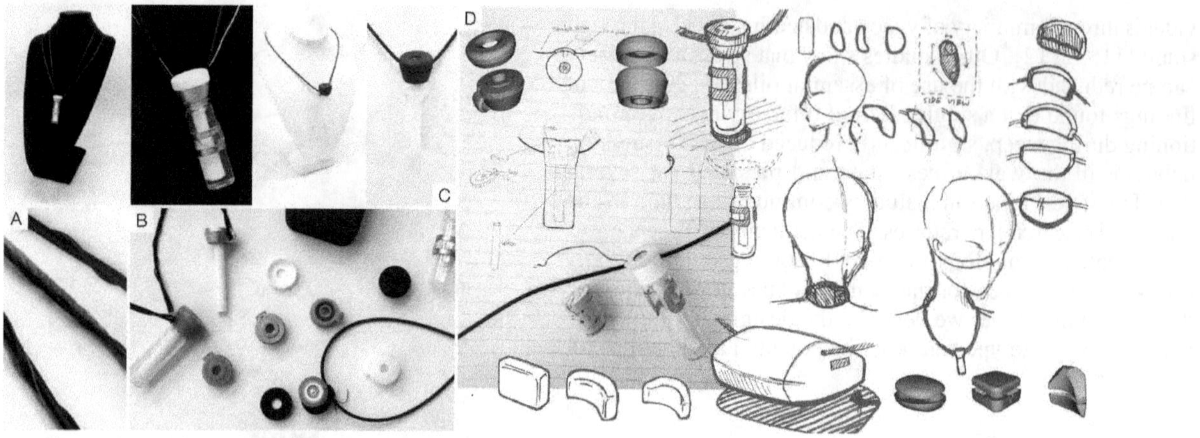

Figure 3. A) Close up of the different braided cables and cords of the Essence necklace (including conductive cord and Vcc/GND cables). The cord is 2mm diameter made of carbon-black impregnated conductive rubber. B) 3D printed results from Shapeways and Formlabs. C) Final design with small decorative gold/bronze-style accessories. The necklace is approximately located 7 inches from the nose (enough to reach the nose and not be too noticeable by the user). D) Design and fabrication of the Essence necklace.

Androstenol, Androstenone and Androsterone [2, 1]. Aside from pheromone perfumes, Essence can also be used with liquid forms of hormones or other types of medicines such as Oxytocin nasal sprays.

Conductive Thread

Usually jewelry string serves only as a decorative element, the materials used for necklaces or other wearable jewelry do not include electronic components or cables. In this prototype we braided two cables (Vcc and GND) with a conductive rubber cord stretch sensor (see Figure 3.A). Therefore, the thread not only serves as a decorative component but also as a connector between the microcontroller and the piezoelectric. The necklace thread is a key element in the design of the wearable since it transfers power and data from the back part of the necklace to the piezoelectric (front part). The sensor measures stretch forces: as you pull on it, the resistance increases. When these values go over a certain threshold the scent is released. The necklace can also release the scent without manual activation and can be controlled to release scent automatically without user involvement, for example based on physiological sensor data.

Wireless Communication

To endow the necklace with communication capabilities to be remotely controlled through the smartphone Android application, we used a microprocessor that controls the whole system and a Bluetooth Low Energy (BTLE) board that implements the wireless communication with the smartphone. When activated, the default values are 1 second of burst of scent every 20 seconds, additionally the user can manually release extra bursts of scent by pulling the necklace down. The system is powered with a 3.7V Lithium Battery. The user can easily charge the necklace through a small USB micro connector and additionally there is a turn on/off button. The microprocessor is an ATmega32u4, the hardware interface to transfer the commands is UART.

Physiological Data and Context Awareness

The system is capable of releasing scent based on context data from the smartphone such as location (GPS), date and current time. We also experimented with releasing scent based on physiological data such as Heart Rate, Electrodermal Activity and brain activity. For the HR and EDA we used the E4 Wristband [16]. In the case of brain activity we used the EEG MUSE Headband [31] to detect the concentration levels accordingly to the brainwave frequency. We detect when the user is emitting Gamma brainwaves - usually seen in states of peak performance, high focus and concentration. These values increase when the user is focused and directs his/her attention with intensity. We mapped the values from 0 to 1 and synchronized them with the burst of scent.

APPLICATIONS

Sleep and Memory

Sleep has been identified as a state that optimizes the consolidation of memories [40, 14]. Neuroscientists conducted laboratory studies that cued new memories in humans during sleep by presenting an odor that had been presented as context during a prior learning episode, and showed that reactivation indeed causes memory consolidation during sleep [14, 6]. These medical studies suggest that the optimal learning point occurs when memories are processed in SWS (Slow Wave Sleep) and REM sleep (Rapid Eye Movement). Work on [5] supports the need for detecting biometric information of the user to ensure that scent are released at a specific point in time.

Using Essence users could benefit from these studies and experiment outside of laboratories, for example while they are sleeping at their homes. The convenience of having a portable device that can be used anywhere will help to deploy the device for larger number of users and make it possible to analyze the biometric data and contextual information collected by the smartphone.

Learning and Cognitive Performance

It has been proved that peppermint scent promotes a general arousal of attention, and that it causes people to stay focused on their task and increases their concentration [39]. It has also been proven that memory recall can be improved by presenting contextual stimuli that were present at the time memories were recorded [7, 17]. Essence can release a specific scent while a user is studying and then help them retrieve the learned facts by releasing the same scent again. Other use cases could potentially help a person concentrate or focus, like when meditating or doing yoga.

Social Interactions and Immersive Environments

When coupled with Virtual Reality or Mixed Reality, the addition of smell significantly enhances the sense of immersion to augment digital experiences and creates a more complete sensorial experience [45]. Beyond immersive systems we could also use Essence as a subtle way of communication among remote users.

In a physical social interaction, people are constantly using their sense of smell. Even though we are not very aware of doing so, our brain is responding to odors [37, 15]. Odor-less scents like pheromones or hormones can be used to remotely intersect users' realities and perceptions [43, 30, 19]. As previously mentioned in this paper, chemical signals communicate human emotions [11, 12, 32]. We secrete different odors depending on the emotional state that we are in, such as the "smell of fear" or "aggression". We may induce pleasurable scents, mask body odors, or may put subjects into a state of high suggestibility. Using olfactory devices like Essence, the user can have complete control over the secreted scent signals that could potentially trigger stronger social responses between subjects.

As mentioned in the "Physiological Data and Context Awareness" section, Essence is capable of using date, location and time information. A remote user could remotely control the necklace and release the scent at a certain location or time of the day as a means of subliminal messaging and notifications as if "I am thinking of you" or "I am worried". For example, if the user goes to the doctor and stress levels go beyond a certain threshold, the remote wearer could sense the "scent of fear", increasing empathy between them. The remote person could then trigger a nice scent to calm the stressed person down, or the system itself could automatically release a burst of scent when the doctor's location is detected.

Wellbeing

There are a variety of application scenarios related to health purposes ranging from using Essence for mindfulness and meditation or as a personal, wearable device for cold and flu treatment, allergies, asthma or other respiratory problems to beauty treatments like face moisturizer for dry skin. In the same way, we could potentially release the scent of lavender or vanilla to reduce stress levels or pain for diseases like cancer. Studies have already shown that stress and anxiety can be reduced with the use of essential oils. Researchers administrated Heliotropin (a vanilla fragrance) to patients undergoing cancer treatment [36]. The results reported that the administration of fragrance was associated with 63% less anxiety versus placebo effect.

TESTS

We conducted a set of tests to evaluate Essence in a mobile, everyday life context. We were mainly interested in testing the robustness and usability of the prototype for long periods of time in multiple scenarios.

4 participants (men, with a mean of 29 years old) were asked to use the necklace during 3 days in 6 different campus locations (3 indoor and 3 outdoor). The participants reported not using accessories or necklaces in their daily life (a drawback that might bias against the study).

The type of scents used were tea tree, peppermint and rose. The smell selection was based on previous studies that examined how "positive" fragrances induce feelings of relaxation, reduced anxiety and alertness [29, 36, 39].

Evaluation

We used computer-based surveys, questionnaires and in-person final interview to gain an understanding of the participants' perception of the system.

Users were asked to fill out a questionnaire and a survey about their experience wearing the necklace for each one of the environments. The questionnaires asked to rank ease of use, satisfaction and comfort of the necklace.

The questions of the surveys were related to the feel of the necklace and the intensity and frequency of the scent to identify opportunities for improvement. Some of the questions related to the olfactory experiences included awareness of the scent and the necklace, intensity, pleasantness, distraction or to what extent the scent helped them relax or focus.

Results

The results of the initial testing of the prototype show that the Essence prototype is robust and usable enough to be used for long periods of time in multiple environments. The necklace successfully worked during all the tests and participants ranked the experience of wearing the Essence necklace very positively Figure 4. The results suggest that users generally found easy and effortless to wear the necklace.

User Experience

When asked to describe the experience of wearing the necklace in different environments, participants mentioned: "Effortless, it was nice to feel the good smell from time to time", "Most of the time I completely forgot it was there, except for some moments when the scent suddenly became more noticeable, either stronger or just different. However even when it was noticeable it was pleasant, it never became an inconvenience." "The scents were pleasant and relaxing and otherwise I hardly noticed it was there." "It was very seamless, and enhanced the environment nicely." "The necklace wasn't too invasive. I did feel some weight of the device in the back of my neck, but quickly forgot about it".

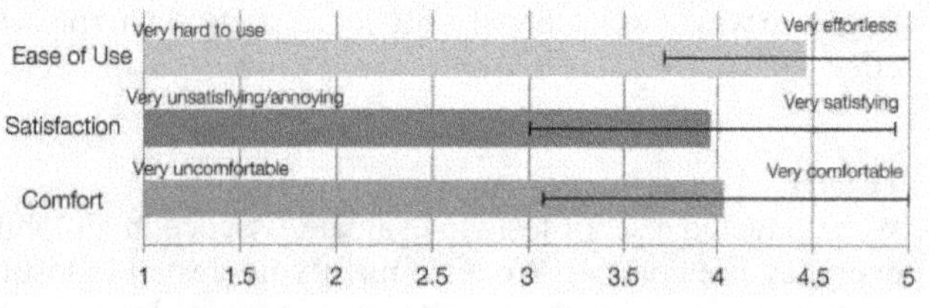

Figure 4. The chart show user feedback (P=4) where 5 = very effortless, very satisfying and very comfortable, suggesting that users found the system easy to use and were satisfied overall with the experience of wearing the necklace. Ease of use (mean = 4.464, std = 0.744), satisfaction (mean = 3.964, std = 0.961), and overall comfort (mean = 4.035, std = 0.961).

Awareness

When asked to rank how aware they were of the necklace, most of the users mentioned that they were not aware (mean of 2, were 1 is "not at all", and 5 is "very much"). However, although the mean was 2, one of the participants ranked negatively the necklace and mentioned he was aware of it all time because the scent was too strong for him, especially the Peppermint (mean of 3.4). Another interesting thing happened with P11, he ranked awareness in all situations "1" - as if he was not aware of the necklace, however in day 2, he ranked the necklace as "5" - very aware, because the scent was "too strong" for him. Interestingly, the type of scent and intensity were exactly the same in day 1, but then he ranked it as "1" - not aware of the necklace. That day, in the report he wrote, "I am almost not aware of the necklace. However, I could smell the scent much less at the beginning. Seems like I need some time to get used to the smell. Maybe it's because I was biking right before doing the study."

Intensity and Frequency of Scent

The prototype released a burst of scent every 20 seconds (1 second per burst). As mentioned in the System Description section of this paper, this is a default duty cycle that can be changed by the user. In the surveys we asked if they would increase or decrease the intensity or timing of every burst of scent. The results were completely different for each person. For example, P10 would increase the intensity of scent in all conditions, whereas for P12 the scents were too strong so he wanted to decrease them. In the same condition, P12 ranked as "decrease intensity during this session. Too strong!", while the rest of participants mentioned "just about right" or "increase". Based on that feedback we confirmed how important was for the user to be able to control the intensity and duration of the scent depending on their preferences.

Use cases and Feedback

In the final survey, participants were asked if they would wear the essence necklace in their daily life and in what kind of cases they would use it. Some participants responded they would use the necklace for meditation sessions, relaxing and concentration. Some users mentioned they would prefer to use it in private spaces since they do not usually wear necklaces in public. Potential improvements people mentioned were the ability to control intensity, and make the back part of the necklace smaller and more compact.

Limitations and Findings

We conducted an initial testing of the prototype with a small number of participants that shows a robust prototype that can be used in every-day life situations. The user tests show an overall comfort, ease of use and satisfaction wearing the necklace. Further study is required, including a larger sample size and increased variety in participants' demographics (olfactory perception differs by gender, age and culture [18]).

In the following paragraphs we provide some of the qualitative findings, limitations and recommendations for future designs of olfactory devices based on users experiences'.

Customizable Bursts

In general, during the study and while interviewing people, we corroborated how different people's perceptions are in regard to smell. While for one person the scent was not strong enough, for the other it was too much. While some of them loved the Peppermint scent, others did not like it at all. The preferences even vary from day to day within the same person. The feedback provided through the final interview and surveys show the importance for future designs of olfactory devices of creating systems that can be controlled by the user depending on their preferences (augmenting/decreasing intensity and frequency of the scent like Essence).

Limitations and Potential Improvements

Some potential limitations of the current prototype are the refilling need and the limit of one scent at a time. Although the refilling need depends on the duty-cycle chosen by the user, it is important to take into account for future designs of olfactory interfaces habituation and desensitization and the limits of intensity and frequency of scent (mentioned in the Scent Release section of this paper).

Promising improvements for future designs of olfactory devices include the miniaturization of the back part of the necklace, the use of flexible materials or soft electronics and to have a design that can accommodate multiple scents in one. These improvements are specially relevant for night usage and to enable use of scent for multiple use cases without the need to replace the container (e.g. peppermint to focus while studying, lavender to relax, and rose for sleep).

CONCLUSION AND FUTURE VISION

We presented Essence, a wearable olfactory display that can be controlled manually or automatically to release subtle bursts of scent. We designed a fashionable and comfortable necklace that can be used in daily life. The results of the tests show that it is important for future olfactory devices to let the users change the default duty cycle and to have a customizable system like Essence.

In future work we would like to deploy several of the Essence prototypes so we can conduct user studies in different environments, for longer periods of time and while the person is awake and sleeping. We also want to further develop the smartphone app so the user can configure biosensor-data based release rules similar to https://ifttt.com/. For example, "if X and Y then release scent for Z intensity and W frequency".

The result could be personal, wearable devices that will promote health and wellbeing in very different ways than today's fitness and sleep trackers. We believe that in the future users will be able to use this kind of systems to facilitate memory consolidation for learning purposes, enhance mood and wellbeing. We hope Essence will encourage discussion within the community and open up contributions in the promising area of olfactory devices for HCI systems.

ACKNOWLEDGMENTS

This work was partially funded by Facebook. The views and conclusions contained herein are those of the authors and should not be interpreted as necessarily representing the official policies or endorsements, either expressed or implied, of Facebook. A full list of acknowledgments can be found in [3].

REFERENCES

1. 2016. Love Scent. (2016). http://love-scent.com/
2. 2016. Raw Chemistry. (2016). https://rawchemistry.com/
3. Judith Amores. 2016. *Essence : Olfactory interfaces for unconscious influence of mood and cognitive performance*. Master's thesis. Massachusetts Institute of Technology. http://hdl.handle.net/1721.1/106061
4. Aromajoin. 2016. AromaShooter. (2016). https://aromajoin.com/
5. A. Arzi, Y. Holtzman, P. Samnon, N. Eshel, E. Harel, and N. Sobel. 2014. Olfactory Aversive Conditioning during Sleep Reduces Cigarette-Smoking Behavior. *Journal of Neuroscience* 34, 46 (2014), 15382–15393. DOI: http://dx.doi.org/10.1523/JNEUROSCI.2291-14.2014
6. Anat Arzi, Limor Shedlesky, Mor Ben-Shaul, Khitam Nasser, Arie Oksenberg, Ilana S Hairston, and Noam Sobel. 2012. Humans can learn new information during sleep. *Nature neuroscience* 15, 10 (2012), 1460–5. DOI: http://dx.doi.org/10.1038/nn.3193
7. Benedict Carey. 2014. *How We Learn: The Surprising Truth About When, Where, and Why It Happens.* Random House, New York, USA.
8. Dipesh et al. Chaudhury. 2010. Olfactory Bulb Habituation to Odor Stimuli. *Behavioral neuroscience* (2010).
9. Parsani R. Pandey A. V. Roman X. Cheok-A. D. Choi, Y. 2013. Light perfume: a fashion accessory for synchronization of nonverbal communication.. In *Leonardo*. 439–444.
10. Yongsoon Choi, Adrian David Cheok, Xavier Roman, The Anh Nguyen, Kenichi Sugimoto, and Veronica Halupka. 2011. Sound Perfume: Designing a Wearable Sound and Fragrance Media for Face-to-face Interpersonal Interaction. In *Proceedings of the 8th International Conference on Advances in Computer Entertainment Technology (ACE '11)*. ACM, New York, NY, USA, Article 4, 8 pages. DOI: http://dx.doi.org/10.1145/2071423.2071428
11. J. H. B. de Groot, M. A. M. Smeets, A. Kaldewaij, M. J. A. Duijndam, and G. R. Semin. 2012. Chemosignals Communicate Human Emotions. *Psychological Science* 23, 11 (2012), 1417–1424. DOI: http://dx.doi.org/10.1177/0956797612445317
12. J. H. B. de Groot, M. A. M. Smeets, M. J. Rowson, P. J. Bulsing, C. G. Blonk, J. E. Wilkinson, and G. R. Semin. 2015. A Sniff of Happiness. *Psychological Science* (2015), 0956797614566318–. DOI: http://dx.doi.org/10.1177/0956797614566318
13. Diffus Design. 2009. Climate Dress. (2009). http://www.diffus.dk/climate-dress/
14. Susanne Diekelmann and Jan Born. 2010. The memory function of sleep. *Nature reviews. Neuroscience* 11, 2 (2010), 114–26. DOI: http://dx.doi.org/10.1038/nrn2762
15. Dina Marie Zemke, Stowe Shoemaker. 2008. A Social Atmosphere: Ambient Scent's Effect on Social Interaction. *Cornell Hospitality Quarterly.* (2008).
16. Empatica. 2016. E4 Wristband. (2016). http://www.smell.dating/
17. Kleinbard Jeff. Erdelyi, Matthew H. 1978. Has Ebbinghaus decayed with time? The growth of recall (hypermnesia) over days . *Journal of Experimental Psychology: Human Learning and Memory* (1978), 275–289.
18. Camille Ferdenzi, S. Craig Roberts, Annett Schirmer, Sylvain Delplanque, Sezen Cekic, Christelle Porcherot, Isabelle Cayeux, David Sander, and Didier Grandjean. 2013. Variability of Affective Responses to Odors: Culture, Gender, and Olfactory Knowledge. *Chemical Senses* 38, 2 (2013), 175–186. DOI: http://dx.doi.org/10.1093/chemse/bjs083
19. Camille et al. Ferdenzi. 2016. Androstadienone's influence on the perception of facial and vocal attractiveness is not sex specific. *Psychoneuroendocrinology* 66 (2016).
20. Inc. with Donat-Pierre Luigi. Jacki Morie. Fabricated by Anthrotronix. 2005. ICT Scent Collar. (2005). http://ict.usc.edu/wp-content/uploads/212/03/ScentCollarBrochure1.pdf
21. Daniel. Kahneman. 2012. *Thinking, Fast and Slow.*
22. E. Amores J. Leigh S. W. Benavides-X. Maes P. Ishii H. Kao, C. Dreshaj. 2015. clayodor : Retrieving Scents through the Manipulation of Malleable Material. *TEI 2015* (2015). DOI: http://dx.doi.org/10.1145/2677199.2688814
23. J. "Jofish." Kaye. 2001. *Symbolic Olfactory Display.* Master's thesis. Massachusetts Institute of Technology, Cambridge, MA.
24. J. "Jofish." Kaye. 2004. Making Scents: Aromatic output for HCI. *Magazine Interactions. Volume 11, Issue 1* (2004), 48–61.

25. Thalma Lobel. 2014. *Sensation: The New Science of Physical Intelligence.*

26. Kevin Lynch. 2015. Subliminal: How Your Unconscious Mind Rules Your Behavior, by Leonard Mlodinow (Vintage Books, 2013). *Journal of Consciousness Studies* 22, 9-10 (2015), 229–234.

27. Rachel S. Herz Mary A. Carskadon. 2004. Minimal olfactory perception during sleep: why odor alarms will not work for humans. *Sleep* (2004).

28. Lucy McRae. 2011. Swallowable Parfum. (2011). http://swallowableparfum.com

29. Tiffany Field Maria Hernandez-reif Saul Schanberg Cynthia Kuhn Mary Galamaga Virginia McAdam Robert Galamaga Miguel A. Diego, Nancy Aaron Jones. 1998. Aromatherapy positively affects mood, EEG patterns of alertness and math computations. *International Journal of Neuroscience* (1998).

30. K Mizuno, N Mizuno, T Shinohara, and M Noda. 2004. Mother-infant skin-to-skin contact after delivery results in early recognition of own mother's milk odour. *Acta Paediatrica* (2004).

31. Muse. 2016. Muse, the brain sensing headband. (2016). http://www.choosemuse.com/

32. Smiljana Mutic, Valentina Parma, Yvonne F. Brünner, and Jessica Freiherr. 2016. You smell dangerous: Communicating fight responses through human chemosignals of aggression. *Chemical Senses* 41, 1 (2016), 35–43. DOI: http://dx.doi.org/10.1093/chemse/bjv058

33. Marianna Obrist, Alexandre N Tuch, and Kasper Hornbaek. 2014. Opportunities for Odor: Experiences with Smell and Implications for Technology. *Proceedings of the SIGCHI Conference on Human Factors in Computing Systems* (2014), 2843–2852. DOI: http://dx.doi.org/10.1145/2556288.2557008

34. Onotes. 2015. Ophone. (2015). http://www.onotes.com/ophone2/

35. Nimesha Ranasinghe, Kasun Karunanayaka, Adrian David Cheok, Owen Noel Newton Fernando, Hideaki Nii, and Ponnampalam Gopalakrishnakone. 2011. Digital Taste and Smell Communication. In *Proceedings of the 6th International Conference on Body Area Networks (BodyNets '11)*. ICST (Institute for Computer Sciences, Social-Informatics and Telecommunications Engineering), ICST, Brussels, Belgium, Belgium, 78–84. http://dl.acm.org/citation.cfm?id=2318776.2318795

36. William H. Redd, Sharon L. Manne, Bruce Peters, Paul B. Jacobsen, and Hilary Schmidt. 1994. Fragrance administration to reduce anxiety during MR imaging. *Journal of Magnetic Resonance Imaging* 4, 4 (jul 1994), 623–626. DOI: http://dx.doi.org/10.1002/jmri.1880040419

37. Regina M. Sullivan, Donald A. Wilson, Nadine Ravel, Anne-Marie Mouly., and Bryan Raudenbush. 2015. Olfactory memory networks: form emotional learning to social behaviors. *Front. Behav. Neuroscience 17* (2015).

38. Scentee. 2013. (2013). http://www.scentee.com/

39. Shannon Barker, Palema Grayhem, Jerrod Koon, Jessica Perkins, Allison Whalen and Bryan Raudenbush. 2003. Improved Performance on Clerical Tasks Associated with Administration of Peppermint Odor. *Perceptual and Motor Skills* (2003), 1007–1010.

40. Robert Stickgold. 2012. To sleep, perchance to learn. *Nature* 15, 10 (2012), 1322–1323. DOI: http://dx.doi.org/10.1038/384037a0

41. Jenny Tillotson and Adeline. Andre. 2005. Smart Second Skin. University of the arts London. (2005). http://ualresearchonline.arts.ac.uk/5570/

42. R. Strong W. Gaver. 1996. Feather, scent, and shaker: Supporting simple intimacy. *Proceedings of CSCW'96* (1996).

43. Claus Wedekind, Thomas Seebeck, Florence Bettens, and Alexander J. Paepke. 1995. MHC-Dependent Mate Preferences in Humans. *Proceedings of the Royal Society of London B: Biological Sciences* 260, 1359 (1995), 245–249. DOI: http://dx.doi.org/10.1098/rspb.1995.0087

44. Anouk Wipprecht and Niccolo Casas. 2012. Smoke Dress. (2012). http://www.niccolocasas.com/SMOKE-DRESS/

45. Tomoya Yamada, Satoshi Yokoyama, Tomohiro Tanikawa, Koichi Hirota, and Michitaka Hirose. 2006. Wearable Olfactory Display: Using Odor in Outdoor Environment. In *Proceedings of the IEEE Conference on Virtual Reality (VR '06)*. IEEE Computer Society, Washington, DC, USA, 199–206. DOI: http://dx.doi.org/10.1109/VR.2006.147

Group Touch: Distinguishing Tabletop Users in Group Settings via Statistical Modeling of Touch Pairs

Abigail C. Evans,[1] Katie Davis,[1] James Fogarty,[2] Jacob O. Wobbrock[1]
[1]The Information School, [2]Computer Science & Engineering
DUB Group | University of Washington
Seattle, WA, USA 98195
{abievans, kdavis78, wobbrock}@uw.edu, jfogarty@cs.washington.edu

ABSTRACT
We present *Group Touch*, a method for distinguishing among multiple users simultaneously interacting with a tabletop computer using only the touch information supplied by the device. Rather than *tracking* individual users for the duration of an activity, Group Touch *distinguishes* users from each other by modeling whether an interaction with the tabletop corresponds to either: (1) a new user, or (2) a change in users currently interacting with the tabletop. This reframing of the challenge as distinguishing users rather than tracking and identifying them allows Group Touch to support multi-user collaboration in real-world settings without custom instrumentation. Specifically, Group Touch examines pairs of touches and uses the difference in orientation, distance, and time between two touches to determine whether the same person performed both touches in the pair. Validated with field data from high-school students in a classroom setting, Group Touch distinguishes among users "in the wild" with a mean accuracy of 92.92% (*SD*=3.94%). Group Touch can imbue collaborative touch applications in real-world settings with the ability to distinguish among multiple users.

Author Keywords
Tabletop; modeling; distinguishing users; "in the wild."

ACM Classification Keywords
H.5.3. Group and Organization Interfaces: Collaborative Computing.

INTRODUCTION
Interactive tabletops can support collaboration because of the large, shared interface that multiple people can interact with together [9,22]. However, with the exception of two systems, DiamondTouch [8] and Fiberio [24], tabletops are limited by their inability to identify users. The capacity to distinguish among users is desirable for a number of reasons, ranging from basic usability (e.g., resolving conflicting gestures carried out by different people [32]), to enabling certain application features (e.g., allowing users to separate personal and shared space on the screen [27,40]), to tracking and evaluating an individual's contributions to a group task [29]. For example, in the domain of collaborative classroom education [12], distinguishing among users can enable interventions that help students improve overall group collaboration (Figure 1).

Figure 1. Group Touch can distinguish among users "in the wild" with a mean accuracy of 92.92% (*SD*=3.94%) using only touch information. Pictured above are high school students in a classroom. The challenge of *distinguishing* among users (i.e., knowing one user's touches are different from another's) is a different challenge than *identifying* them (i.e., knowing to whom each touch belongs).

A number of methods have been proposed for distinguishing among tabletop users, but most existing approaches either rely on external sensors (e.g., [1,29,30,35,36]) or constrain interaction (e.g. [4,21,43]) so that users are prevented from taking full advantage of the tabletop's multi-touch capabilities. In our prior investigation of tabletop collaboration in high school classrooms [12], the need arose for distinguishing among users engaged in unconstrained multi-touch interaction without using external sensors, which were not practical due to the physical constraints of the classroom. No existing approach could meet this need.

This paper describes *Group Touch*, a novel user-independent approach to distinguishing among users that utilizes only the built-in capabilities of the tabletop computer and does not impose restrictions on users. Importantly, existing approaches have generally taken on the goal of trying to *identify* and *track* each user. In this work, we relax and reframe that goal, instead focusing on *distinguishing* one

CHI 2017, May 06-11, 2017, Denver, CO, USA
© 2017 ACM. ISBN 978-1-4503-4655-9/17/05…$15.00
DOI: http://dx.doi.org/10.1145/3025453.3025793

user from the next by determining when subsequent touches are from the same user or different users. We therefore do not achieve the ability to uniquely identify a user (e.g., for authentication purposes), but we do gain the ability to distinguish among multiple users during periods of simultaneous interaction. This reframing of the objective is a key insight that simplifies the problem but still retains many capabilities important for multi-user tabletop interaction scenarios. Use cases for Group Touch include: (1) resolving conflicting input that occurs when multiple people are simultaneously interacting with the same interface; (2) modeling the collaborative processes of small groups working at tabletop computers; and (3) evaluating and informing the design of software to better support small group collaboration at tabletop computers.

We explain how Group Touch works, give example scenarios in which it works, and demonstrate its effectiveness on a collection of field data acquired by groups of high school students collaborating at a Microsoft PixelSense in a classroom setting. Our results show that Group Touch can distinguish among 4-6 simultaneous users of a tabletop computer "in the wild" with an accuracy of 92.92% (*SD*=3.94%).

The contributions of this work are: (1) a novel approach to distinguishing among users at a tabletop computer that does not restrict multi-touch interaction or require additional sensors; and (2) an empirical study of the effectiveness of this approach using touch data collected entirely in a chaotic classroom field setting.

RELATED WORK

Common tabletop computers are vision-based, using either frustrated total internal reflection (FTIR) [19] or diffuse illumination (DI) [38] to detect touches. Existing approaches to distinguishing among users at vision-based tabletops fall into three categories: (1) approaches that augment the tabletop with additional sensors; (2) approaches that require the user to wear or hold external sensors; and (3) approaches that use only the built-in capabilities of the tabletop hardware. We review each of these in turn.

Approaches that augment the tabletop with additional sensors are typically reliable, accurate, and unobtrusive to the user. These approaches make it possible to track individual users for the duration of their time at the tabletop. For example, proximity sensors have been added to the edges of tabletop computers in order to track users' locations around the screen [2,41]. Multiple approaches have used cameras mounted above the tabletop to track users' arms and hands [6,29,34]. Bootstrapper [35] uses a depth camera mounted under the table to track users by their shoes and then match touches to individuals using the touch orientation detected by the tabletop's vision system.

Other approaches augment users with additional sensors, such as rings [36], wristbands [30], gloves [28], or cards [25] that communicate with tabletops' built-in sensors to identify users. Ackad et al. [1] used a combination of users' personal mobile devices and an overhead depth camera.

However, relying on external sensors is not always practical or desirable. For example, our work is motivated in part by the need to distinguish among users in the context of a study of collaborative learning at tabletop computers in authentic classroom settings [12]. The physical constraints of the study sites mean that the tabletop needs to be set up and then removed for each class session, making it impractical to use external sensors such as a depth camera that would need to be fixed in place. This problem has been encountered by other researchers studying tabletops in classroom settings [26]. Augmenting users (high school students) with wearable sensors was ruled out simply because such sensors require additional setup, storage, and maintenance, all of which increase time spent administering a learning activity and the burden of classroom management on the teacher. These factors go against evidence-based best practices and guidance on integrating new technologies into classrooms [3,10,11]. Therefore, deployments like this need an approach to distinguishing among users that does not rely on external sensors.

Several studies have investigated the use of finger orientation and hand contours, captured by vision-based tabletops' on-board cameras, to match touches to hands and users [7,13,42,43,44]. Ewerling et al. [13] developed an image processing technique to match touches to individual hands with four users simultaneously interacting with a tabletop computer. They did not explore the application of their technique to distinguishing users. Dang et al. [7] and Zhang et al. [44] both developed heuristic methods using touch orientation and distances between contact points to map touch points to hands. Mapping touches to hands could potentially improve gesture detection and thereby enhance the interactive experience. Both methods were highly effective at differentiating between the hands of single participants, but neither method was tested with groups or used to extrapolate from hands to users.

Zhang et al.'s [43] *See Me, See You* algorithm used hand contours captured by the vision system to detect finger orientation and handedness. Using touch orientation along with a touch's coordinates, Zhang et al. trained a support vector machine to predict a user's location at the tabletop, thus distinguishing among different users. Their approach, however, does not support multi-touch input, purposefully constraining users to single-point touches in order to make identification possible.

For touchscreens with capacitive sensing capabilities, Harrison et al.'s [21] capacitive fingerprinting technique takes advantage of the natural differences in electrical current passing through individual users. This approach does not restrict how users touch the screen, but a limitation of the prototype tested in Harrison et al.'s study is that it can only handle one touch at a time.

Blažica et al. [4] enable identification of users across all types of tabletop computers using hand biometrics. However, their approach is only able to distinguish among multiple simultaneous users when they place a hand on the screen in a specific position—all five fingers splayed and touching the screen. Therefore, it is not a suitable approach for distinguishing users during "in the wild" tabletop interaction, such as in a high school classroom.

Finally, application-based approaches take advantage of assumed or enforced social protocols. For example, an approach that automatically segments a tabletop interface into territories belonging to individual users [16] draws upon Scott et al.'s [39] findings that groups tend to divide the tabletop into personal and shared territories without any explicit coordination. However, social protocols can vary greatly depending on the context, limiting their generalizability as a means of distinguishing users. For example, research with adults in a lab setting has shown that participants are reluctant to reach into one another's perceived personal space or territory on the tabletop [37], supporting the notion that it is possible to distinguish users by identifying those personal territories. In contrast, children engaged in collaborative learning around a tabletop often break or ignore boundaries of personal space, actually enhancing collaboration [15,33]. Given that our context is tabletop collaboration in authentic high school classrooms, these findings suggest that assuming young users will follow adult social protocols may be unwise.

All of the approaches described above that use only the built-in capabilities of the hardware to distinguish users also impose restrictions on how users can interact with the tabletop. Some researchers argue that there are scenarios where users will be willing to sacrifice unconstrained interaction for the ability to track users [43]. However, this will only hold true when the value added by tracking users outweighs the inconvenience of artificial constraints on interaction. When this is not the case, such as when an application requires true multi-touch input, the above approaches are not suitable. Additionally, these approaches are at risk of failure with young users because it can be difficult to get children and adolescents to comply with behavioral constraints. With Group Touch, we address the problem of distinguishing users without utilizing external sensors and without constraining interaction.

DESIGN AND EVALUATION OF GROUP TOUCH

In order to support unconstrained multi-touch interaction, we forego the goal of *identifying* and *tracking* users (knowing to whom each touch belongs), which has been the focus of many of the aforementioned approaches. Instead, our aim is *distinguishing* among users (knowing one user's touches are different than another's). This means that our approach cannot enable sophisticated personalization of interfaces or authentication, but it can be used to address core usability problems that arise when multiple people interact with a single shared interface, such as determining whether simultaneous touches are by a single person performing a single multi-touch gesture or multiple people performing separate gestures (e.g., to resolve conflicts). Our approach could also be used for modeling collaboration in order to understand group working practices and inform the design of collaborative tabletop applications.

Most approaches to distinguishing among users have tackled the problem at the individual level by trying to match touches to users. By relaxing the goal of tracking and identifying, we reframe the problem at the group level; after all, the need to distinguish among individuals only arises when there are multiple users in a group. This reframing leads us to compare touches to each other instead of attempting to match touches to specific individuals.

Group Touch has two components. The first is a multilayer perceptron (MLP) model trained on touch data collected entirely "in the wild." The model predicts, given a pair of touches, whether they were carried out by the *same* person or *different* people. The second component is an algorithm that uses the predictions of the MLP model to group touches that were likely to have been carried out by the same person. The following sections describe the dataset that was used to develop and evaluate Group Touch and the design of each component in turn.

Creating the Touch Dataset

Group Touch was developed and evaluated using touch data collected "in the wild" during a study of collaborative learning at tabletop computers in classroom settings [12]. Data were collected from high-school students using five distinct multi-touch applications (Figures 2 and 3) on a Microsoft PixelSense in two different educational programs.

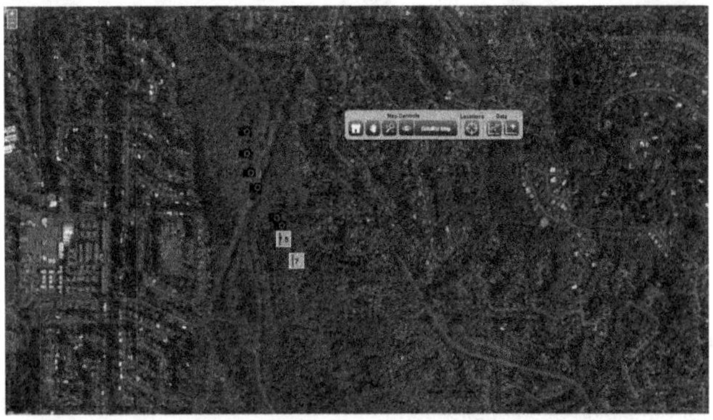

Figure 2. The mapping application used in the classroom. The two blue squares represent locations with available water quality data. Touching the squares opened up graphs and charts of the data. The shown toolbar provided access to additional navigation and settings.

The participants in the first study setting—an after school science program—were eleven 9th to 12th grade students (6 male, 5 female). Figure 2 shows the custom-built mapping application used in this setting. The teachers of the science program had requested an application that would enable students to see stream-monitoring data they had collected laid out on a map of their study area that could be panned and zoomed to different levels of detail. Students could use the map to navigate to various data collection locations and to interact with tables, graphs, and images of data. Students interacted with the application using standard multi-touch gestures such as pinch-to-zoom, swipe-to-pan, and multiple-finger rotation. Four sessions were recorded across two class periods with the students using the computer in groups of five to six for around 30 minutes a session. A total of 1,072 touches were logged in this setting.

Participants in the second study setting—a user-centered design course—were sixteen 10th and 11th grade students (6 male, 10 female). Figure 3 shows screenshots of the applications that were custom-built for this course. The students used each application for 10-15 minutes in groups of three to four over four class sessions. One application (Figure 3, top left) enabled the students to draw on wireframes for their design project. A second application (Figure 3, top right) helped groups brainstorm questions for a usability test. A third application helped students improve their search skills (Figure 3, bottom left) by finding and comparing resources for their projects. These applications were built using the PixelSense's native interface components, which fully support multi-touch. The final application (Figure 3, bottom right) was a multi-touch-enabled browser plugin for finding and annotating, via drag and drop, real-world examples of usability heuristics. Thirteen group sessions were logged in this setting, amounting to 9,255 touches.

Figure 3. The applications used in the second study setting. From left to right, top to bottom, the first three applications used the computer's native SDK. The fourth (bottom right) application was browser-based. All applications supported multi-touch. (See the text for details on each application.)

In both classroom settings, the teacher determined the activities that the students carried out, and students were not given any instructions on how they should interact with the tabletop computer. The students elected to stand while using the computer and chose how to arrange themselves around the screen. They touched freely and rampantly, without any rules imposed on them to take turns or "be polite" to their collaborators. In this way, the environment paralleled many authentic classroom situations.

All 17 sessions across both study sites were video recorded with a single camera and every touch was logged by software on the tabletop. The camera was mounted on a tripod to the side of the table, angled down so that the whole tabletop screen was visible. The purpose of the camera was to enable us to manually label the author of every single touch using the video to obtain ground truth. Manually labeling the touches took around 200 hours.

The touch data collected in both settings proved to be as "messy" as might be expected from unconstrained field settings with high school students. We observed considerable variation in how students carried out standard multi-touch gestures, such as drag and rotation, echoing Hinrich and Carpendale's [23] findings from their study of multi-touch gestures on tabletops "in the wild." Students were free to move around the tabletop and often did, occasionally pushing and shoving each other. Figure 1 shows multiple students simultaneously interacting with the table, which was characteristic of much of the students' time with the table, even though taking turns and adhering to the social protocols of effective collaborative work would have been beneficial for the learning activities. Additionally, a notable proportion of student interactions appeared to be carried out without an obvious task-related purpose. For example, students regularly spun or flicked on-screen objects while engaged in off-task conversation. These behaviors have also been noted in other reports of tabletop use in classroom settings [12,26].

The MLP Model and Feature Selection

The first component of Group Touch, the MLP model, predicts whether a pair of touches was carried out by the same person or different people based on three features (Figure 4): (1) the difference in touch orientations; (2) the pixel distance between the two touches; and (3) the time difference between touches, in milliseconds.

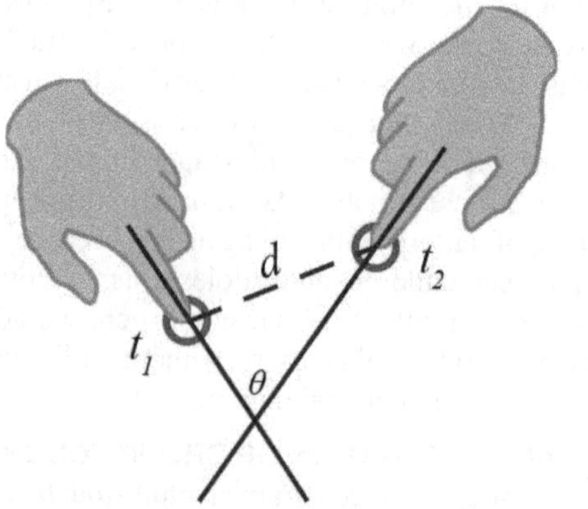

Figure 4. The touch features used to predict whether a pair of touches was carried out by the same user are: (1) the difference θ between the touches' orientations, (2) the distance d between the touch points, and (3) the time between t_1 and t_2.

The three features were selected based on the following reasoning. Consider Figure 5, a raw image captured by the PixelSense's on-board cameras. Even without any context, a human viewer can determine that the two touch points detected by the computer (the brightest points in the image) are being carried out by two different people—we can clearly see two hands in a configuration which would be very difficult for a single person to achieve given the size of the screen (40"). The primary features of the two touch points that enable us to infer that we are seeing the hands of two separate people are the difference in their orientations and the distance between the touch points. Touch orientation refers to the orientation of the finger's contact area detected by the computer's vision system.

Figure 5. A raw image captured by Microsoft PixelSense on-board cameras showing two different people touching the screen.

In Figure 5, the touch points are concurrent, which helps us determine that we are seeing two different people. If the touch points were not concurrent—for example, if the touch on the left of the screen took place 30 seconds after the touch at the top—we would be less confident that we were seeing two people rather than one person who has taken a few steps to their right in order to reach a different area of the screen. Therefore, a third feature, the time that has passed between the touches, is also necessary to make a prediction that the two touches were carried out by the same person or two different people.

Based on the above examples, the three features included in the model are all needed to make a prediction of "same" or "different" but the exact nature of the relationship between them is not clear and is likely non-linear. Although including just three features makes for a simple model, the non-linearity adds complexity. The MLP classifier has been demonstrated to be well-suited for complex problems where the relative importance of each feature is unknown [17], making it a good choice for this work. Our main requirement for classifier selection was that the model output a probability with each classification, as this was necessary for our grouping algorithm, described below. We selected MLP as our classifier after using leave-one-out nested cross validation in Weka [18] to test a number of classifiers that output a probability. The Weka classifiers tested included Logistic Regression, LibSVM, and BayesNet among many others. Our use of a classifier learned from data, instead of a heuristic approach, also means that future versions of Group Touch could incorporate additional touch features found to be predictive.

The MLP Model, Pre-processing, and Training

The purpose of our MLP model is to predict, given a pair of touches, whether or not those touches are carried out by the same or different people. To prepare a touch log to train our model, each touch was processed sequentially.

Pre-processing of the raw touch logs began by converting individual touches into pairs of touches. Each touch pair consisted of a given touch and the previous touch by each user in the session. The values of each of the features—difference in orientation, distance, and time between touches (see Figure 4)—were calculated to form an *instance* with a class label of either "same" or "different." A single instance comprised the new touch and the last touch carried out by the same user (with the class label, "same"). *N*-1 instances comprised the new touch and the last touch carried out by each of the other users in the group (with the class label, "different"). So in a group of *N* users, each new touch resulted in *N* touch pairs, or instances.

Consider, for example, that several of our user groups comprised four students. In these groups, each new touch resulted in four instances (or touch pairs)—one instance formed from the differences between the new touch and the last touch by the *same* person, and three instances describing the differences between the new touch and the last touch by each of the *other* three people.

Creating touch pairs in the aforementioned manner helped to account for differences in how groups of users interact with any given application, as it always produced a similar distribution of instances with the "same" versus "different" class label for a group of *N* users regardless of the activity or the users' working style. For example, a group of four users will always produce three instances with the class label "different" for every instance with the class label "same." This consistency is important to prevent over-fitting the MLP model to a particular application or group working style (e.g., turn-taking versus parallel interactions).

Before training the model, each feature was normalized to the range [0, 1]. For two of the three features, normalization was straightforward as the possible range of values is inherently limited—the difference in orientation can only fall between 0° and 180°, and the maximum distance between two touch points is determined by the length of the screen diagonal. The elapsed time between touches, however, does not have a clear upper limit. We set the upper limit for time between touches to be the 90th percentile for our full dataset, or about 307 seconds, in order to remove outliers. Instances with a greater time between touches were dropped from the training data. Although this upper limit may seem high at just over five minutes, it was fairly common in our dataset for groups to take breaks from interacting with the screen to discuss something, or for some individual users to refrain from interacting for extended periods of time, therefore leading to lengthy gaps between touches by particular users.

We trained and optimized Group Touch's MLP models in Weka using leave-one-out nested cross validation to prevent overfitting. This method resulted in 17 models—each one trained and optimized on the data from 16 of the study sessions and evaluated on the unseen data from the remaining study session.

For every touch logged, as described above, there were more instances generated with the class label "different" than "same," so the data were heavily weighted towards the "different" label (77.40% of instances across all sessions). To avoid overfitting the models to the majority class label, we applied the SMOTE filter [5] to balance the training data, resulting in an almost 50%-50% split between the two labels. MLP models can potentially be sensitive to the order of training instances, so we applied the Randomize filter to shuffle instances before training.

Touch Grouping Algorithm

After a touch pair is categorized with the "same" or "different" label, the next step is to establish groups of touches that are likely to have been carried out by the same user. The goal of Group Touch is to detect when additional users begin touching the screen and *distinguish* among multiple users as they are concurrently interacting with the computer; it is not intended to *track* or *identify* individual users for the duration of an activity. Key to our approach is that a "group" is not synonymous with a "user"—it is a *group of touches* that belong to a single user, representing a period of sustained interaction. Figure 6 illustrates the algorithm used to place touches into groups.

The first touch creates the first group (Figure 6A). For every subsequent touch, a touch pair is created with the last touch in each group established so far. When the MLP model is queried, it returns the probability that the last touch belonged to the same user. If P(same) is less than a specified threshold (p), a new group is started (Figure 6B); otherwise, the touch is assigned to the group with the highest P(same) (Figure 6C).

The value of threshold p can vary between 0.5 and 1.0. Higher thresholds mean that it is more likely a touch group will be made up of touches carried out by only one user because a more confident "same" prediction is required for a touch to be added to an existing group. However, higher thresholds also lead to new groups being created more often, with each group containing fewer touches and lasting a shorter period of time. In contrast, lower thresholds lead to touch groups that last for longer and contain more touches, but also increase the likelihood that touches by different users will be mistakenly grouped together because a weaker "same" prediction is sufficient to add a touch to an existing group.

To evaluate the grouping algorithm and establish a suitable value for threshold p, we tested it on each session of touch data using a leave-one-out procedure. This testing involved

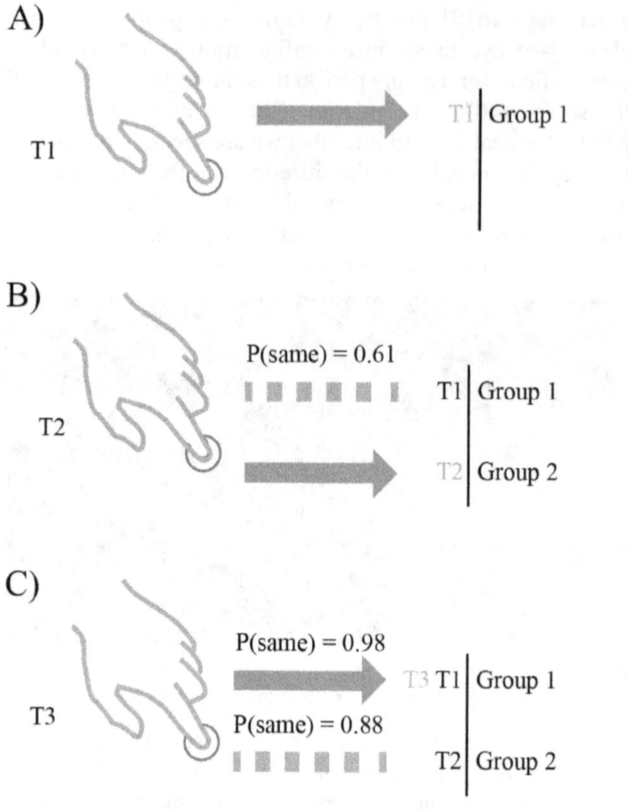

Figure 6. An example of the algorithm to place touches into groups. A) The first touch creates the first group. B) For subsequent touches, we create touch pairs with the last touch of each group, then query the model for each pair. We create a new group if no pairs have a same-author with probability ≥ p, set to 0.80 in this example. C) If multiple touch pairs have a same-author probability ≥ p, we add the touch to the group with the highest probability.

using the algorithm to group the touches in a session according to predictions from the MLP model trained on touch data from the other 16 sessions. As well as being dependent on the performance of the MLP model, the outcome of the grouping algorithm would also be affected by the value of the probability threshold, p. Therefore, we tested the algorithm with a range of probability threshold values from 0.5 to 0.9, in increments of 0.1. This test was repeated with each of the 17 sessions of touch data in order to determine an optimal value of p. We determined that a threshold of 0.80 was suitable for our purposes, a decision that we discuss in more detail in the next section, together with implications of this decision.

Approaches that use touch orientation to match touch points to hands [7,44] have shown thumb touches to be a source of error as the orientation of the thumb can be different from other fingers on the same hand. We anticipated this would also be an issue for Group Touch. Thumb touches are relatively infrequent in general interaction and do not feature in most standard gestures, with the exception of pinch-to-zoom. Thumb touches, however, are heavily used when typing on a virtual keyboard—typically when pressing the spacebar. To remedy this potential problem,

(a) Session - Application	(b) # of Touches	(c) # of Users	MLP Model		(f) Grouping Accuracy (%)
			(d) Accuracy on Test Data (%)	(e) Area under ROC Curve	
1 - Brainstorm	601	5	96.87	0.99	99.44
2 - Heuristics	105	4	89.32	0.96	96.30
3 - Heuristics	328	4	91.49	0.96	95.74
4- Heuristics	241	5	94.29	0.97	98.40
5- Heuristics	240	5	87.81	0.91	89.89
6 - Map	104	5	92.19	0.93	94.74
7 - Map	262	6	91.85	0.94	91.84
8 - Map	519	5	93.85	0.95	91.76
9 - Map	187	5	84.96	0.89	88.97
10 - Resources	285	4	90.50	0.95	94.04
11 - Resources	448	4	89.27	0.95	95.78
12 - Resources	271	5	89.66	0.92	90.10
13 - Resources	296	5	88.28	0.92	89.50
14 - Wireframes	465	5	89.53	0.96	93.07
15 - Wireframes	435	5	89.45	0.96	95.16
16 - Wireframes	241	5	87.54	0.92	83.43
17 - Wireframes	295	4	87.80	0.95	91.49
Mean:	**313.12**	**4.76**	**90.27**	**0.94**	**92.92**
***SD*:**	**138.32**	**0.56**	**2.91**	**0.03**	**3.94**

Table 1. Group Touch results by session. Columns (d) and (e) show how just the MLP model performed on the test data for each session. Column (f) shows the performance of the grouping algorithm with threshold *p*=0.80. Column (f) is therefore the performance of Group Touch.

groups of touches on a virtual keyboard were merged when the same keyboard instance was touched and the touches occurred within 384 ms of each other. This threshold was chosen based on the typing speeds of participants in a study of typing on virtual keyboards [14]; it represents the time between keystrokes for the slowest participant. Touches to the same keyboard within this time could be assumed to have been carried out by the same user.

Our evaluation of Group Touch was carried out offline but was set up as if it was grouping touches interactively at run-time—touches were processed in the order they were received and logged. Accuracy was calculated as the percentage of touches added to a group where the preceding touch correctly had the same user, using the manual labels assigned from the videos as ground truth.

RESULTS

Group Touch's overall accuracy for a session ranged from 83.43% to 99.44%, with a mean of 92.92% (*SD*=3.94%). However, only 2.66% of all touches logged were incorrectly added to a group of touches by a different user. This discrepancy between the overall accuracy and the number of touches added to incorrect groups occurs because our selection of a p threshold of 0.80 means the algorithm favors creating a new group of touches in the absence of a strong prediction of "same user" for any existing group. Therefore, groups of touches associated with a particular user persist for short periods of time but are highly accurate. Table 1 shows the complete results by session.

To test the first component of Group Touch in isolation, the MLP model that predicts whether a pair of touches was authored by the same person or different people, we used leave-one-out cross-validation to evaluate the model, withholding a different session's touch data each time. Within the training data for each fold in the leave-one-out cross validation, we conducted a 10-fold cross validation of the MLP model. These scores were highly consistent across sessions—the mean cross validation score was 89.22% (*SD*=0.29%). When the trained models were then tested on the withheld touch data, the mean accuracy was 90.27% (*SD*=2.91%). Leave-one-out test results for the MLP model are shown in Table 1(c). Figure 7 shows the ROC curves.

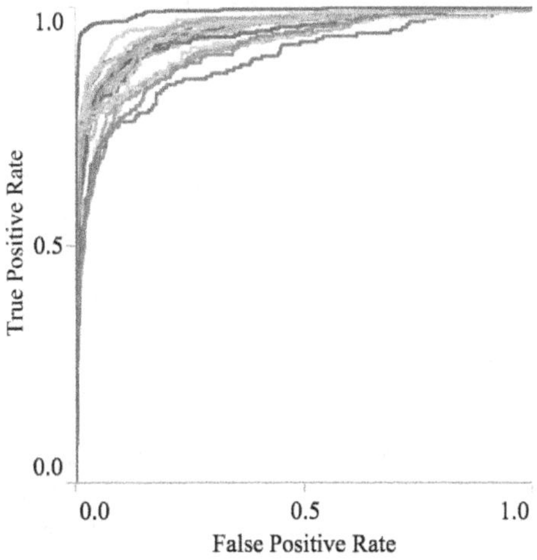

Figure 7. The ROC curves for each MLP model. The area under the curve, listed in Table 1, ranged from 0.89 to 0.99.

The second component of Group Touch, its grouping algorithm, adds a touch to the group for which the MLP model has returned a prediction of "same" person with the highest probability above a threshold p (see Figure 6). We tested threshold values between 0.5 and 0.9 in 0.1 increments and found that mean accuracy increased from 88.83% to

94.23% (Figure 8). At the same time, the median duration of a group—the time elapsed from the first touch in a group to the last—decreased from 7,207 ms to 2,383 ms. Therefore, Group Touch can distinguish among simultaneous users for longer periods of time when the value of *p* is lower but with a tradeoff of lower accuracy within touch groups.

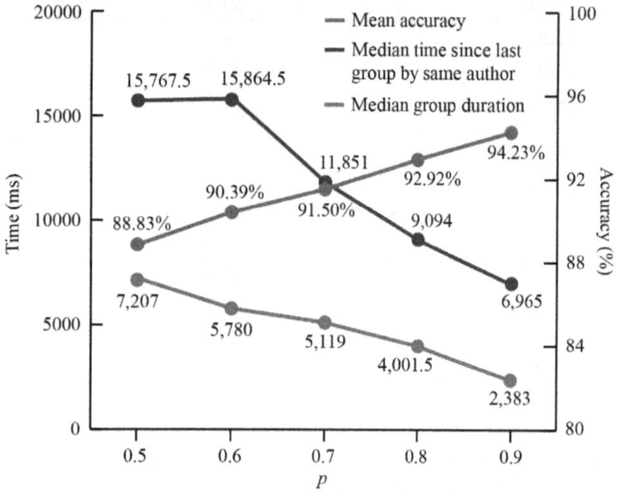

Figure 8. As the value of *p* increases, the accuracy of Group Touch increases. However, the median time since the last group of touches with the same user and the median duration of groups decreases.

To evaluate the threshold values, we also tracked another measure: the time between groups of touches *belonging to the same person* (i.e., the time that elapsed since that person last touched the screen). For example, Figure 8 shows that when *p*=0.8, the median time since the last group by the same user was 9,094 ms. This means that when a new group is started with a touch by user X, a median of 9,094 ms have passed since X last touched the screen. When the time between groups of touches belonging to the same person is brief, the system is being conservative in assigning new touches to existing groups. It therefore becomes more likely that sustained input by a single person will be ascribed to multiple people. Figure 8 shows that, as the value of *p* increased, the median time between groups of touches belonging to the same person decreased. Therefore, although accuracy within groups will be highest when *p*=0.9, longer sequences of related gestures by a single user are more likely to be split into multiple groups than when *p* is lower.

Based on Figure 8, we chose 0.80 as the value of *p*. Although the average accuracy increases to 94.23% when *p*=0.90, both time metrics decrease to a point where Group Touch would only be reliably able to distinguish among users for brief interactions. At *p*=0.90, Group Touch still has valuable use cases (see the Discussion) but at *p*=0.80, Group Touch retains high accuracy and is able to distinguish among simultaneous users over longer periods of time, making it useful for a wider range of applications. When *p* was set to 0.80, the midspread (middle 50%) of groups lasted between 0.65 and 12.02 seconds and contained 2 to 6 touches. The longest group recorded lasted 77.10 seconds and contained 80 touches. Table 1(d) shows the results of the evaluation of the grouping algorithm with the threshold, *p*, set to 0.80.

To understand why Group Touch creates new groups for touches by an existing user, we investigated the differences between touches that resulted in a new group and those that were added to an existing group. Figure 9 shows the average features of touch pairs by the MLP model's probability that a pair was carried out by the same user, P(same). The "New groups created" region shows the average features of false negatives—touch pairs that were actually by the same user (based on the labels assigned manually) but were incorrectly labeled by Group Touch as being by different users, leading to the creation of a new group. For these touch pairs, the MLP model returned a probability, P(same), below our threshold of 0.80 (see Figure 6B). Moreover, 62.41% of false negatives occurred when the MLP model returned P(same) < 0.1, a strong prediction that the touches were carried out by different people. Clear trends emerged for each feature as P(same) increased. Typically, touch pairs with the lowest values of P(same) had large values for time between touches (*M*=162.54 s, *SD*=76.70 s). Difference in orientation (*M*=69.86°, *SD*=47.14°) and distance between touch points (*M*=601.37 px, *SD*=347.47 px) also tended to be higher but there was more variation for these features. These results suggest that extended time between touches results in the creation of a new group when an existing group of touches by the same user is available.

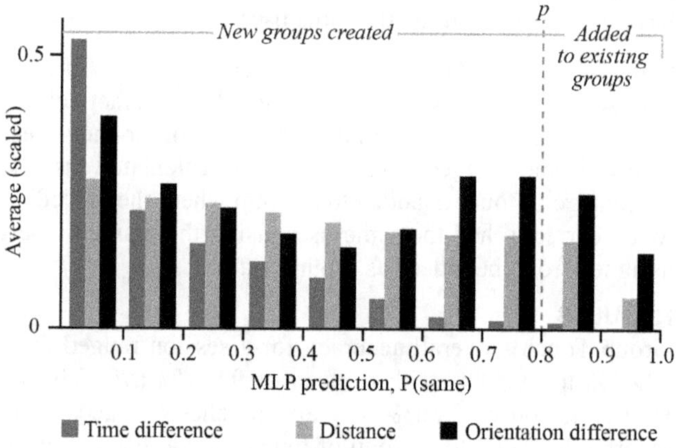

Figure 9. Average features of touch pairs by the probability they were carried out by the same user according to the MLP model.

For comparison, Figure 9, "Added to existing groups," shows the average features of touch pairs that resulted in a touch being added to an existing group. These are pairs where the MLP model returned the highest value of P(same) above our 0.80 threshold (see Figure 6C). 93.58% of these touch pairs were true positives that were correctly assigned—both touches were carried out by the same user. 91.16% of these touch pairs had a P(same) of at least 0.90. The time between touches for pairs with a P(same) of at least 0.90 was brief (*M*=1.03 s, *SD*=1.54 s). Difference in orientation (*M*=25.25°, *SD*=24.75°) and distance between touches (*M*=130.35 px, *SD*=130.79 px) were also at their lowest when P(same) was at least 0.90. This means that a touch was more likely to be correctly added to an existing group when it was close to the last touch in the group in terms of all three features.

DISCUSSION

Group Touch's overall accuracy (Table 1(d)) shows that it was successful at grouping touches that belonged to the same user. There was little variability in the accuracy of both the MLP model (Table 1(c)) and the grouping algorithm (Table 1(d)) across the 17 sessions of touch data collected in five different applications. These results indicate that Group Touch is user-independent and can perform consistently across a range of applications.

Group Touch favors creating a new group of touches when the MLP model does not return a strong prediction of "same user" for any touch pair. This means that group assignments are highly accurate, with only 2.66% of all touches in our dataset being added incorrectly to a group by another user. However, this also means that it is important to understand when and why the model is unable to return a strong prediction of "same user," leading to the creation of new groups. The trends shown in Figure 9 suggest that extended time between touches is a strong reason that new groups are created when an existing group of touches by the same user is available. Therefore, Group Touch is likely to perform better and create groups that persist for longer when users are regularly interacting with the screen, so time between touches is brief. Given that Figure 9 also shows that touches are correctly added to groups when the time and distance between touches are low, Group Touch is probably not suited for applications where users frequently jump around different areas of the screen. This might explain why session 16 had a much lower accuracy than all other sessions at 83.46%, 6.46% lower than the next lowest result. The students in this session spent much of the time flicking the on-screen objects at other objects to make them bounce around the edges, then reaching across the full length of the screen to retrieve the object.

The value of the threshold *p* used to assign touches to groups of touches by the same user impacted the group duration and time between groups by the same user, as well as the accuracy. We selected 0.80 as our value of *p* because it resulted in a high grouping accuracy and the decrease in group duration was much steeper with a *p* above 0.80. However, the value of *p* and the resulting tradeoff between group duration and accuracy affects the potential use cases for Group Touch and therefore should be adjusted depending on how Group Touch is to be used.

The simplest and most generalizable use case for Group Touch is resolving conflicting input that occurs when multiple people are simultaneously interacting with the same interface. For example, without the ability to distinguish among users, the touch input of multiple people attempting to drag an object in different directions will look very much like that of a single user carrying out a pinch-to-zoom action. Another example would be a user attempting to close a window that another user is actively working in [31]. Group Touch makes it possible to resolve these and other conflicts and determine how the application should respond because it is not necessary to know the identity of the users, just whether or not multiple users are interacting with the application concurrently. In this scenario, Group Touch would affect the application's behavior in ways that are visible to users. Therefore, the high accuracy of the top value of *p*, 0.90, would likely be favored over groups that persist for longer, particularly as conflicting gestures will occur with a small number of overlapping touches.

In addition to resolving conflicting gestures, there are numerous application scenarios where the ability to detect when multiple people are attempting to interact with the same object would be useful. For example, in a collaborative document editing application, it would be useful to prevent concurrent interaction in some situations (e.g., one user scrolling a page while another is making edits). Online collaboration tools, such as Google Docs, handle this situation by allowing each user to control navigation of their own view of the document—they can see others' edits as they occur but they can move around their own view of the document independently. This approach would not transfer to a similar application on a shared screen. Group Touch could help in this scenario by making it possible to temporarily block interaction from users other than the person actively working in the document. Additionally, tracking concurrent versus individual edits to a document could make document revision history more useful.

The ability to temporarily block other users from interacting with an object that a user is currently holding could also be used to enforce turn-taking in a collaborative learning environment or as a game mechanic in a competitive game where players have to steal objects from their opponents. Taking the opposite approach to the same incident—only responding to input if multiple people are simultaneously interacting with an object—would make it possible to support cooperative gestures. Cooperative gestures have been shown to be useful for increasing awareness of important functionality and increasing participation in applications for collaborative work and play [31, 32].

Group Touch could also be used to model the collaborative processes of small groups working at tabletop computers. For example, the ability to distinguish when multiple people are interacting with an application makes it possible to detect when users are taking turns, interfering with the actions of others, or working in parallel, all of which have been shown to impact collaborative learning [12,15,20,26,33]. For this use case, it would be important to capture longer interactions that contain more than just a small number of isolated gestures. Therefore, a lower *p* threshold, which creates groups that persist for longer would be preferable to increasing accuracy.

Application designers could also use information about when and where conflicting gestures occur, and how groups use their applications, to evaluate and refine their designs to enable better collaborative use. For example, Group Touch would make it possible to automatically identify areas of the screen where there is typically only one user interacting at a time and those where there tend to be multiple users interacting. This information could be used to determine placement of shared interface elements and how to divide the screen into individual and shared workspaces.

Group Touch offers an enhancement to existing touch-detection on large, multi-user touchscreens that adds a new capability without breaking existing touch functionality when errors occur. For example, Group Touch false positives may cause an application to interpret the touches of multiple users as a single gesture. This outcome is typical of most current commercial tabletops. Therefore, when Group Touch produces a false positive, behavior will be the same as in current systems.

In the case of false negatives, the primary causes are extended time between touches, or touches close together in time that have very different orientations or locations. How false negatives impact a user will largely depend on what an application does with information provided by Group Touch. For example, when detecting and resolving conflicting gestures, false negatives due to touches that are far apart in time are unlikely to produce a conflict in the interface and therefore unlikely to affect the user. In some cases, however, a false negative could cause a zoom gesture to look like two separate pan gestures. These cases occur infrequently and application-level design could help to mitigate any impact.

Limitations

The main limitation of Group Touch is that it does not track or identify users for the duration of an activity, and therefore cannot enable personalization, such as color-coding each user's touches [43], or tracking individual contributions to the group effort [29]. It also cannot be used for authentication [4,24]. However, existing approaches to distinguishing users that are able to provide these features either rely on external sensors or artificially constraining interaction. As stated, Group Touch is intended for situations where such methods are impractical or undesirable.

Additionally, the applications we used to design and evaluate Group Touch all featured highly collaborative tasks in which group members worked with shared objects. We expect accuracy would be about the same for other tasks of this nature. However, we expect that Group Touch may have lower accuracy in situations where individual users frequently interact with objects in very different areas of the screen (e.g., rapidly reaching from the top left corner to the bottom right). Based on our analysis of touch group characteristics (Figure 9), these types of interactions would look like touches carried out by different people. In applications requiring this functionality, Group Touch may not be the best option for distinguishing among users.

Finally, in this work we have not yet identified the exact situations where Group Touch performs poorly. For example, we have not investigated how good Group Touch is at recognizing two-handed input by a single person versus single-handed input. This limitation is because all of our touch data were collected "in the wild" in uncontrolled field settings and extracting these types of specific interactions would be an extremely laborious process. A controlled lab study would likely be necessary to gain this kind of insight.

FUTURE WORK

One avenue for future work would be to address some of the limitations of Group Touch by testing the approach with data collected in less collaborative applications and to conduct a controlled study that can identify the exact types of low-level input that Group Touch is best able to handle.

Additionally, it would be worthwhile to investigate ways to improve Group Touch by combining it with other approaches that focus on finger and hand detection (e.g. [7,44]), which may help make Group Touch even more robust.

In our future work, we intend to use Group Touch to model the processes of collaborative learning with tabletop computers in high school classroom settings using the touch patterns described by Evans et al. [12]. To date, identifying indicators of the quality of collaborative learning processes has required manually labeling touch data using video recordings. Group Touch will make it possible to detect and respond to these touch patterns in real-time.

CONCLUSION

We have presented Group Touch, an approach to distinguishing among multiple simultaneous users by detecting when the users interacting with a vision-based tabletop computer change. Our approach achieved a mean accuracy of 92.92% (*SD*=3.94%). Group Touch is the first approach to distinguishing users that was designed and evaluated using data collected entirely "in the wild." It uses only the built-in capabilities of the tabletop hardware and does not require the use of extra sensors, making it more flexible and easier to deploy than many existing approaches.

Group Touch is not intended to replace existing approaches to distinguishing users, nor is it a suitable approach if individual users need to be identified and tracked for the duration of a session. Instead, it is intended to bring the capability of distinguishing among concurrent users to new settings that other approaches cannot support, namely, settings where use of external sensors is impractical and artificially constraining interaction is undesirable.

ACKNOWLEDGMENTS

This work was supported in part by the National Science Foundation under awards IIS-0952786 and IIS-1053868. Any opinions, findings, conclusions or recommendations expressed in this work are those of the authors and do not necessarily reflect those of the National Science Foundation.

REFERENCES

1. Christopher James Ackad, Andrew Clayphan, Roberto Martinez Maldonado, and Judy Kay. 2012. Seamless and continuous user identification for interactive tabletops using personal device handshaking and body tracking. *Extended Abstracts on Human Factors in Computing Systems (CHI EA '12)*, 1775–1780.
2. Michelle Annett, Tovi Grossman, Daniel Wigdor, and George Fitzmaurice. 2011. Medusa: a proximity-aware multi-touch tabletop. *Proceedings of the ACM Symposium on User Interface Software and Technology (UIST '11)*, 337–346.
3. Katerine Bielaczyc. 2009. Designing social infrastructure: critical issues in creating learning environments with technology. *Journal of the Learning Sciences* 15, 3: 301–329. http://doi.org/10.1207/s15327809jls1503
4. Bojan Blazica, Daniel Vladusic, and Dunja Mladenic. 2013. MTi: a method for user identification for multitouch displays. *International Journal of Human-Computer Studies* 71: 691–702. http://doi.org/10.1016/j.ijhcs.2013.03.002
5. Nitesh V. Chawla, Kevin W. Bowyer, Lawrence O. Hall, and W. Philip Kegelmeyer. 2011. SMOTE: Synthetic minority over-sampling technique. *Journal Of Artificial Intelligence Research* 16: 321–357.
6. Andrew Clayphan, Roberto Martinez-Maldonado, Christopher Ackad, and Judy Kay. 2013. An approach for designing and evaluating a plug-in vision-based tabletop touch identification system. *Proceedings of the Australian Computer-Human Interaction Conference (OzCHI '13)*, 373–382. http://doi.org/10.1145/2541016.2541019
7. Chi Tai Dang, Martin Straub, and Elisabeth André. 2009. Hand distinction for multi-touch tabletop interaction. *Proceedings of the ACM International Conference on Interactive Tabletops and Surfaces (ITS '09)*, 101–108. http://doi.org/10.1145/1731903.1731925
8. Paul Dietz and Darren Leigh. 2001. DiamondTouch: a multi-user touch technology. *Proceedings of the ACM Symposium on User Interface Software and Technology (UIST '01)*, 219–226. http://doi.org/10.1145/502348.502389
9. Pierre Dillenbourg and Michael Evans. 2011. Interactive tabletops in education. *International Journal of Computer-Supported Collaborative Learning* 6, 4: 491–514.
10. Pierre Dillenbourg and Patrick Jermann. 2010. Technology for classroom orchestration. In *New Science of Learning: Cognition, Computers and Collaboration in Education*, M. S. Khine and I. M. Saleh (eds.). Springer, New York, NY, 525–552.
11. Pierre Dillenbourg, Guillaume Zufferey, Hamed Alavi, Patrick Jermann, Son Do-lenh, and Quentin Bonnard. 2011. Classroom Orchestration : The Third Circle of Usability Why is Paper Highly Usable in Classrooms ? *Proceedings of the International Conference on Computer-Supported Collaborative Learning (CSCL '11)*, 510–517.
12. Abigail C. Evans, Jacob O. Wobbrock, and Katie Davis. 2016. Modelling collaboration patterns on an interactive tabletop in a classroom setting. *Proceedings of the ACM Conference on Computer Supported Cooperative Work and Social Computing (CSCW '16)*, 860–871.
13. Philipp Ewerling, Alexander Kulik, and Bernd Froelich. 2012. Finger and hand detection for multi-touch interfaces based on maximally stable extremal regions. *Proceedings of the ACM International Conference on Interactive Tabletops and Surfaces (ITS '12)*, 173–182.
14. Leah Findlater, Jacob O Wobbrock, and Daniel Wigdor. 2011. Typing on flat glass: examining ten-finger expert typing patterns on touch surfaces. *Proceedings of the SIGCHI Conference on Human Factors in Computing Systems (CHI '11)*, 2453–2462. http://doi.org/10.1145/1978942.1979301
15. Rowanne Fleck, Yvonne Rogers, Nicola Yuill, et al. 2009. Actions speak loudly with words: unpacking collaboration around the table. *Proceedings of the ACM International Conference on Interactive Tabletops and Surfaces (ITS '09)*, 189–196. http://doi.org/10.1145/1731903.1731939
16. Fernando Garcia-sanjuan, Javier Jaen, and Alejandro Catala. 2013. Evaluating heuristics for tabletop user segmentation based on simultaneous interaction. *Expert Systems With Applications* 40, 14: 5578–5587. http://doi.org/10.1016/j.eswa.2013.04.011
17. M. W. Gardner and S. R. Dorling. 1998. Artificial Neural Networks (The Multilayer Perceptron)—A Review of Applications in the Atmospheric Sciences. *Atmospheric Environment* 32, 14/15: 2627–2636.
18. Mark Hall, Eibe Frank, Geoffrey Holmes, Bernhard Pfahringer, Peter Reutemann, and Ian H. Witten. 2009. The WEKA data mining software: an update. *SIGKDD Explorations* 11, 1: 10–18.
19. Jefferson Y Han. 2005. Low-cost multitouch sensing through frustrated total internal reflection. *Proceedings of the ACM Symposium on User Interface Software and Technology (UIST '05)*, 115–118.
20. Amanda Harris, Jochen Rick, Victoria Bonnett, et al. 2009. Around the table: Are multiple-touch surfaces better than single-touch for children's collaborative interactions? *International Conference on Computer-Supported Collaborative Learning (CSCL '09)*, 335–344.

21. Chris Harrison, Munehiko Sato, and Ivan Poupyrev. 2012. Capacitive fingerprinting: exploring user differentiation by sensing electrical properties of the human body. *Proceedings of the ACM Symposium on User Interface Software and Technology (UIST '12)*, 537–543.
22. Steven E Higgins, Emma Mercier, Elizabeth Burd, and Andrew Hatch. 2011. Multi-touch tables and the relationship with collaborative classroom pedagogies: a synthetic review. *International Journal of Computer-Supported Collaborative Learning* 6, 4: 515–538.
23. Uta Hinrichs and Sheelagh Carpendale. 2011. Gestures in the wild: studying multi-touch gesture sequences on interactive tabletop exhibits. *Proceedings of the SIGCHI Conference on Human Factors in Computing Systems (CHI '11)*, 3023–3032.
24. Christian Holz and Patrick Baudisch. 2013. Fiberio: a touchscreen that senses fingerprints. *Proceedings of the ACM Symposium on User Interface Software and Technology (UIST '13)*, 41–50. http://doi.org/10.1145/2501988.2502021
25. Paul Jermann, Guillaume Zufferey, and Pierre Dillenbourg. 2008. Tinkering or sketching: apprentices' use of tangibles and drawings to solve design problems. *Proceedings of the European conference on Technology Enhanced Learning (EC-TEL '08)*, 167–178.
26. Ahmed Kharrufa, Madeline Balaam, Phil Heslop, David Leat, Paul Dolan, and Patrick Olivier. 2013. Tables in the wild: lessons learned from a large-scale multi-tabletop deployment. *Proceedings of the SIGCHI Conference on Human Factors in Computing Systems (CHI '13)*, 1021–1030. http://doi.org/10.1145/2470654.2466130
27. Daniel Klinkhammer, Markus Nitsche, Marcus Specht, and Harald Reiterer. 2011. Adaptive personal territories for co-located tabletop interaction in a museum setting. *Proceedings of the ACM International Conference on Interactive Tabletops and Surfaces (ITS '11)*, 107–110. http://doi.org/10.1145/2076354.2076375
28. Nicolai Marquardt, Johannes Kiemer, David Ledo, Sebastian Boring, and Saul Greenberg. 2011. Designing user-, hand-, and handpart-aware tabletop interactions with the TouchID toolkit. *Proceedings of the ACM International Conference on Interactive Tabletops and Surfaces (ITS '11)*, 21–30. http://doi.org/10.1145/2076354.2076358
29. Roberto Martinez, Anthony Collins, Judy Kay, and Kalina Yacef. 2011. Who did what? Who said that?: Collaid: an environment for capturing traces of collaborative learning at the tabletop. *Proceedings of the ACM International Conference on Interactive Tabletops and Surfaces (ITS '11)*, 172–181. http://doi.org/10.1145/2076354.2076387
30. Tobias Meyer and Dominik Schmidt. 2010. IdWristbands: IR-based user identification on multi-touch surfaces. *Proceedings of the ACM International Conference on Interactive Tabletops and Surfaces (ITS '10)*, 277–278. http://doi.org/10.1145/1936652.1936714
31. Meredith Ringel Morris, Anqi Huang, Andreas Paepcke, and Terry Winograd. 2006. Cooperative gestures: multi-user gestural interactions for co-located groupware. *Proceedings of the ACM Conference on Human Factors in Computing Systems (CHI '06)*, 1201–1210. http://doi.org/10.1145/1124772.1124952
32. Meredith Ringel Morris, Kathy Ryall, Chia Shen, Clifton Forlines, and Frederic Vernier. 2004. Beyond "social protocols": multi-user coordination policies for co-located groupware. *Proceedings of the ACM Conference on Computer Supported Cooperative Work*, 1–4. http://doi.org/10.1145/1031607.1031648
33. Taciana Pontual Falcão and Sara Price. 2010. Interfering and resolving: how tabletop interaction facilitates co-construction of argumentative knowledge. *International Journal of Computer-Supported Collaborative Learning* 6, 4: 539–559. http://doi.org/10.1007/s11412-010-9101-9
34. Raf Ramakers, Davy Vanacken, Kris Luyten, Karin Coninx, and Johannes Schoning. 2012. Carpus: a non-intrusive user identification technique for interactive surfaces. *Proceedings of the ACM Symposium on User Interface Software and Technology (UIST '12)*, 35–44.
35. Stephan Richter, Christian Holz, and Patrick Baudisch. 2012. Bootstrapper: recognizing tabletop users by their shoes. *Proceedings of the 2012 ACM annual conference on Human Factors in Computing Systems*, 1249–1252. http://doi.org/10.1145/2207676.2208577
36. Volker Roth, Philipp Schmidt, and G Benjamin. 2010. The IR ring: authenticating users ' touches on a multi-touch display. *Proceedings of the ACM symposium on User Interface Software and Technology (UIST '10)*, 259–262.
37. Kathy Ryall, Clifton Forlines, Chia Shen, and Meredith Ringel Morris. 2004. Exploring the effects of group size and table size on interactions with tabletop shared-display groupware. *Proceedings of the ACM Conference on Computer Supported Cooperative Work (CSCW '04)*, ACM Press, 284–293.
38. Johannes Schöning, Jonathan Hook, Nima Motamedi, et al. 2009. Building interactive multi-touch surfaces. *Journal of Graphics, GPU, and Game Tools* 14, 3: 35–55.
39. Stacey D. Scott, Carpendale Sheelagh, and Kori. M. Inkpen. 2004. Territoriality in collaborative tabletop workspaces. *Proceedings of the ACM Conference on*

Computer Supported Cooperative Work (CSCW '04), 294–303. http://doi.org/10.1145/1031607.1031655

40. Masanori Sugimoto, Kazuhiro Hosoi, and Hiromichi Hashizume. 2004. Caretta: a system for supporting face-to-face collaboration by integrating personal and shared spaces. *Proceedings of the SIGCHI conference on Human factors in computing systems (CHI '04)*, 41–48. http://doi.org/10.1145/985692.985698

41. Cristian Tanase, Radu-daniel Vatavu, Ş Pentiuc, and Adrian Graur. 2008. Detecting and tracking multiple users in the proximity of interactive tabletops. *Advances in Electrical and Computer Engineering* 8, 2: 50–53.

42. Feng Wang, Xiang Cao, Xiangshi Ren, and Pourang Irani. 2009. Detecting and leveraging finger orientation for interaction with direct-touch surfaces. *Proceedings of the ACM Symposium on User Interface Software and Technology (UIST '09)*, 23–32. http://doi.org/10.1145/1622176.1622182

43. Hong Zhang, Xing-Dong Yang, Barrett Ens, Hai-Ning Liang, Pierre Boulanger, and Pourang Irani. 2012. See me, see you: a lightweight method for discriminating user touches on tabletop displays. *Proceedings of the SIGCHI Conference on Human Factors in Computing Systems (CHI '12)*, 2327–2336. http://doi.org/10.1145/2207676.2208392

44. Zhensong Zhang, Fengjun Zhang, and Hui Chen. 2014. Left and right hand distinction for multi-touch tabletop interactions. *Proceedings of the 19th international conference on Intelligent User Interfaces (IUI '14)*, 47–56.

What Makes Live Events Engaging on Facebook Live, Periscope, and Snapchat

Oliver L. Haimson[1,2]
ohaimson@uci.edu
[1]Microsoft Research
Redmond, WA, USA

John C. Tang[1]
johntang@microsoft.com
[2]Department of Informatics
University of California, Irvine
Irvine, CA, USA

ABSTRACT

Live streaming platforms bring events from all around the world to people's computing devices. We conducted a mixed methods study including interviews ($N = 42$) and a survey ($N = 223$) to understand how people currently experience events using Facebook Live, Periscope, and Snapchat Live Stories. We identified four dimensions that make remote event viewing engaging: immersion, immediacy, interaction, and sociality. We find that both live streams and the more curated event content found on Snapchat are immersive and immediate, yet Snapchat Live Stories enable quickly switching among different views of the event. Live streams, on the other hand, offer real time interaction and sociality in a way that Snapchat Live Stories do not. However, the interaction's impact depends on comment volume, comment content, and relationship between viewer and broadcaster. We describe how people experience events remotely using these social media, and identify design opportunities around detecting exciting content, leveraging multiple viewpoints, and enabling interactivity to create engaging user experiences for remotely participating in events.

Author Keywords

Live streams; events; video; user engagement; social media; Facebook Live; Periscope; Snapchat.

ACM Classification Keywords

H.5.m. Information interfaces and presentation (e.g., HCI): Miscellaneous.

INTRODUCTION

In June 2016, thousands watched as U.S. House of Representatives Democrats and C-SPAN used the Periscope live streaming platform to broadcast the Democrats' sit-in to protest gun control political inaction after the official camera feed was turned off [61]. Outside, supporters also used Periscope to live stream their rally. Several weeks later, a Minnesota woman used Facebook Live to live stream the aftermath of a police officer shooting her boyfriend Philandro Castille [53]. In August, a New Yorker's Periscope stream of a man climbing Trump Tower using suction cups reached over 225,000 live viewers [27]. These are just a few well-publicized events in 2016 that demonstrated the rise of live streaming as a tool for sharing exciting or contentious events. Beyond these national stories, many events were live streamed at a smaller scale: concerts, birthday parties, political marches, karaoke nights, gaming conventions, and baseball games, just to name a few.

Snapchat also emerged in 2016 as a major media platform [19,31] both for social sharing and event experiences via the Snapchat Stories feature, recently mimicked by Facebook, Instagram, and others [24]. Snapchat "Live" Stories are not truly live, instead appearing 45 minutes to 16 hours after an event, in our observation. They are human or algorithmic curations of user-submitted video or photo "Snaps." While many breaking news events, such as the House sit-in and Castille's murder, did not appear as Snapchat Live Stories, others, including the Trump Tower climber, did. Snapchat Live Stories tend to focus on planned events like sports games, festivals, and conventions, but do sometimes feature breaking news stories (though not in real time).

While live streams and Snapchat Live Stories offer popular but different experiences for viewing events, together they provide a window into how people use social media to remotely experience events today. To understand this emergent sociotechnical phenomenon, we conducted a mixed methods study including interviews ($N = 42$) and a survey ($N = 223$). We examined how people use the most prominent live streaming tools, Facebook Live and Periscope, along with Snapchat Live Stories, to view and share event experiences. We asked, what is engaging about viewing events live? How do live streamed events compare with viewing Snapchat Live Stories? We define user engagement as a quality of user experience characterized by four of O'Brien and Toms' [41] user engagement attributes that are most relevant to viewing events remotely: focused attention, endurability (i.e., satisfaction), novelty, and felt involvement [39]. By understanding current tools' strengths and limitations, we identify design opportunities for new user experiences around remotely participating in events.

CHI 2017, May 06 - 11, 2017, Denver, CO, USA.

ACM 978-1-4503-4655-9/17/05...$15.00
DOI: http://dx.doi.org/10.1145/3025453.3025642

We find that both live streams and Snapchat Live Stories are engaging for viewers. However, people desire to view a future event via live streams more than Snapchat Live Stories, largely due to the interaction live streams afford with the streamer and other viewers. We contribute an empirical understanding of how people use social media to view events and what makes this experience engaging.

BACKGROUND

Despite the growing popularity of live streams, any individual live stream can be boring. Zooming into any given region on Periscope's or Facebook's live map interface will likely reveal many streams of talking heads, "Untitled" broadcasts of people going about their day or showing their surroundings, and even broadcasts titled "Bored." Even when a viewer's friends' broadcasts show up in their Facebook feed, they may find that friend's commentary or even vacation footage boring.

However, during events, live streams can provide engaging viewing experiences. From the perspective of a person in the stadium, a sports fan can watch her favorite baseball team win the game. An activist can view a political march thousands of miles away, from the perspective of someone in the middle of the crowd. These can be powerful experiences, but may also be punctuated with down times. Perhaps the team has not scored in a few innings. Maybe the protesters are losing steam toward the end of a long march. Something *could* happen at any moment, but the viewer cannot anticipate whether anything *will* happen. This keeps them watching. Live streamed events are engaging but dull.

Snapchat Live Stories, on the other hand, tend to be fast-paced and exciting. Curated to only include videos and photos from lively periods during an event, they give viewers a quick snapshot of event highlights. The sports fan can still watch her favorite team win the game and skip the uneventful innings; however, she can only view the event after the game has already been won. The activist likely cannot view the political march via Snapchat Live Stories unless the march was high-profile enough to be on Snapchat's radar, which many smaller events are not.

We compare these two platform types, live streams and Snapchat Live Stories, to understand how to better design user experiences for remote event viewing. How can a system optimize the engaging parts and work around the dull moments in event live streams? How can it deliver exciting event experiences in real time? We first provide background on the three platforms of interest (see Figure 1), which we chose due to their popularity, making it more likely that they offer multiple streams for events. We detail the state of each of these apps at the time of this writing, which we expect to change with the quick pace of technological development.

Facebook Live

Originally released in 2015 as a platform for celebrities and public figures to broadcast live content, Facebook Live was made available to all U.S. users in January 2016 [9]. While

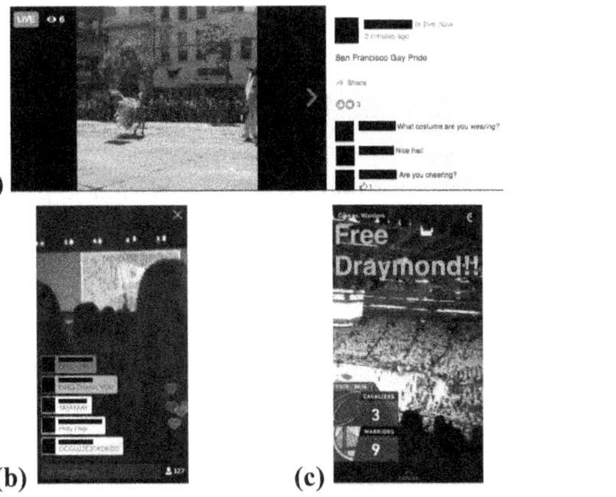

(a) (b) (c)

Figure 1. Screenshots showing user interfaces and interaction types for event viewers on Facebook Live (a), Periscope (b), and Snapchat Live Stories (c). (Please zoom in for detail).

Facebook Live streams can be broadcast publicly, people typically only come across streams broadcast by people they follow, either via notification or when a stream appears in their newsfeed. Users may also find event live streams by browsing using the Facebook Live Map [16]. Facebook Live streams offer several types of interaction: comments, which are persistent and appear to the right of the video for viewers and below the video for broadcasters; and reactions, including Like, Love, Haha, Wow, Sad, and Angry, which, when clicked or touched by the viewer, first show a small photo of the viewer's face which turns into the reaction's emoji while floating across the video screen.

Periscope

Periscope, owned by Twitter, is a live streaming platform launched in March 2015. The app operates separately from Twitter, and users can have separate social graphs on each, but live streams are typically shared publicly on Twitter using #Periscope when the broadcast begins. Event live streams are discoverable by browsing or searching event hashtags on Twitter or within the Periscope app, browsing in the app's map interface, or via notification if the broadcaster is a connection. Periscope live streams allow text comments (though only from the first 100 viewers), which overlay the video starting at the bottom of the screen before floating up and disappearing, and hearts, originating at the bottom right screen corner when the viewer taps and then floating up.

Snapchat Live Stories

Snapchat launched its "Live" Stories feature in June 2014 [11]. The feature allows event attendees to contribute to a collective story that can then be viewed by remote Snapchat users. Live Stories were displayed in the app under the "Live" heading starting in August 2014 [37]. After a user records a "Snap" (a video or photo, sometimes with overlaid annotations) at an event, users may be given the option of sharing to an event story, which appears above the list of people to whom the Snap can be sent. Snapchat then curates a selection of submitted Snaps into an event story, organized in a particular order (usually chronological), sometimes with added contextual information. Each Snap lasts for 10 seconds at most, and viewers can skip to the next by tapping the screen. At the time of this writing, Snapchat Live Stories afford no interactivity, and the Live Story is available for roughly 24 hours before disappearing.

RELATED WORK

Much as video communication tools enable people to share experiences across distance [6], mobile video media allow people to experience events as a group, rather than individually [28,29]. When live events are broadcast to remote audiences, "distributed liveness" occurs as new configurations of audience, broadcasters, and technologies combine various physical and social environments [59]. Live streams can make shared event experiences especially vivid by intertwining physical and digital experiences [12]. To effectively support event spectatorship, technology must be designed to consider people, context, and the event [38]. This is especially important for remote viewers, who lack situational context of an event's physical surroundings.

Yet both present and remote event spectators face challenges. Event spectatorship is tricky, because the closer a spectator is to a particular active area, the more she loses context for the larger event [15]. Live streaming systems can enable broader context via multiple streams from different event areas. Dezuli et al. designed a system that allowed event spectators to share videos of different perspectives with each other [12]; however, users had to already be friends to share content, a limitation that diminishes when content is shared publicly on live stream platforms.

Live event attendees often record event videos as a way both to relive the experience later, and to give a gift to those who could not attend in person; however, videos of live events cannot replace the experience of being there in person [34]. Several studies have capitalized on event audiences' willingness to record video, creating systems for collaborative video productions to enhance crowd-recorded event content [4,49,50].

Live streaming is an important resource for sharing information during political, breaking news, and crisis events, and can be a means for civic engagement [13] and citizen [17,33,48] as well as professional journalism [17]. For political events, live streaming enables what Andén-Papadopoulos [1] calls "citizen camera-witnessing," a means for people to document and spread images of oppression, and what Gregory [20] calls "co-presence," the shared sense of space and time that bridges the gap between event participants and audience. Thus, remote audiences can witness and even participate in events [2,20].

Live streams have become popular in part because of the opportunity for viewers to interact with and participate in streams, and even to build informal, impromptu communities through shared viewing [21,22,55]. Broadcasters appreciate interactivity, and often let viewers' comments influence their streams' content [51,55]. While Twitter offers some interactivity during live events through text [52], live streams offers that interaction in sync with visual event footage.

Two-way interaction between viewers and broadcasters can be powerful, but brings challenges on both sides. Live streamed event experiences suffer when remote audiences do not feel acknowledged by streamers, or when event performers or broadcasters cannot tell whether their audience is engaged [45,59]. Broadcasters could improve live stream experiences for viewers by avoiding repetitive content and making stronger connections with their audiences [46]. Technical challenges also detract from both broadcasters' and viewers' live stream experiences [30], and most streams currently draw few viewers [54].

Viewer experiences are improved when they have multiple live streams to choose from. Tang et al. [55] found evidence of multiple live streams from events, signifying the potential to aggregate multiple streams into a rich event experience for viewers. Hamilton et al. [22] prototyped this idea using Rivulet, a system offering viewers a multiple-stream interface for events, and found that multiple streams engaged users through interaction and a shared experience.

While a large body of literature has examined Facebook as a social network site (e.g., [14,32]), no research has been published yet about Facebook Live as an event-viewing platform. Previous literature on Snapchat has investigated it as a communication platform, to understand types of content people post and how their behaviors relate to self-presentation, privacy, and ephemerality [5,44,47,56–58,62]. Yet no research to date has studied Snapchat Live Stories. We examine Facebook and Snapchat in a new light, along with Periscope, to understand how people use these popular social media platforms to view events remotely.

METHODS

We conducted a mixed methods study involving interviews ($N = 42$) and a survey ($N = 223$) to understand how people use Facebook Live, Periscope, and Snapchat Live Stories to view and share event experiences. We took an iterative approach to the study design, adjusting our methods as we learned from our interview data. The study was approved by the ethics review committee at our institution.

Data Collection: Interviews

Interviews took place in June – August 2016 in three phases. In all phases, interviews were semi-structured to allow participants to focus on topics most salient in their viewing or broadcasting experience. Viewer interviews focused on how viewers experienced events remotely, what they found engaging about event viewing on the different platforms, what was missing from their experience, and how they interacted with broadcasters and other viewers. Each interviewee received a $20 Amazon gift card gratuity.

Phase 1: Within-subjects approach

In this phase, we asked participants ($N = 8$) to view content from one of two popular events (an NBA Finals game and the gaming convention E3 Expo) on each of the three platforms. We chose events that we anticipated would offer multiple live streams as well as a Snapchat Live Story. We matched participants to events based on their interest in recent events they had attended, elicited by a screening survey. Participants were instructed to view 15 minutes total of content within a designated timeframe and to switch between the three platforms as they wished, while making sure to view at least two different live streams of the event on both Facebook Live and Periscope, and the event's Snapchat Live Story. Different participants may have watched different streams, reflecting a realistic user experience in which each chose what appealed most to them. They were also asked to interact with at least one live stream on each platform. To make events as consistently discoverable as possible between Facebook Live and Periscope, we directed participants to use the Facebook Live Map [16] and Periscope's map view to find streams. We then interviewed participants for approximately 30 minutes within 48 hours after their event viewing experience.

Phase 2: Between-subjects approach

Phase 2 was similar to Phase 1, but instead we employed a between-subjects approach, where some participants ($N = 6$) viewed live streamed content and others ($N = 4$) viewed Snapchat Live Stories for two popular events (San Francisco Pride parade and VidCon convention for online video). The between-subjects approach allowed us to understand participants' experiences with the different platforms without them making their own comparisons.

Phase 3: In-the-wild approach

In Phase 3, we interviewed people ($N = 14$) who had chosen to view event live streams "in the wild" (i.e., on their own accord) within the last three weeks. This allowed us to understand viewing motivations and experiences more holistically by focusing on people who were self-motivated to seek out live streamed event content.

Broadcaster interviews

Throughout the three phases, we also recruited and interviewed broadcasters ($N = 10$) from the same events viewed by Phase 1 and 2 viewers, and from events similar to those viewed by Phase 3 viewers.

Recruitment

To recruit, we created a screening survey that we sent out to email lists for interns and full-time employees at our company, shared via our personal networks on Facebook and Twitter, and posted on event and live stream-focused groups on Facebook and forums on Reddit. We chose participants for Phases 1 and 2 based on their interest in the event types we wanted them to view and their willingness to download and use the platforms studied. We chose Phase 3 participants based on the type of events they had viewed or broadcast, aiming to get a wide range of event types. We limited our sample to people between ages 18-44 to capture the demographics common for live streaming platforms [3].

Data Analysis: Interviews

We analyzed interviews using iterative open coding, allowing codes to emerge from the data, and the constant comparative method to develop themes and organize codes within themes [10]. We focused our coding on factors that make live streams and Snapchat Live Stories engaging, limitations to viewing, and differences among the platforms. We quickly learned that live streams and Snapchat Live Stories are vastly different experiences – the former is a way to view events remotely, while the latter is a summary of event content – and we treated them as such for the remaining data collection and analysis. We met regularly to collaboratively discuss the emerging codes and to organize them into larger themes, an iterative process that evolved as we analyzed more data. We ultimately settled on four themes that contribute to viewer engagement and limitations to viewing, and with which we can compare across the different platforms: immersion, immediacy, interaction, and sociality. Each theme included a subset of codes, described in the results section. After reaching saturation, we coded the remaining interview data using this coding scheme.

Data Collection: Survey

Based on the themes and codes that emerged in our interview data analysis, we created a survey instrument to validate the findings among a larger population of live stream viewers. We wanted to quantify user engagement across the platforms and understand which factors contributed most to user engagement. We asked participants to recall a specific event when they viewed one or more live streams. For this event, we measured engagement using a subset of questions from O'Brien and Toms' validated user engagement scale [41] (see Table 1). Additionally, we developed questions to measure the presence of each of the codes within our four themes (immersion, immediacy, interaction, and sociality) for that event. For example, "The [live stream(s)/Snapchat Live Story] enabled me to be one of the first people to see the event" helped us measure the immediacy theme. Users responded on a 5-point Likert scale ranging from Strongly disagree to Strongly agree. Participants were required to

	A Live streams (full sample) $N = 223$	**B** Live streams (those who also viewed Snapchat) $N = 63$	**C** Snapchat Live Stories $N = 63$	Diff. btwn. **A & C**	Diff. btwn. **B & C**
Scale or variable	Mean (Standard deviation)				
Engagement (average of Focused Attention, Endurability, Novelty, Involvement)	3.85 (0.62)	4.06 (0.72)	3.96 (0.72)	†	n.s.
Focused Attention[a]	3.43 (0.98)	3.86 (0.83)	3.68 (0.98)	*	†
Endurability[a] (Satisfaction)	4.02 (0.73)	4.18 (0.75)	4.15 (0.72)	†	n.s.
Novelty[a]	4.07 (0.63)	4.18 (0.64)	4.01 (0.79)	n.s.	n.s.
Involvement[a]	3.88 (0.80)	4.02 (0.79)	3.98 (0.94)	n.s.	n.s.
Wanting to experience a future event via platform	4.22 (0.73)	4.40 (0.61)	4.03 (0.97)	n.s.	*
Immersion[b]	3.82 (0.59)	4.02 (0.51)	3.93 (0.70)	†	n.s.
Immediacy[b]	3.57 (0.58)	3.58 (0.57)	3.48 (0.57)	n.s.	n.s.
Interactivity[b]	3.47 (0.60)	3.63 (0.58)	-	-	-
Sociality[b]	3.75 (0.74)	4.05 (0.75)	-	-	-

[a]subset of questions from [37]

[b]average of responses to several questions about factors associated with theme

† $p < 0.10$; * $p < 0.05$; ** $p < 0.01$; *** $p < 0.001$

Table 1. Descriptive statistics for scales and variables used in survey instrument.

have viewed a live streamed event within the past three weeks. Those who had also viewed a Snapchat Live Story within the past three weeks were given additional questions about that experience. The Snapchat Live Stories survey section did not include questions about interactivity or sociality since the platform does not afford such interactions between event story viewers and those who submit Snaps.

Recruitment

We used SurveyGizmo as an intermediary to recruit panel participants from Cint, a firm specializing in panel recruitment. As with the interview sample, we recruited people ages 18-44. The survey was active for 1.5 weeks in August 2016. We received 376 complete surveys, which we cleaned using both manual inspection and SurveyGizmo's data cleaning tools. We removed 153 responses for one or more of the following reasons: viewing a live stream that was not an event; viewing an event via a platform other than those being studied (e.g., on television); failing our "trap" questions; speeding; straightlining or patterned responses; fake or gibberish text responses. This left 223 completed, clean responses, for which we paid $15 each.

Data Analysis: Survey

We analyzed the quantitative survey data using descriptive statistics and Wilcoxon tests to understand differences in engagement and viewing experience on the platforms. We built linear regression models to identify factors that most contributed to (1) viewer engagement and (2) wanting to experience a future event via live streams. We used a type of backwards feature selection called recursive feature elimination in R's caret package [7] to determine the optimal features to include in the models (see Table 2).

Participant Data

Interview participants

Interview participants were 55% women, 43% men, and 2% genderqueer and had a mean age of 25 (*SD* = 6.15). 76% viewed and/or broadcast on Facebook Live, 64% on Periscope, 50% on both live stream platforms, and 10% on Snapchat only. 64% had viewed a Snapchat event story recently. Because many of the interviews took place in July 2016 during and after the Republican and Democratic National Conventions (which we classified as conventions rather than political rallies or breaking news, though they fit in multiple categories), the convention category is most prevalent at 35%, followed by political rallies, marches, and protests (17%), breaking news (15%), and public social

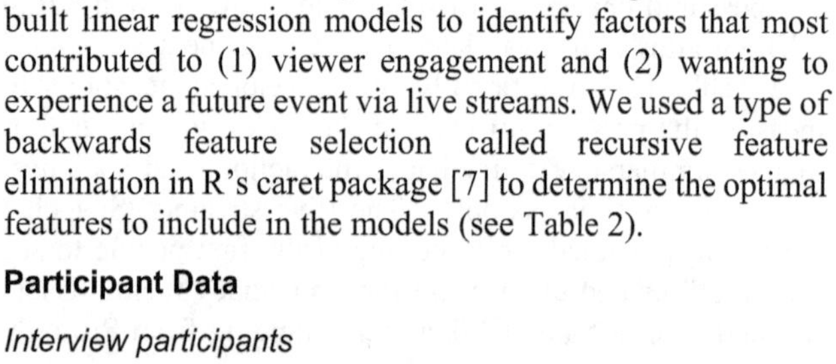

Figure 2. Percent of participants who viewed each event type.

events (15%) (see Figure 2). The interview event type percentages add up to more than 100% because many interview participants had viewed or broadcast more than one type of event, while in the survey we asked participants to recall one particular event.

Survey participants

Survey participants were 63% women and had a mean age of 31 (*SD* = 6.86). After removing major outliers, survey participants had viewed on average 2.91 live streams (*SD* = 2.01, median = 2) for an average viewing time of 38.39 minutes (*SD* = 41.08, median = 25). 93% viewed live streams on Facebook Live, 16% on Periscope, and 9% on both platforms. 28% had also viewed a Snapchat Live Story within the past three weeks. Due to the survey's timing, the most common event type was Olympics-related (22%) followed by concerts/performances (16%), breaking news (16%), and public social events (15%) (see Figure 2).

Limitations

For the survey, we recruited live stream viewers, then asked the subset of them who had viewed Snapchat Live Stories about that experience. Recruiting specifically for Snapchat Live Stories viewers may have led to different results. Additionally, recruiting for some interviewees internally at our institution skewed participants toward being young and tech-savvy; a skew that may also hold for users of the tools we study. For the survey, however, we recruited a more general population via the panel sample, and still found support for our interview findings. Finally, in the regression models we controlled for event type, but particular streams that participants watched may have been more engaging than others, a potential confound.

RESULTS

In this work, we first show that live streamed events, as well as Snapchat Live Stories (a more curated and after-the-fact way to view events), engage viewers. We then detail what makes remote event viewing engaging. We find that while immersion and immediacy make remote event viewing engaging for both live streams and Snapchat Live Stories, live streams are unique in providing interactive and social experiences. Even without interactivity, Snapchat Live Stories are engaging because they offer a simple and concise way to browse through multiple rich pieces of content, a feature currently missing from live stream platforms. Though interactivity is key to engaging live streamed event viewing experiences, interactivity can drive or detract from engagement depending on the content and volume of comments and the relationship between viewer and broadcaster. We elaborate on these results, and present statistical results from the survey and quotes from the interviews.

Remote event viewing is engaging.

Live streams are engaging for most viewers. Live stream engagement was, on average, 3.85 on a 5-point Likert scale (*SD* = 0.62). To add some context, this metric is higher than O'Brien and Toms' user engagement scale [41] in the context of video games (M = 3.66) [60], online shopping (M = 3.38) [42], and multimedia webcasts (M = 3.05 after translating to a 5-point Likert scale) [40], when taking the average of subscales similar to those we used (see Table 1). In our interviews we learned that engagement is a broad construct made up of many dimensions. Beyond engagement more generally, in this section we detail how engagement for live streams compared to engagement for Snapchat Live Stories, and what factors make remote event viewing engaging for viewers.

Live streams are as engaging as Snapchat Live Stories.
To understand how engaged viewers were for live streams compared to Snapchat Live Stories, we conducted a paired Wilcoxon signed-rank test with continuity correction. The Wilcoxon test is a non-parametric statistical test used to compare means for two samples of ordinal data, appropriate for Likert-scale data such as ours. We find no significant difference between live stream engagement ($M = 4.06$, $SD = 0.54$) and Snapchat Live Stories engagement ($M = 3.96$, $SD = 0.72$), $V = 879.5$, $p = 0.24$, for those survey participants who viewed events on both platforms. Thus, we conclude that viewers find live streams, on average, just as engaging as Snapchat Live Stories.

Immersion and immediacy make event viewing engaging.
Four dimensions that make event viewing engaging emerged inductively from our qualitative interview analysis: immersion, immediacy, interactivity, and sociality. Using these dimensions, we can compare and contrast across platforms. While both live streaming platforms in this study (Periscope and Facebook Live) exhibit all four of these characteristics, Snapchat Live Stories do not afford interaction or sociality. Interestingly, both interview and survey participants attributed immediacy to Snapchat Live Stories despite the fact that the stories are not truly immediate. We now discuss immersion and immediacy, the two dimensions that make event viewing engaging for both live streams and Snapchat Live Stories.

Immersion
Immersion is the feeling of "being there," an experience that video systems have attempted to provide for remote parties for a number of years [18,43] and which is significantly associated with event viewing engagement, $r(221) = 0.65$, $p < 0.001$. As one interview participant described her event viewing experience:

You're sort of like being there without necessarily being there. I get really into watching [sports events], and I really like watching the hockey games or the soccer games live so I can be like, 'I was there when he scored.' – Phase 2, F, 20

Watching a sports event remotely via live stream gave an experience immersive enough that this person can recount *being there* when the athlete scored. But what contributes to this sense of being there? We identified five factors that make remote event viewing immersive. First, a viewing experience is immersive if the energy and excitement of the event comes through in the video. Seeing and hearing an excited and energetic crowd is a second, closely related factor that enables immersion for viewers. Getting another person's perspective allows for an immersive experience, as does seeing the event from a privileged or special viewpoint (e.g., front row or backstage). Finally, when a viewer can see multiple views and experience multiple people's perspectives, the event becomes even more immersive.

Variable	**Model 1: Live stream engagement**		**Model 2: Wanting to experience a future event via live streams**	
	Coefficient (Standard error)			
Immersion variables				
Energy and excitement	0.19***	(0.04)	0.24***	(0.07)
Crowd's presence			0.19**	(0.06)
Other people's perspectives	0.14**	(0.04)		
Multiple viewpoints	0.09**	(0.03)		
Immediacy variables				
Unpredictability	0.14***	(0.03)	0.11*	(0.05)
Access to information not available elsewhere	0.14***	(0.03)		
Being the first to see an event	0.09**	(0.03)		
Content not censored or edited			0.08*	(0.04)
Interactivity variables				
Other viewers responded to comments/questions			0.12*	(0.05)
Many comments			-0.11*	(0.05)
Control variables (included in model; none statistically significant; details omitted for space)				
Age; Gender; Time viewed; Used Periscope; Also viewed Snapchat; Event type; Broadcaster relationship to viewer				
Adjusted R^2	0.54		0.29	

† p < 0.10; * p < 0.05; ** p < 0.01; *** p < 0.001

Table 2. Linear regression models examining factors associated with engagement (Model 1) and wanting to view a future event via live streams (Model 2).

In the survey, several of these factors were significantly associated with engagement in Model 1 (see Table 2): energy and excitement (on a 5-point Likert scale, a 1 point increase in a live streamed event's energy and excitement increases engagement by 0.19, $p < 0.001$), access to other people's perspectives, and multiple viewpoints.

Snapchat Live Stories are similarly immersive; an interviewee described gaining other people's perspectives, special viewpoints, and multiple views while watching a Story for a fashion event:

It was not only the designers; it was the models, it was the actual people who were doing the clothes, the fashion artists, the makeup artists, whatever. It was cool because you could see just a lot of perspectives. You could see from the perspective of someone walking on the runway. Then the next story was someone watching the same walk from the audience. So it was really fun. We could see all of the different angles. You could see all of the different stories there. – Phase 3, F, 20

Thus, Snapchat Live Stories enable multiple views in a quick, easy, and exciting user experience.

Immediacy

By virtue of being live, live streams give viewers a sense of immediacy. Viewers can see what is happening in real time, and this immediacy is associated with a more engaging viewing experience, $r(221) = 0.53, p < 0.001$. A major factor of immediacy is unpredictability; that is, the sense that the viewer, and the broadcaster, do not know what will happen next. An interview participant described the unpredictable nature of viewing a Black Lives Matter rally:

You know, we watch so many videos online of things getting out of hand or things turning violent... And so watching it remotely I think there was constantly this sense of what's going to happen. Is something going to go wrong? Is something going to turn violent? – Phase 3, M, 32

Additionally, immediacy involves having access to information that one could not find elsewhere, and being one of the first to learn about an event as it unfolds. Many interview participants described viewing live streamed events, such as political rallies or concerts, that were not covered by mainstream news sources. In these instances, people could stay current on the event's developments via live stream. Because the content was also not censored or edited by any media company, live streams enabled viewers to see "what really happened."

Statistical modeling helps us understand how immediacy factors relate to engagement. In Model 1 (see Table 2), unpredictability, access to information not available elsewhere, and being one of the first to see an event were significantly positively related to live stream engagement.

Although Snapchat Live Stories are not truly live, many interview and survey participants reported viewing them as immediate. They do offer several of the characteristics that we found relate to immediacy: an inability to predict what one will see next, and access to information not available elsewhere. Surprisingly, although content often appears on Snapchat hours after it happens, 62% of survey respondents who had viewed Snapchat Live Stories reported that they enabled them to be one of the first to see an event. Snapchat Live Stories may not be truly immediate, but they are immediate enough for some users, perhaps because some do not check their phone often enough for true immediacy to matter [8]. Snapchat Live Stories also appear unedited and uncensored to 43% of Snapchat-viewing survey participants, despite being professionally or algorithmically edited and curated (a costly and time-consuming endeavor). Snapchat's ability to appear immediate without being truly live gives insight into what makes Snapchat Live Stories so engaging.

The quick switch is important.

Snapchat Live Stories provide an immersive and immediate experience in a very different way than live streams. On Snapchat, the viewer switches between viewpoints very quickly: no video or photo is displayed for longer than 10 seconds, and users can tap the screen even before a Snap ends to get to the next one. On Facebook Live and Periscope, viewers can become immersed in an event experience for a longer timespan without the view switching so quickly. However, to get multiple viewpoints, viewers must exit out of one live stream, interrupting their viewing experience while searching or browsing for another stream. This detracts from immersion and immediacy because people lose concentration and worry that they might miss an important event moment. Thus, many interview participants described desiring a fast, easy way to switch between streams. One interviewee described wanting to switch between live streams as easily as changing television channels:

Imagine that some big event happened and you are surfing channels on the TV. Sometimes if you're watching the news, you would be like, 'This news channel isn't covering enough details about this.' Then you see what the other guys are covering. So I can imagine in my head the same thing playing out [with live streams]. – Phase 3, M, 27

Another interviewee described the importance of being able to switch quickly between different event content on Snapchat, enabling immersion and immediacy:

I love that I can just go back and forth between the content they show. That, to me, is really awesome, especially if ... let's say Xbox and Sony both had their press conferences at the same time. How can I pick? I want to be doing it all at the same time. I think that quick switch is really important. – Phase 1, M, 20

The quick switch is missing from Periscope. Some Facebook Live streams include a subtle arrow (see Figure 1) that allows switching to another stream, but the feature remained undiscovered by participants in our study, and the "next" streams are often unrelated. Providing the ability to quickly switch between different viewpoints of an event, in real time, could be a powerful way to increase user engagement.

People want to experience future events more via live streams than via Snapchat Live Stories.

Despite the absence of a quick switch, people were nonetheless eager to experience future events via live stream. We found that survey participants wanted to experience a future event significantly *more* via live streams ($M = 4.40$, $SD = 0.61$) than they did via Snapchat Live Stories ($M = 4.03$, $SD = 0.97$), $V = 457.5, p < 0.05$. While Snapchat Live Stories offer a compelling way of quickly and easily managing multiple viewpoints, with a sense of immediacy despite not showing content in real-time, we argue that interactivity is the important aspect missing from the Snapchat Live Story experience that leads people to be more likely to turn to live streams for future event viewing. We discuss the exciting and challenging nature of real-time interactivity for designing engaging real-time event experiences in the next section.

Interactivity is key in remote event viewing experiences.

While watching video content is often a passive experience, attending an event is typically interactive: the crowd cheers together for the musician on stage; the people checking out the same booth at a convention make small talk. Thus, to fully experience an event remotely, viewers must have the ability to interact with broadcasters and with other viewers. One interview participant described the excitement and involvement that real time interaction affords:

I am able to ask [a] question through [the broadcaster's] involvement, which is amazing to me, but I also think having that live feed, especially to breaking events or anything that is on the cusp of enacting change or that has personal meaning to me is – it's exciting. – Phase 3, G, 30

In this section we detail what we mean by interaction and sociality in live streamed events, how they relate to user engagement, and some of the challenges in providing interactive viewer experiences.

Live streams are interactive and social in a way that Snapchat Live Stories are not.

Interaction and sociality, two important factors contributing to engagement for live streams, are absent from Snapchat Live Stories. Participants noticed this difference and many (70% of survey respondents who had viewed Snapchat Live Stories) reported wanting to be able to interact with Snapchat Live Stories. As one interviewee stated:

Snapchat's a lot different 'cause Snapchat's like... you can't interact with a story. But with Periscope and Facebook, I think that's something I did enjoy from them. – Phase 2, F, 19

Interaction

Interaction is an important aspect of engagement for live streams, $r(221) = 0.41, p < 0.001$. Fichet et al. [17] found that interactions between live stream viewers and broadcasters importantly allow the audience to participate in crisis events as they unfold, and we find that this is also true for non-crisis events. Interactions on live streams include text comments and questions, to which broadcasters and other viewers often respond. A specific interaction type that people reported was requests, where viewers can often influence the broadcaster's actions at the event. As one interview participant who viewed a gaming expo described:

Someone asked like..., 'Oh, what are the specs on this game?' And then the person there could answer just by looking at the booth display, or... read it to them and just walk up closer. – Phase 1, F, 20

Interactions also include likes and reactions on Facebook Live and hearts on Periscope. Interview participants described these reactions as lightweight ways to show appreciation to broadcasters, particularly after an exciting moment in the stream. Viewer interactions encouraged other viewers to interact with the live streams:

So when that happened, there was tons of hearts, and then I felt like I probably clicked more than I would have because I saw more people commenting and, you know, their comments – or their interactions, rather, in both types – encouraged more interactions on my part. – Phase 1, M, 20

Model 2 (see Table 2) shows that when other viewers responded to comments or questions made on a live stream, survey participants were significantly more likely to want to experience a future event via live stream. This demonstrates the importance of interactivity in the live streaming experience, which was echoed in our interview data. One interview participant described that broadcasters answering viewer questions enabled *"a personal engagement with the individual who is providing that live video" (Phase 3, G, 30)*. Another described how interactions with broadcasters and other viewers led to an immersive experience:

I think questions are very important. It was very cool to be able to see other people's questions, answer them, have the broadcaster answer them. It really feels like you are with them at the moment, if they see what you are saying and they reply. – Phase 2, F, 19

Interactivity is a key difference between event content that is broadcast live in real time, and content that is made available afterwards. Interactive live streams make viewers feel, as one interview participant put it, like *"you actually have a say and you feel like you have a voice that could be heard" (Phase 1, M, 25)*. Interactions on live streams may help explain why live streams are as engaging as Snapchat Live Stories, despite often including long stretches when nothing particularly interesting occurs. Live streams are an active, rather than a passive, means of viewing video.

Sociality

By sociality, we mean the ways that live streams can be social even *without* the viewer interacting in any way. Sociality is positively associated with engagement, $r(221) = 0.59$, $p < 0.001$. Sociality occurs particularly when the broadcaster is a friend of the viewer's, and enables friends to connect remotely. Interviewees described using live streams as a way to remotely attend events with a group of friends, or *"catching up with them, even without greeting them" (Phase 3, M, 27)*.

Even when people did not know other viewers of the same event, live stream viewers sometimes created impromptu, short-term groups of people who were all viewing the same content, as found in previous research [21,22,55]. In this way, people could share the viewing experience with others, further adding to sociality and engagement.

Finally, live stream viewing was often motivated by emotional proximity [26], a term we extend from crisis informatics to apply to events more broadly. Emotional proximity is defined as "an emotional connection to people who were affected by a crisis, or a sentimental association to the crisis location" [26]. Interview participants reported feeling emotionally and socially connected to live streams involving a person or place that they cared about:

It helps that I am from Toledo and that's where [the live stream] was from, so I think there's this kind of emotional connection with growing up and hearing about this special event that happened here. So yeah, definitely kind of felt that emotional connection. – Phase 3, F, 21

Emotional proximity to both Toledo and to her friend who was broadcasting the event compelled this participant to view several songs by a country singer, despite the fact she was not typically a country fan. Other interview participants described feeling motivated to view live streams from the Turkish military uprising because they felt connected to friends from Turkey. Sociality makes live streams emotionally relevant and, together with interactivity, contributes to engaging live stream viewing experiences.

Comment volume and content affects interactivity.

As much as interactivity overall makes live streams engaging, certain interactive aspects can cause challenges. In particular, the volume and content of comments can make interactivity exciting or frustrating, especially on Periscope, where the text comments overlay the video. Many interview participants reported disliking streams with overwhelming amounts of text, which participants described as distracting:

Most of the time it was just all those comments popping up, distracting if I'm really trying to watch it ... if I want to read the comments I'll read them, but I just want to watch a video without distractions. – Phase 2, F, 20

Others remarked on the overwhelming and unruly nature of comments on live streams, often expressing frustration that broadcasters would not get the chance to see or respond to their comment in the sea of text. Even if text overload could be decreased, the problem of which text should be displayed remains. Many interview participants remarked on the boring nature of some comments (e.g., "Hi from [location]!"). While mundane comments can be annoying for viewers, harassing or offensive comments are even worse. Particularly with political events or events celebrating marginalized identities, online harassment occurred in real time, as described by an interview participant:

The one thing I hate, though, about the bubbles just popping up like that is that there were a lot of trolls,... and it being a Pride Festival there was a lot of hate speech, and so... that was kind of ruining the experience on some videos for me. – Phase 2, M, 21

Finding the right balance between a stream that is interactive enough vs. overwhelming text, or a stream with exciting debate vs. online harassment, is a challenge for live stream platform designers and moderators. This difficult balance may account for the fact that in Model 2 (Table 2), more comments on a live stream is negatively associated with wanting to experience a future live streamed event, *coef.* = -0.11, $p < 0.05$. The tradeoffs live stream viewers face between interaction and engagement highlight the need to design for interactive experiences that recognize the nuances of real time commenting. This requires handling comment volume and content in real time, whether through human, crowdsourced, or automated moderation.

Who is broadcasting matters for interactivity.

In addition to nuances around comments, the nature of a viewer's relationship to the broadcaster also affects a live stream's interactivity. Viewers find live streams engaging no matter who is broadcasting; in Model 1 we found no significant effects for broadcaster type. People also desire to view a future event via live streams the same amount no matter who is broadcasting (Model 2). However, when it comes to interaction, the viewer's relationship with the broadcaster matters.

Barriers to interaction arise on live streams. Many viewers are lurkers on social media more broadly, and live streams are no exception. Others reported not knowing a tool's norms well enough to feel comfortable commenting. However, if a broadcaster is a friend, barriers to interaction often dissolve. People liked the opportunity to interact more on live streams broadcast by friends ($M = 4.12$, $SD = 0.82$) than those live streams not broadcast by friends ($M = 3.78$, $SD = 0.85$), $W = 6024.5$, $p < 0.01$. One interview participant described feeling comfortable interacting when she knew the broadcaster:

If it were people that I knew, like someone live streaming a birthday party or something like that,... I would totally interact. That barrier would absolutely be gone. With strangers, that could be like corporations, it feels like there are so many comments and so much traffic that is being generated that whatever you put is just lost in the void almost. – Phase 3, F, 20

This quote highlights the fact that it is not only a viewer's relationship to the broadcaster that encourages interaction; viewers must also be sure that their comments will be seen. Thus, to increase interactivity, live streaming platforms must cleverly manage text volume without making viewers feel that their voices are not being heard.

While a viewer may prefer to interact when a friend is broadcasting, many events that she would want to view are not attended by her friends. It is not realistic to expect that one's friends would be present at, for instance, the Cubs game in Pittsburgh, or the Adele concert in London. Remotely attending these events via live stream would require streams broadcast by strangers or professional sources. Finding ways to increase interaction among strangers might enable live stream platforms to sustain interaction during events, which is key to engaging live stream experiences.

DISCUSSION AND IMPLICATIONS FOR DESIGN

In this work we showed how interaction with broadcasters and other viewers engages viewers of live streamed events. At the same time, though interactivity is missing, people love the experience of viewing events on Snapchat and the way the platform presents an immersive experience without the dull segments often present in live streams. We identify opportunities for designing event viewing tools that offer interactivity *and* exciting, Snapchat-like user experiences. We apply our results to explore how to provide interactive, social, immersive, real-time event viewing experiences.

Detecting exciting content

Snapchat requires skilled content curators, an algorithm that identifies compelling content, or a combination of the two, to deliver Live Stories. Such content curation is costly, and adds a time window between when content is recorded and viewed. In contrast, we suggest that a similarly compelling event experience could be achieved by delivering live streamed, user-generated content in an easily-browseable format, using the crowd to generate and highlight interesting material. The value of interactivity and sociality suggests ways of creating a more satisfying experience. Because most live stream experiences currently focus on individual streams, not the overall event, we need to help people find which stream *within an event* is of most interest to them. Thus, we need to develop digital equivalents for the cues people use to decide what acts in a three-ring circus to attend to: they look to see which act is attracting the biggest crowd (number of viewers) and which is getting the most engagement via applause and laughter (hearts and text comments). As Mostafa et al. [36] found, detecting exciting streams and moments in streams is feasible by analyzing the volume of user actions: views, comments, and likes/hearts. We recommend that designers leverage this crowd-generated information to enable early detection of engaging content, and make it available in an experience in which viewers can quickly discover and switch among different views.

Managing multiple views

Spectators, media sources, and even performers record many videos during events, but this vast collection of content is not well organized or easily consumable by viewers. Even the collection of live streamed content for a particular event on a particular platform (e.g., the Olympics on Facebook Live), is not easy for viewers to discover, browse, and view. Thus, a live streaming tool should allow viewers to easily and quickly browse through different live streams from the same event – the "quick switch" or "surfing channels" approach participants mentioned in interviews. This is something that Snapchat does well, by allowing viewers to tap on the screen to access the "next" Snap. However, when browsing real-time event content, it is less clear how to specify the "next" logical stream. Crowd-generated information, along with geographical proximity, could be used to organize streams into a ribbon of content that viewers could flip back and forth among. Such an approach would increase immersion and decrease the possibility of missing an important event moment by displaying multiple streams in an easy-to-navigate manner and eliminating the need to exit out of one stream and browse for another.

Capitalizing on interactivity

Live streaming enables a new form of "active spectatorship" [29] in which spectators can be geographically remote; thus, live streaming platforms must be designed specifically for a collective, rather than individual, viewing experience. Interactivity is a key component of active spectatorship. We described three limitations to interactivity in live streams: comment volume, comment content, and barriers to interacting with broadcasters who are not friends. To address these issues, we discuss opportunities for creating the right kind of interactions that add to, rather than detract from, immersion and engagement. Live stream platforms should employ clever ways to manage comment streams on popular live streams to tackle comment content and volume issues. One solution is to use crowdsourcing to highlight the most important comments [35]. Another is to segment comments by grouping viewers based on social graphs or shared interests. Our results indicate that interaction increases when the streamer is a friend; thus, grouping viewers according to their social network connections could lead to a more comfortable context for commenting. When watching television remotely with friends and family, social awareness and lightweight messaging makes people feel more involved in viewing [23]. This likely holds for live streams: making small, personal chat channels available for people to view live streams with and interact with friends, family, or existing online communities (rather than strangers) could increase viewer interactivity and engagement. Additionally, providing an interface in which users could add live streams into existing group text or video chats would provide an exciting, personal, and social event viewing experience. Another optimal strategy may be to group commenters by shared interest or allegiance (e.g., Cubs fans in one comment channel and Indians fans in another), with the caveat that this may lead to filter bubbles.

If designed well, live stream platforms that enable multiple views and promote interactivity can meet needs that are not currently met even by physical event attendance, enabling remote event experiences to go "beyond being there" [25]. By highlighting design opportunities, we hope to influence live stream system design to create new, engaging experiences around attending events remotely.

CONCLUSION

We empirically examined people's experiences with viewing videos of remote events across three current platforms. By understanding the dimensions that make live streamed events engaging (immersion, immediacy, interaction, and sociality) and current tools' limitations (the cumbersome nature of finding exciting content, viewing multiple streams, and managing comments), we outline design opportunities for live streaming platforms. With this work, we contribute a nuanced understanding of remote event viewing, and inform the continued emergence of this sociotechnical phenomenon.

ACKNOWLEDGEMENTS

We thank study participants for sharing their experiences with us. We also acknowledge Microsoft Research colleagues (Gina Venolia, Kori Inkpen, Matthew Miller, and Gerard Wilkinson), Nazanin Andalibi, and anonymous reviewers for providing valuable feedback on this work.

REFERENCES

1. Kari Andén-Papadopoulos. 2013. Citizen camera-witnessing: Embodied political dissent in the age of "mediated mass self-communication." *New Media & Society*: 1461444813489863. https://doi.org/10.1177/1461444813489863
2. Kari Andén-Papadopoulos. 2013. Media witnessing and the "crowd-sourced video revolution." *Visual Communication* 12, 3: 341–357. https://doi.org/10.1177/1470357213483055
3. Salman Aslam. 2015. Periscope by the Numbers: Stats, Demographics & Fun Facts. http://www.omnicoreagency.com/periscope-statistics/
4. Tom Bartindale, Guy Schofield, and Peter Wright. 2016. Scaffolding Community Documentary Film Making Using Commissioning Templates. In *Proceedings of the 2016 CHI Conference on Human Factors in Computing Systems* (CHI '16), 2705–2716. https://doi.org/10.1145/2858036.2858102
5. Joseph B. Bayer, Nicole B. Ellison, Sarita Y. Schoenebeck, and Emily B. Falk. 2016. Sharing the small moments: ephemeral social interaction on Snapchat. *Information, Communication & Society* 19, 7: 956–977. https://doi.org/10.1080/1369118X.2015.1084349
6. Jed R. Brubaker, Gina Venolia, and John C. Tang. 2012. Focusing on Shared Experiences: Moving Beyond the Camera in Video Communication. In *Proceedings of the Designing Interactive Systems Conference* (DIS '12), 96–105. https://doi.org/10.1145/2317956.2317973
7. caret. Recursive Feature Elimination. http://topepo.github.io/caret/rfe.html
8. Yung-Ju Chang and John C. Tang. 2015. Investigating Mobile Users' Ringer Mode Usage and Attentiveness and Responsiveness to Communication. 6–15. https://doi.org/10.1145/2785830.2785852
9. Josh Constine. 2016. Facebook Takes On Periscope By Giving Live Streaming To All U.S. iPhoners. https://techcrunch.com/2016/01/28/comfortable-ephemerality-vs-reach/
10. Juliet Corbin and Anselm Strauss. 2008. *Basics of qualitative research: Techniques and procedures for developing grounded theory.* Sage.
11. Jordan Crook. 2014. Snapchat Launches Collaborative Timelines Based On Events. https://techcrunch.com/2014/06/17/snapchat-launches-collaborative-timelines-based-on-events/
12. Niloofar Dezuli, Jochen Huber, Elizabeth F. Churchill, and Max Mühlhäuser. 2013. CoStream: Co-construction of Shared Experiences Through Mobile Live Video Sharing. In *Proceedings of the 27th International BCS Human Computer Interaction Conference* (BCS-HCI '13), 6:1–6:10. http://dl.acm.org/citation.cfm?id=2578048.2578057
13. Audubon Dougherty. 2011. Live-streaming Mobile Video: Production As Civic Engagement. In *Proceedings of the 13th International Conference on Human Computer Interaction with Mobile Devices and Services* (MobileHCI '11), 425–434. https://doi.org/10.1145/2037373.2037437
14. Nicole B. Ellison, Charles Steinfield, and Cliff Lampe. 2007. The Benefits of Facebook "Friends:" Social Capital and College Students' Use of Online Social Network Sites. *Journal of Computer-Mediated Communication* 12, 4: 1143–1168. https://doi.org/10.1111/j.1083-6101.2007.00367.x
15. Mattias Esbjörnsson, Barry Brown, Oskar Juhlin, Daniel Normark, Mattias Östergren, and Eric Laurier. 2006. Watching the cars go round and round: designing for active spectating. In *Proceedings of the SIGCHI conference on Human Factors in computing systems*, 1221–1224. http://dl.acm.org/citation.cfm?id=1124955
16. Facebook. 2016. Facebook Live Map. https://www.facebook.com/livemap
17. Elodie Fichet, John Robinson, Dharma Dailey, and Kate Starbird. 2016. Eyes on the Ground: Emerging Practices in Periscope Use during Crisis Events. In *Proceedings of ISCRAM 2016.* http://faculty.washington.edu/kstarbi/ISCRAM2016_Periscope_FINAL.pdf
18. Robert S. Fish, Robert E. Kraut, and Barbara L. Chalfonte. 1990. The VideoWindow System in Informal Communication. In *Proceedings of the 1990 ACM Conference on Computer-supported Cooperative Work* (CSCW '90), 1–11. https://doi.org/10.1145/99332.99335
19. Sarah Frier. Snapchat Passes Twitter in Daily Usage. *Bloomberg.com.* http://www.bloomberg.com/news/articles/2016-06-02/snapchat-passes-twitter-in-daily-usage
20. Sam Gregory. 2015. Ubiquitous witnesses: who creates the evidence and the live(d) experience of human rights violations? *Information, Communication & Society* 18, 11: 1378–1392. https://doi.org/10.1080/1369118X.2015.1070891
21. William A. Hamilton, Oliver Garretson, and Andruid Kerne. 2014. Streaming on Twitch: Fostering Participatory Communities of Play Within Live Mixed Media. In *Proceedings of the 32Nd Annual ACM Conference on Human Factors in Computing Systems* (CHI '14), 1315–1324. https://doi.org/10.1145/2556288.2557048
22. William A. Hamilton, John Tang, Gina Venolia, Kori Inkpen, Jakob Zillner, and Derek Huang. 2016. Rivulet: Exploring Participation in Live Events Through Multi-Stream Experiences. In *Proceedings of the ACM International Conference on Interactive Experiences for TV and Online Video* (TVX '16), 31–42. https://doi.org/10.1145/2932206.2932211
23. Gunnar Harboe, Crysta J. Metcalf, Frank Bentley, Joe Tullio, Noel Massey, and Guy Romano. 2008. Ambient social tv: drawing people into a shared experience. In *Proceedings of CHI*, 1. https://doi.org/10.1145/1357054.1357056

24. Alex Heath. Here are all the times Facebook copied Snapchat in 2016. *Business Insider*. http://www.businessinsider.com/all-the-times-facebook-copied-snapchat-in-2016-2016-12
25. Jim Hollan and Scott Stornetta. 1992. Beyond Being There. In *Proceedings of the SIGCHI Conference on Human Factors in Computing Systems* (CHI '92), 119–125. https://doi.org/10.1145/142750.142769
26. Y. Linlin Huang, Kate Starbird, Mania Orand, Stephanie A. Stanek, and Heather T. Pedersen. 2015. Connected Through Crisis: Emotional Proximity and the Spread of Misinformation Online. In *Proceedings of the 18th ACM Conference on Computer Supported Cooperative Work & Social Computing* (CSCW '15), 969–980. https://doi.org/10.1145/2675133.2675202
27. Gerald Iorio. 2016. #TrumpClimber. *Periscope*. https://www.periscope.tv/w/1vOxwpkOjYLKB
28. Giulio Jacucci, Antti Oulasvirta, Tommi Ilmonen, John Evans, and Antti Salovaara. 2007. Comedia: Mobile Group Media for Active Spectatorship. In *Proceedings of the SIGCHI Conference on Human Factors in Computing Systems* (CHI '07), 1273–1282. https://doi.org/10.1145/1240624.1240817
29. Giulio Jacucci, Antti Oulasvirta, and Antti Salovaara. 2006. Active construction of experience through mobile media: a field study with implications for recording and sharing. *Personal and Ubiquitous Computing* 11, 4: 215–234. https://doi.org/10.1007/s00779-006-0084-5
30. Oskar Juhlin, Arvid Engström, and Erika Reponen. 2010. Mobile broadcasting: the whats and hows of live video as a social medium. In *Proceedings of the 12th international conference on Human computer interaction with mobile devices and services*, 35–44. http://dl.acm.org/citation.cfm?id=1851610
31. Hope King. 2016. Teens say Snapchat is "most important social network." *CNNMoney*. http://money.cnn.com/2016/04/13/technology/snapchat-instagram-facebook/index.html
32. Cliff Lampe, Nicole Ellison, and Charles Steinfield. 2006. A face(book) in the crowd: social Searching vs. social browsing. In *Proceedings of the 2006 20th anniversary conference on Computer supported cooperative work* (CSCW '06), 167–170. https://doi.org/10.1145/1180875.1180901
33. Ben Lenzner. 2014. The emergence of Occupy Wall Street and digital video practices: Tim Pool, live streaming and experimentations in citizen journalism. *Studies in Documentary Film* 8, 3: 251–266. https://doi.org/10.1080/17503280.2014.961634
34. Jessa Lingel and Mor Naaman. 2012. You should have been there, man: Live music, DIY content and online communities. *New Media & Society* 14, 2: 332–349. https://doi.org/10.1177/1461444811417284
35. Matthew K. Miller, John C. Tang, Gina Venolia, Gerard Wilkinson, and Kori Inkpen. 2017. Conversational Chat Circles: Being All Here Without Having to Hear It All. In *Proceedings of ACM CHI Conference on Human Factors in Computing Systems*.
36. Ahmed E. Mostafa, Kori Inkpen, John C. Tang, Gina Venolia, and William A. Hamilton. 2016. SocialStreamViewer: Guiding the Viewer Experience of Multiple Streams of an Event. In *Proceedings of the 19th International Conference on Supporting Group Work* (GROUP '16), 287–291. https://doi.org/10.1145/2957276.2957286
37. David Nield. 2014. Our Story event streams go live for all Snapchat users. *Digital Trends*. http://www.digitaltrends.com/mobile/story-event-streams-go-live-snapchat-users/
38. Andreas Nilsson, Urban Nulden, and Daniel Olsson. 2004. Spectator Information Support: Exploring the Context of Distributed Events. In *The Interaction Society: Practice, Theories and Supportive Technologies: Practice, Theories and Supportive Technologies*. Idea Group Inc (IGI).
39. Heather L. O'Brien and Elaine G. Toms. 2008. What is user engagement? A conceptual framework for defining user engagement with technology. *Journal of the American Society for Information Science and Technology* 59, 6: 938–955. https://doi.org/10.1002/asi.20801
40. Heather L. O'Brien and Elaine G. Toms. 2010. Is there a universal instrument for measuring interactive information retrieval?: the case of the user engagement scale. In *Proceedings of Information Interaction in Context*, 335. https://doi.org/10.1145/1840784.1840835
41. Heather L. O'Brien and Elaine G. Toms. 2010. The development and evaluation of a survey to measure user engagement. *Journal of the American Society for Information Science and Technology* 61, 1: 50–69. https://doi.org/10.1002/asi.21229
42. Heather Lynn O'Brien. 2010. The influence of hedonic and utilitarian motivations on user engagement: The case of online shopping experiences. *Interacting with Computers* 22, 5: 344–352. https://doi.org/10.1016/j.intcom.2010.04.001
43. Gary M. Olson and Judith S. Olson. 2000. Distance Matters. *Hum.-Comput. Interact.* 15, 2: 139–178. https://doi.org/10.1207/S15327051HCI1523_4
44. Lukasz Piwek and Adam Joinson. 2016. "What do they snapchat about?" Patterns of use in time-limited instant messaging service. *Computers in Human Behavior* 54: 358–367.
45. Stuart Reeves, Steve Benford, Claire O'Malley, and Mike Fraser. 2005. Designing the Spectator Experience. In *Proceedings of the SIGCHI Conference on Human Factors in Computing Systems* (CHI '05), 741–750. https://doi.org/10.1145/1054972.1055074
46. Stuart Reeves, Christian Greiffenhagen, Martin Flintham, Steve Benford, Matt Adams, Ju Row Farr, and Nicholas Tandavantij. 2015. I'D Hide You: Performing Live Broadcasting in Public. In *Proceedings of the 33rd Annual ACM Conference on Human Factors in*

Computing Systems (CHI '15), 2573–2582. https://doi.org/10.1145/2702123.2702257

47. Franziska Roesner, Brian T. Gill, and Tadayoshi Kohno. 2014. Sex, Lies, or Kittens? Investigating the Use of Snapchat's Self-Destructing Messages. In *Financial Cryptography and Data Security*, Nicolas Christin and Reihaneh Safavi-Naini (eds.). Springer Berlin Heidelberg, 64–76. http://link.springer.com/chapter/10.1007/978-3-662-45472-5_5
48. Adam Rugg and Benjamin Burroughs. 2015. Periscope, Live-Streaming and Mobile Video Culture. In *Geoblocking and Global Video Culture*. Institute of Network Cultures, Amsterdam.
49. Marco Sá, David Shamma, and Elizabeth Churchill. 2014. Live mobile collaboration for video production: design, guidelines, and requirements. *Personal & Ubiquitous Computing* 18, 3: 693–707. https://doi.org/10.1007/s00779-013-0700-0
50. Guy Schofield, Tom Bartindale, and Peter Wright. 2015. Bootlegger: Turning Fans into Film Crew. In *Proceedings of the 33rd Annual ACM Conference on Human Factors in Computing Systems* (CHI '15), 767–776. https://doi.org/10.1145/2702123.2702229
51. David A. Shamma, Elizabeth F. Churchill, Nikhil Bobb, and Matt Fukuda. 2009. Spinning Online: A Case Study of Internet Broadcasting by DJs. In *Proceedings of the Fourth International Conference on Communities and Technologies* (C&T '09), 175–184. https://doi.org/10.1145/1556460.1556486
52. David A. Shamma, Lyndon Kennedy, and Elizabeth F. Churchill. 2009. Tweet the Debates: Understanding Community Annotation of Uncollected Sources. In *Proceedings of the First SIGMM Workshop on Social Media* (WSM '09), 3–10. https://doi.org/10.1145/1631144.1631148
53. Catherine E. Shoichet. 2016. Facebook Live video offers new perspective on police shootings. *CNN*. http://www.cnn.com/2016/07/07/us/facebook-live-video-minnesota-police-shooting/index.html
54. Matti Siekkinen, Enrico Masala, and Teemu Kämäräinen. 2016. A First Look at Quality of Mobile Live Streaming Experience: the Case of Periscope. In *Proceedings of Internet Measurement Conference*. http://arxiv.org/abs/1605.04270
55. John C. Tang, Gina Venolia, and Kori M. Inkpen. 2016. Meerkat and Periscope: I Stream, You Stream, Apps Stream for Live Streams. In *Proceedings of the 2016 CHI Conference on Human Factors in Computing Systems* (CHI '16), 4770–4780. https://doi.org/10.1145/2858036.2858374
56. Sonja Utz, Nicole Muscanell, and Cameran Khalid. 2015. Snapchat Elicits More Jealousy than Facebook: A Comparison of Snapchat and Facebook Use. *Cyberpsychology, Behavior, and Social Networking* 18, 3: 141–146. https://doi.org/10.1089/cyber.2014.0479
57. J. Mitchell Vaterlaus, Kathryn Barnett, Cesia Roche, and Jimmy A. Young. 2016. "Snapchat is more personal": An exploratory study on Snapchat behaviors and young adult interpersonal relationships. *Computers in Human Behavior* 62: 594–601. https://doi.org/10.1016/j.chb.2016.04.029
58. Jon M. Wargo. 2015. Spatial Stories with Nomadic Narrators: Affect, Snapchat, and Feeling Embodiment in Youth Mobile Composing. *Journal of Language & Literacy Education* 11, 1. http://files.eric.ed.gov/fulltext/EJ1061110.pdf
59. Andrew M. Webb, Chen Wang, Andruid Kerne, and Pablo Cesar. 2016. Distributed Liveness: Understanding How New Technologies Transform Performance Experiences. In *Proceedings of the 19th ACM Conference on Computer-Supported Cooperative Work & Social Computing* (CSCW '16), 432–437. https://doi.org/10.1145/2818048.2819974
60. Eric N. Wiebe, Allison Lamb, Megan Hardy, and David Sharek. 2014. Measuring engagement in video game-based environments: Investigation of the User Engagement Scale. *Computers in Human Behavior* 32: 123–132. https://doi.org/10.1016/j.chb.2013.12.001
61. Nicky Woolf. 2016. Democrats stream gun control sit-in on Periscope after Republicans turn TV cameras off | US news | The Guardian. https://www.theguardian.com/technology/2016/jun/22/democrats-sit-in-periscope-facebook-live-gun-control
62. Bin Xu, Pamara Chang, Christopher L. Welker, Natalya N. Bazarova, and Dan Cosley. 2016. Automatic Archiving Versus Default Deletion: What Snapchat Tells Us About Ephemerality in Design. In *Proceedings of the 19th ACM Conference on Computer-Supported Cooperative Work & Social Computing* (CSCW '16), 1662–1675. https://doi.org/10.1145/2818048.2819948

Reducing Interruptions at Work: A Large-Scale Field Study of FlowLight

Manuela Züger[1], Christopher Corley[2], André N. Meyer[1], Boyang Li[2], Thomas Fritz[1], David Shepherd[2], Vinay Augustine[2], Patrick Francis[2], Nicholas Kraft[2], Will Snipes[2]

[1]University of Zurich, Zurich, Switzerland
[2]ABB Corporate Research, Raleigh, United States

{zueger, ameyer, fritz}@ifi.uzh.ch, {christopher.corley, boyang.li, david.shepherd, vinay.augustine, patrick.francis, nicholas.a.kraft, will.snipes}@us.abb.com

ABSTRACT

Due to the high number and cost of interruptions at work, several approaches have been suggested to reduce this cost for knowledge workers. These approaches predominantly focus either on a manual and physical indicator, such as headphones or a closed office door, or on the automatic measure of a worker's interruptibilty in combination with a computer-based indicator. Little is known about the combination of a physical indicator with an automatic interruptibility measure and its long-term impact in the workplace. In our research, we developed the FlowLight, that combines a physical traffic-light like LED with an automatic interruptibility measure based on computer interaction data. In a large-scale and long-term field study with 449 participants from 12 countries, we found, amongst other results, that the FlowLight reduced the interruptions of participants by 46%, increased their awareness on the potential disruptiveness of interruptions and most participants never stopped using it.

ACM Classification Keywords

H.5.3. Information Interfaces and Presentation: Group and Organization Interfaces

Author Keywords

Interruption cost; knowledge worker; awareness; physical indicator; automatic interruptibility measure; field study

INTRODUCTION

Knowledge workers are frequently interrupted by their co-workers [13, 10, 29]. While many of these interruptions can be beneficial, for instance to resolve problems quickly [20], they can also incur a high cost on knowledge workers, especially if they happen at inopportune moments and cannot be postponed [4, 22, 8, 24].

CHI 2017, May 6-11, 2017, Denver, CO, USA.

ACM 978-1-4503-4655-9/17/05...$15.00
http://dx.doi.org/10.1145/3025453.3025662

Due to the high cost and the high number of interruptions that knowledge workers experience every day (e.g., [10, 13]), several approaches have been proposed that can roughly be categorized by the interruptions they address: computer-based and in-person. Studies have shown that the cost of computer-based interruptions can successfully be mitigated by automatically detecting a knowledge worker's interruptibility and mediating interruptions by deferring them to more opportune moments (aka. defer-to-breakpoint strategy) [19, 2, 16]. Another strategy to reduce the cost of computer-based interruptions is to indicate a person's interruptibility to co-workers in a contact-list style application on the computer [30, 21, 5]. While these approaches have also been suggested for addressing in-person interruptions, they did not show to have any effect on them, probably since the contact-list style applications can easily be hidden behind other applications and thus forgotten at communication initiation [21, 5, 12, 14].

For in-person interruptions—one of the most costly kind of interruptions due to their high frequency and immediate nature [29, 13, 24]—approaches predominantly rely on manual strategies to physically indicate interruptibility, such as wearing headphones, closing the office door, or using busy lights that have to be set manually [29, 1]. Since manual approaches are cumbersome to maintain, users generally don't update them on a regular basis and their accuracy and benefits are limited [25]. Only very few approaches have looked at a combination of a physical interruptibility indicator with an automatic interruptibility measure to reduce the cost of in-person interruptions [15, 7] and there is no knowledge on the long-term effects of such approaches.

In our research, we developed the FlowLight approach, an approach to reduce the cost of in-person interruptions by combining a physical interruptibility indicator in the form of a traffic-light like LED (light emitting diode) with an automatic interruptibility measurement based on a user's computer interaction. In a large-scale and long-term field study with 449 knowledge workers from 12 countries and 15 sites of a multinational corporation, we evaluated the FlowLight and its effects in the workplace. Over the course of the study, we collected a rich set of quantitative and qualitative data, including self-reported interruption logs of 36 participants, survey responses of 183 participants that used the FlowLight for at least 4 weeks, and in-depth interviews of 23 participants.

Our analysis of the data shows, amongst other results, that the FlowLight significantly reduced the number of interruptions of participants by 46%, while having little impact on important interruptions. Further, the FlowLight increased the awareness on the cost of interruptions within the workplace, participants felt more productive using the FlowLight and most participants continued using the light for up to 13 months by now. Overall, the gained insights on the long-term usage of the FlowLight provide strong support for the benefits of combining a physical interruptibility indicator with an automatic interruptibility measure in the workplace and its significant impact on reducing in-person interruption costs.

RELATED WORK

Related work on managing interruptions can broadly be grouped into strategies for reducing interruptions and disruptiveness, and ways of measuring and indicating interruptibility.

Reducing Interruptions and their Disruptiveness

Knowledge workers have long recognized the detrimental effects of interruptions and have sometimes developed their own techniques for managing them. These techniques include the use of instant messaging to negotiate availability for an interruption beforehand and reduce the disruptiveness for the interrupted person [26], as well as the use of manual and physical indicators, such as headphones or a closed office door to either signal unavailability or tune out distractions [29].

In addition to these informal means, researchers have developed approaches to reduce the negative effects of interruptions. One strategy to reduce the disruptiveness of interruptions is to defer them from moments when the interruptee is in the middle of a task to naturally occurring breakpoints—aka. 'defer-to-breakpoint' strategy. This idea is based on studies finding that the cognitive load drops at task boundaries, and that interruptions at lower cognitive load are less harmful [3, 8]. Iqbal and Bailey developed a system that implements a defer-to-breakpoint policy to reschedule notifications to more opportune moments and found that they caused less frustration and shorter reaction times [19]. Ho and Intille used accelerometers to detect activity transitions and found that messages on mobile devices were better received during transitions compared to random times [16]. While these approaches have been successful at mitigating interruptions from the computer and mobile devices, they do not address the frequent and costly in-person interruptions in workplaces that the FlowLight targets.

A second strategy that builds upon the idea of deferring interruptions to more opportune moments is to indicate a knowledge worker's interruptibility to potential interrupters and thereby implicitly help negotiate the timing of the interruption. In the following, we discuss approaches to measure and to indicate a knowledge worker's interruptibility.

Measuring Interruptibility

Previous research has explored various features to measure a person's interruptibility. For instance, Hudson et al. simulated sensors by coding audio and video recordings into features related to the person's current context, such as the number of people present or the phone being on the hook [18]. While their approach showed promise in measuring interruptibility, the chosen features are difficult to capture automatically.

To automatically detect a person's interruptibility, Stern et al. developed an approach that is based on the person's location and calendar information [28]. Fogarty et al. used speech sensors, location and calendar information and activity on the computer to measure presence and availability [11]; Tani and Yamada measured interruptibility using the pressure applied on the keyboard and mouse [31]; and Coordinate by Horvitz et al. uses user activity and proximity of multiple devices to forecast presence and availability [17].

More recently researchers have also started to use biometric data to measure interruptibility. For instance, Kramer classified interruptibility during a US military training with an electroencephalography (EEG) sensor that captures the electrical activity of the brain [23]. Chen et al. calculated interruptibility based on an electromyography (EMG) sensor that captures heart rate variability and muscle activity [9]. In our previous work, we used various biometric sensors (EEG, electrodermal activity (EDA), skin temperature, and photoplethysmography (PPG)) to predict interruptibility [32]. Overall, research has shown that biometric sensors can be valuable in automatically measuring interruptibility, however, at this point the biometric sensors required to accurately measure interruptibility are generally still too invasive for long-term usage.

The FlowLight builds upon previous research in this area by automatically measuring interruptibility based on a combination of computer activity, calendar information and log-in state. It thereby utilizes a minimally invasive set of features that performs well without compromising the users' privacy or requiring additional body-worn biometric sensors. It further extends previous research in this area by combining the automatic measure with a physical indicator.

Indicating Interruptibility

To indicate a knowledge worker's interruptibility to co-workers, most prior research focused on contact list-style tools that are installed on the user's computer and vary mostly in the data that is used to determine availability/interruptibility. For instance, the ConNexus tool has a contact list view that provides awareness information on a person's device idleness, log-in state and activity history and thus indicates a person's availability to facility communication for the integrated communication channels, such as IM [30]. Awarenex and Lilsys build on ConNexus, adding mobile location tracking and physical presence sensors, respectively. An evaluation of these tools found a qualitative improvement in interruption awareness but no reduction in the number of interruptions [5]. Lai et al.'s MyTeam approach uses information on presence, network connection and mouse and keyboard activity to indicate availability in a contact list. In a small user study, they found that the approach decreased the number of phone calls and voice mails but increased the face-to-face interruptions [21]. Fogarty et al. developed MyVine that integrates with a phone, IM and an email client and uses context information from speech sensors, computer activity, location and calendar information. A four week study revealed that the context information was mainly used as presence indicator and did not prevent interruptions via IM [12]. Overall, study results for these computer-based interruptibility indicators suggest that they can help increase awareness on the disruptiveness of interruptions, which could be a first good step as stated by Beyea[6]. However, the results also suggest that these approaches do not reduce in-person interruption costs, which is what the FlowLight is addressing.

Since in-person interruptions are one of the top causes for interruptions in the workplace and their immediate nature makes them particularly disruptive [29], researchers found that knowledge workers use physical indicators, such as headphones or office doors to indicate interruptibility and reduce interruptions and distraction [29].

Only few researchers examined indicators that are not just visible on a knowledge worker's computer monitor. InterruptMe projects availability cues of possible contacts onto a wall at the time when the interrupter is about to initiate a communication [15, 14]. The MoodLight uses an ambient display connected to an electro-dermal activity (EDA) monitor that indicates the excitement level of one or two individuals [27]. Bjelica et al. developed an automatic interruptibility indicator that displays the status through ambient lighting effects and found in a small and short study that the indicator reduced the number of interruptions [7]. The FlowLight presented in this paper uses a physical traffic-light like LED placed at the desk of each person, such that the person's interruptibility status can be seen by anyone approaching. Thereby, our approach is more direct and prominent than subtle ambient lighting and different to previous research, our large-scale field study examines the long-term effects of such physical indicators.

APPROACH AND IMPLEMENTATION

The FlowLight consists of a computer application to automatically determine a user's interruptibility state and a physical LED light to indicate this state to co-workers. The FlowLight was developed iteratively over more than a year and improved continuously based on feedback from a small developer team that we used for testing, and later on, also based on feedback from study participants.

Physical LED Light. FlowLight uses a physical traffic-light like LED to indicate the interruptibility status to co-workers. This light has evolved throughout the pilots[1]. The first model, which was designed and soldered in-house, is shown in Figure 1a. In Figure 1b the same model light is shown encased in plastic and deployed in an open office space. Finally, Figure 1c shows the blink(1)[2] LED light that we adopted to avoid installation issues with certain drivers immediately after the first major pilot, which was also the first of two pilots in India (denoted as India #1 in Figure 2). Typically, we mounted the LED light on a user's cubical wall or outside a user's office.

The light uses different colors to indicate four states: *Available* as green, *Busy* as red, *Do Not Disturb (DnD)* as pulsating red, and *Away* as yellow. Note that these states and colors mimic the ones used by prominent instant messaging services, in particular the one used by the company under study.

[1]We use the term *pilot* to refer to each individual field study trial with a separate team.

[2]`https://blink1.thingm.com/`

Application. The application features three main components: a *Tracker* to capture events relevant for calculating the interruptibility state, a *Status Analyzer* to analyze the captured events and calculate the user's interruptibility state on the fly, and a *Status Manager* to manage the user's current status, propagating it to the LED light and other applications, in particular instant messaging (IM) clients. The application was implemented to be compatible with the Windows operating system, Skype for Business, an IM and video-conferencing system, and Office 365, a software suite that provides email and calendaring services, amongst others. We chose to tailor our application to these systems and applications due to the IT setup at the target company for our study.

The *Tracker* logs a user's mouse and keyboard interaction. In particular, it collects mouse clicks, movements as pixels moved, scrolling as pixels scrolled and keystrokes (without recording the specific key). This component also logs calendar events to determine meetings and the Skype status.

The *Status Analyzer* uses the tracked keyboard and mouse events to calculate the user's interruptibility status on the fly, i.e., whether the user is available, busy, highly busy (DnD) or away. The algorithms used to calculate the interruptibility status are described below.

The *Status Manager* is notified by the Status Analyzer at every change in the user's interruptibility, and then propagates the updated status to the physical LED light and the user's presence status in Skype for Business. The presence status in Skype for Business can also be changed manually by the user, or automatically by the Office 365 calendar, in case a meeting is scheduled. In case the presence status is changed manually, the Status Manager updates the interruptibility state of the application and the physical LED light.

Algorithms for Status Updates. Over the course of this study, we used three different algorithms to determine and update the interruptibility status automatically, improving them based on critical user feedback as discussed below.

FlowTracker. This algorithm sums up the computer interaction in the past three minutes according to heuristic weights assigned to each type of event, which were tuned based on feedback from early alpha and beta users of the FlowLight. If the value of the sum is in between the top 9% and the top 4% of their activity range—we captured averages over the past days—the user is considered busy. If it is within the top 4%, the user is considered highly busy. In our first pilot study in Bangalore, India (India #1 in Figure 2), we used different thresholds at first, namely 13% and 5% based on a prior study that indicated that knowledge workers are not interruptible for approximately 18% of their day. However, several technical writers (and others) involved in that pilot gave strong feedback that the light switched to the busy state too easily, which is why we lowered the thresholds to the mentioned 9% and 4%.

Smoothing. While the FlowTracker showed promise, many early users complained that it was too sensitive to certain input. For instance, a twenty second burst of typing may cause a user to temporarily be shown as busy. Therefore, the Smoothing algorithm marks users as busy if they were active in each of the

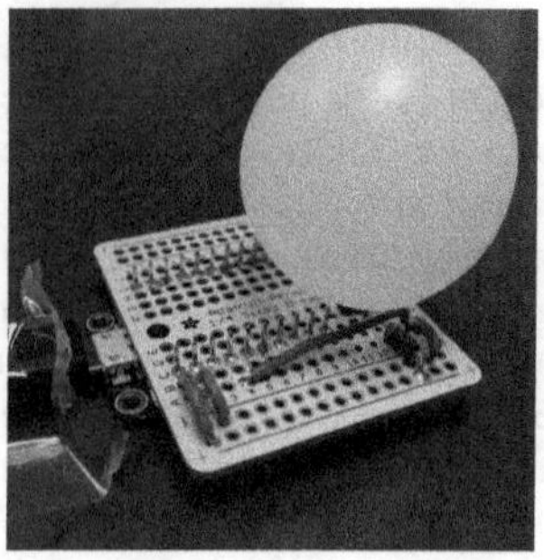

(a) July 2015 - Original Prototype

(b) August 2015 - First Major Pilot (Lights Emphasized with Overlays)

(c) October 2015 - Blink(1) Version with Adhesive Clip

(d) April 2016 - Deployment in Second Pilot in India (India #2)

Figure 1: Evolution of the Physical Indicator of the FlowLight Over Time

last three minutes and exceeded a threshold of 100 combined mouse clicks and key presses in the recent past (between 4 and 7 minutes ago). This algorithm reduces frequent changes by requiring over three minutes of activity to become busy and, once busy, by requiring only one above-threshold minute in the recent past to remain busy. To achieve the highly busy status, users had to be busy at the current point in time and had to be above-threshold for fifteen of the last thirty minutes.

Smoothed FlowTracker. While the Smoothing algorithm leads to fewer status changes, since it relied on a static threshold (i.e., 100 combined mouse clicks and key presses), it did not adapt to individual users' work patterns. For instance, designers working on drawings tended to use mouse clicks almost exclusively, which makes it difficult to exceed the threshold. Thus, we finally combined the FlowTracker algorithm with the Smoothing algorithm to achieve the advantages of both approaches. This algorithm, currently in use, operates as the Smoothing algorithm, but instead of using a static threshold, it utilizes the FlowTracker algorithm to determine above threshold values. This algorithm eliminated all of the most common complaints reported by pilot users. Further refinement of the algorithm is left for future work.

Although our main intent was to use an algorithm to infer interruptibility, we offered participants a "Manual Only" mode since it was requested by some participants, especially those with management roles that needed to be available to others most of the time, and we noticed (and our study confirmed) that our algorithms might not be accurate for everyone or for all activities requiring focus, such as reading or thinking.

EVALUATION

To evaluate the FlowLight, in particular the combination of the physical indicator and the automatic interruptibility measure as well as its effect on knowledge workers, we conducted a long-term and large-scale field study with 449 knowledge workers. For this study, we installed the FlowLight at over 15 locations in 12 countries of one multinational corporation. Over the course of the study, we collected a rich set of data using a combination of experience sampling, a survey, an interview and computer interaction monitoring. Figure 1 illustrates a few pictures of the FlowLight in use in different pilots. Figure 2 indicates the increasing and continuous number of participants

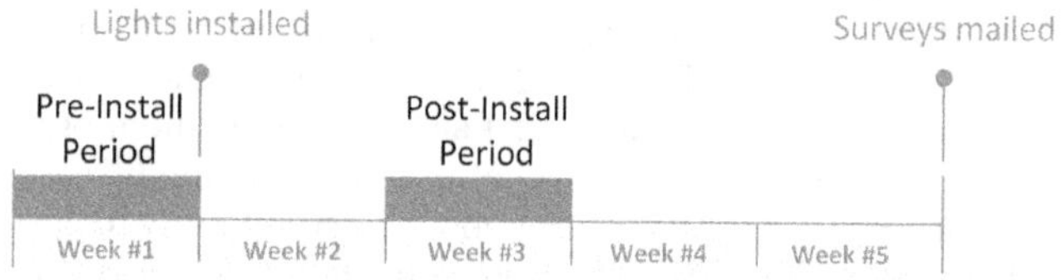

Figure 3: Timeline of Study Procedure

and the major pilots of this study since its beginning and up to September 2016.

Study Procedure

For each team participating in our field study we conducted the same five-week pilot procedure as illustrated in Figure 3. Prior to the start of a pilot, we asked the participants to install the FlowLight application in 'data collection only'-mode.

In *Week #1* of the pilot, users were instructed to use the FlowLight application to manually log the time and severity of each interruption during the five day work week. Our application allowed participants to log interruptions by a click on the taskbar menu or a hotkey combination for minimal invasiveness. As soon as an interruption had been logged, a single modal dialog appeared that asked participants to specify the severity of the interruption on a 5-point Likert scale.

At the beginning of *Week #2*, the physical indicator of the FlowLight was installed and the automatic status update feature for the interruptibility status was activated. To minimize Hawthorne-type effects and have participants and co-workers get used to the FlowLight, we then waited for one week before we gave further instructions.

At the beginning of *Week #3*, we again asked participants to manually log their interruptions for 5 work days. We also reminded participants about the manual logging in Week #1 and #3 to ensure they would not forget.

During *Week #4 and #5* users continued using the FlowLight. Throughout these 5 weeks the application collected anonymized usage data. At the end of *Week #5*, after participants had the FlowLight for four weeks, our application prompted them to complete a survey. The survey took an average of 14.2 minutes to complete and had questions on the

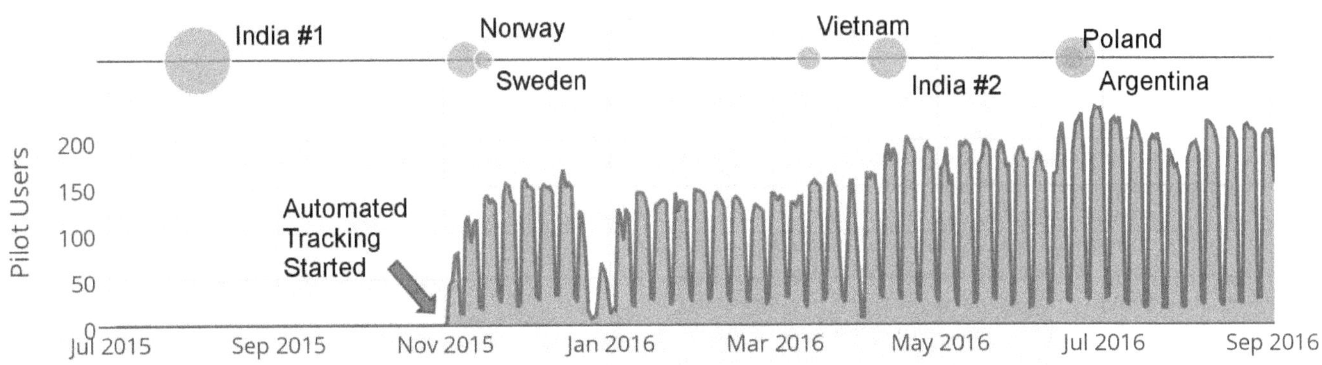

Figure 2: FlowLight Users Over Time (Size of Orange Circles Indicates the Number of Participants; Regular Dips in the Number of Pilot Users Represent Weekends and the Prolonged Dip in December/January 2016 represents the Christmas Break)

FlowLight approach and its impact, in particular on participants' interest in continuing using the approach, its impact on interruption costs, productivity and interaction behavior, on the accuracy of the automatic state detection and manual setting, as well as on general feedback and demographics. After completing the survey, users were asked on the last page of the survey to upload their data collected by the FlowLight application, which included the usage data logs and the logs of the manually captured interruptions.

For a deeper understanding of the long-term usage, experience and effect of the FlowLight, we conducted in-depth interviews with a subset of participants approximately two months after they installed the FlowLight. Interview participants were selected semi-randomly, based on accessibility, availability and willingness to participate in the interview. The interviews were on average 19.5 minutes long and the questions focused on the benefits and limitations participants observed with the FlowLight approach, as well as on how it impacted their own behavior and interactions in the team over the course of the two months since the installation. For instance, we asked participants whether they felt that their colleagues respected their FlowLight or if they noticed situations in which the status was not accurate. Note that the interview and survey questions can be found on our supplemental materials site [3].

Independent of the timeline of the study procedure, we also started to anonymously log the number of people running the FlowLight application each day. For privacy reasons, we only keep track of the number of unique active FlowLight users in the online log.

Participants

Since the beginning of our study 13 months ago, we installed the FlowLight approach with a total of 449 participants from 15 sites, located in 12 different countries, of one multinational corporation. From these 449 participants, we were able to gather:

Survey responses from 183 participants (IDs: S1-S183), 144 male and 39 female, with an average age of 36.0 years (standard deviation, in the following denoted with ±, of 8.7), an average professional experience of 12.0 years (± 8.0), from a variety of work areas, including 77 participants in development, 56 in other engineering, 24 in project management, 15 in other non-engineering, and 11 in testing, and with various job roles, including 70 individual contributors, 36 other, 32 leads, 31 managers, 8 executives, and 6 architects;

Interview transcripts (conducted by us) from 23 participants (IDs: I1-I23), 22 of which were male, 1 female, average age of 36.9 years (± 5.8), average experience of 13.2 years (± 4.7), and with various job roles, including 9 managers, 11 software developers, 1 researcher, 1 product owner, and 1 tester;

Interruption logs (self-reported) from 36 participants across six different countries, 13 from Argentina, 6 from Norway, 5 from Poland, 5 from Switzerland, 5 from Sweden, and 2 from the USA;

Usage data logs from 47 participants (IDs: D1-D47) 20 from Argentina, 18 from India, 4 from Poland, and 5 from Vietnam.

Online logs from all 449 participants that installed the approach (each one had the application running for at least one day after we integrated the logging feature).

Note that due to privacy concerns with the collected data, we did not require participants to identify themselves in each step and/or fill in their demographics, except for the survey, which is why we can only report some demographics for each round and are not able to track the participants across the different methods, for instance the survey and the self-reported interruption logging.

Data Collection and Analysis

Survey and Interview. In total, we collected survey responses from 183 participants after they had been using the FlowLight for at least four weeks, and interview transcripts from the 23 participants after they had been using the FlowLight for approximately two months. To analyze the textual data of the survey and interview responses, we used techniques based on Grounded Theory, in particular open coding and axial coding to determine higher level themes. To establish a common set of codes and themes, two of the authors applied open axial coding to the same subset of interview transcripts and then established a common understanding and defined a structure for the most commonly mentioned concepts. As the topics of the survey and interviews overlap, we used and extended the same coding scheme to analyze the textual survey responses.

[3] https://sites.google.com/site/focuslightonline

To validate the analysis of the survey results, two additional authors extracted their main findings from a subset of the responses independently.

Interruption Logs. Interruption logs capture the self-reported interruptions per participant logged with the FlowLight software. We collected interruption logs with at least two logged interruptions from 102 participants. We down-selected these to 36 logs by applying strict filtering criteria to ensure data validity as follows. We excluded all interruptions in all logs that were accidentally logged during the first five days after the installation of the FlowLight, as interruptions in the period right after the installation are not representative due to Hawthorne-type effects, such as participants getting used to the FlowLight, and co-workers asking curiosity questions. We then excluded all participants, that logged interruptions for fewer than three days in the pre- or the post-installation period. We chose three days as the threshold for each period to ensure a representative sample of work days for comparison without a too strong bias by individual outlier days. Each of the 36 interruption logs captured a combined average of 9.0 work days ($\pm$ 2.2) for pre- and post-period, and contained an average of 28.9 total logged interruptions ($\pm$ 17.0) per participant for the combined time period. We used these interruption logs to compare the impact of the FlowLight on the number of interruptions rated as disruptive by participants.

Usage Data Logs. We captured usage data logs from a total of 179 participants. These logs consist of computer interaction logs, such as mouse and keyboard events, and FlowLight usage data. Since we wanted to analyze user behavior before and after installing the light, we removed any logs that did not include at least two days before and after installing the light. We also excluded logs older than January 2016, as key usage messages were not yet logged by our software, making the analysis infeasible. We ended up with 47 usage data logs containing a total of 1560 work days. These logs consisted of an average of 7.3 work days ($\pm$4.2) prior to light installation and 25.9 work days ($\pm$14.0) after light installation per participant.

We analyzed usage logs in two ways. First, we counted the number of status change events recorded in the log per day per user for the period before and after the light installation event. It is worth noting that we only included usage logs within the five work days and not on weekends. Second, we used the intervals between status change events detected by one of our algorithms to determine how much time was spent in each status, again for before and after light installation. To eliminate inappropriate intervals (e.g., a user did not turn off the workstation after work), we only accumulated the duration within 12 hours per day.

Online Logs. We collected online logs for a total of 305 days from November 2, 2015 until September 2, 2016 and from 449 participants. These logs were used to determine how many users were using the FlowLight on a given day (as shown in Figure 2). We analyzed these logs by summing up the number of unique identifiers that appeared in the log on a given day, which represents the number of active users for that day. Based on participants' feedback during the period of the field study, we deployed the three main variations of the algorithm described earlier to set the status of the Flow-

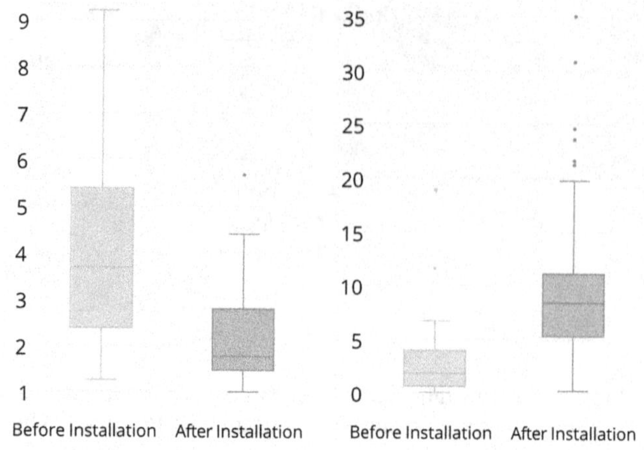

(a) Interruptions per Participant and Day.

(b) Number of State Changes per Participant and Day.

Figure 4: Logged Interruptions and State Changes Before and After Installing the FlowLight.

Light. We analyzed differences between the data sets gathered with the three main variations of the algorithms and found no significant differences between the data collected with any two variations, neither in the collected survey items, nor the interruption logs. In the following, we will therefore present the results aggregated over all variations.

RESULTS

In this section we present the primary findings of our field study. We first examine the effect of the FlowLight on the cost of interruptions before we examine how the FlowLight changed participants' interruption awareness, their interruption-related behavior, and their perception of productivity. Subsequently, we present insights on the costs of the approach, on the influence of its accuracy, on its continued usage by participants and on professional differences.

Reduced Cost of Interruptions

Figure 4a is based on the 36 collected interruption logs and illustrates the distribution of the number of interruptions per day and participant in the period before and the period after participants had been using the FlowLight for one week.

Overall, the number of interruptions decreased after the installation and one week usage of the FlowLight by an average of 1.9 ($\pm$1.6) interruptions (49%) per participant and day, from 4.1 ($\pm$2.1) to 2.2 ($\pm$1.1). A Wilcoxon signed-rank test showed that this reduction is statistically significant (Z =-5.0, p <.000001).

A second Wilcoxon signed-rank test only on the number of severe interruptions (disruptiveness rating of 4 or 5) per day and participant further showed that there is also a statistically significant reduction with p <.001 and Z = -3.2.

An analysis of the survey results (see Figure 5 for more detail) further supports that installing the FlowLight reduced the cost of interruptions. 55.0% of the 182 survey participants that answered the question stated that they either strongly agree, agree or agree somewhat that they were interrupted less than

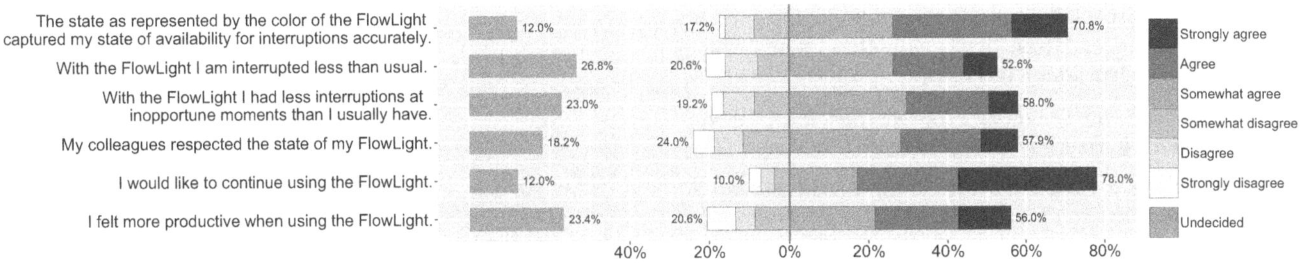

Figure 5: Results of a Subset of the Survey Questions.

usual during their work, while only 20.3% disagreed with it. Even more participants, 59.3%, agreed that they had less interruptions at inopportune moments than usual, whereas only 19.8% disagreed with this statement.

During interviews participants echoed this quantitative evidence. In interview excerpts (full quotes listed in subsequent subsections) participants consistently mentioned that interruptions were reduced. They claimed that the pilot *"..resulted in less interruptions.." (S126)* , eliminated interruptions from colleagues (e.g., *"When [the light]'s red I think they don't interrupt." (I11)*), and *"..didn't stop [interruptions] completely but they surely reduced." (S16)* .

Overall, our findings from the interruption logs, survey questions, and interview questions show strong support that the introduction of the FlowLight reduced the cost of interruptions in terms of the overall number as well as their severity.

Increased Awareness of Interruption Cost

After using the FlowLight for some time, participants developed a high degree of awareness for the cost of interruptions:

"It brings more awareness to what people are doing. Sometimes people take it for granted that people are always interruptible. But there is actually a cost or a penalty when you interrupt someone. So, I think just the concept is good because it reminds people that there is sometimes a good time and a bad time to interrupt people. So, I think just from an awareness campaign, it's valuable as well." (I20)

"The pilot increased the sensitivity to interruption. Team members think more about whether an interrupt is necessary and try to find a suitable time." (S45)

The FlowLight thereby served as a physical reminder for the interruptibility of co-workers in the moment and participants generally respect it and its state:

"It's kind of a like a mood indicator ... so it tells people the state ... of the owner of the light. And then it helps people be more aware or attentive to what my current situation is." (I18)

"I think what really changed is ... a different consciousness about interruptions in our team and also with my colleagues ... I think ... they really respect the light. When it's red I think they don't interrupt." (I11)

Overall, 70% of the 23 interview participants explicitly stated that the FlowLight is respected in their offices and 59.6% of 183 survey respondents agreed that colleagues respected the state of their FlowLight vs. 23.0% that did not (Figure 5).

The increased awareness and respect also triggered participants to change their behavior in a variety of ways, ranging from thinking twice before asking, to deferring the interruption, asking before interrupting and changing to a different communication channel, such as email or instant messaging:

"People ask each other if they are available, even when the light is green, even to people with no light. When I see the colleague I want to ask a question ... has a red light, then I wait a while, or write an email." (S77)

"If it's red, I'll send them a message so that when they're no longer busy or something like that, they'll see the message and they can respond to it then ... so it doesn't require an immediate response" (I19)

Fortunately, participants used common sense when working with FlowLights. If a light was red or red blinking participants would still interrupt if the request was urgent:

"Once I go up there [to the person] and I see the light and then I also see that they're pretty intense then I'll push it off unless I really need to get answered to." (I17)

Feeling of Increased Productivity and Self-Motivation

As a further effect of the FlowLight, 58.5% of the survey respondents felt more productive using it, while only 20.1% disagreed with this (Figure 5). This feeling of increased productivity often stemmed from the fewer interruptions:

"I definitely think it resulted in less interruptions both in person and via Skype. This resulted in more focus and ability to finish work." (S126)

Another reason for the increased productivity is that the FlowLight serves for some participants as a self-monitoring device that motivates them to become or stay focused, which, however, can also be distracting at times:

"Mostly it has helped as a personal monitor only for me. If I see the light red, I sense I am in the flow and I keep working." (I2)

"When I notice that my light is turning yellow, and I'll feel like, 'Oh yeah, I've been idle' and then I do something ... I think the other way, yeah, there's some effect there too. Like, if I see that it's red, or even flashing red, then I'm like, 'Yeah, I've been very active, or productive, I should keep that going.' At the same time, I think it's also a little bit distracting too. Sometimes just because the light is there, I turn around to check it." (I12)

Costs of Using the FlowLight

While people experienced reduced interruption costs and increase in productivity, there are also costs when starting to use the FlowLight. Especially right after installing it the curiosity of co-workers can lead to an increase of interruptions, which, however, diminishes after a few days:

"People walk by, they see it, they ask me questions, 'What's that? How does it work? What's going on?' like this." (I19)

"Initially there were many people just curious to know what the light is about. This increased the number of interruptions but after few days, people started to respect [it]." (S16)

A few participants also experienced situations in which the FlowLight provoked interruptions, as the green color of the light might be misunderstood as an invitation (observed by 26% of the interviewed participants):

"What I definitely notice is that green is more inviting. So it actually encourages people to come by and say, "Hello" for me at least." (I20)

In some cases, changing the interaction culture might require a mandate from higher up or can even be too expensive:

"The more important issue is for it to work, you have to have people committed to following the light rules, which probably requires engagement of some higher management ... and requires introducing the lights to a wider audience." (I6)

"For us ... the main cost of introducing [it is] that you have to change how you are used to interact with people, that you first have to remember to take a look at the light. That's something that's probably too much for the team. [In] our environment .. it's easier to look at the people than at lights." (I8)

If colleagues choose to ignore the light, especially for unimportant interruptions, it can lead to negative emotions:

"So, for us, what we also heard sometimes is that people have the light red, and others still interrupt them, and they're like, 'Oh no, I have this light red, why did they?' Like it bothers them, and it creates negative emotions almost more than it creates positive emotions..." (I17)

Finally, the public disclosure of the interruptibility status might make people feel exposed at times (8% of survey participants agree, 6% strongly agree) or lead to negative feelings:

"Oh, do other people see that my light is yellow? And are they thinking that I'm not working?" (I12)

Like any new technology, there is a cost to adopting the FlowLight. However, most of the identified costs diminish quickly or can be mitigated by clear direction from management. Overall though participants predominantly stated that the colors of the light were interpreted appropriately and were mostly not concerned about being observed.

Automatic State Changes and Accuracy

The algorithm of the FlowLight caused automatic state changes to indicate a user is, for instance, available for interruptions or busy and not interruptible. Figure 4b illustrates the change in distribution of the number of state changes per participant per day before and after installation. A Wilcoxon signed-rank test with Bonferroni-adjusted alpha levels of .01 per test (.05/5) showed a statistically significant change in the number of state changes ($Z = -5.5337$, $p \leq .01$) with an increase in state changes from 1.8 before to 8.4 after. This

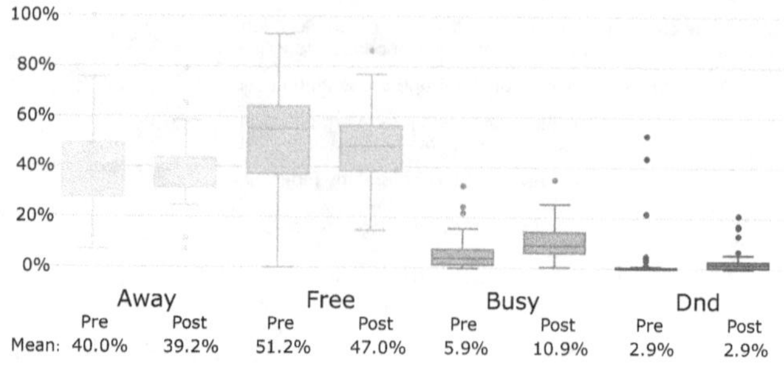

Figure 6: Time Spent in each State Before (Pre) and After (Post) Installation.

increase shows that the automated algorithm is affecting users' availability status in Skype. Figure 6 presents the time spent in each state before and after light installation. Analysis of this data shows a small insignificant decrease in time spent in the available state from 51.2% to 47.0% (Wilcoxon signed-rank test $Z = -1.7143$, $p = .043$) and a significant increase in the time spent in the busy state from 5.9% to 10.9% ($Z = -3.6403$, $p \leq .01$), a very small yet significant difference in do not disturb state ($Z = -3.2093$, $p \leq .01$), and no significant changes to time spent in the away state. Note that during the before-light period the status was already affected by meetings entered in the calendar, which caused the status to change to busy.

Participants generally agreed that the FlowLight captured their state of availability for interruptions accurately:

"I think it [state representativeness] was actually quite good, because what I found is, if I'm not working on a critical task, for example, responding to email which usually isn't critically mind provoking. The light would be green and then people would take that opportunity to stop by and see what they needed to talk about. Whereas if I was in the middle of a meeting or if I was more involved in my work, it would turn red and then at that point they might wait for it to turn green. That's my impression." (I20)

Overall, 71.0% of survey respondents agreed that the FlowLight captures their state accurately while only 15.8% disagreed (Figure 5). This shows that even an interruptibility measure based on a simple algorithm might be accurate enough to be accepted by users and provide value.

At the same time, interview participants and 64% of our survey respondents mentioned that there are situations where the FlowLight was not representative and accurate, partly stemming from limitations in measuring interruptibility solely with computer interaction data:

"The light was mostly green while debugging code. During debugging, I think interrupts hurt a lot. On the other hand, the light was sometimes red when working on documents / e-mails that do not require too much focus." (S45)

"[The] light captures the movements of the mouse and keyboard, and actually, there are times, which I think of a solution separate from the time, which I implement [it] so ... I'm the most occupied when I think something and usually, I write it on a paper or just keep it on my mind." (I4)

In several cases, participants just changed to setting the state manually when it was not accurate and they wanted to indicate to others that they are available or do not want to be disturbed:

"There was a case when I was reading an article, and I needed a 100% concentration on that, so I just manually changed my status to busy. It was helping me a lot. I think my colleagues are also doing the same when they are engrossed in an article and they want free time, they'll just keep their light busy." (I4)

In fact, 32% of our survey respondents reported to have changed their Skype status (which is linked to the FlowLight) more often after the light was installed, 23% less often and 45% had no changes. With the FlowLight installed, 17% of participants reported to change their status at least once a day, 37% one to several times a week, and 46% rarely or never. The job role can also affect the accuracy of the FlowLight, especially for managers, administrative assistants, and sales people. For instance, several managers mentioned that interaction was such a core part of their role that they felt they should always be available and turned off the automatic feature.

Continued Usage of FlowLight

Most participants, 82.6% of the 23 interview participants and 79.1% of the 183 survey participants, stated their intention to keep using the FlowLight even after the pilot period. This sentiment is reflected in actual usage data: two months after installing the FlowLight application 85.5% of users remained active (384/449).

Based on online logging of application instances that we started in November 2015, Figure 2 shows the number of active FlowLight users per day. The Figure also depicts the start date and relative size for the major pilots (e.g., India #1 started in August '15 and had 80 participants, Norway started in November '14 and had 44).

Note that due to holidays in different locales, vacation, sick days, and travel the number of active users per day is consistently about 70% of the number of unique users over the last month (e.g., a measure of 200 active users per day indicates about 315 number of unique users in the last month).

In spite of most users continuing to use the FlowLight, about 20% of users discontinued usage. There were several reasons that we identified from the interviews and surveys that decreased the benefit of the FlowLight, including the office layout and the visibility of the LED light, the company culture and people ignoring the lights, the initial willingness to use such a system, and the accuracy of the state indicated by the FlowLight. In some cases, the decreased benefit also resulted in participants ceasing to use the FlowLight:

"From my perspective that was something I was against from the first day but as I said I decided to join the pilot because I am a team member. ... From time to time I was looking at it but it was a little bit discouraging because the color of the light didn't reflect what I was doing and maybe after one week of using it I gave up totally." (I9)

Professional Differences in Using the FlowLight

An analysis of the survey responses with respect to professional roles shows that developers (including testers) and project managers stated more frequently than participants from other working areas that they wanted to continue using the FlowLight , even though not significantly (82% vs 70% on average) and perceived their state to be significantly more accurate (77% vs 60%, $t = 2.51$, $p = .01$). For project managers, these differences might be explained by the fact that they also reported more often (but not significantly) to manually change their FlowLight status on a daily basis than participants from other work areas (24% vs 16%) and by our experiences gathered during the installation phase, in which managers often asked to disable the automatic mode completely as they wanted to be available for most of their work time. For developers, the differences might be explained by their extensive computer interaction, but future research is needed to confirm this.

DISCUSSION

The results of our large-scale and long-term study show that the FlowLight can reduce the interruption costs for knowledge workers and can increase the awareness, amongst other benefits. In the following, we discuss implications of our findings, in particular with respect to the combination of the physical indicator with the automatic interruptibility measure, the accuracy of the measure, and the cost of not interrupting. Finally, we discuss threats to validity and limitations of our study.

Reasons for FlowLight's Positive Effects

The FlowLight uses a combination of a physical LED light with an automatic measure based on computer interaction to update the user's interruptibility status. The findings show that the approach was well adopted and successfully reduced in-person interruption costs. This poses the question if these effects might after all stem solely either from the automatic interruptibility measure or the physical LED light. With respect to the sole use of an automatic interruptibility measure, prior related work that used an automatic measure to update computer-based contact-list style tools, did not find any or the same level of positive effects as our study on both, cost reduction and awareness [30, 5, 21]. On the other hand, manually maintaining the interruptibility state incurs a high cost as shown by previous research [25] and only very few of our users switched to the manual option in cases the algorithm was not accurate enough or they wanted to ensure some undisrupted time. In addition, our findings show that while participants have a high tolerance for the accuracy of the automatic interruptibility status updates, when inaccuracies happen too often, participants also stop using the approach altogether. Overall, this indicates that the combination of the physical LED light and the automatic interruptibility measure is important to provide significant benefits to knowledge workers to use it in the long-term and that it led to the positive impact on awareness and interruption cost found in our study.

Accuracy of Automatic Interruptibility Measure

Participants' high tolerance for the accuracy of the automatic interruptibility measure of the FlowLight poses the question of how accurate the underlying measure has to be to provide sufficient benefit to the user. Over the course of our field study, we adapted the automatic measure two times to account for early user feedback, yet we did not find any significant differences in the effects on interruption cost and behavior. However, we intend to study the relation between accuracy and the effects on interruption cost further in the future.

Also, while participants had a high tolerance, they reported numerous situations in which they observed the status to be set incorrectly. The most frequent situation in which the status is incorrect occurs when participants "think" about something and experience a high cognitive load, yet do not interact with the computer at all. In future work and with the continuously decreasing invasiveness of biometric sensors, we plan to extend our approach to integrate biometric sensors, to cover these situations more accurately. We further plan to improve our algorithm by integrating application data, which we were not able to collect in this study due to privacy constraints. Knowing the current application might improve the algorithm's accuracy, e.g. one might be less interruptible while working in a development related program and more while being in an email client. As the nature of work and interactions vary across work areas and job roles, tailoring the algorithm accordingly could further improve its accuracy.

Cost of Not Interrupting

As related work has shown, not all interruptions are bad and some are definitely needed, for instance, to unblock co-workers. By physically indicating knowledge workers as not interruptible (Busy and DnD state), the FlowLight might prevent co-workers from interrupting them for important issues, reducing overall team productivity. The findings of our study on the FlowLight provides evidence that this cost is minimal at best for two reasons. First, a data analysis of the usage logs collected for our study shows that the FlowLight ends up having a significant yet small effect on the time that a knowledge worker is indicated as not interruptible (+5% per day). Second, while the FlowLight increases the awareness of the cost of interruptions, participants still interrupt their co-workers regardless of the FlowLight state if they have an important concern to discuss, as also stated by 35% of our interview participants, without being explicitly asked.

Threats and Limitations

A major threat to the validity of our study is the completeness of the collected data. For instance, we were not able to identify participants across different data sets. While we encouraged participants to share their data and ensured them that we only use it for research purposes, we could not demand it due to privacy concerns. We were also not able to collect geographic data due to privacy concerns and thus were not able to analyze geographic differences.

Similarly, the accuracy of the interruption logs might be incomplete or not completely accurate. Since interruption logs are based on self-reports, participants might have forgotten to log some interruptions. Also, the work patterns and habits of the days on which they logged interruptions before and after the installation of the FlowLight might have been significantly different, which makes it more difficult to compare the effect of the FlowLight. We tried to mitigate this risk by only including the logs of participants who logged interruptions for more than three days before and three days after and by regularly reminding them to log their interruptions. Furthermore, different participants might have different criteria and judgement standards for logging interruptions. We tried to mitigate this fact by instructing participants to only log external in-person interruptions at work. In addition, by using a paired test that only compares within subject (Wilcoxon signed rank), we mitigate this effect as long as participants did not change their definition of an interruption over time.

We limited the validity threats related to generalizability across individuals and teams by collecting data from 449 participants from twelve countries and with a variety of job roles. As not all participants are native English speakers, there might be a response bias. We tried to mitigate this risk by providing sufficient instructions, opportunity for contacting us if participants had any questions, and also by visiting each major pilot site to introduce and explain the study. Based on the large number and diversity of participants, we observed that responses were not dominantly distributed to extremes, which would indicate that these knowledge workers were particularly biased based on such difficulties. From our in-person experience we can report that with very few exceptions we perceived similar acceptance, respect and in general a very positive perception of the FlowLight across all locations.

Another threat is the influence of the various algorithms on the study results. Since we wanted to ensure that participants are satisfied with the FlowLight and that we take their feedback serious, we evolved the algorithm two times. To mitigate the risk of a certain bias in the data, we looked for significant differences between populations where we might expect to find them and did not find any.

CONCLUSION

In-person interruptions at the workplace can incur a high cost and consume a lot of a knowledge worker's time, if they happen at inopportune moments. While there are several approaches to possibly reduce the interruption costs, little is known about the impact of a physical and automatic interruptibility indicator. In this paper, we presented FlowLight—an automatic interruptibility indicator in the form of a physical traffic-light like LED—and reported on results from a large-scale and long-term field study with 449 participants from 12 countries. We found that the FlowLight significantly reduced the number of interruptions by 46%. We also observed an increased awareness of the potential disruptiveness of interruptions at inopportune moments, which impacts the interaction culture in a positive way, and that our approach can motivate knowledge workers and make them feel more productive. We discuss the importance of combining the physical indicator with the automatic interruptibility measure and the high tolerance of participants to the accuracy of the approach. Overall, our study provides deep insights and strong evidence on the very positive effects of the long-term usage of the FlowLight, and the continued usage of the approach by most participants indicates the success of the approach.

ACKNOWLEDGMENTS

The authors would like to thank all study participants. This work was funded in part by SNF.

REFERENCES

1. 2016. `http://www.embrava.com/`. (2016).
2. Ernesto Arroyo and Ted Selker. 2011. Attention and intention goals can mediate disruption in human-computer interaction. In *IFIP Conference on Human-Computer Interaction*. Springer, 454–470.
3. Brian P Bailey and Shamsi T Iqbal. 2008. Understanding changes in mental workload during execution of goal-directed tasks and its application for interruption management. *ACM Transactions on Computer-Human Interaction (TOCHI)* 14, 4 (2008), 21.
4. Brian P Bailey and Joseph A Konstan. 2006. On the need for attention-aware systems: Measuring effects of interruption on task performance, error rate, and affective state. *Computers in human behavior* 22, 4 (2006), 685–708.
5. James Bo Begole, Nicholas E Matsakis, and John C Tang. 2004. Lilsys: sensing unavailability. In *Proceedings of the 2004 ACM conference on Computer supported cooperative work*. ACM, 511–514.
6. Suzanne C Beyea. 2007. Distractions, interruptions, and patient safety. *AORN journal* 86, 1 (2007), 109–112.
7. Milan Z Bjelica, Bojan Mrazovac, Istvan Papp, and Nikola Teslic. 2011. Busy flag just got better: Application of lighting effects in mediating social interruptions. In *MIPRO, 2011 Proceedings of the 34th International Convention*. IEEE, 975–980.
8. Jelmer P Borst, Niels A Taatgen, and Hedderik van Rijn. 2015. What Makes Interruptions Disruptive?: A Process-Model Account of the Effects of the Problem State Bottleneck on Task Interruption and Resumption. In *Proceedings of the 33rd annual ACM conference on human factors in computing systems*. ACM, 2971–2980.
9. Daniel Chen, Jamie Hart, and Roel Vertegaal. 2007. Towards a physiological model of user interruptability. In *IFIP Conference on Human-Computer Interaction*. Springer, 439–451.
10. Mary Czerwinski, Eric Horvitz, and Susan Wilhite. 2004. A diary study of task switching and interruptions. In *Proc. SIGCHI*. ACM, 175–182.
11. James Fogarty, Andrew J Ko, Htet Htet Aung, Elspeth Golden, Karen P Tang, and Scott E Hudson. 2005. Examining task engagement in sensor-based statistical models of human interruptibility. In *Proceedings of the SIGCHI conference on Human Factors in Computing Systems*. ACM, 331–340.
12. James Fogarty, Jennifer Lai, and Jim Christensen. 2004. Presence versus availability: the design and evaluation of a context-aware communication client. *International Journal of Human-Computer Studies* 61, 3 (2004), 299–317.
13. Victor M González and Gloria Mark. 2004. Constant, constant, multi-tasking craziness: managing multiple working spheres. In *Proceedings of the SIGCHI conference on Human factors in computing systems*. ACM, 113–120.
14. Juan David Hincapié-Ramos, Stephen Voida, and Gloria Mark. 2011a. A design space analysis of availability-sharing systems. In *Proceedings of the 24th annual ACM symposium on User interface software and technology*. ACM, 85–96.
15. Juan David Hincapié-Ramos, Stephen Voida, and Gloria Mark. 2011b. Sharing availability information with InterruptMe. In *Proceedings of the 13th international conference on Ubiquitous computing*. ACM, 477–478.
16. Joyce Ho and Stephen S Intille. 2005. Using context-aware computing to reduce the perceived burden of interruptions from mobile devices. In *Proceedings of the SIGCHI conference on Human factors in computing systems*. ACM, 909–918.
17. Eric Horvitz, Paul Koch, Carl M Kadie, and Andy Jacobs. 2002. Coordinate: Probabilistic forecasting of presence and availability. In *Proceedings of the Eighteenth conference on Uncertainty in artificial intelligence*. Morgan Kaufmann Publishers Inc., 224–233.
18. Scott Hudson, James Fogarty, Christopher Atkeson, Daniel Avrahami, Jodi Forlizzi, Sara Kiesler, Johnny Lee, and Jie Yang. 2003. Predicting human interruptibility with sensors: a Wizard of Oz feasibility study. In *Proceedings of the SIGCHI conference on Human factors in computing systems*. ACM, 257–264.
19. Shamsi T Iqbal and Brian P Bailey. 2008. Effects of intelligent notification management on users and their tasks. In *Proceedings of the SIGCHI Conference on Human Factors in Computing Systems*. ACM, 93–102.
20. Ellen Isaacs, Steve Whittaker, David Frohlich, and Brid O'Conaill. 1997. Informal communication re-examined: New functions for video in supporting opportunistic encounters. *Video-mediated communication* 997 (1997), 459–485.
21. Jennifer Lai, Sachiko Yoshihama, Thomas Bridgman, Mark Podlaseck, Paul B Chou, and Danny C Wong. 2003. MyTeam: Availability Awareness Through the Use of Sensor Data.. In *INTERACT*.
22. Gloria Mark, Daniela Gudith, and Ulrich Klocke. 2008. The cost of interrupted work: more speed and stress. In *Proceedings of the SIGCHI conference on Human Factors in Computing Systems*. ACM, 107–110.
23. Santosh Mathan, Stephen Whitlow, Michael Dorneich, Patricia Ververs, and Gene Davis. 2007. Neurophysiological estimation of interruptibility: Demonstrating feasibility in a field context. In *In Proceedings of the 4th International Conference of the Augmented Cognition Society*.
24. Daniel McFarlane. 2002. Comparison of four primary methods for coordinating the interruption of people in human-computer interaction. *Human-Computer Interaction* 17, 1 (2002), 63–139.

25. Allen E Milewski and Thomas M Smith. 2000. Providing presence cues to telephone users. In *Proceedings of the 2000 ACM conference on Computer supported cooperative work*. ACM, 89–96.
26. Bonnie A Nardi, Steve Whittaker, and Erin Bradner. 2000. Interaction and outeraction: instant messaging in action. In *Proceedings of the 2000 ACM conference on Computer supported cooperative work*. ACM, 79–88.
27. Jaime Snyder, Mark Matthews, Jacqueline Chien, Pamara F Chang, Emily Sun, Saeed Abdullah, and Geri Gay. 2015. Moodlight: Exploring personal and social implications of ambient display of biosensor data. In *Proceedings of the 18th ACM Conference on Computer Supported Cooperative Work & Social Computing*. ACM, 143–153.
28. Hermann Stern, Viktoria Pammer, and Stefanie N Lindstaedt. 2011. A preliminary study on interruptibility detection based on location and calendar information. *Proc. CoSDEO* 11 (2011).
29. Edward R Sykes. 2011. Interruptions in the workplace: A case study to reduce their effects. *International Journal of Information Management* 31, 4 (2011), 385–394.
30. John C Tang, Nicole Yankelovich, James Begole, Max Van Kleek, Francis Li, and Janak Bhalodia. 2001. ConNexus to awarenex: extending awareness to mobile users. In *Proceedings of the SIGCHI conference on Human factors in computing systems*. ACM, 221–228.
31. Takahisa Tani and Seiji Yamada. 2013. Estimating user interruptibility by measuring table-top pressure. In *CHI'13 Extended Abstracts on Human Factors in Computing Systems*. ACM, 1707–1712.
32. Manuela Züger and Thomas Fritz. 2015. Interruptibility of software developers and its prediction using psycho-physiological sensors. In *Proceedings of the 33rd Annual ACM Conference on Human Factors in Computing Systems*. ACM, 2981–2990.

MyriadHub: Efficiently Scaling Personalized Email Conversations with Valet Crowdsourcing

Nicolas Kokkalis[1], Chengdiao Fan[1], Johannes Roith[1], Michael S. Bernstein[1], Scott Klemmer[2]
[1]Stanford University, [2]UC San Diego
{nicolas, chengdiao, jroith, msb}@cs.stanford.edu, srk@ucsd.edu

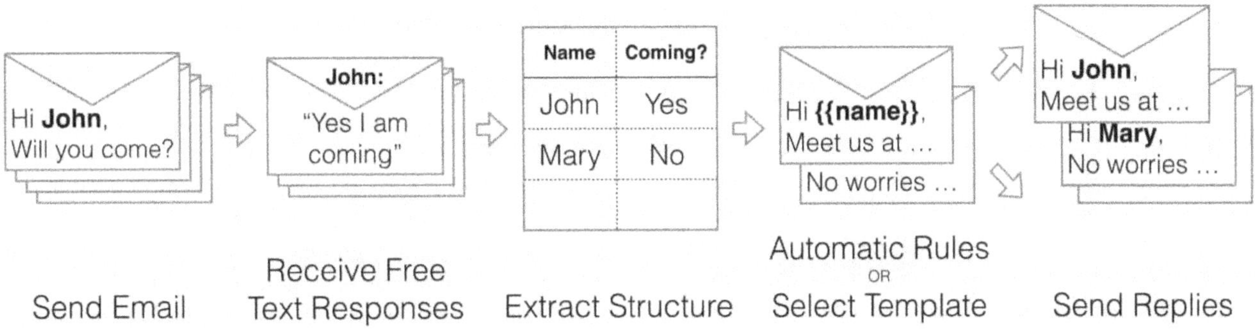

Figure 1. MyriadHub enables users to manage many parallel conversations in a personalized way. To enable reuse, it extracts implicit structure from incoming emails, matches on rules built from previous conversations, then responds.

ABSTRACT

Email has scaled our ability to communicate with large groups, but has not equivalently scaled our ability to listen and respond. For example, emailing many people for feedback requires either impersonal surveys or manual effort to hold many similar conversations. To scale personalized conversations, we introduce techniques that exploit similarities across conversations to recycle relevant parts of previous conversations. These techniques reduce the authoring burden, save senders' time, and maintain recipient engagement through personalized responses. We introduce MyriadHub, a mail client where users start conversations and then crowd workers extract underlying conversational patterns and rules to accelerate responses to future similar emails. In a within-subjects experiment comparing MyriadHub to existing mass email techniques, senders spent significantly less time planning events with MyriadHub. In a second experiment comparing MyriadHub to a standard email survey, MyriadHub doubled the recipients' response rate and tripled the number of words in their responses.

Author Keywords

Mail Merge; Email Overload; Valet Crowdsourcing.

ACM Classification Keywords

H.5.3. Information Interfaces and Presentation (e.g. HCI): Group and Organization interfaces.

CHI 2017, May 06 - 11, 2017, Denver, CO, USA

ACM 978-1-4503-4655-9/17/05...$15.00
DOI: http://dx.doi.org/10.1145/3025453.3025954

INTRODUCTION

Online communication scales our reach: with email, we can broadcast messages to thousands [29]. Unfortunately, online communication does not equivalently scale our ability to carry on those thousands of conversations [26]. For example, suppose a designer wanted to ask users for feedback on a new beta feature. Today this process means managing hundreds or thousands of parallel conversations in a single inbox [24]. Complex task coordination overloads email and hinders coordination effectiveness [11]. Forms and surveys can handle larger numbers of respondents, but they can feel impersonal and have low response rates [3, 19, 31]. Consequently, communicators are forced to choose between personalized contact with a few, or impersonal broadcasts at scale.

However, many conversational turns share content and structure. For example, many customer service requests share nearly-identical responses and follow-up requests [26]. Even discussion forums contain redundancy [34]. Likewise, event planning, student requests, and user feedback each involve far fewer conversational paths than recipients. If it were possible to structure these replies and conversational paths and re-apply them in new threads, a user might be able to hold individual conversations with far more people than possible today.

This paper introduces *MyriadHub* (Figure 1). MyriadHub exploits cross-email commonality to recycle elements of previous conversations in similar new ones. It uses *valet crowdsourcing* [22] to extract metadata from emails so that previous replies can be recycled when new email threads reach the same state. These metadata-annotated examples enable MyriadHub to generate rules and templates. Users, valet crowd workers, or algorithms apply these rules to respond quickly to new incoming messages.

For example, suppose a student sends email requesting an assignment extension for medical reasons. A valet crowd worker [22] extracts the reason (*reason: medical*) from the email, and MyriadHub suggests a response from another thread: ask for the doctor's letter. When the student responds with such a letter, the extracted result (*excused: true*) prompts a positive response. Had the student instead asked for an extension with no reason (*reason: unjustified*), the prompted response might instead be a generic "each student gets two free late days."

The MyriadHub system demonstrates this conversational recycling, helping users see and manage massive parallel email conversations. MyriadHub uses valet crowdsourcing [22] to give crowd workers restricted, accountable access to users' inboxes so they can extract metadata from specific threads and enable the system to suggest relevant replies. MyriadHub, as of writing, includes 336 users, 1,107 campaigns created, and 104,946 emails sent. We describe three such campaigns in detail, including startup founders' introduction requests and student internship applications.

This paper presents two experimental studies of MyriadHub's effectiveness. First, to examine its success in managing responses, we performed a within-subjects experiment comparing MyriadHub to traditional mail merge when planning a simulated event. Participants spent significantly less time and made fewer errors with MyriadHub. Second, to verify that MyriadHub can emulate personalized messages, we performed a between-subjects experiment randomizing whether recipients interacted with MyriadHub or an email survey. Recipients assigned to the MyriadHub condition responded at double the rate and with three times as much in-depth content measured by the number of words in their responses.

MYRIADHUB COMBINES SCALE & PERSONALIZATION

MyriadHub sits atop existing web-mail clients and monitors specific threads to create reusable replies and rules. The user can deploy these rules to send contextualized replies when the next conversation reaches the same state.

Example scenario: Asking users for feedback

Christina is a user experience researcher for a mobile video application. To get feedback on a recent feature launch, she imports 500 users of the application, as well as how many times each person has used the feature, into a Google Spreadsheet. Christina opens MyriadHub in her web browser, links a new campaign to the Google Spreadsheet and authors a query in MyriadHub to select users who have used the new feature at least five times. She writes an initial email asking these users for their feedback. In a separate email, she encourages those who have only used the feature once to try it again and give feedback.

When Christina returns from meetings later that day, forty users have responded. Her valet crowd worker for this email campaign has extracted each user's positive and negative feedback, grouped them into themes and tagged each email thread with those themes in MyriadHub *(Structure extraction with valet crowdsourcing)*. Christina creates a few quick histograms based on extracted data stored in her spreadsheet, then writes a search query (which the system proactively stores as *a rule)* to identify users with the most prevalent negative feedback: wanting to share a subset of a video rather than the whole recording. She composes a template message to those users pointing them to the advanced option that allows them to do so, and asks them if they have tried it *(Scaling conversation through templates and rules)*. She writes replies similarly for other popular responses. Lastly, she groups the long tail of uncommon responses together into a template reply to share all the other popular feedback and ask which they agree with most. MyriadHub learns rules from these searches and responses that it can apply to future messages.

When Christina returns in the morning, she finds many recipients have responded further, and many others responded to her original message. Christina's crowd assistant has extracted metadata from these new responses, and MyriadHub used that data to trigger rules that it captured from her previous responses and propose replies *(Scaling conversation through templates and rules)*. Christina agrees and sends those messages. Short on time, she then skims a few responses to her most recent reply with no template yet, and replies to those users directly using her usual mail client *(Flexible integration with existing tools)*. Her crowd assistant takes those replies and generalizes them into new rules for similar messages. Through MyriadHub, Christina collected large-scale user feedback with similar benefits to holding many personalized conversations in parallel, yet in much less time. Based on the feedback received and structured, she can discover and start new directions of inquiry.

Personalized email conversations at large scale

This scenario illustrates the creation and reuse of an ad-hoc message repository [1] for large-scale email conversations. With MyriadHub, users can recycle past messages to quickly to author contextually-appropriate responses. Additional example scenarios include course staff fielding students' logistical questions, or event planners handling conversations that come up with client after client.

In summary, users log into MyriadHub with their Google account, and begin creating a MyriadHub campaign by connecting a Google spreadsheet of recipients and drafting the initial message templates. The MyriadHub inbox shows the status of who has replied (Figure 3). The email viewing interface has two properties of note. First, along the right is a metadata extraction pane (Figure 2): the user or valet can extract field values. Second, when the user replies, below the clipped bottom of Figure 2, they have the option of saving the current reply as a new template. This template gets saved into the conversation tree (Figure 5). From the MyriadHub homepage, the user or valet can click to see a list of templates, and set up rules that will trigger each template response (Figure 4).

Structure extraction with valet crowdsourcing

For MyriadHub to reuse conversations, it needs to have a computer-understandable representation of each conversation. For example, it needs to know whether each person replied with an agreement to serve on the program committee, or the date by which they have said they can decide. In MyriadHub, email structure refers to the metadata contained in the meanings of incoming email responses, such as an answer of "yes" or "no" to the invitation or the reason for asking an assignment extension. Email structure in MyriadHub is not fixed; rather it can be as flexible as the contents of conversations change, and as the information that different senders care about in the responses varies. For example, in the scenario above, the structure is represented by the fields defined in Christina's spreadsheet and values extracted from her user responses. Email structure extraction is possible via machine learning and natural language processing [10], but it can be noisy, and difficult to bootstrap off a small number of initial messages.

MyriadHub uses valet crowdsourcing to flexibly extract semantic themes from messages. People feel a tension recruiting assistants for managing complex, personal information: they want help, but have reasonable concerns about giving others unfettered access to their personal accounts. *Valet crowdsourcing* [22] provides a limited-access window to personal information (such as email), accompanied with an audit trail of every action for accountability. Its principles can be applied to crowdsourcing (crowd of assistants), outsourcing (one or a few expert assistants), or even local employees or co-workers.

Like a valet car key, valet interfaces seek a dual objective of *Privacy* (through parsimonious access control) and *Accountability* (through transparent access boundaries and activity logging). For privacy, a valet interface parsimoniously gives assistants just enough access to help. For accountability, it makes access boundaries transparent so users have an accurate model of what the assistants can and cannot do, and it causes transgressions to leave fingerprints (for instance, by logging valet assistants' actions). MyriadHub logs all of a valet's actions, and limits their access only to messages labeled with the relevant Gmail label; valets do not have broad access. Because people may be unaware of the valet's existence, it is advised that such systems provide enough *Disclosure* to all relevant parties, for example by adding explanatory text to outgoing emails.

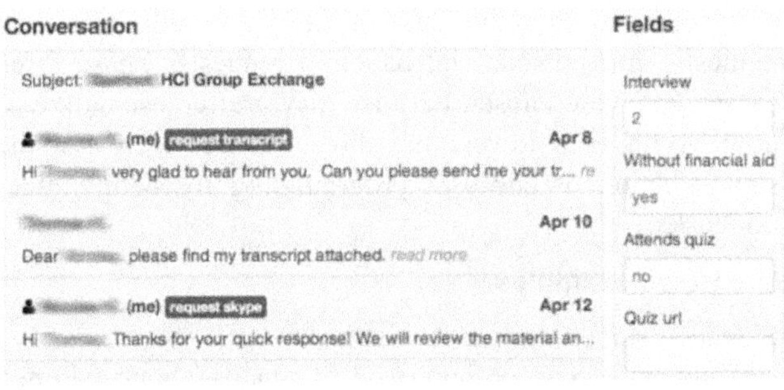

Figure 2. Crowd workers extract fields (right) from the raw thread text (left).

MyriadHub recruits valets from online crowdsourcing marketplaces such as Upwork (www.upwork.com), where workers have experience in relevant domains, such as administrative assistance and data entry. Users pay valets based on their posted rates, often around \$10 per hour. A new assistant can be hired for each campaign, or previous ones can be re-hired. MyriadHub users can also recruit valets from within their organization—such as an administrative assistant or TA—or play the valet role themselves.

The valets' primary role is extracting fields and values from each incoming email (Figure 2). Most fields are determined by the user at campaign creation. More fields can be added by a user or valet as needed. Fields might include the recipient's most salient worry about a feature, their favorite and least favorite design alternative, or positive/negative votes for each proposed conference theme.

To facilitate large-scale conversational tracking and data extraction, MyriadHub separates each recipient into a separate thread. By contrast, many email clients (*e.g.*, Gmail) aggregate everyone who responds to the same initial message into one thread. While this thread aggregation makes sense for many common email tasks, it makes following distinct interleaved conversations difficult.

Scaling conversation through templates and rules

With each message's structure extracted, MyriadHub enables the user to draw on previous messages that were sent in similar circumstances (Figure 3). Crowd assistants generalize one-off responses into templates that can be reapplied to future conversations, building the conversational scaffold through demonstration.

When a message's extracted data matches a search query

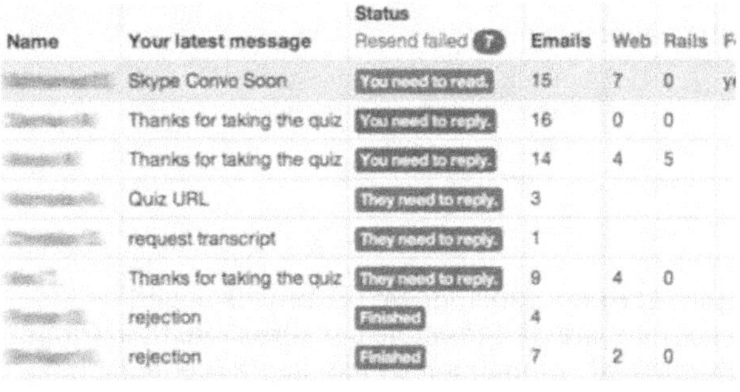

Figure 3. MyriadHub signals recipients' positions in the conversation tree and information extracted

or rule created from a previous message, MyriadHub prepares a reply, inserting values into the template. For example, if a recipient responds to an invitation by accepting the invitation and asking what food to bring, and such a response has been previously sent for the properties [coming: true] and [question: food], MyriadHub can automatically reply with the same response as before or batch the response for the user to customize.

Figure 4 demonstrates rules and associated templates for a campaign. Search queries might filter on a column (e.g., [skype_handle: unknown]), the most recent template sent (e.g., [Last sent message: request transcript]), or status (e.g., [Status = They need to reply]). The user can specify a template to respond with when a rule fires. New matches to a rule who had yet to receive the associated template accrue to a count in a green label in the New Matches column. MyriadHub defaults to asking the user to confirm before responding. Alternatively, the user can opt to allow MyriadHub to auto-respond once the rule matches.

Each message in MyriadHub can be a template and include variables from data extracted using {{variable name}} in the text. Using these variables, a single template message can become many different replies depending on the information extracted from the recipient's previous message.

If MyriadHub has no rule or template for the current message, the user creates one. The user does this through demonstration: replying directly to a message using their normal email client. The crowd assistant generalizes this message by creating field placeholders such as {{name}} and {{paper title}}. They then author a rule for when the template would be applicable (*e.g.*, [agree to review: true]). MyriadHub can also create a new rule whenever the user sends messages to the resulting recipients of a search query. This rule can later be automatically or manually reapplied when new matches appear.

Visualization of Conversation State

Holding multiple conversations at the same time requires

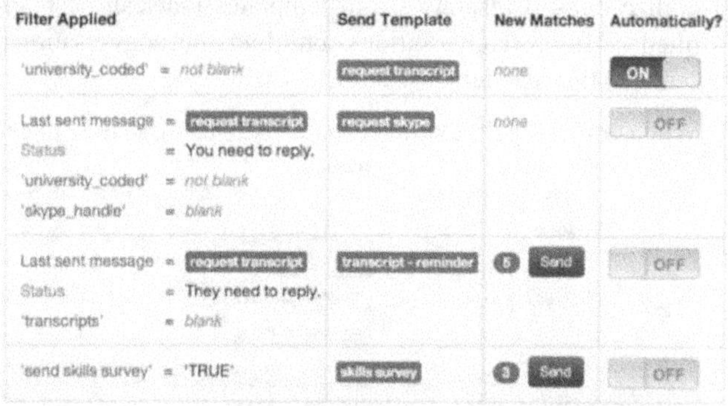

Figure 4: Rules can suggest responses based on the structure extracted from the conversation, then trigger automatically or in batch by the user's request. These four rules are a subset of the twelve used to manage the entire research intern interview campaign.

tracking the state of each conversation, like playing multiple simultaneous games of chess. To help users with this, MyriadHub visualizes each campaign as a tree (Figure 5). Sibling templates in the tree are alternative paths that conversations took, and child templates indicate responses. Labeled numbers next to each template give the user an overview of how many recipients are in each state. While not all conversations have tree structures and other conversational visualizations, such as funnels and milestones, are possible and can be explored in the future, we chose tree structure for now to make it simple for users to understand.

Instead of a traditional read/unread status, MyriadHub denotes the conversation status of each recipient using four states: "you need to read", "you need to reply", "they need to reply" and "conversation finished" (Figure 3). For example, if the user is running a campaign about an event, she would mark all the recipients who declined to come to the event as finished. For each individual recipient, MyriadHub also shows how many emails got exchanged and the last template they received.

Flexible integration with existing tools

MyriadHub integrates with existing tools through synchronization with the user's Google or Google Apps account. Each MyriadHub campaign appears in the user's Gmail account as a single email thread and is associated with a Google Sheet that stores all extracted metadata and can be downloaded or edited. Rows in the spreadsheet represent recipients and columns contain data about each recipient.

While a user typically begins a campaign, MyriadHub integrates with Gmail's labeling system to enable campaigns that are pushed to the user. For example, a researcher may receive ongoing questions about graduate admissions or internships throughout the year. The researcher can create a campaign for these types of messages, tag incoming email in Gmail with the MyriadHub campaign label to associate the message with the campaign, and let MyriadHub take over.

HOW PEOPLE USE MYRIADHUB

As of this writing, MyriadHub has 336 users, 1,107 campaigns created, and 104,946 emails sent. To illustrate the breadth of conversation recycling and how it helps users communicate at scale, we report on three MyriadHub deployments: coordinating student interviews, administrative requests, and personal introduction requests. These three campaigns were chosen because they are representative of how MyriadHub lowers the threshold and increases the sophistication of end-user programming for communication tasks.

Illustrated examples

Selecting student research interns

Dealing with tens or hundreds of emails about an open position for a student summer internship requires effort in tracking each applicant's status and repetitive personalized messaging, e.g. soliciting resume and transcripts, interview instructions and scheduling. MyriadHub lowers the threshold to scale straightforward or formulaic email conversations. A researcher used MyriadHub to recruit and manage the interviews for summer intern applicants. He began by emailing an advertisement to a group of students. The resulting conversations produced a total of 226 emails. The researcher created 33 MyriadHub message templates: 19 were used multiple times; 14 were used once to handle exceptional requests.

Figure 5 shows the evolution of the campaign's conversation tree, including the popular paths and one-offs. The cascading feature of the template tree demonstrates the progress of the application/admission process: greeting, request for transcript and resume, rejection, further interviews, and finally offers. These templates were built and used on different subgroups of the campaign recipients and organized through rules created as the campaign developed.

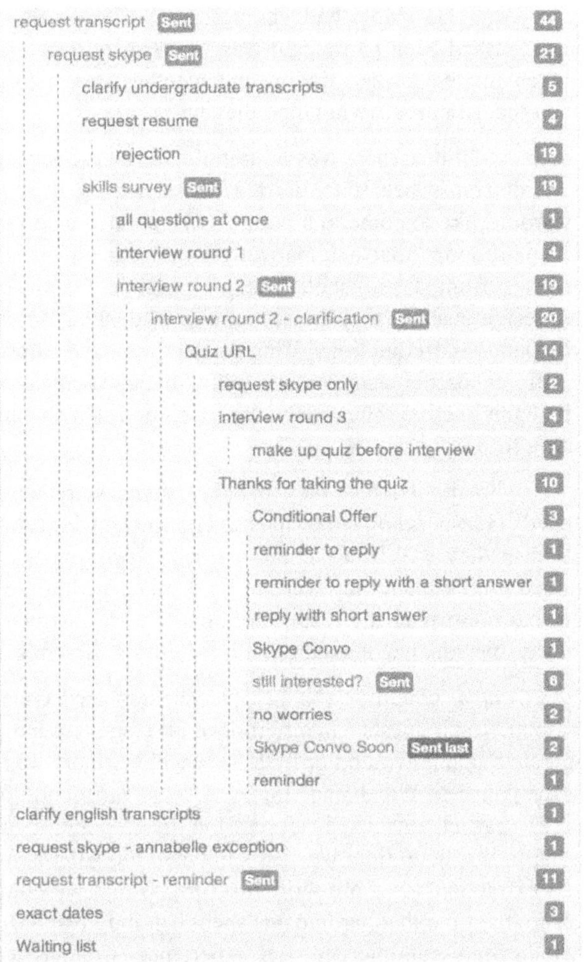

Figure 5. A conversation tree covering over two hundred emails to manage intern interviews, including highly reused templates and branching-out one-offs. Labeled numbers indicate how many recipients received that template most recently.

The campaign began with each student submitting an application through a Google Form. As students applied over time, MyriadHub used an automatic rule applied to the form spreadsheet to initially greet each student and request their transcript and resume. It also handled reminder emails when participants forgot to respond. Integration with Google Docs was used to administer an online quiz by sending a custom quiz URL to each applicant. The quiz results were uploaded into a new field, then later used to send different messages to students with high and low scores. The researcher had three assistants handle the entire campaign. He only wrote seven of the main emails and the rest was fully handled by the assistants on his behalf.

Figure 4 demonstrates a subset of the rules in this campaign. For example, one rule triggers when the "interview" field contained values "no", "1", "2" and "3", corresponding to rejection, first-round interview, second-round interview and third-round interview. This rule sent templates to inform the recipients of their rejection or instructions for the upcoming rounds of interviews. Likewise, the rule [send skills survey: true] has three new matches who have not received the template "skills survey". The user can send these new matches the appropriate messages by clicking the blue button "Send".

The researcher used rules to deal with the irregular timing of new applicants over a period of weeks. For example, when the bulk of the applicants were already in the second round of interviews, new applicants were still arriving. The user routed new applicants into the correct stage of the interview cycle using the spreadsheet; MyriadHub matched them to a rule to send the stage-appropriate message.

Handling incoming student requests

MyriadHub integrates with general-purpose tools and supports recycling of conversations to handle similar incoming requests in daily email. To help with a class that had heavy student administrative requests, a professor used MyriadHub to manage the responses. Unlike the previous case, where the initiator of the conversation was the user, here the user did not start the conversation: the students initiated each thread, but many asked similar questions. The professor assigned each incoming request a Gmail label that MyriadHub created for the campaign, either manually or through automatic Gmail filters. Some labels led to automatic responses. For example, MyriadHub responded to questions about the participation requirements and office hours automatically with an existing MyriadHub template based on a rule. Others were processed by TAs and then generalized into new templates.

Whenever the teaching assistants had insufficient information to respond, they asked the professor for the information, saved his input in a new message template and reused the updated template later when necessary. The message templates and campaign structure also served as a starting point for a FAQ for the next run of the class.

Personal introductions

The previous examples show how MyriadHub lowers the threshold to simple conversations; here, we focus on how MyriadHub raises the ceiling by supporting sophisticated email interactions at scale. A director of a Silicon Valley startup accelerator needed to make introductions for the startups in the program to potential investors. This task involved multiparty coordination: the director needs to collect each founder's targeted investors, determine whether the investor and the founder are a good fit, decide whether he will make the introduction, edit the startup's supplied text so that it is relevant to the potential investor, and send a personalized email to the investors with corresponding relevance to make the introduction. With tens of startups and investors, and each connection requiring different messages for the introduction, this is heavy work.

MyriadHub helped this director with collecting the initial lists from different startup founders, editing the data collected, and sending the final personalized introduction to investors. First, he started a MyriadHub campaign to ask the founders to submit the list of targeted investors through a Google spreadsheet. In the spreadsheet, founders were asked to enter their own names and startups, the investor names and basic information, how relevant the investor was to them, and their company descriptions that they wanted to sent to specific investors. The assistant of this director helped him manage this campaign, collect the incoming lists and compile these spreadsheets into a master spreadsheet.

The director then started a new campaign based on this master spreadsheet. In this spreadsheet, he had an overview of which founder asked for which investor, and he could quickly make a decision whether he would introduce these two by entering *yes* or *no* into a new column. In the meantime, he edited the text written by the founders—the relevance between the company and the funder, and the company description—in his own wording.

When decision-making was finished, he used MyriadHub to query only the connections he agreed to introduce. He drafted a generic email template and personalized them via template variables, e.g. the customized relevance and company description per connection. He made the introductions for all founders all at once, and at the same time.

This process repeats three times a year, when the director makes introductions for about 20 startups. Each startup's list of targeted investors ranges from 10 to 50 people. He reported to us, "MyriadHub saves me at least 20 hours each time I have to make these personalized introductions in batches." In this example, MyriadHub supported multiparty coordination that required personalization at scale.

EVALUATION

Does MyriadHub save time?

The previous examples give some indication of the breadth of scenarios that conversational recycling can cover. MyriadHub was designed to help by accelerating common email flows. However, MyriadHub introduces a fixed cost of creating a template, adding variable fields to it, filtering and sending (which creates and applies rules), within an unfamiliar interface. Given these costs, is the benefit worth the trouble, and by how much? In a within-subjects experiment comparing MyriadHub to the Gmail interface, we measured how much time participants saved when handling a sample conversation. We also measured how many errors users made, for example sending the wrong response or forgetting to respond.

Method: Field Experiment

A within-subjects experiment enrolled 12 participants composed of undergraduate and graduate students at a private West Coast American university and young technology professionals. Most had engineering backgrounds. A scenario asked each participant was to organize a potluck with ten invited guests, finding out whether each person could come, and if so, what food they will bring.

In both conditions, there was an initial mail merge sent on the participant's behalf to the ten guests asking them if they would like to come to a potluck. We created a server-side email script that automatically simulated all guests' responses from a pre-labeled set of possible responses. This design ensured that the scenario was identical across participants and conditions. This script responded almost instantly to participants' emails, allowing us to measure participants' active time rather than confound it with time waiting for responses.

Guests who replied that they couldn't come were to be thanked. Guests who replied positively were to be asked what dish they will bring to the potluck. Once guests responded with a dish, they were to be thanked with a message that confirmed the dish. Participants were instructed to always personalize messages with the guests' first name.

In the *Control* condition (N=12), participants used Gmail to respond to all guests. Gmail grouped all responses into a single thread, and would notify users whenever there was a new response to the thread. In the *MyriadHub* condition (N=12), participants used MyriadHub to respond to all guests. In this condition, we also simulated the valet assistant's extraction via a pre-written script, so that we could measure the time that participants spent handling responses—which represents the end user experience—rather than also measuring the assistants' time. This simulated assistant extracted the columns *coming* (yes/no) and *dish* for the participants. So, participants could use all the filtering and template recycling functionalities of MyriadHub directly, but they had to author all templates and apply rules themselves, just like they would in practice.

We measured the time it took participants to complete their tasks. Specifically, we measured the time between the first invitation and the last email response that the participants sent in each condition.

We asked participants to communicate with a relatively small number of people: only ten, vs. the hundreds or thousands that MyriadHub is designed for. MyriadHub provides time savings that scale as a function of the number of recipients. However, MyriadHub introduces a fixed cost of setting up templates and rules. So, with a small number of recipients, this experiment is a conservative measurement of MyriadHub's benefit. A null hypothesis would suggest that the one-time fixed cost would equal or outweigh the per-conversation benefits with only ten recipients. We hypothesized that, even with a small number of recipients, MyriadHub would result in time savings. If MyriadHub outperforms the Control condition even in this conservative setup, its benefits would be even larger as the number of guests increases, because more redundancy can be reduced using conversational recycling.

Results

MyriadHub saved people time when handling a sample scenario with high redundancy. A pairwise t-test comparing the email processing time of the 12 participants was significant ($t(11)=5.56$, $p<0.001$): participants in the MyriadHub condition spent 32% less time (μ=5.75 mins, std. dev=1.82) to respond to the emails, compared to the Control condition (μ=8.5 mins, std. dev=2.94).

All participants completed the tasks in MyriadHub conditions without any errors, while 7 of 12 participants in the Control condition made mistakes when responding to emails. A two-proportion z-test confirms that the difference is significant ($p<0.05$). Mistakes in the control conditions included (i) sending the wrong response to the wrong scenario (e.g. saying "thanks for coming" to someone who said they are not coming), (ii) forgetting to respond to some guests, and (iii) failing to personalize the message.

Both conditions followed up with a questionnaire to understand participants' experiences and how they spent their time. 6 of 12 participants answered the questionnaire. Control participants reported difficulty tracking guests' status: "[I spent my time] mostly figuring out whether I had already responded to an email or not. It quickly got messy in the long thread… [It's a] very tedious process"; "[I spent my time] checking who I haven't replied to (because the responses don't get grouped together by person [like in MyriadHub]). Realistically, if I were to manage the party like this at this scale, I would create my own spreadsheet to keep track of things, similar to what MyriadHub offers."

Participants' main limiting factor using MyriadHub was creating filters and templates. As one participant reported, "When I found the commands that I needed, the rest was straightforward and fast". MyriadHub clearly had a learning curve: "I think MyriadHub will be better once you get the hang of it." Participants also recognized that templates were not as deeply personalized as individual emails: for example, one simulated guest could not attend due to illness. In the Control condition, many of the participants showed concern for the recipient's health, mentioning something like "hope you feel better soon." Participants tended not to do this when using MyriadHub. With MyriadHub, users either have to handle one-offs in traditional ways or compromise personalization to achieve scale. MyriadHub does not remove the tradeoff between personalization and scale, but it does mitigate this tension. How much it can mitigate depends on how many conversational similarities MyriadHub can exploit and how much redundancy it can reduce.

Limitations

For consistency, the experiment employed simulated responses rather than real conversations. For efficiency, guests' responses arrived immediately. Also, the sample size of this study is relatively small.

Does MyriadHub yield more engagement than surveys?

Myriad's benefits for authors are of little use if recipients don't engage with the messages. To investigate this, a between-subjects experiment examined whether MyriadHub recipients are more likely to respond, and respond at length, than recipients of a typical email survey.

Method: Field Experiment

The second experiment enrolled 172 undergraduate and graduate students, all currently or recently enrolled in a one-unit seminar featuring visiting speakers. Most had engineering backgrounds. The seminar organizer wanted students' feedback on a proposed change to the class requirements that would require each student to participate as a discussant after the main lecture, once during the term.

Participants were randomly divided into two conditions. The stimuli for both conditions were emails sent at the same time, with the same wording except the response method for the instructor's questions. In the *control* condition (N=87), students received an email describing the proposed change and requesting that they fill out a short Google Form. The survey asked three open-ended questions with free text response, a yes/no question asking whether they support the change, and a field to enter their name. Respondents' names were recorded and visible to the instructor in both conditions.

In the *MyriadHub* condition (N=85), MyriadHub sent an email describing the proposed change and then asked the three open-ended questions directly in the email body. Responses were thematically grouped using MyriadHub and responded to via a template. The instructor responded to students based on the extracted structure from their feedback (*e.g.*, one response for everyone suggesting that they would need to see the paper beforehand). As the campaign developed, the researchers extracted message structure, built templates and rules, and applied them as appropriate.

Both participants in the survey and MyriadHub conditions only received one email if they never acted. The content of these questions and requests were identical, except whether the questions were embedded inside a linked survey or requested as a direct response. So, all differences are due to the requested medium for feedback.

Effectiveness measurements included response rate and response length (word count); cost measures included Upwork assistant pay and time. Response rates indicate how compelling the request was; word count suggests how engaged the participant was in the conversation.

For the MyriadHub condition, response rate is calculated by dividing the number of participants who responded to the initial email by the total number of recipients. Word count is calculated by concatenating the body text of each participant's responses. For the survey condition, the response rate was the number of surveys submitted divided by the total number of recipients. Word count is calculated by concatenating all answers to the form. The cost measurements mainly focused on the cost and time of crowd workers hired in the MyriadHub condition to extract metadata from raw email text. Other than that, in both conditions, the user had to spend about equal amount of time on the initial setup (drafting the survey vs. creating a MyriadHub campaign) with no economic cost. We measured MyriadHub crowd worker costs by hiring two remote workers from Upwork to independently, from scratch, extract values for the predetermined fields. To test accuracy, we compared their results against participants' results.

We used chi-squared tests to compare response rates and t-tests to compare word counts. Each condition had one outlier whose word count was several standard deviations longer than the mean (642 words in MyriadHub; 280 in the control). The analysis presented here, as is common, omits these outliers. Omission did not affect the results' significance. Two researchers jointly examined responses to better understand their relevance, quality and style.

Results

Thirteen of 87 participants in the control condition filled out the form, a response rate of 15% (Figure 6). By contrast, 27 out of 85 participants in the MyriadHub condition responded by email, doubling the response rate to 32%. A chi-squared test confirmed that MyriadHub recipients responded significantly more often ($X^2(171)=5.9$, $p<0.05$). Combining all the form text fields, the average word count in the control condition was 39 words (std. dev = 27), whereas the average word count in the MyriadHub condition's emails was three times that—114 words (std. dev.= 69). A t-test comparing the response lengths of the 38 respondents was significant ($t(36)=3.57$, $p < 0.05$): participants in the MyriadHub condition were not only more likely to respond, they also wrote longer responses. This length comparison is notable in that some respondents never got to the second and third questions in the script. We used response rates here not to show a predictable result already established by previous studies [19]: more personalized messages receive higher response rates. Rather, we emphasize that MyriadHub replicates these benefits with less effort than prior work.

Text content, quality and styles also diverged between two conditions. When reacting to the proposed addition to the course requirements, survey participants all replied "no" via a radio button located in the middle of other open-ended questions. The free-text answers generally focused on objections, were negative and blunt in style. For example, "this idea would deter future students from enrolling and they would instead enroll in other seminars"; "I would probably drop the class"; "please don't do this!" In contrast, MyriadHub responses were more positive, constructive and creative. Some MyriadHub respondents liked the proposal. Some expressed their concerns but also supplied specific suggestions on how to modify the proposal to make it more effective. For example, "adding the discussant can be very good for the learning experience in this class. However, I have two pieces of suggestions regarding to the specific implementation of the discussant...." Many of them were even open for further discussions after writing a long message, such as "These are just some initial thoughts, and I'd be happy to discuss them in more detail if you'd like." While it is possible that response bias would positively inflect participants' responses, participants in the MyriadHub condition engaged more with the idea.

In terms of cost, the first Upwork worker charged \$11.11/hour, and spent 100 minutes on completing the data extraction for all email threads, for a total of \$18.52. The second worker charged \$10.00/hour, and spent 60 minutes on the same process, totaling \$10.00. These results correspond to \$0.37 and \$0.69 per thread, typically involving at

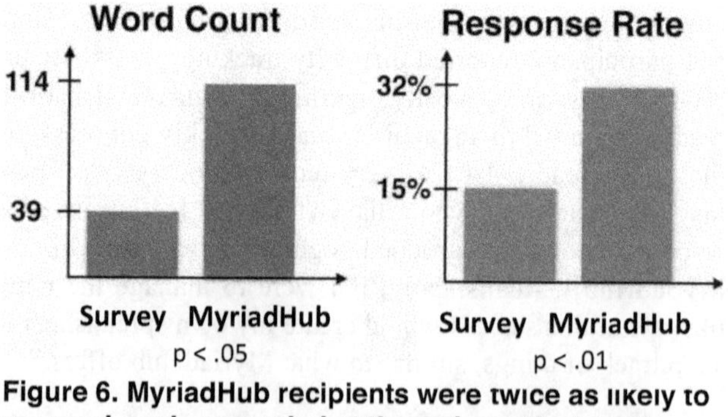

Figure 6. MyriadHub recipients were twice as likely to respond, and responded at three times the length.

least two responses per thread. The first worker agreed with the researchers' manual extractions in 96% of the cases and the second worker agreed 97% of the time. From these results, we suspect that MyriadHub's benefits can be attained using on-demand part time crowd assistants.

Limitations

Surveys are not the only way one can scale feedback solicitation. Custom websites, mailing lists, mobile apps for example could achieve some of that. The study does not prove that personalization is the only cause of the increased response rate and word count; there could be other factors, too. Word count only indirectly measures the depth of response contents. But, we believe that it captures the construct to a first approximation, and a qualitative analysis helps triangulate the effect.

DISCUSSION

Table 1 compares the relative merits of MyriadHub's techniques, surveys and email. In sum, our evaluations suggest that MyriadHub scales online communication without deeply compromising personalization, and increases response rate with a small amount of valet assistance.

The time it takes users to handle email responses with traditional email clients increases linearly with the number, N, of *total* messages they send. Using MyriadHub, the time is a function with complexity dominated by how many *unique* messages the user writes. This is a sub-linear function f(N) that depends on the redundancy that exists in the email responses (*e.g.* could be log(N)). In other words, MyriadHub is O(f(N)) while Gmail is O(N), where f(N) is a sub-linear function. This means that the higher the redundancy, the more time MyriadHub saves its users. In the first experiment, potluck planning with 10 guests, this translated to a 32% improvement. This experiment had high communication redundancy, but also few recipients.

MyriadHub's conversational recycling doubled the response rate and tripled the text written by correspondents. The personal conversation also changed the tone of the discussion: students in the MyriadHub condition were more positive about the proposal to add work to the seminar course than those who filled out a survey. The perceived level of personal touch is the most likely mechanism: MyriadHub emails were originally written by the end user and customized to each circumstance. Mail merge would have only allowed the initial email to be personalized—making follow-ups difficult. However, if it becomes obvious that the conversation is automated, the honest signal [12] would disappear, and this effect might lessen.

	Email	Surveys	Myriad
Communication Scale	↓	↑	↑
Personalization	↑	↓	↑
Response Rate	↑	↓	↑

Table 1. Custom email is highly personalized and attracts higher response rates but is difficult to scale. Surveys are easy to scale but are impersonal and suffer from low responses rates. MyriadHub combines these merits.

Does conversational recycling lie to the recipient about the level of personal attention they are getting? MyriadHub messages often look like they were authored only for the recipient, and this may well contribute to the system's benefits. However, triggering a MyriadHub response rule without tweaking the response can produce an uncanny valley of personalization, where the message looks like it is from a person but is triggered in confusing contexts. MyriadHub offers a middle ground, holding each message as a pending response so the user can tweak it to avoid any potential missteps. This approach retains many benefits of recycling while minimizing the risk of a mistake.

As with many collaborative systems, exceptions are common. Without a mechanism to handle unanticipated situations, users might abandon the system [14]. These unusual circumstances are not actually all that unusual: 14 of 33 templates in the internship interview scenario were used only once (Figure 5).

For MyriadHub to scale, it can't require individually authoring a response. For common queries and responses, the valet/rule can respond with a message from the library. The best way we have observed for MyriadHub users to engage with 'long-tail' responses is through redirection, rather than direct engagement. This is a similar parlor trick to how the 1960s AI psychoanalysis program ELIZA worked: respond to a question with a question. For example, when students provided off-script feedback on the class proposal, the user avoided answering directly by listing other common feedback and asking if any of those ideas resonated.

Conversational remixing layers a lightweight structure onto email conversation, making it useful even for ad-hoc needs. Flexible use of existing tools can beat rigid predesigned systems, especially as rapid prototyping testbeds for information needs. The goal is to ease a transition to custom-built software if the campaign remains popular and the scripts ossify. For example, people often escape structured personal information management tools and instead use *todo.txt* files on their desktop [8], non-profits create their own ad-hoc "homebrew databases" [30], and internet users author lightweight collections of items ranging from cereal boxes to historical timelines [7]. With academic paper reviewing, systems such as EasyChair, Precision Conference, and ManuscriptCentral formalize some parts of the conversation. However, what's formalized is relatively limited – reviewers still do a lot of semi-repetitive work. Furthermore, changing this process is much more difficult than in MyriadHub. Because academic reviewing software is bespoke, making even a small change often requires significant software development.

Future work will focus on supporting more natural responses at larger scales. MyriadHub has no straightforward way to manage emails that trigger components of multiple previous responses. One solution would be to enable a response to inherit from multiple response templates, like a *mix-in* in object-oriented programming. In addition, large campaigns such as the interview deployment can become unwieldy. More automation (*e.g.*, interactive machine learning) could support quicker decisions. In addition, parallelizing multiple crowd assistants might allow individuals to specialize in sub-parts of the campaign structure.

RELATED WORK

Email senders who need to reach a large audience have to choose among impersonal mass messages (*e.g.*, surveys [19, 29] or mailing lists [35]), personalized conversations with only a manageable subset of their audience [26, 3] or intractable, costly parallel conversations with everyone [11, 24]. At the same time, impersonal mass messages make it worse [26] for already overloaded email recipients [13, 15, 33] and suffer from low response rates [3, 31].

A major risk of scaling email communication is overload. Sources of email overload include the volume, email organization, and email handling strategies [13, 11, 32, 33]. MyriadHub mitigates email overload by improving email organization and handling strategies. It threads by recipient instead of by conversation, structures email content and reuses templates and rules with a small amount help from crowd workers, to compensate for the large volume of incoming responses in scaling.

Valet crowd assistants can help users extract structure from users' inboxes as in EmailValet [22]. MyriadHub extends its valet crowdsourcing philosophy. While EmailValet extract the content of choice (tasks embedded in users' inbound emails), MyriadHub adopts the "Programming by a Sample" model [18], in which crowd workers extract metadata from inbound emails and create templates based on users' outbound email examples in the same process.

Structure extraction and summarization are important components of MyriadHub. Crowds can aid with categorization and clustering of qualitative text-based data [2] or extracting tasks from email [22]. Alternatively, machine learning can help summarize messages [28] or forward and reply to messages [19]. MyriadHub demonstrates how thread-specific structure extraction can enable more effective communication: these tasks may be possible for micro-task crowds or machine learning in the future.

Commercially available mass email systems (for example MailChimp.com and iContact.com) generally focus on personalizing the *initial* outgoing email of a campaign, optionally segmenting recipients based on their properties. Their segmentation structure is usually a fixed data input into campaigns, *e.g.* types of customers, rather than flexible structures created as conversations grow in MyriadHub. MyriadHub generalizes this concept to support responses into an entire conversation through recycling relevant conversational parts, as a form of programming by demonstration. This is valuable because targeted, personal emails produce higher engagement [5] and higher perceived personal attention [4, 20].

Customer support software (such as zendesk.com, desk.com, and kayako.com) focuses on building collective reusable knowledge [9] and applying it to specific issues [16]. Publishing past conversations on sites such as on StackOverflow or Quora can transfer one-off knowledge into public memory [23, 25]. However, these organizational memory systems [1] work when the conversation has no conditional branching and the only follow-ups are for clarification [21, 24, 28].

CONCLUSION

Email extends the number of people we can reach, but not our conversational bandwidth. To combine the personal touch of one-on-one email with the large scale of email surveys, we explore MyriadHub: extracting the structure of conversations using valet crowdsourcing and re-applying previous responses when a similar situation recurs with a new conversational partner. MyriadHub allows users to hold conversations with large numbers of people by adapting previous responses to new situations. Holding conversations as usual can bootstrap conversation recycling: crowds generalize each thread and then only ask the user to contribute when a new branch of the conversational tree has been encountered.

Today's narrative around systems research in communication tools focuses on enhancing users' personal information management techniques. This framing highlights email overload [15, 33], email-based tasks [6, 22], and mining communication patterns [17, 27]. Instead, tools might make us better communicators. Could they help us say what we want to say more effectively and with fewer misunderstandings? Could they help us understand when to respond? MyriadHub helps amplify our voice. Future systems might help us improve that voice as well.

ACKNOWLEDGMENTS

We thank Ludwig Schubert for his work on an early draft of this paper, Valentin Costet for his technical contributions and Anika Raghuvanshi for her contributions to the video figure. This work was supported by National Science Foundation award IIS-1351131.

REFERENCES

1. Mark Steven Ackerman and Thomas W. Malone. 1990. Answer Garden: A tool for growing organizational memory. In *Proceedings of the ACM SIGOIS and IEEE CS TC-OA conference on Office information systems* (COCS '90).

2. Paul André, Aniket Kittur and Steven P. Dow. 2014. Crowd synthesis: Extracting categories and clusters from complex data. In *Proceedings of the 17th ACM conference on Computer supported cooperative work & social computing* (CSCW '14). ACM New York, NY, USA. 989-998.
3. William G. Axinn, Thomas E. Fricke and Arland Thornton. 1991. The Microdemographic Community-Study Approach Improving Survey Data by Integrating the Ethnographic Method. In *Sociological Methods & Research* 20.2 (1991): 187-217.
4. Greg Barron and Eldad Yechiam. 2002. Private e-mail requests and the diffusion of responsibility. In *Computers in Human Behavior* 18.5 (2002): 507-520.
5. Gerard Beenen, Kimberly Ling, Xiaoquin Wang, Klarissa Chang and Dan Frankowski. 2004. Using social psychology to motivate contributions to online communities. In *Proceedings of the 2004 ACM conference on Computer supported cooperative work* (CSCW '04). ACM New York, NY, USA, 212-221.
6. Victoria Bellotti, Nicolas Ducheneaut, Mark Howard and Ian Smith. 2003. Taking email to task: the design and evaluation of a task management centered email tool. In *Proceedings of the SIGCHI Conference on Human Factors in Computing Systems* (CHI '03). ACM New York, NY, USA, 345-352.
7. Edward Benson and David R. Karger. 2014. End-users publishing structured information on the web: an observational study of what, why, and how. In *Proceedings of the SIGCHI Conference on Human Factors in Computing Systems* (CHI '14). ACM New York, NY, USA, 1265-1274.
8. Michael Bernstein, Max van Kleek, David Karger and MC Schraefel. 2008. Information scraps: How and why information eludes our personal information management tools. In *ACM Transactions on Information Systems* (TOIS) 26.4 (2008): 24.
9. John H. Boose. 1990. Knowledge acquisition tools, methods and mediating representations. In *Knowledge Acquisition for Knowledge-Based Systems* (Motoda, H. et al., Eds), IOS Press, Tokyo (1990): 123.
10. Simon H. Corston-Oliver, Eric Ringger, Michael Gamon and Richard Campbell. 2004. Integration of Email and Task Lists. In Proc. CEAS.
11. Laura A. Dabbish and Robert E. Kraut. 2006. Email overload at work: an analysis of factors associated with email strain. In *Proceedings of the 2006 20th anniversary conference on Computer supported cooperative work* (CSCW '06). ACM New York, NY, USA, 431-440.
12. Judith Donath. 2007. Signals in social supernets. In *JCMC* 13.1 (2007): 231-251.
13. Danyel Fisher and A.J. Brush. 2006. Revisiting Whittaker & Sidner's email overload ten years later. In *Proceedings of the 2006 20th anniversary conference on Computer supported cooperative* work (CSCW '06). ACM New York, NY, USA, 309-312.
14. Fernando Flores, Michael Graves, Brad Hartfield, and Terry Winograd. 1988. Computer systems and the design of organizational interaction. In *ACM Transactions on Information Systems* (TOIS) 6.2 (1988):153-172.
15. Catherine Grevet, David Choi, Debra Kumar and Eric Gilbert. 2014. Overload is overloaded: email in the age of Gmail. In *Proceedings of the SIGCHI Conference on Human Factors in Computing Systems* (CHI '14). ACM New York, NY, USA, 793-802.
16. Christine A. Halverson, Thomas Erickson and Mark S. Ackerman. 2004. Behind the help desk: evolution of a knowledge management system in a large organization. In *Proceedings of the 2004 ACM conference on Computer supported cooperative work* (CSCW '04). ACM New York, NY, USA, 304-313.
17. Sudheendra Hangal, Monica S. Lam, and Jeffrey Heer. 2011. Muse: Reviving memories using email archives. In *Proceedings of the 24th annual ACM symposium on User interface software and technology* (UIST '11). ACM New York, NY, USA, 75-84.
18. Björn Hartmann, Leslie Wu, Kevin Collins and Scott R. Klemmer. 2007. Programming by a sample: rapidly creating web applications with d. mix. In *Proceedings of the 20th annual ACM symposium on User interface software and technology*. ACM New York, NY, USA, 241-250.
19. Dirk Heerwegh, Tim Vanhove, Koen Matthijs and Geert Loosveldt. 2005. The effect of personalization on response rates and data quality in web surveys. In *International Journal of Social Research Methodology* 8.2..
20. Adam N. Joinson and Ulf-Dietrich Reips. 2007. Personalized salutation, power of sender and response rates to Web-based surveys. In *Computers in Human Behavior* 23.3 (2007): 1372-1383.
21. William Jones. 2007. Personal information management. In *ASIST* 41.1 (2007): 453-504.
22. Nicolas Kokkalis, Thomas Köhn, Carl Pfeiffer, Dima Chornyi, Michael S. Bernstein and Scott R. Klemmer. 2013. EmailValet: Managing email overload through private, accountable crowdsourcing. In *Proceedings of the 2013 conference on Computer supported cooperative work* (CSCW '13). ACM New York, NY, USA, 1291-1300.
23. Lena Mamykina, Bella Manoim, Manas Mittal, George Hripcsak and Björn Hartmann. 2011. Design lessons from the fastest Q&A site in the west. In *Proceedings of the SIGCHI Conference on Human Factors in Computing Systems* (CHI '11). ACM New York, NY, USA, 2857-2866.

24. Donna McAuliffe. 2003. Challenging methodological traditions: Research by email. In *The Qualitative Report* 8.1 (2003): 57-69.
25. Kevin Kyung Nam, Mark S. Ackerman, and Lada A. Adamic. 2009. Questions in, knowledge in?: a study of naver's question answering community. In *Proceedings of the SIGCHI Conference on Human Factors in Computing Systems* (CHI '09). ACM New York, NY, USA, 779-788.
26. Albert Oosterhof. 2000. Creating individualized e-mail to students. In *Journal of Computing in Higher Education* 11.2 (2000): 75-90.
27. Adam Perer, Ben Shneiderman, and Douglas W. Oard. 2006. Using rhythms of relationships to understand e-mail archives. In JASIST 57.14 (2006): 1936-1948.
28. Owen Rambow, Lokesh Shrestha, John Chen, and Chirsty Lauridsen. 2004. Summarizing email threads. In *Proc. NAACL.*
29. Kim Sheehan, and Sally J. McMillan. 1999. Response variation in e-mail surveys: An exploration. In *Journal of Advertising Research.*
30. Amy Voida, Ellie Harmon and Ban Al-Ani. 2011. Homebrew databases: Complexities of everyday information management in nonprofit organizations. In *Proceedings of the SIGCHI Conference on Human Factors in Computing Systems* (CHI '11). ACM New York, NY, USA, 915-924.
31. Herbert F. Weisberg, Jon A. Krosnick, and Bruce D. Bowen. 1996. *An introduction to survey research, polling, and data analysis.* Sage.
32. Steve Whittaker, and Julia Hirschberg. 2001. The character, value, and management of personal paper archives. In TOCHI 8.2 (2001): 150-170.
33. Steve Whittaker and Candace Sidner. 1996. Email overload: exploring personal information management of email. In *Proceedings of the SIGCHI Conference on Human Factors in Computing Systems* (CHI '96). ACM New York, NY, USA, 276-283.
34. Amy X. Zhang, Lea Verou and David Karger. 2017. Wikum: Bridging Discussion Forums and Wikis Using Recursive Summarization. In Proc. CSCW. ACM New York, NY, USA.
35. Amy X. Zhang, Mark S. Ackerman, and David R. Karger. 2015. Mailing Lists: Why Are They Still Here, What's Wrong With Them, and How Can We Fix Them?. In *Proceedings of the 33rd Annual ACM Conference on Human Factors in Computing Systems* (CHI '15). ACM New York, NY, USA, 4009-4018.

"If a person is emailing you, it just doesn't make sense": Exploring Changing Consumer Behaviors in Email

Frank Bentley, Nediyana Daskalova, Nazanin Andalibi
Yahoo
Sunnyvale, CA, USA
[fbentley, nediyana, nazanin]@yahoo-inc.com

ABSTRACT
Much of the existing research literature on email use focuses on productivity or work settings. However, personal use of email has rarely been studied in depth. With the growth of messaging platforms being used for an increasing amount of personal communication, yet email use remaining high, we were interested in learning what Americans are using email for in their daily lives in 2016. To explore this topic, we use qualitative data from over 150 interviews with personal email users as well as quantitative data from several larger survey-based studies. We will show that personal email use is very different from what has been previously studied by workplace researchers and that daily use is largely focused on receiving and viewing B2C messages such as coupons, deals, receipts, and event notifications with personal communication over email diminished to a rarer, less-than-daily occurrence. We discuss the implications of this for the design of email and communications clients and present a design and prototype for an application that seeks to support these more frequent uses of consumer email.

Author Keywords
Email; Consumer; B2C; Deals; Coupons; Communication; Mobile Devices; Messaging.

ACM Classification Keywords
H.4.3 Communications Applications: Electronic Mail; H.5.m. Information interfaces and presentation (e.g., HCI): Miscellaneous

INTRODUCTION
The past ten years have brought many changes to the broader communication landscape. Messaging applications such as WhatsApp and Facebook Messenger, along with SMS, have become the platform of choice for the majority of person-to-person communication. [3, 6] However, email remains a frequent daily habit for billions of people throughout the world. We wanted to gain a better picture of what people are using email for in their everyday lives, outside of work contexts, and to use this information to help design applications that better serve the needs of personal email users.

CHI 2017, May 06-11, 2017, Denver, CO, USA
© 2017 ACM. ISBN 978-1-4503-4655-9/17/05…$15.00
DOI: http://dx.doi.org/10.1145/3025453.3025613

There exists a wide variety of research on email use, going back many years. However, the vast majority of this work focuses on business use of email or productivity and interruption impacts of using email throughout the day in an office setting. Where they exist, studies of consumer email use focus largely on users' organization strategies and not on the types of content sent and received and how email is currently used in everyday life. This lack of an exploration of current email behaviors led us to the following research questions, which motivated the studies presented in this paper:

1) What are the main uses of personal email accounts in people's daily lives?
2) What types of messages do users read and send?
3) What devices are users using to access email, and in particular what causes them to use email on a computer?
4) How are other communications services complementing email use?

We will address these questions through data from over 150 interviews with a wide demographic range of personal email users from San Francisco, Chicago, Champaign, New York City, and Silicon Valley as well as extensive survey data about current practices from representative samples of Americans. Wherever possible we will support our quantitative findings with explanations and quotes from our qualitative interviews as well as go the other way to demonstrate where interview themes generalize to percentages of the larger American population.

With this combination of data, we will show how consumer email has rapidly changed from a person-to-person communication platform, as often studied in the 90s and early 2000s to a business-to-consumer (B2C) platform where users mainly receive a variety of coupons, deals, political subscriptions, receipts, events, confirmations, and other system-generated messages, many of which are extremely useful to them. Where personal communication still exists in email, it is largely professional messages, such as emailing doctors, children's teachers, or applying for jobs. As one of our participants told us, and has been echoed by many others in similar words, "email is all business." We will conclude with implications for the design of consumer email solutions that meet the current needs of people for dealing with the hundreds of commercial messages that they receive per day – use cases very different from what mail products are often designed for (composing messages, viewing personal contacts, etc.) and require different solutions from the inbox as a chronological list that we are used to.

RELATED WORK

As email growth expanded in the 1990s, several researchers began studying email use in corporations where email was quickly becoming a daily task. Early work focused on user's triaging behaviors. Whittaker & Sidner [24] categorized email management into three main types: frequent filer, spring cleaner, and no-filer. The concept of "email overload" first appeared in this paper and referred to all of the tasks one had to accomplish to reply to all of the person-to-person messages in a work Inbox. However, they studied office workers using Lotus NotesMail and not consumers, hence most of the discussion is focused on productivity and work task management. Bälter [1] later divided the no-filer category into folderless cleaner and folderless springcleaner, depending on whether items were deleted from the inbox on a daily basis. Interestingly missing from these categories is someone who lets unread messages pile up and never cleans them, something we will return to in our examination of consumer inboxes.

Revisiting this work in 2006, Fisher et al. [10] found that most workers at Microsoft did not strictly abide by one of these filing or organization strategies, but did something in the middle, with some filing, some deleting, some amount of a piling inbox. We will return to this in our discussion of consumer inbox triage.

In 2005, Belotti et al. [2] continued to explore "email overload" in the work context, where participants were overloaded with a variety of personal communication relating to tasks that must be completed. In particular, they found that tasks where an email response is needed to continue along often led to the greatest stress and feelings of overload when one had many of these messages to respond to. Even with this focus, many of the tactics that they observed are relevant to consumer email, including marking messages unread to follow up on them, filing messages in customized folders, and creating calendar events to remind users to follow up on an email message. Also, their discussion of "rapid response" tasks versus "extended response" tasks is relevant beyond the world of "task-based project management." However, due to their focus on the work context, implications around organizing messages per "task" may not overlap with the majority of current consumer needs, which as we describe below are not necessarily task-based.

Researchers have also studied the likelihood of an email receiving responses. Dabbish et al [9] studied the likelihood for emails to get a reply in a business context, and found that a self-rated "importance" of each message had little correlation with a user's likelihood to respond.

What was most striking to us in our literature review was that all of this literature came from the study of business use of email, much of it studying workers of large software tech companies such as Microsoft or HP. With over 4.3 billion active email accounts in the world [20], there was a large need for studying the use of more typical consumer users. In early research from 1999, Kraut et al [16] explored how consumers were using the Internet, and found that email use for personal communication was a main driver of Internet use in the home, being "more convenient and faster than postal mail." Their conversation around email focuses only on interpersonal use, via direct messages or via topic-based mailing lists. Receiving messages from companies is not mentioned.

A more recent study by Grevet et al [12] in 2014 explored Gmail use for both personal and professional accounts, however focused more on differences in organization styles than in the particular content of messages received. They did discuss "type overload" where people receive a variety of different types of messages in their personal Gmail accounts, yet almost all of the message types discussed are types of personal communication (medical information, clubs, personal communication, etc.). Yet their comment about work email being about managing tasks while personal email is about managing "multiple facets of daily life" was interesting to us, and in need of further investigation to understand exactly what these facets are.

Even as recently as 2011, Farnham and Churchill [10] found that email was still primarily used for communicating with family. "Life management," including topics such as receipts and bank statements, ranked 3rd in terms of usage. However, much has changed in the communications landscape in the past five years since this survey. Other HCI research has discussed the rapid growth of text messaging and instant messaging services, particularly on mobile phones. Grinter et al [13-14] studied the increasing use of text messaging and instant messaging for personal communication, especially with teenagers [15], while Church et al [6] studied the rise of Whatsapp and features that made it popular for individual and group messaging over using email or SMS for personal communication.

Finally, Cecchinato et al [5] explored email search in work compared to personal contexts and discuss that search in a personal account is more likely to be used to find specific information (such as hotel booking information), hinting that email might become a tool for "domestic paperwork." This idea was interesting to us, but was not quantified in any of this earlier work. How are people using their personal accounts day-to-day for a wide variety of tasks, and how many users are abandoning the platform for personal communications?

None of this existing work discusses what has happened to email use while personal communication has been moving to other messaging platforms. The focus of our work over the past year has been to build up a comprehensive set of studies exploring personal email use from a wide variety of angles – from the types of messages received, to the devices it is used on, to the role of email in people's lives. These studies will combine to show how personal email use in 2016 is quite different from the use of email that has been studied in previous work and that this has clear implications for the design of personal email applications.

OUR DATASETS

We have collected a wide variety of qualitative and quantitative data from December 2015 through July 2016 relating to the use of personal email in America. We will briefly describe the datasets before discussing specific themes that we have observed. All studies were approved in advance by our institution.

Qualitative Data

The bulk of our qualitative data comes from interviews with 150 participants (aged 18-67, 53% female) conducted in 2016 as a part of weekly user research sessions. Sessions were held in San Francisco, Champaign-Urbana, Chicago, Silicon Valley, and New York City, in order to capture a wide range of Americans, as well as different types of cities, suburbs, and rural areas. We recruited as broadly as possible for these studies and had participants who were bankers, lawyers, teachers, bail bondsmen, security guards, cooks, actors, stay-at-home parents, construction workers, store clerks, farmers, blacksmiths, and many other diverse occupations.

These sessions each began with a short interview about email use, including the participant's main uses of email, the devices they use and general patterns of use, and a tour of their email accounts including how they manage email, the types of messages that they had in their email that required attention, and their practices of triage.

The audio from these interviews was removed from the archived videos and transcribed. Themes were identified from these transcripts using a grounded theory process. The items of analysis were exact quotes from participants and themes were identified inductively in a team-based grounded-theory analysis until the group reached consensus. Themes were compared to data from the representative surveys to find explanations for the behaviors that we observed in the surveys. This is a common method for data triangulation in mixed-methods studies as data from surveys is more reliable for frequency than counting instances from interviews.

In this paper, we will also use short answer qualitative data from open-ended questions from a variety of surveys that we have conducted. Specific surveys will be discussed below and often included several open-ended questions to elicit deeper feedback from a larger number of participants, from a broader selection of the United States population, on topics of interest. For example, we conducted primarily qualitative surveys to better understand primary uses of email and reasons people create new email accounts. Each of these surveys was deployed to a sample of adults in the United States via diverse SurveyMonkey United States panels or via Amazon Mechanical Turk (AMT) and received participants of wide age ranges from all regions of the country, well-balanced in terms of education, income, and gender as shown in Figure 1. Comparative studies have found these surveys to capture less than a 10% margin of error on technology usage questions when compared to larger, expensive professional market research surveys.

Quantitative Data

Quantitative data in this paper comes from several sources. Over the past seven months, we have conducted a number of larger surveys, as mentioned above, to understand behavior in the wider population and to validate hypotheses that we have observed in our interviews with a larger, more representative sample of Americans. Specific, quantitative-focused surveys investigated email log out behaviors, coupon use, searching email for flights or packages, and motivations for creating new email accounts. Each survey was distributed to a sample of diverse respondents as described above between January and August of 2016. Some questions were also asked in a larger-scale survey deployed to a United States representative sample of 1,000 individuals via a market research firm for further validation. We will clearly state the source of all quantitative data in the findings section below. We realize that email use may be different in other countries, as shown in the business context by Tang et al [22], but chose to focus on America given the large population and ease of conducting larger, representative surveys. We leave the study of current personal email practices in other countries to future work.

Study	N	RQ	Ages	Gender
1. In-person Interviews	150	1,2,3,4	18-67	53% F
2. Market Research Survey	1000	1,2	18-65	50% F
3. Email Use Survey	150	1,2,3,4	19-62	43% F
4. Coupon/Deal Survey	151	1,2,3	19-67	47% F
5. Unsubscribe/Account Survey	120	3	21-75	43% F
6. Notifications Survey	300	3,4	18-65	42% F

Table 1: A summary of the studies presented in this paper. We will refer to studies by number below to make it easier to understand the samples used for each finding.

FINDINGS

By triangulating quantitative and qualitative data from each of the studies mentioned above, we discovered several interesting findings about the changing role of personal email use that we have not found discussed in the literature.

These centered on the changing nature of consumer email from an interpersonal communication platform to a business-to-consumer (B2C) communication platform, the primary role of coupons and deals in consumer email, current organizational practices, and a rapid move towards mobile-only (or mobile vast-majority) access. Most interesting to us is that through these changes from personal to commercial messages, email has not reduced its role in people's lives, and with mobile notifications the frequency of accessing email has only increased over desktop use. We find that the older image of email primarily serving person-to-person communication has almost completely disappeared, with most users sending an email every few days at most, while receiving many dozens or hundreds per day. Specific findings around each of these themes, with data triangulated from multiple methods and studies to support each theme, will be discussed in the remainder of this section.

The shift towards B2C communication

When we think of personal email, we often think of personal messages sent to friends and family, and this is the image of personal email painted by much of the previous work in this area (e.g. [12,16]). However, when we ask our research participants about the last emails that they have sent, they often think for a while and tell us about messages sent weeks or months ago.

We began each of our 150 interviews with a question asking participants to tell us what they use email for before actually opening up their accounts. Rarely will personal correspondence appear in the top items listed. Instead, people discuss using email for finding deals, getting receipts and tracking information, using it to sign up for mailing lists or apps/websites, and finding out about events such as concerts or movies. This represents a vast shift from thinking about email as a personal communications platform, to understanding it as mostly a business to consumer platform, more similar to Facebook Pages than to traditional written communication.

Participants frequently tell us that email is "all business" and personal communication is mostly limited to professors, hiring managers when applying for jobs, doctors, or other professionals. When participants mention that they use email for "personal communication" we ask them to explain that to us. Almost always, the explanation will involve telling us about receiving bank statements, receipts, messages from doctors, etc. For example, an interview participant in Chicago told us that he uses email primarily for "personal" use. When asked what "personal" meant, he explained that it was bills, doctors, shopping, and receiving receipts from companies. A participant from Champaign told us that her email use was for *"everything personal, like buying concert tickets, shopping on amazon, and bank statements."* Another Chicago participant said that she uses email "very rarely" with people that she knows as they won't respond as quickly compared to sending a text message or Facebook message. She used to communicate with family in Mexico via email, but now mostly does this over Whatsapp, similar to findings from Church et al [6].

One area where we continue to see personal messages being sent is in communicating with military service

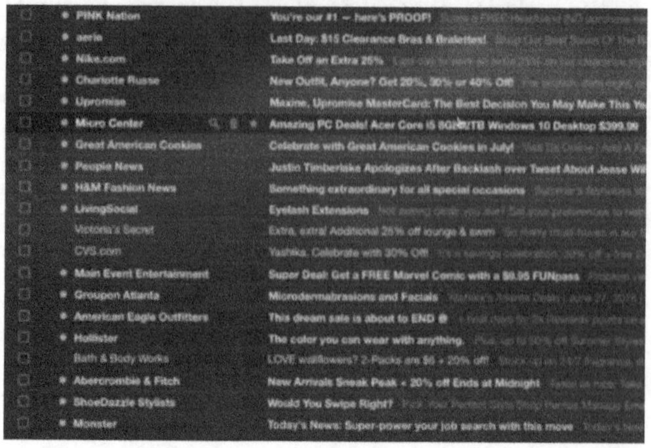

Figure 1: A typical email Inbox as observed in our in-person interviews. Note that there is no personal correspondence visible in these first 20 messages (although this is the participant's main personal account that she also uses to email people), and that the majority of emails will never be opened or deleted. Note that there is no personally identifiable information in this screenshot.

Use of Email	Percent
Receive advertisements/coupons/deals from stores	67%
Send emails to friends/family	66%
Receive receipts or bills	56%
Manage Travel Plans (flight/hotel reservations for you or friends/family)	24%
Participate in group mailing lists	22%
Receive political updates (candidates or current government leaders)	16%
Receive News/Sports updates	15%
Communicate with teachers/professors	14%
Receive local updates (local police, NextDoor, etc.)	11%
Communicate with medical professionals	8%
Other	7%

Table 2: Selections made by 150 participants when choosing their "top three uses" of email (from Study #3).

	25%	50%	75%	100%
Last Sent	10 days	2 days	1 day	0 days
Second to Last Sent	19 days	4 days	2 days	2 days

Table 3: Quartile view of the number of days since a participant sent their last two emails in their primary personal account (from Study #3).

members who are serving overseas. Email is often the most reliable way to reach soldiers who might not have access to mobile phones and networks and have their communication monitored by the government. When asked the last time she sent an email to a person, a participant in Chicago (whose Inbox can be seen in Figure 1) told us, *"Oh, that would have been a while ago. I think it would have been to a friend of mine that just joined the military about a month ago and that's our only way of communicating."*

After hearing stories like this for many weeks in a row in our interviews, we wanted to explore email use from a more representative audience. Perhaps the people who came into our lab were different from the general population in some way that affected the types of messages that they received. We conducted a survey of 150 respondents using a United States panel on Survey Monkey (Study #3 from Table 1) and asked participants to list their top three uses of email (see Table 2). The most selected option was using email to "Receive advertising/ deals/coupons" and the number three choice was to "Receive receipts or bills." Overall, almost two thirds of use cases chosen in participants' top three were "receive" use cases. Sending use cases such as communicating with friends, family, doctors, teachers, etc. only accounted for one third of the responses. We were interested to see that the option "Send emails to friends or family" came in second via this self-reported data. However, when we asked participants to check the last time they had sent an email (to anyone), it was often days or weeks ago. The median date was two days ago (see Table 3), however the mean was 41 days ago, showing a very long tail of email sending behavior from personal accounts. When looking at the second most recently sent message, the median date was four days ago and the mean was 52 days ago. These patterns represent very different usage from the email overload [24] observed in corporate email, with dozens of personally sent messages to respond to every day.

We also explored the subscriptions that participants had in their email. As a part of our interviews with ten participants in the lab, we used a script to scan through the messages in their inboxes to find the message lists that they were subscribed to (messages that had a "List-Unsubscribe" header). Participants had an average of 93 different list subscriptions in their primary email accounts. The majority of these were for stores, including coupons and deals, with other lists coming from political candidates, causes (e.g. change.org, kickstarter.org), community mailing lists, and social websites (e.g. Facebook, Twitter, Tumblr, Next Door, etc.).

To explore this behavior at an even larger scale, we created several questions in the n=1000, US representative, marketing survey discussed above (Study #2 from Table 1). 56% of respondents told us that their email inbox is mostly used for receiving commercial emails. In addition, 56% had looked for a package shipment or receipt in their email in the past week, and 32% had checked travel details in the past week, representing other key uses of commercial and system-generated email.

So if email is being used more for emails from companies to people, how are people communicating with each other? Largely, SMS [12, 14] and messaging applications [6] have taken over this category of communication. In the larger marketing survey (Study #2), 41% of respondents said that email is "not important" for personal communication. This was backed up by qualitative data in the lab. A participant in San Francisco told us: *"If a person is emailing you it just doesn't make sense because it's easier to text them. If I text you I know you got it right away. If I email you, how do I even know it got to you. Texting, I can at least see a dialogue."* A participant in Silicon Valley told us that: *"Text messages is perfect because it's faster. Email is cool, but texting is for right now."* And another participant told us, *"I don't do a lot of friend communication on email anymore. Between Facebook and text, that about covers it."*

We find it interesting that this drastic switch of personal communication has not dramatically reduced email usage. In our large survey (Study #2), only 26% of participants said that they thought they were using email less often when compared to a year ago, and many are using it much more often given the convenience of accessing email on smartphones and the use of push notifications. Through another survey deployed on both Survey Monkey and AMT to 300 smartphone users in the United States (Study #6), we found that 72% of mobile email users had email notifications enabled. Interview participants frequently speak about specific email subscriptions that they love to read, or specific deals that they look out for on a weekly basis as a reason to check email regularly. Email is no less a part of peoples' day-to-day lives, it is just used for different types of communication than it has been in the past.

The role of Coupons and Deals

As discussed above, receiving commercial deals and coupons was cited as a primary use of email for 67% of survey respondents in Study #2. We initially became interested in this topic through qualitative data we were receiving in the lab. In our study in Chicago, we had a participant who was the master coupon organizer for the family. When asked how she used her email, she told us: *"Coupons from stores, I'm really big on that. If there are things that I want, why not sign up for email and promotions from these companies and save a little money? If they have a big sale or something, I want to know what's going on."*

Participants described maintaining a general awareness of the coupons that they had in their inbox by reading the subject lines as they came in (even if not opening the messages). Participants then remembered to look for these coupons when about to purchase something in the future. A participant in San Francisco told us: *"A few weeks ago, I was at Macy's buying something and I remembered that I had seen a coupon in my email, so I went through and searched for it so that I could use it."* Another talked about signing up for a mailing list from a store to get coupons: *"I did a search in my inbox for Forever 21. I was looking for the coupon they had sent since I signed up for their newsletter."* Many participants discuss reading through the subject lines of deal emails daily. A Silicon Valley participant told us: *"I usually look through them in the evenings to see if they are only good for the day. I look through them then because that is when I have a little quiet time to be able to concentrate to surf the Internet and see if there are any deals I want to take advantage of."*

Since coupons and deals emerged as a frequent topic of discussion with participants in the lab, we wanted to quantify their use. We created a few questions in the n=1000 survey (Study #2) to better understand behaviors around emailed deals. In our US-representative sample, we found that 46% of all respondents had **used** a coupon/deal from their email in the past week. This number was quite surprising and we have seen very similar numbers in other follow-up studies using different panels of participants. In fact, 47% of families and 45% of singles told us that they "mainly use" email for coupons/deals. And 49% of all respondents (490/1000) said that email is important for finding out about coupons and deals, more than those who said it was important for personal communication.

We wanted to know more about these coupons and deals, and conducted an n=150 survey to explore couponing behaviors in email (Study #4). In this survey, deployed on SurveyMonkey to a United States sample, 92% of participants reported receiving a coupon or deal in their personal email in the past week, and 45% had used one. The most frequent coupons used were from Target, Groupon, Amazon, Kohl's, Best Buy, Walmart, Papa John's, Newegg, Old Navy, Michael's, Macy's, and eBay – representing a wide variety of both online and offline retailers. 44% redeemed their last-used coupon using a code online, while 23% showed it on a device in a store, and another 22% printed the coupon.

Beyond just using the coupon themselves, in Study #4 we found that 65% of participants discussed sharing coupons from email with others in the past month. A participant in Chicago signed up for sneaker coupons that she would send to her brother whenever there was a particularly good deal and also sent her mom grocery and drug store coupons. She used many coupons herself as well, including using a clothing store coupon on her walk over to the interview.

However, keeping track of coupons is often difficult, and 60% of our survey participants in Study #4 did not organize their coupons in any particular way. However, 25% of participants discussed using specific folders for keeping track of coupons. Users receive far more coupons than they will use, and 62% of respondents discussed deleting unneeded emails with deals/coupons –immediately if they are not needed, after they have expired, or as part of mass purges when they clean their inbox.

Problems that participants faced with coupons were forgetting about coupons and having them expire, receiving too many coupons and not having time to look at them, and feeling overwhelmed with the amount of commercial email that they were receiving. This feeling of being overwhelmed has led to a rapid shift in email organization behaviors, compared to what has been reported in previous work.

Email Organization Behaviors and a Revisit of Email Overload

Email Overload [24] was heavily discussed in the previous work studying email use. However, in a professional context, overload most frequently referred to not being able to respond to all of the messages one was receiving in sufficient time. However, as discussed above, there are very few messages in a consumer inbox that require a traditional written response. The overload that we frequently observe in our interviews and tours of participants' inboxes is observing users who receive too much commercial email for them to manage, often many dozens of coupons or deals a day, in addition to dozens of mailing lists, political messages, and social updates from services such as Facebook, LinkedIn, or Twitter.

Receiving too much email led our participants to several different behaviors. As email becomes too much to manage, users stop marking messages read. About a third of our participants in Study #1 had over 10,000 messages in their primary personal account. They had a mean of 3,504 unread messages .(similar to Grevet et al.'s finding of a mean 4,846 unread messages in their n=19 study in 2014 [12]) with only 35% of participants being "caught up" on their messages with less than 20 unread. This does not mean that users with many unread messages are not "active" users – in fact most check their email dozens of times per day on their phone. However, their practice is to only choose to open the specific messages that they would like to read. For them, the unread count conveys little information, and the messages that are read are often the important ones that they want to return to later on – either to use a coupon, to pay a bill, or to get back to a professor or manager when seeking a job. This is in contrast to the many complex organizational schemes observed in previous studies that mostly focused on work-related email, or personal email that had many interpersonal messages (e.g. [12,24,25]) as findings that messages that are unread are somehow important and need to be attended to [2].

"I don't really manage my email" is a frequent response in the lab when we ask users to show us how they organize their Inboxes. One participant in Silicon Valley even referred to their inbox as *"an explosion."* Selecting all visible messages in the Inbox and pressing delete was a common triaging tactic that we observed with these users, and they frequently discussed going on deletion binges every few months to reduce the unread count. One

participant in Silicon Valley discussed having a "new zero" of 600 messages and that she tries to keep her inbox below that level. If she sees a badge for 602 messages, then she knows that she has two new ones. But many participants have just given up trying to mark messages read, seeing the inbox more as a feed than a list where each item needs action taken.

The large volume of messages that participants receive also leads to unsubscribing from specific email lists. This behavior is quite common with 20% of survey respondents in the larger marketing survey (#2) having unsubscribed from at least one list in the last week, and 27% in the last two weeks.

Frequently, the overload of messages leads users to abandon an account altogether. Research participants frequently discuss abandoning older email accounts because they were receiving too much email. It is easier for them to just start fresh than to try to unsubscribe from everything in their Inbox that they no longer wish to receive. Table 4 shows the top reasons for creating a new account from Study #5, with 25% of people creating an account to escape the large amount of mail that they were receiving in an older account. Note that this is much more common than the 4% of users who created a totally new account for commercial mail purposes only.

Reasons for Creating a new Account	Percentage
To have a more professional sounding username	27%
Old account getting too much spam	25%
Didn't want to give "real" email address to a business	18%
Didn't want to give "real" email address to a person	14%
To Use a Service (e.g. Android/Chrome/Google Docs/Fantasy Sports)	11%
For work/side projects (to keep separate from personal)	10%
Problems with old account (locked out, deleted for non-use, etc.)	6%
To use for giving out to websites/signing up for things/online shopping	4%
To try something new	3%
Graduated from school and needed a new address	2%

Table 4: The top reasons for creating a new email account, asked of 150 respondents. The new "email overload" does not have to do with responding to messages, but with the vast volume of commercial mail that appears in the inbox, drowning out specific messages or deals that a user wants to engage with (from Study #5).

Participants in this survey reported an average of 3.7 active email accounts. Often, these included a main personal account, a main work account, and 1-2 specific accounts for certain services or older addresses no longer used. In our interviews, participants often spoke about having old usernames that they created in middle or high school that they are embarrassed to use today. Yet some mail still goes to that account, so they check it regularly or IMAP it into their main account. Specific services, such as Google Docs, Android, or Yahoo Fantasy Sports require accounts on their respective domains, also causing users to create additional accounts and leading to a general sense of overwhelming effort needed to stay on top of them all.

With one-third of users no longer actively managing their inboxes, and even more who frequently mass delete hundreds of messages at a time, there is an increasing need to develop better tools for users to keep track of the hundreds of messages that they are receiving per day, which range from coupons, deals, receipts, communication with medical professionals, teachers, and the occasional personal message.

The rapid shift towards mobile

Email is quickly becoming a mobile-focused activity. In fact 149 of the 150 participants that we interviewed said that they primarily access email on their mobile phones. This follows an overall industry trend of decreasing desktop use in general, however, we were initially surprised by participants who discussed not having used desktop mail in weeks or months. Reasons for users to go to their email on a computer are: when they are on the desktop anyway for another task, needing to print something, or needing to type a longer response or include a document – such as emailing a real estate or insurance agent.

One participant in Champaign told us that he will only use mail on the desktop a few times a month while he is using his computer for specific work-based tasks. Otherwise, the computer stays off and he only uses the phone, or occasionally a tablet to access email and the Internet. Another participant told us that she only uses her phone for email during the week, but on Saturdays uses a computer at the library to order supplies for her farm and checks email then as well. Another participant told us that she would check her email on desktop only if her phone battery dies.

These behaviors are not just limited to the rural Midwest. We frequently see participants in San Francisco or Sunnyvale discussing broken laptops that they do not care to fix and do not miss at all. Smartphones are becoming primary computing devices for more and more people. PEW has even tracked a 5% uptick over the past two years in households dropping broadband as they switch to mobile-only for Internet [16].

Increasingly participants discuss only turning on a computer if they have a specific task to accomplish. A participant in Chicago told us: *"I only use my laptop for [medical] school stuff. Otherwise it's all on my phone or iPad. And I check my email several times a day on those."*

This move towards mobile means that it cannot be assumed that users will visit email on a computer in a given week or even month. Mobile mail clients need to be as fully featured as their desktop counterparts. An additional challenge on mobile is the smaller screen and increased difficulty in typing, making searching or scrolling for a message more difficult than on a computer. Solutions to help people get to messages that they need to return to are even more important on mobile devices.

DISCUSSION

Through our quantitative and qualitative data, we have shown that personal email use is very different from the business email use that has been frequently studied in the literature. While the study of business email frequently revolves around response times to personal messages or on distraction from a primary task while checking email, consumer email is far less about composing emails and having specific follow-up tasks.

The majority of email that consumers receive is from commercial sources, such as coupons, deals, receipts, confirmations, tracking numbers, etc. People receive so much of this email that they often feel overwhelmed, in a new type of email overload quite different from the one studied by Whittaker [24] in the mid-1990s at HP and a different style of type overload as observed by Grevet et al [12] where the types are almost all different types of business-generated messages.

When one thinks about personal email as a mass B2C communication channel, the design affordances of the past are perhaps not as relevant. Having a single, reverse-chronological list of sender, subject, and date text is likely not the best way to store, browse, and consume large numbers of coupons, receipts, or travel itineraries. Even just having a few chronological lists, such as in Gmail's categorized inbox is missing the larger opportunity. If one were setting out to design a system from scratch that would be a user's main source of accessing coupons, receipts, travel itineraries, and bank statements, a chronological list with a text subject preview hardly seems like the ideal solution.

Systems that actively parse message data could show promise for helping users to make sense of the large amount of messages and structured data that they receive and can help people to feel less overwhelmed with trying to find that one important email from an instructor or bank in a typical list of 10,000+ unread messages.

In fact, it might be this proliferation of commercial messages that contributed to the decline of email use for personal communication. If personal messages are likely to get lost in hundreds of deals and receipts, then it is no wonder that this communication has moved towards dedicated personal communication platforms such as Facebook Messenger or WhatsApp, where communication is aggregated by person, and people serve as the core navigational item.

Given these new trends of personal email use, we will describe design implications and a proposed solution that takes advantage of these opportunities in the next section.

IMPLICATIONS FOR DESIGN

Given the data above, we have been created several Implications for Design to create systems that help people manage the types of emails that they receive in their personal accounts that are important to them. We have also created a concept, CardMail, which organizes email to help with the problem of overload, and lets users quickly get to deals, receipts, tickets, travel itineraries, and subscriptions with one tap, removing the need for manual organization.

Sorting Commercial Mail

Following the finding from Grevet et al [12] that personal email is about managing "multiple facets of daily life," and seeing the variety of different uses that our participants had for the email, we believe that it is important to be able to automatically sort commercial mail by type. Receipts, bills, travel itineraries, tickets and event confirmations, emails from doctors or teachers, and the occasional personal note are all very distinct content types and should be treated as such. Users should be able to quickly find messages of a certain type when entering their email application.

Extracting Actionable Information

Often, emails contain a good deal of extraneous information for the task at hand. If a user wants to find out when their package is arriving, or what time their flight leaves tomorrow, the entire email is not needed. As Cecchinato et al. [5] have shown, search in personal email accounts is often for specific details in a message, such as confirmation numbers, addresses, and times. Email systems should reduce the burden of reading entire messages by extracting relevant details from the messages in the form of rich, actionable cards.

The majority of the time, users would never even have to read the complete message. Cards could show the relevant details for a receipt (e.g. $5.00 on an Uber in San Francisco on 8/15/16), making it easy to quickly scroll through a stream of receipt cards to find the needed information and reducing the need to open and close a large number of messages to find the one with the details that are needed in a particular situation.

Ordering Messages

Finally, messages should not be ordered in the old-fashioned reverse chronological order that was created for personal communications. Messages within categories should be sorted in an order that makes sense for that type of information. Travel can be organized by trip, not by the dates the individual reservations happened to be placed. Events and tickets can be organized by the date of the event. And deals could be grouped by the sender or ordered by the dates that the deals will expire.

This order would make it much faster to find relevant messages, as well as to use lists of messages or cards as a way to see what is coming up and access tickets or

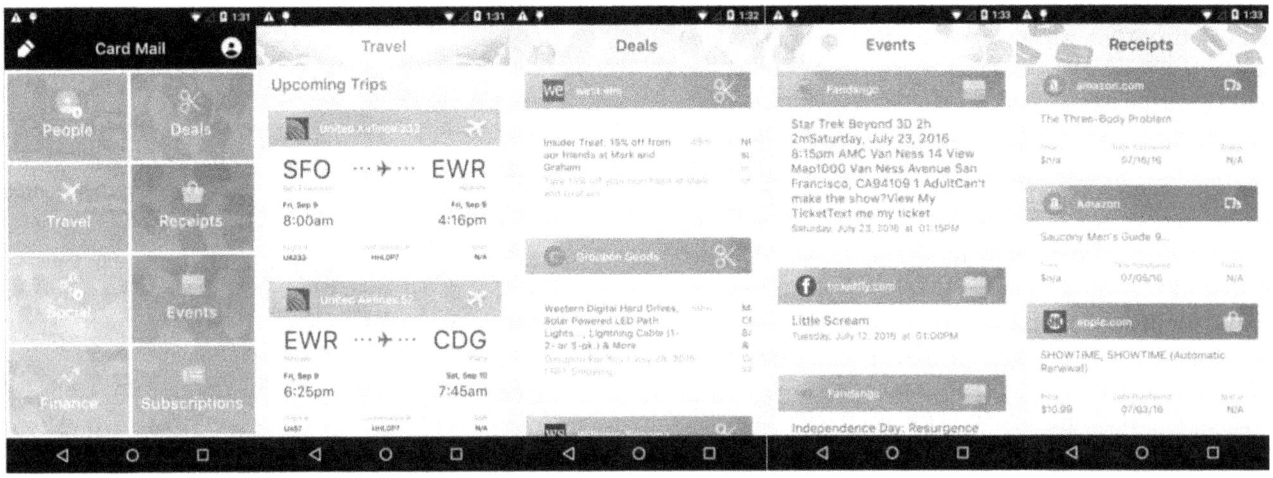

Figure 2: CardMail does away with the Inbox and shows specific categories of messages that people receive. Users can view what they are looking for directly, and do not feel overwhelmed by thousands of unread messages in their inbox.

boarding passes to today's movies or flights without the need to search or scroll through large and cluttered inboxes.

CardMail

Learning from our findings and taking a human-centered approach, the CardMail system aims to address the problem of personal email overload and people's desire to not have to work hard to manage their personal email. The goal of the system is to keep people's mail separated into specific categories, and completely removes the "Inbox" as a concept. If a user wants to view deals, they can tap on Deals and see all of their coupons organized by sender. If they want to see their Receipts or their Travel itineraries, they can tap directly on those sections.

Beyond removing the Inbox, CardMail also does away with a default reverse chronological message list. Messages in each category are organized in the way that makes the most sense. Trips and Events are organized by the date of the relevant flights, hotels, or tickets. Deals are organized based on the expiration date of the offer, and are also aggregated by sender, so that one can find the best deal from a particular merchant when they are about to shop there. In our interviews we found that many people had specific merchants that they had in mind when looking to their Inbox for a deal, making a sender-centric model an easy way to find the best valid deal from a particular merchant without the need to search or manually sort through the dozens of deal messages received per day.

The categorization that we use comes from iterative participatory design research conducted through weekly studies in 2016. We began by conducting card sorts of email, asking participants to create logical groupings of their messages to understand which types of email made sense to group together. We then continued with research on the design of the cards themselves and the information that is most relevant to be shown for a flight or an Amazon receipt by asking participants to discuss recent instances where they had to find information in their email including the types of information that they were looking for and what was useful/irrelevant to them in these specific instances.

Since it was designed, we have shown CardMail to 20 users in the lab using their own accounts, and have received very positive feedback. Participants like that it does not require any manual effort to manage messages and they can easily find the messages that they need in a specific category. Participants frequently discuss liking the deals organized by store. We plan to run a field study to see how it works outside of the lab in the coming months.

Systems like CardMail follow directly from the main uses of email discussed by our users and fits with the types of content that people are receiving in their email accounts in 2016. To build a truly consumer-centric email platform, it helps to start with understanding the specific message types that users receive and value as well as the types of use that exist in real-world accounts.

CONCLUSION

We believe this to be the first comprehensive and quantitative investigation of how consumers are using their email in everyday life in an era where most person-to-person communication has moved to other platforms. In this paper, we have explored the types of messages that users receive, the changing tools for personal communication, how consumers manage coupons and deals, how they organize (or don't) their Inboxes, as well as the rapid shift towards mobile-only or mobile-majority access to email. These dramatic changes provide a very different view of email use from that in the literature, which often studied email practices of tech workers for their work-related messages. Email, in the consumer context, is not the productivity tool that is frequently discussed, but is rapidly becoming the main channel for businesses to interact with consumers – from sending receipts, deals, updates, events, or other types of communication.

Through CardMail, we are showing what it means to design for consumer use cases of email, and we believe that these features are novel as well as extremely useful for people and the ways that they use email in their daily lives. Building a consumer email platform means stepping back from expectations around sending and receiving person-to-person, task-based messages in a work context and understanding people's current behaviors and struggles with their personal email data.

ACKNOWLEDGMENTS

We would like to thank the Yahoo Mail team for their help and collaboration in all of these studies as well as Talia Knobel and Charlotte Sperling for help with the visual design of CardMail. We would also like to thank the UX Research team at Yahoo for supporting this research and for creating an environment that balances academic contributions and practical findings for product teams.

REFERENCES

1. Olle Bälter. Strategies for organizing email messages. Proceedings of HCI 1997, Springer, 21–38.
2. Victoria Bellotti, Nicolas Ducheneaut, Mark Howard, Ian Smith, Rebecca E. and Grinter. Quality versus quantity: E-mail-centric task management and its relation with overload. *Human- Computer Interaction 20*, 1 (2005), 89–138.
3. Frank R. Bentley, S. Tejaswi Peesapati, and Karen Church. 2016. "I thought she would like to read it": Exploring Sharing Behaviors in the Context of Declining Mobile Web Use. In *Proceedings of the 2016 CHI Conference on Human Factors in Computing Systems* (CHI '16). ACM, New York, NY, USA, 1893-1903. DOI: http://dx.doi.org/10.1145/2858036.2858056
4. Ying-Yu Chen, Frank Bentley, Christian Holz, and Cheng Xu. 2015. Sharing (and Discussing) the Moment: The Conversations that Occur Around Shared Mobile Media. In *Proceedings of the 17th International Conference on Human-Computer Interaction with Mobile Devices and Services*(MobileHCI '15). ACM, New York, NY, USA, 264-273. DOI=http://dx.doi.org/10.1145/2785830.2785868
5. Marta E. Cecchinato, Abigail Sellen, Milad Shokouhi, and Gavin Smyth. 2016. Finding Email in a Multi-Account, Multi-Device World. In *Proceedings of the 2016 CHI Conference on Human Factors in Computing Systems* (CHI '16). ACM, New York, NY, USA, 1200-1210. DOI: https://doi.org/10.1145/2858036.2858473
6. Karen Church and Rodrigo de Oliveira. 2013. What's up with whatsapp?: comparing mobile instant messaging behaviors with traditional SMS. In *Proceedings of the 15th international conference on Human-computer interaction with mobile devices and services* (MobileHCI '13). ACM, New York, NY, USA, 352-361. DOI: http://dx.doi.org/10.1145/2493190.2493225
7. Edward Cutrell, Mary Czerwinski, and Eric Horvitz. Notification, disruption, and memory: Effects of messaging interruptions on memory and performance. In *Proc. INTERACT 2001*, IOS Press (2001), 263–269.
8. Laura A. Dabbish and Robert E. Kraut. 2006. Email overload at work: an analysis of factors associated with email strain. In *Proceedings of the 2006 20th anniversary conference on Computer supported cooperative work* (CSCW '06). ACM, New York, NY, USA, 431-440. DOI=http://dx.doi.org/10.1145/1180875.1180941
9. Laura A. Dabbish, Robert E. Kraut, Susan Fussell, and Sara Kiesler. 2005. Understanding email use: predicting action on a message. In *Proceedings of the SIGCHI Conference on Human Factors in Computing Systems* (CHI '05). ACM, New York, NY, USA, 691-700. DOI=http://dx.doi.org/10.1145/1054972.1055068
10. Shelly D. Farnham and Elizabeth F. Churchill. 2011. Faceted identity, faceted lives: social and technical issues with being yourself online. In *Proceedings of the ACM 2011 conference on Computer supported cooperative work* (CSCW '11). ACM, New York, NY, USA, 359-368. DOI=http://dx.doi.org/10.1145/1958824.1958880
11. Danyel Fisher, A. J. Brush, Eric Gleave, and Marc A. Smith. 2006. Revisiting Whittaker & Sidner's "email overload" ten years later. In *Proceedings of the 2006 20th anniversary conference on Computer supported cooperative work* (CSCW '06). ACM, New York, NY, USA, 309-312. DOI=http://dx.doi.org/10.1145/1180875.1180922
12. Catherine Grevet, David Choi, Debra Kumar, and Eric Gilbert. 2014. Overload is overloaded: email in the age of Gmail. In *Proceedings of the SIGCHI Conference on Human Factors in Computing Systems* (CHI '14). ACM, New York, NY, USA, 793-802. DOI: http://dx.doi.org/10.1145/2556288.2557013
13. Rebecca E. Grinter and Margery A. Eldridge. "y do tngrs luv 2 txt msg?." *ECSCW 2001*. Springer Netherlands, 2001.
14. Rebecca Grinter and Margery Eldridge. 2003. Wan2tlk?: everyday text messaging. In *Proceedings of the SIGCHI Conference on Human Factors in Computing Systems* (CHI '03). ACM, New York, NY, USA, 441-448. DOI=http://dx.doi.org/10.1145/642611.642688
15. Rebecca E. Grinter, Leysia Palen, and Margery Eldridge. Chatting with teenagers: Considering the place of chat technologies in teen life. *ACM*

Transactions on Computer-Human Interaction (TOCHI) 13, no. 4 (2006): 423-447.

16. Robert Kraut, Tridas Mukhopadhyay, Janusz Szczypula, Sara Kiesler, and Bill Scherlis. Information and communication: Alternative uses of the Internet in households. *Information Systems Research* 10, no. 4 (1999): 287-303.
17. Gloria Mark, Stephen Voida, and Armand Cardello. 2012. "A pace not dictated by electrons": an empirical study of work without email. In *Proceedings of the SIGCHI Conference on Human Factors in Computing Systems* (CHI '12). ACM, New York, NY, USA, 555-564. DOI=http://dx.doi.org/10.1145/2207676.2207754
18. John Horrigan and Maeve Duggan. Home broadband adoption: Modest decline from 2013 to 2015. PEW Internet. http://www.pewinternet.org/2015/12/21/1-home-broadband-adoption-modest-decline-from-2013-to-2015/ Accessed July, 2016.
19. Bonnie A. Nardi, Steve Whittaker, and Erin Bradner. 2000. Interaction and outeraction: instant messaging in action. In *Proceedings of the 2000 ACM conference on Computer supported cooperative work* (CSCW '00). ACM, New York, NY, USA, 79-88. DOI=http://dx.doi.org/10.1145/358916.358975
20. Sarah Radicati. Email Statistics Report, 2012-2016. http://www.radicati.com/wp/wp-content/uploads/2012/04/Email-Statistics-Report-2012-2016-Executive-Summary.pdf. Accessed July, 2016.
21. Tony Tam, Artur Ferreira, and André Lourenço. 2012. Automatic foldering of email messages: a combination approach. In *Proceedings of the 34th European conference on Advances in Information Retrieval* (ECIR'12), Ricardo Baeza-Yates, Arjen P. Vries, Hugo Zaragoza, B. Barla Cambazoglu, and Vanessa Murdock (Eds.). Springer-Verlag, Berlin, Heidelberg, 232-243. DOI=http://dx.doi.org/10.1007/978-3-642-28997-2_20
22. John Tang, Tara Matthews, Julian Cerruti, Stephen Dill, Eric Wilcox, Jerald Schoudt, and Hernan Badenes. 2009. Global differences in attributes of email usage. In *Proceedings of the 2009 international workshop on Intercultural collaboration*, pp. 185-194. ACM, 2009.
23. Joshua R. Tyler and John C. Tang. "When can I expect an email response? A study of rhythms in email usage." *ECSCW 2003*. Springer Netherlands, 2003.
24. Steve Whittaker and Candace Sidner. 1996. Email overload: exploring personal information management of email. In *Proceedings of the SIGCHI Conference on Human Factors in Computing Systems* (CHI '96), Michael J. Tauber (Ed.). ACM, New York, NY, USA, 276-283. DOI=http://dx.doi.org/10.1145/238386.238530
25. Steve Whittaker, Tara Matthews, Julian Cerruti, Hernan Badenes, and John Tang. 2011. Am I wasting my time organizing email?: a study of email refinding. In *Proceedings of the SIGCHI Conference on Human Factors in Computing Systems* (CHI '11). ACM, New York, NY, USA, 3449-3458. DOI=http://dx.doi.org/10.1145/1978942.1979457

'Maker' within Constraints: Exploratory Study of Young Learners using Arduino at a High School in India

Sowmya Somanath[1], Lora Oehlberg [1], Janette Hughes[2], Ehud Sharlin[1], Mario Costa Sousa[1]
[1]University of Calgary, [2]University of Ontario Institute of Technology
[1]Calgary, [2] Oshawa, Canada,
[1]{ssomanat,lora.oehlberg,ehud,smcosta}@ucalgary.ca, [2]{janette.hughes}@uoit.ca

ABSTRACT

Do-it-yourself (DIY) inspired activities have gained popularity as a means of creative expression and self-directed learning. However, DIY culture is difficult to implement in places with limited technology infrastructure and traditional learning cultures. Our goal is to understand how learners in such a setting react to DIY activities. We present observations from a physical computing workshop with 12 students (13-15 years old) conducted at a high school in India. We observed unique challenges for these students when tackling DIY activities: a high monetary and psychological cost to exploration, limited independent learning resources, difficulties with finding intellectual courage and assumed technical language proficiency. Our participants, however, overcome some of these challenges by adopting their own local strategies: resilience, nonverbal and verbal learning techniques, and creating documentation and fallback circuit versions. Based on our findings, we discuss a set of lessons learned about makerspaces in a context with socio-technical challenges.

ACM Classification Keywords

H.5.m. Information Interfaces and Presentation (e.g. HCI): Miscellaneous

Author Keywords

DIY; Maker Culture; India; Young Learners; Physical Computing; HCI4D

INTRODUCTION

Maker movement-inspired activities in schools (e.g. [26, 27, 37]), and extracurricular outreach (e.g. [32, 36]) has increased and broadened participation in do-it-yourself (DIY) activities among young learners. A general emphasis has been placed on the idea that every child can become an innovator [18, 23, 34]. However, not all children have the resources or support they need to innovate [4]. Contextual challenges [33, 41, 52] or situational traits of unique learner groups [31, 33, 55] hinder young learners from participating in the maker movement.

CHI 2017, May 06-11, 2017, Denver, CO, USA.
 ISBN/978-1-4503-4655-9/17/05...$15.00.
DOI: http://dx.doi.org/10.1145/3025453.3025849

The overarching goal of our research is to explore what happens when there are systematic infrastructural and cultural limitations that inhibit maker culture from taking hold.

An impoverished school in India is a prime example of a context with both economic and rigid education culture constraints that challenge several assumptions of maker culture – for example, easy access to technology, abundant independent learning resources and the intellectual ability of a student to independently select and solve problems [18, 37]. Within these constraints, we explore how young learners in India respond to the innovation and self-directed learning fostered by DIY. Introducing maker culture into formal education in India (e.g. teacher preparation and curriculum design) is a multi-faceted challenge and beyond the scope of this study.

In this paper, we present an observational study of a physical DIY workshop conducted at the Kar school (a pseudonym), a high school in peri-urban Bengaluru, India. Twelve (6 girls, 6 boys) grade 8 students (13-15 years old) participated in our three-day workshop and used the Arduino to prototype beginner level project ideas. We adopted a similar study methodology to what has been previously explored in other DIY workshops (e.g. [11, 31]). We observed, engaged in the participant projects, and conducted informal interviews with the participants. The results of our observations and informal interviews from both during and after the workshop indicate that students at the Kar school face monetary and psychological cost to exploration, have limited independent learning resources, struggle to find the necessary intellectual courage to explore and have technical barriers to engage in DIY physical computing activities. However, students are resilient, adopt traditional learning techniques and make do with the means available to them to overcome some of the challenges.

The primary contributions are: (i) identification of challenges to practicing DIY activities caused by infrastructural and resource limitations and cultural constraints, specifically those prevalent in India; And (ii) observed students' strategies to overcome some of the identified challenges. Based on our observations we discuss a set of lessons learned about makerspaces within technical, infrastructural and social constraints.

IDENTIFYING LIMITATIONS IN THE CONTEXT OF INDIA

The Kar school is a prime example of two forms of limitations prevalent in India, more broadly: 1) infrastructure and educational resource limitations and 2) cultural resistance to non-conforming DIY activities.

Infrastructure and Educational Resource Limitations

DIY activities often assume that technology infrastructure (e.g. computers) and educational resources (e.g. documentation, access to books, instructional videos etc.) are readily available. However, an impoverished school in India may not meet this implied requirement. Several articles highlight that rural schools, and sometimes public and private schools in urban cities, can have very poor or sometimes non-existent educational inputs, teaching material or facilities [15, 28, 42, 45]. For example, limited access to computers (particularly in rural schools) is not uncommon. Pawar et al. [45] pointed out that it is common for several students (sometimes up to ten) to share the same computer. In some schools, a single PC is used as a solo teaching aid; an entire class (30-40 students) crowds around the same computer, ultimately causing the students to lose interest and shift their attention to other things [45]. Similarly, students have limited access to educational resources and thus lack the necessary exposure, confidence and knowledge to participate in self-directed DIY activities. For example, Krishna Kumar's [30] article about "textbook culture" in schools in India notes that resources other than the textbook are not available in the majority of the schools, and where non-textbook resources are available they are seldom used. Teachers fear damaging such resources, and the poor chances of repair or replacement discourage the teacher from using them, in turn limiting students' opportunities to interact with them [30]. These infrastructure and learning resource limitations challenge many of the assumptions of traditional maker culture – that people have the resources they need to independently learn how to create things.

Cultural Resistance to Non-Conforming DIY Activities

Beyond infrastructure and educational resource constraints, India has a rigid education culture that includes non-negotiable curricula, a top-down learning approach, limited interaction with teachers and teacher-centric teaching models. This dominant educational culture actively discourages non-conformist behavior, including innovation and the freedom to explore subjects independently. For example, most schools in India follow a "textbook culture", wherein the textbook is the main source of knowledge for both the teacher and the students [30]. Per this pedagogical approach, the teacher must ensure that students can answer questions based on the textbook without consulting the text during examinations. This examination-driven structure and "textbook culture" encourages rote learning and gaining surface level knowledge, as opposed to deeper analytical or critical knowledge perspectives [15, 30]. Mitra et al. [40] identified the teaching method employed in the majority of schools in India as teacher-centric. A single teacher is in charge of the entire class, and students are not allowed to interact or consult with each other during class time. Students are required to only perform individual learning and complete individual assessments. Mukerjee [41] observed that such teacher-centric, rote-learning is less effective because often students' understanding is limited, distorted or all together wrong. This educational culture is in direct conflict with the student-driven, self-motivated, and discovery-based principles suggested by DIY.

Limitations at the Kar School

We found both infrastructure and resource constraints as well as traditional educational culture in effect at our study site. We conducted a preliminary observation of one of Kar School's several computer science laboratory sessions. We observed an entire 30 minutes' computer science laboratory session of 15 grade 7 students. This observation was conducted prior to the three-day workshop.

For the laboratory session, a computer science teacher instructed the class in Excel. Although the purpose of the laboratory session was to provide students with hands-on training, the predominant discourse was a one-sided teacher-driven theory lecture. The teacher instructed students to take notes and draw screenshots of Excel menu options, as read from a textbook by the teacher (a classic example of "textbook culture" [30]). During the lecture, students appeared disinterested and easily distracted. During the entire session, no students accessed any of the computers. Further conversations with the teacher revealed that because the lab computers were maintained and updated by an individual outside of the school facility, often the teachers were afraid to let students access computers for fear that the students might damage the computers or disturb the installed software. Within these observed resource limitations and the rigid educational culture constraints at the Kar school we wanted to explore how students react to DIY.

RELATED LITERATURE

Similar research exploring ideas of constructionist and project-based learning has been done with impoverished communities in the learning science and education fields [4, 8, 12, 41, 46, 50, 52]. Several researchers' have also explored 'making' with 'at-risk' youth [31, 44, 55, 57], whose participation in the maker movement is hindered by their situational traits. Below we briefly discuss a few of these research works.

Impoverished Communities

Mukherjee [41] explored hands on learning in a school in India and posited that a constructivist approach to learning could benefit students trained in âĂIJtextbook cultureâĂİ. Hands on activities such as BRiCS (build robots create science) was hypothesized as a means to improve practical knowledge and understanding of educational concepts for students who are used to rote-learning [41]. Sipitakiat et al. [51, 52] explored the use of GoGo board, a small autonomous computer with sensing and control abilities, in an economically challenged context (Brazil). From the ethnographic studies conducted using the GoGo board, Sipitakiat et al. [52] found that cost constraints and limited availability of hardware are potential challenges for promoting physical computing activities in impoverished communities of Brazil. The authors suggested locally manufacturing the microcontroller board to reduce costs, and to re-use found and existing materials such as broken electronics to encourage exploration of readily available technology (e.g. clocks and radios). Lin and Shaer conducted a case study to explore how technology toys can promote computational thinking for young children in Cape Town [33]. They explored the use of littleBits [6] with elementary school children from diverse socioeconomic backgrounds. They found the main challenges for South African children to be peer pressure, low self-esteem and unequal treatment from teachers. In contrast to privileged students, children of impoverished communities were observed to exhibit important differences: had a lower frequency of communication and primarily relied on non-verbal communication, affecting the social aspects of making; had less of a gender divide for DIY-based activities; and thanks to littleBits [6], had a new opportunity to develop fine motor skills and practice basic language skills (e.g, using prepositions to describe their circuit).

Unique Learner Groups

Situational traits of 'at-risk' youth hinder their participation in the maker movement; these students tend to quickly give-up, are unwilling to experiment and communicate, and demonstrate less engagement and lack of motivation. Kuznetsov et al. [31] introduced e-textile activities as therapy and for mentoring of 'at-risk' students. They found that the e-textile workshop sessions inspired their participants, who tended to be uninterested and uncooperative in educational activities, to complete interactive projects and engage with workshop volunteers as mentors and peers. Stager [57] introduced the concept of Constructionist Learning Laboratory (CLL) to engage youth in prison facilities. The design goal of CLL was to create an environment that mimics the principles of constructionism [44], wherein, youth engaged with a wide range of low and high-tech materials (e.g. LEGO, Arduino) to build physical artifacts. It was observed that CLL students engaged in learning-by-making and students who were thought to be incapable of learning proved quite capable and even enrolled in college courses while in the CLL. Somanath et al. [55] explored the use of a variety of computational platforms (e.g. Arduino, Makey-Makey and LilyPads) in DIY activities to engage 'at-risk' learners. They observed that in contrast to instruction-based starter kit activities, engaging their participants in open-ended design activities improved participants' self-assessed experiences with circuitry and programming. Based on their observations, they discussed that creative tasks, access to a variety of tools and making the projects relevant to the students could improve students' engagement in DIY activities.

In this paper we explore how students faced with *both* economic and cultural limitations react to DIY activities. Students in India are a unique learner group whose rigid education culture and resource constraints hinder their participation in the maker movement. The situational constraints for students at the Kar school actively discourage innovation and independent exploration. In light of our goal, India presents a unique opportunity to gain insights about 'making' within technical, infrastructural, and social challenges.

STUDY METHOD

Our research team hosted a three-day 'make-a-thon' style [54] physical computing workshop at the Kar School, a private high school in peri-urban Bengaluru, India. Each day, the workshop lasted three hours and students engaged in building simple projects using Arduino and other electronics (sensors, actuators and components). To understand what typical classroom interactions look like at the Kar school we also did a preliminary observation of a computer science laboratory session, as already discussed.

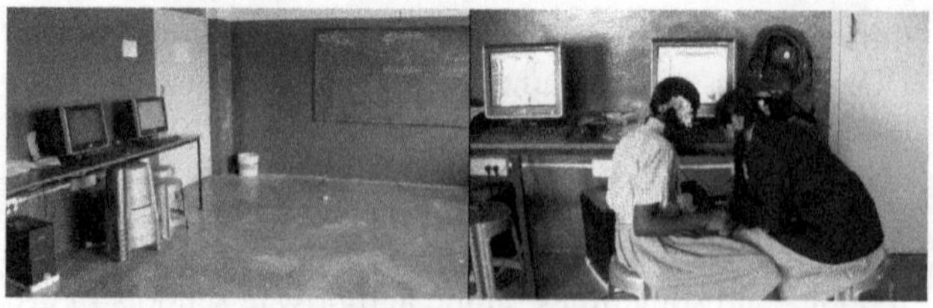

Figure 1. Workshop site: Kar school computer science laboratory.

The Kar school is a low-fee charging institution and hence, affordable to students from low social economic status (SES) backgrounds. We conducted the workshop during school hours (9:00 am - 4:00 pm) at the school's only computer lab facility (Figure 1). There are two reasons why we could not conduct the study as a longer after school program. First, the computer lab facility and the school were shut down after school hours. Second, few students (especially girls) were willing to participate in the workshop after school hours due to security concerns, or lack of parental permission. Electricity availability at the school was also limited and unscheduled outages were a common occurrence during the workshop. Due to unscheduled outages, workshop times had to be flexible. The school's faculty had no prior knowledge of Arduino, or about the maker movement.

Participants

A group of 12 students (6 girls and 6 boys) ages 13-15 years (grade 8) participated in our three-day workshop. The choice of grade 8 students was opportunistic. The school principal selected the 12 participants based on the following criteria. First, because students would miss a total of nine hours of regular class time, the principal wanted to select students who could cope with this break from in-class learning; hence, he chose students who performed academically well among the grade 8 students. Second, we wanted to ensure that the same students could attend all three days of the workshop. As a result, the principal chose students who were also regular attendees at school, ensuring that there was a high probability that all participants would attend the entire workshop series.

From our pre-questionnaire we gathered that all our participants belong to the low SES strata. The participants' parents' occupations can be classified as low-paying jobs that require minimal or no prior education (e.g. building painter, janitor, barber etc.).

All but one participant had experience with computers since grade 5; one participant began using a computer during grade 6. Two of the 12 participants owned a personal computer. The most common use of the computers (as specified on the questionnaire) in the school was for using programs such as MS Access and MS Excel (current curriculum). Beyond computers, students had previously interacted with mobile phones that belonged to other family members and two participants personally owned mobile phones. Participants used them for playing games, calling friends and watching videos. There was no explicit mention of using Internet on the phone. When asked about their prior exposure to programming, programming languages and programmable electronics, 11 out of 12 participants listed English as a programming language. Participants' perception of programming was also quite different from the traditional definition: our participants' equated computer programming to using installed programs on a computer. No participant reported any prior knowledge of electronics and/or programmable electronics.

Setup

To observe how young learners at the Kar school would engage with DIY physical computing activities, we provided the resources for this study: 6 Arduino microcontrollers (one Uno R3 and five Leonardo) and a range of electronic components, sensors and actuators (switches, push buttons, resistors, phototransistors, light sensitive resistors, piezo buzzers, servos, vibration sensors, mini speakers, carbon monoxide sensors, temperature sensors, LEDs and force sensitive resistors). The total cost of the electronics purchased was ~\$400. Most of the electronics used in the study are accessible within urban India, and can be purchased online and are shipped internationally. We also used Arduino's in our workshop because of their affordance to build a wide variety of projects [55] and rich documentation. During the workshop all the electronics were kept on a central table for participants to freely access. At the end of the workshop, the entire package and additional resources (a copy of the Arduino programming notebook [19] and SparkFun Inventor's Guide [56]) were donated to the school for future use by students.

A total of six computers were used during the study to create a 2:1 student-to-computer ratio. Four out of six computers belonged to the school; the researchers provided two additional laptops. Kar school had a total of ten computers, however, six of the computers were not working at the time of the study. Because multiple users cannot simultaneously build circuits using an Arduino, we used the 2:1 student-to-computer ratio. An increased ratio would more likely cause students to crowd around the single Arduino and a computer, resulting in one student becoming the dominant circuit builder and programmer. Other students would become passive onlookers and perhaps ultimately disengage from the activity (similar to single computer use scenario described by Pawar et al. [45]).

We installed the Arduino IDE (line programming) and Ardublocks [3] (graphical programming) on all computers. As the Kar school had no Internet connection, none of the computers used for the study had Internet access. This setback prevented students from accessing online learning resources. To mitigate the lack of Internet access, the researchers provided a word document with basic sample code for each of the electronic components on all the computers. Because the provided sample code could be directly copy pasted into the Arduino IDE as opposed to ArduBlocks, where the participant would have to assemble graphical programming blocks, participants ended up using the Arduino IDE both during and after the workshop.

Workshop

The goal of our three-day workshop was to position the participants as investigators with agency and in turn, to observe how the challenges of the context shaped their DIY experience. The study encouraged discovery-based collaborative learning [2] wherein, the participants worked in small groups of two or three and helped their peers to debug code and circuit connections. Throughout the workshop period the researcher adopted an inquiry-based learning approach [1], guiding students by posing questions or problems rather than presenting solutions without much invested effort. The researcher was also available for help; however, because only one researcher was managing the study, their help was also a scarce resource. Throughout the remaining paper we reference the researcher as R, participant as P and group as G.

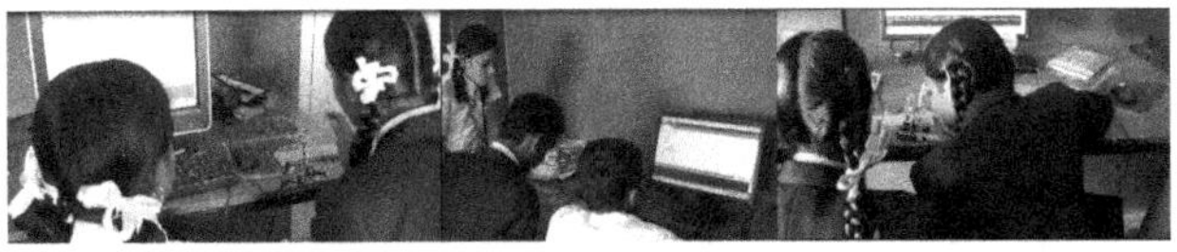

Figure 2. Workshop: Participants working on their projects.

Workshop Day 1. On day one the researcher briefly introduced the participants to basic electronics: what is an electric circuit, what is a breadboard and how to build a circuit. The researcher drew a simple circuit diagram on the blackboard to aid the explanation. The researcher demonstrated a practical example of a circuit using an LED and a coin cell battery, showing how to turn on the LED by pressing the LED legs to the positive and negative side of the battery. To familiarize our participants with the Arduino, the researcher walked the participants through a step-by-step LED blinking exercise. Pairs of participants replicated and extended the exercise by connecting multiple LEDs. Participants used the Arduino sample code *Blink* to program the LED. The researcher demonstrated the use of both Arduino IDE and the Ardublocks IDE. After the LEDs were successfully blinking, the researcher gave participants time to continue exploring the circuit connections. After the circuit exploration phase, each group presented to their peers detailing their experimentation process. The researcher used the presentation sessions to probe students' understanding of hardware and software, and to learn how they thought the LEDs blinked. Following these discussions, it became easier for the researcher to clarify and formalize more technical concepts such as serial connections and functionality of a microcontroller. Example of a question asked by the researcher during the discussion is as follows:

R: *How did the LEDs turn on and off?*
P7 : *The circuit is continuously going. The current is passing from one bulb [LED] to another, so it is glowing and then shut down, then again it is starting.*

The researcher employed a similar inquiry-based approach to break down parts of the code. Participants were asked by the researcher to share their understanding of keywords such as *setup*, *loop* and *delay*. Based on participants' definitions, the researcher explained the corresponding functions in the code. To provoke the participants to think further, the researcher posed logical questions. For example:

R: *How do you think we can make the LED stop blinking?*
P7: *By removing delay?*

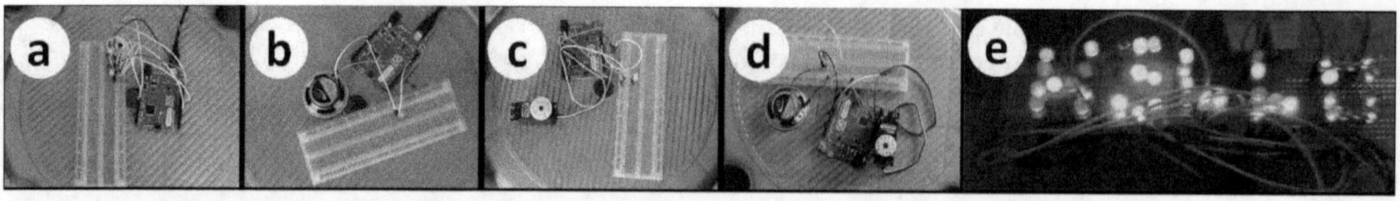

Figure 3. Projects demonstrated at the end of the workshop: (a) LED calculator, (b) Sound and Light, (c) Servo Controlled LED and (d) Servo + LED + Speaker; Project demonstrated at the science fair: (e) "Hello World".

At the end of the session the researcher briefly explained the functionality of the remaining components. In preparation for the 'make-a-thon', the researcher asked the participants to think of simple project ideas for day two. To inspire the participants, the researcher orally discussed examples of projects that participants could build.

Workshop Day 2. On the second day, each of the groups presented their project ideas. Presentations were semi-structured asking students to identify the project they wanted to build and briefly list the initial set of hardware they would need to use. The researcher asked questions during the presentations to better understand the group's goal for the chosen project. Participants spent the remaining workshop time building circuits and programming (Figure 2). The researcher encouraged the participants to collaborate and ask peers for help before approaching the researcher. The researcher would eventually help to move them along. The researcher asked the groups to make notes of their working process and presentations were conducted at the end of the session summarizing their tasks and challenges for the day. Two groups (G3 and G4) discontinued working on their projects during day two and joined other groups.

Workshop Day 3. On the final day, four groups completed their chosen projects. The groups did a final presentation of their projects (Figure 3a-d). The workshop closed with an open-ended discussion with the participants. The discussion covered the following topics: participation experience, participants' view of how they benefited from attending this workshop, what they found challenging, and their thoughts on future possibilities for building other physical interactive prototypes.

Beyond the workshop: Science Fair

Six weeks after the workshop we were informed by the school principal that the school was conducting a science fair. Two workshop participants from G1 demonstrated two electronics projects that they had built at the science fair. The first project demonstrated by G1 was a reconstructed version of their workshop project, a LED calculator (Figure 3a). The second project was a new and independent exploration by G1 (no researcher help) entitled *"Hello World"* (Figure 3e). The student built an array of blinking LEDs arranged to spell "Hello" as seen in Figure 3e. A researcher conducted an unstructured interview during the school science fair to gain insights into the design process and challenges faced by the group.

Data Collection and Analysis

Data sources for this study included the following:

1. **Pre-questionnaire** – asked personal demographic information and a few questions regarding prior technology and programming experience.
2. **Presentation videos** – at the end of each workshop day we video recorded all participant presentations as they summarized their work, detailing the tasks they had accomplished and how they resolved project related issues. In addition, on day two of the workshop we video recorded all the participants as they presented their project ideas.
3. **Individual group videos** – we used the two laptop web cameras to capture conversations and working processes of two groups.
4. **Written notes from students** – at regular intervals (∼2 times per session) each group was asked to write notes about problems they were addressing and a list of any unresolved problems.
5. **Closing discussion video** – at the end of the workshop, we video recorded an informal discussion of the participants' experiences. All workshop participants were part of this discussion.
6. **Informal interview at science fair** - we audio recorded an informal interview with G1 at the school science fair to learn more about their progress after the workshop.

Majority of the collected data was in English. However, parts of the laptop videos were spoken in the local state language (Kannada) and were translated by the researcher (native speaker). Our qualitative analysis methodology is inspired by Walny et al.'s approach [61]. One author (analysis lead) did several passes through the transcribed video and interview data, and identified the sequence of activities performed by each group captured as workflow diagrams (Figure 4). Looking across all group's workflows, the analysis lead created a set of common activity labels. These labels were discussed and revised among three co-authors to arrive at the final set of labels:

A *identify project*: corresponds to the project proposed by the group;
B *identify material*: lists the components chosen by the group for their project;
C *identify behaviour*: describes the expected behaviour of the project as explained by the participants;
D *implement*: summarizes the main steps taken to implement the project;
E *project demonstration*: name of the final project demonstrated.

Using the activity labels, we traced each student groups workshop journey, from project identification to project demonstration. Guided by the workflow diagrams, we returned to our

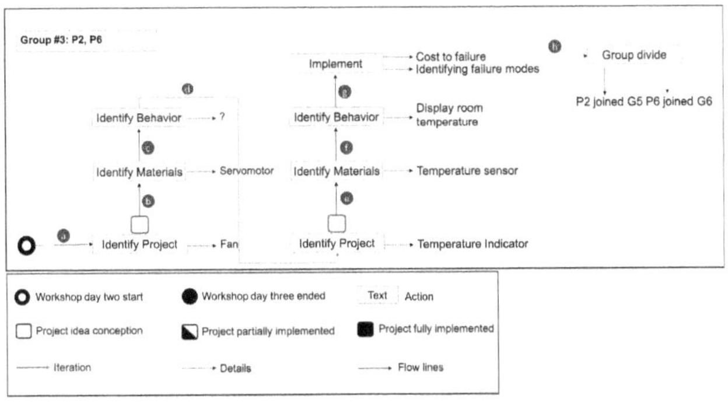

Figure 4. Example workflow diagram (Group 3)

transcribed video and interview data, and student notes data to identify challenges and student strategies.

CHALLENGES TO PRACTISING DIY-BASED ACTIVITIES

Within the known resource limitations and cultural constraints prevalent at the Kar school, we observed monetary, resource and situational challenges for students to engage in DIY physical computing activities.

C1: Monetary and Psychological Cost to Exploration

Exploration and tinkering is common to DIY activities [22, 37]. Failure is common, necessary, and fruitful. During exploration and tinkering, learners may fail to accomplish the desired results, may damage the hardware components or may decide to not use a purchased component. However, in a context like the Kar school, there is a high monetary and psychological cost associated with trial and error.

In our study we observed two instances of fear. G3 wanted to build a project using the Arduino temperature sensor. However, G3's attempts at incorporating the temperature sensor failed. The researcher upon debugging G3's circuit connection found that the temperature sensor was connected incorrectly and was damaged (the program constantly displayed values in the range of 200°C). After realizing they had broken the sensor, the participants could not be motivated to continue their project and did not want to work with another temperature sensor. To keep G3 involved in the workshop the researcher suggested that the members of G3 join other groups whose projects interested them.

This fear is even apparent when coding software, even though there is very low likelihood of causing irreversible damage through failure. For example, upon G2's circuit building success, the researcher advised G2 to explore the sample program code by modifying the program variables. During this process, the participants would only modify the variable as suggested by the researcher and were reluctant to modify the variables' values on their own. Possible reasons for this hesitation is that G2 may have been concerned that they could not go back to the original code, they did not understand the code or that they did not know what could be modified and how it could be modified. However, irrespective of the researcher encouragement and assurance that they could not "damage" code, participants of G2 did not engage in much free-form code exploration. Similar hesitation with modifying code was also observed in the other groups.

C2: Limited Independent Learning Resources

In a typical makerspace (a communal space for practising hands on learning), learners have access to several learning resources that help introduce young learners to new educational and computational technologies. These resources may include online learning resources, specialized after school programs, and qualified mentors (e.g. [9, 20, 37]). However, in a setting like the Kar school, the number of available learning resources is heavily restricted. There was no Internet access available at the Kar school, limiting students from accessing any online documentation. Students did not have any textbooks or guides for physical computing available as a reference. Additionally, teachers at the school were not aware of programmable electronics, and could not mentor or guide the students. The limited availability of independent learning resources challenges several assumptions of how a student can successfully participate in DIY-based activities – How does a novice learner become aware of the idea of DIY? How do novices learn about physical computing technologies such as Arduino, Makey-Makey and littleBits? How do they understand materials and behaviours? Below we illustrate instances of participants having difficulty with: (a) finding sources of inspiration; (b) understanding how to use and work with technology; and, (c) increasing project complexity due to limited independent learning resources.

Use of independent learning resources such as, online videos and pictures is a common way of inspiring ideas [24] and has been used in prior studies (e.g. [55]). However, students in our workshop had difficulty coming up with ideas because they did not have exposure to outside learning resources. Although proposing new ideas for prototyping is a challenge for any novice learner and has been previously observed (e.g. [31]), in our study site it was further emphasized due to limited learning resources. During the workshop 4 out of 6 groups (G1, G3, G5 and G6) proposed to build a fan using a servomotor. Originally the project was proposed by G1, followed by G3, G5 and G6 proposing the same idea. Not having access to resources that could inspire the participants (e.g. showcase of online examples), groups ended up proposing the same ideas. We observed this stagnant ideation again when G5 completed the fan project, but was unable to suggest a new project idea to explore. The researcher had to suggest a new project ("Servo Controlled LED") to allow them to continue exploring.

Understanding hardware and their corresponding behaviour requires some initial documentation input, for example, datasheets or books that explain simple components. Although participants were given a brief introduction to each hardware component being used in the study on day one of the workshop, they had no learning aid that they could use for support. Consulting the researcher was their only source for clarification and learning. Because of this, two groups were seen proposing wrong project ideas. For example, G2 first proposed to build a project titled "Voice Recording", listing FSR and mini speaker as the required electronic components for this project. The identified behavior was to use the speaker to record the FSR input. However, G2 had no understanding of the distinction between an input and an output device resulting in a flawed behavior identification. The participants were not aware that speaker was an output device and could not be used for recording purposes. Clarification had to be provided by the researcher. Similary, G3 attempted to use a temperature sensor, but wrongly interpreted that 200°C was the correct output for a temperature sensor. The researcher had to re-explain what a temperature sensor was and what the expected output value ranges would be.

Limited resources also make it difficult to increase project complexity or scaling up an idea. Participants had been exposed to connecting one LED to their circuit during day one of the workshop. Scaling from one LED connection to multiple LEDs (required for the LED calculator project) was challenging for all groups. For example, G1 initially connected all the LEDs to the same pin of the Arduino and had no control over individual LED states. Without a reference for concepts like serial and parallel circuit connections, participants were constrained to either solve by trial and error, or ask the researcher. Because our participants were novices, the researcher had to guide them to keep the group moving ahead with their project. Scaling up was also an observed issue for programming. Participants had template code to make one LED blink, however, to change the states of the individual LEDs they had to modify the code accordingly. This was found to be a challenging task as participants did not fully understand how to modify the line code (*"...we were having problems in the codes which we were not knowing"* [P7]).

C3: Finding intellectual courage

Unlike students familiar with an interactive collaborative learning context [7], students schooled in rigid educational settings like our study site focus on following the teacher instead of independently exploring an educational concept. Rigid educational paradigms like "textbook culture" expect students to memorize textbook content and follow exactly what the teacher proposes (teacher-centric teaching) [30, 39, 41]. At the Kar school we observed that students sometimes lacked the necessary intellectual courage to freely explore and learn.

An instance of students' unable to find their intellectual courage was observed on day one of the workshop. After the LED demonstration, participants were given time and were encouraged to explore the circuit. While a majority of the groups explored connecting multiple LEDs to their circuit, G3 was an exception. G3 did not modify their one LED circuit connection. When asked if they wanted to connect more LEDs to their circuit, participants of G3 said *"no"*.

While finding the necessary intellectual courage is a limitation among all groups, particularly G3 who refused to follow others in experimentation, G6 demonstrated unusual intellectual courage for the group. From the laptop videos of G6 we observed that P9 was rather experimental in his approach - *"wait I am doing something, even I don't know what I am doing"* [P9]. Unstructured exploration was characteristic of G6 throughout the workshop - G6 continued to add electronics to their circuit with no explicit goal. Even though they were faced with frustration in the process and the participants felt like they should have done a project similar to others (*"we should have also taken LED project"* [P9]), they strived to keep pushing ahead (*"Don't try to hurry, let's keep trying"* [P12]). This was interesting because although they had no set goal, when G6 found the intellectual courage to explore, they discovered several aspects of circuit building and programming in the process of unstructured exploration.

C4: Assumed Language Proficiency

To identify and solve programming errors, students need to understand the syntax of the programming language, and interpret error messages. However, these error messages assume that students have the necessary proficiency with technical English. In places like the Kar school, this assumed language proficiency is yet another barrier for students. This poses a fundamental challenge to practicing DIY-based activities as students who are dealing with unfamiliar English vocabulary will have even more difficulty comprehending the underlying technical concepts behind an error message.

An instance of assumed language proficiency was observed in the video data of G6. Upon uploading the modified template code to the Arduino board, the IDE notified the participants of "precautions" (a compiler notification). However, in order to troubleshoot and isolate the debugger messages the participants have to first understand them. G6 did not understand the meaning of the word precautions (*"let's ask her [the researcher] what is precaution"* [P12]), causing a fundamental block in their progress. Although English is the language of instruction at our study site, this observation shows how technology may prevent people from accessing it when they do not have enough English language proficiency, and much less proficiency in technical language or concepts.

FINDING SUCCESS: STUDENT STRATEGIES

In the previous section we identified some of the challenges that a context like our study site poses for practicing DIY-based activities. In this section we present strategies that students adopted to overcome some of the above challenges. Motivated by Smyth et al.'s [53] argument about needs assessment, we acknowledge that although the above identified challenges are potential roadblocks to practicing DIY inspired physical computing, the identified "needs" or "challenges" may not be as strongly felt by the 'maker' as perceived by an outsider. Below we discuss four strategies that our participants adopted as a way to overcome *some* of the challenges (C1-C4).

S1: Resilience

Resilience, the ability to creatively cope with challenges has been discussed in the context of economically challenged settings (e.g. [43, 52]) and makerspaces (e.g. [49, 58]). *Jugaad*, 'to make do', has been discussed in the context of India as an innovative and improvised solution to resource constraints [47, 48]. Within our study context, being resilient was yet again an emergent strategy. Participants creatively coped with both material unavailability (C1) as well as limited independent learning resources (C2) by being resilient.

During the workshop G2 wanted to use the force sensing resistor (FSR) and a speaker to build a project that would generate audio based on FSR input ("FSR Sound"). However, they could not conveniently include the FSR into their prototype because they did not have a soldering iron. Once the group realized they needed – but did not have – a soldering iron, G2 reconsidered their options and decided to alter the scope of their project. This time they chose to use an LED and proposed altering the LED state based on the audio tone ("Sound Light"). The unavailability of the tool forced the participants to rethink the possibilities of what could be explored and come up with new ideas.

G1 demonstrated resilience at several levels during their after workshop experience, while building the "hello world" project (Figure 3e). First, G1 did not have a resistor that they required for their project. Instead, to keep moving forward with the project goal, P1 used their common sense to use a metal wire as a substitute for a resistor. Although the metal wire may not be the exact solution to a missing resistor, the spirit to keep trying is essential to making. Second, G1 initially built a series circuit for the "Hello world" LED display, but soon realized they did not have enough wires and had to reconsider their circuit building strategy. To overcome this challenge, G1 referenced the textbook that was provided to the school as part of the after-workshop package and found a solution to reduce the number of wires required. Lastly, P1 had forgotten how to code his circuit; instead of being deterred, he involved his friend to get programming help.

S2: Nonverbal and Verbal Learning Techniques

Nonverbal communication is a social learning technique observed in young children [62]. Lin and Shaer [33] observed that children in their workshop in Sourth Africa, also primarily used gestures to communicate with each other. In our study, we observed imitation as a form of nonverbal communication. Within the "textbook culture", rote-learning, and teacher-centric pedagogy practiced in schools in India [30, 39, 41], imitation is an implicit learning technique. Students are trained to memorize textbook content and reproduce the same during examinations. Also, because of the teacher-centric teaching style, students are trained to follow. Therefore, over a period of time, students become accustomed to imitate or copy. While much of "textbook culture" is counterproductive to DIY culture, students adopted this learned skill of imitation as a strategy to overcome the limited learning resources challenge (C2).

On day one of the workshop the researcher guided the participants using an introduction activity that involved building a simple LED circuit. Participants' were given time (30 minutes) to explore the electrical circuit before the workshop was continued further. During this period, G1 took the lead and connected multiple LEDs to their circuit by trial and error. Following this, four other teams (with the exception of G3) imitated them and connected multiple LEDs. This was interesting because they were not following the instructor, instead, they were following their peers. Another instance of imitation was observed during day two and three of the workshop where participants were seen visiting work spaces of other workshop group. Seeing G2 use a mini speaker in their project, G6 was also inspired and decided to include a mini speaker in their circuit. However, it is important to note that while imitation is a successful strategy to overcome the limited resources challenge, imitation as a strategy can fail if there is a problem at the source level. For example, by imitating G1's initial project proposal, four out of six groups (G1, G3, G5 and G6) proposed the "Fan" project. Because G1 was not sure about what they wanted to build for the "Fan" project, all other groups also drew a blank as they did not know what the expected behavior of the "Fan" project should be.

In addition to nonverbal social learning techniques, asking peers or friends for help is a common verbal learning technique employed by students [10]. Although students in India are mostly used to individual learning and are discouraged from consulting or interacting with their peers within a classroom setting [39], within our workshop setting, asking peers for help was an emergent and encouraged strategy. With help from peers and occasionally from the researcher, students managed to build projects and stay involved in the physical computing workshop, as well as after the workshop (where there was no researcher available for help). When P6 from G2 joined G6 (due to temperature sensor burn out), participants of G6 were encouraging of their new group member and got her up to speed by explaining their circuit connections (*"red line is power, black line is ground, and white line is analog. Analog is here, it's analog 0"* [P12]). They were also ready to trust their new member and willing to delegate tasks to her (*"you connect the circuit"* [P9]). We also observed that the group members would often help each other with connecting components and would think together when they were unsure. One member of the group was found to be the dominant circuit builder, while others took on the role of observers and advisers (*"connect to the positive, what you are doing is wrong"* [P12]). Similarly, for programming, since G6 was connecting multiple electronic components to their circuit, merging and debugging code was a challenging task for them. They were observed to be collaboratively dissecting code piece-by-piece to aid understanding. Seeking help of other group members was seen to be a prominent activity of G6. They were observed to validate and correct their own circuit connections by checking those of other groups (*"wait let me think, G1 has done the same"* [P12]). Similarly programming also involved intergroup collaborative effort. Participants were observed to be: (a) clarifying code logic (*"To turn off, turn the code to LOW"* [P7]), (b) clarifying syntax (*"LOW has to be in capital letters"* [P4]) and (c) suggesting possible applications for each other's projects - *"They can create a calculator (LED based) and the speaker can tell the result"* [P7].

S3: Documentation and Fallbacks

The utility of taking notes as a way to help learning is a common practice in schools in general [25]. In our preliminary observation, students took notes as the teacher dictated various aspects of computer software. In our workshop note taking was an emergent strategy students employed to overcome limited learning resources and to create their own documentations and reference points.

Based on our analysis of the collected written notes from all the groups and the post-workshop questionnaire responses, participants documented their current experience by jotting down personal pointers to assist them in their future DIY attempts. Two examples of personal notes are: (1) *"a) Red line is power; b) Blue line is ground; and c) Every circuit has to end in ground line"* [P3]. (2) *"While building the electrical circuit we have to keep the pin codes in mind. After connecting the wires, we have to keep the pin codes in the mind and type in the computer"* [P11].

Unlike the elaborate notes dictated by the teacher from the textbook, the student notes from the workshop are similar in nature to logbooks in engineering and science – i.e. an informal document used for personal record keeping, to serve as a reminder of work-in-progress, recording actions and other people's input [13, 38].

As part of development of understanding (i.e. a broad view of understanding as both a process and an outcome [22]), note taking practices were also extended to physical circuits. Participants were observed to have a fallback circuit version they could go back to when their circuit connections were not working. A common strategy that was observed across all the working groups when their circuit connections did not work was to trace back to a simple one LED circuit, rebuild it, test it, and if found to be working, then they would attempt to reconstruct their current circuit. Having a last working version to fallback on (analogous to software versions) served both as reassurance to continue attempting to build their circuits, as well as, served as a technical base to build upon.

LESSONS LEARNED

Given the general growth in interest in makerspaces and HCI4D, in this section we discuss lessons learned as researchers running a 'maker' workshop, based on the technical, infrastructural, and social challenges observed at the Kar School.

Engaging with the School

We faced two primary challenges when engaging with the school. The first challenge was to gain permission to run a maker workshop in a school in India. We approached several public and private schools in peri-urban areas of Bengaluru, prior to running the workshop at the Kar school. Due to the non-negotiable curricula and the examination-driven structure followed by all the schools [29], convincing the school principal to allow students to participate in an activity that is outside their curriculum was a challenge. School principals were reluctant to let their students miss scheduled in-class learning to learn skills that were not being tested in the examinations. There were several ways we addressed such concerns. First, we had to convince the principal that learning new skills (programming, electronics) could help students in their future education and employment. Second, we had to limit the workshop hours, so that students did not miss several in-class learning hours. Third, we also learned that the school principal needed to be in control of participant recruitment. As already discussed, the principal selected students who performed academically well, as he considered them capable of coping with the break from in-class learning. The biased recruiting strategies can be a challenge for studies which aim to measure students' improved technology literacy.

The second challenge was our limited opportunities for continued observations. After the workshop, we donated the electronics to the school to allow students to continue exploring. One student team built a project for the school science fair after the workshop. However, from an informal interview conducted after the workshop, we gathered that students did not have free access to the electronics – the school principal had securely locked away the electronics to avoid damage and distraction during examinations. As already discussed, the poor chance of repair or replacement, discourages teachers from giving students opportunities for direct interaction [30]. In addition, practising skills outside of the curricula is not favoured. Because students were limited from further hands-on exploration, we as researchers had fewer opportunities for in-the- wild observations.

Supporting Students

We learned two lessons related to supporting students in India-like contexts: (a) peer-support to scaffold self-directed learning is essential, and (b) allow learners to create self-assistance structures.

In impoverished contexts, where there are limited independent learning resources and limited mentor support, we learned that peer-support to scaffold self-directed learning is essential. Learners trained in rigid educational contexts are required to work individually and are not allowed to interact with other students during class [40]. Also, the young learners trained in rigid educational structures are accustomed to teacher-driven learning [40, 41]. However, a fundamental requirement for DIY is self-direction. Alternative to the traditional, students learn self-direction if they are placed in an environment where they are somewhat forced to take ownership over the learning process (as demonstrated by the local student strategies resilience and learning techniques). Peer-support can benefit from technology. For example, creating social support structures – such as online communities of novice learners, a project showcase in school where students can speak about their experiences and student-organized workshops where peers can teach each other – is one way to leverage resilience and non-verbal and verbal learning strategies demonstrated by students [35]. Additionally, creating technology that enables more process-focused rather than end product-focused documentation [59] may help self-directed experimentation.

To overcome the independent learning resources challenge, learners create self-assisting learning resources to help themselves (S3). For example, learners developed informal documentation and circuit fallback plans to assist themselves in the circuit building process and, more generally, problem solving. Technology can help learners to create self-assistance structures that can be referred to when needed. For example, in our workshop students created logbook-like documentation. More widely accessible digital documentation can be created for instance using mobile devices (e.g. [17, 5]) and multimedia-based collaborative note taking tools (e.g. [16, 21]). Such approaches may help young learners to create textual and multimedia reference points for both programming and circuit building (e.g. capturing images of the circuit, capturing videos of circuit building, annotating images, creating list of important pointers) in the absence of rich independent learning sources.

Researcher as a Mentor

In sharp contrast to the teacher-centric and top down schooling environment at Kar-like schools, during the workshop the researcher assumed the role of a mentor. On the first day of the workshop, the mentorship role was guided by the theory of ZPD (zone of proximal development) [60]. The theory of ZPD argues that children will not learn much if they were left to discover everything on their own. The theory suggests that in the beginning the learner should be guided and assisted to help attain the necessary minimal skills. To allow students to ease into the DIY process and to encourage novice participation, methods should be employed that start simple and slowly move towards open-ended activities. For example, starting with a simple guided linear activity (e.g. making an LED blink as used in our study), will provide students an entry point to get a glimpse of what is possible. Following structured exercises, students can be given more freedom to explore possibilities and self-directed ideas. If the introduction activity is simple to follow learners are encouraged by the initial success of completing the activity, easing the transition from the linear activity to open-ended exploration. For example, after the guided single LED blinking activity, 5 out of 6 groups experimented with connecting several more LEDs to their circuit.

We also learned that an inquiry-based approach [1] to mentoring was helpful (especially during the 'make-a-thon'). Students at the Kar school are used to imitation. As already discussed, imitation can be harmful if the students' understanding is limited or all together wrong [41]. However, by guiding students' by asking questions, one can steer the students' towards understanding the problems and exploring alternative course of action. For example, G3 imitated G1 and proposed to build a "Fan". However, upon being asked about the expected behaviour of this project by the researcher, it was found that G3 was unaware of what the "Fan" project entailed.

Maker Tools

From our study we learned that choice of electronics is affected by four variables: availability, transferability of skills, learning curve and learning goals. Conventional DIY electronics like Arduino are the more viable microprocessor option for learners who may need to work with off-the-shelf components, for availability or cost reasons. Arduino-like platforms are also more accessible (the design is open-source). In a spectrum spanning transferability of skills and learning curve, Arduino-like platforms fall on one end of the spectrum [14]. While Arduino has a steep learning curve, it affords learning of traditional electronics skills (e.g., breadboards, wires, components) which are highly transferable compared to self-contained educational platforms (e.g. littleBits or Makey-Makey). In addition, although Arduinos have steep learning curve, they have a "high-ceiling", i.e. with gradual increase in learner's technical competence, the learning is extensible to explore more complex projects [55].

We also learned that there exists a similar trade-off for choice of programming environment: ease of access versus ability to remix code. In our study we introduced participants to both visual programming environment, ArduBlocks, and the more traditional line programming, Arduino IDE. However, we learned that students gravitated towards using an approach that facilitated easy copy-paste and remixing of code (also observed by Kafai et al. [26]). While visual programming is easy to approach, most starter kit books and online resources include non-visual programming sample code, making line coding a more viable option (especially in Kar-like contexts where textbooks are the main source of information).

LIMITATIONS

We conducted a short observational study of students using a single DIY platform, Arduino, in a high school in India. Our study represents one of many possible resource-constrained settings. Our design recommendations may also apply to other communities of learners with similar constraints. Economic constraints and rigid education culture exist in other developing country contexts. For example, Sipitakiat et al. [52] observed economic challenges in Brazil similar to those observed in India which inhibit DIY from taking hold. Lin and Shaer [33] noted that students from impoverished communities in South Africa experience reduced teaching quality, and found that littleBits can help improve students computational thinking. We encourage future researchers to examine how our findings apply to other learner groups with similar constraints.

CONCLUSION AND FUTURE WORK

This paper has contributed to an understanding of how students in an impoverished and rigid education culture context (here, a high school in India) would react to the possibility to practice DIY-based activities. Our study at the Kar school shows that young learners face both resource and psychological limitations for engaging in DIY physical computing activities. However, within the constraints, students were observed to be persistent and strived to overcome some of the challenges by creating local strategies. Based on the results, we discussed a set of lessons learned and challenges faced to inform future researchers exploring makerspaces in contexts with technical, infrastructural and social challenges.

We have several directions for future work. One direction is to realize our technology design recommendations and study the effects on engaging India-like learners via our prototype systems. Second, is to study the effects of our technology design with two different unique learner groups (e.g. India-like learners and 'at-risk' youth) to compare and contrast how technology for DIY should be designed for young learners who are less ready to get involved in DIY. Third, it would be interesting to learn if there is a real improvement in STEM learning when India-like learners are engaged in DIY-based activities in comparison to traditional learning activities.

ACKNOWLEDGMENTS

We would like to thank the Kar school for granting us permission to run our study. We would also like to thank all our participants for taking part in the workshop. This research was supported by the AITF scholarship.

REFERENCES

1. Kathryn Alesandrini and Linda Larson. 2002. Teachers bridge to constructivism. *The Clearing House* 75, 3 (2002), 118–121.
2. WS Anthony. 1973. Learning to discover rules by discovery. *Journal of Educational Psychology* 64, 3 (1973), 325.
3. Ardublock. 2016. Ardublock: a Graphical Programming Language for Arduino. http://blog.ardublock.com/. (2016). [Online; accessed 2016].
4. Angela Calabrese Barton, Edna Tan, and Day Greenberg. 2016. The Makerspace Movement: Sites of Possibilities for Equitable Opportunities to Engage Underrepresented Youth in STEM. *Teachers College Record* (2016).
5. Aaron Bauer and Kenneth Koedinger. 2006. Evaluating the effect of technology on note-taking and learning. In *CHI'06 Extended Abstracts on Human Factors in Computing Systems*. ACM, 520–525.
6. Ayah Bdeir. 2009. Electronics as material: littleBits. In *Proceedings of the 3rd International Conference on Tangible and Embedded Interaction*. ACM, 397–400.
7. Helen Beetham and Rhona Sharpe. 2013. *Rethinking pedagogy for a digital age: Designing for 21st century learning*. routledge.
8. Paulo Blikstein. 2008. Travels in Troy with Freire. *Social justice education for teachers: Paulo Freire and the possible dream* (2008), 205–244.
9. Paulo Blikstein. 2013. Digital fabrication and 'making' in education: The democratization of invention. *FabLabs: Of machines, makers and inventors* (2013), 1–21.
10. Kenneth A Bruffee. 1984. Collaborative learning and the "Conversation of Mankind". *College English* 46, 7 (1984), 635–652.
11. Leah Buechley, Mike Eisenberg, Jaime Catchen, and Ali Crockett. 2008. The LilyPad Arduino: using computational textiles to investigate engagement, aesthetics, and diversity in computer science education. In *Proceedings of the SIGCHI conference on Human factors in computing systems*. ACM, 423–432.
12. David Cavallo, Paulo Blikstein, Arnan Sipitakiat, Anindita Basu, Alexandra Camargo, Roseli de Deus Lopes, and Alice Cavallo. 2004. The city that we want: generative themes, constructionist technologies and school/social change. In *Advanced Learning Technologies, 2004. Proceedings. IEEE International Conference on*. IEEE, 1034–1038.
13. Karin Knorr Cetina. 2009. *Epistemic cultures: How the sciences make knowledge*. Harvard University Press.
14. Joshua Chan, Tarun Pondicherry, and Paulo Blikstein. 2013. LightUp: an augmented, learning platform for electronics. In *Proceedings of the 12th International Conference on Interaction Design and Children*. ACM, 491–494.
15. Gretchen Rhines Cheney, Betsy Brown Ruzzi, and Karthik Muralidharan. 2005. A profile of the Indian education system. *Prepared for the New Commission on the Skills of the American Workforce* (2005).
16. Patrick Chiu, Ashutosh Kapuskar, Sarah Reitmeier, and Lynn Wilcox. 1999. NoteLook: Taking notes in meetings with digital video and ink. In *Proceedings of the seventh ACM international conference on Multimedia (Part 1)*. ACM, 149–158.
17. Liwei Dai, Wayne G Lutters, and Carlie Bower. 2005. Why use memo for all?: restructuring mobile applications to support informal note taking. In *CHI'05 extended abstracts on Human factors in computing systems*. ACM, 1320–1323.
18. Dale Dougherty. 2013. The maker mindset. *Design, make, play: Growing the next generation of STEM innovators* (2013), 7–11.
19. Brian W Evans. 2007. Arduino Programming Notebook. *Publeshed: First Edition August* (2007).
20. Neil Gershenfeld. 2005. Fab: Personal fabrication, fab labs, and the factory in your computer. (2005).
21. Werner Geyer, Heather Richter, Ludwin Fuchs, Tom Frauenhofer, Shahrokh Daijavad, and Steven Poltrock. 2001. A team collaboration space supporting capture and access of virtual meetings. In *Proceedings of the 2001 International ACM SIGGROUP Conference on Supporting Group Work*. ACM, 188–196.
22. Joshua P Gutwill, Nina Hido, and Lisa Sindorf. 2015. Research to Practice: Observing Learning in Tinkering Activities. *Curator: The Museum Journal* 58, 2 (2015), 151–168.
23. Erica Rosenfeld Halverson and Kimberly Sheridan. 2014. The maker movement in education. *Harvard Educational Review* 84, 4 (2014), 495–504.
24. Scarlett R Herring, Chia-Chen Chang, Jesse Krantzler, and Brian P Bailey. 2009. Getting inspired!: understanding how and why examples are used in creative design practice. In *Proceedings of the SIGCHI Conference on Human Factors in Computing Systems*. ACM, 87–96.
25. Michael JA Howe. 1974. The utility of taking notes as an aid to learning. *Educational Research* 16, 3 (1974), 222–227.
26. Yasmin B Kafai, Eunkyoung Lee, Kristin Searle, Deborah Fields, Eliot Kaplan, and Debora Lui. 2014. A crafts-oriented approach to computing in high school: Introducing computational concepts, practices, and perspectives with electronic textiles. *ACM TOCE* 14, 1 (2014), 1.

27. Yasmin B Kafai, Kristin Searle, Eliot Kaplan, Deborah Fields, Eunkyoung Lee, and Debora Lui. 2013. Cupcake cushions, scooby doo shirts, and soft boomboxes: e-textiles in high school to promote computational concepts, practices, and perceptions. In *Proceeding of the 44th ACM technical symposium on Computer science education*. ACM, 311–316.
28. Geeta Kingdon. 1996. The Quality and Efficiency of Private and Public Education: A Case-Study of Urban India. *Oxford Bulletin of Economics and Statistics* 58, 1 (1996), 57–82.
29. Geeta Gandhi Kingdon. 2007. The progress of school education in India. *Oxford Review of Economic Policy* 23, 2 (2007), 168–195.
30. Krishna Kumar. 1988. Origins of India's "textbook Culture". *Comparative Education Review* 32, 4 (1988), 452–464.
31. Stacey Kuznetsov, Laura C Trutoiu, Casey Kute, Iris Howley, Eric Paulos, and Dan Siewiorek. 2011. Breaking boundaries: strategies for mentoring through textile computing workshops. In *Proc. of the SIGCHI*. ACM, 2957–2966.
32. Ladies learning Code. 2016. Digital Literacy for Women and Youth. http://ladieslearningcode.com/program/girls-learning-code/. (2016). [Online; accessed 2016].
33. Veronica Lin and Orit Shaer. 2016. Beyond the Lab: Using Technology Toys to Engage South African Youth in Computational Thinking. In *Proceedings of the 2016 CHI Conference Extended Abstracts on Human Factors in Computing Systems*. ACM, 655–661.
34. Silvia Lindtner, Shaowen Bardzell, and Jeffrey Bardzell. 2016. Reconstituting the utopian vision of making: HCI after technosolutionism. In *Proceedings of the 2016 CHI Conference on Human Factors in Computing Systems*. ACM, 1390–1402.
35. Emily Lovell and Leah Buechley. 2011. LilyPond: an online community for sharing e-textile projects. In *Proceedings of the 8th ACM conference on Creativity and cognition*. ACM, 365–366.
36. Make:. 2016. Make: Education. http://makezine.com/tag/education/. (2016). [Online; accessed 2016].
37. Sylvia Libow Martinez. 2013. Invent To Learn: Making, Tinkering, And Engineering In The Classroom Author: Sylvia Libow Martinez, Gary S. Stager, Publis. (2013).
38. Hamish McAlpine, Ben J Hicks, Greg Huet, and Steve J Culley. 2006. An investigation into the use and content of the engineer's logbook. *Design Studies* 27, 4 (2006), 481–504.
39. Sugata Mitra. 2005. Self organising systems for mass computer literacy: Findings from the 'hole in the wall' experiments. *International Journal of Development Issues* 4, 1 (2005), 71–81.
40. Sugata Mitra, Ritu Dangwal, Shiffon Chatterjee, Swati Jha, Ravinder S Bisht, and Preeti Kapur. 2005. Acquisition of computing literacy on shared public computers: Children and the" hole in the wall". *Australasian Journal of Educational Technology* 21, 3 (2005), 407.
41. A Mukherjee. 2002. Build Robots Create Science–A Constructivist Education Initiative for Indian Schools. *Proceedings of Development by Design, Bangalore, India* (2002).
42. Karthik Muralidharan and Michael Kremer. 2006. Public and private schools in rural India. *Harvard University, Department of Economics, Cambridge, MA* (2006).
43. Dayo Olopade. 2014. *The bright continent: Breaking rules and making change in modern Africa*. Houghton Mifflin Harcourt.
44. Seymour Papert and Idit Harel. 1991. Situating constructionism. *Constructionism* 36 (1991), 1–11.
45. Udai Singh Pawar, Joyojeet Pal, and Kentaro Toyama. 2006. Multiple mice for computers in education in developing countries. In *Information and Communication Technologies and Development, 2006. ICTD'06. International Conference on*. IEEE, 64–71.
46. Leïla Perié, Livio Riboli-Sasco, and Claire Ribrault. 2014. Straight into conflict zones, scientific research empowers the minds. *LISTENING AND EMPOWERING* (2014), 69.
47. Nimmi Rangaswamy and Melissa Densmore. 2013. Understanding Jugaad: ICTD and the tensions of appropriation, innovation and utility. In *Proceedings of the Sixth International Conference on Information and Communications Technologies and Development: Notes-Volume 2*. ACM, 120–123.
48. Nimmi Rangaswamy and Nithya Sambasivan. 2011. Cutting Chai, Jugaad, and Here Pheri: towards UbiComp for a global community. *Personal and Ubiquitous Computing* 15, 6 (2011), 553–564.
49. Kimberly M Sheridan and Abigail Konopasky. 2016. Designing for Resourcefulness. *Makeology: Makerspaces as Learning Environments* 1 (2016), 30.
50. Arnan Sipitakiat. 2001. *Digital technology for conviviality: making the most of students' energy and imagination in learning environments*. Ph.D. Dissertation. Massachusetts Institute of Technology.
51. Arnan Sipitakiat and Paulo Blikstein. 2010. Think globally, build locally: a technological platform for low-cost, open-source, locally-assembled programmable bricks for education. In *Proceedings of the fourth international conference on Tangible, embedded, and embodied interaction*. ACM, 231–232.
52. Arnan Sipitakiat, Paulo Blikstein, and David P Cavallo. 2004. GoGo board: augmenting programmable bricks for economically challenged audiences. In *Proceedings of the 6th international conference on Learning sciences*. International Society of the Learning Sciences, 481–488.

53. Thomas N Smyth, Satish Kumar, Indrani Medhi, and Kentaro Toyama. 2010. Where there's a will there's a way: mobile media sharing in urban india. In *Proceedings of the SIGCHI conference on Human Factors in computing systems*. ACM, 753–762.

54. Sowmya Somanath, Janette Hughes, Ehud Sharlin, and Mario Costa Sousa. 2015. The Concept of DIY as an Education Model for Indian Public Schools. In *CHI'15 Extended Abstracts*. ACM.

55. Sowmya Somanath, Laura Morrison, Janette Hughes, Ehud Sharlin, and Mario Costa Sousa. 2016. Engaging 'At-Risk' Students Through Maker Culture Activities. In *Proceedings of the TEI '16: Tenth International Conference on Tangible, Embedded, and Embodied Interaction (TEI '16)*. ACM, 150–158.

56. SparkFun. 2016. SparkFun Inventor's Kit Guidebook - V3. https://www.sparkfun.com/products/retired/11976/. (2016). [Online; accessed 2016].

57. Gary S Stager. 2013. Papert's prison fab lab: implications for the maker movement and education design. In *Proceedings of the 12th International Conference on Interaction Design and Children*. ACM, 487–490.

58. Joshua G Tanenbaum, Amanda M Williams, Audrey Desjardins, and Karen Tanenbaum. 2013. Democratizing technology: pleasure, utility and expressiveness in DIY and maker practice. In *Proc. of the SIGCHI*. ACM, 2603–2612.

59. Tiffany Tseng and Mitchel Resnick. 2014. Product versus process: representing and appropriating DIY projects online. In *Proceedings of the 2014 conference on Designing interactive systems*. ACM, 425–428.

60. L Vygotsky. 1987. Zone of proximal development. *Mind in society: The development of higher psychological processes* (1987), 52–91.

61. Jagoda Walny, Jonathan Haber, Marian Dörk, Jonathan Sillito, and Sheelagh Carpendale. 2011. Follow that sketch: Lifecycles of diagrams and sketches in software development. In *Visualizing Software for Understanding and Analysis (VISSOFT), 2011 6th IEEE International Workshop on*. IEEE, 1–8.

62. Stephen C Want and Paul L Harris. 2002. How do children ape? Applying concepts from the study of non-human primates to the developmental study of 'imitation' in children. *Developmental Science* 5, 1 (2002), 1–14.

'I Make, Therefore I Am': The Effects of Curriculum-Aligned Making on Children's Self-Identity

Sharon Lynn Chu The StoryLab
Rebecca Schlegel Dept. of Psychology
Francis Quek TEILab
Andrew Christy Dept. of Psychology
Kaiyuan Chen Dept. of Psychology
Texas A&M University
[sharilyn, beccaschlegel, quek, achristy, frostioe]@tamu.edu

ABSTRACT
Prior research investigating the effects of incorporating Making into educational contexts has been limited to snapshot studies. These studies however do not allow for the investigation of aspects that require longer-term development and nurture. We present a longitudinal study that investigates the effects of Making on children's degree of science self-efficacy, identity formation as possible scientists and engineers, and academic performance in science. Designed interactions with Making technology were integrated into the science curriculum of elementary school classrooms in a public school with a high proportion of students from minority populations for a year. Results showed significant differences between the 'Making classrooms' and the control classrooms, and from pre- to post-test on the students' inclination towards science. The results support the promise and potential of incorporating Making into formal schooling on the growth and long-term attitudes of children towards science and STEM in general.

Author Keywords
Making; Maker movement; Children; Education; STEM; Science; Self-identity; Self-efficacy; Learning.

ACM Classification Keywords
H.5.m. Information interfaces and presentation (e.g., HCI): Miscellaneous.

INTRODUCTION
Making broadly refers to the practices surrounding the use of a set of technologies, that include for instance, electronics, 3D printing, programming and microprocessors as despecialized means of prototyping and creation of technology-based artifacts. It is typically associated with values and characteristics such as play, innovation, intrinsic motivation [1] and technological literacy. Many have commented on the potential for Making to support, enliven, change, or even revolutionize children's education in subjects such as science, mathematics and computing.

CHI 2017, May 06-11, 2017, Denver, CO, USA
© 2017 ACM. ISBN 978-1-4503-4655-9/17/05...$15.00
DOI: http://dx.doi.org/10.1145/3025453.3025458

A challenge to the use of Making in formal education is that while Making emphasizes and values discovery and innovation, modern public school systems are driven by scheduled learning goals and accountability [2]. Hence, most Making-oriented programs are conducted in such venues as workshops, community-based Makerspaces, museums, after-school programs, and paid Maker classes. This poses issues of equity as participants are self-selected through parents who see the value of Making, and have the resources to bring their children to these venues.

This paper presents results from a quantitative analysis of variables and interactions of a year-long Making-oriented program implemented in a low socio-economic status public elementary school that serves students from predominantly underrepresented populations. The students engaged in Making activities designed to match their state-mandated existing science curriculum. Our results how our program was related to students' self-efficacy, interest and identity in Making and STEM (Science, Technology, Engineering and Mathematics).

To date, there have been few studies to validate the promise advanced for HCI research in Making, and even fewer have looked at sustained application of Making for the broader population within the framework of public schools that support universal access to learning and development. Insofar as work in HCI is growing rapidly on the design of Maker kits (e.g., Mentjes and Schelhowe's work at the Interaction Design and Children conference 2016 [3]), understanding motivations of Makers (e.g., Hudson et al.'s work in CHI 2016 [4]), the study of Maker cultures (e.g., Lindtner et al.'s work [5] and Taylor et al.'s work [6] in CHI 2016), etc., this paper contributes empirical evidence on the potential impact of Making, thus cementing the 'raison-d'être' of or rationale for such HCI work in Making.

We lead into the rest of this paper with a review of work on Making in education. Our review first describes theoretically and empirically the role of Making in learning, and then overviews investigations that have broached the issue of self-efficacy and self-identity in Making in learning contexts. We then present the theoretical foundation for our work, before describing our study, measures, analysis procedures, and results.

BACKGROUND: MAKING IN EDUCATION
Much has been written about the role of Making in learning. A significant portion of prior work has been in

terms of practical industry and government initiatives. For instance, programs have combined craft technologies with engineering and mathematics education [7], the Laboratory School for Advanced Manufacturing (Lab School), grounded in the premise that students can learn through the design and fabrication process [8], or the FabLab@School worldwide network that allow children to solve their own and the local community problems by making the tools they need [9]. Theoretically, Making and digital fabrication in education have been said to be founded on Papert's constructionism [10] – hands-on learning through the creation of digital and physical artifacts.

However, the integration of Making in learning is challenging. For example, drawing from his observations in digital fabrication workshops with older students, Blikstein [10] reports on the 'keychain syndrome': equipment are trivialized when over time, students become fixated on using them for making only one thing (keychains in his case). Nemorin [11] draws from his ethnographic experiences in 3D printing workshop classes to highlight three issues that may be problematic for the integration of Making into formal schooling: 1) the lack of pragmatic engagement, 2) affective labor, and 3) mediated alienation. Much evidence that show the benefits of Making with regards to learning in the literature is qualitative in nature. In the only published survey paper on empirical studies of Making to date, Papavlasopoulou et al.'s [12] analysis of the 43 studies that met their selection criteria revealed that the majority of the studies (52%) were qualitative, with the rest being either mixed (30%) or purely quantitative (18%). They noted that most of the quantitative studies measured the results of the treatment only through a post-test. Their review also showed that most of the studies had a sample size that was fewer than 50 participants.

Even so, qualitative Making for learning studies reveal that students' experiences in Making scenarios are rich, multi-layered and complex. Flores and Springer [13], for instance, describe the initial experiences of students who followed an inquiry-based curriculum at the Hillbrook Middle School Makerspace. Posch and Fitzpatrick [14] report case study experiences of children aged 10 to 14 years old who attended a workshop at a FabLab that provided instruction on 2D/3D design and fabrication, printed circuit board (PCB) fabrication and assembly, and software programming. Sheridan et al. [15] present a qualitative analysis of the processes that occur in three different Makerspaces when taken as learning environments. Worsley's [16] doctoral dissertation presents results from multimodal analyses of high school and tertiary students engaging in various Making-related activities, with an emphasis on the analysis of reasoning strategies used. Nemorin and Selwyn [17] present an ethnographic investigation of a 3D printing course enacted in an Australian high school.

Existing quantitative results that we found on Making for learning are encouraging. For example, in the Robot Diaries project [18, 19], middle school students designed "affective, programmable tangible communication devices using familiar crafting materials and then use motors, lights and computation in novel ways to animate their creations". The project was tested in a six-day workshop with seven participants. Pre-post tests show that the children improved in both declarative knowledge and general knowledge of technical systems. They identified and correctly labeled on average 4 out of 6 robotic components at pre-test and 5.9 at post-test. More children were able to better identify the parts of a given electronic toy and explain how it works at post-test than at pre-test.

Work on Making in educational settings is growing rapidly, and it can be ascertained from the literature thus far that Making is somewhat positively correlated with the learning of specific subject matter. However, a gap still exists in our understanding of the longer-term effects of Making approaches, especially in formal learning contexts. This gap in knowledge is echoed in Jenkins and Bogost's [20] lament that HCI Making research is hermetic and isolated from the broader world of domain practice. We argue that with a greater focus on the development of the person – the Maker – rather than simply on technology kit development or the transfer of content and skills, HCI Making research can contribute significantly to the development of Makers who have the appropriate mindset and predispositions to venture outside the artificial confines of Maker workshops and planned activities.

THEORETICAL FOUNDATION

Development of a Maker Identity

Literature in Making research that specifically addresses identity or mindset formation is scarce. Halverson and Sheridan [21] define Makers as the "identities of participation that people take on within the Maker movement". What characterizes a Maker identity or who is a Maker? Based on interviews with 17 youth about their conceptions of themselves as Makers, Martin and Dixon [22] put forth that Maker youth espouse 3 themes: "Open community, Active participation"; "Making in control to the normal"; and "Making is integrated across all contexts". Six experts conducted in-depth interviews to construct Maker profiles of the youth presenters of 5 showcased projects at the 2012 World Maker Faire [23], and the profiles show characteristics that echo many of the values identified by others in the adult Maker. In a survey of 2600 adults participating in a range of DIY communities, Kuznetsov and Paulos [24] identified 'open sharing', 'learning', and 'creativity' as important values of the Maker. Based on their ethnographic studies of steampunk practitioners, Tanenbaum et al. [25] highlight 'pleasure', 'utility' and 'expressiveness' as values in the Maker movement. Further, Dougherty has aligned the Maker mindset with the 'growth mindset', a mindset that tolerates risk and failure, and that believes that capabilities can be developed instead of being fixed.

Thus, if a Maker is creative, learning-oriented, open to sharing, risk-taking, and tolerant of failure, does one's engagement in Making impact one's sense of self to incorporate a Maker identity? The answer is not evident as engagement in Making may not lead one to become a Maker, just as anyone can engage in cooking but may not fashion themselves to be cooks. Halverson and Sheridan [21] state it as such: "it is not clear that individuals and groups automatically take on identities of participation within the Maker landscape. Some participants in Making activities may not consider themselves Makers and therefore self-select out of public conversations".

More importantly for our work, *can curriculum-aligned Making in the formal public school context in the United States impact children's identity as a Maker?* The difficulty that formal school contexts add is at least two-fold: first, the characteristics of Making and of the Maker tend to be counter to schooling cultures and frameworks, and second, in the classroom the goal of the teacher is to teach about the specific topic or subject matter of the class (science, language arts, history, etc.). What then is the role of Making in such contexts, and by which pathways may a Maker identity be fostered? Although the constraint of topic learning, e.g., science, is not necessarily present in short-term studies done in informal contexts, such studies have provided indications of potential Maker identity formation through the pathways of increased self-efficacy and interest.

For instance, Katterfeldt et al. [26] draw from decade-long research on digital fabrication workshops for children to present three core ideas that may facilitate Bildung (deep, sustainable learning that leads to 'learning-to-be'): *be-greifbarkeit* (being 'graspable'), *imagineering* (creative approaches to technology), and *self-efficacy* (relating oneself to technology). Qiu et al. [27] conducted three workshops involving middle- and high-school-aged children engaging in computational textiles projects using LilyPad Arduino-based technologies, following a curriculum emphasizing computer science (programming) concepts. They found that the children's perceived self-efficacy increased from pre- to post-surveys on statements such as "I feel comfortable programming computers on my own." The statements however were not drawn from validated scales.

Ornelas et al. [28] present comments that seem to indicate increased technological awareness and confidence in high school students who participated in an afterschool program at the Stanford University FabLab where they engaged in Making and digital fabrication projects. Our own work [29] presenting the approach of a 'means-to-an-end' to integrate Making with learning, has shown that Making has the potential to impact the development of a Maker mindset in a series of workshops with elementary school-aged children. The only longer-term study of Making that we found is Alexander et al.'s [30] who implemented learning activities centered on digital fabrication in 2 fourth-grade and 3 fifth-grade classes across 2 schools for a year. They found that student attitudes were positive in the post-test survey items as compared to the pre-test.

Other studies also suggest that there may be differences in gender in how Making impacts Maker identity formation. Holbert [31] for example, frames Making as being about creating for others, and conducted a five-day workshop with 9 children aged 9 to 10 making 'dream toys' for young PreK children at the same school. The post-interview showed that the children were generally excited about making toys for other children, but findings showed a slight difference between the attitudes of girls versus boys, who "seemed more driven by a personal connection to the toy than to the preK children".

Identity Formation in Science

While theory on Maker identity development is still in its infancy, significant work in social and educational psychology has explored the development of children's motivations and identity development in STEM fields:

Self-efficacy refers to evaluations of one's ability in a given domain [32-34]. A large body of evidence indicates that these evaluations are predictive of many important psychological and educational outcomes. An early study by Bandura and Schunk [35] found that self-efficacy in mathematics was predictive of both objective math performance and self-reported interest in math among 7- to 10-year-olds. More recent work has found that children's self-efficacy is a major predictor of their career aspirations, and the impact of many other factors such as family socio-economic status appears to be mediated by children's self-efficacy [36]. In a similar vein, Wang [37] found that math self-efficacy was predictive of students' decisions to pursue STEM majors in college.

There are biases in terms of race and gender in such science identity development pathways. For example, although many girls express interest in science during their elementary school years, they have increasingly negative views of science, science classes, and science-based careers as they progress through middle and high school [38, 39]. Thus, early self-efficacy in STEM domains seems to be critical to promoting long-term interest and persistence in STEM fields. The period of third- to fifth-grade that we address in our work falls precisely during what Piaget [40] called the 'concrete operational phase', a time when children's social awareness is intensively developing and concepts of self begin to form.

Self-Identification and Self-Concept: Osborne [41] defines self-identification as "the extent to which an individual defines the self through a role or performance in a particular domain." In other words, self-identification refers to the extent to which a person considers the domain in question (STEM, in our case) to be an important and defining part of who they are (their self-concept). A range of theories in social psychology, e.g., cognitive dissonance [42], control theory [43], self-discrepancy [44], self-verification [45], and prototype matching [46], maintain that the self-concept serves an organizing function, such that people generally strive to avoid behaving in ways that are inconsistent with it. Specific to STEM fields, evidence indicates that a major reason for students' lack of interest in STEM is attributable to a dissimilarity between students' own self-concepts and their prototypical concepts of students who like math and science [47]. In other words, a major barrier to student engagement with STEM seems to be that many students simply do not see themselves as the "kind of person" who is interested in STEM fields.

Identity in Making and Science

We put forth that conversely to other kinds of intervention such as curricular changes, teaching strategies, use of novel devices like tablets and Smartboards, etc., the characteristics of Making afford tremendous potential to impact identities, for example: i) Making is hands-on and production-based, and thus require engagement. Many studies have reported on children who continue Making beyond the workshop time allotted (e.g., [48]); ii) Making is integrative. Making projects are not focused on the learning of one specific skill but are cumulative and build upon each other, so that over time the child has greater opportunity to feel that they are approaching mastery; and iii) Making is personal. The 'low threshold, high ceiling' [49] aspect of Making (low barrier of entry with wide possibilities) allows one to easily customize projects. In the words of Kafai, Fields and Searle [50], "the aesthetic component of making affords students the opportunity to bring personal identity into the typically technocratic work of schooling".

In the context of the public school classroom, we hypothesize that a Making intervention will foster students' sense of self-efficacy in Making, and that this increased self-efficacy may in turn cement greater self-identification as a Maker. We also hypothesize that simultaneously, a Making intervention will have positive impact on students' relation with the subject matter of the Making, in our case STEM. The positive impact can be in terms of increased self-efficacy in STEM, which may foster students' self-identification as possible scientists and engineers (or other STEM-related persons), and possibly affecting downstream outcomes such as the students' desire to enter STEM fields.

CURRICULUM-ALIGNED MAKING ACTIVITIES

Our investigation of Making in formal school contexts has necessitated the development of Making kits and activities to be used as part of our Making intervention. We developed 23 Making kits and activities targeted at grades 3, 4 and 5 over the course of a year-long study. The kits and activities were developed by a design team consisting of members with expertise in electrical engineering, computer science, child-computer interaction and design, and education and classroom pedagogy, informed by feedback from the participating teachers. In all the kits, Making was implemented using an interactive arts-and-craft approach in which the students construct their science projects around basic electronic circuits.

Admittedly, prior work in Making has produced a diversity of Maker kits and Making-based implementations tested in workshops or camp settings, e.g., LightUp [49], the MakerCart [51], Chibitronics [52]. Nevertheless, we were interested in Maker kits that are directly aligned with the local curriculum standards, for both pedagogical and practical reasons, thus warranting the development of our own Maker kits. We acknowledge here that, as highlighted by Halverson and Sheridan [21], many questions still remain as to 'what works' for learning through Making, such as "What should students do there (makerspaces)? Should Making supplement current curricula or replace it?". Since the focus of this paper is not to discuss the design of Maker activities in the classroom, we present study results only in the context of our specific Maker kits designed to be aligned with elementary school curricula. We have described the design process of our Maker kits in more detail elsewhere (see [53]). For context in this paper, we present below two examples of the curriculum-aligned Making activities that were deployed in the classrooms.

Example 1:

The first Making week for Grade 5 addressed the science unit of 'Matter and Energy: Mixtures and Solutions'. Specifically, the learning goals of the unit were for students to understand that some mixtures maintain physical properties of their ingredients, such as iron filings and sand, while in solutions, such as salt or Kool-Aid in water, the process of dissolving makes the constitutions harder to separate. On day 1 of the Making week, the students built an electronic mixer (Figure 1 Day 1). The mixer comprised of a basic electronic circuit with a geared rotating motor as the load and a switch made out of card stock and conductive copper tape. A 3D-printed mixer head was attached to the motor through a dowel rod so that the student can insert the head into a container and activate the motor. With their electronic mixer, students mixed glitter with water and made observations about the mixture.

On day 2, the students built an electric sifting tool to separate the individual parts of a mixture (Figure 1 Day 2). This comprised of a simple hand-held sieve with a vibrating motor attached to it. Activating the vibrating motor by depressing the card switch would shake the sieve to separate its contents. On day 3, they built a circuit with a vibrating motor attached to a plastic cup containing glitter and Lego pieces (Figure 1 Day 3). Pressing the switch activates the motor that vibrates the cup, presenting an alternate way to create mixtures. On day 4, the students first constructed their vibrating motor circuit again, and then mixed iron fillings with glitter. They were then tasked to separate the iron fillings from the glitter using a magnet (Figure 1 Day 4). On day 5, the last day of the Making week for the 'Mixtures & Solutions' unit, the students built the same electronic mixer again with the rotational motor circuit, and mixed red Kool-Aid powder with water. They recorded observations on the properties of the solution.

Example 2:
In week 3, the Grade 4 classes engaged in a Making activity aligned with the science unit of 'Earth and Space: Rapid Changes'. The learning goals for the Making week for that unit were to understand that Earth consists of natural resources, its surface is constantly changing, and some changes occur rapidly. Examples of rapid changes include volcanic eruptions, earthquakes, and landslides. The students built a model of a village that sits on a pair of foam-core 'tectonic plates' with vibrating motors attached to its foundations (the plates were placed together in a large plastic box on dowel rod 'pillars' that were attached to the plates with 3D-printed mountings) (see Figure 2). A layer of kitty litter was laid on top of the foam core plates and the students created a village made of decorated origami houses on top of the kitty litter. When the vibrating motors taped to the 'foundation pillars' are activated, the foam-core plates shake and separate, destroying the village and causing some of the kitty litter to fall into the crack of the separated plates. Figure 2 Right shows the students constructing the tectonic plate model.

Other examples of Making activities that the students engaged in included building LED-embedded food chains (see Figure 3 Left), rotating solar system models (see Figure 3 Right), lighted dioramas, reflection and refraction through LEDs, etc.

STUDY DESCRIPTION

Research Questions

The work presented in this paper addressed the following specific questions:

a. *Can Making activities integrated in formal schooling positively influence elementary school students' sense of self-efficacy in Making, interest in Making, and sense of identity as Makers?*
b. *Can Making activities in formal schooling positively influence elementary school students' sense of science self-efficacy, interest in science, and intended career paths?*
c. *Can student participation in curriculum-integrated Making activities positively influence elementary school students' academic performance?*

Study Population

Our study followed third-, fourth-, and fifth-grade classrooms (students aged 8 to 11 years old) of a local elementary school. With consultation from the school's administration, two classes for each grade were selected yielding a total of six classes. The population of the school consists of a majority of students from groups typically underrepresented in STEM fields (72% Latino, 26%

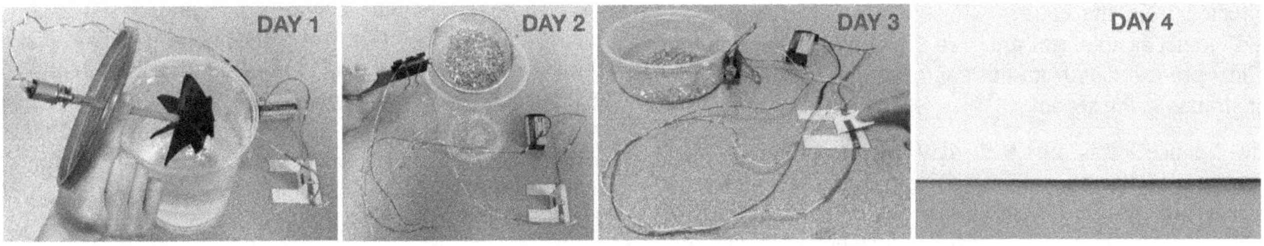

Figure 1. Day-by-day curriculum activities for 'Mixtures & Solutions' Making kit

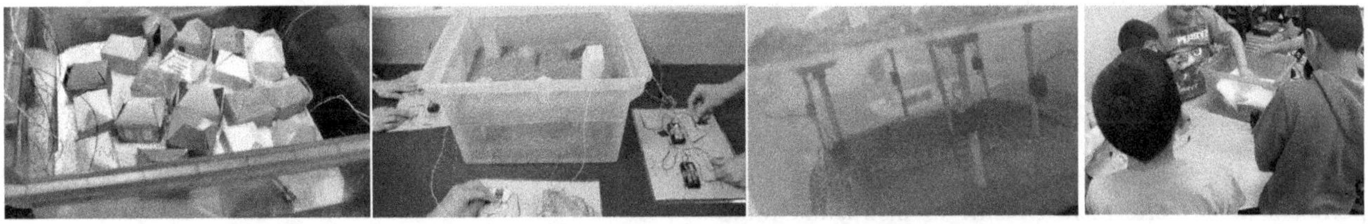

Figure 2. 'Earthquake' Making kit and activity

Figure 3. (Left) LED-embedded food chain; (Right) Rotating solar system model

African American, 96% on reduced lunch programs, >50% Low-English Proficiency). We designed and implemented different Making activities centered on specific learning standards for each grade level for every science unit throughout a 36-week school year. The school system covers six science units over a year in accordance with the state's curriculum. In consultation with the teachers, one week was chosen as the Making intervention week for each of the six science units for each grade. We met with the teachers for each class six weeks prior to the designated week that we would be implementing the interactive Making activities in their classroom to engage them as design informants. In total thus, we worked with six teachers and 121 students across the three grades in our intervention. We also administered surveys at the end of the year to students in the unselected classes (n = 3) to serve as a control group (n = 117 students).

Study Protocol

At the beginning of the academic year, parents provided written informed consent for their child to be observed and recorded during class. A pre-survey questionnaire was administered to the students in all participating classes (n = 114: 63% Hispanic or Latino, 35% Black, <1% Multiracial, <1% White) to evaluate their initial predispositions towards Making and towards science. The same post-survey questionnaire was again administered in the last week of the academic year to all students who remained in the study. Furthermore, for each grade level, the post-test was also collected from the classes who did not participate in the study to act as a control group (n = 61). We were unable to collect pre-test data from this control group because of time constraints in the school.

The science class on each day of the Making week consisted of five main parts: i) initial instruction by the teacher; ii) Making instructions by a member of the design/research team; iii) students' engagement in Making; iv) science experiment; v) post-experiment notetaking and discussion led by either the teacher or the researcher. In the initial instruction, the teacher reviewed content previously covered, and introduced the students to the science concepts of the day. The researcher then took over the class to provide guidance as to how to build the artifact, materials needed, and how the artifact were to be used in the science experiment to be performed. Outside of instruction times during the class, the students were allowed to work relatively autonomously and in free-flow interactions. They were able to ask for help from one or two logistics helpers who were present in the classroom throughout the Making process. The teacher or the researcher provided instruction for the science experiment, after which the students were asked to write down their observations in their notebook, and a classwide discussion was initiated. Figure 4 shows the students engaging in one of the Making activities, as well as the general setup of the classroom during the study.

MEASURES

For our study, we focused on the variables of interest, self-efficacy and self-identity with regard to Making and science, as well as academic performance in science, as measured by state test scores. The general format of the pre- and post-surveys was adapted from The Self Perception Profile for Children (SPPC) [54]. In a "structured alternative format", each child was presented with an affirmative statement about themselves and its negative counterpart. The students were instructed to make an initial choice between the two statements, then they were asked to rate how true the statement chosen was of them (see table 1 for an example). Responses were recoded into a 1 to 4 Likert scale type response, such that higher numbers always indicated more interest, efficacy, and identification. We describe below the sources of our measures for each variable.

Table 1. Sample item used in the surveys

Really true of me	Sort of true of me				Sort of true of me	Really true of me
☐	☐	I want to build or make things	OR	I don't really want to build or make things	☐	☐

Maker identity, Self-efficacy and Interest

Maker identity was measured with a 12-item scale ($\alpha = .48$ in pre-test; $\alpha = .89$ in post-test). The items in the scale were drawn from the Maker Mindset Assessment [55], and were adapted for elementary school-aged children. An example item included the following statements "I like making things with my hands" and "I don't like making things with my hands". *Maker self-efficacy* was measured by one item we developed based on guidelines specified by Bandura [56] for self-efficacy measures. The two statements in this item read, "I am good at building or making things" and "I'm not very good at building or making things". For *Maker interest*, we developed two items with affirmative statements such as "I like to build or make things" and "I want to build or make things". The two items were significantly correlated ($r = .48$ in pre-test; $r = .60$ in post-test), and were collapsed into a single composite.

Science Self-efficacy and Interest

As with Maker self-efficacy, science self-efficacy was similarly measured with two items, with the affirmative statement of the items reading:" I feel I am very good at science" and "Being good at science is an important part of who I am". The two items were again positively correlated (correlation coefficient $r = .29$ in pre-test; $r = .59$ in post-test), and collapsed into a single composite.

To measure science interest, we developed another face valid single item measure. The affirmative statement of the item read: "I like science".

STEM Career Possible Self and Interest

Following the work of Anderman et al. [57], we assessed children's STEM career possible self by having them report how true it would be that someday they might have a job where they "help build things", "discover new things", "make and invent new things", "use technology every day", and also a job that uses "math", "science", "writing". The reliability of the seven items was satisfactory (α = .79, in pre-test; α = .83, in post-test).

For STEM career interest, we adapted a measure used in Robnett and Leaper's study [58]. Each child was asked to indicate how true it is for them that "they want to become a scientist/engineer/science teacher/math teacher/computer programmer/astronaut/doctor) versus "I want to be something different". The seven items for this measure again reached satisfactory reliability (α = .79, in both pre-test and post-test). As a result, we averaged the items to form a composite. Finally, an open-ended question was also included in both the pre- and post-surveys asking the student to write down their first and second choice jobs that they would like to have in the future.

Science Examination Scores

Fifth-grade students typically sit for the state's assessments of academic readiness for various subjects (reading, mathematics, science, social studies) in the last month of the academic year. The science test includes questions from all units covered during the year, and addresses reasoning and content. We obtained the science scores for the students in both the Making group and the control group from the school district. We note that third- and fourth-graders are not tested in science at the state level.

DATA ANALYSIS AND RESULTS

Making Self-Efficacy, Interest and Identity

To address whether the classroom Making activities were related to students' sense of Making self-efficacy and interest in Making, and instilled a sense of identity as Makers, two analyses were done: A) a comparison of mean scores on the corresponding measures between students in the Making and control classrooms at the end of the academic year; and B) a comparison of means at the beginning of the academic year versus means at the end of the academic year for students in the Making classrooms. The SPSS statistical package was used for all analyses. No significant gender differences were found on any of our dependent variables. We were not able to look at any other differences that may arise from other demographic variables such as cultural background as there were not enough participants in each subgroup to make valid comparisons.

For the first analysis, an independent two-tailed t-test was run comparing the Making and control groups' post-test scores on Making self-efficacy, interest in Making and identification as a Maker (Table 2A). Results revealed that students in the Making classrooms reported significantly higher Making self-efficacy and interest in Making than students in the control classrooms ($p < .005$). Students in the Making classrooms also reported a somewhat greater

Figure 4. Students engaging in classroom Making activities

resonance with a Maker identity than students in control classrooms. However, this difference was not significant.

For the second analysis, a dependent two-tailed t-test was run on the Making group students' scores on Making self-efficacy, interest in Making, and identification as a Maker at pre- and post-test (Table 2B). No significant differences were found for any of the three variables. However, the means were relatively high at both time points for this group (all variables were measured on a 4-point scale; with higher numbers indicating more efficacy, interest, and identity). Note that the means here may not match the means in Table 2A given that only students with a complete pre- and post-test could be used in this analysis as it was a within-subject comparison. For the between-subject comparisons reported in Table 2A, all participants with post-test data could be included in the analysis.

Science Self-Efficacy, Interest and Career Paths

We conducted the same two types of analyses on the students' scores on science self-efficacy, interest in science, identification as possible scientists, and likelihood to have a STEM-related career. Overall, the results for these variables were more robust, suggesting that the intervention was effective particularly in boosting science than Making variables. For the first analysis (Table 3A), students in the Making classrooms reported significantly higher levels of science self-efficacy ($p < .005$), science interest ($p < .05$) and interest in STEM careers ($p < .05$) than students in the control class at the end of the academic year. The difference for possible self was marginally significant. For the second analysis, students in the Making classrooms reported significantly higher levels of science self-efficacy ($p < .005$), STEM possible self ($p < .005$), and STEM career interest ($p < .005$) at the end of the academic year relative to the beginning (Table 3B). The only difference that was not significant was for science interest, but these students reported relatively high levels of interest at the beginning of the year as well. Additionally, we found that the science variables were all significantly positively correlated with the Making variables (average r = .44).

Science Attitudes and Academic Performance

An independent two-tailed t-test was run on the scores of the fifth-graders in the Making group and the control group on their end-of-year state science examination. While students in the Making classes had somewhat higher test scores (M = 31.35, SD = 6.40) than students in the control classes (M = 29.75, SD = 6.21), this difference in scores was not statistically significant (p = .35).

Finally, we examined whether the Making and science variables were correlated with the students' scores on their end-of-year state science examination. Results from the tests revealed that Maker possible self (r = .35, p = .004) was significantly correlated with the examination scores. Maker self-efficacy (r = .23, p = .07) and Maker interest (r = .30, p = .07) trended with test scores but did not cross the significance threshold. Of the science variables, both science self-efficacy (r = .25, p = .04) and science interest (r = .25, p = .003) were significantly correlated with the examination scores. Neither STEM possible self (r = .18, p = .16) nor STEM career interest (r = -.01, p = .94), were strongly related to the examination scores.

Since it was still possible for our Making intervention to have increased examination scores via mediation effects of increased interest, self-efficacy and identification with science, we tested five mediation models using Hayes' [59] (model 4) PROCESS macro. For each model, science class type (Control class = 0; Making class = 1) was entered as the independent variable; examination scores were entered as the dependent variable; and a single science or Making variable was entered as the mediating variable. Bias-corrected confidence intervals for the effects in this model were computed based on 5,000 bootstrapped resamples. Results of this analysis revealed a significant indirect effect of science class type on test scores through science interest (b = 1.12, SE = .73, bias-corrected 95% CI = [.04, 3.05]) and science self-efficacy (b = .89, SE = .64 bias-corrected 95% CI = [.07, 2.89]). Maker self-efficacy, Maker possible self and Maker interest were not significant mediators.

Open-Ended Career Choices

We coded the students' responses to the open-ended question about desired career paths using the following process: 1) blank responses or responses that could not be understood were counted as unknowns and were removed from the dataset; 2) the responses were standardized such that phrases referring to the same jobs were coded with a single term (e.g., "cop" and "policeman" were both coded as 'policeman'); 3) the standardized responses were grouped into categories based on field (e.g., "doctor", "nurse", "surgeon", "dentist" were all grouped into the category 'medicine'); 4) we found a large number of responses referring to medicine-related jobs (notably doctor) and veterinarian. We removed these from the dataset as well, although they were STEM-related fields, as they seemed to relate more to a cultural meme rather than actual possible selves; and 5) the rest of the categories were coded as being either STEM-related or non-STEM-related. STEM-related categories were "scientist" (included jobs like scientist, biologist, geologist, etc.), "engineer"

Table 2. Results for Making Self-Efficacy, Maker Interest, and Maker Identity

A. Intervention VS Control			
	Maker Classrooms Post-Test Mean (SD)	Control Classrooms Post-Test Mean (SD)	Independent t-test
Making Self-Efficacy	3.27 (.83)	2.77 (1.08)	t(171) = 3.37, p = .001
Maker Interest	3.27 (.82)	2.85 (1.01)	t(172) = 2.99, p = .003
Maker Identity	3.26 (.64)	3.17 (.60)	t(174) = .38, p = .38
B. Intervention Pre Vs Intervention Post			
	Maker Classrooms Pre-Test Mean (SD)	Maker Classrooms Post-Test Mean (SD)	Dependent t-test
Making Self-Efficacy	3.13 (.86)	3.28 (.80)	t(93) = -1.39, p = .17
Maker Interest	3.46 (.72)	3.32 (.74)	t(93) = 1.46, p = .15
Maker Identity	3.31 (.42)	3.32 (.55)	t(93) = -.22, p = .83

Table 3. Results for Science self-efficacy, Interest, Identity, and Career Interest

A. Intervention VS Control			
	Maker Classrooms Post-Test Mean (SD)	**Control Classrooms Post-Test Mean (SD)**	**Independent t-test**
Science Self-Efficacy	3.31 (.79)	2.81 (.91)	t (172) = 3.80, p < .001
Science Interest	3.49 (.79)	3.13 (.99)	t(170) = 2.58, p = .011
STEM Possible Self Composite	3.10 (.72)	2.88 (.70)	T(173) = 1.91, p = .058
Interest in STEM Career Composite	2.39 (.78)	2.07 (.66)	t(172) = 2.72, p = .007
B. Intervention Pre Vs Intervention Post			
	Maker Classrooms Pre-Test Mean (SD)	Maker Classrooms Post-Test Mean (SD)	Dependent t-test
Science Self-Efficacy	3.01 (.85)	3.33 (.74)	t(93) = -.322, p = .002
Science Interest	3.49 (.81)	3.52 (.72)	t(91) = -.33, p = .74
STEM Possible Self Composite	2.84 (.74)	3.11 (.68)	t(94) = -3.11, p = .002
Interest in STEM Career Composite	2.09 (.79)	2.40 (.79)	t(95) = -3.91, p <.001

(included jobs of engineer, robotics engineer, inventor), and "technology" (that included computer programmer, game developer, etc.).

Table 4 shows the percentage of STEM-related careers relative to non-STEM careers for each of the Making group pre-survey, Making group post-survey, and the control group post-survey. As first career choice, only 4.82% of the students in the Making classes wanted a STEM-related job at the beginning of the year (A1). This rose to 19.54% at year end (A2). In comparison, only 2.22% of the students in the control group (B) expressed STEM-related jobs as first career choice even at year end. Second career choices followed a similar pattern. The Making group saw the percentage of students listing a STEM-related job as second choice rise from 13.40% at year onset to 19.10% at year end. The control group however had only 9.09% of students listing STEM-related jobs at year end as second choice. We note as well that although we did not count 'teacher' as a STEM profession, listings of "teacher" in the pre-survey became more specific in the post-survey with a number of the students listing "science teacher" or "math teacher".

DISCUSSION

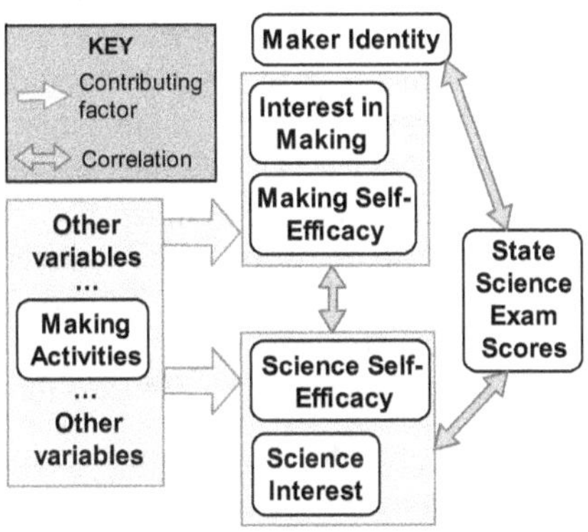

Figure 5. Results illustration

Our work set out to investigate the influences on third-, fourth- and fifth-grade students of consistently integrating Making into the science school curriculum over a year. We were interested in the students' self-efficacy, sustained interest and self-identity as Makers and as individuals with STEM interests. For Making to be able to impact the child outside the 'sandbox' [20] of study settings, it needs to be able to affect such variables that require longer time to develop. We note that we cannot determine true causality of any of the variables in our study given the constraints of our research design.

A summary illustration of our study results is shown in Figure 5. We saw that after a year of curriculum-integrated Making within the scope of the activities that we deployed, the students in the Making group reported greater self-efficacy and interest in Making than the control group at year end. The Making group also had greater self-efficacy in being able to do science, although they were not necessarily more interested in science. As for questions of identity, the students in the Making group did not necessarily feel completely inducted as Makers even after a year. It is highly encouraging though that the Making students' interest in STEM careers and sense of being possible STEM people were greater than the control group and increased over time. This is echoed by the change seen in the students' career choices on the open-ended survey question from the beginning to end of the year.

Table 4. Students' self-reported career choices (A1: Making group pre-survey; A2: Making group post-survey; B: Control group post-survey)

	A1	A2	B
Total Responses	117	115	61
Career Choice 1			
Unknowns	4	8	4
Medicine/Veterinarian	30	20	12
Total Responses Included	83	87	45
STEM careers	4 (4.82%)	17 (19.54%)	1 (2.22%)
Non-STEM careers	78 (95.18%)	70 (80.46%)	44 (97.78%)
Career Choice 2			
Unknowns	9	6	4
Medicine/Veterinarian	11	20	13
Total Responses Included	97	89	44
STEM careers	13 (13.40%)	17 (19.10%)	4 (9.09%)
Non-STEM careers	91 (86.60%)	72 (80.90%)	40 (90.91%)

Science examination scores were correlated with the students' Maker identity, science self-efficacy and science interest. This suggests that confidence and interest in science are important for academic achievement in the subject. More interestingly, the greater a student's identification as a Maker, the better his or her academic science performance was.

To answer our research questions directly thus, our approach to the integration of Making into the school curriculum: i) contributed to changes in Making self-efficacy and interest, and trended toward a Maker identity; ii) contributed to changes in science variables on self-efficacy and identity. No effect was found on science interest, which was already high from the onset; iii) did not lead to significant differences in science examination scores, but the latter co-varied with the students' level of Maker identity, science self-efficacy and science interest; and iv) contributed to qualitative changes in the career choices of a number of students.

These findings highlight key points that we believe add to our knowledge of the potential of curriculum-integrated Making in schools. First, Making may not necessarily increase one's interest in the subject matter of the Making. We found that after our Making intervention, the students had greater confidence in their ability to do science, and thus could possibly see themselves as future scientists. However, they were not significantly more interested in science as a topic. Borrowing Blikstein's 'keychain syndrome' scenario [10], the children making keychains using digital fabrication would be more confident that they know about keychains, and could possibly even see themselves as future keychain makers, but they may not become more interested in the topic of keychains itself. We suggest three possible explanations for this: 1) engagement in Making may be an enabler of science interest, but not a determinant of it as it seems to be for self-efficacy; 2) the increase in self-efficacy may not have crossed a certain threshold needed to produce gains in interest. Lenox and Subich [60] described such a threshold effect for self-efficacy and vocational interests; or 3) our interest measure suffered from a ceiling effect since the pre-test scores were already high and the scale did not allow the students to rate much higher in the post-test.

The significant change in science identity however was also reflected in the career choices that the students listed. More students listed STEM-related jobs as their first career choice after our intervention. These students gained both interest and self-efficacy, i.e., the child is strongly interested in STEM and believes she is able to do that job. More students indicated STEM-related jobs as their second career choice as well at year end. Out of the 17 students, 9 indicated a STEM job for second career choice but not as first choice. These students may have gained self-efficacy, but not necessarily interest. For these students, Making may have expanded their 'toolbox of skills' and broadened their scope of possibilities in life, even though they may not change their career goals to becoming scientists or engineers.

And second, curriculum-integrated Making may not be a direct contributor to academic achievement, but function more in indirect ways. The higher science examination scores for the Making group were not significantly different from the scores of the control group. However, the scores were mediated by science self-efficacy and interest that were both correlated with Making variables, that we affected through our intervention. In the classroom thus, it appears that Making is a multi-step function that may contribute to STEM learning.

Limitations

We acknowledge that our study has several limitations that should be noted. First, we intervened for a week in every unit in the science curriculum. This amounted to a Making week every six weeks for the students in each class over the academic year. It is certainly possible that a continuous Making intervention may lead to amplified effects that we were not able to detect in our study. Second, no fixed guidelines exist currently as to how to integrate Making into an elementary school curriculum. We drew from an interdisciplinary group to design our Making kits and activities that made up the intervention. It is possible that implementation technicalities may have influenced results.

Third, the school ecosystem is very complex. It was not possible for us to account for all the potential confounding variables that may have influenced the students throughout the year, e.g., exposure to outside activities, teaching styles, etc. Although all students were from the same school and neighborhood, and the groups were likely comparable on many accounts, there are dynamics in student selection and classroom and school organization that affect students' ratings and performance. Nonetheless, the study provided important data that may hopefully help us to understand more about how Making may function in public school settings. Finally, although we intervened for only selected learning standards for each science unit in the curriculum, our analysis looked at the impact on overall science examination scores. In future analysis, we will isolate the examination script for questions relating only to the standards covered in our Making intervention.

CONCLUSION

We presented results from a year-long study with over 120 students from three grades in a public elementary school. We evaluated the influence of students engaging in a sustained manner with Making technology integrated with a public school curriculum on their self-efficacy, interest, and self-identity with respect to Making and STEM. Our study results showed that the greatest relationship is with science self-efficacy and identity. We also saw that our intervention approach of using Making as the tool for learning science may influence science examination scores through the students' science self-efficacy and identity. These results are important because children between ages 8 and 11 are beginning to develop their nascent self-identities by discovering what they may be good at. This efficacy and possible identity can support greater resiliency in the study of STEM subjects as they progress through school.

Our work provides a foundation for many other trajectories. For example, future investigations can look at students' interactions with other Making technologies beyond electronics, such as programming with microcontrollers. Our study focused on the third- to the fifth-grade in science. Further research may relate the approach to other K-12 grade levels and to other subjects like mathematics or the language arts. And finally, another potential direction may be to see if Making skills acquired in the course of classroom activity may impact their interest and use of Making beyond the classroom.

ACKNOWLEDGMENTS

We would like to thank the school principal, the curriculum coordinators, the participating teachers, the students and all the staff at Neal Elementary School, Bryan, TX for participating in our program. We also acknowledge the support of the Bryan Independent School District. We also thank the reviewers, particularly the meta-reviewer who helped us refine the paper. This research has been supported by NSF grant #DRL-1433770.

REFERENCES

1. Dougherty, D., *The Maker Mindset*, in *Design, Make, Play: Growing the Next Generation of STEM Innovators*, M. Honey and D.E. Kanter, Editors. 2013, Routledge. p. 7-11.

2. Halverson, E.R. and K.M. Sheridan, *The Maker Movement in Education.* Harvard Educational Review, 2014. **84**(4): p. 495-504.
3. Meintjes, R. and H. Schelhowe. *Inclusive Interactives: the Transformative Potential of Making and Using Craft-Tech Social Objects Together in an After-School Centre.* in *Proceedings of the The 15th International Conference on Interaction Design and Children.* 2016. ACM.
4. Hudson, N., C. Alcock, and P.K. Chilana. *Understanding Newcomers to 3D Printing: Motivations, Workflows, and Barriers of Casual Makers.* in *Proceedings of the SIGCHI Conference on Human Factors in Computing Systems.(To appear).* 2016.
5. Lindtner, S., S. Bardzell, and J. Bardzell. *Reconstituting the utopian vision of making: HCI after technosolutionism.* in *Proceedings of the 2016 CHI Conference on Human Factors in Computing Systems.* 2016. ACM.
6. Taylor, N., U. Hurley, and P. Connolly. *Making community: the wider role of makerspaces in public life.* in *Proceedings of the 2016 CHI Conference on Human Factors in Computing Systems.* 2016. ACM.
7. Bull, G. and R. Berry, *Connected Classroom Classroom Engineering and Craft Technologies.* Learning and Leading with Technology, 2011. **38**(5): p. 26.
8. Bull, G., et al., *An educational framework for digital manufacturing in schools.* 3D Printing and Additive Manufacturing, 2015. **2**(2): p. 42-49.
9. Blikstein, P. and D. Krannich. *The makers' movement and FabLabs in education: experiences, technologies, and research.* in *Proceedings of the 12th International Conference on Interaction Design and Children.* 2013. ACM.
10. Blikstein, P., *Digital Fabrication and 'Making'in Education: The Democratization of Invention.* FabLabs: Of Machines, Makers and Inventors, 2013: p. 1-21.
11. Nemorin, S., *A critical perspective on 'Making'in school: The implementation of 3D printing in high-school settings,* in *FabLearn Conference.* 2015, Stanford University: Palo Alto, CA.
12. Papavlasopoulou, S., M.N. Giannakos, and L. Jaccheri, *Empirical Studies on the Maker Movement, a Promising Approach to Learning: A Literature Review.* Entertainment Computing, 2016.
13. Flores, C. and T. Springer. *Authentic Learning and Assessment in the Self-Directed Environment of a Middle School Maker Space.* in *Workshop on Digital Fabrication in Education at the 12th International Conference on Interaction Design and Children (IDC).* 2013. Bremen, Germany.
14. Posch, I. and G. Fitzpatrick. *First steps in the FabLab: experiences engaging children.* in *Proceedings of the 24th Australian Computer-Human Interaction Conference.* 2012. ACM.
15. Sheridan, K., et al., *Learning in the making: A comparative case study of three makerspaces.* Harvard Educational Review, 2014. **84**(4): p. 505-531.
16. Worsley, M., *Making with Understanding: Research on Studies from a Constructionist Learning Environment,* in *Graduate School of Education.* 2014, Stanford University.
17. Nemorin, S. and N. Selwyn, *Making the best of it? Exploring the realities of 3D printing in school.* Research Papers in Education, 2016: p. 1-18.
18. Hamner, E., et al. *Robot Diaries: Broadening Participation in the Computer Science Pipeline through Social Technical Exploration.* in *AAAI Spring Symposium: Using AI to Motivate Greater Participation in Computer Science.* 2008.
19. Hamner, E., T. Lauwers, and D. Bernstein. *The Debugging Task: Evaluating a Robotics Design Workshop.* in *AAAI Spring Symposium: Educational Robotics and Beyond.* 2010.
20. Jenkins, T. and I. Bogost. *Escaping the Sandbox: Making and Its Future.* in *Proceedings of the Ninth International Conference on Tangible, Embedded, and Embodied Interaction.* 2015. ACM.
21. Halverson, E.R. and K. Sheridan, *The Maker Movement in Education.* Harvard Educational Review, 2014. **84**(4): p. 495-504.
22. Martin, L. and C. Dixon. *Youth Conceptions of Making and the Maker Movement.* in *12th International Conference on Interaction Design and Children (IDC).* 2013. ACM.
23. New York Hall of Science, *Making Meaning (M2).* 2013: New York: New York Hall of Science.
24. Kuznetsov, S. and E. Paulos. *Rise of the expert amateur: DIY projects, communities, and cultures.* in *Proceedings of the 6th Nordic Conference on Human-Computer Interaction: Extending Boundaries.* 2010. ACM.
25. Tanenbaum, J., et al. *Democratizing Technology: Pleasure, Utility and Expressiveness in DIY and Maker Practice.* in *CHI '13.* 2013. Paris, France: ACM.
26. Katterfeldt, E.-S., N. Dittert, and H. Schelhowe, *Designing digital fabrication learning environments for Bildung: Implications from ten years of physical computing workshops.* International Journal of Child-Computer Interaction, 2015.
27. Qiu, K., et al. *A curriculum for teaching computer science through computational textiles.* in *Proceedings of the 12th International Conference on Interaction Design and Children.* 2013. ACM.
28. Ornelas, N.O., G. Calderon, and P. Blikstein. *Makers in Residence Mexico: Creating the Conditions for Invention.* in *Short paper at FabLearn Europe: Digital Fabrication in Education Conference.* 2014.
29. Chu, S.L., et al., *Making the Maker: A Means-to-an-Ends approach to nurturing the Maker mindset in elementary-aged children.* International Journal of Child-Computer Interaction, 2015.
30. Alexander, C., et al. *Piloting innovative learning experiences: Measuring outcomes of digital fabrication activities across five classes.* in *Proceedings of Society for Information Technology & Teacher Education International Conference 2013.* 2013.
31. Holbert, N., *Leveraging cultural values and "ways of knowing" to increase diversity in maker activities.* International Journal of Child-Computer Interaction, 2016.
32. Bandura, A., *Self-efficacy: toward a unifying theory of behavioral change.* Psychological review, 1977. **84**(2): p. 191.
33. Bandura, A., *Self-efficacy mechanism in human agency.* American psychologist, 1982. **37**(2): p. 122.
34. Bandura, A., N.E. Adams, and J. Beyer, *Cognitive processes mediating behavioral change.* Journal of personality and social psychology, 1977. **35**(3): p. 125.
35. Bandura, A. and D.H. Schunk, *Cultivating competence, self-efficacy, and intrinsic interest through proximal self-*

motivation. Journal of personality and social psychology, 1981. **41**(3): p. 586.
36. Bandura, A., et al., *Self-efficacy beliefs as shapers of children's aspirations and career trajectories.* Child development, 2001. **72**(1): p. 187-206.
37. Wang, X., *Why students choose STEM majors motivation, high school learning, and postsecondary context of support.* American Educational Research Journal, 2013: p. 0002831213488622.
38. AAUW, *Shortchanging Girls, Shortchanging America.* 1990, American Association of University Women: Washington DC.
39. Zimmer, L. and S. Bennett. *Gender Differences on the California Statewide Assessment of Attitudes and Achievement in Science.* in *Annual Meeting of the American Educational Research Association.* 1987.
40. Piaget, J., *The language and thought of the child (1923).* 1973, New York: World.
41. Osborne, J.W., *Identification with Academics and Academic Success among Community College Students.* Community College Review, 1997. **25**(1): p. 59-67.
42. Festinger, L., *A theory of cognitive dissonance.* Vol. 2. 1962: Stanford university press.
43. Carver, C.S. and M.F. Scheier, *Control theory: A useful conceptual framework for personality–social, clinical, and health psychology.* Psychological Bulletin, 1982. **92**(1): p. 111-135.
44. Higgins, E.T., *Self-discrepancy: a theory relating self and affect.* Psychological review, 1987. **94**(3): p. 319.
45. Swann, W.B., A. Stein-Seroussi, and R.B. Giesler, *Why people self-verify.* Journal of personality and social psychology, 1992. **62**(3): p. 392.
46. Setterlund, M.B. and P.M. Niedenthal, *" Who am I? Why am I here?" Self-esteem, self-clarity, and prototype matching.* Journal of personality and social psychology, 1993. **65**(4): p. 769.
47. Hannover, B. and U. Kessels, *Self-to-prototype matching as a strategy for making academic choices. Why high school students do not like math and science.* Learning and instruction, 2004. **14**(1): p. 51-67.
48. Beyers, R.N., *Nurturing creativity and innovation through FabKids: A case study.* Journal of Science Education and Technology, 2010. **19**(5): p. 447-455.
49. Chan, J., T. Pondicherry, and P. Blikstein. *LightUp: an augmented, learning platform for electronics.* in *Proceedings of the 12th International Conference on Interaction Design and Children.* 2013. ACM.
50. Kafai, Y., D. Fields, and K. Searle, *Electronic textiles as disruptive designs: Supporting and challenging maker activities in schools.* Harvard Educational Review, 2014. **84**(4): p. 532-556.
51. McKay, C. and K. Peppler. *MakerCart: a mobile fab lab for the classroom.* in *Position Paper at the Interaction Design for Children Conference (IDC).* 2013.
52. Hughes, J., G. Gadanidis, and C. Yiu, *Digital Making in Elementary Mathematics Education.* Digital Experiences in Mathematics Education, 2016: p. 1-15.
53. Angello, G., et al. *Making as the New Colored Pencil: Translating Elementary Curricula into Maker Activities.* in *Proceedings of the The 15th International Conference on Interaction Design and Children.* 2016. ACM.
54. Harter, S., *Manual for the self-perception profile for children.* 1985: University of Denver.
55. The Maker Effect Foundation. *The Maker Mindset Assessment.* 2015 [cited 2015 July]; Available from: http://www.themakereffect.org/maker-research/.
56. Bandura, A., *Guide for constructing self-efficacy scales.* Self-efficacy beliefs of adolescents, 2006. **5**: p. 307-337.
57. Anderman, E.M., L.H. Anderman, and T. Griesinger, *The relation of present and possible academic selves during early adolescence to grade point average and achievement goals.* The Elementary School Journal, 1999: p. 3-17.
58. Robnett, R.D. and C. Leaper, *Friendship groups, personal motivation, and gender in relation to high school students' STEM career interest.* Journal of Research on Adolescence, 2013. **23**(4): p. 652-664.
59. Hayes, A.F., *PROCESS: A versatile computational tool for observed variable mediation, moderation, and conditional process modeling.* 2012: White Paper.
60. Lenox, R.A. and L.M. Subich, *The Relationship Between Self-Efficacy Beliefs and Inventoried Vocational Interests.* The Career Development Quarterly, 1994. **42**(4): p. 302-313.

"It's a Bomb!" – Material Literacy and Narratives of Making

Sophie Landwehr Sydow
Södertörn University &
Stockholm University
Huddinge, Sweden
sophie.landwehrsydow@sh.se

Jakob Tholander
Mobile Life @
Stockholm University
Stockholm, Sweden
jakobth@dsv.su.se

Martin Jonsson
Södertörn University
Huddinge, Sweden
martin.jonsson@sh.se

ABSTRACT

This paper analyses a series of events in which a discarded box found in a garbage room is examined and taken apart in the context of a makerspace. The participants' inquiry provided a rich and multifaceted experience in various settings, including puzzle-solving, exploring physical and digital materials, engaging people with different skills. The social engagements with and around the artifacts brought certain interpretative aspects to the fore. Situated acts of interpretation worked as ways of building a coherent narrative and a meaningful experience. In the paper, we highlight the relationship between on the one hand the subjects' skills and motivations to understand and make sense of the technology at hand which we call *material literacy*, and on the other hand the specific *material qualities* that encourage or trigger certain interpretations and experiences. The qualities we discuss are: opacity, risk, authenticity, uniqueness, age, and hybridity. This study allows us to reposition the contemporary understanding of makerspaces beyond that of being places for innovation and learning.

Author Keywords

Material literacy; Experience; Taking apart; Material qualities; Maker culture.

ACM Classification Keywords

H.5.m. Information interfaces and presentation (e.g., HCI): Miscellaneous.

INTRODUCTION

Vignette: *"Ok, that's enough for today". I gather my things and get ready to leave. When reaching the door, I spot two young men working in a corner of the room. They are sitting close together, talking with low voices. One of them is holding a battered plastic box. His hands are stained with oil and he is wearing a pair of worn-out jeans. I see circuit boards, cables and metal parts sticking out from the box. He is leaning over the other man's shoulder; both are staring at three computer screens with long rows of code.*

CHI 2017, May 06-11, 2017, Denver, CO, USA
© 2017 ACM. ISBN 978-1-4503-4655-9/17/05…$15.00
DOI: http://dx.doi.org/10.1145/3025453.3025529

The man standing wears a dark suit and a tie neatly in place. I walk over to see what is going on:
"What is this?" I ask. One of the men looks at me, "I opened this box and found all this: a microcontroller, cables, this fuse ... and some kind of explosive material. I thought that there is something special about it. Now we are trying to extract information from the code." Another bystander suddenly clears her throat, after a second of silence she says: "Explosives? So ... it's a bomb!?"
I take a step back and feel my heartbeat racing as I realize that we are all trapped in a basement.
"What – really?", I ask. The man looks at me and responds: "We don't know yet, but it's super exciting."

This event captures the essence of what evolved into an explorative journey for two members at a local makerspace. Like reading a well written crime story, this provided a rich experience with many dimensions such as solving a puzzle; handling explosives, deconstructing hardware and software, engaging people with different skillsets, tracing unknown participants and even trespassing private property. The whole experience ranged over a timespan of more than six years, but discoveries along the way led the participants back two decades in time to uncover the origins of the box.

Activities of taking technology apart and various forms of puzzle solving are common throughout the history of human-computer interaction (HCI), and the field provides several potential perspectives from which activities like this could be understood. Studies of similar engagements - maker activities in particular - have emphasized instrumental purposes and foregrounded aspects such as learning [6, 7, 33, 35], innovation [11, 21, 36, 45] and community building [2, 40, 41]. Such aspects were also present in our case, but on closer analysis it became obvious that they did not capture the essential qualities of what the activity was primarily about. Instead, it became salient that the two main participants engaged in these activities for the sake of the experience itself. Here several separate occasions and activities were tied together through the participants' interpretations of a complex mangle of things, materials, technologies, people, and situations, forming a coherent narrative. Central to the activities and to the overall experience that were formed was how the participants made sense of and interpreted the components and situations at hand. We are aware that all maker activities have experiential dimensions in their own right and do not deny any other aspects that come as effects.

The paper foregrounds the experiential dimensions of maker activities without reasoning about their purposes in the form of specific outcomes. To achieve this, our analysis focuses around the participants' processes of interpretation of the artifact, materials, code and electronics involved. This analytical approach has similarities to interpretative processes of reading, allowing us to portray the narrative aspects of the experiential efforts of the participants, putting to the fore how skills of interpretation and reading a narrative out the objects and components played a key role in forming their experience. Thereby, this lens allows us to see the close relationships between the multitudes of different activities, things, and materials, that were part of this case without foregrounding one before the other. This approach ties back to traditions in media and literature studies, where any object can be understood in terms of text, that can be subjected to an analysis in the form of interpretation and reading. A similar kind of practice has recently been introduced to HCI in the form of interaction criticism [3 and 5]. The kind of interpretative practices we discuss here does however not specifically refer to the analytical reading of a critic or a researcher, rather, it relates to the leisurely oriented reading that people engage with for the experience that it provides. The empirical part of this paper offers an ethnographic description of how the blue fiberglass box (figure 1), in the hands of the two men, becomes an object around which they built an individual and social experience and a shared narrative.

Based on the analysis of this case, we offer three main contributions to HCI. First and foremost, the paper suggests a repositioning of maker activities that reach beyond ideas around innovation and learning by focusing on how makerspace activities provide opportunities for co-creating narrative experiences.

Figure 1. The blue fiberglass box closed.

Second, we highlight the relation between the qualities of an artifact (fig. 1), its making and the experience that participants have around these qualities. We thereby contribute to the discussion on the interplay between computational materials and experience. Third, we position our discussion of the participants' skills and abilities within the broader discourse of what literacy - and in particular *material literacy* - can be about in relation to hybrid digital objects and things.

EXPERIENCE AND INTERPRETATION

In Grint and Woolgar's seminal study of the design and use of interactive technology [15] they propose the metaphor of technology as text, which has strongly influenced STS and HCI research. Along with this metaphor follows the idea that the technologies are written by designers and consequently read by users. One central aspect that this metaphor provides is the view of interaction with technology as essentially *interpretative*. Also in work of Akrich and Latour [1] and Suchman [39] related notions of design and interaction as processes of scripting and de-scripting are used to emphasize how certain forms of use cannot be pre-formulated into artifacts, but always goes through processes of subjective de-scription on behalf of the user. Such interpretative perspectives on interaction has strongly influenced HCI research for instance through notions like open-endedness in design [34] and ambiguity [12]. A design-oriented critique of the positions of Grint and Woolgar and other scholars argues that the metaphor of technology as text becomes overly essentialist by suggesting that an artifact could be open to any kind of interpretation [16].

Another way of approaching this is to situate the interpretation of artifacts in a context of narrative and storytelling. McCarthy and Wright [24] explicitly tie the notion of experience to that of narrative. In HCI, narratives have been widely explored, often focusing on creating means and tools for users to create different types of stories. In McCarthy and Wright's conceptualization, they propose that we frame and structure life events in terms of coherent narratives in order to make sense of the world [24]. Thus, the narrative of experience does not necessarily mirror what has occurred, but consist of selective and subjective interpretations constructed for various purposes. This will also be emphasized in our analysis of the participants' interpretations of the components and the disassembly of the blue box, reflecting their tracing of its functionality and origin and how these formed their experience. As substantial interaction design research suggests, the kind of interpretations we can expect users to make from certain artifacts is affected both by the users' different skills and experiences, but of course also by the characteristics of the artifact, in terms of for example affordances, material qualities and constraints [42]. There have been several attempts to conceptualize how the characteristics and behaviors of computational materials affect experience, in terms of for example use qualities [22], or experiential qualities [18, 23, 38]. Related here is also the ongoing discussion in HCI around materiality and the role of physical and digital materials in interaction design. The material discussion in HCI suggests a move away from the idea that things are either physical, digital or computational to instead approach these as primarily material [10, 37, 44]. This move extends our understanding of digital, physical and hybrid materials and provides a common ground from which to explore these issues, a stance that plays well with the case at hand where the participants engage both with physical circuit boards, as well as with digital code. Conceptually the notion of material can here be characterized as *"embodiments through which properties can be experienced and performed"*, be it in physical, temporal form or state of matter [13]. Building on this view, we think that there is need to further explore how materials shape ways of doing and how practice is rooted in the experience of those materials.

To conclude this brief note on experience and interpretation, we note that experiences in engagements with technology emerge out of interplay of a complex set of factors, involving the participants and their previous experiences, certain qualities of the artifacts and materials, and how the separate activities are situated in a larger context.

What is worth pointing out here is however that to understand the unfolding of experience we should examine both the artifacts with its material qualities as well as the acts of subjective meaning making and interpretation. The question of the role of interpretation for the unfolding of experience becomes especially prominent in the case at hand, where the participants do not engage with technology in the way it was designed for. Engagements with technology, that does not fall into the realm of using or playing, are not as easily understood in terms of people's experiences around them. For activities, such as designing, making or (as in the current case) taking things apart, the lenses used to analyze them tend to focus on instrumental qualities and outcomes, such as learning or collaboration benefits.

MAKING AND TAKING APART

Numerous researchers in HCI have previously explored maker culture and the situated practices and activities that making brings to the fore. In current research, the emancipatory and democratizing potential of making and maker culture is regarded as promising, highlighting making as means to rethink educational approaches [6, 30, 35], spark innovation [11, 21, 36, 45], and to increase interest in and participation with technology [2, 40, 41].

Research on makerspace activities tend to focus on *constructive* practices with numerous labels such as making, crafting, tinkering, do-it-yourself (DIY), repair and reuse [7, 25, 30, 31]. As will be shown in our study, all activities taking place in makerspaces are however not about making. There is also a set of activities that is better described as acts of *deconstruction*, including practices such as hacking, un-crafting and reverse engineering [4, 17, 27, 28, 33].

Examples of practices around taking apart and disassembling electronics and computational things and objects have been extensively explored in HCI, foremost notable as means for fostering understanding and learning. Construction and deconstruction as a form of tinkering or bricolage practice are for example central in Papert's seminal works on constructionism and learning-by-making [29]. Another prominent example of how deconstruction is related to learning is the notion of *reverse engineering*, which can be described as an unfolding process that through careful and structured disassembly uncovers the details and the knowledge that is contained within an artifact [19]. Originating from mechanical engineering education it deals with a detailed study of a product including its material, structure, surface, qualities and operating conditions [8]. To learn what a product is made of; reverse engineering is foremost used in cases where blueprints or layouts are missing and when existing artifacts are to be imitated or rebuilt in a later stage. Scholars teaching the practice describe reverse engineering broadly as a process for discovering underlying fundamental principles that enable a device [26].

Another related practice is that of *hacking*, which originally relates to the activity of finding ways to invade or hack systems, and which therefore possess rather negative connotations. However, as Rosner and Bean point out, this meaning changes when transformed from digital computing to the material world [33]. Previous research in this field includes hacking physical materials such as IKEA furniture [33], self-made tools at the hackerspace [4] or as a starting point for reuse and reconfigurations of material [17]. Ames et al. conclude that these practices *"are often celebrated as a more authentic engagement with technology and a return to old 'cherished' and 'more physical' materials"* [2]. The activities of opening and taking apart computational things have also been explored in the context of interaction design processes, where they become an integral part of the design activities [14], to develop a sensitivity and understanding for the design materials at hand, or for reaching common ground and shared understandings within a design team [28]. Recent work also introduces the notion of *un-crafting* as an attempt to provide a coherent approach to engage with the manifold understandings of taking apart objects, devices and materials [27].

The research mentioned above tend to highlight the outcomes of deconstruction activities such as the development of new knowledge and skills, how it aids the creation of novel artifacts, or social purposes such as developing shared understandings as well as fostering collaboration. What have been less explored in HCI research is how taking things apart can be meaningful as an activity you engage in for its own sake. Here we would like to bring to the fore other driving forces that may bring meaning to such activities such as curiosity, the excitement of following traces, or reflecting on interpretations.

METHOD

As part of a half-year ethnography at a local makerspace, this case captured our attention amidst its inquiry process, which is featured as a vignette in the beginning of this paper. The study site is a community driven and crowdfunded makerspace, which was initiated by a group of people in 2013 and located in Northern Europe. The makerspace has more than 100 active paying lab members each month and is in the basement of a startup hub. The six-month long ethnography, conducted by the first author, took place at site with visits between one up to three times a week, observing maker practices and following multiple maker projects, which varied in size and scale. In this case the role of the researcher was the one of an observer, deliberately taking a step back by capturing ongoing activities and practice.

The activities captured in this case, stretch over several months, and the associated narrative has a timeframe that ranges over several years. The presented data is collected using photographs and field notes, taken at site or shortly after the observations. A set of semi-structured interviews was also conducted and recorded, focusing on the participants' recollections of the activities, in order to fill gaps in the story.

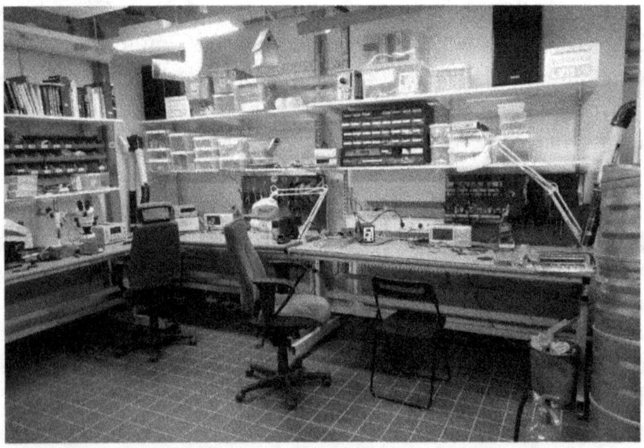

Figure 2. The study site: The Makerspace electronics corner.

THE STORY OF THE BLUE BOX

In the following section, we present how the box (see fig. 1) was found and the subsequent investigation that followed. This series of events is organized and presented in five parts: *The garbage room, the box, the components, the code,* and an *epilogue*. In regards to the timeline, we are interweaving different storylines, which stretch over a period of more than twenty years. As time is an important factor in this presented case, it is relevant to note that the participants' various engagements build the primary chronological arc and our involvement through observation and subsequent analysis can be regarded as a secondary level of capturing the ongoing practice.

Chapter 1 – The Garbage Room

Svante is a twenty-eight-year-old man with interest in technologies and machinery, ranging from tools and apparatus to digital, mechanical and electronic gadgets. He particularly likes to explore things that are strange and unknown to him. Svante has a history of scavenging and fishing up weird objects from open waters or searching through private and secluded places. Some of his earlier findings suggest that Svante does not only want to possess the object, but much like a collector does, he creates meaning by following up the object's history, its original purpose and where it came from. Svante is skilled in fixing motors and vehicles. In the makerspace, he is known as a hands-on guy, with skills and knowledge in engineering and fixing tools and machinery. In a previous account, he mentioned that he is often amused about other makers fearing real machinery, fuel and hands-on dirty work: *"The geeks are so very afraid of the smell of gasoline - like as if something would explode right away or something".*

Back in 2010, while sniffing around in the closed-up garbage room of a large insurance company, trespassing the grounds otherwise closed to the public, he made one particular find. Svante came across a blue box made from fiberglass plastic, measuring approximately 20x35x20 cm. For most people this would seem just like an ordinary robust plastic storage box, of the kind that you would find in any garage or store fishing gear. During the interview with Svante he reflected about his discovery of the box: *"There was a lot of interesting stuff there, but this box just captured my attention. What could it be?"* Only from seeing it lying around amidst garbage, he was drawn to it. Despite being aware of that it would be illegal to take the box with him he could not just leave it there, arguing; "*it was to be thrown away anyhow*". Something in the mere appearance of the box sparked his attention and interest, seeing a possible function of the box from small details on its surface: *"I saw the lid on the box and something that looked like an antenna, ... there was this loop which gained my attention. First I thought it had something to do with measuring radioactive samples".*

Further on, during a later discussion we asked whether the box could be dangerous. Hence this was of importance, as he responded: *"Oh yes, I was scared, but the box was very interesting. You could say that it sparked my interest. And I just couldn't let it go".* These quotes illustrate Svante's ability to read possibilities from small details on the box and how this triggers his fascination and excitement for understanding what the box could be about. His previous experiences together with skills in seeing subtle details form the starting point. The box hereby promised an experience that was worth investing significant time; effort and risk. Forming this experience comes through the interweaving of Svante's interest in exploring technical things, searching the surroundings for potentially exciting and adventurous objects that would take him into detours and places where he is not supposed to be, just to build a personal adventure in his everyday life. It is not just any weird mechanical or electronic thing that captures his attention; it is something in the object that suggests exploring the unknown, with an exciting or dangerous potential. Here the experience emerges and develops in situ, and is continuously constructed through

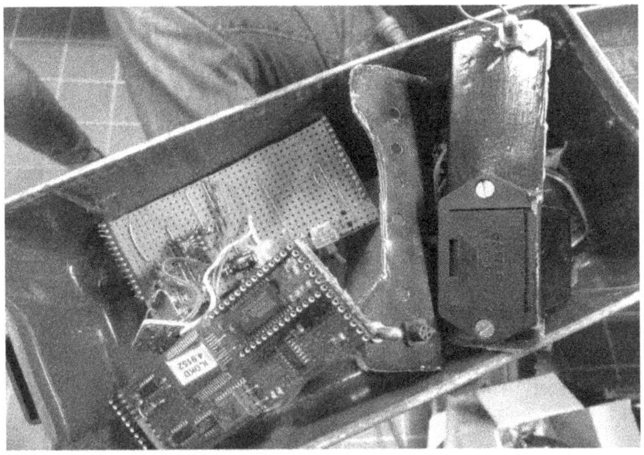

Figure 3. Unsorted components in the blue box

his investigations of the objects characteristics, the place where it is located, and the situational circumstances under which it was found.

Chapter 2 – The Box

Coming back from the scavenger hunt at the garbage room Svante was eager to know what the box would contain. First, he started considering the character surface, trying to find out how it could have been constructed. It had protected areas on the sides and when looking closely he could see that there were things embedded underneath the fiberglass. On closer inspection, he reflected that: *"I could see that the box had protection from each angle. It has reinforced walls, top lock, the base and everywhere else."* He opened the sealed box with tools from his garage. On the question on what would be the worst thing that could happen he responded: *"It could explode or go off in some kind of way. I just hoped it wouldn't have any long-term effects. But even if I would have known that it's dangerous, I would have opened it anyway."* Obviously, this was not the first-time Svante had been opening sealed objects. The fact that it might be dangerous did not make him hesitate to investigate the box further. Instead they seem to be one of the primary motivations for carrying on. However, it turned out that the box in this case was basically empty. There was no explosion, no valuables and no treasure inside. The only thing was that caught his attention were some metal contraptions on each side (shown in fig. 5a). Disappointed that there seemed to be nothing more to it than just an empty box, Svante saw no immediate urge of proceeding. He left the box lying around in his apartment and at some point, it ended up in the back of his wardrobe, and he lost interest for several years. During that time the box served a different purpose such as storing cigarettes. However, it's mere presence reminded Svante of this unsolved mystery. *"But you know this box annoyed me and my friends for a long time. I had it like five years where it was just standing around but always wondered, what its original purpose might have been".* Instead of just tossing that project aside, he kept it and continued having ideas, but still lacking proof he did not know how to proceed.

In this first step of inspection, the visible surface of the box is investigated (fig. 4a), revealing details that contribute to the initial ideas and first assumptions about the construction of the box and its origin. The potential danger and risk that became apparent were fundamental to the experience that he started to build around it. That something might go wrong fuels his curiosity and determination to explore. The opacity of the box and the limited clues of its intended purpose also made it interesting, suggesting a potential challenging investigation. Despite this, at this point he did not see enough potential in where the exploration of the box could take him, leaving it lying about in his apartment serving practical or no apparent purposes. This long and ongoing time period further builds up its status as an unsolved mystery.

Chapter 3 – The Components

In January 2016, Svante decided to bring the box to the makerspace. What sparked him to continue to further investigate the box was a key moment while sitting around with friends in his apartment, and the blue box suddenly caught his attention, he recalls: *"It was the texture and the color, it was exactly the same as CIT boxes have".* The rifled distinctive texture of the box was specific features he recognized (fig. 4a). Realizing that it could be a CIT (cash-in-transit) box turned out to be a big moment for Svante, as he had recently come across a case with similar textures and patterns. This realization motivated him to investigate the artifact again. Now, starting to form and idea of the purpose of the box, made Svante curious about the different parts, and how they were constructed. This time around Svante decided to break into the two metal compartments on each side of the box, revealing a mixture of cables, boards, microcontrollers, lamps and battery components. Figure 3 shows the inside of the box with the components dragged out from their original position. Seeing this spurred his engagement wanting to understand what the box could be about: "*It became really interesting when I discovered the PCB boards and the microcontroller and not just mechanical but also electronic parts*". After closely inspecting the boards several times, Svante discovered that one of the PCB boards carried a vague black imprint from a well-known security company next to the chip (fig. 5b).

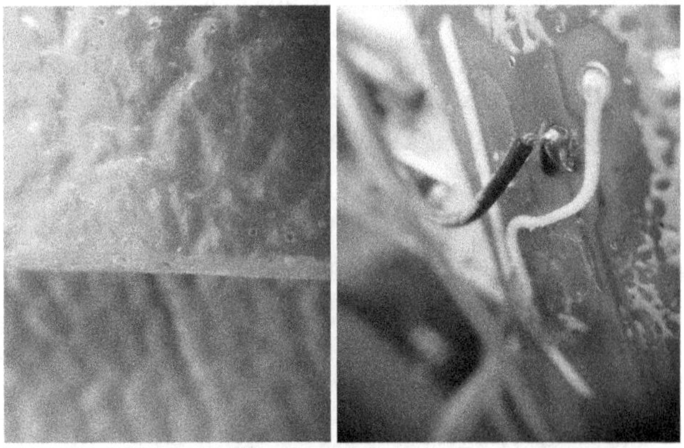

Figure 4. a) Pattern and texture of the box in detail. b) Close-up on soldering on the battered PCB board.

"*Suddenly I was a thousand percent sure that it must be a CIT box. And then I wanted to know so much more!*" These findings triggered Svante to dig deeper not only into how box was constructed and what was for, but also into the larger story around the box, who made it, for what purpose, and why it ended up in that locked up garbage room. The reason for bringing the box to the makerspace in the first place was to ask other members for help and to share the experience. This time he asked a skilled programmer, Ola for help.

In comparison to Svante, Ola is more into software, computer security, and hacking. As both men continued to explore the insides of the box together, and inspecting the different parts more closely, two elements caught their attention: the two PCB boards and the microprocessor. When commenting on the soldering work on the PCB boards (fig. 4b). Ola reflects: "*This looks like a mix between thru hole and surface mount construction, so this may probably have taken place right within the transition phase*". What Ola suggests here is that the dominant construction method for electronics between the 1960's –and 1990's was the thru-hole mount method, which was then replaced by surface mounting. Telling that this form of combination is noticeable in the boards, the electronic construction could be traced back to the mid-90s. In further discussing the properties of the board Svante said: *"Something which is kind of interesting is how much that is made with a proper printed circuit board and how much of is made on a prototype board" (*see fig. 5c*)*.

They also agree that the work on some of the PCB boards is "*impressive soldering*", here switching focus from the materials to relate to the handcrafting skills of the person making the box in the first place. Ola continued that another way of telling apart an old circuit board from a new one is the way in which the angles are drawn in the circuit boards pattern (fig. 5b). He recalls, "*Back in the 1970's people used hand-drawn circuits, which then tended to have no corners at all, but they were replaced by 90 degrees' sharp angles and today we have rounded corners instead. [...] So that is indeed an indicator and gives information how old this object might be"*. When inspecting the board closer, Ola starts arguing that the included chip (visible in fig. 5b) tells a story as well since; "*this chip is socketed which means that it must be removed for programming and that tells us two things: Firstly, it's old because if you compare it to new systems, they use other systems for circuit programming.*

Arriving at this point of the exploration the object was taken apart; the fixture pieces were broken order to gain access to the internal components. Svante got in contact with Ola, and the makerspace electronic corner (shown in fig. 2) served as a space to meet and explore the different electronic, mechanical and computational components. The focus here shifts from looking at the entire object to instead investigate its constituent parts and materials, searching for clues to further their understanding of the box. By inspecting the components in detail, reading from the materials with Svante and Ola's combined skills, they made it possible to start forming two images: One of the functioning of the object through knowledge of the content's various physical and digital qualities and the idea of the box being a prototype which is read out from traces the material provided. Secondly they start to envision the original maker of the box, reflecting on the skills and identity of that person.

Chapter 4 – The Code

At this point Svante is convinced that it is a prototype for a CIT-box they got their hands on. However, the physical explorations still did not provide a complete picture. Svante "*really wanted to know more*", which led them to take a closer look at the digital content. This was the main reason why he asked Ola for help so they could extract information from the chip itself. When discussing the qualities of the chip Ola reflected: "*It was just a matter of knowing that it would store something and then we just needed to find out what*". Using an imported chip reader from China he got hold on some rows of code. "*First it looked like weren't gonna be successful. There was just so little information*". Ola tried different software to access what the chip had stored but several of them failed. Finally, he decided to try and crack the information by using a disassembler, (a piece of software that translates machine code into assembly code). Since each assembly language is specific to a computer architecture this made this procedure challenging, but information on its brand and serial number provided Ola with a clue on where to start (fig. 5b). The software then "*literally disassembles it. It's really an obscure software. It's not something a lot of people need to do, basically it's virus researchers or people that crack applications*". The extracted assembly code provided Ola with a structure he was familiar with and could interpret. In one of the interviews, Ola reflected on the assembly process and explained the steps of the software more thoroughly: "*What it's doing now while working through the program is that it's basically going through all*

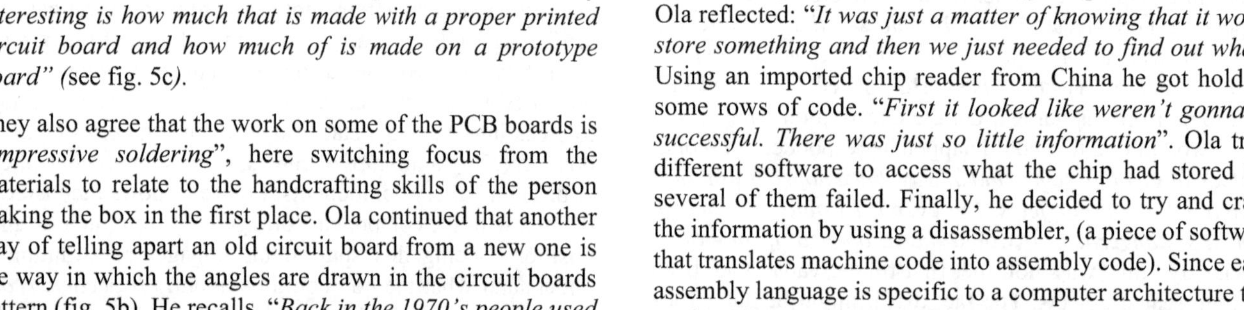

Figure 5. a) Re-assembled box with metal components on each side. b) PCB board with 90 degree sharp angles, also showing the socketed chip and security imprint. c). The prototype board closeup.

those possible parts so that it can work out like all the possible options at all the places the program would go and then it makes a map of this". The assembler code as such is not very user-friendly and demands a certain level of expertise to interpret. The screen then showed long rows of line numbers and data strings: "*In order to find the code you need to scroll down lots and lots*". Ola explained that the program "*is doing a lot of guesswork. But technically if you would run this through a compiler it should actually spit out the original program in the end*". At this point Ola had a quite good picture of the overall workings of the code. However, Svante was curious in finding information that could help him trace the origin of the original maker. Ola explained: "*I looked which one has to do with anti-piracy and these strings had the name of the company in them*". In another string, he also found a date indicating when it was built. Furthermore, an important observation from the reading of code was that it had a lot of blank space: "The *program just didn't take as much room. It kind of makes sense that they were gaps as they normally aren't filled up completely, so it's probably an early prototype.*"

The process of extracting, disassembling and assembling the code from the chip provided two important clues that contributed to Svante's hypothesis about the history and construction of the box. First Ola could read out the year it was created (1996) and a name that could lead to people who built it. Secondly, the fact that there was lots of blank space on the chip strengthened their assumption that the box was an early prototype of something that would later be refined. Here they drew a conclusion that its maker was an individual inventor that had been working on the box on his own. This example also put to the fore the need for specific tools and knowledge. Here Ola's specific skillset came into play; he knew which hardware and software to use and how to read out data from old and discarded systems. By hacking into the system, being able to make meaning of the code and its underlying logic provided the missing pieces of information.

In a similar way as chemists' mixes in other materials (reagents) to spur a chemical reaction that may give clues about the chemical composition of a sample, the code is here "mangled" using a tool to make it give away clues. Additionally, the activities have clear illegal connotations, in regards to how to gain access to presumably pirated and cracked software, how to use them to hack into systems and to read out information. Here the notion of risk-taking and danger reappears, and the fact that the activity is playing with these elements work as a motivator.

Epilogue

"*I found the person who developed the box, I was at his home and actually talked to him yesterday*" Svante exclaims with delight a couple weeks after they could decode the program on the chip. To continue the search Svante had used the information from the program to find the specific company. By searching the Web, he got hold of more information on the company and its owners, realizing that the business, which was founded back in 1989 had been active until just recently. Svante had concluded that as the date of the box's chip dated back to 1996, the company had to be older than twenty years. The search pointed him to different addresses and people, which he had called by phone but without finding the right person. On a last attempt Svante, had decided to visit one of the addresses, but nobody had heard of the company or the owner before. Disappointed he went back to his car, but still convinced that there must be a way to find the origin of the box. As he had "*already come so far*" there was no idea of giving up at this point. Based on the company name he could find yet another address which he decided to try in person instead. After a short drive to a residential area, he found himself in front of a house that was only accessible by key code. He saw an older lady inside, standing on the stairs so he waved enthusiastically. The woman opened the door and with the blue box under his arm he asked for the company and its CEO, who was supposed to live there. "*That's my husband you are looking for*" she responded. Svante had finally discovered Carl, the person he was looking for. Carl was a retired engineer who has been working within the security sector for the past thirty years. "*Carl was more than surprised but also amazed to see the old box again. He said that it has been twenty years since he last saw the piece*". Even though he could just spare a couple of minutes, Carl briefly told Svante the story behind the box.

It turned out to be just like Svante had anticipated; the blue box was a prototype for a CIT case. But not just any prototype: The box was the first prototype of its kind and included novel technology, which then, turned into a series of security cases for many years to come. Carl and his colleague were the first to work with liquid colors in that context: "*These were the first and companies actually still use liquid paint today, but this model is the first CIT case which has been approved and this one was the first prototype, which then later after iterations went into mass production*".

This was the point when Svante finally got all the answers to what the box was made for. The story was hereby tied together when Svante saw Carl's astonishment while confronted with this object from his past. The linking element in this final step here were the *digital traces* that Svante had found online both about the company and the people that had left them. To finish the search and taking the project to its end was critical to his whole endeavor. This allowed him to tie all the different elements of his experience together into a coherent narrative with a coherent ending.

The experience had involved a significant amount of technical explorations and social interactions. Svante drew advantage of the social networks around the makerspace to discuss his findings and ideas and could engage people at the site with different skills to draw out certain clues and discover traces, that finally allowed him to trace the box all the way back to its original maker.

DISCUSSION

A blue fiberglass box that turned out to be a prototype of a CIT-case filled with explosive material, electronics and digital components played a central role in this ethnographic account of unpacking the functions and history of the box. The question we would like to ask is what this story tells us in regards to design research, concerning experiences and interactions with technologies in makerspace settings? We have positioned this as a kind of narrative experience. Clearly, the box was in no way designed or intended to work as an object for someone to build a social and personal experience around. It was built to explode if someone tried to break into it, no more than that. Nevertheless, the dramaturgy provided by the explosive character of the box and the interpretations of the participants provided potential for the experiences that emerged.

The main points that we would like to make from these accounts, regard to how the experiences that are formed and the engaging and exciting story that the participants create for themselves, rely on their abilities and strong motivations to deconstruct and interpret the properties of the objects and materials that they encounter. To use a phrasing of Grint and Woolgar: *"The user is encouraged to find in her dealings with the machine an adequate puzzle for the solution which the machine offers"* [15: p. 73]. In a similar fashion, the participants in our study very much treated the box as a puzzle which could be solved by reading the associations to an overall narrative that could be made by interpreting the various objects and materials. The dramaturgy itself is a driving force and motivator that relates to previous experiences and future expectations. By conceptualizing the participant's abilities of interpreting the box as a form of close reading of its qualities, we aim to foreground essential aspects of what it means to understand, engage with and experience technology.

Just like the ability of reading, interpreting, and writing text is so much more than understanding the words and sentences on pieces of paper, *material literacy* as shown here, is about the ability to deeply engage with, take apart, contextualize, and create rich meaning – even stories – from a technological artifact. Our analysis shows that the complexity of the abilities involved in people's everyday technology encounters cannot be understood merely as "on-off" skills, but are of highly multifaceted and nuanced character depending on actors, settings and technology. An important elaboration of this interpretative process comes from the extended timeframe in which the participants' experiences are situated. These processes cannot merely be understood from what happens at a particular moment, but what needs to be put in relation to events, activities, and memories that extend over longer periods of people's lives.

Just like the interpretation of a piece of text depends on the specific historical and social contexts and situations in which they are encountered, the interpretation of a technological artifact has similar characteristics.

Material qualities

In interaction with technological objects, like the blue box, certain characteristics or *material qualities* emerge that encourage or trigger certain interpretations or experiences in people's engagements with the objects. These qualities are on the one hand inherent to the artifact, but are also *relational*, as the unfolding of experience is highly dependent on the relationship between the subjects' skills and motivations to understand and make sense of the technology, and the specific material qualities of the object at hand. We argue that the concepts of material literacy and material qualities become especially useful when exploring practices such as taking apart, un-crafting, making and hacking hybrid digital-physical objects. Here we identify six central qualities of the artifact and its constituent materials that that we believe were particularly important for how the activity played out. We also believe that these qualities are translatable to other areas of interaction design research:

Opacity – Given the original purposes of the box it was clearly designed to reveal as little as possible about how it was constructed, providing as few clues as possible to anyone wanting to break into it. Its character as a riddle that would be very difficult to solve is one of the primary driving forces that makes Svante curious. For Svante and Ola, the box is however partly transparent, allowing for inspection of the internal electronics and the assembly code, but require a combination of specific skills and tools to interpret. HCI has a history of designing objects for experiences in quite the opposite way; aiming for maximum transparency. Design-wise, this could be understood in terms of a continuum between opacity and transparency that is relational to each subject. The experience is thus shaped by this relationship between opacity and transparency and the nuances that arise from the participants' interpretations. In this case the interpretation by the participants allows them to see enough leads or clues, while still preserving a sense of mystery in the interaction.

Risk – An important attribute of the box is the fact that it contains explosives. The possibility that the box might blow up at any moment introduces an element of danger and risk, which influences the experiences of engaging with the box. Svante is from previous experiences aware of potential risks of tampering with the box, but this does not seem to discourage him from further explorations. Rather on the contrary: the explosives seem to add an element of excitement to the experience. The element of risk as part of an experience has previously been discussed by for example [20] as part of a discussion on the differences between interacting with digital versus physical media. It is noted that interactions in the physical world are associated with a more general sense of risk, as actions cannot be undone, and as you may get physically hurt. Further, risk can be used as a design parameter, since an increased level of risk typically leads to increased engagement and more careful and deliberate actions [20]. What is also notable here is that Svante's expertise and previous experience suggest that he can estimate the potential danger, while the element of risk still becomes an important dramaturgic element in the narrative that is being created.

Uniqueness – In their investigation of the box, Svante and Ola concluded that this object is a prototype, meaning that it is not mass-produced, and probably just exists as one instance, at least in this particular form. Previous discussions on how we appreciate uniqueness in interactive artifacts point to how uniquely crafted objects are always imperfect, and how the uniqueness of the produced outcomes can be linked to the skilled work of the crafts specialist [43]. The insight that the box is a prototype seemed to sustain their interest and made them see more value in the box than if it had been part of a series of identical CIT boxes. This uniqueness and the fact that is a crafted object, signals that someone has invested time, skills and effort into creating a single artifact.

Authenticity – In their study of bookbinding practices Rosner and Taylor discuss how objects gain the attribute of authenticity as a result of use and interactions with the material: "*It is through our continued interactions with material, and the impressions we leave on it, that deeper attachments evolve*" [32: p. 2668]. In our case, Svante and Ola showed an interest and a fascination of the original maker and the context for which the box was aimed for. The box revealed certain traces of these, such as in the "*impressive soldering work*", or in the imprints on the circuit board pointing to a security company. These traces, together with the place of discovery and the specific purpose for which the box was built, contributes to the sense of authenticity and points to a history of previous engagements.

Age – That the box is for a computational object relatively old, is an important ingredient in the engagements with it. The age adds to the sense of mystery and an important part of the inquiry concerns determining the age of the object. Here Svante and Ola can approximate the age of the box, as the circuit boards holds certain signifiers that point to specific time periods. Such age-related properties have previously been described in terms of *material traces* that" concretize *a unique location in time and space and highlighting the humans' role in recognizing that distance*" [31: p. 1651]. Also, as the box no longer fills its original purpose, it can be considered obsolete, or even dead. Nevertheless, through their engagements, Svante and Ola bring it back to life, as it becomes the center of their inquiry. Similarly noted by Jackson and Kang – "*As work with found, broken and obsolete objects makes clear, there are 'lives' to our technologies beyond the contexts and functions for which they were originally designed*" [17: p. 457].

Hybridity – In the presented case, the box is disassembled into its constituent materials, electronics and code. Svante can make sense of most of the electronics, plastics and explosives, but when it comes to the details of the electronics and the software, he needs the specific competences and skills from Ola. The way of approaching artifacts as hybrids, forming compositions of different materials is addressed by for example [44], who uses the term computational composites to describe artifacts that have both digital and physical components. A main argument made is that the composite artifact is more than the sum of its parts, with its own unique qualities. In a similar manner, even though our box can be described in terms of an assembly of materials and components with specific qualities, the unfolding of experience of the two participants needs to be understood in relation to a composite whole. Also, the material qualities outlined in this chapter should not be considered independently, but rather in terms of how they come together forming a hybrid around which the experience is built.

Here we have outlined a set of qualities to help us further the understanding of how the material characteristics of the box interplay with the unfolding experience. Although these identified qualities could potentially aid the design of new interactive artifacts, the point we want to make here is, that the experience is not a direct effect by the specificities of the artifact itself, but rather unfolds in the interplay between the qualities and how the particular subjects engage, interpret and make sense of them in their situational and social context.

Material literacy in Makerspaces

We have framed the participants' engagement with technologies and the social processes around them primarily as an experientially oriented process with similarities to that of interpreting and reading texts. We suggest that this process can be understood through the notion of material literacy, which puts the relation between the interpretation of the objects and materials to the fore, and highlights how such a process contributes to the formation of an overall experience. This is not to say that all the different activities the participants engage in should be understood as a form of reading, but rather it points to the centrality of a kind of meaning making from which the participants build a narrative form of experiencing the activities. By framing users' interpretative activities in this way, we aim to put the rich flora of different objects, things, technologies and constituting materials under scrutiny on an equal level. Rather than treating engagement with a piece of code as essentially different than the analysis of the texture of a fiberglass case, we argue that when processes such as these unfold, we should see the variety of ways of interpreting - and in a sense making 'readings' - of the objects and materials at hand, as part of the same kind of meaning making as in building a coherent narrative experience. Grint and Woolgar formulate this in their discussion of technology as text: "*The organization of the text hinges [...] on associations made available within the text and between the text and reader*" [15: p. 73].

The forms of experiences made possible by interpretative practices in relation to hybrid objects should not be looked upon as a form of linear reading from a literary point of view. Rather this resembles a hyper-text form of reading in which associations of the various elements of objects are meaningfully woven together into a narrative whole. This interpretative practice can be understood in terms of a continuous process in which various pieces of 'text' and material are meaningfully put together [9].

The notion of material literacy provides a means of bridging technology as text and technology as material. Interpreting technology is largely about being able to deal with the technology's hybrid character defined by a multitude of material qualities. This advances a way of thinking about literacy with technological artifacts that opens for new types of engagements, interpretations, and experiences, with consequences not only for maker activities, but also for the understanding of human technology relationships. As we have shown, such deeper engagements with technology may go beyond mere straight-forward interpretations such as prescribed use scenarios. The metaphor of technology as text influences many facets of HCI, especially the development of an interpretative characterization of interaction. However, here we hope to be able to expand what maker and hacking activities are about – through a characterization – that emphasizes elements of interpretation, narrative and hyper-text reading. We find that this provides ground to contribute to the HCI-oriented perspective on the discourse around literacy and digital literacy and how new forms of these may take shape in hybrid digital and physical environments.

As we have argued, a central ability that the participants of our study demonstrate is that of treating the physical and the digital as fundamentally intertwined. Thus, being literate does not imply considering the digital as a domain of its own separated from other objects and things around which we build our interpretations and experiences of the world. As shown in our study, interpretation of such digital and physical hybrid objects may take place in highly social contexts, thereby providing grounds for collaborative forms of actions, ranging from co-reading code, joint explorations of electronics and construction materials, and co-theorizing about how objects are constructed and assembled. Importantly, interpretations of these objects, things and materials then go beyond merely understanding and making sense of them, but include how such processes contributes to the rich variety of experiences of our everyday lives are formed.

CONCLUSION

The overarching aim of this work has been to take a closer look at the activities that takes place at makerspaces, where we propose the notion of *material literacy* as means to further the understanding of how experiences unfolds in the engagements with objects and materials. We hope to have opened a discussion that goes beyond ideas around innovation and learning and to highlight makerspace activities as spaces for co-creating narrative experiences. In doing so we have shown and expanded notions of literacy and how these should be understood in digital and physical contexts. The point that we hope to have reached is that makerspace activities can look very different and relate to a wide variety of things. To understand such activities, and people's relations to artifacts and technologies in such settings we need to widen any pre-conceived notions about what making and hacking is about, and furthermore, about how we invite other kinds of activities that rarely have been the focus of attention. Another set of contributions relates, in a more immediate sense, to interaction and experience design practice.

We identified a set of material qualities; opacity, risk, uniqueness, authenticity, age, and hybridity that were crucial for the unfolding experience and that arguably should be relevant also for similar settings. Our claim is not that these can straightforwardly be translated into design, of for instance new treasure hunt technologies. Rather, we point to the importance of thoroughly considering how such qualities touch upon the personal and social driving forces behind people's engagement in various activities, the wide range of skills and interests that people have, and how those aspects may interplay in the design of new things and technologies.

REFERENCES

1. Madeleine Akrich and Bruno Latour. 1992. A summary of a convenient vocabulary for the semiotics of human and nonhuman assemblies. In *Shaping Technology/ Society Studies in Sociotechnical Change* (pp. 259-264). The MIT Press.
2. Morgan G. Ames, Jeffrey Bardzell, Shaowen Bardzell, Silvia Lindtner, David A. Mellis, and Daniela K. Rosner. 2014. Making cultures: empowerment, participation, and democracy - or not? In *CHI '14 Extended Abstracts on Human Factors in Computing Systems* (CHI EA '14). ACM, NY, USA, 1087-1092. DOI: http://dx.doi.org/10.1145/2559206.2579405
3. Jeffrey Bardzell and Shaowen Bardzell. 2015. Humanistic HCI. *Synthesis Lectures on Human-Centered Informatics* 8.4: 1-185.
4. Jeffrey Bardzell, Shaowen Bardzell, and Austin Toombs. 2014. "Now that's definitely a proper hack": self-made tools in hackerspaces. In *Proceedings of the SIGCHI Conference on Human Factors in Computing Systems* (CHI '14). ACM, New York, NY, USA, 473-476. DOI: http://dx.doi.org/10.1145/2556288.2557221
5. Jeffrey Bardzell. 2011. Interaction criticism: An introduction to the practice, Interacting with Computers, Volume 23, Issue 6, November 2011, Pages 604-621, ISSN 0953-5438, DOI: http://dx.doi.org/10.1016/j.intcom.2011.07.001.
6. Paulo Blikstein and Dennis Krannich. 2013. The makers' movement and FabLabs in education: experiences, technologies, and research. In *Proceedings of the 12th International Conference on Interaction Design and Children* (IDC '13). ACM, New York, NY, USA, 613-616. DOI: http://doi.acm.org/10.1145/2485760.2485884

7. Leah Buechley and Hannah Perner-Wilson. 2012. Crafting technology: Reimagining the processes, materials, and cultures of electronics. *ACM Trans. Computer-Hum. Interact.* 19, 3, Article 21, DOI: http://dx.doi.org/10.1145/2362364.2362369
8. Elliot J. Chikofsky and James H. Cross. "Reverse engineering and design recovery: A taxonomy." *IEEE software* 7.1 (1990): 13-17.
9. Lars Rune Christensen and Pernille Bjorn. 2014. Documentscape: intertextuality, sequentiality, & autonomy at work. In *Proceedings of the SIGCHI Conference on Human Factors in Computing Systems* (CHI '14). ACM, New York, USA, 2451-2460. DOI: http://dx.doi.org/10.1145/2556288.2557305
10. Andy Crabtree and Tom Rodden. 2008. Hybrid ecologies: understanding cooperative interaction in emerging physical-digital environments. *Personal Ubiquitous Comput.* 12, 7 (October 2008), 481-493. DOI: http://dx.doi.org/10.1007/s00779-007-0142-7
11. Verena Fuchsberger, Martin Murer, Manfred Tscheligi, Silvia Lindtner, Shaowen Bardzell, Jeffrey Bardzell, Andreas Reiter, and Pernille Bjorn. 2016. Fabrication & HCI: Hobbyist Making, Industrial Production, and Beyond. In *Proceedings of the 2016 CHI Conference Extended Abstracts on Human Factors in Computing Systems* (CHI EA '16). ACM, NY, USA, 3550-3557. DOI: http://dx.doi.org/10.1145/2851581.2856491
12. William W. Gaver, Jacob Beaver, and Steve Benford. 2003. Ambiguity as a resource for design. In *Proceedings of the SIGCHI Conference on Human Factors in Computing Systems* (CHI '03). ACM, New York, NY, USA, 233-240. DOI=http://dx.doi.org/10.1145/642611.642653
13. Elisa Giaccardi and Elvin Karana. 2015. Foundations of Materials Experience: An Approach for HCI. In *Proceedings of the 33rd Annual ACM Conference on Human Factors in Computing Systems* (CHI '15). ACM, New York, NY, USA, 2447-2456. DOI=http://dx.doi.org/10.1145/2702123.2702337
14. William Goddard and Robert Cercos. 2015. Playful Hacking within Research-through-Design. In *Proceedings of the Annual Meeting of the Australian Special Interest Group for Computer Human Interaction* (OzCHI '15), Bernd Ploderer, Marcus Carter, Martin Gibbs, Wally Smith, and Frank Vetere (Eds.). ACM, New York, NY, USA, 333-337. DOI: http://dx.doi.org/10.1145/2838739.2838802
15. Keith Grint and Steve Woolgar. 2013. The machine at work: Technology, work and organization. John Wiley & Sons.
16. Ian Hutchby. 2001. Technologies, texts and affordances. *Sociology*, *35*(2), 441-456.
17. Steven J. Jackson and Laewoo Kang. 2014. Breakdown, obsolescence and reuse: HCI and the art of repair. In *Proceedings of the SIGCHI Conference on Human Factors in Computing Systems* (CHI '14). ACM, New York, NY, USA, 449-458. DOI: http://dx.doi.org/10.1145/2556288.2557332
18. Martin Jonsson, Anna Ståhl, Johanna Mercurio, Anna Karlsson, Naveen Ramani, and Kristina Höök. 2016. The Aesthetics of Heat: Guiding Awareness with Thermal Stimuli. In *Proceedings of the TEI '16: Tenth International Conference on Tangible, Embedded, and Embodied Interaction* (TEI '16). ACM, New York, NY, USA, 109-117. DOI: http://dx.doi.org/10.1145/2839462.2839487
19. David Kadavy. 2011. *Design for Hackers: Reverse Engineering Beauty*. John Wiley & Sons.
20. Scott R. Klemmer, Björn Hartmann, and Leila Takayama. 2006. How bodies matter: five themes for interaction design. In *Proceedings of the 6th conference on Designing Interactive systems* (DIS '06). ACM, New York, NY, USA, 140-149. DOI=http://dx.doi.org/10.1145/1142405.1142429
21. Silvia Lindtner, Garnet D. Hertz, and Paul Dourish. 2014. Emerging sites of HCI innovation: hackerspaces, hardware startups & incubators. In *Proceedings of the SIGCHI Conference on Human Factors in Computing Systems* (CHI '14). ACM, New York, NY, USA, 439-448. DOI: http://dx.doi.org/10.1145/2556288.2557132
22. Jonas Löwgren. 2006. Articulating the use qualities of digital designs. *Aesthetic computing*. 383-403.
23. Jonas Löwgren. 2007. Fluency as an Experiential Quality in Augmented Spaces. Int. Journal of Design
24. John McCarthy and Peter Wright. 2004. *Technology as experience*. Cambridge, MA: MIT Press.
25. David A. Mellis and Leah Buechley. 2014. Do-it-yourself cellphones: an investigation into the possibilities and limits of high-tech diy. In *Proc. of the SIGCHI Conference on Human Factors in Computing Systems* (CHI '14). ACM, New York, NY, USA, 1723-1732. DOI:http://dx.doi.org/10.1145/2556288.2557309
26. Robert Messler. 2013. Reverse Engineering: Mechanisms, Structures, Systems and Materials. McGraw Hill Professional.
27. Martin Murer, Verena Fuchsberger, and Manfred Tscheligi. 2015. Deconstructivist interaction design: interrogating expression and form. In *Proc. of The Fifth Decennial Aarhus Conference on Critical Alternatives* (AA '15). Aarhus University Press 33-36. DOI: http://dx.doi.org/10.7146/aahcc.v1i1.21313
28. Martin Murer, Mattias Jacobsson, Siri Skillgate, and Petra Sundström. 2014. Taking things apart: reaching common ground and shared material understanding. In *Proceedings of the SIGCHI Conference on Human*

Factors in Computing Systems (CHI '14). ACM, New York, NY, USA, 469-472. DOI: http://dx.doi.org/10.1145/2556288.2557267

29. Seymour Papert and Idit Harel. 1991. "Situating constructionism." *Constructionism* 36: 1-11.
30. Jennifer A. Rode, Anne Weibert, Andrea Marshall, Konstantin Aal, Thomas von Rekowski, Houda El Mimouni, and Jennifer Booker. 2015. From computational thinking to computational making. In *Proceedings of the 2015 ACM Int. Joint Conference on Pervasive and Ubiquitous Computing* (UbiComp '15). ACM, New York, NY, USA, 239-250. DOI: http://dx.doi.org/10.1145/2750858.2804261
31. Daniela K. Rosner, Miwa Ikemiya, Diana Kim, and Kristin Koch. 2013. Designing with traces. In *Proceedings of the SIGCHI Conference on Human Factors in Computing Systems* (CHI '13). ACM, New York, NY, USA, 1649-1658. DOI: http://dx.doi.org/10.1145/2470654.2466218
32. Daniela K. Rosner and Alex S. Taylor. 2011. Antiquarian answers: book restoration as a resource for design. In *Proceedings of the SIGCHI Conference on Human Factors in Computing Systems* (CHI '11). ACM, New York, NY, USA, 2665-2668. DOI: http://dx.doi.org/10.1145/1978942.1979332
33. Daniela Rosner and Jonathan Bean. 2009. Learning from IKEA hacking: i'm not one to decoupage a tabletop and call it a day. In *Proceedings of the SIGCHI Conference on Human Factors in Computing Systems* (CHI '09). ACM, New York, NY, USA, 419-422. DOI: http://dx.doi.org/10.1145/1518701.1518768
34. Phoebe Sengers and Bill Gaver. 2006. Staying open to interpretation: engaging multiple meanings in design and evaluation. In *Proceedings of the 6th conference on Designing Interactive systems* (DIS '06). ACM, New York, NY, USA, 99-108. DOI=http://dx.doi.org/10.1145/1142405.1142422
35. Kimberly Sheridan, Erica R. Halverson, Breanne Litts, Lisa Brahms, Lynette Jacobs-Priebe and Trevor Owens. 2014. Learning in the making: A comparative case study of three makerspaces. *Harvard Educational Review*, *84*(4), 505-531.
36. Adrian Smith, Sabine Hielscher, Sascha Dickel, Johan Söderberg and Ellen van Oost. 2013. Grassroots digital fabrication and makerspaces: Reconfiguring, relocating and recalibrating innovation? *University of Sussex, SPRU Working Paper SWPS, 2.*
37. Petra Sundström, Alex Taylor, Katja Grufberg, Niklas Wirström, Jordi Solsona Belenguer, and Marcus Lundén. 2011. Inspirational bits: towards a shared understanding of the digital material. In *Proc. of the SIGCHI Conf. on Human Factors in Computing Systems* (CHI '11). ACM, New York, USA, 1561-1570. DOI: http://dx.doi.org/10.1145/1978942.1979170
38. Anna Ståhl, Jonas Löwgren, Kristina Höök. 2014. Evocative Balance: Designing for Interactional Empowerment. *International Journal of Design.*
39. Lucy Suchman. 2007. Human-machine reconfigurations: Plans and situated actions. Cambridge University Press.
40. Joshua G. Tanenbaum, Amanda M. Williams, Audrey Desjardins, and Karen Tanenbaum. 2013. Democratizing technology: pleasure, utility and expressiveness in DIY and maker practice. In *Proc. of the SIGCHI Conference on Human Factors in Computing Systems* (CHI '13). ACM, NY, USA, 2603-2612. DOI:http://dx.doi.org/10.1145/2470654.2481360
41. Nick Taylor, Ursula Hurley and Philip Connolly. 2016. Making Community: The Wider Role of Makerspaces in Public Life. In *Proceedings of the Conference on Human Factors in Computing Systems* (CHI '16). ACM, New York, USA, 1415-1425. DOI: http://dx.doi.org/10.1145/2858036.2858073
42. Jakob Tholander, Maria Normark, and Chiara Rossitto. 2012. Understanding agency in interaction design materials. In *Proceedings of the SIGCHI Conference on Human Factors in Computing Systems*. ACM.
43. Vasiliki Tsaknaki and Ylva Fernaeus. 2016. Expanding on Wabi-Sabi as a Design Resource in HCI. In *Proceedings of the 2016 CHI Conference on Human Factors in Computing Systems* (CHI '16). ACM, New York, NY, USA, 5970-5983. DOI: http://dx.doi.org.focus.lib.kth.se/ 10.1145/2858036.2858459
44. Anna Vallgårda and Johan Redström. 2007. Computational composites. In *Proceedings of the SIGCHI Conference on Human Factors in Computing Systems* (CHI '07). ACM, New York, NY, USA, 513-522. DOI: http://dx.doi.org/10.1145/1240624.1240706
45. Tricia Wang and Joseph 'Jofish' Kaye. 2011. Inventive leisure practices: understanding hacking communities as sites of sharing and innovation. In *CHI '11 Extended Abstracts on Human Factors in Computing Systems* (CHI EA '11). ACM, New York, USA, 263-272. DOI: http://dx.doi.org/10.1145/1979742.1979615

MakerWear: A Tangible Approach to Interactive Wearable Creation for Children

Majeed Kazemitabaar[1], Jason McPeak[2], Alexander Jiao[2], Liang He[1], Thomas Outing[1], Jon E. Froehlich[1]
Makeability Lab | Human-Computer Interaction Lab (HCIL)
Department of Computer Science[1], Department of Electrical and Computer Engineering[2]
University of Maryland, College Park
{majeed, jmcpeak, ajiao, lianghe, touting, jonf}@umd.edu

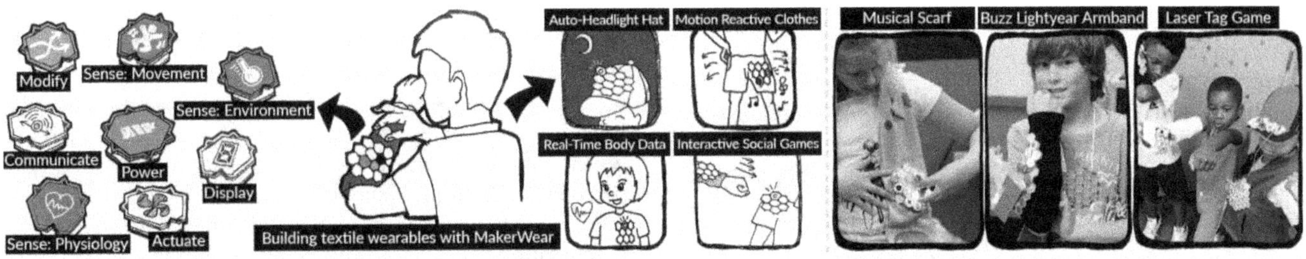

Figure 1: We introduce *MakerWear*, a new wearable construction kit for young children (K-6). By combining tangible, 'plug-and-play' electronic modules on a textile-integrated socket mesh, children can create a wide range of wearable designs from sound reactive clothes to interactive social games.

ABSTRACT
Wearable construction toolkits have shown promise in broadening participation in computing and empowering users to create personally meaningful computational designs. However, these kits present a high barrier of entry for some users, particularly young children (K-6). In this paper, we introduce *MakerWear,* a new wearable construction kit for children that uses a tangible, modular approach to wearable creation. We describe our participatory design process, the iterative development of MakerWear, and results from single- and multi-session workshops with 32 children (ages 5-12; *M*=8.3 years). Our findings reveal *how* children engage in wearable design, *what* they make (and want to make), and *what* challenges they face. As a secondary analysis, we also explore age-related differences.

Author Keywords
Construction kits; e-textiles; wearables; children; STEM

ACM Classification Keywords
H.5.2. User Interfaces – prototyping, user-centered design; K.3 Computers and education

INTRODUCTION
Wearable construction kits such as *LilyPad* [10], *Flora* [3], and *EduWear* [29] have shown promise in attracting underrepresented groups to STEM [13], expanding perceptions of computing [28], and empowering users to create self-expressive and personally meaningful computational designs [25]. These kits, however, require programming, an understanding of circuits, and manual skills like sewing and soldering. Though this complexity allows users to create diverse and increasingly sophisticated designs—fitting Resnick and Silverman's notion of "wide walls" and "high ceilings" [47]—it also presents significant challenges to young children and can impede playful experimentation and rapid prototyping (echoing [18,24]).

CHI 2017, May 06-11, 2017, Denver, CO, USA

ISBN 978-1-4503-4655-9/17/05...$15.00
DOI: http://dx.doi.org/10.1145/3025453.3025887

In this paper, we introduce and examine *MakerWear*, a new wearable construction kit for young children (K-6) that uses a tangible, 'plug-and-play' approach to wearable creation. MakerWear is comprised of two parts: (i) single-function, electronic modules that, when combined, create complex interactive behaviors, and (ii) a flexible, magnetic socket mesh that is either pre-integrated into clothing or attached *post-hoc* like a fabric patch. The mesh provides power, a communication infrastructure, and an easy method to attach and remove modules. By manipulating these tangible modules, children can create a wide range of designs, such as: a '*sound-reactive shirt*' that changes color with music, a '*fitness tracker*' that automatically counts and displays steps, or a new game of '*laser tag*' where children interact together through their designs (Figure 1).

MakerWear is informed and inspired by prior work in digital-physical construction kits [58,59] and robotic kits [6,20] that demonstrate how, with appropriately designed tools, young children can develop basic programs and work with electronic sensors and actuators. Wearables, however, present a fundamentally different creative design context. First, constructions are *worn* and, thus, are inherently social, mobile, and potentially always with the child. Second, the focus of design shifts from electro-mechanical objects to designing for the *self*—children can create designs that react to their movement, physiology, and changing environment. Third, wearable creation pushes computational design outward from the confines of a room or a screen into the context of a child's everyday life (*e.g.*, pretend play, sports). Thus, we see MakerWear not just as a platform for creativity and self-expression but as a way for children to augment meaningful experiences in their lives with computation.

To build MakerWear, we pursued a two-year iterative design process, beginning with participatory design sessions with children, design probe sessions with STEM educators, and iteratively building and pilot testing prototypes with target users. Informed by these experiences, we built our final prototype with a focus on enabling children to leverage the richness of *wearability*—their changing environments, their bodies (*e.g.*, movement, physiology), and social interactions. To examine *what* and *how* children make with MakerWear, what challenges arise, and how (and if) children leverage the unique properties of wearability in their designs, we conducted two single-session and three four-session workshops with 32 children (ages 5-12; *M*=8.3 years). Our findings show how children of all ages were able to build interactive wearable designs and develop understanding of key MakerWear principles (*e.g.*, input/output, sensing, sequencing). The multi-session workshops allowed children to work on their own self-directed projects, which resulted in a broad set of creative designs from fitness trackers to superhero costumes.

In summary, our contributions include: (i) the MakerWear system, including the 'plug-and-play' modules and custom socket design, which dramatically lowers barriers to wearable design; (ii) findings from pilot studies and single- and multi-session workshops characterizing how children engage in wearable design, what they make, and the challenges therein; and (iii) an analysis of age-related differences in MakerWear creation and understanding.

RELATED WORK

We draw on two primary sources to inform our designs: (i) developmental psychology and early childhood education (*e.g.*, [14,42,51]) and (ii) programming tools and creative construction kits for younger children (K-6). We also position our contributions within wearable design tools.

Theoretical Underpinnings

At roughly kindergarten age, there is a well-documented shift in cognitive and physical abilities [56]. Children demonstrate increased attention, self-direction, and logical thinking. Hand and finger control also improves, leading to greater enjoyment of and involvement with fine-motor activities [56]. These children are in what Piaget termed the *preoperational stage* [42,51]. They begin to think symbolically but struggle with abstract concepts like perspective-taking and mental modeling, so often need to rely on *physical representations* to help formulate, test, and revise ideas about how the world works [1,42,53]. By around age 7, children enter the *concrete operational stage*, characterized by the development of logical thought [42,51], but still primarily limited to concrete events or objects rather than abstract ideas. Thus, in our work, we take a *tangible* approach where wearable designs are built and 'programmed' using physical digital manipulatives [45].

Our work is also rooted in Papert's theory of constructionism, which suggests that the best learning experiences occur when children are actively engaged in designing and creating things [27,40]. Constructionism places a critical focus not just on learning through making but on the *social nature* of design—that is, that ideas are shaped by the knowledge of an audience and the feedback provided by others [27]. As an outward facing medium, wearables are uniquely social compared to the more insular contexts of other construction kits, presenting opportunities for diverse feedback across social spheres from peers and parents to teachers and coaches. MakerWear also explicitly supports building social interaction through module behaviors (*e.g.*, sending data to other wearers). Finally, Papert stresses that intellectual engagement is heightened when children work on activities and projects that are personally meaningful and interesting [47]. Our work begins to examine how children, enabled by our toolkit, engage with computational design to augment meaningful experiences and objects in their daily life (*e.g.*, sports, pretend play).

Programming Tools and Construction Kits

A broad set of work exists on building and studying programming tools for children (see reviews [7,33]) though only a small subset is aimed at and evaluated with elementary-age children [43], our target group. For these younger users, two approaches are common: (i) simplified graphical, block-based user interfaces like *Scratch Jr.* [16,54] and *KidSim* [44,52] and (ii) tangible approaches that use physical manipulatives such as *Tern* [21] or *Strawbies* [22]. For either approach, tool designers attempt to reduce literacy and fine-motor requirements (*e.g.*, typing, mouse input), simplify programming constructs (*e.g.*, eliminate variables), and enforce syntactically correct programming statements through block-shaped constraints—compare Scratch Jr. (ages 5-7) *vs.* Scratch (ages 8+) [48], for example.

Our work takes a tangible approach. Tangibles can provide sensory engagement for young children [60], an easy entry-point for novices [53], visibility and concreteness of work [5], and opportunities for peer collaboration [21]. MakerWear builds on work in digital-physical, tangible construction kits, such as *Electronic Blocks* [58,59], *roBlocks/Cubelets* [36,49] and *littleBits* [4,35], where the entire programming experience—both user *input* and *output*—is tangible, without the need for a computer. Despite the popularity of these kits, we could find no empirical examinations with our target age range. One exception is Electronic Blocks (for ages 4-8): two qualitative studies showed that children could build structures with *sensor* and *action* blocks but struggled with *logic* blocks and sequencing. No direct comparisons across ages were made. Though not a purely tangible approach, Marina Bers' extensive work with children (ages 4-7) and robotics also demonstrates that with proper instruction and tools, young children can build and program simple digital-physical constructions, though they struggle with looping, variables, and conditional statements [5,6,30,53,55].

In summary, while not aimed at wearable design, the above studies and tools help demonstrate that even the youngest users in our target range (ages 5-6) are capable of basic programming and working with sensors and actuators. We extend these findings to the context of wearable design.

Wearable Construction Kits

As noted in the Introduction, wearable construction kits such as *LilyPad* [10,13] and *Flora* [2,3] have helped broaden participation in wearable creation but still have high barriers to entry for children. Other wearable toolkits—*Quilt Snaps* [12], *EduWear* [29], *TeeBoard* [37], *i*Catch* [38,39], and *fabrickit* [15]—attempt to address some of these issues but are still designed for older children (10+) or adult hobbyists and, consequently, do not provide developmentally appropriate interfaces or architectures for younger ages. For example, EduWear (for ages 10-14) consists of a small set of pre-made fabric modules and a graphical programming interface for Arduino, but is otherwise similar to LilyPad—it requires sewing, creating circuits, understanding analog and digital I/O, and software programming to build even the simplest designs. MakerWear uses higher-order abstractions with a focus on *behaviors* (*e.g.*, sensing motion, turning on a light) rather than circuits, low-level I/O, and writing code. Moreover, the mesh sockets eliminate the need for sewing.

Closest to our work is i*Catch (for ages 10+), which uses specially designed e-textile clothing with integrated wiring ("host substructure") that interfaces with electronic modules via conductive snap fasteners. While i*Catch eliminates the need for some craft and engineering skills, the approach is still fundamentally *software* driven and requires writing code. Indeed, each of the aforementioned kits attempt to simplify aspects of building wearables but all use a conventional embedded systems model: a one-microcontroller-to-many-peripherals approach that requires interfacing with a computer to write, compile, and download code. In contrast, our approach allows children to build a range of wearable designs *tangibly* by manipulating plug-and-play modules. When a module is placed, creations work instantly to better support tinkering and rapid iteration.

DESIGN PROCESS AND GOALS

To design and build MakerWear, we employed an iterative, human-centered design process that included participatory design activities with children and design probe sessions with STEM educators. We then conducted lab-based and museum-based pilot studies with increasingly refined prototypes before deploying and studying our final prototype in single- and multi-session workshops. Here, we describe the initial participatory process and resulting design goals.

Participatory Design with Children

To gather design ideas and solicit critical feedback, we conducted five participatory design sessions with children. We employed a participatory design method called *Cooperative Inquiry* (CI), where adults and children collaboratively brainstorm, design, develop, and test technology [17]. The sessions spanned the design process, from early ideation and lo-fi prototyping to using and critiquing functional prototypes. In total, 11 children participated (6 female) with an average age of 9.2 (*range*=6-11). Each session included 6-9 children and 3-5 adult co-designers; 8 children participated in more than one session (*M*=2.9 sessions/child).

In the two initial CI sessions, children used low-tech prototyping materials to design and sketch their own interactive clothing and wearable modules. Several recurring themes emerged: (i) reacting to body movement and physical actions; (ii) using the wearer's physiology; (iii) designing custom-built games; (iv) appropriating clothing as a social communication device; and (v) pragmatic designs (*e.g.*, increasing visibility at night for safety). In addition, groups wanted the ability to program their clothing to add new functionality (*e.g.*, using Scratch), combine sensor modules to create custom inputs, and activate multiple output modules simultaneously. In later CI sessions, children helped test initial, semi-functional prototypes, pilot test design activities, and informally use and compare MakerWear to other construction kits like Cubelets and littleBits. From these sessions, children suggested new module types, larger socket meshes, and a greater diversity of clothes. Children also helped co-design the look-and-feel of modules (*e.g.*, changing names like *UV Light Sensor* to *Sunlight Detector*).

Design Probe with STEM Educators

Once we had created initial, semi-functional prototypes, we solicited feedback from two groups of professional STEM educators: staff from an interactive children's museum (*N*=4) and a STEM education consultancy (*N*=8). These sessions lasted roughly 90 minutes and included an introduction, a semi-structured interview about educational experiences and making philosophies, a demonstration of the current prototype, and, finally, a brainstorm session focused on eliciting design ideas and workshop activities. Both groups of educators were generally positive about our prototypes, particularly the 'plug-and-play' and tinkerability aspects, the use of wearables as a design platform (*e.g.*, to support movement-based design experiences), and our use of iconography and color to distinguish the module types. They also suggested ideas for new modules, physical designs, and design activities, such as integrating lo-fi materials and trying to design for universal accessibility. Key concerns included: (i) the *learnability* of modules; (ii) the small *size* of modules, especially for younger children's (ages 4-5) fine motor abilities; (iii) the *robustness* of modules, particularly when involved in vigorous activity like running or jumping.

Wearable Toolkit Design Principles and Goals

Informed by our participatory design sessions, our own experiences building, using, and testing initial prototypes (including early systems [31,32]), and relevant prior work (*e.g.*, [16,47,58]), we synthesized the following key goals for a wearable toolkit aimed at children:

- **Leverage wearability.** Previous wearable toolkits provide basic components largely undifferentiated from robotic kits (*e.g.*, light sensors, LEDs, speakers). In contrast, we aim to

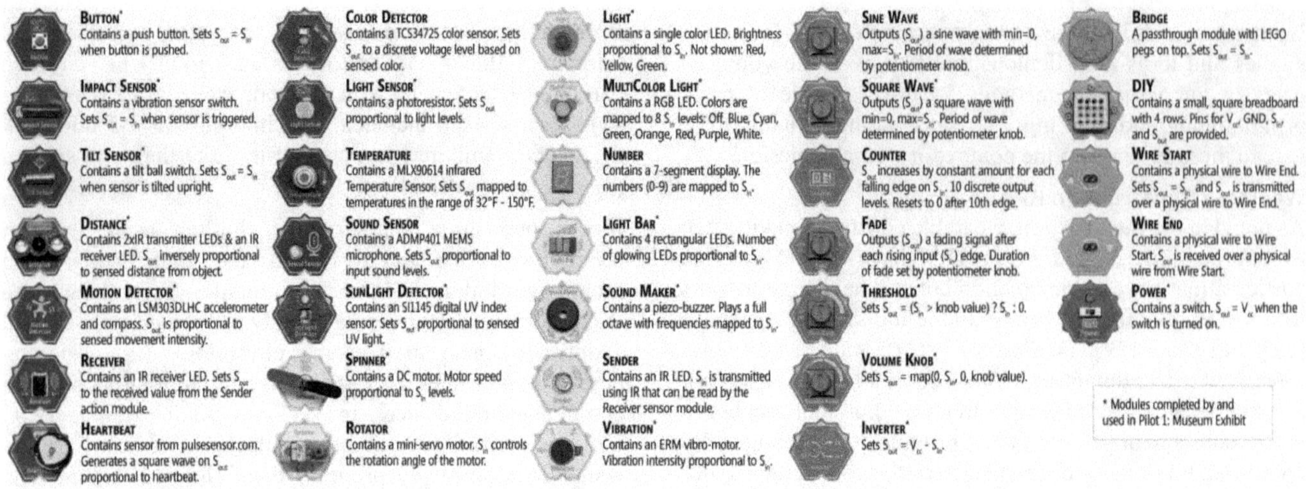

Figure 2. The final MakerWear prototype has 32 modules: 12 sensors (black), 9 actions (white), 7 modifiers (blue), 3 misc (orange), and 1 power (red).

leverage the richness of *wearability* and *mobility*—for example, changing environments, children's bodies (*e.g.*, movement, physiology), and social interaction.

- **Augment daily experiences.** We aim to support designs that are personally meaningful and augment everyday experience, be it socio-dramatic play, soccer practice, or a dance recital.
- **Low floors, high ceilings, wide walls.** Extending from [47], children-oriented wearable toolkits should be approachable but also support the creation of sophisticated, multi-faceted designs as a child gains experience.
- **Tinkerable.** Because of a dual reliance on craft skills and programming, previous wearable toolkits limit children's ability to *tinker* and *rapidly prototype*—two important aspects of the creative making process [46,57]. Wearable toolkits should allow children to easily try out multiple alternatives, to take things apart, and to create new versions.
- **Developmentally appropriate.** An overarching principle is to create developmentally appropriate designs informed by the literature and revised through iterative design.

THE MAKERWEAR SYSTEM

MakerWear is comprised of two parts: (i) single-function, 'plug-and-play' magnetic modules that can be combined to create complex interactive behaviors (Figure 2); (ii) a flexible, magnetic socket mesh that is either pre-integrated into clothing or attached *post-hoc* like a fabric patch (*e.g.*, via a safety pin or iron-on Velcro). The mesh provides power (V_{cc}) via an internal LiPoly battery, ground (*GND*), a communication wire (*Signal*), and an easy method to attach and remove modules. The modules and mesh are hexagonal, enabling creations to extend and branch into non-linear forms that are visually interesting and can adapt to clothing contours. Our architecture is scalable—allowing for large cascading designs—and responsive (*e.g.*, modules work instantly when placed and react within 10ms to input). The MakerWear system is open source, including hardware (schematics and board layout), microcontroller software, and design files: https://github.com/MakerWear.

Module design. Modules are 25.5mm across × 9-30mm in height, depending on the embedded electronics. Each module is colored by type with a laser-etched, child-friendly name and icon on the top layer. There are currently five module types: *power* (red), *actions* (white), *sensors* (black), *modifiers* (blue), and *misc* (orange). *Sensors* modules sense and translate physical phenomena into electronic signals (*e.g.*, light levels, heart rate, physical movement), *actions* translate signals into perceptual forms (*e.g.*, sound, light, vibration), and *modifiers* transform signals into other types of signals (*e.g.*, inverters, faders). *Misc* includes a *DIY* electronic module for building with raw electronic components and a wire module that allows users to jump across sockets or link multiple socket meshes together.

Each module contains a small embedded microcontroller (either an Atmel ATtiny85 or ATmega328), a custom printed circuit board (PCB), electronic components, and a neodymium magnet (Figure 3). The bottom of the module has small, spring-based conductive pins to robustly connect with the mesh. Most modules have one input signal side (S_{in}) and three output sides (S_{out}), indicated by triangular slots and tabs, which fit together like puzzle pieces. In our current prototype, S_{out} is shared (equivalent) on all three sides, but this is not intrinsic to our architecture and future modules could have multiple inputs and outputs. The two remaining sides remain open to prevent accidental connections in tightly packed configurations. While we experimented with

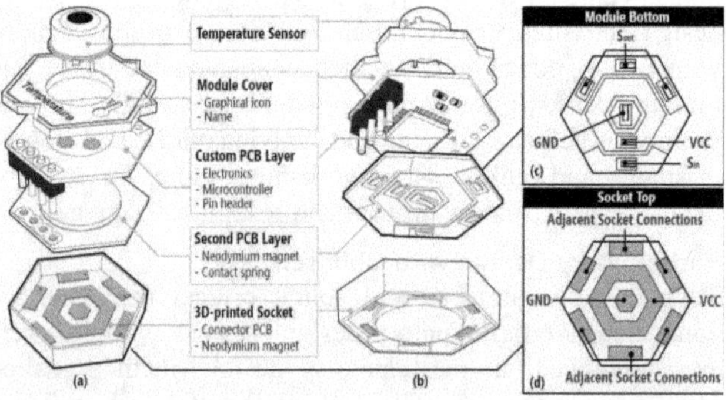

Figure 3. An exploded (a) top-down and (b) bottom-up view of an example MakerWear module and socket as well as overhead views of (c) module and (d) socket connector points. The contact springs ensure a robust connection.

both fabric and flexible PCB designs, current modules use a traditional rigid PCB with a laser-cut top made of matboard.

Module library. Selecting appropriate abstractions and providing a diverse catalog of modules is crucial to any construction kit. In addition to providing standard electronic modules (*e.g.,* LEDs, vibro-motors), we focused on building modules that leveraged the unique opportunities of wearability, particularly: *body movement and physiology, social interaction,* and the *changing environment.* Modules range from low-level behavioral abstractions (*e.g.,* an LED module) to higher-level abstractions (*e.g.,* an accelerometer-based motion detector that outputs values corresponding to movement intensity). We have currently designed and built 32 modules (Figure 2). While a large number of modules can be overwhelming, the tradeoff is that too few modules could constrain creativity, especially as a user gains experience. As a comparison, Scratch Jr. has 25 programming blocks. In our studies, we introduce blocks incrementally, or exclude some more complicated ones altogether depending on age group.

Socket mesh design. The socket mesh serves two primary functions: (i) it provides power, GND, and a communication wire, and (ii) an easy, robust mechanism to attach/detach modules to clothes. Each hexagonal socket is made of a PCB base encased by 0.8mm 3D-printed walls. Similar to a wooden puzzle with precut slots, the sockets provide a strong visual affordance about how and where to place modules. We have created two types of socket meshes: those integrated directly into clothes (*e.g.,* hats, scarves, vests) and a set of self-contained mesh patches that can be attached to clothes or other artifacts (such as backpacks) via safety pins or worn as jewelry. The meshes are individually wired and contain an integrated, rechargeable LiPoly battery. A small recharging cable is hidden in the fabric material. For the purposes of our research, we focused on clothing that could be easily taken on and off, such as hats, sleeves, and vests. Socket counts range from 14 sockets on a sleeve to 23 on a vest.

Creating with MakerWear. Wearable creations are built by placing correctly oriented modules in adjoining sockets on a mesh and adjusting on-module knobs, when available. All programs start with a *Power* module, which has six outputs, all of which set $S_{out} = V_{cc}$. The simplest functional program is thus *power → action*. In this design, if the action module is a *Blue Light*, it would always be on. By adding a sensor, the design becomes interactive. For example, *Power → Tilt Sensor → Blue Light* would turn on the light when in the proper tilt position and *Power → Light Sensor → Inverter → Blue Light* would turn on the light proportional to darkness level. Finally, because each module has three S_{out} connections, creating non-linear designs is straightforward. A single sensor module, for example, can be directly connected to up to three action modules, activating each simultaneously.

How does this work? All module behavior is contingent on its S_{in}, which itself is a function of all preceding modules in the input chain. Action modules forward their S_{in} to their S_{out} ($S_{out} = S_{in}$), while sensor and modifier outputs are a function of two factors: for sensors, $S_{out} = f(S_{in}, \textit{sensing value})$ and for modifiers, $S_{out} = f(S_{in}, [\textit{on-module knob value}])$. We use a hybrid analog-digital design: the analog S_{in} is read in, digitized, and processed by a module's microcontroller and then converted back to analog for S_{out} using pulse width modulation with an RC low-pass filter for smoothing. To ensure that modules with different current consumption (*e.g., Spinner vs. Light*) would not cause brownouts, we isolate each module's S_{in} from the previous module by using an op-amp voltage follower or the microcontroller's ADC pin, which uses a high impedance input (100 MΩ)

Depending on the module, custom code on the microcontroller interfaces with its embedded electronics (*e.g.,* via I2C) smooths out S_{in} using a small sliding window, and/or performs some signal processing. For example, *Counter* increases S_{out} by a set amount every time a falling edge on S_{in} is detected. *Actions* modules either map S_{in} into discrete actions (*e.g.,* the *MultiColor Light* maps S_{in} into 8 different colors) or react proportionally to S_{in}'s voltage (*e.g.,* the *Spinner* or *Vibration*). Similarly, sensors and modifiers either discretize their outputs—*e.g., Color Detector* has 8 and *Counter* has 10 voltage levels—or outputs an analog value between 0-V_{cc}. See Figure 2 for complete descriptions.

PILOT STUDIES

To gain preliminary understanding of *how* and *what* children could build with MakerWear and to uncover usability issues, we conducted two pilot studies: an interactive museum exhibit and a 1.5-hour workshop. Our findings were used to refine our final prototype as well as our workshop approach.

Pilot 1: Museum Exhibit

We hosted a 3-hour interactive MakerWear exhibit at a local children's museum. Though open to all attendees, the exhibit was in a small private room to ensure informed consent by a parent or guardian. We set up three MakerWear stations, two of which had a sleeve (14 sockets each) and one of which had a scarf (9 sockets). In total, 17 children participated (ages 4-16; 5 female) and spent an average of 20 minutes (*SD*=13 mins) using MakerWear. Unlike our later studies, no detailed demographic or questionnaire data was obtained. Two research assistants provided introductory demos to newcomers, answered questions, and facilitated making. At the time of this study, MakerWear had a total of 18 modules, which are marked with a * in Figure 2.

Results. Though time-limited and with minimal training, we observed an iterative process of playful experimentation, creation, and testing. Children made a wide range of designs from a simple, button-activated, light-up scarf to a go-away, sneak-up alarm system. Some children reappropriated lo-fi materials from the museum into their designs. Common challenges included: difficulty comprehending module behaviors (especially modifiers), sequencing issues (placing actions *before* sensors), and some small technical issues (*e.g.,* faulty socket wiring). Younger children tended to create simpler designs, often only using action modules, and had a tendency to fill up every available socket; however, they also seemed to enjoy themselves. For example, a mother commented about her 4-year old son: *"he hasn't been captivated like that for any other activity in this museum."*

Outcomes. Informed by this experience, we made a few key improvements: (i) we provided more explicit support for lo-fi integration by adding LEGO pegs and Velcro to the *Rotator* and *Bridge* and brought lo-fi materials to our sessions; (ii) we increased the number of sockets on MakerWear clothes and introduced a wire module to connect multiple meshes; (iii) we created 12 additional modules to inspire a greater diversity in designs, including the *Rotator*, *Number*, *Heartbeat*, *Temperature*, and *Sender* and *Receiver*. These revisions were made before our next pilot evaluation.

Pilot 2: Single-Session Workshop

To help test the revised MakerWear platform and trial our workshop plan, we conducted a 1.5-hour pilot with 6 children (4 female) ages 5-9 (M=6.8; SD=1.3). At this point, we had 30 modules (everything except *Sound Sensor* and *Bridge*); however, only 20 were used here due to time constraints. Participants could choose from nine pieces of clothing: two vests (23 sockets), two sleeves (14), two hats (15 and 19), one scarf (19), and two fabric patches (19). The session began with a questionnaire and a demonstration then alternated between introducing new modules and playtime.

Results. While more structured than the museum exhibit, our results were, surprisingly, more mixed. Though five of the six participants were able to build basic designs using power and action modules as well as a simple modifier, the *Volume Knob*, only a few were able to confidently build more sophisticated designs (*e.g.*, with sensors). Moreover, sequencing continued to be a challenge, especially for younger participants. Despite these issues, we observed children making connections to their everyday life, being able to accurately describe their designs, and using modules to help problem solve. For example, Zara (girl, age 7) made *Power → Impact Sensor → Light* and said, *"This is exactly how light-up shoes work. When you stomp your shoe, it would light up."* Later, she used a *Light Bar* to visualize the signal between a *Volume Knob* and *Sound Maker* and stated *"I made something to show how much power is going up."*

Outcomes. We identified three key areas of improvement: (i) we appeared to overwhelm the children with content and new modules, which caused confusion and frustration; (ii), unsurprisingly, we found that the two younger children needed more time to play with and understand each module; (iii) finally, some of the new sockets and modules malfunctioned, further inducing frustration and confusion. To address these issues, we rewrote our workshop plans to reduce content, split the workshops into age groups, and implemented a more comprehensive testing procedure to find and fix errors before our deployments.

STUDY 1: SINGLE-SESSION WORKSHOPS

With a refined MakerWear platform and workshop protocol, we ran two single-session workshops at a local children's museum (N=13; ages 5-12). The goals were similar to our pilot studies—to examine the approachability of MakerWear and *how* and *what* children make. A secondary goal was to help inform the design of our multi-session workshops.

Method

Participants were recruited via the children's museum. Sign-ups occurred online with one session for ages 5-7 and one for ages 8+. The workshop was free apart from museum admission ($12). We had five participants (all female) in the younger session and eight (3 female) in the old. See Table 1. Four parents also attended (3 in younger, 1 in older) who provided constructive prompts, helped facilitate making, and offered emotional security, especially to younger children.

N	Age	Gender	Computer Use	Grphical Prgmng Exp.	Electronics Experience
5	*M*=6 *Rnge*=5-7 *SD*=1	5 girls	1 Multiple times a day 4 A few times a week	1 A few times a week 1 A few times a month 3 Never	1 A few times a month
8	*M*=9.9 *Rnge*=8-12 *SD*=1.5	3 girls 5 boys	6 Multiple times a day 1 A few times a week 1 Never	1 Once a day 2 A few times a month 5 Almost never/never	2 A few times a week 2 A few times a month 4 Almost never/never

Table 1. Single-session workshop group sizes and demographics.

Procedure. Sessions lasted just over 1.5 hours and included: a pre-study questionnaire (10 mins), an introduction to MakerWear (5 mins), building/playing with MakerWear (70 mins), and a post-study questionnaire (10 mins). A team of three researchers facilitated each workshop. Based on our pilot studies, we prepared slightly different workshop plans for the two age groups (Figure 4). The older group had a faster pace, which allowed us to introduce additional modules and design challenges. To reduce confusion and provide time for playful exploration, we used only a subset of our module library—10 modules for the younger group and 16 for the older group (Table 2). New concepts and modules were introduced incrementally, starting with *Power* then simple actions. When a module was first introduced, we would either explain and quickly demo the module or ask the children to experiment and figure it out themselves. Children had ~5 minutes of playtime to explore each new module. We used the same clothing as in Pilot 2 but with two new larger sleeves (20 sockets each). Participants selected their clothing at the beginning of the workshop but could switch anytime.

To help assess understanding as well as computational and problem-solving skills, we conducted two design challenges in the ages 5-7 workshop (*Wearable Instrument* and *Dance Freeze*) and three in the 8+ workshop (*Auto-Flashlight Clothes, Buzz Lightyear*, and *Dance Freeze*)—see Figure 5. The workshop ended with a *"Dance Freeze Game"* where children danced wearing their *Dance Freeze* designs- in a game similar to musical chairs. When the music stopped, the children had to stop dancing. They were eliminated if their designs were still flashing lights and making sounds, which

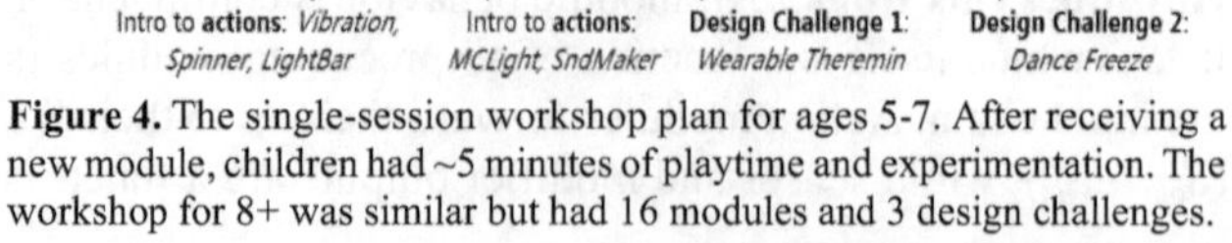

Figure 4. The single-session workshop plan for ages 5-7. After receiving a new module, children had ~5 minutes of playtime and experimentation. The workshop for 8+ was similar but had 16 modules and 3 design challenges.

indicated that they were still moving. During the session, researchers intermittently performed artifact-based interviews [9] to assess understanding and design motivation. Three long mirrors allowed children to see their creations while wearing them.

Ages	Actions	Sensors	Modifiers	Total
5-7	*Light, Vibration, Spinner, Light Bar, MultiColor Light, Sound Maker*	*Distance Sensor, Motion Detector*	*Volume Knob*	10
8+	*+Rotator*	*+Light Sensor, +Tilt Sensor, +Impact Sensor, +Button*	*+Inverter*	16

Table 2. Modules used in our single-session workshops.

Data and Analysis

We used a mixed-methods approach to assess understanding, computational thinking, subjective factors (*e.g.*, enjoyment), as well as to analyze how children made with MakerWear, what they made, and challenges therein. We analyzed session video, design challenge performance, artifact-based interviews, and the pre- and post-study questionnaires. The pre-questionnaire collected demographic data and prior relevant experience. The post-questionnaire asked about how participants felt about MakerWear and their designs as well as questions assessing understanding of module behavior, sequencing, and other computational thinking principles. Questionnaires used a mixture of closed-form, age-appropriate Likert-scale questions [19] as well as free response. For some younger children, questions were individually read by a researcher and responses transcribed.

Multiple video cameras captured how children used MakerWear and their facial expressions, physical movement, and social interactions. To analyze session video, we used a thematic coding approach with a mixture of inductive and deductive codes [8]. Two researchers created an initial codebook based on study goals and pilot study experiences, including for *engagement*, *use of modules*, *troubleshooting behavior*. One researcher coded sample video from the 8+ group, concurrently updating the codebook to support new themes. Two researchers then coded the remaining videos, discussed their findings, and co-interpreted the data.

Findings

We describe key themes and common patterns related to making with MakerWear. For the Likert-scale questions, we report means (*M*) and standard deviations (*SD*)—a score of 5 is best. All names are pseudonyms with (age, gender).

Making with MakerWear. Children across both age groups were engaged in making throughout the workshop. Because of the workshop structure and pace, children did not have time to create their own designs like we observed in the museum exhibit or later in the multi-session workshops. Instead, their focus was on understanding and building with modules and completing the design challenges. In terms of MakerWear clothing: six used sleeves, four used the fabric patches, two used hats, and one used a scarf. Interestingly, rather than affixing the fabric patch to clothes, a child in the younger group adapted it with string to wear it as a necklace.

Two styles of making emerged, which was at least partially influenced by clothing type: seven children spent most of their time iteratively building and testing their designs while *wearing* their clothing (6 sleeves, 1 vest). The other six children primarily built on a table and then infrequently switched to wearing for testing. Of course, some clothing like the two hats made it difficult to build a design while wearing it. Across both groups, children took advantage of the three module outputs and made branching, non-linear designs with interesting visual patterns. While designs with multiple actions were common or even sequences such as *action → sensor → action*, very few children cascaded two sensors together. One exception was: Dmitry (12, boy) who combined a *Button* and a *Tilt Sensor* so that a button press would only work when his design was tilted.

To troubleshoot, children employed three common strategies: (i) they removed and re-added a module either to the same socket or to a neighboring socket that created a functionally equivalent design; (ii) they re-ordered modules around until their design worked as expected—this was the most common solution to solving sequencing issues; and/or (iii) they asked a researcher, parent, or another child for help.

Understanding MakerWear. We analyzed how children understood MakerWear-specific concepts (*e.g.*, actions *vs.* sensors, individual modules) as well as higher-level principles related to computational thinking: sequencing, branching, and logic. When first introduced to MakerWear, children quickly understood basic concepts: a *Power* module is always needed to start a design and that modules had to be in neighboring sockets to be connected. Some children struggled initially with orienting inputs and outputs, which was corrected by facilitators using a puzzle analogy and focusing attention on the I/O triangles. All 13 participants struggled initially with sequencing (*e.g.*, modifiers and sensors must come before actions), particularly in the younger group. This was mostly resolved by the session's end, as evidenced by their design challenge performance and post-study questionnaire responses. For example, on the questionnaire, 12 children (92.3%) correctly fixed a design that had an ordering problem. The one participant who got it wrong (Sayuri, 5, girl) left it blank.

On the post-study questionnaire, all children correctly described action modules—*e.g.*, "*they do something like light or move*" (Brody, 8, boy). In contrast, for the *Volume Knob*, which is a modifier module and therefore potentially more complicated, all of the older children described it properly —*e.g.*, "*it allows you to control how much power gets through to power the other modules'* (Brian, 12, boy) but only two younger children did: "*it controls volume and controls actions'* (Angel, 6, girl). For those who got this wrong, we observed proper use in our video analysis (*e.g.*, to change light color, sound), so the problem may have been in articulating this knowledge on a written questionnaire. Children also exhibited understanding through their artifact-based interviews. For example, when asked to describe her design, which contained three branches, Angel (6, girl) stated "*the power comes from here [points at the Power module] and then it kinda travels here, here and also travels here.*"

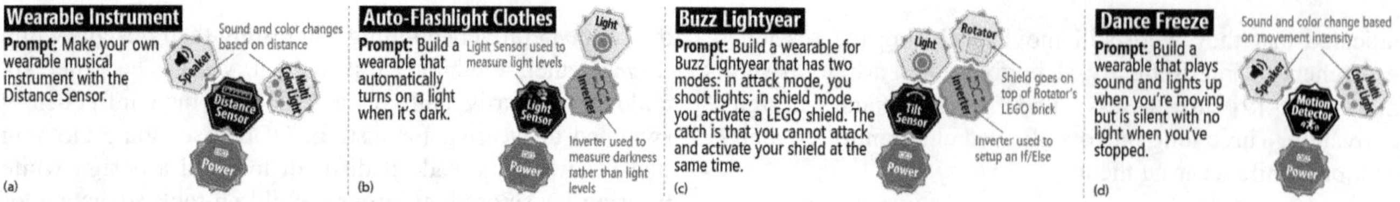

Figure 5. The design challenge descriptions and example solutions used in the single-session workshops.

In summary, children seemed to understand differences between module types, module behaviors, and higher-level principles like sequencing and how a signal traverses through a design; however, they had little exposure to modifiers, multiple sensors, and few opportunities to demonstrate understanding of more complex concepts like conditionals.

Design challenges. Generally, most children were able to complete the design challenges (Figure 5). For the younger group, all five children successfully created their wearable instruments; however, Elise's (5, girl) father helped her determine which modules to use though she placed them correctly herself. For the older group, all eight children were able to make their auto-flashlight clothes; however, one child required some prompting (*e.g., "remember which module allows your design to do the opposite thing"*). For the two harder challenges, *Buzz Lightyear* (only for older group) and *Dance Freeze* (both groups), performance was more mixed but still largely positive. For *Buzz Lightyear* (Figure 5c), seven children built the tilt-based rotating shield but only five were able to create a design that correctly alternated between attack and shield mode. While we used this challenge to examine understanding of the inverter and control structures, two children created unexpected designs that, instead, used two parallel 'threads' extending from *Power*. For example, Ellie (9, girl) created two independent branches: (*Power → Tilt → Rotator*) and (*Power → Button → Light*); however, this is only partially correct because both the shield and attack modes could be activated at the same time.

Finally, for the *Dance Freeze* challenge (Figure 5d), seven children (1 from younger; 6 from older) confidently built and tested a successful design with no assistance. Three children in the younger group and all children in the older group were eventually able to create working designs with minimal prompting (*e.g., "remember, your design should also make sound when you are dancing"*). Two younger children received significant assistance from their parents, so we did not count these in our assessment. Children enjoyed playing the *Dance Freeze Game* with their designs, particularly the older children who asked to play three full rounds.

Overall reactions. In their post-study questionnaires, all 13 children reported wanting to use MakerWear again (M=4.8; SD=0.4) and to bring their design home (M=4.9; SD=0.3). All but one child reported having fun (M=4.4; SD=0.9). The exception was Leiko (7, girl) who marked a '2', but in video analysis was engaged and smiling, and quickly and successfully completed her design challenges. Finally, all but one child reported being proud of their creations (M=4.3; SD=1.1). The exception was Angel (6, girl) who selected 5's on all other Likert questions. When asked to select a favorite module, action modules were selected most frequently, including the *Sound Maker* (N=5 votes) because '*you can change the sound*' (Hiroka, 7, girl), the *MultiColor Light* (N=3) because '*it changes color*' (Ellie, 9, girl), and the *Distance Sensor* (N=2) because '*it's like magic*' (Jay, 9, boy). When asked to describe the coolest thing about the workshop, 10 of the 13 children mentioned something that they made such as *Buzz Lightyear* or *Dance Freeze*.

Summary. In summary, our findings show that children across age groups were able to understand basic principles such as power, I/O orientation, and sequencing and apply these to build with MakerWear. However, the workshops were time-constrained and focused primarily on basic modules (with the exception of the *Inverter* in the 8+ group).

STUDY 2: MULTI-SESSION WORKSHOPS

To gain deeper insight into how children use and understand MakeWear over longer periods of time with a wider variety of modules, we conducted three four-day workshops in after-school programs at two local community centers.

Method

Participants were recruited through the after-school programs and informed consent was obtained before the first workshop. We had 19 participants in total, who were split into different sessions by age: youngest (M=6.3 years), middle (M=8.8), and oldest (M=10.2)—see Table 3.

Procedure. Sessions lasted ~1.5 hours and roughly followed the single-session format, intermixing the introduction of new modules with design challenges; however, the multi-sessions covered more content, allowed for more open playtime, and, following Bers *et al.'s TangibleK* robotics curriculum [6,55], included a final design project (Days 3 and 4). Children completed a pre-study questionnaire at the beginning of the first day. All subsequent sessions started with two 'fix-it' design challenges where children were given pre-made designs with a problem and told to fix it. Each day ended with a ~10-minute post-study questionnaire.

The final project design process was open-ended. Children brainstormed, sketched, and implemented their ideas with intermittent feedback from peers and workshop facilitators. Lo-fi materials like fabric, pipe cleaners, ping pong balls, and LEGOs were provided. On Day 4, projects were presented to family members and peers at an informal exhibition. Overall, we introduced 21 modules in the youngest group—most of the actions and sensors but only two modifiers (*Volume Knob* and *Inverter*)—and 31 in the middle and oldest groups (no *DIY* module because covering circuits was beyond the workshop scope). At least two researchers and one program

Figure 6. A subset of final projects, including: **(a)** Omar's wrecking-ball superhero armband, **(b)** Sarah's sneak attack lacrosse alarm system, **(c)** Kevin's sound-reactive armband, **(d)** Amelia's jogging clothes, **(e)** Jake's fitness tracker, and **(f-g)** Austin's wireless Pokémon. See supplementary video.

staff helped facilitate sessions. We used the same mixed-methods approach as Study 1 to analyze Study 2 data.

Findings

We present findings uniquely afforded by the multi-day evaluation: (i) what children designed and built for themselves with their final projects; (ii) age-related differences; and (iii) how children progressed in their understanding and use of MakerWear.

Final projects. Unlike the built artifacts from the single-session workshops, the final projects (Figure 6) allow us to understand what children *can* and *choose* to create after gaining experience with MakerWear. For analysis, we focused on project themes, how children used modules in their designs, and the complexity of the artifacts themselves (*e.g.,* number of modifiers). The most common theme was sports/fitness (6 designs), followed by role-play characters like superheroes (5), socio-dramatic play (2), and decoration (2). Two children brought materials from home to use in their designs: a lacrosse stick and a Pokémon doll. In terms of sensing, children most commonly sensed: movement (7 designs), physical actions like pressing or twisting (5), the environment (4), physiology (3), or social interactions (2). Seven designs used at least one modifier, four used more complex control structures with *Inverters* and *Thresholds*, and all but one design integrated lo-fi materials.

For the designs themselves, the sports projects included both equipment and clothing augmentation. For example, Sarah (9, girl) added a *Distance Sensor* to her lacrosse stick along with *MultiColor Lights* and a *Sound Maker* to warn her when someone was about to take the ball. Amelia (10, girl) created intricate jogging clothes that included four meshes: a left sleeve that tracked and beeped on every heart beat by using a *Heartbeat Detector,* a *Counter,* a *Number* display, and a *Sound Maker*, a right sleeve with two *Spinner* fans controlled by a *Volume Knob* to cool her down, and a safety vest and hat that lit up in the dark using a *Light Sensor* and *Inverter.* Finally, Jake (11, boy) made a fitness tracker to count steps and, using a *Threshold,* reward the wearer with flashing lights and sounds if they reached 900 steps.

N	Age	Gender	Computer Use	Grphical Prgmng Exp.	Electronics Experience
7	*M*=6.3 *Rnge*=5-7 *SD*=0.8	3 girls 4 boys	6 At least once per day 1 A few times a week	4 Indicated some exp. 3 Never	4 Indicated some exp. 3 Never
6	*M*=8.8 *Rnge*=8-9 *SD*=0.4	1 girl 5 boys	4 At least once per day 1 A few times a week 1 A few times a month	1 A few times a week 2 A few times a month 3 Almost never/never	2 A few times a week 2 A few times a month 2 Almost never/never
6	*M*=10.2 *Rnge*=8-12 *SD*=1.3	4 girls 2 boys	3 At least once per day 2 A few times a week 1 A few times a month	3 A few times a week 2 A few times a month 1 Almost never	3 A few times a week 1 A few times a month 2 Almost never/never

Table 3. Multi-session workshop group sizes and demographics.

Role-play characters were more fantastical. For example, Omar (6, boy) made a wrecking-ball superhero armband that lit-up, made sound, and moved a ping-pong ball and pipe cleaners via a *Rotator* when a button was pressed, while Dan (7, boy) made a ninja armband that vibrated and flashed lights when he performed an uppercut. Finally, as an example of socio-dramatic play, Sean (10, boy) made a *Harry Potter Sorting Hat* that could tell if someone belonged to Gryffindor or Slytherin. This hat had a social element: one child held the hat while another wore a scarf. The scarf detected what color the person wore (an "evil" or "good" color) and transmitted the data to the hat, which in turn lit up to indicate Slytherin or Gryffindor. These examples illustrate the range of creative possibilities that MakerWear was able to support. See our supplementary video.

Age-related differences. We analyzed differences related to how children built with MakerWear, the modules they used, the sophistication of their projects, and their understanding of key principles. A quantitative analysis of final projects is shown in Table 4. Unsurprisingly, as age increases, children used not only more modules in their final projects but also more complex modules like modifiers with sophisticated structures (*e.g.,* using *Inverters* or *Thresholds*). Interestingly, the opposite appears true with integrating lo-fi materials—the two younger groups, on average, used about two pieces of lo-fi material each while the older group used less than one piece. In the most extreme case, one child (Kayla, girl, 6) made her final project, a puppet, entirely out of lo-fi materials without any modules. Younger children were also more likely to use simple sensors like *Buttons* to create interaction compared with older children.

Using fix-it challenge and questionnaire data, we analyzed sequencing, branching, and complex cascading (*e.g., sensor* → *sensor* or *modifier* → *sensor*). We had four fix-it 'sequencing' challenges on Days 2 and 4. The youngest group successfully solved 81% of the challenges while the two older groups solved 100%. Interestingly, while we asked similar questions on end-of-day questionnaires—*e.g.,* by showing a picture of a design with an ordering problem—*all* children performed worse here: the youngest group scored 44% and the middle and oldest groups ~90%. For branching, we showed two

Group	# Modules	# Sensors	# Modifiers	# Ctrl Strctrs	# Branches	# Lo-Fi
5-7	5.8 (3.7)	0.8 (0.4)	0 (0)	0 (0)	0.6 (0.9)	2.0 (1.3)
8-9	9.3 (4.7)	1.2 (0.8)	1.0 (0.5)	0.5 (1.2)	1.3 (1.0)	2.3 (2.1)
8-12	18.1 (14.2)	2.7 (1.5)	3.7 (1.5)	1.0 (0)	2.0 (3.1)	0.7 (1.2)

Table 4. A quantitative analysis of final projects with format. Cells show average/design and SD. *Ctrl Strcrs*=Control structures refers to designs that used thresholds or inverters to setup conditionals. Branches refers to the number of times more than one output of a module was used.

functionally equivalent designs on Day 4, one using linear branching and one using non-linear branching. All of the older children correctly stated that the two designs do *not* behave differently but only two (33%) in the youngest group did. Finally, we observed only one child in the youngest group use complex cascading—LeShawn (7, boy) who used *Tilt Sensor* → *Inverter* to complete a design challenge; these structures were far more common in the two older groups.

In summary, all children were able to create designs with MakerWear and generally understood basic concepts (*i.e.*, I/O orientation, sequencing). The younger children, however, created simpler designs, had difficulty with more complex concepts, and a few struggled even on Day 4 with some basic-to-intermediate principles like branching.

Progressions. We also examined how children's use and understanding of MakerWear changed over the four days as they acquired more experience and more modules were available. Children demonstrated learning both through how they made designs and their questionnaire responses. For example, on Day 1 only 47% of children answered sequencing questions correctly; this jumped to 77% on Day 4. Keisha (6, girl) said, "*I remembered that if you put the lights with power, it's just gonna stay on but if you put it after the distance, it will change.*" For the *Threshold* module, which was only used in the older group, 20% of children correctly answered questions on Day 3, rising to 78% on Day 4. Two children used a *Threshold* in their final projects. Finally, introducing new modules opened new opportunities for learning and design. For example, children used the *Wire* module not just to skip sockets, as expected, but also to connect across meshes and to spread out their designs (*e.g.*, to isolate an *Impact Sensor* from reacting to *Vibration*).

Overall reactions. When asked what they thought of MakerWear on the end-of-study questionnaire, all but two participants selected '5' (M=4.9; SD=0.4). When asked to describe their favorite activity, the most common response was the final project (N=7): "*My lacrosse stick, because it represented me and what I like to do*" (Sarah, 9, girl), "*my own super hero thing*" (Mike, 9, boy), and "*my final project because it was hard to use and fun to make*" (Keisha, 6, girl).

DISCUSSION AND CONCLUSION

This paper contributes a new tangible, modular approach to wearable design called MakerWear. Our findings show that children across our target range (K-6) were able to successfully create a wide variety of wearable designs, actively apply computational thinking (*e.g.*, I/O, sequencing, logics), and create artifacts of which they were proud. In the multi-session workshops, children designed and built final projects that both leveraged the unique properties of wearability and augmented meaningful experiences and objects in their lives (*e.g.*, sports, fictional characters).

Design tradeoffs. While the MakerWear platform lowers barriers to wearable design compared to previous kits, there are tradeoffs. First, the role of craft and aesthetics—which is not just a key part of fashion but also touted as one reason why previous wearable toolkits have been successful in broadening participation in CS [26,28,50]—is deemphasized in MakerWear. Future work should explore how to better integrate craft opportunities, perhaps by involving children in socket creation and/or by providing more modules, like the *Rotator*, that easily interface with craft materials. Second, while the textile-integrated socket mesh enables our tangible, plug-and-play approach, the mesh itself is not fabric, is relatively heavy, and requires expertise to build. The socket mesh patch (visible in Figure 6f) may offer a nice compromise; it provides the benefits of tangible wearable design but can be attached to any material. A flexible kit should provide the option of specialized clothing or patches to allow for retrofitting of existing clothes.

Third, the sole reliance on a tangible, modular approach limits designs to available modules in contrast to completely open kits (*e.g.*, [41]). To address this concern, we are currently exploring a hybrid tangible-graphical approach [20] that will allow older children or more experienced users to program modules via a touchscreen interface. Moreover, the *DIY* module, which we did not evaluate in this paper, provides another opportunity for more open-ended projects by allowing children to create their own modules from raw electronic components. Modules like *DIY* may serve as introductory pathways to more complex kits like LilyPad.

Robustness and power. At this stage in our research, we focused on usability, engagement, and enabling creative design rather than addressing pragmatic wearable concerns such as weight, robustness, and power. While our STEM educators raised concerns about the robustness of an early MakerWear prototype, we did not see a single module fall off during evaluations; however, a few modules did break with use (primarily magnets becoming detached). In terms of power analysis, individual modules draw between 9-96mA (M=24.8mA) for sensors to 5-80mA (M=46.5mA) for actions. A 14-socket mesh completely filled with the highest current-drawing action modules in their fully-on states draws ~644mA, while a more average design draws half that. Most children's creations, however, include interactivity so are not always fully on, reducing power consumption.

Study limitations. We evaluated MakerWear using a workshop-based study methodology that, while common for construction kit research [11,23,29,34], makes it difficult to assess the effect of curriculum and adult facilitation on outcomes. More research is needed to examine how children would use MakerWear in less-structured environments and for longer periods. Moreover, while we provided both a qualitative and quantitative assessment of age-related differences in using MakerWear, the latter was limited by the content and modules introduced in each workshop, which was imbalanced (the youngest group used 20 modules, the two older groups 30). We have recently partnered with two organizations to examine more longitudinal uses of MakerWear—specifically, in the context of children creating wearables for sports programs and community theatre.

REFERENCES

1. Edith Ackermann. 1996. Perspective-taking and object construction. In *Constructionism in practice: Designing, thinking, and learning in a digital world*, Yasmin B. Kafai and Mitchel Resnick (eds.). Lawrence Erlbaum Associates, Mahwah, NJ, 107–123.
2. LLC Adafruit Industries. FLORA: A wearable Arduino-compatible electronics platform. Retrieved March 14, 2015 from https://www.adafruit.com/products/659
3. LLC Adafruit Industries. 2012. Announcing the FLORA, Adafruit's wearable electronics platform and accessories. Retrieved July 1, 2015 from https://blog.adafruit.com/2012/01/20/announcing-the-flora-adafruits-wearable-electronics-platform-and-accessories/
4. Ayah Bdeir and Ted Ullrich. 2011. Electronics as material: littleBits. *Proceedings of the fifth international conference on Tangible, embedded, and embodied interaction - TEI '11*, ACM Press, 341–344.
5. M. U. Bers and Michael S. Horn. 2010. Tangible programming in early childhood: Revisiting developmental assumptions through new technologies. In *High-tech tots: Childhood in a digital world.* Information Age Publishing, Greenwich, CT, 49–72.
6. Marina Umaschi Bers, Louise Flannery, Elizabeth R Kazakoff, and Amanda Sullivan. 2014. Computational Thinking and Tinkering: Exploration of an Early Childhood Robotics Curriculum. *Comput. Educ.* 72: 145–157. http://doi.org/10.1016/j.compedu.2013.10.020
7. Paulo Blikstein. 2013. Gears of Our Childhood: Constructionist Toolkits, Robotics, and Physical Computing, Past and Future. *Proceedings of the 12th International Conference on Interaction Design and Children*, ACM, 173–182. http://doi.org/10.1145/2485760.2485786
8. Virginia Braun and Victoria Clarke. 2006. Using thematic analysis in psychology. *Qualitative Research in Psychology* 3, 2: 77–101. http://doi.org/10.1191/1478088706qp063oa
9. Karen Brennan and Mitchel Resnick. 2012. New frameworks for studying and assessing the development of computational thinking. *Proceedings of the 2012 annual meeting of the American Educational Research Association, Vancouver, Canada.*
10. Leah Buechley and Michael Eisenberg. 2008. The LilyPad Arduino: Toward Wearable Engineering for Everyone. *IEEE Pervasive Computing* 7, 2: 12–15.
11. Leah Buechley, Mike Eisenberg, Jaime Catchen, and Ali Crockett. 2008. The LilyPad Arduino: using computational textiles to investigate engagement, aesthetics, and diversity in computer science education. *Proceeding of the twenty-sixth annual CHI conference on Human factors in computing systems - CHI '08*, ACM Press, 423–432.
12. Leah Buechley, Nwanua Elumeze, Camille Dodson, and Michael Eisenberg. 2005. Quilt Snaps: A Fabric Based Computational Construction Kit. *Proceedings of the IEEE International Workshop on Wireless and Mobile Technologies in Education*, IEEE Computer Society, 219–221. http://doi.org/10.1109/WMTE.2005.55
13. Leah Buechley and Benjamin Mako Hill. 2010. LilyPad in the Wild: How Hardware's Long Tail is Supporting New Engineering and Design Communities. *Proceedings of the 8th ACM Conference on Designing Interactive Systems - DIS '10*, ACM Press, 199–207.
14. Carol Copple and Sue Bredekamp (eds.). 2009. *Developmentally Appropriate Practice in Early Childhood Programs Serving Children from Birth through Age 8.* National Association for the Education of Young Children, Washington, DC, USA.
15. fabrickit. Fabrick Kit. Retrieved June 1, 2016 from http://www.fabrick.it/index.html
16. Louise P Flannery, Brian Silverman, Elizabeth R Kazakoff, Marina Umaschi Bers, Paula Bontá, and Mitchel Resnick. 2013. Designing ScratchJr: Support for Early Childhood Learning Through Computer Programming. *Proceedings of the 12th International Conference on Interaction Design and Children*, ACM, 1–10. http://doi.org/10.1145/2485760.2485785
17. Mona Leigh Guha, Allison Druin, and Jerry Alan Fails. 2013. Cooperative Inquiry revisited: Reflections of the past and guidelines for the future of intergenerational co-design. *International Journal of Child-Computer Interaction* 1, 1: 14–23.
18. Sibel Deren Guler and Michael Everett Rule. 2013. Invent-abling: Enabling Inventiveness Through Craft. *Proceedings of the 12th International Conference on Interaction Design and Children*, ACM, 368–371. http://doi.org/10.1145/2485760.2485801
19. Lynne Hall, Colette Hume, and Sarah Tazzyman. 2016. Five Degrees of Happiness: Effective Smiley Faced Likert Scales for Evaluating with Children. *Proceedings of the ACM SIGCHI Interaction Design and Children Conference.*
20. Michael S Horn, R Jordan Crouser, and Marina U Bers. 2012. Tangible Interaction and Learning: The Case for a Hybrid Approach. *Personal Ubiquitous Comput.* 16, 4: 379–389. http://doi.org/10.1007/s00779-011-0404-2
21. Michael S Horn and Robert J K Jacob. 2007. Designing Tangible Programming Languages for Classroom Use. *Proceedings of the 1st International Conference on Tangible and Embedded Interaction*, ACM, 159–162. http://doi.org/10.1145/1226969.1227003
22. Felix Hu, Ariel Zekelman, Michael Horn, and Frances Judd. 2015. Strawbies: Explorations in Tangible Programming. *Proceedings of the 14th International Conference on Interaction Design and Children*, ACM, 410–413. http://doi.org/10.1145/2771839.2771866
23. Jennifer Jacobs, Mitchel Resnick, and Leah Buechley. 2014. Dresscode: Supporting Youth in Computational Design and Making. *Constructionism and Creativity*. Retrieved from http://constructionism2014.ifs.tuwien.ac.at/papers/3.2_1-8520.pdf
24. Yasmin B. Kafai, Deborah A. Fields, and Kristin A. Searle. 2012. Making Technology Visible: Connecting the Learning of Crafts, Circuitry and Coding in Youth e-Textile Designs. *Proceedings of the 10th International Conference of the Learning Sciences (ICLS)*, 188–195.

25. Yasmin B. Kafai, Eunkyoung Lee, Kristin Searle, Deborah Fields, Eliot Kaplan, and Debora Lui. 2014. A Crafts-Oriented Approach to Computing in High School. *ACM Transactions on Computing Education* 14, 1: 1–20.
26. Yasmin B. Kafai and Kylie A. Peppler. 2014. Transparency Reconsidered: Creative, Critical, and Connected Making with E-textiles. In *DIY Citizenship: Critical Making and Social Media*, Matt Ratto, Megan Boler and Ronald Deibert (eds.). MIT Press, 179–188.
27. Yasmin B. Kafai and Mitchel Resnick. 1996. Introduction. In *Constructionism in Practice: Designing, Thinking, and Learning in A Digital World* (1st Editio), Yasmin B. Kafai and Mitchel Resnick (eds.). Routledge, 1–8.
28. Yasmin Kafai, Deborah Fields, and Kristin Searle. 2014. Electronic Textiles as Disruptive Designs: Supporting and Challenging Maker Activities in Schools. *Harvard Educational Review* 84, 4: 532–556.
29. Eva-Sophie Katterfeldt, Nadine Dittert, and Heidi Schelhowe. 2009. EduWear: Smart Textiles As Ways of Relating Computing Technology to Everyday Life. *Proceedings of the 8th International Conference on Interaction Design and Children*, ACM, 9–17. http://doi.org/10.1145/1551788.1551791
30. Elizabeth R Kazakoff and Marina Umaschi Bers. 2014. Put Your Robot in, Put Your Robot out: Sequencing through Programming Robots in Early Childhood. *Journal of Educational Computing Research* 50, 4: 553–573. http://doi.org/10.2190/EC.50.4.f
31. Majeed Kazemitabaar, Liang He, Katie Wang, Chloe Aloimonos, Tony Cheng, and Jon E Froehlich. 2016. ReWear: Early Explorations of a Modular Wearable Construction Kit for Young Children. *Proceedings of the 2016 CHI Conference Extended Abstracts on Human Factors in Computing Systems*, ACM, 2072–2080. http://doi.org/10.1145/2851581.2892525
32. Majeed Kazemitabaar, Leyla Norooz, Mona Leigh Guha, and Jon E Froehlich. 2015. MakerShoe: Towards a Wearable e-Textile Construction Kit to Support Creativity, Playful Making, and Self-expression. *Demo Proceedings of the 14th International Conference on Interaction Design and Children*, ACM, 449–452. http://doi.org/10.1145/2771839.2771883
33. Caitlin Kelleher and Randy Pausch. 2005. Lowering the Barriers to Programming: A Taxonomy of Programming Environments and Languages for Novice Programmers. *ACM Comput. Surv.* 37, 2: 83–137. http://doi.org/10.1145/1089733.1089734
34. Winnie W Y Lau, Grace Ngai, Stephen C F Chan, and Joey C Y Cheung. 2009. Learning Programming Through Fashion and Design: A Pilot Summer Course in Wearable Computing for Middle School Students. *Proceedings of the 40th ACM Technical Symposium on Computer Science Education*, ACM, 504–508. http://doi.org/10.1145/1508865.1509041
35. littleBits Electronics Inc. littleBits. Retrieved June 25, 2015 from http://littlebits.cc
36. Modular Robotics. Cubelets. Retrieved July 1, 2015 from http://www.modrobotics.com/cubelets
37. Grace Ngai, Stephen C.F. Chan, Joey C.Y. Cheung, and Winnie W.Y. Lau. 2009. The TeeBoard: an education-friendly construction platform for e-textiles and wearable computing. *Proceedings of the 27th international conference on Human factors in computing systems - CHI 09*, ACM Press, 249. http://doi.org/10.1145/1518701.1518742
38. Grace Ngai, Stephen C.F. Chan, Hong Va Leong, and Vincent T.Y. Ng. 2013. Designing i*CATch: A multipurpose, education-friendly construction kit for physical and wearable computing. *ACM Transactions on Computing Education* 13, 2: 1–30.
39. Grace Ngai, Stephen C.F. Chan, Vincent T.Y. Ng, et al. 2010. i*CATch: a scalable plug-n-play wearable computing framework for novices and children. *Proceedings of the 28th international conference on Human factors in computing systems - CHI '10*, ACM Press, 443–452.
40. Seymour Papert. 1993. *Mindstorms: Children, Computers, and Powerful Ideas*. Basic Books, Inc., New York, New York.
41. Hannah Perner-Wilson, Leah Buechley, and Mika Satomi. 2011. Handcrafting textile interfaces from a kit-of-no-parts. *Proceedings of the fifth international conference on Tangible, embedded, and embodied interaction - TEI '11*, ACM Press, 61.
42. Jean Piaget. 1952. *The origins of intelligence in children*. International Universities Press, New York.
43. Dylan J Portelance and Marina Umaschi Bers. 2015. Code and Tell: Assessing Young Children's Learning of Computational Thinking Using Peer Video Interviews with ScratchJr. *Proceedings of the 14th International Conference on Interaction Design and Children*, ACM, 271–274. http://doi.org/10.1145/2771839.2771894
44. Cyndi Rader, Cathy Brand, and Clayton Lewis. 1997. Degrees of Comprehension: Children's Understanding of a Visual Programming Environment. *Proceedings of the ACM SIGCHI Conference on Human Factors in Computing Systems*, ACM, 351–358. http://doi.org/10.1145/258549.258793
45. Mitchel Resnick, Fred Martin, Robert Berg, et al. 1998. Digital manipulatives: new toys to think with. *Proceedings of the SIGCHI conference on Human factors in computing systems - CHI '98*, ACM Press, 281–287.
46. Mitchel Resnick and Eric Rosenbaum. 2013. Designing for Tinkerability. In *Design, Make, Play : Growing the Next Generation of STEM Innovators*, Margaret Honey and David E Kanter (eds.). Routledge, 182–199.
47. Mitchel Resnick and Brian Silverman. 2005. Some reflections on designing construction kits for kids. *Proceeding of the 2005 conference on Interaction design and children - IDC '05*, ACM Press, 117–122.
48. Mitchel Resnick, Brian Silverman, Yasmin Kafai, et al. 2009. Scratch: Programming for All. *Communications of the ACM* 52, 11: 60. http://doi.org/10.1145/1592761.1592779
49. Eric Schweikardt and Mark D Gross. 2006. roBlocks: A Robotic Construction Kit for Mathematics and Science Education. *Proceedings of the 8th International Conference on Multimodal Interfaces*, ACM, 72–75. http://doi.org/10.1145/1180995.1181010

50. Kristin A. Searle, Deborah A. Fields, Debora A. Lui, and Yasmin B. Kafai. 2014. Diversifying high school students' views about computing with electronic textiles. *Proceedings of the tenth annual conference on International computing education research - ICER '14*, ACM Press, 75–82.

51. Robert S. Siegler, Judy S. DeLoache, and Nancy Eisenberg. 2010. *How Children Develop.* Worth Publishers.

52. David Canfield Smith, Allen Cypher, and Jim Spohrer. 1994. KidSim: Programming Agents Without a Programming Language. *Commun. ACM* 37, 7: 54–67. http://doi.org/10.1145/176789.176795

53. Amanda Strawhacker and MarinaU. Bers. 2014. "I want my robot to look for food": Comparing Kindergartner's programming comprehension using tangible, graphic, and hybrid user interfaces. *International Journal of Technology and Design Education*: 1–27. http://doi.org/10.1007/s10798-014-9287-7

54. Amanda Strawhacker, Melissa Lee, Claire Caine, and Marina Bers. 2015. ScratchJr Demo: A Coding Language for Kindergarten. *Proceedings of the 14th International Conference on Interaction Design and Children*, ACM, 414–417. http://doi.org/10.1145/2771839.2771867

55. Amanda Sullivan and Marina Umaschi Bers. 2016. Robotics in the early childhood classroom: learning outcomes from an 8-week robotics curriculum in pre-kindergarten through second grade. *International Journal of Technology and Design Education* 26, 1: 3–20. http://doi.org/10.1007/s10798-015-9304-5

56. Heather Biggar Tomlinson. 2009. Developmentally Appropriate Practice in the Kindergarten Year—Ages 5-6. In *Developmentally Appropriate Practice in Early Childhood Programs Serving Children from Birth through Age 8* (Third Edit), Carol Copple and Sue Bredekamp (eds.). National Association for the Education of Young Children, Washington, DC, USA, 187–216.

57. Shirin Vossoughi and Bronwyn Bevan. 2014. *Making and Tinkering: A Review of the Literature.* Retrieved from http://www.sesp.northwestern.edu/docs/publications/1926024546baba2b73c7.pdf

58. Peta Wyeth. 2008. How Young Children Learn to Program With Sensor, Action, and Logic Blocks. *Journal of the Learning Sciences* 17, 4: 517–550. http://doi.org/10.1080/10508400802395069

59. Peta Wyeth and Gordon F Wyeth. 2001. Electronic blocks: Tangible programming elements for preschoolers. *IFIP TC. 13 International Conference on Human-Computer Interaction*, 496–503.

60. Oren Zuckerman, Saeed Arida, and Mitchel Resnick. 2005. Extending Tangible Interfaces for Education: Digital Montessori-inspired Manipulatives. *Proceedings of the SIGCHI conference on Human factors in computing systems - CHI '05*, ACM Press, 859–868. http://doi.org/10.1145/1054972.1055093

Self Harmony: Rethinking Hackathons to Design and Critique Digital Technologies for Those Affected by Self-Harm

Nataly Birbeck[1], Shaun Lawson[2], Kellie Morrissey[1], Tim Rapley[3], Patrick Olivier[1]

[1] Open Lab, Newcastle University, Newcastle upon Tyne, UK, {nataly.birbeck, kellie.morrissey, patrick.olivier} @newcastle.ac.uk

[2] Northumbria University, Newcastle upon Tyne, UK, shaun.lawson@northumbria.ac.uk

[3] Institute of Health & Society, Newcastle University, Newcastle upon Tyne, UK, tim.rapley@newcastle.ac.uk

ABSTRACT

In this paper we explore the opportunities, challenges and best practices around designing technologies for those affected by self-harm. Our work contributes to a growing HCI literature on mental health and wellbeing, as well as understandings of how to imbue appropriate value-sensitivity within the digital design process in these contexts. The first phase of our study was centred upon a hackathon during which teams of designers were asked to conceptualise and prototype digital products or services for those affected by self-harm. We discuss how value-sensitive actions and activities, including engagements with those with lived experiences of self-harm, were used to scaffold the conventional hackathon format in such a challenging context. Our approach was then extended through a series of critical engagements with clinicians and charity workers who provided appraisal of the prototypes and designs. Through analysis of these engagements we expose a number of design challenges for future HCI work that considers self-harm; moreover we offer insight into the role of stakeholder critiques in extending and rethinking hackathons as a design method in sensitive contexts.

Author Keywords

Self-harm; mental health and wellbeing; hackathons.

ACM Classification Keywords

H.5.m. Information interfaces and presentation: Miscellaneous;

INTRODUCTION

Good mental health and wellbeing is integral to quality of life, and enables people to cope with the complexities of everyday activities, to work productively, and to maintain fulfilling relationships [35]. In the UK, it is reported that one-in-four people experience at least one mental health problem in any one year, and that one-in-six are experiencing a problem at any given time [23]. Statistics around mental health in younger people give further cause for concern: one-in-five young adults show signs of an eating disorder, and one-in-twelve deliberately harm themselves [38]. Self-harm describes the situation in which a person physically, and deliberately, injures or harms himself or herself without the intent of committing suicide. Self-harm is not a mental health condition in itself, but is symptomatic of other wellbeing issues, and often indicative of a range of co-morbid mental health challenges. Although frequently associated with younger people, self-harm can affect people of any age: estimates in the UK indicate that, in the population overall, 400 in 100,000 people are self-harming [22].

Though the human-computer interaction community has increasingly engaged with issues related to mental health and wellbeing, [2,12,30,31,34] there has been little research that has specifically considered the use of digital technologies for individuals affected by self-harm. Some previous research at the intersection of technology and self-harm (rather than mental health more generally), has been conducted outside of HCI, largely by healthcare practitioners and clinicians, whilst there has also been work relating to self-harm and eating disorders by researchers from public health, psychiatry, and youth studies [7, 25, 28]. Such work has mostly focused on explorations of online discussion in self-harm forums, and the analysis of self-harm content on social media platforms [7,9,10,13,16]. Owens et al [27] however highlight the need to involve service-users in digital intervention design in order to uncover and incorporate unmet needs into the design process. The nature of self-harm, lack of public awareness, and issues of social acceptability and taboo, however, mean traditional approaches to participatory healthcare design are particularly difficult to configure.

We set out to address these challenges through the design and execution of a research process which explicitly sought involvement from a variety of stakeholders involved with those affected by self-harm. These included service-providers and the wider public, as well as people with lived

CHI 2017, May 06-11, 2017, Denver, CO, USA
ACM 978-1-4503-4655-9/17/05.
http://dx.doi.org/10.1145/3025453.3025931

experience of self-harm. This two-stage process engaged these stakeholders in an exploration and critique of digital technologies within the context of self-harm, involving: (i) a hackathon to deliberately design for those affected by self-harm, and (ii) a series of stakeholder engagements in which participants critiqued concepts from the hackathon. We discuss the motivation, design and value-sensitive considerations of the hackathon, and how these informed the ideation and iteration of ideas for design and application of digital technologies. We then detail the stakeholder critiques with service providers, and the process of the engagements in which we sought to unpack the feasibility, acceptability and potential of the concepts for users.

Our reflections on this fieldwork highlight key considerations for designing within the context of self-harm, including: (i) the necessity of considering the appropriateness of nuance or simplicity of technologies for different care pathways and the effect that responsibility-sharing via technology can have on a self-harmer's support network; and (ii) the tensions and discrepancies between the concerns of clinicians and charity workers when discussing the implications of technologies and self-harm. This work reveals important challenges for interaction design to address self-harm specifically, and offers insights into how extending and rethinking the hackathon process with stakeholder critiques is a valuable tool for design in sensitive settings more generally. Our wider contribution lies in the unique integration of Value Sensitive Design (VSD) approaches to conduct a hackathon in difficult contexts, and dissemination and synthesis of our experiences regarding the engagement of service providers outside of the hackathon as an integral part of a more inclusive, considered, and longitudinal design process.

BACKGROUND

Self-harm is usually considered to be a way of expressing emotional distress, creating a sense of control, or escaping traumatic memories. It encompasses behaviors ranging from cutting, excessively exercising, punching or hitting oneself, misuse of alcohol or drugs, and eating disorders (ED) [22]. Self-harm is typically symptomatic of other mental health issues, including depression, anxiety, or borderline personality disorder (BPD). The conventional form of treatment or intervention that is decided for those who self-harm very much depends upon an individual's own reasons for self-harming. Treatment can include Cognitive Behavioral Therapy (CBT) and prescription of anti-depressants or anti-psychotics. In extreme instances individuals might also be subjected to a compulsory legal order committing them to a psychiatric hospital.

Self-harmers have been finding ways to connect with one another and share their experiences. This experience-sharing is mostly occurring through social media platforms like Tumblr, Twitter and Instagram, but also through mental health and self-harm apps that facilitate talking, such as 7 Cups of Tea [1] and Happier [14]. Whilst some of these apps engender mutual support and reinforce positive behaviors, many of the forums allow self-harm behaviors to be propagated by individuals through providing tips for harming and keeping the practice hidden. The current use of technology by self-harmers to connect with one another allows us to consider how the design of digital and social technologies can affect change in the lives of those experiencing self-harm.

Self-harm, mental health and HCI

The majority of academic work on computing and mental health behaviors in the past has taken a broad approach to the issue, often lacking the nuance that accurately reflects the complexity of human mood and behavior. There are three main areas of work in the HCI field in relation to mental health: 1) designing wearables in order to elicit behavioral signals, with a view to improve diagnosis, management and prevention of mental health issues; 2) creating online communities to facilitate support for those facing similar mental health issues; and 3) designing to foster positive mental health and wellbeing; developing factors like mindfulness and gratitude [8]. In the majority of research at the intersection of HCI and mental health, the mental illness is foregrounded, and the experience of the individual is largely overlooked.

Engagement by the HCI community with self-harm is limited. If we use a wider definition of self-harm, however, then there is work that considers eating disorders (EDs) and online communities [28, 29]. Systematic reviews of social media in these contexts identify both the beneficial and detrimental effects for young people discussing deliberate self-harm and ED [7,10,13]. For many individuals, online platforms can provide a sense of community and facilitate the support necessary to help and guide those experiencing self-harm [15, 29]. However, Chancellor et al [10] explore the detrimental nature of lexical variations on moderated hashtags in pro-ED communities, and Pater et al [28] discuss the ways in which online ED communities misappropriate technology for negative health purposes. Related work highlights the value of anonymous online discussion for those that self-harm, and the importance of health professionals understanding this value, despite the perceived detrimental effects on individuals' behavior [15]. The significance of involving both service providers and service users in a critical and sensitive dialogue about the design of self-harm interventions was also identified [27], but is often overlooked.

Hackathons

An increasingly popular approach to innovation that involves co-creation with stakeholders is to use open design, and maker, events, such as hackathons. [3]. This is particularly true for the use of issue-oriented problems – events focused on finding 'solutions' to social concerns – which have been widely deployed by advocates of civic technology innovation, but also as a means for traditionally remote or conservative institutions to engage (or be seen to engage) with the wider public. However, as an instrumental or social phenomena they are still largely underexplored. Indeed, while Trainer et al. [36] consider the trade-off between the value to participants of social tie formation with technical achievement, Lodato & Di Salvo understand them simply as "events which draw together various people, objects, and resources, for the purpose of articulating issues, as a kind of material participation" [18].

Hackathons in Sensitive Contexts

An increase in the interest of hackathons as a design thinking method has seen some organizers turn towards challenging or difficult topics. Health-related hackathons have gained significant attention: MIT Hacking Medicine [24], MedHacks 2.0 [21] and LiftOff Health [17] have all used hackathons to explore the intersection of technology and health with a view to transforming healthcare provision. Empowerment of refugees, health technologies in resource-limited settings, and homelessness are just a few examples of the sensitive areas that hackathons are addressing. Despite the increasing popularity of hackathon events, they have been criticized for their transient nature. Often the end of the event signals the dispersion of ideas, concepts and publics. Mantzavinou and Ranger [19] acknowledge that hackathons can generate short-lived excitement but lack a way to find sustainable solutions that create real impact. They understand hackathons as a 'launching point' to inspire further work and collaboration, and we endeavored to ensure that our hackathon was a launching point, as opposed to a fleeting event.

The sensitivity of the topics previously mentioned frequently makes hackathons *prosocial* events. While some hackathon participants are motivated by competition, demonstrating skills, or meeting future employers, other attendees exhibit altruistic behaviors, with the intention of creating digital tools to aid a particular community. In the context of our event, the majority of applicants were keen to disclose that they wished to attend in order to enhance their own understanding of self-harm, and work with those affected by it in order to create tools that would positively affect their futures. The notably prosocial nature of this event may have affected the design outcomes. It is worth noting that if the participants had been motivated by less altruistic reasons, the outputs may have been very different.

OVERALL STUDY DESIGN

Motivated by the lack of literature that considers how to design technologies for, and with, those affected by self-harm, we conducted a hackathon to foreground individuals who would be involved in the use of these technologies. Given that hackathons have been criticized for generating short-lived solutions, we sought to extend the conventional format to demonstrate that the event itself can be imagined as the beginning of a more powerful design process.

Our approach was influenced by elements of VSD that emphasize the ethical values of direct and indirect stakeholders in the design process. This approach to ethics and technology considers that the outcomes of design processes are value-laden and that we should situate moral questions at the beginning of the design process. VSD advocates that designers identify stakeholders in the conceptual phase, how their values might be impacted by the technology, and subsequently involve these stakeholders in the research and technical phases of a design process [6]. We endeavored to do this by holding engagements with those who had experience of self-harm throughout the entire research process of this study, and incorporated their life experiences and suggestions into our overall study design. Self-harm is a particularly sensitive topic due to the stigmatization of the term and practice, coupled with its psychiatric connotations [9]. The juxtaposition of a collaborative environment and the sensitive nature of self-harm made for a particularly challenging setting. Therefore, preceding the event we met with charity workers, and individuals who had experienced self-harm, and discussed the challenges and ethical considerations of the event. Guest speakers, timetable and resources were also set through these engagements. These sense-checking activities allowed us to ensure that the event would be run in a sensitive manner. It was our goal to engage end-user stakeholders in the design process at the hackathon, and then service providers in a conversation that would surface design challenges for HCI, but also for the implications of service provision in this context.

In the next section we will discuss how, through value-sensitive activities, we carefully reconfigured the conventional hackathon format to account for the sensitivities of our participants. We outline a detailed description of the hackathon we coordinated, including the idea generation, expert feedback, and documentation of the concepts. Then we describe the digital designs that 7 teams produced, explaining the concepts, motivations, and imagined users. Following this, we will outline the process of the stakeholder critiques and findings from these critical discussions. We conclude with interaction design challenges for self-harm, and insights into the valuable role of stakeholder critiques in the reconfiguration of hackathons in sensitive and challenging contexts.

PHASE ONE: THE HACKATHON

We approached the design of Self Harmony, our hackathon, as an opportunity to bring together communities who would not usually collaborate on technology creation within the context of self-harm. We endeavored to create a safe but structured space in which there was a unique opportunity to work in collaboration with a diverse community; an environment in which engagement with technology could be used to provide digital solutions in a particularly sensitive and challenging context.

Participant Recruitment

As a university based event, we particularly targeted attendees from the student body (approx. 20,000 undergraduate and postgraduate students), the local healthcare and voluntary sector, as well as the general public. Participants were recruited through local and national mailing lists and a website designed to promote the event. The website explained the threefold mission of the hackathon: 1) to aid in emotional coping, not only for those individuals who self-harm, but also their support networks; 2) to raise awareness of the term and practice, and dispel common misconceptions; and 3) to explore the concept of harm reduction. Potential participants were then able to browse the website and apply to attend the event through an online form. There were also advertisements within a local newspaper and posters distributed in university buildings and local public places. Participation was accepted on a first-come-first-served basis. All participants were offered compensation for travel costs, and food and refreshments were provided for the entire weekend.

45 participants attended the two-day (weekend) event. Participants' backgrounds varied widely, from senior medical trainees (n=4), health researchers (n=4), technologists (n=15), designers/makers (n=5), charity workers (n=5), members of the public (n=4), and individuals with lived experience of self-harm (n=8). Expert speakers were invited to inspire the participants and were chosen to cover a wide range of experiences and expertise within the context of mental health: a senior medical trainee with lived experience of self-harm, a professor of mental health, a mental health activist (and leader of a voluntary organization); and a facilitator of a self-injury support group.

The Event Itself

As the concept of Self Harmony was sensitive and unexplored territory for a hackathon, it was important that we guided the participants and discussed the scope and context of the issue so that conceptualization was appropriate. Given that self-harm is a behavior, rather than a mental disorder in itself, we aimed to provide participants with accounts of self-harm behaviors and experiences so that they could create actionable designs and prototypes. Inspiration packs attempted to guide the initial ideas for prototypes through the setting of three challenges:

1. How might we design a technology to be used by people who self-harm that will support them during their times of need?
2. How might we design a technology that will provide emotional support and guidance for the people around those that self-harm?
3. How might we design a technology that will improve our understanding of the patterns and causes of self-harm, on either a regional or national level?

These challenges directly related to our three themes of harm reduction, emotional support, and raising awareness, respectively. It was explained to participants that these challenges were set to guide them in a novel and unfamiliar area, and that it would be useful for teams to document how these challenges subsequently shaped their idea generation.

The first morning of the weekend was filled with context-setting talks and presentations from experts in self-harm who were there to provide inspiration for teams. Participants were given the opportunity to participate in a Q&A panel with all presenters and ask questions regarding the key challenges presented at the hackathon and the feasibility of ideas that participants raised. The presenters, along with others with lived experience of self-harm (n=3), a mental health charity worker (n=1), a technologist (n=1), an HCI academic (n=1), and a mental health researcher (n=1) acted as mentors throughout the hackathon. The mentors were asked to be present for the duration of the weekend in order to sense-check ideas with teams, and provide continuous critique to engender an iterative design process [23]. The regular feedback from the mentors was intended to constructively aid the teams throughout the process and ensure that teams sensitively engaged with the topic.

Documentation of the Event

The activity of participants at Self Harmony was captured in various ways in order to document the event and the various ideation processes that teams experienced and constructed. Teams were asked to use Slack in order to evidence aspects of their design concepts such as potential user base, inspiration, challenge addressed, and possible collaborators for development and deployment. Participants were encouraged to use Slack throughout the event to show how their ideas progressed as a team and outline what informed their ideation process. Furthermore, the keynote presentations, team feedback sessions and mentors' critiques were also captured on video. Selected elements of this documentation were later used in the presentation to stakeholders to engage them in a critical dialogue in order to reveal key concerns and strengths of the technologies.

Building a Safe Environment at the Hackathon

Full ethical approval was obtained from our internal institutional ethics committee. On application for Self Harmony, potential participants were emailed and informed that by attending the hackathon they would be agreeing to partake in a research study that was investigating the potential for digital technology in the context of self-harm. Participants were then able to submit an online form that specified if they consented to attending the hackathon and being part of the research study. Subsequently, on arrival at the event, all attendees (participants, mentors and presenters) was briefed and consented to participate in the research for the duration of the weekend. At the hackathon, participants were made to feel as comfortable as possible. There was a separate 'safe space' to the rear of the building that was for participants to relax and have discussions if they felt upset or triggered by anything brought up. On the second day this room was occupied by volunteers from a national charity who were there to provide emotional support for participants.

The configuration and design of the event was conducted bearing in mind the vulnerable population and the potential risk to attendees. For this reason, we held regular meetings with local mental health organizations in order to sense-check and ensure that we were creating a sensitive space that would facilitate innovation in a tactful and comfortable manner. It was in one of these meetings that an editor of a national mental health magazine stressed the importance of a space where participants could relax and speak to mental health professionals who were on hand to provide support when needed.

Design outcomes

The hackathon teams produced seven designs. In order to give an accurate sense of both the diversity of these, and also the commonalities, we briefly describe each below. As we explain later (Phase 2), we initially engaged stakeholder participants with all seven designs, but gravitated towards the three that solicited the most engaged responses.

Paperchain

Paperchain (Figure 1) is a mobile app that is based upon traditional chain analysis, which is a commonly used technique in dialectal behavior therapy (DBT). This form of therapy is particularly common with those that are experiencing self-harm. The app is a digital iteration of a paperchain, and allows users to track their moods and emotions by coloring in the chain. The app facilitates zooming in and out in order to gain perspective of how their moods have fluctuated over significant periods of time. It is also possible to share the digital paperchain with significant others and create codes between individuals that signify how someone is feeling at a particular time.

Digital Distraction Box

The Digital Distraction Box (Figure 2) is a physical, electronically locked box that holds self-harm tools. On top of the box is a digital screen that the user must interact with before the box will unlock. The screen can be configured in various ways by the user: it may display positive images, distraction games, and/or a way to audio record the reasons why somebody is self-harming, with the aim of retrospectively identifying triggers for the behavior. The box can also be configured so that it automatically unlocks after being shaken for a prolonged period of time. This concept was created not as a self-harm intervention, but to reduce the amount of harm caused.

Squeeze

Squeeze (Figure 3) is a crocheted, digital stress ball that is controlled by an Arduino single board microcontroller. As the user practices breathing techniques and mindfulness,

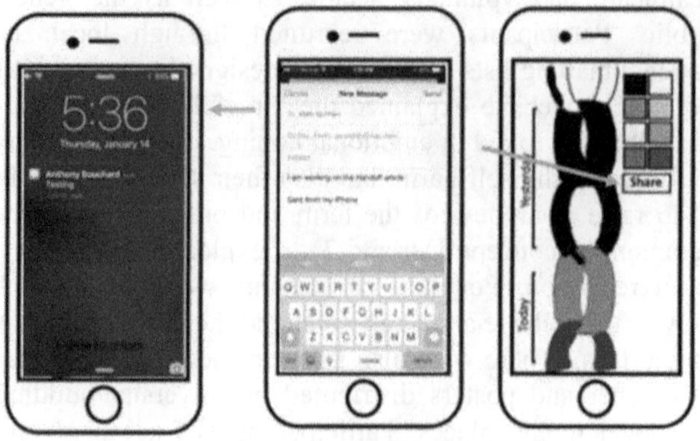

Figure 1. Paperchain App

Figure 2. Digital Distraction Box

they receive digital feedback from the stress ball. Squeeze was made to allow the user to feel an element of control over their own body and thoughts. The team identified the potential for communities to come together and create the Squeeze with a physical toolkit and an online repository.

Wavelength

When a user arrives at the web-based interface, they can decide whether to be a speaker or a listener. Speakers are presented with a pool of images from which they can choose three to represent how they are feeling. They are then able to annotate their chosen images to explain why they are relevant to their current mood. Once they have annotated their images they will be connected to a random listener in order to have a peer-to-peer conversation about how they are feeling.

Harmonize

An individual who self-harms writes a blog post and invites their friends and family to comment on it. To allow multiple perspectives to be shown, friends and family are able to blur out lines to indicate they did not know something was happening, comment, and highlight pieces to draw attention to them. If everyone that has been involved in the blog post feels happy with it, the blog can be uploaded to a website as an interactive blog. This concept is based on evidence that writing can improve outcomes of those self-harming. The team members saw this design as one that could be used as part of a family-

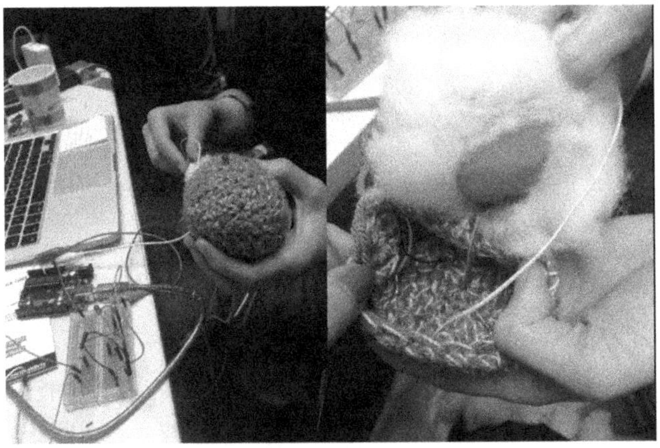

Figure 3. Squeeze Prototype.

based intervention, aimed at those who are nearing the end of a care pathway.

Speak Up

Speak Up is a web-based tool for the community of caregivers around those who self-harm. When a user is on the platform they are able to disclose whether they self-harm or if they know somebody who self-harms. They can then browse the platform and read information that other people have posted and select whether they found that information 'helpful' or 'unhelpful' to their situation. These selections will remain private, but will contribute to a personalized set of ratings for all of the posters on the forum. That way, when a user logs in to their account, they will be able to see whose posts they have previously found most helpful, and will have the opportunity to speak to them in a private conversation.

Good Vibes

Good Vibes is a mobile app and wearable that are intended to promote positivity and remind a user of what they like about themselves. A user can create a 'support network' where chosen loved ones will have the app and wearable. Everybody in the support network is able to input positive messages, comments and photos about themselves and the original user. If somebody is in crisis or feels that they need some positivity, they can squeeze their wearable that will send an alert to their network's wearables and prompt them to input a positive message.

PHASE TWO: FOLLOW UP STAKEHOLDER CRITIQUES

In the second phase of the research process we used our documentation of the outputs of Self Harmony to engage stakeholders (statutory and voluntary service providers) in discussions as to their appropriateness and potential for positive impact (as digital 'interventions'). We conducted stakeholder critiques with a range of individuals who worked in the area of mental health or self-harm specifically (see Table 1).

Each critique lasted approximately one hour and was held either at our research lab or the participants' place of work. At each engagement a number of the seven concepts from Self Harmony were presented to participants via various photos, video clips and other fragments of documentation collected at the event. The researcher began by presenting the outcomes to participants, explaining the digital concepts, their imagined users, and sources of inspiration in turn. Throughout this process, stakeholders were prompted to discuss the perceived usability and potential impact of each concept. Each stakeholder critique built upon the previous one, changing the order and length of the concept descriptions in order to scaffold a more critical dialogue.

Stakeholder participant	n = x
Student Wellbeing Services	3
Clinical Psychology Team	3
Third Sector Volunteers	3
Statutory Service Provider (and General Practitioner)	1
Self-Harm Nurse	1

Table 1 - Participant Information

It was explained to participants that the lead researcher had not been involved in the design or creation of the concepts, with the intention of engendering more critique. Participants were encouraged to be critical of each of the concepts in order to uncover the key concerns and implications of designing digital technologies in the context of self-harm.

Results

Although there were seven teams who conceptualized and prototyped seven different outcomes, here we present three outcomes that accurately represent the variety of outputs that were created. Furthermore, these three outcomes dominated the stakeholder discussions, engendering the most critique and therefore highlighting challenges for future work.

Digital Distraction Box

The Digital Distraction box was the most divisive concept out of the seven that were presented to stakeholders. Interestingly, it was also the concept that received the most affirmation from the participants at the hackathon who had lived experience of self-harm. These participants felt that it was the most useful concept, as although it was taking an interventionist approach, it did not ignore the fact that self-harm is an effective coping mechanism for many individuals.

In the stakeholder critiques the Digital Distraction Box sparked revealing conversations around the physicality of the box. Clinicians suggested that there was no need for a physical box when the behavioral techniques that the box prompted – such as distraction, reflection and trigger identification – are portable. The clinicians involved recognized that the box was best suited for self-harming individuals that used physical tools, but asserted that if the purpose of the concept is to create "barriers" to self-harming, these barriers can be created and recreated anywhere. One General Practitioner said, *"I don't think you have to have... You don't have to carry your blade with you in a portable device all the time for it to be effective, if it was a blade".* It was important for all of the clinicians that the behavioral techniques patients learned were accessible at all times, rather than the tools they were able to use to self-harm.

The team of clinical psychologists was disappointed with the physical box and also imagined a concept that was more portable. *"But I still really like the idea of having it on the phone".* The idea that the distractions could be portable for the individual, and on hand to negate the urge to self-harm, was crucial for the clinicians. The psychologists felt that their patients had acquired the skills to practice 'distraction' and 'grounding' techniques and those would be all that was necessary to stop the urge to self-harm. The psychologists then began to imagine how the portability of such a digital tool could be re-imagined in order to facilitate their ideas of what a 'good' digital tool would be. They imagined *"a little map, like a little treasure map, that would be good".* This imagined treasure map would display various positive images and activities configured personally by the user, which would meaningfully delay the act of self-harming.

The psychology team explained that they would be unable to incorporate the digital box into the care pathway of their patients: *"Well there's no way we could use that here, for example. We take a real positive risk taking approach. As in people have access to their hair straighteners and razors and stuff, as and when they feel able to manage that safely".* This revealed why the respondents were unable to identify the box as a useful tool for self-harmers. They later went on to explain that they are a recovery-focused program and that the emphasis is upon 'healthy coping mechanisms', and whilst recognizing that self-harming is a very real coping strategy for most individuals, they felt that it was an option that they no longer wanted to be available. For this particular group of psychologists, the discomfort evoked by the box is tied to their philosophy of care, but also where the individual is within their recovery pathway. As their care is situated within an individual's recovery pathway, their philosophy states that they should not have any access to tools they could harm themselves with, unless those involved in the recovery feel they are ready.

The physicality of the box seemed to evoke discomfort and unease in other clinicians, too. One therapist explained *"there's something that makes me feel a bit uncomfortable about someone putting them in a place with the specific purpose of accessing them [the tools]".* The Student Wellbeing team considered the idea of keeping the tools in one place and creating hurdles to overcome before reaching them as 'reinforcing' and 'rewarding' self-harming behavior.

Interestingly, the issue of portability was not a key concern for a charity worker who had experience of working with young people who self-harmed. When discussing with a charity worker whether the box needed to be portable, he explained that from his experience, the urge to self-harm only ever arises within an individual's home:

"I think also part of that is probably to do with I think people want to feel safe. I know it sounds silly but you know what I mean. People want to be safe when they are self-harming because it is not about ending their life. If they were to go by themselves in the middle of nowhere in some woods and self-harm probably I would say that is very, very unlikely to happen because there is a huge risk there. They don't want to end their life so why would they do it somewhere that is risky?"

This quotation, though not explicitly discussing the design concept, reveals and unpacks some common misconceptions about self-harming behavior. It is interesting that both a charity worker, and the self-harmers, could see the practical value of the box and share an understanding of the lived work of self-harm. Whilst it brought about unease in clinicians, because of the perceived risk to an individual; for those that self-harm, and the charity workers, it became obvious that it did not evoke the same discomfort. The charity worker and those with lived experience were able to see past the initial risks of self-harming behavior to the protective factors that the box facilitated. He explains that individuals who self-harm do not always do so as they intend to end their lives. People tend to self-harm in their homes, as they want to feel safe and secure. Although self-harming is widely considered a risky, dangerous behavior, for many individuals it is the opposite of that; it is a way to personalize, ground, and make them feel safe.

Paperchain

Paperchain seemed to be accepted more widely by clinicians throughout the engagements, as it was in line with the traditional methods that are encouraged to prompt behaviour change. This said, there were some key concerns that surfaced in relation to the digital paperchaining mobile app. All of the clinicians were concerned that the app may be too simplistic, or reductive, in that there are only eight different colours available for users to represent their moods or behaviours. This was made particularly obvious by a key informant involved in the commissioning of local health services: *"I think it might be too unsubtle, too reductionist... You can imagine my clinical psychologists might say, 'It's a bit too reductionist'".* Psychologists felt that the app was not nuanced enough, as they wanted their patients to go further than mood acceptance and identification. They wanted the app to explore the nuances of the moods that led to self-harming and trigger identification, and the subsequent methods used to delay and distract from those urges.

This was echoed by the therapists from a student wellbeing service: *"I think we're not trying to encourage people to just change their mood. We're trying to encourage them to accept what their mood is. So there needs to be something there that either is looking at the triggers, or looking at the chain as it stands"*. There was a consensus that although the Paperchain app had the potential to be effective, in that its grounding in traditional methods of chain analysis was well-evidenced, it did not go far enough in its prompting of behavioural change. The clinicians approached about the app wanted there to be an iteration of the design that facilitated signposting, trigger identification and more colours in order to represent more nuanced moods.

Third sector volunteers were less concerned about the simplistic nature of the app and the implications for behaviour change, and focused on issues of accessibility and privacy. *"But what if you don't have a Smartphone or you don't have your own laptop? If you want to go on the internet you have to go on your mum's computer or whatever"*. Charity workers were concerned with a more encompassing critique arc about the technologies in that they required a laptop or smartphone. It was important that individuals who needed the app had access to their own technologies in order to maintain a sense of privacy when logging their behaviours. The demographic of individuals that mental health charities were working with often did not have access to these devices due to their economic status, which could lead to difficult conversations with family and friends.

The potential for a support network to be notified about behavior paperchains and the configuration and sharing of personal codes evoked concerns about responsibility and onus. It was felt that although support networks are an integral part of the recovery and journey of those self-harming, that their involvement should be approached with a certain amount of scepticism. One clinical psychologist observed *"what if the family haven't logged in or if they miss it and then there's a bit of a blame or, "Well I did tell you because it's on my chain"'*. Whilst sharing codes had the potential to create meaningful and valuable relationships between loved ones, it could also mean that people are held accountable for not noticing or purposefully ignoring information input by those self-harming.

Squeeze

Overall, Squeeze evoked positive reactions from both clinicians and charity workers alike. Clinical psychologists were able to scaffold conversation around the digital stress ball by relating it back to the distress tolerance boxes that their patients used. This comparison to similar techniques used in-house facilitated an interesting discussion in which participants were able to reimagine the tangible and collaboratively design a new iteration of it: *"And maybe, as you go up, you could get a new thing that you could make on it as well, or stick on it? Or maybe you could sew on a star or something, when you get better?"*. This enthusiasm and shared imagining was typical of concepts that engendered little criticism, as respondents were able to concentrate on how to improve the designs, rather than explore their concerns for them.

This design was received so positively that three of the engagements were characterised by participants imagining different iterations of the tool that could be deployed at the same time: *"You might have two models, you might have them readymade, and then for those people who have enjoyed the readymade and want to do something for a friend, they might decide to knit one for a friend."* It was decided that the DIY nature of this concept may be anxiety-inducing for those individuals who are not creative and so there should be a readymade version, too. This off-the-shelf version would also mean that individuals who were not in the correct 'headspace' or did not have the time and effort to invest could still try it.

On the other hand, it was felt that there is something valuable about investing the time to personally create the Squeeze ball. One respondent said: *"Yes, it's a lot to ask but I think maybe if you made a thing out of it. Then if they've gone through building it then they've invested...they've got that ownership of it"*. The process of creating the tool itself, whilst practising mindfulness and breathing techniques, coupled with the therapy of making, was seen as a powerful process in itself.

DISCUSSION

Following the critical engagements with stakeholders in the context of self-harm, we offer several challenges for the design of digital technology and services in this area. These challenges relate to designing within a relationship of care, appropriately leveraging behavioral techniques, and striving for a common language between stakeholders in the design process.

Responsibility Sharing in Connected Networks of Care

Many of the design concepts were designed to facilitate conversations about self-harm across a support network. One of the challenges at the hackathon was to create a technology for the support network around a self-harming individual, given that caregivers often face conflicting demands, and can need their own form of support [5]. However, rather than designing *for* the support network, participants tended to only consider how the caregivers could *support* those self-harming. Several of the teams decided to design concepts that allowed friends and family to communicate with the self-harmers and support them throughout their experiences. This well-intentioned notion of responsibility-sharing caused concern within the stakeholder critiques. One clinician expressed worry for the potential recipients of the digital paperchain. It became apparent that poor wellbeing of one family member, coupled with the responsibility of care, could result in the poor mental health of another.

This concern regarding onus was mirrored in the discussions held by the team of clinical psychologists. Whilst acknowledging the necessity of mutual support for individuals experiencing mental health challenges, they also recognised the negative effects that caring for a self-harmer could have on oneself. The psychologists felt that if somebody was experiencing low mood and was then constantly prompted to positively respond to somebody in distress, then their own mental health could suffer.

Furthermore, stakeholders were concerned not only about the fact that the mental health of the support network could be negatively affected, but also that an element of blame could occur. Clinicians were concerned that by involving loved ones in the self-harming individual's 'app network', there would be an element of 'blame' that would occur if friends or family did not respond. It became apparent that when designing for those affected by self-harm, we must consider not only the mental health of the individual, but also the mental health of the support network around the individual [11].

Baumgarten acknowledges that within ecologies of care – dementia in particular - often the caregiver will begin to suffer from mental health issues [5]. When designing within such a sensitive context, it is important that we consider how technology can allow individuals to support one another, without imposing an onus on caregivers and exacerbating any mental health issues. It is imperative that within HCI, there is a greater consideration of how technology can affect not only those who need care, but their caregivers. For inspiration concerning designing within caring relationships surrounding mental health challenges, we can turn to existing HCI work on caregivers for people with dementia. Wallace [37] used bespoke probes to empathically engage a couple living with dementia, and aid their design of digital jewellery to reflect upon their sense of personhood. In her work, she did not just focus on the person with dementia, but instead positioned her design response within the relationship between Gillian and John. When designing for such a sensitive context, we should ensure that we consider not only the person who is self-harming but also the caregiver's sense of self.

Nuance and Simplicity in Caring Technologies

Another concern that pervaded the stakeholder critiques was a perceived lack of nuance which stakeholders thought failed to represent the different behaviors and moods of the users. Particularly with Paperchain there was a sense that the eight different colors available were not varied enough to represent the infinite amount of moods an individual may experience in one day. The clinicians explained that they encouraged their patients to accept their moods by identifying and exploring their emotions in detail.

An individual involved in the commissioning of statutory health services echoed the importance of considering nuance in technologies for those experiencing mental health difficulties, but also acknowledged the benefit that some people may find in having simplistic tools to express their emotions. For some clinicians, it was more important that the users were able to express their emotions in any way, whether through words, visual images, or colors. The notion that an individual could identify and express the moods, emotions and events that led to the act of self-harming was more important than *how* they are expressed, and to what degree.

When designing technologies for those who self-harm, it is imperative to consider how to *appropriately* leverage behavior change techniques, or whether they are even appropriate at all [4,20]. Although it would be appropriate within some care pathways to design an element of nuance into a digital technology, for others it is more important to facilitate a simplistic conversation. This speaks to the wider implication of designing not just for one community of those who self-harm, but multiple communities.

The notion of behavior change was fundamental for clinicians, and there is an opportunity for future work that explores how traditional methods can be individualized and therefore augmented by technology. However, behavior change should not be implemented without critical forethought given the sensitive context in which we are deploying these technologies.

Conflict in Design Processes

The language which was used, and the way in which stakeholders responded to the concepts from Self Harmony differed between the clinicians and the individuals who worked for mental health charities. The clinical psychologists and therapists from the wellbeing service were concerned about how the digital technologies prompted behavior change and facilitated 'barriers' to self-harming behaviors that would ultimately result in more positive mental health behaviors.

Through a process of shared reflection that made use of past experiences with patients who displayed self-harming behaviors, the clinicians were able to reveal their concerns for the Self Harmony concepts. The technologies that raised concerns were the ones that were felt to reinforce self-harming behaviors. The clinicians felt that the concepts should facilitate positive behavior change and enhance the traditional methods that are currently in practice. All of the clinicians explained that their desired iterations of the apps would work upon aiding trigger identification, mood reflection and distraction techniques.

The clinicians raised more concerns regarding the Self Harmony outputs than the charity sector respondents. The clinical psychologists and therapists used a language that engendered ideas of prevention and a creation of 'barriers' and 'hurdles' to the act of self-harming. Whilst there was a positivity regarding all of the designs, clinicians expressed concerns that some of the technologies had the potential to reinforce negative behaviors. Particularly with the 'Digital Distraction Box', there was a discomfort from healthcare providers that arose from the perceived 'accessibility' of self-harming tools that existed in the box. This discomfort was also present due to the perceived potential for the act of self-harming to be rewarded, or reinforced, by the tools within the box.

Whilst clinicians noted concerns regarding the implications of designing for a perceived vulnerable population, charity workers were worried about more practical issues, such as use in-situ and whether the target population would be able to gain access to the technologies. The conversations with the charities revealed something about the subjective realities of those affected by self-harm. It was acknowledged that despite the 'undesirable' and often dangerous nature of self-harm, for many individuals this is an acceptable and very real coping mechanism for processing and dealing with emotions.

Revealing stakeholder conflicts in this way means that HCI work can concentrate upon striving towards a shared language in the design of technologies that will affect different communities in the context of mental health. Our research identifies the presence of conflicting agendas within a complex, challenging and sensitive setting. There is a wider question here, when working with a number of diverse stakeholders, about how to ensure that no one voice is prioritized, and the design process is configured appropriately and equally by all.

Extending the Conventional Hackathon Format

Motivated by the criticism that conventional hackathons do not create lasting impact [19], and only generate short-lived attention, we extended and rethought the traditional hackathon format. By holding a series of engagements with stakeholders after the hackathon, we have been able to scaffold the conventional hackathon format so that expert stakeholders who could not attend the event were able to maintain a valuable involvement in appraising the design outcomes, and provide further ideas and imagine more appropriate design iterations for the self-harm context.

Despite the increasing popularity of hackathons, they still tend to attract a majority of technologists, and those with no technological expertise feel that they do not possess the skillset to attend and make valuable contributions to idea generation and prototype development [19]. By extending the hackathon with the stakeholder critiques, we ensured that non-technologists were able to have a tangible involvement in the design outcomes. Moreover, we were able to sustain an interest in the projects that resulted from the hackathon, which will lead to a reiteration of the outcomes with the expert stakeholders.

Furthermore, the critical engagements allow us to consider how we could reconfigure future hackathons in challenging and sensitive contexts. It is of utmost importance to involve those with lived experience in the design of the outcomes at the hackathon. However it is equally important to ensure that experts have the opportunity to engage in critiques of these outcomes from a later, more objective perspective, as they possess an expertise that can be seen as integral to how these design outcomes could be successfully integrated into self-harm care pathways. By engaging with a diverse set of expert stakeholders, we are able to imagine how design outcomes from hackathons can be appropriately redesigned for different individuals and different care pathways within the context of self-harm. Appropriate consideration must be given to how the participation of stakeholders – including those who self-harm and healthcare practitioners – is scaffolded, and how their contributions are appropriately accounted for. Though some aspects of the hackathon could be considered 'conventional', the contribution of this work lies in the integration of VCD approaches of conducting a hackathon in a sensitive setting, and a subsequent engagement of practitioners, clinicians and users in a more inclusive, considered and longitudinal design process.

Our own future work will see the documentation from Self Harmony, and the critiques from stakeholders, inform a competition commissioning platform that will facilitate open sourcing ideas for designing and developing digital tools for mental health. The platform will facilitate an online conversation between individuals with lived experience of self-harm, software developers, and healthcare professionals, which will result in the proposal of ideas for apps, and the subsequent deployment of the winning app into the local community. Through this continued extension of the conventional hackathon format we strive for a greater level of inclusion in the design processes and the creation of sustainable digital tools to support mental health and wellbeing.

CONCLUSION

Motivated by existing literature, we configured and ran a hackathon to design technologies for those affected by self-harm. We extended the conventional hackathon format by holding a series of critical engagements where experts were asked to critique the design outcomes. Through an analysis of these engagements, we unpack key concerns and challenges for research in digital mental health that considers self-harm: responsibility-sharing in networks of care; nuance in caring technologies; stakeholder conflicts; and extending the conventional hackathon format. Moreover, we identify how rethinking and extending the conventional hackathon format can be a valuable design method in sensitive settings.

ACKNOWLEDGEMENTS

We wish to thank all of the hackathon participants, as well as Sophie Buckle, Teresa Almeida and Rehaan Ansari for helping to organize the event. The research was funded through the EPSRC Centre for Doctoral Training in Digital Civics and Newcastle University (EP/L016176/1) and the EPSRC - NIHR HTC Partnership Award Network Grant (EP/M000206/1) "Social Computing and Mental Health Research Network". Data supporting this publication is openly available under an 'Open Data Commons Open Database License'. Additional metadata are available at: http://dx.doi.org/10.17634/138138-1.

REFERENCES

1. 7 cups of tea. 2016. Someone to Talk To, Online Therapy and Free Counseling. *7 Cups of Tea.*

Retrieved August 21, 2016 from https://www.7cups.com/

2. Bert Arnrich, Venet Osmani, and Jakob Bardram. 2013. Mental health and the impact of ubiquitous technologies. *Personal and Ubiquitous Computing* 17, 2: 211–213. http://doi.org/10.1007/s00779-011-0464-3

3. Jessica A Artiles and David R Wallace. 2013. Borrowing From Hackathons : Overnight Designathons As a Template for Creative Idea Hubs in the Space of Hands-on Learning , Digital Learning , and Systems Re-Thinking. *World Engineering Education Forum*: 8. Retrieved from http://www.acofipapers.org/index.php/acofipapers/2013/paper/viewFile/491/154

4. Eric P.S. Baumer and M. Six Silberman. 2011. When the implication is not to design (technology). In *Proceedings of the 2011 annual conference on Human factors in computing systems - CHI '11*, 2271. http://doi.org/10.1145/1978942.1979275

5. Mona Baumgarten, Renaldo N. Battista, Claire Infante-Rivard, James A. Hanley, Rubin Becker, and Serge Gauthier. 1992. The psychological and physical health of family members caring for an elderly person with dementia. *Journal of Clinical Epidemiology* 45, 1: 61–70. http://doi.org/10.1016/0895-4356(92)90189-T

6. Alan Borning and Michael Muller. 2012. Next steps for value sensitive design. In *Proceedings of the 2012 ACM annual conference on Human Factors in Computing Systems - CHI '12*, 1125. http://doi.org/10.1145/2207676.2208560

7. Dina L G Borzekowski, Summer Schenk, Jenny L. Wilson, and Rebecka Peebles. 2010. E-Ana and e-Mia: A content analysis of pro-eating disorder web sites. *American Journal of Public Health* 100, 8: 1526–1534. http://doi.org/10.2105/AJPH.2009.172700

8. Rafael A. Calvo and Dorian Peters. 2013. Promoting psychological wellbeing: Loftier goals for new technologies [opinion]. *IEEE Technology and Society Magazine 32*, 19–21. http://doi.org/10.1109/MTS.2013.2286429

9. Stevie Chancellor, Zhiyuan Lin, Erica L. Goodman, Stephanie Zerwas, and Munmun De Choudhury. 2016. Quantifying and Predicting Mental Illness Severity in Online Pro-Eating Disorder Communities. In *Proceedings of the 19th ACM Conference on Computer-Supported Cooperative Work & Social Computing - CSCW '16*, 1169–1182. http://doi.org/10.1145/2818048.2819973

10. Stevie Chancellor, Jessica Annette Pater, Trustin A Clear, Eric Gilbert, and Munmun De Choudhury. 2016. #thyghgapp: Instagram Content Moderation and Lexical Variation in Pro-Eating Disorder Communities. In *Proceedings of the 19th ACM Conference on Computer-Supported Cooperative Work & Social Computing - CSCW '16*, 1199–1211. http://doi.org/10.1145/2818048.2819963

11. Patrick Corrigan. 2004. How Stigma Interferes With Mental Health Care. *American Psychologist* 59, 7: 614–625. http://doi.org/10.1037/0003-066X.59.7.614

12. David Coyle and Gavin Doherty. 2009. Clinical evaluations and collaborative design. In *Proceedings of the 27th international conference on Human factors in computing systems - CHI 09*, 2051. http://doi.org/10.1145/1518701.1519013

13. Michele P. Dyson, Lisa Hartling, Jocelyn Shulhan, et al. 2016. A systematic review of social media use to discuss and view deliberate self-harm acts. *PLoS ONE* 11, 5. http://doi.org/10.1371/journal.pone.0155813

14. Happier. 2016. Gratitude Journal, Meditation and Celebrating the Good Around You. Retrieved July 13, 2016 from https://www.happier.com/

15. R. Jones, S. Sharkey, T. Ford, et al. 2011. Online discussion forums for young people who self-harm: user views. *The Psychiatrist* 35, 10: 364–368. http://doi.org/10.1192/pb.bp.110.033449

16. Stephen P Lewis, Nancy L Heath, Jill M St Denis, and Rick Noble. 2011. The scope of nonsuicidal self-injury on YouTube. *Pediatrics 127*, e552–e557. http://doi.org/10.1542/peds.2010-2317

17. LiftOffHealth. 2016. LiftOffHealth. Retrieved June 14, 2016 from http://liftoffhealth.com/

18. T. J. Lodato and C. DiSalvo. 2016. Issue-oriented hackathons as material participation. *New Media & Society* 18, 4: 539–557. http://doi.org/10.1177/1461444816629467

19. A. Mantzavinou and J.B. Ranger. 2016. *Health hackathons drive affordable medical technology innovation through community engagement.* Retrieved from http://cooperation.epfl.ch/files/content/sites/cooperation/files/Tech4Dev 2016/1265-Mantzavinou-SE07-MED_Full Paper.pdf

20. Mark Matthews, Saeed Abdullah, Geri Gay, and Tanzeem Choudhury. 2014. Tracking mental well-being: Balancing rich sensing and patient needs. *Computer* 47, 4: 36–43. http://doi.org/10.1109/MC.2014.107

21. Medhacks 2.0. 2016. MedHacks 2.0. Retrieved August 14, 2016 from http://medhacks.org/

22. Mental Health Foundation. 2016. Self-Harm. *Mental Health Foundation*. Retrieved August 13, 2016 from https://www.mentalhealth.org.uk/a-to-z/s/self-harm

23. Mind. 2013. How many people have mental health problems? *Mind*. Retrieved January 21, 2016 from http://www.mind.org.uk/information-support/types-of-mental-health-problems/statistics-and-facts-about-mental-health/how-common-are-mental-health-problems/

24. MIT Hacking Medicine. 2016. MIT Hacking Medicine. Retrieved August 4, 2016 from http://hackingmedicine.mit.edu/

25. Stuart B. Murray, Scott Griffiths, Leila Hazery, Tori Shen, Tom Wooldridge, and Jonathan M. Mond. 2016. Go big or go home: A thematic content analysis of pro-muscularity websites. *Body Image* 16: 17–20. http://doi.org/10.1016/j.bodyim.2015.10.002

26. NHS England. 2016. Self-Harm. *NHS Choices*. Retrieved June 6, 2016 from http://www.nhs.uk/conditions/self-injury/Pages/Introduction.aspx

27. Christabel Owens, Paul Farrand, Ruth Darvill, Tobit Emmens, Elaine Hewis, and Peter Aitken. 2011. Involving service users in intervention design: A participatory approach to developing a text-messaging intervention to reduce repetition of self-harm. *Health Expectations* 14, 3: 285–295. http://doi.org/10.1111/j.1369-7625.2010.00623.x

28. Jessica A Pater, Oliver L. Haimson, Nazanin Andalibi, and Elizabeth D Mynatt. 2016. "Hunger Hurts but Starving Works:" Characterizing the Presentation of Eating Disorders Online. In *Proceedings of the 19th ACM Conference on Computer-Supported Cooperative Work & Social Computing - CSCW '16*, 1183–1198. http://doi.org/10.1145/2818048.2820030

29. V. Prasad and D. Owens. 2001. Using the internet as a source of self-help for people who self-harm. *Psychiatric Bulletin* 25, 6: 222–225. http://doi.org/10.1192/pb.25.6.222

30. Mashfiqui Rabbi, Shahid Ali, Tanzeem Choudhury, and Ethan Berke. 2011. Passive and In-Situ assessment of mental and physical well-being using mobile sensors. In *Proceedings of the 13th international conference on Ubiquitous computing - UbiComp '11*, 385. http://doi.org/10.1145/2030112.2030164

31. Stefan Rennick-Egglestone, Sarah Knowles, Gill Toms, Penny Bee, Karina Lovell, and Peter Bower. 2016. H,ealth Technologies "In the Wild." In *Proceedings of the 2016 CHI Conference on Human Factors in Computing Systems - CHI '16*, 2124–2135. http://doi.org/10.1145/2858036.2858128

32. Stephen M Schueller, Ricardo F Munoz, and David C Mohr. 2013. Realizing the potential of behavioral intervention technologies. *Current Directions in Psychological Science* 22, 6: 478–483. http://doi.org/10.1177/0963721413495872

33. S. Sharkey, R. Jones, J. Smithson, et al. 2011. Ethical practice in internet research involving vulnerable people: lessons from a self-harm discussion forum study (SharpTalk). *Journal of Medical Ethics* 37, 12: 752–758. http://doi.org/10.1136/medethics-2011-100080

34. Anja Thieme, Ashur Rafiev, Cassim Ladha, et al. 2016. Challenges for Designing new Technology for Health and Wellbeing in a Complex Mental Healthcare Context. In *Proceedings of the 2016 CHI Conference on Human Factors in Computing Systems - CHI '16*, 2136–2149. http://doi.org/10.1145/2858036.2858182

35. Anja Thieme, Jayne Wallace, Thomas D. Meyer, and Patrick Olivier. 2015. Designing for mental wellbeing. In *Proceedings of the 2015 British HCI Conference on - British HCI '15*, 1–10. http://doi.org/10.1145/2783446.2783586

36. Erik H. Trainer, Arun Kalyanasundaram, Chalalai Chaihirunkarn, and James D. Herbsleb. 2016. How to Hackathon: Socio-technical Tradeoffs in Brief, Intensive Collocation. In *Proceedings of the 19th ACM Conference on Computer-Supported Cooperative Work & Social Computing - CSCW '16*, 1116–1128. http://doi.org/10.1145/2818048.2819946

37. Jayne Wallace, Peter C. Wright, John McCarthy, David Philip Green, James Thomas, and Patrick Olivier. 2013. A design-led inquiry into personhood in dementia. In *Proceedings of the SIGCHI Conference on Human Factors in Computing Systems - CHI '13*, 2617. http://doi.org/10.1145/2470654.2481363

38. YoungMinds. 2016. Self-Harm. Retrieved July 3, 2016 from http://www.youngminds.org.uk/for_children_young_people/whats_worrying_you/self-harm

Changing Moods: How Manual Tracking by Family Caregivers Improves Caring and Family Communication

Naomi Yamashita[1], Hideaki Kuzuoka[2], Keiji Hirata[3], Takashi Kudo[4], Eiji Aramaki[5], Kazuki Hattori[2]

[1] NTT Communication Science Labs.
[2] University of Tsukuba.
[3] Future University Hakodate.
[4] Osaka University Department of Psychiatry.
[5] Nara Institute of Science and Technology.

ABSTRACT

Previous research on healthcare technologies has shown how health tracking promotes desired behavior changes and effective health management. However, little is known about how the family caregivers' use of tracking technologies impacts the patient-caregiver relationship in the home. In this paper, we explore how health-tracking technologies could be designed to support family caregivers cope better with a depressed family member. Based on an interview study, we designed a simple tracking tool called Family Mood and Care Tracker (FMCT) and deployed it for six weeks in the homes of 14 family caregivers who were caring for a depressed family member. FMCT is a tracking tool designed specifically for family caregivers to record their caregiving activities and patient's conditions. Our findings demonstrate how caregivers used it to better understand the illness and cope with depressed family members. We also show how our tool improves family communication, despite the initial concerns about patient-caregiver conflicts.

Author Keywords

Caregiving; informal caregiver; depression; family communication; healthcare technology; tracking technology

ACM Classification Keywords

J.3. Life and Medical Sciences, Health, Medical Information Systems

INTRODUCTION

The onset of mental illness in a family causes a significant burden and stress on its members [3,6,29]. In most cases, mental illness—and its medication—causes unexpected behaviors in sufferers. For example, they might become demanding and disruptive or express extremely negative attitudes or rage [18,24,42]. When family caregivers face such circumstances, they often become puzzled and do not know how to react. In addition to the difficulty of coping with such unexpected behaviors, social stigma is often attached to such illnesses, making it difficult for family caregivers to consult with others [10]. Under such circumstances, most family caregivers prefer to gather information about the illness themselves [29]. However, finding useful information is also complicated due to the huge individual differences among symptoms. Consequently, family caregivers generally have little choice but to rely on discoveries based on their own experiences [29].

CHI 2017, May 06 - 11, 2017, Denver, CO, USA

ACM 978-1-4503-4655-9/17/05…$15.00
DOI: http://dx.doi.org/10.1145/3025453.3025843

Despite the significant impact of mental illness on families, much HCI/CSCW work on mental illness has focused on either the patient or clinician, aiming for better patient care. Little research has focused on supporting family caregivers.

Our goal is to design a tool that helps family caregivers develop strategies to improve their interaction with care recipients. In this paper, we focus on tracking technology and explore its potential to aid family caregivers. For example, by tracking the care recipient's moods and caregiving activities, family caregivers may be able to experiment new coping strategies and reflect on them by analyzing how their behavior affected the care recipient's moods/symptoms [34]. Such experimentation and optimization of coping strategies might lead to better caregiver-care recipient relationships. Family caregivers' private use of tracking technology also aligns with caregivers' current practices where they opt to develop coping strategies on their own [29].

However, previous research also warns that family caregivers' use of tracking technologies to monitor care recipients' health may create caregiver-care recipient conflicts caused by the care recipients' perception of being under surveillance [20,41]. Since individuals suffering from mental illness tend to have a high awareness of surveillance [28], we need to be cognizant of its risks and pay extra attention to how tracking technologies affect domestic relationships.

In this paper, which is an initial attempt to reach our goal, we explore the following research issues: (1) how a tracking technology might assist family caregivers' development of coping strategies, and (2) how it affects the relationships between family caregivers and care recipients. We investigate these research issues by focusing on caregivers who look after homebound depressed family members.

To answer these research questions, we first conducted a preliminary interview study to determine the tracking items family caregivers wish to follow and the family caregivers' concerns about using tracking technologies at home. Based on this interview study, we developed a technology probe [22], which is a web-based tracking tool, and deployed it with 14 family caregivers of depressed family members. During the deployment study, the family caregivers recorded their caregiving activities and their care recipient's behaviors/moods for six weeks. The deployment study focused on investigating the impact of tracking technology on the family caregivers' development of coping strategies and the relationships between family caregivers and care recipients.

In the rest of our paper, we first frame this work by introducing previous works. We then present the findings of our preliminary interview study, which revealed the design requirements of our tracking tool. Next, we present our tracking tool and report its deployment study. Finally, we discuss design implications and future directions.

BACKGROUND

Caregiving for a Depressed Family Member

Research shows that depression causes a variety of behavioral changes in its sufferers. For example, the reactions of depressed sufferers tend to be negative, lethargic, and offensive [18,28,42]. Such attitudes of sufferers often negatively affect others. Family caregivers are no exception. Family caregivers who are living with depression sufferers are generally exposed to these behaviors, since sufferers typically withdraw from social activities and seclude themselves at home during depressive episodes [3,24,42].

Such behavioral changes caused by depression tend to deviate from the sufferer's original personality [24,42]. In such cases, those behaviors seem to create a gap between the caregiver's expectations and the sufferer's actual behaviors [43]. The family caregivers have difficulty understanding such behaviors, especially whether they arose from the depressive symptoms, and do not know how to deal with them. For instance, when caregivers experience extreme sufferer attitudes or behaviors, many seem to get confused whether they should criticize the sufferer or suppress their reactions to avoid exacerbating the depressive symptoms.

Another notable characteristic of depression is its high recurrence rate [26,42]. The risk of future recurrences dramatically increases once a sufferer experiences one recurrence; another recurrence happens 70% of the time, and a second happens 90%. Such recurrent nature of depression may create anxiety in family caregivers who are concerned with triggering a recurrence by their own words/behaviors [23,31].

What also complicates family caregivers is the social stigma surrounding depression [3]. Many family caregivers miss their own companionships from before the depression [3,25] and also tend to avoid mental health clinics [23,43]. While many family caregivers seek useful information from the web to learn how to interact with depression sufferers, such attempts are often unsuccessful due to the large variance in symptoms and family situations [43]. Consequently, most family caregivers struggle to develop coping strategies by themselves.

Technological Support for Mental Healthcare

If technology could help family caregivers develop strategies for coping with care recipients, it might ameliorate the interaction between family caregivers and care recipients.

Yet few technologies have been designed to support family caregivers or to improve the relationships between family caregivers and care recipients. HCI research on healthcare has focused almost exclusively on designing technologies for better patient care [14,16]. For example, researchers studying depression (or mental healthcare) have focused on designing technologies that improve access and engagement with traditional treatments/services, such as electronic contact, online self-help manuals, and online interventions [4,5,10,11,15,36]. Even though some technologies are designed for caregiver use, their primary focus is on facilitating effective treatment of patients. For example, systems are being developed to enable caregivers to monitor patient activities from distant locations [17,39] and improve coordination with other caregivers for better patient care [8,40].

Less research has addressed the needs of caregivers or focused on improving the relationship between caregivers and care recipients [6,12,32]. Yamashita et al. studied the burden on family caregivers of depressed individuals and suggested building social/emotional support networks that exclude those who have close connections with the care recipient so that caregivers can share their feelings without worrying about the potential impact on care recipients [43]. While previous studies focused on providing emotional support to family caregivers, they did not support building better relationships with care recipients.

Health tracking Technologies

Health tracking technologies are a growing trend in e-health studies [27,33,34]. As represented in the Quantified Self movement, advancements in web technologies, mobile technologies, and smart home technologies are encouraging researchers to develop a wide range of applications, including tools for managing chronic conditions or achieving better health [27,38].

These tools have mainly been developed for individuals to better understand their own illness and promote desired behavioral changes. Few examined the family caregivers' use of health tracking tools or focused on its impact on family communication [19,21,38,41]. Furthermore, the studies that focus on family communication report somewhat contradicting results: while some studies show that automatically detecting care recipients' heath information and sharing it with family members create caregiver-care recipient conflicts [20], others suggest that a properly designed tracking technology can keep family relationship healthy or even improve family communication [21,41]. For example, Toscos et al.'s work on children with type I diabetes argued how a poorly designed tracking technology could exacerbate parent-child conflict [41]. Huber et al. studied the impact of in-home monitoring technologies on family relationships, and showed that the technology enhanced communication between independently-living older adults and their informal caregivers [21]. Grimes et al. studied how tracking technologies can facilitate family health discussions [19]. Overall, these studies argue the importance of understanding the potential impact of health tracking technologies on family dynamics.

Our idea of exploiting caregiver tracking to improve family communication was hinted from these previous works. However, it has not been studied in the domain of mental healthcare. In our case, we must keep in mind that family caregivers who are looking after a depressed family member are having trouble communicating with their care recipients. Thus, careful design considerations must address how to include the care recipients in the system. Introducing a poorly designed tool into homes might severely damage family relationships.

PRELIMINARY INTERVIEW STUDY

To identify the ways in which tracking technologies could be designed to support family caregivers cope with care recipients who are experiencing depression, we interviewed 14 family caregivers looking after a depressed family member. From interviews, we identified the basic design requirements of our tracking tool.

Data Collection

We recruited through a consumer marketing company 14 family caregivers (12 females and 2 males, age: min = 24, max = 48, mean = 41.8) who had been caregiving for a depressed family member within the last two years. The care recipients had their initial onset about six years earlier (min=1 year, max=16 years). At the point of recruitment, four had experienced relapses, but all started working/going to school again within the last two years. Ten still regularly saw a doctor and took antidepressant pills daily. All of the caregivers were the spouses of the care recipients and held primary responsibility for looking after them. Four were full-time homemakers, four worked part time, five had full-time jobs outside the home, and one worked at home. The interviews with the family caregivers lasted approximately 1 to 1.5 hours each. For the interview manuscript, we drafted semi-structured interviews in collaboration with the psychiatrist on our research team. The interviews focused on the following themes:

- The current practices adopted for tracking records and their effects on family caregivers: e.g., if care recipients tracked their own health conditions, to what extent did the family caregivers find the records useful? Did family caregivers ever take notes about their care recipients' health conditions or their caregiving activities?
- The items considered by family caregivers important or relevant to understand the illness and to help them develop strategies for better interaction with the care recipients.
- Finally, family caregivers' concerns about using tracking technologies at home.

All of the data were audio-recorded and transcribed for analysis. The transcripts were analyzed using an iterative approach. Participant comments were extracted from each interview and grouped into categories, which were discussed, reorganized, and integrated by the researchers until they reached agreement.

Summary of Interview Findings

Current Practices. Some family caregivers seemed to keep a caregiving journal, although none wrote in it on a regular basis. In their journal, they only wrote about calamitous events, such as big fights with the care recipient, and described their own feelings about those events to let off steam. Although they sometimes reviewed their journals, they felt that the practice was discouraging and futile because it was filled with negative and emotional descriptions.

According to the family caregivers, some care recipients also kept a diary about their health conditions as part of therapy or treatment suggested by their doctors. However, many family caregivers seemed to perceive such self-reports as unreliable because patients become forgetful during depressive episodes [13].

Items to Record. When family caregivers were asked what items they wanted to track, they listed a range of things that could be consequential to care recipient moods: weather, medication, amount of sleep, outdoor activities, meals, drinking, their own caregiving activities, and unexpected events such as phone calls from a friend or fighting. In fact, most of these items are asked when diagnosing depression using Diagnostic and Statistical Manual of Mental Disorders (DSM-IV-TR) [1]. The articulation of "unexpected events" is expected to increase their understanding of the illness [35].

Concerns about Possible Conflicts. Although many participants showed interest in developing strategies to cope better with their care recipients, they also expressed concerns about using tracking technologies at home. Consistent with previous literature [19,20,41], many worried that care recipients might feel paranoid that they were under surveillance if they were recorded. However, when asked whether they would use the system without the consent of their care recipients, most disagreed, expressing a desire to get permission for recording their data. On the other hand, when asked about the possibility of tracking and reflecting with their care recipients, all preferred *not* to do so for fear of fights/conflicts. For example, they worried about offending the care recipients or that the care recipients' frequent negative reactions might inhibit them from generating constructive/positive reflection. Indeed, most of the family caregivers mentioned that they actually avoided discussing the illness at home. Note that the psychiatrist in our team also recommended not forcing the care recipients to reflect with a non-professional (i.e., family caregiver) because it could lead to fatal consequences.

Technology Requirements. The preliminary interview suggest that our system should:

- promote unbiased recording (i.e., not just bad events) to support positive self-reflection by the family caregivers.
- let family caregivers record and reflect on the logged data (including care recipients' health information) on their own after getting permission from the care recipients.
- include the following recording items: weather, medication, amount of sleep, outdoor activities, meals, drinking, their own caregiving activities, and unexpected events.

TRACKING TOOL

Based on our interviews and suggestions from the psychiatrist on our research team, we developed a web-based tracking tool called the Family Mood and Care Tracker: FMCT.

Design

The design of our tracking tool was speculative. We designed our tool as a technology probe [22] and kept its design as simple as possible because we wanted to explore the family caregivers' attitudes toward the technology in a real-world setting before further complicating the system.

FMCT consists of two sections: recording and reviewing. The recording section allows the family caregivers to record data, and the reviewing section facilitates reflective analysis by family caregivers by visualizing the recorded data in a chart.

Recording Section

The recording section allows the family caregivers to record all of the items identified above in the preliminary interview study: patient mood, medication, amount of sleep, outdoor activities, meals, drinking, their own caregiving activities, and unexpected events.

Figure 1 shows a page of the recording section. To minimize the family caregivers' input burden, most recording items consist of multiple-choice questions. For example, for patient sleep, the caregivers select the amount from four choices: long, normal, short, and unknown. The weather information (atmospheric pressure, highest/lowest temperatures, and actual weather conditions) is automatically retrieved from a weather information site. For medication, the caregivers first register their care recipient's prescribed medicines and usual doses from a menu. After

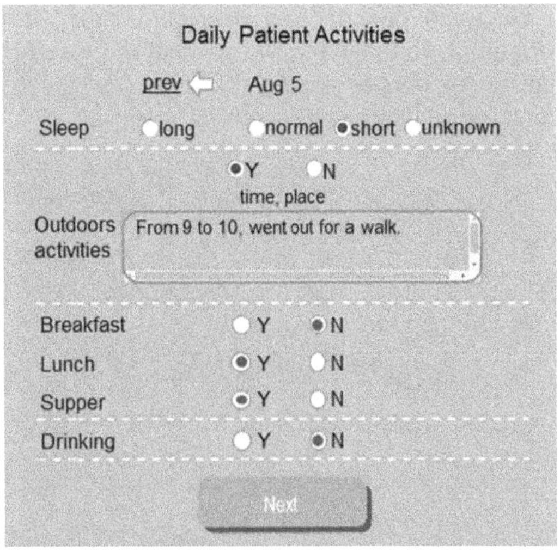

Figure. 1 User interface of recording section (translated into English)

that, they enter the data (i.e., adding or deleting medicines) only when there is a change in the daily medicine intake.

Based on previous research, the patient mood was recorded on a scale of 1–10 [2,14,16,37]. Note that the family caregivers rated the care recipients' moods based on their appearances. Even though the family caregivers' ratings might be different from the care recipients' actual mood, we assume that this subjective value remains useful for developing coping skills.

Free-form text boxes were provided for three items: outdoor activities, own caregiving activities, and unexpected events. For outdoor activities, the caregiver enters the details of where the care recipient went and for how long. For own caregiving activities, three free-form text boxes were prepared as prompt input for the positive and negative outcomes of their caregiving activities as well as lessons learned. We expected these three items to facilitate caregivers' unbiased reflections on their own daily caregiving activities and help them develop future coping strategies. Finally, a free-form text box was provided to facilitate reflection about unexpected events. Since such events happen sporadically, the data input for this field was optional.

Reviewing Section

The reviewing section displays a chart that facilitates caregiver reflections on caregiving activities and care recipient conditions (Figure 2). All data were displayed in a single chart so that caregivers can holistically explore them [30]. The chart shows the patient mood (red line) and the caregiver burden (blue line) as graphs, weather information, and other data as icons. Family caregivers can also see the unexpected events and the caregiving activities recorded on a particular day by clicking on a date, which makes a textbox pop up and show the record. Another textbox for the details of outdoor activities also pops up by clicking on the shoe icon. We expect such a chart to help family caregivers identify health condition patterns and develop coping strategies. From Figure 2, for example, we see that the care recipient tends to stay indoors or skip breakfast/lunch when he is in a bad mood (as highlighted by green rectangles).

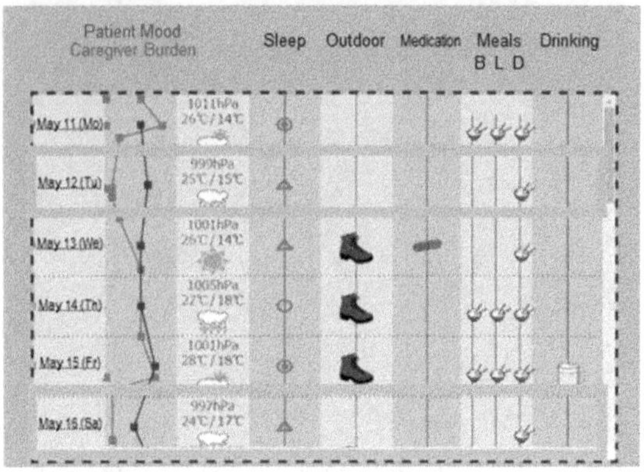

Figure 2. User interface of reviewing section (translated into English)

DEPLOYMENT STUDY

We ran a six-week deployment study with FMCT to investigate how family caregivers' tracking behaviors impacted their caregiving activities and interaction with their care recipients. The study was reviewed and approved by the ethical committee of the first author's organization (ethics review ID: H27-011).

Participants: Family Caregivers

We recruited 15 family caregivers (12 females and 3 males, mean age = 43.0) for the deployment study from the same consumer marketing company in our preliminary interview study. Upon recruitment, we excluded family caregivers who were themselves diagnosed with a major depression and recruited 15 family caregivers who were currently looking after a family member who was experiencing depression. Nine caregivers were spouses of care recipients, three were parents, two were daughters, and one was a sibling. All of the caregivers lived with the care recipient and held primary responsibility for looking after them. Six caregivers were full-time homemakers, six had full-time jobs outside the home, and two worked at home.

Procedure

Before the study, we explained it to the family caregivers by telephone. The family caregivers filled out surveys and gave informed consent before the study began. The surveys included questions about the care recipient's socio-demographic data and mental conditions. Agreement from care recipients was also required for participation.

Once the study started, the family caregivers used FMCT for six weeks in their homes. The family caregivers were asked to use it every single day, if possible. One dropped out because another family member was hospitalized during the study. After six weeks of deployment, we individually interviewed the family caregivers in 1-hour sessions.

Conditions of Care Recipients

The ages of the care recipients ranged from 24 to 59 (mean=43.1). Eight were male, and six were female. On average, the care recipients had their initial onset about eight years earlier (min.=1 year, max.=19 years). At the point of recruitment, nine had experienced relapses. All of the care recipients held jobs or went to college before getting depressed, but none had returned to society at the point of recruitment – they were all homebound. Two returned to work during the deployment study. All regularly saw a doctor and took antidepressant pills daily.

Data Collection

Log Data: All data entry to FMCT was made by the family caregivers. We gathered all of the data entries during the six-week study. Each entry was stored with a user ID and a timestamp.

Post-study Surveys: In post-study surveys, the family caregivers rated whether they perceived themselves becoming more attentive to their care recipients' moods/behaviors or more careful with their own attitudes/behaviors toward their care recipients. They also rated the workload caused by FMCT and evaluated the usefulness of each recording item.

Semi-structured Interviews: Similar to the preliminary interview study, we drafted semi-structured interviews through collaboration with our research team's psychiatrist. The interviews explored the family caregiver's experiences with FMCT by focusing on the following central themes and questions: How did they incorporate FMCT as part of their daily routine? Did they find self-reflection useful in terms of developing their own coping strategies? If so, how? Did they notice anything different or new about their care recipient or their caregiving activities from using FMCT? Did using it change their own caregiving activities? If so, how? Did the relationships between the family caregiver and care recipient change after using FMCT? If so, how?

The interview data were all audio-recorded, transcribed, and analyzed using inductive qualitative methods [9]. The first author arranged the quotes into an affinity diagram and inductively generated high-level themes in the data. The themes were then discussed by the researchers to iteratively refine the codes. The findings below emerged from this collaborative analysis.

RESULTS

Although the design of our tool was speculative, our tracking tool received a surprisingly high evaluation from the family caregivers. Indeed, most participants (twelve) noted in interviews that they became more actively engaged in the care, gained better control over the moods of their care recipients, and increased/improved communication with them. Below, we analyze how such changes were made through the data obtained by FMCT.

The results are presented in three parts. We start by reporting the family caregivers' general usage patterns of FMCT,

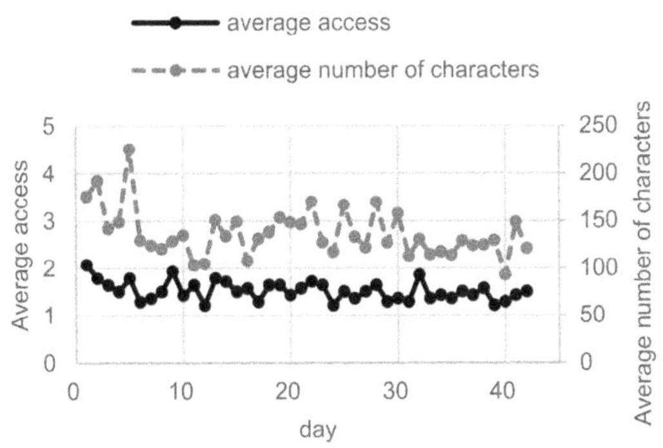

Figure 3. Average number of accesses and Japanese characters entered per person

followed by its usability issues; we then present the findings from our semi-structured interviews, which explored whether providing family caregivers with a simple tracking tool assisted the development of coping strategies with care recipients and how it impacted the relationships between family caregivers and care recipients.

General Usage Patterns

During the deployment study, seven participants used smart phones, four used personal computers, six used a family-shared computer, and one used a tablet (including multiple use devices).

Figure 3 shows the average number of accesses and Japanese characters entered in the free-form textboxes per person over time. The system was stably accessed by the participants throughout the deployment period. They accessed FMCT an average of 1.52 times per day per person, ranging from 0 to 6 times per day. Overall, the system received stable input throughout the deployment period. Participants entered an average of 137 characters per day per person, ranging from a 0 to 940 characters.

Usability Issues of FMCT

Input Burden

Although we were concerned about the family caregivers' burden of manual tracking [7], their perceived workload was not as high as we expected. In post-study surveys, the participants rated their burden on a 5-point Likert scale: 1=very high, 5=no burden at all. Their scores ranged from 2=moderately high to 5=no burden at all, and their average score was M=3.5 (SD=0.94). Some participants who perceived a high workload explained that they felt anxious when they had nothing to write in the free-text forms. Others without a mobile device to access FMCT complained about the inconvenience of sharing a computer, since they sometimes had to wait for access.

Evaluation of Recording Items

In the post-study surveys, the participants evaluated the usefulness of each recording item on a 5-point Likert scale: 1=very useful, 5=not useful at all.

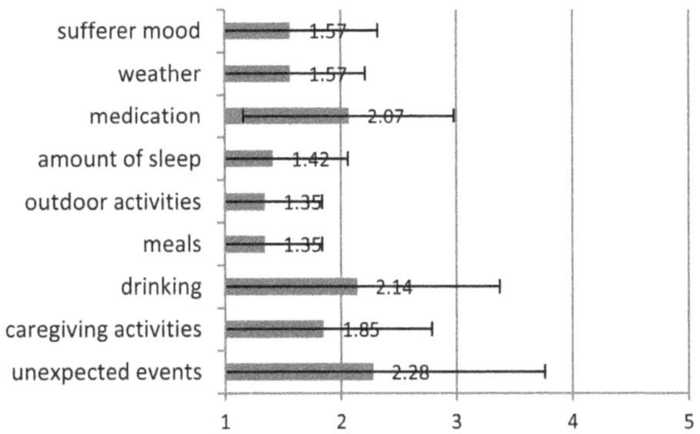

Figure 4. Perceived usefulness of recording items (1=very useful, 5=not useful at all)

The family caregivers in our study generally found FMCT's recording items useful (Figure. 4). However, some asked for adjustments in the recording items. For example, family caregivers whose care recipients did not drink wanted to omit this item. As for "unexpected events," some family caregivers complained about the inability to record the event's time. Since FMCT did not allow them to specify the time, the family caregivers tried to record them immediately after the event, which they found inconvenient. Finally, some caregivers suggested adding a few more patient behaviors to the recording items: snacks, taking a bath, and amount of communication.

Interview Findings

Six themes emerged from the interview coding. The prevalence of each theme was: 18 times over 12 participants for "Becoming attentive to care recipient's behaviors", 35 over 12 for "Making better sense of care recipient's behavior", 22 over 12 for "Developing concrete action plans", 19 over 9 for "Changing views on care recipients", 13 over 7 for "Being generous to care recipients", and 34 over 13 for "Better communication with care recipients".

Becoming Attentive to Care Recipient's Behaviors

In general, the survey results showed that family caregivers perceived themselves as becoming more attentive to their care recipient's behaviors (M=1.93, SD=0.65 on a 5-point Likert scale: 1=became very attentive, 5=did not become attentive at all.) One participant described how using FMCT produced greater attentiveness toward her care recipient's moods and behaviors:

[ID 7, full-time employee, daughter of care recipient] Since I'm always busy in the morning, I didn't really care whether she was in a good or bad mood. But after I started to use this [FMCT], I paid more attention to her condition to find something to record. Like her mood while eating breakfast and her tone of voice.

Another participant, whose husband experienced a relapse two years ago, mentioned that she started to pay extra attention to his medication:

[ID 1, homemaker, wife of care recipient] I feel more involved with my husband's illness. I started to watch him more carefully, and I realized that he often forgot to take some of his medication.

Although the family caregivers' access to FMCT was limited (1.52 times per day), the family caregivers perceived themselves as getting more attentive to the moods and behaviors of their care recipients. In particular, the recording items seemed to remind them of aspects to which they should pay attention when they were with their care recipients. Such attentiveness often led them to new findings about their care recipient's behaviors.

Making Better Sense of Care Recipient's Behavior

By becoming more attentive to their patients' moods and behaviors, family caregivers seemed to notice subtle things that they had previously overlooked. These details provided cues for better understanding of mood changes and behavioral patterns. For example, one participant realized that her mother's mood was greatly affected by the weather:

[ID 2, full-time employee, daughter of care recipient] I wasn't even aware that the weather affected my mother's moods. During the study, I realized a couple of times, that when she was out of sorts, the weather was also bad.

As with *ID 2*, many family caregivers realized that there are underlying reasons for the mood changes of care recipients. Although our study gathered no concrete evidence that their individual discoveries were true, the family caregivers seemed to feel that they could make better sense of their care recipients' behaviors by recording and reviewing their moods and activities every day.

Developing Concrete Action Plans

Such discoveries of care recipient moods/behaviors affected the family caregivers in multiple ways. For example, the discoveries helped them develop concrete action plans to effectively support their care recipients. In other words, the family caregivers gained a clearer sense of what they should and should not do/say to them. *ID 1*, whose husband often forgot to take his medicine, described how she came to provide help:

[ID 1, homemaker, wife of care recipient] I talked to my husband when I noticed that he hadn't taken all of his medication. I thought he knew, but to my surprise, he didn't. Since he is a well-organized person, I had been assuming that he could manage by himself. But I realized that there were certain things that he couldn't manage. I decided to support him in these areas.

Other family caregivers reviewed the FMCT graph and searched for clues to cope better with their care recipients. For example, one family caregiver described how she successfully handled her mother's unexpected behavior by reviewing the FMCT record:

[ID 7, full-time employee, daughter of care recipient] My mother was in a good mood while eating supper, but she suddenly got very quiet and toned down. I wondered why and reviewed the [FMCT] record. While tracking back, I started to wonder what things made her happy. Then I found a case where my mom became happy when I praised her cooking. I instantly thought this might be the case. I realized that I had just eaten silently without praising her cooking. I went to her and said, "Your cooking was so delicious that I completely forgot to thank you." I was relieved to see her returning to normal.

As with *ID 7*, some caregivers reviewed the FMCT record during bad periods for their care recipients, developed a hypothesis and an action plan to improve the situation, and tested it. Again, we do not claim to know that *ID 7*'s hypothesis was correct; the care recipient may have had different reasons for her tone down. However, the important point is that FMCT appeared to provide family caregivers useful clues for developing new coping strategies. By experimenting those coping strategies, family caregivers started to see some connections between their own behavior and the care recipients' mood/behavior. Some family caregivers even noticed patterns between the two:

[ID 4, full-time employee, husband of care recipient] Previously, I couldn't understand why she was so moody. Although I had a feeling that I'd said something wrong, it quickly faded from my memory. By tracking and reviewing every day, I noticed certain patterns. Similar things happened over and over. Somewhere in my mind, I knew that praising her was good, but I came to realize just how important it was to praise her, as a real experience.

Such discoveries seemed to help the family caregivers realize that there are certain things that they as family caregivers can do to improve the current situation. According to the family caregivers, the "lessons learned" section was particularly useful for tracking the trial-and-error results of their hypotheses and finding better coping strategies. The holistic view of the care recipients' mental state and caregiving activities also seemed to help them analyze the connection between the two and to devise new coping strategies. Throughout the process, many family caregivers perceived themselves as more attentive to their own behaviors (M=2.28, SD=0.78 on a 5-point Likert scale: 1=became very attentive, 5=did not become attentive at all).

Changing Views on Care Recipients

The family caregivers' discoveries about care recipient moods/behaviors also seemed to affect their views of the care recipients. Many said that they had been making incorrect assumptions about their care recipients. For example, one family caregiver who had experienced depression himself described how he realized that advising his daughter based on his own experience could be inappropriate:

[ID 10, working at home, father of care recipient] I recently realized that my daughter's experience with depression might be different from mine. Hers is seasonal, but not mine. I knew that for a fact, but I didn't actually understand the difference. (...) I tended to give her advice based on my own experience. I guess I was being over-possessive at times. (...) While reviewing the graphs, I noticed a correlation between the weather and her moods, and I started to understand that her depression might be totally different from mine.

Some also mentioned that their views about the care recipients gradually changed as they entered the "positive outcomes" field of their daily caregiving activities:

[ID 11, full-time employee, wife of care recipient] I realized that he himself is making an effort. For example, one day when he went to the library, he borrowed a book for me because he thought I might like it. By keeping records, I realized how much he cares about me, the small things that I would normally pay no

attention to. (...) I used to think that it was always me, the caregiver, who provides support, but after using this tool, I felt that we could care for each other.

Overall, the FMCT recording items (particularly filling out the "positive outcomes" field) seemed to facilitate positive self-reflection of the family caregivers' caregiving activities. It provided them a chance to reconsider their caregiving habits and how they had been communicating with their care recipients. As a result, many family caregivers became aware that their views on care recipients had been one-sided or/and judgmental, which helped them avoid negative assumptions about their care recipients.

Being Generous to Care Recipients

According to the family caregivers, such changes in their views also changed their attitudes and made them more generous toward their care recipients:

[ID 10, working at home, father of care recipient] I don't think this [FMCT] tool is really that critical, but it does have its uses. It changed the way I communicate with my daughter. I used to push her away and criticize her opinions. But I started to feel that I should be more generous: to listen to her until she was finished without criticizing her, even when I think she's wrong.

[ID 11, full-time employee, wife of care recipient] I can now see that the disease is the troublemaker, not him. (...) I started to avoid saying negative things to him.

Consequently, FMCT seemed to give family caregivers breathing room to take a step back and communicate with their care recipients in a more relaxed manner.

Better Communication with Care Recipients

Finally and most importantly, although we were concerned that the family caregivers' use of FMCT might create patient-caregiver conflicts, none of the family caregivers reported such an effect. In fact, most reported the opposite:

[ID 7, full-time employee, daughter of care recipient] Previously, when my mom was feeling down, I would just avoid talking with her and go back to my room. By tracking her moods, I realized that there are certain reasons which make her feel unhappy. Then I felt perhaps I could help her eliminate those causes. (...) Since I recorded the topics that she liked to talk about, I could start a conversation on those topics and ask things like "What happened after that?" I think asking these questions shows that I remember what she said in the past and I care about her, which is important.

As with ID 7, some family caregivers seemed to find a way to communicate with the care recipients even when they were in bad mental states. Furthermore, some family caregivers mentioned that asking the care recipients about their health improved their communication:

[ID 2, full-time employee, daughter of care recipient] The amount of communication with my mom definitely increased. Previously, communication often started with a complaint, like "Why did you do this or that?," and so our communication tended to be aggressive. (...) During this study, I had to ask her some questions to record her daily activities. After I returned from work, I asked her about her day, whether she had lunch, how she was feeling, etc. There was no reason to become aggressive about these questions. I could ask them in a normal tone. My mom also looked pleased when I asked them. I think she felt cared for.

Some even reported that the care recipients became more proactive when talking about their health conditions.

[ID 3, homemaker, wife of care recipient] To record his condition, I often asked him some questions, like whether he slept well last night and so on. Gradually, he started to talk about his condition before I even asked him. (...) Previously, it was like, "I'm tired" or "I'm exhausted," and nothing else. But he started to elaborate on his conditions and show that he is thinking about the future. (...) I felt like he was indirectly participating in the study. It's good to have a common goal, collaborating to keep the record and fight the disease.

As with *IDs 2* and *3*, although family caregivers initially asked questions of the care recipients (e.g., whether they had lunch) to maintain the FMCT records, those questions seemed to please the care recipients and introduced thoughtful communication between care recipients and family caregivers. Overall, the recording items sometimes served as tickets to start safe conversations. Together with the family caregivers' relaxed attitudes, such conversations seemed to lead them to a positive communication cycle.

DISCUSSION

In summary, most participants reported that FMCT positively affected their daily lives, although two participants did not seem to notice any change; one became ill during the study, and another didn't seem to care whether her husband recovered. All other participants seemed to feel that they became more actively engaged in the care, gained better control over their care recipients' moods, and increased/improved communication with them.

Strategies for Better Coping with Care Recipients

Our deployment study showed how tracking technologies could help family caregivers develop coping strategies. One possible scenario is that family caregivers first became more attentive to their care recipients' moods/behaviors by manually filling out the FMCT forms every day [31]. Through observations, they started to catch subtle cues that triggered patient mood changes and behavioral patterns. These discoveries seemed to help the family caregivers make better sense of their care recipients' illness or/and unexpected behaviors, which also helped them develop strategies for coping with their care recipients.

While this finding coincides with previous research where health-monitoring technologies facilitated user reflections and active engagement in care [32,41], it remains quite surprising if we consider that all the data (including sufferer's condition) was manually captured by the family caregivers. That is, the care recipient's actual health condition may be different from the family caregiver's subjective observations. Consequently, the individual discoveries of the family caregivers based on such logging could be misleading or even incorrect. Despite such shortcomings, the family caregivers did seem to find FMCT helpful for tracking their trial-and-error processes of their caregiving activities and clarifying a sense of what they should and should not do/say to their care recipients.

What seemed relevant and critical to the family caregivers was the recording activity itself. The family caregivers' direct engagement with data collection facilitated careful observation of the care recipients, which helped them realize aspects and details they would not have noticed otherwise. As suggested by previous works, such an effect would probably have been reduced or non-existent if the data were automatically retrieved by sensors [7,31].

With regards to the risk of family caregivers forming false beliefs about what causes mood changes of the sufferers, the psychiatrist in our team argue that the risk of caregivers' false beliefs to cause fatal consequences should be low because i) the false beliefs of the caregivers are unlikely to affect medical treatment of the care recipients, and ii) the tool directly affects family caregivers who wish to better cope with the care recipients.

In terms of recording the FMCT items, the selected recording items seemed to help the family caregivers efficiently clarify the source of their reflections. For some family caregivers, some of the items introduced new perspectives on what to watch for when observing the care recipients (e.g., *ID2*). In addition, the "positive outcome" field apparently facilitated positive reflections on caregiving. Indeed, all of the participants who took notes about their caregiving activities before joining the study (7 of 14) mentioned that their notes tended to be emotional and negative, whereas FMCT provided an opportunity to take a step back and think of the positive aspects of their caregiving activities. This resembles previous studies that argued for the importance of providing positive feedback to encourage positive behavioral changes [e.g., 19].

Overall, through the process of filling out the daily FMCT entries, many family caregivers seemed to realize that their views about the care recipients had been one-sided, and they became more generous and considerate to them. It also seemed to help them realize that they could devise steps or plans themselves to improve their current situations.

Impact on Family Communication

Many family caregivers in our study also reported that their communication with their care recipients increased and improved. Such an effect was evident for those who often asked the care recipients about their conditions. Even though the family caregivers initially asked questions to maintain the FMCT records, the care recipients seemed pleased to be asked about their health conditions. For the family caregivers, recording mundane events functioned as a ticket to initiate safe or even amiable conversation with their care recipients. For some caregivers, asking care recipients about their health condition for filling out the FMCT forms became a habit (e.g., *ID 3*). According to the caregivers, some care recipients gradually started to actively provide information about their health and activities. For those families, care recipients became collaborators in fighting depression, rather than a target at which to throw care. This is significant progress, considering that the family caregivers had avoided talking about the illness with their care recipients.

This finding is particularly interesting because previous literature suggested that family caregivers who are monitoring the health of care recipients might create conflicts. Our interviews suggest two factors that might cause this positive effect. First, family caregivers who exhibit concern by asking the care recipients about their conditions seemed to generate a positive cycle between the two parties (e.g., *ID2, ID3*). Second, the coping strategies that family caregivers developed during the deployment study seemed to successfully improve communication (e.g., *ID7*).

However, note that the first factor did not emerge in all of the family caregivers, especially siblings of care recipients who seemed reluctant to ask about health conditions because they did not want to annoy their care recipients. Thus, the factors that contribute to better caregiver-care recipient relationships might depend on their own family relationships.

Design Considerations and Future Directions

Based on our findings, next we discuss how health monitoring technologies might be designed to assist family caregivers' development of coping strategies and improve caregiver-care recipient relationships.

Providing Balanced and Non-Sensitive Recording Items

To facilitate unbiased self-reflection, we suggest providing family caregivers with a balanced set of recording items. Since family caregivers are generally feeling anxious and tend to focus on negative events, a semi-structured format that induces positive reflections on caregiving is important.

Furthermore, to trigger safe and amiable communication between family caregivers and care recipients, we suggest to record mundane events because it seemed to function as a ticket to initiate safe and amiable conversation with their care recipients. We particularly suggest avoiding sensitive items such as the degree of forgetfulness or increased lethargy or listlessness. Although these items are closely related to the symptoms of depression, broaching them can lead to conflict.

Appreciating the Advantages of Manual Input

Another design recommendation is to allow caregivers to manually input care recipients' conditions. Despite the various challenges of manual input (e.g., high burden for logging data, lack of scientific rigor), our findings showed two clear advantages in the context of family caregiving: (1) it facilitated careful observation of care recipients, which led them to discover effective coping strategies, and (2) it triggered thoughtful communication between family caregivers and care recipients. The first advantage is consistent with previous works, which showed that self-reports (i.e., manual tracking) increase self-awareness and engagement [7,31]. Even though the overall trend of health-tracking technologies is toward passive tracking where the data of health-related behaviors are automatically collected, our study provides additional evidence to appreciate the advantages of manual tracking.

While manual input afforded the above advantages, it certainly posed the family caregivers burden of capturing data. Previous works noted that people have difficulty maintaining manual tracking [7,27]. However, the family caregivers in our study seemed to maintain engagement with our system. One possible explanation is that family caregivers gradually manifested their care to the care recipients by using the system. Since the care recipients knew that the family caregivers were using the system to improve their support at home, such use reflected that they cared about them. Particularly for those whom it became a habit to ask the care recipients about their health condition (e.g., *ID 3*), entering the FMCT records became important because it was built into their communication.

Considering the Effects of Excluding Care Recipients

Finally, we suggest the designers of mental healthcare technologies to consider the option of excluding the care recipients from the design space. Existing systems, which allow family caregivers to monitor the care recipients' health conditions, often include care recipients by either automatically detecting the care recipients' physiological/behavioral data or leveraging their self-tracked data [19,20,41]. However, we excluded the care recipients from our system because family caregivers in our preliminary interviews expressed strong resistance to reflect on the data with their care recipients. It is risky to force the care recipients to reflect with the family caregivers particularly in a sensitive home setting where family members avoid talking about the illness. At the same time, consistent with previous work [19], family caregivers in our study expressed resistance to track their health information without the consent of the care recipients. Getting permission by explaining the purpose of the system (i.e. to better support the care recipients) appeared to be a good way to address this tension because family caregivers could record data on the care recipients without feeling that they are holding secrets.

Even with the consent of the care recipients, we were still concerned that the family caregivers' use of the system may create caregiver-care recipient conflicts because individuals experiencing depression tend to have a high awareness of surveillance [28]. Despite our concerns, most of our family caregivers reported that their communication with their care recipients increased and improved. It is important to note that the side effect of excluding care recipients from the system contributed to this result. By not allowing the care recipients to contribute to the data logging, the family caregivers often had to ask the care recipients for their health information, which eventually created a positive communication cycle. Although previous research valued the importance of sharing health information and transparency with family members [19], our study shows a new way of facilitating family communication in a sensitive home setting.

It is also worth noting that the psychiatrist in our team pointed to another possible advantage of caregiver tracking. Despite our concerns that caregiving tracking might deviate from the patient's actual condition, caregiver tracking may provide more objective data than patient self-tracking because patients during depressive episodes tend to be forgetful or have difficulties objectively recording their own conditions [42].

Future Directions

Our experiences deploying FMCT sparked two promising research areas. First, the family caregivers in our study expressed the desire to share their tracking records with other family caregivers so that they could learn from others. Since such a sharing function and communication between users has also been recommended in previous literature [12,32], we are planning to provide a sharing function in FMCT. Of course, we need to exert extra caution in developing such a function. For example, providing family caregivers a channel to communicate with others might impose an extra burden on them, e.g., by making them feel obligated to respond to others. It also risks shifting the relationships between family caregivers and care recipients into that of "family caregivers vs. care recipients" by allowing family caregivers to bond.

Second, we are interested in investigating the impact of FMCT on the care recipients. While many family caregivers in our study reported that their relationships with their care recipients improved, we are interested in learning whether the care recipients had same impressions.

CONCLUSION

This paper showed the potential of tracking technologies to support family caregivers for better interaction with a depressed family member. The deployment study of our simple tracking tool revealed that the system effectively supported the caregivers to develop coping strategies. The manual input of care recipient's moods/behaviors by family caregivers promoted higher attentiveness to the care recipients and the selected recording items introduced new perspectives to them. The most significant finding is that the family caregivers' data entry served as a trigger to introduce a conversation with their care recipients. The results from this study identified three design decisions which were crucial for helping family caregivers develop coping strategies and improving communication between family caregivers and care recipients: 1. family caregiver's manual input of care recipient's moods/behaviors and own caregiving activities, 2. barring the care recipients from contributing, 3. balanced and non-sensitive recording items. We believe our study will open up new ways of using tracking technologies in the field of mental healthcare.

ACKNOWLEDGMENTS

This work is partially supported by Grant for Scientific Research (B) 70396141 from Japan Society for the Promotion of Science (JSPS).

REFERENCES

1. American Psychiatric Association. 2000. *Diagnostic and Statistical Manual of Mental Disorders, 4th Edition, Text Revision (DSM-IV-TR)*, American Psychiatric Association.
2. Jakob E. Bardram, Mads Frost, Károly Szántó, Maria Faurholt-Jepsen, Maj Vinberg, and Lars Vedel Kessing. 2013. Designing mobile health technology for bipolar disorder: a field trial of the monarca system. In *Proceedings of the SIGCHI Conference on Human Factors in Computing Systems* (CHI '13), 2627-2636. http://dx.doi.org/10.1145/2470654.2481364
3. Nili R. Benazon and James C. Coyne. 2000. Living with a depressed spouse. *J Fam Psychol* 14, 1: 71-79.
4. Timothy W. Bickmore, Suzanne E. Mitchell, Brian W. Jack, Michael K. Paasche-Orlow, Laura M. Pfeifer, and Julie O'Donnell. 2010. Response to a relational agent by hospital patients with depressive symptoms, *Interact Comput* 22, 4: 289-298.
5. Gianluca Castelnuovo, Andrea Gaggioli, Fabrizia Mantovani, and Giuseppe Riva. 2003. New and old tools in psychotherapy: The use of technology for the integration of traditional clinical treatments. *Psychotherapy: Theory, Research, Practice, Training* 40, 1-2: 33-44.
6. Yunan Chen, Victor Ngo, and Sun Young Park. 2013. Caring for caregivers: designing for integrality. In *Proceedings of the 2013 Conference on Computer Supported Cooperative Work* (CSCW '13), 91-102. http://dx.doi.org/10.1145/2441776.2441789
7. Eun Kyoung Choe, Nicole B. Lee, Bongshin Lee, Wanda Pratt, and Julie A. Kientz. 2014. Understanding quantified-selfers' practices in collecting and exploring personal data. In *Proceedings of the 32nd annual ACM conference on Human factors in computing systems* (CHI '14). 1143-1152. http://doi.acm.org/10.1145/2556288.2557372
8. Sunny Consolvo, Peter Roessler, Brett E. Shelton, Anthony LaMarca, Bill Schilit, and Sara Bly. 2004. Technology for care networks of elders. *Pervasive Comput* 3, 2: 22-29.
9. Juliet Corbin and Anselm Strauss. 2014. *Basics of qualitative research: Techniques and procedures for developing grounded theory.* Sage publications.
10. David Coyle, Gavin Doherty, Mark Matthews, and John Sharry. 2007. Computers in talk-based mental health interventions. *Interact Comput* 19, 4: 545-562. http://dx.doi.org/10.1016/j.intcom.2007.02.001
11. Shannon L. Currie, Patrick J. McGrath, and Victor Day. 2010. Development and usability of an online CBT program for symptoms of moderate depression, anxiety, and stress in post-secondary students. *Comput Hum Behav* 26, 6: 1419-1426. http://dx.doi.org/10.1016/j.chb.2010.04.020
12. Sara J. Czaja and Mark P. Rubert. 2002. Telecommunications technology as an aid to family caregivers of persons with dementia. *Psychosom Med* 64, 3: 469-476.
13. Pedro L. Delgado, and Jason Schillerstrom. 2009. Cognitive difficulties associated with depression: what are the implications for treatment? *Psychiatr Times* 26, 3. Retrieved January 6, 2017 from http://www.psychiatrictimes.com/cognitive-disorders/cognitive-difficulties-associated-depression-what-are-implications-treatment
14. Robert F. Dickerson, Eugenia I. Gorlin, and John A. Stankovic. 2011. Empath: a continuous remote emotional health monitoring system for depressive illness. In *Proceedings of the 2nd Conference on Wireless Health* (WH '11), Article 5, 10 pages. http://dx.doi.org/10.1145/2077546.2077552
15. Gavin Doherty, David Coyle, and Mark Matthews. 2010. Design and evaluation guidelines for mental health technologies. Interact. Comput. 22, 4: 243-252. http://dx.doi.org/10.1016/j.intcom.2010.02.006
16. Gavin Doherty, David Coyle, and John Sharry. 2012. Engagement with online mental health interventions: an exploratory clinical study of a treatment for depression. In *Proceedings of the SIGCHI Conference on Human Factors in Computing Systems* (CHI '12), 1421-1430. http://dx.doi.org/10.1145/2207676.2208602
17. John Duncan, L. Jean Camp, and William R. Hazelwood. 2009. The portal monitor: a privacy-enhanced event-driven system for elder care. In *Proceedings of the 4th International Conference on Persuasive Technology* (Persuasive '09), Article 36, 9 pages. http://dx.doi.org/10.1145/1541948.1541995
18. Ian H. Gotlib. 1992. Interpersonal and cognitive aspects of depression. *Current Directions in Psychological Science* 1, 5: 149-154.
19. Andrea Grimes, Desney Tan, and Dan Morris. 2009. Toward technologies that support family reflections on health. In Proceedings of the ACM 2009 International Conference on Supporting group work (GROUP '09), 311-320. http://dx.doi.org/10.1145/1531674.1531721
20. Gillian R. Hayes, Lamar M. Gardere, Gregory D. Abowd, and Khai N. Truong. 2008. CareLog: a selective archiving tool for behavior management in schools. In *Proceedings of the SIGCHI Conference on Human Factors in Computing Systems* (CHI '08), 685-694. http://dx.doi.org/10.1145/1357054.1357164
21. Lesa Huber, Kalpana Shankar, Kay Conelly, Kelly E. Caine, L. Jean Camp, Beth Ann Walker, and Lisa Borrero. 2013. How In-Home Technologies Mediate Caregiving Relationships in Later Life. *Int J Hum-Comput Int* 29, 7:441-455.
22. Hilary Hutchinson, Wendy Mackay, Bo Westerlund, Benjamin B. Bederson, Allison Druin, Catherine Plaisant, Michel Beaudouin-Lafon, Stéphane Conversy, Helen Evans, Heiko Hansen, Nicolas Roussel, and Björn Eiderbäck. 2003. Technology probes: inspiring design for and with families. In *Proceedings of the SIGCHI Conference on Human Factors in Computing Systems* (CHI '03), 17-24. http://dx.doi.org/10.1145/642611.642616
23. Miriam Jacob, Ellen Frank, David J. Kupfer, and Linda L. Carpenter. 1987. Recurrent depression: An assessment of family burden and family attitudes. *J Clin Psychiatry* 48, 10: 395-400.
24. Thomas E. Joiner and James C. Coyne. 1999. *The Interactional Nature of Depression.* American Psychology Association, Washington, DC.

25. Gabor I. Keitner, Christine E. Ryan, Ivan W. Miller, and Robert Kohn. 1995. Role of the family in recovery and major depression. *Am J Psychiatry* 152, 7: 1002-1008.

26. Martin B. Keller. 1999. The long-term treatment of depression. *J Clin Psychiatry* 60, Suppl 17: 41-45.

27. Predrag Klasnja, Wanda Pratt. 2012. Healthcare in the pocket: Mapping the space of mobile-phone health interventions. J Biomed Inform 45, 1: 184-198.

28. Donald F. Klein, Paul H. Wender. 1993. *Understanding depression: A complete guide to its diagnosis and treatment.* Oxford University Press.

29. Harriet P. Lefley. 1996. Family caregiving in mental illness. *Family caregiver applications series*, v. 7. Sage Publications.

30. Ian Li, Anind K. Dey, and Jodi Forlizzi. 2011. Understanding my data, myself: supporting self-reflection with ubicomp technologies. In *Proceedings of the 13th International Conference on Ubiquitous Computing* (UbiComp '11), 405-414. http://dx.doi.org/10.1145/2030112.2030166

31. Ian Li, Anind K. Dey, and Jodi Forlizzi. 2012. Using context to reveal factors that affect physical activity. *ACM Trans Comput-Hum Interact* 19, 1: 21 pages.

32. Leslie S. Liu, Sen H. Hirano, Monica Tentori, Karen G. Cheng, Sheba George, Sun Young Park, and Gillian R. Hayes. 2011. Improving communication and social support for caregivers of high-risk infants through mobile technologies. In *Proceedings of the ACM 2011 Conference on Computer Supported Cooperative Work* (CSCW '11), 475-484. http://dx.doi.org/10.1145/1958824.1958897

33. Leslie S. Liu, Patrick C. Shih, and Gillian R. Hayes. 2011. Barriers to the adoption and use of personal health record systems. In *Proceedings of the 2011 iConference* (iConference '11), 363-370. http://dx.doi.org/10.1145/1940761.1940811

34. Deborah Lupton. 2016. The diverse domains of quantified selves: self-tracking modes and dataveillance. *Economy and Society* 45, 1: 101-122.

35. Lena Mamykina, Elizabeth Mynatt, Patricia Davidson, and Daniel Greenblatt. 2008. MAHI: investigation of social scaffolding for reflective thinking in diabetes management. In *Proceedings of the SIGCHI Conference on Human Factors in Computing Systems* (CHI '08), 477-486. http://dx.doi.org/10.1145/1357054.1357131

36. Gabriela Marcu, Jakob E. Bardram, Silvia Gabrielli. 2011. Framework for Overcoming Challenges in Designing Persuasive Monitoring and Feedback Systems for Mental Illness. In *Proceedings of Pervasive Computing Technologies for Healthcare (PersuasiveHealth)*, 1-8.

37. Mark Matthews and Gavin Doherty. 2011. In the mood: engaging teenagers in psychotherapy using mobile phones. In *Proceedings of the SIGCHI Conference on Human Factors in Computing Systems* (CHI '11), 2947-2956. http://dx.doi.org/10.1145/1978942.1979379

38. Sun Young Park, Hee Young Jeong, and John Zimmerman. 2008. ESURE: Support for Parents in Managing their Children's Health. In *Proceedings of Design and Emotion*, 13 pages.

39. Robert Percevic, Michael J. Lambert, and Hans Kordy. 2004. Computer supported monitoring of patient treatment response. *J Clin Psychol* 60, 3: 285-299.

40. Karen P. Tang, Sen H. Hirano, Karen G. Cheng, and Gillian R. Hayes. 2012. Balancing caregiver and clinician needs in a mobile health informatics tool for preterm infants. In *Proceedings of Pervasive Computing Technologies for Healthcare* (PervasiveHealth), 1-8.

41. Tammy Toscos, Kay Connelly, and Yvonne Rogers. 2012. Best intentions: health monitoring technology and children. In *Proceedings of the SIGCHI Conference on Human Factors in Computing Systems* (CHI '12), 1431-1440. http://dx.doi.org/10.1145/2207676.2208603

42. U.S. Department of Health and Human Services, National Institutes of Health, National Institute of Mental Health. 2015. *Depression* (NIH Publication No. 15-3561). U.S. Government Printing Office.

43. Naomi Yamashita, Hideaki Kuzuoka, Keiji Hirata, and Takashi Kudo. 2013. Understanding the conflicting demands of family caregivers caring for depressed family members. In *Proceedings of the SIGCHI Conference on Human Factors in Computing Systems* (CHI '13), 2637-2646. http://dx.doi.org/10.1145/2470654.2481365

Modeling and Understanding Visual Attributes of Mental Health Disclosures in Social Media

Lydia Manikonda*
School of Computing, Informatics, and Decision Systems Engineering
Arizona State University
lmanikonda@asu.edu

Munmun De Choudhury*
School of Interactive Computing
College of Computing
Georgia Tech
munmund@gatech.edu

ABSTRACT
Content shared on social media platforms has been identified to be valuable in gaining insights into people's mental health experiences. Although there has been widespread adoption of photo-sharing platforms such as Instagram in recent years, the role of visual imagery as a mechanism of self-disclosure is less understood. We study the nature of visual attributes manifested in images relating to mental health disclosures on Instagram. Employing computer vision techniques on a corpus of thousands of posts, we extract and examine three visual attributes: visual features (e.g., color), themes, and emotions in images. Our findings indicate the use of imagery for unique self-disclosure needs, quantitatively and qualitatively distinct from those shared via the textual modality: expressions of emotional distress, calls for help, and explicit display of vulnerability. We discuss the relationship of our findings to literature in visual sociology, in mental health self-disclosure, and implications for the design of health interventions.

Author Keywords
social media; mental health; Instagram; visual attributes

ACM Classification Keywords
H.4 Information Systems Applications: Miscellaneous

INTRODUCTION
Social media platforms have emerged to be conducive means of social exchange and support seeking around stigmatized concerns like mental health. The benefits of such practices are situated in the literature on self-disclosure—*the "process of making the self known to others"* [11]. Self-disclosure can be an important therapeutic ingredient and is linked to improved physical and psychological well-being [30]. Moreover, since many social media platforms, like Instagram, Tumblr or Reddit allow anonymous or semi-anonymous discourse, they have come to be adopted widely in helping cope with mental health challenges [13, 4]; conditions known to be associated with high social stigma.

*Authors contributed equally to this work

CHI 2017, May 06-11, 2017, Denver, CO, USA

DOI: http://dx.doi.org/10.1145/3025453.3025932

Self-disclosure can happen via the adoption of many diverse interaction modalities. For instance, expressive writing is identified to play a prominent role in supporting mental health therapeutic processes [43]. In fact, recent research has studied mental health disclosures through the lens of social media [3, 10, 14], and has largely explored the ways in which linguistic attributes, such as affect, cognition, and linguistic style may reveal cues about one's psychological state. We note that other modalities of mental health disclosure, such as visual imagery shared on social media, are under-explored.

The rich literature in visual sociology situates imagery to be a powerful means of enabling emotional expression related to mental illnesses, especially those feelings and experiences that individuals may struggle to express verbally or through written communication [45]. It has been found that the parts of the brain that process visual information are evolutionarily older than the parts that process verbal information [33]. Thus, visual imagery are likely to evoke deeper elements of psychological consciousness than do words or writing. Mental health disclosures based on words alone utilize less of the brain's capacity than do those in which the brain is processing imagery as well as words. Given these considerations, sharing and reflecting on visual narratives are a known psychiatric approach to tackle mental illness [26].

Extracting and characterizing the expressive meanings conveyed in the imagery shared around mental health disclosures on social media can provide rich information grounded in individuals' everyday experiences and interactions. Thus these approaches could raise the quality of language-only studies of mental health disclosures. We leverage the recent uptake of photo sharing practices on different social media platforms, such as Instagram and Tumblr to investigate this research problem [15]. We are observing a shift in online user-generated content from predominantly text-based data to richer forms of image-based media. As Tifentale and Manovich [51] rightly noted, these image sharing practices open up fascinating opportunities for the study of "digital visual culture". Our broad research goal in this paper revolves around investigating *how social media disclosures of mental health challenges could be characterized via shared visual imagery*. Specifically, we address the following three research questions:

(RQ 1) What *visual features* characterize images of mental health disclosures shared on social media?

(RQ 2) What are the kinds of *visual themes* manifested in these images, and what is the nature of *emotional expression* associated with these visual themes?

(RQ 3) How do visual themes of mental health images complement and contrast with themes manifested in the language of these social media posts?

To address these research questions, we leverage a large dataset of over two million public posts associated with ten mental health challenges shared on Instagram. We present some of the first quantitative insights into the nature of visual features, themes and emotion expressed in these images. For the purpose, we employ computer vision techniques of image analysis and unsupervised machine learning methods to identify visual and linguistic themes.

Our findings indicate the prominence of a visual channel supporting candid and disinhibited social exchange around mental health. Specifically, we find that the visual and emotional markers of mental health images capture unique characteristics of self-disclosure, beyond those expressed via the sharing of linguistic content. These include, expressions of distress, personal struggles, explicit graphical content, as well as calls for help, and supportive advice toward improved well-being. We find that many of these markers align with forms of self-disclosure reported in the psychology literature.

We situate our findings in literature on visual sociology and the role of visual narratives in mental well-being. We discuss how our work can inspire further research on visual cues of mental health disclosures on social media. We also present design and ethical considerations toward building human-centered technologies and tools to provide support and scaffolding around this new self-disclosure medium.

BACKGROUND AND RELATED WORK

Self-Disclosure and Mental Health

Goffman posited the importance of "sympathetic others" in helping people cope with difficult experiences, as well in enabling self-disclosure [22]. Self-disclosure has been widely investigated both in the psychology and the computer mediated communication (CMC) literature. This body of work has argued self-disclosure to be beneficial: having been linked to trust and group identity, as well as playing an important role in social interactions by reducing uncertainty [2, 11, 30].

In the context of mental health, Ellis [16] reported that discourse on emotionally laden traumatic experiences can be a safe way of confronting mental illness. Jourard [32] also reported that self-disclosure was a basic element in the attainment of improved mental health. This is because, painful events that are not structured into a narrative format, may contribute to the continued experience of negative thoughts and feelings that underlie many mental illnesses. Self-disclosure facilitates a sense of resolution, which results in less rumination and eventually allows disturbing experiences to subside gradually from conscious thought. A seminal work [42] found that participants assigned to a trauma-writing condition showed immune system benefits. Self-disclosure has also been associated with reduced visits to medical centers and psychological benefits in the form of improved affect [48].

Our work builds on these observations and examines the manner in which individuals might be appropriating the photo-sharing capability of social media platforms like Instagram to self-disclose about mental health challenges.

Visual Methods and Visual Sociology

Visual methods have widely been employed in the study of psychosocial aspects of health and well-being [25, 45]. According to Harrison [26], 'visual methods' describe any research design, which utilizes visual evidence, including the use of photographs, video recordings, drawings, and art. Often, these approaches connect "core definitions of the self" to society, culture and history via the examination of imagery. In fact, Harrison [26] distinguished between the visual as *topic* (i.e. the visual itself as the subject of investigation) and the visual as *resource* (i.e. the visual as a means of accessing data about other topics of investigation).

Visual methods have been found to be very powerful, since certain emotions, thoughts, feelings, experiences, events, and relationships are more easily or variously expressed in a visual, rather than verbal form (see Gillies et al. [21]). They can also act as a tool for an individual's identity and communication [47]. In particular, positive affect manifested in visual imagery can be indicative of an individual's well-being, as well as provide insight into their social, cognitive, and behavioral tendencies and responses [33]. Imagery is also known to help portray stories or narratives relating to the intimate dimensions of the social—family, or one's own body [47].

In our work, we leverage the observation that vulnerable individuals might be taking on to social media platforms to engage in mental health self-disclosure via visual imagery. We aim to examine some of the complexities typically explored through qualitative visual methods, via large-scale characterization of such mental health imagery shared on social media.

Social Media Imagery Analysis

Users of social media platforms are sharing large volumes of images around their daily lives, personal life events, or opinions, often in the form of personal photographs, selfies, memes, gifs and so on. Recently, a growing body of research has examined and characterized such imagery to identify sentiment and emotion [31], societal happiness [1], geographic landmarks [34], abusive behaviors such as alcohol use [41], public health challenges such as obesity [19], and fitness [52].

Many of these works combine both text and imagery features toward the problem domain under consideration. For instance, Pang et al. [41] mined markers of underage drinking by first inferring age and gender of users from their Instagram profile pictures, and then analyzing the associated hashtags to discover the existence of drinking patterns in terms of time, frequency and location. Similarly, Abdullah et al. [1] developed a measure of population-scale happiness, known as Smile Index, by analyzing the visual cues of Instagram images, and then went on to validate it against text-only measurements as well as self-reported happiness. Another interrelated line of research [6, 39] has also examined visual features present in these images, for instance, color palettes, and their relationship to social engagement. In this paper, we borrow several computational social media image analysis methodologies employed in the above body of research, in order to extract and characterize visual cues relating to mental health disclosures on Instagram.

Social Media and Mental Well-being

Recently, a growing body of research has focused on understanding how large-scale social media activities can be used to understand, infer, and improve the wellbeing of people, including mental health concerns [12, 13, 27]. A common thread in this research is how computational techniques may be applied to naturalistic data, that people share on today's online social platforms, to make sense of their health behaviors and related experiences.

However, these works have primarily focused on the computational analysis of text and language for the purpose: including psycholinguistic analysis, topic modeling, and supervised and unsupervised language modeling. As noted earlier, many social media platforms today allow sharing of rich media objects, such as images, beyond text. We extend current state-of-the-art by examining the nature of mental health related visual cues manifested in Instagram posts.

Another complementary line of research has also examined how content, primarily text, shared on social media and online communities may enable self-disclosure and help seeking, specifically toward facilitating wellbeing [17, 29, 18]. In this light, approaches to community building have been proposed [53], and the role of participation and self-disclosure in such communities toward promoting health recovery and coping has been examined in domains as cancer, diabetes, and drug abuse [37, 38, 46]. In the mental health domain, Balani and De Choudhury [7] developed a classifier to automatically infer levels of self-disclosures in different mental health forums, whereas in [13], the authors found that self-disclosure around a stigmatized condition like mental illness tends to be higher in platforms that allow anonymity.

Close to our work are the works of Andalibi et al. ([3, 4]) and Reece et al. ([44]). In the former work, Instagram images shared on #depression were analyzed through qualitative coding and did not study the visual cues of the images. In the latter work, Instagram user profile data collected through responses to a standardized clinical depression survey were utilized to reveal predictive markers of depression. However, these works did not characterize mental health disclosures facilitated uniquely by the visual modality. We employ computational methods to examine themes emerging out of the visual content of images spanning different mental health disorders. Thus our work extends this larger body of work by characterizing a form of online content, visual imagery, hitherto under-investigated in the context of mental health.

DATA

Data Collection

We utilized Instagram's official API[1] to obtain the dataset used in this paper. Each post in this dataset is public and contains post-related information, such as, the image, caption, likes, comments, hashtags, filter and geolocation, if tagged.

[1]https://www.instagram.com/developer/

anxiety	depression	mentalillness
bipolar	bpd	schizo
selfharm	paranoia	anorexic
depressed	bingeeatingdisorder	thinstagram
socialanxiety	unwanted	blades

Table 1: Sample tags used to obtain our Instagram dataset.

Referring to prior literature [10], we adopted an iterative approach to first identify a set of appropriate, distinguishing hashtags around different prominent mental illnesses prevalent in social media. With the seed tags, we performed an initial data collection of 1.5 million posts shared on Instagram between Dec 2010 and Nov 2015. Then by leveraging an association rule mining approach, we compiled the top k (k = 39, frequency $\geq$ 5000) co-occurring tags in the 1.5M posts, and then appended them to the original seed tag list for further data collection. Table 1 lists a sample set of tags used to crawl the dataset.

This final list of 45 tags was thereafter passed on to a psychiatry researcher to be categorized into different disorder types. For tags that described experiences or symptoms cross-cutting across different conditions (e.g., "anxiety"), they were counted toward each disorder type. Table 2 gives a list of the ten different disorders identified in our data. We additionally consulted the Diagnostic and Statistical Manual of Mental Health Disorders (DSM-V [5]), that indicates these disorders to be prominent mental health challenges in populations. This categorization of the mental health challenges was conducted to ensure that our data used in the ensuing analysis focused on well-validated and clinically recognized conditions. At the same time, it allowed us to focus on a diverse range of disorders expressed on social media, rather than specific ones studied in prior work [12, 13, 27]; thus enabling us to discover generalized patterns in visual disclosures of mental health challenges in social media. Our final crawl included 2,757,044 posts from 151,638 users spanning these disorders.

Anxiety Disorder	Depressive Disorder	PTSD
Bipolar Disorder	Panic Disorder	Suicide
Eating Disorder	OCD	Schizophrenia
Non-suicidal Self-injury		

Table 2: Disorder Categorization.

Data Reliability

Next, we assessed the suitability and reliability of our collected corpus of Instagram posts and users for our later analyses. For the purpose, we extracted n-grams (n=3) from the profile biographies of users. The top 10 *uni-*, *bi-* and *tri-*grams are shown in Table 3. They show that users are appropriating Instagram to seek and provide social and emotional support around different mental health concerns ("need someone talk", "feel free dm"). There are also explicit mentions of specific psychological challenges around mental health ("depression anxiety", "telling suicidal kids"), including warnings for profile visitors ("trigger warning"), and personal experiences of the condition ("alone alone alone").

We corroborated these observations with a licensed psychiatrist, and concluded that the users in our dataset are engag-

Trigrams	Bigrams	Unigrams
need someone talk	days clean	love
just another depressed	report just	follow
ever need talk	self harm	like
depression self harm	secret account	account
telling suicidal kids	stay strong	days
feel free dm	mental health	need
one dat time	depression anxiety	one
dm need talk	need talk	years
report just unfollow	just block	depression
mine unless stated	trigger warning	dm

Table 3: Top mentioned tri-, bi- and uni-grams of bios extracted from user profiles sharing mental health posts.

ing in genuine mental health disclosures, tend to demonstrate disinhibition towards sharing their mental health experiences, and are appropriating the platform specifically for this purpose via the chosen account.

METHODS

Visual Features. Towards our first research goal RQ 1, to examine the visual features of images relating to mental health disorders, we employ the extraction of color profiles, i.e., *grayscale histograms* [50]. Grayscale histograms provide us intuition about the brightness, saturation, and contrast distribution of images. In these histograms, images with high contrast pixels are binned in bins with lower numbers (near 0), whereas images with brighter pixels are binned in higher number bins (near 255). We utilize the OpenCV library[2] to extract these color histograms of images in our dataset.

We also assess the *visual saliency* of images (using OpenCV) – a distinct subjective perceptual quality that makes some images stand out from their neighbors [24]. A typical image in our dataset is of size 612px × 612px, so by using a saliency metric, we obtain a 612 × 612 grid matrix. For each image in these three visual feature categories, we obtain an empirical threshold that ensures $1/3^{rd}$ of the pixels will be greater than this value, when sorted based on their saliency.

Visual Themes. Identifying meaningful themes from images is known to be challenging as they contain richer features compared to text [23]. To examine the themes manifested in different mental health images that is posed as RQ 2, we used a 2-step human-machine approach. The first step employed automated computer vision techniques to perform initial clustering. The second step involved human raters to refine and label the automatically generated clusters, wherein they independently reorganized the clusters to obtain coherent descriptor labels. Our human-machine methodology is motivated by two observations: Human coding can help extract semantically meaningful and contextually relevant image themes, but is difficult to scale in the face of datasets as large as ours. Automated clustering techniques can address the issue of scalability, but, on their own, may not provide reliable or meaningful themes. We describe our two step method below:

Step I. In the first step, we used OpenCV to extract the Speeded Up Robust Features of the mental health images (SURF: [8]). SURF is a speeded-up local feature detector and descriptor that is good at handling images with rotation and blurring. More elaborately, the method uses a blob detector based on the Hessian matrix to find points of interest. It then develops a unique and robust description of an image feature, e.g., by describing the intensity distribution of the pixels within the neighborhood of the point of interest. It is typically used to locate and recognize objects, people or faces, to make 3D scenes, to track objects and to extract points of interest. Thus, these are likely to be helpful in characterizing the visual attributes of our mental health image data.

The extracted SURF vectors for all images are of 64 dimensions. Following the standard image vector quantization approach (i.e., SURF feature clustering) [8], we obtained the codebook vector for each image[3]. Finally, we used the k-means clustering algorithm (with Euclidean distance metric) to obtain 20 clusters, where we determine k in an empirical data driven manner, that improves cluster consistency.

Step II. Next, with the help of two researchers familiar with mental health content on social media, the images in the 20 clusters and the affinity of themes were independently examined, so as to refine the clusters, as well as develop semantic descriptors characterizing them. The researchers adopted a semi-open coding approach, borrowing from the literature on mental health self-disclosure [30, 2, 11] and recent work in characterizing mental health images shared on different social media platforms [3, 4]. The annotators first independently coded all of the 20 clusters. Then following mutual discussion and resolution of inconsistencies, they merged the 20 clusters and readjusted them (shifting some images to other appropriate clusters) to eventually identify six major visual themes of mental health images.

Linguistic Emotions of Visual Themes. Next, we employ the psycholinguistic lexicon LIWC (http://liwc.wpengine.com/) on the text associated with our mental health images spanning the different visual themes. We use the following five emotional attributes, motivated from prior work on mental health and social media [13, 7] – *anger, anxiety, sadness, positive affect* and *negative affect*, and a measure of attributions to loss of life, indicated by the *death* category.

Linguistic Themes. Finally, to complement the visual themes (our research goal RQ 3), we identify themes from the captions and hashtags (textual data) associated with the Instagram images in our dataset. We refer to these latent topics as *linguistic themes*. Existing literature [42] emphasizes the importance of studying language, since it reflects a variety of thoughts, functions as a signal of identity, and emphasizes the social distance. We believe the linguistic themes may therefore help us contrast the visual themes around how individuals engage in mental health disclosure on Instagram.

We used TwitterLDA[4] to extract these linguistic themes. This method was developed for topic modeling of short text cor-

[2]https://opencv-python-tutroals.readthedocs.io/en/latest/

[3]For a given image I, it can have 96 SURF features corresponding to the different segments of an image. These features are expressed in terms of the codebook vector (of size n) as I = <$C_1 : f_1, C_2 : f_2, C_3 : f_3, dots, C_n : f_n$> where, C_1 is the cluster of all features about specific characteristic of an object in the image.

[4]https://github.com/minghui/Twitter-LDA

	Anxiety	Bipolar	Depression	ED	NSSI	OCD	PD	PTSD	Schizophrenia	Suicide
Proportion of High contrast images	0.101	0.113	0.12	0.08	0.122	0.073	0.104	0.092	0.106	0.116
Proportion of High saturation images	0.58	0.644	0.577	0.669	0.481	0.751	0.601	0.733	0.63	0.577
Proportion of High brightness images	0.32	0.243	0.30	0.25	0.396	0.175	0.295	0.1743	0.263	0.306

Table 4: Proportion of different mental health category posts belonging to the three color (pixel) distributions. Here ED=Eating Disorder; NSSI=Non-suicidal Self-injury; PD=Panic Disorder. All columns sum to 100%.

pora for mining the latent topics. As typically done in topic modeling, we pre-processed the data by removing a standard list of stop words, words with very high frequency (> 0.25× datasize), and words that occur fewer than five times. Since LDA is an unsupervised learning approach, identifying the correct number of topics is challenging. We used the default hyper-parameter settings and 10 topics, which we determined based on the value of average corpus likelihood over ten runs.

These 10 topics constituted what is known as lifted forms of linguistic vocabulary [54]. On these extracted linguistic vocabulary, to arrive at interpretative descriptions (we call them linguistic themes), we adopted a similar semi-open coding approach as the visual themes that involved the same two researchers as above. The raters referred to the mental health literature [2, 11, 30], and identified the best possible description that characterized the tokens in the linguistic vocabulary corresponding to each of the 10 linguistic topics.

To characterize and represent each of these visual and the linguistic themes, we propose a measure of visual diversity. This measure estimates how coherent images are with respect to the each other in a theme. To measure the diversity in terms of the latent visual features, images are expressed in terms of their principal components within a theme. In the component space, distance between a pair of images are computed by employing the cosine theta similarity function. To perform these set of operations, we utilize the Python *scikit-learn* library[5].

RESULTS

RQ 1: Visual Features

Toward our first research goal, we examine a variety of visual features manifested through the mental health imagery shared on Instagram. First we explore the types of color profiles (grayscale histograms) of the mental health images. In Figure 1 we show histogram plots associated with three categories: images of high contrast, those with high saturation, and those with high brightness.

	Contrast	Saturation	Brightness
saliency	45302 (45340)	59500 (55027)	41995 (42650)
hashtags	13 (13.4)	6 (10.2)	10 (12)

Table 5: Median (and mean) values of saliency and hashtag counts of images associated with the three color categories.

Next in Table 4 we show the proportion of posts belonging to the three color categories. We observe that a large number of images across the disorders are of high saturation (48-75%), i.e., these images contain different types of colors. However a considerable fraction *does* belong to the extreme ends as well, i.e., the high contrast and high brightness categories (25-52%). Thus, unlike prior findings where 90% of Instagram images were observed to *not* have dominant colors [39], in our case, we observe a contrasting pattern.

We further find that (Table 5) the high saturation mental health images have higher saliency compared to the other categories ($\chi^2(2) = 19.7; p < 10^{-15}$; eta-squared estimate of effect size $E_r^2 = .52$, based on a Kruskal-Wallis test). This implies that these mental health images are likely to trigger greater cognitive and perceptual stimulus to viewers [24]. Further, high contrast and high brightness images tend to have more hashtags attached ($\chi^2(2) = 13.6; p < 10^{-15}; E_r^2 = .35$), indicating that the authors of these posts attempt to engage with the Instagram audience by associating their posts with a wide range of topics and content indicators. We conjecture this might be a way for the authors of these posts to increase their likelihood of discoverability and visibility on Instagram.

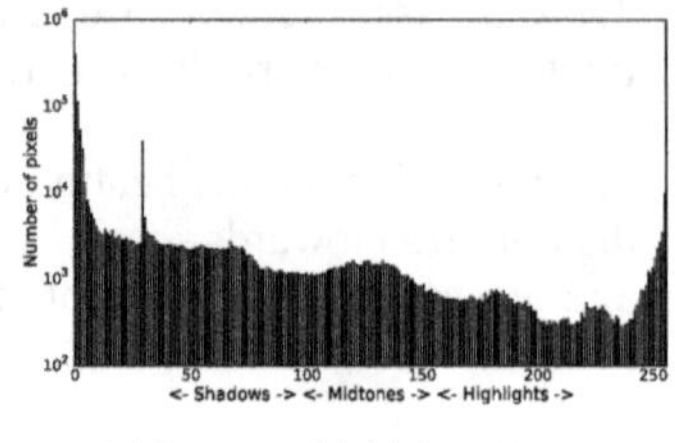

(a) Images with high contrast.

new line)

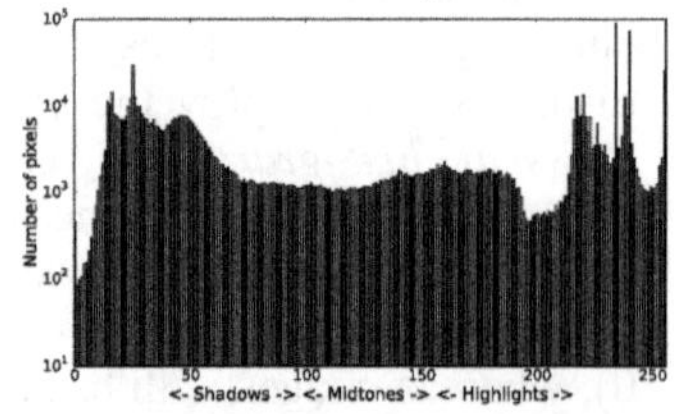

(b) Images with high saturation.

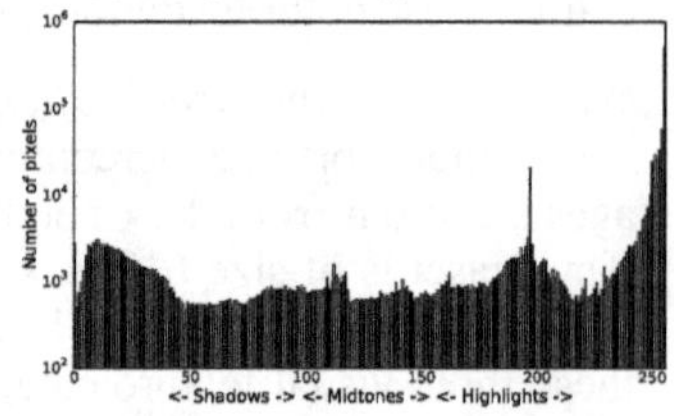

(c) Images with high brightness.

Figure 1: Example images corresponding to the three color categories obtained by extracting grayscale histograms of mental health images.

RQ 2a: Visual Themes

Next, per RQ2, we examine the types of visual thematic content present in mental health images in our Instagram dataset. Figure 2 gives heat map visualizations of all images that were clustered into six different visual themes; the heatmaps were generated from a dimensionality reduced (via Principal Component Analysis) representation of the images in each visual cluster. Specifically, we considered each heatmap as a symmetric matrix with the row and column corresponding to two images from a given visual theme. The pixel value to a given row and a column represents the visual diversity value between the two images that are marked on the axes. For a given set of images, visual diversity is thus computed for all possible combinations of image pairs in a visual theme. Alongside the heatmaps, we also include the manually curated labels of the themes, and their percentage representation in our Instagram dataset. We find that within the themes themselves, there is

[5]http://scikit-learn.org/stable/

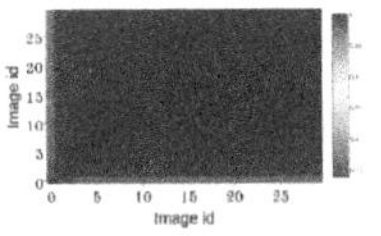

(a) **Captioned Images** (images with embedded text, motivational words and quotes) [52%]

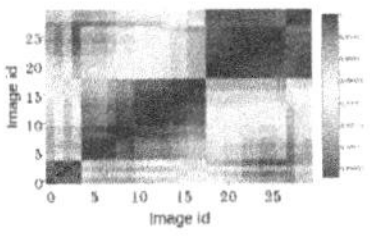

(b) **Selfie Images** (self-portraits; only one human face is present in the image) [17%]

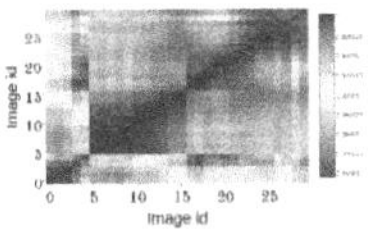

(c) **Social** (users posing with others; at least two human faces are in the image) [11%]

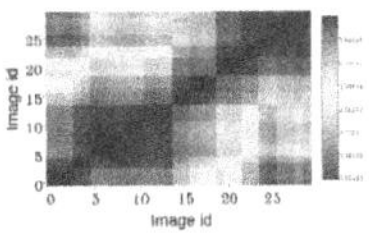

(d) **Food** (images about food, recipes, diet, drinks etc.) [10%]

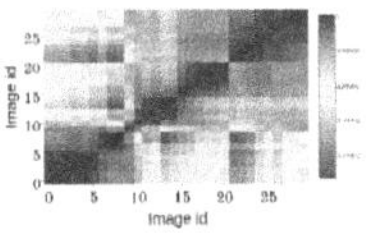

(e) **Physical Perceptions** (images of explicit body parts in high detail) [5%]

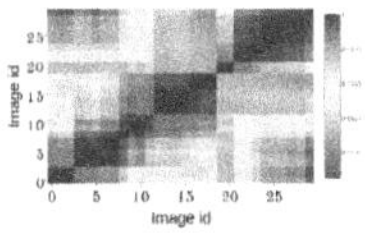

(f) **Graphic Images** (images with explicit, self-destruction or self-harm content) [2%]

Figure 2: Heatmap representations of images in the six visual themes. We use an RGB scale, meaning that red indicates high visual diversity, whereas blue indicates the reverse. Percentage of images belonging to the theme are provided in square brackets.

Visual Theme	Top Tags
Captioned Images	depression, anxiety, depressed, suicide, suicidal, sad, anorexia, selfharmmm, ana, alone, bipolar, worthless, bulimia, broken, anorexic, selfhate, ptsd, pain, schizophrenia, lonely, recovery, killme, sadness, love, death, hurt, help, quotes, suicidalthoughts, emo, depressionquotes
Selfie Images	depression, anxiety, depressed, suicide, suicidal, bipolar, anorexia, selfharmmm, ana, bulimia, ocd, schizophrenia, fat, ptsd, mia, ugly, anorexic, grunge, recovery, panicattack, love, blithe, ednos, secret_society123, bulimic, emo, ed, mentalillness, mentalhealth, eatingdisorder
Social	depression, anxiety, depressed, suicide, suicidal, anorexia, ocd, panicattack, ana, ptsd, bipolar, bulimia, mia, worthless, recovery, anorexic, emo, love, eatingdisorder, ednos, mentalillness, blithe, schizophrenia, grunge, mentalhealth, depressing, bulimic, skinny, ed, death
Food	depression, anxiety, depressed, suicide, sad, bipolar, suicidal, ptsd, ana, ocd, anorexia, schizophrenia, mentalhealth, alone, mia, broken, mentalillness, fat, ugly, bulimia, recovery, panicattack, anorexic, eatingdisorder, bulimic, calories, help, emo, sue, fitness
Physical Perceptions	depression, depressed, suicide, suicidal, anorexia, anxiety, ana, bulimia, sad, mia, anorexic, fat, bulimic, eatingdisorder, ed, worthless, skinny, ugly, blithe, lonely, broken, purge, mentalillness, ednos, pain, emo, ptsd, hurt, thin, workout
Graphic Images	depression, depressed, anxiety, suicide, suicidal, cutting, selfharmmm, blithe, cuts, suicidalthoughts, cut, starve, sad, blood, secret_society123, triggerwarning, f4f, fat, pathetic, empty, blades, numb, depressing, bruise, brain, razors, alternative, boyscanbedepressedtoo, scared, hated

Table 6: Top 30 tags associated with each of the six visual themes.

low visual diversity, as expected, based on a cosine similarity metric (CS) ≥ 0.98. Among the visual themes, *Social* has lowest ($CS \geq 0.99$) and *Captioned images* has highest ($CS \geq 0.90$) visual diversity with $H = 1254$, $p < 10^{-15}$.

What kind of textual cues characterize these visual clusters? In Table 6 we present the top 30 tags associated with each of these themes. We do not observe as much difference across them. For instance, inspection of the content of these tags across the visual themes reveals that many of these top tags include the tags we used to collect our data around the 10 mental health disorders ("depression", "anxiety", "eating disorder", 'suicide"). Moreover, tags like "pain", "broken", "lonely", "'death" appear consistently across multiple themes, likely because the content associated with the different themes relate to the topic of mental health concerns. Our observations can further be quantified through the high value of the mean Spearman rank correlation (ρ=.21 (σ=.19), $p < .001$; ref. Table 7) between the tags and their frequency ranks in each visual theme.

We now present a descriptive analysis of the visual themes:

Captioned Images. First, we find that more than half (52%) of the mental health images contain embedded textual data. We conjecture that individuals use this medium as a way to share motivational and encouraging thoughts, quotes and ideas, such as calls for support. One such embedded text image says: *Life is way too short to spend another day at war with yourself.* Additionally, use of tags like "warrior" and "dontgiveup" in images of this theme indicate individuals' desire to express their opinions and thoughts relating to tackling mental health challenges.

Nevertheless, we do also observe people to share confessions in this theme, or as a way to converse with or reach out to an audience: *It is starting to hurt, too much again*; *You killed what was left of the good in me.* The tags associated with this theme include "broken", "lonely", "help". Our inspection of images in this theme reveals high self-focus and self-preoccupation i.e., most of the embedded text are in first person singular pronouns and concern one's personal thoughts and experiences. These observations align with prior work that analyzed social media language relating to mental health [14].

Selfie Images. Next, although selfie images are observed to be a visual theme in our study, they span less than a fifth of all types of mental health images (17%). On the contrary, in generic Instagram images, prior work reports selfies to be one of the most notable types [28].

Marwick [40] found that selfies shared by Instagram users show glimpses of their lives to others, connect with audiences, and receive instant feedback. While these motivations are likely still present in the mental health communities on Instagram, the images in this visual theme tend to share considerable negative perspectives or signs of distress: e.g., tags like "ugly", "mentalillness", "anxiety", "fat", "selfharmmm". These tags contrast the typical tags appearing in generic self-

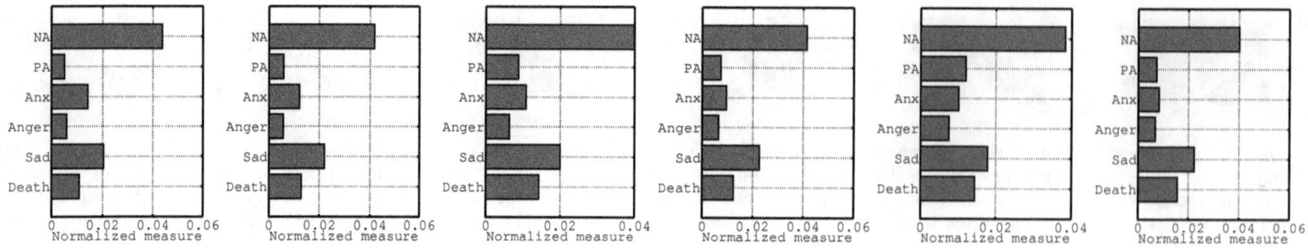

(a) Captioned Images (b) Selfie Images (c) Social (d) Food (e) Physical Perceptions (f) Graphic Images

Figure 3: Distribution of emotions for each of the six visual themes extracted in this study.

	Captioned	Selfie	Social	Food	Phys Perc	Graphic
Captioned	1	0.189	0.272	0.107	0.282	0.217
Selfie		1	0.674	0.091	0.260	0.247
Social			1	0.249	0.141	-0.165
Food				1	0.161	-0.056
Phys Perc					1	0.459
Graphic						1

Table 7: Spearman rank correlation coefficients ρ comparing the most frequent tags across all pairs of visual themes.

ies [28]. Further, Tifentale and Manovich [51] noted that by sharing their selfies, Instagram users construct their identities and simultaneously express their belongingness to a certain community. Hence, usage of the variety of mental health tags in the images of this theme might be a mechanism for individuals to find communities that relate to similar difficult to disclose experiences, or as a way for them to define their identity around stigmatized conditions.

Social Images. The third largest visual theme (11%) in our dataset is found to visualize social settings in people's everyday lives. The post images associated with this theme all tend to have more than one human face present in the same frame. This indicates that some individuals in our data may be choosing to share public information about their social contexts or their association with friends or family. Our conjecture stems from observing tags like "happy", "support" and "people" that appear frequently in images of this theme. It is known that feelings of social isolation and loneliness are predominant in individuals with mental health concerns [48].

Food. The fourth visual theme spans 10% of the image posts, and revolves around aesthetic visuals of plated food. While many generic mental health tags tend to be associated with this theme, we observe the presence of distinctive tags relating to dietary practices and physical health ("fat", "fitness", "calories"). Some of the mental health disorders we consider in this paper relate specifically to unusual or dangerous dietary habits, such as eating disorders and anorexia. This may explain the presence of diet or ingestion specific tags. Contrastively, tags like "recoveryfood", "healthyfood", "highprotein", "plantstrong", "foodisfuel" in the images associated with this time may indicate recovery trajectories or intentions to cope with these mental health challenges.

Physical Perceptions. Next, the visual theme around "physical perceptions" (5%) includes content that elucidate detailed perspectives about one's own body. Tags in this cluster include "skinny", "ugly", "thin". It is known that mental health conditions like eating disorders and anorexia are associated with manifestation of a desire to be unusually skinny, by adhering to normative perceptions of body image [20]. Thus, certain individuals might be appropriating the visual communication channel of Instagram to craft, reinforce, advocate or share particular body image perceptions. This observation is further supported in the usage of various tags that illustrate injurious attitudes and beliefs about one's body, such as "face", "fatfatfatfat", "notskinnyenough", "fatty", "overweight".

Graphic Images. Finally, despite being a smaller share (2%), we observe a noted visual theme of highly graphic images, wherein individuals share images of damaging their own body. Tags like "cut", "blood", "blades", "bruise" uniquely appear in the images associated with this theme. While the specific intent behind the sharing of these images needs further investigation, usage of tags like "pathetic", "empty", "numb", "hated" does indicate the range of self-deprecating thoughts that characterize images in this theme. The visual expressivity of Instagram may be providing individuals with an outlet to showcase and release their emotional pain [35].

RQ 2b: Emotions Manifested in Visual Themes

Next, we present the expression of emotions in the mental health images spanning the six visual themes. Figure 3 summarizes the distributions of the measures of six emotions across each visual theme described above.

Broadly, the different visual themes express diverse emotions. Expectedly, levels of Negative Affect (NA), Anger, Anxiety, Sadness and Death are relatively higher in all themes, compared to Positive Affect (PA). However, we observe notable differences in how specific emotions are expressed in the different visual themes. We discuss them below:

First, NA is consistently the largest emotion expressed in all the six visual themes ($H(1433663, 6) = 5.7; p < .001$ based on a Kruskal Wallis test). It is highest in the Graphic Images visual theme (+8.7%), followed by Captioned Images (+8.0%). We note similar trends for Sadness; it is higher by +28% in the Captioned Images theme, compared to others. As observed earlier (also see Table 6), the images associated with the Captioned Images tend to act as an outlet of deep-seated feelings and emotional distress—this can explain the high measures of NA and Sadness in it.

Anxiety is the highest in the Social theme (+60%; $H(1433663, 6) = 6.4; p < .001$); its second highest value is observed for the Graphic Images theme (+48%). Since per Table 6, many of the tags associated with Graphic Images relate to self-injurious behaviors known to be commonly associated with anxiety challenges [35], we see that manifested via the Anxiety measure.

Next, we find that Anger is highest in the Food and Social themes (+18% and +12% respectively; $H(1433663, 6) = 2.7; p < .01$). Recall that our data consists of images associated with the topics of eating disorders and anorexia; hence the manifested anger in the Food theme may indicate self-conflicting thoughts about diet and food. On the other hand, high Anger in the Social theme may be attributed to limited access to social support; an aspect that characterizes many mental health related content on social media [14].

Somewhat surprisingly, we observe that the Food theme also includes the highest manifestation of PA (+108%; $H(1433663, 6) = 10.5; p < .0001$). This shows that, for some individuals, sharing Food related content may relate to a desire to adopt healthy and functional dietary habits, and positive perspectives towards physical health. Moreover, many individuals in mental health recovery tend to share diet images as a way to identify with this behavior change process (ref. tags in Table 6). This might also be the underlying reason behind high PA. Next, PA is lowest in the Graphic Images (-52%; $H(1433663, 6) = -5.9; p < .001$). Due to the large volume of images in the Graphic Images theme relating to deliberate harm to one's bodies, the emotion expressed in these images tends to be of largely negative tonality (and thus low PA). Finally the theme of Physical Perceptions stands out from the rest of the themes with respect to the expression of Death related emotions (+50%; $H(1433663, 6) = 6.2; p < .001$).

RQ 3: Linguistic Themes

As a final analysis (per RQ 3), we present and contrast the observations gleaned from the visual themes and their emotions, with linguistic themes obtained from the same set of mental health images. The extracted 10 linguistic themes and their associated vocabulary is presented in Table 8.

All of the linguistic themes are highly semantically coherent within themselves, as noted from the themes' annotations in Table 8. Further, none of the linguistic themes overlap conceptually with any of the visual themes, as noted in the human annotations. In fact, mean Spearman rank correlation between the top 100 tags of each linguistic and visual theme is only .14 ($p < .01$), indicating that the sets of themes provide complementary perspective in understanding the different mental health disclosures of individuals on Instagram.

Going deeper into specific linguistic themes, we notice two themes (7 and 8) specifically expressing positive and negative emotion respectively. Example tags for the two themes include "sadness", "emo", "emogirl" and "good", "happy", "fun", "beautiful" respectively. Expectedly, two themes (2 and 5) relate to specific mental health challenges, ranging from anorexia and self-harm (tags like "blithe", "selfhate", "anorexia") to expressions of suicidality ("cutting", "worthless", "killme"). (Table 7).

At the same time, we find the presence of a few linguistic themes that do not particularly relate to mental health issues. For instance, theme 6 spans content shared with the typical

Topic	Top Words
1	[non-English posts] con, amo, por, para, feliz, dia, pra, mais, meu, minha, mi, na, nao, los, amor, vida, em, como, narcissist, mas
2	[anorexia and body image] suicide, anorexia, ana, bulimia, mia, anxiety, anorexic, sad, fat, blithe, worthless, selfhate, sue, ugly, ednos, scars, skinny, ed, secret_society123
3	[fitness and workout] mentalhealth, ptsd, health, fitness, motivation, thinstagram, inspiration, workout, fitspo, veterans, fit, healthy, awareness, gym, support, weightloss
4	[everyday feelings and updates] feel, people, life, time, day, me, make, today, good, hate, anxiety, make, back, things, it, love, sad, fucking, mentalhealth, im, hope, hard, school
5	[self-hatred, self-harm and suicidality] sad, cutting, worthless, selfharm, broken, selfhate, lonely, ugly, cut, scars, fat, sadness, scars, pain, killme, death, hurt, dead
6	[general Instagram audience oriented content] love, instagood, follow, followme, photooftheday, tagsforlikes, beautiful, picoftheday, girl, cute, instadaily, fashion, happy, smile
7	[negative emotion] grunge, emo, sad, bands, tumblr, scene, ana, selfharm, music, softgrunge, punk, alternative, goth, bmth, sadness, pastel, ptv, pale, piercetheveil, emogirl
8	[positive emotion] love, happy, day, lol, good, birthday, tbt, time, night, fun, beautiful, family, baby, work, great, cute, snow, morning, selfie, friends, miss, home, made
9	[art, poetry, memes] art, dankmemes, drawing, memes, anime, fnaf, poetry, emo, bipolar, autism, sketch, filthyfrank, artist, kidzbop, sad, selfharmmm, feminism, love, dank, lol
10	[mental health recovery] depression, anxiety, recovery, anorexia, bulimia, ednos, eatingdisorder, edrecovery, ed, ana, hope, suicide, staystrong, anorexiarecovery, mia

Table 8: Linguistic theme distributions generated using the Latent Dirichlet Allocation (LDA). The human annotations of the topics are included inside the square brackets.

Instagram audience [28] (note tags like "instadaily", "smile", "bestoftheday", "instamood", "selfie", "tagsforlikes"). Another example is theme 4 that expresses feelings and thoughts around everyday activities and experiences (example tags include "life", "people", "today", "good", hope", school"). Together, these themes indicate that despite primarily maintaining mental health focused accounts on Instagram (ref. Table 3), certain individuals do involve themselves in generic discourse as well. Again, this is in contrast to the visual themes, where we observed some mental health challenge manifested in every theme.

Finally, we find two linguistic themes that relate specifically to more uplifting content, such as relating to fitness (theme 3) and mental health recovery (theme 10). The former consists of tags like "workout", "healthy", "support", "motivation", "gym", "exercise" and "mentalhealthawareness". This indicates that the posts associated with this theme encourage and promote behaviors around improved physical health, known to bear links to better mental well-being [49]. Theme 10 includes majority of content around recovery from eating disorder behaviors, as observed through tags like "anorexiarecovery", "eatingdisorderrecovery" and "staystrong". By sharing the posts associated with this theme, individuals may be aiming to seek and provide emotional support, or to share their personal stories and experiences. Further inspection reveals that some of the posts associated with these two themes (3 and 10) tend to also be generated by a range of mental health support groups on Instagram. We note that such recovery related information was not discoverable through the visual themes.

DISCUSSION

Relationship of Findings to Visual Sociology

Our work indicates the adoption of the visual modality of photo-sharing social media platforms for mental health disclosure. In fact, many of the shared mental health images bear specific visual signatures, such as with high brightness or high contrast pixels. To explain this finding, we draw on Berger [25]: *"black-and-white photography is paradoxically more evocative than colour photography. It stimulates a faster onrush of memories because less has been given, more has been left out"*. Individuals might be choosing these minimalist visual techniques to draw attention to their psychological state. The specific visual signatures may also indicate that the individuals want their emotions and experiences to be *visible* to others [45], beyond linguistic descriptions, although displaying these emotions can make them susceptible to both judgment and encouragement.

Further, through the analysis of visual themes, we found that images with a variety of distinct visual cues serve as a vehicle of expression of distress, helplessness and social isolation to certain individuals. From the theme "Physical Perceptions", we can learn that shared visual imagery on Instagram may be allowing some individuals to seek feedback on atypical perceptions of their own physical image [20]. Further, we observed the use of imagery in sharing graphic content (theme: "Graphic Images"). Research identifies many underlying reasons behind such physically damaging graphic expression, such as normalization of behavior as a way to deal with emotional distress [9].

At the same time, we observed mental health images on Instagram also being mobilized to seek and provide psychosocial support and as "safety valves" [21]. This is observable in the theme Captioned Images, that includes explicit calls for help. Goffman [22] posited the desire of individuals with socially stigmatized experiences to look for "sympathetic others". Adopting the visual modality, individuals may be intending to bond around mental health topics.

One of our less expected findings is that the visual and the linguistic themes were considerably distinct. These differences can be ascribed to the ways that the themes capture not just different forms of mental health disclosures on Instagram. They also capture the disinhibiting nature of people's discourse with their audiences, as well as in expressing aspects of their experiences that may not be easily communicated via either of the modalities. For instance, the presence of the visual themes, Graphic Images and Physical Perceptions indicates that individuals are taking to the photo-sharing affordance of Instagram as a way for emotional release around a distressful experience. As Keltner noted, such tendencies of emotional expression via the visual modality are a known attribute of many mental health sufferers [33].

At the same time, linguistic themes provide us with contextual groupings around the shared visual imagery. We found the presence of a linguistic theme around mental health awareness and recovery, and others around specific positive and negative emotions. Together, the two modalities provide us a comprehensive picture of the characteristics of social media based mental health disclosure practices.

Implications for HCI and Design

An important goal of this paper has been to open up new discussions in the social media and mental health research communities about the role of image-sharing behaviors on social media in addressing mental health challenges. Can we develop mechanisms that can sense, based on one's shared visual imagery, their vulnerability, and extend timely, tailored and helpful support to those in need? We discuss HCI and design implications relating to intervention tool development, technologies for emotional self-reflection, and capabilities that enable access to social and emotional support, in the light of mental health challenges.

(Semi)-automated intervention tools, or automated tools that use domain expert help, can be built leveraging our visual theme extraction method. These tools can trigger a warning, in a privacy-honoring way, to individuals when imagery with visual signatures related to unusual physical and mental vulnerability are shared. This can include imagery relating to the themes "Physical Perceptions" or "Graphic Images", that contained many vulnerable tags ("selfharmmm"), and expressed high negative emotion. Note that the role of visual cues is critical here, since the usage of linguistic cues alone may not reveal the nuances of one's mental health disclosure—the tag "depression" can appear in a variety of posts, ranging from the naïve to those that can describe potentially dangerous behaviors. In fact, combining the characteristics of the visual and linguistic cues, psychologists can assess the gravity or severity of the mental health disclosures made on social media platforms, including understanding their temporal trends in the larger community.

Although Instagram and other social media platforms have put in place some intervention policies to bring help to those users who engage in mental health disclosure, at best, they can be called "blanket" strategies. This is because the interventions are neither tailored to the individual or the context, nor do they leverage nuanced and subtle cues manifested in shared content. For instance, Instagram bans certain mental health tags (e.g., 'suicide', 'thinspiration'), whereas Tumblr issues a public service announcement for all searches on a set of terms (e.g., "depressed", 'proana'). Our methods can help improve such efforts by discovering, analyzing, and characterizing the diverse range of information shared in visual imagery, aside from textual data.

Technologies for self-reflection. Leveraging our methods of characterizing visual and linguistic attributes of mental health disclosures, we believe that social media platforms can provide individuals with capabilities for emotional self-reflection. These capabilities can include personal visualizations and displays: individuals can analyze historical trends of the different visual themes manifested through their shared social media content, and associated linguistic constructs. For instance, temporal patterns of themes like "Physical Perceptions", "Graphic Images", or "Selfies" can be shown to end users, alongside the associated tags and the expressed levels of PA, NA, Anger, Anxiety, Sadness and Death, derived via our emotion extraction method. Interpretable summaries of the visual features of shared images can also be included in these self-reflection enabling systems—such as, color or saliency based information that compare one's social media visual signature with typical Instagram content. Those intending to cope with or manage mental health challenges can especially benefit from such self-awareness.

Capabilities to avail social and emotional support. Exclusive mechanisms to seek support around mental health issues can also be developed utilizing our visual and linguistic content characterization framework. Individuals who engage in consistent sharing of imagery with negative body image perceptions, graphic images or content associated with extreme negative emotion can be algorithmically recommended to access recovery related content shared on the same platform, that may be residing outside of their "echo chambers". Additionally, pointers to help resources can be incorporated, such as ways to avail online therapy, pop-ups to reach out to a friend, or a self-care expert.

Ethical Considerations

Due to the sensitivities around the topic of investigation in this paper, there are many important ethical implications to consider. For this work, we used public posts shared on Instagram, and we did not have any interaction with the users. Therefore our work did not qualify for approval from the relevant Institutional Review Board.

Nevertheless, we acknowledge that employing our proposed methods and approaches in the design of the above outlined interventions presents some ethical challenges. How can these automated approaches, that are themselves prone to errors, be made to act fairly, as well as secure one's privacy, their rights on the platforms, and their freedom of speech? Further, how can we address potential risks of these automated approaches misinterpreting and misrepresenting any of the shared visual or linguistic cues? To address these ethical challenges we propose the following guidelines to be incorporated in the design and deployment of the above proposed interventions and tools: a) Seeking voluntary consent from the population being studied and those likely to benefit from the technologies. b) Partnership with a trained domain expert, e.g., a clinical psychologist or a psychiatrist so as to ensure that the tools bear potential to extend help and support to individuals engaging in significant mental health disclosures. c) Including extensive privacy and security protocols to protect the individuals being studied, starting from collection of social media data, to its analysis and modeling, and then during the development of the interventions and tools. And d) Adoption of user centered design approaches in intervention and technology development, to investigate specific needs and constraints of the target users, as well as their acceptability, utility, and interpretability.

Limitations and Future Work

We acknowledge that there are some limitations to our work, as the analysis and the inferences obtained are purely data-driven and relied on public posts shared on Instagram around mental health challenges. Specifically, to obtain disclosures of mental health issues, we utilized tags attached to posts. We presume self-selection biases in users who make public posts and link them to different mental health hashtags. We caution against applying our methods to arbitrary contexts.

Moreover, although users might be voluntarily relating themselves to one of the mental health disorder categories, it is unclear to what extent this constitutes an online identity construction activity. Importantly, it is challenging to assess the gravity of a given user's health condition using these posts or images alone, or more specifically if they are actually experiencing a clinical mental health concern. On a related note, although the tags we employed for obtaining our mental health data were verified through consultation with a licensed psychiatrist, we do not claim our methods reveal symptoms or diagnostic markers of mental illness in individuals. Therefore the methods we developed in this paper were not evaluated for their effectiveness in discovering mental health concerns, but rather as a principled and quantifiable way to understand the nature of mental health disclosures shared on social media. Putting it together, our findings should not be interpreted to be diagnostic claims about one's mental health. To do so, we advocate for collaboration between clinicians and HCI researchers, along with voluntarily consenting patients. This constitutes one of our future research directions.

Finally, qualitative methods would lend a deeper understanding of the motivations behind appropriating a public social media outlet for vulnerable and sensitive exchange. We also emphasize that the analyzed visual and linguistic patterns on Instagram are not the only patterns that can help study self-disclosure. Indeed, current advancements in machine learning approaches like deep learning [36] have created a new thread of research in image classification, where image classification problems once difficult to solve, can now be solved very efficiently. We believe such methods can be incorporated to study mental health imagery shared on social media.

CONCLUSION

In this paper, we presented one of the first quantitative analyses of visual imagery shared on the photo-sharing social media Instagram around a variety of mental health challenges. We characterized different forms of self-disclosure as enabled via the visual imagery medium, and contrasted them with that enabled via linguistic expression. We found that individuals were appropriating photo-sharing affordances of Instagram to vent their discontentment around mental health challenges, seek support, and to disclose sensitive and vulnerable information about their emotional distress. We believe our approach and findings can influence the design of new health interventions that leverage the rich information embedded in visual imagery of mental health disclosures.

ACKNOWLEDGMENTS

This research is supported in part by grants to Kambhampati (Manikonda's advisor), including a Google research award and the ONR grants N00014-13-1-0176 and N00014-15-1-2027. De Choudhury was partly supported through NIH grant #1R01GM11269701. We thank members of the SocWeB lab and the reviewers for their valuable feedback.

REFERENCES

1. Saeed Abdullah, Elizabeth L Murnane, Jean MR Costa, and Tanzeem Choudhury. 2015. Collective smile: Measuring societal happiness from geolocated images. In *Proc. CSCW*. 361–374.
2. Irwin Altman and Dalmas A Taylor. 1973. *Social penetration: The development of interpersonal relationships.* Holt, Rinehart & Winston.
3. Nazanin Andalibi, Pinar Ozturk, and Andrea Forte. 2015. Depression-related Imagery on Instagram. In *CSCW'15 Companion*.
4. Nazanin Andalibi, Pinar Ozturk, and Andrea Forte. 2017. Sensitive Self-disclosures, Responses, and Social Support on Instagram: the case of #depression. In *Forthcoming in Proc.CSCW*.
5. American Psychiatric Association and others. 2013. *Diagnostic and statistical manual of mental disorders (DSM-5®)*. American Psychiatric Pub.
6. Saeideh Bakhshi Bakhshi, David Shamma, Lyndon Kennedy, and Eric Gilbert. 2015. Why We Filter Our Photos and How It Impacts Engagement. In *Proc. ICWSM*.
7. Sairam Balani and Munmun De Choudhury. 2015. Detecting and characterizing mental health related self-disclosure in social media. In *Proc. CHI Extended Abstracts*. 1373–1378.
8. Herbert Bay, Tinne Tuytelaars, and Luc Van Gool. 2006. Surf: Speeded up robust features. In *Proc. ECCV 2006*.
9. Jay Callahan. 1996. A specific therapeutic approach to suicide risk in borderline clients. *Clinical Social Work Journal* 24, 4 (1996), 443–459.
10. Stevie Chancellor, Zhiyuan Jerry Lin, Erica L Goodman, Stephanie Zerwas, and Munmun De Choudhury. 2016. Quantifying and Predicting Mental Illness Severity in Online Pro-Eating Disorder Communities. In *Proc. CSCW*.
11. Paul C Cozby. 1973. Self-disclosure: a literature review. *Psychological bulletin* 79, 2 (1973), 73.
12. Munmun De Choudhury, Scott Counts, Eric Horvitz, and Aaron Hoff. 2014. Characterizing and Predicting Postpartum Depression from Facebook Data. In *Proc. CSCW*.
13. Munmun De Choudhury and Sushovan De. 2014. Mental Health Discourse on reddit: Self-disclosure, Social Support, and Anonymity. In *Proc. ICWSM*.
14. Munmun De Choudhury, Michael Gamon, Scott Counts, and Eric Horvitz. 2013. Predicting depression via social media. In *Proc. ICWSM*.
15. Maeve Duggan, Nicole B Ellison, Cliff Lampe, Amanda Lenhart, and Mary Madden. 2015. Social media update 2014. *Pew Research Center* 19 (2015).
16. Darren Ellis and John Cromby. 2012. Emotional inhibition: A discourse analysis of disclosure. *Psychology & health* 27, 5 (2012), 515–532.
17. Gunther Eysenbach, John Powell, Marina Englesakis, Carlos Rizo, and Anita Stern. 2004. Health related virtual communities and electronic support groups: systematic review of the effects of online peer to peer interactions. *Bmj* 328, 7449 (2004), 1166.
18. Robert Douglas Ferguson, Michael Massimi, Emily Crist, and Karyn Moffatt. 2014. Craving, Creating, and Constructing Comfort: Insights and Opportunities for Technology in Hospice. In *Proc. CSCW*.
19. Venkata Rama Kiran Garimella, Abdulrahman Alfayad, and Ingmar Weber. 2016. Social Media Image Analysis for Public Health. In *Proc. CHI*.
20. David M Garner and Paul E Garfinkel. 1982. Body image in anorexia nervosa: Measurement, theory and clinical implications. *The International Journal of Psychiatry in Medicine* 11, 3 (1982), 263–284.
21. Val Gillies, Angela Harden, Katherine Johnson, Paula Reavey, Vicky Strange, and Carla Willig. 2005. Painting pictures of embodied experience: The use of nonverbal data production for the study of embodiment. *Qualitative research in psychology* 2, 3 (2005), 199–212.
22. Erving Goffman. 2009. *Stigma: Notes on the management of spoiled identity*. Simon and Schuster.
23. Jacob Goldberger, Hayit Greenspan, and Shiri Gordon. 2002. Unsupervised image clustering using the information bottleneck method. In *Joint Pattern Recognition Symposium*. Springer, 158–165.
24. Jonathan Harel, Christof Koch, and Pietro Perona. 2006. Graph-based visual saliency. In *Proc. NIPS*.
25. Douglas Harper. 2002. Talking about pictures: A case for photo elicitation. *Visual studies* 17, 1 (2002), 13–26.
26. Barbara Harrison. 2002. Seeing health and illness worlds–using visual methodologies in a sociology of health and illness: a methodological review. *Sociology of Health & Illness* 24, 6 (2002), 856–872.
27. Christopher M Homan, Naiji Lu, Xin Tu, Megan C Lytle, and Vincent Silenzio. 2014. Social structure and depression in TrevorSpace. In *Proc. CSCW*.
28. Yuheng Hu, Lydia Manikonda, and Subbarao Kambhampati. 2014. What We Instagram: A First Analysis of Instagram Photo Content and User Types. In *Proc. ICWSM*.
29. Jina Huh and Mark S Ackerman. 2012. Collaborative help in chronic disease management: supporting individualized problems. In *Proc. CSCW*.
30. Adam N Joinson and Carina B Paine. 2007. Self-disclosure, privacy and the Internet. *The Oxford handbook of Internet psychology* (2007), 2374252.
31. Dhiraj Joshi, Ritendra Datta, Elena Fedorovskaya, Quang-Tuan Luong, James Z Wang, Jia Li, and Jiebo Luo. 2011. Aesthetics and emotions in images. *Signal Processing Magazine, IEEE* 28, 5 (2011), 94–115.

32. Sidney M Jourard. 1959. Healthy personality and self-disclosure. *Mental Hygiene. New York* (1959).

33. Dacher Keltner. 2004. Ekman, emotional expression, and the art of empirical epiphany. *Journal of Research in Personality* 38, 1 (2004), 37–44.

34. Lyndon Kennedy, Mor Naaman, Shane Ahern, Rahul Nair, and Tye Rattenbury. 2007. How flickr helps us make sense of the world: context and content in community-contributed media collections. In *Proc. ACM MM*.

35. E David Klonsky. 2007. The functions of deliberate self-injury: A review of the evidence. *Clinical psychology review* 27, 2 (2007), 226–239.

36. Alex Krizhevsky, Ilya Sutskever, and Geoffrey E Hinton. 2012. Imagenet classification with deep convolutional neural networks. In *Proc. NIPS*.

37. Diana MacLean, Sonal Gupta, Anna Lembke, Christopher Manning, and Jeffrey Heer. 2015. Forum77: An Analysis of an Online Health Forum Dedicated to Addiction Recovery. In *Proc. CSCW*.

38. Lena Mamykina, Andrew D Miller, Elizabeth D Mynatt, and Daniel Greenblatt. 2010. Constructing identities through storytelling in diabetes management. In *Proc. CHI*.

39. Lydia Manikonda, Vamsi Meduri, and Subbarao Kambhampati. 2016. Tweeting the Mind and Instagramming the Heart: Exploring Differentiated Content Sharing on Social Media. In *Proc. ICWSM*.

40. Alice E Marwick. 2015. Instafame: Luxury selfies in the attention economy. *Public Culture* 27, 1 75 (2015), 137–160.

41. Ran Pang, Agustin Baretto, Henry Kautz, and Jiebo Luo. 2015. Monitoring adolescent alcohol use via multimodal analysis in social multimedia. In *Proc. IEEE Big Data*.

42. James W Pennebaker. 1990. *Opening up: The healing power of confiding in others*. William Morrow.

43. James W Pennebaker and Cindy K Chung. 2007. Expressive writing, emotional upheavals, and health. *Foundations of health psychology* (2007), 263–284.

44. A. G. Reece and C. M. Danforth. 2016. Instagram photos reveal predictive markers of depression. *ArXiv e-prints* (aug 2016).

45. Michael Rich, Jennifer Patashnick, and Richard Chalfen. 2002. Visual illness narratives of asthma: explanatory models and health-related behavior. *American journal of health behavior* 26, 6 (2002), 442–453.

46. Meredith M Skeels, Kenton T Unruh, Christopher Powell, and Wanda Pratt. 2010. Catalyzing social support for breast cancer patients. In *Proc. CHI*.

47. Brian K Smith, Jeana Frost, Meltem Albayrak, and Rajneesh Sudhakar. 2006. Facilitating narrative medical discussions of type 1 diabetes with computer visualizations and photography. *Patient Education and Counseling* 64, 1 (2006), 313–321.

48. Joshua M Smyth. 1998. Written emotional expression: effect sizes, outcome types, and moderating variables. *Journal of consulting and clinical psychology* 66, 1 (1998), 174.

49. Thomas Stephens. 1988. Physical activity and mental health in the United States and Canada: evidence from four population surveys. *Preventive medicine* 17, 1 (1988), 35–47.

50. Markus A Stricker and Markus Orengo. 1995. Similarity of color images. In *IS&T/SPIE's Symposium on Electronic Imaging: Science & Technology*. International Society for Optics and Photonics, 381–392.

51. Alise Tifentale and Lev Manovich. 2015. Selfiecity: Exploring photography and self-fashioning in social media. In *Postdigital Aesthetics*. Springer, 109–122.

52. Ingmar Weber and Yelena Mejova. 2016. Crowdsourcing Health Labels: Inferring Body Weight from Profile Pictures. In *Proc. ACM Digital Health*.

53. Paul Wicks, Michael Massagli, Jeana Frost, Catherine Brownstein, Sally Okun, Timothy Vaughan, Richard Bradley, and James Heywood. 2010. Sharing health data for better outcomes on PatientsLikeMe. *Journal of medical Internet research* 12, 2 (2010).

54. Wayne Xin Zhao, Jing Jiang, Jianshu Weng, Jing He, Ee-Peng Lim, Hongfei Yan, and Xiaoming Li. 2011. Comparing Twitter and Traditional Media Using Topic Models. In *Proc. ECIR*.

The Social Lives of Individuals with Traumatic Brain Injury

Jessica L. Feuston, Charlotte G. Marshall-Fricker, Anne Marie Piper
Northwestern University
Evanston, IL
{jes.feuston, CharlotteMarshallFricker2018}@u.northwestern.edu, ampiper@northwestern.edu

ABSTRACT
Traumatic Brain Injury (TBI) can affect all aspects of an individual's life, including physical ability, communication, and mental health, and present chronic health conditions that persist throughout the lifespan. Although prior work documents a decrease in social interaction following brain injury, little is known about how individuals with TBI engage in social behavior during their recovery, how others in their lives participate, and how these interactions occur in both online and offline contexts. We examine these issues through an interview study involving individuals with TBI, as well as caregivers and social contacts of individuals with TBI. Our analysis identifies the concept of social re-emergence, a non-linear process of developing a new social identity that involves withdrawing from social life, developing goals for social participation, disclosing health information for social support and acceptance, and attaining social independence.

Author Keywords
Traumatic brain injury; social interaction; recovery.

ACM Classification Keywords
H.5.m. Information interfaces and presentation (e.g., HCI): Miscellaneous

INTRODUCTION
A growing body of work in human-computer interaction (HCI) examines the role of technology in recovery and management of chronic health conditions. Sharing health experiences face-to-face and online can facilitate social support, which is accepted as a positive influence on health outcomes [21, 63]; however, some health conditions, such as stroke and brain injury, can significantly challenge an individual's ability to communicate and participate socially. Complications to social life associated with other significant health conditions and long-lasting illnesses have been examined in various contexts, including maintaining normalcy and supporting disease management [26, 42]. However, questions remain concerning how people negotiate their post-injury social lives in the context of recovery, symptom management, and the participation of others. This paper reports on an interview study with individuals with Traumatic Brain Injury (TBI) and caregivers and social contacts of individuals with TBI as a way of understanding these questions.

CHI 2017, May 06 - 11, 2017, Denver, CO, USA

ACM 978-1-4503-4655-9/17/05...$15.00
DOI: http://dx.doi.org/10.1145/3025453.3025784

TBI impacts millions of Americans each year [22] and can affect motor ability, memory, speech, mental health, and other aspects of wellbeing [16, 29, 37, 39]. Although often viewed as a health event requiring treatment and rehabilitation [48], TBI can lead to chronic health conditions that persist across the lifespan [12, 13, 48]. The impact of injury on cognitive functioning and mental health, in particular, can lead to decreased social connectedness due to challenges communicating with others and maintaining and building relationships [16, 51, 69]. As a survivor of TBI said: *"Brain injury is a minimizer. It makes the world a lot smaller for a lot of folks. Many folks with brain injuries can't drive. Many are not ambulatory at all. There are a lot of us that are dual diagnosed with TBI and PTSD (post-traumatic stress disorder), which means going out in crowds can be absolutely terrifying and overwhelming."*

These challenges have the potential to reduce the number and intimacy of social contacts, which can cause feelings of isolation and depression [5, 55]. Although there is hope that survivors can recover through therapy, medical treatment, and time [29, 53], the concept of recovery implies returning to pre-injury functioning, including resuming prior patterns of social activity. Some literatures examine social activity through a lens of psychosocial recovery, which assesses social interaction in interpersonal relationships, employment, and independent living skills [19, 51, 54]. Through this perspective, a survivor's social recovery is defined clinically by a series of outcome measures (e.g., frequency of social interactions outside of the home) with their life before injury as a baseline [67]. This places the burden of recovery on the survivor, neglects the larger social context in which this individual exists and interacts, and presents a survivor's prior social life as a point of comparison to 'measure' recovery.

In contrast to this view, we articulate the concept of *social re-emergence* as the process through which individuals reassemble and negotiate their social lives following a significant health event. Social re-emergence is a nonlinear process of developing a new social identity where individuals may withdraw from social life, develop goals for social participation, disclose health information for social support and acceptance, and attain social independence. Regaining social life after TBI involves navigating functional communication challenges and social situations set against a backdrop of stigmatized and potentially invisible health conditions (e.g., cognitive impairment, depression). Survivors participate "in the capacity" that they can and carefully manage disclosure of their experience. However, interactions with caregivers and social contacts assuming caregiving duties can disempower survivors and their goals for social independence. The notion of social re-emergence reveals several tensions that play out in the online and offline lives of individuals with TBI, specifically: social life is a force that pushes and pulls on wellbeing; social support requires balancing disclosure of health-related information with stigma and social acceptance; and social interaction involves power dynamics between survivors and others within their social ecosystem. These tensions highlight design considerations for technology aimed at supporting recovery and a process of social re-emergence for individuals with TBI.

RELATED WORK

Analyzing the experience of individuals with TBI joins and extends literatures on how people use technology to manage health conditions and how people negotiate online interaction in the context of health and recovery.

Living with Chronic Health Conditions

A growing body of literature examines the ways in which technology can support the experience of living with chronic health conditions and surviving various health events. This literature emphasizes understanding an individual as a person rather than a patient [45, 46] and creating information systems that position the individual at the center [61]. There is also a growing awareness of the broader social context in which health management occurs. For example, Park and Chen [58] describe migraine management as involving communication with family, friends, and coworkers through a process of social recognition and assistance during migraine episodes. The unpredictable but recurring nature of migraines, in which individuals must identify and then call attention to their condition, parallels the experience of some individuals with TBI, many of whom also experience chronic health conditions that interfere with day-to-day living [12]. Further, apart from very young children, older adolescents and young adults (i.e., ages fifteen to twenty-four years old) are most likely to sustain a TBI resulting in an emergency department visit [22]. Many of these survivors may still live with their parents or move back in with parents or other family members following injury. Managing chronic conditions in the context of a parent-child caregiving relationship presents challenges to how care is negotiated and how parents empower their adult children to be an active participant in their care [25].

Online Interaction and Health and Recovery

Interacting online, often through online groups and forums, is a way in which people experiencing chronic conditions and recovering from health events share experiences and information, discuss symptoms, seek resources, and connect [26, 28, 41, 44, 66]. Though people are engaging in online activity associated with their health conditions, these interactions tend to remain separate from social interactions on other popular platforms (e.g., Facebook, Twitter). While individuals may be hesitant to share health information online due to the potentially public nature of many social platforms [57], sharing on Facebook groups can assuage privacy concerns for some (e.g., new mothers [23]). Newman et al. explain that some people want to share information about their health online to connect with others and seek social support, but that posting this information conflicts with impression management goals [52]. Specifically, people often manage how certain audiences perceive them by selectively sharing information and attempting to regulate what others share [17, 36, 40].

Issues of social support and online disclosure become more complex in the case of highly sensitive or stigmatized health issues, such as mental health (e.g., depression, anxiety). Understanding online interactions involving individuals with mental health conditions is a growing topic of interest. While some researchers question whether disclosure of these conditions on social media is aimed at seeking support or "[promoting] dangerous actions" [7], others raise awareness of the stigma associated with mental health and suggest we focus on mental wellbeing as a holistic approach to understanding and designing for mental health conditions [70]. Mental wellbeing can be affected by TBI [33, 38, 65], and the present paper helps fill some of the gaps around how and why individuals seek social support while negotiating disclosure of sensitive and potentially stigmatizing experiences.

Technology for Individuals with TBI

Limited prior work within HCI addresses the unique experience of individuals with TBI, and the work that does exist focuses predominantly on functional challenges following TBI. For instance, researchers have designed applications to support cognitive impairment associated with TBI (e.g., memory loss, planning, problem solving) in the form of an activity planner that helps individuals, with support from a caregiver, plan and track activities [43]. Others have examined the adoption of smartphone reminder applications among individuals with brain injury, noting issues of social acceptability [30]. Putnam and colleagues examined games to motivate individuals with brain injury to engage in rehabilitation tasks [10, 62]. Still other work involves interactive learning simulators to help teenagers gain empathy and understanding toward parents who have TBI [20]. Adjacent literature to TBI understands the role of technology in stroke recovery, including functional rehabilitation [1], augmentative communication [60], and the wider social context in which rehabilitation occurs [2].

While related work has focused on physical and cognitive rehabilitation associated with TBI and stroke, far less is known about the role of technology in social aspects of recovery. Scholars in related disciplines present technology as a way of helping promote social interaction following TBI [71], and a review of the literature found that usage of social media by survivors is associated with reduced feelings of social isolation [5]. However, these researchers also note many remaining questions, including how people with TBI use social media and the role of online interaction in rehabilitation.

METHOD

We conducted semi-structured interviews with 14 adults with TBI (ages 22–65; *M*=44 years; 7 female), three informal caregivers, and two social contacts (i.e., a friend and a family member not taking on primary caregiving duties) of adults with TBI (ages 25–38; *M*=30 years; 3 female). Additionally, we conducted informal interviews with four clinicians who provide services for individuals with TBI (3 speech-language pathologists, 1 occupational therapist). Clinician interviews informed the design of our study and were not included in formal data analysis. Our goal of incorporating this diversity of stakeholders is to understand the sociotechnical system surrounding survivors from multiple perspectives, experiences, and values. We distinguish between caregivers and social contacts to describe differences between individuals providing primary assistive support and individuals who may provide support in social contexts. The inclusion of these individuals is not to invalidate survivors' experiences. These perspectives demonstrate how interpretations of survivors' social lives may conflict with actual survivor perspectives.

Fifteen of the 19 adults with TBI spoken to or about had been injured in a motor vehicle accident; others sustained TBI during falls or athletic accidents. At the time of diagnosis, injury severity included mild to severe TBI [32]. This diversity may account for dissimilarities between our study and others involving individuals with TBI, which often focus on survivors of severe TBI and report reduced social activity [18, 68]. Participants were recruited using websites, such as Craigslist, forums, and personal blogs or websites, and the research team's interpersonal connections. Due to the broad nature of our online advertisements, we provided a series of screening questions prior to scheduling an interview. All participants self-reported mild or moderate TBI at the time of the study and were able to consent independently.

Interviews were conducted in person, over the phone, and through text-based mediums (i.e., email and instant messaging). We incorporated remote methods of interviewing (i.e., phone and text) to extend the reach of the study, in particular for individuals who did not feel comfortable meeting in person or communicating verbally. We developed interview questions by drawing from relevant literature and input from clinicians informing our research. Our interview protocol focused on the short- and long-term impacts of TBI, the recovery process, and stigma associated with brain injury. We also asked participants about their use of technology and interaction on social network sites and online forums. For in-person interviews, we asked participants to show and discuss their social media usage. In-person and phone interviews lasted approximately an hour and participants received $30 in appreciation of their time. We audio recorded and transcribed all interviews for data analysis.

Data Analysis

Our process of data analysis followed a constructivist grounded theory approach [8]. We developed emergent themes through iterative coding, memo writing, and constant comparison of data to our emerging concepts. Our research team frequently discussed emergent concepts and iteratively revised the interview protocol to delve into areas needing conceptual refinement. Our analysis focuses on the experience of individuals with TBI and their social contacts but draws on insights from clinicians as a way of further understanding TBI and the process of recovery. Throughout our analysis, we reflected on the ways in which TBI, which is typically defined as a health event, resembled the long-term nature of chronic conditions [12, 48]. We viewed recovery as a continuous, non-linear process rather than a state periodically assessed through surveyable outcomes [4, 15, 34, 74]. Additionally, we use the word "survivors" to refer to adults with TBI, which is common terminology among participants and community advocates. In place of participants' actual names, we use S*x* to refer to survivors, C*x* to refer to caregivers, and SC*x* to refer to social contacts.

FINDINGS

We briefly describe participant experiences to give a sense of the diverse and complex nature of TBI. Some survivors, such as S1, "*went to an urgent care the next day*" or a few days following injury; others were *"rushed by an ambulance... to the nearest trauma center,"* as S2 described. Time spent at hospitals and rehabilitation centers varied with injury severity. Some survivors were *"instantly knocked into a coma,"* such as S3, and remained in a hospital for weeks, while others were *"in and out the same day,"* as S2 commented.

Survivors described the impacts of TBI as reaching across physical, cognitive, and mental health aspects of wellbeing. Physical impacts included difficulty with verbal communication, walking, and sleeping, as well as visual sensitivities (such as to bright light), fatigue, and chronic pain. S4, a retired police officer injured while on active duty, *"couldn't walk, couldn't feed myself, all that good stuff,"* and S3 described a *"separated left shoulder... broken clavicle, nose, and cheek."* Many participants received therapy services to address these aspects of injury. In our sample, survivors of severe TBI were most likely to have long-lasting physical impacts, such as motor and verbal impairments. Survivors also discussed cognitive changes following injury; particularly changes to executive functioning and memory loss. S5, a survivor of severe TBI and former professional baseball player, described a slow ascent back to awareness: *"I didn't remember anything until about [a month after the accident]. I came to standing in front of a mirror... I came out of darkness through a fog."* Injury also impacted mental health. S6 described an increase in anxiety and depression: *"My anxiety and depression, they were bad. They weren't that great before, but now they're off the charts."* Many described a sense of not knowing when, if ever, they would fully recover.

Recovery from TBI does not necessarily occur linearly [13] nor have a definitive end destination or plateau [12, 48]. Participants shared how the impact of their TBI changed over time, and not always for the better. Describing TBI as "devastating," S6 mentioned how *"new things (symptoms) come and go all the time. It's terrifying."* Similarly, S2, who was injured while cycling, shared, *"Two months after the accident I lost my ability to read. I couldn't recognize text and characters anymore."* Focusing on healing physically, S7, a student injured while studying abroad, only *"started noticing I was going through some emotional phases, like deep depression and anxiety, and stuff that I'd never, ever felt before"* months following injury.

The changing symptoms following TBI impact all facets of survivors' lives, from coursework and careers to relationships. Across these experiences, we uncovered a complex and nuanced picture of the social lives of individuals following injury. Below we analyze how survivors navigate their experience in a social context and attempt to regain social life – particularly with respect to the role of technology – as well as how their social contacts and caregivers participate in this process.

An Active Process of Social Withdrawal

Following TBI, many of our participants experienced an abrupt disturbance to their daily routines. One significant change participants described involved a period of social withdrawal. For some, social withdrawal was necessitated by injuries requiring lengthy hospital stays or rehabilitation. Survivors, particularly of severe TBI, remained in hospitals, rehabilitation centers, or their homes until they reached a point of functional independence – which was months or years after their injury or, for some, indefinitely. We found similar patterns of social withdrawal among survivors not requiring the same extent of functional recovery. A week following a fall that resulted in mild TBI S8 "*stayed home the whole time. Just feeling exhausted really quickly."* Similarly, S7, another survivor of mild TBI, felt *"incapacitated for about a whole month. I couldn't leave the house. You know – black eye – and it was really ugly."* Withdrawing to the home was based on the need for physical recovery as well as social privacy regarding injury and social familiarity regarding environment.

Out of necessity and choice, survivors described being unable to attend school, work, or other events providing social opportunities. For many individuals – particularly those with mild TBI – withdrawal was an active process motivated by mindfulness around recovery. Participants described new perspectives regarding social interaction and a reprioritization of other aspects of life over social activities. S3, a survivor of severe TBI, talked about his decision to socially withdraw by describing how he *"wanted to focus on 'me' for a while, and then begin rebuilding my life outside of that."* S9, another survivor, described, *"Time is very important to me...therefore I like to make sure that my time is used in ways that will benefit me or others. I generally don't like to just 'hang out'. I don't feel this is...productive..."* S7 also explained:

"I've been focusing on school, and I've been focusing on different parts of my life. Before...I was able to have a social life; take pictures with people, and then post it. But, then, I would still get my school stuff done. Now, I'm really just focusing on one area of my life that I'm trying to get better, instead of trying to balance everything."

Others can interpret turning inward as disinterest in social interaction. C1 described how her brother *"didn't want to be bothered with anybody."* She suggested that his feelings may have been compounded by insecurities around physical and speech impairments. Another family member, SC1, discussed her brother's decreased social drive, describing how he would sometimes speak with friends online, *"but when it comes to face-to-face, I don't know. But he just doesn't do it."* SC1 perceived her brother's withdrawal from face-to-face interactions as an ambiguous decline in social activity. However, survivors may choose to intentionally limit their own social interaction. S8, injured while training for a marathon, discussed going *"home versus [going] out...to just make sure that I was able to rest my eyes and my brain."* S1 also finds opportunities to disengage from social situations while in them: *"I would go out to dinner with friends and suddenly I just couldn't function. I'd just be like, 'Sorry... I just need to kind of shut down for a bit.'"*

While some survivors actively disengage from social interaction following injury, others described a slow awareness of changes in their social life. S10 said, *"It was just an isolating kind of time. It seemed like the world around me had changed. It took me easily a year before I really recognized that it was me who had changed."* For some participants, this led to decreased effort at relationship maintenance. S10 described how many of her relationships languished, and she found herself with fewer social contacts and opportunities for interaction. Further, other survivors described the impact of memory loss on their ability to recall prior social behavior. S11 noted that social contacts perceived differences in her behavior, though she did not: *"People would...say, 'Well, that's not how you were before.' 'Oh, I miss the old you' or 'I like the new you.'"*

In addition to these in-person contexts, tensions between survivors' 'old' social lives and present experiences contributed to social withdrawal in online settings. S3 *"quit Facebook...for over a year. I had things I wanted to accomplish and it was only distracting me with a bunch of crap I didn't care about anymore from my 'old' life."* SC1 also described how her brother was offline for several months: *"When he came back home, he was still adjusting. It took some months to start getting back into that type of stuff (social media)."*

Survivors may face challenges regaining their social lives following social withdrawal. S3 explained, *"I'm trying to work on [my social life] currently. Nobody is going to give me a social life. I have to go and 'take' it."* Going and taking it, however, often requires that survivors work toward regaining functional communication and understanding nonverbal social nuances (i.e., body language), which can be affected by TBI [49, 50].

Regaining Social Communication and Participation

Interacting in social situations, both in person and online, following TBI can present many challenges. In terms of face-to-face communication, survivors in our study described struggling with memory and attention, which introduced challenges to social communication such as maintaining conversation and applying information from previous conversations to new ones. S5 described his experience with memory loss; saying, *"When I was going through...memory loss my friends would come over and I couldn't remember their name... The harder I tried to remember their name, the more impossible it was."* S9 also wrote about his long-term memory loss: *"When I woke up from the coma I had forgotten who my mother was. I also had forgotten my other family members."* Though not severely impacted by memory impairment, S7 also noted challenges to maintaining focus in conversation.

Environmental factors, such as fluorescent lighting and ambient noise, can also present challenges to communication in certain social contexts. S9 explained his difficulty focusing on conversation while in crowds: *"There is much more sensory stimulation that my brain has to handle and process. This makes it more difficult for me..."* He also succinctly described his preference for quiet locations and small-scale interactions: *"I prefer to keep the sensory stimulation to a minimum."*

Survivors also discussed reduced confidence in face-to-face social interactions due to stigma associated with physical and communicative impairments. S3 described speech production challenges; saying, *"I've noticed that I can be the 'silent type' now. I am too self-conscious, especially about my speech, and I get reluctant to make conversation."* Similarly, C1 said of her brother: *"When we're in public he doesn't really talk as much, 'cause it still bothers him that he has the impediment, even though it's not bad... It's obvious when you have a speech impediment or you're walking with a cane and you're only seventeen. Those type of things bothered him."*

Further, communicative challenges can be unrelated to speech production and memory. S9 explained social pressure to spontaneously react with an appropriate emotional response. Speaking about his post-injury emotional lability, which has impacted his ability to "control" his emotions, he said, *"I sometimes feel embarrassed – especially [if I become angry] in a public setting like a movie theatre."*

Regaining social participation is a process that occurs in stages. S3 feels comfortable speaking with friends and family, but is still *"trying to get out of my little bubble with strangers... That all just comes down to self-confidence...and that's coming."* When survivors feel ready to re-enter social life, they participate "in the capacity" that they can, S8 explained. This involves creating communication strategies and reconfiguring social expectations around their participation. For example, some participants need to take breaks cognitively, even when out with friends, and have strategies for "shutting down" temporarily, as S1 described. Others discussed using notecards to support their memory and engagement in face-to-face situations. S9 described how these situations are less difficult when he can prepare responses in advance and has familiarity with whom he is speaking. He also *"[writes] things down for future reference and then [tries] to memorize appropriate responses for different situations and settings,"* such as responses to questions about weekend activities. S10, with help from her partner, *"had two reminders that we would use to remind me to at least pretend [to use social cues], so that I could make eye-contact, sit up straight. So, it looked like I was paying attention, even if I didn't have the energy..."*

Survivors also described adapting technology to support their social communication needs. For example, S9 takes to his blog and to email, which allow for revision and reflection before contributing to a conversation. Additionally, S9 explained how in written communication *"there is generally a communication trail that I can refer to that helps me remember what was discussed. This greatly reduces the possibility of me feeling embarrassed and self-conscious."* S3, who also described verbal communication challenges, frequently uses text messaging when he wants to be easily understood – often during negatively charged social interactions. He explained, *"When I'm excited or angry I become near incomprehensible. [Using text], I can get sentences out a whole lot more fluently..."*

In addition to using technology to communicate effectively, survivors use technology to seek online social spaces in which they feel accepted and comfortable. S3 described feeling comfortable online because *"I don't feel like anyone would know I'm disabled unless I told them... I just hate being disabled, but...I'm stuck with it, so I'm trying to make the best of it."* Similarly, C1 explained that *"social media was helpful"* for her brother *"because he didn't have to have face-to-face interaction. I think that's what was easier for him in a sense because he didn't feel judged."*

Some survivors found online TBI forums and support groups helpful in providing resources and acting as a safe space for accessing and regaining social interaction. C1's brother used forums to regain comfort interacting with others, particularly those who shared similar experiences. Some survivors, however, described TBI forums as challenging due to the diverse experience of living with TBI. Further, S6, a survivor of severe TBI, described online TBI groups as "depressing after a while" and as "dead ends." He explained, *"Nobody got better. Or you would see new people with concussions come and go as they got better, and you'd just get depressed."* His experience with irregular activity on TBI forums also presented challenges to building and maintaining relationships. *"There are some [people] that are regular, but not regular in the way that you chat back and forth. People leave a post and run."* He turned to political forms as a source of social interaction; saying, *"I've made friends. If it wasn't for those boys, if it wasn't for chat boards to give me some company – I made a few friends off of them – who knows where I'd be?"*

We learned that survivors relying heavily on online communities for social interaction may feel unsatisfied with the medium of their primary social activity. S3 explained, *"Online interactions are sorta social in my eyes. It's social, but social-ness you can do in your PJs."* Further, some caregivers and social contacts described how they provided social opportunities for survivors. *"We invite them over,"* SC1 emphasized when speaking about her brother's friends. Transportation was a key barrier to face-to-face social interaction for several participants. SC2 explained, *"If [survivor] wants to come to my house, he cannot drive by himself. His mom has to drive him."* S3 also described how his lack of a car limits social opportunities: *"I've had very little in the way of a social life since my accident, I've become a loner without trying."* He continued, *"When [my friends] can hang out they do not want to come and shuttle me..."* Therefore, online social interactions, although perceived as less social than "getting out of the house," are an important aspect of survivors' social lives as a whole.

Managing Disclosure for Support and Acceptance

Given the complexity of injury and recovery, survivors have an abrupt influx of health information to manage following TBI. In addition to formal medical settings, information management occurs in a variety of social contexts. Survivors may share explicit experiences, raise general awareness, and excuse behavior perceived as socially inappropriate. Survivors are mindful about the perception of their injury, and carefully consider the impact of stigma prior to sharing experiences and disclosing information. For example, survivors described disclosing information in face-to-face social contexts to raise awareness and gain support. S12 explained: *"I don't have any problem telling people that I have a TBI... I definitely emphasize that it's definitely a silent disability. It's one of those things that people can't see...but...impacts your life the same way being an amputee can...."*

Similarly, S10 talked about disclosing health information *"because there are flukes about me. Quirks that otherwise look odd... It's better for people to know."* S12 mentioned that she does act differently *"as far as the way I think about things and approach things,"* but wants her social contacts to be aware that *"people can still be normal even though they've had a TBI."* Disclosure in face-to-face contexts may occur repeatedly if a survivor's injury is not visible. S7 talked about having to *"explain myself over and over again, because [my friends] do forget."* She described how *"they just think, 'Oh, the same old [S7] as before.' Well, yes and no. I am, but a lot has changed..."* Survivors may also disclose health information in face-to-face social contexts where they perceive an increase in the visibility of their injury. S4 described a time at the bank: *"I feel it's necessary to tell them that I have a brain injury, so they don't think I'm just stupid or something."* S2 described a similar impulse to increase awareness: *"I wish there were times that I had a t-shirt...that said, 'You know I'm handicapped'... So that when I'm...trying to remember...my four-digit pin...you might be a little bit more patient..."*

Survivors also described feeling comfortable sharing experiences with other survivors who, presumably, have an intimate understanding of the impact of TBI. S8 connected with a former educator upon learning they had a shared experience through TBI. *"She would kind of be the resource of the emotional; [the] friend resource of someone who's gone through it,"* she explained. *"She understood the severity of it."* Support groups also offer in-person spaces where survivors can connect to share experiences and receive support. S2 described his first support group experience: *"It was the very first time I didn't feel alone. It was just an amazingly cathartic, emotionally overwhelming, emotionally validating experience... And the challenge that we faced is we only saw each other once a month. So, I started a smaller Facebook group."*

Brain injury online support groups and forums offer additional opportunities for survivors to seek and share experiences; although they do not necessarily portend social connection or relationship building. S12 talked about losing her *"sense of smell, which has been the most depressing long-term effect of the TBI"* and looking *"for people on Reddit with that similar problem."* In addition to seeking symptom-specific experiences, survivors may join online communities to connect with others who share a similar recovery experience. C1 explained how her brother and other survivors on a brain injury forum *"[bonded] over trying to do things or... Just talking about whatever...they say stuff like... 'I used to be able to do this and now it's difficult.'"* Survivors may connect with other survivors on forums unrelated to brain injury. S6 described how, on a political forum, he *"joked... 'What [do you expect] from me? I got a brain injury.' And somebody asked if it was true and... before you know it, you meet two or three people (with brain injuries)."* Survivors may also share experiences on forums or in groups "to help other people," as S12 explained, though this sharing may never be acknowledged. S2 explained, *"My experience has value, and I can use my experience within this social space to maybe lift somebody else higher; offer them hope."*

Participants described their disclosure practices in TBI communities as distinct from their behaviors on other social platforms, particularly platforms that include an audience of social peers without TBI [52]. C2 explained that his brother used to post a lot of pictures of himself on Facebook and Instagram, but now "*doesn't post pictures of himself at all. I think it's because he's just insecure about the way he looks...*" S7 described being *"very, very, very hesitant to [make an announcement regarding her injury on Facebook] because... I'm not a showy person. I don't do things for likes..."* In fact, announcing or calling specific attention to an injury on social platforms such as Facebook, Instagram, and Twitter was not common among participants, although some posted recovery-related status updates to reach a broad audience at a single time. SC1's brother, for example, *"every now and then"* will say *"'I'm doing fine.'... I think he does that because so many people try to talk to him about, 'How you doing?'"* Many survivors keep health information off their social media accounts due to the public nature of these platforms. S8 explained, "*I debated [posting an announcement] for a while... I just didn't want people probing. It was a very confusing and personal thing that happened to me."* She also talked about the expectation for responding to condolences: *"I didn't want a random person... [commenting] 'I'm worried about you'... How am I supposed to continuously update?"*

Mindfulness of health information disclosure to non-survivors also occurs in offline contexts. C1 described how her brother was *"starting to feel more comfortable"* talking about his injury in face-to-face situations. Similarly, C3 mentioned how her cousin told most people that *"he was 'busy,'"* but did disclose to a few closer friends that he was *"'having these health problems, so I'm taking a leave of absence.'"* Discussing stigma associated with brain injury, S7 said, *"sometimes [TBI] scares people away. Like, 'Oh, she's got problems'... I really [reserved] who I tell this to, 'cause not everyone needs to know things about my life."*

Attending to both the words and actions of others, survivors are mindful of how their brain injury is perceived in certain social contexts. For example, dating can introduce challenges to disclosure and acceptance. Speaking about the depression and anxiety she experienced following her brain injury, S7 said, *"I feel that that is kind of a taboo in society... A lot of guys think, 'Okay, girls are prone to being psycho girlfriends.'"* Additionally, prior to dating his current wife, S4 was acutely aware of how he could be perceived in a romantic situation: *"You're damaged goods. And who wants to marry somebody that's taking a lot of medicine and can't do anything?"*

Concern regarding support and acceptance impacts to whom survivors disclose health information and in which contexts they share this information. However, once information is disclosed, caregivers and social contacts may feel they have a right to act on it – often in ways conflicting with a survivor's preference for disclosure.

Negotiating Social Support and Independence

Many survivors described having supportive caregivers, social contacts, and strong support networks following injury. Talking about her friends, S7 explained, *"If they didn't wanna be my friends, they probably would have been gone a long time ago... They understand me, and I understand them, and we have a great time."* Similarly, SC2 discussed how *"[survivor's] still my friend, but it's really different"*; noting how his friend had changed following TBI. Further elaborating, he said, *"[Survivor] has a group of people that really care about him, and took care of him in his bad times."*

Caregivers often "pushed" survivors towards functional independence. S11 described how her mother did not have *"any limitation in what she felt that I would be able to do or what she felt I would be able to accomplish... It left me knowing that I could achieve more than the doctors were saying."* SC2 discussed how his friend's mom, who acted as his friend's primary caregiver, *"had to be in class with [survivor] at the same time"* because his friend would call professors inappropriate names. *"His mom had to say, '[Survivor], shut up. Control.'"* Support from caregivers may seem "tough." S10, a survivor, described her wife's approach to caregiving: *"You (survivors) never recognize that anything's wrong, and they don't advance. They don't improve. So, you need somebody who lets you burn dinner every night, but doesn't let you burn the house down."* However, achieving balance between support and independence is challenging [25].

Caregivers and social contacts may be supportive without knowing how to appropriately demonstrate that support to survivors. C1 expressed pride and enthusiasm over her brother's recovery, but disregarded his continued need for certain assistive technologies (e.g., speech-based text entry) by saying, *"He was always a little bit lazy."* Further, S6 described an aunt who *"thinks I'm a drug addict"* and *"stands by me for the wrong reasons."* When individuals are supportive of a survivor's recovery, they may *"want to help; they just don't know how,"* S5 explained. Many survivors discussed similar sentiments. S10 described how people's *"way of helping me out is to speak very loudly."* She finds these situations humorous, knowing "it's meant well," even if these actions are not actually helpful.

Caregivers and social contacts can act in unsupportive ways because they do not understand the long-lasting impact of TBI on cognitive functioning and mental health, particularly when physical symptoms are no longer apparent. S2 described how individuals have said, *"'You look normal. You sound kinda normal...it's just bullshit. You're just making it all up.'"*

The complex and potentially 'invisible' nature of brain injury further complicates how other people interpret and act on a survivor's need for support. While caregivers and social contacts may be well-intentioned, they may also act in ways that stifle social independence. C2 discussed his brother's new "behavioral issues" with his brother's employer: *"I said, 'If there's behavioral issues with him, please let us know immediately so we can address it.' Versus just letting him fly on anything."* Continuing, C2 explained how this disclosure resulted in his brother's employer limiting his brother's social interaction at work as a way of preventing inappropriate outbursts or socially aggressive behavior.

Survivors may feel that their caregivers and social contacts are infringing on their social independence as an adult. S3 described how his father *"is a little overprotective. I feel like he treats me like I'm a kid...because of my injury."* S1, a graduate student, described how, in the middle of a seminar, a professor inappropriately *"grabbed me by the arm and said, 'You really need to lie down...' She just took me to this [faculty] restroom."* SC2 talked about how *"[survivor's mom] usually just leaves him at my house, and you have a small kid with you. She tells me, 'You should not let him drink. Watch out with what he does. Let me know when to pick him up.'"* These instances illustrate the complex relationship between supporting and limiting a survivor's social interactions and, ultimately, their social independence.

As indicated in prior work [59], caregivers and social contacts may track and monitor the behavior of survivors. C3 described asking her cousin questions about his activities to *"get a sense of where he's going."* Tracking survivor behavior occurs in online spaces, as well. C2 talked about monitoring his brother's online activity by checking his Facebook feed to "*see what he's looking at...*" Specifically, he installed *"a parental control tracker, so you can monitor what he's been looking at... We haven't blocked any sites for him... it's just monitoring."*

Some survivors may not be aware of measures taken by their caregivers and social contacts. Others, however, described how these actions introduced tensions to relationships. Talking about how her mother had been granted "legal temporary guardianship," S11 described, *"When I realized that, I got really ticked off... I was twenty-one years old. There's no reason that my mother should be telling me what I can and can't do..."* S10, a survivor and professor of medicine, explained how her relationship with her wife was *"no longer equal partners. All of a sudden you've taken this marriage and you've turned it into a parent-child relationship."* She described resentment on both sides: *"You really have really horrid judgment [due to TBI], trust me, but that doesn't mean that you don't resent that someone else is telling you what to do. And they resent that they have to, and they resent the loss of relationship."*

Many of the caregivers and social contacts in our study also discussed these changing roles and relationship dynamics. C3 described how she was no longer *"just [survivor's] friend or cousin"* because of the duties she adopted following her cousin's accident. Similarly, C2 talked about how his relationship with his older brother had become *"like the relationship you have with your parents. They used to take care of you and, then when they get old, you end up taking care of them."*

Power dynamics created through changing roles played out in the ways caregivers and social contacts disclosed information about survivors or forced survivors to disclose information to others. C3 *"told [survivor] that he had to tell his best friend [about his injury]"* or she was going to disclose the information. Social contacts and caregivers may not only disclose information about a survivor's injury when it first occurs; they may update or remind others about it, often to excuse or apologize for behavior perceived as socially inappropriate. C2 described a time when his brother "was really upset" during a family gathering and acted in a manner that was perceived as inappropriate. C2 said, *"We talked to my uncle, and my grandparents, and...explained the situation. They knew that he had an accident...we just reminded them that a lot of [his behavior] is probably because of that."* SC2 talked about disclosing information about his friend online: "*If I had friends, [survivor] would add them on Facebook and talk to them on Facebook. And I'd tell them, 'He had a brain injury and he might say weird stuff.. If you don't want to talk to him, you don't have to talk to him.'*"

Similarly, S11 mentioned a time when her mother told another individual, *"'Oh, don't pay attention to [survivor]. She just had a brain injury; she doesn't know what she's talking about.'"* As these examples illustrate, some caregivers and social contacts disclose information in ways that further highlight stigma associated with TBI in an attempt to excuse and normalize a survivor's social behavior. This disclosure may be related to stigma-by-association, in which individuals feel implicated by the disability and mental health of another [56].

As survivors regain independence, the need for assistance and support from caregivers and social contacts may change. Power dynamics, however, may transition more slowly. While some relationships get "much better" with time, as C1 explained, others remain tense or damaged by the abrupt transition from social equal to an individual involved or implicated in the social care of another. C3 described *"periods where [survivor] hasn't been talking to me for a couple days, because he sussed out that I was intruding,"* even though that has not been the case recently. Trust can also be difficult to regain for survivors. S10 talked about how rebuilding trust was "a slow transition." Her family *"need[ed] the help of outside people to help them recognize what some of [my] strengths are, and what some of [my] achievements are."* Yet, sometimes relationships are unsalvageable. S6 felt abandoned by many of his friends: *"Forget most friends, period. Everything's gone when you get a brain injury. Nobody can understand and everybody walks away, except for family, and [my partner], and my cat."*

Social contacts and caregivers may have difficulty understanding the lasting impact of TBI, further contributing to relationship tensions emerging throughout recovery. Survivors may actively assess the benefits of others' support and the ways in which this support can conflict with re-entering social life, including managing disclosure of their personal experience in tandem with the complications of a lifelong health condition.

DISCUSSION

Recovery from significant health events can drastically impact all aspects of an individual's health and wellbeing. While related studies understand social interaction for survivors in specific contexts (e.g., employment [73], conversation [49]) and assess recovery by measuring social outcomes (e.g., frequency of interactions [4, 74]), our analysis illustrates social life as far more nuanced. We offer the concept of social re-emergence as a way of understanding the complex process of social interaction in the context of recovery and symptom management following TBI. Our analysis uncovers social interactions between survivors and family members, friends, and colleagues in informal caregiving roles and contexts. Survivors must negotiate these relationships in offline and online contexts while progressing toward recovery and independence. Further, we describe social re-emergence as an individual process that reveals tensions between various facets of social life and wellbeing. We discuss these tensions below and then reflect on how the concept of social re-emergence informs technology design.

Social Life Pushes and Pulls on Wellbeing

Some recent TBI literature references the positive nature of social support during recovery and rehabilitation [14, 35]. Similarly, a growing body of work within HCI views technology as a way of providing social support during recovery and management of health conditions [24, 26, 27]. Discussions of social support, however, rarely consider how social life can be both a positive *and* negative force on recovery. As a nonlinear process, social re-emergence supports ebbs and flows in social life, including survivors' active engagement in social withdrawal as part of their broader recovery. Social withdrawal may involve spending extended periods of time at home, "shutting down" while out with friends, or temporarily leaving social media. The act of turning inward may not be indicative of a decreased social drive; rather, it may indicate that survivors need time and privacy to tend to their health and wellbeing.

When changes due to TBI are not readily visible (e.g., cognitive fatigue, memory loss, anxiety) caregivers and social contacts may not understand a survivor's needs regarding social interaction. Others may misinterpret an individual's choice to withdraw and attempt to encourage, facilitate, or even force a survivor into social situations based on that individual's previous patterns of social activity. These actions, though often well-intended, may be at odds with survivors' own goals for participation. A focus on social re-emergence rather than recovery helps counter the comparison between a survivor's past and present social self, and, as part of an ongoing process, enables survivors to re-emerge to social life with a new sensitivity towards interaction in terms of how they are perceived, their unique needs for communication (e.g., prompting memory, social cueing), and their goals for social participation.

Seeking Social Support

While some survivors described feeling self-conscious about their physical appearance following injury (e.g., black eyes, scarring, using a cane to walk), many also described experiencing stigma and challenges to social acceptance regarding *invisible* disabilities (i.e., cognitive impairment and mental health), many of which can persist long after physical symptoms diminish. Throughout the process of social re-emergence, survivors weigh the benefits of disclosure for social support with stigma associated with brain injury. Survivors described disclosing their experiences through online forums and in-person encounters to raise awareness about TBI, self-advocate, and gain social support and acceptance. However, health information disclosure may also involve normalizing actions perceived as discrepant from previous social interactions or from socially normative behavior when survivors perceive their injury has become visible (e.g., feeling they have said something "stupid").

Some survivors may not disclose health information or may limit what they share, particularly with social contacts met post-injury. Given the prominence TBI has in many survivors' lives, individuals want to be perceived as more than just "a brain-injured person." Social re-emergence may involve navigating disclosure to minimize injury as a new social identity develops. Stigma adds a new dimension to the disclosure process for survivors; it does so, as well, for their caregivers and social contacts.

Power Dynamics in Social Interaction

Our analysis of social life following TBI revealed complex power dynamics that survivors navigated as part of the process of social re-emergence. Despite a survivor's effort to carefully manage sharing their experience, we learned that caregivers and social contacts often overstepped boundaries and threatened privacy by disclosing information about a survivor's condition to others in their social network. These actions can conflict with how the survivor chooses to manage disclosure in the context of stigma and social support (e.g., being forced to tell a best friend). Additionally, caregivers and social contacts did not always disclose information that was supportive or empowering of a survivor. Some forms of disclosure trivialized or entirely rejected the survivor's experience.

Caregivers and social contacts sometimes acted in ways that impeded a survivor's ability to regain social independence, despite intending to support and protect survivors. The transition from parent, spouse, sibling, or social peer to a caregiving role, even in strictly social contexts, presents complex challenges [9, 11, 25]. However, from the survivor's perspective, social re-emergence involves negotiating these relational changes in a broader social context, and tensions can arise when survivors begin to seek independence in their social life. Many social contacts beyond caregivers were implicated in social-facing caregiving behaviors, such as monitoring a survivor's whereabouts, activity at a party, or computer use (similar to [59]). Therefore, a survivor's social contacts may attempt to protect and support the individual, while stifling the survivor's ability to regain social independence.

Designing for Social Re-Emergence

The concept of social re-emergence questions the assumption that social interaction is an inherently positive force on recovery. HCI research and design tend to view social interaction related to health and recovery from this perspective, though some recent research calls into question the impact of social media use on wellbeing [6, 7]. Survivors negotiate their social lives in nonlinear ways (i.e., social withdrawal) that may be viewed as apathy or inconsistency by others. While abstaining from social media has been connected to religious observance or seeking a healthy lifestyle [64], we find that similar behaviors also occur as part of the broader recovery process. Technology that pushes social interaction on survivors without understanding their idiosyncratic needs could pose additional stressors and distract from the recovery process. For example, user-retention features among many social platforms (e.g., email notifications of social updates) encourage people to re-engage with aspects of social life through the platform, and may be harmful to survivors actively engaging in social withdrawal.

Social re-emergence accepts that a survivor's network and patterns of social activity may never return to what they were previously; nor is that the goal. The concept of social re-emergence suggests refinement of the social self in both online and offline contexts [72]. System design could support the shifting social needs of survivors by allowing users to reconfigure their social network relationships and privacy settings in ways that suit their current goals for social participation (e.g., rehabilitation, dating) without necessarily reminding them of their past social life. Although social comparison often occurs in the context of others online [31], technologies that exploit a history of social interaction (e.g., Facebook On This Day feature) have the potential to invoke unproductive, and potentially distressing, comparisons with an individual's prior social life. Emphasizing events in the present over events from the past may help survivors develop appropriate, post-injury goals for social participation.

Further, in online contexts prone to context collapse [47], tensions also arise between seeking social support and needing to disclose potentially stigmatizing information about TBI. Survivors of TBI, however, are not alone in this experience; others with significant health conditions face tradeoffs between seeking social support and broadcasting a private experience to their social networks [52, 66]. Increased user control over social network organization and information accessibility is not the only way to address this challenge. Social re-emergence highlights a larger issue of systems being ill-equipped to support the negotiation of multiple goals for social participation within a singular platform and to adapt as these goals change throughout the course of a health condition.

In addition to designing for survivors, research in HCI should take into account the social ecosystem in which these individuals interact and exist. Particular design consideration should be paid to caregivers and social contacts who may be involved in a survivor's recovery process. Some research points to the importance of integrating caregiver observations of a survivor's mental health and subjective behaviors (e.g., personal hygiene) to inform treatment during recovery [3]. However, technology that promotes tracking survivor behavior without providing a means to modify this activity over time may invalidate a survivor's experience, introduce tensions to relationships, and present yet another obstacle to a survivor's ability to regain social independence.

CONCLUSION

TBI is a complex and diverse health event that can have lasting impacts on all aspects of a survivor's life. Survivors grapple with questions of when, if ever, they will recover, and experience a range of physical, cognitive, and mental health changes that impact their social lives. The notion of recovery in the context of social life misses the nuance of picking up the pieces and reconfiguring social interaction to support a new, post-injury reality. Underlying this process are challenges of navigating social situations with changed abilities and living with stigma associated with cognitive impairment and mental health conditions. While caregivers and social contacts try to help survivors regain social participation and independence – often by performing social-facing caregiving behaviors – they can invalidate a survivor's experience, and also experience associated stigma. There are many opportunities to design technology to support the dynamic and nonlinear process of social re-emergence. A sensitivity towards the experience of a renewed social self – rather than a return to an 'old' social life – is at the center of this issue.

REFERENCES

1. Gazihan Alankus, Amanda Lazar, Matt May, and Caitlin Kelleher. *Towards customizable games for stroke rehabilitation.* ACM, City, 2010.
2. Madeline Balaam, Stefan Rennick Egglestone, Geraldine Fitzpatrick, Tom Rodden, Ann-Marie Hughes, Anna Wilkinson, Thomas Nind, Lesley Axelrod, Eric Harris, and Ian Ricketts. *Motivating mobility: designing for lived motivation in stroke rehabilitation.* ACM, City, 2011.
3. Greg Barish, Patricia Lester, William R. Saltzman, and Eric Elbogen. *Beyond sensors: reading patients through caregivers and context.* ACM, City, 2014.
4. Marilyn Bergner, Ruth A. Bobbitt, William B. Carter, and Betty S. Gilson. The Sickness Impact Profile: development and final revision of a health status measure. *Medical care* (1981), 787-805.
5. Melissa Brunner, Bronwyn Hemsley, Stuart Palmer, Stephen Dann, and Leanne Togher. Review of the literature on the use of social media by people with traumatic brain injury (TBI). *Disability and rehabilitation*, 37, 17 (2015), 1511-1521.
6. Moira Burke, Cameron Marlow, and Thomas Lento. *Social network activity and social well-being.* ACM, City, 2010.
7. Stevie Chancellor, Tanushree Mitra, and Munmun De Choudhury. *Recovery Amid Pro-Anorexia: Analysis of Recovery in Social Media.* ACM, City, 2016.
8. Kathy Charmaz. *Constructing grounded theory.* Sage, 2014.
9. Yunan Chen, Victor Ngo, and Sun Young Park. *Caring for caregivers: designing for integrality.* ACM, City, 2013.
10. Jinghui Cheng, Cynthia Putnam, and Doris C. Rusch. *Towards Efficacy-Centered Game Design Patterns For Brain Injury Rehabilitation: A Data-Driven Approach.* ACM, City, 2015.
11. Juliet M. Corbin and Anselm Strauss. *Unending work and care: Managing chronic illness at home.* Jossey-Bass, 1988.
12. John D. Corrigan and Flora M. Hammond. Traumatic brain injury as a chronic health condition. *Archives of physical medicine and rehabilitation*, 94, 6 (2013), 1199-1201.
13. John D. Corrigan, Kip Smith-Knapp, and Carl V. Granger. Outcomes in the first 5 years after traumatic brain injury. *Archives of physical medicine and rehabilitation*, 79, 3 (1998), 298-305.
14. Barbara M. Dausch and Sheila Saliman. Use of family focused therapy in rehabilitation for veterans with traumatic brain injury. *Rehabilitation Psychology*, 54, 3 (2009), 279.
15. Ed Diener, Robert A. Emmons, Randy J. Larsen, and Sharon Griffin. The satisfaction with life scale. *Journal of personality assessment*, 49, 1 (1985), 71-75.
16. Sureyya S. Dikmen, Joan E. Machamer, Janet M. Powell, and Nancy R. Temkin. Outcome 3 to 5 years after moderate to severe traumatic brain injury. *Archives of physical medicine and rehabilitation*, 84, 10 (2003), 1449-1457.
17. Joan Morris DiMicco and David R. Millen. *Identity management: multiple presentations of self in facebook.* ACM, City, 2007.
18. Jacinta Douglas. Elizabeth Usher Memorial Lecture: Placing therapy in the context of the self and social connection. *International journal of speech-language pathology*, 17, 3 (2015), 199-210.
19. Kristy Draper, Jennie Ponsford, and Michael Schönberger. Psychosocial and emotional outcomes 10 years following traumatic brain injury. *The Journal of head trauma rehabilitation*, 22, 5 (2007), 278-287.
20. Jean E. Dumas, Nicolas Szilas, Urs Richle, and Thomas Boggini. Interactive simulations to help teenagers cope when a parent has a traumatic brain injury. *Computers in Entertainment (CIE)*, 8, 2 (2010), 10.
21. Gunther Eysenbach, John Powell, Marina Englesakis, Carlos Rizo, and Anita Stern. Health related virtual communities and electronic support groups: systematic review of the effects of online peer to peer interactions. *Bmj*, 328, 7449 (2004), 1166.
22. Mark Faul, Likang Xu, Marlena M. Wald, and Victor G. Coronado. Traumatic brain injury in the United States. *Atlanta, GA: national Center for injury Prevention and Control, Centers for disease Control and Prevention* (2010).
23. Lorna Gibson and Vicki L. Hanson. *Digital motherhood: How does technology help new mothers?* ACM, City, 2013.
24. Hwajung Hong, Eric Gilbert, Gregory D Abowd, and Rosa I. Arriaga. *In-group questions and out-group answers: Crowdsourcing daily living advice for individuals with autism.* ACM, City, 2015.
25. Matthew K. Hong, Lauren Wilcox, Daniel Machado, Thomas A. Olson, and Stephen F. Simoneaux. *Care Partnerships: Toward Technology to Support Teens' Participation in Their Health Care.* ACM, City, 2016.
26. Jina Huh and Mark S. Ackerman. *Collaborative help in chronic disease management: supporting individualized problems.* ACM, City, 2012.
27. Jina Huh, Leslie S. Liu, Tina Neogi, Kori Inkpen, and Wanda Pratt. Health vlogs as social support for chronic illness management. *ACM*

Transactions on Computer-Human Interaction (TOCHI), 21, 4 (2014), 23.

28. Jina Huh and Wanda Pratt. *Weaving clinical expertise in online health communities*. ACM, City, 2014.
29. Grant L. Iverson. Outcome from mild traumatic brain injury. *Current opinion in psychiatry*, 18, 3 (2005), 301-317.
30. Matthew Jamieson, Marilyn McGee-Lennon, Breda Cullen, Stephen Brewster, and Jonathan Evans. *Issues influencing the Uptake of Smartphone Reminder apps for People with Acquired Brain Injury*. ACM, City, 2015.
31. Adam N. Joinson. *Looking at, looking up or keeping up with people?: motives and use of facebook*. ACM, City, 2008.
32. Cathy Jones. Glasgow coma scale. *AJN The American Journal of Nursing*, 79, 9 (1979), 1551-1557.
33. Ricardo E. Jorge, Robert G. Robinson, David Moser, Amane Tateno, Benedicto Crespo-Facorro, and Stephan Arndt. Major depression following traumatic brain injury. *Archives of general psychiatry*, 61, 1 (2004), 42-50.
34. Robert Allen Keith, Carl V. Granger, Byron B. Hamilton, and Frances S. Sherwin. The functional independence measure. *Adv Clin Rehabil*, 1 (1987), 6-18.
35. Rebecca Koehler, Erin Wilhelm, and Ira Shoulson. *Cognitive rehabilitation therapy for traumatic brain injury: evaluating the evidence*. National Academies Press, 2012.
36. Airi Lampinen, Vilma Lehtinen, Asko Lehmuskallio, and Sakari Tamminen. *We're in it together: interpersonal management of disclosure in social network services*. ACM, City, 2011.
37. Harvey S. Levin. Neurobehavioral outcome of closed head injury: implications for clinical trials. *Journal of neurotrauma*, 12, 4 (1995), 601-610.
38. Harvey S. Levin, Felicia C. Goldstein, and Ellen J. MacKenzie. *Depression as a Secondary Condition Following Mild and Moderate Traumatic Brain Injury*. City, 1997.
39. Muriel D. Lezak and Kevin P. O'Brien. Longitudinal study of emotional, social, and physical changes after traumatic brain injury. *Journal of Learning Disabilities*, 21, 8 (1988), 456-462.
40. Eden Litt, Erin Spottswood, Jeremy Birnholtz, Jeff T. Hancock, Madeline E. Smith, and Lindsay Reynolds. *Awkward encounters of an other kind: collective self-presentation and face threat on Facebook*. ACM, City, 2014.
41. Leslie S. Liu, Jina Huh, Tina Neogi, Kori Inkpen, and Wanda Pratt. *Health vlogger-viewer interaction in chronic illness management*. ACM, City, 2013.
42. Leslie S. Liu, Kori M. Inkpen, and Wanda Pratt. *I'm Not Like My Friends: Understanding How Children with a Chronic Illness Use Technology to Maintain Normalcy*. ACM, City, 2015.
43. Edmund LoPresti, Ned Kirsch, Richard Simpson, and Debra Schreckenghost. *Solo: interactive task guidance*. ACM, City, 2005.
44. Haley MacLeod, Kim Oakes, Danika Geisler, Kay Connelly, and Katie Siek. *Rare world: Towards technology for rare diseases*. ACM, City, 2015.
45. Julie Maitland and Matthew Chalmers. *Self-monitoring, self-awareness, and self-determination in cardiac rehabilitation*. ACM, City, 2010.
46. Lena Mamykina, Elizabeth D. Mynatt, and David R. Kaufman. *Investigating health management practices of individuals with diabetes*. ACM, City, 2006.
47. Alice E. Marwick. I tweet honestly, I tweet passionately: Twitter users, context collapse, and the imagined audience. *New media & society*, 13, 1 (2011), 114-133.
48. Brent E. Masel and Douglas S. DeWitt. Traumatic brain injury: a disease process, not an event. *Journal of neurotrauma*, 27, 8 (2010), 1529-1540.
49. Skye McDonald and Sharon Flanagan. Social perception deficits after traumatic brain injury: interaction between emotion recognition, mentalizing ability, and social communication. *Neuropsychology*, 18, 3 (2004), 572.
50. Skye McDonald, Sharon Flanagan, Jennifer Rollins, and Julianne Kinch. TASIT: A new clinical tool for assessing social perception after traumatic brain injury. *The Journal of head trauma rehabilitation*, 18, 3 (2003), 219-238.
51. Alvin McLean Jr., Surreyya S. Dikmen, and Nancy R. Temkin. Psychosocial recovery after head injury. *Archives of physical medicine and rehabilitation*, 74, 10 (1993), 1041-1046.
52. Mark W. Newman, Debra Lauterbach, Sean A. Munson, Paul Resnick, and Margaret E. Morris. *It's not that i don't have problems, i'm just not putting them on facebook: challenges and opportunities in using online social networks for health*. ACM, City, 2011.
53. Thomas A. Novack, Amy L. Alderson, Beverly A. Bush, Jay M. Meythaler, and Kay Canupp. Cognitive and functional recovery at 6 and 12 months post-TBI. *Brain Injury*, 14, 11 (2000), 987-996.
54. Michael Oddy, Michael Humphrey, and David Uttley. Subjective impairment and social recovery after closed head injury. *Journal of Neurology, Neurosurgery & Psychiatry*, 41, 7 (1978), 611-616.
55. John H. Olver, Jennie L. Ponsford, and Carolyn A. Curran. Outcome following traumatic brain injury:

a comparison between 2 and 5 years after injury. *Brain injury*, 10, 11 (1996), 841-848.
56. Margareta Östman and Lars Kjellin. Stigma by association. *The British Journal of Psychiatry*, 181, 6 (2002), 494-498.
57. Carolyn E. Pang, Carman Neustaedter, Bernhard E. Riecke, Erick Oduor, and Serena Hillman. *Technology preferences and routines for sharing health information during the treatment of a chronic illness*. ACM, City, 2013.
58. Sun Young Park and Yunan Chen. *Individual and Social Recognition: Challenges and Opportunities in Migraine Management*. ACM, City, 2015.
59. Anne Marie Piper, Raymundo Cornejo, Lisa Hurwitz, and Caitlin Unumb. *Technological Caregiving: Supporting Online Activity for Adults with Cognitive Impairments*. ACM, City, 2016.
60. Anne Marie Piper, Nadir Weibel, and James D. Hollan. *Introducing multimodal paper-digital interfaces for speech-language therapy*. ACM, City, 2010.
61. Wanda Pratt, Kenton Unruh, Andrea Civan, and Meredith M. Skeels. Personal health information management. *Communications of the ACM*, 49, 1 (2006), 51-55.
62. Cynthia Putnam, Jinghui Cheng, Fang Lin, Sai Yalla, and Stephanie Wu. *Choose a Game": Creation and Evaluation of a Prototype Tool to Support Therapists in Brain Injury Rehabilitation*. City, 2016.
63. Shelly Rodgers and Qimei Chen. Internet community group participation: Psychosocial benefits for women with breast cancer. *Journal of Computer-Mediated Communication*, 10, 4 (2005), 00-00.
64. Sarita Yardi Schoenebeck. *Giving up Twitter for Lent: how and why we take breaks from social media*. ACM, City, 2014.
65. Jonathan M. Silver, Rachel Kramer, Steven Greenwald, and Myrna Weissman. The association between head injuries and psychiatric disorders: findings from the New Haven NIMH Epidemiologic Catchment Area Study. *Brain Injury*, 15, 11 (2001), 935-945.
66. Meredith M. Skeels, Kenton T. Unruh, Christopher Powell, and Wanda Pratt. *Catalyzing social support for breast cancer patients*. ACM, City, 2010.
67. Margaret A. Struchen, Monique R. Pappadis, Angelle M. Sander, Christina S. Burrows, and Katherine A. Myszka. Examining the contribution of social communication abilities and affective/behavioral functioning to social integration outcomes for adults with traumatic brain injury. *The Journal of head trauma rehabilitation*, 26, 1 (2011), 30-42.
68. Robyn L. Tate, G Anthony Broe, Ian D. Cameron, Adeline E. Hodgkinson, and Cheryl A. Soo. Pre-injury, injury and early post-injury predictors of long-term functional and psychosocial recovery after severe traumatic brain injury. *Brain Impairment*, 6, 02 (2005), 75-89.
69. Nancy R. Temkin, John D. Corrigan, Sureyya S. Dikmen, and Joan Machamer. Social functioning after traumatic brain injury. *The Journal of head trauma rehabilitation*, 24, 6 (2009), 460-467.
70. Anja Thieme, Jayne Wallace, Thomas D. Meyer, and Patrick Olivier. *Designing for mental wellbeing: towards a more holistic approach in the treatment and prevention of mental illness*. ACM, City, 2015.
71. Theodore Tsaousides, Yuka Matsuzawa, and Matthew Lebowitz. Familiarity and prevalence of Facebook use for social networking among individuals with traumatic brain injury. *Brain injury*, 25, 12 (2011), 1155-1162.
72. Sherry Turkle. *The second self: Computers and the human spirit*. Mit Press, 2005.
73. Paul Wehman, Pam Targett, Mike West, and John Kregel. Productive work and employment for persons with traumatic brain injury: what have we learned after 20 years? *The Journal of head trauma rehabilitation*, 20, 2 (2005), 115-127.
74. Barry Wilier, Kenneth J. Ottenbacher, and Mary Lou Coad. The Community Integration Questionnaire: a comparative examination. *American journal of physical medicine & rehabilitation*, 73, 2 (1994), 103-111.

User-Guided Synthesis of Interactive Diagrams

John Sarracino
UC San Diego
jsarraci@cs.ucsd.edu

Odaris Barrios-Arciga
Scripps College
obarrios1585@scrippscollege.edu

Jasmine Zhu
Harvey Mudd
jizhu@hmc.edu

Noah Marcus
Harvey Mudd
nmarcus@cs.hmc.edu

Sorin Lerner
UC San Diego
lerner@cs.ucsd.edu

Ben Wiedermann
Harvey Mudd
benw@cs.hmc.edu

ABSTRACT

Interactive diagrams are expensive to build, requiring significant programming experience. The cost of building such diagrams often prevents novice programmers or non-programmers from doing so. In this paper, we present user-guided techniques that transform a static diagram into an interactive one without requiring the user to write code. We also present a tool called EDDIE that prototypes these techniques. We evaluate EDDIE through: (1) a case study in which we use EDDIE to implement existing real-world diagrams from the literature and (2) a usability session with target users in which subjects build several diagrams in EDDIE and provide feedback on EDDIE's user experience. Our experiments demonstrate that EDDIE is usable and expressive, and that EDDIE enables real-world diagrams to be implemented without requiring programming expertise.

Author Keywords

Interactive Diagrams; Program Synthesis

ACM Classification Keywords

H.5.m. Information Interfaces and Presentation (e.g. HCI): Miscellaneous; I.2.2. Automatic Programming: Program synthesis

INTRODUCTION

Interactive diagrams are animated diagrams that users can interact with using a computational device such as a computer or tablet. For example, an interactive physics diagram with pulleys and weights might allow the user to move the pulleys and vary the weights, while observing the physical simulation that ensues.

Developing an interactive diagram requires programming expertise with technologies like JavaScript, HTML5 and server-side databases, and diagram authors might not have the level of programming ability required to make an interactive diagram.

CHI 2017, May 06 - 11, 2017, Denver, CO, USA

ISBN 978-1-4503-4655-9/17/05...$15.00

DOI: http://dx.doi.org/10.1145/3025453.3025467

In this paper, we present USER-GUIDED INTERACTION SYNTHESIS, a technique that bridges this gap by enabling users to build good interactive diagrams without requiring any programming knowledge. Instead of writing code directly to implement an interactive diagram, users first make a static version of the diagram and then our technique *synthesizes* (i.e., adds) interactivity automatically. This technique also allows the author to visualize alternative interactivity models, so the author can quickly explore the space of possible interactive diagrams, and select and/or refine the ones that are the most appropriate for the specific goals.

The main challenges in making program synthesis-based techniques work are twofold: (1) usability/expressiveness and (2) computational tractability. For the former, the synthesis langauge must be expressive and general enough to implement a variety of interaction models, while succinct enough to be amenable to synthesis and usable by non-programmers. For the latter, even with a succinct intermediate representation the search space is extremely large and underconstrained as the number of possible programs that implement interactive diagrams is unbounded and metrics for suitable interactions vary among diagrams.

To address these problems, USER-GUIDED INTERACTION SYNTHESIS makes use of the following two key ideas:

- **Constraint-based formalism**: This technique expresses and runs interactive diagrams using a constraint-based formalism with dynamically-adjusted constraints. This additional structure more effectively explores the search space of programs that implement interactive diagrams: instead of looking at all possible *programs*, the search looks at all possible *constraints* over a set of clearly defined variables. Furthermore, dynamic constraints offer a succinct and natural way of capturing the variation in interactivity across diagrams.

- **User-guided preview-based synthesis**: This technique employs a user-guided and interactive synthesis technique for programs in the constraint-based formalism. It does not rely on programming knowledge. Instead it uses a *preview-based* approach where the diagram author is shown previews of various interaction modalities, from which the author can pick the best one. The preview-based technique drastically reduces the user's manual effort while also narrowing down the search space.

Using the above ideas, we built a diagram editor called EDDIE (screenshot in Figure 1a) that implements USER-GUIDED INTERACTION SYNTHESIS. To demonstrate feasibility on a real-world application of interactive diagrams, we picked the domain of physics education. As benchmarks we used the interactive diagrams from the Physics Education Technology project (PhET) [42]. We performed our evaluation along three dimensions, *expressiveness*, *utility*, and *usability*.

For expressiveness and utility, we performed a case study in which we used EDDIE to re-implement a variety of existing PhET diagrams. Of the 11 existing PhET diagrams on gravity, springs, and pendulum motion, EDDIE was able to generate analogous versions for 9 of these 11 diagrams. Making these diagrams with EDDIE took a few minutes of human effort each. By comparison, these 11 benchmarks as implemented in PhET each required an average of roughly 5000 lines of expertly-written code.

For usability, we recruited a group of science teachers to author two diagrams using EDDIE and provide feedback on their experience. All of the participants were able to complete the task within an hour, and none of the participants required direct aid from the authors.

Our experiments demonstrate that EDDIE is usable and expressive, and that USER-GUIDED INTERACTION SYNTHESIS allows real-world diagrams to be authored with much less effort than the original diagrams.

In summary, our contributions are as follows:

- USER-GUIDED INTERACTION SYNTHESIS, a technique that transforms a static diagram into an interactive one without requiring the user to write code. The technique is summarized in the **Overview** section.
- A constraint-based formalism for interactive diagrams, summarized in the **Interactive Diagrams using Constraints** section.
- A user-guided, preview-based synthesis engine for interactive diagrams in the constraint-based formalism language, discussed in the **User-Guided Diagram Synthesis** section.
- An implementation of USER-GUIDED INTERACTION SYNTHESIS in a diagram editor named EDDIE, discussed and evaluated in the **Prototyping and Evaluation** section.
- An evaluation of EDDIE on a case study of PhET interactive physics diagrams, discussed in the **Case Study** subsection.
- An evaluation of EDDIE on a user insight survey of science educators, discussed in the **Usability: Teacher Usage and Insights** subsection.

RELATED WORK

Visual Editors. There is a long and rich line of work on visual editors for diagrams, for example [29, 10, 26, 17, 55, 31, 52, 32, 51, 50]. To understand how our work fits into this broad line of research, it's important to first note that the vast majority of prior editors (including all those cited above) support either *static* or *animated* diagrams, but not authoring of *interactivity* for the viewer, which is our main goal.

Much fewer editors support authoring of interactivity – Kitty [30] and Apparatus [1] are the main examples in this space. Our work is different from these editors in two ways. First, our approach of encoding diagrams using constraints and synthesizing the constraints automatically is novel. Second, our tool requires much less expertise to use than prior approaches. Consider for example Apparatus [1], which is a direct-manipulation editor for authoring interactive dataflow diagrams. While Apparatus is a powerful and sophisticated system, to use Apparatus the author must first become familiar with the tool's dataflow programming paradigm. Consider as another example Kitty [30], which is sketch-based project for professional authoring of interactive animations. While Kitty enables the diagram author to add end-user interactivity to an animation, the author in Kitty must correctly express a global interactivity modality as the composition of pairwise element functional relationships.

In contrast to prior work, in our tool, the author must only: (1) draw a static, non-animated diagram, in a style that is familiar to many computer users (2) select between self-animating previews. This is a substantially lower cognitive burden: in our tool, the author has only two concepts to cognitively process (static diagrams and previews of dynamic diagrams) whereas in prior tools, the author must also process the language/mechanism for expressing interactivity (note that we have such a mechanism—the constraint language—but we *generate* the constraints automatically). We validate in our experiments that users with no prior knowledge can quickly generate interactive diagrams after just seeing a 15 minute demo.

There is however a key tradeoff here: while our approach reduces the cognitive burden required to build interactive diagrams, we don't provide the same expressiveness as prior approaches (as we will discuss in the Limitations and Future Work section). As such, our work complements prior work: we provide good automation for a subset of all possible diagrams, and authors can go to more complex techniques/approaches for the rest.

Constraints in User Applications. Constraints have been used for visual layout for many years, dating back to SketchPad [47]. More recent work uses constraints for GUI builders [39, 38, 49], for user interactions [48], and as programming paradigms [40, 18]. The DeltaBlue project [19] coined the notion of an *incremental* constraint solver, which can dynamically resolve a system when constraints are added or removed. Our work presents an application of constraint solving to the domain of interactive diagram synthesis: indeed, our implementation uses Cassowary [4, 12], an incremental constraint solver also used in Mac OS X.

Inference of Layout Constraints. Closely related to our work is research on layout editors that use constraints in the back-end, for example the work on Programming by Manipulation for Layout [25] and The Auckland Layout Editor for GUIs [54]. Our work is different in that, instead of just inferring layout constraints, our work also infers (with the help of a human) the constraints for *interactivity*: what happens when control points in a diagram are dragged by a user.

Program Synthesis. Program Synthesis infers a program from a partial program or a specification [21]. Synthesis is hard because the search space is large, which is typically addressed by limiting the domain language [22, 23, 46, 28, 41], cleverly enumerating programs [33, 53], or asking the human for help [45]. The primary difference in our work is that we apply synthesis-inspired techniques to the domain of interactive diagrams. We narrow the search space by (1) considering a constraint-based formalism whose structure we can exploit and (2) asking the human to make key decisions.

Programming by Demonstration. Programming by Demonstration (PbD), also know as Programming by Example, builds programs from example input-output pairs [15, 37]. PbD is used in a variety of settings, such as generating web scripts [34], building visual tutorials [20], and creating multi-touch interactions [35]. In contrast to PbD, our approach does not use example program input-output pairs.

Interactive Technical Diagrams. There has been a lot of recent interest in digitizing figures and diagrams for STEM education [24, 3]. A large and successful project integrating computers with education is the Physics Education Technology (PhET) project [42], which builds and evaluates interactive diagrams for K-12 [8, 36, 43]. PhET's diagrams require significant programming expertise to build. The project employs 4 full-time software developers and states that each diagram typically involves a software developer, a scientist, and an educator [6]. Our contribution is to enable users with no programming expertise to directly build interactive diagrams.

Interactive Diagram Toolkits. Kitty [30] is a sketch-based project for professional authoring of interactive animations. Kitty's model of interaction is that of *functional relationships* with one parameter, e.g., variable A as a function of variable B. The functional relationship model fits well within the domain of sketch-based animation authoring; however, many useful diagrammatic relationships involve more than two variables and so can't be expressed with Kitty's functional relationships. In addition, users of Kitty must specify the functional relationship between each diagram element and the remaining diagram elements, which leads to a quadratic growth in the number of user-provided relationships. In contrast, our use of constraints enables the technique to not only encode many useful relationships between more than two variables, but to do so very succinctly, without having to explicitly state pair-wise relationships between all diagram elements.

Sketch-based Simulation Inference. Sketching is a body of work focused on recognizing a simulation or animation from a user's diagrammatic sketch. By relying on properties of particular domains, sketching has been applied effectively to mechanical systems [10, 11], vector spaces [14], and fluid simulations [55]. In addition, more general sketching systems have also been developed [17, 27]. With the exception of Kitty [30], sketching work builds non-interactive diagrams: in contrast, we use program synthesis techniques to build interactive diagrams.

OVERVIEW

We begin with an overview of how EDDIE works through an example. There are two kinds of people who interact with EDDIE: users who *build* interactive diagram, which we will refer to as *authors* from now on; and users who *interact* with interactive diagrams, which we will refer to as *viewers* from now on. For a single diagram, EDDIE displays both perspectives simultaneously (screenshot in Figures 1a) using two panes, a left pane for the editing perspective of the author and a right pane for previewing the perspective of the viewer. The left author pane is akin to a traditional editor perspective, whereas the right pane provides a live interactive preview that is continuously updated.

For our running example, suppose that an author wants to build an interactive physics diagram depicting a platform with a weight on top of a spring, as shown in Figures 1a and 1b. The author places a weight (using an image link), a spring, a rectangle for the platform, and a rectangle for the base in the diagram by clicking the respective buttons in the "Shapes" and "Physics" dropdown menus. Once the shapes are in the diagram, the author uses the left pane of EDDIE to place the shapes in the desired configuration (as shown in Figures 1a and 1b). As the shapes are moved in the left author pane, the shapes in the right viewer pane follow.

The author next adds viewer interactivity to the diagram. EDDIE enables viewer interactivity through draggable points called *drag points*. Drag points are visible in the viewer's perspective (the right pane) and are draggable by the viewer. For this diagram, the author desires two viewer interactions through two drag points. First, when the viewer drags the *middle of the platform*, the following should happen: (1) the platform translates, but only in the Y dimension (2) the base remains in place (3) the weight translates and (4) the spring compresses/extends. Second, when the viewer drags the *middle of the base*, the entire diagram should translate in both dimensions.

To add these interactions, the author must first specify where drag points are located. This is done by clicking "Interaction", which displays all candidate drag points in the author pane. The author can then enable the desired drag points by clicking on them (clicking again disables the drag point). In the running example, the author selects the two desired drag points, in the middle of the weight and in the middle of the base, as shown in Figure 1b.

For each enabled drag point in the author pane, EDDIE automatically generates a tentative interaction modality. At this point, the author can interact with the diagram in the viewer pane and see what interaction modalities EDDIE has picked. Interacting with the diagram, the author notices that the drag point on the base translates the entire diagram, exactly as the author intended. The drag point on the weight moves the weight and platform and stretches the spring in both the X and Y dimensions, which—although a valid interaction—is *not* what the author intended. Instead, the author intended the weight and platform to ignore viewer input in the X dimension, i.e., to only translate and stretch in the Y dimension.

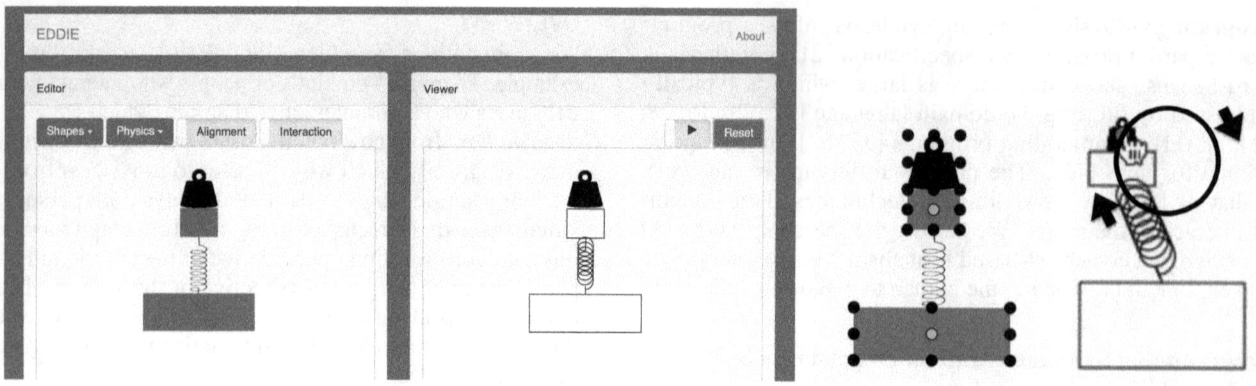

(a) (b) (c)

Figure 1: Screenshots of EDDIE: (a) the main view, with left editing pane and right preview pane (b) drag point selection view, with selected points in orange and unselected ones in black (c) animated preview pane—this particular interaction adjusts the spring's height and width to match the movement of the platform.

To change the interaction of the drag point on the weight, the author right-clicks the drag point in the author pane. EDDIE generates a list of valid interaction modalities for this drag point and displays this list in a preview window. The preview window shows an *animated preview* of the currently selected modality, along with "left" and "right" arrows to navigate through the list of animated previews. Each animated preview is *self-animating*, in that it shows what would happen if a viewer were to drag the drag point in a circular pattern. Figure 1c shows a static snapshot of such a self-animating preview. The circle and arrows are not part of the preview – they are used in Figure 1c to explain what path the drag point takes during the animation. These self-animating previews enable the author to quickly flip through many possible viewer interactions. In the running example, the author clicks "right" several times until the correct version is shown. The author then clicks "accept" to use this interaction modality.

The author now interacts again with the diagram in the viewer pane, and sees that the drag point on the base has the desired viewer interactivity. Furthermore, the author also tries the simulation component of the diagram in the viewer pane (the spring contains its own physical properties), and makes sure that the diagram works as intended. The diagram is now complete.

Overview of USER-GUIDED INTERACTION SYNTHESIS. So far, this overview focused on a description of EDDIE from the perspective of the author and omitted technical details of the technique underlying EDDIE. EDDIE uses a technique we call USER-GUIDED INTERACTION SYNTHESIS, which broadly speaking works as follows. First, interactive diagrams are represented in an intermediate language in two parts: a symbolic description of the shapes and a constraint-based formulation of interaction modalities. Second, given a static diagram, which contains shape descriptions and locations of drag points (with no interactivity), a synthesis algorithm generates an ordered list of interaction modalities for each drag point, in which each interaction modality is represented by a set of constraints governing that point's motion. Third, the author is able to preview all the interaction modalities by right-clicking on a drag point, and selecting from a list of animated previews. The rest of this paper explains these technical details in more depth. The next section (Interactive Diagrams Using Constraints) shows how to encode interactive diagrams using constraints, and the following section (User-Guided Diagram Synthesis) describes our synthesis algorithm and previewing approach.

INTERACTIVE DIAGRAMS USING CONSTRAINTS

USER-GUIDED INTERACTION SYNTHESIS uses a constraint formalism to encode interactive diagrams. We first present background material on constraint systems and then we show how to use constraints to encode a given interactive diagram.

Background on Linear Constraint Systems

A *linear constraint* is a linear equality over variables, in this case floating-point variables. For example, $y = 3x$ and $t = 2$ are linear constraints, while $x^2 + y^2 = 3$ is not. A *linear constraint solver* takes a set of linear constraints and attempts to produce a valuation of constraint variables that satisfies the input constraints. If the input constraints are not solvable, e.g., $x = 2$ and $x = 3$, the constraint solver produces a variable valuation that minimizes an error metric, typically a weighted sum of violated constraints. Linear constraint solving is an example of linear programming, which is typically solved using Dantzig's classic simplex algorithm [16] or a variant thereof.

This work uses a specific kind of constraint solver, namely an *incremental constraint solver* [19]. Such constraint solvers are designed specifically for interactive domains, including graphical applications, and are typically used in the following way. First, the layout of graphical objects on the screen is encoded using a set of constraints. Then, each time the viewer moves an object on the screen, the constraints are solved again to re-compute the layout of objects. A prominent example of such a constraint solver is the Cassowary [12] constraint solver, which we use in our implementation of EDDIE (and which is also used in the layout engine for Mac OS X).

Interactive constraint solvers have two features specifically designed for interactive graphical applications: *stay* constraints and *edit* constraints.

A *stay* constraint is a constraint of the form $Stay(v)$, where v is a variable. This constraint tells the constraint solver that the next time it is invoked to solve the constraints, the variable v should remain the same as its old value. This is useful because in most cases there are many solutions to the constraints, and the *stay* constraints enable an algorithm to state that for certain variables, all else being equal, they should remain unchanged.

An *edit* constraint is a constraint of the form $Edit(v = c)$ where v is a variable and c is a numerical constant. This constraint acts exactly like the regular constraint $v = c$, except that after the solver is done solving the constraints, it *deletes* the edit constraint. Edit constraints are used to encode changes due to viewer input. For example, if the viewer moves an object horizontally on the screen to a new position, one would create an edit constraint to temporarily set the X variable for that object to be the new position. The solver then solves the constraints (including the edit constraint) to find a new layout, after which the edit constraint is automatically removed. At this point the viewer's input has been incorporated into the current values of the variables, and so there is no need to keep the edit constraint around.

Finally, constraint solvers also have a way of *prioritizing constraints*. This is typically done by assigning constraints weights, and the constraint solver tries to minimize the sum of the weights of violated constraints. This prioritization feature is a side effect of the fact that these solvers typically use Simplex, which similarly solves constraints by minimizing the weighted sum of violated constraints. Despite being an implementation detail of the solver's algorithm, prioritization can be useful for interactive user applications.

Interactive Diagrams using Constraints

Now that we have covered background material on constraint systems, we show how to encode a *particular interactive diagram* using constraints. At this point, we are not yet concerned with synthesis of interactive diagrams (i.e., synthesis of the constraints)—we are simply showing how to encode a single interactive diagram using constraints. In the **Synthesis** section, we will show how to *synthesize* an interactive diagram by exploring a set of interactive diagrams and selecting the best one using feedback from the author.

In our technique, interactive diagrams have two components: (1) a shape description section, which states what shapes are in the diagram, and (2) a constraint section, which describes relationships between shapes as linear constraints. Figure 2 shows some examples of the shape primitives used in the shape description section, along with their graphical representation. The parameters to these shape primitives are constraint variables, which we call *control variables*; the relationships between these control variables are stated by equations in the constraint section.

We now describe the three different kinds of constraints and how they are used.

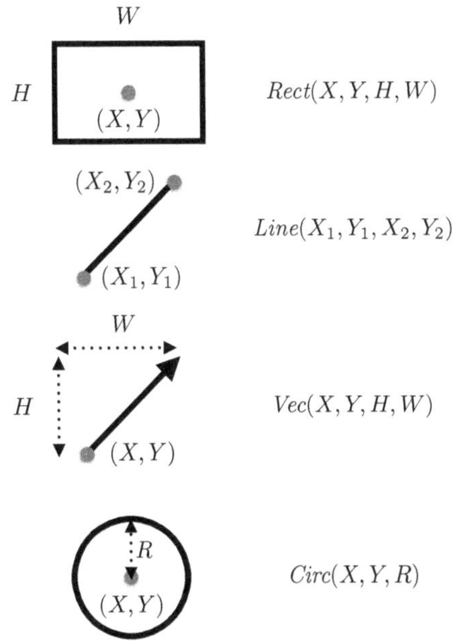

Figure 2: Example primitives for the shape description section. EDDIE also supports Images and Springs, which are analogous to Rectangles and Vectors respectively.

Layout Constraints. Layout constraints are linear equations over control variables which encode layout invariants that must remain true as the diagram is re-configured based on viewer actions. For example, one could state that two rectangles are always centered at the same location by equating their X and Y control variables; one could state that a spring is connected to the corner of a rectangle by equating the spring's end-point to an expression that corresponds to the rectangle's corner.

Taken in isolation, the layout constraints are usually *under-constrained*, meaning that there are many possible solutions. We address this in the standard way by adding *stay* constraints over all control variables. Although staying *all* control variables seems like it might pin the diagram and prevent it from moving, we will next describe how interactive changes happen to the diagram.

Interactivity Constraints. Whereas layout constraints capture layout invariants that must always be met, interactivity constraints are *edit* and *stay* constraints that capture interaction modalities. A viewer can interact with a diagram through *drag points*, which we capture using a primitive *Drag(X,Y)*, where X and Y are constraint variables. Intuitively a drag point *Drag(X,Y)* is simply a point that captures mouse events and sets X and Y to the mouse's position using edit constraints.

In prior work, when edit constraints were added to the system, all existing stay constraints would remain in effect. Although this might seem to lead to a system with no solution (since some points will be constrained to stay and to move at the same time), the edit constraints can be *prioritized* higher than the stay constraints, with the intention of having edit constraints over-ride stay constraints. However, to get this to work in

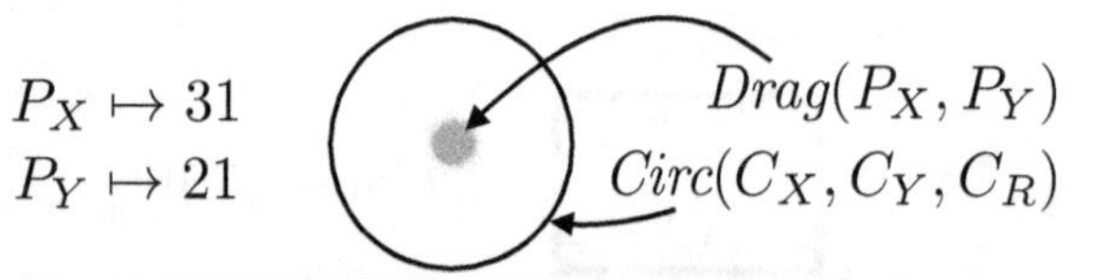

	Initial	Drag update	Result
Layout	$P_X = C_X$ $P_Y = C_Y$	$P_X = C_X$ $P_Y = C_Y$	$P_X = C_X$ $P_Y = C_Y$
Interactivity	$Stay(P_X)$ $Stay(P_Y)$ $Stay(C_X)$ $Stay(C_Y)$ $Stay(C_R)$	$Stay(C_R)$ $Edit(P_X = 31)$ $Edit(P_Y = 21)$	$Stay(P_X)$ $Stay(P_Y)$ $Stay(C_X)$ $Stay(C_Y)$ $Stay(C_R)$
Solver State	$P_X = 30$ $P_Y = 20$ $C_X = 30$ $C_Y = 20$ $C_R = 10$	$P_X = 30$ $P_Y = 20$ $C_X = 30$ $C_Y = 20$ $C_R = 10$	$P_X = 31$ $P_Y = 21$ $C_X = 31$ $C_Y = 21$ $C_R = 10$

Figure 3: Solver state before, as a result of, and after a drag update of (P_X, P_Y) to $(31, 21)$.

practice requires a very careful selection of weights to get the right prioritization.

Instead, we take a different approach, in which we do not depend on any prioritization. In particular, we explicitly temporarily "unstay" the variables that we want to allow to move. Every drag point has a *free* set, which is a set of variables whose stay constraints will be temporarily removed when the drag point is moved.

Figure 3 shows an example of how this works. This example has a circle C and a drag point P at the middle of the circle. The free set for the drag point is $\{P_X, P_Y, C_X, C_Y\}$. The example shows what happens when the drag point is dragged from (30,20) to (31,21). The table at the bottom of Figure 3 shows the solver state (layout constraints, interactivity constraints, and current values of all variables) at three different points in time: (1) "Initial": before the drag happens (2) "Drag Update": after the drag happens and after the constraints are updated to reflect the drag, but before the solver has solved the new constraints (3) "Result": after the solver has solved the constraints to reflect the drag. Note how the stay constraints for the free set of P, namely $\{P_X, P_Y, C_X, C_Y\}$ are temporarily removed, and then added back in.

Note that in this example if the drag point's free set had instead been $\{P_X, C_X\}$, then the stay constraints for P_Y and C_Y would have remained in effect throughout. Since this approach prioritizes stay constraints *over* edit constraints, this would make the Y-position of the circle remain the same, while still allowing the X-position to change to 31. In essence, the final result would be that the circle would only be allowed to move in the X-direction, even if the edit constraint (i.e., the viewer moving the mouse) would try to move the circle in the Y-direction. Note also that the prioritization of stay constraints over edit constraints is precisely the opposite of what prior work has done. This can be done without problems because this approach explicitly removes stay constraints for the variables that should be allowed to be free.

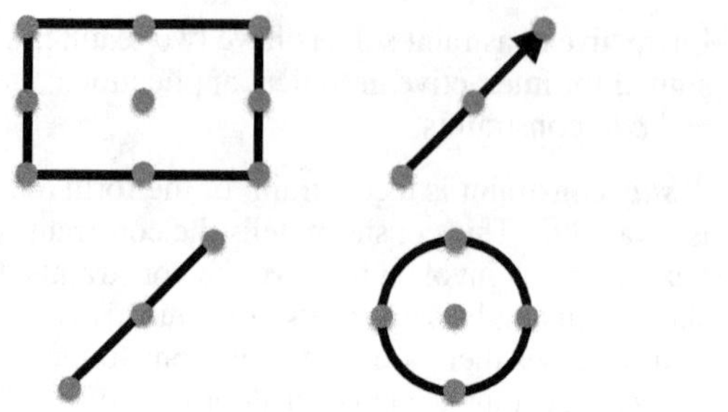

Figure 4: Snap points for our shape primitives. Images and Springs are analogous to Rectangles and Vectors.

USER-GUIDED DIAGRAM SYNTHESIS

Now that we have described how to encode a *single* interactive diagram using constraints, we can now present how interactivity synthesis works. The key insight in this synthesis approach is that it is *user-guided*: during synthesis this approach will ask the author for help with certain decisions that the author is best equipped to do. This collaboration between human and computer enables USER-GUIDED INTERACTION SYNTHESIS to avoid expensive work and incorrect results, while also reducing the work that the author needs to do.

Generating Layout Constraints

After the author draws the static diagram, USER-GUIDED INTERACTION SYNTHESIS first generates layout constraints. Layout constraints capture adjacency relationships, invariants such as "a spring connects P and Q", or "X lies right next to Z". To do so, we first define *snap points* for each of our shape primitives and express the snap point coordinates in terms of shape control variables. Recall that shape control variables are the constraint variables passed as parameters to shape primitives like *Rect*. Figure 4 shows the snap points for several of our shape primitives. For example, given a vector rooted at (X, Y) and with height H and width W, an expression for the midpoint of the vector is $(X + W/2, Y + H/2)$. This expression calculates the midpoint regardless of updates to any of the underlying variables. We call such expressions *snap point expressions*.

Now that we have defined snap points, this approach starts with the *static* diagram that is provided by the author. For each snap point the algorithm now has two things: (1) as mentioned above, it has a snap point expression stating the snap point's coordinates in terms of control variables, for example $(X + W/2, Y + H/2)$ for the mid-point of a vector; (2) it also has the snap point's concrete coordinates in the static diagram, for example $(10, 20)$.

This technique now searches the static diagram for *contact points*, which are two snap points that have the same concrete coordinates in the static diagram—in other words two snap points that are located at the same exact position. This algorithm assumes that a pair of overlapping snap points is not

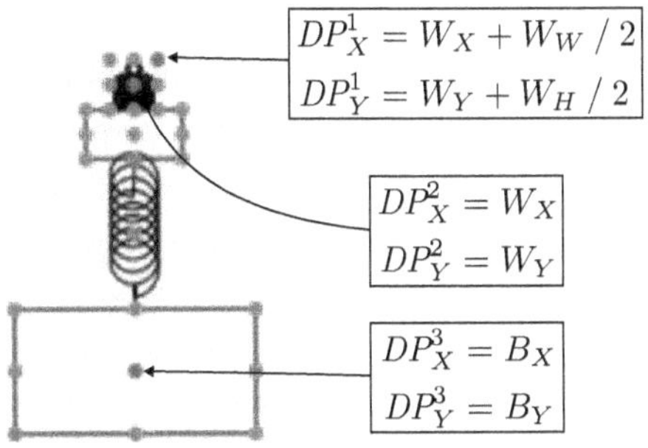

Figure 5: Drag points and their generated linear constraints.

accidental, but rather indicates that the two shapes should be connected at that point. So, for each such pair of overlapping snap points in the static diagram, the point is considered to be a *contact point*, and this technique adds a constraint to keep the two snap points co-located by equating their (X, Y) snap point expressions.

Selecting Drag Points

After generating layout constraints, the next step is to select drag points, which are the points that viewers can drag around on the screen. A drag point is a snap point (as defined previously) which the author has decided to make interactive (recall that each shape has many snap points, as shown for example in Figure 4).

One approach for selecting drag points is to exhaustively search through all subsets of snap points, make them interactive drag points, prune non-sensical results, and then have the author go through these results. However, this approach is both expensive and likely to generate an overwhelming number of options, when in fact the author in most cases already knows precisely which points should be interactive.

Instead, we have decided to let the author make this decision upfront by stating directly which snap points to turn into drag points. The author can click on "Interactions", which displays all candidate points that can be made into drag points. The author can then click on the points that should be interactive. Figure 5 shows this interface after the author has selected three drag points, which have become green to indicate they are selected. At any point later in the editing, the author can go back to this view and select additional drag points, or disable previously selected drag points.

USER-GUIDED INTERACTION SYNTHESIS now needs to generate layout constraints for the newly created drag points. For each snap point P that the author has selected to become a drag point, the technique creates control variables for the drag point's X and Y coordinates, and creates constraints equating those control variables to P's snap point expressions. These constraints have two purposes. (1) When the underlying shape moves/resizes because of other changes in the diagram, the drag point also moves—consider for example a drag point in the corner of a box for resizing, which should move with the shape. (2) When the drag point is moved, it will have an effect on the shape itself.

Generating Interactivity Constraints

Now that the author has chosen drag points, what remains is to generate the constraints that govern the interactivity of these drag points. Recall that interactivity of drag points is governed by the free set of each drag point. This free set captures those variables which will be allowed to change when a given drag point is dragged. Thus, this algorithm must generate a free-set map M from drag points to sets of variables. Our general approach will again leverage human interaction: the engine generates free-set maps and orders them heuristically, and finally displays animated previews to the author showing what interactions look like under these different free-set maps. The author will then be able to quickly find their desired interactivity.

Pruning by Validity. First, we show how to significantly narrow down the search space of free-set maps before even displaying them to the author. We define a notion of validity for the free-set map, so that the search only needs to look at valid maps, instead of all maps. To understand where this notion of validity comes from, let's return to constraint solvers.

There are two situations where constraint solvers give results that are difficult to predict. The first is when the constraints are *underspecified*, in which case there are many solutions, and the constraint solver just picks one. The second is when the constraints are *overspecified*, in which case the constraint solver uses weights to figure out which constraints to violate. In both of these situations the results are hard to predict and are very sensitive to small changes in constraint weights. Instead, the synthesis algorithm will keep constraints *exactly specified*, where there is a single solution. The notion of validity for a free-set map M will *guarantee* that the constraints are always exactly specified, so that the solution depends only on the constraints, and not on internal details of the solver or brittle weights.

At first, one might think that there is a simple way to define validity, which is to require that the number of variables is equal to the number of constraints. Although in linear systems this guarantees no more than one solution (i.e., it avoids being underspecified), it doesn't guarantee a solution (i.e., it *does not* avoid being overspecified).

Instead, we define an algorithmic definition of validity. In particular, for each drag point and the free set in M for the drag point, the algorithm constructs the edit constraints that would be built at runtime if the drag point were dragged, and then uses a simple traversal through the constraints starting at the edited variables to make sure that all variables can be solved for exactly. To begin, the algorithm initially marks as *determined* all the variables that have changed (i.e., mentioned in edit constraints) and all other variables that are constrained to stay unchanged (i.e., mentioned in a stay constraint). Next, each time it sees a linear constraint where all but one of the variables is determined, the last variable is marked as determined (which works because linear constraints provide a unique solution for the last undetermined variable in an equation). We repeat this process until no more variables can be marked as determined. If during this process each variable is marked as determined *exactly once*, this drag point and its associate free set leads to a single unique solution when dragged. If this process succeeds for all drag points and their associated free sets in M, we say that M is valid.

Narrowing down to only valid maps is really important: for a drag point in our most complex benchmark, there are 28 shape control variables for roughly 268 million possible free-set maps but only 3 of these maps are valid. The above definition of validity can be applied directly using a naïve approach that enumerates all possible free sets for each drag point, and then applies the validity definition to only maintain valid maps. While this approach works, it is also very expensive and indeed, intractible in practice. We have developed an optimized dynamic-programming computation which builds the valid free sets bottom-up efficiently.

Preview Ranking and Visualization. Empirically the number of valid maps for a given drag point is relatively small (on average 14.5). As a result, for each drag point the algorithm generates all valid free sets and ranks the results with several heuristic aesthetics functions.

This ranking function encodes numerically the following four aesthetic observations: (1) changes in response to viewer interaction tend to involve only a handful of shapes, and so we favor interactions with fewer number of shapes; (2) shapes tend to respond to changes the same way in both dimensions, e.g., resizing in one dimension but translating (not resizing) in another is very unusual; (3) drag points on the corners of shapes tend to control stretching, while drag points in the middle of shapes tend to control translation; (4) drag points that move in one dimension are much less common than points that move in multiple dimensions.

Once the free sets are ranked, the top-ranking free set for each drag point becomes the default for that drag point. The author can now interact with the diagram in the viewer pane. If any drag point does not interact in the intended way, the author can right-click on the drag point and see an ordered list of all available interaction modalities. Each modality is previewed automatically through a self-animating diagram, showing the author what would happen if the drag point were moved in a circular motion. The author can flip through the different previews, and pick the one that captures the correct interactivity. Figure 1c in the Overview section depicts an automatically-animated preview. The preview adds an image of a hand to indicate exactly which part of the diagram is being dragged. There is also an "Accept" button (not shown) that allows the author to accept the current preview, and selection arrows (not shown) that allow the author to move between different previews.

By ordering the interactivity modalities heuristically, using the top-ranked modality as the default, and allowing the author to change modalities through previews, this technique leverages the computer's ability to quickly narrow down millions of modalities into a short ordered list, and also leverages the human's ability to quickly pick among a list of self-animating previews.

PROTOTYPING AND EVALUATION

To evaluate USER-GUIDED INTERACTION SYNTHESIS, we built a diagram editor named EDDIE that implements our approach. We wanted EDDIE to be easily accessible and so implemented EDDIE as a client-side HTML5/JavaScript web application. For the static diagram editor, we slightly modified the FabricJS [2] library.

To demonstrate feasibility on a real-world application of interactive diagrams, we picked the domain of physics education. We evaluate EDDIE on diagrams in the Physics Education Technology (PhET) project, a library of interactive educational technical diagrams [42]. PhET has received many awards and accolades and has provided empirical evidence for its educational effectiveness [6, 36, 13, 9]. In addition to being interactive, PhET's diagrams include a simulation modelling the technical topic. As a proof of concept we extended EDDIE with a naïve physics engine to model a subset of PhET's physical diagrams.

We evaluate EDDIE along three dimensions: (1) *Expressiveness*, which looks at what kinds of interactive diagrams EDDIE can build (2) *Cost Savings*, which looks at how good EDDIE is at reducing a user's effort of authoring interactive diagrams and (3) *Usability*, which looks at how usable the tool is in practice. The first two dimensions (expressiveness and costs savings) are evaluated through a case study in which we ourselves implement several real-world diagrams. The third dimension (usability) is evaluated by asking thirteen educators to use EDDIE to build two PhET diagrams.

Case Study. In our case study, we looked at all interactive PhET physics diagrams for the following three topics: (1) simple spring mechanics, (2) gravity and planetary motion, and (3) pendulum motion. We discuss the physical and interactive properties of diagrams within each of these topics in turn.

- **Simple Spring Mechanics:** these diagrams study the dynamics of idealized, massless springs with one end fixed and the other subject to an applied force, for example a weight or another spring. The drag point is connected to the free end and controls the displacement of the spring. Springs can be connected end-to-end, in *series*, or side-by-side, in *parallel*. This category contains five diagrams: 1 spring, 2 springs, 2 series springs, 2 parallel springs, and a weight on a spring.
- **Gravity and Planetary Motion:** these diagrams study the force of gravity and its application to planetary motion. These diagrams have a number of spheres representing planets, as well as overlaid vectors representing velocity. PhET uses drag points in two ways: to determine the placement of a planet, and to determine the value of a velocity vector. This category contains four diagrams: a gravity lab, 2 planets, 3 planets, and 4 planets.
- **Pendulum Motion:** this diagram studies the motion of a simple pendulum subject to gravity and air resistence. The shapes consist of spheres representing the pendulum base and weight and a line between the spheres. A drag point controls the position (and by extension, angular displacement) of the pendulum weight. This category contains two

diagrams, one with two pendulums and one with a single pendulum.

Across the three categories above, there are a total of 11 interactive diagrams. EDDIE is able to generate nine of these diagrams with very little human interaction, requiring at most five minutes of effort by the authors. Before we show the benefits that EDDIE provides in these nine diagrams compared to the traditional way of building these diagrams, we first explain the two diagrams that EDDIE cannot generate.

The first unsupported diagram is a series spring simulation in which the drag point simultaneously translates and compresses one of the springs. Our system limits updates to a single variable and so does not support this interaction. To support such interactions, we could extend EDDIE to use ranking functions on stay-constraints.

The second unsupported diagram is a spring simulation in which the viewer can drag-and-drop weights onto a platform attached to a spring. This action consists of two different layout configurations, one in which the weight is free-floating and one in which the weight is attached to the spring. Our framework currently assumes the layout constraints always hold for a given diagram and so can't support this functionality. To support such interactions, EDDIE would need to add support for conditional layout constraints and drag-and-drop features.

Cost Savings. We now evaluate the manual effort required by the author to make diagrams in EDDIE compared to the traditional approach. The baseline we use is the PhET implementation of the nine benchmarks we also implemented in EDDIE. In general, PhET benchmarks require a large amount of effort to build, and the builder needs to have a lot of programming experience. At the time of this writing, the project employs four full-time software developers [6]. Each diagram requires between 3800 and 5700 lines of handwritten JavaScript and Flash. Figure 6 shows the different benchmarks, along with the lines of codes required to implement each benchmark in PhET (column "PhET LoC").

In EDDIE, authoring a diagram requires two efforts. First, the author generates a static representation of the diagram. We have not formally quantified this effort, but most static diagrams have only a handful of shapes, and creating and aligning those shapes takes on the order of minutes.

Second, the author specifies drag points and drag point interactions in the diagram. Figure 6 shows the effort required for this in three columns: "P" shows the number of drag points that the author must select; "V" shows the total number of previews (that the author must view across all drag points for that benchmark (note that the V count includes the view that the author accepts for each drag point, meaning that V cannot be smaller than P); "VPP" (which stands for *views per point)* shows the total number of previews that the author must view per drag point, in other words VPP = V/P (VPP cannot be smaller than 1).

The VPP metric captures the effectiveness of this technique's heuristic for ordering interactivity models (through ranking of free-set maps). A VPP of 1 corresponds to EDDIE always choosing the right interactivity model first, while a high VPP corresponds to showing many undesired interactivity models before the author finds the right one.

Category	Phet LoC	Name	P	V	VPP
Springs	5278	1 spring	1	3	3
		2 springs	2	6	3
		parallel	1	8	8
Orbits/Gravity	5628	lab	2	4	2
		2 body	4	4	1
		3 body	6	6	1
		4 body	8	8	1
Pendulum	3821	1 mass	1	1	1
		2 masses	2	2	1

Figure 6: Comparison of programming effort between PhET and EDDIE for a variety of PhET physics diagrams. "P" is the number of points present in the diagram, "V" is the number of candidate interactions viewed by the user, and "VPP" is our metric of "Views-Per-Point", "V"/"P". EDDIE significantly reduces the effort of authoring diagrams, requiring one or two views per point for most diagrams.

The VPP results demonstrate that EDDIE ranks interaction modalities well: in most cases, the correct interaction modality is in the top 3. Only one benchmark required 8 views per point, but even in this case, because the previews are self-animating, the viewer can very quickly browse through 8 previews, usually in less than one minute. As a whole, this case study demonstrates that EDDIE can express a variety of real-world diagrams and further, requires little effort by a power user (i.e., one of the authors of this paper).

Usability: Teacher Usage and Insights. To collect feedback and evaluate usability on the target audience of nonprogrammers, we introduced EDDIE during a higher-education computer science pedagogy class for K-12 teachers. We recruited eleven science teachers (three female) aged 25-55 and two male science professors aged 45-60. Participants were first given a brief 15-20 minute presentation on interactive diagrams and the features of EDDIE.

Next, the participants were given an instructional page about EDDIE and two interactive PhET diagrams to replicate within EDDIE. For each diagram, the organizer demonstrated the desired functionality of the specific diagram. The organizer did not directly aid the participants after participants started using EDDIE.

All participants replicated the two diagrams within an hour. The first diagram, consisting of a weight on the end of a spring [7], took the participants roughly 35-45 minutes to replicate. The second diagram was simpler, consisting of two pendulums hanging from a common pivot [5] and took roughly 5-20 minutes to replicate.

After completing both diagrams, the participants answered some qualitative questions about their experience using EDDIE. We asked participants for both positive and negative feedback about the tool, in a free form manner. We did not prompt the participants to discuss any particular feature of EDDIE, and we did not tell them what part of EDDIE was novel.

On the positive side, 8 out of 13 participants mentioned that EDDIE was easy to use and one explicitly mentioned that the side-by-side panes were useful for simultaneously displaying the author's and viewer's perspectives. Finally, 5 out of 13 participants mentioned that they liked EDDIE's static editing capabilities, which are mostly inherited from the existing FabricJS framework.

On the negative side, EDDIE performs a lot of work for the user and as a consequence several participants experienced a steep learning curve—3 out of 13 participants were at times surprised by the output of their actions. However, all three participants overcame the learning curve by referring to the help pages and all three completed both exercises. Furthermore, 3 out of 13 participants were at first confused by the functionality of the left/right buttons in the interface that enables users to select interaction modality. This confusion was resolved after viewing the help page and all three participants completed the diagrams. EDDIE's visualization and presentation of the list is tangential to our research contribution and was picked for ease of implementation. There are other mechanisms to make this interface clearer, for example displaying a swiping animation when previews are switched, replacing the left/right buttons with a single "next" button, or replacing the left/right buttons with a touch/swipe interface.

Finally, the participants used their own machines, which resulted in a wide variety of platforms (e.g., tablets, netbooks, and laptops) and web browsers (e.g., Firefox, Chrome, Safari, Internet Explorer, Edge). A significant number of these environments experienced some performance problems, for example lagging and jittery animated previews. Unfortunately, we did not discover these problems before the study because we had developed and tested EDDIE on a higher-end laptop, on which performance was not an issue. Still, despite these performance problems, EDDIE was ultimately usable and all participants finished their tasks quickly. Furthermore, we have not yet done any significant performance optimizations or extensive cross-browser testing. With further tuning and testing, we believe we can bring good performance to EDDIE across a wide variety of environments.

Insights and Lessons Learned. Through our usage and evaluation of EDDIE, we found that EDDIE's design works well for a variety of reasons.

First, the side-by-side view is useful because it gives immediate feedback on how generated diagrams work. Task-switching is well-known to require measurable cognitive effort [44]. EDDIE's side-by-side panes likely incur less cognitive load than alternating between two different views, because the panes in EDDIE are always visible at the same position.

Second, the self-animated previews are effective at quickly allowing authors to see different interaction modalities, but without having to do any actual manual interaction. This makes the selection process for interaction modalities very quick and easy to use.

Third, the approach of reducing the search space (by pruning underconstrained modalities) and then ordering the top candidates is effective because it narrows the author's attention to only the most promising interaction modalities. While developing EDDIE, prior to adding the ordering heuristics, we experienced frustration at having to navigate many incorrect interactions. After adding the aesthetic heuristics, the experience was much improved.

Limitations and Future Work. There are clear opportunities for future work on expanding our expressiveness and automation to get closer to the expressiveness of more manual tools like Kitty [30] or Apparatus [1], including: continuous locations for drag points, user-defined adjacency relationships, conditional relationships, and nonlinear relationships. Still, despite these limitations on expressiveness, our formalism of shapes and drag points connected by linear adjacency relationships can capture about 67% of the interactivity present in PhET diagrams, a real-world set of interactive diagrams that domain experts actually wanted to build.

In addition, our physics engine is relatively simplistic and as a consequence, there are many diagrams in PhET for which EDDIE can support the interactive portion but not the domain-specific chemical, mathematical, or physical components. To fully support these diagrams, an expert programmer would have to extend EDDIE's implementation by adding domain-specific primitives for these uncovered topics. Once this is done, diagram authors could then use the newly added primitives to reproduce these (currently unsupported) diagrams, without writing any additional code.

Summary. Our case study demonstrates that EDDIE can express and implement a broad variety of real-world diagrams. EDDIE only requires a handful of clicks to generate a complete interactive diagram and does not require any coding experience. In contrast, the original benchmarks require a large amount of programming expertise, which prevents many content experts from directly authoring diagrams. In addition, we demonstrated that EDDIE is usable by non-programming users and gathered some valuable target audience feedback about diagram construction using EDDIE.

CONCLUSION

We presented USER-GUIDED INTERACTION SYNTHESIS, a technique that transforms a static diagram into an interactive one without requiring any code to be written. We also presented an implementation in a tool called EDDIE, which we show is expressive and usable. By drastically reducing the cost of making interactive diagrams, this line of research opens up the possibility for experts who have domain knowledge (e.g., teachers who know about STEM) to build animated diagrams that they would otherwise not be able to build. This provides an exciting avenue not only for future research, but also for eventual impact on the adoption of interactive diagrams.

Funding: This work was funded by NSF grant 1423517.

REFERENCES

1. 2016. Apparatus: a hybrid graphics editor and programming environment for creating interactive diagrams. Website. (2016). Accessed on 2016-04-12 from http://aprt.us.
2. 2016. FabricJS JavaScript Canvas Library. Website. (2016). Accessed on 2016-09-19 from http://fabricjs.com/.
3. 2016. Interactive Mathematics: Learn math while you play with it. Website. (2016). Accessed on 2016-04-08 from http://www.intmath.com.
4. 2016. Overconstrained: Cassowary projects and its community. Website. (2016). Accessed on 2016-04-11 from http://overconstrained.io.
5. 2016. Pendulum Lab – Motion, Pendulum, Simple Harmonic Motion – PhET. Website. (2016). Accessed on 2016-09-19 from https://phet.colorado.edu/en/simulation/legacy/pendulum-lab.
6. 2016. PhET: Interactive Simulations for Science and Math. Website. (2016). Accessed on 2016-04-11 from https://PhET.colorado.edu.
7. 2016. Resonance – Resonance, Harmonic Motion, Oscillator – PhET. Website. (2016). Accessed on 2016-09-19 from https://phet.colorado.edu/en/simulation/legacy/resonance.
8. Wendy K. Adams, Sam Reid, Ron LeMaster, Sarah McKagan, Katherine Perkins, Michael Dubson, and Carl E. Wieman. 2008a. A Study of Educational Simulations Part II Interface Design. *Journal of Interactive Learning Research* 19, 4 (October 2008), 551–577. https://www.learntechlib.org/p/24364
9. Wendy K. Adams, Sam Reid, Ron LeMaster, Sarah B. McKagan, Katherine K. Perkins, Michael Dubson, and Carl E. Wieman. 2008b. A Study of Educational Simulations Part I - Engagement and Learning. *Journal of Interactive Learning Research* 19, 3 (July 2008), 397–419. https://www.learntechlib.org/p/24230
10. Christine Alvarado and Randall Davis. 2004. SketchREAD: A Multi-domain Sketch Recognition Engine. In *Proceedings of the 17th Annual ACM Symposium on User Interface Software and Technology (UIST '04)*. ACM, New York, NY, USA, 23–32. DOI: http://dx.doi.org/10.1145/1029632.1029637
11. Christine Alvarado and Randall Davis. 2006. Resolving ambiguities to create a natural computer-based sketching environment. In *ACM SIGGRAPH 2006 Courses*. ACM, 24.
12. Greg J. Badros, Alan Borning, and Peter J. Stuckey. 2001. The Cassowary linear arithmetic constraint solving algorithm. *ACM Transactions on Computer-Human Interaction* 8, 4 (dec 2001), 267–306. DOI: http://dx.doi.org/10.1145/504704.504705
13. Julia M. Chamberlain, Kelly Lancaster, Robert Parson, and Katherine K. Perkins. 2014. How guidance affects student engagement with an interactive simulation. *Chem. Educ. Res. Pract.* 15 (2014), 628–638. Issue 4. DOI: http://dx.doi.org/10.1039/C4RP00009A
14. Salman Cheema and Joseph J LaViola Jr. 2010. Applying mathematical sketching to sketch-based physics tutoring software. In *International Symposium on Smart Graphics*. Springer, 13–24.
15. Allen Cypher and Daniel Conrad Halbert. 1993. *Watch what I do: programming by demonstration*. MIT press.
16. George B Dantzig, Alex Orden, Philip Wolfe, and others. 1955. The generalized simplex method for minimizing a linear form under linear inequality restraints. *Pacific J. Math.* 5, 2 (1955), 183–195.
17. Richard C. Davis, Brien Colwell, and James A. Landay. 2008. K-sketch. In *Proceeding of the twenty-sixth annual CHI conference on Human factors in computing systems - CHI '08*. ACM Press, New York, New York, USA, 413. DOI: http://dx.doi.org/10.1145/1357054.1357122
18. Tim Felgentreff, Alan Borning, Robert Hirschfeld, Jens Lincke, Yoshiki Ohshima, Bert Freudenberg, and Robert Krahn. 2014. *ECOOP 2014 – Object-Oriented Programming: 28th European Conference, Uppsala, Sweden, July 28 – August 1, 2014. Proceedings*. Springer Berlin Heidelberg, Berlin, Heidelberg, Chapter Babelsberg/JS, 411–436. DOI: http://dx.doi.org/10.1007/978-3-662-44202-9_17
19. Bjorn N Freeman-Benson, John Maloney, and Alan Borning. 1990. An incremental constraint solver. *Commun. ACM* 33, 1 (1990), 54–63.
20. Floraine Grabler, Maneesh Agrawala, Wilmot Li, Mira Dontcheva, and Takeo Igarashi. 2009. Generating Photo Manipulation Tutorials by Demonstration. In *ACM SIGGRAPH 2009 Papers (SIGGRAPH '09)*. ACM, New York, NY, USA, Article 66, 9 pages. DOI: http://dx.doi.org/10.1145/1576246.1531372
21. Sumit Gulwani. 2010. Dimensions in program synthesis. In *Proceedings of the 12th international ACM SIGPLAN symposium on Principles and practice of declarative programming*. ACM, 13–24.
22. Sumit Gulwani, Susmit Jha, Ashish Tiwari, and Ramarathnam Venkatesan. 2011a. Synthesis of loop-free programs. In *Proceedings of the 32nd ACM SIGPLAN conference on Programming language design and implementation - PLDI '11*. ACM Press, New York, New York, USA, 62. DOI: http://dx.doi.org/10.1145/1993498.1993506
23. Sumit Gulwani, Vijay Anand Korthikanti, and Ashish Tiwari. 2011b. Synthesizing geometry constructions. *ACM SIGPLAN Notices* 46, 6 (jun 2011), 50. DOI: http://dx.doi.org/10.1145/1993316.1993505
24. Markus Hohenwarter and Karl Fuchs. 2005. Combination of dynamic geometry , algebra and calculus in the

software system GeoGebra. *Computer algebra systems and dynamic geometry systems in mathematics teaching conference 2004* 2002, July (2005), 1–6. `http://www.geogebratube.org/material/show/id/747`

25. Thibaud Hottelier, Ras Bodik, and Kimiko Ryokai. 2014. Programming by manipulation for layout. In *Proceedings of the 27th annual ACM symposium on User interface software and technology - UIST '14*. ACM Press, New York, New York, USA, 231–241. DOI: `http://dx.doi.org/10.1145/2642918.2647378`

26. Takeo Igarashi, Satoshi Matsuoka, and Hidehiko Tanaka. 2007. Teddy: a sketching interface for 3D freeform design. In *Acm siggraph 2007 courses*. ACM, 21.

27. Joaquim Jorge and Faramarz Samavati. 2010. *Sketch-based interfaces and modeling*. Springer Science & Business Media.

28. Sean Kandel, Andreas Paepcke, Joseph Hellerstein, and Jeffrey Heer. 2011. Wrangler: Interactive Visual Specification of Data Transformation Scripts. In *Proceedings of the SIGCHI Conference on Human Factors in Computing Systems (CHI '11)*. ACM, New York, NY, USA, 3363–3372. DOI: `http://dx.doi.org/10.1145/1978942.1979444`

29. Alan Kay and Adele Goldberg. 1977. Personal dynamic media. *Computer* 10, 3 (1977), 31–41.

30. Rubaiat Habib Kazi, Fanny Chevalier, Tovi Grossman, and George Fitzmaurice. 2014a. Kitty: sketching dynamic and interactive illustrations. *Proceedings of the 27th annual ACM symposium on User interface software and technology - UIST '14* (2014), 395–405. DOI: `http://dx.doi.org/10.1145/2642918.2647375`

31. Rubaiat Habib Kazi, Fanny Chevalier, Tovi Grossman, Shengdong Zhao, and George Fitzmaurice. 2014b. Draco: Bringing Life to Illustrations with Kinetic Textures. *Proceedings of the SIGCHI Conference on Human Factors in Computing Systems* (2014), 351–360. DOI: `http://dx.doi.org/10.1145/2556288.2556987`

32. Rubaiat Habib Kazi, Tovi Grossman, Nobuyuki Umetani, and George Fitzmaurice. 2016. Skuid: Sketching Dynamic Illustrations Using the Principles of 2D Animation. In *Proceedings of the 2016 CHI Conference on Human Factors in Computing Systems*. ACM, 4599–4609.

33. Vu Le, Sumit Gulwani, and Zhendong Su. 2013. SmartSynth. In *Proceeding of the 11th annual international conference on Mobile systems, applications, and services - MobiSys '13*. ACM Press, New York, New York, USA, 193. DOI: `http://dx.doi.org/10.1145/2462456.2464443`

34. Gilly Leshed, Eben M Haber, Tara Matthews, and Tessa Lau. 2008. CoScripter: automating & sharing how-to knowledge in the enterprise. In *Proceedings of the SIGCHI Conference on Human Factors in Computing Systems*. ACM, 1719–1728.

35. Hao Lü and Yang Li. 2012. Gesture Coder: A Tool for Programming Multi-touch Gestures by Demonstration. In *Proceedings of the SIGCHI Conference on Human Factors in Computing Systems (CHI '12)*. ACM, New York, NY, USA, 2875–2884. DOI: `http://dx.doi.org/10.1145/2207676.2208693`

36. Emily B. Moore, Timothy A. Herzog, and Katherine K. Perkins. 2013. Interactive simulations as implicit support for guided-inquiry. *Chem. Educ. Res. Pract.* 14 (2013), 257–268. Issue 3. DOI: `http://dx.doi.org/10.1039/C3RP20157K`

37. B. A. Myers. 1986. Visual Programming, Programming by Example, and Program Visualization: A Taxonomy. In *Proceedings of the SIGCHI Conference on Human Factors in Computing Systems (CHI '86)*. ACM, New York, NY, USA, 59–66. DOI: `http://dx.doi.org/10.1145/22627.22349`

38. Brad A. Myers. 1990. Creating User Interfaces Using Programming by Example, Visual Programming, and Constraints. *ACM Trans. Program. Lang. Syst.* 12, 2 (April 1990), 143–177. DOI: `http://dx.doi.org/10.1145/78942.78943`

39. Dan R. Olsen, Jr. and Kirk Allan. 1990. Creating Interactive Techniques by Symbolically Solving Geometric Constraints. In *Proceedings of the 3rd Annual ACM SIGGRAPH Symposium on User Interface Software and Technology (UIST '90)*. ACM, New York, NY, USA, 102–107. DOI: `http://dx.doi.org/10.1145/97924.97936`

40. Stephen Oney, Brad Myers, and Joel Brandt. 2012. ConstraintJS: programming interactive behaviors for the web by integrating constraints and states. In *Proceedings of the 25th annual ACM symposium on User interface software and technology*. ACM, 229–238.

41. Eleanor O'Rourke, Erik Andersen, Sumit Gulwani, and Zoran Popović. 2015. A Framework for Automatically Generating Interactive Instructional Scaffolding. In *Proceedings of the 33rd Annual ACM Conference on Human Factors in Computing Systems (CHI '15)*. ACM, New York, NY, USA, 1545–1554. DOI: `http://dx.doi.org/10.1145/2702123.2702580`

42. Katherine Perkins, Wendy Adams, Michael Dubson, Noah Finkelstein, Sam Reid, Carl Wieman, and Ron LeMaster. 2006. PhET: Interactive Simulations for Teaching and Learning Physics. *The Physics Teacher* 44, 1 (dec 2006), 18. DOI: `http://dx.doi.org/10.1119/1.2150754`

43. Noah S. Podolefsky, Katherine K. Perkins, and Wendy K. Adams. 2009. Computer simulations to classrooms: tools for change. *AIP Conference Proceedings* 1179, 1 (2009), 233–236. DOI: `http://dx.doi.org/10.1063/1.3266723`

44. Robert D Rogers and Stephen Monsell. 1995. Costs of a predictible switch between simple cognitive tasks. *Journal of experimental psychology: General* 124, 2 (1995), 207.

45. Leonid Ryzhyk, Adam Walker, John Keys, Alexander Legg, Arun Raghunath, Michael Stumm, and Mona Vij. 2014. User-guided device driver synthesis. In *11th USENIX Symposium on Operating Systems Design and Implementation (OSDI 14)*. 661–676.

46. Armando Solar-Lezama, Liviu Tancau, Rastislav Bodik, Sanjit Seshia, and Vijay Saraswat. 2006. Combinatorial Sketching for Finite Programs. *SIGOPS Oper. Syst. Rev.* 40, 5 (Oct. 2006), 404–415. DOI: http://dx.doi.org/10.1145/1168917.1168907

47. Ivan E Sutherland. 1964. Sketch pad a man-machine graphical communication system. In *Proceedings of the SHARE design automation workshop*. ACM, 6–329.

48. Brad Vander Zanden. 1992. Languages for Developing User Interfaces. A. K. Peters, Ltd., Natick, MA, USA, Chapter An Active-value&Mdash;Spreadsheet Model for Interactive Languages, 183–209. http://dl.acm.org/citation.cfm?id=131302.131313

49. Bradley T. Vander Zanden, Richard Halterman, Brad A. Myers, Rob Miller, Pedro Szekely, Dario A. Giuse, David Kosbie, and Rich McDaniel. 2005. Lessons Learned from Programmers' Experiences with One-way Constraints: Research Articles. *Softw. Pract. Exper.* 35, 13 (Nov. 2005), 1275–1298. DOI: http://dx.doi.org/10.1002/spe.v35:13

50. Haijun Xia, Bruno Araujo, Tovi Grossman, and Daniel Wigdor. 2016. Object-Oriented Drawing. In *Proceedings of the 2016 CHI Conference on Human Factors in Computing Systems*. ACM, 4610–4621.

51. Jun Xing, Rubaiat Habib Kazi, Tovi Grossman, Li-Yi Wei, Jos Stam, and George Fitzmaurice. 2016. Energy-Brushes: Interactive Tools for Illustrating Stylized Elemental Dynamics. In *Proceedings of the 29th Annual Symposium on User Interface Software and Technology*. ACM, 755–766.

52. Jun Xing, Li-Yi Wei, Takaaki Shiratori, and Koji Yatani. 2015. Autocomplete hand-drawn animations. *ACM Transactions on Graphics (TOG)* 34, 6 (2015), 169.

53. Kuat Yessenov, Shubham Tulsiani, Aditya Menon, Robert C. Miller, Sumit Gulwani, Butler Lampson, and Adam Kalai. 2013. A Colorful Approach to Text Processing by Example. In *Proceedings of the 26th Annual ACM Symposium on User Interface Software and Technology (UIST '13)*. ACM, New York, NY, USA, 495–504. DOI: http://dx.doi.org/10.1145/2501988.2502040

54. Clemens Zeidler, Christof Lutteroth, Wolfgang Sturzlinger, and Gerald Weber. 2013. The Auckland Layout Editor: An Improved GUI Layout Specification Process. In *Proceedings of the 26th Annual ACM Symposium on User Interface Software and Technology (UIST '13)*. ACM, New York, NY, USA, 343–352. DOI: http://dx.doi.org/10.1145/2501988.2502007

55. Bo Zhu, Michiaki Iwata, Ryo Haraguchi, Takashi Ashihara, Nobuyuki Umetani, Takeo Igarashi, and Kazuo Nakazawa. 2011. Sketch-based Dynamic Illustration of Fluid Systems. *ACM Transactions on Graphics* 30, 6 (dec 2011), 1. DOI: http://dx.doi.org/10.1145/2070781.2024168

Peripheral Popout: The Influence of Visual Angle and Stimulus Intensity on Popout Effects

Carl Gutwin[1], **Andy Cockburn**[2], **and Ashley Coveney**[1]

[1]Department of Computer Science
University of Saskatchewan
Saskatoon, Canada
gutwin@cs.usask.ca

[2]Computer Science and Software Engineering
University of Canterbury
Christchurch, New Zealand
andy@cosc.canterbury.ac.nz

ABSTRACT

By exploiting visual popout effects, interface designers can rapidly draw a user's attention to salient information objects in a display. A variety of different visual stimuli can be used to achieve popout effects, including color, shape, size, motion, luminance, and flashing. However, there is a lack of understanding about how accurately different intensities of these effects support popout, particularly as targets move further from the center of the visual field. We therefore conducted a study to examine the accuracy of popout target identification using different visual variables, each at five different levels of intensity, and at a wide range of angles from the display center. Results show that motion is a strong popout stimulus, even at low intensities and wide angles. Identification accuracy decreases rapidly across visual angle with other popout stimuli, particularly with shape and color. The findings have relevance to a wide variety of applications, particularly as multi-display desktop environments increase in size and visual extent.

Author Keywords

Information visualization; popout; peripheral vision.

ACM Classification Keywords

H.5.m. Information interfaces and presentation (e.g., HCI).

INTRODUCTION

Popout is a phenomenon in visual perception in which an object is immediately distinguishable from a field of distractor objects because of its unique visual properties [16,21,35]. For example, a red circle in a field of blue circles "pops out" and is immediately noticeable (Figure 1). Popout occurs because of the ability of the human visual system to process visual features in an entire scene without conscious attention [21,35]. This broad parallel processing ability means that popout occurs very quickly (within 200-250ms [16]), and is independent of the number of distractors – a red circle pops out whether there are 10 or 100 blue circles.

CHI 2017, May 06 - 11, 2017, Denver, CO, USA

ACM 978-1-4503-4655-9/17/05…$15.00
DOI: http://dx.doi.org/10.1145/3025453.3025984 .

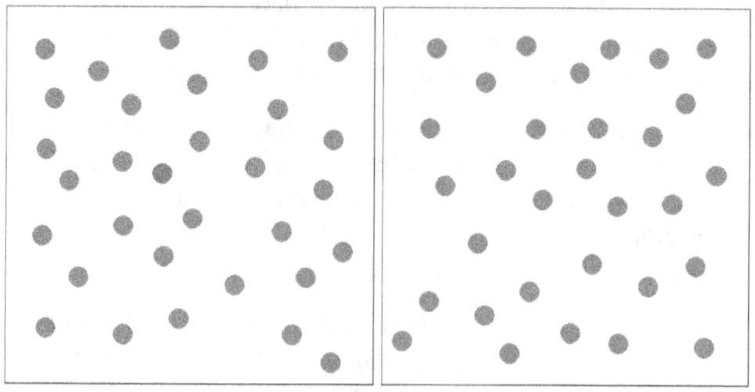

Figure 1. Popout of a red circle in a field of blue circles. Left: target present. Right: target not present. From Healey [16].

Popout can be very useful in the design of visual information presentations, because the effect can be used to draw the user's attention to important items in the display. Since the user's visual focus is limited to a small region of a screen, popout can provide visual notification from other areas, without requiring that the user continuously scan the display. As Raj and Rosenholtz state, "an alert that 'pops out' will draw our attention, and can easily be noticed even if we are not looking right at it" [32, p. 89].

The fact that popout draws attention "even if we are not looking right at it" is a critical part of its value for information presentation – but the degree to which popout works if a target is located further into peripheral vision is not well studied (despite a great many studies on different aspects of popout in general). Understanding how the distance from visual focus affects popout is important, because display environments are becoming larger and larger – with triple-monitor setups, curved widescreen panels, and large-format displays now common. In these settings, objects could appear far from the user's focus, and it is not clear whether popout will continue to draw the user's attention when it appears at a large visual angle from the focus point.

In addition, it is likely that the different visual variables that have been shown to pop out (e.g., Healey [16] discusses hue, luminance, shape, motion, flashing, orientation, and size) could be affected differently by increasing angle, because of the characteristics of the peripheral visual field. The distribution and density of cone, rod, and ganglion cells in the retina means that peripheral vision has lower acuity and is less able to see color, but has good sensitivity to luminance, contrast, and motion [1,5,37,39].

To determine whether popout works in peripheral vision, we carried out a laboratory study that tested people's ability to see popout targets that were represented using six visual variables and five levels of difference between the target and the distractors (termed 'intensity'). The visual variables (hue, luminance, size, shape, motion, and flashing) have all been shown in previous research to exhibit popout effects [9,18,19,21,27,36]. The study used a three-monitor setup that allowed targets to be shown up to 62° from center in either direction. Participants were shown a field of distractor objects (and possibly a popout target) for 240ms, and were asked to indicate whether there was a target present. Our study considered two main questions: whether increasing horizontal angle reduces people's sensitivity to popout; and how the six different visual variables differ across their five levels of intensity. We also looked at other issues such as differences between the left and right visual fields, and whether the monitor bezel reduces performance.

The study provides several novel findings about people's ability to perceive popout effects in the periphery:

- For visual variables *hue*, *shape*, and *size*, there were strong negative effects of increasing angle (e.g., at level 3 of hue and shape, accuracy fell from 90% at ±6° to less than 20% at ±26°).
- At wider angles for lower levels of several variables, accuracy was near zero; this suggests that attempts to use subtle effects to attract attention are likely to be unnoticed for users with large displays.
- For *motion*, *luminance*, and *flashing*, increasing angle had less of an effect (e.g., accuracy above 70% even at 62° and level 3 of the variable); however, there were still substantial effects at the lowest levels of intensity.
- A preliminary follow-up study suggested that the effects of individual variables may be additive (i.e., it may be possible to combine variables to achieve larger pop-out).

Our study provides new understanding of how popout works across the large display settings that are now common, and shows that some approaches to achieving popout are unlikely to work in many scenarios. Our work provides valuable baseline information for designers who wish to use popout in large-scale information presentations.

RELATED WORK

Peripheral vision

The human visual field covers approximately 135° vertically and 210° horizontally (Figure 2), and is often divided into regions based on evidence about visual performance [14,40].

- *Central* vision is the region at the user's visual focus, and is characterized by high acuity and good color discrimination, due to the presence and density of cone cells in the fovea. The central region covers 5° of visual angle (2.5° on each side of center).
- *Paracentral* vision is the region immediately outside the foveal central region, and covers 8° of the visual field (4° on each side of center). Paracentral vision has a higher acuity than peripheral vision, although it does not have the cone-cell density of the central region.
- *Near-peripheral* vision is the region between 8° and 30°, based on evidence of a of a drop in acuity and color perception at 30° [14]. The near-peripheral region has a higher density of rod cells than other areas of the retina, with rod density declining rapidly towards the central region, and more graduadually away from it.
- *Mid-peripheral* vision covers the region from 30° to 60° from center, and defines the approximate limit of upwards peripheral vision.
- *Far-peripheral* vision covers the region from 60° to the boundary of the visual field (approximately 105° from center horizontally, and 70° downwards).

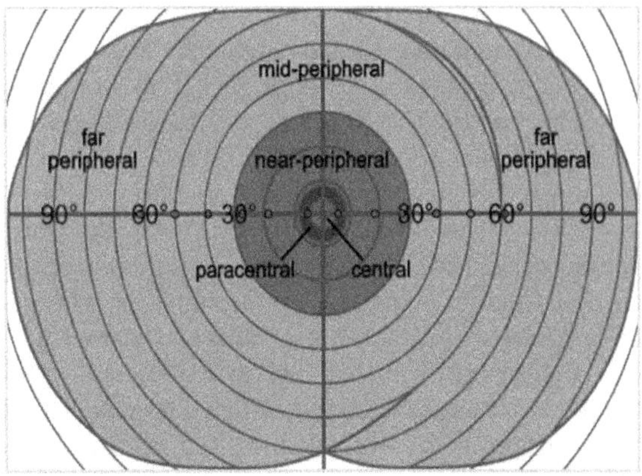

Figure 2. Regions in the human visual field (redrawn from [40]). Red dots indicate target locations in study.

Perception of stimuli in peripheral vision

Many studies have considered people's abilities to detect different types of stimuli in the peripheral visual field, although these have not considered the specific phenomenon of popout. Some tests have been consolidated into standard diagnostic procedures in optometry – for example, *perimetry* is the measurement and mapping of light sensitivity in the visual field, and involves testing a patient's ability to detect static or moving lights of different intensity at different locations in peripheral vision.

Researchers have also looked at other stimuli in addition to light intensity. Color is commonly considered: studies using constant-size stimuli show a decrease in hue discrimination in peripheral vision (e.g., [26]), but other studies that adjust the size of the stimulus proportional to the density of cones have shown that people can successfully differentiate hues [1]. Letter recognition has also been tested – early studies showed that response times significantly increased beyond 3° from the center of vision [10]. Response to motion also differs across the visual field. Studies have shown that for slowly-moving targets, response time and error in estimation of speed both increased with increasing angle from central vision; however, for fast-moving targets, response time and accuracy were unaffected [37].

Popout as a perceptual phenomenon

The observation that some visual features can be detected very rapidly has been made by numerous researchers in vision, perception, and visual attention. The processing of these visual features was initially called "pre-attentive" because detection of these stimuli appears to occur before focused attention can take place (i.e., less than the 200-250ms it takes to change visual focus [16]). Early studies coined the term *popout* because objects with unique visual properties seem to "pop out of the display" [35], regardless of the number of distractor objects – that is, visual search time is constant, not linear in the number of distractors.

Researchers have found that several different features (or *visual variables*) can pop out – in a review of the area, Healey [16] identifies sixteen different features (orientation, length, closure, size, curvature, density, number, hue, luminance, intersection, terminators, 3D depth, flicker, motion direction and velocity, and lighting direction) that have all been shown in prior studies to create popout effects. In addition, numerous studies have considered variations on the basic question – such as whether popout occurs when the target is composed of a combination of visual features (conjunction search), or whether popout occurs in situations where there are multiple kinds of distractors. Studies of popout use two main methods to test perception: either participants are asked to visually search a scene until they find a target object (here completion time is the dependent measure), or participants are shown a field of objects for 100-250ms, and are asked to state whether the field contained the target (here, accuracy is the dependent measure).

Several theories have been proposed to explain popout (for details, see Healey's review [16]). For example, Triesman's Feature Integration Theory [35] suggests that the human visual system maintains a set of feature maps for different visual attributes (such as color or shape). These maps are encoded and accessed in parallel, leading to the fast response time and the independence from the number of distractors. Another theory suggests that our early visual system is able to identify textural features called "textons," which are blobs with visual properties such as hue and shape, plus line terminations and crossings [21]. A third theory ("guided search") suggests that we process visual scenes using both bottom-up maps (similar to Triesman's) and top-down maps that encode user interest in specific properties (e.g., if a person is trying to find a blue item) [41].

An important aspect of several different theories is the recognition that the degree of popout is affected by the difference between the target object and the distractor objects for a specific visual variable. For example, "a long vertical line can be detected immediately among a group of short vertical lines, but a medium-length line may take longer to see" ([16], p. 1173). Duncan and Humphreys [7] identify two different types of similarity that can affect the perception of popout: first, as similarity between targets and non-targets increases, search efficiency decreases; and second, as the similarity between different non-target objects decreases (i.e., the distractors have a wider range of visual features), search efficiency also decreases.

There have been only a few studies of how perception of popout varies with distance from visual focus, and these have considered only small angular distances. Experiments by Carrasco and colleagues looked at popout in a conjunction search (using line orientation and hue), where a field of up to 36 objects was shown on a single monitor for either 62ms or 104ms [4]. They compared accuracy when the popout targets appeared at angles of 0.7° – 3.5° from the fixation point, and found that accuracy decreased significantly as angular distance increased. A later study (using line orientation as the visual variable and an 84ms presentation, again on a single monitor) tested angles of 4°, 8°, and 12° from center, and showed a similar degradation of accuracy [27].

Popout in information visualization

The popout effect is well known in the field of information visualization, and several guides to designing visualizations discuss how the effect can be used [25,39]. The attention-drawing capability of popout is frequently mentioned in these guides: for example, Munzner states "An example of preattentive processing is the visual popout effect that occurs when a single yellow object is instantly distinguishable from a sea of grey objects, or a single large object catches one's eye. Exploiting pre-cognitive processing is desirable in a visualization system so that cognitive resources can be freed up for other tasks" ([28], p. 5). Similarly, Ware's textbook on information visualization suggests that popout is a useful technique for attracting the user's attention (for example, in visual monitoring tasks): "In displaying information, it is often useful to be able to show something 'at a glance.' If you want people to be able to instantaneously identify some mark on a map as being of type A, it should be differentiated from all other marks in a pre-attentive way" ([39], p. 165).

Several prototype and commercial systems have been built that use the idea of popout [18,19,24,34]. For example, the Popout Prism web browser [34] uses color highlighting and magnification to enhance the visibility of keywords specified by the user; and Gajos's Visual Popout interface highlighted recently-used items in pink [24]. In addition, several recent web and PDF viewers implement visual effects for text searches that can allow items to pop out. Figure 3 shows an example from the Firefox browser – in the figure, the user has searched for "England," and all text matches are highlighted in pink, which pops out from the mostly-black text. In addition, one match is considered to be the "current" match (and moves forward by pressing Control-G) – and this text is highlighted in green, with the intention that the large difference in color will be enough to draw the user's attention to the location of the text.

However, despite these implementations, and despite the field's statements that popout can be useful for drawing the user's attention (which implies that the effect is occurring outside of foveal vision), few guidelines discuss the issue of how perception of popout changes when the target is in the user's peripheral vision. Some texts, such as Ware's, state general principles indicating that sensitivity to color and small targets is reduced in the periphery, so other modes such as motion or auditory cues should be used instead [39] – but there are few details about exactly where and how people's sensitivity to different visual variables diminishes. Therefore, in the study described next, we set out to determine this information for a range of visual variables.

Figure 3. Using color difference to show the next match.

STUDY METHODS

We carried out a laboratory study to determine the effects of visual angle and stimuli intensity on people's ability to perceive different types of popout effects. Participants were shown a visual field of objects for 240ms, after which it was hidden from view. In 60% of trials a single target object was present in the visual field (with some type and intensity of popout stimulus applied), and in 40% of trials no target was present (all objects were visually identical). Immediately following the presentation of the visual field, participants responded to a yes/no question asking whether they had seen the target or not. The presentation of targets was experimentally controlled to test six different types of popout, each at five different levels of intensity, and at different angles from the center of the display.

Visual variables and intensity levels

We chose six visual variables that have been shown in previous research to show popout effects, and that are either commonly used in information visualization (hue, shape, size) or likely to be visible in the periphery (luminance, flashing, motion). These variables (and the levels of each variable) are shown in Figure 4 (in the study described below, all objects were shown on a black background).

We created five versions of each visual variable to examine increasing levels of difference between the target and the distractors – we term these levels of difference as 'intensity'. For some of the visual variables, the range was constrained at both ends (e.g., there is a fixed range of hues between red and blue); for other variables, the range was constrained only at one end (e.g., size can range from the size of the distractors to an arbitrary upper end). The levels for each variable are shown in Figure 4 and Table 1.

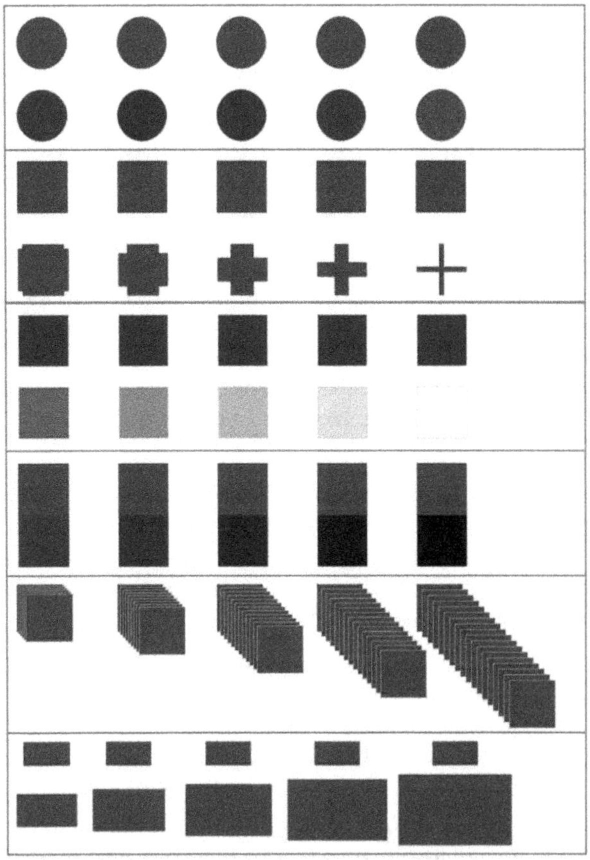

Figure 4. Visual variables and intensity levels. Rows 1-3: Color, Shape, Luminance (distractors upper, targets lower). Row 4: Flashing (upper and lower indicate alternating frames). Row 5: Motion (all frames shown). Row 6: Size (distractors upper, targets lower).

	D	1	2	3	4	5
Color (RGB)	R: 0 G: 0 B: 250	R: 29 G: 0 B: 200	R: 58 G: 0 B: 150	R: 88 G: 0 B: 100	R: 117 G: 0 B: 50	R: 146 G: 0 B: 0
Shape (line width)	50	41	32	23	14	5
Luminance (grey value)	50	91	132	173	214	255
Flashing ("off" color)	B: 250	B: 214	B: 173	B: 132	B: 91	B: 50
Motion (move/frame)	0px	1px	2px	3px	4px	5px
Size (width x height) = Area	25x50 =1250	32x65 =2080	40x80 =3200	47x95 =4465	55x110 =6050	62x125 =7750

Table 1. Values for intensity levels of the visual variables (D = value for distractor; 1-5 = target value for that level)

Color. Distractors and targets were circles of 50 px diameter. Target hues were equally spaced in RGB from isoluminant values of 'red' and 'blue' (using the luminance calculation in [38]). Maintaining equal luminance meant that the red end of the scale was RGB(146,0,0), and the blue distractors were RGB(0,0,250). Although RGB is not a perceptually-uniform color space, our approach still provides levels that are perceptually distinct (see Figure 4) and that increase towards a maximum isoluminant hue difference.

Shape. Distractors were 50px blue squares. Targets were an identical color, but their shape deviated from the square by an amount of intrusion at each corner (becoming a cross). The degree of intrusion varied across levels in increments of 9 pixels, from 9 px at level 1 to 45 px at level 5.

Luminance. Distractors were 50px gray squares with color RGB(50,50,50). Target brightness was chosen from five equally-spaced points (increments of 41) on a greyscale ranging from the color of the distractors (50) to white (255).

Flashing. Distractors were 50px static blue squares. Flashing targets abruptly changed hue every 60ms during the 240ms presentation of the object field. For the largest intensity (level 5), the target changed from blue to black (the color of the background); other levels changed between blue and an equally-spaced color in the range from blue to black.

Motion. Distractors were 50px static blue squares. Targets were animated using 17 frames during the 240ms presentation of the object field. Figure 4 shows the distance moved per frame for each level (from 1px at level 1 to 5px per frame at level 5); the movement direction was diagonal, with the displacement applied equally to x and y axes.

Size (Area). Distractors were 50×25px blue rectangles. Target dimensions on each axis were multiplied by $1 + (0.3 \times \textit{level})$ to generate a larger rectangle. At level 5, the target dimensions were therefore 2.5× those of the distractor (i.e., 125×62 pixels; 7750 pixels total vs 1250 pixels total).

Visual angles to target locations

We chose six horizontal target locations (duplicated for left and right), organized into two groups according to the regions of the visual field (Figure 2). Three locations cover the near peripheral region (±6°, ±18°, and ±26°), and three cover the mid-peripheral region (±38°, ±50°, and ±62°). Angles were measured from the center vertical line. We placed targets at ±8° from the center horizonal (upper and lower locations were collapsed for analysis).

Participants and apparatus

Twenty-two participants were recruited from the local university community (14 male, 8 female, mean age 27.7 years). Participants were all experienced with mouse-and-windows desktop computers (more than 10 hrs/wk).

The study used a three-monitor setup with three Dell 25-inch HD LCD panels (Figure 5) to provide a visual workspace of 5760x1080 pixels with a physical size of 65x13 inches. Monitors used identical settings for brightness, contrast, gamma, and white balance. The monitors were arranged in a curve such that the user was 70cm from the center of all three monitors. All three monitors were driven from a single NVidia graphics card and a Windows10 PC. We built a custom experimental system for the study that presented all trials (in full-screen mode) and recorded performance data. All questionnaire data was recorded on web-based forms.

Study procedure

Participants completed informed consent forms and demographic questionnaires. They were then assigned to a random order of presentation of the visual variables (hue, shape, luminance, flashing, motion, and size). Participants carried out a series of trials for each intensity level of the first visual variable, in order from most intense to least intense. This ordering was chosen because prior sensitization to visual stimuli can improve detection, and we wanted this factor to be consistent (and to ensure that low-visibility stimuli were not missed simply because they were presented first). Once all of the levels were complete for a visual variable, participants proceeded to the next visual variable.

For each intensity level, there were two blocks, with each block containing 24 target locations: 12 horizontal angles (6 in each direction), and 2 vertical locations for each angle. At the start of each intensity level, the system showed the specific target that would be used for that level; this target had exactly the same appearance for all 48 trials of a level.

Each trial asked the participant to state whether they saw a target object (with particular visual properties specific to the condition) after a 240ms presentation of a field of objects. The 240ms time period was chosen to be within the 200-250ms period for pre-attentive processing [13], and to allow our motion and flashing effects time to be seen. Participants started each trial by focusing on a fixation cross at the center of the middle monitor. After a random interval of 1-2 seconds (to avoid anticipatory action), a field of objects was presented for 240ms (Figure 5). The field contained 104 distractors, distributed quasi-randomly across the three monitors (avoiding overlaps), and possibly one target object. In 60 percent of trials, a popout target was present, and in 40 percent, no target was present. The 60/40 split was chosen through iterative testing to maximize the number of positive trials without participants realizing that there were more of one type (which could have led to effective guessing); as discussed below, the split was successful in preventing a substantial false positive rate.

After the 240ms presentation, the visual field was hidden, and the participant was asked to state whether they saw the target – e.g., "Did you see a more-red circle among the blue circles?" They answered by pressing the '1' key for "yes" and the '0' key for "no." As soon as they had answered, the fixation cross appeared and the next trial started. Participants were asked to be as accurate as possible about whether they had seen the target, but were not asked to answer quickly.

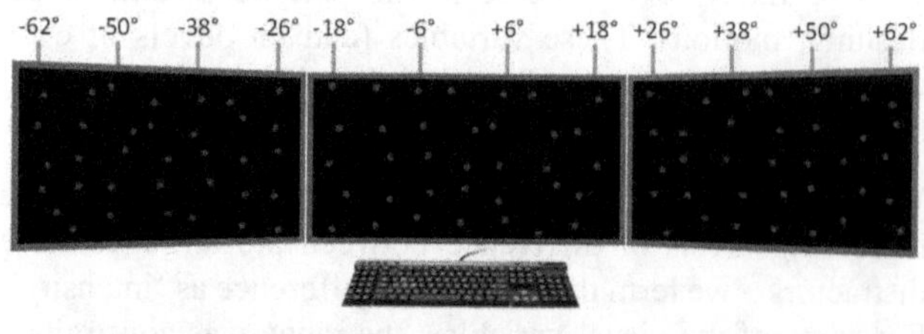

Figure 5. Object field presented to participant for one trial.

After each level, participants filled out a web-based effort questionnaire based on the NASA-TLX survey; they then returned to the study system and continued with the next level. With two blocks of 48 trials for each of 5 levels, each visual variable condition contained 240 trials; a single condition took approximately 20 minutes to complete.

Data analyses and design

Because each visual variable condition took approximately 20 minutes, not all participants were able to complete all six conditions. Therefore, we assigned later participants to balance the number of people per visual variable (11 people per condition). The fact that there is an incomplete mapping between participants and conditions, however, prevents the creation of a standard linear model for ANOVA. Therefore, our analysis uses a Hierarchical Mixed Model (HMM), which provides a similar model but allows for missing data from some participants [11]. The analysis was carried in R using the *nlme* library, using participant as a random factor.

The study therefore used a mixed between/within repeated-measures design, with three factors:

- *Variable*: the visual variable used to create the popout effect (hue, shape, luminance, flashing, motion, size)
- *Angle*: the horizontal visual angle from the center of the screen to the target (left: -6°, -18°, -26°, -38°, -50°, -62°; right: +6°, +18°, +26°, +38°, +50°, +62°)
- *Level*: the amount of difference in the visual variable between the target and the distractors (i.e, intensity); each condition used five levels as shown in Figure 4.

The dependent measure was accuracy (the proportion of responses in which participants correctly identified the presence of the target, using only the "target present" trials). For perception of effort, the dependent measures were the subject's responses to the TLX-style questionnaire.

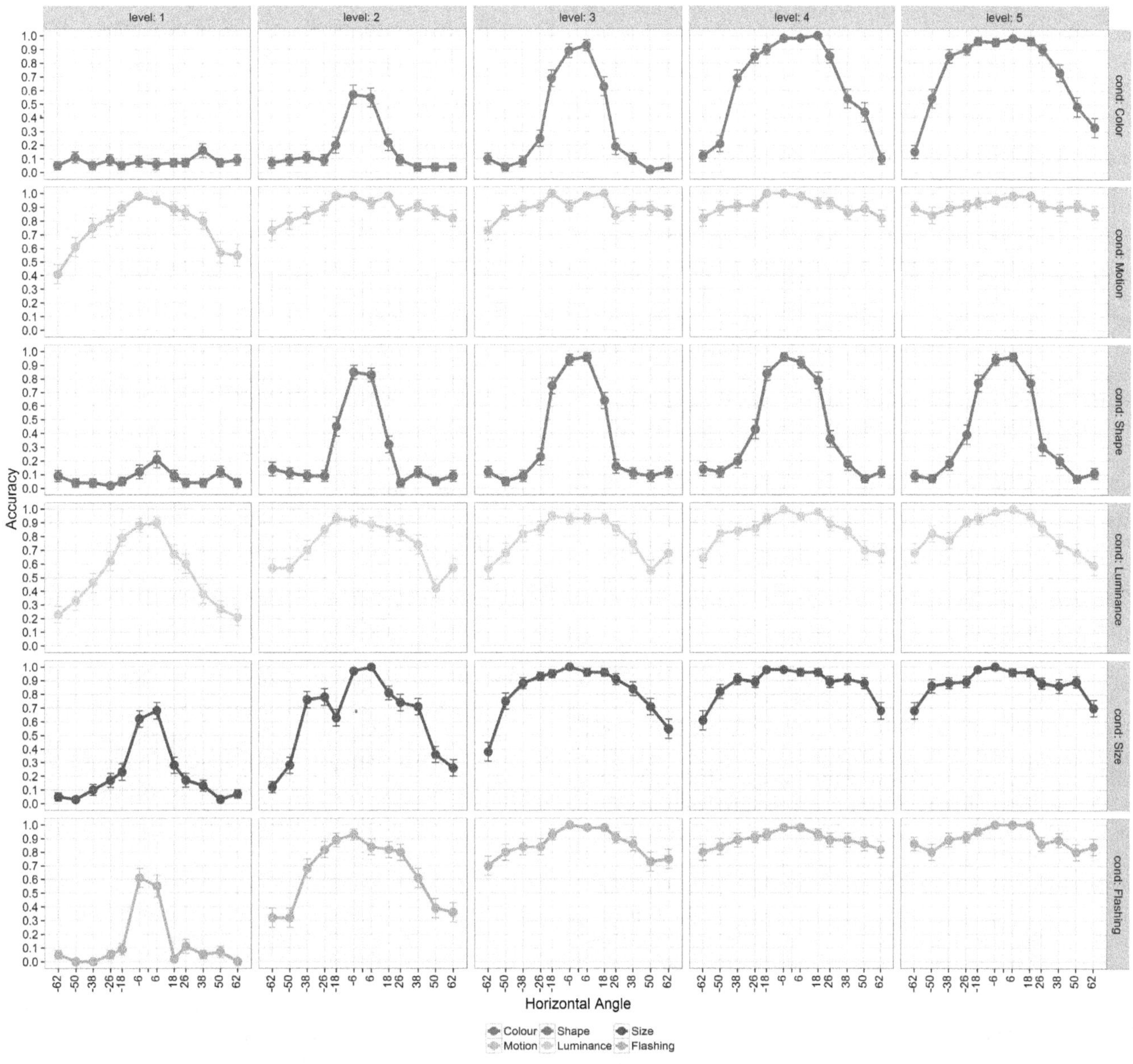

Figure 6. Accuracy ±s.e. by Variable (rows), Intensity Level (columns), and Angle (x-axis). Target-present trials only.

RESULTS

Data check: performance on target-not-present trials

Participants could, in theory, have answered 'yes' or 'no' to all trials, regardless of the presence or absence of the actual stimuli. To test the veracity of each participant's responses, we calculated the mean accuracy for trials where the target was *not* present. Accuracy in these trials for all visual variables was above 90%, suggesting that participants were in fact answering honestly and to the best of their ability.

Main effects of Angle, Variable, and Level on accuracy

Overall, there was a substantial drop in perception accuracy as visual angle increased – from 86% at ±6° from center to less than 40% at ±62° (Figure 6). The Hierarchical Mixed Model (HMM, see Data Analyses section above) showed a strong effect of *Angle* on accuracy ($F_{11,17447}$=396.76, p<.0001). The effect of *Angle* was essentially symmetrical across left and right angular deviations, with the HMM showing no significant effects of *Side* ($F_{1,17803}$=0.07, p=0.80), and no interactions of *Side* × *Angle* ($F_{1,17803}$=1.77, p=0.18) or *Side* × *Variable* ($F_{1,17795}$=1.63, p=0.15).

The HMM showed strong effects on accuracy for both *Variable* ($F_{5,17447}$=908.90, p<.0001) and *Level* ($F_{4,17447}$= 1415.29, p<.0001). Averaged across all levels, accuracy means varied from 87% for Motion, 74% for Luminance, 69% for Flashing, 67% for Size, 38% for Color, down to 29% for Shape. Follow-up oneway analyses of the pairs in this sequence (Bonferroni corrected) showed differences between each contiguous pair (all p<0.0001) except for Flashing→Size (p=.036). A similar follow-up analysis of *Level* showed significant differences between pairs of intensity levels (p<0.0001) except for level 5 → 4 (p=.22). However, the main effects of *Variable* and *Level* must be considered in light of the interactions described below.

Interactions between Angle, Variable, and Level

The HMM showed significant two-way interactions between *Angle* and *Variable* ($F_{55,17447}$=16.84, p<.0001) and between *Angle* and *Level* ($F_{44,17447}$=5.68, p<.0001); there was also a three-way interaction ($F_{220,17447}$=8.07, p<.0001).

These interactions are illustrated in Figure 6. Accuracy with different visual variables responded differently to increasing angle. Accuracy with Motion was relatively constant and high across *Angle*, whereas accuracy with Shape or Color followed a bell-shaped curve across *Angle*. The different levels for each variable also performed differently across angle – e.g., accuracy with Color and Shape vary from a floor effect (near ~7% across angle) at level 1 to a rounded-hill shape at level 3 and above, with maximum accuracy over 90%; in contrast, Luminance varies from a peak shape at level 1 (with a maximum at 90%) to a near-flat ceiling effect at level 4 and higher. The interpretation of these interactions is considered further in the Discussion below.

Does the bezel reduce perception of popout?

We were interested in whether the visual discontinuity of the bezels in our three-monitor setup influenced people's ability to perceive popout. From inspection of the overall results by angle (Figure 7), there appears to be a slightly steeper decrease from ±18° to ±26° (which includes the monitor bezels) than would be suggested by the overall curve of the data. In addition, the 18-26° angular range is within the near-peripheral region of the visual field – so there are no obvious physical changes in the eye that might explain this steeper gradient (compared, for example, to the changes observed beyond 30°); the blind spot is located in the 12-15° region and should therefore not influence identification here.

This partial finding suggests that target proximity to display edges *may* adversely affect the accuracy of popout perception. If this is case, it might arise from the lack of uniformity in the visual field near the display edge (i.e., the display edge and bezel adds visual stimuli that are not present within the body of the display). However, the effect of the bezel is small (corresponding to the limited impact of bezels seen in other work, e.g., [41]), and further research is necessary to explore this issue.

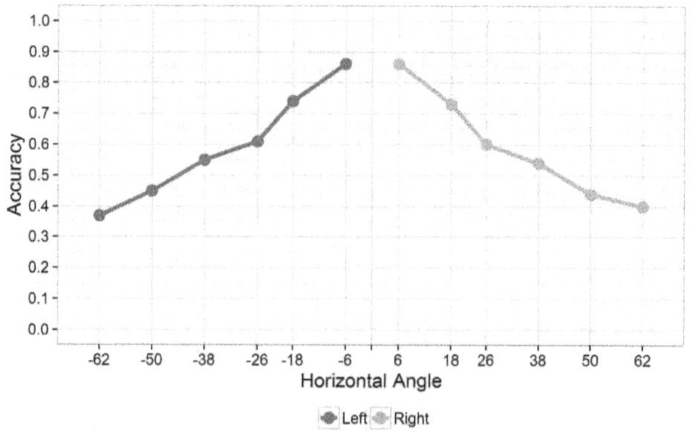

Figure 7. Overall accuracy (±std.err), by Angle.

Perception of Effort

After each intensity level, participants completed a NASA-TLX effort questionnaire. Mean results from this survey are shown in Figure 8 – although the mixed design of the study meant that we did not carry out statistical analyses of these data. However, Figure 8 shows that there were substantial overall differences in perceived effort, which approximately follow the performance results. For example, perceived effort for Motion and Luminance is consistently less than that for Color and Shape, which mirrors participant accuracy with these visual variables. In addition, for Luminance, Size, and Flashing, perceived effort scores increase as the visual intensity lessens (i.e., moving from right to left in the chart).

We also asked two additional questions for each level and condition: "How visible was the target?" and "How accurate were you in locating the target?" Results from these questions are shown in Figure 9.

The two main findings from these analyses are that Shape required relatively high effort, resulted in low levels of perceived success, visibility, and accuracy, and that these perceptions were relatively uniform across intensity level. Motion, in contrast, showed low levels of effort, and high levels of perceived success, visibility and accuracy. These positive results for motion were also relatively stable across intensity. Other variables showed a clear increase in perceived visibility and accuracy across intensity.

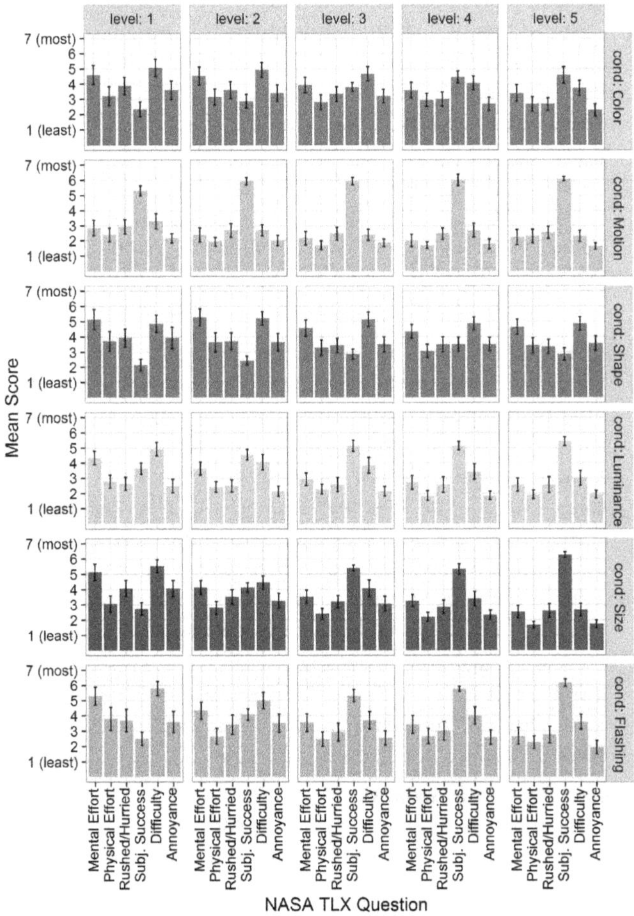

Figure 8. Mean responses (±s.e.) to NASA-TLX questions, by intensity and visual variable.

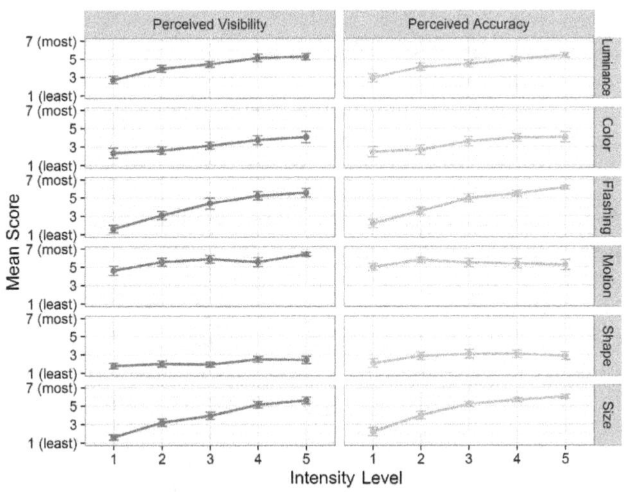

Figure 9. Mean responses (±s.e.) to questions about visibility and accuracy, by intensity level and visual variable.

FOLLOWUP STUDY: ADDITIVE EFFECTS

The study described above tested visual variables in isolation – however, several real-world interfaces enhance the presentation of a highlighted item using more than a single visual variable. For example, the Mac OS/X preview application highlights the next item in a search with an animation that uses both hue change and an increase in size (Figure 11). This raises questions of whether the effects described above are additive – that is, whether accuracy with an effect that uses two variables would be the sum of the performance for each variable on its own.

To provide some preliminary data on performance with combinations of popout cues, we carried out a small exploratory study as a follow-up, with four new participants. We asked participants to complete tasks similar to those described above, but in a set of conditions designed to allow examination of specific combined popout cues. First, we tested their accuracy with Color at level 3 and Motion at level 1 – and then tested the combination of Color and Motion. Second, we tested Luminance at level 2, Size at level 2, and then combined Luminance and Size.

Results are shown in Figure 10. For Color and Motion, the effect of combining the variables was not entirely clear. For targets presented on the right side of the display, there appeared to be a positive additive effect, with the 38, 50 and 62° combined data points much higher than Color or Motion alone. However, data on the left of the display did not show the same outcome, with the combined effects resulting in similar accuracy to Motion alone. The combination of Luminance and Size showed a clearer advantage both for left-side and right-side targets. Accuracy for angles ±(18° to 38°) ranged from 10%-70% with either Luminance or Size alone, but was above 90% with both variables. Again, in some cases the combination was better than the sum of the components.

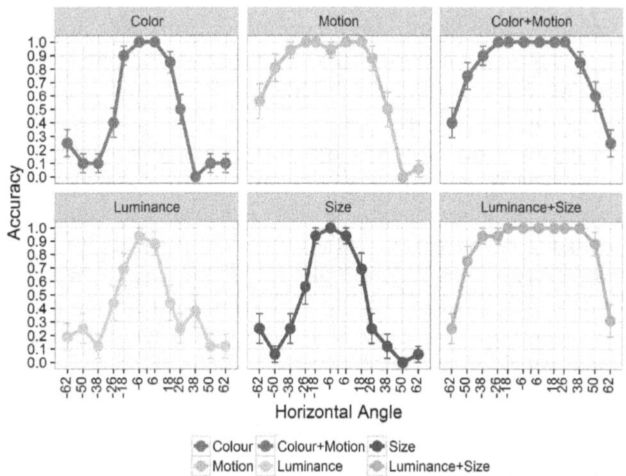

Figure 10. Additive effects. Top: Color level 3, Motion level 1, and Color+Motion. Bottom: Luminance level 2, Size level 2, and Luminance+Size.

This study is highly preliminary and involved only four people. Therefore, our limited results suggesting that combinations of effects can increase noticeability must be explored further with additional studies.

DISCUSSION

Summary of findings

The main findings are summarized in Figure 6. The key observation from the figure is that there are substantial differences between visual variables in how the accuracy of popout identification decreases as targets appear further from the center of vision – some variables support stronger peripheral popout than others.

At intensity level 3 and above, all of the visual variables allowed high accuracy at the center of the visual field (90% and higher, following a presentation that lasted only 240ms). However, accuracy dropped off steeply as the angle from center increased with Shape and Color, whereas accuracy remained comparatively high across angle with dynamic methods (Motion and Flashing). Motion was particularly accurate at wide angles, even when the movement was small. Subjective assessments of visibility and accuracy (Figure 9) mirrored the accuracy results, with high perceived accuracy and visibility for Motion, and low values for Shape.

Reasons for results

Perceptual factors

Properties of the human visual system help explain some of the results. For example, the distribution of cone cells, which detect color, is dense in the central visual field, but sparse beyond it, which explains why the accuracy of Color deteriorates abruptly beyond central target placement. The lower density of cones beyond the parafoveal region means that humans are much less sensitive to color in the periphery, so hue-based popout primarily occurs when a saccade brings the target into the parafovea (unless targets are large [1]).

Accuracy with Shape also dropped off rapidly with angle. It is possible that physical attributes of the eye contribute to this finding. For example, the differential distribution of certain types of ganglion cells across the retina [7] might make elemental visual features, such as edges or corners, less prominent at the periphery. Alternatively, it is also possible that shape interpretation is best achieved subsequent to inclusion of an object within the parafoveal region. The possibility of a saccade within the 240ms presentation in our experiment was low, but the bell-shaped curves for Shape accuracy may reflect the probability that a saccade from a central location includes the target within the presentation period. Further research on perceptual feature extraction is required to properly explain the cause of the Shape results.

Finally, prior research on visual perception strongly suggests that the high accuracy findings for Motion, Luminance, and Flashing (across broad angles) stem from the selective firing of ganglion cells in response to input from rods and cones (see [5] for a review).

Experimental factors

We designed the experiment with the intention that the intensity levels of each visual variable would provide roughly equivalent increments in the distinction between distractor and target. Although we described our manipulations in a replicable manner, it is possible that our findings are influenced by the exact manipulations tested. One important issue is that there were different ranges of intensities possible with each visual variable – as described above, levels of Color are limited by the distance between the colors of the distractors and the target, whereas other variables have a larger possible range (e.g., Luminance, Motion, and Size). It is difficult to equalize the perceptibility of different intensities for different visual variables, so to some degree the variables must be treated as independent.

Other factors could be considered as well. It is possible (though we believe unlikely) that our findings for Shape would be different if a different form for Shape targets was used. For example, the different levels of Shape might instead transition between a square (distractor) and a perfect circle (level 5) with intermediate levels of rounded corners. Similarly, it is possible that results for Luminance or Color would differ if a white, rather than black, background was used. Further experimental work is required to cross-validate and generalize these findings. In addition, considering our results using computational models of visual attention (e.g., [21]) may provide additional predictive and explanatory power about the mechanisms that led to different results for different stimuli.

Implications for designers

Interface designers often need to address tradeoffs between the desirability of drawing the user's attention to a salient data item and the risks of distracting the user from their current tasks [2]. While findings from this research improve our basic understanding of visual characteristics that draw the user's attention to objects placed at different locations across the visual field, we have not addressed issues of unintended distraction caused by popout effects (and we note that motion and flashing are often criticized as being distracting in many information presentations). We intend to examine the correspondence between noticeability and distraction for different visual variables in upcoming work.

A first and unsurprising implication of the results is that popout effects are more reliable if the target object is placed near to the center of the visual field. This was evident for all levels of our popout stimuli except level 1 of Color, which had low accuracy even with central placement. We assume that the stimulus chosen for level 1 Color was close to the just-noticeable-difference level for color discrimination from the distractor. While some interaction contexts may prohibit or discourage placing a popout target near the center of the display, others will permit it (e.g., "find" functionality in a browser might scroll the view to present the target near the center of the display). If the visual field does not allow scrolling, another possibility involves tracking the user's visual focus in order to calculate an ideal popout effect for the specific location of the target. It is likely that eye trackers will become common in some display environments, and camera-based gaze tracking is becoming feasible [19]. Eye tracking can also be used to compare the approach of peripheral popout to that of Bailey and colleagues, who used subtle modulations of the peripheral visual field to draw the user's visual attention [2].

A second design implication is that motion effects are highly accurate even at wide angles and at subtle levels. At level 1, our tested motion effects involved movements of only a few pixels on the screen (~1mm of movement), yet they enabled better accuracy than higher levels with other visual variables. Subjective responses including workload measures and perceived accuracy were also better for motion effects than other visual variables. Motion, then, is a powerful popout cue at high angles and at low movements. Yet some commercial examples of Motion popout cues are highly exaggerated, and possibly unnecessarily so; for example, the icon bounce effect in the Mac OS/X Dock involves animated vertical movements of ~80 pixels, but our results indicate a subtler effect would be sufficient to make users aware of the alert.

Our results can be applicable in a number of contexts. First, previous work has shown that alerts are often difficult to see in multi-display environments (e.g., [12]), which is a substantial problem for control rooms or systems for emergency response. Designers can use the findings from our study to help ground the design of multi-display systems on empirical evidence. Second, our study provides a better understanding of different methods for visual feedback. For example, feedback during "Find" tasks in different PDF viewers provides an interesting contrast between commercial approaches to the design of popout effects. Figure 11 (top) shows "Find" results in Apple's Preview application (v8.1), which over 400ms scrolls the next occurrence into view, highlights it with a yellow background, and then briefly zooms the text. This effect – combining flashing, luminance, hue, and motion – appears to be much more effective than that used in the Chrome PDF viewer (Figure 11 bottom), which scrolls the next item into view and highlights it with a low luminance blue-grey highlight. When not in the visual focus, the lack of movement or other strong stimuli may be insufficient to induce a desired popout effect.

Figure 11. Commercially deployed highlighting techniques that are used to popout text targets in PDF viewers: Apple's Preview (top) and Chrome's PDF viewer (bottom).

Limitations and future work

This research has generated a set of empirical characterizations of the effectiveness of different pop-out visual variables at different levels of intensity and at different angles from the center of the visual field. However, there are abundant opportunities for extending these findings and for validating them with different stimuli, intensities and angles. For example, we plan to test accuracy when participants do not see the stimuli in the most-visible to least-visible pattern used in our study – it is possible that changing this order will reduce accuracy (because participants will not be sensitized to low-visibility stimuli). Another opportunity is the examination of other motion effects than the simple diagonal displacement used in our studies. Harrison and colleagues examined the broad opportunities for designers working with kinetic icons, presenting an initial 'kineticon vocabulary' [15]. It is likely that different styles and patterns of motion will induce different popout outcomes in humans. For example, studies might examine the different impact of motion frequency, shape (e.g., pulse versus jiggle), and abruptness (e.g., slow-in/slow-out versus instant velocity changes). Analogous manipulations of other visual variables and their combinations also needs further examination.

A third area for future work will build on our preliminary results regarding the potential additive effects of combined visual variables. For example, different combinations may allow the benefits of different variables to be exploited. Our results show that motion effects are highly accurate in prompting accurate popout, but continued motion after initial popout may impair overall performance (e.g., reading moving text will be harder than reading static text, and selecting a moving object could be frustrating). By combining motion with other variables (such as luminance, hue, or shape), users may be able to gain from an initial popout induced by a brief burst of motion, followed by static presentation that is temporally enduring but uses less distracting stimuli with other visual variables that remain effective because they lie within the center of view.

CONCLUSIONS

Visual popout effects allow users to rapidly identify one item among a field of many candidates. Interface designers can use a variety of popout visual stimuli to alert users to objects that need attention. The results presented in this paper demonstrate that different popout visual stimuli vary significantly in their effectiveness as target items are displayed further from the center of the visual field. While nearly all of the evaluated techniques allowed high levels of target identification accuracy when presented at high intensities near the display center, some also maintained high levels of accuracy at the periphery (such as Motion, Flashing, and Luminance) while others did not (Color and Shape). These findings are particularly relevant as the size and extent of display environments increase, and they contribute to a growing vocabulary for the application of visual stimuli in interface design.

ACKNOWLEDGMENTS

This work was supported by the Natural Sciences and Engineering Research Council of Canada.

REFERENCES

1. I. Abramov, J. Gordon, and H. Chan (1991) Color appearance in the peripheral retina: effects of stimulus size. *Journal of the Optical Society of America A*, 8 (2): 404–414. DOI:10.1364/JOSAA.8.000404.
2. Reynold Bailey, Ann McNamara, Nisha Sudarsanam, and Cindy Grimm. 2009. Subtle gaze direction. *ACM Trans. Graph.* 28, 4, Article 100 (September 2009), 14 pages. DOI:dx.doi.org/10.1145/1559755.1559757
3. L. Bartram, C. Ware, and T. Calvert. Moticons: Direction, distraction, and task. *International Journal of Computer-Human Studies* 58, 5 (2003), 515–545.
4. M. Carrasco, D. Evert, I. Chang, and S. Katz (1995) The eccentricity effect: Target eccentricity affects performance on conjunction searches, *Perception & Psychophysics*, 57, 1241-1261.
5. C.W. Clifford and M. Ibbotson, Fundamental mechanisms of visual motion detection: models, cells and functions, *Progress in Neurobiology*, 68 (6), December 2002, 409-437, DOI:dx.doi.org/10.1016/S0301-0082(02)00154-5.
6. C. Curcio, K. Sloan, R. Kalina, and A. Hendrickson (1990) Human photoreceptor topography. *Journal of Comparative Neurology*, 292(4), 497-523.
7. James J. DiCarlo, Davide Zoccolan, Nicole C. Rust, How Does the Brain Solve Visual Object Recognition?, *Neuron*, 73(3), February 2012, 415-434.
8. J. Duncan, and G. Humphreys, Visual search and stimulus similarity. *Psychological Review*, 96(3), 1989, 433–458.
9. J. T. Enns, Three-dimensional features that pop out in visual search. In D. Brogan (ed.), *Visual Search*, Taylor & Francis, 1990, 37–45.
10. C. Eriksen and D. Schultz (1977) Retinal locus and acuity in visual information processing. *Bulletin of the Psychonomic Society*, 9(2), 81-84.
11. A. Field, J. Miles, and Z. Field, *Discovering Statistics using R*, Sage, 2012.
12. Juan E. Garrido, Victor M. R. Penichet, Maria D. Lozano, Aaron Quigley, and Per Ola Kristensson. 2014. AwToolkit: attention-aware user interface widgets. *Proceedings of the Conference on Advanced Visual Interfaces* (AVI '14). 9-16. DOI:dx.doi.org/10.1145/2598153.2598160
13. K. Grill-Spector and R. Malach (2004) The human visual cortex. *Ann. Rev. Neurosci.*, 27, 649-677.
14. T. Hansen, L. Pracejus, L., and K. Gegenfurtner, Color perception in the intermediate periphery of the visual field, *Journal of Vision*, 9(4):26, 2009, 1-12.
15. Chris Harrison, Gary Hsieh, Karl D.D. Willis, Jodi Forlizzi, and Scott E. Hudson. 2011. Kineticons: using iconographic motion in graphical user interface design. *Proceedings of the SIGCHI Conference on Human Factors in Computing Systems* (CHI '11). 1999-2008. DOI=http://dx.doi.org/10.1145/1978942.1979232
16. C. Healey and J. Enns (2012) Attention and visual memory in visualization and computer graphics. *IEEE Transactions on Visualization and Computer Graphics, 18*(7), 1170-1188.
17. C. Healey, K. Booth, and J. Enns, Harnessing preattentive processes for multivariate data visualization. *Proceedings of Graphics Interface 1993*, 107–117.
18. C. Healey and J. Enns, Large datasets at a glance: Combining textures and colors in scientific visualization. *IEEE Transactions on Visualization and Computer Graphics* 5, 2 (1999), 145–167.
19. Michael Xuelin Huang, Tiffany C.K. Kwok, Grace Ngai, Stephen C.F. Chan, and Hong Va Leong. 2016. Building a Personalized, Auto-Calibrating Eye Tracker from User Interactions. *In Proceedings of the 2016 CHI Conference on Human Factors in Computing Systems (CHI '16)*, 5169-5179. http://dx.doi.org/10.1145/2858036.2858404
20. D. Huber and C. Healey, Visualizing Data with Motion. *Proc. Visualization 2003*, 527–534.
21. L. Itti and C. Koch (2001) Computational modelling of visual attention. *Nature reviews neuroscience*, 2(3), 194-203.
22. B. Julész and J.R. Bergen, Textons, the fundamental elements in preattentive vision and the perception of textures. *Bell System Technical Journal* 62, 6 (1983), 1619–1645.
23. B. Julesz (1984) Toward an axiomatic theory of preattentive vision. In G. Edelman, W. Gall & M. Cowan (eds.), *Dynamic Aspects of Neocortical Function*, 585-611.
24. Krzysztof Z. Gajos, Mary Czerwinski, Desney S. Tan, and Daniel S. Weld. 2006. Exploring the design space for adaptive graphical user interfaces. *Proceedings of the working conference on Advanced visual interfaces - AVI '06*, 201–208. DOI:dx.doi.org/10.1145/1133265.1133306
25. C. Malamed (2011) *Visual Language for Designers: Principles for Creating Graphics that People Understand*, Sage, 2011.
26. D. McKeefry, I. Murray, and N. Parry (2007) Perceived shifts in saturation and hue of chromatic stimuli in the near peripheral retina. J*ournal of the Optical Society of America A*, 24, 3168–3179.
27. Cristina Meinecke, Mieke Donk, Detection performance in pop-out tasks: Nonmonotonic changes with display size and eccentricity, *Perception*, 2002, 31, 591–602.

28. T. Munzner, *Interactive Visualization of Large Graphs and Networks*, PhD dissertation, Stanford University, 2000.

29. A.L. Nagy, R. Sanchez, and T. Hughes, Visual search for color differences with foveal and peripheral vision. *Journal of the Optical Society of America A*, 7(10), 1990, 1995–2001.

30. A.L. Nagy and R. Sanchez, Critical color differences determined with a visual search task. *Journal of the Optical Society of America A*, 7(7), 1990, 1209–1217.

31. R. Rosenholtz, J. Huang, A. Raj, B. Balas, and L. Ilie, (2012) A summary statistic representation in peripheral vision explains visual search. *Journal of vision*, 12(4), 14-14.

32. A. Raj and R. Rosenholtz (2010) What your design looks like to peripheral vision. *Proceedings of the 7th Symposium on Applied Perception in Graphics and Visualization*, 89-92.

33. D. Sagi and B. Julész, Detection versus discrimination of visual orientation. *Perception*, 14, 1985, 619–628.

34. B. Suh, A. Woodruff, R. Rosenholtz, and A. Glass (2002) Popout prism: adding perceptual principles to overview+ detail document interfaces. In *Proceedings of the SIGCHI conference on Human factors in computing systems*, 251-258.

35. Anne Treisman and Stephen Gormican, Feature analysis in early vision: Evidence from search asymmetries. *Psychological Review*, 95(1), 1988, 15-48. http://dx.doi.org/10.1037/0033-295X.95.1.15

36. Anne Treisman, Search, similarity, and integration of features between and within dimensions. *Journal of Experimental Psychology: Human Perception & Performance* 17, 3 (1991), 652–676.

37. P. Tynan and R. Sekuler (1982) Motion processing in peripheral vision: Reaction time and perceived velocity. *Vision research* 22(1), 61-68.

38. W3C, *Techniques for Accessibility Evaluation and Repair Tools*, https://www.w3.org/TR/AERT#color-contrast, retrieved September 18, 2016.

39. C. Ware, Information Visualization: *Perception for Design*. Morgan Kaufmann, 2000.

40. Wikipedia, *Peripheral Vision*, https://en.wikipedia.org/wiki/Peripheral_vision

41. James R. Wallace, Daniel Vogel, and Edward Lank. 2014. Effect of Bezel Presence and Width on Visual Search. *Proceedings of the International Symposium on Pervasive Displays (PerDis '14)*, ACM, 6 pages. DOI=http://dx.doi.org/10.1145/2611009.2611019

42. J. Wolfe, Guided Search 2.0: A revised model of visual search. *Psychonomic Bulletin & Review* 1, 2 (1994), 202–238.

Attention Allocation Aid for Visual Search

Arturo Deza* Dynamical Neuroscience UC Santa Barbara deza@dyns.ucsb.edu

Jeffrey R. Peters Mechanical Engineering UC Santa Barbara jrpeters@engineering.ucsb.edu

Grant S. Taylor U.S. Army Aviation Development Directorate, USA grant.s.taylor.civ@mail.mil

Amit Surana United Technologies Research Center, USA suranaa@utrc.utc.com

Miguel P. Eckstein Psychological and Brain Sciences, UC Santa Barbara eckstein@psych.ucsb.edu

ABSTRACT

This paper outlines the development and testing of a novel, feedback-enabled *attention allocation aid (AAAD)*, which uses real-time physiological data to improve human performance in a realistic sequential visual search task. Indeed, by optimizing over search duration, the aid improves efficiency, while preserving decision accuracy, as the operator identifies and classifies targets within simulated aerial imagery. Specifically, using experimental eye-tracking data and measurements about target detectability across the human visual field, we develop functional models of detection accuracy as a function of search time, number of eye movements, scan path, and image clutter. These models are then used by the AAAD in conjunction with real time eye position data to make probabilistic estimations of attained search accuracy and to recommend that the observer either move on to the next image or continue exploring the present image. An experimental evaluation in a scenario motivated from human supervisory control in surveillance missions confirms the benefits of the AAAD.

ACM Classification Keywords

H.1.2 [Models and Principles]: User/Machine Systems–Human factors, Human information processing; H.4.2 [Information Systems Applications]: Types of Systems–Decision Support; H.m [Miscellaneous]; I.6.4 [Simulation and Modeling]: Model Validation and Analysis; General Terms: Experimentation, Human Factors, Verification

Author Keywords

Attention; cognitive load; decision making; visual search.

[0]All authors of the paper are also affiliated with the Institute for Collaborative Biotechnologies.

CHI 2017, May 6-11, 2017, Denver, CO, USA.

http://dx.doi.org/10.1145/3025453.3025834

INTRODUCTION

The maturation of visual sensor technology has steadily increased the amount of real-time data that is available in modern surveillance mission scenarios ranging across military, homeland security and commercial applications. In many cases, it is the job of a human operator to ensure that this data is processed quickly and accurately. For example, *supervisory systems* involving collaboration between human operators and unmanned vehicles often require the sequential processing of imagery that is generated by the autonomous vehicles' onboard cameras for the purpose of finding targets, analyzing terrain, and making key planning decisions [39]. The incredible volume of data generated by modern sensors, combined with the complex nature of modern mission scenarios, makes operators susceptible to information overload and attention allocation inefficiencies [9], which can lead to detrimental performance and potentially dire consequences [44]. As such, the development of tools to improve human performance in visual data analysis tasks is crucial to ensuring mission success.

This article focuses on the development and experimental verification of a novel, attention allocation aid that is designed to help human operators in a sequential visual search task, which requires the detection and classification of targets within a simulated landscape. Our study is primarily motivated by surveillance applications that require humans to find high value targets within videos generated by remote sensors, e.g., mounted on unmanned vehicles; however, the presented method is applicable to a variety of application domains.

Specifically, the main contribution of this paper is the introduction and experimental verification of a real-time and feedback-enabled *attention allocation aid* (AAAD), which optimizes the operator's decision speed when they are engaging in target search, without sacrificing performance. The motivating observation is that humans have imperfect awareness of the time required to acquire all task-relevant visual information during search, and thus are generally inefficient at administering their time when scrutinizing the data sets. The proposed aid makes real-time automated search duration recommendations based on three key metrics: 1) visual search time, 2) number of eye movements executed by the observer, and 3) an estimated target detectability based on prior measurements of both the target visibility across the visual field and the observer's fixations during search. In particular, these metrics are used by the aid to estimate the time required for the operator to acquire the visual information that is necessary to support the search decisions, and subsequently indicate when this time has elapsed via a simple indicator on the user interface. We experimentally evaluate the AAAD in a simulated surveillance scenario motivated by human supervisory control, and found a factor of $\times 1.5$ increase in user efficiency in detecting and classifying targets in realistic visual imagery from a slowly moving sensor. The AAAD pipeline is generic and can readily be extended and applied to other sources of images, i.e., satellite images, astronomical images [6], x-rays for medical imaging [1, 13] or security scanning [5], and video surveillance [45] which include a human-in-the-loop [53, 52].

Our rigorous development of the AAAD also includes a number of secondary contributions, including: definition of detectability surfaces based on eye-tacking measurements, incorporation of image clutter effects, creation of a composite exploration map, and utilization of a probabilistic framework for decision making when computing overall search satisfaction based on time, eye movements, and detectability scores.

PREVIOUS WORK

Research in human computer interaction has capitalized on basic vision science research by including samples of the the visual environment through eye movements (active vision) within a larger modeling framework that includes cognitive, motor, and perceptual processing involved in visual search (Tseng and Howes, 2015 [48] and Halverson and Hofson, 2011 [20] which expands on the work of Kieras and Meyer, 1997 [32]). Such models have been proposed for potential use for computer interface evaluation and design.

Another line of research has focused on how to augment human capabilities in coordinating multiple tasks. For example, models have been used to optimize how observers split their attentional resources when simultaneously conducting two different visuo-cognitive tasks [36].

Attention allocation aids have been studied in the context of human supervisory control of large data acquired by multiple automated agents (e.g., [46, 9]). Such scenarios present the challenge of a human having to inspect large data sets with possible errors due to visual limitations, attentional bottlenecks, and fatigue. The use of advanced physiological sensing through eye-tracking technology has become a viable option for both the assessment of the operator cognitive state, and the evaluation of operator performance in a number of realistic applications, e.g. [49]. One line of research attempts to use eye-tracking measurements to detect physiological and cognitive precursors to behavior such as perceived workload, fatigue, or situational awareness. Indeed, objective measures such as blink rates [51], pupil diameter [50, 31] , and fixation/saccade characteristics [2], all have correlations to cognitive processing, although the use of such measurements as reliable indicators of operator mental states is not fully understood [12]. If undesirable states can be accurately anticipated with physiological measures, then they can be used to drive automated aids that mediate operator resources through, e.g., optimization of task schedules [38] or adaptive automation schemes [22, 43].

Other researchers have utilized eye tracker technology to show increased efficiency of human search by relying on a "divide and conquer" collaborative search [57, 7]. In such schemes, multiple observers (usually two) engage in target search simultaneously with real-time updates of their partners' gaze and access to voice communication.

A novel approach investigated in the current work is the design of an attention allocation aid that uses eye-tracking data to make real time inferences of the attained target detection accuracy and critically, the time to achieve asymptotic accuracy. Such estimates, which we will refer to as search satisfaction time, are utilized by the attention allocation aid to recommend that the user end the current search and move on to the next data set. In addition, if the observer completes search prior to the search satisfaction time, the eye position data can also be utilized to assess whether some area of the image remains unexplored, and suggest that the observer to further explore that area.

The success of the proposed approach requires an adequate understanding of the relation between fixational eye-movements and the accumulation of sensory evidence supporting task performance. A critical component to understanding the contribution of eye movement to task performance is the dependence of target detectability with its distance from the point of fixation, commonly referred to as *retinal eccentricity* [11, 37, 33, 10]. Indeed, this relationship can be used to build attention-based models for predicting performance [24]. Often, dynamic sensory evidence accumulation models are also dependent upon the nature of the stimuli. Our attention allocation aid relies on a set of experiments measuring how accuracy in detecting the target of interest varies with distance from fixation (retinal eccentricity) and as a function of the presentation time of the image data. These measurements are then used to implement the AAAD and validate its utility in optimizing search. To our knowledge the current approach for the AAAD and thorough experimental validation is novel to the field.

We also note that a key difference of our work in comparison to existing literature, is that our attention allocation aid is essentially a back-end search optimizer, which tells the observer *when* to stop search; rather than advising the observer *where* to look (it does not compute fixation cue's or saliency-like maps [23, 8]).

MOTIVATION AND HYPOTHESIS

Humans have difficulty assessing when adequate visual information has been acquired during challenging search tasks and optimally allocating their fixations over different parts of the image [55]. The purpose of the AAAD is to utilize in real time the temporal dynamics of the eye-position data and the information acquisition process to recommend to the observers that either all information has been acquired and search can be terminated, or further exploration of the image is required. The AAAD is expected to reduce both premature image search termination and long periods of image search when no target is present without compromising the search task performance, i.e. detection and false alarm rates. Thus, the AAAD should ideally improve observer's efficiency in completing more sequential search tasks in a given allotted time period with a level of detection accuracy that is as good or better than search without the AAAD.

In what follows, we present a series of experiments in order to develop, calibrate, and test the effectiveness of the AAAD in a visual target search/classification task. Subjects were asked to search for people within simulated aerial images, and subsequently classify whether or not the person was holding a weapon. The stimuli and eye-tracking apparatus used in all of our experiments are described below.

Stimuli Creation: A total of 273 videos were created, each with a total duration of 120 seconds, where a 'birds eye' point-of-view camera rotated slowly around the center. While the video was in a rotating motion, there was no relative motion between any parts of the video. From a repeated subset of the original 273 videos, a total of 1440 different short clips were created, which were subsequently divided into the 4 groups (stimuli sets) that were used in subsequent experiments. Half of the clips had person present, while the other half had person absent. These short and slowly rotating clips were used instead of still images in our experiment, to simulate imagery from a moving sensor in a surveillance scenario. All clips were shown to participants in a random order. The stimuli used in all our experiments present varying levels of zoom (high, medium, low) and clutter (high, medium, low).

Apparatus: An EyeLink 1000 system (SR Research) was used to collect eye-tracking data at a frequency of 1000 Hz. Each participant sat at a distance of 76 cm from a LCD screen on gamma display, so that each pixel subtended a visual angle of $0.022\,deg/px$. All video clips were rendered at 1024×760 px (22.5 deg $\times 16.7$ deg) and a frame rate of 24 fps. Eye movements with velocity over 22 deg/s and acceleration over 4000 deg/s^2 were qualified as saccades. Every trial began with a fixation cross, where each subject had to fixate the cross with a tolerance of 1 deg.

DEVELOPING THE ATTENTION ALLOCATION AID (AAAD)

This section presents details about the development and calibration of the AAAD. Here, preliminary experiments were run to estimate perceptual performance curves (PPCs) (describing the relationship between detection accuracy and each of three metrics: time, number of eye movements, and detectability) under various levels of image complexity (clutter and zoom levels). These PPCs allow the identification of asymptotic detection accuracy, which is the primary criterion used by the AAAD to estimate expected detection accuracy in real time.

Experiment 1: Psychometric Data Collection

We performed two preliminary studies to generate the time, eye movement, and detectability PPCs: a forced fixation search (no eye movements allowed) and a free search experiment. The free search data is directly used to compute the relevant PPCs, while the forced fixation data is used to calculate detectability surfaces that allow for the computation of the detectability PPC. See Figure 1 for experimental flow.

Forced Fixation Search

A total of 13 subjects participated in a *forced fixation search* experiment where the goal was to search within the visual periphery to identify if there was a person present or absent (yes/no task; 50% probability of person presence) and, in addition, to identify if there was a weapon present or absent (yes/no task; 50% probability of weapon presence contingent on person present). Participants had variable amounts of time (100, 200, 400, 900, 1600 ms) to view each clip. Clips were presented in a random order, with the person at a variable degree of eccentricity (1 deg, 4 deg, 9 deg, 15 deg) from point of fixation. Subjects were not made aware of the eccentricity values used in each trial. They were then prompted with a Likert scale that required them to rate from 1-10 (by clicking on a number) their confidence of person presence. A value of 1 indicated strong confidence of person absent, and a value of 10 indicated a strong confidence of person present – intermediate values represented different levels of uncertainty. Values of 1-5 were classified as person absent, and 6-10 were classified as person present. A second rating scale (identical to the first) was then presented, requiring the subject to rate their confidence regarding weapon presence. Participants had unlimited time for making their judgments, although no subject ever took more than 10 seconds per judgment. There was no response feedback after each trial.

Each subject participated in 12 sessions that consisted of 360 clips each. There were 4 stimuli sets (each set consisted of unique images), and each participants viewed each set 3 times in random order without being aware that the images were repeated (4 sets $\times$ 3 times = 12 sessions). Every set also had the images with aerial viewpoints from different vantage points (Example: set 1 had the person at 12 o'clock – as in North, while set 2 had the person at 3 o'clock – as in East). To mitigate fixation bias, all subjects had a unique fixation point for every trial associated with each particular eccentricity value. All clips were rendered with variable levels of clutter. Each session took approximately one hour to complete. The person,i.e. search target, was of size 0.5 deg $\times$0.5 deg, 1 deg$\times$1 deg, 1.5 deg$\times$1.5 deg, depending on the zoom level. If a subject fixated outside of a 1 deg radius around the fixation cross during the trial, then the trial was aborted.

Free Search

A total of 11 subjects participated in a *free search* experiment where the goal was to detect and classify the person. Although eye movements were allowed, subjects were not explicitly told to foveate at the person (although they usually chose to do so). Participants had twice the amount (200 ms, 400 ms, 800 ms, 1800 ms, 3200 ms) of time than in the Forced Fixation Search. All observers began each trial with a fixation at center of the screen. They then proceeded to scan the scene to find a person and determine if the person was holding a weapon. Once the trial time was over, they were prompted with a "Person Detection" and "Weapon Detection" rating scale, and had to rate from 1-10 by clicking on a number reporting how confident they were on detecting/classifying the person. Similar to the forced fixation experiment, participants had unlimited time to make their judgments and did not receive any feedback after each trial. No trials were aborted.

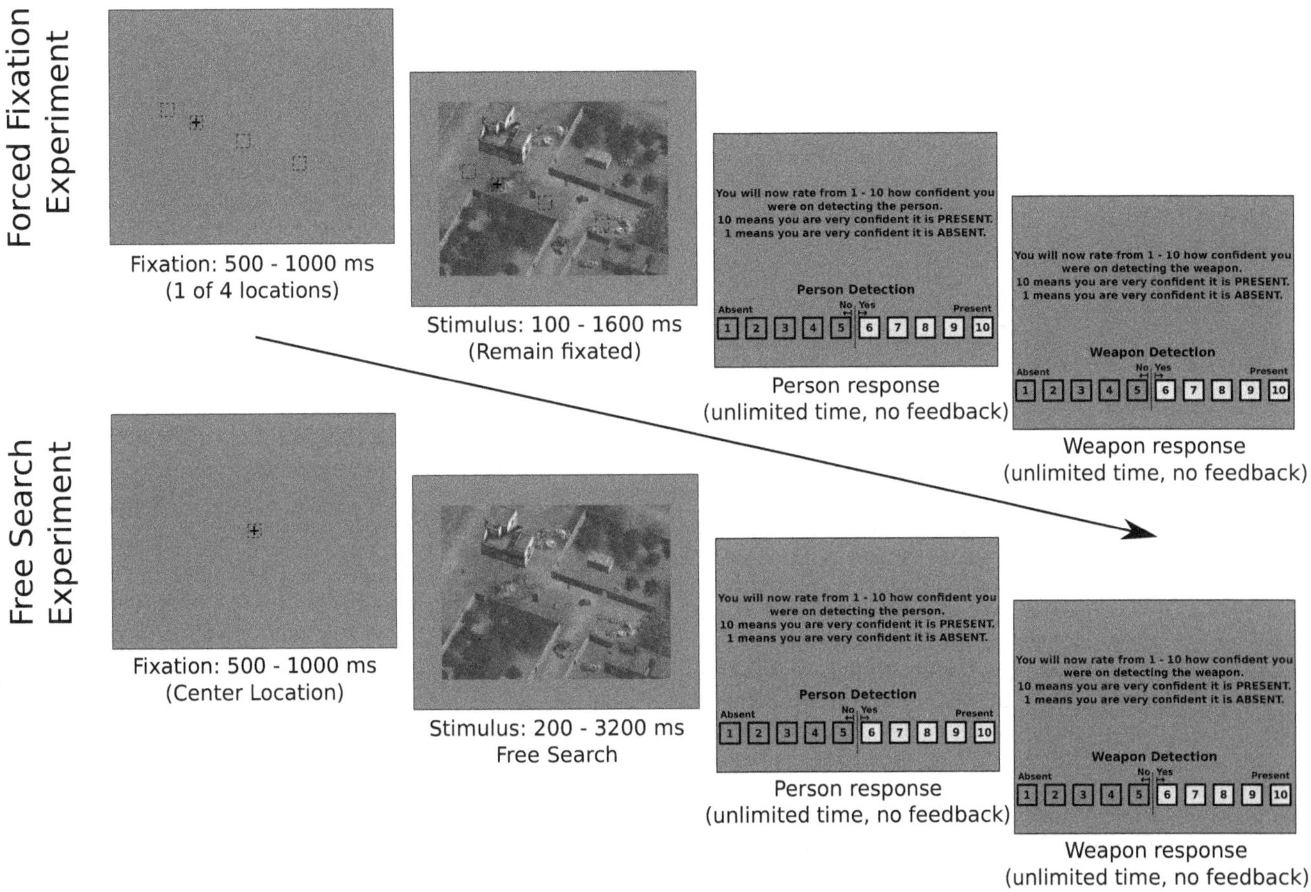

Figure 1. Experiment 1: The forced fixation (top) and free search (bottom) experiments to obtain the time, eye movements, and detectability PPCs.

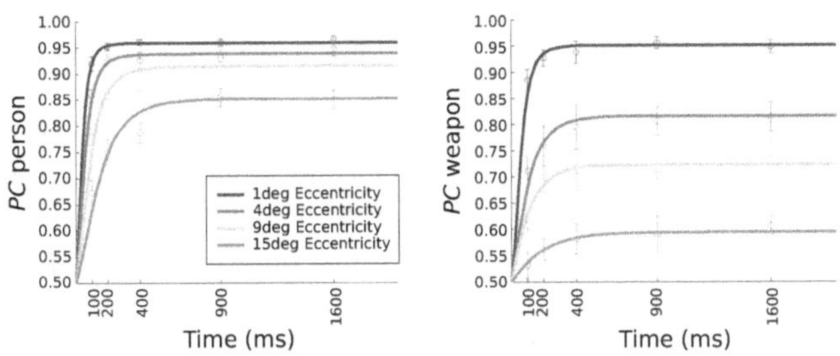

(a) Person and weapon detection proportion correct (PC)

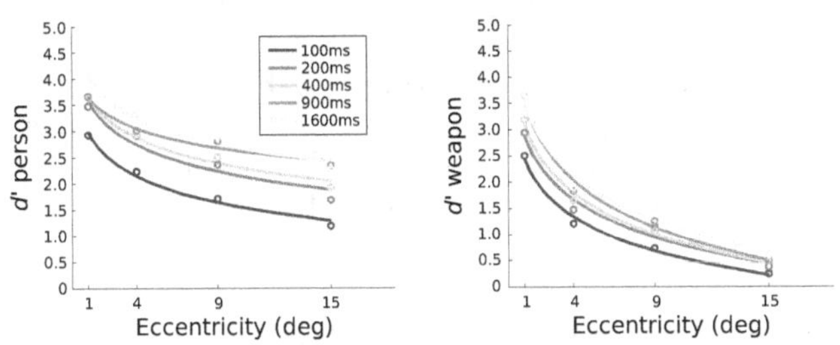

(b) Person and weapon detectability curves (d')

Figure 2. Person and weapon detection performance in proportion correct (PC) and d' space from the forced fixation search experiment. Notice that (a) and (b) are dual representations of each other. The bottom curves in d' space will be used to generate a detectability surface.

Each subject in the free search experiment participated in 6 sessions that consisted of two sets of 360 unique images. In these sessions, each subject viewed one of the two sets of images, and each set was presented 3 times leading to a total of 6 sessions. Subjects were not made aware that the sessions were repeated.

Fitting Perceptual Performance Curves (PPCs)

Motivation of PPCs

PPCs were constructed to relate performance to each of three different metrics. The first metric is visual search time, since it is well known that time affects visual search accuracy [15] – the main intuition being that the more time a subject spends scanning an image, the higher the likelihood of detecting the target (person or weapon). The second metric is the number of eye movements a subject performs while engaging in target search. Typically, time will pass on as more eye movements are produced, but there are some cases where scrutiny in classifying or detecting a target is needed by spending long periods of fixation. As an example, one could imagine an *exploitation vs exploration* search scenario where a subject spends 1000 ms on a single fixation, given the difficulty to *classify* the target (exploitation), as opposed to a scenario where the same subject makes 3 sparse and exploratory fixations in the same 1000 ms time window to *find* the target (exploration). For this

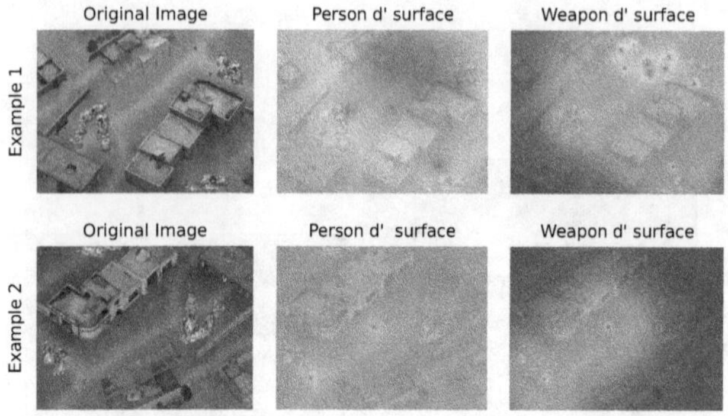

Figure 3. Sample person and weapon fixation maps generated from the forced fixation search experiment (Fig. 2(b)). These fixation maps are projections of Detectability Surfaces as described in the Supp. Mat.

reason we chose to make time and eye movements independent metrics for our AAAD system. The third and last metric is detectability. Here, a detectability score is constructed by generating a pixel-wise map that quantifies localized information aggregation in different parts of the image (as indicated by eye movements), and subsequently combining the result to quantify the target's overall detectability. Following our previous example, one could imagine that even if an observer spends the allotted 1000 ms searching for a target and making *e* number of eye movements in a small spatial vicinity, it might not be a good strategy compared to spreading fixations across the image. See Figure 3 for an example of such fixations overlayed on different images.

We are interested in successful observer detection of the person and the weapon targets. Given that our results show that the weapon requires more time to detect than the person, the AAAD recommendation to end search was based on the PPCs corresponding to the detection of the weapon. Basing the AAAD on the PPCs for the person detection would likely compromise the detection of the weapon.

Computing PPCs

To model the target detection accuracy, we use the observer hit rate (the proportion of trials that the observer indicated that a target is present, given that a target is actually present in the trial stimuli) and false alarm rate (the proportion of trials that the observer indicated that the target is present, given that no target is actually pesent in the trial stimuli). Hit rates and false positive were represented as an empirical detectability index (d') and a decision criterion (λ) using an equal variance normal Signal Detection Theory (SDT) model (Green & Swets) [18]. We then fit the resulting data with curves to model the functional relationship between the detectability indices and each of the relevant performance metrics. The best fit functions were then utilized with the equal variance SDT model to generate estimates of attained accuracy in terms of proportion correct (PC). Notice that proportion correct and hit rate are different since proportion correct takes into account both the hit rate and the correct rejection rate (proportion of trials in which the observer correctly decided that the target is absent).

For a fixed condition and setting (assuming Gaussian signal and noise distributions), the general equations to compute (d', λ) are [54]:

$$d' = Z(\text{Hit Rate}) - Z(\text{False Alarm Rate}) \quad (1)$$

$$\lambda = -Z(\text{False Alarm Rate}) \quad (2)$$

where $Z(\circ)$ is the inverse of the normal cumulative Gaussian distribution, and the hit/false alarm rates are calculated at the given experimental condition and setting. Consider as an example a condition and setting for the forced fixation search experiment: Condition = $(4 \text{ deg}, 200 \text{ ms})$, Setting = $(\text{high zoom}, \text{low clutter})$. Likewise, a sample condition and setting for the free search experiment: Condition = 400 ms, Setting = $(\text{medium zoom}, \text{high clutter})$.

For the Time and Eye-Movements PPCs, we used a straightforward regression to find an exponential relation of the form $d'(x) = \alpha(1 - e^{-\beta x})$, where $x : \{\text{Time, Eye Movements}\}$ and β is constant, to obtain a continuous approximating function for the collection of points d' within a given setting.

To compute final Time and Eye Movements PPC curves, recall that there exists a function $g(\circ)$ that estimates PC, i.e., $PC(x) = g(d'(x), \lambda(x))$, where:

$$PC(x) = m(x)(\text{Hit Rate}) + n(x)(1 - (\text{False Alarm Rate})) \quad (3)$$

and

$$\text{False Alarm Rate}(x) = Z^{-1}(-\lambda(x)) \quad (4)$$

$$\text{Hit Rate}(x) = Z^{-1}(d'(x) - \lambda(x)) \quad (5)$$

where $m(x)$ and $n(x)$ are variables that are contingent on the number of signal (i.e. person/weapon) present and signal (i.e. person/weapon) absent trials ($m(x) + n(x) = 1, \forall x$), and the hit/false alarm rates are estimates of the true values at x. Here, curves are fitted in d' space, rather than directly from PC space, to deal with possible unbalanced datasets with signal present/absent trials (See Discussion).

In order to obtain the detectability PPC (Figure 4 (right)), we perform a binned regression across all trials between the respective PC performance from the free viewing task in Experiment 1 and the values of a composite detectability score D' for each image. The score D' in each trial was computed by first generating a *detectability surface* from the user's fixations and the detectability curves (Figure. 2(b)), and subsequently performing a spatial average. We note that the detectability PPC is the only curve that is regressed directly to PC given that the argument of our regression function is in a d'-like space, thus $\lambda, m(x), n(x)$ need not be calculated. The training data we have for this regression is from the free search experiment.

Further details regarding the generation of the Time PPC, Eye Movements PPC, and Detectability PPC is provided in the Supplementary Material.

Performance Criteria and AAAD Functionality

The AAAD was designed to integrate three different inputs to compute search satisfaction. The three previous PPC in-

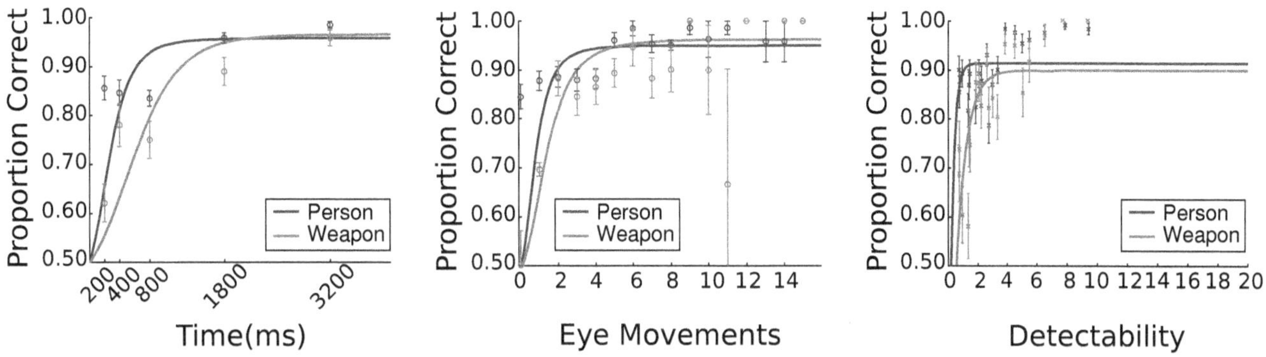

Figure 4. Perceptual Performance Curves (PPCs) for time (left), eye movements (center), and detectability (right) for a (low zoom, high clutter) setting. In general it takes higher time, eye movements, and detectability scores to achieve asymptotic performance for weapon detection *vs* person detection. Also shown are the error bars along each curve. Recall they have been fitted in d' space, and have been re-plotted in PC space (Eq. 3).

puts can be seen as individual metrics on their own, and are computed independently in the system.

Search Satisfaction Model

For computing general search satisfaction we require that all three of the following conditions are simultaneously satisfied:

$$Pr[(PC^T_{max} - PC(t)) < \varepsilon] > \eta, \tag{6}$$

$$Pr[(PC^E_{max} - PC(e)) < \varepsilon] > \eta, \tag{7}$$

$$Pr[(PC^D_{max} - PC(D')) < \varepsilon] > \eta, \tag{8}$$

where $PC^T_{max}, PC^E_{max}, PC^D_{max}$ are the (fixed) asymptotic values of PC with respect to the time, number of eye-movements, and detectability PPCs given a (zoom, clutter) setting, resp. $PC(t), PC(e), PC(D')$ are the current estimated values of PC as calculated by the time, number of eye-movements, and detectability PPCs, respectively, and ε, η are fixed thresholds.

An image is only said to have been adequately searched if *all* criteria (6), (7), and (8) are simultaneously satisfied. Also notice that the criteria (6), (7), and (8) are all non-decreasing in their respective arguments (which are monotonically increasing in time); thus a condition will never revert to being "unsatisfied" after being satisfied. We will refer the above search satisfaction criterion as *PC general satisfaction*.

Our motivation for using the above mentioned probabilistic framework is to take into account the error bars of each time, eye movements, and detectability curves that are zoom and clutter level dependent. We include these error bars as Gaussian standard deviations σ in our probabilistic computation:

$$Pr[(PC_{max} - PC) < \varepsilon] \rightarrow 1 - Z^{-1}(\frac{PC_{max} - PC - \varepsilon}{\sigma}). \tag{9}$$

The above strategy can be thought of centering a gaussian $(\mu_x, \sigma_x) := (PC, \sigma)$ at every point in the PPC curves, and computing how far away the asymptotic performance PC_{max} is from every point in the curve. Thus, we will find and select the minimum point in the curve that fulfills this condition for each time, eye movements, and detectability PPC. These are the threshold PPC's that once all of them are reached in real-time on the AAAD system, the AAAD will trigger "On". A value of $\eta = 0.025, \varepsilon = 0.02$ was selected for our experiments.

Attention Allocation Aid Design

The Attention Allocation Aid system is designed to run in the background of the simulation interface (see Figure 5). The AAAD system starts by computing the clutter and zoom level of the input image from the slowly evolving video clip in each trial. It is assumed that the level of zoom (high, medium, or low) can be obtained from ground truth settings, given that a pilot can control a camera's zoom level, while the clutter level can be computed from the input image/video [56, 41, 35]. For our main experiments, we assumed that ground truth was provided to classify images based on clutter, since our main goal is to prove that the AAAD system works under ideal conditions[1]. A thorough investigation of the use of clutter models as ground truth predictors is left to future work.

As the trial progresses, the three PC *vs* {Time, Eye Movements, Detectability} curves (Figure 4) are updated in real-time using gaze location, fixation time, and saccade information obtained from the eye-tracker. The Time PPC is updated at each frame. The Eye Movements PPC is updated with an interruption-based paradigm – contingent on the eye-tracker detecting an eye movement. The Detectability PPC is updated only after every eye movement event, given that we have the fixation position and time. Each of the PC Satisfaction conditions (see Eq. (6, 7, 8)) is monitored independently, and once all criteria are satisfied, the AAAD systems switches from an "Explore" to a "Move On" state, where observers are encouraged to cease search, and make a decision.

Parallel to this, an *Exploration* map is computed in real-time in the back-end. The goal of the Exploration map is to inform the searcher where he/she has already searched, and to indicate the highly cluttered regions where a person is likely to be. The Exploration map has no knowledge of a target present/absent, and only uses image clutter and observer fixations.

If an observer attempts to advance to the next image while the AAAD system state is in "Explore" state, the Exploration map appears for ~ 120 ms. The map is weighted by previously explored regions (computed via the detectability surface; see Supplementary Material), such that, highly

[1]If we did *not* assume *oracle-like* inputs for zoom and clutter levels, then not finding a significant effect, could be due to poor clutter modeling, rather than poor AAAD system design.

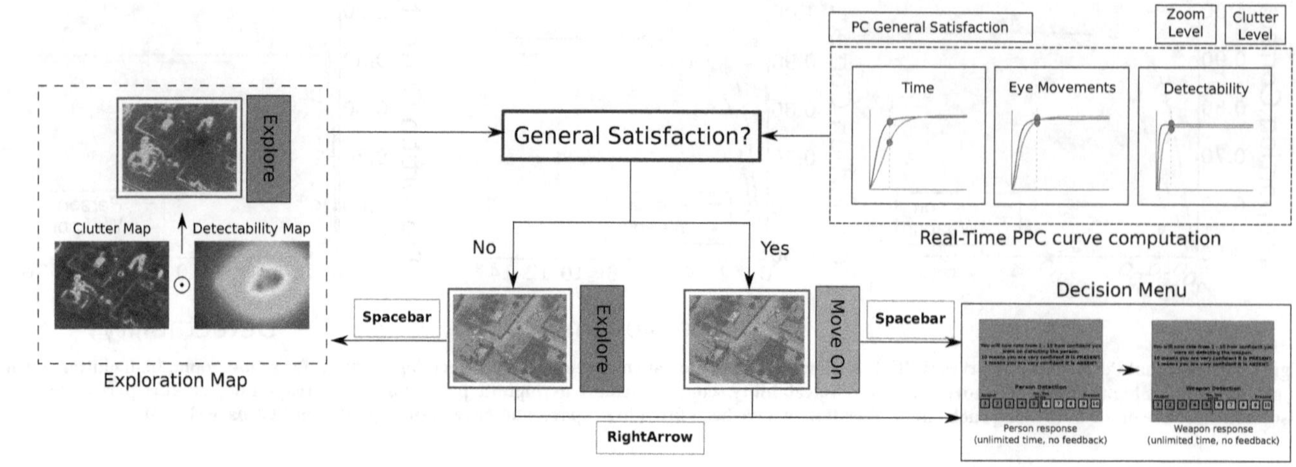

Figure 5. Attention Allocation Aid (AAAD) system diagram. From the start of each trial, the PPC curves are updated in real-time in the back-end, waiting for General Search Satisfaction to be achieved. Possible user inputs (highlighted in magenta) are the space bar and the right arrow. The right arrow takes the user directly to the decision menu terminating the trial, regardless of Satisfaction. The spacebar will lead the observer to the Exploration Map, and later back to the original stimuli if Satisfaction is not achieved, or to the decision menu otherwise

cluttered and non-explored regions are highlighted. The Exploration map is computed as follows: Exploration map $=$ FC $\odot (1 - \text{Detectability Surface})$, where FC is the *feature congestion* [41] dense clutter map, $\odot$ is the element-wise multiplication operator, and the detectability surface is normalized to lie in the interval $[0,1]$.

Notice that the only inputs (to the system) that the observer can produce while performing a trial (besides passively providing eye movements), are by pressing the right arrow key, which forces the trial to terminate and the subject to make a decision, irrespective of PC general satisfaction being achieved (for both AAAD, and non-AAAD experimental sessions); or by pressing the space bar, which activates the Exploration map if PC general satisfaction is not achieved, and terminates the trial if otherwise.

EVALUATING THE ATTENTION ALLOCATION AID

In this section we summarize a second experiment used to evaluate the effectiveness of the AAAD. Two experimental conditions were considered: A person and weapon search and classification experiment with and without AAAD. The goal of this experiment is to objectively measure any improvements in the search task performance when the subjects are assisted by the AAAD. Since it was the first time for all of our second group of subjects to participate in an eye tracking experiment, we decided to add two additional practice sessions (twenty minutes each) where we would verbally explain the non-AAAD and AAAD system.

After the practice sessions, half of the subjects were tested starting with the AAAD condition and the other half started without the AAAD condition. We counterbalanced our participants to reduce possible learning effects. The group of participants involved in Experiment 2, did not participate in and were not aware of Experiment 1. The completion of the first 2 practice sessions plus Experiment 2 with both conditions (counterbalanced) took an estimate of 2 hours for each subject. The same person and weapon present/absent statistics of Experiment 1 were used for Experiments 2 and 3. Figure 6 illustrates the design of the search task without (top stream) and with (bottom stream) the AAAD.

Experiment 2: AAAD Evaluation

Condition 1: Target search without AAAD

A total of 18 subjects participated in a non-AAAD target search experiment where the goal was to complete as many trials as possible in a 20 minute interval without sacrificing task performance, where the task per trial was to correctly detect and classify the target in the minimum amount of time.

Target detection involved reporting if the person was present or absent in the scene, and target classification involved reporting whether or not the person had a weapon. Although eye movements were allowed, subjects were not told explicitly to foveate at the target (although this was usually the case). In other words, it was possible for the subject to move on to the next trial by detecting the target in the periphery [10]. A fixation cross was placed at the center of the screen for uniform starting conditions across participants. After terminating search, subjects were prompted with a "Person Detection" rating scale where they had to rate their confidence in a person's presence on a scale from 1-10 by clicking on a number. A "Weapon Detection" rating scale then appeared where subjects also had to rate their weapon detection confidence from a scale from 1-10. Participants had unlimited time for making their judgments, though no subject took more than 10 seconds per judgment. There was no response feedback, i.e., whether their detection responses were correct after each trial.

Condition 2: Target search with AAAD

The same 18 subjects participated in a target search experiment in presence of the AAAD where the goal was same as in the previous condition. In this experiment, the AAAD was visibly turned on for the participants. They saw a text message above the center stimuli with a caption: "Explore" or "Move On", and there was a colored square below the stimuli that

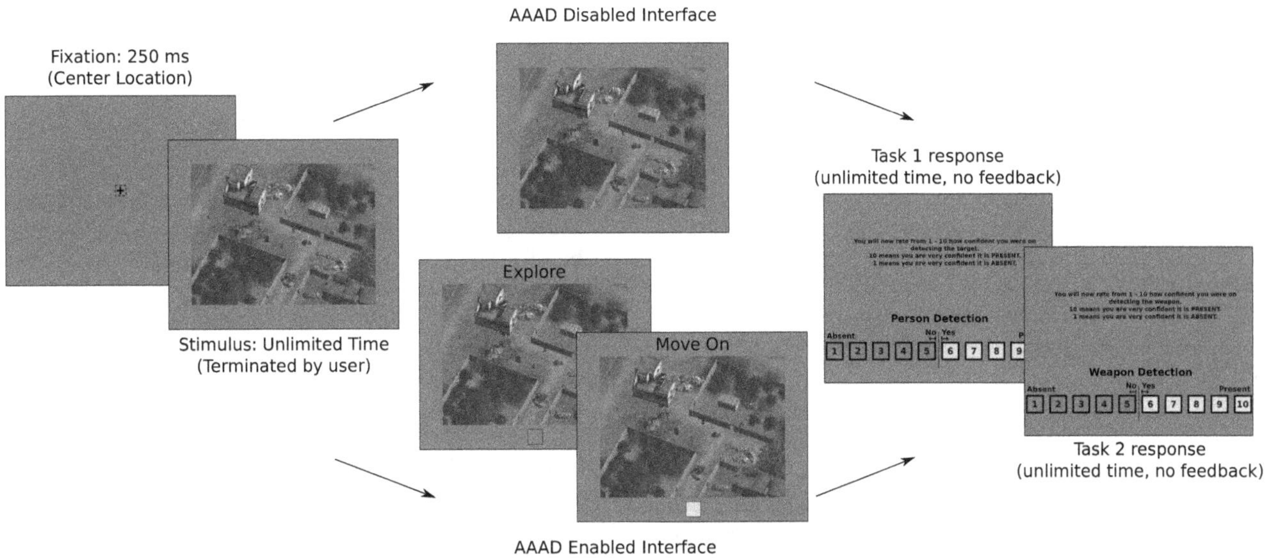

Figure 6. Experimental flow for Experiment 2 where we test the Attention Allocation Aid (AAAD) for condition 1 (AAAD off; top) and condition 2 (AAAD on; bottom). The top stream illustrates the non-AAAD condition, while the bottom stream illustrates the AAAD condition. Notice that the text and color in the AAAD enabled interface are coupled together: "Explore" = red, "Move On" = green. The red and green colors in the decision menus are independent of the AAAD colors.

	System Evaluation	
	Non-AAAD	**AAAD**
Average Trial Number (#)	54.33 ± 2.26	$\mathbf{57.94 \pm 1.74}$
Average Mean Time per Trial (s)	2.88 ± 0.42	$\mathbf{1.94 \pm 0.18}$
Person Hit Rate (%)	96.39 ± 1.42	$\mathbf{96.94 \pm 0.88}$
Weapon Hit Rate (%)	89.37 ± 2.92	$\mathbf{92.35 \pm 2.30}$
Person False Alarm Rate (%)	2.88 ± 2.63	$\mathbf{2.42 \pm 2.04}$
Weapon False Alarm Rate (%)	8.19 ± 5.54	$\mathbf{7.15 \pm 4.70}$
Person Miss Rate (%)	3.61 ± 1.42	$\mathbf{3.06 \pm 0.88}$
Weapon Miss Rate (%)	10.63 ± 2.92	$\mathbf{7.65 \pm 2.30}$
Person Correct Rejection Rate (%)	97.12 ± 2.63	$\mathbf{97.58 \pm 2.04}$
Weapon Correct Rejection Rate (%)	91.81 ± 5.54	$\mathbf{92.85 \pm 4.70}$
Mean Trial time *vs* Time Trigger (s)	2.32 ± 0.10	$\mathbf{1.37 \pm 0.05}$
Mean Trial time *vs* EyeMvmt Trigger (s)	2.35 ± 0.10	$\mathbf{1.37 \pm 0.05}$
Mean Trial time *vs* Detect. Trigger (s)	2.70 ± 0.13	$\mathbf{1.10 \pm 0.06}$
Mean Trial time *vs* General Trigger (s)	2.70 ± 0.13	$\mathbf{1.10 \pm 0.06}$

Table 1. General results of the systems evaluation without and with AAAD. It should be noted that subjects were counterbalanced (half-split) to start with or without the AAAD during evaluation to compensate for learning effects. Average refers to the mean computed across observers.

was colored red or green depending on the AAAD status. Participants were told to think of the AAAD as a stoplight: when it was red they should keep looking for the person/weapon, and should only move on to the next trial if the light turned green or if they were confident that they had either found the person/weapon or there was no person/weapon present.

RESULTS

Table 1 summarizes the results of both conditions in the second experiment. There is a significant increase in number of trials per person ($M = 3.61$, $SD = 5.69$, $t(17) = 2.813$, $p = 0.015$, two-tailed), as well as a significant decrease in mean trial time ($M = -0.31$, $SD = 1.36$, $t(17) = -2.613$, $p = 0.009$,two-tailed) between AAAD conditions. Overall performance is stable, though slight improvement is seen with the AAAD. Significant differences of trial *vs* trigger times are also found. The AAAD was ran in the back-end (but not visible to the observers) in the non-AAAD condition, to compute these measures. Notice that there is a virtual speed-up factor of: $\times 1.5$, in terms of average mean time per trial across observers when using the AAAD.

In addition we performed a related samples t-test (for person t_P and weapon t_W detection) between the hit rates ($M_P = 0.54$, $SD_P = 3.65$, $t_P(17) = 0.497$, $p = 0.626$, two-tailed; $M_W = 2.97$, $SD_W = 12.42$, $t_W(17) = 1.016$, $p = 0.324$, two-tailed), false alarm rates ($M_P = -0.46$, $SD_P = 2.98$, $t_P(17) = -0.655$, $p = 0.521$, two-tailed; $M_W = -1.03$, $SD_W = 6.42$, $t_W(17) = -0.684$, $p = 0.503$, two-tailed), misses ($M_P = -0.54$, $SD_P = 4.65$, $t_P(17) = -0.497$, $p = 0.625$, two-tailed; $M_W = -2.97$, $SD_W = 12.42$, $t_W(17) = -1.016$, $p = 0.323$, two-tailed), and correct rejections ($M_P = 0.46$, $SD_P = 2.98$, $t_P(17) = 0.655$, $p = 0.521$, two-tailed; $M_W = 1.03$, $SD_W = 6.42$, $t_W(17) = 0.684$, $p = 0.503$, two-tailed), and found no significant differences between non-AAAD and AAAD conditions. This last finding is somewhat ideal as the AAAD is intended to either preserve or improve these measures.

Finally, we decided to compare the trigger times of the time, eye movements, detectability, and general satisfaction conditions of the non-AAAD sessions with the AAAD sessions. For comparison, we subtract the final trial time minus the respective trigger time. As such, these times can be thought of as offsets. Note that although the non-AAAD condition does not show any visible assistant to the observer, the PPCs are still being computed in the back-end for the purposes of comparative data analysis. We performed four independent samples t-tests (Time: t_T, Eye Movements: t_{EM}, Detectability: t_D, General: t_G) collapsing all trials across all observers for these times and found significant differences for all trigger case scenarios, supporting the utility of the AAAD: $t_T(1920) =$

−8.46, $p < 0.0001$, two-tailed; $t_{EM}(1900) = -9.03$, $p < 0.0001$, two-tailed; $t_D(1192) = -11.52$, $p < 0.0001$, two-tailed; $t_G(1190) = -11.56$, $p < 0.0001$, two-tailed.

DISCUSSION

Extensions of model validity beyond current scenarios: Our results show the potential of a new approach in attention allocation aids that optimizes human search performance by utilizing real time fixational eye movements with prior measurements of target visibility across the visual field and as a function of time. However, there are various potential questions about the generalization of the model across search scenarios.

Our development of the AAAD assumed a target that is present in 50% of the images. A logical question arises as to whether the framework can generalize to real scenarios in which the target is present less frequently. Our model fits herein are performed using signal detection theory metrics (Green and Swets, 1967 [18]) that partition performance into an index of detectability, which is invariant to target prevalence, and a decision criterion, which has an optimal value (maximizing proportion correct) that varies with target prevalence. The model curves, which are utilized to make recommendations to the user, specify proportion correct as a function of time, eye movements, etc. and will vary with target prevalence. However, the model can generalize such curves to varying estimated target prevalence assuming an optimal decision criterion for the given prevalence. Although, we have not tested the generalization experimentally, the theory accommodates such scenarios and generalizations.

For simplicity, our current work used a single target when developing the AAAD. Another natural question to ask is whether the proposed AAAD can still be used if there is the possibility of multiple targets within a given image. Indeed, it could be the case that multiple targets could change how the aid operates within a given application. In some multiple-target scenarios where the detection of *even one* target is sufficient to trigger a decision, our strategy may still apply. For example, for some medical applications, such as screening mammography, finding at least one suspicious target triggers a follow-up diagnostic mammogram. In other applications, localization of each individual targets is important and might require additional development of multiple target model curves to use in conjunction with a prior distribution of the number of targets within the images.

Impact of computer vision developments on proposed AAAD framework: The recent advanced in computer vision might seem to diminish the contributions of the proposed scheme if one assumes that all human search will eventually be replaced by machines. This is yet another reasonable question to ask, since vision has thrived in recent years, in part due to significant advances of Deep Learning [27, 26]. State of the art object recognition algorithms [47, 40, 21] have achieved high performance on certain datasets (MNIST [28], CIFAR [25], ImageNet [42]). However, the images in these datasets typically present ideal scenes with large objects at the center of an image and, currently, the ability of state of the art algorithms to find small or occluded objects in cluttered scenes (MSCOCO [29]) remains well-below that of humans. Moreover, computers often show glaring errors that humans would not make in what have been called *adversarial* examples [17] in the computer vision community (e.g. by rigging individual pixel values in an image which 'hacks' a classifier, a computer can wrongly predict that a white noise-like image is a school bus with 99% confidence [34]). Furthermore, there is still a fundamental lack of understanding with regard to the effects of computer-aided detection aids as a substitute for human observers in many application domains. For example, computer automated detection is prevalent in some countries to flag potential locations for radiologists scrutinizing x-ray mammograms. Yet there is no consensus about its contributions to improving radiologists' diagnosis accuracy (e.g. Eadie, Taylor, & Gibson, 2012 [14]). As a result of these deficiencies, human observation is still heavily relied upon in a number of applications. As a result, there are many ongoing efforts to reduce errors and optimize human visual search in life-critical tasks from military surveillance [3], to security baggage screening [19], and medical imaging [4].

What is quickly becoming prevalent across many applications is the use of a computer aid that assists humans in localizing potential targets [16]. The proposed AAAD framework does not take into account the presence of a computer aid flagging potential target locations. In some cases, the presence of a computer aid is known to guide search with the risk of leading to over-shortened searches and missed targets that are not flagged by the computer aid [30]. The underlying model in the proposed AAAD allows calculation of an estimated observer accuracy given a pattern of fixations, time and the target visibility across the visual field. In principle, the model could be used to predict if an observer is short-cutting their search (due to the presence of the computer aid) and to alert the observer to further search the image/s. Thus, the developed AAAD framework could be potentially integrated with a computer aid, although its main contribution would likely shift from reducing search times to reducing missed targets.

Potential contribution beyond current application: Although the presented work introduces an AAAD within the context of a very specific task and images, our work serves as a proof of concept for a decision aid design approach that can potentially be applied to a variety of other applications including baggage screening and medical imaging. The model within the AAAD predicts performance on any given trial as a function of time and pattern of fixations and could be potentially used for quantifying the probability that a target was missed on a given image given the observers' search pattern. Such probabilities of error could be stored with the images and used later to identify images that require secondary inspection by an additional 2nd human observer.

Arguably, the main limitation of the AAAD is that the model relies on empirically measured curves describing the detectability of the target across the visual field and as a function of time. We are currently investigating how to predict target detectability by analyzing image properties such as clutter in real time, which would greatly benefit the application of the model to broader domains.

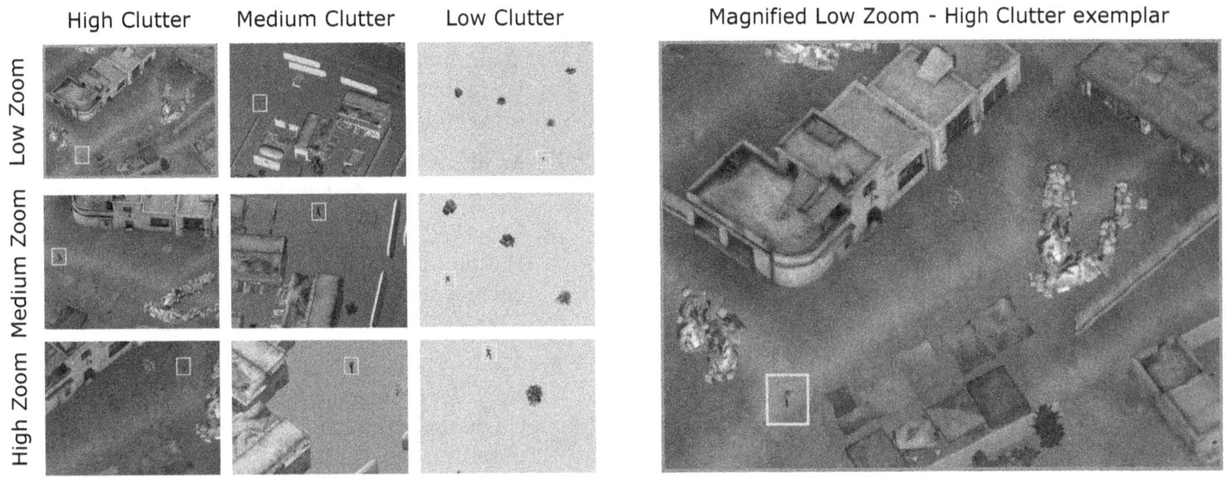

(a) Sample Person Present and Weapon Present Stimuli.

Figure 7. Sample Stimuli of Experiments 1 and 2. Left: we show random samples of person present, and weapon present in multiple clutter and zoom conditions. Right: we show a magnified version of the (Low Zoom, High Clutter) setting. The box in green has been overlayed on each subimage to reveal the location of the person and weapon when applicable.

CONCLUSION

Our experiments show evidence that our real-time enabled support decision system dubbed *AAAD* optimizes user efficiency in terms of an increase in the number of trials done as well as a decrease in time spent per each trial, while maintaining performance such as target hit rate and false alarm rate. Thus, the AAAD system has successfully integrated asymptotic performance of search time, eye movements and target detectability. We have described how to fully implement such system through an initial psychometric experiments to find perceptual performance curves for target search, as well as two consequent experiments that verify the benefits of the AAAD. Future computer-human interaction based systems could benefit from implementing AAAD-like systems where having a human-in-the-loop is critical to finding a target even beyond surveillance systems, e.g., medical imaging, astronomical data imagery and remote sensing.

ACKNOWLEDGEMENTS

This work has been sponsored by the U.S. Army Research Office and the Regents of the University of California, through Contract Number W911NF-09-D-0001 for the Institute for Collaborative Biotechnologies, and that the content of the information does not necessarily reflect the position or the policy of the Government or the Regents of the University of California, and no official endorsement should be inferred.

REFERENCES

1. Craig K. Abbey, Frank W. Samuelson, Adam Wunderlich, Lucretiu M. Popescu, Miguel P. Eckstein, and John M. Boone. 2015. Approximate maximum likelihood estimation of scanning observer templates. In *SPIE Medical Imaging*. International Society for Optics and Photonics, 94160O–94160O.
2. Ulf Ahlstrom. 2005. Subjective workload ratings and eye movement activity measures. (2005).
3. Sea Applications Center Air, Land. 2006. FM 3-04.15, Tactics, Techniques, and Procedures for the Tactical Employment of Unmanned Aircraft Systems (UAS). (2006).
4. Kate Alexander. 2010. Reducing error in radiographic interpretation. *The Canadian Veterinary Journal* 51, 5 (2010), 533.
5. Adam T. Biggs and Stephen R. Mitroff. 2015. Improving the efficacy of security screening tasks: A review of visual search challenges and ways to mitigate their adverse effects. *Applied Cognitive Psychology* 29, 1 (2015), 142–148.
6. Katherine L. Bouman, Michael D. Johnson, Daniel Zoran, Vincent L Fish, Sheperd S Doeleman, and William T Freeman. 2015. Computational Imaging for VLBI Image Reconstruction. *arXiv preprint arXiv:1512.01413* (2015).
7. Susan E Brennan, Xin Chen, Christopher A Dickinson, Mark B Neider, and Gregory J Zelinsky. 2008. Coordinating cognition: The costs and benefits of shared gaze during collaborative search. *Cognition* 106, 3 (2008), 1465–1477.
8. Zoya Bylinskii, Adrià Recasens, Ali Borji, Aude Oliva, Antonio Torralba, and Frédo Durand. 2016. Where should saliency models look next?. In *European Conference on Computer Vision*. Springer, 809–824.
9. Mary L. Cummings, Sylvain Bruni, and Paul J. Mitchell. 2010. Human supervisory control challenges in network-centric operations. *Reviews of Human Factors and Ergonomics* 6, 1 (2010), 34–78.
10. Arturo Deza and Miguel P. Eckstein. 2016. Can Peripheral Representations Improve Clutter Metrics on Complex Scenes?. In *Neural Information Processing Systems*.
11. Ivan Diaz, Miguel P Eckstein, Anaïs Luyet, Pierre Bize, and François O Bochud. 2012. Measurements of the

detectability of hepatic hypovascular metastases as a function of retinal eccentricity in CT images. In *SPIE Medical Imaging*. International Society for Optics and Photonics, 83180J–83180J.

12. Birsen Donmez, Patricia E Pina, and ML Cummings. 2009. Evaluation criteria for human-automation performance metrics. In *Performance Evaluation and Benchmarking of Intelligent Systems*. Springer, 21–40.
13. Trafton Drew, Melissa Le-Hoa Vo, Alex Olwal, Francine Jacobson, Steven E Seltzer, and Jeremy M Wolfe. 2013. Scanners and drillers: Characterizing expert visual search through volumetric images. *Journal of vision* 13, 10 (2013), 3–3.
14. Leila H Eadie, Paul Taylor, and Adam P Gibson. 2012. A systematic review of computer-assisted diagnosis in diagnostic cancer imaging. *European journal of radiology* 81, 1 (2012), e70–e76.
15. Miguel P. Eckstein. 2011. Visual search: A retrospective. *Journal of Vision* 11, 5 (2011), 14–14.
16. Maryellen L Giger. 2014. Medical imaging and computers in the diagnosis of breast cancer. In *SPIE Optical Engineering+ Applications*. International Society for Optics and Photonics, 918908–918908.
17. Ian J Goodfellow, Jonathon Shlens, and Christian Szegedy. 2014. Explaining and harnessing adversarial examples. *arXiv preprint arXiv:1412.6572* (2014).
18. DM Green and JA Swets. 1966. Signal detection theory and psychophysics. 1966. *New York* 888 (1966), 889.
19. Kelly S Hale, Katie Del Giudice, Jesse Flint, Darren P Wilson, Katherine Muse, and Bonnie Kudrick. 2015. Designing, developing, and validating an adaptive visual search training platform. In *International Conference on Augmented Cognition*. Springer, 735–744.
20. Tim Halverson and Anthony J Hornof. 2011. A computational model of âĂIJactive visionâĂİ for visual search in human–computer interaction. *Human–Computer Interaction* 26, 4 (2011), 285–314.
21. Kaiming He, Xiangyu Zhang, Shaoqing Ren, and Jian Sun. 2015. Deep residual learning for image recognition. *arXiv preprint arXiv:1512.03385* (2015).
22. David C. Klein. 2014. *Using Adaptive Automation to Increase Operator Performance and Decrease Stress in a Satellite Operations Environment*. Ph.D. Dissertation. Colorado Technical University.
23. Kathryn Koehler, Fei Guo, Sheng Zhang, and Miguel P Eckstein. 2014. What do saliency models predict? *Journal of vision* 14, 3 (2014), 14–14.
24. Ian Krajbich and Antonio Rangel. 2011. Multialternative drift-diffusion model predicts the relationship between visual fixations and choice in value-based decisions. 108, 33 (2011), 13852–13857.
25. Alex Krizhevsky. 2009. Learning multiple layers of features from tiny images. (2009).
26. Alex Krizhevsky, Ilya Sutskever, and Geoffrey E Hinton. 2012. Imagenet classification with deep convolutional neural networks. In *Advances in neural information processing systems*. 1097–1105.
27. Yann LeCun, Yoshua Bengio, and Geoffrey Hinton. 2015. Deep learning. *Nature* 521, 7553 (2015), 436–444.
28. Yann LeCun, Léon Bottou, Yoshua Bengio, and Patrick Haffner. 1998. Gradient-based learning applied to document recognition. *Proc. IEEE* 86, 11 (1998), 2278–2324.
29. Tsung-Yi Lin, Michael Maire, Serge Belongie, James Hays, Pietro Perona, Deva Ramanan, Piotr Dollár, and C Lawrence Zitnick. 2014. Microsoft coco: Common objects in context. In *European Conference on Computer Vision*. Springer, 740–755.
30. David Lyell and Enrico Coiera. 2016. Automation bias and verification complexity: a systematic review. *Journal of the American Medical Informatics Association* (2016), ocw105.
31. Sandra P. Marshall. 2002. The index of cognitive activity: Measuring cognitive workload. In *Human factors and power plants, 2002. proceedings of the 2002 IEEE 7th conference on*. IEEE, 7–5.
32. David E Meyer and David E Kieras. 1997. A computational theory of executive cognitive processes and multiple-task performance: Part I. Basic mechanisms. *Psychological review* 104, 1 (1997), 3.
33. Jiri Najemnik and Wilson S. Geisler. 2005. Optimal eye movement strategies in visual search. *Nature* 434, 7031 (2005), 387–391.
34. Anh Nguyen, Jason Yosinski, and Jeff Clune. 2015. Deep neural networks are easily fooled: High confidence predictions for unrecognizable images. In *2015 IEEE Conference on Computer Vision and Pattern Recognition (CVPR)*. IEEE, 427–436.
35. Aude Oliva, Michael L. Mack, Mochan Shrestha, and Angela Peeper. 2004. Identifying the perceptual dimensions of visual complexity of scenes.
36. Misha Pavel, Guoping Wang, and Kehai Li. 2003. Augmented cognition: Allocation of attention. In *System Sciences, 2003. Proceedings of the 36th Annual Hawaii International Conference on*. IEEE, 6–pp.
37. Eli Peli. 1990. Contrast in complex images. *JOSA A* 7, 10 (1990), 2032–2040.
38. Jeffrey R. Peters and Luca F. Bertuccelli. 2016. Robust Task Scheduling for Multi-Operator Supervisory Control Missions. *AIAA Journal on Aerospace Information Systems* (2016). To Appear.
39. Jeffrey R. Peters, Vaibhav Srivastava, Grant S. Taylor, Amit Surana, Miguel P. Eckstein, and Francesco Bullo. 2015. Human supervisory control of robotic teams: integrating cognitive modeling with engineering design. *IEEE Control Systems* 35, 6 (2015), 57–80.

40. Shaoqing Ren, Kaiming He, Ross Girshick, and Jian Sun. 2015. Faster R-CNN: Towards real-time object detection with region proposal networks. In *Advances in neural information processing systems*. 91–99.

41. Ruth Rosenholtz, Yuanzhen Li, and Lisa Nakano. 2007. Measuring visual clutter. *Journal of vision* 7, 2 (2007), 17–17.

42. Olga Russakovsky, Jia Deng, Hao Su, Jonathan Krause, Sanjeev Satheesh, Sean Ma, Zhiheng Huang, Andrej Karpathy, Aditya Khosla, Michael Bernstein, and others. 2015. Imagenet large scale visual recognition challenge. *International Journal of Computer Vision* 115, 3 (2015), 211–252.

43. Mark W. Scerbo. 2001. Adaptive Automation. In *Neuroergonomics: The Brain At Work*, Raja Parasuraman and Matthew Rizzo (Eds.). 239–252.

44. Thom Shanker and Matt Richtel. 2011. In New Military, Data Overload Can Be Deadly. The New York Times. (January 16, 2011).

45. Karthikeyan Shanmuga Vadivel, Thuyen Ngo, Miguel Eckstein, and B.S. Manjunath. 2015. Eye tracking assisted extraction of attentionally important objects from videos. In *Proceedings of the IEEE Conference on Computer Vision and Pattern Recognition*. 3241–3250.

46. Thomas B. Sheridan. 1992. *Telerobotics, Automation, and Human Supervisory Control*. MIT press.

47. Karen Simonyan and Andrew Zisserman. 2014. Very deep convolutional networks for large-scale image recognition. *arXiv preprint arXiv:1409.1556* (2014).

48. Yuan-Chi Tseng and Andrew Howes. 2015. The adaptation of visual search to utility, ecology and design. *International Journal of Human-Computer Studies* 80 (2015), 45–55.

49. US Air Force. 2010. *Report on technology horizons, a vision for Air Force Science And Technology during 2010–2030*. Technical Report. AF/ST-TR-10-01-PR, United States Air Force. Retrieved from http://www.af.mil/shared/media/document/AFD-100727-053.pdf.

50. François Vachon and Sébastien Tremblay. 2014. What Eye Tracking Can Reveal about Dynamic Decision-Making. In *Int. Conference on Applied Human Factors and Ergonomics*. Kraków, Poland, 3820–3828.

51. Marlies E. van Bochove, Lise Van der Haegen, Wim Notebaert, and Tom Verguts. 2013. Blinking predicts enhanced cognitive control. *Cognitive, Affective, & Behavioral Neuroscience* 13, 2 (2013), 346–354.

52. Carl Vondrick, Donald Patterson, and Deva Ramanan. 2013. Efficiently scaling up crowdsourced video annotation. *International Journal of Computer Vision* 101, 1 (2013), 184–204.

53. Carl Vondrick and Deva Ramanan. 2011. Video Annotation and Tracking with Active Learning. In *NIPS*.

54. Thomas D. Wickens. 2001. *Elementary signal detection theory*. Oxford university press.

55. Jeremy M. Wolfe. 2012. When do I quit? The search termination problem in visual search. In *The influence of attention, learning, and motivation on visual search*. Springer, 183–208.

56. Chen-Ping Yu, Wen-Yu Hua, Dimitris Samaras, and Greg Zelinsky. 2013. Modeling clutter perception using parametric proto-object partitioning. In *Advances in Neural Information Processing Systems*. 118–126.

57. Yanxia Zhang, Ken Pfeuffer, Ming Ki Chong, Jason Alexander, Andreas Bulling, and Hans Gellersen. 2016. Look together: using gaze for assisting co-located collaborative search. *Personal and Ubiquitous Computing* (2016), 1–14.

Steering Through Sequential Linear Path Segments

Shota Yamanaka
Meiji University and JSPS
Nakano, Tokyo, Japan
stymnk@meiji.ac.jp

Wolfgang Stuerzlinger
Simon Fraser University
Vancouver, Canada
w.s@sfu.ca

Homei Miyashita
Meiji University
Nakano, Tokyo, Japan
homei@homei.com

ABSTRACT

The steering law models human motor performance and has been verified to hold for a single linear and/or circular path. Some extensions investigated steering around corners. Yet, little is known about human performance in navigating joined linear paths, i.e., successions of path segments with different widths. Such operations appear in graphical user interface tasks, including lasso operations in illustration software. In this work, we conducted several experiments involving joined paths. The results show that users significantly changed their behavior, and that this strategy change can be predicted beforehand. A simple model summing the two indexes of difficulty (*ID*s) for each path predicts movement time well, but more sophisticated models were also evaluated. The best model in terms of both of R^2 and *AIC* values includes the *ID* of the crossing operation to enter the second path.

Author Keywords

Steering law; graphical user interfaces; pointing; human performance; modeling; motor control.

ACM Classification Keywords

H.5.2. [Information interfaces and presentation]: User Interfaces - Input devices and strategies.

INTRODUCTION

The steering law was derived to model complicated tasks, such as writing a character, drawing a line, and navigating a path [1]. As one of the more robust models for human motor performance, the steering law has been verified to hold with various types of computer input devices [2, 25], various conditions such as 3D operations [7, 18] and even virtual reality car driving [31].

One goal of our work is to test the generality of the steering law. For example, it is interesting to see if it holds across different age groups [23] or to study the effects of the dominant hand [15]. In this paper, we investigate how well the steering law predicts sequences of path segments, i.e., joined paths. Except for a few studies, previous work usually conducted user experiments with a single linear and/or a circular tunnel. The only exploration beyond this focused on path segments joined at a corner. We could not find any study focusing on the application of the steering law for collinear paths with different widths. While navigating through paths that change width is an operation that occurs in graphical user interface (GUI) applications, no one has investigated how well the steering law predicts performance for such tasks.

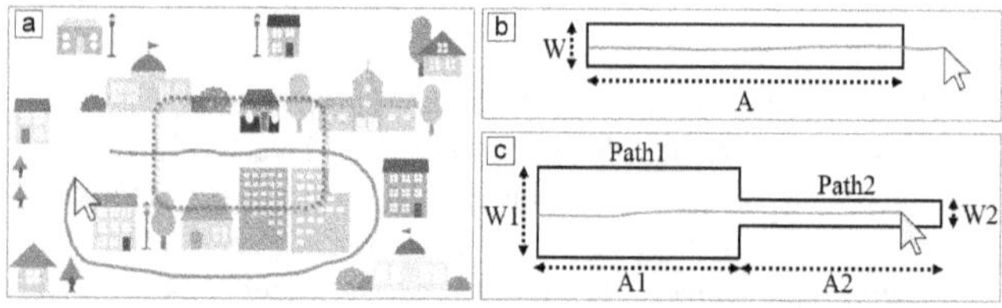

Figure 1. (a) A lasso operation (shown) as a green line. The part of the stroke highlighted in red traverses a tunnel with changing width (wide-to-narrow). (b) The steering law models strokes through a constant-width path. (c) Our work investigates steering through joined linear path segments with different widths, such as a wide-to-narrow path.

A more general form of a steering task is selecting objects in a drawing application through a lasso operation as shown in Figure 1a. When a user lassoes several objects, s/he must perform a sequence of steering operations through paths of varying widths and corners. Most previous literature on the steering law has focused on navigation through a single path segment, as shown in Figure 1b. User behaviors and strategies for navigation through more than one path segment (apart from corners) have not been analyzed in detail. As a first step towards a more general form of the steering law, we conduct several experiments for steering tasks involving two joined linear path segments (Figure 1c). The contributions of our work are as follows:

1) Based on a speed profile analysis of cursor trajectories, we identify that users change their movement strategies (a) in the presence of a path joint and (b) based on the width difference between two path segments.

2) We observed high fitness values in our experiments for a simple model that sums the two indexes of difficulty (*ID*s) for each segment to model the movement time (*MT*) for the entire path. Yet, taking the crossing operation to enter the second path segment (path2) into account improves the model fitness in both terms of R^2 and Akaike information criterion (*AIC*) values.

CHI 2017, May 06-11, 2017, Denver, CO, USA
ACM 978-1-4503-4655-9/17/05.
http://dx.doi.org/10.1145/3025453.3025836

3) We also show that even when the two path segments have different lengths, the structure of the steering law automatically balances the weights for each segment on the entire *ID*.

RELATED WORK

While we introduced a lasso operation as an example of various types of stroking motions, in this paper we focus only on steering through two joined linear path segments. In this section and afterwards, *a*, *b*, *c*, and *d* in equations are empirically determined constants.

Steering Law Model

Laws of steering have been proposed by Rashevsky [20, 21] for car driving and Drury [11] for pen drawing. For GUI operations, Accot and Zhai represents a relationship between the movement time *MT* required to traverse a path with length *A* and width *W* [1]:

$$MT = a + b\frac{A}{W} \tag{1}$$

and *A*/*W* is also known as the index of difficulty (*ID*). This relationship was first confirmed using an indirect-input pen tablet [1] and subsequently for other computer input devices [2, 25]. Changes of the motor scale [3], start position [32], temporal constraint (time limit) [33], and path angle [27] were also tested. 3D manipulations [7, 18] and car driving [31] follow the steering law too.

Accot and Zhai also proposed that the average cursor speed *v* in the path linearly increases as its width increases [1]:

$$v = a + bW \tag{2}$$

where the *v* is *A*/*MT*.

A circular path with radius *r* can be modeled by replacing *A* with $2\pi r$ in Equation 1 [2, 3]. Models for linearly-narrowing paths [1], widening spiral paths [1], and the *MT* difference between linearly-narrowing and widening paths [30] have been presented. In this paper, we investigate only constant-width linear path segments.

Other Models for Steering Tasks

Modeling Steering Tasks with Pointing

When a user selects an item in cascading menus, s/he has to move the cursor within the boundaries and then click the intended item. This is called a targeted steering motion [9, 17, 24]. We discuss three models for such motions in detail, because we will later derive new models for joined paths from them in the discussion.

For pointing tasks, selecting a target of size *S*, which lies a distance *A* away, requires a movement time *MT*:

$$MT = a + b\log_2\left(\frac{A}{S} + 1\right) \tag{3}$$

and $\log_2(A/S + 1)$ is also called the *ID* of Fitts' law [12]. Dennerlein et al. proposed a model for targeted steering tasks with separated terms for the *ID* of the steering (ID_S) and pointing (ID_P) components [9]:

$$MT = a + bID_S + cID_P \tag{4}$$

Their results showed good fits with $R^2 \geq 0.98$. Kulikov and Stuerzlinger proposed a simpler model which sums ID_S and ID_P directly [17]:

$$MT = a + b(ID_S + ID_P) \tag{5}$$

This model was created to reduce the number of parameters in Dennerlein's model. Even for a model with few parameters, any extra free parameter naturally increases correlation but introduces overfitting [8, 17, 26], resulting in potentially inaccurate predictions of *MT*.

Senanayake et al. showed that ID_S and ID_P affect the total *MT* differently and thus simple sum of two *ID*s in Dennerlein's and Kulikov's methods cannot model more general path/target parameters [24]. They then proposed a model which separates the steering and the pointing phases, and which weighs *ID*s on the entire *MT*. In this model, a user is predicted to move the cursor without hitting the boundaries of the path for a distance of $(A - nW)$ at first, and then directly points to the final target, which lies a distance of $(nW + S/2)$ away, as illustrated in Figure 2:

$$MT = a + b\left(\frac{A - nW}{W}\right) + c\log_2\left(\frac{2(nW + S/2)}{S}\right) \tag{6}$$

In their results, $n = 5$ was an appropriate choice, based on Thibbotuwawa et al. [28] results. In Thibbotuwawa et al.'s work, they tested various combinations of *A* and *W* values, and confirmed that users do not need to perform the closed-loop steering phase when *A*/*W* is less than 5 [28]. Based on this observation, Equation 6 was derived, which models that users switch to target pointing at a distance of $5 \times W$ from the end. The *ID* for the pointing phase in Senanayake's model is based on a different formulation of Fitts' law:

$$MT = a + b\log_2\left(\frac{2(A + S/2)}{S}\right) \tag{7}$$

Senanayake et al. found that Equation 6 models targeted steering tasks better than Dennerlein's and Kulikov's work.

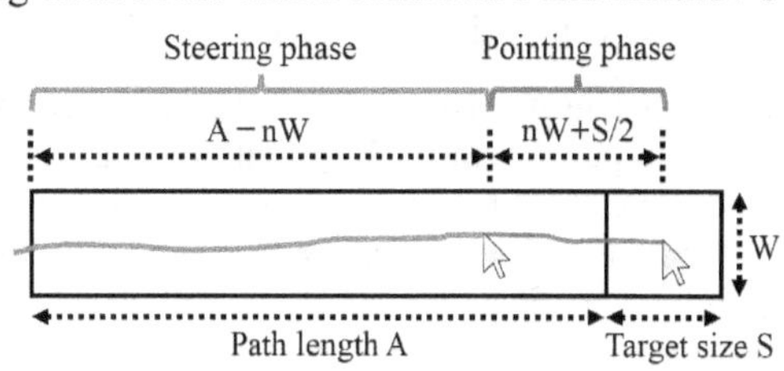

Figure 2. Two-phase model for targeted steering motion by Senanayake et al. [24].

Modeling Steering Tasks with Steering

Pastel found that when navigating a path with a corner in the middle, users steered in the first path segment, then stopped at the corner, and then steered again in the second path segment [19]. Hence, passing through a tunnel whose center bends at a certain angle (45°, 90°, and 135°) can be predicted to require the time *MT*:

$$MT = a + bID_S + cID_P \tag{8}$$

where ID_P uses *A*/2 for the target distance. Pastel's experiment did not include conditions where the two path segments had different widths. In addition, this work did not verify model generality for the case of angle = 0°. We assume that a path with no bending (a 0°-corner) does not follow Pastel's model because users will not perform a stopping operation during their traversal of such a path.

Bateman et al. conducted steering law experiments in a racing video game [5]. The racing courses included three straight tracks connected by two 90° corners. Although they were aware of Zhai et al.'s driving experiments [31], they unfortunately did not show or discuss the fit of the steering law for their data.

In summary, navigating two linear path segments with different widths connected in a straight line (i.e., at 0° bend) cannot be directly expressed by previous models. The simplest way involving the least additional parameters would be to add the *ID* of the first (ID_1) and the second path segment (ID_2), similar to Kulikov's method:

$$MT = a + bID_{2SS} \tag{9}$$

$$ID_{2SS} = ID_1 + ID_2 \tag{10}$$

We call this the ID_{2SS} model, as it includes two free parameters for a combination of a steering and a steering task. This model can also be derived from the global form of the steering law [1]:

$$MT = a + b\int_0^A \frac{dx}{W(x)} \tag{11}$$

where *A* is the total path length, *x* is a position in the path, and *W*(*x*) is the path width at *x*. According to this global law, the total *ID* of joined path segments is the sum of each *ID* of all the paths. If the ID_{2SS} model does not fit to the experimental data, we have to consider other models or additional free parameters. The comparison with other possible models will be discussed in *Overall Discussion*.

We assume that users' strategies could be different from that in a single path segment. E.g., with only a single path segment, the speed in the tunnel is expected to be constant per the steering law. The instantaneous speed *v* in a path is then determined by the path width *W*, as follows [1]:

$$v = \frac{W}{\tau} \tag{12}$$

where τ is the empirically determined time constant. On the other hand, if two path segments are joined, where the first path segment (path1) width W_1 is 50 pixels and the second (path2) width W_2 is 25 pixels (*narrowing* condition), a user has to decelerate in advance of the joint because the speed in path1 is faster than that of path2 according to Equation 12. The opposite condition (*widening*) might show different characteristics than *narrowing*. This asymmetric behavior cannot be predicted through the original steering law. Thus, the relationship of *MT* and *ID* might not hold for joined path segments with different widths. To address this potential shortcoming, we present here several experiments and, based on the results, discuss suitable steering models.

BASELINE EXPERIMENT 1: LINEAR PATH NAVIGATION

To establish a *baseline* for later comparisons of user strategies and behaviors, we first conducted a traditional steering law experiment involving a single linear path.

Apparatus

The PC was a Sony Vaio Z (Intel Core i7-5557U, 3.1 GHz; Intel Iris 6100; 16 GB; Windows 10). The input device and display was a Wacom Cintiq 27 QHD Touch DTK-2700/K0 (27" diagonal, 2560 × 1440 resolution, 596.7 × 335.6 mm active input area, 4.29 pixels/mm). The experimental system implemented with Hot Soup Processor 3.4 used full-screen mode. The system reads and processes input at approximately 125 times per second. The pen tablet was positioned on a table in "stand" mode (20 degrees, Figure 3). All participants wore a cotton artist glove to reduce friction. Participants were informed that their palms could touch the surface, as we had disabled finger touch sensing.

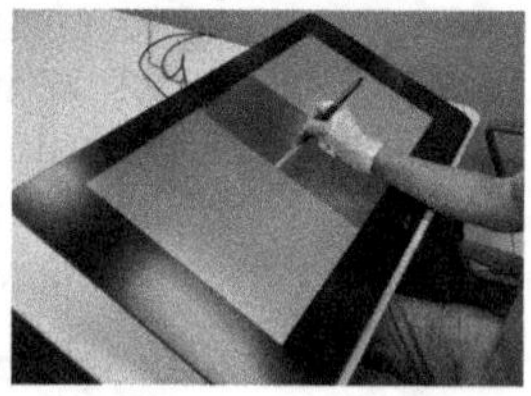

Figure 3. Experimental setting.

Participants

Thirteen volunteers participated in the experiment, of which three were female and ten male. The average age was 21.9 years (*SD* = 2.15). All participants had normal or corrected-to-normal vision and were right-handed. Three participants had 1 to 7 years of experience with using a stylus habitually.

Task

We reused the color scheme from previous work for the task areas: a blue starting area, a white path, and a green end area [16, 30]. The participants made a stroke within the white path as quickly and accurately as possible. A crosshair cursor left a trace from the moment of pen contact until lift-off. A bell sound was made when the cursor crossed the end line. A beep sounded when the cursor went over the path constraint. Then the participant had to retry the same task again. Going across the boundaries was counted as a steering error [3, 30], but lifting the pen tip during a trial was not considered an error. Still, if a user lifted the pen tip, the trial was suspended, and the participant had to redo the task again. Re-starting within a path or hovering was not permitted.

Design and Procedure

Two movement distances (*A* = 480 and 640 pixels, or 112 and 149 mm respectively) and four path widths (*W* = 15, 23, 33, and 45 pixels, or 3.50, 5.36, 7.69, and 10.5 mm respectively) were tested. The total number of combinations of the parameters was $2(A) \times 4(W) = 8$. *ID*s ranged from 10.7 to 42.7 bits. One *block* consists of a random order of the 8 conditions. Participants first performed one practice block, and then ten blocks for data collection. Movement direction was always to the right. The recorded data for the actual tasks were 8 conditions × 10 blocks × 13 participants = 1040 trials. Participants took 6 to 7 minutes from the instructions to the completion of all tasks.

Results

After excluding lifting-pen instances (six trials), the total number of trials was 1079, with 39 steering errors (3.61%). Following previous work [1, 2, 3, 3029], we analyzed only error-free trials via repeated-measures ANOVA with a Bonferroni post hoc test. The speed profiles for experiment 1 will be analyzed with the results of experiment 2 later.

Movement Time MT

Figure 4a-c show the average *MT*. We observed main effects for *A* ($F_{1,12} = 87.607$, $p < .001$) and *W* ($F_{3,36} = 48.130$, $p < .001$). The post hoc test shows that navigation time increases as *A* increases ($p < .001$) and *W* decreases ($p < .001$ for all *W* pairs). We also observed a significant interaction of $A \times W$ ($F_{3,36} = 33.095$, $p < .001$); the *MT* difference between two *A* values decreases as *W* increases (Figure 4c). These tendencies are consistent with previous steering law studies with a stylus.

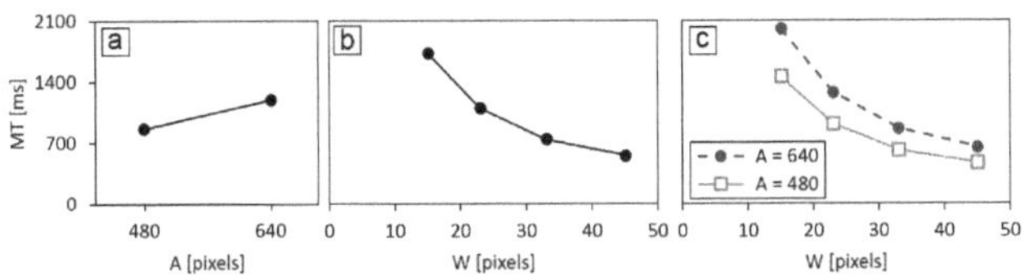

Figure 4. *MT* for (a) *A*, (b) *W*, and (c) *A* × *W* values.

Errors

We observed main effects for *A* ($F_{1,12} = 10.749$, $p < .01$) and *W* ($F_{3,36} = 9.768$, $p < .001$). We also observed a significant interaction of $A \times W$ ($F_{3,36} = 9.141$, $p < .001$). Averaged error rates were 1.52 and 5.63% for $A = 480$ and 640 pixels; 4.24, 2.80, 0.192, and 0% for $W = 15$, 23, 33, and 45 pixels, respectively.

Model Fitting

Figure 5a and b show that steering law held with excellent fits of $R^2 > 0.99$ for *MT* (Equation 1) and *v* (Equation 2) forms using eight $A \times W$ data points. This means that the experimental conditions of *A* and *W* values, and device, were all suitable for steering law tasks.

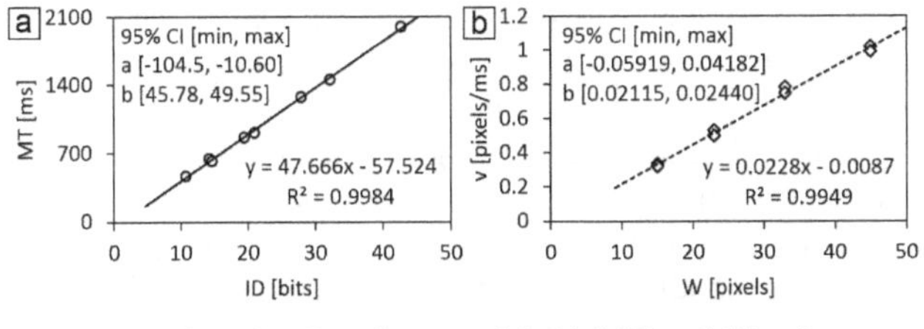

Figure 5. Steering law fitness with (a) *MT* and (b) *v* forms.

EXPERIMENT 2: NAVIGATING TWO JOINED PATH SEGMENTS WITH SAME LENGTHS AND DIFFERENT WIDTHS

The purpose of this experiment was to observe the effects of a joint between two path segments on users' behaviors and model fitness. To increase internal validity, we simply connected two paths used in the experiment 1. This study was conducted directly after experiment 1 using the same apparatus and the same 13 participants.

Design and Procedure

The same values of *A* and *W* were used in this experiment; *A* (A_1 and A_2) = 480 and 640 pixels, and *W* (W_1 and W_2) = 15, 23, 33, and 45 pixels. A_1 and A_2 were always the same value, while W_1 and W_2 were always different values, which excludes the (relatively uninteresting) condition of a normal (equal width) steering task. The total combinations of the parameters were $2(A) \times \{4(W_1) \times 4(W_2) - 4$ (excluding $W_1 = W_2)\} = 24$ conditions = 1 block. Participants first performed half a block (12 trials) in random order as a practice session, and then performed five blocks of actual trials. Movement direction was always to the right. The recorded data for the actual tasks were 24 conditions × 5 blocks × 13 participants = 1560 trials. The total time taken was 15 or 20 minutes. Two paths were connected at their centers on the y-axis as illustrated in Figure 1c, and the path segment joint was always located at the center of the display.

Results

After omitting lifting-pen instances (22 trials), the total number of trials was 1703, with 143 errors (8.40%). Below, we first analyze model fitness and present analyses of *MT* and error rates later.

Model Fitting

At first, we check whether the steering law holds for each of the two path segments (path1 and path2) separately. We then check whether the simple sum of two *ID*s (ID_{2SS}, Equation 9) model user performance for the entire path well.

With six data points, Figure 6a shows that the steering law held well for narrowing path sequences (i.e., $W_1 > W_2$). Figure 6b shows that the *widening* condition follows the law too. The fit without separating tunnel type (*narrowing* or *widening*) is not as good ($R^2 > 0.91$, Figure 6c). Thus, our hypothesis for a need to create a steering law for joined path segments is not strongly supported for the tested configurations. Figure 7a-c show the results of path2, and Figure 8a-c show the model fitness using the ID_{2SS} model.

Note that, the *"no separation"* graphs in Figure 6c, Figure 7c, and Figure 8c did not merge *MT* data with the same *ID* values. For example, in path1 (Figure 6), the times on *ID* = 19.4 bits were 1295 and 1037 ms for (a) *narrowing* and (b) *widening* respectively. If we use one merged point for *narrowing* and *widening* conditions on the same *ID* value, the *MT* for *no separation* is 1209 ms. The merged data is not the average of the two tunnel types, due to the different number of data points. The results for *no separation* using merged *MT* on the same *ID* are as follows:

Path1 time $MT = +294.2 + 45.92 \times ID$, with $R^2 = 0.981$

Path2 time $MT = -17.94 + 46.94 \times ID$, with $R^2 = 0.992$

Total time $MT = -137.3 + 55.51 \times ID$, with $R^2 = 0.995$

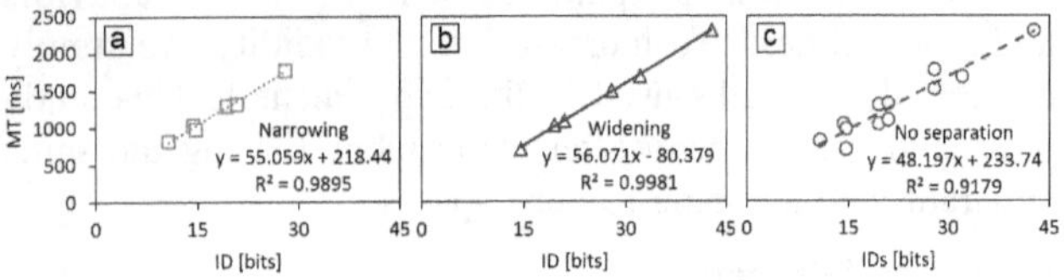

Figure 6. Model fitness of path1 in conditions of (a) narrowing, (b) widening, and (c) no separation of tunnel types.

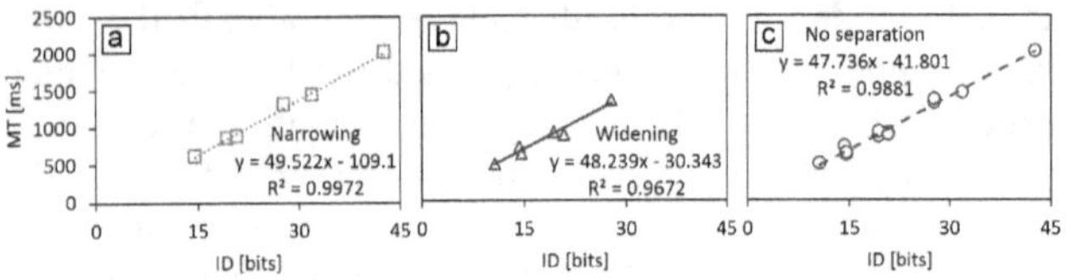

Figure 7. Model fitness of path2 in each condition.

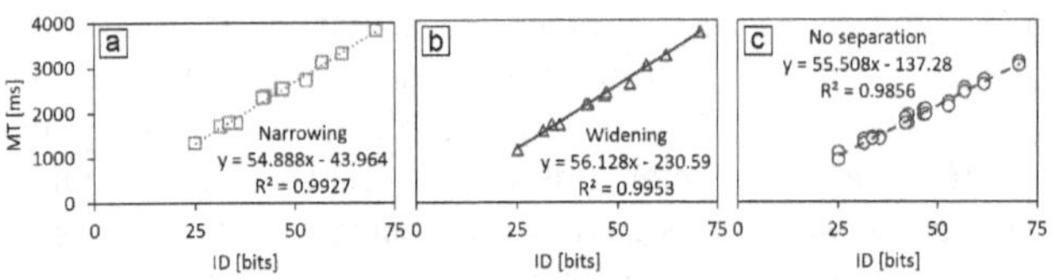

Figure 8. Model fitness of total times for each condition.

Movement Time MT

Because of the combinations of tunnel parameters, we cannot use an ANOVA with A, W_1, and W_2 as independent variables. For example, a condition of $W_1 = 15$ does not have $W_2 = 15$. In addition, (path1 × *narrowing*) and (path2 × *narrowing*) have different *ID* values (see Figure 6a and Figure 7a), and thus an ANOVA for separating path1 and path2 cannot use *ID* values as an independent variable. Therefore, we analyze only the total time using *tunnel type* (*narrowing* or *widening*) and ID_{2SS} as independent variables.

We observed main effects for *tunnel type* ($F_{1,12} = 15.405$, $p < .01$) and *ID* ($F_{11,132} = 41.969$, $p < .001$). The post hoc test shows that navigation for *narrowing* requires longer times, 2456 ms, compare to *widening*, 2326 ms ($p < .01$). The time required tends to grow with larger *ID* values.

Errors

We observed main effects for *tunnel type* ($F_{1,12} = 9.302$, $p < .05$) and *ID* ($F_{11,132} = 6.156$, $p < .001$). The post hoc test shows that the error rate for *narrowing*, 54/834 = 6.47%, is less than for *widening*, 89/869 = 10.2% ($p < .05$). The error rate tends to increase with larger *ID* values.

Discussion with Speed Profile Analysis

As shown in Figure 6-8, the steering law held reasonably well for all conditions in experiment 2. Hence, we wanted to analyze if users' strategies had not changed compared to those in experiment 1. To verify this question, we analyze the speed profiles for experiments 1 and 2 together.

A red line in Figure 9a shows the average speed profile on the x-axis for all participants under the condition of $A = 480$, $W_1 = 23$, and $W_2 = 15$ pixels in experiment 2. Because the raw data at the 8 ms sampling rate were very noisy and because we want to focus on the path segment joint, we re-sampled the cursor trajectories at every 40 pixels on the x-axis. The time for path1 ($W_1 = 23$) was 1323 ms, and for path2 ($W_2 = 15$) was 1444 ms. The two blue lines in Figure 9a show speeds in experiment 1 with the same width as path1 and path2 of experiment 2. The average times were 911 ms for $W = 23$ and 1451 ms for $W = 15$. The times for path2 in experiment 2 had only a small difference from the corresponding tasks in experiment 1 (7 ms, 0.77% longer), while the same correspondence in path1 shows a marked difference (412 ms, 45% longer).

A red line in Figure 9b shows the speed for the *widening* condition of $A = 480$, $W_1 = 15$, and $W_2 = 23$ pixels. Similar to the *narrowing* condition, the time for path1 of 1688 ms was significantly longer than that of experiment 1 (237 ms, 16% longer), while path2 with 890 ms was less than in experiment 1 (21 ms, 2.3% shorter).

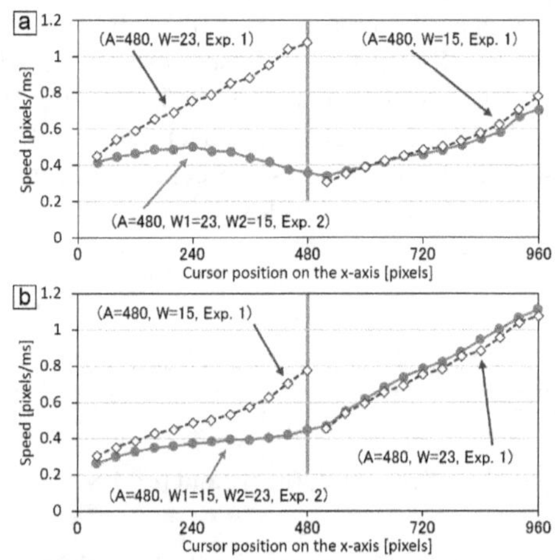

Figure 9. Red lines show the average speed profiles under the condition of $A = 480$, $W = 23$ and 15 for (a) *narrowing* and (b) *widening* path segments in experiment 2. Blue lines show the data from experiment 1. The green line at the center is the path joint. The speed at the start line is undefined.

At the start point of a path, it is natural that the speeds are slower than the top-speed for both *narrowing* and *widening*, because many users touched the surface with the stylus just before the start line and then gradually increased the speed. However, the speed at the first plot point in experiment 2 is slower than the speed at the start of experiment 1. This means that users anticipated the following path and they tried to limit their top speed at or even before the start. In addition, users changed their steering behaviors in the first path segment (path1) in the presence of a second path segment. Although the speed gradually increased until the end in experiment 1 (blue lines), in experiment 2 the speed began to decrease at x = 240 (the center of path1) for *narrowing* conditions. Furthermore, the top speed did not reach the same speed for a path with a width of 23 pixels compared to the speed of experiment 1. To be specific, users decreased the speed at around 0.36 pixels/ms before the joint as shown in Figure 9a. In the second path segment, they easily reached and then exceeded that speed. Thus, we speculate that users decreased their speed *more than necessary* in path1 in the presence of a second path segment.

Why did the users significantly reduce their speed in the presence of a subsequent path segment? Here, we explain these behaviors through referring to work outside of HCI, namely several studies of similar conditions in the psychophysics field: When a person walks on a path and has to pass through a gate, s/he rotate the shoulders if the gate width is less than 1.3 × shoulder width [29]. Obviously, there is no concern of hitting the gate for such a gate width, even if subtle movements of the body during walking are considered, but we still naturally rotate the body. Humans anticipate and prepare more than necessary in advance in order to avoid an accident. We fundamentally want to avoid errors and put in effort, even if the effort may be wasted later. Higuchi et al. performed another study on gate passing [14] where participants answered that they could pass through the gate at 2.8 m in front of the gate. They predicted that they could not pass through the gate if the width was less than 1.15 × shoulder width. Hence, they could not perfectly predict the gate width, and if that width would require shoulder rotation.

In summary, humans change their actual behavior to avoid errors, and the necessity of the behavior change is partially determined in advance. In our experiment 2, the excess speed reduction for the *narrowing* condition might occur to avoid going over the boundaries when entering path2. The long distance of the deceleration in advance of the segment joint can also be explained through the analogy with Higuchi et al.'s study; users reliably anticipate and determine whether they should change their later behavior (i.e., reduce their speed).

For other tunnel parameters not shown in Figure 9 we observed similar tendencies; speeds in path2 are close to the results of experiment 1; those in path1 for *narrowing* follow an inverted "U" shape; and speeds in path1 for *widening* gradually increase, but slower than for experiment 1.

Although users exhibited significantly different behaviors, the steering law still held for any conditions in experiment 2. Hence our results demonstrate an aspect of generality of the steering law: we can accurately predict the total time for the two joined two path segments.

However, this still poses additional questions. First, does the steering law fit hold for conditions with different path segment lengths, i.e., $A_1 \neq A_2$? Experiment 2 included only conditions with $A_1 = A_2$ because our purpose was to analyze the effects of the path segment joint in isolation. The simple sum of two *ID* values was sufficient to model the total performance for $A_1 = A_2$ conditions, but this might only hold if the weights of two *ID* values are equivalent. If the balance is broken, for example, $A_1 = 100$ and $A_2 = 400$ pixels, some appropriate weights could be needed, such as:

$$\frac{A_1}{A_1 + A_2} \times ID_1 + \frac{A_2}{A_1 + A_2} \times ID_2 \tag{13}$$

or,

$$A_1 \times ID_1 + A_2 \times ID_2 \tag{14}$$

Another question is if the steering law ID_{2SS} model applies for conditions with $W_1 = W_2$? Such conditions were omitted in experiment 2 to test only paths with a joint. If the results of constant-width path differ from those with a joint, we have to predict times with a separate model. To analyze the generality of the steering law for such conditions, we conducted another experiment.

EXPERIMENT 3: NAVIGATING TWO JOINED PATH SEGMENTS, INCLUDING CASES WHERE LENGTHS ARE DIFFERENT AND WIDTHS ARE EQUAL

The purpose of this experiment was to validate the applicability of the steering law for two joined path segments, including cases where lengths are different and widths are equal (i.e., one linear path). The same 13 participants joined, and the same apparatuses were used. Depending on each participant this study was conducted 12 to 20 days after experiment 1 and 2.

Design and Procedure

Figure 10 shows the path parameters in this experiment. Five A_1 values (150, 250, 400, 600, and 800 pixels, or 35.0, 58.3, 93.2, 140, and 186 mm respectively) and three W values for both W_1 and W_2 (15, 23, and 39 pixels, or 3.50, 5.36, and 9.09 mm respectively) were tested. A_2 was always 400 pixels. Thus, the ratio of A_1/A_2 was 0.375, 0.625, 1.00, 1.50, and 2.00, respectively. In this experiment we included conditions with the same values of W_1 and W_2. The total combinations of the parameters were $5(A_1) \times 1(A_2) \times 3(W_1) \times 3(W_2) = 45$ conditions = 1 block. Participants first performed 20 trials from these 45 conditions in random order as a practice session, and then performed four blocks as actual trials. Movement direction was always to the right. The recorded data for the actual tasks were 45 conditions × 4 blocks × 13 participants = 2340 trials. The total time taken was 20 or 25 minutes. The condition of *tunnel type* (*narrowing*, *widening*, and *constant*) was defined by the combination of W_1 and W_2. The two paths were joined at the centers on the y-axis, and the path joint always located at the center of the display.

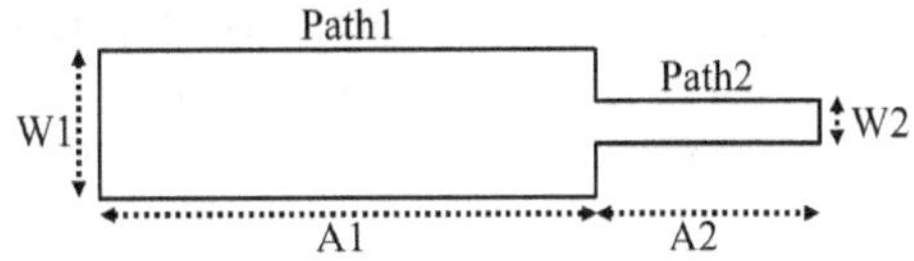

Figure 10. Parameter definition for experiment 3 with two joined path segments with unequal length. This image illustrates a condition with $A_1 > A_2$, and $W_1 > W_2$.

Results

After omitting lifting-pen instances (3 trials), the total number of trials was 2582, with 242 steering errors (9.37%). We cannot analyze the data using ID_{2SS} as an independent variable because the three *tunnel types* had different *IDs*. Hence, we compare *MT* and error rates using only *tunnel types*.

Movement Time MT

We observed a main effect of *tunnel type* ($F_{2,24} = 10.950, p < .001$). The average *MT* was 1735, 1643, and 1551 ms for *narrowing*, *widening*, and *constant* respectively. The post hoc test shows that navigation for *narrowing* requires longer times than constant ($p < .01$). The other pairs show no significant difference.

Errors

We observed no main effect of *tunnel type* ($F_{1,12} = 0.057, p = .945$). The results were 81/861 = 9.41% for *narrowing*, 79/859 = 9.20% for *widening*, 82/862 = 9.51% for *constant*.

Model Fitting

Figure 11a-c show that steering law held using 15 data points for each *tunnel type* ($R^2 > 0.95$), and Figure 11d shows a good fit using all 45 data points ($R^2 > 0.96$).

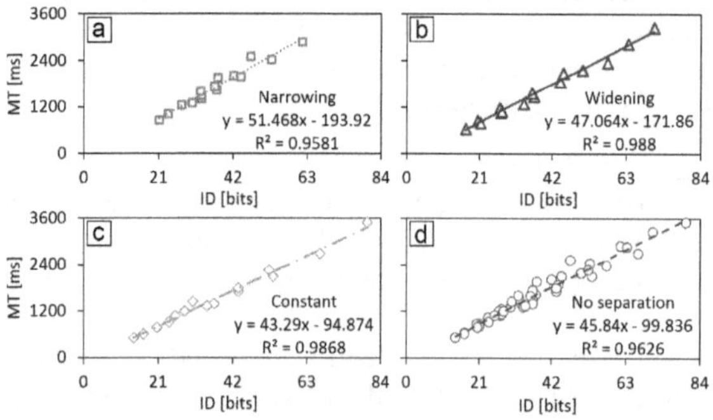

Figure 11. Model fitness in conditions of (a) *narrowing*, (b) *widening*, (c) *constant*, and (d) *no separation*.

Discussion with Speed Profile Analysis

Figure 12 shows the average speed profiles. We re-sampled at every 50 pixels as a common divisor of the five A_1 values, after confirming 25 pixels still showed noisy lines.

Figure 12a shows that users could not accelerate in the first path segment (path1) due to the extremely short distance. Also, the speed in path1 seems to adjust to an appropriate value to enter path2. This can be also confirmed by comparing to Figure 12e; the maximum speed in $A_1 = 800$ was 0.620 pixels/ms, while that in $A_1 = 150$ was 0.477 pixels/ms (23% slower). This means that the users cannot accelerate the cursor before the path ends, if A_1 is too short. Senanayake et al. [25] and Thibbotuwawa et al. [28] observed similar behaviors for a single linear path.

In joined path segments, the speed could not reach the appropriate value in the first segment, while the speed in the second one reached the appropriate value for W_2. Thus, users' performance seemed not to follow the steering law predicted by Equation 12. This breaks the consistency between path1 and path2. Furthermore, the average speed in path1 for *narrowing* condition differed strongly depending on the value of A_1. The speeds in path1 calculated via $A_1/(MT$ for path1) were 0.360, 0.393, 0.422, 0.432, 0.432 pixels/ms for $A_1 = 150$ to 800 pixels, respectively. The speed reached a constant value around $A_1 = 400$ or 600 pixels. On the other hand, for *widening* conditions, the speeds were 0.341, 0.358, 0.323, 0.338, 0.308 pixels/ms in path1 of $W_1 = 15$, which show no clear tendency of acceleration/deceleration with increasing A_1.

For the *constant* condition, as expected, the speeds generally increased like the results of experiment 1. In summary, clear differences are caused by the conditions of *tunnel type*, path length, and path width. Still, the steering law showed excellent fits for any situations in experiment 3. Therefore, we confirmed an aspect of generality of the steering law; in two joined linear path segments, the steering law holds regardless of the differences of path length and width, including equivalent lengths and widths.

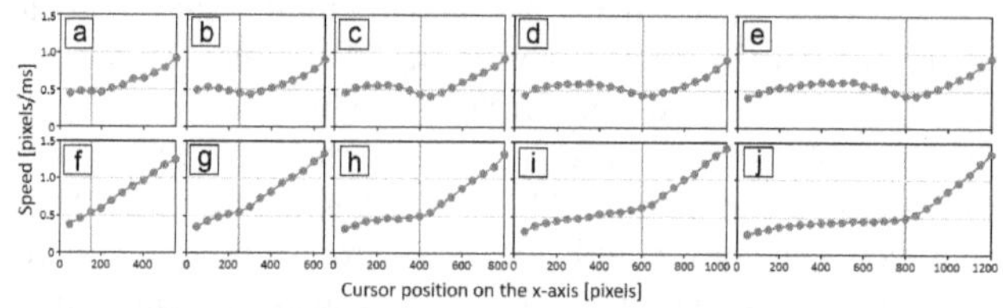

Figure 12. Average speed profiles under the condition of W = 23 and 15 for (top) *narrowing* and (bottom) *widening* conditions. (left to right) A_1 = 150 to 800 pixels respectively. Green lines at the center show the path joint.

OVERALL DISCUSSION

Auto-weight Function in Steering Law Structure

According to the results of experiments 2 and 3, the steering law ID_{2SS} held for two joined linear path segments. For a range of 0.375 to 2.00 for A_1/A_2, the robustness of the law was confirmed through accurate model fits. We speculated initially that the balance of ID_1 and ID_2 would break if the path lengths were different, but this hypothesis was not supported. Again, summing the two *IDs* means $ID_{2SS} = A_1/W_1 + A_2/W_2$. We consider that the structure of this sum itself has weights. For example, in a condition of $A_1 = 800$ and $A_2 = 400$ pixels, weights of 2:1 might be required. However, the ID_{2SS} model of $800/W_1 + 400/W_2$ already has appropriate weights through the two A factors. In hindsight, this "auto-weighting" function is inevitable due to the structure of the steering law. Yet this function had not been documented in the literature, likely because steering tasks with joined path segments have been not analyzed in detail.

Anticipation of the Following Path

Our hypothesis of that users change their behaviors affected by a path joint was strongly supported (Figure 9 and 12). Users determined the need to accelerate or decelerate by anticipating the following path segment being narrower/wider/equivalent compared to the current one.

Anticipation behaviors can be seen in the *narrowing* conditions more easily than the other ones. In a condition of $W_1 = 23$, $W_2 = 15$, and $A_1 = 600$ and 800 pixels in experiment 3, users began to decelerate about 250 pixels in advance of the joint (Figure 12d and e). Other parameter combinations of W and A showed different peak points (Figure 12a, b, and c). Can we define this peak-to-joint distance as the *anticipation distance* for entering the second segment? Yet, we can even observe that users determined the strategy to enter path2 *before* entering path1. As shown in Figure 9, users' behaviors in path1 were significantly affected by the presence of path2 compared to without it. Therefore, *anticipation distance* is not an appropriate name for the distance of peak-to-joint, which we term D_{PJ}.

How is this D_{PJ} determined by users? According to Equation 12, D_{PJ} depends on the paths widths; the current speed is proportional to the current width, and the distance to decelerate increases as the difference between the appropriate speeds in path1 and path2 becomes greater. To confirm this, we reanalyze the data of experiment 2, which tested four W values. Figure 13 shows conditions with W_2 = 15 pixels. We assumed that the peak in path1 appears earlier as W_1 increases, but the results do not show a clear relationship between D_{PJ} and W_1. Although deriving a model for the relationship between them would pose an interesting contribution to the field of human performance modeling, none of models we derived fitted the actual data of experiments 2 and 3 well. One reason is that a sampling distance of 40 or 50 pixels is comparatively coarse for path widths of 15 to 45 pixels. A finer sampling could reveal the speed characteristics for each condition better, but when data is noisy (spiky) it is harder to define a true peak.

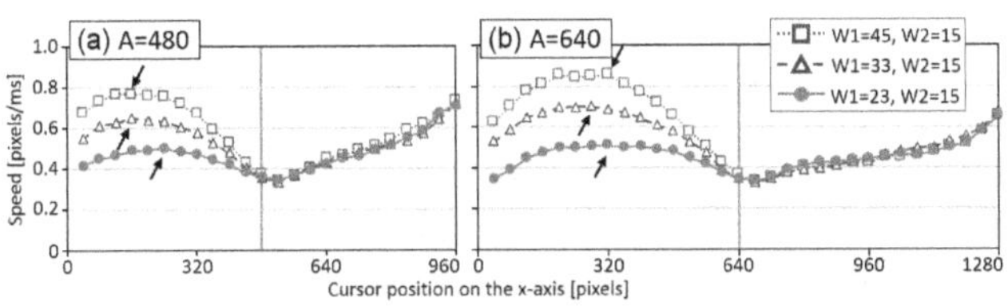

Figure 13. Average speed profiles of the *narrowing* condition in experiment 2. (a) A_1 = 480 and (b) A_2 = 640 pixels. Green lines show the path joint on the x-axis. Arrows indicate peaks in path1.

If A_1 is short, D_{PJ} has different characteristics. In the condition with $W_1 = 23$, $W_2 = 15$, and $A_1 = 150$ pixels, users had to set the speed for W_2 at the start (or even before the start) of path1, otherwise they would cause errors. Therefore, even if a model for D_{PJ} from path parameters is derived, the model could only adapt to conditions with sufficiently large values for A_1.

Although our experiments did not include a condition with various A_2 values, behaviors in path1 could also be affected by the value of A_2. Imagine an extreme condition: $A_2 = 30$ pixels for a *narrowing* condition. Here, users do not have to reduce the speed in path1 to pass through path2, and the task becomes close to a combination of a steering and a crossing [4] task.

Comparison with Other Models

The ID_{2SS} model accurately modeled steering through two joined paths segments. However, according to the speed profiles, user behaviors in joined paths were different from those in a single segment. Thus, we explore a model which reflects human behavior better than a sum of two ID values.

Weighted Models

The fitness of the weighted models are as follows: for experiment 2, R^2 = 0.986 and 0.908 (Equation 13 and 14, respectively), and for experiment 3, R^2 = 0.913 and 0.910. We assume that the reason behind the reduced fitness is that these models do not consider the user behaviors shown in Figure 9. Therefore, more sophisticated models are required to explain the users' behaviors.

Deriving Better Models for Users' Behaviors

Predictive model fitness cannot be discussed only through comparing R^2 values, because a complex model with many free parameters naturally increases the fit. Hence, we also compare with the Akaike information criterion (*AIC*) [6]. This statistics method balances the complexity of the model (i.e., number of free parameters) and the fitness, and determines the comparatively best model. As a brief explanation, a model with (a) lower *AIC* value is a better one, (b) $AIC \leq (AIC_{\text{minimum}} + 2)$ considers comparisons with better models, and (c) $AIC \geq (AIC_{\text{minimum}} + 10)$ is safely rejected. This analysis method was also used for selecting a pointing task model by Ren et al. [22] and Chapuis and Dragiceivc [8].

Another alternative candidate model is to use three free parameters for two steering *IDs*, similar to Dennerlein [9]:

$$ID_{3SS}\text{ model: } MT = a + b\left(\frac{A_1}{W_1}\right) + c\left(\frac{A_2}{W_2}\right)$$

and we call this the ID_{3SS} model. Next, we adapt Senanayake's model [24] to our experimental tasks. When a user navigates a single path, s/he can gradually accelerate and escape from the path (see blue lines in Figure 9). However, when s/he navigates two joined path segments, the speed in path1 cannot reach a speed comparable to that in a single path for both *narrowing* and *widening* conditions to correctly enter path2. Another way to state this is to say that a user reduces the speed to pass through the "gate" before entering the second segment. The preparation time to adjust the speed before entering the path2 is not modeled by the original steering law, and hence, the deceleration and longer times are unique characteristics of paths with joined segments. To take the time to enter the gate into account, it is reasonable to add a crossing time [4]. As illustrated in Figure 14, this motivates us to derive a model with three different performance phases. The core of this idea is that a user transits to a crossing operation for W_2 at a distance ($n \times W_1$) in advance of the joint (n is same as Senanayake's model). To cross a line of width W which lies at a distance A, we use the same formula as Fitts' law (Equation 3). Our new model for a combination of a steering, a crossing, and a steering task is:

$$MT = a + b\left(\frac{A_1 - nW_1}{W_1}\right) + c\log_2\left(\frac{nW_1}{W_2} + 1\right) + d\left(\frac{A_2}{W_2}\right)$$

	Model	a	b	c	d	R^2	AIC
Experiment 2	ID_{2SS}	-137.3 [-277.4, 2.883]	55.51 [52.54, 58.47]	—	—	0.986	290
	ID_{3SS}	-137.3 [-243.0, -31.51]	51.77 [48.88, 54.67]	59.24 [56.35, 62.13]	—	0.992	277
	ID_{4SCS}	-319.0 [-674.8, 36.90]	60.99 [53.32, 68.66]	187.5 [40.37, 334.7]	49.73 [41.85, 57.62]	0.994	272
	ID_{3SCS}	-67.71 [-189.0, 53.61]	55.45 [53.41, 57.48]	80.02 [47.30, 112.7]	—	0.996	272
Experiment 3	ID_{2SS}	-99.84 [-213.6, 13.92]	45.84 [43.06, 48.62]	—	—	0.963	578
	ID_{3SS}	-111.8 [-249.1, 25.46]	45.62 [42.48, 48.75]	46.75 [40.42, 53.08]	—	0.963	580
	ID_{4SCS}	-261.4 [-428.1, .94.70]	49.84 [47.03, 52.65]	228.3 [147.3, 309.3]	31.14 [23.82, 38.47]	0.979	556
	ID_{3SCS}	-115.1 [-295.1, 64.92]	45.97 [43.44, 48.49]	91.84 [33.66, 150.0]	—	0.970	571

Table 1. R^2 and AIC values for four candidate models. a, b, c, and d are constants with 95% CI values [min, max] in the models. Colored cells show the best values for each analysis method.

and we call this the ID_{4SCS} model. The difference from Senanayake's model is that a line to be crossed has no depth size S, as in pointing tasks. Another option is to add the two steering ID values as in the ID_{2SS} model:

$$MT = a + b\left(\frac{A_1 - nW_1}{W_1} + \frac{A_2}{W_2}\right) + c\log_2\left(\frac{nW_1}{W_2} + 1\right)$$

and we call this the ID_{3SCS} model.

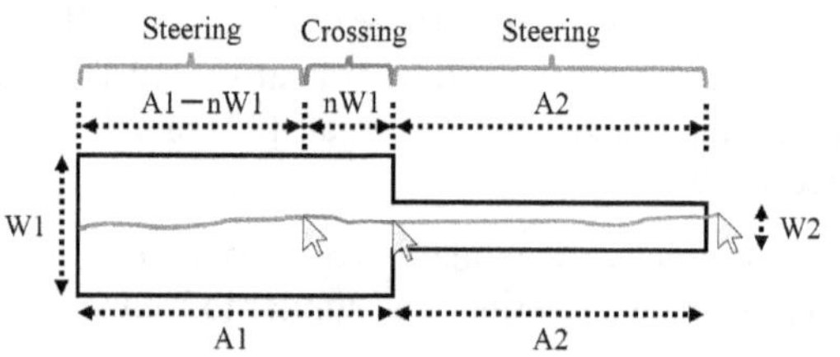

Figure 14. A model of two steering and one crossing phases.

As we explore models for the relationship between the total MT and path parameters, we analyze the composite of all data for experiments 2 and 3 (*no separation* conditions in Figure 8 and 11). Senanayake et al. showed that the fitness improved by changing the Fitts' ID model depending on target distances, and by changing the steering ID model when the ID was less than eight [24]. These alternatives were based on the fact that Fitts and steering IDs only depend on the distance A when A is small [13, 28]. However, for a fair comparison with the other models, we only use basic models of ID_{4SCS} and ID_{3SCS} models without changing the form of the ID. In our analysis, we fixed the n value to 5 as in previous work [24]. We observed that $(A_1 - nW_1)/W_1$ was sometimes negative in our ID_{4SCS} and ID_{3SCS} models, e.g., $A_1 = 150$, $W_1 = 39$, $n = 5$ results in –1.15. This can be explained by that users anticipated the joint even before the cursor entered path1. Because n was fixed, it was not counted as a free parameter in the AIC calculation.

Table 1 shows the result. Overall, the SCS models showed better fits than SS models. For SS models, 2SS showed a worse fit than 3SS for both R^2 and AIC values in experiment 2, and close fits in experiment 3. For SCS models, the difference in R^2 values was less than 1% in experiments 2 and 3. Yet, the AIC difference between 4SCS and 3SCS was more than 10 in experiment 3, with 4SCS being the better choice according to the AIC threshold criterion. In summary, although the SS models show good fits, taking the crossing operation between two steering operations into account provides even better predictions, with ID_{4SCS} being the best choice.

We also analyzed if the choice of n = 5 affected the outcome of our work. If we optimize n in the SCS models to maximize the R^2 value and to minimize the AIC value, their optimized values have little difference from those for n = 5. As these changes do not affect the overall conclusion on the model comparisons above, we conclude that the SCS models are not that sensitive to the n value, and this result justifies a previous study [24] which fixed the n value to 5.

Still, we initially believed that we could identify the true anticipation distance from the n value which optimizes the R^2 and AIC values. However, we found it quite difficult to clearly separate the steering and crossing phases, potentially because a steering operation can be interpreted as a sequence of crossing operations [1, 31]. Although determining the anticipation distance to pass through the gate is difficult, we conclude that adding a crossing term between two steering motions still improves model fitness.

While the SCS models explain the acceleration/deceleration behavior better, the difference in terms of ID between the SS and SCS models is small for experiment 2 and 3. Even when the crossing-ID was inserted, the replaced ID values were less than 3.5 bits, while experiment 3 explored IDs up to 80 bits. We assume that reason behind the small improvement of the model fitness comes from this small replacement of ID values.

Effects of Learning, Scaling, and Fatigue

In our study, user performance could be affected not only by A and W. For example, experiment 1 and 2 were performed first, and then experiment 3 was designed based on the results of these experiments. Thus, the order was not balanced, and learning effects could exist in our data

Another potential effect is scaling [3]. Experiment 1 involved (max) 149-mm lengths, which required mainly wrist movements with a forearm extension, while Experiment 3 included (max) 279.2-mm lengths, which can require upper-arm movements. Such greater motor movements could degrade the steering performance [3].

Fatigue can also have an effect. It took seven minutes for experiment 1 and 25 min for experiment 3. For these reasons, the validity of direct data comparisons (e.g., for performance or speed) is somewhat limited in our study.

Application

Based on the speed profile, a support system could predict if a user wants to enter a narrow path. Thus, forward objects could be shrunk temporarily during lassoing when a user decelerates. Figure 15 shows the procedure; a) when a user decelerates to enter a narrow path during making a lasso stroke, b) the forward objects shrink to decrease steering difficulty. If the user would not like to enter the narrow path (e.g., the user just wants to stop there to finish the lasso), the shrinking effect does not have a negative effect on the operation. We will evaluate this idea in the future.

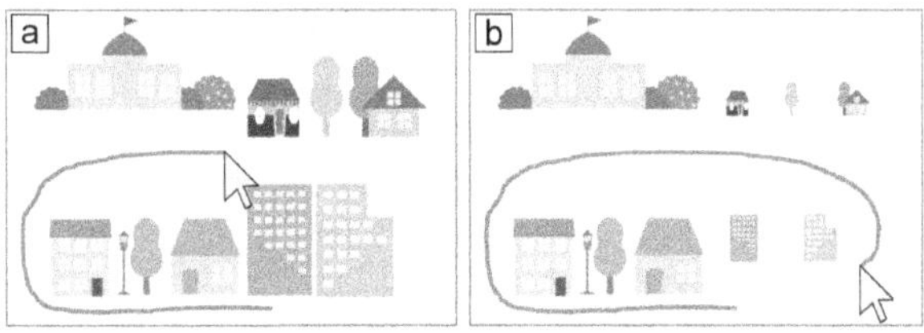

Figure 15. Facilitation system for lassoing tools. (a) When a user decelerates to enter the narrow path, (b) this system shrinks the objects in the (predicted) direction of the path.

Limitations and Future Work

The conditions tested in our experiments are still somewhat limited. Paths were only linear in shape and always connected at the center on the y-axis. Thus, the best strategy was moving the pen tip in the middle of the paths on the y-axis. If the two paths were connected at different positions, e.g., at the top as illustrated in Figure 16a, users' strategies would need to change. Here, some users might always navigate closely to the top boundary to reduce the total movement distance in the path like Figure 16a-(i). Others might navigate along the middle of path1, and then transit to the middle of path2 to avoid errors like Figure 16a-(ii).

The number of path segments is another limitation. We only tested two path segments with a single joint. In a condition where more paths are joined, different behaviors might be observed. As an extreme scenario, Figure 16b shows a sequentially connected repeated sequence of path1 (A_1, W_1) and path2 (A_2, W_2). Can we calculate the entire ID as (A_1/W_1 + A_2/W_2) × (number of path1 and path2), even if A_1 is short, e.g., 30 or 40 pixels? We assume that the entire ID becomes closer to the (entire length)/W_2 as A_1 becomes shorter, because the wider width of W_1 cannot be effectively used. Drewes presented this problem and made the same assumption [10]. Our experimental results support this hypothesis as follows: users have to avoid errors to accomplish steering tasks, and thus the speed in path1 must decrease to enter path2, based on the anticipatory behavior that we observed. If A_1 is short, because users anticipate the next path in advance of a joint, users have to continuously adjust the speed at the appropriate value for W_2, and thus the path width is expected to be always close to W_2. Further work is required to validate this hypothesis.

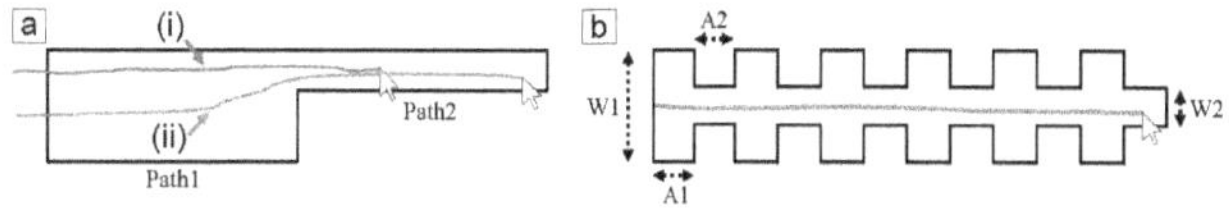

Figure 16. Two cases that our current work cannot describe adequately: (a) Steering through paths connected off-axis. (b) Steering through a sequence of six pairs of wide-to-narrow paths.

The four models derived in this paper accurately predict MT based on data for joined path segments. However, these models cannot predict MT for joined path segments from data for a single path, because slopes and intercepts of single and joined path segments are not similar (see Figure 5a and Table 1). To predict MT in joined path segments, we have to 1) measure MTs with various IDs in joined path segments, 2) regress the data (like Figure 11), and 3) use that to predict MT for a given ID value. We cannot predict MT from single path segment data, as the crossing-motion occurs only in joined path segments.

Our future work will also investigate a more general steering model that covers, e.g., linear, joined, and curved paths. In it, we might consider human-focused parameters, such as Higuchi et al.'s work on anticipation [14] and Zhou and Ren's work on subjective operational biases [34]. To achieve this goal, much more experimental work is needed.

CONCLUSION

We conducted several steering law experiments to investigate performance for steering tasks with two joined linear path segments. Users' behaviors significantly changed in the presence of a path joint, but a simple sum of two IDs for each path was enough to model the performance well. Four possible models were compared by the fitness using R^2 and AIC, and we identified model ID_{4SCS}, to be the best overall, as it takes account of the crossing operation required for entering the following path.

The speed profiles in joined path segments have not been studied before, nor have the speed differences from a single path segment and the reasons behind them been explored. Especially the deceleration data for narrowing conditions identifies fundamentally different behaviors relative to previous work. Our results thus provide a better understanding of steering motions, in particular for error avoidance strategies and anticipation of the successive path segment, which can be observed only in path sequences. In the future, we will investigate more complex conditions, including combinations of paths with changing widths and corners, towards a more general version of the steering law.

ACKNOWLEDGEMENTS

This work was supported by JSPS KAKENHI #15J11634. The first author also thanks his present affiliation, Yahoo Japan Corporation.

REFERENCES

1. Johnny Accot and Shumin Zhai. 1997. Beyond Fitts' law: models for trajectory-based HCI tasks. In *Proceedings of the SIGCHI Conference on Human Factors in Computing Systems* (CHI '97), 295–302. http://dx.doi.org/10.1145/258549.258760
2. Johnny Accot and Shumin Zhai. 1999. Performance evaluation of input devices in trajectory-based tasks: an application of the steering law. In *Proceedings of the SIGCHI Conference on Human Factors in Computing Systems* (CHI '99), 466–472. http://dx.doi.org/10.1145/302979.303133
3. Johnny Accot and Shumin Zhai. 2001. Scale effects in steering law tasks. In *Proceedings of the SIGCHI Conference on Human Factors in Computing Systems* (CHI '01), 1–8. http://dx.doi.org/10.1145/365024.365027
4. Johnny Accot and Shumin Zhai. 2002. More than dotting the i's --- foundations for crossing-based interfaces. In *Proceedings of the SIGCHI Conference on Human Factors in Computing Systems* (CHI '02), 73–80. http://dx.doi.org/10.1145/503376.503390
5. Scott Bateman, Andre Doucette, Robert Xiao, Carl Gutwin, Regan L. Mandryk, and Andy Cockburn. 2011. Effects of view, input device, and track width on video game driving. In *Proceedings of Graphics Interface* (GI '11), 207–214.
6. Kenneth P. Burnham and David R. Anderson. 1998. Model selection and multimodel inference: a practical information-theoretic approach. Springer. http://dx.doi.org/10.1002/sim.769
7. Géry Casiez, Patricia Plénacoste, and Christophe Chaillou. 2004. Does DOF separation on elastic devices improve user 3D steering task performance? In *Proceedings of the Asia Pacific Conference on Computer Human Interaction* (APCHI '04), 70–80. http://dx.doi.org/10.1007/978-3-540-27795-8_8
8. Olivier Chapuis and Pierre Dragicevic. 2011. Effects of motor scale, visual scale, and quantization on small target acquisition difficulty. *ACM Transactions on Computer-Human Interaction* (TOCHI), Vol.18, No.3, Article 13. http://dx.doi.org/10.1145/1993060.1993063
9. Jack Tigh Dennerlein, David B. Martin, and Christopher Hasser. 2000. Force-feedback improves performance for steering and combined steering-targeting tasks. In *Proceedings of the SIGCHI Conference on Human Factors in Computing Systems* (CHI '00), 423–429. http://dx.doi.org/10.1145/332040.332469
10. Heiko Drewes. 2013. A lecture on Fitts' law. http://www.cip.ifi.lmu.de/~drewes/science/fitts/A%20Lecture%20on%20Fitts%20Law.pdf
11. Colin G. Drury. 1971. Movements with lateral constraint. *Ergonomics*, Vo.14, No.2, 293–305. http://dx.doi.org/10.1080/00140137108931246
12. Paul M. Fitts. 1954. The information capacity of the human motor system in controlling the amplitude of movement. *Journal of Experimental Psychology*, Vol.47, No.6, 381–391. http://psycnet.apa.org/doi/10.1037/h0055392
13. Khai-Chung Gan and Errol R. Hoffmann. 1988. Geometrical conditions for ballistic and visually controlled movements. *Ergonomics*, Vol.31, No.5, 829–839. http://dx.doi.org/10.1080/00140138808966724
14. Takahiro Higuchi, Hajime Takada, Yoshifusa Matsuura, and Kuniyasu Imanaka. 2004. Visual estimation of spatial requirements for locomotion in novice wheelchair users. *Journal of Experimental Psychology: Applied*, Vol.10, No.1, 55–66. http://psycnet.apa.org/doi/10.1037/1076-898X.10.1.55
15. Errol R. Hoffmann. 1997. Movement time of right- and left-handers using their preferred and non-preferred hands. *International Journal of Industrial Ergonomics*, Vol.19, No.1, 49–57. http://dx.doi.org/10.1016/0169-8141(95)00092-5
16. Sergey Kulikov, I. Scott MacKenzie, and Wolfgang Stuerzlinger. 2005. Measuring the effective parameters of steering motions. In *Extended Abstracts of the SIGCHI Conference on Human Factors in Computing Systems* (CHI '05), 1569–1572. http://dx.doi.org/10.1145/1056808.1056968
17. Sergey Kulikov and Wolfgang Stuerzlinger. 2006. Targeted steering motions. In *Extended Abstracts of the SIGCHI Conference on Human Factors in Computing Systems* (CHI '06), 983–988. http://dx.doi.org/10.1145/1125451.1125640
18. Lei Liu, Jean-Bernard Martens, and Robert van Liere. 2011. Revisiting path steering for 3D manipulation tasks. *International Journal of Human-Computer Studies*, Vol.69, Issue 3, 170–181. http://dx.doi.org/10.1016/j.ijhcs.2010.11.006
19. Robert L. Pastel. 2006. Measuring the difficulty of steering through corners. In *Proceedings of the SIGCHI Conference on Human Factors in Computing Systems* (CHI '06), 1087–1096. http://dx.doi.org/10.1145/1124772.1124934
20. Nicolas Rashevsky. 1959. Mathematical biophysics of automobile driving. *Bulletin of Mathematical Biophysics*, Vol.21, No.4, 375–385. http://dx.doi.org/10.1007/BF02477896
21. Nicolas Rashevsky. 1970. Mathematical biophysics of automobile driving IV. *Bulletin of Mathematical Biophysics*, Vol.32, No.1, 71–78. http://dx.doi.org/10.1007/BF02476794

22. Xiangshi Ren, Jing Kong, and Xing-Qi Jiang. 2005. SH-model: a model based on both system and human effects for pointing task evaluation. *IPSJ Journal*, Vol.46, No.5, 1343–1353.
23. Xiangshi Ren and Xiaolei Zhou. 2011. An investigation of the usability of the stylus pen for various age groups on personal digital assistants. *Behaviour & Information Technology*, Vol.30, No.6, 709–726. http://dx.doi.org/10.1080/01449290903205437
24. Ransalu Senanayake, Errol R. Hoffmann, and Ravindra S. Goonetilleke. 2013. A model for combined targeting and tracking tasks in computer applications. *Experimental Brain Research*, Vol.231, No.3, 367–379. http://dx.doi.org/10.1007/s00221-013-3700-4
25. Ransalu Senanayake and Ravindra S. Goonetilleke. 2016. Pointing device performance in steering tasks. *Perceptual and Motor Skills*, Vol.122, No.3, 886–910. http://dx.doi.org/10.1177/0031512516649717
26. R. William Soukoreff, I. Scott MacKenzie. 2004. Towards a standard for pointing device evaluation, perspectives on 27 years of Fitts' law research in HCI. *International Journal of Human-Computer Studies*, Vol.61, No.6, 751–789. https://doi.org/10.1016/j.ijhcs.2004.09.001
27. Namal Thibbotuwawa, Ravindra S. Goonetilleke, and Errol R. Hoffmann. 2012. Constrained path tracking at varying angles in a mouse tracking task. *Human Factors*, Vol.54, No.1, 137–149. http://dx.doi.org/10.1177/0018720811424743
28. Namal Thibbotuwawa, Errol R. Hoffmann, and Ravindra S. Goonetilleke. 2012. Open-loop and feedback-controlled mouse cursor movements in linear paths. *Ergonomics*, Vol.55, No.4, 476–488. http://dx.doi.org/10.1080/00140139.2011.644587
29. William H. Warren Jr. and Suzanne Whang. 1987. Visual guidance of walking through apertures: body-scaled information for affordances. *Journal of Experimental Psychology: Human Perception and Performance*, Vol.13, No.3, 371–383. http://psycnet.apa.org/doi/10.1037/0096-1523.13.3.371
30. Shota Yamanaka and Homei Miyashita. 2016. Modeling the steering time difference between narrowing and widening tunnels. In *Proceedings of the SIGCHI Conference on Human Factors in Computing Systems* (CHI '16), 1846–1856. http://dx.doi.org/10.1145/2858036.2858037
31. Shumin Zhai, Johnny Accot, and Rogier Woltjer. 2004. Human action laws in electronic virtual worlds: an empirical study of path steering performance in VR. *Presence*, Vol.13, No.2, 113–127. http://dx.doi.org/10.1162/1054746041382393
32. Xiaolei Zhou, Xiangshi Ren, and Yue Hui. 2008. Effect of start position on human performance in steering tasks. In *Proceedings of the International Conference on Computer Science and Software Engineering* (CSSE '08), Vol.2, 1098–1101. http://dx.doi.org/10.1109/CSSE.2008.1310
33. Xiaolei Zhou, Xiang Cao, and Xiangshi Ren. 2009. Speed-accuracy tradeoff in trajectory-based tasks with temporal constraint. In *Proceedings of the IFIP International Conference on Human Computer Interaction* (INTERACT '09), 906–919. http://dx.doi.org/10.1007/978-3-642-03655-2_99
34. Xiaolei Zhou and Xiangshi Ren. 2010. An investigation of subjective operational biases in steering tasks evaluation. *Behaviour & Information Technology*, Vol.29, No.2, 126–135. http://dx.doi.org/10.1080/01449290701773701

Modeling User Performance on Curved Constrained Paths

Mathieu Nancel[1,2,4] **& Edward Lank**[1,3]
[1]Cheriton School of Computer Science, University of Waterloo, Canada
[2]Aalto University, Helsinki, Finland
[3]University of Lille & [4]Inria Lille, France
mathieu.nancel@inria.fr, lank@uwaterloo.ca

ABSTRACT

In 1997, Accot and Zhai presented seminal work analyzing the temporal cost and instantaneous speed profiles associated with movement along constrained paths. Their work posited and validated the *steering law*, which described the relationship between path constraint, path length and the temporal cost of path traversal using a computer input device (e.g. a mouse). In this paper, we argue that the steering law fails to correctly model constrained paths of varying, arbitrary curvature, propose a new form of the law that accommodates these curved paths, and empirically validate our model.

ACM Classification Keywords

H.5.2 User Interfaces

Author Keywords

Steering Law; Movement; Models.

INTRODUCTION

In Human-Computer Interaction (HCI) research, performance models, i.e. mathematical models that characterize the temporal or kinematic properties of actions, [1, 3, 6, 8, 15, 17], are a common area of inquiry. Models from psychology such as Fitts's Law [9] and the Hick Hyman Law [19] have been used to describe selection time (pointing or choice) in interfaces. HCI researchers have extended and leveraged these models in various ways: for example, models have been adapted to describe pointing time for bivariate targets [3], to characterize novice-to-expert transitions in interface manipulation [8], and to describe the behavior of pointing facilitation techniques [4]

In 1997, Jon Accot and Shumin Zhai [1, 2] developed a novel, temporal model that described the cost of traversing constrained paths, the *steering model*. The steering model relates the time taken to traverse a path to the length of the path and the tolerance, or width, of the path, i.e.

$$t = a + b\left(\frac{A}{W}\right) \qquad (1)$$

CHI 2017, May 06 - 11, 2017, Denver, CO, USA

ACM 978-1-4503-4655-9/17/05âĂę$15.00
DOI: http://dx.doi.org/10.1145/3025453.3025951

Here, A represents the length of the path and W represents the width of the path. The constant a represents additive factors in starting and stopping [15], and b is the reciprocal of the index of performance, a measure of the effectiveness of the input device. Accot and Zhai demonstrate that the steering model effectively predicts the temporal cost of straight, circular and spiral paths.

While the steering model is an appropriate representation of straight and circular paths, one open question is whether it can be generalized to represent paths of varying curvature. As Accot and Zhai note in their work leveraging the Steering Model to analyze paths [2], "One dimension that may affect steering difficulty but not modeled yet in the steering law is tunnel shape." Past work in psychology [12, 22, 21] and HCI [14] argues that variation in curvature has a non-linear effect on movement speed, and, by implication, time.

In this paper, we derive a generalization of the steering model designed to incorporate both variations in curvature and in width (or tolerance) that allows prediction of both the instantaneous speed and the overall temporal cost of paths of arbitrary width and curvature. Through our experiments we show high correlation with temporal cost and instantaneous speed for both touch and mouse input.

Is there call for a generalized steering model? We argue that there is, primarily because of the rise in popularity of touchscreen displays. Modern multi-touch tablets support two different input touches: taps and strokes. While unconstrained strokes have been effectively modeled, not every input stroke is unconstrained: In a cluttered display contacting other interface objects can cause movement or other disruptions that require rearrangement. From intelligent selection [14], to shape tracing [26], to difficulty measures in games [5], understanding movement models under constraint can be a useful tool to design interaction techniques or overall applications. As a result, we argue that the modeling of constrained, arbitrary paths represents a useful enhancement of our ability to model generalized input on computer displays.

The remainder of this paper is organized as follows. We first review the steering model formulation and related psychology and HCI work that models curved trajectories. Next we present a mathematical model of expected time for paths of arbitrary width/curvature combinations. We then describe our experiments and data, before concluding with a discussion of the implications of our work.

RELATED WORK

Steering Model

When moving toward a target along an unconstrained trajectory, movement follows a ballistic profile [10]. When constrained by endpoint, the kinematics [16, 18] and temporal cost of movement is described by Fitts's Law [9]:

$$t = a + b\log\left(\frac{A+W}{W}\right) \quad (2)$$

In this expression, the logarithmic term is known as the index of difficulty, the index of performance is the reciprocal of b [2, 15], and the constant a represents additive factors. Additive factors include initiation or *planning time* at the beginning of a movement and time at the end of a movement between target acquisition and task delimitation (e.g. the time it takes between stopping and clicking) [15].

Leveraging Fitts's Law, Accot and Zhai [1] derived a theoretical steering law by representing a constrained path as an infinite series of targeting tasks along the trajectory. Given an infinite set of targeting tasks, each individual distance, A, shrinks to a vanishingly small distance, ds, and, at each location, a constraint on the direction of movement is specified, $W(s)$. By integrating over the entire path, S, we are left with an expression of the form:

$$t = a + b\int_S \log\left(\frac{ds}{W(s)} + 1\right) \quad (3)$$

Performing a Taylor expansion on the logarithmic term and noting that $W(s) \gg ds$, yields:

$$t = a + b\int_S \frac{ds}{\ln 2 \times W(s)} + \varepsilon \cong a + \frac{b}{\ln 2}\int_S \frac{ds}{W(s)} \quad (4)$$

For a tunnel of fixed width, $W(s)$ is constant, yielding the simplified equation in the introduction. As well, because b and $b/\ln 2$ differ only by a constant factor $\ln 2$, without loss of generality we will replace $b/\ln 2$ by b, taking it as understood that it will represent the slope of the straight-line equation in *ID* and that its reciprocal is a function of input device performance, i.e. *IP*.

Alongside their work analyzing time, Accot and Zhai also note that an instantaneous law for speed of motion can be derived simply by noting that time equals distance divided by speed, i.e.:

$$t = a + \int_S \frac{ds}{v(s)} \quad (5)$$

Moving constant b into the integral, this implies that:

$$v(s) = \frac{1}{b}W(s) = IP \times W(s) \quad (6)$$

While the simplified form of the steering law in the introduction is intuitive and easily understood, it is also the case that the simplified form of the steering law presented in the introduction, Equation (1) derived from Equation (4) with constant width, becomes significantly more complex as aspects of the tunnel change. For example, for uniformly narrowing or widening tunnels, Equation (4) becomes:

$$t = a + b\frac{A}{W_L - W_0}\ln\frac{W_L}{W_0} \quad (7)$$

Here W_0 is the width at the beginning of the tunnel, and W_L is the width at the end of the tunnel.

Accot and Zhai also begin an analysis of a generalized steering law for arbitrary paths, leveraging, in particular, spiral paths. Here, the equation for a spiral path is again more complex:

$$t = a + b\int_{2\pi}^{2\pi(n+1)} \frac{\sqrt{(\theta+\omega)^6 + 9(\theta+\omega)^4}}{(\theta+2\pi+\omega)^3 - (\theta+\omega)^3} d\theta \quad (8)$$

In this equation, the numerator represents the length of a widening spiral of n loops, and the denominator represents the gradually widening width of the spiral. In summary, Equation (1) represents only one type of tunnel: a fixed width tunnel. Equations (7), (8), and, in the general case, Equation (4), represent a much more accurate view of the complexities inherent in any representation of temporal complexity of path.

Challenges to the Steering Law

More recently, even the theoretically satisfying aspects of Equation (4) has failed to fully account for irregular tunnels. Yamanaka and Miyashita [24, 25] examine the temporal complexity of narrowing and widening tunnels. They note that widening tunnels take significantly less time than narrowing tunnels and introduce a free weight, k, to correct the movement time as follows:

$$t = a + b\left(\frac{A}{W_L - W_0}\ln\frac{W_L}{W_0} + \frac{A(W_L - W_0)}{kW_L W_0}\right) \quad (9)$$

In their Discussion of their result, Yamanaka and Miyashita note that the addition of a free weight parameter is unsatisfactory, and that a more accurate analysis of user behavior in light of a feed-forward model of constraint might explain the variation one sees in widening versus narrowing tunnels. In support of this, they point to speed profiles through their narrowing tunnel paths that demonstrate that, approximately 100 pixels prior to the end of the tunnel, participants' speed levels out and then begins to increase such that, at the region of highest constraint, participant speed is significantly faster than it was earlier in the tunnel despite the fact that the tunnel has decreased in width ([24], Figures 13, 14).

Second, Equation 4 does not model curvature as a component of the model. This is not a significant problem if curvature is constant over a path, but does become a problem if curvature varies. To understand the effects of curvature on time, consider the instantaneous speed model by Accot and Zhai, Equation 6. This equation predicts that speed is a function of width. However, what happens if curvature varies? Does this have an impact on speed? Consider Figure 1, taken from work on sloppy selection by Lank and Saund [14]. If curvature were unimportant, then the speed (vertical axis) should be constant over the path through the oval, but it is not. As predicted by the steering law, Figure 1 shows that path width affects speed

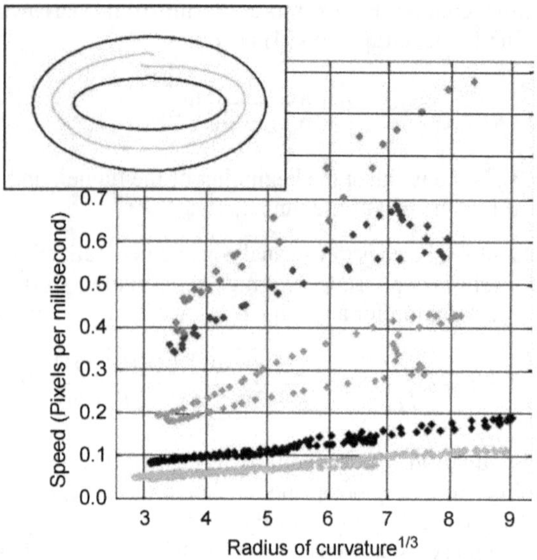

Figure 1. Speed profile of 10, 20, 40, 60, and 80-pixel constrained elliptical paths (from Lank & Saund[10]).

in that narrower paths require users to go more slowly, but we also see an effect of varying curvature on speed: users move more slowly at locations of small radius of curvature and more rapidly at locations of high radius curvature (when the path is less curved).

Most of the work on the steering law has focused on time, not speed. However, we feel that it is important to understand both speed and time profiles for two reasons. First, variations in speed affect the time it takes to traverse a tunnel. If speed is related to tunnel width *and* tunnel curvature, then both of these effects combine to produce a cost model because time is simply distance divided by speed. Second, beyond the effect on cost models, a link between speed profiles and path constraints has implications for designing interaction techniques such as smart scissors, for the assessment of care in moving and drawing, and for difficulty measures in gaming, to name only a few examples. While Accot and Zhai only analyze straight-line, circular and spiral paths, they highlight the importance of a more generalized model for arbitrary paths in their work [2].

Speed vs Curvature: The 2/3 Power Model

One obvious conclusion that can be drawn from Lank and Saund's work on sloppy selection is that path width is insufficient to fully represent variations in speed, and therefore time, for the oval paths. As shown in Figure 1, there is a possible linear relationship between speed and the cube-root of radius of curvature alongside a linear increase in slope as a function of width or tolerance.

Lank and Saund draw inspiration for their analysis of trajectory models from studies of human performance in psychology. In this field, researchers note that curved trajectories typically follow a power law relationship, commonly called the 2/3 power law [13, 22, 21] and formulated by Lacquaniti et al. [13] as follows:

$$A(s) = \kappa\,[c(s)]^{2/3} \tag{10}$$

In this equation, $A(s)$ represents the angular velocity in radians per second at point s = (x,y) along a path, $c(s)$ is the curvature of the path at that point s (the inverse of the radius of an arc that corresponds to the path), and κ is a constant called the velocity gain factor[1].

Our interest is not in angular velocity but in instantaneous speed. Transforming angular velocity, $A(s)$, to speed requires that we multiple angular velocity by the path radius, $R(s)$. Multiplying by radius at point s, $R(s)$, and recognizing that curvature, $c(s) = 1/R(s)$, yields an equation for speed versus a path's radius of curvature, $R(s)$:

$$v(s) = \kappa\,[R(s)]^{1/3} \tag{11}$$

One challenge with interpreting the 2/3 power law is the velocity gain factor, κ. If instantaneous speed is measured in m/s, then κ has units of $m^{2/3}/s$ [13]. While unintuitive, the unusual units are a result of the motor control processes that bias toward smooth movement [10] and of the complex link between speed and acceleration of a curved path in Cartesian coordinates and the path's radius of curvature [21]. Increasingly, researchers in HCI have leveraged the 2/3 power law relationship to model movement (e.g. [6, 14]. However, beyond the work cited above on sloppy selection, we are unaware of any generalization of the steering model for paths of arbitrary curvature.

FORMULATING A GENERALIZED STEERING MODEL

Leveraging past work by Lank and Saund [14], Viviani and others [21], and Accot and Zhai [1], a straightforward formulation of a steering law for generalized paths would incorporate both aspects of path constraint and curvature, i.e.:

$$t = a + \int_S \frac{ds}{v(s)} = a + b' \int_S \frac{ds}{W(s) \times R(s)^{1/3}} \tag{12}$$

Alongside this equation for the temporal cost of an arbitrary path, one can also calculate instantaneous speed along the path as:

$$v(s) = \frac{1}{b'} W(s) \times R(s)^{1/3} \tag{13}$$

In this equation, the term $1/b'$ is the product of the index of performance (Equation (6) above) and the velocity gain factor, κ, from the 2/3 power law, Equation (11). The term $W(s)R(s)^{1/3}$ is our model parameter, and we will call the value that this term takes *model units* for the remainder of this paper.

[1]In many formulations of the 2/3 power law, there exists a parameter $\alpha = [0, 0.1]$. α is a function of speed: for open-loop movement tasks such as scribbling, which are high speed, it's value approaches 0.1. For careful drawing tasks – of the kind found in, for example, tunnel traversal, where speed is slow and movement control is closed loop – its value = 0, allowing us to ignore it. More information can be found in [21].

Overall, at this point, we have two different hypothetical models to describe a generalized steering law. First, from Accot and Zhai, we have a model of the form of Equation (4), which incorporates only tunnel width and does not include curvature. Alongside this, we have a hypothesized model, Equation (12), which includes both tunnel width and curvature. We reproduce each of these models here, both for completeness and to simplify later contrasts for the reader.

Hypothetical Model 1 (Accot and Zhai, cf Equation 13 in [1]):

$$t = a + b \int_S \frac{ds}{W(s)} \quad (4)$$

Hypothetical Model 2 (proposed by this paper):

$$t = a + b' \int_S \frac{ds}{W(s)R(s)^{1/3}} \quad (12)$$

Alongside these temporal models we have two speed models that correspond directly to instantaneous forms of these speed models. The two speed models are Equations (6) and (13), respectively:

Hypothetical Instantaneous Speed Model 1 (Accot and Zhai, cf Equation 20 in [1]):

$$v(s) = \frac{1}{b} W(s) \quad (6)$$

Hypothetical Instantaneous Speed Model 2 (proposed by this paper):

$$v(s) = \frac{1}{b'} W(s) \times R(s)^{1/3} \quad (13)$$

MODEL VALIDATION

To contrast the above models, two options present themselves. First, one can leverage the total traversal time of a path to analyze whether the temporal cost model is correct, contrasting Equations (4) and (12). Alongside this, and more revealing, one can analyze the speed profiles, Equations (6) and (13). Our experiment evaluated the ability of the model to predict speed during constrained steering tasks on a touch input display. While we believe that a generalized model of steering under paths of varying curvature is most relevant to touch input, it is also important to evaluate modifications of the steering law using a mouse as an input device for experimental consistency with the original work on steering law by Accot and Zhai [1].

Experimental Task

Our experimental task was a steering task using paths depicted in Fig. 2-bottom. Paths were displayed on the screen in cyan over a black background. Participants, using a designated input device (touch or mouse), began movement outside the constrained path near the red half-circle shown at the bottom right, entered the path by crossing the red half-circle, and then were required to traverse the path without exiting from end indicated by the red half-circle to the unmarked end of the path. The paths were unidirectional as shown in Fig. 2-bottom, i.e. paths had their start and endpoint at opposite sides of the screen offset by arbitrary angles; these paths would typically not result in occlusion as their unidirectional nature would allow a participant to position him or herself such that their arm did not block the path during path traversal, reducing any confounds that repositioning to address occlusion [23] might create in the captured data.

Apparatus

The study was implemented in Java 7 and run on a first generation Microsoft Surface Pro tablet running Windows 8. The display is 23.4 × 13.1 cm (208 DPI) with an input rate of 126 Hz. Input was captured using both the multi-touch display of the Surface Pro (for touch modality) and using a generic, USB computer mouse (for mouse modality).

Participants

12 participants (7 males, mean age 28) participated in the experiment. All were right handed.

Procedure

The experiment was completed in two blocks, with at least one week between blocks to prevent learning effects. In the first block, all participants completed the task using the multi-touch display with their finger as the input device. In the second block, six of the participants returned and repeated the same paths using the mouse as the input device.

For each block, participants traversed 11 constrained paths. Each block of the experiment proceeded as follows. First, participants were introduced to (or reminded of) the steering task. Similar to directives provided to participants in Fitts's Law tasks, participants were asked to drag the input device inside the path as fast as they could without moving outside of the path. A red half-disc represented the beginning of the path, the point at which they had to start. All participants were presented with the same set of paths. The order of the paths was randomized, and the first two paths were considered training and not logged.

To allow users to validate their movements, the trace of the finger's actual movement was represented as a blue line on the display. If the participant crossed the path boundary, the trace would turn red; this was considered an error and, when it happened, a 'Restart' button was shown and participants were instructed to tap it to restart the trial. Participants were given three attempts to successfully complete a path, after which the next trial started. If any path was not completed successfully within three attempts, that path was presented a final time at the end of the study for a single, final attempt. The study lasted about 20 minutes for each participant.

Path Generation

The 11 paths were generated randomly before the study began in four steps. The process for generating paths is shown in Figure 3, and occurs as follows:

1. A guiding line is defined crossing the center of the screen and starting from a random point located 5 to 15 mm away from the lateral edges, and at least 5 mm away from the top and bottom edges (Fig. 2-a).
2. A set of N points (6 to 10) is defined along the guide, with random distances between them, and with uniform noise

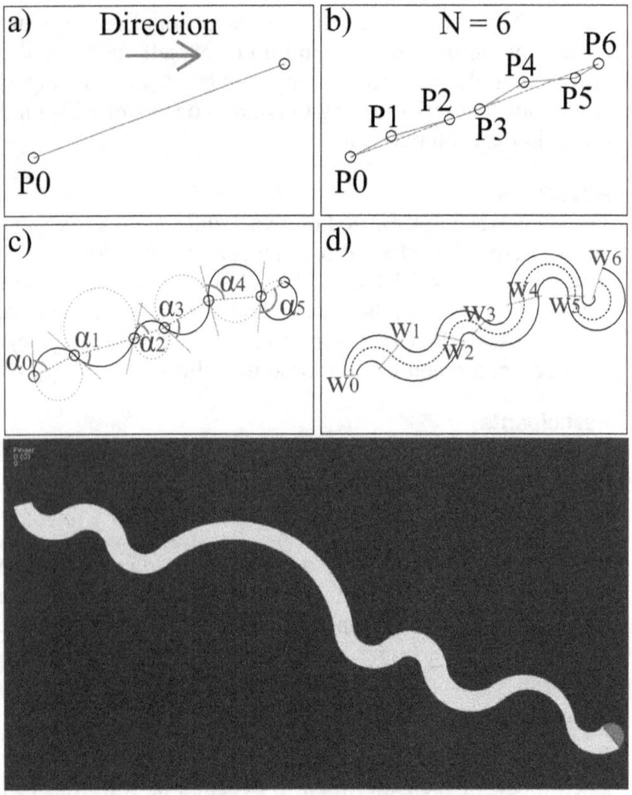

Figure 2. Creating a linear path from P_0 to P_6, modeled as 6 arcs with 6 smoothly varying width constraints. At the bottom, a path from the experiment.

($[-1,1]$ mm) added to their coordinates (Fig. 2-b) to offset them from the guiding line in step 1.

3. The actual trajectory is defined. An initial angle α_0 is chosen randomly within $[-\pi/2.5, -\pi/5] \cup [\pi/5, \pi/2.5]$ radians at the defined starting point P_0 (left- or rightmost) and an arc is generated from the starting point to the next point P_1, its center equidistant from P_0 and P_1 and its tangent at P_0 matching α_0. The tangential angle α_1 of this arc at P_1 is then used to compute the next arc to P_2, and so on until P_N is reached (Fig. 2-c).

4. The final path is generated by randomly selecting widths for every point P_n (within $[3,13]$ mm for the width for each point, P_n, and interpolating width to width variation linearly between P_n and P_{n+1} (Fig. 2-d).

Our measurements above result in path widths that vary between 3mm and 13mm and radii of curvature that vary between 6mm and 41mm. Considering width, in the original experiment of Accot and Zhai [1], pixel measurements were used to describe tunnel width, not mm. Our selection of path size was inspired by results in Accot and Zhai's work on input device performance, in particular their data (see Figure 9 in [2]) which shows nonlinearity effects that appear in mouse/touchpad/stylus data at 70 pixels in path width on their hardware configurations (i.e. just under 18mm). While we use touch and mouse, not touchpad, wider path non-linearity [2] might impact the performance of models, so we wanted to be below the 70 pixel cut-off they used. Our path widths correspond to pixel widths of 10 to 50 pixels on Accot and Zhai's hardware configuration [1].

Speed Calculation and Model Parameter Specification

For each sample, we capture position time data over the course of the user's trajectory. Position is in screen coordinates (x, y) in millimeters, and time is captured in milliseconds. Given this initial data, our goal is to plot speed against model parameters of width (Eq. 6) and width × cube-root of radius of curvature (Eq. 13).

To calculate speed from participant input data, we perform a second degree polynomial regression of x(t) and y(t) data as described by Lank and Saund [14] at each input point on each path for each participant. To calculate speed in this fashion, we first had to decide how many data points to include in the regressions. Calculating speed and acceleration using three data points results in a signal containing a significant amount of sampling noise, while using too many points results in over-smoothing. We analyzed second-order polynomial regressions for a range of time-window sizes (0 to 4 s), shown in Figure 3 on the vertical axis. Using a window of 1200 ms, we find that we can eliminate high frequency noise that results from neurophysiological factors [11, 20] and sampling idiosyncrasies [14] while still preserving speed fluctuations on the order of 100 ms (10 Hz).

Research Questions

There are two primary research questions that we explore with our study.

First, given recent work on narrowing versus widening tunnels, and, in particular, observations from Yamanaka and Miyashita [24, 25] on feedforward modeling of movement (see figures 13 and 14 from [24]), we first explore whether or not our participants pre-plan, and what that window pre- planning is. We expect that the free weight value is a direct result of path planning; if one examines the derivation of the free weight parameter in Yamanaka and Miyashita, they use path segments of short length to define an ID modifier, ID_{gap}, for their tunnel segments. The question then becomes: What is the length of this short segment?

Second, an open question is which model correlates better with observed movement data, Equation (6) or Equation (13). To address this question, we perform a fit over both models and analyze the results.

RESULTS

Result 1: Do Users Pre-Plan?

Given our data, there exists an initial question motivated by Yamanaka and Miyashita: At what point do width and radius of curvature constrain speed? Is it the current point, i.e. motion planning results in near perfect coordination of constraint and movement? Or is it some point slightly ahead of movement (in the future), i.e. the user anticipates the oncoming constraint and plans ahead?

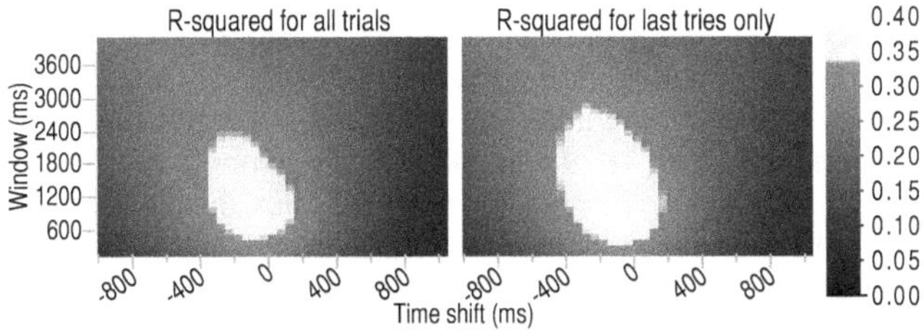

Figure 3. A heat map of correlations between speed and model parameters. We find that participants plan approximately 100 ms into the future, i.e. about 0.1 s.

To perform this analysis, we use exactly the same technique as Yamanaka and Miyashita leverage in their paper, namely we explore r^2 values over time and space.

Figure 3 depicts this analysis along the horizontal axis. Analyzing the linear fit of speed against model values, we found that correlation is maximized if we consider constraint from a point 100 ms and 200 ms into the future. There is no difference in the minimization function for either model. Essentially, from our data it appears that, for steering tasks, reaction to constraint occurs on a time interval of approximately 0.1-0.2 s prior to the constraint. This value correlates well with past work in motor planning [16, 18, 20].

Alongside temporal pre-planning, it is also possible that pre-planning occurs over a fixed distance versus a fixed time interval. In analyzing movement, we find that pre-planning distance varies. For narrower tunnels, participants' pre-planning distance is shorter than for wider tunnels, and this distance seems to correlate with on-coming width. Given the linear relationship between width and speed predicted by both models, it seems clear that users pre-plan over a temporal interval, i.e. the pre-planning is predicated on the need to have time to react to impending constraint. We use a pre-planning interval of 150 ms during our analysis.

Result 2: Model Correlation

Any movement data will have significant neurophysiological noise. The standard approach to this, typified by analysis in Fitts's Law experiments, is to average speed values over a large set of data points for multiple users to produce an overall model of time against ID values for movement [7] Averaging is challenging with data when the independent variable is continuous. In typical Fitts's Law laboratory experiments, because discrete values are used for ID, averaging is simplified. In real-world pointing tasks where ID varies continuously, averaging must be handled differently.

To average our data points, we used a technique inspired by Chapuis et al. [7] in their analysis of real world Fitts-style movement data. We binned data into ranges for width and ranges for radius of curvature, specifically, in our case, 10 different width bins and 3 different radius of curvature bins, yielding 30 data bins overall. We chose these bins because 10 different bins of width corresponds to 1mm per bin width (width varies from 3mm to 13mm). Radius of curvature ranges from 6mm to 41mm; when taking the cube root, this yields numerical values between 1.8 and 3.4.

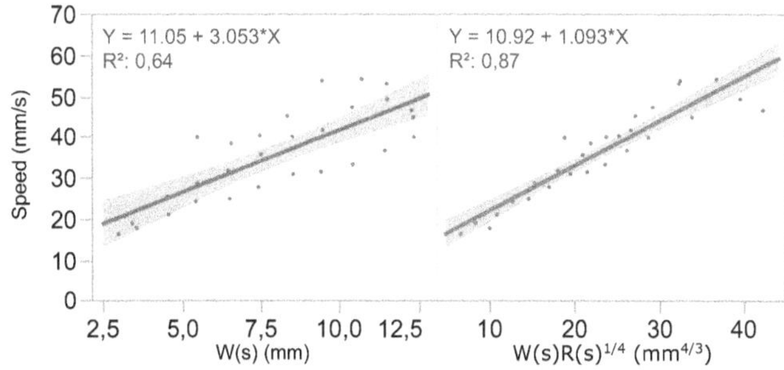

Figure 4. Plot of binned data values for Accot and Zhai (left) and for our model (right) on 30 data points for touch data. Note that incorporating curvature data results in much less variability in data with respect to the straight-line fit.

To replicate Fitts's style analysis, we calculated an average (model unit, speed) value for each data bin and an average (width, speed) data point for each bin for each participant. Similar to Fitts's Law analysis [4, 7], we also took a "mean-of-means" measure, i.e. the average of participant values for each bin to create an overall best-fit line. Once averaged by participant and overall, we treated all data values identically; this is commonly done in Fitts-style analysis [7], where average time is plotted in unweighted form against ID and correlations are typically performed treating all averaged data points with equal weight.

To determine which model most accurately represents data, two options present themselves: either the radius of curvature term will improve the correlation, r^2, or it will not. We performed a linear fit of the data using both model parameters (proposed by this paper) and width values (Accot and Zhai's model) on the 30 averaged data points per user and averaged across all users. For our model, data points were $(W(s)R(s)^{1/3}, v(s))$ averaged per bin; for Accot and Zhai, data points were $(W(s), v(s))$ values again averaged per bin.

Touch Data

Table 1 depicts r^2 values for the model proposed by this paper and for the Accot and Zhai model using our touch input data.

	Accot and Zhai			Proposed Model		
	a	b'	r^2	a	b	r^2
P1	4.29	3.76	.61	4.62	1.32	.80
P2	3.80	5.85	.77	9.34	1.84	.81
P3	24.65	2.28	.35	24.37	0.83	.49
P4	10.80	3.65	.71	12.82	1.22	.82
P5	11.80	4.16	.39	4.24	1.80	.78
P6	7.23	2.50	.40	4.74	0.99	.67
P7	2.80	3.76	.56	0.92	1.42	.84
P8	4.25	2.99	.71	4.63	1.05	.91
P9	27.42	2.54	.47	27.09	0.91	.65
P10	27.15	1.91	.41	27.89	0.65	.50
P11	21.95	1.72	.37	21.31	0.64	.54
P12	13.26	2.24	.46	12.99	0.81	.63
Overall	11.05	3.05	.64	10.92	1.09	.87

Table 1. Comparison of coefficients (a or y-intercept and b'/b or slope) and correlation (r^2) for our model and for Accot and Zhai's model for touch data.

Overall correlations of 0.87 and 0.64 are both statistically significant on 30 data points (for our model, $r^2 = 0.87, p < 0.0001$; for Accot and Zhai, $r^2 = 0.64, p < 0.0001$). This is unsurprising; width is an important component of both models. However, given two models, both with statistically significant correlations, a higher r^2 value represents a more encompassing model, i.e. our model accounts for more of the variability present in the data (basically 87% for our model versus 64% for theirs). Measuring whether our model represents a significant improvement on the data can be done using pairwise t-tests of correlation values for each participant ($p < 0.0001$ for pairwise, two-tailed t-test). The strong statistical signal is unsurprising, given an observation of the pairwise samples: for every participant, correlation improves for our model versus Accot and Zhai's model.

Mouse Data

While touch data provides a strong indication of the advantage of our model, one question we had was whether touch input might differ from mouse-based input, i.e. it is important to check that input device characteristics were not unfairly biasing against Accot and Zhai's model. Using the same method described above to produce Fitts's style data points, we performed an analysis of six of our study participants on mouse data. Table 2 depicts correlations for both our model and Accot and Zhai's model on mouse data. Similar to touch data, our model significantly outperforms Accot and Zhai both per user and overall (our model's $r^2 = 0.96$ vs Accot and zhai's model $r^2 = 0.77$).

	Accot and Zhai			Proposed Model		
	a	b'	r^2	a	b	r^2
P1	6.96	2.13	.84	9.31	0.65	.84
P2	11.21	3.38	.62	10.24	1.24	.88
P3	-1.17	4.32	.72	-0.59	1.50	.93
P6	5.86	2.09	.72	6.85	0.70	.85
P7	-0.32	2.61	.73	0.20	0.91	.91
P8	4.82	2.23	.67	4.77	0.80	.88
Overall	4.02	2.75	.77	4.71	0.95	.96

Table 2. Comparison of correlation coefficients, r^2, for our model and for Accot and Zhai's model for mouse data. Note, again, the significant reduction in variability with respect to the best-fit line.

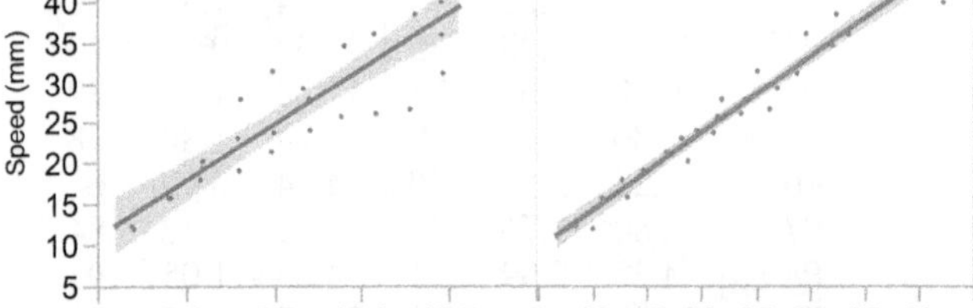

Figure 5. Mouse data plot of best-fit line (mean-of-means) for Accot and Zhai (left) and our model (right). Note, again, the reduction in variability when radius of curvature is represented in the model.

Width Effects and Touch Data

In our analysis of Accot and Zhai's original work, one issue that came to the fore was the discontinuities in path constraint. Accot and Zhai note that their model only holds for path widths of less than 80 pixels on a 1024 × 768 pixel display. Furthermore, as we noted earlier, if one examines Figure 9 in Accot and Zhai, 1999 [2], Accot and Zhai note nonlinearity effects that become present in the data at values even as low as 70 pixels (16mm when converting from their experimental setup to SI units). The challenge is as follows (from the original Accot and Zhai steering law):

- For path widths of less than 80 pixels, Accot and Zhai propose the steering law.
- For unconstrained paths, Fitts's Law predicts a temporal cost.
- For path widths between 80 pixels and unconstrained (weakly constrained), a model discontinuity exists that has yet to be resolved. We are aware of no work that addresses the discontinuity between 80-pixel paths and unconstrained paths.

While mouse correlations are very high for our model, touch data has strong but slightly lower overall correlation values. To determine whether discontinuities were impacting the fit (r^2) of our touch data, we analyzed lower model units (narrower curved paths) versus higher model units (wider curved paths) by segmenting the data into two halves, lower and higher values, along the x-axis for each model. Table 3 shows the corresponding values for r^2 for both models for touch data. In this table, the first two rows represent a split using our model units and the second two rows represent a split using width, i.e. based on their model. Of significance in this table is correlation for Accot and Zhai's model at high model units/high widths, where their correlation is no longer statistically significant. Essentially, this indicates that for wider paths in our touch data, larger than 8mm, width is no longer a significant factor in performance. While our model also degrades, because curvature continues to affect speed, our model still retains some ability to explain variations in data. This trend is also apparent in Figure 4.

Split	Model	Low model units r^2	High model units r^2
$W(s)R(s)^{1/3}$	Our model	**0.85**	0.36
	Accot and Zhai	0.48	0.00 (ns)
$W(s)$	Our model	**0.91**	0.62
	Accot and Zhai	0.60	0.08 (ns)

Table 3. Examining correlation coefficients for lower-model-values and for higher-model-values for hypothesized model and Accot and Zhai with touch data. Note that, as expected, for weakly constrained paths, Accot and Zhai's model does not correlate with movement time or speed.

Examining high versus low values for our model and for width for mouse data (see Table 4 we find that width continues to have some affect on behavior for high model units (though r^2 values for our model continue to outperform their correlations).

Error Effects

In our experimental method, participants were given three successive attempts to successfully traverse a path, plus one

Split	Model	Low model units r^2	High model units r^2
$W(s)R(s)^{1/3}$	Our model	**0.94**	0.79
	Accot and Zhai	0.76	0.17 (ns)
$W(s)$	Our model	**0.94**	0.89
	Accot and Zhai	0.75	0.33

Table 4. Examining correlation coefficients for lower-model-values and for higher-model-values for hypothesized model and Accot and Zhai with mouse data. Note that, as expected, for weakly constrained paths, Accot and Zhai's model does not correlate with movement time or speed.

additional attempt at the end of the study if they failed three times. We hypothesized that multiple errors, each requiring a user to restart a given path, might result in users becoming ever-more careful, which, in turn, might result in changes to kinematic properties of movement. If kinematics change, that change might invalidate any model. We therefore ran our analyses with two path sets:

1. All: Analyze all paths generated by participant.
2. Last: Only the last attempt for a given path for each participant is analyzed (regardless of success or failure).

Table 5 depicts the r^2 values for model fits for both all and last. Correlations were virtually identical for All and Last, leading us to conclude that errors did not affect the performance of our model in steering tasks.

Errors	Touch		Mouse	
	r^2	p	r^2	p
All	0.87	< 0.0001	.96	< 0.0001
Last	0.86	< 0.0001	.94	< 0.0001

Table 5. Correlation and significance for average movement speeds taking all paths versus last attempts.

Towards an Instantaneous Model

One aspect of our model (and of Accot and Zhai's speed versus constraint model) that is interesting to consider is its ability to serve as a real-time model, i.e. to explore how well the competing models fit every available data point. This would be akin to measuring correlation between index-of-difficult and time for every single discrete pointing task in a Fitts's Law experiment, rather than taking user means and then mean of user means. Given the amount of neurophysiological noise in target acquisition tasks, one would expect very low correlations [7]. Table 6 shows these correlations and Figure 6 plots all data for both models. The model incorporating curvature outperforms Accot and Zhai's width-only model in all cases.

	Accot and Zhai			Proposed Model		
	a	b'	r^2	a	b	r^2
P1	4.99	3.03	.25	2.42	1.34	.35
P2	-0.16	5.99	.59	2.74	2.15	.62
P3	22.28	2.11	.16	19.16	1.00	.28
P4	16.90	2.64	.23	15.04	1.12	.34
P5	11.53	3.02	.28	7.29	1.45	.43
P6	5.70	1.94	.27	3.58	0.89	.41
P7	2.08	3.19	.40	-0.35	1.40	.56
P8	3.31	2.86	.43	3.28	1.10	.50
P9	26.52	2.29	.10	24.55	0.98	.16
P10	25.60	1.80	.18	24.34	0.77	.25
P11	18.81	1.83	.20	17.98	0.75	.29
P12	11.66	2.08	.24	11.29	0.83	.31
Overall	9.99	2.77	0.22	8.36	1.78	0.30

Table 6. Comparison of correlation coefficients, r^2, for our model and for Accot and Zhai's model for touch data on approximately 7000 data points per user and 82965 data points for overall data.

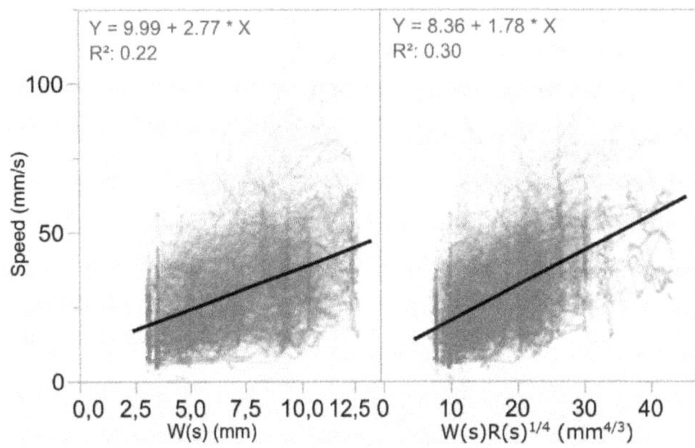

Figure 6. Plot of fitting parameters on all data points (n = 82965).

DISCUSSION

Model Comparison

We observe significantly higher correlation between our model, that incorporates curvature, compared to Accot and Zhai's.

The one challenge with our model and with Accot and Zhai's model is the discontinuities that exist between models and unconstrained movement. There are also discontinuities possible when individual constraints are adjusted instantaneously, i.e. tunnel widths are defined by discontinuous values rather than varying smoothly over time. The closest model currently available to model movement between varying constraints is the minimum jerk model of goal directed movement [10]. The premise of this movement is that human motor control values movement that minimizes abrupt changes in acceleration. One could, therefore, model varying constraints through a piecewise function, such that, where constraints are continuous, users vary smoothly between constraints using constrained path models (Accot and Zhai for straight-line paths; ours for more arbitrary paths). Where discontinuities occur, users leverage minimum jerk speed adjustments to transition from one constraint to the next.

There exists some justification for a piecewise approach to aimed movement. Cao and Zhai [6] propose a temporal model of character formation that breaks pen strokes into three different substrokes: line segments, corners, and curves. A character consisting of a line segment and a curve segment, for example a 'J' is modeled as a straight segment with a curved segment, and two different models define the temporal cost of the two different substrokes.

Trajectory Cost Models and Implications

The steering law [1], as formulated by Accot and Zhai, was primarily considered a model of the temporal cost of path traversal, though, as they note, an instantaneous speed variant can easily be deduced. In our enhanced model of steering through irregular paths, our focus has, to this point, been primarily on the correlation between expected speed values at any specific point along the path and path parameters of width and radius of curvature.

Given the very highly statistically significant correlations between model parameters and instantaneous speed (all p-values < 0.001 in experiments both on the tablet form factor and on the larger display with both touch and mouse input), it is obvious that the correlations that we hypothesize exist. Given the strength of the r^2 values between average speed across many trials at specific model points, it is also obvious that our model accurately characterizes the factors affecting expected speed.

One benefit of the speed model we provide is that it can easily be used either as a performance model to evaluate speed, a cost model to evaluate time, or a constraint model to evaluate perceived constraint for any given path. First, to model expected performance at a given point, our model accurately characterizes expected speed at that point. This satisfies the first implication, a characterization of the expected performance at any point along a trajectory.

To understand the use of this model to describe overall temporal cost, consider the relationship between speed, distance, and time commonly captured in introductory physics textbooks:

$$v(s) = \frac{ds}{dt} \implies dt = \frac{ds}{v(s)} \implies t = c + \int \frac{ds}{v(s)}$$

Thus, our model can easily be used to calculate expected cost of any arbitrary constrained path simply by evaluating the integral described above. If it proves impractical to calculate the integral, a summation can serve as an approximation, provided Δs is set sufficiently small to ensure a good approximation to the integral:

$$t = c + \int \frac{ds}{v(s)} \approx c + \sum \frac{\Delta s}{v(s)}$$

Finally, as noted by Lank and Saund [14], a model that links speed to constraint and curvature can be used to infer the perceived constraint of a path being traversed by a user in a graphical user interface. Given the widespread adoption of multi-touch as an input modality, gestural input, both constrained and unconstrained is commonplace. From a gesture, speed and curvature can be calculated – the speed directly using numerical differentiation using an appropriate technique such as the polynomial regression described above and curvature (the inverse of radius of curvature) from parameters of movement via the formula:

$$curvature = \frac{|v_x a_y - v_y a_x|}{(v_x^2 + v_y^2)^{3/2}}$$

The one challenge with an instantaneous model is that there exists significant neurophysiological noise in real-time input as we saw in Table 6, a result of users behavior deviating from the optimal due. These deviations are likely due to small errors in submovements [16, 18] and the need to iteratively correct those small errors. On the other hand, it is also the case that we do not necessarily need to predict instantaneous speed or infer instantaneous constraint at a pixel or millisecond level. If we group points together, perhaps over 10mm or 20mm of user movement, or we infer based on a slower sampling rate such as 5Hz we can use averaged data points to infer overall constraint within a region, similar to a sliding window filter. An appropriate averaging window will be task-specific; techniques such as sloppy selection, intelligent scissors, or difficulty assessment for gaming tasks can select appropriate averaging intervals based on the fidelity of measure needed.

CONCLUSION

In this paper, we propose an extension of the original steering law work of Accot and Zhai [1], modifying it to take into account the effect of arbitrary variations of curvature along constrained paths. Our new formulation models the temporal cost of constrained path traversal via the following formula:

$$t = a + b' \int_S \frac{ds}{W(s) \times R(s)^{1/3}}$$

We also provide a model of instantaneous speed of the form:

$$v(s) = \frac{1}{b'} W(s) \times R(s)^{1/3}$$

We empirically validate this model and discuss its relationship to past work.

ACKNOWLEDGMENTS

This research underwent ethics review by the Office of Research Ethics at the University of Waterloo. Funding for this research was provided by the Natural Science and Engineering Research Council of Canada, by The European Research Council (ERC) Horizon 2020 Innovation and Research Program (Grant Agreement 637991) and by La Région Nord-Pas-de-Calais, France.

REFERENCES

1. Johnny Accot and Shumin Zhai. 1997. Beyond Fitts' Law: Models for Trajectory-based HCI Tasks. In *Proceedings of the ACM SIGCHI Conference on Human Factors in Computing Systems (CHI '97)*. ACM, New York, NY, USA, 295–302. DOI: http://dx.doi.org/10.1145/258549.258760
2. Johnny Accot and Shumin Zhai. 1999. Performance Evaluation of Input Devices in Trajectory-based Tasks: An Application of the Steering Law. In *Proceedings of the SIGCHI Conference on Human Factors in Computing Systems (CHI '99)*. ACM, New York, NY, USA, 466–472. DOI: http://dx.doi.org/10.1145/302979.303133
3. Johnny Accot and Shumin Zhai. 2003. Refining Fitts' Law Models for Bivariate Pointing. In *Proceedings of the*

SIGCHI Conference on Human Factors in Computing Systems (CHI '03). ACM, New York, NY, USA, 193–200. DOI:http://dx.doi.org/10.1145/642611.642646

4. Ravin Balakrishnan. 2004. âĂIJBeatingâĂİ FittsâĂŹ law: virtual enhancements for pointing facilitation. *International Journal of Human-Computer Studies* 61, 6 (Dec. 2004), 857–874. DOI: http://dx.doi.org/10.1016/j.ijhcs.2004.09.002
5. Daniel Boutros. 2008. Difficulty is Difficult: Designing for Hard Modes in Games. (2008). http://www.gamasutra.com/view/feature/3787/difficulty
6. Xiang Cao and Shumin Zhai. 2007. Modeling Human Performance of Pen Stroke Gestures. In *Proceedings of the SIGCHI Conference on Human Factors in Computing Systems (CHI '07)*. ACM, New York, NY, USA, 1495–1504. DOI: http://dx.doi.org/10.1145/1240624.1240850
7. Olivier Chapuis, Renaud Blanch, and Michel Beaudouin-Lafon. 2007. *Fitts' Law in the Wild: A Field Study of Aimed Movements*. Technical Report. https://hal.archives-ouvertes.fr/hal-00612026 LRI Technical Repport Number 1480, Univ. Paris-Sud, 11 pages.
8. Andy Cockburn, Carl Gutwin, and Saul Greenberg. 2007. A Predictive Model of Menu Performance. In *Proceedings of the SIGCHI Conference on Human Factors in Computing Systems (CHI '07)*. ACM, New York, NY, USA, 627–636. DOI: http://dx.doi.org/10.1145/1240624.1240723
9. Paul M. Fitts. 1954. The information capacity of the human motor system in controlling the amplitude of movement. *Journal of Experimental Psychology* 47, 6 (1954), 381–391. DOI: http://dx.doi.org/10.1037/h0055392
10. T. Flash and N. Hogan. 1985. The coordination of arm movements: an experimentally confirmed mathematical model. *Journal of Neuroscience* 5, 7 (July 1985), 1688–1703. http://www.jneurosci.org/content/5/7/1688
11. D. M. Green and J. A. Swets. 1966. Signal detection theory and psychophysics. 1966. *New York* 888 (1966), 889.
12. P. L. Gribble and D. J. Ostry. 1996. Origins of the power law relation between movement velocity and curvature: modeling the effects of muscle mechanics and limb dynamics. *Journal of Neurophysiology* 76, 5 (Nov. 1996), 2853–2860. http://jn.physiology.org/content/76/5/2853
13. Francesco Lacquaniti, Carlo Terzuolo, and Paolo Viviani. 1983. The law relating the kinematic and figural aspects of drawing movements. *Acta Psychologica* 54, 1âĂŞ3 (Oct. 1983), 115–130. DOI: http://dx.doi.org/10.1016/0001-6918(83)90027-6
14. Edward Lank and Eric Saund. 2005. Sloppy selection: Providing an accurate interpretation of imprecise selection gestures. *Computers & Graphics* 29, 4 (Aug. 2005), 490–500. DOI: http://dx.doi.org/10.1016/j.cag.2005.05.003
15. I. Scott MacKenzie. 1992. Fitts' Law As a Research and Design Tool in Human-computer Interaction. *Hum.-Comput. Interact.* 7, 1 (March 1992), 91–139. DOI: http://dx.doi.org/10.1207/s15327051hci0701_3
16. David E. Meyer, Richard A. Abrams, Sylvan Kornblum, Charles E. Wright, and J. E. 1988. Optimality in human motor performance: Ideal control of rapid aimed movements. *Psychological Review* 95, 3 (1988), 340–370. DOI:http://dx.doi.org/10.1037/0033-295X.95.3.340
17. Robert Pastel. 2006. Measuring the Difficulty of Steering Through Corners. In *Proceedings of the SIGCHI Conference on Human Factors in Computing Systems (CHI '06)*. ACM, New York, NY, USA, 1087–1096. DOI: http://dx.doi.org/10.1145/1124772.1124934
18. Réjean Plamondon. 1995. A kinematic theory of rapid human movements. *Biological Cybernetics* 72, 4 (March 1995), 295–307. DOI: http://dx.doi.org/10.1007/BF00202785
19. Steven C. Seow. 2005. Information Theoretic Models of HCI: A Comparison of the Hick-Hyman Law and Fitts' Law. *Hum.-Comput. Interact.* 20, 3 (Sept. 2005), 315–352. DOI: http://dx.doi.org/10.1207/s15327051hci2003_3
20. Reza Shadmehr and Steven P. Wise. 2005. *The computational neurobiology of reaching and pointing: a foundation for motor learning*. MIT press.
21. Paolo Viviani and Tamar Flash. 1995. Minimum-jerk, two-thirds power law, and isochrony: converging approaches to movement planning. *Journal of Experimental Psychology: Human Perception and Performance* 21, 1 (1995), 32–53. DOI: http://dx.doi.org/10.1037/0096-1523.21.1.32
22. Paolo Viviani and Roland Schneider. 1991. A developmental study of the relationship between geometry and kinematics in drawing movements. *Journal of Experimental Psychology: Human Perception and Performance* 17, 1 (1991), 198–218. DOI: http://dx.doi.org/10.1037/0096-1523.17.1.198
23. Daniel Vogel and Ravin Balakrishnan. 2010. Occlusion-aware Interfaces. In *Proceedings of the SIGCHI Conference on Human Factors in Computing Systems (CHI '10)*. ACM, New York, NY, USA, 263–272. DOI:http://dx.doi.org/10.1145/1753326.1753365
24. Shota Yamanaka and Homei Miyashita. 2016a. Modeling the Steering Time Difference Between Narrowing and Widening Tunnels. In *Proceedings of the 2016 CHI Conference on Human Factors in Computing Systems (CHI '16)*. ACM, New York, NY, USA, 1846–1856. DOI: http://dx.doi.org/10.1145/2858036.2858037
25. Shota Yamanaka and Homei Miyashita. 2016b. Scale Effects in the Steering Time Difference Between Narrowing and Widening Linear Tunnels. In *Proceedings*

of the 9th Nordic Conference on Human-Computer Interaction (NordiCHI '16). ACM, New York, NY, USA, 12:1–12:10. DOI: http://dx.doi.org/10.1145/2971485.2971486

26. Stanislaw Zabramski, Suman Shrestha, and Wolfgang Stuerzlinger. 2013. Easy vs. Tricky: The Shape Effect in Tracing, Selecting, and Steering With Mouse, Stylus, and Touch. In *Proceedings of International Conference on Making Sense of Converging Media (AcademicMindTrek '13)*. ACM, New York, NY, USA, 99:99–99:103. DOI: http://dx.doi.org/10.1145/2523429.2523444

Free the Hands! Enhanced Target Selection via a Variable-Friction Shoe

Daniel Horodniczy, Jeremy R Cooperstock
Centre for Intelligent Machines, McGill University
Montreal, Canada
danielh | jer@cim.mcgill.ca

ABSTRACT

While several foot-controlled pointing devices have been explored as alternatives to conventional interfaces, we are interested in whether such devices can achieve higher performance with the addition of variable friction. Users wore our variable-friction prototype shoe on their right foot, which they slid on a low-friction surface to control a mouse cursor. Two interface modes were evaluated: constant (CF) and variable friction (VF), under the ISO 9241-9 standard for pointing device evaluation. For the variable-friction modality, target regions were high friction to provide sliding resistance cues. Our findings confirmed that variable-friction foot-controlled pointing can achieve throughput competitive with a range of hand-controlled devices. This suggests the potential for taking advantage of foot input for simple pointing tasks, in particular when the hands are overloaded. With respect to other foot-controlled pointing systems, our implementation offered improved performance and comparable error rates. In addition, the analysis provided further insight into the design of foot-controlled input devices.

Author Keywords

Variable Friction; Haptic Feedback; Foot-Controlled Input; Fitts' Law.

ACM Classification Keywords

H.5.2 User Interfaces: Haptic I/O; Input devices and strategies; Interaction styles.

INTRODUCTION

The foot is an underutilised resource as an interaction tool or peripheral manipulator. There are numerous situations where our feet are left to act as a simple supporting mechanism while our hands are overloaded. In such situations, the feet could perform secondary tasks, thereby relieving load on the hands and potentially achieving greater efficiency. Ultimately, the question we address is whether pointing performance of the foot, manipulated on a 2D plane while sitting, can be improved by friction modulation applied on the contact face of the shoe sole. Target pointing is a common and essential task in the desktop environment. When such pointing is done by foot, previous studies reported a lack of fine-grained dexterity [17]. However, the literature indicates that variable friction can be used to augment pointing performance on touch screens in a sliding context [9]. This motivated the study reported here, investigating whether variable friction, applied to the foot, might allow for effective pointing performance when the hands are overloaded.

CHI 2017, May 6–11, 2017, Denver, CO, USA

ISBN 978-1-4503-4655-9/17/05 $15.00
DOI: http://dx.doi.org/10.1145/3025453.3025625

RELATED WORK

Variable Friction

The literature shows that the objective of variable friction, in general, is to augment simulations or interfaces by adding a degree of controlled tactility, specific to slippage [3, 9]. However, variable friction has not yet entered the mainstream of commercial devices (e.g., smartphones), as have vibration feedback and 3D touch capabilities. Applications include virtual environment augmentation and haptics-driven enhancement of user experience, usability, and pointing performance.

From a haptics standpoint, variable friction has been demonstrated to improve pointing performance [1, 5, 4, 9] and may be used in conjunction with vibration stimuli to further enrich perceptual experiences [10]. Haptic feedback is quite common in mobile devices and we anticipate that the porting of variable friction to these interfaces is simply a matter of time.

Foot-Controlled Pointing

The foot has been studied from an HCI perspective as early as the 1960s [6]. Early work investigated the ideal ergonomic and functional design of foot-controlled interfaces intended to augment pointing performance and experience in the desktop environment [6, 13, 14]. However, given the greater dexterity of fingers than toes, it comes as no surprise that hand-controlled devices significantly outperform their foot-controlled counterparts, as demonstrated in Table 2. The difference in performance is manifested in both movement time and accuracy, since it takes the foot approximately twice as long as the hand to complete equivalent movements [12, 8].

Garcia and Vu compared the performance of a hand-controlled trackball and a foot-controlled mouse in word processing tasks over ten sessions to investigate the effects of learning.

Trackball performance was superior, but performance quickly plateaued, whereas foot mouse performance continually improved over the sessions. This suggested an inherent bias in comparisons between hand- and foot-operated pointing devices due to experience with hand pointing. It also suggested that further practice may help to meet or exceed conventional mouse pointing performance, necessitating further research on the topic [7, 18].

A Variable-Friction Shoe

The prototype friction-varying mechanism used in this work (shown in Figure 2) attaches to one's shoe sole at the heel [10]. Both high- and low-friction materials are used on a single face of contact between the mechanism and the floor. Friction is modulated by controlling the position of the high-friction material, thereby regulating the normal force experienced at the heel. To facilitate relative continuity in friction variation, an elastic element is placed between the high-friction material and the position control element. Low-friction material is used at the shoe sole face and in regions where the high-friction material may protrude. When the elastic element is uncompressed, the high-friction material does not contact the floor, resulting in an experience of low-friction. The concept is illustrated in Figure 1. The prototype has a mass of approximately 850 g.

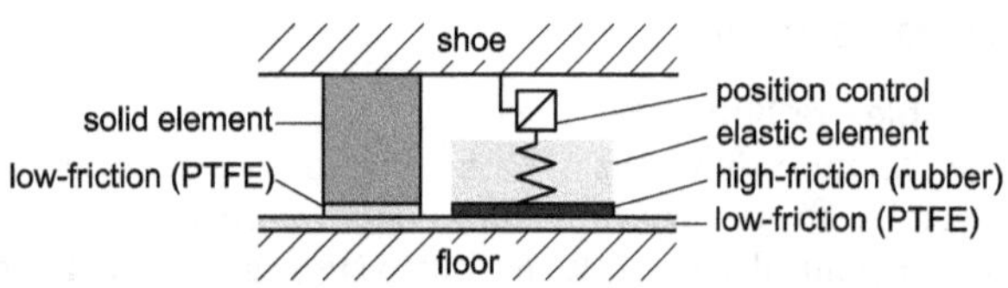

Figure 1. A diagram illustrating the mechanism of friction variation employed by the prototype.

Assuming Coulomb's model of dry friction and that the mass of the device is negligible with respect to a user's mass, the effective COF is described mathematically as follows [10]:

$$F_{\text{human}} = F_{\text{lf}} + F_{\text{hf}} \tag{1}$$

$$F_{\text{hf}} = E_{\text{el}} S_{\text{el}} \varepsilon_{\text{el}} \tag{2}$$

$$\mu_{\text{eff}} = \frac{\mu_{\text{lf}} F_{\text{lf}} + \mu_{\text{hf}} F_{\text{hf}}}{F_{\text{lf}} + F_{\text{hf}}} \tag{3}$$

$$\mu_{\text{eff}} = \mu_{\text{lf}} + (\mu_{\text{hf}} - \mu_{\text{lf}}) \frac{E_{\text{el}} S_{\text{el}} \varepsilon_{\text{el}}}{F_{\text{human}}} \tag{4}$$

F_{human} is the downward force applied by the user on the shoe sole. F_{lf} and F_{hf} are the ground reaction forces experienced by the high- and low-friction materials. E_{el} is Young's modulus of the elastic element, ε_{el} its percentage strain and S_{el} its cross-sectional area (of the high-friction material). The COFs of the high- and low-friction materials are μ_{hf} and μ_{lf}, respectively. When the elastic elements are uncompressed (i.e., $\varepsilon_{\text{el}} = 0$), then $\mu_{\text{eff}} = \mu_{\text{lf}}$. Compression of the elastic element increases the force applied to the high-friction material F_{hf} by an amount equal to the decrease of force applied to the low-friction material F_{lf}. If F_{hf} reaches the total force F_{human}, the low-friction material is no longer in contact with the floor and $\mu_{\text{eff}} = \mu_{\text{hf}}$.

The prototype mechanism consists of a set of brake pads, composed of a rigid element (aluminum), elastic element (EVA foam) and high-friction material (Santoprene rubber), which are translated orthogonally with respect to the sole to modulate friction. The sole of the shoe is polytetrafluoroethylene (PTFE) because of its low self-contact COF. The actuator driving the brake pads is a thin-profile stepper motor. Rotational motion from the motor is transferred by a gear train to lead screws, which are fastened by thread on to the rigid element of the brake pads. Brake pad extension was tracked by an optical rotary encoder sensing the rotation of the gear train. The brake is controlled by simple thresholding, i.e., actuation ceases when the desired position is reached. On the bottom of the mechanism, PTFE tabs protrude as the supporting low-friction material. Preliminary tests determined that the shoe could render COFs over a range of approximately 0.11–0.4 for a mass range of 0–11.4 kg.

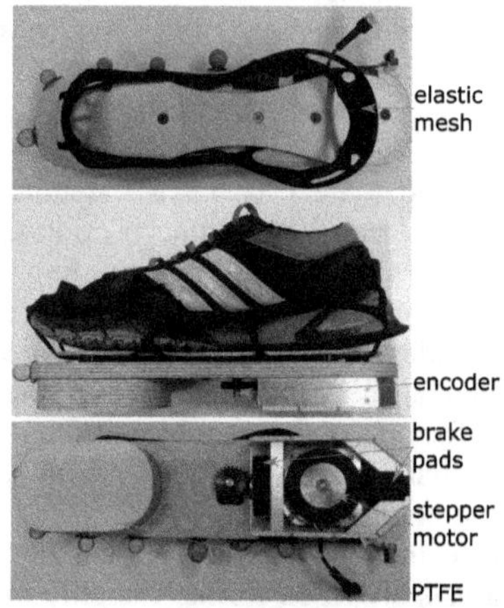

Figure 2. Top, side and bottom pictures of the prototype with annotations. The prototype fastens to subject's shoes using an elastic mesh.

FOOT-CONTROLLED POINTING

Method

Our experiment used Wobbrock et al.'s *FittsStudy*,[1] where subjects were evaluated using constant low friction (CF), and with high friction over target regions, but low friction elsewhere (VF), to complete 1D and 2D tasks for nine movement conditions. The movement conditions had amplitudes $A = \{300, 600, 1000\}$ and widths $W = \{20, 60, 128\}$, which gave an index of difficulty range of $ID = \{1.74 - 5.67\}$. Each movement condition included a total of fifteen trials, of which the first four were discarded to mask learning effects, resulting in 396 recorded movements per subject. To ensure suppression of learning effects, a number of other measures were taken. The presentation of each combination of interface and dimensionality was based on a Latin squares design and the order of movement conditions within each task was randomized. Before each subject began, they would complete three trials for each combination of interface, task dimensionality and movement condition. To mask the sound of motor actuation, subjects listened to pink noise, played through earbuds, and in addition, wore sound suppression earmuffs during all phases of the experiment.

[1] https://depts.washington.edu/aimgroup/proj/fittsstudy/

In order to guarantee that target regions were high-friction, both proximity and velocity thresholds were used to determine the point in time to extend the shoe's brake pads. Actuation time lasted approximately 180 ms and resulted in an estimated change in COF of approximately 0.25.

Apparatus and Procedure

The apparatus consisted of the prototype, a slanted PTFE surface, three motion capture cameras (OptiTrack Flex:V100R2), a 24-inch 1920 × 1080 LCD monitor and an ASUS TP500LN laptop computer (Intel® Core™ i7-4510U CPU @ 2 GHz, 8 GB RAM, Windows 10) with a mouse. The motion capture cameras, sampled at 100 Hz, tracked the position of the subject's right foot during the evaluation, which was streamed via USB to a modified version of *FittsStudy* as cursor position input. Subjects wore the prototype on their right foot, which they slid on the slanted PTFE surface to control the mouse cursor. The position of the foot on the PTFE surface was mapped directly to screen coordinates (i.e., absolute positioning). Subjects used a conventional mouse left-click to indicate a selection since our interest was specifically focussed on the human ability to control cursor position. Subjects were instructed to move the cursor to each target as quickly and accurately as possible, with emphasis on speed.

Before each subject's participation, the PTFE surface and prototype sole were sanded with 600 and 1000 grit sandpaper and subsequently cleaned with isopropyl alcohol. Between each of the four blocks experimental conditions, i.e., the pairing of interface (CF or VF) and dimensionality (1D or 2D), the prototype sole and the PTFE surface were wiped clean of PTFE flakes. Figure 3 shows the physical layout of the experimental setup. Before and after the experiment, subjects were required to complete a questionnaire. The pre-experiment questionnaire collected personal data (i.e., age, gender), while the post-experiment questionnaire enquired about interface-specific information such as the subject's levels of comfort, effort, fatigue, perception of variable friction, dimensionality preferences, strategies employed, and difficulties encountered.

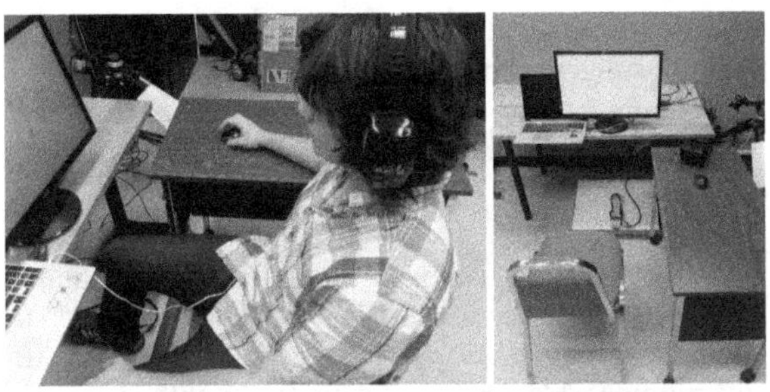

Figure 3. Apparatus used in the foot-controlled pointing Fitts' characterization. The PTFE surface was set on an incline to facilitate a greater range of motion when sliding the foot while sitting.

Results

A total of twelve subjects (6F / 6M) aged 20–33 ($\mu = 24.3$, $\sigma = 3.8$), voluntarily consented to participate in the study, which received approval from the McGill Research Ethics Board. Experimentation lasted an average of 45 minutes and subjects were compensated $10. The pre-experiment questionnaire revealed that eleven of the subjects were right-foot dominant, while the other was ambidextrous. Three of the subjects encountered foot-operated interfaces (e.g., car driving, piano/organ playing) less than once per week, but the remaining nine dealt with them on a consistent basis (i.e., more than twice per week). Table 1 summarizes the Fitts' models and their associated coefficients of determination as well as the mean throughputs (TP) and percentage errors for each combination of interface and dimensionality.

Table 1. Fitts' law movement time models, their coefficients of determination and associated TPs and error rates.

Interface	Movement Model	R^2	TP (bits/s)	% Error
1D CF	$MT = ID \times 341 - 7$	0.74	3.04	6.38
1D VF	$MT = ID \times 271 - 156$	0.74	3.22	6.40
2D CF	$MT = ID \times 619 - 363$	0.76	2.09	10.93
2D VF	$MT = ID \times 470 - 22$	0.80	2.21	8.19

A two-factor repeated measures ANOVA was used to analyze the TP data, revealing significant effects of both friction interface ($F_{1,11} = 21.31, p < 0.001$) and task dimensionality ($F_{1,11} = 350.40, p < 0.001$). No interaction was found between these two factors ($F_{1,11} = 0.53, p = 0.48$). Application of Mauchly's test confirmed that the assumption of sphericity had not been violated ($F = 0.72, p = 0.68$). Further inspection, comparing the TPs of constant and variable friction with respect to task dimensionality reveal significant differences between the interfaces for the 1D ($F_{1,11} = 10.87, p < 0.01$) and 2D tasks ($F_{1,11} = 5.07, p < 0.05$). Graphical illustration of the TPs can be seen in Figure 4.

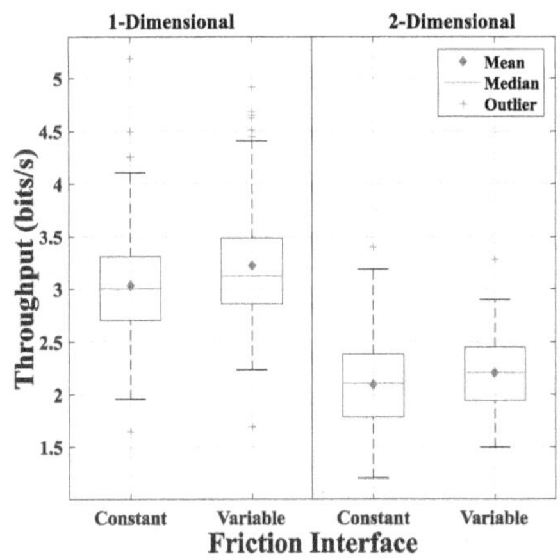

Figure 4. Box plots of all four combinations of friction interface and task dimensionality.

Discussion

Movement Models

As is apparent from the slopes of the 1D and 2D models, the additional dimension nearly doubles the required movement time for pointing tasks with the same ID. We note that longer movement times are especially prevalent for small target widths. A peculiarity seen in the 2D CF case is its low intercept, which we believe to be attributed to the inherent difficulty of accurate 2D foot-pointing on a slippery surface. While reduced friction minimizes the effort required to move the foot, a lack of accurate fine motor control was observed.

Subjects had the tendency to overshoot targets by a small distance, and subsequently attempt correction, only to overshoot again, spending considerable time in the process of repeated corrections. The same characteristic is not seen in the 1D CF case, most likely due to heel rotation, which subjects often employed.

Throughput

Although this is, to our knowledge, only the second foot-controlled pointing system analyzed using ISO 9241-9, a clear difference in performance is seen between our implementation and that of Velloso et al. [17]. We note that while our foot-based interface cannot achieve the same performance as the best hand-controlled devices, it is nevertheless competitive, as shown in Table 2. Similarly, observed error rates are comparable to that of conventional pointing devices. We attribute the relatively strong performance of the foot-based interface primarily to the inclined, low-friction surface used in our experiment. Minimal effort in sliding, and the use of sticky targets, greatly simplify foot-controlled pointing. We hypothesize that with practice, improved TPs and reduced error rates would be seen and establish the system as a clear competitor with touchpads and trackballs.

Table 2. Reported throughputs and error rates of hand and foot-operated pointing devices evaluated using ISO 9241-9 on 2D tasks.

Hand-Controlled Device	Throughput (bits/s)	Error (%)
Mouse [16]	3.7 – 4.9	11.0
Trackball [16]	3.0	8.6
Touchpad [16]	0.99 – 2.9	7.0
Wiimote [11]	2.59	10.2
Joystick [16]	1.6 – 2.55	9.6
Wii Classic Controller [11]	1.48	6.58
Foot-Controlled Device	**Throughput (bits/s)**	**Error (%)**
2D VF	**2.21**	**8.19**
Depth Camera [17]	1.16	7.64

Post-Experiment Data

Likert Scales

With regards to ease of use, comfort, and smoothness, users indicated a clear appreciation for the interface. We believe this was owed largely to the low-friction surface and possibly the use of familiar mouse clicks as a selection modality. The midrange values of physical effort scores can be explained by the lengthy duration of the experiment and lack of experience with the body kinematics associated with foot pointing. We attribute the mental effort scores to the inherent concentration required when performing Fitts' tasks. Lastly, we note that subjects only indicated initial fatigue, at a low level, after more than thirty minutes of continuous pointing activity. This result is likely helpful for the adoption of new peripherals.

Perceptions, Preferences, Strategies and Challenges

Seven of the subjects reported perceiving the friction modulation, five of whom felt vibration in addition to increased sliding resistance. Only two of these subjects actually preferred the variable-friction interface, despite its superiority in performance. Those who disliked variable friction complained

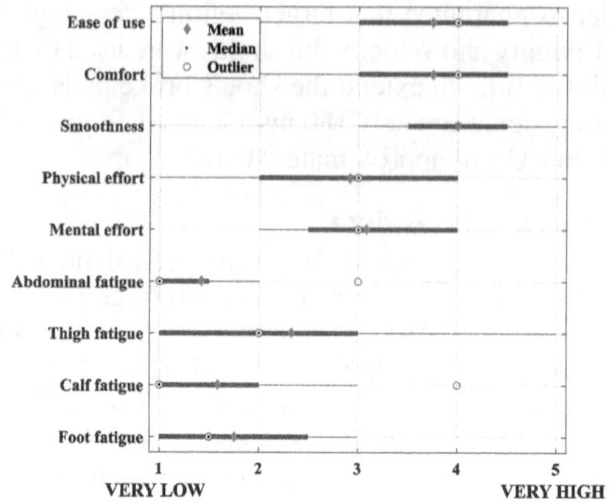

Figure 5. Box plots of the Likert scale data collected in the post-experiment questionnaire.

of feeling a lack of control and difficulty in manipulation as desired. Given the improved results of the variable friction modality, we hypothesize that subjects merely perceived a lack of control, due to the increased sliding resistance, rather than having actually experienced one. Four subjects preferred the 2D task for its challenge, while the remainder enjoyed the simplicity of a single dimension. The most preferred direction of movement was diagonal, along the *northwest/southeast* axis, where north is located at the toe and south is located at the heel. We presume this preference can be credited to a physiological predisposition, as similar findings are seen in other publications [2].

Fine motor control, with respect to small-target pointing, was reported as the most challenging aspect of the experiment. Two specific strategies were noted: firm placement of the left foot for superior control, and heel rotation for improved accuracy. Only two of the subjects cited firm foot placement, but all utilized heel rotation. Subjects generally employed heel rotation in low amplitude 1D tasks because of the ease of this movement.

Subjects' recommendations were widely varied, but consisted mostly of suggested physical improvements, described below.

- Subjects wanted to configure the device's friction levels to their preference. This would negate the feeling of lacking control and allow users to fine tune the device as desired.
- Adding vibration feedback was suggested by a number of subjects. Given the inconsistency in sliding friction perception, we hypothesize that this feedback may cause users to overcompensate and perhaps undershoot their targets.
- Modification of the mapping type from an absolute one to a rate-based implementation (i.e., first-order control) may be assistive in low-amplitude movements due to the smaller displacements for reduced speeds.

Potential Applications

A number of potential applications have been envisioned for use with our current implementation. Primarily, these employ variable friction to indicate a change in gradient, e.g., a volume slider whose friction increases with volume, or modulated friction to create virtual "bumps", e.g., detents in a rotational menu, similar to the alarm clock of Levesque et al. [9], but driven by foot. High-friction borders around grouped regions, e.g., individual paragraphs, could facilitate movement through text documents by foot, leaving the user's hands free to manipulate the keyboard as desired. Simeone et al. [15] offer at least two scenarios where variable friction would be beneficial, such as during a swipe gesture to create a bump indicating that the user has passed over an object or menu item, or to create a friction gradient providing feedback of a parameter level during a control operation.

CONCLUSION

Constrained, low-friction surfaces are comfortable, easy to manipulate and generate little fatigue when used for foot pointing over extended periods of time. We found further evidence that the foot may compete with traditional hand-operated pointing devices. The notion that the foot is better suited to coarse grained, non-accurate tasks is supported by evidence from this experiment, but the analysis clearly indicates that assistive techniques (i.e., variable friction), can make our feet effective in tasks requiring precision.

Evaluation of foot-controlled pointing systems against other pointing devices should be performed with tasks requiring simultaneous cursor control and keyboard manipulation to demonstrate the improved efficiency foot pointing may offer. In addition, the effects of practice require further exploration [18]. Lastly, variable-friction pointing systems should be evaluated with distracting targets [9] to ensure their effectiveness in more realistic use cases.

REFERENCES

1. Motoyuki Akamatsu and I Scott MacKenzie. 1996. Movement characteristics using a mouse with tactile and force feedback. *International Journal of Human-Computer Studies* 45, 4 (1996), 483–493.
2. Jason Alexander, Teng Han, William Judd, Pourang Irani, and Sriram Subramanian. 2012. Putting your best foot forward: investigating real-world mappings for foot-based gestures. In *Proceedings of the SIGCHI Conference on Human Factors in Computing Systems*. ACM, 1229–1238.
3. Olivier Bau, Ivan Poupyrev, Ali Israr, and Chris Harrison. 2010. TeslaTouch: electrovibration for touch surfaces. In *Proceedings of the 23nd annual ACM symposium on User interface software and technology*. ACM, 283–292.
4. Andy Cockburn and Stephen Brewster. 2005. Multimodal feedback for the acquisition of small targets. *Ergonomics* 48, 9 (2005), 1129–1150.
5. Jack Tigh Dennerlein, David B Martin, and Christopher Hasser. 2000. Force-feedback improves performance for steering and combined steering-targeting tasks. In *Proceedings of the SIGCHI conference on Human Factors in Computing Systems*. ACM, 423–429.
6. William K English, Douglas C Engelbart, and Melvyn L Berman. 1967. Display-selection techniques for text manipulation. *Human factors in electronics, IEEE Transactions on* 1 (1967), 5–15.
7. Fredrick P Garcia and Kim-Phuong L Vu. 2011. Effectiveness of hand-and foot-operated secondary input devices for word-processing tasks before and after training. *Computers in Human Behavior* 27, 1 (2011), 285–295.
8. Errol R Hoffmann. 1991. A comparison of hand and foot movement times. *Ergonomics* 34, 4 (1991), 397–406.
9. Vincent Levesque, Louise Oram, Karon MacLean, Andy Cockburn, Nicholas D Marchuk, Dan Johnson, J Edward Colgate, and Michael A Peshkin. 2011. Enhancing physicality in touch interaction with programmable friction. In *Proceedings of the SIGCHI Conference on Human Factors in Computing Systems*. ACM, 2481–2490.
10. Guillaume Millet, Martin J-D Otis, Daniel Horodniczy, and Jeremy R Cooperstock. Design of Variable-Friction Devices for Shoe-Floor Contact. *submitted for publication to Mechatronics* (????).
11. Daniel Natapov, Steven J Castellucci, and I Scott MacKenzie. 2009. ISO 9241-9 evaluation of video game controllers. In *Proceedings of Graphics Interface 2009*. Canadian Information Processing Society, 223–230.
12. Toni Pakkanen and Roope Raisamo. 2004. Appropriateness of foot interaction for non-accurate spatial tasks. In *CHI'04 extended abstracts on Human factors in computing systems*. ACM, 1123–1126.
13. Glenn Pearson and Mark Weiser. 1986. Of moles and men: the design of foot controls for workstations. In *ACM SIGCHI Bulletin*, Vol. 17. ACM, 333–339.
14. Glenn Pearson and Mark Weiser. 1988. Exploratory evaluations of two versions of a foot-operated cursor-positioning device in a target-selection task. *ACM SIGCHI Bulletin* 19, 3 (1988), 70–75.
15. Adalberto L Simeone, Eduardo Velloso, James Alexander, and Hans Gellersen. 2014. Feet movement in desktop 3D interaction. In *3D User Interfaces (3DUI), 2014 IEEE Symposium on*. IEEE, 71–74.
16. R William Soukoreff and I Scott MacKenzie. 2004. Towards a standard for pointing device evaluation, perspectives on 27 years of Fitts' law research in HCI. *International journal of human-computer studies* 61, 6 (2004), 751–789.
17. Eduardo Velloso, Jason Alexander, Andreas Bulling, and Hans Gellersen. 2015a. Interactions under the desk: A characterisation of foot movements for input in a seated position. In *Human-Computer Interaction–INTERACT 2015*. Springer, 384–401.
18. Eduardo Velloso, Dominik Schmidt, Jason Alexander, Hans Gellersen, and Andreas Bulling. 2015b. The Feet in Human–Computer Interaction: A Survey of Foot-Based Interaction. *ACM Computing Surveys (CSUR)* 48, 2 (2015), 21.

To Miss is Human: Information-Theoretic Rationale for Target Misses in Fitts' Law

Julien Gori, Olivier Rioul and Yves Guiard
LTCI, CNRS, Telecom ParisTech
Université Paris-Saclay
Paris, France
firstname.lastname@telecom-paristech.fr

ABSTRACT

In usual Fitts' law experiments the outcome of a pointing act can be either measured as an error, i.e., a distance from endpoint to target center, or categorized in an all-or-none way as a hit versus a miss. Information theory offers a useful distinction between transmission errors (the received symbol is wrong) and erasures (the received symbol is empty). Although Fitts' law research has been very much inspired by the information theoretic rationale, the error/erasure distinction has escaped attention so far: Target misses have always been treated as normally-distributed errors, through the effective index of difficulty ID_e. The paper introduces a new index of difficulty based on the simple observation that a target miss conveys zero bit of information, i.e., it is an erasure. Not only is the new index more consistent with the fundamentals of information theory, it is much simpler to derive than the ISO-recommended ID_e.

ACM Classification Keywords

H.5.2. Information Interfaces and Presentation: User Interfaces; Theory and Methods

Author Keywords

Information Theory; Fitts' Law; Human Performance Models

INTRODUCTION

Fitts' law is a well documented rule [13] that predicts the time MT it takes to reach a target of width W located at distance D. The law conveniently reduces the two-parameter task (D,W) to a single parameter called the index of difficulty ID [12]:

$$ID = \log_2\left(1+\frac{D}{W}\right) \quad \text{bit}^1.$$

[1]This form of the ID is known as the Shannon ID [11]. Other well-known forms are the Welford $ID = \log_2(\frac{1}{2}+\frac{D}{W})$ [18] and the Fitts $ID = \log_2(\frac{2D}{W})$ [4].

CHI 2017, May 6-11, 2017, Denver, CO, USA.

http://dx.doi.org/10.1145/3025453.3025660

Movement time MT has been found empirically to be linearly related to ID:

$$MT = a+b\cdot ID. \quad (1)$$

The experimental paradigm introduced by Fitts [4] consists of measuring MT, which participants try their best to minimize, at various levels of ID. Ideally, movement endpoints must always fall within the prescribed tolerance interval of width W—or at least with very few misses. Unfortunately, the paradigm faces a serious difficulty: As has been observed ever since Fitts [4], the percentage of target misses tends to increase systematically, along with MT, as ID is raised, meaning that experimenters face two effects of the same manipulation, which is one too many. Different participants may also have different biases towards speed or accuracy (see e.g. [6] for further discussion on the innate bias in psycho-physical experiments).

The currently received—and actually standardized [10, 17]—solution is to adjust the ID by computing an *effective* index of difficulty ID_e in the place of the prescribed or *nominal* ID. The adjusted index takes into account the empirical standard deviation σ of the endpoint distribution:

$$ID_e = \log_2\left(1+\frac{D}{W_e}\right) = \log_2\left(1+\frac{D}{4.133\sigma}\right) \quad \text{bit.} \quad (2)$$

Historically, Fitts' law emerged in a specific context: Information Theory was booming[2], and at the time many psychologists (e.g., [1, 9, 14]) were trying to apply its operational results to human behaviour. One concept crucial to most researchers, Fitts included, was the *channel capacity*, namely, the maximum rate at which information can be reliably transmitted in a communication system. The expression for ID shown in Equation (1) is based on Shannon's formula for the capacity of the Gaussian channel [3, 4, 12].

Errors vs. Erasures

In this paper, we call attention to the distinction made in Information Theory between two sorts of transmission mistakes: *errors* vs. *erasures*. We will show that this classic distinction, which apparently has escaped the attention of Fitts' law students, opens the way to an elegant theoretical solution to

[2]Shannon himself believed it was even ballooning [16].

the problem raised in the Fitts paradigm by the non-constant frequency of target misses.

In communication engineering, an *error* is said to have occurred when the received symbol differs from that originally sent. For example, the word BUTTER is received in the place of the sent word BATTER, the A having been accidentally replaced by an U. But suppose that the received word is B?TTER, with the question mark signaling a missing character: This is what is called an *erasure*. One important difference between an error and an erasure is that the former conveys wrong information whereas the latter conveys no information at all.

How does the error/erasure distinction apply to Fitts' target-reaching paradigm? Below we will argue that the option most consistent with the logic of this paradigm is to model target misses as erasures, rather than errors.

MEASURING ACCURACY IN FITTS' PARADIGM

The goal of a Fitts' law experiment being to observe and study the speed-accuracy tradeoff described by Woodworth [20], the choice of the metrics used to measure *speed* and *accuracy* is fundamental. While there has been unanimous agreement in the literature that movement time provides a satisfactory measure of speed [8], the measure for accuracy defined by Equation (1) has been controversial from the outset [3]. It is only recently that the adjustment for errors was standardized by ISO [10, 17].

In a Fitts' law experimental setup[3], the task of the participant is to aim for a target of predefined width as fast as possible while making as few mistakes (target misses) as possible. There are three different ways of handling these mistakes: simply ignoring them, measuring the error rate (a percentage), or measuring the spread of endpoints (typically a standard deviation).

- *Ignoring the mistakes.* Fitts, who did not measure actual amplitudes, classified the movements in an all-or-none way as hits and misses. Although he did tabulate the (variable) error rates he obtained in his experiments, he felt in a position to leave them aside because of the "small incidence" of target misses [4, p. 265].
- *Taking the error rate into account.* To our knowledge, Crossman [3] was the first to try to incorporate the error rate information into his *ID* measure, leveraging the standard Gaussian distribution model.
- *Taking the spread of endpoints into account.* This is the standardized way of measuring accuracy in Fitts' law [10, 17]. Recourse to the standard deviation as a measure of accuracy has the implication that the amplitude of the mistake matters in the upcoming analysis: if the target is missed, the farther from the edge of the interval, the worse the performance. It also implies that there is equivalence between two movements hitting the target if and only if they end up at exactly the same distance from the center of the target.

[3]While Fitts's time-minimization paradigm is widespread in HCI, it is important to bear in mind that it is not the only workable paradigm for studying the speed-accuracy trade-off of aimed movement [7, 8, 15].

The ISO standard and Fitts' law literature in general treats mistakes as *errors*, by referring to the standard deviation of the endpoints distribution—either by direct estimation or through a calculation from error rates. Thus in the *error* concept, the accuracy depends on the (continuous) distance between the movement endpoint and the target center.

There seems to be a contradiction between this approach and the all-or-none logic of Fitts' experimental paradigm: Since the only instruction for participants is to *hit* the target about 96% of the time (i.e., *miss* it about 4% of the time), all movements that end up inside the W interval should be considered equivalent, in keeping with the observation that in a real-world interface, what matters is not precisely *where* the click takes place, but rather *whether or not* the click falls in the intended area. This corresponds to the information-theoretic concept of *erasures*.

Besides this conceptual mismatch between errors and mistakes, ID_e suffers from at least three further deficiencies.

INFORMATION-THEORETIC CRITIQUE OF ID_e

The detailed expression of the effective width W_e in Equation (2) as given in [17] is as follows. Let σ denote the standard deviation of the end-point distribution, and ε the error rate, i.e., the proportion of target misses:

- If σ is available:

$$W_e = 4.133\sigma. \tag{3}$$

- Otherwise:

$$W_e = \begin{cases} W \cdot \frac{2.066}{z(1-\varepsilon/2)} & \text{if } \varepsilon > 0.0049\% \\ 0.5089 \cdot W & \text{otherwise.} \end{cases} \tag{4}$$

The received justification is as follows [12, Section 2]:

> "The entropy (H), or information, in a normal distribution is $H = \log_2((2\pi e)^{1/2}\sigma) = \log_2(4.133\sigma)$, where σ is the standard deviation in the unit of measurement. Splitting the constant 4.133 into a pair of z-scores for the unit-normal curve (i.e., $\sigma = 1$), we find that the area bounded by $z = \pm 2.066$ represents about 96 % of the total area of the distribution. In other words, a condition that target width is analogous to the information-theoretic concept of noise is that 96 % of the hits are within the target and 4 % of the hits miss the target [...]. When an error rate other than 4% is observed, target width should be adjusted to form the effective target width in keeping with the underlying theory."

We see three issues with ID_e:

1. The computation of W_e as 4.133σ as well as the computation leading to Equation (4) presumes a Gaussian distribution of endpoints [17], but the validity of this hypothesis has been questioned empirically, e.g., [4] [19].
2. To our knowledge Information Theory provides no justification to the relation $W_e = 4.133\sigma$. When Crossman [3] calculated the expression for W_e from the area under the standard normal curve, he took the 5% value as an arbitrary "permissible" error rate. McKenzie [12] noticed that

by changing the arbitrary rate from 5% to 3.88% (approximately 4%), the entropy of the rectangular distribution of width W_e would equal the entropy of the Gaussian distribution of standard deviation σ (see Appendix), but this is no more than a nice coincidence: we can see no information-theoretic reason to equalize these two entropies.[4].

3. The threshold of error rate placed at 0.0049% is arbitrary. Even if considering a Gaussian distribution for the endpoints, the one-to-one relationship between standard deviations and error rates is only true for strictly positive error rates. Indeed, when the error rate is vanishing, the standard deviation is also vanishing, so ID_e tends to infinity! To prevent this from happening, [17] recommends that below a certain error rate (0.0049%), ID_e should be kept constant. The justification of the threshold error rate of 0.0049% is that it "rounds to 0.00". As shown below, the existence of such a threshold is in fact adverse to the theory.

The standardized index of difficulty ID_e is thus questionable. It relies on the unsafe Gaussian hypothesis, two arbitrary constants, and one coincidence. Even more importantly, it has never been shown to be the correct expression of the capacity of a human-motor channel—the expected rationale behind Fitts' law.

We now propose a new effective index $ID(\varepsilon)$ that is compliant with Fitts' experimental design, does not need the Gaussian hypothesis and is justified theoretically as a channel capacity.

A COMPLIANT INDEX OF DIFFICULTY: $ID(\varepsilon)$

We have already noted that treating target misses as errors is not adapted to Fitts' paradigm—these events should rather be viewed as erasures. Indeed, the design of the experiment entails a binary decision: there is a target and the movement either finishes inside (a hit) or outside (a miss). This is consistent with the instruction "try to hit the target" as opposed to "try to aim for the center of the target". In this section we build a model for a channel which allows erasures, and obtain a new index of difficulty $ID(\varepsilon)$ through Shannon's concept of channel capacity.

Consider a channel that oscillates randomly between a good (G) state and a bad (B) state, with probability ε of being in state B and probability $1-\varepsilon$ of being in state G. When the channel is in its good state, it corresponds to the typical channel of capacity $\log_2(1+\frac{D}{W})$ described by McKenzie [12], which we refer to as the *Fitts channel*. However, when the channel is in its bad state it can only produce erasures—we call it an *erasure channel*. This configuration (Figure 1) is known as a *compound* channel [5].

We now evaluate Shannon's *capacity* of such a channel as a common ground to compare the performance of different participants operating at different accuracy levels (with different values of ε). The channel capacity corresponds to the maximum transmission rate that the participants would have achieved with an arbitrarily small error rate, as if they never missed the target. Shannon's capacity of the compound channel of Figure 1 is given by the following theorem.

[4]Incidentally, these entropies can both be negative. Information Theory distinguishes the (discrete) entropy of a discrete random variable, which is non-negative and serves as a measure of information, and the (so-called *differential*) entropy of a continuous random variable such as a normal random variable, which is positive for large variances and negative for small variances and thus cannot be interpreted as a measure of information [2]

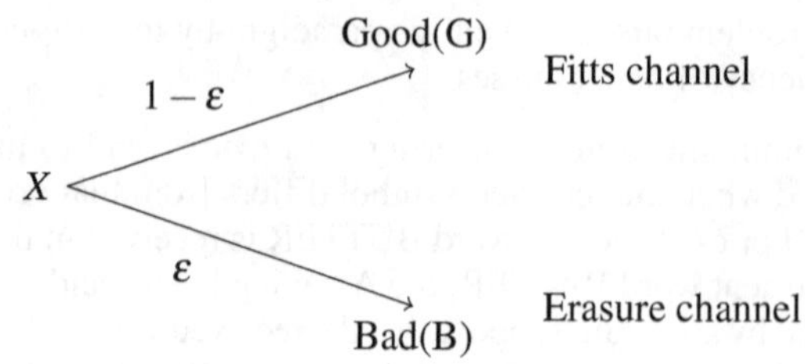

Figure 1. Compound channel for an aiming task with target misses.

THEOREM (COMPOUND CHANNEL CAPACITY). *Consider a compound channel as in Figure 1, with probability ε of being in state B and probability $1-\varepsilon$ of being in state G. The capacity of such a channel is given by*

$$C = (1-\varepsilon)\log_2\left(1+\frac{D}{W}\right).$$

As expected, the obtained capacity is lower than the capacity $\log_2(1+\frac{D}{W})$ that would have been achieved with 100% hitting accuracy ($\varepsilon = 0$).

The formal information-theoretic proof is known [2] and summarized in the Appendix for completeness, but is easy to sketch in order to understand the reasoning: The participant is effectively time sharing both channels. With Fitts' channel, the transmitted information is $\log_2\left(1+\frac{D}{W}\right)$ bits and with the erasure channel the transmitted information is 0 bit, so that, on average, $C = (1-\varepsilon)\times\log_2\left(1+\frac{D}{W}\right)+\varepsilon\times 0$. In line with Fitts' parallel between capacity and ID, our new effective index is

$$ID(\varepsilon) = (1-\varepsilon)\log_2\left(1+\frac{D}{W}\right)$$

where ε is no other than the traditional 'error rate' (more cautiously designated here as the percentage of target misses).

COMPARING THE TWO INDICES

We now provide an analytical comparison of ID_e and $ID(\varepsilon)$. The behavior of the standardized ID_e for vanishing error rates is problematic. Indeed, the inverse Gauss error function (see Appendix) $\mathrm{erf}^{-1}(1-\varepsilon)$ tends to $+\infty$ as ε vanishes, so that we would normally have

$$\lim_{\varepsilon\to 0} ID_e = \infty.$$

Due to the 0.0049% bounding, however, instead we obtain

$$\lim_{\varepsilon\to 0} ID_e = \log_2\left(1+\frac{D}{0.5089W}\right) \simeq \log_2\left(1+\frac{2D}{W}\right)$$
$$= 1+\log_2\left(\frac{1}{2}+\frac{D}{W}\right),$$

which is equivalent to the Welford index of difficulty [18]. The particular choice to bound the index at the 0.0049% rate results in the index coincidentally tending to the Welford ID, not the Shannon ID. Therefore, there is no continuity as epsilon approaches zero for ID_e.

In contrast, $ID(\varepsilon)$ *does* have the property of continuity towards zero since obviously $ID(0) = ID$.

Figure 2 shows the two indices $ID(\varepsilon)$, ID_e as well as the unbounded $u\text{-}ID_e$ (for which the 0.0049% distinction is not made) for $D/W = 15$ as a function of ε in the interval $[0-1]$. The difference $ID_e - ID(\varepsilon)$ between ID_e and $ID(\varepsilon)$ is lowest around $\varepsilon = 0.1$. With higher values of ε, the difference increases but such high errors rates are not common. However, for very small values of ε, $ID(\varepsilon)$ can be up to 1 bit smaller then ID_e. It can be noted that this difference accounts for very careful participants which are well handled by $ID(\varepsilon)$.

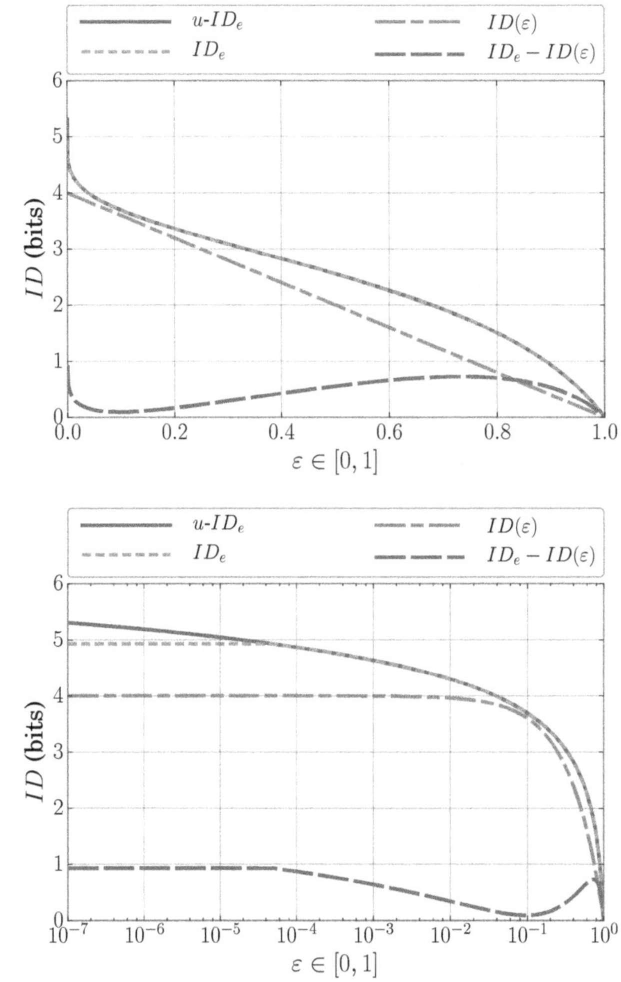

Figure 2. Comparison of $ID(\varepsilon)$ and ID_e for erasure rate in $[0,1]$, for $\frac{D}{W} = 15$. $u\text{-}ID_e$ refers to ID_e where the 0.0049% distinction is not made. The scale is lin-lin above and lin-log below.

IMPLICATIONS FOR HCI

As we have seen, there remains room in Fitts' law research to improve the theory. We feel that the erasure-channel notion has promise to improve our conceptual grasp of accuracy, the Achilles heel of Fitts' experimental paradigm.

Capitalizing on the fact—so far unrecognized, to our knowledge—that the target misses that take place in Fitts' time-minimization paradigm can be interpreted as erasures in the language of Information Theory, we have derived a new effective index of difficulty which has a number of desirable properties: not only is it theoretically safer than the ISO index as it does not presuppose a Gaussian distribution of endpoints, it is also theoretically more relevant, having been proven to measure a capacity in Shannon's strict sense. It is also more convenient in practice for two reasons: (a) it is continuous towards the zero-error rate region, thus allowing the researcher to dispense with an arbitrary treatment of the 0 percent miss case; and (b) it is a great deal simpler to compute than the ID_e traditionally used in HCI by Fitts' law practitioners.

This is a purely theoretical note and obviously more research is needed to seriously evaluate all the implications of our result. The reader might feel that perhaps the above-described index is just a better tool to obtain essentially the same results, but there is nothing so practical as a good theory, and there is reason to think that a conceptually neater and practically easier ID should help the HCI researchers who routinely exploit Fitts' law to obtain safer results.

ACKNOWLEDGMENTS

The authors would like to thank Michel Beaudouin-Lafon for his precious help during the preparation of the manuscript.

APPENDIX

PROOF FOR W_e. Consider the endpoint location Y about the target center, assumed normally distributed $\mathcal{N}(0, \sigma^2)$. The event $|Y| > \frac{W}{2}$ defines a target miss. Then target width W and error rate ε are related by:

$$\varepsilon = 1 - \text{erf}\Big(\frac{W}{2\sqrt{2}\sigma}\Big) \tag{5}$$

which allows to link W and W_e. Equalizing $\log_2 W_e$ to the Gaussian entropy $H = \log_2(\sqrt{2\pi e}\sigma)$ gives $W_e = 4.133\sigma$, which from Equation (5) amounts to choose $\varepsilon = 3.88\%$. □

PROOF OF THE THEOREM. The channel capacity [2] is defined as the maximized value of mutual information $I(X;Y)$. Let S ($= G$ or B) be the channel state. Since observing the output Y already determines the state, one has $I(X;Y) = I(X;(Y,S))$. By the chain rule for mutual information [2], one has

$$\begin{aligned} I(X;(Y,S)) &= \mathbb{P}(S=G)\cdot I(X;Y|S=G) + \mathbb{P}(S=B)\cdot I(X;Y|S=B) \\ &= (1-\varepsilon)\cdot I(X;Y|S=G) + \varepsilon\cdot I(X;Y|S=B). \end{aligned}$$

Here $I(X;Y|S=G)$ is the mutual information computed for the Fitts channel, and $I(X;Y|S=B) = 0$ bit since for bad state, only an erasure can be output. Thus $I(X;Y) = (1-\varepsilon)I(X;Y|S=G)$. Maximizing over the input distribution gives the result. □

REFERENCES

1. F. Attneave. 1959. *Applications of information theory to psychology: A summary of basic concepts, methods, and results.* Henry Holt.
2. T. M. Cover and J. A. Thomas. 2012. *Elements of information theory.* John Wiley & Sons.
3. E. R. F. W. Crossman. 1957. The speed and accuracy of simple hand movements. *The nature and acquisition of industrial skills* (1957).
4. P. M. Fitts. 1954. The information capacity of the human motor system in controlling the amplitude of movement. *Journal of experimental psychology* 47, 6 (1954), 381.
5. E. N. Gilbert. 1960. Capacity of a Burst-Noise Channel. *Bell system technical journal* 39, 5 (1960), 1253–1265.
6. D. M. Green and J. A. Swets. 1966. Signal detection theory and psychophysics. 1966. *New York* 888 (1966), 889.
7. Y. Guiard, H. B. Olafsdottir, and S. T. Perrault. 2011. Fitt's law as an explicit time/error trade-off. In *Proceedings of the SIGCHI Conference on Human Factors in Computing Systems.* ACM, 1619–1628.
8. Y. Guiard and O. Rioul. 2015. A mathematical description of the speed/accuracy trade-off of aimed movement. In *Proceedings of the 2015 British HCI Conference.* ACM, 91–100.
9. W. E. Hick. 1952. On the rate of gain of information. *Quarterly Journal of Experimental Psychology* 4, 1 (1952), 11–26. DOI: http://dx.doi.org/10.1080/17470215208416600
10. ISO9241. 2000. 9241-9 Ergonomic requirements for office work with visual display terminals (VDTs)-Part 9: Requirements for non-keyboard input devices (FDIS-Final Draft International Standard), 2000. *International Organization for Standardization* (2000).
11. I. S. McKenzie. 1989. A note on the information-theoretic basis for Fitts' law. *Journal of motor behavior* 21, 3 (1989), 323–330.
12. I. S. McKenzie. 1992. *Fitts' law as a performance model in human-computer interaction.* Ph.D. Dissertation. University of Toronto.
13. I. S. McKenzie. 2002. Bibliography of Fitts' law research. (2002). http://www.yorku.ca/mack/RN-Fitts_bib.htm [Online; last update: June 25, 2002].
14. G. A. Miller. 1956. The magical number seven, plus or minus two: some limits on our capacity for processing information. *Psychological Review* 63, 2 (1956), 81–97.
15. Richard A Schmidt, Howard Zelaznik, Brian Hawkins, James S Frank, and John T Quinn Jr. 1979. Motor-output variability: a theory for the accuracy of rapid motor acts. *Psychological review* 86, 5 (1979), 415.
16. C. E. Shannon. 1956. The bandwagon. *IRE Transactions on Information Theory* 2, 1 (1956), 3.
17. R. W. Soukoreff and I. S. McKenzie. 2004. Towards a Standard for Pointing Device Evaluation, Perspectives on 27 Years of Fitts' Law Research in HCI. *Int. J. Hum.-Comput. Stud.* 61, 6 (Dec. 2004), 751–789. DOI: http://dx.doi.org/10.1016/j.ijhcs.2004.09.001
18. A. T. Welford. 1960. The measurement of sensory-motor performance: Survey and reappraisal of twelve years' progress. *Ergonomics* 3, 3 (1960), 189–230.
19. A. T. Welford, A. H. Norris, and N. W. Shock. 1969. Speed and accuracy of movement and their changes with age. *Acta psychologica* 30 (1969), 3–15.
20. R. S. Woodworth. 1899. Accuracy of voluntary movement. *The Psychological Review: Monograph Supplements* 3, 3 (1899), i.

Implications for Adoption

Joseph Lindley
Imagination
Lancaster University
j.lindley@lancaster.ac.uk

Paul Coulton
Imagination
Lancaster University
p.coulton@lancaster.ac.uk

Miriam Sturdee
HighWire CDT
Lancaster University
m.sturdee@lancaster.ac.uk

ABSTRACT

In this paper we explore the motivations for, and practicalities of, incorporating 'implications for adoption' into HCI research practice. Implications for adoption are speculations which may be used in research projects to scrutinize and explore the implications and requirements associated with a technology's potential adoption in the future. There is a rich tradition within the HCI community of implementing, demonstrating, and testing new interactions or technologies by building prototypes. User-centered design methods help us to develop prototypes to and move toward designs that are validated, efficient, and rewarding to use. However, these studies rarely shift their temporal focus to consider, in any significant detail, what it would mean for a technology to exist *beyond* its prototypical implementation, in other words how these prototypes might ultimately be adopted. Given the CHI community's increasing interest in technology-related human and social effects, the lack of attention paid to adoption represents a significant and relevant gap in current practices. It is this gap that the paper addresses and in doing so offers three contributions: (1) exploring and unpacking different notions of adoption from varying disciplinary perspectives; (2) discussing why considering adoption is relevant and useful, specifically in HCI research; (3) discussing methods for addressing this need, specifically design fiction, and understanding how utilizing these methods may provide researchers with means to better understand the myriad of nuanced, situated, and technologically-mediated relationships that innovative designs facilitate.

Author Keywords

Adoptability; Prototyping; Design Fiction; Implications for Adoption.

ACM Classification Keywords

I.m. Computing Methodologies: Miscellaneous.

CHI 2017, May 06 - 11, 2017, Denver, CO, USA

ACM 978-1-4503-4655-9/17/05···$15.00
DOI: http://dx.doi.org/10.1145/3025453.3025742

INTRODUCTION

The motivation that led us to create this paper came from a very specific requirement: as part of a long-term research project it was necessary to develop a framework for working with the concept of 'adoption' in the context of technological research and development. As regular contributors to the CHI conference, and being well-aware of the huge breadth of perspectives on emerging technology in that community, we were immediately drawn to the corpus of HCI literature to begin our inquiry. Our initial literature search, specifically within SIGCHI conferences, yielded surprisingly few articles of relevance from the field. In one of the few articles we located that directly addresses adoption in a HCI context, a salient question was raised by Chilana et al. They ask whether doing "good science" will help us pass on what we discover in our research to users or consumers, or alternatively, is adoption beyond the scope of what we should be concerned with? "In short", they ask, "must we care?" [17].

Whilst Chilana et al. raise the question several times, they do not offer any concrete answers as to whether we (HCI researchers) should care about the potential future adoption of the interfaces and technologies we are researching. However, our argument is that we *should* care about adoption, an assertion naturally accompanied by questioning *why* should this be the case. By attempting to provide answers to these questions, we establish a motivation for researchers to consider potential future adoption of the technologies and prototypes they are working with. Once this motivation is established we describe how design fiction, among other methods, is well suited tool for incorporating 'implications for adoption' into research projects.

The paper is structured as follows, broadly fitting into three sections. First we review a range of literature from several disciplines in order to showcase the diversity of research relevant to the core idea being discussed (the potential adoption of emerging technology). The review's purpose is to explore a series of different logics for considering any technology's potential future adoption. In the second section, we focus on HCI literature in order to make the case as to why potential future adoption is of particular relevance and importance to HCI. At this point we will have established that speculating about adoption *could* be a useful endeavor, and also forwarded specific HCI-centric reasons for *why* this is the case. In the final section of the paper we describe and discuss strategies for *how* researchers may apply the ideas presented in this paper to their work, and discuss possible trajectories for further research in this area.

YOU SAY POTATO, I SAY POTAHTO

Disciplinary boundaries pervade academic endeavors, but HCI in particular sits at a disciplinary confluence [8,62]. Because of this positioning, different terms for similar phenomena or similar terms for differing phenomena, are commonplace. Therefore, it is useful to introduce and explore a few differing disciplinary perspectives and terminologies for concepts related to adoption of emerging technologies. It would be impossible to review each of these areas exhaustively and instead this section aims to make clear the *breadth* of existing perspectives on adoption and also introduce those perspectives which later on in the paper directly support the proposition that we conclude with; the incorporation of implications for adoption within research projects. Clarifying the diversity of perspectives serves two purposes. While it is important to simply acknowledge that these ways of looking at adoption exist, more significantly in terms of the paper's argumentation it is important that we demonstrate the gap in existing practices. By making the nature of this gap clear, the proposal to include implications for adoption in HCI research projects, is explicated with as much context and clarity as is possible. The first area we review concerns moving technology research out of academic environments and towards commercialization.

The practice of developing not-for-profit research so that it can be commercially exploited is an area of interest and study that was formerly referred to as 'technology transfer' but in modern terms is usually referred to as 'technology exchange'. This could involve a research organization imparting to a commercial organization a prototype to be refined and marketed, an idea that can be developed into a new product, an idea that can improve an existing product, an idea to help mitigate failure for an in-progress project, or practices that make operations more efficient [33]. The defining factor in such activities is the bipartite relationship: there is always a research entity and a commercial entity that are required to work together [37]. The change in terminology, from transfer to exchange, reflects the realization that the relationship between the two entities is rarely linear, requires knowledge to flow back and forth between partners, and envisioning it as a simple one-way flow can be harmful. Chilana et al pose a series of intriguing questions in their CHI paper that studies the transfer of technology from a University research project into a startup company. With awareness that HCI research is usually assessed in terms of feasibility, novelty, and generalizability, and noting that "many researchers believe in making research contributions for the sake of advancing knowledge alone", they ponder "Even if commercialization is not the eventual goal, a focus on adoption might still be helpful for reflecting on design choices and research questions" [17]. One intention of this paper is to reconcile these two perspectives (the first being that research is done for the sake of knowledge alone, the second being that considering adoption may help reflect on design and research questions) and in doing so pose a rhetorical argument that exploring the potential adoption of an emerging technology, may, in itself, contribute to the advancement of knowledge *and* help to refine design and research questions. While studies of efficient technology exchange may offer some insights that are eventually applicable to adoption, for the most part the research in this area is about relationships between people. Foley points out "People, not papers, transfer technology" and that "fully understanding the product development cycle, academicians, will gain a more realistic view of their roles in the process" [33]. Both sentiments are indicative of how technology exchange does not, in isolation, explore or research how a particular technology may be adopted, or what the implications of its adoption may be. Rather studies in this area explore how to cushion the blows of this "contact sport" [33], or how to manage the exchange process. There is an implicit assumption that if the exchange is done well, then adoption 'should happen', but little effort to explore what that adoption's impact might be.

Another school of thought when considering adoption, prevalent in studies of Management Science and Information Systems, is the Technology Acceptance Model (TAM). TAM extends the Theory of Reasoned Action, an idea grounded in social psychology [32], which quantifies and balances various factors related to potential users of a system (e.g. their beliefs, attitudes, and intentions). Although primarily studied and applied in workplace settings, and hence its 'home' disciplines being management-centric, TAM frequently extends sideward into marketing studies [47]. Aiming to understand how the factors integral to the Theory of Reasoned Action interact vis-à-vis technologies in the workplace, TAM looks at the relationship between perceived usefulness, ease of use, and how these may impact potential future usage of a yet-to-be-implemented technology system. TAM attempts to provide managers with an opportunity to intervene and improve a system before it is implemented, thus avoiding the costly pitfalls of developing or implementing a system that either is not useful, or will not be accepted by users [24].

Although widely used, TAM is not without shortcomings. For example recent research suggests that constant reformulation of the model, which is necessary to keep pace with technological progress, has left TAM, and its many decedents, in a state confusion [6]. The original research proposing the model has significant empirical support, which has been successfully replicated, however neither the original model nor the replications successfully take account of a number of phenomena that are very likely relevant to conclusions based on the model: "It may be that a variety of factors, such as user experience, type or sophistication of system use, or other task and user characteristics may mediate the relationship between ease of use and usage" [1]. Hence, while it is accepted as a useful tool, and bootstrapped by strong empirical foundation, TAM is not a definitive approach for understanding a system's potential for acceptance. As Segars and Grover point out with regards to ease of use and usefulness, central to any prediction based on TAM, "no absolute measures for these constructs exist across varying technological and organizational contexts", going on to hint at *why* this may be the case they add "it seems plausible that both task and user characteristics alter the nature and important perceptions that explain technology use" [68]. Legris et al also note that empirically TAM can be shown to be effective in certain contexts, but that most of the data that form the empirical base for the model come from artificially sterile environments, for example based largely on students, self-reported data, and a narrow scope of contexts and technology types [45]. When the true complexities of socio-technical relationships are taken into account TAM's ability to present meaningful views into the future is drastically reduced. TAM's focus is on whether a system *can* be used, and sidelines the potential *implications* for its use. Hence while it is relevant to our inquiry into adoption, it seems that TAM-derived answers are constrained to a relatively tightly scoped set of questions.

The anthropologist Lucy Suchman's concept of 'situated action' describes a complex and mutually interdependent assemblage of action, context, social and technological factors [75]. It is this type of complexity that approaches such as TAM struggle to meaningfully account for, hence we turn to the work of Suchman and other social scientists in search of more nuanced perspectives on these factors. The diverse variety among the sites of inquiry that social scientists draw upon is in stark contrast to the relatively concise domains of inquiry that studies of technology exchange and TAM frequent. Technology exchange is limited to commercializing research-backed technologies – which naturally limits which technologies (i.e. those that have a potential market) and which organizations studies of transfer are relevant to. Meanwhile TAM tries to ensure new systems will be seamlessly incorporated into businesses (usually large corporations) at minimal cost and without resistance from the workers. In contrast, *social* studies of technology observe a vast range of different users, environments and technologies and these are used to form theories that are relevant to a multitude of complex questions (e.g. how innovations are anticipated, transferred, accepted, adopted, and domesticated) [58]. In the following we offer an overview of some of these ideas and approaches from the social sciences that are relevant to the notion of adoption.

The social construction of technology (SCOT) was the first step toward superseding an outdated view that cast users as inert entities in their relationship with technology. Moving beyond the view that users are simply consumers of technology, Pinch and Bijker explore the notion of 'interpretive flexibility' in order to develop their perspective on SCOT. Interpretive flexibility can be reduced to the idea that an emerging technology can be interpreted differently by different social groups. A famous example is the pneumatic bicycle tire, a cutting-edge technology of the 1890s. Before the technology was adopted, engineers developed their own perspectives on what pneumatic tires could be for: as a means to reduce vibration, as a way to increase speed, or to increase comfort. All the while, skeptics suggested that they were dangerous, prone to deflation, and ugly [61]. The bicycle study is just one of many such examples, usually looking back at technologies that have been adopted. They tend to point to patterns of changes as more people are exposed to, and begin to use, new technologies. Firsthand practical knowledge amasses, consensus emerges, and diversity of opinion about the technology's possible applications and meanings, reduces. In other words, adoption causes the interpretive flexibility to decrease, and as a result a socially constructed understanding of the technology stabilizes. An interesting facet of this process is that often the stabilized 'meaning' of the technology as it has been socially constructed is quite different to the original purpose [61]. Although early SCOT studies focused on how early adopters shaped the meaning of the technologies, later studies showed that in some circumstances users are able to reconstruct apparently stable technologies too [41].

In addition to SCOT there are a whole host of other sociologies which may be used to shed light on the adoption of technology. While the multitude of differing perspectives can be useful, they also highlight the lack of any cohesive or unifying theory. Woolgar describes users as 'readers' (inferring that technologies may be considered as text) and uses this as a means to understand any given device or machine's interpretive flexibility [80:60]. He describes how machines 'configure' their users with meaning that is 'encoded' within the designs. For some scholars this formulation appears one-dimensional and neglects the 'decoding' process: any reader of a novel, after all, has the agency to interpret the text on the page [52]. Hence we can say that while designers encode meaning which configures users, users themselves have the potential to influence designers (this is somewhat similar to Buchanan's argument about design *itself* being rhetoric [14]), designers, then, re-encode new meanings into their designs, which of course are intended to be adopted by users and hence the cycle repeats. Akrich employs a similar metaphor, this time describing a given technology's relationship with potential users it in the same terms that an actor relates to a film script [2]. Just as actors interpret a script they are performing, users of a technology interpret the technology. While both film actors and technology users are unavoidably influenced by what the scriptwriter put on the page (or the designer designed), they also have the ability to enact the script (or the technology) in their own style. "We have to go back and forth continually between the designer and the user, between the designer's envisioned users and the real users, between the world inscribed in the object and the world described by its displacement" [2]. Acknowledging this cyclical and reciprocal relationship between entities in technology adoption is echoed by domestication theory too. Domestication theory, which although called a theory is primarily an analytical model, describes how technologies are integrated into everyday life, users and contexts adapt to the new condition (as modified by the technology), these adaptations are then folded back into the innovation cycle. Rooted in studies of technology in household settings, the theory has since been applied outside the home too, but introduces its own terminology and style [70]. Actor network theory, media and cultural studies, feminist perspectives – to name a few – offer their own nuanced accounts of how technology and people collide, and how those collisions sometimes result in widespread adoption of the technologies [58]. Although all of these delicately different perspectives are fascinating, and for the conscientious scholar can provide valuable insight, an in depth study of them is not viable in the context of this paper. Nor is such an in depth exploration of them *necessary* to galvanize the core of our argument. For the most part, an awareness of SCOT, interpretive flexibility, the co-evolution of meaning as a product of environment, technology, design and users, will suffice.

With that said, we want to acknowledge there are a number of other related concepts we have not discussed in detail, including anticipation ('the sociology of expectations' [3,13]), foresight [64,65] (generating and interpreting future policy ideas, for example), and scenario planning [59,67] (constructing shared narratives about possible futures). There have also been interesting attempts to unify psychological approaches such as TAM with other theories of acceptance and methods such as user-centered design [25]. Although each area of study has its own properties, as with the differences between sociological perspectives, for the purposes of *our* argument we can assume that they are variations on those we have already introduced. To briefly recap, technology exchange explores the dynamics of how research, done purely for the sake of knowledge, may be transferred to a commercial setting. TAM provides managers with tools to reduce the risk of a yet-to-be-implemented technology system being difficult to use and therefore being rejected by users. The range of sociological lenses describe, for example, how technologies are shaped by users, that designs contain encoded meanings, and that technologies are usually adapted and interpreted in order for interpretive flexibility to stabilize and the technology to become domesticated.

While all the areas reviewed have individual focal points, a single concept that unites all of these endeavors is an attempt to understand the what a particular technology's adoption *means* (albeit with different perspectives on how meaning may manifest itself or be relevant). If we return to the question 'should we care about the potential future adoption of the interfaces and technologies that we are researching?' then we might extrapolate that each of these modes of inquiry indicate reasons why the answer could, in circumstances, be yes. Perhaps, 'yes, because the prototype may be commercialized later'. Maybe 'yes, because we want to ensure that the system will be accepted by users'. Or, 'yes, because if *people* do use this system, it could impact upon them, their lives, society in general, and perhaps future technologies too'. Finally, we may consider 'yes, so as to align with research impact agendas' (a factor that is increasingly relevant). If any of these factors are of relevance to HCI research, which is likely the case, then it should be clear that adoption *is* a material concern.

Before we discuss HCI-specific literature and elaborate on *why* we consider adoption to be particularly relevant to our field, we wish to refer to Gartner's famous 'hype cycle' concept and diagram. We were somewhat reticent to refer to the diagram because despite its familiarity to researchers and commercial innovators alike, there is scant empirical support for its applicability in any given domain or context [38,46]. Despite such potential for criticism we note the compelling nature of the diagrams rhetoric in technology research and development and thus elected to include it. For the purposes of the paper the diagram should be taken as a figurative aid for conceptualizing where the various concepts discussed sit in relation to each other.

The hype cycle places technologies on a graph of time (x-axis) against expectations and/or exposure (y-axis). Starting with a technology trigger exposure and expectations grow quickly to a 'peak of inflated expectations'.

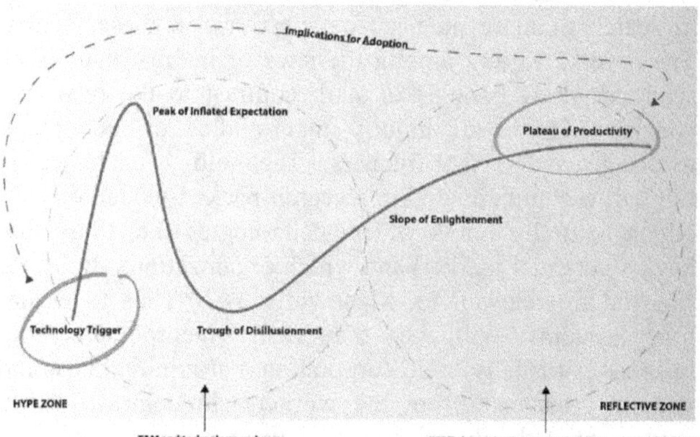

Figure 1. Adapted version of hype cycle illustrating where different approaches may be relevant, and the gap that 'implications for adoption' intends to bridge.

This initial hype, quickly, falls away leading into a 'trough of disillusionment'. Exposure and expectations then grow again, this time more slowly, up the so-called 'slope of enlightenment'. Finally, the technology stabilizes at the 'plateau of productivity'. These phrases provide a temporal spectrum upon which the various ideas and concepts discussed in this paper can now be mapped. For instance, drawing upon ideas introduced thus far, an invocation of TAM would almost definitely take place somewhere on the left-hand side of the diagram (which we have labelled the 'hype zone'). TAM is employed here in an attempt to make the route to the right-hand side of the diagram (which we have labelled the 'reflective zone') as flat as possible, avoiding peaks and troughs. TAM and similar approaches, act on the left, in order to tame the right. Conversely, if we think about SCOT, interpretive flexibility, domestication, and the other sociological perspectives discussed, the studies that inform these views may take place at any point on the diagram, but the point at which technologies stabilize, have reduced interpretive flexibility, and may be considered 'domesticated', invariably sits them on the plateau of productivity. At various junctures in the subsequent sections of the paper, our augmented version of the hype cycle is referred to. It is not intended to be reductive, but rather an efficient vehicle for metaphorically unifying the disparate components parts of our argument.

In the following, we focus on HCI-specific literature, discussing ideas including proximate futures, HCI as 'inter-discipline', and the role of user-centered design methods. Together these factors develop a robust argument for *why* HCI researchers should carefully consider adoption as part of their research endeavors.

HOW WE LEARNED TO STOP WORRYING ABOUT SCIENCE AND LOVE THE PROXIMATE FUTURE

The "proximate future" referred to in the section header is that described by Bell & Dourish, who used the phrase to articulate how 25 years of Ubiquitous Comptuing (ubicomp) research has invariably framed the technologies and concepts being researched as 'out of reach' or 'just around the corner' [5]. This rhetoric was inherited from ubicomp's foundational texts, largely attributed to Mark Weiser [78], yet over the intervening 25 years the same sentiments persist, despite much of what was contained in Weiser's original vision having *already* been achieved. One critique of ubicomp's tendency towards the temporal extrapolation that Bell & Dourish draw attention to, is that future framing in this way appears to encourage researchers to shirk responsibility for *actually implementing* the technologies that they design and develop. In ubicomp texts, implementation is effectively externalized as "someone else's problem", inferring that innovation and research should exist in its own walled garden, completely away from the 'messiness' that a vision which accepts the social construction of technological adoption in everyday life would necessitate. Arguably, in doing so, this trope of ubicomp research texts devalues the research itself, by unnecessarily segregating the knowledge production endeavor from the real world [5]. Another way to consider what we argue is the *inherently* proximately futuristic quality of ubicomp and HCI, can be found by peering into HCI's alleged 'big hole'.

The so-called big hole was exposed by Liu et al through a bibliometric analysis of 20 years of CHI publications [51]. Their findings conclude, based a co-word analysis [16], that researchers contributing to CHI pursue relatively short-lived and diverse technical trends as opposed to focusing on a small number of core themes and studying them over a longer period of time (what the authors call 'motor themes'). One of the authors, Kostakos, reflects critically on the analysis and makes the observation that in the HCI field, researchers do "not systematically get behind a small number of topics to advance them sufficiently into the mainstream" and that we "simply roll from topic to topic, year after year, without developing any of them substantially" [42]. If we refer back to the hype cycle and try and place this type of HCI research on it, the "bandwagon" themes that Liu et al and Kostakos are referring to align very much with what we termed the 'hype zone'. According to the co-word analysis very few HCI research programs stick with a theme until the associated technology has been domesticated, instead they jump from emerging technology to emerging technology *without* considering the products of their research on a continued journey towards the 'plateau of productivity'. Kostakos describes this as a "very worrying prospect for a scientific community" [42], but that sentiment can also be cast in a less negative light. In the subsequent paragraphs we take a view on the nature of the HCI discipline, consider how that disciplinary status relates to HCI's 'motor', and ask what the motor's relationship to the proximate future is.

Blackwell suggests that if we consider HCI an 'inter-discipline' then the tendency to not settle on motor themes is actually a definitional feature [8]. In Blackwell's view the lack of a 'stable core' in HCI is not a concern at all, but rather is an inevitability for a field that pulls influences from, and contributes to, an array of other disciplines. He states that, as opposed to other more traditional areas of academic inquiry, HCI's purpose should not be to maintain a steady mass of knowledge, but to act as a *catalyst for innovation*. The use of the adjective 'motor' to describe the themes that Liu et al identified as missing in HCI, is no accident, but the 'motor' is of course metaphorical. As with an automobile, the motor is what provides power and drive to move things forward. Blackwell argues that the metaphorical motor of HCI *is* in fact present. He says the lack of stable long term themes, which *are* present in other disciplines (e.g. medicine or psychology), would not be expected with such a catalyst for innovation. Hence, we would *expect* Liu et al's search for these 'motor themes' to be fruitless (and, arguably, perhaps the search was misplaced in the first place). Reeves' reflection on the 'big hole' dissects the same argument eloquently, surmising that in order to posit the big hole's existence, some bold assumptions are frequently made about HCI's disciplinarity; the very concept of HCI as a 'discipline' is problematic in the first place; and these problems are deepened by considering HCI a *scientific* discipline [62]. Reeves' perspective seems in agreement with Blackwell's.

If we consider HCI an inter-discipline, then the 'motor' of HCI is the desire to innovate and to forge new ground. In particular forging new ground in the space between various facets of innovation including technical, human, and social aspects. From this perspective, then, arguably the 'proximate future' is actually a key component in what *defines* HCI. While ubicomp always *intended* to look at what was lurking over the horizon of the near future, for HCI-as-inter-discipline it is an *implicit* and definitional feature. By following these new trends HCI acts as a catalyst and driver of innovation. Returning to our adapted hype cycle, we can place the work of many HCI researchers on the left hand side of the diagram, researching and working with technologies that are very new and have limited exposure. Whether you subscribe to Kostakos' assertion that researchers 'roll from topic to topic, year after year', or if you prefer to see this positioning in terms of Blackwell's inter-discipline innovation motor, *or* if you see a consonance between Bell & Dourish's observations of ubicomp and HCI's futurity, all of these views place much of the work emerging from our field towards the left hand side of our adapted hype cycle.

If this proximate quality is central to the endeavor of HCI research, as it seems to be, then we suggest heeding Bell & Dourish's warnings about these perpetually-arriving proximate futures. Rather than using the inevitable messiness that occurs when the technologies we research interact with the realities of everyday life as an excuse to *avoid* thinking about adoption, we should use it as a strong motivator *for considering* adoption. Unifying concerns about the proximate future, worries about HCI researchers' tendency to jump to the 'next big thing', and connecting them with the notion of HCI as inter-discipline, is the overarching theme cementing together this paper's premis. Describing this in terms of our modified hype cycle, the purpose of this paper's thesis is to provide researchers with an efficacious means to bridge the gap between hype zone and reflective zone by leveraging 'implications for adoption'. Although its foundation is now established, in the following paragraphs we introduce a series of resonant perspectives to buttress and brace our argument with addition HCI-centric perspectives.

In their paper introducing the notion of 'research products' Odom et al observe that "a growing portion of the HCI community has moved beyond designing for efficient use to investigating complex matters of human-technology relations that often involve messy, intimate, and contested aspects of everyday life". This sentiment immediately resonates with our modified hype cycle, 'designing for efficiency' which they refer to has synergy with usability studies that take place while technologies are in the hype zone, meanwhile the 'complex matters of human-technology relations' emerge with respect to technologies which have taken some steps towards domestication. Their argument continues: when adopting an artifact-based design response to the 'messy, intimate, and contested' questions that the HCI community is increasingly interested in considering, it is useful to frame the interactions people have with research artifacts "predicated on *what it is* as opposed to what it *might become*" [57]. By this they mean that research products are presented as 'finished' articles, as opposed to being defined by the inherent contingency imported by referring to the research artifacts as 'prototypes'. Research products, though, are not defined solely by reframing the artifact as 'final'. Another definitive factor is that they are installed in 'real' environments (such as research participants' homes) as opposed to being confined to laboratory contexts. Despite this, the properties of what delineates a research product from a research prototype are very subtle, and could likely be disputed. However, for the purposes of this paper, these definitional nuances of research products are inconsequential. Rather, our motivation to refer to this work lies in the reasons *why* research products seem useful: because they look beyond usability studies of prototypical implementations and work towards simulating situated proximate futures (incidentally projects falling under the banner 'research in the wild' have similar motivations and methods [21]). As the authors point out the motivation for moving towards understanding *situated* phenomena stems from HCI's increasing interest in the intricate, entangled, and intimate messiness of individual and societal relationships with technology. If we relate this to our core argument, then the proximate futures which are so common in HCI research are increasingly about *people and technology together*, about how people use technology, and about how technology is adapted *by* people. Research products attempt to provide a means for researchers to shift their focus from the hype zone, and into the reflective zone, where technologies are beginning to become domesticated.

Arriving at findings that resonate with the motivation behind research products, Greenberg & Buxton critique how empirical usability evaluations became a status quo in HCI research. They emphatically make the case that user-centered design (UCD) techniques, specifically usability evaluations, have major and significant role to play for HCI. Their full position is more critical though, they argue that we should be aware that non-empirical methods alongside empirical ones may help to deliver findings that are more representative of reality, depending on circumstance. While they assert that usability testing is often the best method available to understand a new system or interface, they qualify this by saying that it applies 'in many cases, *but not all cases*'. They suggest that combining a variety of methods "will likely help triangulate and enrich the discussion of a system's validity". The bottom line in their critique of usability evaluations is that they "may incorrectly suggest a design's scientific worthiness rather than offer a meaningful critique of how it would be adopted and used in everyday practice". Finally, as well as misrepresenting the complexity of how technologies become situated outside of research and development contexts, it is also noted that usability studies can actually stifle innovation by 'muting' concepts that do not conform to established norms and 'quashing' radical new designs that rely on immature technologies [35]. In his article on 'activity centered design' Don Norman, perhaps one of the most famous proponents of UCD, comes to similar conclusions, suggesting that while UCD can help develop good products it can also make "improvements to bad ones" [55]. Elaborating on the same idea, Norman and Verganti discuss how "meaning change" can be a key driver to take more radical designs out of the hands of early adopters, and into the mainstream [56]. Mapping these thoughts to our adapted hype cycle, we suggest that UCD, and incremental design improvements may help a specific technology to flourish within the realm of the hype zone, however to branch out and beyond, 'meaning change' can be engendered by *considering* implications for adoption.

Greenberg & Buxton, Norman, and Odom et al are all observing the unavoidable mess of *'doing stuff in the world'*. When technologies encounter people, and people interact with the technologies in real environments, then a Pandora's box of possibility is opened. Strategies for how to contain and harness the contents of that box are not straightforward to locate, and less so to utilize. Norman's notes on activity centered design include the observation that people adapt to technology just as much as technology adapts to people, if this is the case, how do we account for it in our designs? He points out that UCD does not have all of the answers. Odom et al respond to the quagmire of complexity by crafting artifacts, and placing those artifacts into the world, usually around people. Through close observation of both the design process and the domestication process that the artifacts and people go through, they discern deeper insights about the interplay between technology and users. Greenberg & Buxton's contribution is framed as a warning against blindly assuming a usability evaluation is the right thing to do in all circumstances, but also includes a number of practical steps to avoid the pitfalls they identified. They suggest paying attention to 'getting the right design before getting the design right' by sufficient use of what they call 'sketching'. They also advocate for using a range of design-led research methods alongside empirical methods [35].

For these perspectives to make sense in the broader scheme of the CHI community while we must allow our field to covet and pursue "appropriate rigour" we should not get hung up on what is or is not "scientific" [63]. What is more, the rigor our community is able to deliver, as per Liu et al's analysis and Kostakos' subsequent critique, almost certainly *does not* sit within the 'big hole' that they called 'quadrant 1' (stable, mainstream, motor themes) [42,51]. Instead the rigor that we can collectively draw upon, and that strengthens HCI's kernel, requires the use of appropriate methods for appropriate tasks [35], must appreciate that our field is a catalyst for innovation, is only defined by its relationships to other fields [8,62], and that HCI, for better or worse, has an intrinsic relationship with the proximate future [5]. Concluding his response to Liu et al, Blackwell says "HCI is not about static knowledge, but ways of deploying and engaging with knowledge in a technological setting" [8]. *Our* thesis is about strengthening HCI's design discourse by demonstrating why and how to explore the potential future adoption of the emerging technologies that are the subject of HCI research. In our concluding section, we describe a proposal for using design fiction in such a way that it can be applied in HCI research contexts to generate or explore 'implications for adoption'.

IMPLEMENTING IMPLICATIONS FOR ADOPTION

The title of our paper makes reference to 'Implications for Design', a trope in HCI research papers which makes particularly regular appearances in research based upon ethnographic fieldwork. In short, implications for design sections try to surmise the findings of field studies into easy-to-interpret, and perhaps generalizable, findings that other researchers (and/or designers) can utilize and build upon. How researchers, interpretations of ethnographic methods, and review processes, inform the inclusion, production, and relevance of implications for design continues to be a contested space [22,26,42,66] – and is not an area that this paper intends to encroach upon in any significant way. However, there *is* commonality between our proposal and discussions related to implications for design. The common ground, and why we saw fit to title this work 'implications for adoption', is that implications for design sections attempt to package insights, which are invariably complex and nuanced (or based upon work that is), into a relatively palatable and succinct delivery mechanism. Consonantly, our call is for packaging *speculations* about the potential future adoption of a currently emerging technology into a relatively digestible and concise delivery mechanism. Perhaps emphasizing this common ground further, the ethnographically informed studies which often result in implications for design are imbued with a 'situated' [22,75] quality that, as will be discussed below, a quality implications for adoption should embody too (insofar as speculations ever *can* be situated).

In the following paragraphs, we discuss how researchers might create and incorporate implications for adoption into HCI research, however our proposals are intended to be suggestive rather than prescriptive in order to avoid the pitfalls of what Dourish referred to as "genre conventions" [26]. Although we are at pains to make it clear our position is not reductive or dogmatic – i.e. there are undoubtedly other ways to appreciate implications for adoption – because it appears to be exceptionally well aligned with our conception of implication for adoption, we pay special attention to design fiction.

Aligning with Design Fiction

The concept of design fiction, originally a term coined by the writer Bruce Sterling [73] but significantly further developed by designer and researcher Julian Bleecker [9], is a method of speculative design which focuses on building fictional worlds [20]. Design fictions contain users, environments, and technologies. The technologies they contain may often be 'real' insofar as they exist in some early or prototypical form in the present, however they are 'fictional' in the way they are diegetically [cf. 35] presented in a fabricated future. Although the HCI corpus includes magical [23,31], ironic [11] and humorous [15,40] design fictions, oftentimes they are built around speculations which attempt to trace plausible trajectories [4]. Among this class of plausible design fiction, building fictional worlds using familiar media and using those media to describe mundane use cases in everyday situations [49], has historically demonstrated design fiction's propensity for effectively suspending disbelief [19]. By suspending disbelief in this way design fiction opens a potential to deeply consider the potential implications of an emerging technology.

Our proposal is to utilize design fiction for implementing implications for adoption, however that suggestion should not be taken without acknowledging a broader discussion which includes caveats and appreciates alternatives. For example, we note that design fiction has been applied broadly in HCI for many other purposes, including to generate ideas [53], prototype interactions [36,74], question solutionist tendencies [12,31,43], scrutinize research agendas [40,50], and to encapsulate or communicate research findings [12,44]. As diverse as the *purposes* for which they are created, design fictions are not media specific, and have appropriated a variety media and presentation formats, for example video [54,79], text [10,15,31], and illustration [44,74]. Design fictions worlds, therefore, can be built using virtually any media artifact or combinations thereof. It is important to remember that these two diversity attributes of design fiction mean although we do feel design fiction may be employed as a useful tool for exploring implications for adoption, given the diversity of practice, of course not *all* design fictions will necessarily be so well matched. Put metaphorically, be mindful that just because some human-computer interfaces are good for inputting text, does not mean that *all* interfaces good for inputting text.

It is also worth noting that across the huge gamut of techniques employed by HCI researchers (particularly design led approaches to reflexivity and futures) there are numerous similar-but-related practices which collectively include some of the same attributes as design fiction. These include approaches such as scenarios [81], research products [57], conceptual design proposals [34], critical design [28], counter-functional design [60], reflective design [69] and propositional objects [77]. Whilst these approaches have merits when considering how to implement implications for adoption, design fiction is, in fact, *uniquely* positioned. Design fiction can leverage world building [cf. 20] to create plausible, mundane, and speculative futures, within which today's emerging technologies may be prototyped as if they are domesticated and situated – two properties with direct relevance to implications for adoption. However, for clarity, we must stress that as with all design fiction, the speculations are not intended to be predictions or premonitions. Rather, they are provocations to serve as lenses to focus the plurality of multiple possible futures that are before us, such that they appear sharper and thus can be better viewed, and critiqued, from our vantage point in present [cf. 18,29].

This general discussion about design fiction is intended to demonstrate how elements of the practice are naturally aligned to the needs of implications for adoption. Specifically, design fictions depict emerging or nascent technological concepts [e.g. 26,41,45,70]. Design fiction allows these concepts to be prototyped as if they have become domesticated. Resonant with HCI's increasing refocusing on human-technology relationships, design fictions represent situated assemblages of environments, users and technologies. These factors demonstrate how design fiction can be an effective bridge from the left-hand side of our adapted hype cycle to the right-hand side. Using design fiction, 'technology triggers' can be explored as if they are already on the 'plateau of productivity' and this can be done in such a way that the technological sensibilities of sociological lenses for understanding future technology (such as SCOT) can be meaningfully 'analogued' for the proximate future. While it is beyond the scope of this paper to include an original demonstration, in the following we refer to examples of design fiction which include speculations congruent with our characterization thus far.

In *PeriodShare* Søndergaard and Hansen created a design fiction world utilizing several elements (physical prototype, crowd funding campaign, a petition for future users, and a performative intervention) that explores a future where wearable technologies facilitate the collection, sharing, and monetization of data pertaining to menstruation. The technology required to facilitate sharing and monetization of menstruation data is contemporarily available (indeed several apps already collect this kind of data, although the presence or lack of a monetization aspect is unclear). The use of design fiction creates a broader and self-consistent world within which menstruation, through its monetization, is more desirable (by implication, 'than it is today') and acts as a vehicle to explore the domestication of that technology. Unfortunately, as the authors acknowledge, "PeriodShare opens up a space for discussions that are deeper and wider than initially explored in this note" [71]. Perhaps as a limitation of publishing conventions that their note was restricted to, Søndergaard and Hansen's work does not, in isolation, complete the leap from the left to the right-hand side of the hype diagram. Communicating the depth of a given design fiction's world within the confines of a research paper (or even a *section of* a research paper) is likely a substantive challenge in using design fiction to implement implications for adoption.

In making the case for creating design fictions as 'fictional papers' [49] in a previous CHI publication we referred to

Game of Drones [48]. Game of Drones explores the practicalities of a drone-based civic enforcement system. As well as touching upon the usability of such as a system, our claim was that it also intends to provoke considerations related to "wider societal and ethical issues of technological futures in which drones might be widely adopted" [48]. Although predating our current inquiry into 'adoption' the fact we used the word 'adopted' reflects our intention to explore the 'implications for adoption' of the technology concept in question. By inventing the details of a user trial to study how drone-enabled civic enforcement could work, the design fiction we built for Game of Drones went further towards concretely stimulating implications for adoption than, for instance, PeriodShare. With that said, it seems implausible to suggest that researchers should be expected to create fictional papers to go alongside 'real' research papers: the burden of additional work would be impractical. A possible antidote to this burden would be to utilize the design fiction trope that inspired the fictional paper approach; 'imaginary abstracts' [10]. As with fictional papers, imaginary abstracts pastiche and imitate their factual counterparts. Creating imaginary abstracts which hint at the implications of future adoption within the context of a research project, is a much more digestible proposition than creating a full fictional paper. However, as has been previously pointed out, with imaginary abstracts what is gained in accessibility is lost in potential depth when compared to fictional papers [49].

A raft of other design fictions feature compelling provocations which showcase ways in which researchers can move towards implications for adoption. A small selection of these are included here to provide the reader with a wider body of work to consider what implications for adoption may become. *Uninvited Guests* showcases one possible domestication of health monitoring devices, specifically focusing on the ways in which the user circumvents the devices' intended uses [76]. *A Toaster for Life* utilizes 3D modeling and product design techniques to unpack the nuances of a modular and connected toaster. In doing so Stead explores the broader implications for adoption vis-à-vis internet of things devices, suggesting uptake of these domestic connected devices may pivot around making elements of them recyclable, modular, and trackable [72]. *Sans Duty* explores a 'transparent tax zone', including a Tinder-style app which allows citizens to 'swipe right' to show how they would like to see their tax contributions spent. Among others, adoption implications that the project conveys include the exclusion of citizens without smartphones and an increase in selfishness resulting from the electronic 'participatory budgeting' system, such as the one depicted [27]. Edwards et al used a collaborative and iterative writing process to produce a series of design fictions which build from contemporary beekeeping practices and folklore, and in doing so exploring the implications of monetized-bee populations and micro-drone technologies [30]. In part what the diversity of approaches and domains shows us, is that there is no *specific* formular describing how to use design fiction to probe the significance of a technology's future adoption.

So far, in our discussion relating to implementing implications for adoption, we have advocated for design fiction as a well-suited approach. This is rooted in a natural alignment between the needs of implications for adoption, and some of the commonly-leveraged attributes of design fiction. In addition to that core argument it may be worth noting that while attention for design fiction in the context of HCI research has grown significantly in recent years, there is arguably a lack of consensus around the precise coordinates of what its role 'should' be. In aligning our characterization of implications for adoption with design fiction perhaps we concretize one *possible* use of design fiction and therefore contribute, in a small way, to disambiguating design fiction's role for HCI. However, implementing implications for adoption using design fiction is certainly not straightforward, an observation supported by those examples we have drawn upon. Although the examples show how design fiction touches upon the right-hand side of our adapted hype cycle, and therefore the space which this paper's thesis aims to address, they conspicuously *don't* fit in to any kind of convention that could be succinctly appropriated as 'the' method for 'doing' implications for adoption. Unfortunately, a more profound inquiry into the details of how design fiction may be used to implement implications for adoption is beyond this paper's scope. In lieu, in the following we further unpack the practicalities of implementing implications for adoption, with a view to supporting and informing future research in this area.

DISCUSSION

We would like to repeat that, despite forwarding design fiction as a potential response to our call to incorporate implications for adoption into HCI research projects, our position is certainly not intended to be domineering or remissive with respect to *other* possible approaches. Put differently, the 'need' laid out in the first two sections of this paper stands independently from any possible solutions, and we commend *any* potentially workable responses to the argument. Each of the alternate approaches listed previously (including scenarios, research products, conceptual design proposals, critical design, etc) have merit and we encourage researchers to consider these as possible responses. With that said design fiction *does* appear to have attributes that are worthy and fitting with respect to what is needed to meaningfully consider implications for adoption. For the argument presented in this paper to become broadly relevant for the field and to mature further inquiry is necessary to refine and test possible means to incorporate implications for adoption into research projects.

As per our references to Liu et al [51] and Blackwell [7,8] earlier, the HCI field is inherently interdisciplinary and diverse. The range of research conducted in the field that is published as part of CHI (as well as related conferences such as CSCW and DIS) is remarkably broad. With that breadth in mind it should come as no surprise that, although we posit that implications for adoption are a missing but important part of HCI research practice, that position is *not* a universal one encompassing the entire field. We do not wish to suggest that *all* HCI research *must* consider implications for adoption in order to be good research. Hence, to narrow down the categories of research implications for adoption could be particularly relevant to is a question that would benefit from experimentation (from researchers working in varied areas) and additional investigation. However, despite being a question that deserves deeper discussion, as a starting point we suggest that any research that can be placed on the left of the hype cycle (i.e. that is or may become a 'technology trigger'), should arguably consider the implication of that research or technology's future adoption. As such research projects aligning to this category should be mindful of this paper's thesis.

The final question we wish to explore in this discussion is, what do implications for adoption 'look' like? For those scholars who are keen to embrace the argument in this paper, and are appreciative of our endorsement of design fiction; how should they proceed to implement implications for adoption in their next publication? Further, given their potential dangers, how could or indeed *should*, a 'genre convention' [cf. 25] around implications for adoption be established? In short, we feel that to develop nuanced answers to these questions, a practical exploration of the ideas we have presented is necessary. The argument we present is a theoretical one, but comes packaged with the addition of some signposting towards design fiction as a suitable method, and indeed specific examples of design fiction which include features relevant to implications for adoption. However, as Odom et al's eloquently describe in their discussion of research products [57], our position must not be reductive or prescriptive, but hopes to open the concept for further development. Critiquing implications for design Kostakos writes "these are extremely polished pieces of text that do a wonderful job of not providing any reusable data, theory, or tools, yet manage to convince us that the implications are important" [42]. This sentiment is, perhaps, the most succinct explication of what researchers recognizing the importance of implications for adoption should aim to achieve.

CONCLUSION

In this paper, we aimed to deliver three contributions. First, we reviewed a variety of literature describing different ways of considering what we refer to as technological adoption. In doing so we highlighted a space which researchers may leverage in order to contextualize the potential implications of the technologies they research when (or if) they eventually become adopted. Second, we referred to a range of HCI-centric literature in order to build an argument for *why* considering adoption in this way is not only relevant to our community, but is arguably *essential* in order to galvanize the field's substance as a driver of innovation. These introductory contributions lay the rhetorical foundation for implications for adoption. With the case established, the third and final contribution the paper offers hinges on design fiction. The paper proposes design fiction is a fitting response to the need laid out in the first two thirds of the paper, and discusses the challenges and opportunities of practically implementing implications for adoption using design fiction. In this paper we argue that by considering 'implications for adoption' HCI researchers may be better equipped to design, critique, and contribute to the proximate future which our community both creates, and thrives in.

ACKNOWLEDGEMENTS

This work was made possible by the RCUK Cyber Security for the Internet of Things Research Hub PETRAS (petrashub.org) under EPSRC grant EP/N02334X/1 and the RCUK Digital Economy Programme's Doctoral Training Centre HighWire (highwire.lancaster.ac.uk) under EPSRC grant EP/G037582/1. We would like to extend our gratitude and thanks to the anonymous reviewers who provided us with objective, insightful, and non-partisan feedback which helped us improve and craft this paper into its final form.

REFERENCES

1. Dennis A. Adams, R. Ryan Nelson, and Peter A. Todd. 1992. Perceived Usefulness , Ease of Use , and Usage of Information Technology: A Replication. *MIS Quarterly* 16, 2: 227–247. http://doi.org/10.2307/249577
2. Madeline Akrich. 1992. The De-scription of Technical Objects. In *Shaping Technology/Building Society: Studies in Sociotechnical Change*. The MIT Press, Cambridge, MA, 205–224.
3. Carla Alvial-Palavicino. 2016. The Future as Practice. A Framework to Understand Anticipation in Science and Technology. *TECNOSCIENZA: Italian Journal of Science & Technology Studies* 6, 2: 135–172.
4. James Auger. 2013. Speculative design: crafting the speculation. *Digital Creativity* 24, 1: 11–35.
5. Genevieve Bell and Paul Dourish. 2007. Yesterday's tomorrows: notes on ubiquitous computing's dominant vision. *Personal and Ubiquitous Computing* 11, 2: 133–143. http://doi.org/10.1007/s00779-006-0071-x
6. Izak Benbasat and Henri Barki. 2007. Quo vadis, TAM? *Journal of the Association for Information Systems* 8, 4: 211–218. http://doi.org/10.1586/erd.10.82
7. Alan Blackwell. 2015. Filling the big hole in HCI research. *Interactions* 22, 6: 37–41. http://doi.org/10.1145/2830317
8. Alan F Blackwell. 2015. HCI as an Inter-Discipline. *Extended Abstracts of the ACM CHI'15 Conference on Human Factors in Computing Systems* 2: 503–

516. http://doi.org/10.1145/2702613.2732505

9. Julian Bleecker. 2009. Design Fiction: A short essay on design, science, fact and fiction. *Near Future Laboratory*.

10. Mark Blythe. 2014. Research through design fiction. *Proceedings of the 32nd annual ACM conference on Human factors in computing systems - CHI '14*, ACM Press, 703–712. http://doi.org/10.1145/2556288.2557098

11. Mark Blythe and Enrique Encinas. 2016. The Co-ordinates of Design Fiction: Extrapolation, Irony, Ambiguity and Magic. *Proc. GROUP'16*: 345–354. http://doi.org/10.1145/2957276.2957299

12. Mark Blythe, Jamie Steane, Jenny Roe, and Caroline Oliver. 2015. Solutionism, the Game. *Proceedings of the 33rd Annual ACM Conference on Human Factors in Computing Systems - CHI '15*, ACM Press, 3849–3858. http://doi.org/10.1145/2702123.2702491

13. Mads Borup, Nick Brown, and Kornelia Konrad. 2006. The Sociology of Expectations in Science and Technology. *Technology Analysis & Strategic Management* 18, September: 285–298.

14. Richard Buchanan. 1985. Declaration by Design: Rhetoric, Argument, and Demonstration in Design Practice. *Design Issues*, 2, 1: 4–22.

15. Laura Buttrick and Conor Linehan. 2014. Fifty Shades of CHI : The Perverse and Humiliating Human-Computer Relationship. 825–833. http://doi.org/10.1145/2559206.2578874

16. M. Callon, J. P. Courtial, and F. Laville. 1983. From translations to problematic networks: An introduction to co-word analysis. *Social Science Information* 22, 2: 191–235.

17. Parmit K Chilana, Andrew J Ko, and Jacob Wobbrock. 2015. From User-Centered to Adoption-Centered Design. *Proceedings of the 33rd Annual ACM Conference on Human Factors in Computing Systems - CHI '15*: 1749–1758. http://doi.org/10.1145/2702123.2702412

18. Paul Coulton, Dan Burnett, and Adrian Gradinar. 2016. Games as Speculative Design: Allowing Players to Consider Alternate Presents and Plausible Futures. *Proceedings of the 50th Design Research Society Conference*: 1–17.

19. Paul Coulton, Joseph Lindley, and Haider Ali. 2016. Design Fiction: Does the search for plausibility lead to deception? *Proceedings of DRS 2016, Design Research Society 50th Anniversary Conference*.

20. Paul Coulton, Joseph Lindley, Miriam Sturdee, and Michael Stead. 2017. Design Fiction as World Building. *Proceedings of the 3nd Biennial Research Through Design Conference*.

21. Aaron Crabtree, Alan Chamberlain, M Davies, et al. 2013. Doing Innovation in the Wild. *Proceedings of the Biannual Conference of the Italian Chapter of SIGCHI*: 1–9. http://doi.org/10.1145/2499149.2499150

22. Andrew Crabtree, Tom Rodden, Peter Tolmie, and Graham Button. 2009. Ethnography considered harmful. *Proceedings of the 27th international conference on Human factors in computing systems - CHI 09*, October 2015: 879. http://doi.org/10.1145/1518701.1518835

23. Nicholas S. Dalton, Rebecca Moreau, and Ross K. Adams. 2016. Resistance is Fertile: Design Fictions in Dystopian Worlds. *Proceedings of the 2016 CHI Conference Extended Abstracts on Human Factors in Computing Systems - CHI EA '16*: 365–374. http://doi.org/10.1145/2851581.2892572

24. Fred Davis, Richard Bagozzi, and Paul Warshaw. 1989. User Acceptance of Computer Technology: A Comparison of Two Theoretical Models. *Management Science* 35, 8: 982–1003.

25. Andrew Dillon and Michael G Morris. 1996. User Acceptance of Information Technology:Theories and Models. *Annual Review of Information Science and Technology*.

26. Paul Dourish. 2006. Implications for design. *Proceedings of the SIGCHI conference on Human Factors in computing systems - CHI '06*: 541. http://doi.org/10.1145/1124772.1124855

27. James Duggan and Joseph Lindley. 2015. *Sans Duty - Making Tax Visisble*.

28. Anthony Dunne. 2006. *Hertzian Tales: Electronic Products, Aesthetic Experience, and Critical Design*. The MIT Press.

29. Anthony Dunne and Fiona Raby. 2013. *Speculative Everything*. The MIT Press, London.

30. Liz Edwards, Deborah Maxwell, Toby Pillatt, and Niamh Downing. 2016. Beebots-a-lula, Where's My Honey? *Proceedings of the 9th Nordic Conference on Human-Computer Interaction - NordiCHI '16*, ACM Press, 1–10. http://doi.org/10.1145/2971485.2993924

31. Enrique Encinas and Mark Blythe. 2016. The Solution Printer : Magic Realist Design Fiction. *CHI Extended Abstracts on Human Factors in Computing Systems*, July 2015: 387–396.

32. M Fishbein and I Ajzen. 1975. *ZEN, Belief, Attitude, Intention and Behavior: An Introduction to Theory and Research*. Addison-Wesley, Reading, MA.

33. Foley, Jim. 1996. Technology Transfer from University to Industry. *Communications of the ACM* 39, 9. http://doi.org/10.1145/514236.514264

34. Bill Gaver and Heather Martin. 2000. Alternatives. *Proceedings of the SIGCHI conference on Human factors in computing systems - CHI '00*, ACM Press, 209–216. http://doi.org/10.1145/332040.332433

35. Saul Greenberg and Bill Buxton. 2008. Usability evaluation considered harmful (some of the time).

Proceeding of the twenty-sixth annual CHI conference on Human factors in computing systems - CHI '08: 111. http://doi.org/10.1145/1357054.1357074

36. Felix Heibeck, Alexis Hope, and Julie Legault. 2014. Sensory Fiction : A Design Fiction of Emotional Computation. 35–40.
37. Ellen A Isaacs and John C Tang. 1996. Technology transfer: so much research, so few good products. *Communications of the ACM* 39, 9: 23–25. http://doi.org/10.1145/234215.234463
38. H. Järvenpää and S. J. Mäkinen. 2008. Empirically detecting the Hype Cycle with the life cycle indicators: An exploratory analysis of three technologies. *2008 IEEE International Conference on Industrial Engineering and Engineering Management, IEEM 2008*: 12–16. http://doi.org/10.1109/IEEM.2008.4737823
39. D. Kirby. 2010. The Future is Now: Diegetic Prototypes and the Role of Popular Films in Generating Real-world Technological Development. *Social Studies of Science* 40, 1: 41–70. http://doi.org/10.1177/0306312709338325
40. Ben Kirman, Conor Linehan, Shaun Lawson, and Dan O'Hara. 2013. CHI and the future robot enslavement of humankind: a retrospective. *CHI '13 Extended Abstracts on Human Factors in Computing Systems on - CHI EA '13*: 2199. http://doi.org/10.1145/2468356.2468740
41. Ronald Kline and Trevor Pinch. 1996. Users as Agents of Technological Change: The Social Construction of the Automobile in the Rural United States. *Technology and Culture* 37, 4: 763. http://doi.org/10.2307/3107097
42. Vassilis Kostakos. 2015. The big hole in HCI research. *interactions* 22, 2: 48–51. http://doi.org/10.1145/2729103
43. Shaun Lawson, Ben Kirman, Conor Linehan, et al. 2015. Problematising Upstream Technology through Speculative Design: The Case of Quantified Cats and Dogs. 2663–2672.
44. Shaun Lawson, Ben Kirman, and Conor Linehan. 2016. Power, participation, and the dog internet. *interactions* 23, 4: 37–41. http://doi.org/10.1145/2942442
45. Paul Legris, John Ingham, and Pierre Collerette. 2003. Why do people use information technology? A critical review of the technology acceptance model. *Information & Management* 40, 3: 191–204. http://doi.org/10.1016/S0378-7206(01)00143-4
46. Harro Van Lente, Charlotte Spitters, and Alexander Peine. 2013. Comparing technological hype cycles: Towards a theory. *Technological Forecasting and Social Change* 80, 8: 1615–1628. http://doi.org/10.1016/j.techfore.2012.12.004
47. Chien-Hsin Lin, Hsin-Yu Shih, and Peter J. Sher. 2007. Integrating technology readiness into technology acceptance: The TRAM model. *Psychology and Marketing* 24, 7: 641–657. http://doi.org/10.1002/mar.20177
48. Joseph Lindley and Paul Coulton. 2015. Game of Drones. *Proceedings of the second ACM SIGCHI annual symposium on Computer-human interaction in play*.
49. Joseph Lindley and Paul Coulton. 2016. Pushing the Limits of Design Fiction. *Proceedings of the 2016 CHI Conference on Human Factors in Computing Systems - CHI '16*, ACM Press, 4032–4043. http://doi.org/10.1145/2858036.2858446
50. Conor Linehan, Ben J. Kirman, Stuart Reeves, et al. 2014. Alternate endings. *Proceedings of the extended abstracts of the 32nd annual ACM conference on Human factors in computing systems - CHI EA '14*, ACM Press, 45–48. http://doi.org/10.1145/2559206.2560472
51. Yong Liu, Jorge Goncalves, Denzil Ferreira, Bei Xiao, Simo Hosio, and Vassilis Kostakos. 2014. CHI 1994-2013: mapping two decades of intellectual progress through co-word analysis. *CHI '14 Proceedings of the SIGCHI Conference on Human Factors in Computing Systems*, 3553–3562. http://doi.org/10.1145/2556288.2556969
52. Wendy E Mackay. 2000. Responding to cognitive overload : Co-adaptation between users and technology. *Intellectica* 30: 177–193.
53. Thomas Markussen and Eva Knutz. 2013. The poetics of design fiction. *Proceedings of the 6th International Conference on Designing Pleasurable Products and Interfaces - DPPI '13*: 231.
54. Eran May-Raz and Daniel Lazo. 2012. Sight. Retrieved October 27, 2014 from http://vimeo.com/46304267
55. Donald a. Norman. 2005. Human-centered design considered harmful. *interactions* 12, 4: 14. http://doi.org/10.1145/1070960.1070976
56. Donald A Norman and Roberto Verganti. 2014. Incremental and Radical Innovation: Design Research vs. Technology and Meaning Change. 30, 1. http://doi.org/10.1162/DESI
57. William Odom, Ron Wakkary, Youn-kyung Lim, Audrey Desjardins, Bart Hengeveld, and Richard Banks. 2016. From Research Prototype to Research Product. *Proceedings of the 2016 CHI Conference on Human Factors in Computing Systems - CHI '16*: 2549–2561. http://doi.org/10.1145/2858036.2858447
58. Nelly Oudshoorn and Trevor Pinch. 2003. *How Users Matter: The Co-Construction of Users and Technology*. The MIT Press, Cambridge, MA.
59. Garry D Peterson, Graeme S Cumming, and Stephen R Carpenter. 2003. Scenario Planning: a Tool for Conservation in an Uncertain World. *Essay 358 Conservation Biology Conservation Biology* 17, 2: 358–366.

http://doi.org/10.1046/j.1523-1739.2003.01491.x

60. James Pierce and Eric Paulos. 2015. Making Multiple Uses of the Obscura 1C Digital Camera: Reflecting on the Design, Production, Packaging and Distribution of a Counterfunctional Device. *Proceedings of the 33rd Annual ACM Conference on Human Factors in Computing Systems*: 2103–2112. http://doi.org/10.1145/2702123.2702405
61. Trevor J Pinch and Wiebe E Bijker. 1984. The Social Construction of Facts and Artefacts: or How the Sociology of Science and the Sociology of Technology might Benefit Each Other. *Social Studies of Science* 14, 3: 399–441. http://doi.org/10.1177/030631284014003004
62. Stuart Reeves. 2015. Locating the " Big Hole " in Hci. August: 1–8.
63. Stuart Reeves. 2015. Human-computer interaction as science. *5th Annunal Aarhus Conference on Critical Alternatives*. http://doi.org/10.7146/aahcc.v1i1.21296
64. Ahti Salo and Kerstin Cuhls. 2003. Technology foresight - Past and Future. *Journal of Forecasting* 22, 2–3: 79–82. http://doi.org/10.1002/for.846
65. Ahti Salo, Tommi Gustafsson, and Ramakrishnan Ramanathan. 2003. Multicriteria Methods for Techonology Foresight. *Journal of Forecasting* 22: 235–255. http://doi.org/10.1002/for.850
66. Corina Sas, Steve Whittaker, Steven Dow, Jodi Forlizzi, and John Zimmerman. 2014. Generating implications for design through design research. *Proceedings of the 32nd annual ACM conference on Human factors in computing systems - CHI '14*, ACM Press, 1971–1980. http://doi.org/10.1145/2556288.2557357
67. Paul J H Schoemaker. 1995. Scenario Planning: A tool for Strategic Thinking. *Sloan Management Review* 36, 2: 25–40.
68. Albert H Segars and Varun Grover. 1993. Re-examining perceived ease of use and usefulness. *MIS Quarterly* 17, 4: 517–525.
69. Phoebe Sengers, Kirsten Boehner, Shay David, and Joseph "Jofish" Kaye. 2005. Reflective Design. *Proceedings of the 4th decennial conference on Critical computing: between sense and sensibility*: 49–58. http://doi.org/10.1145/1094562.1094569
70. Roger Silverstone. 2006. Domesticating domestication. Reflecting on the life of a concept. In *Domestication Of Media And Technology*, Thomas Berker, Maren Hartmann, Yves Punie and Katie Ward (eds.). Open University Press, 229–247.
71. Marie Louise Juul Søndergaard and Lone Koefoed Hansen. 2016. PeriodShare. *Proceedings of the 9th Nordic Conference on Human-Computer Interaction - NordiCHI '16*, ACM Press, 1–6. http://doi.org/10.1145/2971485.2996748
72. Michael Stead. 2016. A Toaster For Life : Using Design Fiction To Facilitate Discussion On The Creation Of A Sustainable Internet of Things. *Proceedings of DRS 2016, Design Research Society 50th Anniversary Conference*: 1–20.
73. Bruce Sterling. 2005. *Shaping Things*. The MIT Press.
74. Miriam Sturdee, Paul Coulton, Joseph G. Lindley, Mike Stead, Haider Ali, and Andy Hudson-Smith. 2016. Research Fiction: How to Build a Voight Kampff Machine. *Proceedings of the 2016 CHI Conference Extended Abstracts on Human Factors in Computing Systems - CHI EA '16*, ACM Press, 375–386. http://doi.org/10.1145/2851581.2892574
75. Lucy Suchman. 1987. *Plans and situated actions: the problem of human-machine communication*. Cambridge University Press.
76. Superflux. Uninvited Guests. Retrieved September 17, 2015 from http://www.superflux.in/work/uninvited-guests
77. Stuart Walker. 2013. Imagination's Promise: Practice-Based Design, Research for Sustainability. In *The Handbook for Design Sustainability*, Stuart Walker and Jacques Giard (eds.). Bloomsbury, London & New York, 460–461.
78. Mark Weiser. 1999. The computer for the 21 st century. *ACM SIGMOBILE Mobile Computing and Communications Review* 3, 3: 3–11. http://doi.org/10.1145/329124.329126
79. Richmond Y Wong and Deirdre K Mulligan. 2016. When a Product Is Still Fictional : Anticipating and Speculating Futures through Concept Videos. 121–133.
80. S Woolgar. 1991. Configuring the user: The case of usability trials. In *A Sociology of Monsters*, John Law (ed.). Routledge.
81. Richard M. Young and Phil Barnard. 1987. The use of scenarios in human-computer interaction research. *ACM SIGCHI Bulletin* 18, 4: 291–296. http://doi.org/10.1145/1165387.275645

UX Design Innovation: Challenges for Working with Machine Learning as a Design Material

Graham Dove, Kim Halskov
CAVI, Aarhus University
Aarhus, Denmark
graham.dove@cc.au.dk, halskov@cavi.au.dk

Jodi Forlizzi, John Zimmerman
HCII, Carnegie Mellon University
Pittsburgh PA, USA
forlizzi@cs.cmu.edu, johnz@cs.cmu.edu

ABSTRACT
Machine learning (ML) is now a fairly established technology, and user experience (UX) designers appear regularly to integrate ML services in new apps, devices, and systems. Interestingly, this technology has not experienced a wealth of design innovation that other technologies have, and this might be because it is a new and difficult design material. To better understand why we have witnessed little design innovation, we conducted a survey of current UX practitioners with regards to how new ML services are envisioned and developed in UX practice. Our survey probed on how ML may or may not have been a part of their UX design education, on how they work to create new things with developers, and on the challenges they have faced working with this material. We use the findings from this survey and our review of related literature to present a series of challenges for UX and interaction design research and education. Finally, we discuss areas where new research and new curriculum might help our community unlock the power of design thinking to re-imagine what ML might be and might do.

Author Keywords
UX practice; design material; machine learning; interaction design;

ACM Classification Keywords
H.5.m. Information interfaces and presentation (e.g., HCI): Miscellaneous;

INTRODUCTION
Technology often enters the market in the form of a technical advance, and without much concern for design. As the technology matures, designers work to re-understand it and to invent new forms not imagined when the technology was first invented. Music players offer a simple example of maturing technology. A relatively simple turntable will play vinyl records, but design innovation brought the Radiogram as a centerpiece for living rooms, the Dansette to define teenage bedrooms, and Technics SL1200s to drive club culture. Similarly, cassette recorders offered an advance over reel-to-reel, making media easier to handle and more stable during use. Designers helped to innovate this advance by bringing to life boom boxes, auto tape decks, and the Walkman. Further technical advances led to the first solid-state media players, followed by many different MP3 players. Design innovation brought about the combined experience of the iPod and iTunes service; followed by all of the devices that paired with the iPod. Technical advances in networking led to streaming media that enabled broadcasting across the Internet. Designers are now helping develop many new forms of music player including services like Apple Music, Pandora and Spotify; that challenge the idea of owning music at all. In each of these cases, a technical advance triggered an opportunity for design innovation to generate a wealth of new products.

We see machine learning (ML) as a not so new technology that is ready for design innovation. ML is neither arcane nor obscure, with numerous textbooks [21,54], introductory articles [16] and online resources [24] covering the topic. It has been an area of active research for at least fifty years [47,48]. News articles on "Big Data," the digitization of industries like healthcare, the increasing use of analytics in business and politics [e.g. 20], the spate of recent articles about the impending driverless car future, and recent developments in techniques such as deep learning [29], have raised ML's public profile. This, combined with an increasing number and popularity of online services and mobile applications that leverage ML to offer exciting new services, has led some user experience (UX) commentators to speculate that ML is the new UX [6], and to highlight ML algorithms as being "where the action is" [12]. Apps and online services regularly detect and filter spam, rank or curate media feeds, make predictions such as estimated driving times, translate speech to text, and autocorrect people's typing through the use of ML. It is no longer enough for UX designers to only improve user experience by paying attention to usability, utility, and interaction aesthetics. Instead, the best user experiences may come from services that automatically personalize their offers to the user and context, and systems that leverage more detailed understandings of people and the world in order to provide new value.

CHI 2017, May 06-11, 2017, Denver, CO, USA
 ISBN 978-1-4503-4655-9/17/05…$15.00
DOI: http://dx.doi.org/10.1145/3025453.3025739

Because ML is becoming an increasingly commonplace feature of new interactive systems, we should now expect UX designers to regularly instigate innovative products and services. They should be generating many new forms that have not been imagined by the engineers who focus on making the technology work. However, in our experience to date, we have rarely seen a UX team conceive of an entirely new way to use ML and then taken this to a development team to implement. It has been our perception that UX design teams are simply "putting lipstick on the pig" [13:7]. So we sought to better understand UX designers' participation in the creation of new intelligent products and services; and to identify where potential obstacles to this may lie.

We suspect that one reason we might see less design innovation with ML than with previous technology is that ML is a more difficult design material to work with. Unlike heuristic driven systems, ML is very different from human intelligence. It applies statistical methods to produce output that can be difficult to explain, and that make seemingly bizarre errors due to a lack of common sense [60,61]. UX designers may therefore struggle to make designs that bridge the ML and human perspective. Another reason might be the lack of education on how to envision products and services that exploit ML. UX design education programs and UX design practice resources almost all talk about designing for mobile as distinct from desktop. However, these programs and resources make little if any mention of how designers should work with ML. UX designers also lack prototyping tools for working with ML. They have tools for prototyping responsive web services and tools that make it easy to simulate the behavior of an app on a smartphone, but they have nothing that helps them quickly prototype and understand the UX impact of false negative and false positive responses from a ML service. Finally, it might be that UX designers lack a clear understanding of what ML is and what it can do. Recent UX articles on the web, where UX designers talk about ML, often reveal huge misconceptions around what ML can actually do, with many designers treating it way too much like magic.

We believe that ML currently represents an under-explored opportunity for ideation and innovation led by UX design. UX design practitioners and researchers should pay closer attention to the possibilities ML offers as a new *design material*. In suggesting this, our objective is to initiate an innovative research and education agenda for UX design that explores what ML might be from a design perspective.

As a first step, we chose to investigate the state of the art in UX practice. We wanted to better understand if UX designers are regularly working with ML, if they are offering ideas for what it might be, and if they are encountering problems that make ML difficult to design with. Through an online survey of fifty-one UX practitioners, we found that 63% of designers work with ML and that most work collaboratively with ML software developers and engineers. Designers working with ML expressed frustration about the difficulty of prototyping with ML, and highlighted difficulties in understanding and expressing the capabilities, limitations and potential of ML. Our findings highlight a clear need for research on new tools and techniques that make it easier for designers to ideate, sketch and prototype what new forms ML might take, and new contexts in which ML might be appropriate. In addition, this research reveals a need to develop educational resources to teach interaction designers about ML as a design material.

In this paper, we present a review of how HCI has addressed ML and its intersection with design. We describe our survey, including its design and findings. Finally, we present a series of ML related challenges for UX and interaction design, and discuss areas where new research and new curriculum might help our community unlock the power of design thinking to re-imagine what ML might be and might do.

RELATED LITERATURE

Evidence for the growing interest in the intersection of ML and UX can be seen in the number of recent articles published on the subject in popular online sources [e.g. 45]. A similar interest, in the intersection of ML and HCI, can be seen in recent CHI workshops covering the topic [23,51]. With this in mind, we undertook a review of HCI literature with particular focus on design innovation and ML. This revealed three themes: 1) technical HCI advances that improve interaction via the application of ML; 2) research to surface and address the challenges in working with "intelligent" technology; 3) work discussing challenges when designing with new or less well understood design materials. We summarize literature related to each theme below.

Technical HCI and ML

The technical side of HCI has been working with ML for many, many years to improve interaction. We do not provide a thorough review here, but instead point out several of the main capabilities and abilities this work has developed. HCI researchers have used ML to increase interaction possibilities. These range from turning people's skin into a touch interface [27] to gesture recognition [50]. They have used it to create adaptive interfaces that reduce users' efforts and automate tasks [36]. They have used ML to infer people's states, like their interruptablity [31], their routines [14], and other important contextual information [11], which can mediate computer interaction. Researchers have also used it to infer things about users. This work ranges from intelligent tutors [35] to recommenders [28] to systems that can detect things like the onset of depression [17]. Other research helped to unlock many new ways ML can improve people's interactions with technology. Our work builds on this success by probing how UX designers can apply their strength in problem reframing and opportunity finding to envision new forms for ML to take and many new ways it might deliver value to people.

The Challenges of "Intelligent" Technology

HCI has a growing body of research focused on design challenges around systems that seem "intelligent." In general, this work does not differentiate whether the underlying technology uses heuristics, more classic AI, or if it uses ML. Instead it has probed the breakdown in understanding and the many misunderstandings between users and these systems.

The challenge of integrating "intelligent" technologies into people's lives can be distilled into the automation debate between 'do it for me' and 'do it myself', or the challenge of when automation is desirable and when people want to feel in control. This debate around what makes a good user experience touches back on some of the early debates about direct manipulation and the value of users taking control vs. agents and the value of saving time and attention [49]. This is not necessarily an either/or choice, and knowledge of both is likely indispensable for a T-shaped UX designer [25,53]. Here we present an overview of HCI research that touches on this point, and on research investigating how people perceive and create expectations of intelligent systems.

HCI research into agents highlights the social nature of human-computer relationships [41], showing this is not necessarily anthropomorphic [2], but that embodiment should be based on a deep understanding of conversational function [10]. Intention recognition, effective turn taking, and effectiveness under uncertainty are deemed to be important for successful interaction [1]. As agents often have an implied, digitized or physical body, design choices like gender and ethnicity also affect the way users respond to agents. This can affect perceived task suitability [22], following stereotypical gender roles [4], influence engagement with agents [32], and affect perceived attractiveness [33]; thereby having an impact on how people perceive the intelligent system.

Intelligent systems sometimes encourage unrealistic expectations, leading to some reluctance to use them in complex or sensitive contexts [38,55]. They may inadvertently display an inability to understand the intent behind users' behavior, which results in "intelligent" features being perceived as useless and unintuitive [57]. Interaction design researchers have explored different ways systems can communicate their awareness and understanding of a user [15,58]. Research into human-robot interaction shows that physical proximity, organizational status, and task structure can alter people's experiences [34], and that expectancy setting and recovery strategies help mitigate error [37]. Also, studies of autonomous and semi-autonomous vehicles show that human behavior is highly responsive to differences in real and perceived levels of control, creating the potential for misalignment [9].

One commonality is that the majority of this work explores intelligent agents that have a presence or virtual form. This is great for services like Siri or Amazon Echo, but it does not translate to lower level services, such as search results, travel time estimators, or activity trackers, all of which work more invisibly. Another shortcoming in this body of literature is that it lacks a rich description of specific challenges of interacting with ML systems. For example, we did not see research investigating issues such as the impact of false positive and false negative responses from agents, or the need to collect ground truth labels, which might negatively impact UX.

Working with Less Well Understood Design Materials

The challenge of working with new or less well understood materials is a recurring theme in some UX research. Buxton talks about the "experience" part of user experience as a difficult material, and he notes the lack of tools that allow designers to sketch and rapidly explore a range of experiential possibilities [8]. Design value comes from instilling particular products and services with the quality of experience that sets them apart from the everyday; and without good tools, designers struggle to explore the space of possibilities.

Here, we present examples from literature in which methods and tools for exploring the experience of new technologies in use have been a key part of HCI research. Innovations range from cooperative lo-fi prototyping, in which designers work with users and technology experts to sketch out possible futures using scenarios [19], to experience prototypes where users and designers can quickly get a feel for the intended experience [7], to user enactments that offer users small sips of many possible futures [42]. Additionally, some UX research has probed the challenge of working with haptics as a design material [40]. Other work has developed sets of interactive textiles to communicate a range of possibilities designers can use in developing sensitizing concepts to support design ideation [52]. Design researchers have also discussed software as an immaterial material, noting the challenge of often needing to use developers as a prosthetic to touch the material they want to explore [43]. They have noted the challenges of working with peoples' personal data to imagine what it might be [18], and created toolkits for generating robots' social behaviors [30]. Recently, some work has explored the challenge of UX designers working with ML, and it has offered a set of mobile interaction patterns to help show designers key points where ML might add value [56].

This list is not exhaustive, but highlights some key aspects of the challenges presented by working with less well understood design materials. Again, what seems missing from this literature are methods and tools more specific to the challenges of interacting with ML systems. We saw only very limited research investigating ML specific issues like how to prototype interactions that may follow an unpredictable course.

SURVEY METHOD

We wanted to assess where the UX design community currently is in terms of ML's technology breakthrough to design innovation. In addition, we wanted to understand whether the difficulty of working with ML as a design material might be inhibiting the design response to this not so new technology. We therefor conducted a survey of professional UX design practitioners. Our intention in selecting a survey to gather data for this study was that it would allow us to quickly gain insight on the state of current practice, and to gain a broad overview of what is now emerging as a prescient area of study.

We used an iterative process to develop the survey: generating sets of questions, piloting them on ourselves and colleagues, and then making changes to address issues of ambiguity or in response to new insights that emerged after each iteration. This resulted in a nine question survey. We asked if participants worked in research or practice, if they had formal design training, if they had been exposed to machine learning as part of their design education, if they had worked on UX projects involving machine learning based services, and if yes, then to provide a short description of the project.

To understand the state of practice, we asked participants who had worked on ML projects to consider their most recent project and classify the relationship between the developers and UX team by selecting one of the following:

- The UX design team gave an interactive form to a machine learning idea that came from others (e.g. software developers or engineers)
- The UX design team generated a novel design concept utilizing machine learning, which was presented and then selected for integration into a new product or service
- The UX design team collaborated with engineers, product managers or others, and jointly developed an idea for a new product or service that utilizes machine learning

To gain insights on the types of challenges they faced when working with ML as a design material, we asked participants who had worked on ML projects to list the three biggest challenges they have faced when working with ML.

We deployed this as an online survey using SurveyMonkey. The survey was promoted via mailing lists for the Interaction Design Association, User Experience Professionals Association, and CHI. It was also listed on interaction design groups at LinkedIn and Reddit, promoted via Twitter and Facebook, and circulated to alumni of interaction design degree courses at our present and former universities. We also requested that respondents forward the survey to other UX or interaction design practitioners in their networks. All responses were anonymous. Because of the self-selecting nature of our recruitment process, we do not make strong claims with regards to how representative a sample of UX practitioners this survey represents. However, because it was widely promoted in the US, the UK and Denmark, we believe that at the very least it offers an informative snapshot of current UX practice.

The survey was available online for a period of two weeks, during which time we received fifty-one completed responses. The survey contained five multiple-choice selection questions and four questions requesting a free text response. Respondents were able to skip individual questions if they so wished. To analyze the results, we collated the responses and performed simple statistics on the quantitative data provided by the multiple-choice questions. To analyze the free text responses, each of which was typically somewhere between a couple of lines of text and a short paragraph in length, we performed a simple thematic analysis [5] to identify patterns across the data and extract key ideas. We then sought agreement across our individual interpretations. In the following section, we discuss each of the questions in turn and present the main findings from our analysis of the responses received.

FINDINGS

Thirty-nine of fifty-one respondents described their work as UX or interaction design practice in a commercial or government setting (see Table 1 for details). Of the five respondents who selected "Other", four have degrees in UX or design (see Question 2 below). They listed their jobs as product manager, user researcher, service experience designer, and experience strategy. Because our aim with this survey is to investigate the way in which ML is encountered in UX design practice rather than research, we have restricted the remainder of our analysis to these forty three respondents, i.e. the thirty nine that self-identified as professional UX practitioners and the four "others" whose self-described work practice fell within our area of interest.

Of the forty-three respondents who practice UX commercially, thirty seven (86%) reported having a degree in UX or some form of design including: interaction design, industrial design, communication design, and service design. Of these thirty-seven, only three (8%) said they had had any exposure to machine learning or machine learning concepts in school. Specific details about these concepts and courses were sketchy. One thought the subject had come up, but not as a dedicated class; one mentioned exposure to pattern recognition algorithms and the third mentioned the school they had graduated from, without giving any more information regarding specific classes.

Of the forty-three respondents that practice UX, twenty seven (63%) claimed to have worked on a project integrating ML into the UX of a commercial product or service. As Table 2 shows, respondents most commonly describe their work generating ideas for ML products or services as being *collaborative* with other professions.

Type of UX Design Work	#	Design Degree
UX or Interaction Designer working on commercial or government products and services	39	33
Interaction Design researcher working on scholarly research	3	2
HCI researcher working on scholarly research	4	2
Other	5	4

Table 1: Area of survey respondents' work

Type of Involvement	#
The **UX design team collaborated with engineers**, product managers or others, and jointly developed an idea for a new product or service that utilizes machine learning	12
The **UX design team gave an interactive form** to a machine learning idea that came from others (e.g. software developers or engineers)	8
The **UX design team generated a novel design concept** utilizing machine learning, which was presented and then selected for integration into a new product or service	7

Table 2: Involvement of UX team in generating ideas for novel ML products

Fifteen respondents were able to provide further details of the most recent projects they worked in that incorporated ML. These included recommendation engines for a variety of industries, face and object recognition for smart phone applications, agent interfaces, filtering of content for a variety of domains, intelligent media monitoring and advertising, and displaying search engine results. Respondents' involvement in these projects included: helping to define the logic, providing interaction design assistance, and providing insights about users' responses to the systems. Across these projects, respondents highlighted that they most frequently used ML to make sense of user actions. In consumer facing projects this most commonly took the form of recommendation engines, and in one case a fraud detection system. Agent interfaces were associated with decision support.

When defining ML, as they understand it, respondents listed features such as personalization, customization, prediction, and recommendation, often referring to the way that ML systems improve over time and through use, reflecting the findings from our previous question. These responses overlapped with an understanding of ML as having the capacity to learn or be trained without explicit programming and to adapt to user input or contextual change. Typical of this view, one respondent stated: "*Machine learning is the broad capability of technology systems to respond, react, and sometimes predict to users' actions and stated desires.*" Similarly, respondents described ML as having the ability to identify patterns in data and then respond to these patterns. For example, one response started: "*At a very high level, ability to identify meaningful data patterns that can surface preferences or problems and perhaps also predict future performance or outcomes.*" Respondents did not typically discuss ML with reference to any technical details, nor mention that ML techniques are rooted in statistical analysis.

When discussing how ML has made an impact on their own practice, respondents indicated that ML is seen as something that is now just beginning to be important, and which will be more important in the future. One respondent stated that: "*Applications of this capability are just starting to make their way into my projects, though it has been present as a meaningless buzzword for many years. The initial applications are very simple as machine learning is still seen as a silver bullet for all problems by laymen.*" There was a general degree of excitement about the possibilities that ML might offer for UX. However, there were also concerns raised. For example, one respondent pointed out that: "*You have to be acutely aware, though, of when users start to perceive anticipation to be interference.*" Another stated that poorly performing natural language interfaces can undermine the way a system is perceived, making people think it is dumber than it really is, saying that: "*...when the machine learning (Natural Language Understanding or Natural Language Processing) is off then patients and even providers lose trust immediately.*"

Challenges When Working With ML

Thirty respondents provided us with details of the three biggest challenges that UX designers face in working with ML. When we looked at their responses, several patterns emerged: first, respondents discussed challenges in envisioning what ML might be; second, they discussed challenges working with ML as a design material; third, they expressed concern in designing with ML as a "black box", raising ethical questions about the purposeful use of ML.

Difficulties in understanding ML and its capabilities

Participants uniformly described difficulties in understanding what ML was and how it worked. One respondent noted, "*We designers do not understand the limits of machine learning and what it can/can't do. Machine learning experts often complain to me that designers act like you can just sprinkle some data science onto a design and it will become automatically magical.*"

Another stated that, *"It is black magic to designers. ...Designers don't understand the constraints of the technology and how to employ it appropriately."* This should not be too surprising if UX designers are only now starting to see ML transition from a buzzword to a real practice concern, and if as we see in earlier responses they did not receive directly applicable education.

Challenges with ML as a design material

Participants also mentioned challenges in working with ML as a design material. One noted, *"I think we just have yet to see its full potential in commercial products. Perhaps that's because UX/interaction designers don't know its potential..."* Another stated, *"The technical complexity is a challenge as is the need to better understand and design for that complexity. It can get deep and unfamiliar very quickly, and designers need some level of expertise to function and contribute to the work at hand."* Inherent in these responses is the idea that designers lack a clear understanding of ML technology, and how to envision uses that don't yet exist, perhaps suggesting they need to see examples first; and perhaps consequently explaining why UX designers have not brought their expertise to bear in the use of ML in today's commercial products. This also reflects the nature of the ML projects that UX designers told us they have been involved in. In essence, these projects use ML in ways that would be totally familiar to ML researchers. Entity identification, object classification, personal recommendation, and agent interaction are classic ML topics, and the use-cases that respondents describe seemed quite typical.

In the same vein, respondents described difficulties in prototyping ML, expressing ML ideas, and noted the need for designers to collaborate with skilled technologists. One noted, *"Machine learning is hard to prototype. Machine learning requires highly skilled collaborators, when a lot of companies are only able to hire 'warm bodies'."* Additionally, another respondent stated, *"...making interactive prototypes that incorporates machine learning is hard (haven't found a way to do that yet in an easy fashion),"* and another indicated that UX designers make statements such as *" ...inputs come in ...some magic happens ...and all your business needs are met!"* Clearly, in order to effectively leverage ML as a design material, designers currently feel that collaborations are essential.

Challenges with the purposeful use of ML

A third frequently mentioned challenge was how to purposefully use AI and ML in systems that respondents might design. This highlighted a desire to bring a human-centered perspective to bear on ML. One respondent summarized the situation well by saying, *"While ML as an enabling technology is still in the early stages, we're likely to be one step behind the engineers that create it... changing this relationship to being one that is design-led, or at least an equal partnership will be important — we need to shift the conversation from technology to people — we'll need to bring the ethical and human centered voice to the algorithms that make it all a reality."* Another wondered who would be accountable if a system driven by ML made an error: *"If machine learning is utilized, how 'deep' does it go? If it makes a (grievous) error, who is held accountable? ....can it be trusted to make decisions or take actions on its own?"* Others talked about the necessity of holding a concern for people as a critically important value: *"Making sure it's not creepy and keeps a human element to it."* *"...map out the right user stories and use cases, to enable effective machine learning."*

DISCUSSION

Our goal here is to initiate a research and education agenda for the UX and interaction design communities. We have observed that ML represents an underexplored opportunity, and that for UX designers ML offers as yet unknown potential as a design material. As a first step, we culled the literature for evidence of the overlap of ML and interaction design. We also surveyed UX design practitioners about their experiences working with ML.

Limitations of the Survey

Inevitably, the richness and depth of the data gathered through surveys is limited in comparison to that we may have gained from interviewing UX designers. Our intention here is to first gain a broad overview before digging in to investigate the particular concerns of a small selection of designers. Our hope with this survey is to lay a foundation that will enable other researchers to pick up this research thread and investigate the challenges associated with working with ML as a design material.

Our survey only reached a small number of UX practitioners; however, it had a broad geographical spread of respondents. We promoted the survey widely throughout networks in the US, UK and Scandinavia, and we targeted UX designers for whom ML is a current or foreseeable topic of concern. We believe that this offers a diversity and representativeness that may not have been present had it been slightly larger but more geographically restricted.

Key Findings From the Survey

Drawing collectively from our literature review, our investigation on the state of the art in UX and ML, and our survey responses, we present other key findings:

First, it is clear that the UX design community understands ML broadly, but not specifically. Nearly two decades of research covered in our literature review revealed generalizations about this technology, but few specifics about what is needed to design with it. This finding was echoed in the survey of UX professionals, in the descriptions of what ML means and how it impacts designers' work. Answers were in broad brushstrokes rather than detailed answers with specific examples. Similarly, when respondents discussed the challenges ML presents, a difficulty in understanding ML was repeatedly highlighted. The difficulties expressed in understanding and therefore ideating and innovating with ML is a clear challenge for designers. However, the literature also points to examples where the development of effective tools and techniques has released the potential for better, more sophisticated design with other complex technologies. We can only imagine that the same will happen for ML in the next decade.

Second, we believe that current interaction design, UX, and even HCI design education cannot prepare the next generation of design graduates to incorporate ML into their work. This is evidenced by the finding that only three respondents had taken a class that they considered had taught them how to integrate ML into the UX design of products and services. Moreover, of the three that did respond positively to this question none provided particular details regarding the class in question. It is further evidenced by the absence of this topic from major UX and interaction design course textbooks [e.g. 13,46]. Finally, the stated difficulties that practicing designers express with regards to understanding and communicating ML suggests they have not been sufficiently prepared in this regard.

Third, while ML clearly pushes the boundaries of design, the balance of collaboration with engineers and software developers is currently such that design-led innovation is still rare. We find evidence for this when we look at designers' descriptions of how the ML projects they have been involved in unfolded. Only 25% of these were classified as the UX design team leading the generation of a novel design concept. It is also evidenced in the challenges respondents described. The technical complexity of ML is a theme that was repeated, as was the need for collaborative expertise.

Finally, our collective research efforts showed that prototyping with ML is difficult. In the era of industrial and product design, designers created prototypes in the form of sketches, plans, and physical models made of paper, cardboard, or foam [26]. The era of UX design added skills from storytelling, narrative, and film to the prototyping process. Designers relied on stories, film techniques, digital video, and stagecraft to construct situations where experiences could be evaluated, particularly with products that do not yet exist [7,42,59].

ML clearly demands a new type of prototyping, one that does not yet exist. We believe that there are a number of reasons for this. First, "learning" implies that the system and data will change over time. Designers are not accustomed to designing a form for data that is dynamic at a large scale. Second, the way in which ML and designers treat data is quite different from each other. Designers mostly visualize data and look for correlations and patterns that "make sense;" that fit with their understanding of how the world should and does work. ML in contrast finds machine-recognizable correlations and patterns in data. It applies no common sense; thus correlations can appear simplistic and even stupid to a person trying to make sense of the patterns. These two efforts are often at odds. Finally, a prototype that relies on ML data will most likely be inordinately complex, and may have many possibilities and a high degree of uncertainty. It may also require an unwieldy amount of ML data to create a functional prototype. This challenges the general idea of prototyping; of making just enough of a system to assess if this is the right direction to go. ML seems to require a much higher level of commitment; perhaps conflicting with UX mantras like "fail fast, fail often."

Challenges for UX Design

The survey results showed that ML is considered to be technically complex and challenging. It was also described as having ethical implications, being potentially expensive, and largely falling outside the scope of smaller projects. Respondents described difficulties in understanding and therefore expressing the capabilities, limitations and potential of ML within a UX design context. They considered interactions with ML difficult to prototype because such interactions are dynamic, and their outcomes are potentially unpredictable. This creates a risk that users might be prevented from achieving the things they want or need to do. They also identified potential difficulties in gathering enough user data for successful ML, and in drawing useful insights from these data. Respondents believed that mental models of ML are often poor, and highlighted a need for good user research to provide a human-centered focus and ensure ML is incorporated in a thoughtful way, rather than interfering or being "creepy". Education, experience and training do not currently prepare designers for working with ML, and they highlighted the potential benefits of working with skilled technologists, engineers and programmers.

These findings have led us to consider some initial challenges for UX design research and education, with regards to working with ML as a design material. We don't suggest that this is an exhaustive list of the challenges that designers face when working with ML, nor even that these will end up being considered the most critical challenges. This is instead an *initial* list of challenges. The motivation for each of these challenges is well grounded in our research data, and we believe they form a solid starting ground. We therefore challenge ourselves, and our community, to investigate how we might:

- Consider the interplay between ML statistical intelligence and human common sense intelligence
- Envision opportunities to apply ML in less obvious ways
- Represent ML's dependency on data in early prototypes
- Foreground ethical considerations of ML

Consider the Interplay of ML and Human Intelligences

Our survey indicated that prototyping with ML presents a significant challenge for UX designers. One reason respondents stated for this is that interactions with ML systems can seem unpredictable, and therefore be difficult to clearly express. It is hard to effectively imagine what the experience will be, or the likely performance errors, until the system is built; therefore making it difficult to assess potential value versus "creepiness". The statistical intelligence displayed by ML may result in a very different interpretation of the same data than common sense human intelligence. This can make performance errors seem bizarre and hard to explain, resulting in potentially dissonant user experiences. To mitigate this, UX designers should consider interactions not only from the more familiar human perspective, but also the perspective of statistical inference, and crucially how these two perspectives might interact. We invite UX and interaction design researchers to build on the examples outlined in our literature [e.g. 15,30], and develop tools and techniques for considering this interplay. So that, for example, we might better anticipate, mitigate or account for ML statistical errors, such as false positives or negatives, or design for perceptive qualities. One area where this may play out is in ML based agents, such as those found in virtual assistants like Amazon Echo and Google Home. Currently, these require somewhat awkward voice commands to initiate interactions. However, the perceptual awareness explored in [15] points in a direction that designers might explore to fundamentally reassess the UX qualities such products aspire to.

Envision Opportunities to Apply ML In Less Obvious Ways

Our survey data indicates that identifying opportunities to apply ML in novel and interesting ways, that respond to emerging trends and uncover unforeseen desires, is currently challenging for designers. Identifying and ideating around these opportunities is a key aspect of the design-led innovation that is apparently common elsewhere, and yet currently missing for systems designed with ML. This is likely because designers' understanding of ML is at a relatively broad-brush scale, making it difficult to ideate, sketch and elegantly prototype ML concepts. We hope that UX and interaction design researchers can build on the examples in our literature review [e.g.7,42] and develop tools and techniques that help envision how ML can be applied in less obvious ways.

An example of applying ML in a less obvious way might be to reevaluate how recommender systems, such as those used in ecommerce or media platforms, are conceived. These represent one of the most familiar forms ML takes, and one that has remained largely unchanged for the last two decades. Most recommenders rank items in order to narrow the apparent choices to a subset of those most likely to result in user selection. The UX design associated with these is an add-on, an afterthought to the classification capabilities of the underlying algorithms. A design-led innovation in recommender systems might overturn this and start from the experiences of the most enthusiastic collectors of books, music or film. It might consider pleasure in the effort of discovery, and the knowledge gained along the way. Designers might explore what makes these search efforts meaningful; and how to enable a more nuanced view of the way in which different individuals' tastes develop, and how they differ from or intersect with the crowd. This design-led exploration might also find ways to mitigate the dissonance caused by inappropriate suggestions, which currently remain all too familiar. The challenge for researchers is not only to undertake such reimagining but also to develop the tools that allow us to explore the results with potential users.

Represent ML's Dependency on Data in Early Prototypes

Our survey data indicates that UX designers may not clearly understand the dependent relationship ML has with data and ground truth. This is also the impression gained from a series of online UX articles that were part of our literature review, and in which designers and commentators treat ML as if it were some type of magic. We therefore challenge UX designers to be more open about the difficulties in planning for data gathering and labeling, like [56], and to develop tools and techniques for prototyping the interdependencies between data and UX early-on when working with ML

Foreground Ethical Considerations

Our survey found that one of the main challenges identified by UX designers with regards to ML is to consider its ethical implications. These responses fit in with a long tradition in design of the concern of the designer in creating something that is ethical, purposeful, and pragmatic [e.g. 39,44], but also in computer science traditions [e.g. 3]. Our hope is that the UX and interaction design communities continue to contribute to this conversation by keeping the needs and desires of people at the forefront of everything that they design.

CONCLUSION

Machine learning (ML) is now a fairly established technology, and user experience (UX) designers have begun to integrate ML services into the things that they design. This paper presents a survey conducted with current UX practitioners to understand how well ML is understood and operationalized in design practice. Our findings show that the design community is only beginning to understand this technology and its application. We expand on these findings to present a series of challenges for UX and interaction design research and education.

ACKNOWLEDGMENTS

We thank all the participants who took the time to complete our survey. This research was supported by The Danish Innovation Foundation grant 1311-00001B, CIBIS.

REFERENCES

1. James F. Allen, Curry I. Guinn, and Eric Horovitz. 1999. Mixed-initiative interaction: *IEEE Intelligent Systems and their Applications*: 14-23.
2. Robbert-Jan Beun, Eveliene De Vos, and Cilia Witteman. 2003. Embodied conversational agents:

effects on memory performance and anthropomorphisation. In *International Workshop on Intelligent Virtual Agents*, 315-319.

3. Nick Bostrom, and Eliezer Yudkowsky. 2014. The ethics of artificial intelligence. In *The Cambridge Handbook of Artificial Intelligence*, Keith Frankish and William M Ramsey (eds), Cambridge University Press, Cambridge: 316-334
4. Sheryl Brahnam, and Antonella De Angeli. 2012. Gender affordances of conversational agents: *Interacting With Computers*: 139-153.
5. Virginia Braun, and Victoria Clarke. 2006. Using thematic analysis in psychology: *Qualitative research in psychology* 3, 2: 77-101.
6. John Brownlee. 2015. *Apple finaly learns AI is the new UI.* Retrieved August 1, 2016 from http://www.fastcodesign.com/3047199/apple-finally-learns-ai-is-the-new-ui
7. Marion Buchenau, and Jane Fulton Suri. 2000. Experience prototyping. In *Proceedings of the 3rd conference on Designing interactive systems: processes, practices, methods, and techniques*, 424-433.
8. Bill Buxton, 2007. *Sketching user experiences.* Morgan Kaufmann,.
9. Stephen M Casner, , Edwin L Hutchins, and Don Norman. 2016 The challenges of partially automated driving. *Communications of the ACM* 59, 5: 70-77.
10. Justine Cassell. 2000. Emboddied conversational interface agents. *Communications of the ACM* 43, 4: 70-78.
11. Guanling Chen and David Kotz. 2000 *A survey of context-aware mobile computing research.* Dept. of Computer Science, Dartmouth College, Dartmouth.
12. Giles Colborne. 2016. *Interaction design in the age of algorithms.* Retrieved August 8, 2016 from https://www.cxpartners.co.uk/our-thinking/interaction-design-in-the-age-of-algorithms/
13. Alan Cooper, Robert Reimann, David Cronin, and Christopher Noessel. 2014. *About face: the essentials of interaction design.* John Wiley & Sons,.
14. Scott Davidoff, Brian D Ziebart, John Zimmerman, and Anind K Dey. 2011. Learning patterns of pick-ups and drop-offs to support busy family coordination. In *Proceedings of the SIGCHI Conference on Human Factors in Computing Systems.*(CHI'11): 1175-1184.
15. Eva Deckers, Pierre Levy, Stephan Wensveen, Rene Ahn, and Kees Overbeeke. 2012. Designing for perceptual crossing: Applying and evaluating design notions. *International Journal of Design* 6, 3: 41-55.
16. Pedro Domingos. 2012. A few useful things to know about machine learning. *Communications of the ACM* 55,10: 78-87.
17. Afsaneh Doryab, Jun Ki Min, Jason Wiese, John Zimmerman, and Jason I Hong. 2014. Detection of behavior change in people with depression. In *Proceedings of AAAI Workshop on Modern Artificial Intelligence for Health Analytics (MAIHA)*.
18. Graham Dove, and Sara Jones. 2014. Using information visualization to stimulate creativity in service design workshops.In *Proceedings of the fourth Service Design and Service Innovation Conference.* (ServDes14): 281-290.
19. Pelle Ehn, and Morten Kyng. 1991. Cardboard computers. In *Design at Work*, Joan Greenbaum and Morten Kyng (eds) Lawrence Erlbaum Associates: 169-197.
20. Harry Enten. 2016. *Election update: where polls and demographics disagree.* Retrieved September 14, 2016 from http://fivethirtyeight.com/features/election-update-where-polls-and-demographics-disagree/
21. Peter Flach. 2012. *Machine learning: the art and science of algorithms that make sense of data.* Cambridge University Press.
22. Jodi Forlizzi, John Zimmerman, Vince Mancuso, and Sonya Kwak. 2007. How interface agents affect interaction between humans and computers. In *Proceedings of the 2007 conference on Designing pleasurable products and interfaces*: 209-221.
23. Marco Gillies, et al. 2016. Human-centered machine learning. In *Proceedings of the 2016 CHI Conference Extended Abstracts on Human Factors in Computing Systems* (CHI'16): 3558-3565.
24. Google. 2016. *Breakthroughs in Machine Learning - Google I/O 2016.* Retrieved August 1, 2016 from https://www.youtube.com/watch?v=sphFCJE1HkI
25. Jonathan Grudin. 2006. Turing maturing: the separation of artificial intelligence and human-computer interaction. In *Interactions*: 54-57.
26. Bjarki Hallgrimsson. 2012. *Prototyping and modelmaking for product design.* Laurence King,.
27. Harrison, Chris, Desney Tan, and Dan Morris. "Skinput: appropriating the body as an input surface." *Proceedings of the SIGCHI Conference on Human Factors in Computing Systems.* Atlanta: ACM, 2010. 453-462.
28. Jonathan L Herlocker, Joseph A Konstan, and John Riedl. 2000. Explaining collaborative filtering recommendations. In *Proceedings of the 2000 ACM conference on Computer supported cooperative work.* (CSCW): 241-250.

29. Geoffrey E Hinton. 2007. Learning multiple layers of representation. *Trends in Cognitive Science* 11,10: 428-434.
30. Chien-Ming Huang, and Bilge Mutlu. 2012. Robot behavior toolkit: generating effective social behaviors for robots. In *Proceedings of the seventh annual ACM/IEEE international conference on Human-Robot Interaction.* (HRI'12): 25-32.
31. Scott E Hudson, et al. 2003. Predicting human interruptibility with sensors: a wizard of oz feasibility study. In*The CHI 2003 New Horizons Conference Proceedings: Conference on Human Factors in Computing Systems.* (CHI'03): 257-264.
32. Francisco Iacobelli, and Justine Cassell. 2007. Ethnic identity and engagement in embodied conversational agents. In *International Workshop on Intelligent Virtual Agents*: 57-63.
33. Rabia Kahn and Antonella De Angeli. 2009. The attractiveness stereotype in the evaluation of embodied conversational agents. *IFIP Conference on Human-Computer Interaction* (INTERACT 2009): 85-97.
34. Yunkyung Kim, and Bilge Mutlu. 2014. How social distance shapes human-robot interaction. *International Journal of Human-Computer Studies* 72: 783-795.
35. Kenneth R Koedinger, and A Corbett. 2006. Cognitive tutors. In *The Cambridge handbook of the learning sciences*, Keith R Sawyer (ed) Cambridge University Press: 61-77.
36. Pat Langley. 1997. Machine learning for adaptive user interfaces. In *Annual conference on Artificial Intelligence*: 53-62.
37. Min Kyung Lee, Sara Kiesler, Jodi Forlizzi, Siddhartha Srinivasa, and Paul E Rybski. 2010. Gracefully mitigating breakdowns in robotic services. In *5th ACM/IEEE International Conference on Human-Robot Interaction* (HRI): 203-210.
38. Ewa Luger, and Abigail Sellen. 2016. Like having a really bad PA: the gulf between user expectation and experience of conversational agents. In *Proceedings of the 2016 CHI Conference on Human Factors in Computing Systems* (CHI'16): 5286-5297.
39. Media Lab Helsiki. *A quick primer for ethics in design.* Retrieved September 15 2016 from http://mlab.uiah.fi/polut/Yhteiskunnalliset/lisatieto_ethics_primer.html
40. Camille Mousette, and Richard Banks. 2011. Designing through making: exploring the simple haptic design space. In *Proceedings of the fifth international conference on Tangible, embedded, and embodied interaction*: 279-282.
41. Clifford Nass, Jonathan Steuer, and Ellen R Tauber. 1994. Computers are social actors. In *Proceedings of the SIGCHI conference on Human factors in computing systems.* (CHI'94): 72-78.
42. William Odom, John Zimmerman, Scott Davidoff, Jodi Forlizzi, Anind K Dey, and Min Kyung Lee. 2012. A fieldwork of the future with user enactments. In *Proceedings of the Designing Interactive Systems Conference.* (DIS'12): 338-347.
43. Fatih Kursat Ozene, , Miso Kim, John Zimmerman, Stephen Oney, and Brad Myers. 2010. How to support designers in getting hold of the immaterial material of software. In *Proceedings of the SIGCHI Conference on Human Factors in Computing Systems.* (CHI'10): 2513-2522.
44. Victor Papanek. 1995. *The Green Imperative: Ecology and Ethics in Design and Architecture*. Thames and Hudson.
45. Pamela Pavliscak. 2016. *Algorithms as the new material of design.* Retrieved September 14th 2016 from http://www.uxmatters.com/mt/archives/2016/06/algorithms-as-the-new-material-of-design.php
46. Jenny Preece, Helen Sharp, and Yvonne Rogers. 2015. *Interaction design: beyond human-computer interaction.* John Wiley & Sons.
47. Frank Rosenblatt. 1961. *Principles of neurodynamics. perceptrons and the theory of brain mechanisms.* Cornell Aeronautical Lab.
48. Arthur L Samuel,.1959. Some studies in machine learning using the game of checkers. *IBM Journal of research and development* 3, 3: 210-229.
49. Ben Shneiderman, and Patti Maes. 1997. Direct manipulation vs. interface agents. *Interactions*: 42-61.
50. Yale Song, David Demirdjian, and Randall Davis. 2012. Continuous body and hand gesture recognition for natural human-computer interaction. *ACM Transactions on Interactive Intelligent Systems* 2, 1: 5.
51. Aaron Spaulding, , Krzystof Z Gajos, Anthony Jameson, Per Ola Kristensson, Andrea Bunt, and Will Haines. 2009. Usable intelligent interactive systems. In *CHI'09 Extended Abstracts on Human Factors in Computing Systems.*
52. Swedish ICT. Retrieved September 15th 2016 from https://www.tii.se/projects/ittextiles
53. Terry Winograd. 2006. Shifting viewpoints: artificial intelligence and human-computert interaction. *Artificial intelligence*: 1256-1258.
54. Ian Witten, Eibe Frank, and Mark Hall. 2011. *Data mining: practical machine learning tools and techniques.* Morgan Kauffman.
55. Allison Woodruff, Sally Augustin, and Brooke Foucault. 2007. Sabbath day home automation: it's like mixing technology and religion. In *Proceedings of the*

SIGCHI conference on Human factors in computing systems. (CHI'07): 527-536.

56. Qian Yang, John Zimmerman, Aaron Steinfeld, and Anthony Tomasic. 2016. Planning adaptive mobile experiences when wireframing. In *Proceedings of the 2016 ACM Conference on Designing Interactive Systems*. (DIS'16): 565-576.
57. Rayoung Yang, and Mark W Newman. 2013. Learning from a learning thermostat: lessons for intelligent systems for the home. In *Proceedings of the 2013 ACM international joint conference on Pervasive and ubiquitous computing*: 93-102.
58. Rayoung Yang, Mark W Newman, and Jodi Forlizzi. 2014. Making sustainability sustainable: challenges in the design of eco-interaction technologies. In *Proceedings of the SIGCHI Conference on Human Factors in Computing Systems*. (CHI'14) 823-832.
59. John Zimmerman. 2005. Video Sketches: Exploring pervasive computing interaction designs. *IEEE pervasive computing* 4, 4: 91-94.
60. John Zimmerman, , et al. 2007. VIO: a mixed-initiative approach to learning and automating procedural update tasks. In *Proceedings of the SIGCHI Conference on Human Factors in Computing Systems*. (CHI'07) 1445-1454.
61. John Zimmerman, Kaushal Kauapati, Anna L Buczak, Dave Schaffer, Srinivas Gutta, and Jacquelyn Martino. 2004. TV personalization system. In *Personalized Digital Television*, Liliana Ardissono, Alfred Kobsa and Mark Maybury, (eds) Kluwer Academic Publishers: 27-51.

Technology Maintenance: A New Frame for Studying Poverty and Marginalization

Amy Gonzales
Indiana University
Bloomington, IN
gonzaamy@indiana.edu

ABSTRACT
This paper offers a new theoretical frame for those interested in poverty and design. As digital access rates peak, *technology maintenance* argues that the digital divide will increasingly manifest in the (in)ability to stay connected. As a novel and conservative test, open-ended data from a 748-person university student survey of technology maintenance were analyzed. Use and ownership were ubiquitous, but students demonstrated variability in *coping with the inevitable*; disconnection was more burdensome for low-resourced students. Findings extend technology maintenance and are leveraged as a starting point for three calls for action in HCI: 1) the CHI community should research the burdens of poverty in poor *and* wealthy contexts; 2) new HCI projects should accommodate inconsistent access; and, 3) new design choices should minimize disruption and optimize stability. This requires action at the individual and organizational level as designers create products that consider marginalization but also use expertise to influence policy.

Author Keywords
Digital divide; poverty; technology maintenance; access

ACM Classification Keywords
H.1.2 User/Machine Systems

INTRODUCTION
The digital design community has long been interested in human welfare [e.g. 9], as exemplified by robust bodies of scholarship on design for disability, global development, and environmental sustainability. However there are notable gaps in the literature on design and socio-economic marginalization within wealthy countries, though recent scholarship may signal a change in this regard [15, 23]. Aims to broaden the scope of prosocial HCI research may thus be aided by the application of a new theoretical lens.

Technology maintenance argues that, as the divide in access and use closes, the digital divide will manifest as the inability for low-income and marginalized groups to *maintain* access [10, 11]. Maintaining access for the poor is complicated by reliance on technology that is more likely to be broken, shared, and *dependably unstable:* cycling through regular periods of disconnection (e.g. prepay cell phones that are regularly without minutes [12]). Maintenance involves constant upkeep of financial, technical, and relational resources, such as balancing phone and gas bills when money is tight or maintaining social ties that can loan a back-up phone. These phenomena are especially insidious in wealthy countries where representative data gives the appearance of widespread ownership and use [e.g. 27]. A handful of studies at CHI and elsewhere have found evidence of chronic 'underconnectedness' in the US [28, 29, 41], but have not yet used a theoretical frame to explore the issue.

A shift in the digital divide poses new challenges for policy makers and new opportunities for technologists and designers. This paper situates this new frame within existing HCI research by leveraging unexplored qualitative findings from the first quantitative survey of technology maintenance in a socio-economically varied population: university students. After evidencing indicators of often overlooked disparities, I then pose three calls to action to designers interested in social change. My aim is to channel prosocial efforts that have focused on non-Western poverty and environmental concerns to think about sustainable HCI from the perspective of economic justice worldwide.

HCI and poverty
There is a long tradition of relevant research on poverty and digital technology in poor countries (i.e. ICTD). Mobile technologies in particular have been embraced for addressing problems like rural economic development, e.g. [26], health promotion [8], and democratic political involvement [37]. Although some projects show more promise than others [4], this work reflects the design community's commitment to improving quality-of-life in non-Western contexts. Along the way researchers have urged restraint from pushing Western agendas onto people with less money and darker skin [15, 17, 23]. This 'post-colonial' approach is more culturally sensitive and may better optimize design success and scalability [2, 4, 17, 39].

CHI 2017, May 06-11, 2017, Denver, CO, USA
 ISBN 978-1-4503-4655-9/17/05...$15.00
DOI: http://dx.doi.org/10.1145/3025453.3025475

There is also a small but important body of extant research at the intersection of digital technology and poverty in wealthy countries. Examples include location-based systems to support food assistance programs [7], or the role of banking and employment technologies for the unemployed [21, 35]. There is also work on digital media use by the homeless, and organizations that serve the homeless [23, 24]. This work has done a good job of recognizing that successful intervention should move "*toward* a sustainable *process* of developing and refining attachments to different socio-technical resources and *away* from focusing simply on co-creating a temporally and materially fixed *artifact* (italics his)" [23, p.1352]. In other words, access to digital technology is not a permanent or categorical state but rather an ongoing experience of labor, negotiation, and coping. These findings are echoed in the handful of HCI studies that explore how low-income and racial minorities in the US struggle with access [29, 41]. Technology maintenance may facilitate new projects for those interested in poverty, especially in places where initial access is achieved but maintenance is a continuous struggle.

Theoretical contextualization

Technology maintenance research originated from interviews with public housing residents in the US [10]. Although those low-income residents ostensibly *had* cellphones, their access mirrored the disruptions described by residents in poorer countries. One key difference between maintenance problems in wealthy and poor countries, however, is that institutions in wealthy countries (e.g. schools, work, government services) expect reliable communication with most residents. Subsequent studies have found that, because the majority of low-income US Americans no longer have a landline telephone [3], disrupted cellphone access disrupts communication with healthcare providers, employers, and much needed personally supportive ties [11, 12]. Low-income US Americans overwhelmingly report technology ownership and Internet use, but are often unable to pay monthly bills and own slow, broken, or shared devices [28]. In other words, because those in the US are increasingly expected to have ICT access, frequent disruptions or 'underconnection' may have serious yet underappreciated consequences, potentially exacerbating inequalities [34, 36].

The idea that digital access is now about maintenance speaks to existing theoretical constructs in HCI. For example, work on *infrastructure* assumes that digital technology is more than a bounded device or system, but rather an amalgam of resources, including stable access to electricity, education, political stability, personal health, community participation, etc. [2, 31]. Another related concept, *obsolescence,* highlights the fragility of digital technology and the patterns of casual waste that we have come to expect in a global society [33]. This literature is often motivated by concerns for environmental costs, but rarely addresses the human cost when people struggle to maintain access; a technology maintenance lens refocuses this phenomenon on economic justice. Finally, research on repair and reuse proposes an epistemological opportunity for rethinking the "crude functionalism of the technology field" by acknowledging and investigating moments of digital breakdown [18, 19, 20]. Like technology maintenance, this work builds on scholarship in anthropology and philosophy that stresses the importance of repair as necessary, inevitable, and political [13]. However, most of this work in HCI has focused on middle-class repair in wealthy countries [e.g. 30], and repair by the poor in poorer countries [e.g. 1, 39]. Technology maintenance also appreciates the struggles of poor communities in wealthy societies as an opportunity for broadening ideas of and solutions for digital instability.

A conservative test

Previous research on technology maintenance has explored disconnection low-income adult populations, primarily as it influences health [10, 12]. But Hargittai [14] notes that assumptions about universal access for young adults makes the consequences of disconnection for youth particularly pernicious. A more stringent test of technology maintenance, then, is to examine maintenance problems in a younger *and* more socio-economically diverse sample where use and ownership are likely to be pervasive. Evidence of technology maintenance phenomena within this sample would broaden the framework to a new, education context and better demonstrate its breadth. I thus ask: how does socio-economic status affect students' abilities to stay connected and the consequences of disconnection?

METHODS AND ANALYTIC APPROACH

Students from a large midwestern university participated in a survey for credit over three semesters between 2014-2015 mostly from a 350-person course on social media. The final sample included 748 students, 51% were self-reported female, 46% freshman and 73% were White. These data were collected as the first quantitative operationalization of previous qualitative findings [10, 11, 12]. As part of the study, survey participants were also asked open-ended questions about whether "problems with technology (e.g. broken, inaccessible, malfunctioning software or hardware)" had ever affected students' ability to "complete coursework on time" or "caused problems in personal relationships." Although the data here are modest in scope they provide a window into an aspect of technology maintenance that is important for student quality of life and may shape social inequality. Quantitative findings are being reviewed elsewhere, but these findings offer important insights on student experiences in their own words.

Of students surveyed, 359 students described having problems with late assignments and 124 students had problems in relationships because of technology disruption. Responses were sorted using a standardized index of socio-economic status (SES): mother's education (6-item scale), father's education (6-item scale), and parent tuition support (3-item scale), (M = .005, SD = .76; *Med.* = .16). As education and income are common metrics of SES, parent tuition support is used as a proxy for income (α = .63). Using techniques common to sociological analysis of qualitative interviews, such as grounded theory, open-ended responses were then critically read and analyzed to detect common themes across participants and between low and high-SES using a median split [5, 6]. Supplemental notes were analyzed, with the final analysis focused on summarizing core themes and identifying disconfirming evidence that suggests that low-SES and high-SES students have different technology maintenance experiences. A dominant theme emerged that further builds on the technology maintenance lens, and is explored below.

RESULTS

Coping with the inevitable

Across SES, problems with laptops and the internet frequently affected students' ability to complete assignments on time. However, low-SES students had more ongoing problems and greater difficulty regaining access. In other words, *coping with the inevitable,* was the theme that emerged across respondents, but in very different forms.

Temporarily disrupted internet and printer access in particular was an equalizer across SES: students of all SES noted loosing access in the middle of completing or submitting an assignment. One student noted: "*literally while attempting to answer this question I lost internet connection using [campus wi-fi].*" Many reported stress (e.g. "*panic and run to the library,*" "*I cried, and then I used someone else's computer...*") and, as one middle-SES student noted, some received lower grades:

"when I lived at my parents house freshman year I occasionally turned assignments in late because of trouble with the internet (too slow, not connecting, etc). I couldn't really do anything about it; I just had to accept a lower grade."

Computer crashes were the other frequent cause of late-assignments. Computer crashes occurred for low and high-SES students, and students in both groups often turned to a friend or campus-resources when problems arose. Low-SES students (26ppl), however, had difficulty regaining stable personal access than high-SES students (11ppl). To illustrate, a high-SES student noted:

"during finals week last semester my Apple computer would not turn on so I had to take it into the store. Thankfully, I had insurance and it was fixable; however, it was a rough week. I had to borrow my friend's laptop or basically live in a computer lab on campus to study and get my work done. My apple computer was fixed within a few days."

In contrast, a lower-SES student wrote, *"over the summer my laptop broke down and I couldn't get it fixed until after summer classes ended."* Temporary problems were universal, but reconnection was harder for lower-SES students, and, as the previous student went on to note, "*set my coursework back.*" Low-SES students were also more likely to report persistent problems:

"my computer is rather trashy because it came without any protection on it and got a virus the very first day I got it. It sometimes works and then randomly on some days will just not go to websites and stays loading a page for hours so I go to the computer lab in my dorm."

This example of technology maintenance underscores the fact that ownership does not ensure access, which is a never-ending process rather than a categorical state, even for university students. More importantly, disparities in reliable connections may exacerbate social inequalities if low-income students have a harder time completing assignments, which could affect long-term academic success and future job prospects.

As with schoolwork, there were also reports of relationship stress because of technology problems, in this case, phone or Skype disconnection and poor cell service. Again, students faced similar problems across SES, but the source of these problems differed (e.g. remote vacation location v. lack of money), as did the solutions. Some high-SES students used back-up technologies when access was compromised (11 ppl). As one high-SES student wrote,

"I spent the summer somewhere where the internet access was very low and there was no cell phone service...I would call my family once a week from a landline and talk to my friends and family using Facebook chat...Overall, it was actually nice to 'unplug'."

Low-SES students were less likely to reference alternative communication when personal communication was disrupted (7ppl). For example, one low-SES student wrote:

"broken phones and technology get costly very fast. I broke a smartphone one time by accident and didn't have a replacement while I was at IU, and my mom at home couldn't help until I came back home. Then it became very costly to fix the problem, and this is difficult when there are other things to pay for. The problems with broken technology get solved, but those problems come with a bigger price not everyone is able to pay."

As this poignant quote conveys, both high and low-SES students were ultimately able to maintain digital access, but low-SES students often pay a higher price for maintenance because additional resources were limited and extenuating circumstances (e.g. illness, foreclosure) complicated solutions. Thus, the core finding from the first analysis of technology maintenance in a socio-economically diverse sample is that SES informs students' ability to *cope with the inevitable*, the consequences of which touch facets of both academic and personal life.

DISCUSSION

These data posed a more stringent test of technology maintenance, previously only examined in low-SES adult samples. Findings reveal that even some of the most connected individuals worldwide—US college students—cannot consistently depend on technology. Moreover, those with fewer resources have a more difficult time regaining access and, for them, the costs of disconnection may be greater. This work elaborates on technology maintenance research describing low-SES citizens in wealthy countries slipping through the cracks of wired social and political institutions (i.e. healthcare, employment, education, etc.) [10, 11, 12]. Findings that students must *cope with the inevitable,* offer a glimpse into disparities even within a hyper-connected segment of the global population. Although disheartening, this transition from disparities in use and ownership to disparities in access maintenance provides new opportunities for designers. Following are three calls to action for those interested in mitigating this evolving digital divide.

Design to understand disruption

First, I echo previous scholars that call for more HCI work on the poor and other marginalized groups within the US and other wealthy countries [15, 41]. Of course, studies on socio-political marginalization from across the globe are important. But we should ask ourselves: why do HCI scholars study poverty in other parts of the world and not the poverty that abounds in the wealthy countries most of us call home? Why are we uncomfortable or uninterested in economic inequality around us? There is a lot of room to build on the small extant body of investigative studies [e.g. 29, 41] and HCI interventions [e.g. 7, 21] that aim to reduce the suffering and experience of poverty and marginalization closer to home. The HCI community should ask questions that bring attention to and mitigate the consequences of poverty in those contexts as well.

Design to accommodate disruption

Second, HCI researchers should accommodate disruption in the plethora of design and evaluation studies taking place. This is especially true when designing for the poor and marginalized, but research on any new system should account for inevitable disruption and maintenance. As the results above indicate, nearly all people experience short-term disruption. How effective can a new doctor-patient portal be if the sickest patients own computers too slow to use? What happens when a new-student welcome app is inaccessible to the lowest-SES students? As Yardi et al. point out, "HCI should attend to socioeconomic factors like race, income and education of its users…otherwise it risks conflating study results with socioeconomic factors" [41, p.3049].

Studies that have successfully done this have found that the need to share devices in communities of color limits the reach of educational computing resources [29, 41]. In Nairobi, the need to conserve expensive phone minutes prompted recommendations of more prominent display of remaining airtime and rethinking services that put callers 'on hold' [39]. But these studies are the exception rather than the rule. If technologists design without accounting for and accommodating disruption, further embedding technology into daily life will only amplify existing disparities [25, 34].

Design to reduce disruption

Finally, technologists are in a position to reduce disruption with hardware and software design. These recommendations have been made before, often with a focus on the environment [16, 19, 22], but in most cases sustainable design would also serve the poor by minimizing costs. This includes investing in modular design of mobile and laptop parts that can be replaced without purchase of an entirely new device [16, 22], or making those devices repairable by using non-soldering techniques (http://www.verdantelectronics.com/). Users might also benefit from promotion of secondary IT markets for selling, sharing and repair—a specialized 'Craigslist' that allows technicians, consumers, and vendors to interface—thus sustaining the life of second-hand devices. Campaigns to inform non-profits about how to help clients sustain access might also be useful (e.g. pbdd.org). These are just some of the ways that those in HCI can design to help reduce disrupted access. Much more work here is needed as well.

CONCLUSION AND POLICY IMPLICATIONS

This paper introduces a new frame to the HCI community and elaborates on previous technology maintenance findings. There is much to learn from extant research, especially in sustainable HCI and HCI4D, that can mitigate the costs of unstable access. Technology maintenance can facilitate that investigation, especially as disparities in maintenance widen over coming decades.

As access rates of computer and mobile use plateau in wealthy countries, the HCI community is in an extraordinary position. Although innovation may always amplify social inequality [34], we are at a point in history, as ICT policy becomes fixed, to decide who can fully take advantage of groundbreaking digital innovations and who must make due with systems that are out-dated, costly, impossible or illegal to repair, and dependably unstable. Researchers who care about poverty and marginalization must therefore get involved at multiple levels of 'infrustructure' design. This includes leveraging technical expertise to collaborate and share best practices with organizations that serve the poor (e.g. nten.org). It could also involve lobbying governments to institute policies that promote access to marginalized users (i.e. see recent FCC proposals to subsidize broadband access), and coming up with incentives for ICT corporations to optimize product longevity. As Suchman [32] wrote, "innovation and change are inevitably costly undertakings, and require associated commitments to their ongoing, long-term development." Over the next decade the need for this commitment from the HCI will only come further into relief.

REFERENCES

1. Syed Ishtiaque Ahmed, Steven J. Jackson, Md. Rashidujjaman Rifat. 2015. Learning to fix: Knowledge, collaboration and mobile phone repair in Dhaka, Bangladesh. In *Proceedings of the Seventh International Conference on Information and Communication Technologies and Development* (ICTD '15).
2. Syed Ishtiaque Ahmed, Nusrat Jahan Mim, Steven J. Jackson. 2015. Residual mobilities: Infrastructural displacement and post-colonial computing in Banglgadesh. In *Proceedings of the SIGCHI Conference on Human Factors in Computing Systems* (CHI '15), 437-446.
3. Stephen J. Blumberg and Julian V. Luke. 2015. Wireless substitution: early release of estimates from the National Health Interview Survey, July–December 2012. June. National Center for Health Statistics. Available at: http://www.cdc.gov/nchs/data/nhis/earlyrelease/wireless201512.pdf.
4. Ruy Cervantes, Mark Warschauer, Bonnie Nardi, and Nithya Sambasivan. 2011. Infrastructures for low-cost laptop use in Mexican schools. In *Proceedings of the SIGCHI Conference on Human Factors in Computing Systems* (CHI '11), 945-954.
5. Kathy Charmaz. 2006. *Constructing grounded theory*. London: Sage.
6. Juliet Corbin and Anselm Strauss. 2008. *Basics of qualitative research*, 3rd. Thousand Oaks, CA: Sage.
7. Lynn Dombrowski, Jed R. Brubaker, Sen H. Hirano, Melissa Mazmanian, Gillian R. Hayes. 2013. It Takes a Network to Get Dinner: Designing Location-Based Systems to Address Local Food Needs. In *Proceedings of the International Joint Conference on Pervasive and Ubiquitous Computing* (UbiComp '13), 519-528.
8. Jonathan Donner and Patricia Mechael. 2013. *mHealth in practice: Mobile technology for health promotion in the developing world.* Bloomsbury.
9. Batya Friedman, Peter H. Kahn Jr. and Alan Borning. 2008. Value Sensitive Design and information systems. In *The Handbook of Information and Computer Ethics.* eds. K. Himma and H. Tavani. John Wiley & Sons, Inc.
10. Amy Gonzales. 2014. Health benefits and barriers to cell phone use in low-income US neighborhoods: Indications of technology maintenance. *Mobile Media & Communication,* 2: 233–248.
11. Amy Gonzales. 2016. The contemporary US digital divide: From initial access to technology maintenance. *Information, Communication & Society,* 19: 234-248.
12. Amy Gonzales, Lindsay Ems, & Ratandeep Suri. 2014. Cell phone disconnection disrupts access to healthcare and health resources: A technology maintenance perspective. *New Media & Society.* Advance online publication. doi:10.1177/1461444814558670
13. Stephen Graham and Nigel Thrift. 2007. Out of order: Understanding repair and maintenance. *Theory, Culture, & Society, 24,* 1–25.
14. Eszter Hargittai and Amanda Hinnant. 2008. Digital inequality: Differences in young adults' use of the internet. *Comm Research*, 35: 602–621.
15. John Harvey, David Golightly, and Andrew Smith. HCI as a means to prosociality in the economy. 2014. In *Proceedings of the SIGCHI Conference on Human Factors in Computing Systems* (CHI '14), 2955-2964.
16. Elaine M. Huang and Khai N. Truong. 2008. Breaking the Disposable Technology Paradigm: Opportunities for Sustainable Interaction Design for Mobile Phones. In *Proceedings of the SIGCHI Conference on Human Factors in Computing Systems* (CHI '08), 323-332.
17. Lilly Irani, Janet Vertesi, Paul Dourish, Kavita Philip, and Grinter, Rebeeca E. Grinter. 2010. Postcolonial computing: a lens on design and development. In *Proceedings of the SIGCHI Conference on Human Factors in Computing Systems* (CHI '10).
18. Steven J. Jackson. 2014. Rethinking repair. In *Media technologies: Essays on communication, materiality, and society,* Tarleton Gillespie, Pablo Boczkowski, and Kirstin Foot (eds.). The MIT Press, Cambridge, Massachusetts, 221-308.
19. Steven J. Jackson, Syed Ishtiaque Ahmed, and Md. Rashidujjaman Rifat. 2014. Learning, Innovation, and Sustainability among Mobile Phone Repairers in Dhaka, Bangladesh. In *Proceedings of the Designing Interactive Systems Conference* (DIS '14), 905-914.
20. Steven J. Jackson and Laewoo Kang. 2014. Breakdown, obsolescence and reuse: HCI and the art of repair. In *Proceedings of the SIGCHI Conference on Human Factors in Computing Systems* (CHI '14), 449-458.
21. Benjamin Jen, Jashanjit Kaur, Jonathan De Heus, and Tawanna R. Dillahunt. 2014. Analyzing employment technologies for economically distressed individuals. In *Proceedings of the SIGCHI Conference on Human Factors in Computing Systems* (CHI '14), 1945-1950.
22. Rob Lawlor. 2015. Delaying obsolescence. *Sci Eng Ethics,* 21: 401-427.
23. Christopher Le Dantec. 2012. Participation and publics: Supporting community engagement. In *Proceedings of the SIGCHI Conference on Human Factors in Computing Systems* (CHI '12), 1351-1360.
24. Christopher Le Dantec and W. Keith Edwards. 2008. Designs on dignity: Perceptions of technology among the homeless. *Proceedings of the SIGCHI Conference*

on Human Factors in Computing Systems (CHI '08), 627–636.

25. Bonnie Nardi. 2014. Designing for the future- but which one? *Interactions,* 26-33.
26. Neil Patel, Deepti Chittamuru, Anupam Jain, Paresh Dave, and Tapan S. Parikh. 2010. Avaaj Otalo: a field study of an interactive voice forum for small farmers in rural India. In *Proceedings of the SIGCHI Conference on Human Factors in Computing Systems* (CHI '10), 733–742.
27. Pew Research Center. (2016). [Key indicator demographic highlight report]. *Pew Research Center Internet Project Survey, Three Technology Revolutions.* Retrieved from http://www.pewinternet.org/three-technology-revolutions/
28. Victoria Rideout and Vikki Katz. 2016. *Opportunity for all? Technology and learning in lower-income families.* A report of the Families and Media Project. New York: The Joan Ganz Cooney Center at Sesame Workshop.
29. Parisa Khanipour Roshan, Maia Jacobs, Michaelanne Dye, and Betsy DiSalvo. 2014. Exploring How Parents in Economically Depressed Communities Access Learning Resources. *Proceedings of the 18th International Conference on Supporting Group Work* (GROUP '14), 131-141.
30. Daniela Rosner and Fred Turner. 2014. Theaters of Alternative Industry. In *Design Thinking Research* eds. C. Meinel and L. Leifer. Springer.
31. Susan L. Star and Karen Ruhleder. 1996. Steps Toward an Ecology of Infrastructure: Design and Access for Large Information Spaces. *Info Systems Rsch,* 7(1): 111-134.
32. Lucy A. Suchman. 2002. Practice-Based Design of Information Systems: Notes from the Hyperdeveloped World. *The Information Society*, 18: 139-144.
33. Babette Tischleder and Sarah Wasserman, eds. 2015. *Cultures of Obsolescence: History, Materiality, and the Digital Age*. Springer.
34. Kentaro Toyama. 2011. Technology as amplifier in international development. *iConference,* 75-82.
35. John Vines, Paul Dunphy, and Andrew Monk. 2014. Pay or Delay: The Role of Technology When Managing a Low Income. In *Proceedings of the SIGCHI Conference on Human Factors in Computing Systems* (CHI '14), 501-510.
36. Kasisomayajula Viswanath and Matthew W. Kreuter. 2007. Health disparities, communication inequalities, and e-health: a commentary. *American Journal of Preventive Medicine,* 32, 5 Suppl: S131.
37. Herman Wasserman. 2011. Mobile phones, popular media, and everyday African democracy: Transmissions and transgressions. *Popular Communication* 9: 146-158.
38. Susan Wyche. 2015. Exploring mobile phone and social media use in a Nairobi slum: A case for alternative approaches to design in. In *Proceedings of the SIGCHI Conference on Human Factors in Computing Systems* (CHI '15).
39. Susan Wyche, Tawanna R. Dillahunt, Nightingale Simiyu, and Sharon Alaka. "If God gives me the chance I will design my own phone": Exploring Mobile Phone Repair and Postcolonial Approaches to Design in Rural Kenya. In *Proceedings of the International Joint Conference on Pervasive and Ubiquitous Computing* (UbiComp '15), 463-473.
40. Susan P. Wyche and Laura L. Murphy. 2012. "Dead China-make" phones off the grid: Investigating and designing for mobile phone use in rural Africa. In *Proceedings of the Designing Interactive Systems Conference* (DIS '12), 186-195.
41. Sarita Yardi and Amy Bruckman. 2012. Income, race, and class: Exploring socioeconomic differences in family technology use. In *Proceedings of the SIGCHI Conference on Human Factors in Computing Systems* (CHI '12), 3041-3050.

All about Acceptability? Identifying Factors for the Adoption of Data Glasses

Marion Koelle [1]*, Abdallah El Ali [1], Vanessa Cobus [2], Wilko Heuten [2], Susanne CJ Boll [1]
[1] Media Informatics and Multimedia Systems, University of Oldenburg, Oldenburg, Germany
[2] Interactive Systems Group, OFFIS - Institute for IT, Oldenburg, Germany
{firstname.lastname}@uol.de, {firstname.lastname}@offis.de

ABSTRACT
Innovations often trigger objections before becoming widely accepted. This paper assesses whether a familiarisation over time can be expected for data glasses, too. While user attitudes towards those devices have been reported to be prevalently negative [14], it is still unclear, to what extent this initial, negative user attitude might impede adoption. However, in-depth understanding is crucial for reducing barriers early in order to gain access to potential benefits from the technology. With this paper we contribute to a better understanding of factors affecting data glasses adoption, as well as current trends and opinions. Our multiple-year case study (N=118) shows, against expectations, no significant change towards a more positive attitude between 2014 and 2016. We complement these findings with an expert survey (N=51) investigating prognoses, challenges and discussing the relevance of social acceptability. We elicit and contrast a controversial spectrum of expert opinions, and assess whether initial objections can be overwritten. Our analysis shows that while social acceptability is considered relevant for the time being, utility and usability are more valued for long-term adoption.

ACM Classi cation Keywords
K.4.0 Computers and Society: General

Author Keywords
Data Glasses; Augmented Reality; Technology Adoption; Social Acceptability; User Acceptance; Public Experiences;

INTRODUCTION
On their market entry, *data glasses*, light-weight head-worn computing devices (e.g., `Google Glass`, `Meta Pro` or the `Atheer one`), triggered a wave of criticisms. One cause for objections was their ability to unobtrusively record video imagery of their environment; seen as a threat to privacy [6].

Over the years, observations of technology adoption have shown that technical innovation often triggers fear, anxiety and objections [4]. However, it has also been noted that initial indignations often fade away and public opinion may change. Both Hosokawa's "Walkman Effect" [10] and the dissemination of consumer photography [2] show how users of a mobile gadget can attract criticism and be accused of rudeness and disrespect of other people's privacy. Albeit, the Walkman, which was predecessor to a whole line of portable music devices, including the iPod, and portable (digital) cameras have found their way into our daily life.

This paper investigates whether this effect also applies to data glasses, which we define according to [14] as class of mono- or binocular head-worn displays that resemble prescription glasses, not limited to a specific device type or brand[1]. Up to now the roles of familiarisation over time and social acceptability are not clear, as data glasses are different from earlier innovations. They differ in terms of form factor and display paradigm, but also in terms of (online) media coverage and exposure [19]: with only 1% of data glasses owners in the US[2], the majority of potential users did not come in contact with actual devices, before they became aware of the publicly hyped discussion. This paper looks at factors that are decelerating data glasses acceptance from both, a retrospective (user study-based) and a prospective (expert-based) point of view.

We retrospectively discuss the adoption of data glasses to date, based on a multiple-year case study (N=118) and investigate prognoses from a survey amongst 51 experts on data glasses, HCI and technology adoption from industry and academia. Our research questions are:

(A) *Can an alteration of user attitudes similar to the "Walkman Effect" be already observed for data glasses?*,

(B) *Do experts expect an alteration of user attitudes within the next ten*[3] *years?*, and

(C) *What factors impede an alteration in user attitudes?*

We contribute quantitative results of a multiple-year study on user attitudes towards data glasses, which is to the best of our knowledge, the first one reported. We surveyed at three distinct points in time, supplementing a study of 2014 (c.f. [14]) with

*Part of the data collection of the presented case study has been carried out by Marion Koelle as part of her doctoral studies at the University of Passau, Germany (2013-2016).

[1]Examples of commercially available data glasses announced or launched between 2014 and 2016: https://www.wareable.com/headgear/the-best-smartglasses-google-glass-and-the-rest, accessed 15/12/2016

[2]c.f.: Vision Voice Newsletter. Google Glass Awareness in the US, http://east.visionexpo.com/Press/Vision-Voice-Newsletter/Google-Glass-Awareness-in-the-US/, accessed 15/12/16

[3]c.f. Years to mainstream adoption for **AR**, Gartner, http://www.gartner.com/newsroom/id/3412017, accessed 15/12/16

CHI 2017, May 06 - 11, 2017, Denver, CO, USA

ISBN 978-1-4503-4655-9/17/05...$15.00
DOI: http://dx.doi.org/10.1145/3025453.3025749

surveys in 2015, and 2016. Our user study's results are complemented with an expert survey identifying weak spots and eliciting a prioritisation of challenges for data glasses adoption. We highlight notions regarding social acceptance, spectator attitudes and (un)obtrusiveness of the device. With our work we contribute to a better understanding of factors that impede or support data glasses becoming habitual in real-life scenarios.

RELATED WORK

We outline theories and models of two relevant research areas: the dissemination of a technology from niche applications into society and the adoption of technology by individuals.

Technology Diffusion into Society

Mensvoort's "Pyramid of Technology" [25] describes the different levels a technology attains from being envisioned (level 1) until becoming naturalised (level 7) and omnipresent. Characteristically, many technologies only climb the lower half of the pyramid, i.e. *applied* (level 3) or *accepted* (level 4), before they stabilise or are replaced by newer technologies. Innovation diffusion models [22] illustrate that initial judgements, though made without any prolonged use of the technology, serve as a filter and either result in non-appropriation or adoption of a new technology. In consequence, initial user attitudes, as we assessed in our case study, are crucial for the success or failure of a particular technology's adoption.

This work focuses on the transition (or "disruption") between an *applied* and an *accepted* technology, c.f. Cisco's Media Disruption Map[4]. Data glasses have attained the *applied* level by taking the step out out of the lab. Our work looks closely on the preconditions of an alternation to an *accepted* technology, i.e., to being "part of our daily life" [25], which we consider achieved if a society's majority has moved from being *excluded* on to being *core* or *peripheral* users [23].

Technology Adoption by Individuals

Davis' well-known Technology Acceptance Model (TAM) [5] defines the adoption of new technologies by individuals based on two main factors: usefulness and perceived ease-of-use. Derivate models add subjective norms and social influence [16, 26], and share the assumption that individuals tend to consult their social network in order to reduce anxiety towards an innovation [11]. Building upon this theoretical ground work, we investigate the characteristics of data glasses adoption, particularly looking into cross-relationships of different factors and provide a device-specific ranking of relevant factors.

An in-depth investigation of smart watch adoption in the context of TAM has been presented by Kim et al. [13]. They investigate "subcultural appeal", i.e. smart watches being a fashion statement, in addition to traditional TAM patterns. Buenaflor et al. [3] assess human factors, including social, physical and demographic aspects of the acceptance of wearable computing devices. A stream of research conducted by Rauschnabel et al. takes a managerial perspective on data glasses adoption. They look into social norms and functional benefits [18], fashion [19] as well as perceived usefulness, ease-of use and both user's and bystander's privacy [20]. While prior work determined factors that influence data glasses adoption, our work goes further and estimates the precedence of improvements based on expert opinions.

MULTIPLE-YEAR CASE STUDY

We present a multiple-year observation of user attitudes towards data glasses, complementing a previously published survey [14]. Unlike in the preceding study, which focused on factors that influence user attitudes, the present study assesses changes in user attitudes over time using the original semantic differential and scenarios to assess the user attitude at *three distinct points in time*, i.e., 04/2014, 04/2015, and 04/2016.

Methodology

We conducted repeated measurements (2014, 2015, and 2016) following the study design and procedure described in [14]. Participants were asked to rate a set of 56 scenarios (28 involving data glasses, 28 smart phones) based on a semantic differential (c.f. Table 1). They indicated their subjective perception using a slider, comprising a range of -5 to +5 with a resolution of 1.0 (11-pt. Likert Scale). The questionnaire was filled out on a desktop computer in a quiet lab environment using a neutral survey platform.

	negative		positive	
negative	tense	⟵⟶	serene	positive
	threatened	⟵⟶	safe	
	unsure	⟵⟶	self-confident	
	observed	⟵⟶	unobserved	
	skeptic	⟵⟶	outgoing	

Table 1. Semantic differential with pairs of adjectives.

All participants were recruited via a regional recruitment platform, which, in contrast to online recruitment, allowed to rule out sampling errors due to changes in popularity of social networks or fluctuation of mailing list subscriptions. Thus sampling stability and a more reliable and valid between-subjects comparison can be achieved. Repeated participation of an individual participant in multiple runs was ruled out during recruitment. Monetary compensation according to the platform's convention (€ 10 /h) was disbursed after the study in a separate room and by personnel different from the experimenter. We analysed the results based on the following hypothesis:

H_1: There was a signi cant alternation in user attitudes towards data glasses between 2014 and 2016.

Participant pro le

Distributed over three distinct samples, 118 participants, aged between 18 and 58 ($\bar{x} = 23$, $\sigma = 4$), 47% female, participated in our study (c.f. demography in Table 3.2). Professional backgrounds/study subjects were diverse with their distribution corresponding to the faculty-wise distribution of study subjects at the whole university (i.e. no IT surplus).

Year	N	Female	Mean Age	Age Range	σ
2014	38	16 (42%)	23	18–38	4
2015	41	18 (44%)	22	20–31	3
2016	39	22 (56%)	23	20–56	6
Overall	118	56 (47%)	23	18–56	4

Table 2. Demography; Age profile and gender distribution.

[4]Gottlieb Duttweiler Institute. From Innovation to Disruption, http://www.gdi.ch/i2d/index.html, accessed 15/12/16

Analysis and Results

With our study we replicated the study presented in [14], and re-conducted it twice over a period of two years. For analysis participants were grouped according to their year of participation. We evaluated the questionnaires reliability based on Cronbach's Alpha ($\alpha \in [0.95; 0.98]$[5]), which accounts for a high consistency within individual measurements [15]. The answers to the semantic differential (11-pt., ordinal scale) were analysed for each scenario and each pair of adjectives individually. Medians were determined and analysed for significance (Kruskal-Wallis test, $df = 2$, adjusted for ties). With no statistically significant differences (all $p > .01$) found, the null hypothesis (H_0), stating that there is no significant alternation in user attitude between 2014 and 2016, has to be accepted.

Limitations

The case study's results confirm the (prevalently negative) user attitude towards data glasses and their influencing factors found in [14]. On top of this, the repeated study shows that there has been no significant change in user attitudes over the three years of investigation. While our findings are applicable to the student population in Passau, Lower Bavaria[6], Germany, our results might not be fully generalisable. Particularly, more progressive user groups (e.g., early adopters) or regions (e.g., silicon valley, metropolises) might already show first signs of an alteration in user attitudes, not captured by our study.

EXPERT SURVEY

Starting from those results we subsequently assess (based on expert opinions) whether those negative attitudes entail a lack of social acceptance and if benefits from data glasses usage are capable of overwriting initial objections. With our expert survey we assess prognoses for the adoption of data glasses, and identify open issues and disagreements.

Expert Profile	Count
UX/IxD Practitioner (min. 2 years experience*)	27 (53%)
Researcher (before PhD*)	11 (22%)
Researcher (Post-doc**, Professor**)	33 (65%)
Early Adopters (min. 1 month experience)	10 (20%)
Author, Journalist or Blogger†	7 (14%)
PR, Marketing, Sales (AR or HmDs)	3 (6%)
Developer (Data glasses HW/SW)	17 (33%)
Other	2 (4%)

* Areas of expertise: User Experience Design, Interaction Design, User-Centered Design or similar.
* Areas of expertise: data glasses, head-worn displays, Augmented Reality, or similar.
** Areas of expertise: Human-Computer Interaction, Technology Adoption Research, Information Ethics, or similar.
† with at least one published article or blog entry covering wearable devices, data glasses, smart contact lenses or other future, head-worn technologies.

Table 3. Predefined expert profiles, participants were presented with brief descriptions (including level of expertise) and asked for self-assessment, multiple selections were possible.

Methodology

We deployed our expert survey online via a neutral survey platform (i.e., not associated with a brand or manufacturer) to prevent sponsor bias. Its main part consisted of 2 two-tiered questions (6-pt. Likert scale with free text explanatory statement: Q1, Q3) and one asking the participants to rank improvement criteria by relevance (Q2).

Q1 Within the next 10 years: do you expect data glasses to be worn by people as a matter of routine?

Q2 What would have to be improved such that data glasses can become a tool used by people in their everyday lives? Please provide us with a ranking. (Options based on [27], c.f. figure 2)

Q3 To what extent do you think that social acceptance will be relevant for the success of data glasses?

The survey explicitly targeted participants that had prior experience with data glasses (e.g., as developer, researcher or early adopter) or expert knowledge in the field of HCI/ICT. For recruitment we used snowball sampling in addition to purposive sampling via email and social networks based on pre-defined expert criteria (c.f. Table 3). Out of 90, 51 experts (15 female), aged 24 to 54 ($\bar{x} = 35$, $\sigma = 7$) submitted completely filled out questionnaires. The majority of participants live and work in Europe (39, 76%) and the US/Canada (10, 20%), followed by Middle East/North Africa (1, 2%) and Asia (1, 2%). There was no compensation paid for participation.

Results and Discussion

The participants' qualitative statements were analysed independently by two coders with regard to re-occurring themes and arguments. Following the procedure of inductive category development [17] results were categorised and summed up (occurrences denoted as n). In the following we highlight the key findings and relate them to prior work.

Prognoses The majority of participants estimate data glasses to be worn as a matter of routine within the next 10 years (Median=3, σ=1.3); also shown in Figure 1. While participants value the advantage of hands-free interaction (n=5), situated information access (n=7), as well as natural interaction (n=4) they also name both technological and societal issues that would have to be solved before wide adoption becomes possible. Particularly, opinions diverge regarding the pervasiveness of adoption and prerequisites that would have to be met. Participants expect data glasses to be successful in specialised application areas (n=18), such as the work place (n=15) or sports (n=4). Opinions were divided whether adoption by consumers for casual usage is likely (n=6) or unlikely (n=7).

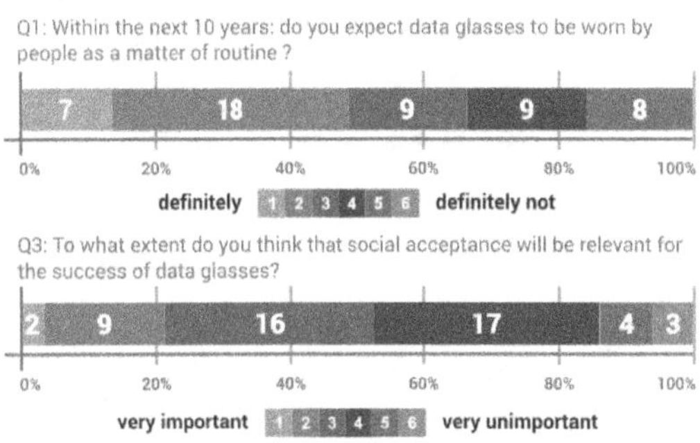

Figure 1. Answers to Q1 (top, Median=3, σ=1.3) and Q3 (bottom, Median=3, σ=1.2), measured on 6-pt. Likert Scales.

Prerequisites for Adoption Subsequently, we highlight the most frequently named factors that impede the adoption of data glasses. Overall, a lack of suitable use cases and useful applications (*Utility*, n=12) was discerned. Participants agreed that overcoming the current lack of utility is crucial for adoption: *"So given we come up with suited application scenarios,*

[5]Cronbach's α determined separately for each perspective (1st person, 2nd person) and device (smart phone, data glasses)

[6]Details on the regions demographics available from `https://www.statistik.bayern.de/veroeffentlichungen/`, accessed 15/12/16

data glasses will become ubiquitous." (P71) Furthermore, participants criticised a lack of wearing comfort and named *Ergonomic Issues* (n=13) as hindrance for adoption. P40 states *"Form Factors are too cumbersome and do not outweigh the provided utility."* This critique is also backed by previous results by Motti et al. [9] who note a lack of "Wearablity" of current devices. Moreover, *Pricing* will have to decrease (n=4) for data glasses to become more affordable. In addition, *Usability* (n=3) has been raised as issue: *"They do not yet present a superior means of communicating information to a user, because the interface is not nimble to manipulate."* (P24) Perceived awkwardness and social shaming (*Social Image*, n=18), as well as *Privacy* (n=7), and *Ethical Issues* (n=9) have been also noted to impede the adoption of data glasses.

Need for Improvements Q2 asked the participants to rank given areas of improvements according to their relevance for the adoption of data glasses. Figure 2 illustrates the overall ranking (middle, dark blue, N=51) along with rankings by subsamples that rated social acceptability either more important (N=27), i.e. below the median or less important (N=24) , i.e. above the median. Rankings were determined based on aggregated scores (Borda count). Differences between sub-groups are significant ($\chi^2(48, N{=}421) = 148.17$, $p < .001$, $V = 0.45$). Usefulness, functionality, and usability, along with compatibility with daily routines have been concordantly identified as most important areas for improvement, as also reflected by the qualitative statements outlined above. Those results are further backed by Shackel's acceptability equation [24].

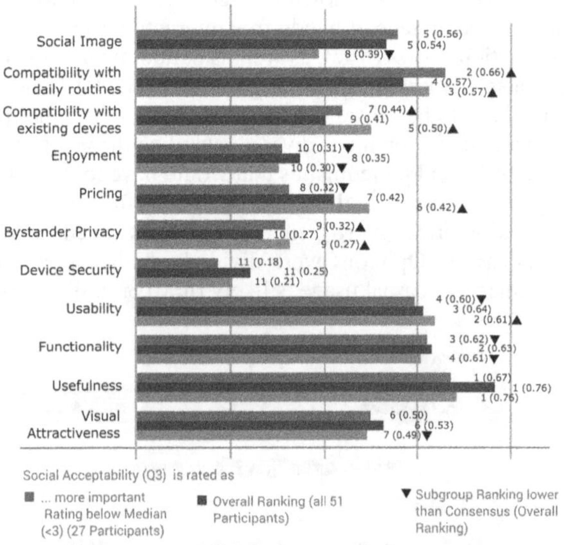

Figure 2. Ranking of required improvements for long-term adoption based on aggregated scores (normalised Borda count, in brackets), changes in ranks indicated by arrows.

How Relevant is Social Acceptance? Along with the improvement of the *Social Image* that was subordinated in Q2 (c.f. Figure 2), only a small majority indicates social acceptance to be slightly important (3) or important (2, Median=3, σ=1.2, c.f. Figure 1) for the adoption of data glasses. Interestingly, participants were in disagreement whether social acceptance is a matter of time (n=5) and exposure (n=2) or if it results from weighing benefits (n=4). Participants also stated that social acceptance comes naturally (n=2), and one participant challenged whether social acceptance can be supported by design: "After all, how can you design for social acceptability?" (P12); Also addressed by Kim et al. [12], who propose Acceptability Engineering as an extended research discipline.

Which Level of (Un)obtrusiveness? While appealing design (n=17), along with the *"Coolness Factor"* (n=4) was frequently named as prerequisite for adoption (Q1), multiple participants consider the resemblance to prescription glasses as crucial. They believe that miniaturisation and unobtrusiveness (n=7) will result in a higher social acceptability. P71 states *"Once we hit the point where data glasses are looking just like normal glasses [...] adoption will increase drastically."*. However, increasing the unobtrusiveness of data glasses might intensify a different set of problems. While the user becomes less prone to objections and social shaming, issues of (bystander) privacy (n=7) arise: it is unclear whether a device with camera is present and/or recording. The question whether interactions with a mobile device shall be unobtrusive [1, 7] or candidly communicated [8] has been adressed in earlier research (e.g., by Reeves at al. [21]) and also raised by P26: *"There is also the issue that the manipulations are highly visible, but the effects are not [...]"*. Finding the "right" level of (un)obtrusiveness challenge for future research; a tightrope walk, requiring to balance a trade-off between being unsuspicious and straightforward: they require *"[s]ubtle design that allows them to stand out, but not so obviously different"* (P76)

CONCLUSION

In this paper we investigated factors impeding and supporting data glasses adoption. Based on a 2014 to 2016 case study, we demonstrated that user attitudes have been stable and prevalently negative over the last three years. However, our survey amongst 51 experts shows that an alteration in user attitudes as well as an adoption of data glasses is expected until 2026. While social acceptability is considered relevant for the time being, experts expect it to be overwritten by more fundamental factors on the long run. They identify **(1) Usefulness, (2) Functionality** and **(3) Usability** as most crucial to long-term adoption. Moreover, the unobtrusive design (**Unobtrusiveness**) is named as a key strategy for improving the social image and acceptability.

Our present work demonstrates that data glasses, though already launched to public and widely discussed, still pose manifold challenges to (HCI) research and will not be accepted without efforts. In order to create utile applications (**Usefulness**) we require more user research, involving in-depth requirements analysis, and deep understanding of specialised (professional) use cases. Novel or improved hardware capabilities, powerful tracking methods, will be prerequisite to providing the needed services and functions (**Functionality**). Current usability issues (**Usability**) will be a challenge not only to usability research but particularly to those looking into novel, advanced interaction methods and visualisation techniques. Finally, design disciplines, e.g., interaction design, will be challenged to determine the the "right" level of unobtrusiveness for data glasses devices and interactions.

ACKNOWLEDGEMENTS

This work reports results of two studies carried out between 2014 and 2016, namely a multiple-year case study and an expert survey. The case study was conducted by Marion Koelle while she was a PhD student at the University of Passau (2013-2016), while the expert survey was conducted at the University of Oldenburg in 2016. The latter has been supported by the BMBF project ChaRiSma under grant number 16I1665.

REFERENCES

1. Fraser Anderson, Tovi Grossman, Daniel Wigdor, and George Fitzmaurice. 2015. Supporting Subtlety with Deceptive Devices and Illusory Interactions. In *Proceedings of the 33rd Annual ACM Conference on Human Factors in Computing Systems (CHI 15)*. ACM, New York, NY, USA, 1489–1498. DOI: http://dx.doi.org/10.1145/2702123.2702336
2. Angela Berkley. 2015. Snapshot Seeing: Kodak Fiends, Child Photographers, and Henry James's What Maisie Knew. *MFS Modern Fiction Studies* 61, 3 (2015), 375–403. https://muse.jhu.edu/article/594732
3. Cherrylyn Buenaflor and Hee-Cheol Kim. 2013. Six Human Factors to Acceptability of Wearable Computers. *International Journal of Multimedia and Ubiquitous Engineering* 8, 3 (2013), 1–8. http://www.sersc.org/journals/IJMUE/vol8_no3_2013/10.pdf
4. Daniel Castro and Alan McQuinn. 2015. *The Privacy Panic Cycle: A Guide to Public Fears About New Technologies*. The Information Technology & Innovation Foundation, Washington, DC, USA. http://www2.itif.org/2015-privacy-panic.pdf
5. Fred D. Davis Jr. 1986. *A technology acceptance model for empirically testing new end-user information systems: Theory and results*. Dissertation. Massachusetts Institute of Technology. http://hdl.handle.net/1721.1/15192
6. Tamara Denning, Zakariya Dehlawi, and Tadayoshi Kohno. 2014. In situ with Bystanders of Augmented Reality Glasses: Perspectives on Recording and Privacy-mediating Technologies. In *Proceedings of the 32rd Annual ACM Conference on Human Factors in Computing Systems (CHI 14)*. ACM, New York, NY, 2377–2386. DOI: http://dx.doi.org/10.1145/2556288.2557352
7. David Dobbelstein, Philipp Hock, and Enrico Rukzio. 2015. Belt: An Unobtrusive Touch Input Device for Head-worn Displays. In *Proceedings of the 33rd Annual ACM Conference on Human Factors in Computing Systems (CHI 15)*. ACM, New York, NY, USA, 2135–2138. DOI: http://dx.doi.org/10.1145/2702123.2702450
8. Barrett Ens, Tovi Grossman, Fraser Anderson, Justin Matejka, and George Fitzmaurice. 2015. Candid Interaction: Revealing Hidden Mobile and Wearable Computing Activities. In *Proceedings of the 28th Annual ACM Symposium on User Interface Software and Technology (UIST 15)*. ACM, New York, NY, USA, 467–476. DOI: http://dx.doi.org/10.1145/2807442.2807449
9. Vivian Genaro Motti and Kelly Caine. 2014. Understanding the Wearability of Head-mounted Devices from a Human-centered Perspective. In *Proceedings of the 2014 ACM International Symposium on Wearable Computers (ISWC 14)*. ACM, New York, NY, USA, 83–86. DOI: http://dx.doi.org/10.1145/2634317.2634340
10. Shuhei Hosokawa. 1984. The Walkman Effect. *Popular Music* 4 (1984), 165. DOI: http://dx.doi.org/10.1017/S0261143000006218
11. Elena Karahanna, Detmar W. Straub, and Norman L. Chervany. 1999. Information Technology Adoption Across Time: A Cross-sectional Comparison of Pre-adoption and Post-adoption Beliefs. *MIS Q.* 23, 2 (June 1999), 183–213. DOI: http://dx.doi.org/10.2307/249751
12. Hee-Cheol Kim. 2015. Acceptability Engineering: The Study of user Acceptance of Innovative Technologies. *Journal of Applied Research and Technology* 13, 2 (2015), 230–237. DOI: http://dx.doi.org/10.1016/j.jart.2015.06.001
13. Ki Joon Kim and Dong-Hee Shin. 2015. An acceptance model for smart watches. *Internet Research* 25, 4 (2015), 527–541. DOI: http://dx.doi.org/10.1108/IntR-05-2014-0126
14. Marion Koelle, Matthias Kranz, and Andreas Möller. 2015. Don't Look at Me That Way!: Understanding User Attitudes Towards Data Glasses Usage. In *Proceedings of the 17th International Conference on Human-Computer Interaction with Mobile Devices and Services (MobileHCI 15)*. ACM, New York, NY, USA, 362–372. DOI: http://dx.doi.org/10.1145/2785830.2785842
15. Kate Miriam Loewenthal. 2001. *An Introduction to Psychological Tests and Scales (2nd Edition)*. Psychology Press, New York, NY, USA.
16. Yogesh Malhotra and Dennis F. Galletta. 1999. Extending the Technology Acceptance Model to Account for Social Influence: Theoretical Bases and Empirical Validation. In *Proceedings of the Thirty-Second Annual Hawaii International Conference on System Sciences (HICSS 99)*. IEEE Computer Society, Washington, DC, USA, 1006–1019. http://dl.acm.org/citation.cfm?id=874068.875913
17. Philipp Mayring. 2014. *Qualitative Content Analysis: Theoretical Foundation, Basic Procedures and Software Solution*. SSOAR, Klagenfurt, Germany. 143 pages. http://nbn-resolving.de/urn:nbn:de:0168-ssoar-395173
18. Philipp A. Rauschnabel, Alexander Brem, and Bjoern S. Ivens. 2015. Who will buy smart glasses? Empirical results of two pre-market-entry studies on the role of personality in individual awareness and intended adoption of Google Glass wearables. *Computers in Human Behavior* 49 (2015), 635–647. DOI: http://dx.doi.org/10.1016/j.chb.2015.03.003

19. Philipp A Rauschnabel, Daniel W.E Hein, Jun He, Young K. Ro, Samir Rawashdeh, and Bryan Krulikowski. 2016. Fashion or Technology? A Fashnology Perspective on the Perception and Adoption of Augmented Reality Smart Glasses. *i-com* 15, 2 (2016), 179–194. DOI: http://dx.doi.org/10.1515/icom-2016-0021

20. Philipp A. Rauschnabel and Young K. Ro. 2016. Augmented reality smart glasses: An investigation of technology acceptance drivers. *International Journal of Technology Marketing* 11, 2 (2016), 123. DOI: http://dx.doi.org/10.1504/IJTMKT.2016.075690

21. Stuart Reeves, Steve Benford, Claire O'Malley, and Mike Fraser. 2005. Designing the Spectator Experience. In *Proceedings of the SIGCHI Conference on Human Factors in Computing Systems (CHI 05)*. ACM, New York, NY, USA, 741–750. DOI: http://dx.doi.org/10.1145/1054972.1055074

22. Everett M Rogers. 2010. *Diffusion of Innovations (4th Edition)*. Free Press, Simon and Schuster Inc., New York, NY, USA.

23. Neil Selwyn. 2003. Apart from Technology: Understanding People's Non-use of Information and Communication Technologies in Everyday Life. *Technology in sSociety* 25, 1 (2003), 99–116. DOI: http://dx.doi.org/10.1016/S0160-791X(02)00062-3

24. Brian Shackel. 2009. Usability - Context, Framework, Definition, Design and Evaluation. *Interact. Comput.* 21, 5-6 (Dec. 2009), 339–346. DOI: http://dx.doi.org/10.1016/j.intcom.2009.04.007

25. Koert M. van Mensvoort. 2013. *Pyramid of Technology: How Technology becomes Nature in Seven Steps.* Technische Universiteit Eindhoven, Eindhoven, the Netherlands. https://pure.tue.nl/ws/files/3805415/760124.pdf

26. Viswanath Venkatesh and Michael G. Morris. 2000. Why Don't Men Ever Stop to Ask for Directions? Gender, Social Influence, and Their Role in Technology Acceptance and Usage Behavior. *MIS Q.* 24, 1 (March 2000), 115–139. DOI:http://dx.doi.org/10.2307/3250981

27. Heetae Yang, Jieun Yu, Hangjung Zo, and Munkee Choi. 2016. User Acceptance of Wearable Devices: An extended Perspective of Perceived Value. *Telematics and Informatics* 33, 2 (2016), 256–269. DOI: http://dx.doi.org/10.1016/j.tele.2015.08.007

Someone to Read with: Design of and Experiences with an In-Home Learning Companion Robot for Reading

Joseph E Michaelis,[1,2] **Bilge Mutlu**[1]
(1) Department of Computer Sciences, (2) Department of Educational Psychology
University of Wisconsin–Madison, Madison, WI
jemichaelis@wisc.edu, bilge@cs.wisc.edu

ABSTRACT
The development of literacy and reading proficiency is a building block of lifelong learning that must be supported both in the classroom and at home. While the promise of interactive learning technologies has widely been demonstrated, little is known about how an interactive robot might play a role in this development. We used eight design features based on recommendations from interest-development and human-robot-interaction literatures to design an in-home learning companion robot for children aged 11–12. The robot was used as a technology probe to explore families' ($N = 8$) habits and views about reading, how a reading technology might be used, and how children perceived reading with the robot. Our results indicate reading with the learning companion to be a way to socially engage with reading, which may promote the development of reading interest and ability. We discuss design and research implications based on our findings.

ACM Classification Keywords
H.1.2. **Models and Principles**: User/Machine Systems—*human factors, software psychology*; H.5.2. **Information Interfaces and Presentation**: User Interfaces—*evaluation/methodology, user-centered design*

Author Keywords
Human-robot interaction; interest development; reading education; educational robots; design probes

INTRODUCTION
Reading has long had an important and established place in education, and developing literacy and reading proficiency is considered a basic and essential element of learning [25, 12]. While classroom instruction for younger readers is an important part of this process, practicing and engaging with reading at home is also crucial for these students [4]. With drastic technological advances in the last decade, using robots as educational agents to support learning both in classrooms and in the home has become increasingly viable [5]. These educational robots can act as learning companions, tutors, or instructional agents that can provide individually tailored instruction to children [27]. When used in the home, robots promise to support student learning and skill-building to supplement classroom instruction.

CHI 2017, May 06-11, 2017, Denver, CO, USA
© 2017 ACM. ISBN 978-1-4503-4655-9/17/05...$15.00
DOI: http://dx.doi.org/10.1145/3025453.3025499

Figure 1. A study participant reads *Eyes on the Goal* to Minnie, our learning companion robot and technology probe designed to investigate how an interactive robot might support interest development in reading.

One type of instructional support that has proven beneficial to both learning outcomes and student engagement is the development of *interest* in a domain [15], and supporting this development can be particularly useful for young readers [17]. However, little is known about how an in-home learning companion robot might provide students with support for interest and engagement in reading. The goals of the work presented here are to explore how young readers currently engage in reading at home and how they imagine technologies such as robots could enhance this activity; to observe how they interact with a robot designed as an in-home learning companion for reading; and to explore their beliefs about how they might use and benefit from a robot as a learning companion. To pursue these goals, we developed an in-home learning companion robot, named "Minnie," to use as a technology probe [16].

In the following sections, we report on the use of Minnie, a robot designed with guidelines derived from prior research in interest development and human-robot interaction, as a probe to gain a better understanding of how a learning companion robot may be used in a child's home and how our design features will be perceived by the child and their family. After providing a brief background on the research that guided our work, we describe how the robot was developed and used as a technology probe. We then detail our data collection methods and results, discuss the implications of these results, and finally conclude with theoretical and practical contributions to both interest development and human-robot interaction.

BACKGROUND

Our work is inspired by prior research that has highlighted the educational promise of robots and their role as social agents. Prior research has found children to readily interact with robots in social ways and utilized this connection to improve pre-school literacy [20] and vocabulary [36]. This body of work has shown that, when compared to other learning technologies, robots have a more dramatic social impact. For example, Han et al. [14] found that a home robot promoted engagement, interest, and learning in English, and users considered the robot to be friendlier than other learning media. These benefits may be due to the robot's ability to better connect socially with its user and perform behavioral strategies more appropriately than other computerized agents [6], as social interactions between humans have been found to positively influence interest and learning in a task [35]. Other studies in human-robot interaction have found robots to be more engaging and life-like [19]; appealing, perceptive, and helpful [38]; and positive and natural [3] than other computerized agents. This social nature of human-robot interaction motivates our exploration of robots as learning companions rather than other computerized agents or alternative learning technologies for reading.

Prior work studying social interaction with robots has identified a specific interplay between human-like features used in the design of the robot and people's attributions of human characteristics to the robot. At a high level, the use of human-like features in the physical design of a robot can promote social interaction [11], and a robot with at minimum an animated head that includes eyes and a mouth can achieve this effect [24]. Children seem particularly prone to social connections due to these anthropomorphic tendencies [37]. This phenomena appears to peak at 9–12 years of age and begins to diminish by age 15 [18], indicating that children may particularly benefit from the integration of human-like features in the design of a learning companion robot.

Our investigation draws on research in interest development as well as in human-robot interaction to identify guidelines for supporting student engagement and interest in a reading task. Interest-development researchers distinguish between *situational interest*, a psychological state characterized by increased focus and attention, and *individual interest*, a predisposition to reengage with specific content [21]. The Four-phase Model of Interest Development proposed by Hidi and Renninger [15] further refines the situational-individual interest distinction into four progressive phases of interest: Triggered Situational, Maintained Situational, Emerging Individual, and Well-Developed Individual. In this model, interest is characterized as increasing positive affect, value, and knowledge for the domain [34].

Promoting situational interest by successfully *triggering* (or catching) and then *maintaining* (or holding) a student's interest during successive interactions can promote the development and maintenance of individual interest [15, 28]. Guidelines for catching and holding interest from this area of research include providing students with autonomy in choosing educational materials [17]; setting and monitoring reading goals [7]; providing materials that align with student topic interests [1] and with which students believe they have the ability to be successful; providing social partners who demonstrate interest in the activity [35]; and reading out-loud to a social partner [33].

Findings from human-robot interaction studies also provide several guidelines for increasing user engagement in human-robot interaction, including the robot making direct eye contact when speaking to its user [30, 31] as well as averting it's gaze while it is "thinking" [2]; providing tailored recommendations for content [23]; and making reference to previous interactions [22]. By incorporating these design guidelines into its behavior, we believe that a learning companion robot may serve as a powerful tool for supporting interest and engagement in reading for young readers. This work explores this promise toward addressing a gap in our understanding of how children interact socially with a robotic learning companion while reading at home and how this social interaction might impact the development of interest for reading.

DESIGN OF THE TECHNOLOGY PROBE

For this study, we first developed a learning companion robot, Minnie, based on the design guidelines discussed in the previous section. Following design research practices from prior work, such as work by Odom et. al [32], we then conducted short in-home visits with families to use the learning companion robot as a *technology probe* [16] for discussion and reflection on how a reading technology might impact current reading habits in each home. Hutchinson et al. [16] describe the technology probe approach as a method with three goals—understanding the user's needs and feelings about the technology, field-testing a technology, and reflection on new possibilities for the technology—that reflect our aims for this study. At this stage of development, our prior understanding of the intended user may not be sufficient, which may limit our view of what the learning companion robot should do and how. The introduction of the learning companion into the home may uncover unknown user needs and expectations as well as inspire new thoughts on and possibilities for the learning companion's use. We intend to explore these ideas to inform design modifications to the learning companion robot prior to empirical testing. Thus, our field testing of the robot is conducted concurrent to deep exploration of the design space through the eyes of the user. In short, we will study the user, the technology, and their interaction all at the same time.

We began the in-home visit by asking one child (referred to as the *main child*) to complete a short survey on individual interest in reading, followed by an interview (pre-) with the family. After the pre-interview, we introduced our learning companion robot to the family and asked the main child in the home to interact with it for a short period of time (approximately 30 minutes). Following the interaction, we completed a second interview (post-) with the family. In the spirit of using the technology as a probe, we did not limit the discussion or interaction with the robot to our preconceived ideas about how, when and where the learning companion should and would be used. Rather, we allowed families to explore ideas about how they would like to or would use this or another technology for reading. The following paragraphs describe this data collection method and subsequent analysis in more detail.

Development of the Robot Platform

Our initial design of the learning companion robot was guided by a desire to leverage the power of social interaction to promote interest and engagement in reading. Based on prior work [11], we determined that a small, desktop humanoid robot with multiple methods of interaction and non-verbal expression would be appropriate for interaction with a child over the activity of reading. We also felt that the robot should be built on a simple, modifiable, and inexpensive platform in order to model the type of constraints inherent in an affordable commercially available robot. This intuition led us to create the robot using a modified version of a freely available 3D-printable robot design from Hello Robo[1] called Maki. A more expensive pre-made robot such as the popular Nao platform by SoftBank Robotics,[2] while possibly offering a more reliable and polished experience, is not flexible in its physical and hardware design, and the cost would preclude many families from actual use in the their homes. The original robot from Hello Robo stands 13.5 inches and has a static torso without any movable appendages (see Figure 2). The head and neck of the robot contain five servo controlled motions, including two closing eyelids, a pair of eyes that move laterally together, and vertical and horizontal head movements. These motion options allowed us to create specific robot behaviors to provide a life-like feel (e.g., blinking eyes) and non-verbal communication (e.g., looking directly at the child).

To perform the necessary computation and facilitate human-robot communication, we modified the original robot design by Hello Robo by adding four pieces of hardware to the robot. First, we integrated a Raspberry Pi 2 Model B[3] microcomputer running the Debian 7 operating system[4] to perform the sensing, actuation, and computation necessary for the robot's functioning and interaction with the child. Integration of the microcomputer also required us to modify the 3D model of the robot, and thus we extended the back wall of the robot's torso in the shape of a small "backpack" that would house the computer and provide us or the end users with easy access to the hardware. Second, we embedded a speaker in each of the ear pieces to allow the robot to utilize text-to-speech responses to the child. Third, we included an RFID reader in the lower front of the robot to allow the child to respond to the robot with four color coded, pre-programmed RFID cards. Roughly, the cards allowed the child to *say* "yes/continue," "no/stop," "pause," and "repeat" to the robot. Fourth, we added a USB camera to achieve two purposes: allowing video input to process facial recognition, which we used for facial tracking, and reading visual tags (AprilTags[5]) placed within books. Each

Figure 2. Image of the learning companion robot, Minnie, used in the study as well as the introductory "Talking with Minnie" book, RFID topic and interaction cards, and books augmented with AR tags. The robot's camera is the red circle on the upper torso. The RFID reader is below the camera and indicated by a red light when the robot is on.

time an RFID card or an AprilTag is scanned, Minnie blinks and makes a distinct beep to let the child know that the scan was registered. The robot platform allows us to implement the eight design elements we identified from our literature review.

Interaction Design of the Robot

The interaction design of our technology probe utilizes the eight guidelines, identified from research in interest development and human-robot interaction to support student engagement and interest in reading, in the following design elements:

*DE*1. Providing students with autonomy in choosing educational materials [17];

*DE*2. Setting and monitoring reading goals [7];

*DE*3. Providing materials that align with student topic interests and with which students believe they have the ability to be successful [1];

*DE*4. Providing a social partner that demonstrates interest in the reading activity [35];

*DE*5. Reading out loud to a social partner [33];

*DE*6. Having the robot maintain eye contact when speaking and averting its gaze while it is "thinking" [29, 2];

*DE*7. Providing tailored recommendations for content [23];

*DE*8. Making references to previous interactions [22].

Design of the Interaction Flow

During the interaction, Minnie, the learning companion robot, uses facial recognition to track the child's position and turn its head and eyes toward the child to establish eye contact (*DE*6). However, to prevent long durations of eye contact from eliciting discomfort, the robot makes idle head and eye movements and engages in gaze aversion. The robot also continually uses pre-scripted dialog based on an interaction flow, described below, which we developed through iterative design and testing.

[1]Hello Robo: http://www.hello-robo.com/
[2]SoftBank Robotics: https://www.ald.softbankrobotics.com/en
[3]Raspberry Pi: https://www.raspberrypi.org/
[4]Debian: https://www.debian.org
[5]AprilTags: https://april.eecs.umich.edu/wiki/AprilTags

Figure 3. Image of a child working with Minnie during the introductory process. The child is holding a topic interest card and has placed the "Talking with Minnie" book on the floor in front of Minnie. The books available for the child to read appear on the right of the image. An example of a green RFID card (top) and a topic interest card with an April tag (bottom) are superimposed on the right of the figure.

Introduction – The interaction flow begins with Minnie saying "hello" to the child and providing a brief backstory on why the robot is there (i.e., the robot tells the child that she is a reading coach in training). The child is then instructed to scan and read a book, "Talking with Minnie," that was written by the authors of this work and is used to teach the child how to interact with the robot. This book is written as a story, but the content guides the child through the use of each interactive tool (e.g., how to scan the RFID cards and AprilTags, as well as what they mean) and how to work with Minnie (e.g., read out loud and scan AprilTags). The robot then asks the child to complete a topic-sort activity using 10 topic interest cards (e.g., mystery, art, science, and/or sci-fi/fantasy) labeled with AprilTags. For this activity, Minnie instructs the child to scan all the topics they like followed by any topics they do not like. The robot stores these preferences in the user profile for the child and later uses this as part of a book suggestion algorithm. Figure 3 illustrates a child working during the introduction process.

Goal Setting – After completing the initial introduction phase, Minnie begins the process of setting reading goals and selecting books. During this process, Minnie informs the child of a goal for reading time that day (*DE*2)—for this study, standardized at 20 minutes in length—before each reading session, and begins tracking the time spent reading after a book is chosen. The learning companion robot will then check the user profile for a current book (i.e., a previously read book that has not been finished), and if one exists, Minnie will remind the child of what they were last reading and the page number they were on (*DE*8). The child has the option to continue or not. If no current book is found, Minnie suggests three books (from a set of the 16 available) to the child that they may like.

The robot's suggestions for books are based on a selection method that uses the child's reading ability, interest in reading, usual daily reading time, and topic interests to recommend books to the child (*DE*3). Books are first filtered by reading difficulty to include books at an appropriate reading and interest level *(DE3)*. To define this filter, we begin with the child's Lexile[6] score, a system of estimated reading ability levels for children and matching difficulty levels for books (scale range: $0 - 2000$), modify this score for children with high ($+100$) or low (-100) interest in reading, and define an ideal difficulty range as the modified Lexile score $\pm$ 100. The filter selects books in our library that fall in this range. These books are then further filtered based on page length by multiplying the child's average daily reading time by five to estimate the length of a book they might complete in a week and selecting books that are $\pm$ 20 pages of this value. Finally, the program assigns each book listed in the library a topic match score. To calculate this score, each book is assigned up to five topic labels by one of our researchers. Points are added to the book's topic match score for any topic that was indicated as a "like" by the user, and points are subtracted for each "disliked" topic. A priority cue is made using the filtered books by placing the highest scoring book at the front of the cue. The top three books in the priority cue are offered to the child as suggested titles (*DE*7). The child may chose any book they wish (*DE*1) and scan the AprilTag placed on the back of the book they choose to indicate their selection. The robot then updates the user profile to store the selected book as the child's current book; the robot confirms the title of the book with the child; and the child is asked to begin reading on page one, which marks the beginning of the reading phase.

Reading – In the reading phase, the child is asked to read *out loud* to Minnie (*DE*5). Minnie is designed to make semi-randomized movements during the reading phase, which include blinking, moving its eyes, and small turns of its head in order to appear engaged in the reading (*DE*4). As the child reads, AprilTags will appear roughly every three to six pages of each book, and the child is instructed to scan these tags when they encounter them. The tag ID is linked to a specific comment, written by our research team, related to what is currently happening in the book (*DE*4). When a scan is received by Minnie, it blinks, makes a distinct *beep*, and delivers the comment via text-to-speech. Each time a book tag is scanned, the user profile is updated to store that page as the current page. During the reading phase, the child may continue to read, scan the *yellow* RFID to pause reading, or scan the *red* RFID to quit reading. This phase continues until the child chooses to quit, or scans the last age of the book. At that point, Minnie enters the "end reading" phase.

End Reading – The end of the reading phase is triggered by either the child choosing to quit reading or when a book has been completed. In both cases, Minnie will compare the time spent reading to the reading goal previously set (*DE*2). If the child has met the reading goal for the day, Minnie will congratulate the child and begin the shut-down process. Shutting down consists of thanking the child for the time spent reading, encouraging them to read more the next day, and telling the child that the learning companion robot is going to sleep. If the reading goal has not been met, the robot will let the child know how much time is remaining to reach the goal and ask whether or not they should continue reading. If the child chooses to continue reading, Minnie asks if the

[6]Lexile: http://www.lexile.com

child would like to read the same book or a new one and then re-enters the reading phase. Otherwise, Minnie initiates the shut-down procedure.

Updating User Profile – When a child scans the last page of a book, Minnie will ask the child whether they liked the book, and the child can respond with *yes* (green card), *no* (red card), or *a little* (yellow card). This response is stored in the user profile and is used to trigger a recalculation of book topic match scores. For books the child liked, the topics associated with that book will be given a higher score rating, which will move books with similar topics up the priority cue. The opposite is true for books that the child dislikes. In this way, Minnie takes the child's feedback about the books they've read together into consideration for future book recommendations (*DE*7, *DE*8).

By addressing the eight design features identified from previous work, we believe that the interaction with the robot may be capable of promoting interest in reading. We next discuss specific methods of interaction that were utilized in this study.

TECHNOLOGY PROBE STUDY

Several methodological choices were made in order to best utilize our learning companion robot as a technology probe during a brief in-home visit. These choices involved strategically choosing the place of the interaction, engaging the parent(s) and the child in the process of setting up the probe, and interrupting the child during their reading in order to facilitate further exploration of Minnie's features. We also asked the child to behave as if the experimenters were not present during the interaction in order to facilitate as authentic an interaction as possible. The experimenter intervened only when technical difficulties posed a barrier to their ability to proceed.

The placement of the robot was chosen after the family was introduced to the learning companion robot. The child was asked where in their home they would likely read with the robot. Of the suggestions made by the child, we asked the parent(s) which of these areas they would be most comfortable with us conducting the robot interaction and chose to work there. This process helped us establish a more authentic interaction between the child and the robot while maintaining the comfort and trust of the parent(s).

The previous section outlined the general interaction design of the learning companion robot. However, in the context of its use as a technology probe, it was unlikely that the child would encounter many of its features due to the short duration of the interaction. To address this limitation, each child was interrupted after approximately 10 minutes of reading and told that they should pretend they were tired of reading the current book. The child scanned the red card to quit reading that book and were instructed to follow Minnie's prompts. Since the reading goal would not have been met, Minnie would tell the child that they had not met their goal and offer to continue reading. Each child was instructed to choose another book and continue reading. Each child was allowed to read for a maximum of 40 minutes before being asked to end their reading session.

Participants

We recruited families ($N = 8$) from the greater Madison, Wisconsin area to participate in the study through flyers posted around coffee shops, grocery stores, and community centers and through word of mouth. Most often one parent and one child participated, one family included two parents, and one younger sibling was present in two families. For each family, one main child (mean age = 11.6; age range: 11–12; male = 5, female = 3) was asked to interact directly with the learning companion robot. All other family members were included in pre- and post-interviews. All parents involved in the study were asked to review and sign a consent form, and the children were asked to read and express their agreement with an assent form as a part of the study protocol reviewed and approved by the Institutional Review Board (IRB).

Data Sources

During the course of our study, we collected data from three major sources. The first type of data source were two separate surveys. One survey was completed by parents as a pre-visit questionnaire on their child's reading ability and habits. The other was the Four-phase Interest Development Reading Scale (FID-RS), an individual interest in reading survey, completed by the child prior to working with the learning companion robot. The reliability of the individual interest scale was measured using Cronbach's alpha, with an alpha value of 0.7 or greater indicating, by convention, a reasonably reliable construct [10]. The second data source was from transcriptions of video-recorded semi-structured interviews conducted before (pre-) and after (post-) the robot interaction. Both interviews were approximately 20 minutes in length, with the post-interview ($M = 19.9$ minutes, $SD = 2.1$ minutes) being slightly longer than the pre-interview ($M = 18.7$ minutes, $SD = 2.3$ minutes). Finally, the third data source comes from coding segments of video recordings made during the robot interaction of about 30–40 minutes ($M = 37.11$ minutes, $SD = 3.18$ minutes)). The following paragraphs discuss each data source in more detail.

Survey

Prior to the in-home visit, one parent from each family was asked to complete a questionnaire to collect overview information about the main child. We asked the parent to describe, to the best of their knowledge, their child's reading ability, the amount of time their child spends reading non-school work each week, their (the parent's) satisfaction with the amount of time their child spends reading, as well as basic demographic information, such as age and grade.

During the in-home visit, the main child was asked to complete the 10-item FID-RS survey to assess the child's individual interest in reading prior to their interaction with the learning companion robot. This survey was developed by rewording items from a previous individual interest survey, developed by Michaelis and Nathan [26], with language from the reading motivation section of the Motivation for Reading Questionnaire, developed by Wigfield and Guthrie [39]. The survey is comprised of Likert-style items, which asked students to rate their level of agreement with statements using a scale from 1 (*strongly disagree*) to 7 (*strongly agree*). Scores were calculated by averaging the scores from all items ($M = 5.8$, $SD = 0.82$). The high Cronbach's alpha ($\alpha = 0.81$) indicates it has a high internal reliability.

Interview and Robot Interaction
Two sources of video data were captured: two interviews with the family (pre- and post-) and the main child's interaction with the robot. For the semi-structured interviews, a pre-determined set of questions was used as a focus for the interaction. However, the interviewer pursued ideas from the family members in a conversational style and encouraged them to elaborate on their comments. Both interviews were transcribed verbatim and segmented by idea unit [9].

We video recorded a semi-structured pre-interview with the family about their current reading habits (e.g., "How often do you read?"); what motivates their child to read (e.g., "What systems do you have in place to encourage your child to read?"); and the family's familiarity with, experience with, and thoughts about working with technology for reading (e.g., "If you had a technology that worked with you while you read, what would it do?"). After the pre-interview, the main child was introduced to the robot and instructed on how to begin working with the robot. Once they were ready to begin, we video recorded their entire interaction. After the robot interaction was completed, we conducted a second semi-structured interview (post-) with the family. This interview was about the family members' view of the robot as a partner (e.g., "Did it feel like Minnie was alive?"), their likes and dislikes about the interaction with the robot (e.g., "Are there any things you would change about Minnie?"), and whether they thought the robot would be a useful tool for the home (e.g., "If the robot were released to the market today, would you be interested in buying one for your child?").

Grounded Theory Analysis
All video data was transcribed, coded, and analyzed following a Grounded Theory approach [13, 8]. The analysis began with an open-coding step where numerous informal codes were used to summarize significant idea units in the interview transcripts. These informal codes were evaluated to find emerging themes within the transcripts, and twenty-four formal codes were identified and applied to the transcripts. We examined the reliability of the coding by comparing inter-rater reliability between coders on 10% of the data and found it to be very high (Cohen's $\kappa = 0.79$). We then developed eight axial codes that combined the formal codes to refine our coding scheme into broader categories, and these categories were further organized into four major themes. The findings below present details of each of the major themes and are followed by a discussion of our interpretation of these findings.

FINDINGS
In this section, we report on the findings from our in-home visits with eight participating families. We discuss four main themes that emerged from our analysis. We first describe what we found to be the relationship with reading for each of our main children: their habits, ability, and interest phase. We will then detail the three remaining themes that emerged. Each theme is supported with evidence from interview and/or robot-interaction data. Figure 4 describes each of the major themes of our findings.

Relationship with Reading

Each of the children described their relationship to reading that was consistent with one of the phases of the Four-phase Model of Interest Development.

Development of Interest

Children describe their interaction with the robot as enjoyable, valuable, and capable of improving their ability—all characteristics of *interest development.*

Attribution of Human Characteristics

Children often attributed human characteristics, including emotions and thought, to the robot.

Social Companionship

Children in the study refer to the robot in terms of having "someone else there" to read with.

Figure 4. Summary of each of the themes emerging from our analysis.

Throughout the description of our findings, families are numbered 1 through 8 with each member identified as "MC" for the main child in the study, "P" for the parent, and "OC" for another child present during interviews. For example, the main child in family number seven is labeled as "MC7", and the parent for family 4 is labeled as "P4". The researcher conducting the interviews is labeled as "R" throughout. Non-verbal actions, such as nodding their head in agreement, appear between double parenthesis, e.g., ((nods head "yes")), and paraphrasing is indicated by words surrounded by brackets.

Relationship with Reading
In recruiting for our study, we initially intended to enroll children with a variety of interest levels in reading. During a short, online, pre-screening questionnaire, we included a question that asked a parent to estimate the amount of time their child spent on reading each week. We believed that this measure would prove useful for inferring a relative interest level but realized soon after we began our visits that this estimate was often not very accurate. Thus, we chose not to make any recruitment decisions based on pre-screening. We instead used pre-interview descriptions of the child's view and habits towards reading to identify what phase of interest in reading they were likely in. While we do not believe that any of our participants are categorized in the first and lowest phase of interest development, *triggered situational interest*, we classified two participants (MC1 and MC2) in phase two, *maintained situational interest*; three (MC3, MC4, and MC5) in phase three, *emerging individual interest*; and three (MC7, MC6, and MC8) in the highest and fourth phase, *well-developed individual interest.* These evaluations were supported by results from each child's FID-RS individual interest survey score. We found that our *phase two* readers had the lowest and third lowest scores (4.5 and 5.4), the *emerging individual interest* readers fell in

a middle range between 5.3 and 5.9, and the *well-develop individual interest* readers had all three of the highest scores that ranged from 6.3 to 7.0 (the scale maximum). Based on information gathered during our pre-interviews, we now turn to describing the children at each level of interest in reading.

Phase 4: Well-developed Individual Interest

Of the three well-developed individual interest readers, one, MC8, had an extreme interest in reading. MC8 reads an exceptional amount (300 or more pages per day), and was described by his parent, P8, as "off the charts." He is such an avid reader that the local bookstore supplies him with "a lot of advanced readers of books each month" to have him "give them an opinion on the books." He described having very little need for a reading technology and struggled to find ideas of what one might do, because he felt no need to support improving his reading ability or motivation to read.

Our two other high interest readers, MC6 and MC7, described themselves as having high reading ability, and that they were an "avid reader," and "always loved to read," respectively. While they felt that they were very good readers, they both indicated that they would like to continue to develop their reading ability. To support this development, they both thought a technology might suggest new books for them to read. MC6 also added a desire for a technology that would track their reading and provide some level of motivational support, while MC7 mentioned an interest in reading out loud.

Phase 3: Emerging Individual Interest

Our three emerging individual interest readers read between 30 to 60 minutes on an average day and find that they can become engrossed in the right book. However, they often struggle to find new books that interest them and are continually seeking out new material. For example MC4 said, "I go out and try to find new books but I don't, like, find that many books appealing to me." This behavior may be due to being reluctant to invest in reading new books, which leads them to re-read many of the books they already have several times. They value reading as a way to learn, believe that they are "okay" readers and would like to "practice and get better," and appreciate ways of being supported in developing their ability. They also recognize a need for some external motivational support, particularly when they do not connect with a book right away (even if it is just a "nagging mom"). MC3 did not suggest anything he would want a reading technology to do. However, both MC4 and MC5 would like a technology to help them understand and pronounce words while they read and to give them feedback about the book as they read.

Phase 2: Maintained Situational Interest

Both of our maintained situational interest readers described themselves as capable readers. While both said that they only "like reading a little," they reported enjoying reading when they really like a book. However, they reported different amounts of time spent reading; MC1 reads 30 minutes a day, because this is the goal her parents set for her, while MC2 reads very little outside of what is required for school. They both felt that reading is something that they should do more of but did not prioritize among other activities. Thus, they did not seek out reading unless required. For MC2, this conflict of feeling

Participant	Phase #	Phase of Interest	FID-RS Score
MC1	2	*maintained situational*	4.5
MC2	2	*maintained situational*	5.4
MC3	3	*emerging individual*	5.4
MC4	3	*emerging individual*	5.3
MC5	3	*emerging individual*	5.9
MC6	4	*well-developed individual*	6.7
MC7	4	*well-developed individual*	7.0
MC8	4	*well-developed individual*	6.3

Table 1. Phase of interest for main child participants. The FID-RS score is a measure of individual interest in reading. Note that no participants were found to be in phase 1.

that he should read more but not really making the time for it appeared in our interview when describing that it is hard for him to find a book. He said, "Yeah I am like looking right now. Well I am trying to get time to look for books. Well I mean I have got a lot of time but...," indicating that while he feels that he should be looking for an interesting book, he is not actively doing so. Both children mention that tracking their reading with a log has been an effective method of motivation, although MC2 no longer uses any tracking, and both said that logging and tracking would be welcome features in a reading technology. MC1 also added that she would like a technology that would "Listen to [her] and tell [her] what it thought of the book or what [they] read." MC2 indicated that he would like a technology that could support understanding by adding illustrations to depict what was happening in the text. Both of their parents mentioned motivational support as something they would like a technology to offer.

This multi-method approach provides theoretically grounded empirical support for the Four-Phase Model of Interest Development that has been called for in the literature [34]. Table 1 summarizes these findings. We now begin describing themes that emerged from observations of the children interacting with the robot and their post-interviews.

Development of Interest

Our initial design of the learning companion robot was heavily influenced by interest development theory, and our analysis found that the children in our study describe much of their interaction in terms of the characteristics of interest development: *positive affect* (i.e., enjoyment), *value* for the interaction, and increasing ability or *knowledge* as a result of the interaction. They also mention all of our specific design elements during interviews and often referenced these in relation to experiencing interest development characteristics. Positive affect was generally mentioned across all participants. All said that they liked something about their interaction with Minnie and described the interaction as "nice," "fun," and "cool." Positive affect was attributed equally across all eight of the design elements that the children mentioned. For example:

> **MC5:** I liked how she could recommend books and she commented during the book about different parts.

Among Phase 2 and 3 children, all eight of our design elements were also described as having value to them. They describe specific aspects of the interaction with the learning companion robot as "helpful" or "important", and these comments were also evenly distributed across all the elements mentioned. In contrast, phase 4 children were much less likely than those in phase 2 or 3 to talk about their interaction with the learning companion robot as a helpful or valuable experience.

In contrast to children referencing many different features of the robot interaction when describing positive affect and value, only two features were mentioned in reference to improving reading ability. Families believed that Minnie providing comments during the reading (*DE*4) helped to improve reading comprehension. Children felt that Minnie's comments were a way of "recapping" or helping them see the story from "a different perspective." Reading out loud (*DE*5) was an element of the interaction that children described as potentially improving their reading skills (e.g., vocabulary and pronunciation). For example, when MC4 was asked about the process of reading out loud, she said that it "helped [her] pronounce [words] better" and this would make her "better at reading."

Describing the interaction with Minnie as a way to develop reading ability was almost entirely done by phase 3 readers. Children in phase 2 and phase 4 each only mention improving reading ability once and focus more on liking the learning companion robot and how the interaction was helpful to the process of reading but not necessarily their ability to read. This behavior may indicate that the support provided by Minnie to improve reading ability is a good match for children who feel they are good readers but need a little help with both comprehension and reading skill. When we asked our families about improvements or changes they would make to the learning companion robot, those in phase 2 focused on changing the interaction to better support reading ability, while those in other phases mentioned ways of improving ease of use. The detail of this distinction can be seen by contrasting MC4's (phase 3) statement above, that the act of reading out loud would be sufficient practice for her to improve her pronunciation, with MC1's (phase 2) belief that they would want to add features to Minnie that support pronunciation. MC1 said she would want to add this type of feature:

> **MC1:** If it was a chapter book, at the end of the chapter [it] would tell you all the words that you got wrong and [you] had to say them.

In comparing children across the three phases of interest, only those in phase 3 (emerging individual interest) seemed to feel their wants and needs for supporting their development of reading ability were met. However, families made many suggestions for additional features to address knowledge and skill building. Some of these focused on improving reading, such as an option to "mostly do reading in [their] head", or "sentences about what happened in the full chapter". Families also often suggested that Minnie be programmed with the capability to provide additional support for other subjects–particularly math and science.

We now assess how well *interest* may be developed as a result of interacting with Minnie by comparing the experiences of children across differing phases of interest in reading. We find that Minnie, as designed, may be best suited for those in an emerging individual phase of interest (phase 3). These children expressed experiencing support for all three characteristics of interest development—positive affect, value, and knowledge or ability development—as a result of their interaction with Minnie, and support across all these areas is important for developing interest at this phase. Minnie may also be appropriate for our maintained situational interest (phase 2) and well-developed individual interest (phase 4) participants, although its benefits for those at extreme levels of interest (i.e., MC8) would likely be limited. Their interest in reading did seem to be triggered by their enjoyment of the interaction and the value they found in working with Minnie—both important factors in developing interest in a domain.

Attribution of Human Characteristics

In order to best promote reading engagement and interest, we designed our learning companion robot to act in a social way. Our participants' attribution of various human characteristics to Minnie indicated that this goal was achieved. The families described the robot as being able to "look," "listen," "talk," and "understand" as well as having personality characteristics such as being "jolly," "pleasant," and "funny." They also attributed thoughts and feelings to the robot such as feeling "happy," making "connections" to what you were reading, appearing to have "liked the book", and seeming to "[have] something to say." When asked why they got this impression, many referenced the feedback and comments as well as the physical movements made by the robot.

Notions about Minnie's feelings and personality came from both physical and software design. Specifically, Minnie's physical shape (e.g., enlarged rounded head and large eyes) seemed to influence perception of her personality, and it's speech capabilities that were tied to the specific context seemed to give the appearance of thoughts and feelings.

One feature of the learning companion robot that had a significant impact on this impression of human characteristics appeared to be the continuous face tracking during the interaction. The robot was designed to orient its head toward each face detected and include intervals of randomized movements in other directions. MC6 noted that it felt like the robot was "looking" at her, and while MC1 worked with Minnie, her sibling, sitting near them, noted that Minnie would point her head directly at each of them and other places in the room.

> **OC1:** It like looked around the room and saw stuff, and it was looking at me and MC1 a lot.

Feeling that Minnie could understand was often attributed to what the learning companion robot would say. Families felt that Minnie "knew your name" because she would use the child's name when saying hello. They also saw her comments during the reading phase to be an indication that she could comprehend the story.

> **MC6:** She talked about the whole thing you've read and the chapter, cause after I read how someone in one book put up a sign on their door she asked like 'Oh I wonder why was there a sign on the door?'

This attribution of human characteristics to the robot is consistent with prior work in the field [11], and we intentionally integrated social behavior in order to further our goals of improving engagement in reading with the robot. We were, however, surprised to find that the social interaction tapped into a strong desire for social companionship while reading.

Social Companionship

The combination of the social behavior of the robot with the children's desire to socially engage while reading produced an effect that we describe as *social companionship*. We did not expect the children in the study to express a desire to socially engage while reading, as it is commonly characterized and pursued as an individual activity. However, the idea of social companionship was touched on by most families, with the exception of MC3 and MC8, during our interviews. For the families who spoke about reading *with* someone, a lack of social companionship was cited as a reason that reading could be boring, and reading together was a habit in which many of our families currently engaged. Since Minnie was designed to behave socially, this behavior seemed to help children find social companionship while they read with it.

Social companionship was not only positively discussed by almost all of our families during our interviews but also appeared to be beneficial across all phases of interest. Both of our phase 2 readers felt that it helped them engage with the reading activity. MC1 had complained that reading is usually boring, but she said that Minnie "encouraged [her]," and reading with it was enjoyable because there was someone else there. She also stated that she "liked the company," because she would "usually read alone."

Our other phase 2 reader, MC2, also seemed to find having Minnie there as a social companion while reading to stimulate his motivation to read.

> **MC2:** Because I mean she helps, it is pretty much like having someone there helping you read. So like if I am home alone, I can have it sit out and I can, it can help me with my stuff while I am reading.
>
> **R:** So, I will come back and I wonder then, so you said a lot of time with reading, you don't really have time for it. Do you think Minnie would make you feel, would you make more time?
>
> **MC2:** Yes.

The social companionship of reading with Minnie also seemed to be a positive experience for our phase 3 and 4 readers as well, although it took different forms; MC4 liked that reading with Minnie felt like reading to someone younger.

> **MC4:** It was a fun change.
>
> **R:** Okay. How so? What do you mean by that?
>
> **MC4:** Umm like I found it, like, that... my, the voice in my head that I use when I'm reading to myself sounds different than when I read out loud... It felt like I was reading to a little kid, and, like, helping them understand.

MC5 related the experience to the positive feelings they had while reading with their family, because it "felt like it was another person listening and like I could communicate with her." MC6 found that the social companionship led to better reading, because:

> **MC6:** It . . . kind of just listened to you instead of just you reading by yourself . . . You actually tried to do really good.

Finally, MC7 found that, through the comments while reading, Minnie took on a social companion role similar to MC7's friends who read the same books as her.

> **MC7:** Umm well, like, at the end of the, like, end of the thing when you scanned, like, she would, like, kind of comprehend what you were reading it seemed like. And she would, like, make connections just like a friend would do.

As discussed above, the social aspects of our learning companion robot were not intended to allow Minnie to provide social companionship. We found, however, that this experience was common for our participants and was an effect across all phases of interest. There is also evidence that the added social companionship of reading with our learning companion robot addresses each of the major areas of interest development: increases in positive affect, value, and knowledge and skills in the domain.

DISCUSSION

The four themes that emerged from our Grounded Theory analysis suggest two major design implications for designing a learning companion robot for reading: providing support for interest development across all phases of interest and intentionally designing for social companionship. The findings may also be applied to other academic domains, such as math or science education, and could prove valuable as design considerations for pedagogical agents and other educational technologies. In this section we will discuss these design implications as well as limitations to the study and potential future work.

Supporting Interest Development

While generating positive affect for a task or area of study is important, researchers note that supporting students to find value in a domain (e.g., reading) and improving knowledge and ability in the task are also critical to interest development. As we looked for emerging themes from our data, positive affect, value, and knowledge building were often referenced by families. We found that interacting with Minnie was generally well-liked by all of the families that we visited across all phases of interest. This positive experience was attributed to all of the design elements of the learning companion robot. Our phase 2 and phase 3 children also often expressed finding value in the interaction, much of which was related to the value they felt from increased motivation to read (phase 2) and supporting the development of their reading ability (phase 3). Phase 4 children did not discuss the value of the interaction to them to the same extent, which may be because they value being able to develop reading abilities at a higher level than our learning companion robot was able to support.

We feel that our eight design elements serve as a good starting point for designing a learning companion robot, or other technology, for reading. The lack of addressing the reading ability development needs of phase 2 and phase 4 learners appears to be the root cause of not fully supporting their interest development. Therefore, to improve future revisions of our robot and to inform the design of other learning technologies that intend to support interest and engagement in reading, we suggest providing a wider variety of deliberate support for improving reading. Suggestions from our families included adding chapter summaries, comprehension questions, and direct vocabulary support for phase 2 readers. Support for phase 4 readers may include the option to read silently with Minnie and to connect the reading experience outside of the book. Future work should test how adding this additional knowledge support affects the child's experience. Other work might also test the effectiveness of this type of learning companion robot in other domains such as math or science.

Designing for Social Companionship

While previous work studied the benefits of social robots in educational settings, our study offers new evidence that a robot might play a role as a social companion situated in the home to support reading. We were surprised to find how many of our children simply enjoyed the presence of Minnie as "someone else there to read with." Most of the children found the interaction with the robot to be very motivating, and our lowest phase of interest readers found that it made reading less boring. Children also attributed increased focus and attention to their reading, improved reading comprehension as a result of reading out loud, and a desire to include Minnie and the feeling of social companionship in other parts of their education and home lives. We believe the ease with which the children in our study felt a social companionship with Minnie was due in part to the strong attribution of human characteristics to the robot. Our families described Minnie as fun, pleasant, and nice, and they could picture including the robot in family reading time. They felt that she could see and understand them and knew what they were reading about. This finding suggests that when designing a social robot as a learning companion, it may be beneficial to more deliberately leverage the benefit of the social companionship that can result. However, further study is needed to better understand this phenomena and the influence it has on a child's engagement in an educational task.

Limitations

While we present findings that help to better understand the use of a learning companion robot for reading, there are several limitations to our study. First, the generalizability of our findings is limited due to the small size of the sample and the geographical region from which it was drawn. A significant limitation is a lack of children at the lowest phase of interest in our participant group, which precludes us from drawing conclusions across the entire spectrum of interest development. Future studies should deliberately seek to include these very low interest students to better understand how to design for this population. We also only conducted our study with children aged 11–12, and our results may differ for different age groups. We recognize that having only interacted with the robot for a short period of time and only allowing one child to directly interact with Minnie may have influenced how our users report their experience. Therefore, we recommend that future studies increase the *breadth* (i.e., a larger sample, from a larger area, made of a broader range of ages and interest phases) and *depth* (i.e., longer period of interaction with the robot including more family members) of this investigation. Finally, the robot was only studied in one educational domain, in one medium (a robot), and in the homes of our families. Theory and practice would benefit from observing the experience of using this type of learning companion in other areas of study, using other forms of educational agents, and in other education settings (e.g., classrooms or informal learning environments).

CONCLUSION

Educational use of robots is a rapidly expanding area of study and has the potential to provide powerful and personalized support to learners from a wide variety of backgrounds, ages, abilities, and interests. To further explore these possibilities, we designed Minnie, a learning companion robot, as a technology probe to examine the reading habits of children and how this type of technology might be used by families in their homes. We asked children to interact with Minnie during an in-home visit and asked families to participate in pre- and post-interaction interviews in order to delve into these ideas, to help evaluate our initial design, and to inspire ideas for future design. Four major themes emerged from our Grounded Theory analysis: (1) the reading habits of our participants aligns with specific phases of the Four-phase Model of Interest Development; (2) interaction with the robot provided support for the development of interest in reading; (3) several human characteristics were attributed to the robot, including emotions and thought; and (4) the robot was embraced as a social companion during the act of reading.

Based on our findings, we recommend the use of the eight design elements described in this study for similar learning technologies. We also recommend that future designs include additional support for improving reading ability that better address the needs of children with a wider range of phases of interest and ability. Finally, our finding of the social role of the learning companion robot and its potential impact as a mechanism for developing interest in reading requires further investigation. This study provides practical design recommendations for the creation of educational robots and may also inform research and design in other areas of educational technology. We also contribute the notion of a robot acting as a social companion to children engaged in an educational task in their home, which has implications for both interest development and human-robot interaction literatures. We hope that this work inspires future exploration of the social role that technology plays in interest development in a variety of areas.

ACKNOWLEDGMENTS

We would like to thank Zhi Tan for the development of an initial version of our robot platform, Rafael Zanetti, Bruno Zarpellon, and Rahul Mehta for their contributions to further development, Catherine Steffel for proofreading our manuscript, and Micheala Jagemann, Angela Siegel, Laura Herzog, Nicole Jagemann, and Molly Matthiesen for their research assistance. This work was supported by the National Science Foundation award 1149970.

REFERENCES

1. Mary Ainley, Suzanne Hidi, and Dagmar Berndorff. 2002. Interest, learning, and the psychological processes that mediate their relationship. *Journal of Educational Psychology* 94, 3 (2002), 545–561.
2. Sean Andrist, Xiang Zhi Tan, Michael Gleicher, and Bilge Mutlu. 2014. Conversational gaze aversion for humanlike robots. In *HRI'14*. Bielefeld, Germany.
3. Wilma A. Bainbridge, Justin W. Hart, Elizabeth S. Kim, and Brian Scassellati. 2011. The benefits of interactions with physicallly present robots over video-displayed agents. *International Journal of Social Robotics* 3 (2011), 41–52.
4. Linda Baker, Deborah Scher, and Kirsten Mackler. 1997. Home and family influence on motivations for reading. *Educational Psychologist* 32, 2 (1997), 69–82.
5. Fabiane Benitti. 2012. Exploring the educational potential of robotics in schools: A systematic review. *Computers and Education* 58 (2012), 978–988.
6. LaVonda Brown, Ryan Kerwin, and Ayanna M. Howard. 2013. Applying behavioral strategies for student engagement using a robotic educational agent. In *2013 IEEE International Conference on Systems, Man, and Cybernetics*. 4360–4365.
7. Consuelo Cabral-Marquez. 2015. Motivating readers: Helping students set and attain personal reading goals. *Reading Teacher* 68, 6 (2015), 464–472.
8. Kathy Charmaz and Linda Liska Belgrave. 2012. Qualitative Interviewing and Groudned Theory Analysis. In *The SAGE Handbook of Interview Research: The Complexity of the Craft*, Jaber F. Gubrium, James A. Holstein, Amir B. Marvasti, and Karyn D. McKinney (Eds.). Sage, Thousand Oaks, CA, 347–366.
9. Michelene T. H. Chi. 1997. Quantifying qualitative analyses of verbal data: A practical guide. *The Journal of Learning Sciences* 6, 3 (1997), 271–315.
10. Linda Crocker and James Algina. 2009. *Introduction to classical and modern test theory*. Cengage, Mason, OH.
11. Brian R. Duffy. 2003. Anthropomorphism and the social robot. *Robotics and Autonomous Systems* 42, 3-4 (2003), 177–190.
12. Paulo Freire and Loretta Slover. 1983. The importance of the act of reading. *The Journal of Education* 165, 1 (1983), 5–11.
13. Barney G. Glaser and Anselm L. Strauss. 1967. *The Discovery of Grounded Theory: Strategies for Qualitative Research*. Aldine, Chicago.
14. Jeonghye Han, Miheon Jo, Sungju Park, and Sungho Kim. 2005. The educational use of home robots for children. In *ROMAN 2005. IEEE International Workshop on Robot and Human Interactive Communication, 2005*. 378–383.
15. Suzanne Hidi and K. Ann Renninger. 2006. The four-phase model of interest development. *Educational Psychologist* 41, 2 (2006), 111–127.
16. Hilary Hutchinson, Wendy Mackey, Bosse Westerlund, Benjamin B. Bederson, Allison Druin, Catherine Plaisant, Michel Beaudouin-Lafon, Stephane Conversy, Helen Evans, Heiko Hanson, Nicolas Roussel, Bjorn Eiderback, Sinna Lindquist, and Yngve Sundblad. 2003. Technology probes: Inspiring design for and with families. In *CHI 2003*. Ft. Lauderdale, FL, 17–24.
17. Troy Jones and Carol Brown. 2011. Reading engagement: A comparison between e-books and traditional print books in an elementary classroom. *International Journal of Instruction* 4, 2 (2011), 5–22.
18. Peter H. Kahn Jr., Takayuki Kanda, Hiroshi Ishiguro, Nathan J. Freier, Rachel L. Severson, Brian T. Gill, Jolina H. Ruckert, and Solace Shen. 2012. "Robovie, you'll have to go into the closet now": Children's social and moral relationships with a humanoid robot. *Developmental Psychology* 48, 2 (2012), 303–314.
19. Sara Kiesler, Aaron Powers, Susan R. Fussell, and Cristen Torrey. 2008. Anthropomorphic interactions with a robot and robot-like agent. *Social Cognition* 26, 2 (2008), 169–181.
20. Jacqueline Kory and Cynthia Breazeal. 2014. Storytelling with robots: Learning companions for preschool children's language development. In *2014 RO-MAN: The 23rd IEEE International Symposium on Robot and Human Interactive Communication*. Edinburgh, 643–648.
21. Andreas Krapp. 1999. Interest, motivation and learning: An educational-psychological perspective. *European Journal of Psychology of Education* 14, 1 (1999), 23–40.
22. Iolanda Leite, Carlos Martinho, Andre Pereira, and Ana Paiva. 2009. As time goes by: Long-term evaluation of social presence in robotic companions. In *The 18th IEEE International Symposium on Robot and Human Interactive Communication*. Toyama, Japan, 367–374.
23. Gi Hyun Lim, Seung Woo Hong, Inhee Lee, Il Hong Suh, and Michael Beetz. 2013. Robot recommender system using affection-based episode ontology for personalization. 155–160.
24. Molly C. Martini, Rabia Murtza, and Eva Wiese. 2015. Minimal physical features required for social robots. *Proceedings of the Human Factors and Ergonomics Society Annual Meeting* 59, 1 (September 2015), 1438–1442.
25. Kathleen McCormick. 1994. *The culture of reading and the teaching of English*. Manchester University Press, Manchester, UK.
26. Joseph E. Michaelis and Mitchell J. Nathan. 2015. The four-phase interest development in engineering survey. In *American Society of Engineering Education (ASEE 2015) Educational Research Methods Division*. Seattle, WA.

27. David P. Miller, Illah R. Nourbakhsh, and Roland Siegwart. 2008. Robots for education. In *Springer Handbook of Robotics*, Bruno Siciliano and Oussama Khatib (Eds.). Springer, Berlin, 1283–1298.

28. Mathew Mitchell. 1993. Situational interest: Its multifaceted structure in the secondary school mathematics classroom. *Journal of Educational Psychology* 85, 3 (1993), 424–436.

29. Bilge Mutlu. 2011. Designing embodied cues for dialogue with robots. *AI Magazine* 32, 4 (2011), 17–30.

30. Bilge Mutlu, Jodi Forlizzi, and Jessica Hodgins. 2006. A storytelling robot: Modeling and evaluation of human-like gaze behavior. In *2006 6th IEEE-RAS International Conference on Humanoid Robots*. IEEE, 518–523.

31. Bilge Mutlu, Takayuki Kanda, Jodi Forlizzi, Jessica Hodgins, and Hiroshi Ishiguro. 2012. Conversational gaze mechanisms for humanlike robots. *ACM Transactions on Interactive Intelligent Systems (TiiS)* 1, 2 (2012), 12.

32. William Odom, Richard Harper, David Kirk, Sian Lindley, and Abigail Sellen. 2012. Technology heirlooms? Considerations for passing down and inheriting digital materials. In *CHI 2012*. Austin, TX, 337–346.

33. Timothy V. Rasinski. 2003. *The fluent reader: Oral reading strategies for building word recognition, fluency, and comprehension*. Scholastic, New York.

34. K. Ann Renninger and Suzanne Hidi. 2011. Revisiting the conceptualization, measurement, and generation of interest. *Educational Psychologist* 46, 3 (2011), 168–184.

35. Carol Sansone and Dustin B Thoman. 2005. Interest as the missing motivator in self-regulation. *European Psychologist* 103, 3 (2005), 175–186.

36. Samuel Spaulding, Goren Gorden, and Cynthia Breazeal. 2016. Affect-aware student models for robot tutors. In *Proceedings of the 15th International Conference on Autonomous Agents and Multiagent Systems (AAMAS 2016)*. Singapore, 643–648.

37. Fang-Wu Tung. 2016. Child perception of humanoid robot appearance and behavior. *International Journal of Human-Computer Interaction* 32, 6 (2016), 493–502.

38. Joshua Wainer, David J. Feil-Seifer, Dylan A. Shell, and Maja J. Mataric. 2007. Embodiedment and human-robot interaction: A task-based perspective. In *16th IEEE International Conference on Robot and Human Interactive Communication*. Jeju, Korea, 872–876.

39. Allan Wigfield and John Guthrie. 1997. Relations of children's motivation for reading to the amount and breadth of their reading. *Journal of Educational Psychology* 89 (1997), 420–432.

Robotic Telepresence at Scale

Irene Rae*
Data Platforms Group
Microsoft
Redmond, WA, USA
irener@microsoft.com

Carman Neustaedter
School of Interactive Arts and Technology
Simon Fraser University
Surrey, BC, Canada
carman@sfu.ca

ABSTRACT
Telepresence robots offer a relatively new way for people to project their presence remotely. However, these experiences have only been studied in controlled or small scale installations. To broaden our understanding of the successes and limitations of telepresence robots in large-scale venues, we conducted a study at CHI 2016 where five factors increased over past research: (1) number of local attendees; (2) ratio of remote users to systems; (3) variety of activities; (4) time zone differences; and, (5) environment size. Our results reveal that unlike small-scale venues and situations, remote users take a more socially isolated and functional approach to remote attendance while combating challenges around scheduling and large navigational spaces. Our results reveal new opportunities for thinking about the design of robot personalization, availability, and navigation for systems targeted at large-scale public contexts.

ACM Classification Keywords
H.5.3. Information Interfaces and Presentation: Group and Organization Interfaces - CSCW

Author Keywords
Telepresence; robots; academic conferences

INTRODUCTION
Telepresence robots—physically independent videoconferencing systems that allow a user to autonomously move in a remote environment—have expanded in the commercial space over the past five years. As these systems have become more affordable, they have been installed in a variety of contexts, including medical facilities [5], workplaces [11, 25], schools [30], museums [14], stadiums [10] and professional conferences [17]. While each of these installations is envisioned to enable remote users to realistically experience a distant environment, our understanding of the factors influencing their success is still in its early stages.

*Author now at Google, irenerae@google.com

CHI 2017, May 06–11, 2017, Denver, CO, USA.

http://dx.doi.org/10.1145/3025453.3025855

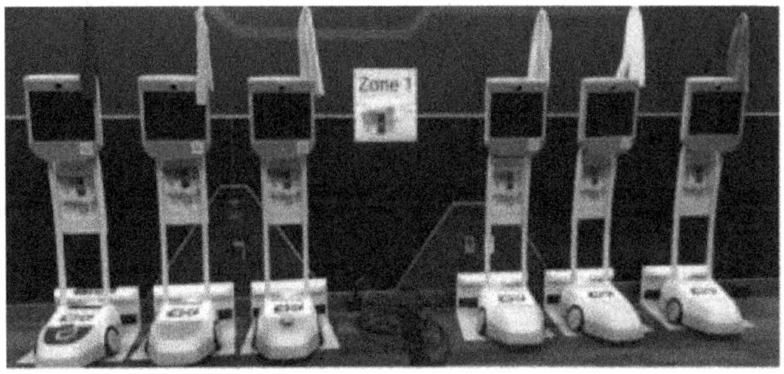

Figure 1: Beams at CHI 2016 at one of two main dock zones.

Research to date has examined these systems to build a grounding of minimal requirements for success [3] and identify how some of these system characteristics may contribute to collaborative outcomes [7, 19]. Work has also examined how these requirements might change outside of controlled laboratory and work settings, such as in the home [2], at restaurants [20] or at academic conferences [13]. While these studies have contributed to our knowledge of how robotic telepresence systems operate, they have typically focused on small scale or confined usage. For example, they have been in controlled or domestic settings [1, 7], the number of users has been relatively small [13], or most users have been close to the remote location (in or near the same time zone) [7, 19, 13]. As a result, whether the knowledge from these studies is generalizable to use cases outside of these circumstances has yet to be explored.

In this study, our goal was to investigate telepresence robots outside of workplace or private interactions, with a particular focus on extending prior work by observing the use of these systems in the context of large-scale events. Attending a concert, visiting a famous museum across the world, or going to a tradeshow, all operate at a larger scale than research has thus far observed along several dimensions. For example, the number of users and bystanders present, the possibility of access to the system as a scarce resource, the need to transition between a variety of activities in a single experience, the difference in distance and time zone, and the varying terrain that remote users encounter, may all be significantly increased in such scenarios over what prior work has observed. Additionally, in these shared system contexts, access to the system before and after use is likely to be limited, constraining the ability to customize the system for identification purposes [11, 13, 27].

To explore the generalizability of past work as these dimensions increase, we conducted a study of 33 remote attendees from across the world within one type of large-scale event, an academic conference. These remote attendees shared access to ten telepresence robots called Beam Pros (Beams) to participate in the ACM Conference on Human Factors in Computing 2016 (CHI) in San Jose, CA, USA (Figure 1). In our study, the number of participants, ratio of remote users to available systems, time zone differences, variety of activities, and spatial challenges were all increased beyond the scope of prior work by at least a factor of two (e.g., increasing the number of bystanders from ~800 to ~3700). Our research goal was to understand the effects that increased scale—growth in size to accommodate larger events—has on: navigation between locations; social interactions; the scheduling of telepresence robot usage, identity representation; and privacy—all research topics that have been studied in small-scale deployments.

Our study contributes to the validation of prior research by highlighting the generalizability of past findings, such as robotic telepresence increasing both positive and negative social attention and navigational difficulties in crowded spaces. We also extend these findings by providing new insights into the emergence of targeted functional behavior over socializing as a means of optimizing the experience for remote users. Our results suggest that telepresence robots, in their current form, may not be the most ideal medium for attendance at large-scale events. In contrast, other design solutions that adapt to changing needs as various factors are increased may be more appropriate. This broadens our understanding of using robotic proxies, and provides insights for the design of future systems.

RELATED WORK

Since the concept of using technology to remotely interact with others was proposed decades ago, shifting from audio [22] to video [15] to robotics [16], the efficacy of such channels has been subject to study [22]. As robotics has emerged as a viable addition to these systems, research has primarily been conducted in one of three settings, controlled laboratory experiments, dedicated semi-private settings—such as at a company, school, or in the home—or at a public venue, such as a museum, restaurant, or conference. Next, we describe work from each of these contexts.

Telepresence Robots in the Lab

Lab work on robotic telepresence has focused on understanding how a variety of design choices affect collaborative outcomes between remote users and those local to the system (locals). In this area, discoveries have been made about the effects that varying system capabilities have, for example, greater range of vision increasing accuracy and confidence in a collaborative task [7] and connection latency on the ability to navigate [3]. Additional work has examined how the presence and appearance of the system embodiment influences user interactions, such as the strength of the embodiment increasing trust development [19], awareness of the physical appearance decreasing enjoyment [23], and taller systems increasing levels of cooperation over shorter systems [19].

These studies have contributed to the design and implementation of current robotic telepresence systems, providing a starting point for understanding their use in semi-structured and real world settings.

Telepresence Robots in Dedicated, Semi-private Settings

In addition to lab work, robotic telepresence has been studied in the wild in early adopter, semi-private settings. For example, the medical field has experimented with using telepresence robots, showing that they can be successfully deployed to provide timely medical care in areas where stroke specialists may be unavailable [28] and to reduce disruption when high levels of traffic may interrupt patient care [9]. Research has also provided insight into how these systems can facilitate positive outcomes in educational settings, such as allowing hospitalized children [30] or remote students [6] to attend school with their classmates. Findings from studies in workplace settings have extended this knowledge, showing that robotic telepresence enables remote users to engage in opportunistic interactions [11] and have greater participation in hub-and-satellite teams [27]. In home settings, researchers have explored situations where telepresence robots may aid in providing home care [12] or help those with mobility needs [1, 26].

This prior work has laid a solid foundation for understanding the effects of robotic telepresence in a variety of contexts. However, in all of these cases, systems were assigned exclusively to single or relatively few users, without challenges or negotiations to gain system access. Additionally, these studies were unable to explore the effects of large time zone differences (e.g., greater than 10 hours) on users.

Telepresence Robots in Public Spaces

As robotic telepresence systems have matured, research has begun to move outside of controlled or semi-private settings into public spaces, such as museums, restaurants, and conferences. Although relatively nascent, work in this area has developed a framework to understand the tradeoffs and requirement differences between varying contexts and environments [20]. In this framework, factors such as the physical and social environments are described as changing between contexts, suggesting that the needs of specific scenarios require different solutions. This work also posited that the framework may be used to predict such needs, facilitating informed design choices in future systems [20]. Further research has continued to explore how differences in context shape system requirements by looking at academic conference attendance (Ubicomp/ISWC 2014). Their results highlighted the link between personalization and identity, privacy challenges due to the difference in remote and local contexts, and the difficulties that missed social cues can cause [13]. Yet this research has only explored small-scale usage of telepresence robots—seven people using dedicated systems—in an event of moderate size (~800 local attendees and 3 parallel sessions) and has suggested the need for further research where these factors are increased.

Our study extends this work and tests its generalizability for a large-scale event. By doing so, our goal is to identify whether increasing factors, such as the ratio of users to each system, may reveal additional insights, change where breakdowns or challenges in usage occur, or alter the effects seen in smaller, more controlled contexts.

STUDY METHODOLOGY

The goal of our research was to extend our understanding of the telepresence robotics space in large-scale, public venues. We were interested in understanding the role that scale may play in affecting navigation between locations, resource negotiations, identity representation, and privacy—all research topics that have been focused on in small-scale deployments, but not large-scale ones. To explore these topics, we increased the scale of the event by five factors:

(1) Number of People: The largest setting explored by prior work was at Ubicomp/ISWC 2014, with local attendance of approximately 800 people [13]. We increased this number by hosting the study at CHI, the flagship conference for human-computer interaction research. For CHI 2016, in-person attendance was approximately 3700 people at the San Jose Convention Center.

(2) Ratio of Users to Available Systems: We had 33 people (18 female) attend via telepresence where remote attendees shared access to 10 Beams. Prior work has generally only studied a one-to-one ratio of remote user to robot in work and home contexts [1, 11, 26]. At Ubicomp/ISWC 2014, seven participants used six Beams [13] and recommendations were made to increase the number of users to require time-sharing of systems. In all of these prior situations, there was little need for schedule coordination because of the low number of remote users when compared to the number of available robots.

(3) Variety of Activities: The largest number of activities seen in previous studies limited participants to three parallel conference tracks and coffee breaks, with one person attending the conference reception [13]. In contrast, telepresence attendance at CHI supported 16 parallel tracks, multiple video-streamed plenary talks, workshops, breaks, poster sessions, interaction showcases, lunches, and receptions.

(4) Time Zone Differences: Remote attendees participated in CHI from a variety of countries, with 17 from North America, 8 from Europe, 4 from Asia, and 4 from Australasia. As such, time zones varied from no differences to 19 hours, compared to prior work where the largest difference was 9 hours [13].

(5) Environment Size: The conference activities took place in a variety of settings, including presentations at the front of the room with audiences between several hundred and several thousand in size, small discussions conducted at group tables, hallway space divided into a variety of exhibits, and a large expo hall with booths and posters. These settings were distributed across three floors of the conference center. To provide context, the largest environments examined by prior work were multiple sessions in 10,000 sq. ft. (929 m^2) at a hotel [13] and a single activity at a museum across approximately 93,750 sq. ft. (8709 m^2) [20]. Our study had multiple activities taking place over 143,000 sq. ft. (13,285 m^2), shown in Figure 2 and described in more detail in the following section.

Participants

Remote participants were recruited via the CHI conference website, mailing list, and social media. Those interested in attending remotely completed an online questionnaire describing their motivations, location, affiliation, and number of times attending CHI in the past. We prioritized applications that faced travel restrictions or had accessibility needs. Using these criteria, all but two people were accepted (these two were local to the conference area). During the conference, we added several additional participants as circumstances arose that warranted remote attendance (e.g., changes in last minute travel plans).

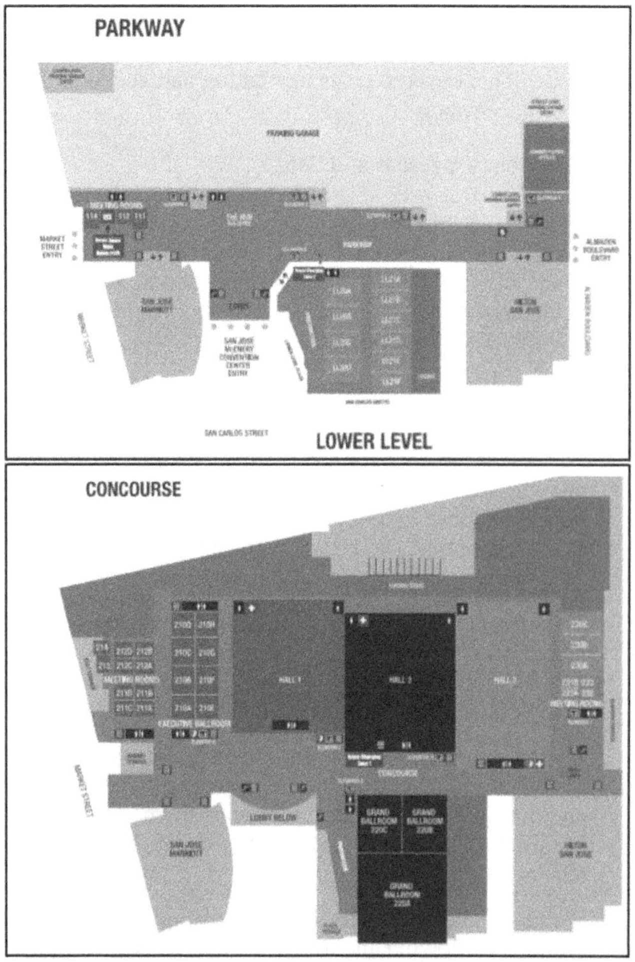

Figure 2: Maps of the convention center given to participants. Bright purple areas were docking stations for the Beams.

Remote attendees had a variety of backgrounds, including 15 faculty members, 13 graduate students, 4 industry practitioners, and 1 post-doctoral researcher. Attendees had a mixture of experience attending CHI, ranging from six first time attendees to one participant who had attended more than 10 times. Five remote attendees faced accessibility challenges (e.g., mobility issues, new baby). Three participants only attended a workshop, two attended a workshop plus the main conference, and the rest all attended various portions of the main conference (e.g., parallel tracks and receptions). Six people attended one day of CHI, 12 attended two days, 9 attended three days, and 6 attended all four conference days.

Remote attendees selected the days that they wanted to attend and then paid \$75 USD per day as a registration fee. This was approximately 1/4 of the normal registration cost and reflected the experimental nature of remote attendance. Remote attendees were asked to complete a short training session with Event Presence, the Beam rental company, prior to the conference. This covered basic navigation and social skills for telepresence robots.

Telepresence System and Setup

We used 10 Beam Pros (Beams) as the telepresence robots (Figure 1). Beams are navigable using a keyboard/mouse or an Xbox controller and contain two cameras, one facing forward and one facing down at the ground. These Beams were connected to a dedicated Wi-Fi network at the conference that was hidden from other attendees.

We integrated design recommendations from prior literature in several ways to test their effects:

1. To address the need for personalization and to test feelings of ownership [11, 13, 27], we assigned a unique color (red, orange, yellow, bright green, dark green, teal, light blue, dark blue, purple, and brown) to each Beam and augmented each system with a flag of that color.
2. To integrate past design recommendations that systems be uniquely identifiable from the side or at a distance, the flags stood at approximately 6'8" (2m) in height, making them easily visible from all angles and in a crowd [13]
3. A photograph of the flag-decorated Beams was provided to remote attendees via an informational website before and during the conference to provide them with an understanding of their appearance when using the system [23, 13]
4. We designated the color of each system on the attendee schedule, allowing them to choose their system, to test whether remote attendees would develop a sense of ownership [13] toward specific colors or would choose to identify themselves by consistently using the same colored system.
5. We attached a map of the convention center, shown in Figure 2, to the Beam to instruct physically present attendees on how to help abandoned Beams (with no one logged in) by pushing them to the nearest charging station [13].

Convention Center Layout

The conference took place in the San Jose Convention Center and spanned three floors: the Concourse, which contained the plenary talks, workshops, and parallel tracks (Figure 2, top); the Parkway, which contained the registration desk and a small number of parallel track sessions (Figure 2, bottom); and the Lower Level, which contained parallel tracks (Figure 2, bottom). The Lower Level was a small section of the Parkway that required additional stairs or an elevator to reach. We placed Beam charging stations on each level, shown in purple on the maps, near either an elevator or high traffic area. It took approximately five minutes to drive a Beam—at top speed, with no local attendees present and without being stopped by people for interactions—from one end of the Concourse level to the other end.

Scheduling

Remote attendees received the maps shown in Figure 2 as recommended by prior work [13] and we posted a schedule online that allowed them to pre-select times that they wanted to connect into the conference with a priority rating. After participants had requested time slots, we modified the schedule to optimize for people's highest priority requests and the availability of Beams, assigning ten people at most to any single time slot. Times with fewer than ten high priority requests were left open and remote attendees were allowed to sign up and log in on a first-come first-serve basis. Included in the schedule was a listing of all ten Beams, each identified by their unique color, and their last known location. Remote attendees were asked to update the location each time they disconnected. Our goal was to allow remote attendees to see where the Beams were docked, in case they wanted to pick a Beam in a certain location (e.g., near the talk they were about to go to). When a participant's time slot came up, they could connect into their reserved Beam. They were told to return the Beam to one of the docking stations after their usage. Beam batteries lasted between 6 and 8 hours, so this was necessary to ensure that they had enough charge to last the full day. It also created several common locations to find the Beams when connecting.

Management and Technical Support

Telepresence was managed and supported by the two telepresence co-chairs and two on-call student volunteers (SVs) that rotated every two to four hours depending on the time of day. We created a backchannel in Skype for conversations, monitored by both the co-chairs and the student volunteers, where remote attendees were told that they could ask for technical support or converse with other remote attendees. The level of involvement and commitment varied by the SVs. Some were highly proactive and moved around the conference venue to find and help remote attendees. Others were passive and waited for problems to arise, at which point they would respond. In addition to monitoring the backchannel, the co-chairs and the student volunteers also did regular rounds of the convention center to recover Beams that had lost connection or to help remote attendees that seemed stuck.

DATA COLLECTION AND ANALYSIS

Due to the scale of the venue and number of potential activities that remote attendees might be engaged in, we chose to collect data in several ways.

Pre-Conference Survey or Interview

Participants were asked to complete a pre-conference survey so we could gauge their expectations prior to the conference. For example, we asked them what they planned to do at CHI, how they were preparing for the conference, and if they had any concerns before attending. Sixteen participants completed the survey and we asked the same questions in semi-structured interviews with an additional four participants to gain a deeper understanding of a select group of attendees. For these interviews, we purposely picked four participants with different geographic locations, affiliations, and work positions.

Daily Online Survey

We created an online survey that participants were asked to complete at the end of each day of their conference attendance. The survey asked open-ended questions about any difficulties they had experienced, preparations or accommodations they had made, and about their choice of system. For example, "Did the size of the convention center or volume of people affect your experience? If so, please explain." "Did you find it beneficial to have Beams parked in various locations? Why or why not?" and "Did you take any special care with the way that you appeared to others at the conference? If so, what did you do?"

Twenty-six of the 33 participants completed the daily survey. The median number of daily survey completions per participant was one with a maximum of four. We used open, axial, and selective coding to analyze the daily survey responses where we looked for main and recurring themes and categorized them.

Field Notes and Observations

We observed the remote attendees throughout the conference, taking field notes and comparing them between experimenters each day. Due to the venue size and number of systems in use, observations were largely opportunistic, varying between fly-on-the-wall and direct interactions. Observations took place in the hallways, conference talks, and exposition areas where we noted where Beams were located and parked, how they interacted with local attendees, and how they navigated through the environment. We analyzed our observations and field notes in conjunction with our interview responses as part of a coding process where our observations yielded a more detailed understanding of the interview results.

Focus Groups

We held two focus groups, one Wednesday in the late afternoon and one Thursday morning (the main conference sessions ran from Monday-Thursday). We invited all remote attendees to join these groups to discuss their experiences, hosting a Skype call for those who were not scheduled for a Beam. We chose the varying start times to accommodate attendees in different time zones.

The goal of the focus groups was to probe more deeply into participants' experiences and build on the daily survey responses. Discussions and questions focused around navigation, personalization, interactions with local attendees, and the conference venue. Only one person attended the first focus group and five people attended the second. Each focus group lasted approximately one hour where we were able to more deeply engage with the select group of remote participants about their experiences. We performed a thematic analysis on transcripts from the focus groups to draw out key insights.

Backchannel

We logged the Skype backchannel and performed coding line-by-line. We also identified and categorized the (most likely) intended recipient of the message and subject of the post. Our goal was to understand how the backchannel was used, including the conversational focus and participants.

CHI Attendee Survey

In addition to the daily surveys completed by remote attendees, we asked two questions in the post-conference CHI survey, requesting that participants describe how they felt about having the Beams available and why they may or may not recommend using them in the future. We received 369 qualitative responses and performed a thematic analysis to understand local attendee perspectives.

Next we discuss our findings for each of the factors that were increased in scale. In each section, we first provide context for our observations in relation to prior work, then highlight additional key insights. Some results occur as a result of multiple scaling factors and, in these instances, we point to the new insights in multiple sections to highlight the factor-specific findings. Quotes list the data source of the quote, followed by P#, where the # denotes the remote participant's ID.

(1) NUMBER OF PEOPLE

In prior work, remote users have operated in environments with multiple users, such as workplaces [11], museums [20], restaurants [20], and conferences [13]. These studies have surfaced insights into the effects that robotic telepresence may have on the behaviors of locals as well as people who are not directly interacting with the remote user (bystanders). We describe how these findings manifested at CHI, along with additional insights.

Validation: Novelty Effect and Local Disruption

Past research has illustrated that in public settings, an increased number of bystanders—people that are not directly interacting with the remote participant—also increases the amount of disruption caused by the presence of the system [13, 20]. This novelty effect [8, 13] draws attention to the remote user and can invoke a variety of feelings. Some people enjoy the additional attention they receive, while others feel self-conscious and sometimes dislike it [20]. We found this to be consistent with the experience at CHI, with 44 open responses from local attendees saying they felt the Beams were disruptive and most remote attendees voicing concerns:

> *"It's real work. It's really difficult. I really like that I have the feeling that I'm at the conference as a person. On the other hand, I feel like an alien because everyone wants to take a picture with me, and everyone talks to me, and it's ... I don't know. It's very strange, and I have mixed feelings about it."* – Focus group, P1

New Insight: Pranking and Abuse

Although research has briefly touched upon the possibility of pranking being directed at remote users of robotic telepresence systems [13], our study is the first to observe and report this behavior:

> *"4 times in one day, a guy would step on my Beam to stop it from moving, and then titter amongst his friends. They always travelled in a gaggle, and seemed to think it was funny. That the SV on two occasions voiced the attitude that "boys will be boys" didn't help. Does that tell us they aren't seeing it as a person? Or that it's more ok to bully when telepresence is involved (we know that!)."* – Daily survey, P6

Remote participants seemed to experience increased levels of harassment as the conference continued:

> *"I also noticed that the attendees were less patient with me today than other days; again, I got the impression that I was an annoyance and inconvenience, which is not a great feeling when trying to participate in a conference. People seemed to feel free today to push my Beam around and in general to act as though I was a piece of furniture rather than an attendee. Not good."* – Daily survey, P22

We also observed local attendees jumping on or kicking charging stations and remote attendees' Beams during sessions. The severity of these cases seemed to increase over time, escalating to reports of vandalism, where remote attendees reported someone ripping the colored flag and antennae off of their Beam, and defacement, where people plastered all of the Beams with stickers from their university's research group.

New Insight: People as Obstacles

Although prior work has cited some difficulties with physical obstacles and maneuvering through crowds [13], our study is the first to report observations where people presented serious obstacles and collisions. Of the 194 comments about use of the Beams by local attendees, ten reported being run over or hit by a robot; however, although remote participants said they were worried about hitting people, none reported awareness of collisions. People became obstacles not only in the break areas between sessions [13], but also in the transitional hallway spaces between talks and the expo halls. For example, a number of the parallel sessions were overcrowded, with attendees spilling out into overflow areas outside of the rooms. In these crowds, many local attendees sat on the floor. These factors increased the number of places where remote attendees had difficulty navigating. Participants also reported having difficulty attracting the attention of locals:

> *"I really want Ben Hur spike wheels – or a way to nudge ppl out of the way, OR that "beep beep" noise that trucks make when they are backing up or that airport carts make – anything to get ppl out of the way. Esp. when ppl are busy looking at their mobile phones – they walk right in front of oncoming robots...even in party mode [sound setting], they either can't always hear me or they are just too focused TO hear...I did YELL "BEEP BEEP" but that didn't always work."* – Daily survey, P6

Similar to prior research [13], we observed remote users finding workarounds, such as positioning themselves in the back of presentation rooms, giving up on seeing the slides and choosing to just listen to talks. A new solution that remote users engaged in was dedicating part of each coffee break to pre-position their Beam, described next.

New Insight: Pre-positioning Breakdowns

A combination of all five of the factors we explored created conditions where a new workaround behavior emerged among remote users. The obstacles presented by the number of attendees, venue size, and environment complexity added to the time required to maneuver between locations. The scarcity of systems constrained options for the placement of Beams. Activities happening in one's local time zone were sometimes misaligned with the conference time zone making it hard to get to a session at the 'right' time.

As remote users became accustomed to these constraints, they began to adapt their behavior, logging in early or using coffee breaks to pre-position the Beam at their next session:

> *"I want to go to Part 1 and 2 of UI Design in Agile later this pm. Can I just leave Beam in the room (210G) during the break? I have it signed out. (I am in CT- will need to eat dinner and feed a baby, so 40 minutes is already cutting it close)"* – Backchannel, P10

Student volunteers noticed this behavior during the first day while doing routine checks for systems that had disconnected in session rooms. In each case, we would check on a Beam to find that a remote participant was there, often sitting by themselves in the room, waiting for the next session to start. Some participants mentioned in the backchannel that they had pre-positioned a Beam to prevent it from being moved by others:

> *"Just parked the Light Blue 2 in LL21F for the next session in a front position, would be great if you can leave it there"* – Backchannel, P12

We witnessed several breakdowns that occurred as a result of this type of behavior.

Scheduling collisions. Although some participants had requested contiguous time slots throughout the day, many had prioritized attending events that occurred at sporadic times. This meant they only had access to a Beam at certain times in the day and these were often not contiguous. When participants either had difficulties getting out of crowded talk rooms to return to the docks or attempted to log in before their reservation to pre-position the Beam, systems would sometimes become overbooked and remote attendees with reservations would not be able to log in. These problems surfaced in the backchannel, when Beams were abandoned away from the charging docks:

> *"I used Dark Blue few minute ago but I'm sorry I can't go back to dock in time. I didn't reserve Beam for current session. Now I signed off. Please use this Beam, if you want."* – Backchannel, P18

Unintentional eavesdropping. The combination of system scarcity and participants pre-emptively positioning systems meant that once a remote attendee had moved a Beam, they sometimes did not want to log out for fear of the Beam being taken or moved by another user. This often meant that remote attendees were left sitting in an empty room waiting for the break to end. During this time, some remote attendees walked away from their computers or covered their cameras to signal that they were unavailable, similar to strategies found in prior work [13]. However, unlike prior findings where balancing public and private environments resulted in locals overhearing information from remote participants' private lives [13], we found remote attendees eavesdropping on unaware locals:

> *"I was in the digital civics thing. I put this [paper up to block my camera]. As soon as I put this thing on, I was sitting at some table with, I think it was <name removed> actually, and he said, "oh yah, let's unplug her." There was another woman there and she kicked me. Not hard,*

but lightly, and she said, "yeah, unplug her." And I was like what the hell is going on here. Let's turn it off, and I just turned it off. I was like, "whatever." Did they feel threatened? I don't know. It was bizarre." – Focus group, P9

In other cases, the remote attendee would suddenly react or interrupt a conversation without having been visible, introducing an awkward element to the exchange. In one case, the remote attendee did not verbally or visually engage, but instead periodically placed a comical image on the screen, resulting in the disruption and abrupt disengagement of the local conversation.

(2) RATIO OF USERS TO AVAILABLE SYSTEMS

Unlike prior work, remote attendees shared access to a limited number of telepresence robots. We observed that participants tended to stay on the same Beam until the end of their time slot and that the scarcity of Beams led to low numbers of no-shows and high participation.

New Insight: Hierarchy of Telepresence Needs

One of the surprising insights was the priority system that remote attendees used to choose a Beam.

"I chose based on floor, and how well the beam was working (i.e. one had low battery, another audio that cut out) and what was available." – Daily survey, P11

From the observed patterns and interview responses, it was clear that participants had a hierarchy of telepresence needs dictating how they were selecting a telepresence robot. At a basic level, participants had to ensure that a working Beam was available to connect into. Following that, they cared about conveniences such as the proximity of the Beam to a desired location and its battery life. Only after those needs were achieved, which sometimes did not happen, did remote attendees think about the personalization of the Beam and their ability to self-project their identity.

Utility over personalization. A number of past studies in robotic telepresence have explored the advantages of personalizing the system and illustrated that users may develop a sense of ownership over time [11, 13, 27]. Informed by this work, we equipped each Beam with a uniquely colored flag to allow remote attendees to personalize their system choice.

We found that although prior literature suggested that a unique appearance, being able to visually distinguish the system from all angles, and awareness of how the system appeared would increase usability, we found that remote attendees prioritized convenience (e.g., location and charge) over identity construction (e.g., colored flags), as shown in Figure 3.

System hopping. Participants on workshop days capitalized on available systems by "hopping" from system to system to jump across the convention center, thus avoiding the need to navigate:

"It was convenient to be able to beam to the coffee station. But that might not be possible on a weekday when all Beams are being used. It would have been nice if there was a sign next to the docking stations so you knew where you were." – Daily survey, P21

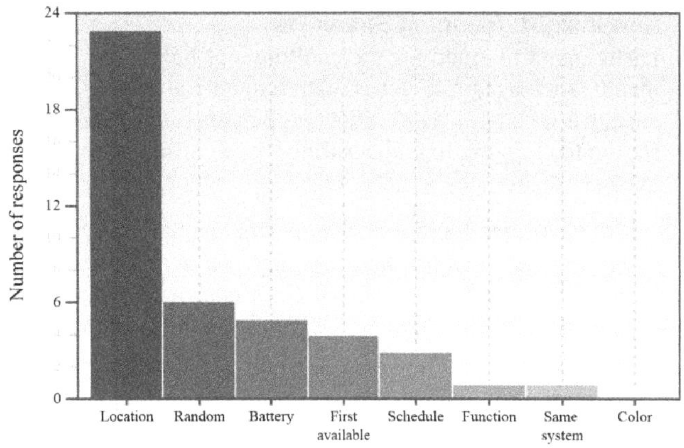

Figure 3: Criteria remote participants prioritized in choosing what system to use.

While this could have theoretically been done at any point during the conference, the scarcity of the Beams and the fact that they were fully booked during the main conference program meant that this valuable and timesaving strategy for navigating the large conference venue was only possible on workshop days (only three people attended workshops).

Coordinating system swaps. Although they weren't able to hop between systems during crowded times, participants compensated by attempting to coordinate with others (from the previous timeslot) in the backchannel, trying to match their desired location with others who were trying to log out. However, this broke down when the system was intercepted by an unintended user:

P14: *"is (sic) anyone beaming out on the second floor? i need to go to 220B"*
P24: *"I'm heading ot the hallway then I'll Beam Out...Drak Green available...or at least I'm not in there anymore"*
P28: *"hey i signed on to the dark green. hope thats ok? gotta get to a demo"* – Backchannel

(3) VARIETY OF ACTIVITIES

Similar to prior work, we found that participants enjoyed the ability to participate in interactive sessions [13]. Beyond this work, we saw an increase in the variety of activities that remote users attended.

Validation: Going Rogue

Prior work had one participant "go rogue" during the conference, using the system outside of the organized parameters [13]. We experienced a similar situation with several remote attendees at CHI; however, the number of systems that this occurred for and the area that they were distributed in was increased over past findings.

(4) TIME ZONE DIFFERENCES

Insights from prior work in remote telepresence at an academic conference identified some of the challenges faced by remote users in balancing the demands of their local job with their remote attendance [13]. Over the course of the conference, we observed a number of strategies and adaptations.

New Insight: Planning Strategies

Participants planned for the challenge of balancing local demands, such as family needs, with remotely attending a conference in a variety of ways. Some participants set up a dedicated station for logging in and ensuring that a sufficient connection existed:

> *"Yes, because I was worried my wifi connection at home was not sufficient for the Beam, I stayed at the office until the end of my Beam sessions. On Monday, this was until 3:30 am. On Tuesday and Wednesday, this was until 1:30 am."* – Daily survey, P28

Other participants took time off from their regular work:

> *"Actually because I was doing this I actually said, "I'm not coming in to work," because during those two days, I'm going to be working at home at night going to the conference. It wasn't bad. I rearranged my schedule around it. It does get tiring. At midnight, I'm pretty much pooped."* – Focus group, P9

While some participants planned these changes ahead of time, others adapted as they grew more experienced:

> *"I'm on an eight hour time difference. On the first day, I tried to come to the university and do work in the morning and then do the conference, so I was at the interactivity grand opening which ended at 3:30am. The next day I just decided that I'm going to treat this as work and start my day later and end my day later."* – Focus group, P28

Large time zone differences had varying effects on participants. Many remote attendees in Europe took advantage of their time zone differences to log in after their workday:

> *"Time zone difference was very convenient. Used the Beam from 14:00-1:00 which works nicely with my weekend schedule."* – Daily survey, P21

Participants with extreme time zone differences, such as the Australasia region, made adjustments to sleep schedules:

> *"Everything between 2am and 6am for me, which is the bulk of the day in San Jose."* – Daily survey, P9

One participant with a 16 hour time zone difference put in a full day of work and spent her entire night remotely attending the conference for three days straight, napping for 1-2 hours between shifts:

> *"Time zone of San Jose is quite different from that of Japan, but I attended events all night. Actually, I'm sleepy now."* – Daily survey, P18

New Insight: Unexpected Logins

The time zone differences also resulted in unexpected logins by remote attendees at odd hours. We found that during the night, some systems had been accessed despite being in a locked up area and at least one remote attendee stated that he had logged in to practice driving.

(5) ENVIRONMENT SIZE

Work in teleoperation [4] and robotic telepresence [7, 13] has focused on the disorientation and difficulties with navigation for remote operators. While we saw manifestations of similar difficulties, we also observed several new challenges.

Validation: Disorientation and Navigation Challenges

Although we followed design recommendations from prior work by providing remote attendees with a map of the venue [13], participants still reported difficulty orienting themselves:

> *"It takes quite a while to 'walk' from one level to another! At one point I got lost in the big exhibit hall. I'm finding it very difficult to keep my bearings in the big open spaces; I simply could not find the exit and ended up asking a group of students to help me to get out."* – Daily survey, P2

The number of remote attendees and the inconsistencies in participants updating the location when logging out increased the disorientation experienced when at login:

> *"I had a very hard time matching the Beam dock to the map–very disorienting to suddenly appear and not know where I am and which direction to go!"* – Daily survey, P2

New Insight: Shared System Disorientation

The scarcity of systems, size of the environment, and technical glitches occasionally meant that Beams were abandoned in random places. Remote attendees commented on how disorienting it was to log into a system in unexpected locations:

> *"I just found a beam in an elevator. Does it belong to someone?"* – Backchannel, P11
> *"<name removed>, did you just leave brown somewhere? I Beamed in, but it is not at a dock, so not sure where I am ??"* – Backchannel, P10

New Insight: Focus on Navigation and Utility

Remote attendees felt that having the Beams in different areas was helpful and it facilitated their choice of system. In particular, having charging stations on each floor allowed many participants to avoid the elevator, where they needed to request help.

> *"I really like the fact that there are upstairs and downstairs beams. This makes it much easier to get around. However, the downstairs beams are close to session rooms but the upstairs beams are not. IT (sic) would be nice to have a shorter 'walk' to rooms since one has to get there so early. The downstairs beams also seem to be close to the main stairway attendees use, which makes them great for serendipitous bumping into folks. I don't know if that is true of the upstairs ones."* – Daily survey, P11

This focus on navigation and utility is reflected in the earlier Section: Hierarchy of Telepresence Needs.

New Insight: De-emphasis on Opportunistic Interactions

Literature in robotic telepresence systems has heavily emphasized that having a physical embodiment increases the frequency of opportunistic interactions—taking advantage of a chance encounter to engage in an unplanned interaction [11, 27]. These interactions are usually cited as taking place while transitioning through the local environment [11, 27]. However, we observed that as remote users navigated through the environment, they optimized for different outcomes. The strategies of pre-positioning, schedule pre-planning, and shifting to a priorities based on a hierarchy of telepresence needs led to participants sometimes perceiving opportunistic interactions as obstacles:

> *"I want to get to somewhere before the talk starts. I want to be there early so I can actually get into a good spot, but I couldn't because I kept getting stopped by people to take selfies."* – Focus group, P26

As remote attendees adapted to the additional challenges of interruptions caused by abuse and increased attention due to the Beams' novelty factor, the priority placed on navigation and pre-positioning above socializing became increasingly apparent.

DISCUSSION

While our results support the generalizability of findings from a number of previous studies, they also highlight the need for careful consideration of how these effects evolve as they grow to meet large-scale event demands. For example, while literature has touched on the possibility of pranking targeted at remote users [11], we observed instances of abuse that became more severe over the course of the conference. This effect may be tied to the phenomena of crowd psychology [21], where being part of a larger group may grant a sense of anonymity and loss of a sense of responsibility. Such a shift suggests that venues with large populations (e.g., sports events or larger conferences) may not be a good fit for the use of robotic telepresence systems, as there may be an increased threat of systems being permanently damaged or rendered unusable. Or, if telepresence robots are used in such settings, designs should provide increased mechanisms to promote additional security (e.g., cameras to easily see behind the robot, location tracking of robots) such that people may be deterred from such negative acts.

Prior work has also examined strategies for time-shifted globally distributed teams and found that people work hard to align their calendars with remote colleagues, including shifting their schedules and sometimes working from home to accommodate others [24]. Although our findings had some similarities, the circumstances in our study differed in a number of ways. For example, our participants attended a limited time event with an inflexible schedule and high number of parallel tracks. Additionally, remote participants shared access to the telepresence systems and the interactions at the conference were not expected to be sustained over a long-term collaborative project. As a result, remote attendees in our study were willing to engage in arguably unsustainable strategies to compensate for time zone differences, such as staying up all night or taking days off of work.

Although little can be done to temporarily change time zones, future systems could be designed to provide a bidirectional shared context. For example, telepresence robots might be able to display contextual information about the remote attendee such as where they are and what time it is in their location so that local attendees can understand their context better and adjust social expectations accordingly. This might be done through simple on-screen visualizations showing a timeline or map.

During the conference, we also observed new situations, such as three remote attendees using their lack of physical presence to attend the Diversity Lunch. Despite having not signed up for the lunch, they were able to participate, possibly because they did not need food, a seat, or any of the 'SWAG', as they were not actually physically there. This concept of leveraging the lack of physical presence opens up new opportunities for future research and design innovation. For example, explorations into how a physical proxy may alter social norms or making design changes to allow remote users to transition in and out of embodied form to match the level of interactivity required. This might involve changing the representation of the user on the telepresence robot's display, or even altering the physical form of the robot in some way. For example, a robot that can fold or compact itself when not in use might become unfolded into a standing form when in use.

Last, our new insights into the prioritization of needs and observed workarounds suggest that robotic telepresence, as currently designed, may not be an optimal solution for remotely attending large-scale public events. Participants found some successes, such as leveraging their ability to jump between systems to circumvent physical limitations and improve their experiences, yet, overall, one could argue that remote attendees did not use the telepresence robots in a way that maximized the physical presence of the system. Rather than the Beams providing a physical proxy, akin to the experience of attending a conference in person, many of the features designed to enable remote users in smaller, more controlled situations, were correlated with additional obstacles or breakdowns when environmental factors were scaled up. Instead of using the robots as social proxies of themselves, remote attendees focused their behaviors around achieving specific tasks where the tasks most often targeted viewing technical content over socializing with others. Participant responses also supported a growing body of literature suggesting that effective telepresence systems may require a divergence from designing to simulate physical presence and that a context-specific approach may provide a better experience [20, 18]. We explore the design implications of this point in the next section.

Design Implications

The insights drawn from our research suggest that as various factors, such as population, remote users, activities, time zone differences, and venue size increase, new behaviors and user strategies may emerge. These behaviors have implications for the design of future systems.

For example, the added complexity of large numbers of people, activities, and space suggests a need for investing effort into supporting better tracking of systems. Such systems might show the location of telepresence robots within the conference center on a map as well as other contextual cues such as when a person logged in last. The increase in levels of disorientation as the number of remote users grows suggests a new focus on creating a less abrupt login experience, an area where little attention has been spent to date. For example, designers may want to consider ways of easing remote users into the system environment by gradually fading in the audio/video or providing snapshots of the surroundings at the login page.

Additionally, the design of current systems has largely been binary in the status that they have afforded remote users: either connected or disconnected. While the Beam does have a hold feature, this proved insufficient in our study where remote attendees engaged in a strategy of pre-positioning their Beams and leaving their camera view on. Future systems targeted at large-scale public events with a variety of activities or multiple pauses (e.g., a sporting event) may require additional options, such as allowing users to flag a system as reserved, facilitating a way for users to make positional requests when systems are shared between users, and giving remote users a way to signal a status of being within earshot while not visible.

Our findings highlight that in large-scale events where activities and contexts may vary dramatically, changes to various factors, such as venue size or number of users sharing a system, may result in behavioral shifts. Our results support recommendations for individual systems, such as the ability to connect into a multitude of stationary displays placed in key locations with audio and video streaming capabilities to promote social mingling. Presentation situations or activities where the remote participant is a passive viewer may be better supported through online streaming since few, if any, social interactions happen while remote attendees are listening to talks (except for the question/answer period). Other large-scale events may require other design solutions, such as creating stationary systems that provide better audio in crowds and support body movement to participate in cheering for sporting events.

While changes may be made to current telepresence systems to more effectively target them at particular activities, the variety of activities, obstacles, and ever-changing contexts we observed suggest that a single one-size-fits-all system may not be the optimal solution for large-scale events. Instead, we propose that a more effective approach may be a group of telepresence technologies that allow remote users to transition between them. For example, allowing remote attendees to migrate between life-sized situated displays that maintain a visibly available presence in crowded mingling environments, robotic telepresence in interactive sessions where mobility is critical to the experience, and livestreaming combined with a summative video display for activities where the remote participant is a passive viewer, may facilitate a better user experience and allow users to more gracefully adjust to the shifting needs of large-scale events. While our results largely highlight new behaviors and insights in academic conferences, they also reveal opportunities for a new generation of research and design in telepresence for large-scale events.

LIMITATIONS AND GENERALIZABILITY

Although our study successfully increased five factors from prior work and placed remote attendees in a large-scale public event, it was not without limitations. The large space, number of activities, higher attendance, and time zone differences made it impossible to observe all of the interactions that took place. While we used multiple data sources, we were unable to report a ground truth on the frequency and rate of adoption of many behaviors. As a result, we were not able to report precise numbers for some of the reported insights. Although we collected responses from the post-CHI survey, the limit of two questions also meant we were not able to gain a nuanced understanding of local attendee perspectives. Additionally, the novelty of having robotic telepresence systems may have affected participant behaviors and further research is required to ascertain whether the behaviors we observed would continue in situations where such systems are commonplace.

Last, our work looked at one type of large-scale event, an academic conference with a technology focus. Large museums and tradeshows are likely quite similar to portions of academic conferences like CHI. They both have a large volume of local attendees, are housed in large venues, and have exhibitions or booths that share characteristics with the poster presentations and demonstrations at CHI. People may also connect from around the world. However, the types of people that would attend these events would likely be much broader than the technology researchers and practitioners that attend CHI. This may create different reactions to telepresence robots. Large-scale events like concerts would also resemble CHI in the volume of attendees, venue size, and breadth of geographic locations that people may attend from. Yet the environment could be quite different with loud noise and greater difficulties with positioning oneself to see the view of the stage, as compared to seeing a speaker at a conference. Thus, although our findings share many characteristics with a variety of large-scale events, further study is required to test the generalizability of our insights.

CONCLUSION

Research in robotic telepresence has largely taken place in small, semi-private settings using dedicated systems. However, robotic telepresence systems are envisioned to empower users beyond these contexts, helping them to attend large-scale public events such as concerts, sports games, museums, and professional conferences. Our study tested the generalizability of prior findings by increasing five factors to more closely match the needs of large-scale events: (1) number of people; ratio of users to available systems; (3) variety of activities; (4) time zone differences; and (5) environment size. Our results showed that as the scale on such factors increased, remote users altered their behaviors to prioritize functional utility. Our findings raise new considerations for how the users of these systems should be treated and highlight opportunities for optimizing the design of these systems for large-scale public venues.

ACKNOWLEDGMENTS

We thank all of the student volunteers, CHI committee members, and conference staff, for their help in supporting telepresence at CHI. We also gratefully acknowledge Juliana Shei for her help in the design of the color personalization of the systems.

REFERENCES

1. Jenay M. Beer and Leila Takayama. 2011. Mobile Remote Presence Systems for Older Adults: Acceptance, Benefits, and Concerns. In *Proceedings of the 6th International Conference on Human-robot Interaction (HRI '11)*. ACM, New York, NY, USA, 19–26. DOI: http://dx.doi.org/10.1145/1957656.1957665
2. Jed R. Brubaker, Gina Venolia, and John C. Tang. 2012. Focusing on Shared Experiences: Moving Beyond the Camera in Video Communication. In *Proceedings of the Designing Interactive Systems Conference (DIS '12)*. ACM, New York, NY, USA, 96–105. DOI: http://dx.doi.org/10.1145/2317956.2317973
3. M. Desai, K. M. Tsui, H. A. Yanco, and C. Uhlik. 2011. Essential features of telepresence robots. In *2011 IEEE Conference on Technologies for Practical Robot Applications*. 15–20. DOI: http://dx.doi.org/10.1109/TEPRA.2011.5753474
4. Terrence Fong and Charles Thorpe. 2001. Vehicle Teleoperation Interfaces. *Autonomous Robots* 11, 1 (2001), 9–18. DOI: http://dx.doi.org/10.1023/A:1011295826834
5. InTouch. 2016. InTouch Vita. Website. (5 September 2016). Retrieved September 5, 2016 from http://www.intouchhealth.com/our-solutions/patient-access/#vita.
6. Clarissa Ishak, Carman Neustaedter, Dan Hawkins, Jason Procyk, and Michael Massimi. 2016. Human Proxies for Remote University Classroom Attendance. In *Proceedings of the 2016 CHI Conference on Human Factors in Computing Systems (CHI '16)*. ACM, New York, NY, USA, 931–943. DOI: http://dx.doi.org/10.1145/2858036.2858184
7. Steven Johnson, Irene Rae, Bilge Mutlu, and Leila Takayama. 2015. Can You See Me Now?: How Field of View Affects Collaboration in Robotic Telepresence. In *Proceedings of the 33rd Annual ACM Conference on Human Factors in Computing Systems (CHI '15)*. ACM, New York, NY, USA, 2397–2406. DOI: http://dx.doi.org/10.1145/2702123.2702526
8. K. Lee Koay, D. S. Syrdal, M. L. Walters, and K. Dautenhahn. 2007. Living with Robots: Investigating the Habituation Effect in Participants' Preferences During a Longitudinal Human-Robot Interaction Study. In *The 16th IEEE International Symposium on Robot and Human Interactive Communication (RO-MAN '07)*. 564–569. DOI: http://dx.doi.org/10.1109/ROMAN.2007.4415149
9. R Latifi, RS Weinstein, JM Porter, M Ziemba, D Judkins, D Ridings, R Nassi, T Valenzuela, M Holcomb, and F Leyva. 2007. Telemedicine and telepresence for trauma and emergency care management. *Scandinavian Journal of Surgery* 96, 4 (2007), 281–289.
10. Dave Lee. 2014. Cheering robots replace real fans at Korean baseball. Website. (25 July 2014). Retrieved September 5, 2016 from http://www.bbc.com/news/technology-28484536.
11. Min Kyung Lee and Leila Takayama. 2011. "Now, I Have a Body": Uses and Social Norms for Mobile Remote Presence in the Workplace. In *Proceedings of the SIGCHI Conference on Human Factors in Computing Systems (CHI '11)*. ACM, New York, NY, USA, 33–42. DOI: http://dx.doi.org/10.1145/1978942.1978950
12. Francois Michaud, Patrick Boissy, Daniel Labonte, Helene Corriveau, Andrew Grant, Michel Lauria, Richard Cloutier, Marc-André Roux, Daniel Iannuzzi, and Marie-Pier Royer. 2007. Telepresence Robot for Home Care Assistance.. In *AAAI Spring Symposium: Multidisciplinary Collaboration for Socially Assistive Robotics*. California, USA, 50–55.
13. Carman Neustaedter, Gina Venolia, Jason Procyk, and Daniel Hawkins. 2016. To Beam or Not to Beam: A Study of Remote Telepresence Attendance at an Academic Conference. In *Proceedings of the 19th ACM Conference on Computer-Supported Cooperative Work & Social Computing (CSCW '16)*. ACM, New York, NY, USA, 418–431. DOI: http://dx.doi.org/10.1145/2818048.2819922
14. National Museum of Australia. 2016. Robot Tours. Website. (5 September 2016). Retrieved September 5, 2016 from http://www.nma.gov.au/engage-learn/robot-tours.
15. Gary M. Olson and Judith S. Olson. 2000. Distance Matters. *Human-Computer Interaction* 15, 2 (Sept. 2000), 139–178. DOI: http://dx.doi.org/10.1207/S15327051HCI1523_4
16. Eric Paulos and John Canny. 1998. PRoP: Personal Roving Presence. In *Proceedings of the SIGCHI Conference on Human Factors in Computing Systems (CHI '98)*. ACM Press/Addison-Wesley Publishing Co., New York, NY, USA, 296–303. DOI: http://dx.doi.org/10.1145/274644.274686
17. Event Presence. 2016. Smart presence for events. Website. (5 September 2016). Retrieved September 5, 2016 from http://eventpresence.com.
18. Irene Rae. 2015. *How Telepresence Robots Shape Communication*. Ph.D. Dissertation. The University of Wisconsin-Madison, Madison, WI, USA.
19. Irene Rae, Leila Takayama, and Bilge Mutlu. 2013. In-body Experiences: Embodiment, Control, and Trust in Robot-mediated Communication. In *Proceedings of the SIGCHI Conference on Human Factors in Computing Systems (CHI '13)*. ACM, New York, NY, USA, 1921–1930. DOI: http://dx.doi.org/10.1145/2470654.2466253
20. Irene Rae, Gina Venolia, John C. Tang, and David Molnar. 2015. A Framework for Understanding and Designing Telepresence. In *Proceedings of the 18th ACM Conference on Computer Supported Cooperative Work & Social Computing (CSCW '15)*. ACM, New York, NY, USA, 1552–1566. DOI: http://dx.doi.org/10.1145/2675133.2675141

21. Stephen Reicher. 2001. The psychology of crowd dynamics. *Blackwell handbook of social psychology: Group processes* (2001), 182–208.
22. François C. Stoll, Douglas G. Hoecker, Gerald P. Krueger, and Alphonse Chapanis. 1976. The Effects of Four Communication Modes on the Structure of Language Used During Cooperative Problem Solving. *The Journal of Psychology* 94, 1 (1976), 13–26. DOI: http://dx.doi.org/10.1080/00223980.1976.9921390
23. Leila Takayama and Helen Harris. 2013. Presentation of (Telepresent) Self: On the Double-edged Effects of Mirrors. In *Proceedings of the 8th ACM/IEEE International Conference on Human-robot Interaction (HRI '13)*. IEEE Press, Piscataway, NJ, USA, 381–388. http://dl.acm.org/citation.cfm?id=2447556.2447684
24. John C. Tang, Chen Zhao, Xiang Cao, and Kori Inkpen. 2011. Your Time Zone or Mine?: A Study of Globally Time Zone-shifted Collaboration. In *Proceedings of the ACM 2011 Conference on Computer Supported Cooperative Work (CSCW '11)*. ACM, New York, NY, USA, 235–244. DOI: http://dx.doi.org/10.1145/1958824.1958860
25. Suitable Technologies. 2016. Beam Pro. Website. (5 September 2016). Retrieved September 5, 2016 from https://suitabletech.com/beampro/.
26. K. M. Tsui, M. Desai, H. A. Yanco, and C. Uhlik. 2011. Exploring use cases for telepresence robots. In *2011 6th ACM/IEEE International Conference on Human-Robot Interaction (HRI) (HRI '11)*. 11–18. DOI: http://dx.doi.org/10.1145/1957656.1957664
27. Gina Venolia, John Tang, Ruy Cervantes, Sara Bly, George Robertson, Bongshin Lee, and Kori Inkpen. 2010. Embodied Social Proxy: Mediating Interpersonal Connection in Hub-and-satellite Teams. In *Proceedings of the SIGCHI Conference on Human Factors in Computing Systems (CHI '10)*. ACM, New York, NY, USA, 1049–1058. DOI: http://dx.doi.org/10.1145/1753326.1753482
28. Paul M Vespa, Chad Miller, Xiao Hu, Val Nenov, Farzad Buxey, and Neil A Martin. 2007. Intensive care unit robotic telepresence facilitates rapid physician response to unstable patients and decreased cost in neurointensive care. *Surgical neurology* 67, 4 (2007), 331–337.
29. Jun Wei, Xuan Wang, Roshan Lalintha Peiris, Yongsoon Choi, Xavier Roman Martinez, Remi Tache, Jeffrey Tzu Kwan Valino Koh, Veronica Halupka, and Adrian David Cheok. 2011. CoDine: An Interactive Multi-sensory System for Remote Dining. In *Proceedings of the 13th International Conference on Ubiquitous Computing (UbiComp '11)*. ACM, New York, NY, USA, 21–30. DOI: http://dx.doi.org/10.1145/2030112.2030116
30. Patrice L. (Tamar) Weiss, Carolynn P. Whiteley, Jutta Treviranus, and Deborah I. Fels. 2001. PEBBLES: A Personal Technology for Meeting Educational, Social and Emotional Needs of Hospitalised Children. *Personal Ubiquitous Computing* 5, 3 (Jan. 2001), 157–168. DOI: http://dx.doi.org/10.1007/s007790170006

Movement Matters: Effects of Motion and Mimicry on Perception of Similarity and Closeness in Robot-Mediated Communication

Mina Choi,[1] **Rachel Kornfield,**[2] **Leila Takayama,**[3] **Bilge Mutlu**[4]
(1) Department of Communication Arts, University of Wisconsin–Madison
(2) School of Journalism and Mass Communication, University of Wisconsin–Madison
(3) Department of Psychology, University of California
(4) Department of Computer Sciences, University of Wisconsin–Madison
mchoi33@wisc.edu, rkornfield@wisc.edu, takayama@ucsc.edu, bilge@cs.wisc.edu

ABSTRACT
In face-to-face interaction, moving with and mimicking the body movements of communication partners has been widely demonstrated to affect interpersonal processes, including feelings of affiliation and closeness. In this paper, we examine effects of movement and mimicry in robot-mediated communication. Participants were instructed to get to know their partner, a confederate, who interacted with them via a telepresence robot. The robot either (a) mimicked the participant's body orientation (mimicry condition), (b) mimicked pre-recorded movements of another participant (random movement condition), or (c) did not move during the interaction (static condition). Results showed that mimicry and random movement had similar effects on participants' perceptions of similarity and closeness to their partners and that these effects depend on the participant's gender and level of self-monitoring. The findings suggest that the social movements of a telepresence robot affect interpersonal processes and that these effects are shaped by individual differences.

ACM Classification Keywords
H.4.3. Information Systems Applications: Communications Applications—*computer conferencing, teleconferencing, and videoconferencing*

Author Keywords
Robot-mediated communication; telepresence robots; nonverbal behavior; movement; mimicry; affiliation; similarity; closeness

INTRODUCTION
Communication technologies have radically transformed how people communicate at a distance. From written letters and phone-calls to e-mail, instant messaging, and videoconferencing, communication media have been developed to achieve more effective and efficient information exchange, especially among long distance communication partners. Recently, telepresence robots have been introduced as another option in distance communication. Telepresence robots, sometimes called mobile robotic presence (MRP) systems, are comprised by a video conferencing system mounted on a moving, physical robotic base [29]. By allowing operators to achieve a physical embodiment and freedom of motion in a remote location, these systems augment video conferencing or audio communication [29, 46] and provide long-distance communicators with a stronger sense of presence [43].

CHI'17, May 06–11, 2017, Denver, CO, USA

DOI: http://dx.doi.org/10.1145/3025453.3025734

Figure 1. We explore how the bodily movements of a telepresence robot, including movements that mimic those of the local user, shape affiliation between local and remote users in robot-mediated communication.

In organizations, telepresence robots provide a new platform for dynamic communication in various settings including business, education, and medicine [36, 58]. For example, corporations use telepresence robots for remote collaboration or to attend conferences at a lower cost compared to the expense of travel (e.g., flight, hotel, and rental car) [40]. In education, homebound or hospitalized students use telepresence robots to join the class in real time, interact with other students, and participate in group discussion [17]. Telepresence robots have been shown to be more efficient compared to communication channels that have become conventional (e.g., phone calls, videoconferencing) [26, 35, 40].

Along with its possibilities and potential for enriching remote communication, the emergence of robot-mediated communication also introduces many unknowns regarding how telepresence robots may support essential interpersonal processes that ensure the effectiveness of face-to-face communication. One component of effective communication is *rapport*, defined as relationships of affinity and trust within a group or between a dyad [6]. Building rapport is important in both our personal and professional lives. Personal relationships are easier to develop and maintain when there is greater rapport between the parties involved [57]. Workplace relationships involve rapport in the sense that frequent informal communication builds coordination and commitment between members of a team [63]. In healthcare contexts, rapport ensures that patients are willing to disclose relevant health information and are receptive to clinicians' care and guidance [7]. Rapport builds, in part, through nonverbal cues [11, 13], especially in informal interactions. For telepresence robots to contribute to effective communication across these contexts, users must be able to build rapport and a sense of affiliation.

In this paper, we study a specific nonverbal process that affects rapport between communication partners, *movement*. We present the design of and findings from a laboratory experiment that examined whether telepresence robots' movements affect how local users affiliate themselves with and perceive remote users in conversational interactions (Figure 1). As telepresence robots replicate many aspects of face-to-face communication, remote users may experience mediated interactions using telepresence robots as though they were "really there" with their communication partners and vice versa [55, 58]. We expect that the nonverbal cues underlying rapport and affiliation in a face-to-face context will also contribute to rapport between interactants in a robot-mediated context.

Background

This section reviews related work addressing the importance of nonverbal communication processes and provides a rationale for examining movement in robot-mediated communication.

Nonverbal Cues in Robot-Mediated Communication

Literature suggests several nonverbal factors that facilitate higher quality interpersonal communication using telepresence robots. Research shows that both physical embodiment and locus of system control–local vs. remote user– have an impact on interpersonal trust in mediated communication [45]. Specifically, granting the local user more control over the configuration of the telepresence unit led to greater trust between the communication partners. Height of the telepresence robot also affected the local user's perception of the remote partner [46]. When the telepresence system was shorter than the local partner, partners behaved in ways that showed more dominance, and they perceived the remote users to be less persuasive than when the telepresence system was taller than them [46]. This finding is consistent with interpersonal communication literature showing that taller people are viewed as more competent and are more likely to emerge as leaders [54, 65, 66]. In addition, spatial configuration, including body orientation of a telepresence robot toward the partner, can enhance interaction quality [30, 31, 33]. The researchers found that the robot's body rotation affects how people arrange themselves, which, in turn, affects how they perceive interaction quality with the robot [33]. The robot's full body rotation was found to be more effective than head rotation only.

The decoration of telepresence robots also influences local users' perceptions of remote users [44, 59]. After a robot-mediated interaction, local participants perceived the remote user of the telepresence robot as more similar to themselves and as more trustworthy when the system has been decorated by the participant compared to when the system was undecorated [44]. Decorating the telepresence robot with an assigned group color created a sense of membership between the local and remote users. These findings all suggest that nonverbal processes involving telepresence robots affect how partners come to view one another after a mediated interaction. It may be possible to enhance relationship building via telepresence robots through further attention to issues of spatial configuration and embodiment.

Mimicry in interpersonal communication

In face-to-face interpersonal communication, a number of embodied processes support affiliation. These processes can operate even without our conscious awareness, such as when we automatically imitate the body postures, mannerisms, and facial expressions of our partners [10, 24]. Nonconscious mimicry plays a key role in building social relationships, with tendencies toward mimicry increasing when partners are more concerned with the feelings of others, or seeking to enhance the closeness of their relationships with others [34]. Experimental studies have also shown that liking can increase when confederates deliberately mimic the behavior of their communication partners, typically without the partners ever becoming aware of the imitation [9]. These effects have been replicated for a number of behaviors including facerubbing, foot-shaking, playing with an object, body orientation, or style of spoken language (e.g., particular phrases and tone of voice) [10, 22, 41, 47, 62]. One mechanism of these effects is perceived similarity. When partners engage in greater mimicry, they are viewed as being more similar to oneself, which increases rapport [60]. As automatic mimicry allows individuals to successfully build social relationships, a tendency toward this behavior would have eventually become widespread in an evolutionary context [34].

While our physical apparatus for automatic mimicry emerged in the context of face-to-face interaction, some recent work suggests that it is possible to achieve mimicry in agent-based communication. Bailenson and Yee [5] conducted an experiment in which participants, representing themselves through avatars in a virtual environment, communicated with computer-based agents. These agents, also represented as human characters, were programmed either to automatically replicate the head movements of participants (i.e., mimicry condition), to move a similar amount without mimicking to the participants' orientation (i.e., random movement condition), or not to move (i.e., static condition) during the interaction. Results indicated that mimicry increased participants' ratings of the agents' positive qualities and persuasiveness more than other conditions. Given these findings, some have proposed that the principles of mimicry should be applied more broadly to design of human-like agents and robots in order to improve user experience [37].

While some prior work has explored interpersonal processes in robot-mediated communication, physical mimicry remains unexplored. For telepresence robots to become broadly acceptable in distance communication, including for informal communication, it is important to understand how telepresence robots can support liking and rapport between partners. Mimicry plays an important role in such processes. Prior work has shown that linguistic mimicry can operate in mediated communication, enhancing liking [21, 47]. Historically, however, mediated communication has not been conducive to perceiving and replicating partners' physical movements. By combining a real-time video feed with an embodied presence, telepresence robots may overcome this impoverishment, enabling operators to perceive the subtle movements of their partners and physically imitate them.

In this paper, we aim to better understand how movements of a telepresence robot influence perceived affiliation between local and remote users and to examine how individual differences play roles in such effects. We present a laboratory study where participants interact with a remote confederate using a telepresence robot in a conversational task (Figure 1).

Individual differences

Research also indicates that the effects of mimicry correspond to individuals' social orientations. Snyder [52] introduced the theory of self-monitoring to describe trait differences in the modulation of expressive behavior to achieve social goals. Self-monitoring refers to the extent to which an individual adjusts his or her behavior to situational demands [52]. Whereas low self-monitors present themselves in the same way regardless of social context, high self-monitors act as a kind of social chameleons, habitually monitoring their environments in order to tailor their performances of self [52]. Self-monitoring therefore relies on a number of preconditions: sensitivity to social cues, ability to infer contextually–specific social norms, and capacity and inclination to manipulate one's expressive behavior accordingly [16, 52]. Self-monitoring can therefore be highly relevant to perceiving and interpreting nonverbal behavior such as movement.

HYPOTHESES

To better understand the effects of different forms of movement in robot-mediated communication and the role of individual differences, we formulated two research questions and four hypotheses regarding local users' perceptions of remote users, drawing on prior research in face-to-face and computer-mediated communication.

Does movement matter?

Movement and embodied presence are key features of telepresence robots that distinguish them from videoconferencing systems [43]. Prior research in both face-to-face and mediated-communication suggests that these features predict rapport, including judgments of attractiveness, similarity, and closeness of partners [1, 29], and this even operates when movements are subtle or uncoordinated to the partner [39]. Thus, we first make the following prediction to examine the effect of robot movement regardless of its coordination to the partner:

H1. Local users will perceive greater affiliation with a remote user that communicates with them via a telepresence robot that displays movement cues than one that is stationary.

While we expect movement in general to positively shape affiliation in robot-mediated communication, literature on face-to-face, agent-based, and mediated communication suggest that, when movements of communication partners are aligned, e.g., through *mimicry* [5, 60, 32], these communicative outcomes are even stronger. Thus, we posit the following hypothesis.

H2. Local users will perceive greater affiliation with remote users who communicate with them via a telepresence robot that mimics their behavior than a telepresence robot that moves but does not mimic.

Do individual differences matter?

We further examine how the predicted effects of robot movements articulated in H1 and H2 vary across individuals, particularly across personality and sex-based individual characteristics. According to literature on personality-based differences, particularly self-monitoring [16, 52], high self-monitors attend and respond to subtle movement cues including mimicry more than low self-monitors do. Thus, we propose that self-monitoring also plays a role in nonverbal processes in the robot-mediated communication context.

H3. The effects of robot movement on local users' affiliation with remote users will depend on local users' level of self-monitoring.

Another key individual characteristic that shapes face-to-face [14] and mediated [23] communication is gender. Some prior work has found strong gender effects in the production [12] and perception [64] of mimicry, which we also expect to see in robot-mediated communication. Studies also indicate that males and females perceive technologies differently [44, 56], and therefore may respond differently to robot-mediated movement. Thus, while we predict user gender to play a role in perceptions of remote partners, we do not have sufficient evidence to predict a particular direction for the effect.

H4. The effects of robot movement on local users' affiliation with remote users will depend on user gender.

METHOD

To test the hypotheses described above, we designed a laboratory study that compared participants' affiliation with and perceptions of a remote confederate who communicates with them via a telepresence robot across several styles of movement. The paragraphs below detail our participants, study design, procedure, manipulation, measures, and analysis.

Participants

A total of 36 participants (18 male, 18 female), stratified by gender within each condition, took part in our study. All participants were recruited from the university of Wisconsin–Madison campus. Participants were aged 18–44 years ($M = 22.83, SD = 5.82$). Participants were compensated $5 USD for their participation. The UW–Madison Institutional Review Board (IRB) approved this research.

Study Design

Following the movement manipulations used by Bailenson and Yee [5], we examine the effects of interactions where the telepresence robot (1) mimics the participant's orientation, (2) displays random movements not coordinated to the participant, or (3) is stationary. The experiment features a 3 × 1 (movement: mimicry, random, vs. static) between-participants design in which a participant completed a "get-to-know-you" conversation task with a female confederate (the "communicating confederate") over a telepresence robot. Participants were told that the confederate was another participant assigned to the same time slot. To control for the large interpersonal variability in factors eliciting social processes, such as physical attractiveness and communication style, the same confederate communicated with participants in all three conditions. To enable the communicating confederate to focus on interacting with the participant and to minimize interference between the interaction task and the task of controlling the robot, the telepresence robot was operated by another female experimenter (the "operating experimenter") who sat at a separate monitor next to the communicating confederate and was out of sight of the participant. A Beam Pro system, a professional-grade telepresence robot designed and manufactured by Suitable Technologies,[1] was used for the experiment.

Procedure

Participants were invited to the lab and told that the purpose of the study was to examine how people interact with a stranger, another participant, over a telepresence robot system. The participants were told that the other participant was located in another building across campus and would use the control interface for the telepresence system to communicate with him or her. Then, they signed a consent form and provided answers to a pre-experiment questionnaire including personality measures. For the experimental task, we used a "get-to-know-you" exercise [19] in which participants were instructed to get to know their partner (the communicating confederate, whom they were led to believe was another participant) in five minutes and to talk about anything they wanted. The telepresence robot entered the room to begin the interaction. After the interaction, the telepresence robot left the room, and participant provided answers to a post-experiment questionnaire about the interaction and debriefed.

Manipulation

Three study conditions varied the movement of the robot during the get-to-know-you interaction. The operating experimenter either (1) did not move the telepresence robot ("static" condition) or moved it by referencing (2) a live-streamed video of the current participant ("mimicry" condition) or (3) a video recording of the former participant in the mimicry condition ("random movement" condition), as was done by Bailenson and Yee [5]. More specifically, in the static condition, the robot remained stationary during the interaction beyond entering and leaving the room. In the remaining two conditions, the operating confederate moved the robot left and right at a speed of 1.5 mph using the keyboard commands "left" and "right." In the mimicry condition, the operating experimenter moved the robot to mirror the participants' upper body posture and movement, capturing both orientation and speed. That is, if the participant moved his/her head or upper body to the right, the operating experimenter would "mirror" this behavior by turning the robot to the left. Finally, a third, random movement condition replicated the same level of movement as the mimicry condition but in a way that was not aligned with the movement of the participant. Instead, the robot mimicked the recorded movement of a previous participant. Specifically, the operating confederate responded to movement cues from a video recording of the prior participant in the mimicry condition, whereas the communicating confederate saw live video feed of the current participant.

In the two movement conditions, the telepresence robot mimicked the participant's movements with an approximate average delay of 500 ms the sources of which included the response time of the operating confederate, network latency, and inherent delays in robot actuation. Across all three conditions, the robot maintained an approximate distance of five feet from the participant, consistent with prior research establishing it as a comfortable conversational distance [15]. While participants were not given any instruction regarding movement, they rarely moved forward or backward beyond a couple inches, and this distance was maintained across the interactions. Participants instead moved their arms, head, and body orientation, which the telepresence robot imitated by rotating to the left or right. During the interactions, the communicating confederate was instructed not to change her body orientation or to move her arms into the video frame (which could have revealed that she was not controlling the movements of the robot). While her facial expressions and conversation topics were not strictly controlled, she was blind to study condition, and we expect variability in her movements and conversation topics to spread randomly across the conditions.

Measures

To measure local participants' affiliation with and perceptions of the remote confederate and their individual characteristics, we used following measures.

[1] Suitable Technologies Beam Pro: http://suitabletech.com

Perceptions of the Remote Partner

Drawing on literature on interpersonal communication, we operationalize rapport with and affiliation toward the remote user as involving (1) perceived *similarity* to and (2) interpersonal *closeness* felt toward the remote confederate [42, 53]. To measure participants' perception of similarity toward a remote user, we used a well-validated Perceived Homophily scale developed by McCroskey [38]. The scale is one of the most widely used measures of perceived similarity. It consists of nine items, and each item was measured on a seven-point scale (1 = strongly disagree, 7 = strongly agree) (Cronbach's $\alpha = 0.72$). The negative items were reversed and summed across the responses ($M = 39.50$, $SD = 6.59$). To measure participants' feelings of closeness toward the remote user, we adopted one item from the Inclusion of Other in the Self (IOS) scale [3]. The item asks participants to rate how close they felt to their partner and provides Venn-like diagrams depicting five degrees of overlap between two circles [61]. The item is widely used to measure perceived closeness ($M = 2.75$, $SD = 1.20$). Three open-ended questions prompted participants to elaborate on aspects of the interaction that they liked and did not like and provide any additional comments about their experience.

Individual Characteristics

Participants filled out a questionnaire measuring levels of *self-monitoring* in the initial survey, which was measured using the 25-item Self-Monitoring Scale developed by Snyder [52]. The original version of the scale used a true-false response scheme, which we modified into a Likert-type scale for psychometric purposes. After reversing negative items, we took the average of item responses ($M = 4.08, SD = 0.51$, Cronbach's $\alpha =$ 0.68). The alpha coefficient reported by Snyder [51, 52] for the scale was $0.66 - 0.70$. Participants' familiarity with robots, $M = 3.58, SD = 1.00$, and comfort with videoconferencing, $M = 2.69, SD = 0.89$, were measured by two single items: "How familiar are you with robots?" and "How comfortable are you with videoconferencing?" using seven-point rating scales (1 = not at all, 7 = very much). At the end of the study, participants filled out a questionnaire asking demographic information including gender, age, and ethnicity.

Analyses

To test our hypotheses, we used analyses of variance (ANOVA) and analyses of covariance (ANCOVA). To test H1 and H2, we used the same ANOVA model with experimental manipulation as the only independent variable. For H3, we used an ANCOVA with experimental manipulation, self-monitoring, and their interaction as independent variables and perceived similarity and closeness as the dependent variables. Testing for H4 involved ANOVA with experimental manipulation, gender, and their interaction as independent variables and perceived similarity and closeness as the dependent variables. Our analysis employed Bonferroni correction to control for Type I errors in all contrast tests and pairwise comparisons (used in the testing of H1 and H2) and *post hoc* pairwise comparisons (used as exploratory analyses following the testing of H4).

RESULTS

Manipulation Check – We first conducted manipulation checks to establish that participants in mimicry and random movement conditions noticed higher levels of robot movement relative to the static condition. A one-way ANOVA was conducted to determine if participants in the mimicry and random movement conditions reported higher levels of movement in the robot compared to those in the static condition. Results showed that the movement manipulation had a significant effect on how much robot movement was reported by the participants, $F(2,33) = 4.83, p = 0.015$. As we expected, participants in the mimicry condition, $M = 4.17$, $SD = 1.75$, and the random movement condition, $M = 4.00$, $SD = 1.86$, reported higher levels of robot movement than those in the static condition, $M = 2.33$, $SD = 1.07$. Pairwise comparisons revealed that the difference between the mimicry and static conditions was statistically significant, $p = 0.025$, as was the difference between the random and static conditions, $p = 0.046$, but the difference between the mimicry and random conditions was not significant, which is expected since both conditions feature similar levels of movement.

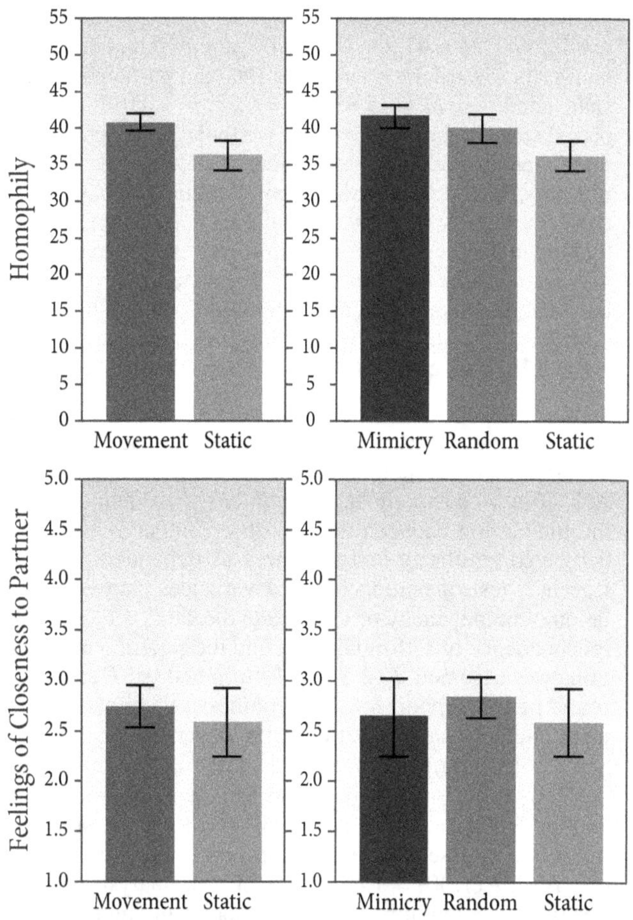

Figure 2. The effects of movement and movement type on measures of affiliation including homophily and feelings of closeness to partner. Our analysis shows that local users report greater homophily toward partners communicating through a robot that displays movement than they do toward partners communicating through a static robot. Error bars represent standard error of the mean.

Testing for H1 and H2– H1 predicted that participants would report increased affiliation with remote users, specifically rating them to be closer and more similar to themselves, when they communicated with them using a telepresence robot that moved rather than a static robot. In H2, we predicted that participants would rate remote users to be closer and more similar to themselves when they communicated with them using a telepresence robot that mimicked their body orientations than a robot that displayed random movements. To test H1 and H2, we conducted a one-way ANOVA followed by planned contrasts between movement (random and mimicry) and static conditions for H1 and between random and mimicry conditions for H2. Additionally, we report on pairwise comparisons between each individual movement condition and the static condition to provide a fuller picture of our data.

Shapiro-Wilk tests show that the data in each condition were normally distributed ($p > 0.05$); Levene's test showed no violation of homogeneity of variance in the data ($p > 0.05$). Results showed a significant effect of the robot movement on participants' perceived similarity, $F(2,33) = 3.50$, $p = 0.042$, $\eta^2 = 0.18$, but not on their perceived closeness, $F(2,30) = 0.16$, $p = 0.85$, $\eta^2 = 0.01$. Planned contrast tests showed that participants in the movement conditions (mimicry and random conditions), $M = 41.33$, $SD = 6.06$, reported higher levels of similarity toward the remote user than did participants in the static condition, $M = 35.83$, $SD = 6.28$, $p = 0.017$, providing partial support for H1. However, we found no support for H2; there was no statistically significant difference between the mimicry, $M = 42.33$, and random conditions, 40.33, in perceived similarity, $p > 0.05$. Additional comparisons showed that the difference between the mimicry and static condition was statistically significant, $p = 0.014$, and the difference between the random and mimicry conditions was marginally significant, $p = 0.083$. Figure 2 illustrates data used for testing H1 and H2 on the graphs on the left and right, respectively.

Testing for H3 – H3 predicted that self-monitoring would moderate the effects of robot movement on local users' perceptions of the remote user. To test H3, we conducted an ANCOVA with experimental conditions, self-monitoring, and the interaction between them as independent variables and perceived similarity and closeness as dependent variables. Levene's test of homogeneity of variances showed no violation of homogeneity of variance in the data ($p > 0.05$). The independence of self-monitoring and the experimental conditions was assumed, $F(2,33) = 1.46$, $p > 0.05$. Our analysis found partial support for this hypothesis; there was a significant interaction effect between the movement manipulation and self-monitoring on perceived similarity, $F(2,30) = 4.22$, $p = 0.024$, $\eta^2 = 0.22$, but not on perceived closeness to the partner, $F(2,30) = 0.80$, $p > 0.05$, $\eta^2 = 0.05$. No significant main effect of self-monitoring on perceived similarity was observed, $F(1,30) = 1.42$, $p > 0.05$. Our analysis showed a positive association between self-monitoring and perceived similarity in the mimicry condition, $B = 3.63$, $SE = 3.15$, and in the random movement condition, $B = 8.43$, $SE = 4.77$, but a negative one in the static condition, $B = -5.05$, $SE = 3.15$. While the slopes for the mimicry and random movement conditions did not significantly differ, $p > 0.05$, the slopes for the mimicry and static conditions were marginally different, $p = 0.072$, and the slopes for the random movement and static conditions were significantly different, $p = 0.008$. Figure 3 shows perceived similarity measurements across the three movement conditions and self-monitoring levels.

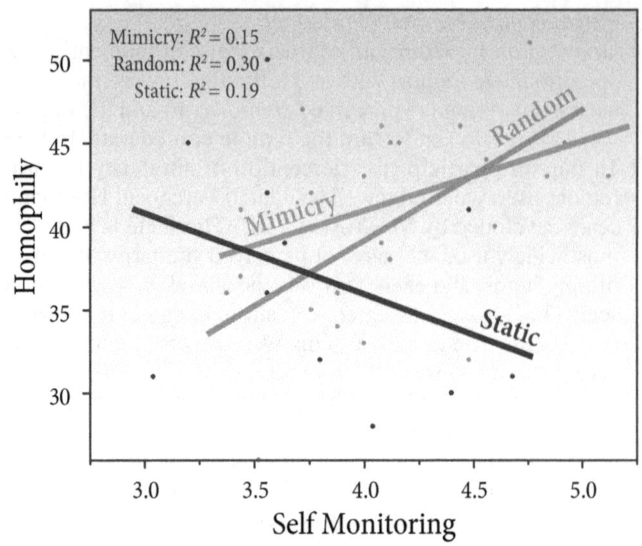

Figure 3. The effects of individual differences, particularly self monitoring, on perceived homophily across the different movement types. We found that high self-monitors rated greater affiliation in the two movement conditions and reduced affiliation in the static condition.

Testing for H4 – Finally, H4 predicted that gender would moderate the effects of robot movement on local users' perceptions of the remote user. To test the moderating effect of gender, we conducted an ANOVA with the movement manipulation, gender, and interaction between the movement manipulation

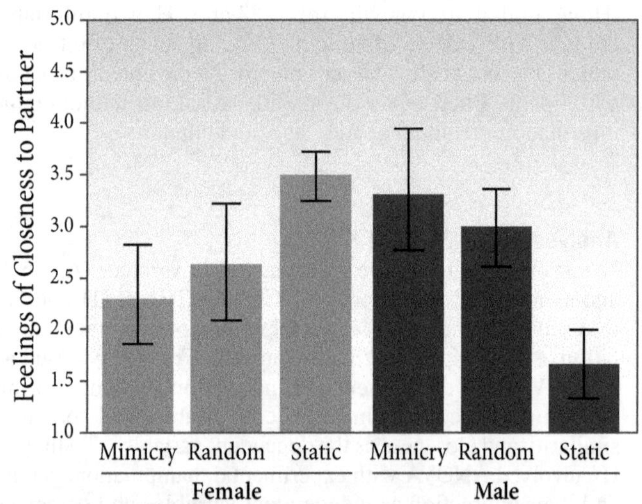

Figure 4. The effects of the movement manipulation on feelings of closeness across females and males. Our analysis found a significant interaction effect between movement type and participant gender, indicating that movement affects how females and males affiliate themselves with partners differently. Error bars represent standard error of the mean.

and gender as independent variables and perceived similarity and closeness as dependent variables, respectively. Levene's test of homogeneity of variances showed no violation of homogeneity of variance in the data ($p > 0.05$). Our analysis found a significant interaction effect between the movement manipulation and gender on perceived closeness, $F(2,30) = 5.36$, $p = 0.010$, $\eta^2 = 0.26$ (Figure 4), but not on perceived similarity, $F(2,30) = 2.89$, $p > 0.05$, $\eta^2 = 0.16$, providing partial support for H4. We further inspected reported levels of perceived closeness across conditions for each gender group using *post hoc* analysis. For males, participants' perceived closeness scores (reported as mean $\pm$ standard deviation) in the mimicry condition (3.33 ± 1.51) were higher than those in the random movement condition (3.00 ± 0.89), which were higher than their scores in the static condition (1.67 ± 0.82). Females' ratings of perceived closeness showed the opposite pattern; their ratings in the mimicry condition (2.33 ± 1.21) were lower than those in the random movement condition (2.67 ± 1.37), which were lower than their ratings in the static condition (3.50 ± 0.55). *Post hoc* pairwise comparisons showed that differences between the movement conditions were not statistically significant for either gender group.

Qualitative Analyses – Review of open-ended items included in the exit survey revealed various specific responses to and interpretations of the robot's movement. While most participants did not remark on the movement, those who did ($n = 8$) typically had positive responses. In the mimicry condition, one participant commented on the naturalism of the movement, writing that the movement of the robot "made it seem more human in the way that humans move slightly when they talk... The robot and screen seemed to embody a human without hands/arms." Another noted that the confederate seemed able to exert agency through movement: "she maintained control of the robot and could rotate and move herself if needed." Two participants in the static condition as well as one participant in the random movement condition remarked on the robot's lack of movement as a disadvantage in the interaction.

Some negative aspects of the robot's movement and positioning were also reported in open-ended responses. One participant in the random movement condition wrote, "sometimes the machine wasn't directly facing me which made it awkward." Another participant in the random movement condition noted that he would have liked to move and gesture more himself but was worried that he wouldn't remain in the robot's field of view. Finally, several participants indicated that they would have preferred to interact while seated.

DISCUSSION

Telepresence robots provide an opportunity to replicate an important aspect of face-to-face communication—physical movement and mimicry—while communicating from a distance. Our results suggest that both mimicry and random movement can be accomplished via a telepresence robot and can affect perceptions of the communication partner; however, this effect depends on individuals' social orientations and gender. Specifically, those more inclined to adapt behaviors to the social context, high self-monitors, viewed their partners as being more similar in both movement conditions relative to the static condition. Males felt closer to their partner in the movement conditions relative to the static condition, whereas in contrast, females felt closer to their partner in the static condition relative to the movement conditions. Broadly, our findings suggest that, as in face-to-face interactions, individual differences shape the effects of nonverbal processes in robot-mediated communication.

This research has theoretical and practical implications on several fronts. First, it offers insight into whether the effects of nonverbal processes in interpersonal communication persist when communication is mediated through telepresence robots. Second, by considering telepresence robots' movements in an informal communication setting, it advances the robot-mediated communication literature, which, to date, has mostly been applied to task-related, collaborative scenarios. Lastly, it offers practical implications for designing communication technologies. These contributions are discussed below.

MOVEMENT MATTERS

Our findings showed that local users felt more similar to remote users when communicating with them via a moving telepresence robot than via a stationary robot. It is likely that the robot's movement enhanced the presence of the remote user so that people felt more engaged in the movement conditions [39, 50]. Future work may measure perceived presence to examine a potential mediating effect. While we found no significant differences between the mimicry and random movement conditions in perceived similarity toward the remote user, pairwise comparisons also showed that only mimicry achieved a statistically significant difference from the static condition on the same outcome. These results suggest that movement matters, especially when movement mimics the partner's body orientation. This finding is similar to prior work in which an embodied agent mimicking the head movements of participants was reported as more persuasive and likable than an agent utilizing recorded movements [5]. However, the telepresence robots' mimicking behavior through the orientation of its frame may not be as high-fidelity a cue as an embodied agent's head movements, and true mimicry is hard to achieve through the bodily affordances of the robot, as would explain the limited differences between our two movement conditions. The telepresence robot's movements are limited because its head and body are connected into a single frame and do not move independently while the virtual agent can mimic three dimensions of the participants' head movements.

Participants in the movement conditions felt more similarity with a remote user than participants in the static condition, and perceived similarity is known to be one of the strong predictors of liking toward the communicative partner [2, 18, 25]. It is possible that participants perceived the robot's subtle motions, regardless of coordination, as reflecting engagement and responsiveness in the interaction. Future research should develop a more detailed mapping between the space of possible robot movements and how they shape local users' perceptions of the remote user. Such investigation will require extending the investigation to other telepresence robot platforms with additional affordances for bodily expression.

Individual Differences Matter

One of the important goals of this study was to examine the role of individual differences in building rapport in conjunction with the movements of a telepresence robot. Our study found differences in the effects of movement related to self-monitoring and gender, both of which may influence participants' orientation toward building relationships with their partner. We observed the effect of robot movements on perceived similarity is moderated by participants' level of self-monitoring. In both movement conditions, high self-monitors perceived more similarity with a remote user than low self-monitors, although this increase in similarity was significant only in the random movement condition. In the static condition, similarity ratings significantly decreased as levels of self-monitoring increased. Consistent with prior work, this finding suggests that high self-monitors pay close attention to nonverbal processes in forming impressions of their partners. In the absence of the robot's movement, high self-monitors felt less similar to their partner than low self-monitors did, as underlined by negative relationship between perceived similarity and self-monitoring observed in the data from the static condition. It is unclear based on our findings whether the robot's movement itself led to higher perceived homophily among high self-monitors or whether high self-monitors actually accommodated to the robot's movement by imitating it themselves, generating homophily through their own imitation. It will be essential for future research to further explore the mechanisms of how self-monitoring shapes perceptions of movement in robot-mediated communication. In this study, we did not find an interaction effect between self-monitoring and the experimental conditions on perceived closeness. Perhaps the robots' movements can shape the perception of similarity among high self-monitors but a five-minute interaction is too short for them to establish closeness.

The present study also found a moderating effect of gender on perceived closeness. While some prior research has suggested that females have an advantage in interpreting nonverbal behavior [8, 20], our results show that, in fact, it was only among men that robot movement amplified feelings of closeness to the remote partner. For women, feeling of closeness was lower in the movement conditions than in the static condition, although these differences did not achieve statistical significance. Additional processes may therefore be at play. First, given that we used the same female confederate in all interactions, it is possible that our results reflect that same-gender or mixed-gender dyads were formed for female and male participants, respectively. The interpretation of the robot's movement may change depending on the gender composition of the dyad, with movement perhaps suggesting romantic interest from an opposite sex partner, as has been found in prior research in a face-to-face context [27]. Another possibility is that females tried to focus on the actual person operating the robot (i.e., through the video feed) and found the relatively unnatural movements of the robot distracting [49], whereas males may have been more attentive to the behaviors conveyed by the embodiment. The potential mechanisms of the observed gender effect should be tested in future research. For instance, adding a male confederate would also allow us to investigate the hypothesis that males' positive response to mimicry is specific to the context of a gender-mixed dyad. The moderating effect of gender, however, was not observed on perceived similarity. Across females and males, participants felt more similarity with a remote user when communicating over a moving robot compared to when communicating over a static robot. Perhaps similarity is a more gender-neutral concept compared to closeness to the partner which could be more directly associated with interpersonal attraction.

Design implications

Our findings suggest that an embodied telepresence robot's physical movements have a positive influence on interpersonal outcomes. According to our findings, whether the robot moved in accordance with the local user or not did not make a big difference. This finding suggests that enabling even general, uncoordinated movements during interactions can enhance interpersonal processes. Such subtle movements can also be easily automated and utilized in interaction without any burden on the remote user. Additionally, while this study did not find an effect specific to mimicry, we speculate that this is at least partly because of the limited motions available with the current telepresence robot systems. We therefore highlight the need for designing telepresence robot systems with a broader range of bodily cues and capabilities for movement. For example, enabling independent head movements can avoid whole body orientations that may be distracting during interactions.

Limitations

As with any single experiment, our study has several limitations. First, while we used a state-of-the-art, high-end telepresence robot system designed for professional use, the system had a limited repertoire of movements (orienting or moving forward, backward, left, or right). These possible movements can only roughly approximate the substantially richer and subtler human body motions (e.g., shaking a hand, shrugging, fidgeting, leaning). Furthermore, the delay between participant movements and the robot movements, introduced by a combination of operator response time, network latency, and robot actuation delays, may have affected perceptions of the mimicked movement. However, our qualitative observations suggest that this delay was not noticeably different from delays and variability that naturally occur in face-to-face nonverbal mimicry. Nonetheless, even given this limited repertoire and our small sample size, we were able to identify effects of movement on similarity and closeness. A second limitation of this study is that, during the interactions, the communicating confederate viewed a video feed of the participant from the perspective of the camera mounted on the telepresence robot, and therefore she could have herself been influenced by the robot's movement. With that said, the robot's motions tended to be subtle and, given that the operating experimenter moved the robot, the conditions were experienced very similarly by the communicating confederate, limiting the possibility of experimenter effects.

Future Directions

Our results suggest promising areas for future research. First, our study highlights the important role individual differences play in perceptions of movement in robot-mediated communication. We also know from prior mimicry literature that orientation to relationship building can be affected by social roles and situational factors. For instance, individuals are inclined to engage in mimicry when interacting with higher status individuals since they may have more to gain through creating positive impressions [4]. Research also suggests that equivocal situations call for availability of a greater range of cues [11], as do situations involving exchange of affective information [28, 48]. Mimicry might have a particularly important role for interactions that are even more affectively charged than those presented here, such as in interactions with close others. Future research is necessary to understand how the nonverbal movements of embodied communication technologies shape the perception of others in different relational communication contexts.

While we found encouraging effects of embodied movement on perceptions of the partner, our study design did not compare these effects to those of nonverbal behaviors found in face-to-face communication. Relatedly, we also do not know, based on our study, the effects that on-camera mimicry (e.g., of facial expressions) might have had on the studied processes. Because on-camera mimicry should have been consistent across conditions, we only know that embodied movement had additional, independent effects. Future research may examine the relative strength of movement and mimicry via the video feed versus the embodied movements of the telepresence robot and may compare these effects to face-to-face mimicry.

CONCLUSION

Nonverbal behaviors are essential cues that shape interpersonal communication, and their importance in computer-mediated communication and robot-mediated communication has been highlighted by prior research. The results from this study advance our understanding the role movement and mimicry play in robot-mediated communication. The present study shows that individuals build positive perceptions of a distant partner communicating through a telepresence robot, which makes slight movements during the interaction, and these effects are similar whether or not movements mimic the partner's body orientation. Furthermore effects of movement are moderated by individual characteristics. We conclude that even with limited cues available with the present telepresence robot systems, nonverbal behaviors play an important role in robot-mediated communication. Our study sheds light on our theoretical understanding of nonverbal processes via telepresence robots and offers implications for the future design of communication technologies through a more detailed understanding of user experience with movement as a design element.

ACKNOWLEDGMENTS

We would like to thank Olivia Zhao, Faye Golden, and Erica Lewis for their help with conducting the study, National Science Foundation for financial support under award #1117652, and Suitable Technologies, Inc. for the loan of the Beam Pro telepresence robot system.

REFERENCES

1. Sigurdur O Adalgeirsson and Cynthia Breazeal. 2010. MeBot: a robotic platform for socially embodied presence. In *Proceedings of the 5th ACM/IEEE international conference on Human-robot interaction*. IEEE Press, 15–22.
2. David M Amodio and Carolin J Showers. 2005. 'Similarity breeds liking'revisited: The moderating role of commitment. *Journal of Social and Personal Relationships* 22, 6 (2005), 817–836.
3. Arthur Aron, Elaine N Aron, and Danny Smollan. 1992. Inclusion of Other in the Self Scale and the structure of interpersonal closeness. *Journal of personality and social psychology* 63, 4 (1992), 596–612.
4. Claire E Ashton-James and Ana Levordashka. 2013. When the Wolf Wears Sheep's Clothing Individual Differences in the Desire to be Liked Influence Nonconscious Behavioral Mimicry. *Social Psychological and Personality Science* 4, 6 (2013), 643–648.
5. Jeremy N Bailenson and Nick Yee. 2005. Digital chameleons automatic assimilation of nonverbal gestures in immersive virtual environments. *Psychological science* 16, 10 (2005), 814–819.
6. Frank J Bernieri. 2005. The expression of rapport. *The sourcebook of nonverbal measures: Going beyond words* (2005), 347–359.
7. Mary Klein Buller and David B Buller. 1987. Physicians' communication style and patient satisfaction. *Journal of health and social Behavior* (1987), 375–388.
8. Linda L. Carli, Suzanne J. LaFleur, and Christopher C. Loeber. 1995. Nonverbal behavior, gender, and influence. *Journal of personality and social psychology* 68, 6 (1995), 1030–1041.
9. Tanya L Chartrand and John A Bargh. 1999. The chameleon effect: The perception–behavior link and social interaction. *Journal of personality and social psychology* 76, 6 (1999), 893–910.
10. Tanya L Chartrand and Rick Van Baaren. 2009. Human mimicry. *Advances in experimental social psychology* 41 (2009), 219–274.
11. M Robin DiMatteo. 1979. A social-psychological analysis of physician-patient rapport: Toward a science of the art of medicine. *Journal of Social Issues* 35, 1 (1979), 12–33.
12. Ulf Dimberg and Lars-Olov Lundquist. 1990. Gender differences in facial reactions to facial expressions. *Biological psychology* 30, 2 (1990), 151–159.
13. P Duggan and L Parrott. 2001. Physicians' nonverbal rapport building and patients' talk about the subjective component of illness. *Human Communication Research* 27, 2 (2001), 299–311.
14. Alice H Eagly. 2013. *Sex differences in social behavior: A social-role interpretation*. Psychology Press.
15. Hall Edward and others. 1966. The hidden dimension. *Doubleday, Garden City* 14 (1966), 103–124.

16. Sarah Estow, Jeremy P Jamieson, and Jennifer R Yates. 2007. Self-monitoring and mimicry of positive and negative social behaviors. *Journal of Research in Personality* 41, 2 (2007), 425–433.

17. Deborah I Fels, Judith K Waalen, Shumin Zhai, and P Weiss. 2001. Telepresence under exceptional circumstances: Enriching the connection to school for sick children. In *Proceedings of the IFIP TC13 Interact '01*. 617–624.

18. Andrew T Fiore and Judith S Donath. 2005. Homophily in online dating: when do you like someone like yourself?. In *CHI'05 Extended Abstracts on Human Factors in Computing Systems*. ACM, 1371–1374.

19. Mark G Frank and Thomas Gilovich. 1989. Effect of memory perspective on retrospective causal attributions. *Journal of personality and social psychology* 57, 3 (1989), 399–403.

20. Robert Gifford. 1994. A lens-mapping framework for understanding the encoding and decoding of interpersonal dispositions in nonverbal behavior. *Journal of Personality and Social Psychology* 66, 2 (1994), 398.

21. Amy L Gonzales, Jeffrey T Hancock, and James W Pennebaker. 2009. Language style matching as a predictor of social dynamics in small groups. *Communication Research* (2009), 1–17.

22. Nicolas Guéguen, Angélique Martin, and Sébastien Meineri. 2011. Mimicry and helping behavior: An evaluation of mimicry on explicit helping request. *The Journal of Social Psychology* 151, 1 (2011), 1–4.

23. Susan C Herring. 2000. Gender differences in CMC: Findings and implications. *Computer Professionals for Social Responsibility Journal* 18, 1 (2000), 0.

24. Cecilia Heyes. 2011. Automatic imitation. *Psychological bulletin* 137, 3 (2011), 463–483.

25. Ted L Huston and George Levinger. 1978. Interpersonal attraction and relationships. *Annual review of psychology* 29, 1 (1978), 115–156.

26. Steven Johnson, Irene Rae, Bilge Mutlu, and Leila Takayama. 2015. Can you see me now?: How field of view affects collaboration in robotic telepresence. In *Proceedings of the 33rd Annual ACM Conference on Human Factors in Computing Systems*. ACM, 2397–2406.

27. Johan C Karremans and Thijs Verwijmeren. 2008. Mimicking attractive opposite-sex others: The role of romantic relationship status. *Personality and Social Psychology Bulletin* (2008), 1–12.

28. Ronald C Kessler and Jane D McLeod. 1984. Sex differences in vulnerability to undesirable life events. *American sociological review* (1984), 620–631.

29. Annica Kristoffersson, Silvia Coradeschi, and Amy Loutfi. 2013. A Review of Mobile Robotic Telepresence. *Advances in Human-Computer Interaction* 2013, Article 3 (Jan. 2013), 1 pages.

30. Annica Kristoffersson, Silvia Coradeschi, Amy Loutfi, and Kerstin Severinson-Eklundh. 2014. Assessment of interaction quality in mobile robotic telepresence: An elderly perspective. *Interaction Studies* 15, 2 (2014), 343–357.

31. Annica Kristoffersson, Kerstin Severinson Eklundh, and Amy Loutfi. 2013. Measuring the quality of interaction in mobile robotic telepresence: A pilot's perspective. *International Journal of Social Robotics* 5, 1 (2013), 89–101.

32. Wojciech Kulesza, Zofia Szypowska, Matthew S Jarman, and Dariusz Dolinski. 2014. Attractive Chameleons Sell: The Mimicry-Attractiveness Link. *Psychology & Marketing* 31, 7 (2014), 549–561.

33. Hideaki Kuzuoka, Yuya Suzuki, Jun Yamashita, and Keiichi Yamazaki. 2010. Reconfiguring Spatial Formation Arrangement by Robot Body Orientation. In *Proceedings of the 5th ACM/IEEE International Conference on Human-robot Interaction (HRI '10)*. IEEE Press, Piscataway, NJ, USA, 285–292.

34. Jessica L Lakin, Valerie E Jefferis, Clara Michelle Cheng, and Tanya L Chartrand. 2003. The chameleon effect as social glue: Evidence for the evolutionary significance of nonconscious mimicry. *Journal of nonverbal behavior* 27, 3 (2003), 145–162.

35. Mathis Lauckner, Dejan Pangercic, and Serkan Tuerker. 2015. Evaluation of a Mobile Robotic Telepresence System in a One-on-One Meeting Scenario. In *Proceedings of the Tenth Annual ACM/IEEE International Conference on Human-Robot Interaction Extended Abstracts*. ACM, 57–58.

36. Min Kyung Lee and Leila Takayama. 2011. Now, I have a body: Uses and social norms for mobile remote presence in the workplace. In *Proceedings of the SIGCHI Conference on Human Factors in Computing Systems*. ACM, 33–42.

37. Tamara Lorenz, Astrid Weiss, and Sandra Hirche. 2016. Synchrony and Reciprocity: Key Mechanisms for Social Companion Robots in Therapy and Care. *International Journal of Social Robotics* 8, 1 (2016), 125–143.

38. James C McCroskey, Virginia P Richmond, and John A Daly. 1975. The development of a measure of perceived homophily in interpersonal communication. *Human Communication Research* 1, 4 (1975), 323–332.

39. Hideyuki Nakanishi, Yuki Murakami, Daisuke Nogami, and Hiroshi Ishiguro. 2008. Minimum movement matters: impact of robot-mounted cameras on social telepresence. In *Proceedings of the 2008 ACM conference on Computer supported cooperative work*. ACM, 303–312.

40. Carman Neustaedter, Gina Venolia, Jason Procyk, and Daniel Hawkins. 2016. To Beam or not to Beam: A study of remote telepresence attendance at an academic conference. In *Proceedings of the 19th ACM Conference on Computer-Supported Cooperative Work & Social Computing*. ACM, 418–431.

41. A Pentland, J Curhan, R Khilnani, M Martin, N Eagle, R Caneel, and A Madan. 2004. A negotiation advisor. In *ACM Symposium on User Interface Software and Technology*. Citeseer.
42. Tal-Chen Rabinowitch and Ariel Knafo-Noam. 2015. Synchronous rhythmic interaction enhances children's perceived similarity and closeness towards each other. *PloS one* 10, 4 (2015), e0120878.
43. Irene Rae, Bilge Mutlu, and Leila Takayama. 2014. Bodies in motion: mobility, presence, and task awareness in telepresence. In *Proceedings of the 32nd annual ACM conference on Human factors in computing systems*. ACM, 2153–2162.
44. Irene Rae, Leila Takayama, and Bilge Mutlu. 2012. One of the gang: supporting in-group behavior for embodied mediated communication. In *Proceedings of the SIGCHI Conference on Human Factors in Computing Systems*. ACM, 3091–3100.
45. Irene Rae, Leila Takayama, and Bilge Mutlu. 2013a. In-body experiences: embodiment, control, and trust in robot-mediated communication. In *Proceedings of the SIGCHI Conference on Human Factors in Computing Systems*. ACM, 1921–1930.
46. Irene Rae, Leila Takayama, and Bilge Mutlu. 2013b. The influence of height in robot-mediated communication. In *Proceedings of the 8th ACM/IEEE international conference on Human-robot interaction*. IEEE Press, 1–8.
47. Lauren E Scissors, Alastair J Gill, and Darren Gergle. 2008. Linguistic mimicry and trust in text-based CMC. In *Proceedings of the 2008 ACM conference on Computer supported cooperative work*. ACM, 277–280.
48. John Short, Ederyn Williams, and Bruce Christie. 1976. The social psychology of telecommunications. (1976).
49. David Sirkin and Wendy Ju. 2012. Consistency in Physical and On-screen Action Improves Perceptions of Telepresence Robots. In *Proceedings of the Seventh Annual ACM/IEEE International Conference on Human-Robot Interaction (HRI '12)*. ACM, New York, NY, USA, 57–64.
50. David Sirkin, Gina Venolia, John Tang, George Robertson, Taemie Kim, Kori Inkpen, Mara Sedlins, Bongshin Lee, and Mike Sinclair. 2011. Motion and attention in a kinetic videoconferencing proxy. In *IFIP Conference on Human-Computer Interaction*. Springer, 162–180.
51. Mark Snyder. 1974. Self-monitoring of expressive behavior. *Journal of personality and social psychology* 30, 4 (1974), 526–537.
52. Mark Snyder. 1987. *Public appearances, private realities: The psychology of self-monitoring*. WH Freeman/Times Books/Henry Holt & Co.
53. Susan Sprecher, Stanislav Treger, Joshua D Wondra, Nicole Hilaire, and Kevin Wallpe. 2013. Taking turns: Reciprocal self-disclosure promotes liking in initial interactions. *Journal of Experimental Social Psychology* 49, 5 (2013), 860–866.
54. Ralph M Stogdill. 1948. Personal factors associated with leadership: A survey of the literature. *The Journal of psychology* 25, 1 (1948), 35–71.
55. Leila Takayama. 2015. Telepresence and Apparent Agency in Human–Robot Interaction. *The Handbook of the Psychology of Communication Technology* (2015), 160–175.
56. Leila Takayama and Janet Go. 2012. Mixing metaphors in mobile remote presence. In *Proceedings of the ACM 2012 conference on Computer Supported Cooperative Work*. ACM, 495–504.
57. Linda Tickle-Degnen and Robert Rosenthal. 1990. The nature of rapport and its nonverbal correlates. *Psychological inquiry* 1, 4 (1990), 285–293.
58. Katherine M Tsui, Munjal Desai, Holly A Yanco, and Chris Uhlik. 2011. Exploring use cases for telepresence robots. In *2011 6th ACM/IEEE International Conference on Human-Robot Interaction (HRI)*. IEEE, 11–18.
59. Katherine M Tsui, Adam Norton, Daniel J Brooks, Eric McCann, Mikhail S Medvedev, Jordan Allspaw, Sompop Suksawat, James M Dalphond, Michael Lunderville, and Holly A Yanco. 2014. Iterative design of a semi-autonomous social telepresence robot research platform: a chronology. *Intelligent Service Robotics* 7, 2 (2014), 103–119.
60. Piercarlo Valdesolo and David DeSteno. 2011. Synchrony and the social tuning of compassion. *Emotion* 11, 2 (2011), 262–266.
61. John Venn. 1880. I. On the diagrammatic and mechanical representation of propositions and reasonings. *The London, Edinburgh, and Dublin Philosophical Magazine and Journal of Science* 10, 59 (1880), 1–18.
62. Frank MF Verberne, Jaap Ham, Aditya Ponnada, and Cees JH Midden. 2013. Trusting digital chameleons: The effect of mimicry by a virtual social agent on user trust. In *International Conference on Persuasive Technology*. Springer, 234–245.
63. Steve Whittaker, David Frohlich, and Owen Daly-Jones. 1994. Informal workplace communication: What is it like and how might we support it?. In *Proceedings of the SIGCHI conference on Human factors in computing systems*. ACM, 131–137.
64. Barbara Wild, Michael Erb, and Mathias Bartels. 2001. Are emotions contagious? Evoked emotions while viewing emotionally expressive faces: quality, quantity, time course and gender differences. *Psychiatry research* 102, 2 (2001), 109–124.
65. Nick Yee and Jeremy Bailenson. 2007. The Proteus effect: The effect of transformed self-representation on behavior. *Human communication research* 33, 3 (2007), 271–290.
66. Thomas J Young and Laurence A French. 1996. Height and perceived competence of US presidents. *Perceptual and Motor Skills* 82, 3 (1996), 1002–1002.

A Simple Nod of the Head: The Effect of Minimal Robot Movements on Children's Perception of a Low-Anthropomorphic Robot

Cristina Zaga, Roelof A.J. de Vries, Jamy Li, Khiet P. Truong, Vanessa Evers
Human Media Interaction, University of Twente, Enschede, The Netherlands
{c.zaga, r.a.j.devries, j.j.li, k.p.truong, v.evers}@utwente.nl

ABSTRACT
In this note, we present minimal robot movements for robotic technology for children. Two types of minimal gaze movements were designed: *social-gaze movements* to communicate social engagement and *deictic-gaze movements* to communicate task-related referential information. In a two (social-gaze movements vs. none) by two (deictic-gaze movements vs. none) video-based study (n=72), we found that social-gaze movements significantly increased children's perception of animacy and likeability of the robot. Deictic-gaze and social-gaze movements significantly increased children's perception of helpfulness. Our findings show the compelling communicative power of social-gaze movements, and to a lesser extent deictic-gaze movements, and have implications for designers who want to achieve animacy, likeability and helpfulness with simple and easily implementable minimal robot movements. Our work contributes to human-robot interaction research and design by providing a first indication of the potential of minimal robot movements to communicate social engagement and helpful referential information to children.

ACM Classification Keywords
H.5.2. User Interfaces (e.g. HCI): Prototyping-User-centered design

Author Keywords
human-robot interaction design; non-anthropomorphic robot; children; nonverbal communication; robot behavior

INTRODUCTION AND RELATED WORK
In many classrooms, children's rooms and playgrounds, we are starting to find robotic products designed to interact with children. Research has shown that robots hold tremendous promise for children's education and socio-emotional development [8, 9, 12, 14, 17, 21, 29] paving the way not only for research, but also for consumer robots for children. While the application domains vary – from educational learning like the Dash and Dot Robots[1] to child therapy with the Leka Robot[2] – common attributes of these robotic products are simple aesthetics, minimal actuation, and nonverbal communication.

Robots designed for children that do not fall in the classic humanoid shape and that rely on nonverbal behavior have clear design advantages: (i) children's expectations of interaction [39] are minimized (e.g., a humanoid face might raise the expectation that the robot is able to understand and produce natural language which is often not the case [41]), (ii) robustness and reliability of the robotic system *in the wild* is maximized (e.g., robot-limb-based locomotion can be complex and is rarely reliable outside laboratory and industrial settings), and (iii) the Uncanny Valley effect is avoided [24, 35]. However, limiting the anthropomorphic robot appearance and reducing the range of communicative modalities available has the disadvantage of leaving interaction designers with fewer degrees of freedom to work with to design robot behaviors. Increasingly, a solution to this disadvantage is to carefully design nonverbal behavior that *'buys the designer valuable expressive power of which other aspects of the robot's design can be relieved'* [13].

Researchers have been exploring design solutions for nonverbal communication of low and non-anthropomorphic robots by focusing on body movements, gaze and other nonverbal behaviors. Body movements and locomotion enable low-anthropomorphic robots to communicate their intentions, internal states, and emotions, contributing to people's comprehension and acceptance of the robot [13, 18, 19]. The importance of a robot's *movements* has been shown by Takayama et al. [36], who demonstrated that by adding simple movements displaying forethought and reaction, the readability and fluency of human-robot interaction were increased. In a similar vein, Sirkin et al. [32] unveiled how robot movements alone are sufficient to convey intention and coordination of joint actions. Fink et al. [10] evaluated the interplay between reactive and proactive engagement-seeking movements, sounds and lights for a robotic toy box to motivate young children to tidy up their room. Interestingly, the proactive nonverbal behaviors were less effective than the reactive ones, distracting the children

CHI 2017, May 06–11, 2017, Denver, CO, USA
© 2017 ACM ISBN 978-1-4503-4655-9/17/05...$15.00
DOI: http://dx.doi.org/10.1145/3025453.3025995

[1]https://store.makewonder.com/
[2]https://www.indiegogo.com/projects/leka-an-exceptional-toy-for-exceptional-children-autism#/

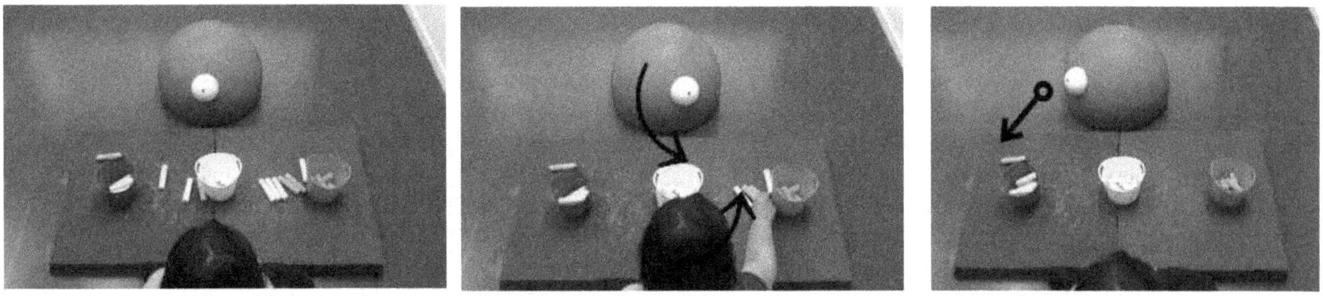

a) b) c)

Figure 1. Figure a) the robot and the actor at the beginning of the sorting task; b) the robot exhibiting social-gaze movement towards the actor; c) the robot exhibiting deictic-gaze movement to provide helpful referential information.

from the tidying up activity. *Gaze* is a powerful nonverbal behavior that greatly supports human-agent interaction [2, 6, 11, 25]. Even though eye gaze and head gaze can be challenging to realize in robots without a clearly distinguishable head and actuated eyes, there is evidence that the communicative power of gaze can also be achieved in low-anthropomorphic robots. For example, results on the role of affiliative and referential gaze from literature on virtual agents [3] can be reproduced in non-humanoid robots. In fact, Lehmann et al. [20] showed that low-anthropomorphic robot's gaze-shift-like movements synchronized with a user's movements positively shaped the interaction in an object-oriented task.

However, two crucial open questions for interaction designers are *how* to design nonverbal robot behavior for low-anthropomorphic robots and what *effect* the robot's behavior will have on the user's perception of the robot. This holds particular importance in child-robot interactions (cHRI), as children bring unique challenges related to the attribution of agency and perception of interaction affordances [16, 37].

In our research, we address the challenge of designing appropriate nonverbal behavior for cHRI. We explore how a low-anthropomorphic robot can communicate social engagement and task-related referential information during a playful joint activity, thereby communicating as a life-like goal-directed agent, a prerequisite in these kind of interactions [27, 38]. The communication is achieved relying only on minimal movements of the robot's whole body (i.e., rotation of the base of the robot) which are simple, technologically not costly and easily implementable. To this end, we designed *social-gaze movements*, synchronous movements shifting toward the interaction partner. To provide helpful task-related referential information, we designed *deictic-gaze movements* shifting the robot's body orientation to an object of interest for the task.

We evaluated the legibility of the minimal movements and children's perception of animacy, likeability and helpfulness of the robot's behavior in a video-based study (VHRI). Animacy is one of the crucial features in children's robot perception [7, 26], as it is a prerequisite to attribute states and qualities to a robot and it maps onto concepts of agency and perceptual causality, which are key concepts in children's perception of agents [1, 26, 27]. Discerning how social-gaze movements and deictic-gaze movements affect children's perception of **animacy** is important to assess the viability of using minimal movements. We measured **likeability** of the robot because positive impressions (e.g., kind, friendly) are important aspects in robot design for children [4, 5]. We measured **helpfulness** since we want to know how our minimally designed social and deictic-gaze movements shape children's perception of helpfulness. Drawing from literature [3, 20], we expect that,
H1: Minimal robot movement resembling social gaze will increase children's perception of animacy (H1a) and likeability (H1b) of the robot.
H2: Minimal robot movement resembling deictic gaze will increase children's perception of helpfulness (H2a) of the robot, and will increase the effect of children's perception of social-gaze movements on animacy (H2b) and likeability (H2c) of the robot.

MINIMAL ROBOT MOVEMENTS: DESIGN AND EVALUATION METHOD

From a methodological perspective, our research follows a combination of human-robot interaction (HRI) design methodologies that has been shown to yields impactful findings [13, 31, 33] also with our population [26]. Our research focus is on designing minimal communicative robot movements during joint activities (e.g., playing together). Our approach is to evaluate our designs in video-based studies and follow-up with *in-person* and *in-situ* behavioral studies. In this note, we present our VHRI study, wherein we exposed children to videos of a robot's social-gaze and deictic-gaze movements to evaluate children's perceptions of animacy, likeability and helpfulness of the robot's behavior. To test our hypotheses, we conducted a two (social-gaze movements vs. none) by two (deictic-gaze movements vs. none) between-subjects video experiment. For each condition, we recorded a movie slightly over one minute in length. In the video, a female actor sits in front of a grey mat where colored chalks were (seemingly) randomly scattered next to three colored baskets (Figure 1a). The robot is positioned on the opposite side of the mat facing the actor and it was controlled remotely by another researcher. We chose the same camera perspective as [20], i.e., over-the-shoulder of the actor (only arms and back of the head visible) to minimize the 3rd person perspective [30]. We asked each participant to watch the movie and to respond to an online questionnaire on SurveyMonkey[3] administered via tablet computers.

[3]https://www.surveymonkey.com/

Robot, scenario and minimal movements design

The robot used is a Festo Robotino[4], a mobile robotic system with three omnidirectional wheels. The robot is covered with a low-fidelity Styrofoam semi-spherical shell. The only anthropomorphic element is a white sphere with a black dot that resembles an eye, not actuated. The robot only rotated (1 degree of freedom).

In our scenario, the robot interacted with an actor during a simple sorting task, i.e., sorting chalks by color. As the robot could not fully participate in the object manipulation task (it does not have arms or grippers), we framed its role as a reactive, but engaged co-player. The robot exhibited social engagement by attentively following the co-player's actions (i.e., social-gaze movements) and provided helpful referential information for the completion of the task (i.e., deictic gaze), by *'pointing'* at the location of the last missing chalk outside the co-player's field of vision.

The design of the robot's minimal movements is derived from virtual agents' and robot's gaze literature [3, 20] and follows principles of animacy [16, 27]. To design social-gaze and deictic-gaze movements, we used solely motion. The minimal robot movements consist of lateral shifts of its base, adapted to the degree of freedom of the robot. The resulting robot behaviors included whole-body (i.e., robot base) shifts (right or left) within an angle of 30 degrees to maximum 120 degrees. Social-gaze movements are devised as robot base shifts aligned to the actor and following face and body orientation of the actor throughout the task (i.e., looking where the actor is looking). The social-gaze shifts start with a minimal latency when the actor moves her head or arm. They are timed to be positively synchronous and they are contingent on the actor's actions (i.e., robot follows the movements and actions of the actor, generating the impression of being socially engaged). Deictic-gaze movements are devised as robot base shifts oriented towards an object. In our case, the robot points once towards the last chalk at the end of each sorting task session (Figure 1b, 1c).

Participants

The study was conducted with 72 participants recruited among 4 classes coming from international elementary schools in Manchester (UK) and Hengelo (NL), where the language of instruction is English. Their age ranged between 8 and 12 years (M = 9.63, SD = .95, $Median$ = 10); 55.6% of the participants were female (N = 40, M = 9.75, SD = .92, $Median$ = 10) and 44.4% was male (N = 32, M = 9.47, SD = .98, $Median$ = 9). 81% of the participants had seen a robot in real life before and 55.6% reported to have played at least once with a robot.

Independent variables

We manipulated social-gaze movements and deictic-gaze movements of the robot between subjects. The resulting conditions are: (i) *social and deictic-gaze movements condition* (i.e., the robot exhibited social-gaze movements since the beginning of the sorting task and the deictic-gaze movements only to indicate where the missing chalk is); (ii) *social-gaze movements condition* (i.e., the robot exhibited social-gaze movements from the beginning of the sorting task and does not exhibit deictic-gaze movements to indicate the missing chalk); (iii) *deictic-gaze movements condition* (i.e., the robot only *'pointed'* at the missing chalk) and (iv) *static condition* (i.e., no social nor deictic-gaze movements).

[4] http://www.festo-didactic.com/int-en/services/robotino/

Manipulation and legibility check

To check the manipulation of social-gaze and deictic-gaze movements a single multiple choice item (i.e., a factual question about how the children understood the robot's behavior) was inserted. This question also allowed us to assess the legibility of the robot's behavior in the scenario. The item was: *What do you think the robot was doing? a) The robot was only pointing at the missing chalk, b) The robot was following what the person was doing and pointing at the missing chalk, c) The robot was standing still doing nothing with the person, d) The robot was only following what the person was doing*. The manipulation was successful and the legibility of the robot's behavior satisfactory. Participants were able to correctly recognize the actions underlying the robot's minimal gaze movements above chance ($\chi^2(d = 9) = 145.166$, $p < .001$).

Dependent variables

We measured perception of animacy and likeability with three items for each construct (both constructs reach high reliability, Cronbach's alpha animacy = .77, and likeability = .88) of the corresponding dimension of the Godspeed questionnaire [4], an HRI validated measure of participants' perceptions in a semantic scale. We designed a 5-point Smiley-o-meter [28] scale item like [22] (*How helpful do you think the robot was*) anchored from *Not helpful at all* to *Very Helpful* to assess the perception of helpfulness of the robot.

Setup and procedure

Participants received a brief introduction, thereafter they were randomly assigned to one of four experimental conditions, which resulted in sub-sample sizes of n = 17 for social and deictic-gaze movements, n = 19 for social-gaze movements, n = 19 for deictic-gaze movements, and n = 17 for the static condition. Each participant sat at a table equipped with a tablet, i.e., Apple iPad, with the browser open on the questionnaire page. An activity facilitator was instructed to support the participants in case of problems and to debrief them upon completion of the questionnaire.

RESULTS AND DISCUSSION

A two-way analysis of variance (ANOVA) was conducted to evaluate the effects of social-gaze and deictic-gaze movements on children's perception of animacy, likeability and helpfulness of the robot.

Perception of animacy

The results of perception of animacy of the robot support H1a, but they partially support H2b. We found an interaction effect of social and deictic-gaze movements on the perceived animacy of the robot ($F(1,68) = 7.168$, $p = .009$, $\eta^2 = .005$). Simple effect analysis of social-gaze movements shows that social-gaze movements play a great role in the perception of the robot as '*life-like*' and '*socially engaged*'. Social-gaze movements significantly ($F(1,58)$, $p < .001, \eta^2 = .042$) contribute to the perception of animacy both in combination with deictic-gaze movements (M = 3.75, SD = 0.68) or not (M = 3.68, SD = 0.64). However, simple effect analysis of deictic-gaze movements show that they do not play a significant role in the perception of animacy (i.e., no significant difference).

Perception of likeability

The results for perceived likeability support H1b, but not H2c. We found no interaction effect of social-gaze and deictic-gaze movements on perceived likeability of the robot. We found that social-gaze movements ($F(1,68) = 4.847$, $p = .031$, $\eta^2 = .06$) had a main effect on the perceived likeability of the robot, which significantly increased (social gaze: $M = 4.17$, $CI[3.922-4.409]$; no social gaze: $M = 3.79$, $CI[3.542-4.029]$), while deictic-gaze movement did not have an effect on likeability, even though deictic-gaze movements were expected to contribute to the perception of likeability by delivering referential information in the task.

Perception of Helpfulness

The results of perceived helpfulness support H2a, but present an additional result. We found no interaction effect of social-gaze and deictic-gaze movements on perceived helpfulness. From main effect analysis though, deictic-gaze movements (hypothesized) and social-gaze movements (not hypothesized) both had a main effect and increased the perception of helpfulness of the robot (social gaze; $F(1) = 43.811$, $p < .000$, $\eta^2 = .33$ no deictic gaze: $M = 2.90$, $CI[2.637-3.156]$, deictic gaze: $M = 4.12$, $CI[3.855-4.374]$, deictic gaze; ($F(1) = 5.427$, $p = .023$, $\eta^2 = .004$ no social gaze: $M = 3.29$, $CI[3.031-3.551]$, social gaze: $M = 3.72$, $CI[3.406-3.908]$). From pairwise comparison and estimates analysis, we found that deictic-gaze movements are fundamental to perceive the robot as helpful, but it is when deictic-gaze and social-gaze movements are combined that perceived helpfulness increases the most (i.e., yields the highest rating for perceived helpfulness, $M = 4.12$, $CI[3.855-4.374]$).

CONCLUSION, LIMITATIONS AND FUTURE WORK

In this note, we explored the design of minimal robot movements resembling social and deictic gaze and we evaluated how they affect children's perception of animacy, likeability and helpfulness of the robot's behavior. We show that minimal robot social-gaze movements and deictic-gaze movements communicate social engagement and helpful referential information and affect children's perception of animacy, likeability and helpfulness. Specifically, we found that the perception of animacy and likeability significantly increases with social-gaze movements, but not with deictic-gaze movements. Although perception of helpfulness significantly increases with deictic-gaze movements, it is when both deictic and social-gaze movements are used that perceived helpfulness increases the most. Our results are relevant for interaction design and have design implications. In particular, social-gaze movements deliver social engagement in a task and have a compelling communicative power. They can be employed, alone or in combination with other minimal movements (in our case, deictic gaze), to achieve animacy and influence likeability of the robot. These movements potentially enable a set of easily implementable robot behaviors for low-anthropomorphic robots. Deictic-gaze movements deliver task-related referential information and affect the perception of helpfulness, but to reach the maximum effect on perception of helpfulness, designers should combine social and deictic-gaze movements. Moreover these findings lay the ground for *in-person* follow-up studies. Building upon our results, we will hone in to understand children's behavioral responses to social-gaze and deictic-gaze movements. Although adopting a VHRI method might pose some limitations (e.g., ecological validity and reliability of the results) [34], a large number of studies have shown that VHRI studies yield similar results as live HRI [20, 26, 33, 36, 40]. We chose a methodology that allowed us to address our hypotheses in a more controlled way. VHRI guaranteed uniformity of the stimuli and we can be relatively certain that the effects obtained are caused by our experimental variables and not by contextual factors, resulting in high internal validity. In addition, VHRI allowed us to reach a relatively large sample size, which is uncommon in cHRI [5]. Another potential drawback of the adopted VHRI is that participants did not experience a live robot, but a video from a 3rd person perspective [30]. Despite the fact that 3rd person and indirect interaction appear to yield reliable results in cHRI [26], we carefully mitigated 3rd person perspective drawbacks by using an over-the-shoulder camera view: participants were able to focus on the robot, not distracted by contextual information (e.g., actor's age, gender or ethnicity). This was also expected to address the limited immersiveness [15] of VHRI. We focused the scope of our VHRI study to our robot platform, but it is possible that our minimal movements can be adapted to other platforms by virtue of their practicality and simplicity for robot design. We focused on children, however, we imagine that adults could also respond to minimal robot movements in a similar manner, by virtue of the simplicity of the movements. We leave empirical evaluation of this as future work. Despite the fact that VHRI normally allows researchers to examine large design spaces with many variables, we investigated only a limited set of variables and measures that were instrumental to our investigation. We believe that this adds to a higher reliability of children's responses, as for children it is often hard to understand and differentiate between too many constructs [23].

To conclude, our work contributes to HRI and design literature by showing the potential of minimal robot movements to communicate social engagement and helpful referential information. In particular, social-gaze movements and to a lesser extent deictic-gaze movements, have compelling communicative power, positively affecting children's perception of animacy, likeability and contributing to the perception of helpfulness of the robot. Our results will strengthen future *in-situ* evaluations and *in-person* studies.

ACKNOWLEDGMENTS

This work is funded by EU FP7 SQUIRREL (Clearing Clutter Bit by Bit) grant number 610532. We thank the anonymous reviewers whose feedback was invaluable to improve our note.

REFERENCES

1. Edith K Ackermann. 2005. Playthings that do things: a young kid's incredibles!. In *Proceedings of the 2005 conference on Interaction design and children*. ACM, 1–8.
2. Sean Andrist, Bilge Mutlu, and Adriana Tapus. 2015. Look Like Me: Matching Robot Personality via Gaze to Increase Motivation. In *Proceedings of the 33rd Annual ACM Conference on Human Factors in Computing Systems (CHI '15)*. ACM, New York, NY, USA, 3603–3612. DOI:http://dx.doi.org/10.1145/2702123.2702592
3. Sean Andrist, Tomislav Pejsa, Bilge Mutlu, and Michael Gleicher. 2012. Designing Effective Gaze Mechanisms for Virtual Agents. In *Proceedings of the SIGCHI Conference on Human Factors in Computing Systems (CHI '12)*. ACM, New York, NY, USA, 705–714. DOI: http://dx.doi.org/10.1145/2207676.2207777
4. Christoph Bartneck, Elizabeth Croft, and Dana Kulic. 2009. Measurement instruments for the anthropomorphism, animacy, likeability, perceived intelligence, and perceived safety of robots. *International Journal of Social Robotics* 1, 1 (2009), 71–81. DOI: http://dx.doi.org/10.1007/s12369-008-0001-3
5. Tony Belpaeme, Paul Baxter, Joachim de Greeff, James Kennedy, Robin Read, Rosemarijn Looije, Mark Neerincx, Ilaria Baroni, and Mattia Coti Zelati. 2013. *Child-Robot Interaction: Perspectives and Challenges*. Springer International Publishing, Cham, 452–459. DOI: http://dx.doi.org/10.1007/978-3-319-02675-6_45
6. Allison Bruce, Illah Nourbakhsh, and Reid Simmons. 2002. The role of expressiveness and attention in human-robot interaction. In *Robotics and Automation, 2002. Proceedings. ICRA'02. IEEE International Conference on*, Vol. 4. IEEE, 4138–4142.
7. Álvaro Castro-González, Henny Admoni, and Brian Scassellati. 2016. Effects of form and motion on judgments of social robotsŒş animacy, likability, trustworthiness and unpleasantness. *International Journal of Human-Computer Studies* 90 (2016), 27–38.
8. David Feil-Seifer and Maja Mataric'. 2008. Robot-assisted Therapy for Children with Autism Spectrum Disorders. In *Proceedings of the 7th International Conference on Interaction Design and Children (IDC '08)*. ACM, New York, NY, USA, 49–52. DOI: http://dx.doi.org/10.1145/1463689.1463716
9. Ylva Fernaeus, Maria Håkansson, Mattias Jacobsson, and Sara Ljungblad. 2010. How Do You Play with a Robotic Toy Animal?: A Long-term Study of Pleo. In *Proceedings of the 9th International Conference on Interaction Design and Children (IDC '10)*. ACM, New York, NY, USA, 39–48. DOI: http://dx.doi.org/10.1145/1810543.1810549
10. Julia Fink, Séverin Lemaignan, Pierre Dillenbourg, Philippe Rétornaz, Florian Vaussard, Alain Berthoud, Francesco Mondada, Florian Wille, and Karmen Franinović. 2014. Which Robot Behavior Can Motivate Children to Tidy Up Their Toys?: Design and Evaluation of "Ranger". In *Proceedings of the 2014 ACM/IEEE International Conference on Human-robot Interaction (HRI '14)*. ACM, New York, NY, USA, 439–446. DOI:http://dx.doi.org/10.1145/2559636.2559659
11. Maia Garau, Mel Slater, Simon Bee, and Martina Angela Sasse. 2001. The Impact of Eye Gaze on Communication Using Humanoid Avatars. In *Proceedings of the SIGCHI Conference on Human Factors in Computing Systems (CHI '01)*. ACM, New York, NY, USA, 309–316. DOI:http://dx.doi.org/10.1145/365024.365121
12. Victor Girotto, Cecil Lozano, Kasia Muldner, Winslow Burleson, and Erin Walker. 2016. Lessons Learned from In-School Use of rTAG: A Robo-Tangible Learning Environment. In *Proceedings of the 2016 CHI Conference on Human Factors in Computing Systems (CHI '16)*. ACM, New York, NY, USA, 919–930. DOI: http://dx.doi.org/10.1145/2858036.2858454
13. Guy Hoffman and Wendy Ju. 2014. Designing robots with movement in mind. *Journal of Human-Robot Interaction* 3, 1 (2014), 89–122. DOI: http://dx.doi.org/10.5898/JHRI.3.1.Hoffman
14. Sooyeon Jeong, Kristopher Dos Santos, Suzanne Graca, Brianna O'Connell, Laurel Anderson, Nicole Stenquist, Katie Fitzpatrick, Honey Goodenough, Deirdre Logan, Peter Weinstock, and Cynthia Breazeal. 2015. Designing a Socially Assistive Robot for Pediatric Care. In *Proceedings of the 14th International Conference on Interaction Design and Children (IDC '15)*. ACM, New York, NY, USA, 387–390. DOI: http://dx.doi.org/10.1145/2771839.2771923
15. Carey Jewitt. 2012. An introduction to using video for research. (2012).
16. Susan C Johnson. 2003. Detecting agents. *Philosophical Transactions of the Royal Society B: Biological Sciences* 358, 1431 (2003), 549–559.
17. Peter H Kahn, Heather E Gary, and Solace Shen. 2013. Children's Social Relationships With Current and Near-Future Robots. *Child Development Perspectives* 7, 1 (2013), 32–37. DOI: http://dx.doi.org/10.1111/cdep.12011
18. Heather Knight and Reid Simmons. 2014. Expressive motion with x, y and theta: Laban effort features for mobile robots. In *The 23rd IEEE International Symposium on Robot and Human Interactive Communication*. IEEE, 267–273.
19. Heather Knight, Ravenna Thielstrom, and Reid Simmons. 2016. Expressive path shape (swagger): Simple features that illustrate a robot's attitude toward its goal in real time. In *Intelligent Robots and Systems (IROS), 2016 IEEE/RSJ International Conference on*. IEEE, 1475–1482.
20. Hagen Lehmann, Joan Saez-Pons, Dag Sverre Syrdal, and Kerstin Dautenhahn. 2015. In Good Company? Perception of Movement Synchrony of a Non-Anthropomorphic Robot. *PloS one* 10, 5 (2015), e0127747. DOI: http://dx.doi.org/10.1371/journal.pone.0127747
21. Daniel Leyzberg, Samuel Spaulding, Mariya Toneva, and Brian Scassellati. 2012. The physical presence of a robot tutor increases cognitive learning gains. (2012).
22. Manja Lohse, Niels van Berkel, Elisabeth MAG van Dijk, Michiel P Joosse, Daphne E Karreman, and Vanessa Evers. 2013. The influence of approach speed and functional noise on users' perception of a robot. In *2013 IEEE/RSJ International Conference on Intelligent Robots and Systems*. IEEE, 1670–1675.
23. Panos Markopoulos, Janet C Read, Stuart MacFarlane, and Johanna Hoysniemi. 2008. *Evaluating children's interactive products: principles and practices for interaction designers*. Morgan Kaufmann.
24. Masahiro Mori, Karl F MacDorman, and Norri Kageki. 2012. The uncanny valley [from the field]. *IEEE Robotics & Automation Magazine* 19, 2 (2012), 98–100.
25. Bilge Mutlu, Toshiyuki Shiwa, Takayuki Kanda, Hiroshi Ishiguro, and Norihiro Hagita. 2009. Footing in Human-robot Conversations: How Robots Might Shape Participant Roles Using Gaze Cues. In *Proceedings of the 4th ACM/IEEE International Conference on Human Robot Interaction (HRI '09)*. ACM, New York, NY, USA, 61–68. DOI: http://dx.doi.org/10.1145/1514095.1514109
26. Sandra Y Okita and Daniel L Schwartz. 2006. Young children's understanding of animacy and entertainment robots. *International Journal of Humanoid Robotics* 3, 03 (2006), 393–412.
27. David H Rakison and Diane Poulin-Dubois. 2001. Developmental origin of the animate–inanimate distinction. *Psychological bulletin* 127, 2 (2001), 209. DOI: http://dx.doi.org/10.1037/0033-2909.127.2.209
28. Janet C Read, SJ MacFarlane, and Chris Casey. 2002. Endurability, engagement and expectations: Measuring children's fun. In *Interaction design and children*, Vol. 2. Shaker Publishing Eindhoven, 1–23.
29. Martin Saerbeck, Tom Schut, Christoph Bartneck, and Maddy D. Janse. 2010. Expressive Robots in Education: Varying the Degree of Social Supportive Behavior of a Robotic Tutor. In *Proceedings of the SIGCHI Conference on Human Factors in Computing Systems (CHI '10)*. ACM, New York, NY, USA, 1613–1622. DOI: http://dx.doi.org/10.1145/1753326.1753567
30. Leonhard Schilbach, Bert Timmermans, Vasudevi Reddy, Alan Costall, Gary Bente, Tobias Schlicht, and Kai Vogeley. 2013. Toward a second-person neuroscience. *Behavioral and Brain Sciences* 36, 04 (2013), 393–414.

31. David Sirkin and Wendy Ju. 2014. Using embodied design improvisation as a design research tool. In *Proceedings of the international conference on Human Behavior in Design (HBiD 2014), Ascona, Switzerland.*

32. David Sirkin, Brian Mok, Stephen Yang, and Wendy Ju. 2015. Mechanical Ottoman: How Robotic Furniture Offers and Withdraws Support. In *Proceedings of the Tenth Annual ACM/IEEE International Conference on Human-Robot Interaction (HRI '15)*. ACM, New York, NY, USA, 11–18. DOI: http://dx.doi.org/10.1145/2696454.2696461

33. Vasant Srinivasan and Leila Takayama. 2016. Help Me Please: Robot Politeness Strategies for Soliciting Help From Humans. In *Proceedings of the 2016 CHI Conference on Human Factors in Computing Systems*. ACM, 4945–4955.

34. Megan Strait, Cody Canning, and Matthias Scheutz. 2014. Let Me Tell You! Investigating the Effects of Robot Communication Strategies in Advice-giving Situations Based on Robot Appearance, Interaction Modality and Distance. In *Proceedings of the 2014 ACM/IEEE International Conference on Human-robot Interaction (HRI '14)*. ACM, New York, NY, USA, 479–486. DOI: http://dx.doi.org/10.1145/2559636.2559670

35. Megan Strait, Lara Vujovic, Victoria Floerke, Matthias Scheutz, and Heather Urry. 2015. Too Much Humanness for Human-Robot Interaction: Exposure to Highly Humanlike Robots Elicits Aversive Responding in Observers. In *Proceedings of the 33rd Annual ACM Conference on Human Factors in Computing Systems (CHI '15)*. ACM, New York, NY, USA, 3593–3602. DOI: http://dx.doi.org/10.1145/2702123.2702415

36. Leila Takayama, Doug Dooley, and Wendy Ju. 2011. Expressing Thought: Improving Robot Readability with Animation Principles. In *Proceedings of the 6th International Conference on Human-robot Interaction (HRI '11)*. ACM, New York, NY, USA, 69–76. DOI: http://dx.doi.org/10.1145/1957656.1957674

37. Michael Tomasello. 1999. The cultural ecology of young children's interactions with objects and artifacts. *Ecological approaches to cognition: Essays in honor of Ulric Neisser* (1999), 153–170.

38. Ryan Wistort. 2010. Only Robots on the Inside. *interactions* 17, 2 (March 2010), 72–74. DOI: http://dx.doi.org/10.1145/1699775.1699792

39. Sarah Woods, Kerstin Dautenhahn, and Joerg Schulz. 2004. The design space of robots: Investigating children's views. In *Robot and Human Interactive Communication, 2004. ROMAN 2004. 13th IEEE International Workshop on*. IEEE, 47–52.

40. Sarah N Woods, Michael L Walters, Kheng Lee Koay, and Kerstin Dautenhahn. 2006. Methodological issues in HRI: A comparison of live and video-based methods in robot to human approach direction trials. In *ROMAN 2006-The 15th IEEE International Symposium on Robot and Human Interactive Communication*. IEEE, 51–58. DOI: http://dx.doi.org/10.1109/ROMAN.2006.314394

41. Selma Yilmazyildiz, Robin Read, Tony Belpeame, and Werner Verhelst. 2016. Review of Semantic-Free Utterances in Social Human–Robot Interaction. *International Journal of Human-Computer Interaction* 32, 1 (2016), 63–85. DOI: http://dx.doi.org/10.1080/10447318.2015.1093856

My Student is a Robot: How Schools Manage Telepresence Experiences for Students

Veronica Ahumada Newhart
University of California Irvine
School of Education
Irvine, CA, USA
vnewhart@uci.edu

Judith S. Olson
University of California Irvine
Department of Informatics
Irvine, CA, USA
jsolson@uci.edu

ABSTRACT
Homebound students, those who can learn but have a serious health issue (e.g. cancer, heart disease, immune deficiency) that prevents physical attendance at school, are now able to go to school using telepresence robots. Telepresence robots are generally video conferencing units on remote-controlled robots. Previous research has shown that using these robots allows homebound students to interact with classmates and teachers as if they are physically present. But, what does this mean for teachers and administrators? We present a qualitative study of 22 teachers and school administrators who worked with telepresent students and 4 who decided against adopting the robot. Our goal was to learn how decisions are made to adopt the robot, what issues arise in its use, and what would make adoption easier. This study contributes new insights on teacher and administrator perspectives on what is needed for effective use of this technology in educational settings.

Author Keywords
telepresence; education; robots.

ACM Classification Keywords
H.5.m. Information interfaces and presentation (e.g., HCI): Miscellaneous

INTRODUCTION
Due to advancements in pediatric medicine, many previously fatal childhood diseases are now chronic illnesses [5,10,16]. As a result, millions of children and adolescents in the US now live with chronic illnesses such as cancer, sickle cell anemia, asthma, etc. [1]. This has led to a growing population of children who are unable to physically attend school but still need to grow socially and learn. Traditional services for these students consist of 4-5 hours of home instruction per week. Unfortunately, traditional home instruction services are not designed to fully support these students' needs and do not provide any avenue for the students to establish or maintain social connections to their school communities. Studies show that inclusive educational practices result in better outcomes for students [4,9], yet current educational practices reinforce the exclusion of some children with chronic illness from school.

Recently, technology has created the opportunity to include the homebound child in school. Videoconferencing has been used in schools, [6–8] but very few studies have explored the use of this technology for homebound children with chronic illness. Some studies examined a technology solution for hospital-bound children, using a non-mobile telepresence robot, PEBBLES [2,17], shown on the left of Figure 1. The "face" of the robot showed the hospital-bound child's face, and the "head" could move to view different parts of the classroom, allowing others to know what the hospital-bound student was looking at. Since PEBBLES did not have independent mobility, it needed assistance when moving from one classroom to another, incurring a social debt to the helpmates.

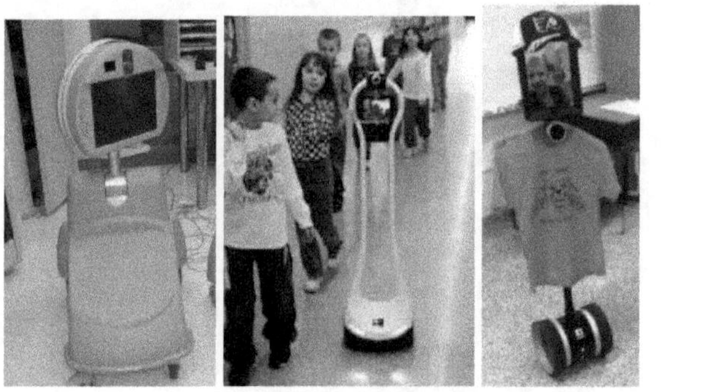

Figure 1.From left to right, PEBBLES, VGo, and Double Robots used in schools

More recently, mobile telepresence robots, originally built to allow adults to work at a distance, have now been introduced into classrooms for homebound children. Both the VGo and Double (shown on the right in Figure 1) have videoconferencing on a screen and allow the homebound child to control both the camera and the wheel/s from home. The child can move the robot around the classroom and is also able to go to lunch, music classes, assemblies and even field trips.

CHI 2017, May 06-11, 2017, Denver, CO, USA

DOI: http://dx.doi.org/10.1145/3025453.3025809

Our research on these robots is guided by Deci and Ryan's self-determination theory (SDT). SDT argues that all humans have universal, innate psychological needs (i.e., competence, autonomy, relatedness) and that if these needs are met, people will function and grow optimally. However, in order for humans to actualize their inherent potential, the social environment must nurture these needs. Our research focuses on the social-contextual conditions of telepresence robot use in classrooms. More specifically, we look at how these conditions facilitate learning and contribute to improved well-being for homebound students. In this study, we examine the factors that facilitate the use of this technology from the perspectives of teachers and administrators as these are the people at the front line of implementing this practice in existing school systems. Without these educators, the robots cannot reach the students.

In our initial study, five students found themselves fully capable of using the robot, offering them feelings of competence and autonomy, two of the three universal and innate psychological needs that are central to psychological health and well-being [11,13,15]. All students claimed to feel included in class; classmates referred to the robot by the homebound child's name as opposed to calling it a device or a robot. And, parents noted significant increases in their children's interest and happiness at being with their friends, fulfilling the third need for psychological health and well-being, relatedness [15]. In one striking case, before a child was offered the robot, his mother attributed the child's decreasing energy level to his worsening heart condition. She even worried that he wouldn't have enough energy to use the robot. But from the first day of going to school on the robot, he attended school 6-7 hours a day, five days a week. He was not only motivated to do well in his regular classes, but he also auditioned for and made it into the school choir using the robot. The child's earlier low energy was later attributed to depression. In addition, the teachers consistently talked about the child returning to school, which gave the homebound child hope and motivation to do well.

This case study also provided information about what features of the robot, originally designed for use by adults in an office setting, would better fit the needs of children in a classroom with classmates and teachers [12]. We highlight some of these design feature recommendations in this paper, as it is important for educators to understand some of the most common challenges to using this technology in schools. Key to robot functioning is Wi-Fi connectivity, which is often spotty when the child is driving the robot in the school halls. Batteries are occasionally limited, requiring the child to interact only from the docking station. A better solution for connectivity would involve equipping the robot with a hotspot.

The robot's audio is key; video is secondary to its presence in the classroom, but essential for the homebound child to see. A wide field of view is important especially in navigation. The user interface for the homebound child was not a problem, since both the VGo and Double use a mouse, track pad, or arrow keys to move. The interface is simple, but one child complained of pain in his finger from hitting the arrow key so much throughout the school day. We recommend a game interface for movement, something most children are familiar with. A number of other recommended features emerged in these cases and the full paper [12] contains many more details and the incidents that drove the recommendations.

Questions remain, however, about the settings in which these robots reside: The school and the home. The previous literature does not cover how the ***school*** should make decisions about allowing a child to come to school on a robot, what to do about the fact that schools are now ***connected*** to spaces outside the school, and what features would help the ***teachers***, who are already burdened with work, to accommodate the student attending school via robot. Schools are complex social settings where many different groups (e.g., teachers, students, administrators, and parents) interact to shape a child's life experiences. There is no research to inform the creation of guidelines for how to make the decision to offer the telepresence robot to a homebound student for school attendance. There is also no research that reveals the special issues surrounding the bridge from school to an outside place, the home or hospital. As the telepresence robot industry expands into schools, the information provided to educators varies by robot manufacturer. In order to successfully support the use of this technology for vulnerable students who are homebound, the HCI and education communities must pioneer the efforts to establish guidelines for educators based on formal objective studies. By interviewing teachers and school administrators, we sought to explore practices and design features that would help make adoption easier. This paper focuses on the following three questions:

- What line of decision making in the school system leads to successful adoption of the telepresence robot?
- What issues arise because the classroom and the home (or hospital) are now accessible to the other via the telecommunications link?
- What would make the adoption smoother for teachers?

METHOD

We conducted interviews of 14 teachers and 8 administrators in 9 different schools who had experience with telepresence robots being used by homebound students to attend schools. The homebound students were in the following grades: K, 2, 3, 5, 6, and 9. In addition, we interviewed 2 administrators and 2 teachers who explored the use of the robots and declined to use them, one even after having purchased it. All interviews were semi-structured and lasted 20 to 60 minutes. Interview topics included the administrative decision-making process for allowing a robot in school, how the robot was introduced to the school and classmates, teacher/administrator perspectives on robot use, and any reports of resistance to using the robot.

Interviews were recorded, transcribed and coded to identify patterns, similarities, and dissimilarities across the cases. We used open coding with iterative labeling of sections of data with testing of the labels across all data sets until they settled into a consistent set [3]. The constant revision allowed for some codes to be subsumed under broader and more abstract categories.

RESULTS

Although there were a number of findings, we focus on the three research questions: The decision making process that led to successful adoption, the issues that arise because the robot provides a "bridge" between the classroom and the home or hospital, and ideas that would make the adoption smoother for teachers.

The Decision Process

Three major stakeholders were identified in all successful cases of robot deployment—parents, teachers and administrators. Any one of the stakeholders could veto the adoption. In the 9 schools where we conducted interviews, a school district administrator initiated 3 of the robots, a hospital administrator initiated 3 of the robots, 1 was initiated by a teacher, 1 by a former teacher, and 1 by a parent.

Getting Parent Support

All participants agreed that for the homebound student to use the robot, parent support was key. Administrators and teachers could initiate the idea, but the full support and cooperation of the parents/guardians was credited for success. All 22 participants who accepted the robot were strong supporters of the technology and were "excited," "thrilled," and "happy," that the child would be able to attend school via robot.

Gaining Board Approval

Once parents approved of the use of the robot for their child, district or school board approval was required. One school principal took a creative approach to gaining support from her district board. To demonstrate the potential of the robot as a participant in a learning environment, she attended the district board meeting via the robot. She rolled in as a robot and participated throughout the entire meeting as she normally would. She then made the formal request for one of her students to attend school via the robot. After the board gave her an "eye test" (i.e., made her go to the back of the room and read the board) and a "hearing test" (i.e. also made her go to a back corner of the room to see if she could still hear them), they approved the use of the robot.

Getting Teacher Support

Having parental support and district approval are two steps on the road to deploying a robot for a student. The third step is gaining support from teachers who will be interacting with the robot on a daily basis. Although all teachers were enthusiastic about the robot, one teacher reported feeling "nervous" and a little "scared." When questioned what motivated her to move ahead and do it, she replied, "I knew it was what he [her student] needed, so I did it." Her hesitations centered on being physically responsible for the robot and not knowing how to control it.

In schools where the decision was made to NOT use the robots, privacy concerns were cited as the main reason. In one school where two teachers were offered the opportunity to use a robot for a 1st grader with cancer, the teachers were strongly resistant. The student had been in their classrooms before diagnosis and they were not willing to reintroduce him to the classroom via the robot. Their main cause for resistance was fear that use of the robot would also allow the mother and other adults in the home to witness what happened in the classroom; posts about what they heard or saw might be made on social media sites. They knew that the mother of the child was active on Facebook and not always in positive ways. At another school, the deployment of a purchased robot was postponed indefinitely due to administrator concerns over a similar fear of the child's mother having access to the classroom and posting what she saw or heard on social media. We elaborate on this point in the next section about the "bridge" between classroom and home or hospital.

The Bridge Between Home and School

The robots used for students to attend school were off-the-shelf robots designed for use in offices and medical settings in the adult world. The only privacy/security features are the login password, an encrypted link, and the inability to video or audio record. There is nothing that ensures that only the student is seen in the classroom or that others in the home or hospital cannot see the classroom. One principal felt that her teachers needed what she called "safe space," echoing the major concern of the schools that did not adopt the robot.

Once the telepresence bridge between home and school is made, then aspects of the home (other children, dogs, parents, their objects and tidiness, etc.) are visible in school. Likewise, the bridge may allow for more people than just the homebound student to see and hear what is happening in school. Privacy of both settings is potentially violated.

Safe Space for Teachers and Classmates

One school created a safe space for teachers and classmates by requiring the at-home parent or adult to fulfill all the requirements and follow the school guidelines for a parent volunteer in the classroom. School administrators did not want to be excessively restrictive with the homebound parent so they transitioned the parent into the existing school structure of a classroom aide. By officially taking this role, it allowed the at-home adult to effectively 'enter' the classroom. In this role, the adult needs to be trustworthy and working within the parameters of school and teacher expectations to maintain student privacy and not discuss, verbally or online, what is observed in the classroom. In addition to officially becoming a classroom aide, the at-home parent/adult also had to agree that when the homebound student was attending school, the student would be seated where no one else in the home could view the classroom. We recommend that, when others are present in the home, the student wear headphones so others cannot hear the teacher or classmates and that the homebound student self-mute to minimize home noises from disrupting the class.

Safe Space for Homebound Students and Families

Viewed from the reverse direction on the bridge, classmates, teachers, and other school personnel now have access to the remote student's home. Most school children do not visit the homes of all their peers but the robots create an open bridge straight into that child's living room, dining room, bedroom, etc. It is just as important to have a safe space for the homebound student where items that are viewed or conversations that are overheard are not repeated or commented on. The VGo screen is fairly small and not much can be viewed beyond the student's head but other robot models, including the Double, have larger screens and may provide increased views of household items and people. In addition to visuals coming through the screen, sounds come through speakers and classmates in our study were aware of siblings, pets, and general household noises. An administrator made the recommendation that a curtain or screen be used behind the at-home student to prevent classmates and school personnel from seeing personal objects and to free parents from the pressures of "having visitors" view their house every day.

How To Make Adoption Easier for Teachers

Most educators have had little training on the needs of children with medical conditions in the classroom [14]. Teachers in our study were also not given much training on the function of the robot and no instruction on how to deal with the social complexities of the robot. One of the teachers who was excited to try it found herself "afraid to touch it" after it arrived. She was not sure what all the buttons were for or if she would inadvertently disconnect the student. One substitute teacher was unaware that a student would be logging in to the robot and turned it off against the homebound student's wishes. This prompted the homebound student to say he "hated" her. Most teachers found the physical robot fairly easy to accommodate in the classroom, not requiring any special arrangements beyond what a student in a wheelchair would need.

Experience with the robot led to a number of suggestions for design changes, which are detailed in Newhart and Olson [12]. Key for the teachers was the fact that the battery life was not sufficient for the student to stay connected for six hours of the day and to have the full mobility they needed. Inadequate battery life required intermittent docking throughout the school day. And, the Wi-Fi connectivity was often lost at router transition points, requiring the robot to be moved by hand to the next area. A teacher mentioned that "in between the hallways there were dead spots so that we would have to like push the robot a little to get it going again."

The VGo is equipped to announce its presence when it is first connected and its departure when disconnected. These announcements were annoying when they occurred because the robot inadvertently disconnected and then reconnected during lessons. This occupancy awareness feature could be replaced with a visual feature that goes on when the robot is occupied and turns off when it is not.

One frustration with everyday tasks for the teacher was that if there was a handout like a quiz or worksheet that was not delivered to the student at home in their box with the upcoming week's worth of material, it was difficult to include the homebound student in the exercise. One student cleverly helped the homebound student take a quiz by putting on earphones to hear the homebound student's answers as she read the questions to him. The ability to fax material back and forth would be a welcome addition.

The placement of the camera near the projected eyes on the face of the robot was important for keeping the student engaged, especially younger ones. One teacher reported that she made every attempt to keep the remote student engaged by "looking at his eyes and making sure he saw my eyes." When questioned about this practice she said it was what she did for all of her 2nd graders.

Several teachers expressed worry that they would be held responsible for any damage to the robot. To continue the theme of "safe space" for the teachers and increase teacher buy-in, administrators should make clear that the physical and financial responsibility for the robot lies with the school or district and not the individual teacher. Of all 14 teachers interviewed, no one knew who paid for the robot, who paid the monthly robot access fee, or who paid for the student's laptop or tablet. Transparency on financial responsibility of the program may ease teacher worries about an expensive piece of technology that is being placed in their classroom.

Schools should have clear guidelines on the selection criteria for use of the robot in order to provide equitable access to the technology. Once selection is made, how a robot is introduced to the school should be tailored along parent and student preferences. While a large production at a school assembly where the robot is rolled out and introduced to the entire school may suit some students, other students do not like being in the spotlight. One student in our study returned her robot because she "didn't like all the attention." The robot physically represents the student in her school community; how she meets and engages with peers should also socially represent the student.

RECOMMENDATIONS

From the descriptions above, we have recommendations for the social practices surrounding the adoption of the telepresence robot for including a homebound child in class.

For The Parents

We know that the parents' cooperation and support of the robot's use is key. Sometimes the parent has to be the initiator, advocating because they believe that having their child attend school on a robot will contribute to their child's well-being [15].

We recommend that the parent and child place the computer that the child will be using in a location that does not violate the household's privacy. Often this is the dining room or a study, not in the living room where there is a lot of traffic and visibility. We recommend that the child communicate with headphones and a microphone so that the classroom activities are not broadcast to others in the household and household activities are not broadcast to the classroom. Privacy is important for both home and school.

In addition, we recommend that the parents go through training as a classroom aide, so that they are aware of what appropriate behavior is for adults in the classroom. In particular, they are not to breach the privacy of their child, the teacher, or their classmates on social media. In many ways, the parent who is near the homebound child on the computer is like a parent attending the class.

For The School Administrators

The school administrators should bring the parents and teachers together to make the decision of whether the homebound child can attend school on a robot. Together, they will come to an understanding of the ground rules as well as the responsibilities and opportunities available. By working it out, they can become a model of inclusion for others.

The school administrators should make sure that the robot's communication path between the school and the home is encrypted, and that the parent has gone through training as a classroom aide. In addition, school administrators should take physical and financial responsibility for the robot, and communicate that to teachers.

School administrators should also plan for equitable access to the technology and how to introduce the robot to the school community and perhaps to the parents of classmates. Some homebound children welcome the attention; some do not. The robot introduction should include the needs and wishes of the parents, homebound children, and teachers.

For The Teachers

Like the parents and administrators, successful adoption requires the teachers' buy-in. But to make the teachers comfortable, they need the assurances from the school administrators that they are *not* responsible if something happens to the robot.

The teachers should be informed about the homebound student's capabilities and schedule. Some homebound children are undergoing therapy treatments, for example, and will need lesson schedules adapted for them when possible.

Teachers need to be trained on how to operate the controls on the robot itself. They need to know how to adjust the speaker volume, how to turn it on and off, how to move it if it gets disconnected, and how to dock it for power. These instructions should remain in the classroom in case a substitute teacher comes and needs to work with the robot.

Before formal introduction of the robot in the classroom, the child should have a special session with the teacher to determine the best placement of "the desk" so the child can see and be seen, hear and be heard adequately. If the child needs to move from room to room, this early session can include a guided tour of where they have to go (e.g. to the music room or the lunch room) and the student should be provided with a map of the school. The student can plot on the map where the connectivity is spotty so the teacher is aware of problem areas and the student can avoid those areas until the connectivity issues are resolved.

To support the inclusion of the child in spontaneous new lessons that involve handouts or quizzes, the school and the home should include fax machines or comparable transmission of tangible documents.

CONCLUSIONS

There is mounting evidence that using a telepresence robot to include homebound children in school is important for their social as well as academic development. In other papers, we have focused on the experience of social inclusion of the child, and design recommendations for modifying a robot so that it is a better fit for children in schools. In this paper, we focused on what school professionals can do to make the appropriate decisions about whether to attempt this intervention, and if so, what to do to prepare. Teachers and parents need adequate training on the technology and provision of safe spaces both in the home and school. We believe through better understanding of teacher and administrator perceptions and attitudes, more children with chronic illness will have the opportunity to experience school attendance via robot. Providing the opportunity for this practice is the first step towards conducting future studies to evaluate the effectiveness of this practice and improve the standard of educational services afforded to homebound students.

ACKNOWLEDGMENTS

This work is supported by the National Science Foundation, under grant ACI-1322304, a Focused Faculty Research Award from Google, and the Children's Hospital of Orange County, Hyundai Cancer Institute.

REFERENCES

1. Bruce E. Compas, Sara S. Jaser, Madeleine J. Dunn, and Erin M. Rodriguez. 2012. Coping with chronic illness in childhood and adolescence. *Annual Review of Clinical Psychology* 8: 455–480. http://doi.org/10.1146/annurev-clinpsy-032511-143108.Coping

2. Deborah I Fels, Judith K Waalen, Shumin Zhai, and Patrice Tamar Weiss. 2001. Telepresence under exceptional circumstances : enriching the connection to school for sick children. In *Proceedings of Interact*, 617–624.

3. Barney G. Glaser and Anselm L. Strauss. 1967. *The Discovery of Grounded Theory*. Weidenfield & Nicholson, London.

4. James G. Gurney, Kevin R. Krull, Nina Kadan-Lottick, et al. 2009. Social outcomes in the childhood cancer survivor study cohort. *Journal of Clinical Oncology* 27, 14: 2390–2395. http://doi.org/10.1200/JCO.2008.21.1458

5. Neal Halfon, Kandyce Larson, and Shirley Russ. 2010. Why Social Determinants. *Healthcare Quarterly* 14, October: 8–20.

6. Susan B. Hopper. 2014. Bringing the World to the Classroom through Videoconferencing and Project-based Learning. *TechTrends* 58, 3: 78–89.

7. Jukka Hussa. 2012. Distance education in the school environment: Integrating remote classrooms by video conferencing. *Journal of Open, Flexible, and Distance Learning* 2, 1: 34–44.

8. Tony Lawson, Chris Comber, Jenny Gage, and Adrian Cullum-Hanshaw. 2010. Images of the future for education? Videoconferencing: A literature review. *Technology, Pedagogy and Education* 19, 3: 295–314. http://doi.org/10.1080/1475939X.2010.513761

9. Gary R. Maslow, Abigail A. Haydon, Annie-Laurie McRee, Carol Ann Ford, and Carolyn Tucker Halpern. 2011. Growing up with a chronic illness: Social success, educational/vocational distress. *Journal of Adolescent Health* 49, 2: 206–212. http://doi.org/10.1016/j.jadohealth.2010.12.001

10. Lidwine B. Mokkink, Johanna H. Van Der Lee, Martha A. Grootenhuis, Martin Offringa, and Hugo SA Heymans. 2008. Defining chronic diseases and health conditions in childhood (0-18 years of age): National consensus in the Netherlands. *European Journal of Pediatrics* 167, 12: 1441–1447. http://doi.org/10.1007/s00431-008-0697-y

11. Veronica Ahumada Newhart. 2014. Virtual inclusion via telepresence robots in the classroom. In *CHI'14 Extended Abstracts on Human Factors in Computing Systems*, 951–956. http://doi.org/10.1145/2559206.2579417

12. Veronica Ahumada Newhart and Judith S. Olson. 2016. Going to school on a robot: A case study to illustrate important design considerations of telepresence robots. *Manuscript in Preparation.*

13. Veronica Ahumada Newhart, Mark Warschauer, and Leonard S. Sender. 2016. Virtual inclusion via telepresence robots in the classroom: An exploratory case study. *The International Journal of Technologies in Learning* 23, 4: 9–25.

14. Ardis L. Olson, A. Blair Seidler, David Goodman, Susan Gaelic, and Richard Nordgren. 2004. School professionals' perceptions about the impact of chronic illness in the classroom. *Pediatrics & Adolescent Medicine* 158, 1: 53–58. http://doi.org/10.1001/archpedi.158.1.53

15. Richard M. Ryan and Edward L. Deci. 2000. Self-determination theory and the facilitation of intrinsic motivation, social development, and well-being. *The American psychologist* 55, 1: 68–78. http://doi.org/10.1037/0003-066X.55.1.68

16. Sandra B. Sexson and Avi Madan-Swain. 1993. School reentry for the child with chronic illness. *Journal of Learning Disabilities* 26, 2: 115–125, 137. http://doi.org/10.1177/002221949302600204

17. Jason Yeung and Deborah I. Fels. 2005. A remote telepresence system for high school classrooms. In *Canadian Conference on Electrical and Computer Engineering*, 1465–1468.

How Do System Administrators Resolve Access-Denied Issues in the Real World?

Tianyin Xu, Han Min Naing, Le Lu, and Yuanyuan Zhou
University of California, San Diego

ABSTRACT

The efficacy of access control largely depends on how system administrators (sysadmins) resolve access-denied issues. A correct resolution should only permit the expected access, while maintaining the protection against illegal access. However, anecdotal evidence suggests that correct resolutions are occasional—sysadmins often grant too much access (known as security misconfigurations) to allow the denied access, posing severe security risks. This paper presents a quantitative study on real-world practices of resolving access-denied issues, with a particular focus on how and why security misconfigurations are introduced during problem solving. We characterize the real-world security misconfigurations introduced in the field, and show that many of these misconfigurations were the results of trial-and-error practices commonly adopted by sysadmins to work around access denials. We argue that the lack of adequate feedback information is one fundamental reason that prevents sysadmins from developing precise understanding and thus induces trial and error. Our study on access-denied messages shows that many of today's software systems miss the opportunities for providing adequate feedback information, imposing unnecessary obstacles to correct resolutions.

ACM Classification Keywords

H.1.2 User/Machine Systems: Human factors; D.4.6 Security and protection: Access controls; K.6.5 Management of computing and information systems: Security and Protection

Author Keywords

Security; access control; configuration; log messages

INTRODUCTION

Motivation

> "Access control doesn't work—40 years of experience says so. The basic problem [is]: its job is to say 'No.' This stops people from doing their work, and then they relax the access control. [There is] usually too much [access], but no one notices until there's a disaster." [31]
>
> —Butler Lampson, Perspectives on Security (2015)

CHI 2017, May 6-11, 2017, Denver, CO, USA.
Copyright © 2017 ACM ISBN 978-1-4503-4655-9/17/05 ...$15.00.
DOI: http://dx.doi.org/10.1145/3025453.3025999

Access control is constantly reported to be "profoundly broken" in real-world system administration practices [33,45,57]. The blame is mainly placed on its side effects, *access-denied issues* where expected access is falsely denied. Anecdotal evidence suggests that in order to resolve such issues, system administrators (sysadmins) often grant too much access, known as *security misconfigurations.* Today, misconfigurations have become a major cause of security failures such as data thefts and system compromises [24,45,67]. For example, the misconfigurations of a database server at an insurance company allowed its data to be publicly accessible, causing massive breach of customers' account information in 2014 [21].

The challenge of correctly resolving access-denied issues lies in the requirement of precise configurations—those only permit expected access while maintaining the protection against illegal access. This is non-trivial in modern software systems, where access to resources is typically restricted by complex, heterogeneous access-control configurations at multiple layers. For example, to access a web page hosted on a web server, an HTTP request is typically checked through access control of firewalls, web authentication/authorization, file permissions, and OS kernel security modules. Correct resolutions need to understand not only already complex access-control configurations of each system component, but also their interactions.

Currently, resolving access-denied issues is mainly through human-centered problem-solving, in which sysadmins reason about missing permissions and devise resolutions. Insecure resolutions are notoriously hard to detect, as security misconfigurations do not manifest through symptoms of failures or anomalies [71]. A few existing tools focus on either predefined bad values [19,37] or inconsistencies among settings [8,9,15,78]. However, as noted in [15], given frequent configuration changes and the ad-hoc, one-off nature, it is very difficult for automated tools to deduce the exact and complete list of security misconfigurations. The correctness of access-control configurations mainly relies on sysadmins' practices.

Equipping sysadmins to correctly resolve access-denied issues requires the understanding of their problem-solving practices: how do sysadmins resolve access-denied issues? what are the obstacles to correct resolutions? how are security misconfigurations introduced? Without answering these fundamental questions, it is difficult for research and development efforts to focus on effective directions and build practical solutions. Unfortunately, few studies have provided answers. Sometimes, we simply lay the blame on sysadmins' attitude and hope for better education, which rarely worked in the past [31,40].

Contribution

This paper presents a quantitative study on real-world practices of resolving access-denied issues, with a particular focus on how and why security misconfigurations were introduced during problem-solving. The objective is to identify and understand the fundamental obstacles faced by sysadmins, as well as the implications for better design of software systems and tool support for access-control configurations.

To this end, we study 486 real-world access-denied issues from four widely-used software systems collected from mailing lists and web forums. For each case, we examine the symptom, root cause, and problem-solving practices. Specially, we deduce the security impact of the configurations introduced by sysadmins in the field. We flag security misconfigurations if the new settings permit too much access.

The study shows that security misconfigurations were commonly introduced as workarounds for access-denied issues—they occurred in 38.1% of the studied cases in different software systems. The most common security misconfigurations were completely disabling access-control modules, voiding all the protection against malice. Ironically, 49.7% of the security misconfigurations introduced in the field failed to work around the issues, mostly because the misconfigurations, as blind attempts, were irrelevant to root causes of the denials.

One contributing factor of such significant prevalence is that security misconfigurations were frequently suggested as potential resolutions on web forums and mailing lists; 48.6% of these suggested security misconfigurations were adopted by sysadmins who were eager to allow the denied access. We observe that voting-based moderation, though commonly used by web forums, is ineffective in suppressing insecure suggestions.

We show that many security misconfigurations were the results of trial-and-error practices commonly adopted for problem-solving: sysadmins tried to allow the denied access by relaxing certain access-control configurations, without precise understanding of root causes—the missing permissions. We show that 70.3% of these misconfigurations were associated with sysadmins' futile configuration attempts that were irrelevant to the root causes. These useless configurations included working on wrong security modules and wrong parameters.

We argue that the lack of adequate feedback is one fundamental reason that prevents sysadmins from developing precise understanding and thus induces trial and error. Typically, the feedback information (mainly via log messages) is too coarse-grained or acts as generic notifications, which is unhelpful for reasoning out the missing permissions.

To quantitatively understand existing feedback information, we study access-denied messages in six mature, widely-used software projects. We show that many of these software systems miss the opportunities for providing specific, precise, and complete feedback to assist correct resolutions. First, access denials occasionally have specific messages: many of them come with generic notifications. Second, root-cause configurations are rarely included in message content, even when the software holds precise knowledge. Third, many messages lack critical details such as subject, access type, and object.

MySQL server fails to start with the following error messages:

```
[ERROR] Can't find file: './mysql/plugin.frm' (errno: 13)
[ERROR] Can't open the mysql.plugin table. Please run
        mysql_upgrade to create it.
```

attempts:

1. restore `plugin.frm` ("This file does exist and is readable!"); [useless]
2. restart the server; [useless]
3. change all MySQL system files to be world readable, writable, and executable. [harmful] [useless]

suggestions:

1. upgrade MySQL version (run `mysql_upgrade`); [useless]
2. check if startup scripts override the configurations. [useless]

root cause & correct resolution:

The file access was denied by AppArmor (a Linux kernel security module) and returned `errno 13`. The resolution is to configure the AppArmor policies to allow MySQL to access the file.

(a) Access denied by an OS security module

Apache web server rejected legitimate access (403 forbidden) with the following error message:

```
[authz_core:error][client:127.0.0.1:38873] AH01630:
client denied by server configuration: /home/remix/
```

attempts:

1. set `"allow from all"`; [useless]
2. allow IPs in `/etc/hosts`; [useless]
3. restart Apache via new user `remix` (changed from `nobody`); [useless]
4. change `/home/remix` to be world executable. [harmful] [useless]

suggestions:

1. check directory permission; [useless]
2. change `/home/remix` to be world executable. [harmful] [useless]

(adopted)

root cause & correct resolution:

The client access is denied by Apache's internal authorization module (mod_access_compat). To resolve the issue, use the `require` configuration parameter to grant necessary access.

(b) Access denied by Apache's internal configurations

Figure 1. Real-world examples of resolving access-denied issues that introduced security misconfigurations in MySQL and Apache [52, 64].

We hope these results to raise the awareness of the importance of assisting access-denied issues, and motivate better feedback and tool support towards usable access control.

Real-world Examples

Figure 1 illustrates two representative real-world examples of resolving access-denied issues that introduced security misconfigurations (selected from our study). In both cases, the sysadmins applied the trial-and-error approach for problem solving—trying various configurations to allow the denied access, without understanding of the root-causes of the denials. In Figure 1(a), the sysadmin failed to reason out the root cause to be the configurations of AppArmor (a Linux kernel security module). Even after the sysadmin recursively configured the most permissive file permissions for MySQL's system files, the expected access was still denied. In Figure 1(b), the access was denied by Apache's internal authorization configurations. However, most of the attempted and suggested configurations targeted on wrong access-control modules (e.g., network-level access control and file permissions) and thus were useless.

Note that the feedback information given by the systems was inadequate in both of the examples. In Figure 1(a), the message content did not even clearly point out access control as the root cause (except the `errno`). In fact, `errno 13`[1] merely means "`permission denied`" and does not reveal any specific information. In Figure 1(b), the error message "`client denied by server configuration`" was too generic to be helpful—it did not pinpoint which security modules and configuration parameters denied the access. Due to the large, complex configuration space, it is not surprising that the sysadmins failed to shot the root-cause configurations in the dark via trial and error.

METHODOLOGY

We study 486 randomly sampled, access-denied cases reported on four software systems collected from mailing lists and sysadmin-oriented web forums. Each case starts with the descriptions of a real-world issue, followed by online discussions and collaborative problem-solving efforts. In order to resolve the reported issues timely, sysadmins were willing (and required [41]) to describe detailed information in the field, including the software versions, system feedback, configurations related to access control, diagnostic/fixing attempts, etc. This provides the opportunity for understanding the reported issues: their root causes, the field practices of problem-solving, and the security impact of the attempted configurations.

For each case considered, two inspectors independently investigated the case report and recorded the information of interest, including the root-cause configurations, observed system feedback, configurations introduced during problem-solving, suggestions of resolutions, etc. The information was recorded in specially designed spreadsheets with detailed written classifications. The two inspectors then compared their results with each other until consensus was reached. For some tough cases, we checked the source code and reproduced the issues to ensure correct understanding. We observed inconsistent results in less than 4% of cases, with early setups of the definitions, categorization, and examples of security misconfigurations. Most inconsistencies were due to one inspector missing security risks of the new configurations; after the other inspector explained the risks, consensus was reached.

Target users: system administrators

Our study focuses on system administrators (sysadmins), a special type of software users [4]. We follow the definition in [5], where *sysadmins* are broadly referred to as "*those who use their technical, social, and organization skills to architect, configure, administer, and maintain computer systems, including operating systems, networks, security systems, databases, web servers, and applications.*" Note that the definition is not limited to full-time IT professionals; thus we also include sysadmins of other occupations (e.g., developers) who managed their own infrastructure consist of the studied software.

Compared with ordinary users, sysadmins are known to be technical inclined [5,28]. Specially, they are expected to take an active role in managing system security, as one primary concern of the systems they manage. Moreover, unlike end users whose access is restricted to avoid disclosure of sensitive information (e.g., internal access-control policies), sysadmins are the policy makers and implementers, with highest privileges.

[1]Linux's manpage lists more than three cases that could result in `errno 13` (`EACCES`) and does not include kernel security modules.

Software	Description	Lang.	Studied cases	
			Period	Total (#)
Apache	Web server	C	2001–2016	126
MySQL	Database	C++	1999–2016	117
Hadoop	Data processing	Java	2009–2016	101
CentOS	Linux distribution	Multiple	2005–2016	142

Table 1. The studied software systems, and the period; total number of real-world access-denied cases studied for each system in this paper.

Also, it is known that today's sysadmins have diverse backgrounds and skill sets—"*there is no single path to becoming a system administrator [...] many system administrators enter the field by self-taught*" [73]. In fact, even within one organization, security administration is often distributed across multiple sysadmins, each being responsible for different aspects of it, e.g., web, databases, operating systems [10].

Target software: server and operating systems

The studied issues were reported on four open-source software systems: Apache, MySQL, Hadoop, and CentOS[2] (c.f., Table 1). We selected these systems for the following reasons. First, all these systems are server and operating systems that are usually managed by sysadmins instead of ordinary end users. Second, all the systems require intensive access-control configuration, as security is one primary aspect of the system administration—the impact of security misconfigurations is severe. Third, all these software systems are mature, actively maintained, and widely used; their access control represents the state-of-the-art design and implementation. Fourth, we intend to cover diverse types of systems in terms of functionalities, programming languages, and system architectures.

Data collection

We collected real-world access-denied cases from the official mailing lists of the target software systems [2,13,23,39] and sysadmin-oriented web forums including ServerFault [46] (for all the studied systems), Database Administrator [16] (only for MySQL), StackOverflow [58] (only for Hadoop[3]), and CentOS official forum [12]. As each studied system had hundreds of thousands of cases, in order to efficiently collect relevant cases, we used keywords related to access denials, including "access denied", "access control", "security", "permission", "privilege", and their variations. From the thousands of cases that contained at least one keyword, we *randomly* selected a thousand case reports with clear and detailed descriptions. Then, we manually examined them to make sure that the cases were really access-denied issues. We only selected *resolved* cases (those confirmed by the original reporters) to ensure correct understanding of the root causes and resolutions. To ensure the representativeness of sysadmins, we collected *one case per reporter* (identified by user IDs and emails).

[2]CentOS is selected over other OS distributions (e.g., Windows and Mac OS) because it is an enterprise-class distribution commonly used as servers. Few CentOS cases are about kernel configurations; most are related to configurations of system utilities (e.g., `mount`) and installed program packages. There are 64 unique programs appearing in the CentOS cases, providing a large, diverse OS software set.

[3]StackOverflow is the primary forum for Hadoop administration (likely because many Hadoop sysadmins are developers).

Table 1 shows the period and number of cases included in this study for the target software. All the cases are public available at: https://github.com/tianyin/access_denied_datasets.

Threats to Validity

As with all characteristic studies, there is an inherent risk that our study may be specific to the target software systems. While we cannot establish representativeness categorically, we have taken care to select diverse software projects that are mature and widely used (Table 1). Note that our study only focuses on system software; we do not intend to draw any conclusion about other types of software such as desktop and mobile apps.

Another concern is the representativeness of the studied access-denied issues. First, novice sysadmins are more likely to report problems, compared with experts. Unfortunately, it is hard to objectively differentiate between novices and experts. In fact, with new and major revisions of software being deployed in the field, there are always novice sysadmins. Second, we only collect cases that were reported by sysadmins and resolved at the time of the study. It is possible that the non-reported and non-resolved cases might have different characteristics.

Another potential source of bias is that the case reports may not record every single configuration action done by the sysadmins. This may affect the statistics of security misconfigurations and useless configurations. According to our experience, most of the sysadmins who reported the access-denied issues described their problem-solving efforts in details to help pin down the root causes efficiently. Therefore, we believe that the reported numbers well represent the general characteristics.

Still, we remind our readers that the results and findings should be taken with the target software and data sources in mind. At the same time, we urge the readers to focus more on the overall trends and implications rather than the absolute numbers.

PROFILES OF ACCESS-DENIED ISSUES

Access-control configurations

Both application- and OS-level access-control configurations are included in the studied cases. Many of the studied software systems implement access-control mechanisms to protect application-specific objects. For example, MySQL provides 32 different privileges for defining access to different objects such as database, table, columns, view, etc. Apache has 15 different authentication and authorization modules which can be used in combination by `RequireAny` and `RequireAll` directives. Besides their own access control, the software programs interact with OS-level access control when requesting OS resources. The common OS-level access control in our study includes file permissions, SELinux, and firewalls (e.g., iptables).

Notably, all access-control configurations in our study were under discretionary or mandatory models. None of the cases used role-based access control (RBAC). SELinux is perhaps the only one that supports RBAC, but in most Linux distributions it is not enforced by default and is rarely enabled.

Patterns of denied access

The denied access falls in two patterns: (1) the software program denied incoming access (e.g., issued by end users' SQL queries) based on its internal access-control configurations; and (2) the software program tried to access OS resources (e.g., files) but was denied by OS-level access controls, e.g., when the Apache web server was fetching HTML files to serve users' HTTP requests. Both the first and second patterns contribute to significant percentages (42.6% and 57.4% respectively).

Unlike application-level access-control configurations which was specific to each application software, 88.2% of the OS-level access-denied issues were related to file access; 67.9% of the denied file access was not caused by the basic three permission triads (denoted as `rwxrwxrwx`) of the accessed files. One common mistake was lacking search permissions on one parent directory of the accessed file (many sysadmins only checked the permissions of the accessed files). Besides file permissions, in many cases the access was denied by other OS security modules (e.g., SELinux and AppArmor) or security policies (e.g., Windows 7 disallows application-level programs to create symbolic links by default [60]).

Log messages as main feedback information

Sysadmins mainly rely on the software's log messages to understand the root causes of denied access. Among all the 486 case reports, 87.0% of the sysadmins examined the logs of the studied software and included them in the case reports (including log files and console log messages); 91.3% of them extracted the log messages specific to the denied access from the entire logs. Besides the logs of the studied software, 5.6% of the sysadmins also examined OS logs for certain types of issues. A common case was checking `audit.log` for SELinux-related issues. Guided by the log messages, most of the sysadmins also examined access-control configurations in configuration files or returned by status-checking commands (such as "`ls -lZ`" for file permissions and security contexts).

Only eight (1.6%) sysadmins checked the software's source code during problem solving (all of them were from Hadoop cases); none used any debuggers (e.g., GDB) to examine execution. This again shows that sysadmins, even with the developer occupation, are *users* of the systems they manage. They mainly rely on the system's feedback information instead of trying to understand the implementation or runtime execution.

Tool support for problem-solving

In the studied access-denied cases, the problem-solving was mostly through manual configuration efforts with few automated tooling support. Very few of the studied software applications provided tool support for automatically pinpointing the missing permissions or suggesting resolutions—sysadmins changed access-control configurations by editing configuration files or using commands (e.g., `GRANT` in MySQL). Similarly, all the file permissions were done with Unix shell commands, such as `chmod`, `chown`, `setfacl`, etc. The only tool support observed in our study was from SELinux (a Linux kernel security module). In certain cases related to SELinux, the sysadmins used `sealert` and `audit2allow` to automatically troubleshoot and generate SELinux policy configurations, which could permit the denied access recorded in audit logs. Note that utilities like `audit2allow` are not the panacea for SELinux denial issues [68]—the common resolutions were still manually editing security labels and boolean parameters.

SECURITY MISCONFIGURATIONS AS INCORRECT RESOLUTIONS

To understand real-world security misconfigurations, we deduce security impact of the access-control configurations introduced by the sysadmin in the studied cases. We determine security misconfigurations if the introduced configurations granted too much access—more than what is necessary and should be permitted. Note that we do *not* measure the absolute security of the configuration values; instead, we leverage the original configurations as the baseline to check if the newly introduced configurations produced appropriate access.

Security misconfigurations are commonly introduced

Our study reveals significant prevalence of security misconfigurations in the field—they were introduced as resolutions among in 38.1% of the studied access-denied cases across different software systems (c.f., Table 2). These results advocate for the importance of studying the usability of access control from the aspects of access-denied issues.

Essentially, access-control configurations are not a one-time effort, but need constant changes to adapt the dynamic nature of information sharing. The enforcement of "security by default" is insufficient to maintain protection of access control in the long term, if sysadmins cannot resolve access-denied issues with correct, secure configurations. Unfortunately, our study shows that the real-world practices of resolving access-denied issues are prone to security misconfigurations.

Common types of security misconfigurations

We categorize the security misconfigurations into three types based on how the access-control configurations were incorrectly loosened. Table 3 gives the definitions of each type and provides real-world examples selected from our study. Table 4 shows the distribution of different types of security misconfigurtions among the studied cases containing misconfigurations.

Disabling the protection by access control of a specific security module was the most common type of security misconfigurations: 74.6% of the cases of security misconfigurations fall in this category. This is likely because disabling the entire module was considered as a quick way to work around the denials (compared with setting correct configurations).

The distribution of the other two types of security misconfigurations mainly depends on the access-control model of the studied software. For example, MySQL implements privilege-based access control—to access a database or a table, the database users need to be granted corresponding privileges. Therefore, over-granting privileges was the common security misconfigurations in MySQL. Apache, as a web server, intensively interacts with the filesystems to fetch files such as web pages, images, and Javascripts. Downgrading file permissions was a common misconfiguration to obtain file access.

Blind misconfigurations cannot permit the denied access

Ironically, 49.7% of the security misconfigurations failed to work around the reported access-denied issues: they were not only harmful (imposing security risks) but also useless. Such lose-lose situation was typically caused by security misconfigurations performed on wrong security modules or configuration parameters which were irrelevant to the root causes of the denials, as exemplified by Figures 1. We discuss the useless configurations in details in the later sections.

Software	# Cases incl. security misconfigurations		Total
	Performed	Suggested	
Apache	42.9% (54)	18.3% (23)	126
MySQL	32.5% (38)	20.5% (24)	117
Hadoop	36.6% (37)	15.8% (16)	101
CentOS	39.4% (56)	6.3% (9)	142
Total	38.1% (185)	14.8% (72)	486

Table 2. Prevalence of security misconfigurations. The percentage (number) of access-denied cases in which security misconfigurations were introduced by the sysadmins and suggested as potential resolutions.

Type	Definition & Example	
Disable protection	**Def.:**	Disable all the protection of the security module
	Ex.1:	Set file permissions to `rwxrwxrwx` [49,53]
	Ex.2:	Disable OS security modules (e.g., SELinux) [55]
	Ex.3:	Remove firewalls (e.g., ModSecurity) [50]
	Ex.4:	Turn off application-level permission checks [59]
Over-grant privileges	**Def.:**	Grant unnecessary privileges to the subject
	Ex.5:	Grant users the access to all the database tables (`"GRANT ALL *.* TO $user"` in MySQL) [54]
	Ex.6:	Add regular users in the administrator group [48]
Downgrade permissions	**Def.:**	Downgrade permissions of the object unnecessarily
	Ex.7:	Give up one type of file permissions (e.g., execution permission by `"chmod a+x $file"` [47])
	Ex.8:	Allow any groups (*) to submit jobs to Hadoop only for allowing one specific user [62]

Table 3. Definitions and examples of different types of security misconfigurations that lead to more access than what is necessary and should be permitted.

Software	Disable protection	Over-grant privileges	Downgrade permissions	Total
Apache	66.7% (36)	9.3% (5)	35.2% (19)	54
MySQL	63.2% (24)	52.6% (20)	2.6% (1)	38
Hadoop	81.1% (30)	13.5% (5)	5.4% (2)	37
CentOS	85.7% (48)	3.6% (2)	12.5% (7)	56
Total	74.6% (138)	17.3% (32)	15.7% (29)	185

Table 4. Distribution of different types of security misconfigurations. The three types are defined in Table 3. Note: some cases introduced more than one types of security misconfigurations.

Security misconfigurations are frequently suggested

As shown in Table 2, among 14.8% of the studied cases security misconfigurations were suggested as potential resolutions on the web forums and mailing lists across the studied systems. Worse, 48.6% of these suggested security misconfigurations were adopted by sysadmins who were eager to allow the denied access on these systems. This partially explains the prevalence of security misconfigurations.

Unlike misconfigurations that result in functionality or performance issues, security misconfigurations are not manifested immediately; also their impact is hard to measure. It could be challenging to understand the security impact of the suggested resolutions, especially when the configurations are complex or unfamiliar to the sysadmins. This calls for future research to help sysadmins evaluate and validate the security of suggestions from untrusted sources.

Interestingly, the characteristics of insecure suggestions are quite different across web forums, as shown in Table 5. Among the studied cases, CentOS Forums and DBA had no security

Web sites	% Cases w/ misconfiguration suggestions (adoption rate of misconfigurations)
StackOverflow [58]	22.4% (76.8%)
Mailing lists [2,13,23,39]	16.7% (14.4%)
ServerFault [46]	14.7% (60.5%)
DBA [16]	0.0% (0.0%)
CentOS Forums [13]	0.0% (0.0%)

Table 5. The percentage of cases where security misconfigurations were suggested (and their adoption rate) on different web sites.

Software	# Cases incl. useless configs		Total
	Performed	Suggested	
Apache	50.8% (64)	48.4% (61)	126
MySQL	41.9% (49)	30.8% (36)	117
Hadoop	32.7% (33)	28.7% (29)	101
CentOS	54.2% (77)	40.8% (58)	142
Total	45.9% (223)	37.9% (184)	486

Table 6. The percentage (number) of studied cases that include useless configurations attempted by sysadmins and suggested by the other users.

misconfiguration suggestions, mainly because in these two sites the reported issues were answered and moderated by a small number of experts (e.g., the designated moderators in CentOS Forums) who were cautious in giving suggestions and were responsible for editing suggestions posted by other users.

On the other hand, we find that voting-based moderation [65], though commonly adopted by web forums, is ineffective in suppressing insecure suggestions. Among all the suggestions that contained security misconfigurations on ServerFault and StackOverflow, only 6.6% of them were down-voted, while 50.8% of them had up-votes.[4] Worse, 32.7% of these misconfiguration suggestions had at least two up-votes, i.e., these insecure suggestions had already influenced other sysadmins besides the reporter. Security misconfiguraions were up-voted because they can work around the denials, and thus considered useful. This again shows that completely relying on sysadmins to correctly evaluate security risks cannot be expected.

Type	Definition & Example
Blind restore	**Def.:** Blindly attempt irrelevant things **Ex.1:** The sysadmin rebooted the system or reinstalled the software [53]
Wrong problem	**Def.:** Fail to recognize access control as the root cause **Ex.2:** The sysadmin was confused by the log messages showing `ClassNotFoundException`, but the root cause was insufficient file permissions [61].
Wrong module	**Def.:** Work on wrong security modules **Ex.3:** The sysadmin changed filesystem permissions, but the file access was denied by SELinux [64]
Wrong param.	**Def.:** Work on wrong configuration parameters **Ex.4:** The sysadmin changed `SecRequestBodyLimit` setting (in `ModSecurity`), but the request was denied by `SecRequestBodyAccess` [51]
Wrong setting	**Def.:** Set wrong access-control configuration values **Ex.5:** The sysadmin granted the `ALL` privilege to the database user, but "`LOAD DATA`" required the `FILE` privilege (`ALL` does not include `FILE`) [17]

Table 7. Definitions and examples of different types of useless configurations that failed to resolve the access-denied issues.

Security misconfigurations through trial and error

We further examine sysadmins' problem-solving practices and observe that many of the introduced security misconfigurations were the results of trial-and-error based problem-solving: sysadmins tried to allow the denied access by loosening certain access-control configurations, without precise understanding of the root causes—the missing permissions. In one case [63], the sysadmin commented on the workaround,

> "This was a terrible work around and I do not recommend it. ~~but~~ I changed the permission of the `/home/hadoop` directory to `777`[5] and it works. I couldn't find where `TokenizedMapper[.class` file] resided in my user file. [I know] This is a terrible option but I am accepting it in order to close the question."

Trial and error is featured by useless configuration efforts that are irrelevant to the root causes and thus cannot resolve the issues. In 70.3% of the studied cases that contained security misconfigurations, sysadmins attempted futile configurations, indicating that the sysadmins failed to reason out the precise root causes of the denials. The following comments describe the typical difficulties encountered by sysadmins during the trial-and-error process,

> "I'm totally stuck. I'm reading other guides and trying random configurations here and there, but I'm clueless."

We shall point out that *trail and error is a terrible problem-solving practice for any security issues* because of its solution-oriented and non-optimal nature—trial and error makes no attempt to discover why a solution works (merely that it is a solution); trial and error only attempts to find a working solution, rather than the best (secure) one. This explains why trial and error often leads to security misconfigurations. To make the matter worse, many of the security-misconfiguration "trials" are not easy to revert—the new configurations could overwrite previous settings or permanently change the system states, e.g., recursively `chmod` a directory in Figure 1(a).

Unfortunately, trial and error appears to be a common problem-solving practice adopted by sysadmins for access-denied issues. As shown in Table 6, a significant percentage (45.9%) of *all* the studied access-denied cases included useless configuration attempts. In a similar percentage (37.9%) of the cases, useless configurations were suggested as potential resolutions by the other users on mailing list and web forums. This shows that precisely understanding the root causes of access-denied issues is a common difficulty.

There are other security misconfigurations due to sysadmins' being incapable of access-control configurations. Typically, the security modules were originally installed and configured by other sysadmins or by default. In one of such cases [50], the sysadmin disabled ModSecurity (a web application firewall) and commented: *"There seems to be a frustratingly large amount of ModSecurity documentation, but I don't have weeks to read through hundreds of documentation [pages] just to find out how to make it play nice with SVN."*

[4] ServerFault and StackOverflow encourages their registered users to up or down vote the suggested solutions. Only votes from users with enough "reputation scores" are counted for the posted vote scores.

[5] A file permission of `777` (i.e., `rwxrwxrwx`) allows everyone in the system to read, write, and execute the file.

Software	Blind restore	Wrong problem	Wrong module	Wrong parameter	Wrong setting	Total
Apache	7.8% (5)	7.8% (5)	48.4% (31)	34.4% (22)	9.4% (6)	64
MySQL	10.2% (5)	24.5% (12)	57.1% (28)	12.2% (6)	14.3% (7)	49
Hadoop	9.1% (3)	12.1% (4)	48.5% (16)	42.4% (14)	6.1% (2)	33
CentOS	5.2% (4)	15.6% (12)	49.4% (38)	28.6% (22)	22.1% (17)	77
Total	7.6% (17)	14.8% (33)	50.7% (113)	28.7% (64)	14.3% (32)	223

Table 8. Distribution of different types of useless configurations (defined in Table 7). Note: some cases had more than one types of useless configurations.

Useless configuration attempts

We categorize the useless configurations based on the error patterns. Table 7 describes the definitions and gives examples of each category. Note that the categories are *exclusive*—wrong configuration parameters means correct security modules and wrong settings indicates correct parameters. Each useless configuration belongs to only one category; but some cases included multiple different types of useless configurations.

Table 8 shows that working on wrong modules and wrong parameters contribute to most of the useless configurations. They were introduced in 50.7% and 28.7% of the studied cases, respectively. In comparison, wrong configuration values was less common. Moreover, in 14.8% of the cases, the sysadmins even did not realize the root causes were related to access control, but chased completely wrong directions, e.g., manipulating the Java classpath for the access-denied issues (Table 7: Ex2). The results show that sysadmins had difficulties in locating the root-cause modules and configuration parameters, not to mention the concrete settings.

Discussion

We argue that one fundamental reason behind the wide adoption of trial and error for problem-solving lies in the lack of adequate feedback information. Typically, the feedback information (mainly via log messages) is too coarse-grained or merely acts as generic notifications. This imposes significant obstacles for sysadmins to develop precise understanding of the root causes and to reason out the missing permissions. In the studied cases, it not uncommon to see sysadmins complaining the feedback messages, for example,

> "Apache's error logs simply say I don't have permission to access the file, [and] isn't telling me anything more useful, and my searches have all told to ensure the permissions are set correctly."

> " I don't even see a mention of the group in this exception message. Do group permissions just not work?"

We believe good feedback messages is essential to assist correct resolutions for access-denied issues. Designing good log messages and improving existing ones would require software developers and tool builders to carefully evaluate the message content. Different from debugging and auditing logs, access-denied messages should be designed from the perspectives of resolving access-denied issues with secure configurations.

INSPECTION OF LOG MESSAGES

To quantitatively understand the feedback information provided by today's software systems, we study access-denied log messages in the latest versions of six mature, widely-used system software projects (Apache, MySQL, Lighttpd, VSFTP, Hadoop, and HBase). The study is based on inspecting the source code via two steps: (1) identifying the program points that deny access in the source code of the studied software program, and the corresponding log messages; (2) evaluating whether the message content satisfies the design principles.

We include the two common access-denied patterns: (1) the software program denies incoming access based on its internal access-control configurations; and (2) the access to external resources (e.g., files) is denied by OS-level access-control configurations. For access to OS resources, we focus on *file* access which dominates external access-denied issues, as revealed in the profiles of access-denied issues.

Note that few work has studied access-denied log messages from the aspect of correctly resolving the issues (prior studies mainly focus on logs for auditing [1, 14] and failure diagnosis [26, 76, 77, 79]). Therefore, we start with presenting the methodology of identifying and evaluating the log messages.

Methodology

Identify access-denied log messages

We identify access-denied log messages by searching the program signatures of access-denied points in the source code; we then validate each point by inspecting related code.

Internal access denials. As different software programs have different access-control implementations, there is no common signature of access denials across software. Fortunately, within each software, denials are manifested through globally defined error code or exceptions. For example, in Apache the error code that would result in 403 Forbidden HTTP status includes `HTTP_FORBIDDEN`, `AUTHZ_DENIED`, and `AUTH_DENIED`; Hadoop throws `AccessControlException` when denying access. These error code and exceptions can be viewed as program signatures of access denials. Starting from the program points that assign the error code or throw the exceptions, we record the log messages specific to the denied access by tracking the propagation of the error code or exception.

File access denials. Access to files is through system/library APIs such as `open`, `fopen`, and `FileInputStream`, where error code (`EACCES`) and exceptions (`IOException`) would be returned for the denied access. We start with file APIs in `libc` and Java SDK. We only include APIs related to access control configurations, and exclude file read/write APIs. In our inspection, we observe that developers seldom check return values and `errno` of two access patterns: (1) deleting files created by them; (2) the file access is checked early (e.g., via `stat` to check accessibility and file types). We exclude these two patterns (including them would result in larger number of unlogged cases).

Most of the studied systems implement customized file APIs that wrap around basic system/library APIs with same semantics and error code, such as `apr_file_open`, and `my_open` for `open`

```
/* hadoop: hadoop-hdfs-project/.../server/namenode/FSPermissionChecker.java
   (commit 0398db5...48896fa) */
  throw new AccessControlException(
-         "Permission denied");
+         "Permission denied. user="
+         + user + " is not the owner of inode=" + inode
  );
```

(a) **The specific and precise principles:** the message was improved by explaining the denial and including root-cause configurations.

```
/* httpd: server/request.c (revision 99781; revision 1301504) */
  } else if (APR_STATUS_IS_EACCES(rv)) {
    ap_log_rerror(APLOG_MARK, APLOG_ERR, rv, r,        added in v2.4.2
                  "access to %s denied ",
+                 "(filesystem path '%s') ",
+                 "because search permissions are missing "
+                 "on a component of the path",
-                 r->uri);                              added in v2.4.1
+                 r->uri, r->filename);
    return r->status = HTTP_FORBIDDEN;
  }
```

(b) **The complete principle**: the log message was improved by including details of the denied access

Figure 2. Demonstration of three design principles of access-denied messages (real-world postmortem improvements for usability issues).

in Apache and MySQL. Thus, besides the basic APIs (defined in `fcntl.h`, `unistd.h`, `stat.h`, `stdio.h`, `java.io`, and `java.nio`), we include customized file APIs for each studied system and track their error returns. Further, if the return values and error code are propagated to higher-level APIs, we recursively treat these APIs as customized file APIs. The method is similar as error-code propagation analysis [44], but with the special focus on identifying the log messages for the denied access.

Principles of access-denied messages

We study access-denied messages based on the following three principles. In essence, the messages should present specific, precise and complete information to help sysadmins understand missing permissions and resolve issues correctly.

Specific: Every access denial should have specific messages for explaining the root causes of the denial. Generic notification messages such as "`permission denied`" are not helpful for problem-solving [34,75].

Precise: When denying access, the software should print precise messages to pinpoint root-cause configurations (e.g., the parameters or missing permissions). This is considered the key to enabling sysadmins to resolve configuration problems [70,72,74,79].

Complete: The messages should include critical details of the denied access to enable sysadmins or automated tools to reproduce the issue and reason out the root causes. To deduce the missing permissions, one needs to know "'who' can do 'what' to 'which' things [14,30,32].

Figure 2 demonstrates these three principles using real-world examples where the messages were improved by the developers as postmortem improvements for usability issues.

Denied access occasionally has specific messages

Table 9 shows the percentage of access denials that has specific explanatory messages. In the studied C/C++ systems, only 66.5% of the program points that deny access have specific

Software	Internal denials		File access denials	
	w/ specific logs	Total	w/ specific logs	Total
Apache	63.7% (56)	88	88.2% (180)	204
MySQL	85.1% (40)	47	80.9% (313)	387
Lighttpd	63.2% (12)	19	71.4% (50)	70
VSFTP	44.0% (11)	25	78.4% (29)	37
Hadoop	100.0% (49)	49	88.0% (271)	308
HBase	100.0% (36)	36	86.7% (26)	30

Table 9. Program points of access denials that have specific log messages.

```
/* httpd-2.4.20: modules/aaa/mod_authz_core.c */
authz_status method_check_authorization(request_rec *r, ...) {
  ...                       <- check access w/ method-based ACL configs
  return AUTHZ_DENIED;      <- no log in this function
}

authz_status ip_check_authorization(request_rec *r, ...) {
  ...                       <- check access w/ IP-based ACL configs
  return AUTHZ_DENIED;      <- no log in this function
}

authz_status host_check_authorization(request_rec *r, ...) {
  ...                       <- check access w/ host-based configs
  return AUTHZ_DENIED;      <- no log in this function
}

int authorize_user_core(request_rec* r, ...) {
  ...                       <- call the above check functions
  if (auth_result == AUTHZ_DENIED) {
    ...
    ap_log_rerror(APLOG_MARK, APLOG_ERR, 0, r, APLOGNO(01631)
                  "user %s: authorization failure for %s:",
                  r->user, r->uri);
}
```

Figure 3. An examples of denying access without giving specific messages in Apache: access denied with different causes (`method`, `IP`, and `host`) all comes with the same generic notification.

```
/* mysql-5.7.13: storage/innobase/row/row0import.cc */
FILE* file = fopen(name, "rb");
if (file == NULL) {
  /* If there is no cfp file, return directly */
  import.m_cfp_missing = true;
  return DB_SUCCESS;               Silently ignoring the denied access
} ...
```

Figure 4. An example of denied file access without any log messages in MySQL: the denial is treated as file non-existence and is silently ignored.

messages to explain the denials; the remaining ones typically fall into generic notifications, such as "`authorization failure`" in the example of Figure 3. As shown in the study of real-world access-denied issues, such generic notification messages cause difficulties for sysadmins to nail down the root-cause configurations, and thus lead to trial-and-error based problem-solving. In the studied Java systems, the denied access is manifested through exceptions such as `AccessControlException` in Hadoop and `AccessDeniedException` in HBase. The software developers are enforced to write a specific message in order to initialize the exception objects (required by the constructor of the exception class). As a result, all the access-denied points in the studied Java programs have specific messages.

The majority (83.9%) of file access have log messages upon denials, while the rest silently ignore the denied access (c.f., Table 9). Most of the unlogged file access denials are treated as file non-existence, as exemplified in Figure 4. Some of them are attributed to the underlying library APIs. In fact,

Software	Pinpoint root-cause config	Internal denials
Apache	87.5% (49)	56
MySQL	17.5% (7)	40
Lighttpd	33.3% (4)	12
VSFTP	0.0% (0)	11
Hadoop	38.8% (19)	49
HBase	13.9% (5)	36
Total	41.2% (84)	204

Table 10. The percentage of messages that pinpoint root-cause configurations when the software denies access.

Software	Error code	Subject	Operation	Object	Total
Apache	71.1% (128)	0.0% (0)	54.4% (98)	81.1% (146)	180
MySQL	56.2% (176)	0.0% (0)	62.0% (194)	81.8% (256)	313
Lighttpd	76.0% (38)	0.0% (0)	46.0% (23)	90.0% (45)	50
VSFTP	3.4% (1)	0.0% (0)	48.3% (14)	65.5% (19)	29
Hadoop	59.8% (162)	0.0% (0)	93.4% (253)	95.2% (258)	271
HBase	92.3% (24)	0.0% (0)	100.0% (26)	96.2% (25)	26
Total	60.9% (529)	0.0% (0)	70.0% (608)	86.2% (749)	869

Table 11. Characteristics of log messages for denied file access. Many log messages miss critical details such as error type, subject, file operation, and file object.

```
/* hadoop-2.7.2: hadoop-hdfs-project/.../server/datanode/DataNode.java */
  throw new AccessControlException(
      "Can't continue with getBlockLocalPathInfo() " +
      "authorization. The user " + currentUser + " " +
-     "is not allowed to call getBlockLocalPathInfo");
+     "is not configured in " +              // Root-cause parameter
+     "dfs.block.local-path-access.user");
```

Figure 5. An example of messages that do not pinpoint the root-cause configurations, and our patch to improve it (accepted by the developers).

```
/* hadoop-2.7.2: hadoop-common-project/.../util/RunJar.java */
System.err.println("Not a valid JAR: " +
                   file.getCanonicalPath());
```

(a) Missing error code: it is hard to infer the root cause of the denied access.

```
/* vsftpd-3.0.3: logging.c */
die("chroot");
```

(b) Missing file object: the log message does not record the target root directory.

```
/* mysql-5.7.13: plugin/innodb_memcached/.../daemon/memcached.c */
log(EXTENSION_LOG_WARNING, NULL, "Failed to open %s: %s\n",
    temp_portnumber_filename, strerror(errno));
```

(c) Missing access type (file operation): the message is printed only when the file is not *writable*.

Figure 6. Different types of inadequate log messages for the denied file access in the studied software programs.

several Java's built-in libraries and APIs equalize denied access and file non-existence. For example, in Java's built-in library `java.io`, all the denied access is manifested through `FileNotFoundException`; APIs like `exists` (in both `java.io` and `java.nio`) do not differentiate between permission errors and file non-existence. Such practice commonly results in confusion when the access is denied for files that do exist [38].

Root-cause configurations are rarely pinpointed

Next we study the content of each specific access-denied message. We focus on the log messages when the software denied access internally. In this case, the software has the opportunity to pinpoint the root-cause configurations (either the relevant parameters or the missing permissions). However, only 41.2% of log messages follow this principle, as shown in Table 10. One main reason behind such inadequate messages is that software developers do not design message content with helping sysadmins in mind; instead, they often assume that sysadmins understand the implementation, as exemplified by Figure 5.

Some of the log messages, though referring to specific denied access, are still in the form of generic notifications. For example, all the denied access to tables in MySQL come with the following notorious message:

"`%s command denied to user %s for table %s`"

As shown in our study, many database administrators cannot figure out the exact missing permissions when their operations are denied, and consequently choose to grant `ALL` privileges as workarounds. This is quite understandable, given that MySQL has 32 distinct privileges and 12 of them apply to tables.

Messages for denied file access miss critical details

We then study the log messages for each denied file access. Assisting resolutions for file access denials needs complete information of the subject, access type, and file object. Moreover, as the denied file access is manifested through `errno` or exceptions in the same way as other types of I/O errors such as disk errors (the file `open` system call can return 21 different `errno`, each representing a unique error type), the log messages should include `errno` or exceptions. Unfortunately, our evaluation shows that many of the log messages for denied access miss these critical details.

Table 11 characterizes the log messages for file access denials. Only 60.9% and 70.0% of messages include `errno`/exceptions and access types, respectively. Compared with C/C++ systems, the studied Java systems have more complete messages because many Java file APIs throw exceptions with stack traces upon the denied access, and thus automatically include the file objects and the operations. In C/C++ systems all these messages were manually written by the software developers. However, Java also provides C/C++ style APIs such as `mkdir` and `renameTo` (`java.io.File`) that use `false` returns to indicate all types of errors. Most of the studied log messages include the denied file objects in the content (but still 13.8% inadvertently miss the information). Figure 6 shows the three types of inadequate file-access messages in the studied software.

Notably, none of the file access denied messages include the subject (against whom access is denied), likely because the subject is not concerned in the other types of access errors (e.g., invalid file names, insufficient memory, and disk errors). However, subject information is critical for access control. In our study, there are several cases in which the sysadmins had difficulties in obtaining subject information, especially when the programs use `setuid` or `setgid`.

IMPLICATIONS

Improving usability of access control requires efforts of both software systems and tooling support. Our results show that current design and implementation of access control are far from adequate to assist correct, secure configurations. One fundamental cause of this situation is that software designers and developers often assume that sysadmins are so expert that the usability of access control is not a concern for them. Our study invalidates this assumption—without adequate feedback and tooling, sysadmins introduce misconfigurations and pose security risks. Our study draws following design implications.

Design of software systems. Our results show that current system feedback via log messages is far from adequate to assist resolving access-denied issues with correct configurations. The feedback messages should be designed with the goal of helping sysadmins to correctly resolve the denied access; they should follow the usability principles—being specific, precise, and complete. It is important to educate developers and raise the awareness that access-denied messages should be designed differently from log messages for other usages (e.g., debugging logs are mostly used by developers themselves). We hope that our work can serve this purpose.

Automated tools for evaluating and enhancing access-denied messages can significantly improve the quality of feedback information. Most of the existing log-enhancement techniques focus on reconstructing execution paths [77] and failure-site information [76] to improve software diagnosability. There are techniques for detecting inadequate log messages for configuration errors that result in functionality issues [79]. These approaches can be extended to detect inadequate access-denied messages based on the usability principles of access control.

Design of tool support. The ultimate tool support is to automate the resolutions for access-denied issues, thus avoiding human errors. This is not impossible: though setting complicated access-control configurations is difficult for human administrators, it is straightforward for automated programs. In fact, SELinux's utilities like `audit2allow` have demonstrated the feasibility to automatically generate correct access-control configurations to allow denied access. In our study of CentOS cases (CentOS enables SELinux by default), we observe that `audit2allow` significantly improves the usability and increases the adoption of SELinux. This approach should be generalized and implemented in other software systems.

Furthermore, tool support for articulating security impact of access-control configurations is highly desired. Our study reveals that one common difficulty of sysadmins is to understand the impact of configuration changes, e.g., who obtains more access after the change. Informing and visualizing such information would help sysadmins make more reasonable and cautious access-control decisions. For common resources such as Unix files and SQL databases, generic tools can be made based on their semantics, while application may need specific implementations for their own access-control mechanisms.

RELATED WORK

The previous studies on access control mainly focus on authoring and visualizing access-control policies. Bauer et al. examined the physical access-control policies and found that users' intended policies were better matched with a flexible access-control system [6]. In another study, Bauer et al. identified three sets of requirements either ignored or inadequately addressed for implementing access-control policies [7]. They reported that policy makers were often distinct from policy implementers; the separation raises challenges of ensuring that the actual configurations correctly implement policies. Sinclair et al. studied access control practices of three organizations and reported that access control was profoundly broken in real-world practices due to over-simplified or wrong assumptions [56,57]. The consequences include frequent over-entitlement (granting too much access) and constant under-entitlement that leads to access-denied issues. Reeder et al. argued that the traditional list-of-rules model is deficient in displaying policies when multiple rules interact, as it cannot convey the interactions amongst rules to policy authors [42]. In another study, Reeder et al. demonstrated that the conflict-resolution method for ALLOW and DENY rules had significant usability impact on the implementation of access-control policies [43]. Adage is one of the first authorization services that place usability at the center of its design [80].

This paper concerns about a complementary aspect of access-control usability—resolving access-denied issues. Certainly, the ultimate solutions is creating perfect configurations to allow access to all authorized requests. However, due to a number of practical challenges, in reality many sysadmins still have to manually resolve access-denied issues on an as-needed basis. As shown in this paper, resolving access-denied issues is critical to the correctness of access control.

Other works have studied access control of various end-user applications, including personal/home data sharing [35, 36], web applications [3, 11], social network services [18, 27], and mobile apps [20]. End-user access control is completely different from security administration of system software studied in this paper. It mainly focuses on protecting the privacy and security of the individuals who are less technical and less motivated [25, 69]; end users do not manage server/OS software in which security is one primary concern. Also, the feedback information for end users needs to balance usability and disclosure of sensitive information [29]; this is less a concern for sysadmins who are policy makers and implementers and usually have highest privileges. Lastly, GUI-based techniques designed for end users are not applicable to system software which typically are not managed via GUIs [5, 22, 66].

CONCLUDING REMARKS

This paper advocates the importance of assisting correct resolutions for access-denied issues—a critical but often ignored aspect of access control usability. We show that the common problem-solving practices based on trial and error are prone to security misconfigurations, and are inefficient in allowing the denied access. Consequently, security misconfigurations are commonly introduced as workarounds in the field, imposing significant security risks. Our study reveals that security misconfigurations are often the results of lacking precise understanding of the root causes (the missing permissions), due to inadequate feedback information and tool support provided by today's software systems. Our future work includes exploring automated approaches to resolving access-denied issues under different access-control models, and deducing security implications of sysadmin's resolutions (e.g., unauthorized access incorrectly granted by their configurations).

REFERENCES

1. Sepehr Amir-Mohammadian, Stephen Chong, and Christian Skalka. 2016. Correct Audit Logging: Theory and Practice. In *Proceedings of the 5th International Conference on Principles of Security and Trust (POST'16)*. Eindhoven, The Netherlands.
2. Apache Users Mailing List. 2016. http://mail-archives.apache.org/mod_mbox/httpd-users/. (2016).
3. Dirk Balfanz. 2003. Usable Access Control for the World Wide Web. In *Proceedings of the 19th Annual Computer Security Applications Conference (ACSAC'03)*. Las Vegas, NV, USA.
4. Rob Barrett, Yen-Yang Michael Chen, and Paul Maglio. 2009. System Administrators are Users, Too: Designing Workspaces for Managing Internet-Scale Systems. In *Proceedings of the 27th ACM Conference on Human Factors in Computing Systems (CHI'03)*. Boston, MA, USA.
5. Rob Barrett, Eser Kandogan, Paul P. Maglio, Eben Haber, Leila A. Takayama, and Madhu Prabaker. 2004. Field Studies of Computer System Administrators: Analysis of System Management Tools and Practices. In *Proceedings of the 2004 ACM Conference on Computer Supported Cooperative Work (CSCW'04)*. Baltimore, MD, USA.
6. Lujo Bauer, Lorrie Faith Cranor, Robert W. Reeder, Michael K. Reiter, and Kami Vaniea. 2008. A User Study of Policy Creation in a Flexible Access-Control System. In *Proceedings of the 26th ACM Conference on Human Factors in Computing Systems (CHI'08)*. Florence, Italy.
7. Lujo Bauer, Lorrie Faith Cranor, Robert W. Reeder, Michael K. Reiter, and Kami Vaniea. 2009. Real Life Challenges in Access Control Management. In *Proceedings of the 27th ACM Conference on Human Factors in Computing Systems (CHI'09)*. Boston, MA, USA.
8. Lujo Bauer, Scott Garriss, and Michael K. Reiter. 2008. Detecting and Resolving Policy Misconfigurations in Access-Control Systems. In *Proceedings of the 13th ACM Symposium on Access Control Models and Technologies (SACMAT'08)*. Estes Park, CO, USA.
9. Lujo Bauer, Scott Garriss, and Michael K. Reiter. 2011. Detecting and Resolving Policy Misconfigurations in Access-Control Systems. *ACM Transactions on Information and System Security (TISSEC)* 14, 1 (May 2011), 1–28.
10. David Botta, Rodrigo Werlinger, André Gagné, Konstantin Beznosov, Lee Iverson, Sidney Fels, and Brian Fisher. 2007. Towards Understanding IT Security Professionals and Their Tools. In *Proceedings of the 2nd Symposium on Usable Privacy and Security (SOUPS'07)*. Pittsburgh, PA, USA.
11. Xiang Cao and Lee Iverson. 2006. Intentional access management: making access control usable for end-users. In *Proceedings of the 2nd Symposium on Usable Privacy and Security (SOUPS'06)*. Pittsburgh, PA, USA.
12. CentOS Forums. 2016. https://www.centos.org/forums/. (2016).
13. CentOS Mailing Lists. 2016. https://lists.centos.org/pipermail/centos/. (2016).
14. Anton Chuvakin and Gunnar Peterson. 2010. How to Do Application Logging Right. *IEEE Security & Privacy* 8, 4 (Jul. 2010), 82–85.
15. Tathagata Das, Ranjita Bhagwan, and Prasad Naldurg. 2010. Baaz: A System for Detecting Access Control Misconfigurations. In *Proceedings of the 19th USENIX Security Symposium (USENIX Security'10)*. Washington, DC, USA.
16. Database Administrators. 2016. http://dba.stackexchange.com. (2016).
17. Database Administrators #127003. 2016. Can't access MySQL database with created user through dll. http://dba.stackexchange.com/questions/127003/cant-access-mysql-database-with-created-user-through-dll. (Jan. 2016).
18. Serge Egelman, Andrew Oates, and Shriram Krishnamurthi. 2011. Oops, I Did it Again: Mitigating Repeated Access Control Errors on Facebook. In *Proceedings of the 29th ACM International Conference on Human Factors in Computing Systems (CHI'11)*. Vancouver, BC, Canada.
19. Daniel Farmer and Eugene H. Spafford. 1990. *The COPS Security Checker System*. Technical Report CSD-TR-993. Purdue University, Department of Computer Science.
20. Adrienne Porter Felt. 2012. *Towards Comprehensible and Effective Permission Systems*. Ph.D. Dissertation. University of California at Berkeley, Electrical Engineering and Computer Sciences.
21. Jeff Goldman. 2014. Misconfigured Server Causes Massive Data Breach at MBIA. http://www.esecurityplanet.com/network-security/misconfigured-server-causes-massive-data-breach-at-mbia.html. (Oct. 2014).
22. Eben M. Haber and John Bailey. 2007. Design Guidelines for System Administration Tools Developed through Ethnographic Field Study. In *Proceedings of the 1st ACM Symposium on Computer Human Interaction for Management of Information Technology (CHIMIT'07)*. Cambridge, MA, USA.
23. Hadoop User Mailing Lists. 2016. http://mail-archives.apache.org/mod_mbox/hadoop-user/. (2016).
24. Hewlett Packard Enterprise. 2015. HP Cyber Risk Report 2015. http://www8.hp.com/h20195/v2/GetPDF.aspx/4AA5-0858ENN.pdf. (Feb. 2015).

25. Adele E. Howe, Indrajit Ray, Mark Roberts, Malgorzata Urbanska, and Zinta Byrne. 2012. The Psychology of Security for the Home Computer User. In *Proceeding of the 33rd IEEE Symposium on Security & Privacy (S&P)*. San Francisco, CA, USA.

26. Weihang Jiang, Chongfeng Hu, Shankar Pasupathy, Arkady Kanevsky, Zhenmin Li, and Yuanyuan Zhou. 2009. Understanding Customer Problem Troubleshooting from Storage System Logs. In *Proceedings of the 7th USENIX Conference on File and Storage Technologies (FAST'09)*. San Francisco, CA, USA.

27. Maritza L. Johnson. 2012. *Toward Usable Access Control for End-users: A Case Study of Facebook Privacy Settings*. Ph.D. Dissertation. Columbia University, Computer Science.

28. Eser Kandogan and Eben M. Haber. 2005. Security Administration Tools and Practices. *Security and Usability, O'Reilly Media, Inc.* (Aug. 2005).

29. Apu Kapadia, Geetanjali Sampemane, and Roy H. Campbell. 2004. Know Why Your Access Was Denied: Regulating Feedback for Usable Security. In *Proceedings of the 11th ACM Conference on Computer and Communications Security (CCS'04)*. Washington, DC, USA.

30. Butler Lampson. 2009. Usable Security: How to Get It. *Commun. ACM* 52, 11 (Nov. 2009), 25–27.

31. Butler Lampson. 2015. Perspectives on Security. SOSP History Day. (Oct. 2015). http://sigops.org/sosp/sosp15/history/.

32. Butler W. Lampson. 1974. Protection. *ACM SIGOPS Operating Systems Review* 8, 1 (Jan. 1974), 18–24.

33. Butler W. Lampson. 2004. Computer Security in the Real World. *IEEE Computer* 37, 6 (Jun. 2004), 37–46.

34. Paul P. Maglio and Eser Kandogan. 2004. Error Messages: What's the Problem? *ACM Queue* 2, 8 (Nov. 2004), 50–55.

35. Roy A. Maxion and Robert W. Reeder. 2005. Improving User-Interface Dependability through Mitigation of Human Error. *International Journal of Human-Computer Studies* 63, 1-2 (Jul. 2005), 25–50.

36. Michelle L. Mazurek, J. P. Arsenault, Joanna Bresee, Nitin Gupta, Iulia Ion, Christine Johns, Daniel Lee, Yuan Liang, Jenny Olsen, Brandon Salmon, Richard Shay, Kami Vaniea, Lujo Bauer, Lorrie Faith Cranor, Gregory R. Granger, and Michael K. Reiter. 2010. Access Control for Home Data Sharing: Attitudes, Needs, and Practices. In *Proceedings of the 28th ACM International Conference on Human Factors in Computing Systems (CHI'10)*. Atlanta, GA, USA.

37. Microsoft Baseline Security Analyzer. 2016. http://www.microsoft.com/technet/security/tools/MBSAHome.mspx. (2016).

38. MySQL Bug #80542. 2016. Should notify users when ignoring their option files. http://bugs.mysql.com/bug.php?id=80542. (Feb. 2016).

39. MySQL General Discussion Mailing List. 2016. https://lists.mysql.com/mysql. (2016).

40. Peter G. Neumann. 2015. Reminiscences on the 25th SOSP's History Day Workshop. http://sigops.org/sosp/sosp15/history/12-neumann.pdf. (2015).

41. Eric Steven Raymond and Rick Moen. 2014. How To Ask Questions The Smart Way. http://www.catb.org/~esr/faqs/smart-questions.html. (2014).

42. Robert W. Reeder, Lujo Bauer, Lorrie Faith Cranor, Michael K. Reiter, Kelli Bacon, Keisha How, and Heather Strong. 2008. Expandable Grids for Visualizing and Authoring Computer Security Policies. In *Proceedings of the 26th ACM Conference on Human Factors in Computing Systems (CHI'08)*. Florence, Italy.

43. Robert W. Reeder, Lujo Bauer, Lorrie Faith Cranor, Michael K. Reiter, and Kami Vaniea. 2011. More than Skin Deep: Measuring Effects of the Underlying Model on Access-Control System Usability. In *Proceedings of the 29th ACM International Conference on Human Factors in Computing Systems (CHI'11)*. Vancouver, BC, Canada.

44. Cindy Rubio-González, Haryadi S. Gunawi, Ben Liblit, Remzi H. Arpaci-Dusseau, and Andrea C. Arpaci-Dusseau. 2009. Error Propagation Analysis for File Systems. In *Proceedings of the 30th Annual ACM SIGPLAN Conference on Programming Language Design and Implementation (PLDI'09)*. Dublin, Ireland.

45. Bruce Schneier. 2009. Real-World Access Control. https://www.schneier.com/blog/archives/2009/09/real-world_acce.html. (2009).

46. ServerFault. 2016. http://serverfault.com. (2016).

47. ServerFault #235376. 2011. Apache/PHP writing to a user's home folder. http://serverfault.com/questions/235376/apache-php-writing-to-a-users-home-folder. (Feb. 2011).

48. ServerFault #287508. 2011. Apache Permission denied problem on OS X. serverfault.com/questions//apache-permission-denied-problem-on-os-x. (Jul. 2011).

49. ServerFault #396036. 2012. Apache httpd permissions. http://serverfault.com/questions/396036/apache-httpd-permissions. (Jun. 2012).

50. ServerFault #401115. 2012. Apache Mod SVN Access Forbidden. http://serverfault.com/questions/401115/apache-mod-svn-access-forbidden. (Jun. 2012).

51. ServerFault #402630. 2012. HTTP Error: 413 Request Entity Too Large. http://serverfault.com/questions/402630/http-error-413-request-entity-too-large. (Jun. 2012).

52. ServerFault #418101. 2012. Apache "Client denied by server configuration", despite allowing access to directory (vhost configuration). http://serverfault.com/questions/418101/apache-client-denied-by-server-configuration-despite-allowing-access-to-direc. (Aug. 2012).
53. ServerFault #421633. 2012. Cannot write file with apache despite 777 permissions on Directory. http://serverfault.com/questions/421633/cannot-write-file-with-apache-despite-777-permissions-on-directory. (Aug. 2012).
54. ServerFault #507914. 2013. Mysql working remotely but not localy. http://serverfault.com/questions/507914/mysql-working-remotely-but-not-localy. (May 2013).
55. ServerFault #65362. 2009. Is there a work around for the "Permission denied" error from urllib2.urlopen? http://serverfault.com/questions//is-there-a-work-around-for-the-permission-denied-error-from-urllib2-urlopen. (Sep. 2009).
56. Sara Sinclair. 2013. *Access Control In and For the Real World*. Ph.D. Dissertation. Dartmouth College, Department of Computer Science.
57. Sara Sinclair and Sean W. Smith. 2010. What's Wrong with Access Control in the Real World? *IEEE Security & Privacy* 8, 4 (Jul. 2010), 74–77.
58. StackOverflow. 2016. http://stackoverflow.com. (2016).
59. StackOverflow #13542384. 2012. Setting permissions for cloudera hadoop. http://stackoverflow.com/questions/13542384/setting-permissions-for-cloudera-hadoop. (Nov. 2012).
60. StackOverflow #22664268. 2014. Error on map reduce example of Hadoop 2.2.0. http://stackoverflow.com/questions/22664268/error-on-map-reduce-example-of-hadoop-2-2-0. (Mar. 2014).
61. StackOverflow #29438893. 2015. Hadoop jar execution failing on class not found. http://stackoverflow.com/questions/29438893/hadoop-jar-execution-failing-on-class-not-found. (Apr. 2015).
62. StackOverflow #30926357. 2015. Oozie on YARN - oozie is not allowed to impersonate hadoop. http://stackoverflow.com/questions/30926357/oozie-on-yarn-oozie-is-not-allowed-to-impersonate-hadoop. (Jun. 2015).
63. StackOverflow #33358339. 2015. Hadoop "error while writing TokenizerMapper permission denied". http://stackoverflow.com/questions/33358339/hadoop-error-while-writing-tokenizermapper-permission-denied. (Jun. 2015).
64. StackOverflow #473789. 2013. mysql doesn't start after relocating data dir. http://serverfault.com/questions/473789/mysql-doesnt-start-after-relocating-data-dir. (Jan. 2013).
65. StackOverflow Help Center. 2016. Why is voting important? http://stackoverflow.com/help/why-vote. (2016).
66. Leila Takayama and Eser Kandogan. 2006. Trust as an Underlying Factor of System Administrator Interface Choice. In *CHI '06 Extended Abstracts on Human Factors in Computing Systems (CHI EA'06)*. Montréal, Québec, Canada.
67. The Open Web Application Security Project. 2013. OWASP Top 10: The Ten Most Critical Web Application Security Risks. http://owasptop10.googlecode.com/files/OWASP%20Top%2010%20-%202013.pdf. (2013).
68. Dan Walsh. 2013. Audit2allow should be your third option not the first. http://danwalsh.livejournal.com/63137.html. (2013).
69. Ryan West. 2008. The Psychology of Security. *Commun. ACM* 51, 4 (Apr. 2008), 34–40.
70. Tianyin Xu, Long Jin, Xuepeng Fan, Yuanyuan Zhou, Shankar Pasupathy, and Rukma Talwadker. 2015. Hey, You Have Given Me Too Many Knobs! Understanding and Dealing with Over-Designed Configuration in System Software. In *Proceedings of the 10th Joint Meeting of the European Software Engineering Conference and the ACM SIGSOFT Symposium on the Foundations of Software Engineering (ESEC/FSE'15)*. Bergamo, Italy.
71. Tianyin Xu, Xinxin Jin, Peng Huang, Yuanyuan Zhou, Shan Lu, Long Jin, and Shankar Pasupathy. 2016. Early Detection of Configuration Errors to Reduce Failure Damage. In *Proceedings of the 12th USENIX Conference on Operating Systems Design and Implementation (OSDI'16)*. Savannah, GA, USA.
72. Tianyin Xu, Jiaqi Zhang, Peng Huang, Jing Zheng, Tianwei Sheng, Ding Yuan, Yuanyuan Zhou, and Shankar Pasupathy. 2013. Do Not Blame Users for Misconfigurations. In *Proceedings of the 24th Symposium on Operating System Principles (SOSP'13)*. Farmington, PA, USA.
73. Tianyin Xu and Yuanyuan Zhou. 2015. Systems Approaches to Tackling Configuration Errors: A Survey. *ACM Computing Surveys (CSUR)* 47, 4 (Jul. 2015).
74. Zuoning Yin, Xiao Ma, Jing Zheng, Yuanyuan Zhou, Lakshmi N. Bairavasundaram, and Shankar Pasupathy. 2011. An Empirical Study on Configuration Errors in Commercial and Open Source Systems. In *Proceedings of the 23rd ACM Symposium on Operating Systems Principles (SOSP'11)*. Cascais, Portugal.
75. Ding Yuan. 2012. *Improving Failure Diagnosis with Better Logging Design and Analysis*. Ph.D. Dissertation. University of Illinois Urbana-Champaign, Department of Computer Science.
76. Ding Yuan, Soyeon Park, Peng Huang, Yang Liu, Michael M. Lee, Xiaoming Tang, Yuanyuan Zhou, and Stefan Savage. 2012. Be Conservative: Enhancing Failure Diagnosis with Proactive Logging. In *Proceedings of the*

10th USENIX Conference on Operating Systems Design and Implementation (OSDI'12). Hollywood, CA, USA.

77. Ding Yuan, Jing Zheng, Soyeon Park, Yuanyuan Zhou, and Stefan Savage. 2011. Improving Software Diagnosability via Log Enhancement. In *Proceedings of the 16th International Conference on Architecture Support for Programming Languages and Operating Systems (ASPLOS'11).* Newport Beach, CA, USA.

78. Jiaqi Zhang, Lakshmi Renganarayana, Xiaolan Zhang, Niyu Ge, Vasanth Bala, Tianyin Xu, and Yuanyuan Zhou. 2014. EnCore: Exploiting System Environment and Correlation Information for Misconfiguration Detection. In *Proceedings of the 19th International Conference on Architecture Support for Programming Languages and Operating Systems (ASPLOS'14).* Salt Lake City, UT, USA.

79. Sai Zhang and Michael D. Ernst. 2015. Proactive Detection of Inadequate Diagnostic Messages for Software Configuration Errors. In *Proceedings of the 2015 International Symposium on Software Testing and Analysis (ISSTA'15).* Baltimore, MD, USA.

80. Mary Ellen Zurko, Rich Simon, and Tom Sanfilippo. 1999. A User-Centered, Modular Authorization Service Built on an RBAC Foundation. In *Proceedings of the 20th IEEE Symposium on Security and Privacy (S&P).* Oakland, CA, USA.

User Interactions and Permission Use on Android

Kristopher Micinski, Daniel Votipka, Rock Stevens, Nikolaos Kofinas, Michelle L. Mazurek, and Jeffrey S. Foster
University of Maryland, College Park
{micinski, dvotipka, rstevens, nkofinas, mmazurek, jfoster}@cs.umd.edu

ABSTRACT
Android and other mobile operating systems ask users for authorization before allowing apps to access sensitive resources such as contacts and location. We hypothesize that such authorization systems could be improved by becoming more integrated with the app's user interface. In this paper, we conduct two studies to test our hypothesis. First, we use AppTracer, a dynamic analysis tool we developed, to measure to what extent user interactions and sensitive resource use are related in existing apps. Second, we conduct an online survey to examine how different interactions with the UI affect users' expectations about whether an app accesses sensitive resources. Our results suggest that user interactions such as button clicks can be interpreted as authorization, reducing the need for separate requests; but that accesses not directly tied to user interactions should be separately authorized, possibly when apps are first launched.

ACM Classification Keywords
H.5.m Information Interfaces and Presentation (e.g. HCI): Miscellaneous

Author Keywords
Android; Permissions; Contextual Security; Apps

INTRODUCTION
Android has a *permission system* that asks users for authorization before an app uses sensitive resources such as contacts or GPS location. A key challenge in such authorization systems is balancing user interruptions with making sensitive resource use transparent. We hypothesize that Android's existing authorization systems (install-time permission lists or run-time dialog boxes, depending on the version) could achieve a better balance by integrating with the app's user interface (UI), because the UI deeply informs the user's mental model of the app's behavior, including security-relevant behavior.

In particular, in this paper we ask whether *user interactions*—button clicks, page changes, dialog boxes, etc.—can be taken as evidence of authorization to use certain sensitive resources. If so, this could reduce the need for separate authorization requests. Conversely, we ask whether sensitive resource use without an associated interaction suggests a need for additional authorization requests. Note that while our studies are heavily influenced by Android, we believe our results will generalize to related mobile OS's and similar settings like web apps.

CHI 2017, May 06–11, 2017, Denver, CO, USA.

ACM 978-1-4503-4655-9/17/05 ... $15.00
DOI: http://dx.doi.org/10.1145/3025453.3025706

To answer these questions, we conducted two related studies. First, we reviewed 150 popular Android apps to determine whether sensitive resource uses are related to user interactions in existing apps. If so, an authorization mechanism integrated with the UI could work well with existing app designs. To carry out this study, we developed AppTracer, a dynamic analysis tool that instruments Android apps to log UI actions and resource uses, and then visualizes the logs as graphs that show temporal ordering of logged events. We used AppTracer to determine whether each observed resource use in each app was *interactive*, meaning either it was immediately preceded by a related UI event (e.g., accessing contacts after clicking a button marked "contacts"), or it was the main focus of the current screen (e.g., using location on a map screen).

We found that, across our subject apps, several resources (microphone, camera, external storage, and calendar) are used almost exclusively interactively; several others (including bluetooth and phone state) are used mostly non-interactively (which we call in the *background* even if the app itself is on screen); and several resources (most notably contacts and location) exhibit a mix of interactive and background uses. These results suggest interactive and background uses may call for different authorization mechanisms, and that these mechanisms cannot necessarily be divided strictly by resource.

These results informed the design of our second study, a 961-participant online survey investigating participants' expectations about interactive and background permission uses. Each participant viewed a slideshow of two usage scenarios for a mock mobile app, where each scenario shows a short interaction (e.g., launching the app, clicking a button, etc.) and then asks if the participant expects microphone, location, and/or contacts to be used after the interaction. We chose these resources to reflect a range of interactivity as measured in our app study. We aimed to gain insight into how different factors affect user expectations, and therefore which authorization mechanisms might be appropriate for different usage patterns.

As we anticipated, we found that users are much more likely to expect resources to be accessed after a related interaction than in the background. However, we also found that seeing one interactive use does not prime the user to expect a future background use, indicating a potential weakness in the Android M request-on-first-use authorization model. In contrast, our findings show that an authorization request at launch does increase expectations for both interactive and background accesses, perhaps because it better conveys the idea that the resource could be accessed at any time.

Drawing on the results of our studies, we make three design recommendations. First, resource uses should be made after associated interactions as much as possible. Given the current makeup of apps, this should be achievable for many commonly used resources without extensive effort. Second, separate authorization dialogs might be unnecessary for resources that are accessed mostly interactively (see, e.g., [27]). Finally, authorization for background resource uses should be distinct from authorization for interactive uses, and these background authorizations may be most effective when the app is launched.

BACKGROUND AND RELATED WORK

In earlier versions of Android, users were presented with a list of permissions requested by an app at install time. The user could then either grant the app full use of those permissions or not install the app at all. This model had a number of problems: few users comprehended or even read the list of permissions [12], and many apps requested more permissions than they used [10]. Because of these issues, Android M [14] switched to a model where apps ask for a permission the first time it is needed; the permission is then granted indefinitely.

In our work, we ask whether authorization systems similar to Android's can be improved by taking the user interface into account. Note that our work is orthogonal to the question of whether permissions are at the right level of granularity [6, 17] or protect the right resources [11].

Contextual Security on Mobile Devices

The motivation for our work, that authorization can be better integrated with the UI, exemplifies *contextual security* [22], which suggests security decisions should take the context into account. Several researchers have studied contextual security on mobile devices. Almuhimedi et. al [3] showed users historical data about how apps accessed their locations. They found 95% of users reassessed the apps' need for location, with 58% of those users further restricting location access. King [19] found users are more likely to expect sensitive resource accesses when suggested by the context. Felt et. al [1] proposed a process for deciding the appropriate authorization mechanism for a permission based on the a permissions' use in context. Several researchers [5, 13, 33] found users are surprised by some sensitive resource accesses that occur when apps are in the background. Most closely related to this paper, in a field study Wijesekera et al. [33] found that context is an important factor in determining expectation of resource use. Our work builds on this finding by using a controlled experiment to distinguish how different contextual factors, including consecutive interactions, contribute to user expectations.

The works just mentioned mainly define context as whether the app is on or off the screen. In contrast, we use a much richer notion of context based on sequences of UI actions.

Enforcing Contextual Security

Many systems have been proposed to enforce contextual security in apps. Chen et. al [8] present Pegasus, a static analysis system for analyzing apps and enforcing policies based on *permission event graphs* (PEGs). For example, Pegasus can check that contacts are only accessed after clicking a certain button. PEGs inspired the design of AppTracer. However, AppTracer uses dynamic (rather than static) analysis to reduce issues of false positives—every behavior AppTracer logs occurred in an actual run, whereas static analysis may report sensitive resource accesses that can never actually occur.

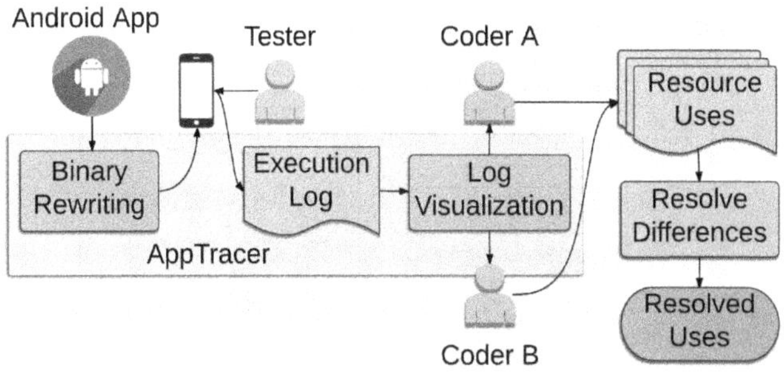

Figure 1: App Measurement Survey Procedure.

Yang et al. [34] presented AppIntent, which uses symbolic execution to determine sequences of UI events that lead to information leakage. Micinski et. al [21] use symbolic execution to enforce secure information-flow properties based on UI events. While both systems are promising, in practice symbolic execution is difficult to run at scale on Android apps due to the complexity of modeling the Android framework.

Stiegler et al. developed CapDesk [30] and later Polaris [29], two capability-based desktop system that utilize user interaction to drive access control. However, CapDesk and Polaris's focus is limited to file access. Roesner et. al [27] expand user-driven access control with *Access Control Gadgets* (ACGs), which tie resource accesses to certain UI elements, e.g., an ACG might allow location to be used only after a specific button is clicked. ACGs were later expanded to work on Android, with and later without modifying the operating system [25, 26]. The original ACG paper includes a user study measuring expectations related to interactive permission uses; our work expands on this idea to study a broader variety of factors and use cases. While the current paper does not directly implement or measure ACGs, our findings do support the use of ACGs.

APP MEASUREMENT SURVEY METHODOLOGY

In our first study, we reviewed a set of popular Android apps to determine how UI actions and resource uses are related. Figure 1 gives a high-level overview of our review process, which ultimately produces a set of *resource use codes* that indicate, for each resource use, what event (if any) caused the use. For example, we might determine that in some app, contacts were accessed just after a button click, or location was used immediately when the app launched.

The next subsections walk through the review process in detail.

Binary Rewriting and Execution Logging

The first step of our process uses AppTracer, a dynamic analysis tool we developed. AppTracer instruments the subject app

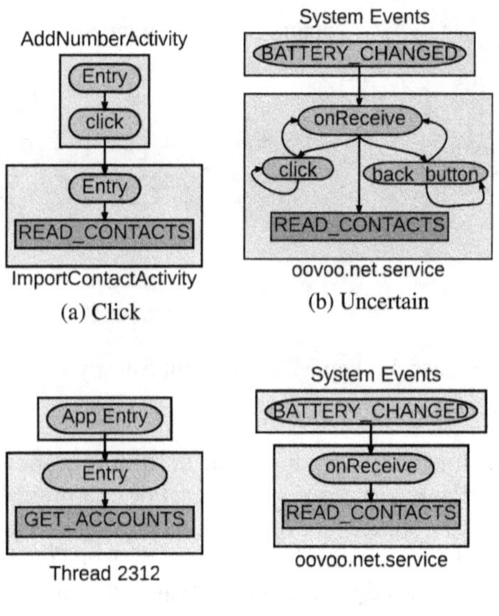

(a) Click (b) Uncertain (c) Startup (d) Background-External

Figure 2: AppTracer graphs and corresponding resource access patterns in our codebook.

so that, when run, it writes a log of UI events and permission uses. AppTracer adds instrumentation using Redexer [17], a rewriting tool for Dalvik bytecode (the language to which Android apps are compiled). Generally speaking, AppTracer instruments code by appending a log method to the bytecode and inserting calls to log at the beginning of UI-related callbacks (e.g., onClick handlers for button events) and just before calls to permission-protected methods (e.g., getLastLocation).

We identified methods associated with the UI using the Android documentation. We identified permission-protected methods using the PScout dataset [4], which attempts to list every security-sensitive method and its associated permission. PScout also includes information about sensitive content providers, intents, etc. Note that while PScout is reasonably thorough, we found several cases it missed. For example, we observed several visual indicators of SD card use that had no corresponding log entry AppTracer. After investigating the apps' decompiled code, we found the SD card was used via Java IO methods omitted by PSCout. Whenever we found such cases, we added the missing methods to our copy of the PScout database and reran our evaluated apps.

Once an app has been instrumented, a tester runs it to generate a log. (Note that one log is usually sufficient because in most apps, any app state is reachable from any other app state.) We elide the details of the log, but at a high level, for each UI event, AppTracer records the type of event and the corresponding parameters (e.g., what button was clicked, which menu option was selected, etc.). For each permission use, AppTracer logs the name of the called method and its arguments.

Log Visualization

After the tester produces a log, the next step is log visualization. Figures 2a–2b show example portions of AppTracer's graph-based visualization, redrawn for compactness and to omit most package names. Here, light blue boxes represent *activities*, which are the "screens" of the app. Within each activity, gray ovals represent the beginning of that activity ("entry," which usually corresponds to the onStart handler), UI events (e.g., "click"), or system events (e.g., BATTERY_CHANGED). Red rectangles indicate calls to methods protected by the named permission. There is an edge from node A to node B if A occurs immediately before B in the log. For example, in Figure 2a, contacts were read immediately after the ImportContactActivity activity was started.

Since logs can be quite lengthy, AppTracer heuristically merges nodes that arise from the same position in the bytecode. This sometimes results in ambiguity. For example, in Figure 2b, the single onReceive node actually represents calls to an Android broadcast receiver that AppTracer coalesced. We discuss this more below.

Finally, AppTracer also allows the user to directly view the log file entries corresponding to a node in the graph. This is useful to retrieve more detailed information about the node. For example, when reviewing Figure 2a, we looked in the log to determine that the clicked button had text associated with contacts. As another example, we used the logs to distinguish SD card accesses to user files from accesses to the app's own storage. We do not count the latter as a sensitive resource access because it accesses data owned by the app.

Resource Uses

The next step is to examine the AppTracer graph and record a set of codes that accurately categorize various resource accesses. More precisely, for each red node in the graph, the coder assigns a pair of the form (*resource*,*pattern*), where *resource* indicates what is protected by the permission and *pattern* is one of six different UI patterns, discussed next.

To keep our results understandable, we grouped together resources according to Google's permission groups [24]. For example, the single SMS resource includes more fine-grained permissions such as READ_SMS and SEND_SMS.

We developed an initial codebook for UI patterns based on our knowledge of Android app development. We then iteratively applied our codebook to sets of five apps (not in our evaluation set) at a time and adjusted the codes as necessary. After evaluating a total of twenty apps, we felt we had reached a codebook with a minimal set of orthogonal patterns.

The six access patterns in our codebook are grouped into three categories. First are the *interactive* patterns *Click* and *Page*. The code *Click* indicates resource use preceded by a UI event (including non-clicks such as swipes). For example, in Figure 2a, we coded READ_CONTACTS as *Click* because the contacts were accessed on a straight-line path from the click of a button labeled as importing contacts. *Page* codes uses that are clearly associated with an activity but are not associated with exactly one click. For example, *Page* would code the use of location during an activity that shows a list of nearby stores.

Second, in the *background* patterns *Startup*, *Bg-App*, and *Bg-Ext*, the resource use has no obviously connected user action.

Startup codes a resource accessed right after app launch but before any screen appears (and is thus disjoint from *Page*), e.g., the use of accounts in Figure 2c, which occurs in a thread created at app launch. *Bg-App* codes a resource used while the app is in the foreground, but with no clearly related user action. For example, a graph similar to Figure 2a would be coded as *Bg-App* if a button labeled for importing contacts was followed by the GET_ACCOUNTS permission rather than READ_CONTACTS. *Bg-Ext* denotes a resource used due to a system event, meaning it would be used whether or not the app is on screen. For example, in Figure 2d, accounts are read after the BATTERY_CHANGED system event.

Finally, *Uncertain* denotes a resource access that did not fit any of the previous patterns. In Figure 2b, we see a path from a system event to onReceive to READ_CONTACTS, which should be coded as *Bg-Ext*. But, the onReceive node also has an incoming edge from the click handler and the back button. These uses would be coded as *Bg-App*. (The *Click* and *Page* codes do not apply because the associated buttons do not indicate contacts will be used.) Because there are multiple possibilities, we code this case as *Uncertain*.

If desired, an AppTracer user can subsequently review the logs to try to resolve the uncertainty. For example, here the log entry associated with BATTERY_CHANGED is followed by a call to onReceive and then READ_CONTACTS. Thus, the permission use is coded as *Bg-Ext*. We then separately looked at the log entries for click and back_button, and found they were followed by an onReceive that was *not* followed by READ_CONTACTS. Thus, examining the logs allowed us to distinguish paths that we merged in AppTracer.

Note that for each app we only count each $(resource, pattern)$ pair once, no matter how often it occurs in the log. A stronger notion of frequency would be hard to interpret, since it would depend on how AppTracer heuristically coalesces graph nodes as well as to how the tester explored the app.

Coding Apps and Resolving Differences

Coding the resource uses of an app is inherently complex. Thus, two coders reviewed apps independently in sets of 15 and met after each set to resolve differences. Coders took approximately 10–20 minutes to code each app, and resolving differences for a set of 15 apps took approximately 30 minutes.

Most differences between coders were due to one coder overlooking a path or a resource in the AppTracer graph. In almost all such cases, when the other coder pointed out the omission, the first coder would quickly reach the same conclusion as the other coder. The remaining differences were caused by disagreements about whether the resource use was interactive. For example, one app read a user's accounts within an activity for filling a form. One coder recorded this as *Click*, since the accounts were read after a click. The other coder recorded this as *Bg-App*, because there was no observable use of the account data, such as pre-filling the form with data from the user's existing accounts. After encountering several such cases, the coders decided on a general principle of coding uses as *Bg-App* unless the UI explicitly mentioned that the resource could be used—hence, this example was resolved as *Bg-App*.

Inter-rater reliability between our coders for the non-visualization-error disagreements was Krippendorff's $\alpha = 0.897$, indicating close agreement [15].

App Selection

We drew our subject apps from a larger set comprising the 20 top downloaded free apps[1] from the 27 non-gaming categories on Google Play. We excluded gaming apps because they typically use native code that AppTracer cannot analyze. This yielded 503 apps (note there is overlap between categories).

We then randomly selected 150 apps to evaluate, subject to the constraint that no more than two apps were from the same developer. (We wanted to avoid bias due to overrepresentation of apps coded in the same style.). We excluded any apps that could not be run with AppTracer, replacing them with new randomly drawn apps to maintain an evaluation set of 150.

We excluded 48 apps because Redexer fails when rewriting them and 23 apps because either they refuse to run if modified (due to internal or system signature checks) or they are primarily implemented in native code. In most cases, we created accounts when signup was required to fully exercise an app, but we excluded 16 apps because they require accounts that are hard to set up online or require a fee (e.g., bank accounts).

Limitations

There are several potential limitations to this study. First, the tester may miss some app behavior, leading to a log that omits some possible resource uses and contexts. We tried to alleviate this concern by exercising as much of the app as possible. However, we did not use app features that required payment.

Second, AppTracer has limitations mentioned above: it may miss UI events or permission-protected methods, and it merges nodes that correspond to the same position in the bytecode. We tried to address the former issue by looking for cases where we expected an event to be in a log but it was not, and then adding the missing events or methods. We addressed the latter issue by manually disambiguating some of the uncertain cases.

Third, our study reviewed only popular Android apps. Observing that a resource is already accessed interactively in popular apps would indicate that changing the Android framework or system to implement interactivity-related protections for those accesses may be reasonable. These apps also represent the common case and likely help to set user expectations about apps and permissions. However, we note that the apps we examine likely differ from the long tail of other apps in important ways; popular apps are likely implemented to high standards and unlikely to be malicious. We leave similar measurements on a broader set of apps as future work.

APP MEASUREMENT SURVEY RESULTS

Figure 3 summarizes the resource use patterns we found. For example, across all apps, the camera was used in the *Click* pattern 57 times. Orange-shaded bars indicate interactive use patterns, and blue shades represent background uses. Resources are sorted by percent of interactive patterns.

[1] as of June 11, 2016

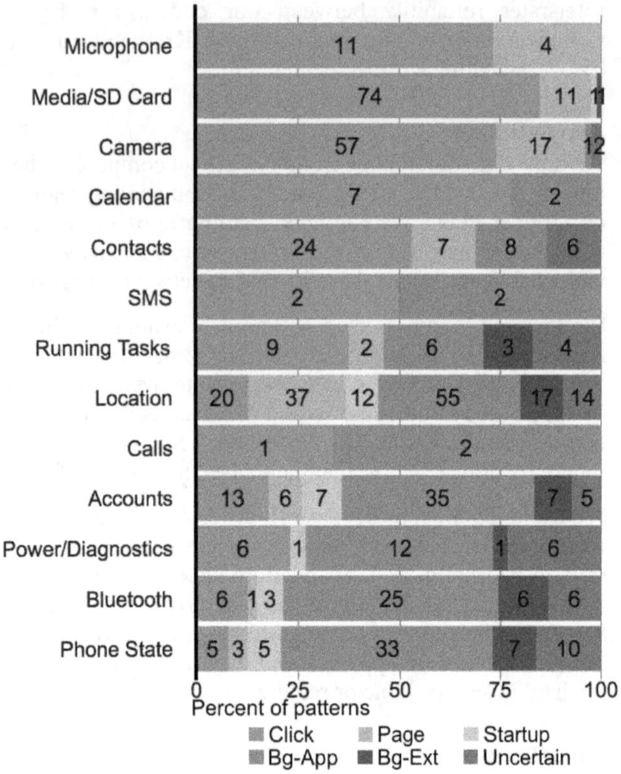

Figure 3: Percent of observed patterns of each type, per resource. Bar labels indicate how many apps we observed using each pattern, non-normalized.

We see that, to a rough approximation, the more sensitive the resource the more likely it is used interactively. Indeed, microphone, media, camera, and calendar were accessed almost exclusively interactively. We investigated the background and *Uncertain* uses for these resources. One calendar use and the two SD card uses were due to periodic background tasks (calendar syncing or scanning for files). One camera use took a picture after the passcode was entered incorrectly three times. One camera use and one calendar use did not seem to access sensitive resources—the camera use accessed configuration information, and the calendar use got the current date (which could be done without accessing the calendar). Finally, after disassembling and reading the bytecode, we found one *Uncertain* camera use could actually only happen interactively.

We next see that contacts, SMS, tasks, location, and calls are used in a mix of interactive and non-interactive ways. We investigated the background and *Uncertain* uses of these resources as well. Contacts were used in the background mainly to pre-fetch or sync the contact list. Two apps used SMS in the background to listen for a registration code after the user signed up for an account. Currently running tasks were polled in the background to monitor battery usage, scan for malicious apps, look for apps by the same developer (to communicate with them), or for analytics and tracking purposes. Call-related permissions were used in the background to block calls from a user-supplied blacklist. While there were too many background location uses to examine them all, those we did examine frequently had no obvious reason (as expected [3, 13]), even in apps that elsewhere used location for a clear purpose.

Resource	# Apps	Resource	# Apps
Location	75	Microphone	14
Media/SD Card	69	Tasks	13
Camera	69	Power/Diag.	12
Phone State	43	Calendar	5
Accounts	39	SMS	4
Bluetooth	31	Calls	2
Contacts	30		

Table 1: Number of apps that used each resource.

Finally, four resources—accounts, power, bluetooth, and phone state information—were mostly accessed in the background. We believe this is either because developers believe users care less about these accesses [11], the uses are hard to explain clearly to non-experts, or the uses are not naturally associated with an immediately preceding interaction.

Looking in more detail at the breakdown between *Click* and *Page*, we see that for most resources, *Click* is a clear majority of the interactive uses. The exception is location, which has more *Page* uses. This was mostly due to location use for map screens or lists of nearby places. Breaking down the background uses, we see the use of resources at *Startup* and in *Bg-Ext* becomes much more common lower in the chart.

Resource Usage Across Apps

We also measured the number of apps that used each resource at least once, as a rough approximation for how familiar each resource is to users. Table 1 shows the results. We found a wide range across resources, with little correlation between frequency of appearance in apps and usage patterns. For example, location was used frequently, and Figure 3 shows that it was often used in the background, whereas media/SD card was also used frequently, but was rarely seen in the background.

Discussion

The results of our app survey suggest several possibilities. Given the large amount of interactive resource use overall, there seems to be a clear opportunity for better integrating authorization into the UI. However, the question remains to what extent interactions make resource use apparent to users. We try to answer this question in the next two sections.

Our app survey also shows that many resources are used in the background, and many of these uses seem reasonable, at least to the authors. Moreover, apps sometimes use the same resource both in the foreground and in the background, to different purposes. This suggests interactive and background uses should be authorized separately. Thus, in the next two sections, we also try to answer questions about how background uses should be authorized, and about whether users' expectations of interactive and non-interactive uses are related.

USER EXPECTATIONS STUDY METHODOLOGY

After our app survey, we conducted an online study to elicit users' expectations about resource use as different user actions

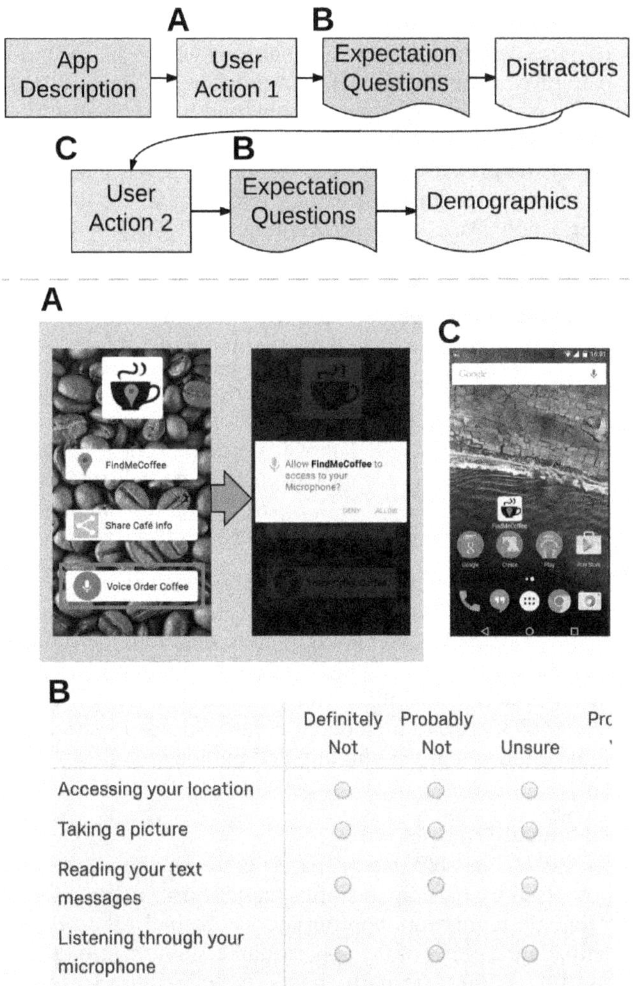

Figure 4: User expectations study procedure. Lower portion shows partial examples of user actions and survey questions.

are performed on a smartphone. Our goal was to understand to what extent user expectations align with the interactivity patterns we observed in our app study. Concretely, our user study examined the following three hypotheses:

H1. Users are more likely to expect resource accesses with an interactive use pattern than without.

H2. The more apps that use a resource (as measured in our app survey), the more likely users are to expect less-interactive uses of that resource.

H3. Users are more likely to expect resource accesses they have seen before.

Note that *H1* and *H3* have implications for the Android M permission system. Specifically, if *H1* is true, users already expect a resource to be accessed due to user action, so an explicit authorization request may be unnecessary. Additionally, if *H3* is false, then users granting authorization for a resource in one access pattern does not cause them to expect that resource to be used later in a different pattern. Thus, requesting authorization only on first use may be insufficient.

H2 is a proxy for a more general hypothesis: that users are more likely to expect accesses to resources with which they are familiar. Familiarity is likely affected by many factors including how many apps use the resource and how often they do so, whether passive notifications are present (as for location), coverage in the news media, etc. For simplicity, we use the frequencies in Table 1 as a metric of familiarity.

Study Overview

We recruited participants through Amazon's Mechanical Turk crowdsourcing service. All participants were at least 18 years old and located in the United States. Participants were paid $1.00 for completing the survey. The survey was approved by the University of Maryland IRB. Participants were instructed that we wanted their opinions about an app; privacy and sensitive resources were not explicitly mentioned.

Figure 4 gives a flowchart of the procedure followed by each study participant. First, the participant reads a short description of an app. We used two mock apps in our study: FindMeCoffee (*Coffee*) and HealthyFit Tracker (*Fitness*). FindMeCoffee locates nearby coffee shops, allows users to share the location of favorite coffee shops with friends, and supports ordering coffee via voice command. HealthyFit Tracker tracks workouts, allows sharing workouts with friends, and allows posting audio "smack talk" on the user's profile. Note while these apps demonstrate different categories, we do not attempt to fully study the effect of app type on user perceptions.

Next the participant views one sequence of user interactions with the app, shown as a slideshow of app screenshots. To avoid confusion with terminology in the next section, we refer to such a sequence as a *user action*. For example, in the user action in Figure 4A, the user clicks the bottom-most button (outlined in red), and the app then displays an authorization request dialog. In Figure 4C, which is only shown partially, the user exits the app and returns to the device home screen.

After viewing a user action, the participant answers five-point Likert questions such as those in Figure 4B, which ask whether a resource is "Definitely not" to "Definitely yes" accessed immediately after the user action. To avoid priming the user, the survey asks about camera, SMS, flashlight, "accessing credit card information," and "looking up coffee shop reviews" (*Coffee*) or "reading your heart rate" (*Fitness*) as well as the three resources we study.

Next, the participant answers five distractor questions, views another user action, and answers the same Likert questions about the second user action. The distractors are designed to induce a cognitive break and ensure the two access patterns are treated as separate events. For example, one distractor asks users "Which button would you press if you wanted to find a new coffee shop?" We did not measure the effectiveness of distractors. The participant concludes the survey by answering demographic questions. Participants took 4 minutes and 45 seconds on average to complete the survey.

To understand the effect of resource access patterns on user expectation, we analyze responses about the first user action each participant viewed. We use responses about the second user action to examine how prior exposure affects expectation.

Conditions

Participants were assigned round-robin to one of 42 conditions, which varied across four variables: the *app*, the *resource* being accessed, the *authorization pattern*, and the pair of *interaction (int) patterns*.[2] Table 2 lists possible values for each variable, and conditions comprise one value from each column.

As mentioned earlier, our study used two mock apps, FindMe-Coffee and HealthyFitTracker, and three resources, chosen to cover a range of int. patterns observed in our app survey: Microphone (*Mic*, only interactive accesses observed), Contacts (*Con*, mixed interactive and background uses observed), and Location (*Loc*, also mixed).

Our study considered three different authorization patterns. First use (*Fst*) mimics Android M, presenting an authorization dialog during the first user action but not the second. Launch (*Lch*) presents an authorization dialog immediately after the app's home page is shown, but before any further screenshots. We noticed anecdotally that a few apps in our study used this strategy. Never (*Nvr*) does not show any authorization dialog at run time. This mimics older versions of Android.

We examined three different int. patterns, also drawn from the app survey: Button Click (*Clk*), Background with Notification (*Bn*, uses a resource without interaction, but displays an icon and short message in the notification drawer indicating some condition is met, such as being located near a coffee shop) and Background Only (*Bg*, uses a resource in a way not clearly shown in the UI). We can order these from most (*Clk*) to least (*Bg*) interactive. We always label the button clearly for its use (no deception). We do not test UI widgets besides buttons.

Regardless of a participant's assigned condition, the survey always asks about expectations for all resources and auxiliary actions. As a result, we implicitly collect data about users' expectations for the *Bg-Bg* int. pattern pair, with authorization pattern *Nvr*, for the two non-targeted resources in each condition. For example, a participant assigned to the *Coffee-Mic-Fst-Clk-Clk* condition also answers Likert questions about contacts and location that are analyzed within the *Coffee-Con-Nvr-Bg-Bg* and *Coffee-Loc-Nvr-Bg-Bg* conditions.

Testing the full-factorial combination of all variables was infeasible, so we eliminated conditions that were redundant or less relevant to our hypotheses, resulting in 42 final conditions. In more detail: We exclude conditions where the second int. pattern is more interactive than the first, as we assume the participant's second expectation would be dominated by the second int. pattern, rather than by the combination of patterns. We use *Bn* only in the first user action, because we are primarily interested in its effect on user expectations for the second user action. We assume expectations for *Bn* itself will depend entirely on whether the participant notices the passive cue, a topic that has been well studied [28, 31] but is somewhat orthogonal to our work. These two rules limit the int. pattern pairs we study to those in the last column of Table 2.

We exclude *Nvr-Bg-Bg* conditions because they provide no evidence of resource use, and are therefore identical to the implicit scenarios discussed above. We also exclude *Fst-Bg-Bg* because, in our experimental design, they are indistinguishable from *Lch-Bg-Bg*. In Table 2, *Bg-Bg* is highlighted in blue to indicate that it is only used with the *Lch* authorization pattern.

Because we do not comprehensively consider the effect of app type, we limit *Fitness* conditions to those we anticipated would have the largest variation in expectations. Specifically, we consider only *Loc* and *Mic* and only conditions where the two user actions exhibit different int. patterns. The *Fitness* scenarios therefore include all combinations of variables in Table 2 that not are not highlighted in blue or yellow.

[2]Through this section we will use the abbreviation int. pattern to avoid confusion with the interactions in our regression analysis.

App	Resource[1]	Authorization[2]	Int. Patterns[3]
Coffee	*Mic*	*Fst*	*Clk-Clk* [4]
Fitness	*Con* [4]	*Lch*	*Clk-Bg*
	Loc	*Nvr*	*Bn-Bg*
			Bg-Bg [4,5]

[1] *Mic* - Microphone, *Con* - Contacts, *Loc* - Location
[2] *Fst* - First, *Lch* - Launch, *Nvr* - Never
[3] *Clk* - Click, *Bn* - Background w/Notif., *Bg* - Background Only
[4] Only used with *Coffee*
[5] Only used with *Lch*

Table 2: Possible values for each variable in tested conditions.

Statistical Analysis

To test *H1* and *H2*, we primarily consider the expectations expressed by participants after the first user action. We use a logistic regression, appropriate for ordinal Likert data, to estimate the effect of the app, resource, authorization pattern, and int. pattern on participants' expectation. To test *H3*, which concerns the effect of the prior user action, we also use a logistic regression, with participants' expectation for the second user action as the outcome variable. We use the same input factors as before, this time including both int. patterns.

Each regression includes multiple observations of each participant: the explicit condition plus two implicit *Nvr-Bg-Bg* responses. As is standard, we include a mixed-model random effect that groups observations from the same participant [16].

Our initial model for each regression included the input variables plus all possible two-way interaction terms. To prevent overfitting, we tested all possible combinations of these inputs and selected the model with minimum Akaike Information Criterion (AIC), a standard measure of model quality [2]. We present only the final model for each regression.

Ecological Validity and Limitations

We use a controlled experiment with mock apps. While this limits ecological validity, it allows us to reason statistically about the effect of specific factors on participants' expectations, and to disregard factors such as participants' history with an app or reputation of the app's developer. In a study environment, participants may be less suspicious than if their real data were at risk. To partially account for this, we ask about expectation rather than comfort level [23].

By limiting our survey to two apps and restricting the int. patterns and resources tested, we likely miss factors, and particularly combinations of factors, that influence expectations. As one example, users likely expect SMS and Calls to have different usage patterns, and these expectations may vary with app type. However, based on the results of our app survey, we believe the variables chosen still provide useful insights.

Each participant sees two user actions in a relatively short time period. We do not study the effect of longer sequences of actions or long-term use (e.g., over days or weeks) of an app.

As is typical for online studies and self-reported data, some participants may not take the survey seriously, and some may try to complete the survey multiple times. We limit repeat participants using MTurk ID and browser cookies. While MTurk has generally been validated for high-quality data [7, 9, 20, 32], U.S. MTurkers are somewhat younger and more male, tech-savvy, and privacy-sensitive than the general population, which may limit the generalizability of our results [18].

These limitations apply similarly across all conditions; we therefore consider comparisons among conditions to be valid.

USER EXPECTATIONS STUDY RESULTS

We now present the results of our online user study. We found that *H1* holds: users were the most likely to expect a resource use when shown a more interactive int. pattern. In contrast, we observed that while resource type does affect user expectation, *H2* was not strongly supported. Finally, we found that *H3* does not hold. However, our results indicate that both background notification (*Bn*) and on-launch authorization requests (*Lch*) increase user expectation of future resource accesses.

For each of our hypotheses, we present key findings from our regression analysis. Summaries of our regressions are shown in Tables 3 and 4. Each table shows the included input variables and their values. Each variable includes a *base case* value (identified by dashes in the remaining columns). The odds ratio (OR) shows the observed effect of each value relative to the base case, measured as odds of expectation increasing one unit on our Likert scale. We also provide the 95% confidence interval (CI) and *p*-value for each measurement.

For example, the third row of Table 3 shows that switching from *Bg* to *Clk* in the first user action, all other variables held constant, is associated with a 106.3× likelihood of increasing one unit of expectation. The CI expresses 95% confidence that the "true" odds ratio is between 63.6 and 177.7. A *p*-value less than 0.05 is interpreted as statistically significant.

The second half of each table shows interactions between value pairs, given as the two values separated by a colon. These odds ratio indicate the change in likelihood when the two variables co-occur, relative to considering them independently. For example, the *Loc*:*Clk* odds ratio of 0.2 in Table 3 suggests the combined effect of these two values is *subadditive*: only 20% as strong as predicted by their individual effects.

Demographics

A total of 961 participants completed the study. Participants' ages ranged from 18 to 70+ years, with 37% age 18-29. Fifty-three percent reported being male and 47% female. ("Prefer not to answer" and "other" options for gender were provided.) Participants were required to be from the United States. Forty-five percent of participants reported holding a college degree, and 25% reported having "far above average" smartphone expertise. Each condition had at least 20 unique participants. Twenty people dropped out partway through the survey, distributed evenly across conditions.

Variable	Value	Odds Ratio	CI	*p*-value
App	*Coffee*	–	–	–
	Fitness	1.3	[0.96, 1.78]	0.086
Int	*Bg*	–	–	–
	Clk	**106.3**	**[63.6, 177.7]**	**< 0.001***
	Bn	**4.1**	**[2.6, 6.7]**	**< 0.001***
Res	*Mic*	–	–	–
	Loc	**17.5**	**[13.4, 22.9]**	**< 0.001***
	Con	0.8	[0.6, 1.0]	0.056
Auth	*Nvr*	–	–	–
	Fst	**2.2**	**[1.2, 4.0]**	**0.008***
	Lch	**1.9**	**[1.2, 3.2]**	**0.008***
App:Res	*Coffee:Mic*	–	–	–
	Fitness:Loc	**0.4**	**[0.3, 0.6]**	**< 0.001***
	Fitness:Con	1.1	[0.8, 1.7]	0.546
Res:Auth	*Mic:Nvr*	–	–	–
	Con:Lch	**3.2**	**[1.5, 6.7]**	**0.002***
	Con:Fst	1.5	[0.6, 3.6]	0.41
	Loc:Lch	0.8	[0.4, 1.6]	0.487
	Loc:Fst	0.5	[0.2, 1.3]	0.166
Res:Int	*Mic:Bg*	–	–	–
	Loc:Bn	**2.4**	**[1.2, 5.0]**	**0.021***
	Con:Bn	**5.0**	**[2.3, 11.3]**	**< 0.001***
	Loc:Clk	**0.2**	**[0.1, 0.4]**	**< 0.001***
	Con:Clk	**0.2**	**[0.1, 0.4]**	**< 0.001***

*Significant effect – Base case (OR=1, definitionally)

Table 3: Summary of regression over participant expectations after the first user action.

H1 – Interactivity v. Expectation

We found that *H1* holds: the more interactive the int. pattern, the more likely the user is to expect the resource access. In fact, interactivity (specifically *Clk*) is the strongest indicator of expectation we measured.

Table 3 shows that both *Clk* and *Bn* significantly increase the likelihood the user expects a resource access compared to *Bg*. The effect of *Clk* is particularly strong (OR 106.3, $p < 0.001$). Because the confidence intervals of *Clk* and *Bn* do not overlap, we can also conclude *Clk* generates significantly more expectation than *Bn*. Table 4 confirms that the strong association between *Clk* and expectation holds for the second user action as well (OR 810.4, $p < 0.001$). Figure 5a illustrates this finding, showing that 90% of participants who saw a *Clk* int. pattern first definitely or probably expected the associated resource use, compared to 72% for *Bn* and 25% for *Bg*.

Explicit authorization, which is by definition interactive, is also associated with a significant increase in expectation. Compared to *Nvr*, both *Fst* and *Lch* have odds ratio effects of about

Variable	Value	Odds Ratio	CI	*p*-value
Int 2	*Bg*	–	–	–
	Clk	**810.4**	**[352.2, 1864.9]**	**< 0.001***
Int 1	*Bg*	–	–	–
	Clk	1.0	[0.8, 1.4]	0.9
	Bn	**2.1**	**[1.5, 2.8]**	**< 0.001***
Res	*Mic*	–	–	–
	Loc	**20.0**	**[15.5, 25.9]**	**< 0.001***
	Con	1.0	[0.8, 1.3]	0.768
Auth	*Nvr*	–	–	–
	Fst	1.4	[0.9, 2.4]	0.174
	Lch	**1.7**	**[1.1, 2.7]**	**0.027***
Res:Auth	*Mic:Nvr*	–	–	–
	Con:Lch	**4.4**	**[2.2,8.5]**	**< 0.001***
	Con:Fst	2.1	[1, 4.5]	0.056
	Loc:Lch	0.8	[0.4, 1.5]	0.445
	Loc:Fst	**0.5**	**[0.2, 0.9]**	**0.029***
Res:Int 2	*Mic:Bg*	–	–	–
	Loc:Clk	**0.1**	**[0.03, 0.3]**	**< 0.001***
	Con:Clk	**0.03**	**[0.01, 0.1]**	**< 0.001***

*Significant effect – Base case (OR=1, definitionally)

Table 4: Summary of regression over participant expectations after the second user action.

$2\times$ for the first user action (Table 3), both significant. This result makes intuitive sense, as the dialogs for both (*Fst* and *Lch*) occur very closely in time to the first int. pattern.

H2 – Real-World Frequency v. Expectation

We observed an inconsistent relationship between real-world frequency and expectation. Location was the most frequently seen resource in the app study (75 apps according to Table 1) and was also the most expected resource we tested. As shown in Tables 3 and 4, *Loc* was associated with 17-22$\times$ higher likelihood of expectation compared to *Con* (seen in 30 apps) or *Mic* (seen in 14 apps). Non-overlapping CIs and *p*-values less than 0.05 indicate these effects are significant. This is consistent with *H2*; however, as our frequency measurement is only a very rough approximation of user familiarity, we note that this effect could relate to existing passive notifications for location, the higher volume of academic and media coverage of the location permission, or other factors.

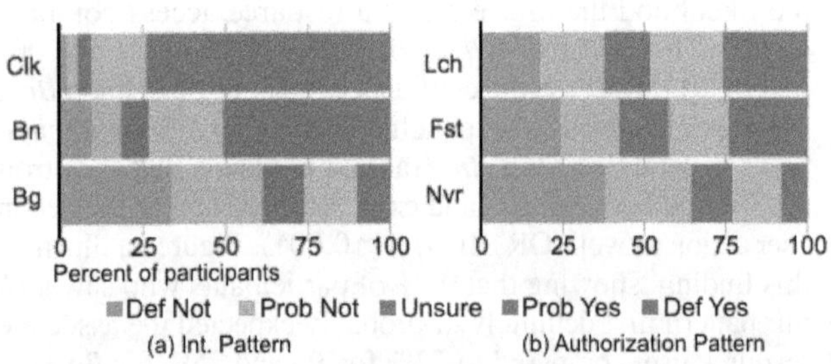

Figure 5: Likert-scale expectation responses for (a) the first user action, organized by int. pattern, and (b) the second user action, organized by authorization pattern.

However, *H2* does not hold when comparing *Con* and *Mic*. While *Con* was seen about twice as often in the app study, there was no significant difference in expectation between the two resources, at either the first or second user action. This could be because our app frequency metric does not sufficiently capture differences (or in this case, similarities) in users' overall exposure to each resource.

While there was no significant difference between the main effects of *Con* and *Mic*, we found evidence that users rarely expected *Mic* to be used with *Bg*. Looking at the *Res:Int* interaction in Table 3, *Loc*:*Bn* and *Con*:*Bn* both show significant superadditive results, indicating that these combinations are even more expected, relative to the baseline *Mic*:*Bg* combination, than those factors' main effects would predict. We hypothesize this difference is driven more by low expectation for background microphone access than high expectations for the other combinations. The interactions involving *Clk* are significantly subadditive, but we suspect this is a ceiling effect: expectations for *Clk*, which as shown in Figure 5a are very high, cannot increase beyond the end of our Likert scale. We see similar effects for the *Clk* interactions in Table 4.

H3 – Effect of Previously Seen Accesses

To examine the effects of prior accesses on participants' expectations, we focus on Table 4. Overall, we find that *H3* does not hold: participants are not more likely to expect resource accesses they have seen before. In particular, the int. pattern variable *Int1:Int2* does not appear in the final model, suggesting the combination of int. patterns does not meaningfully influence expectation at the second user action.

However, participants did appear more likely to expect a background access if they had previously seen an indication that background accesses might be used. Table 4 shows expectation at the second user action was significantly higher when the first int. pattern was *Bn* (OR 2.1, $p < 0.001$) or the *Lch* authorization request was shown (OR 1.7, $p = 0.027$), both of which indicate that background access may occur. Figure 5b illustrates this finding, showing that in the second user action, more participants definitely or probably expected resource usage in *Lch* conditions (47%) than in *Fst* (42%) or *Nvr* (22%). Additionally, the superadditive relationship between *Lch* and *Con* in both regressions may suggest a *Lch* request primes users to expect non-interactive accesses to contacts.

In contrast, we found evidence that the authorization pattern *Fst* implies only a single access. Table 4 shows that *Fst* did not have a significant effect ($p = 0.174$) compared to *Nvr*, indicating that an authorization associated with the first user action is no more effective than no authorization when thinking about a second user action. The subadditive relationship between *Loc* and *Fst* (OR 0.5, $p = 0.029$) also suggests that authorization requests associated with a specific event train users to only expect a resource access after an authorization request. This decreases the otherwise relatively high expectation of background location access. These relationships, while not particularly strong, are notable because they imply that the Android M model may in some cases be counterproductive; we explore this further in the Discussion section below.

App v. Expectation

Finally, we observed that the app type did have some effect on the way other variables were perceived. We found no significant difference between the two mock apps with respect to the first user action ($p = 0.086$), and app effects did not appear in the final model for the second user action, suggesting no meaningful relationship with expectation. However, we do observe in Table 3 a significant, subadditive relationship between *Fitness* and *Loc*, indicating that location accesses were less expected in the fitness app than the coffee app. We expect that across a wider variety of apps, further relationships between app type and expected resource usage would be observable.

CONCLUSIONS AND DESIGN RECOMMENDATIONS

Based on our app survey and user study, we propose several ways to improve Android's and similar authorization systems.

Access Resources As Interactively As Possible

Our app study found that camera, microphone, media, and calendar are already used almost exclusively interactively in popular apps. Moreover, our user study found that users overwhelmingly expect resource access after an explicit click on a related item. We speculate that users would also have higher expectations of resource access under other interactive uses.

Thus, we recommend expecting (or perhaps even requiring) most or all accesses to these four resources to be interactive. Other resources are more frequently used in the background, and it is not always obvious how to associate their uses with a foreground interaction. However, we argue that developers should prioritize (and the Android framework should encourage) making background uses more interactive when possible. For example, a social media app that periodically pulls the user's contacts to recommend new friends could tie this background access to a foreground interaction by asking the user to "turn on" this feature at launch and provide a settings menu where the user could turn the feature off at a later time. While this design is similar to the authorization mechanism provided by Android M, implementing it in the app provides context, which we have found is important to decision making.

We also recommend that when resources that are more typically used interactively will be used in the background, these uses should be documented explicitly in the app's description or a similar user-visible location.

Use Interactions to Grant Authorization

Our results further suggest that if a resource use is interactive, then a separate authorization dialog can be eliminated. We speculate that removing explicit authorization requests in these cases could reduce potential user confusion (e.g., "I just clicked 'Import Contacts,' why is it asking me if I want the app to access contacts?"). In addition, removing these requests could reduce annoyance and habituation, potentially helping the user to focus on other, less clear authorization decisions. Eliminating request dialogs for interactive use cases could also help motivate developers to prioritize interactivity, as mentioned above. Of course, to handle potentially malicious apps we must be sure the preceding interaction is clearly related to the resource use. For example, clicking on a location icon should not cause the camera to be used.

We envision two main approaches to enforce this principle. One idea is access-control gadgets [26, 27], which we discussed with Related Work. Another approach would be to leave apps as they are, but use a program analysis to ensure they conform. For example, we could use AppTracer to do so, in one of two possible modes. AppTracer could be run ahead of time, e.g., by an app market gatekeeper, to examine app behavior. Even though it would not necessarily observe all app behavior, results from analyzing behaviors users actually encounter would still be useful. AppTracer could also be used for auditing: power users and security experts could use AppTracer to log an app's behavior as they use it and then retroactively check the AppTracer graphs for any suspicious behavior, which could then be reported to the broader public.

Handle background authorization separately

We found that users were much less likely to expect background resource access if authorization dialogs were presented after a prior user action or were not presented at all. Thus, we recommend requesting authorization separately and explicitly for background uses. Based on our study, it may be preferable to do so when apps are first launched. However, because our study showed the increase in expectation is small (especially compared to the expectation after a click), it may be important to also show background notifications of use (which also increased expectation) so users remain aware. We note that while authorization on launch informs many users that background accesses should be anticipated, Figure 5 suggests there are others who do not recognize this possibility. Further research into the best approach is still needed.

Resources that have a broad mix of interactive and background uses—such as contacts—might particularly benefit from separate background authorization and limited requests for interactive uses. This could help avoid potential misconceptions about interactive uses being the only uses.

Future work could shed light on how differences in background use cases affect user expectations and preferences. For example, users might be expected to react differently when contacts are accessed in the background for pre-fetch (a use case identified in our app survey) compared to advertising. We also expect that the frequency of access will impact the user's decision. For example, it may be possible to tie high-frequency background uses to some foreground passive notification (e.g., a notification tray icon), similarly to the design presented by Balebako et al. for informing the user of data leakage [5]. This could make the user aware of the accesses without requiring additional authorization effort. Program analysis tools such as AppTracer could potentially be used to separate these cases and apply different authorization policies accordingly.

ACKNOWLEDGMENTS

We thank the anonymous reviewers, Sascha Fahl, Yasemin Acar, and members of HCIL for their helpful feedback. This research was supported in part by NSF CNS-1064997, a UMIACS contract under the partnership between the University of Maryland and DoD, and a Google Research Award.

REFERENCES

1. 2012. How to Ask for Permission. In *Presented as part of the 7th USENIX Workshop on Hot Topics in Security*. USENIX, Berkeley, CA. https://www.usenix.org/conference/hotsec12/workshop-program/presentation/Felt
2. Hirotugu Akaike. 1974. A new look at the statistical model identification. *Automatic Control, IEEE Transactions on* 19, 6 (06 Dec. 1974), 716–723. DOI: http://dx.doi.org/10.1109/tac.1974.1100705
3. Hazim Almuhimedi, Florian Schaub, Norman Sadeh, Idris Adjerid, Alessandro Acquisti, Joshua Gluck, Lorrie Faith Cranor, and Yuvraj Agarwal. 2015. Your Location Has Been Shared 5,398 Times!: A Field Study on Mobile App Privacy Nudging. In *Proceedings of the 33rd Annual ACM Conference on Human Factors in Computing Systems (CHI '15)*. ACM, New York, NY, USA, 787–796. DOI: http://dx.doi.org/10.1145/2702123.2702210
4. Kathy Wain Yee Au, Yi Fan Zhou, Zhen Huang, and David Lie. 2012. PScout: Analyzing the Android Permission Specification. In *Proceedings of the 2012 ACM Conference on Computer and Communications Security (CCS '12)*. ACM, New York, NY, USA, 217–228. DOI: http://dx.doi.org/10.1145/2382196.2382222
5. Rebecca Balebako, Jaeyeon Jung, Wei Lu, Lorrie Faith Cranor, and Carolyn Nguyen. 2013. "Little Brothers Watching You": Raising Awareness of Data Leaks on Smartphones. In *Proceedings of the Ninth Symposium on Usable Privacy and Security (SOUPS '13)*. ACM, New York, NY, USA, Article 12, 11 pages. DOI: http://dx.doi.org/10.1145/2501604.2501616
6. Sven Bugiel, Stephen Heuser, and Ahmad-Reza Sadeghi. 2013. Flexible and Fine-grained Mandatory Access Control on Android for Diverse Security and Privacy Policies. In *Proceedings of the 22nd USENIX Security Symposium (USENIX Security '13)*. USENIX, Washington, D.C., 131–146. https://www.usenix.org/conference/usenixsecurity13/technical-sessions/presentation/bugiel
7. Michael Buhrmester, Tracy Kwang, and Samuel D. Gosling. 2011. Amazon's Mechanical Turk: A New Source of Inexpensive, Yet High-Quality, Data? *Perspectives on Psychological Science* 6, 1 (2011), 3–5. DOI: http://dx.doi.org/10.1177/1745691610393980
8. Kevin Zhijie Chen, Noah M. Johnson, Vijay D'Silva, Shuaifu Dai, Kyle MacNamara, Thomas R. Magrino, Edward XueJun Wu, Martin Rinard, and Dawn Xiaodong Song. 2013. Contextual Policy Enforcement in Android Applications with Permission Event Graphs. In *20th Annual Network and Distributed System Security Symposium, NDSS 2013*. Internet Society, San Diego, California, USA. http://internetsociety.org/doc/contextual-policy-enforcement-android-applications-permission-event-graphs
9. Julie S. Downs, Mandy B. Holbrook, Steve Sheng, and Lorrie Faith Cranor. 2010. Are Your Participants Gaming the System?: Screening Mechanical Turk Workers. In *Proceedings of the SIGCHI Conference on Human Factors in Computing Systems (CHI '10)*. ACM, New York, NY, USA, 2399–2402. DOI: http://dx.doi.org/10.1145/1753326.1753688
10. Adrienne Porter Felt, Erika Chin, Steve Hanna, Dawn Song, and David Wagner. 2011. Android Permissions Demystified. In *Proceedings of the 18th ACM Conference on Computer and Communications Security (CCS '11)*. ACM, New York, NY, USA, 627–638. DOI: http://dx.doi.org/10.1145/2046707.2046779
11. Adrienne Porter Felt, Serge Egelman, and David Wagner. 2012a. I've Got 99 Problems, but Vibration Ain't One: A Survey of Smartphone Users' Concerns. In *Proceedings of the Second ACM Workshop on Security and Privacy in Smartphones and Mobile Devices (SPSM '12)*. ACM, New York, NY, USA, 33–44. DOI: http://dx.doi.org/10.1145/2381934.2381943
12. Adrienne Porter Felt, Elizabeth Ha, Serge Egelman, Ariel Haney, Erika Chin, and David Wagner. 2012b. Android Permissions: User Attention, Comprehension, and Behavior. In *Proceedings of the Eighth Symposium on Usable Privacy and Security (SOUPS '12)*. ACM, New York, NY, USA, Article 3, 14 pages. DOI: http://dx.doi.org/10.1145/2335356.2335360
13. Huiqing Fu, Yulong Yang, Nileema Shingte, Janne Lindqvist, and Marco Gruteser. 2014. A field study of run-time location access disclosures on android smartphones. In *Workshop on Usable Security (USEC)*. Internet Society, San Diego, California, USA.
14. Google 2016. *Requesting Permissions at Run Time*. Google. https://developer.android.com/training/permissions/requesting.html
15. Andrew F Hayes and Klaus Krippendorff. 2007. Answering the call for a standard reliability measure for coding data. *Communication methods and measures* 1, 1 (2007), 77–89. http://dx.doi.org/10.1080/19312450709336664
16. Donald Hedeker. 2008. Multilevel models for ordinal and nominal variables. In *Handbook of multilevel analysis*. Springer, 237–274. http://link.springer.com/chapter/10.1007/978-0-387-73186-5_6
17. Jinseong Jeon, Kristopher K. Micinski, Jeffrey A. Vaughan, Ari Fogel, Nikhilesh Reddy, Jeffrey S. Foster, and Todd Millstein. 2012. Dr. Android and Mr. Hide: Fine-grained Permissions in Android Applications. In *ACM CCS Workshop on Security and Privacy in Smartphones and Mobile Devices (SPSM)*. ACM, Raleigh, NC, USA, 3–14.
18. Ruogu Kang, Stephanie Brown, Laura Dabbish, and Sara Kiesler. 2014. Privacy Attitudes of Mechanical Turk Workers and the U.S. Public. In *Proceedings of the 23rd*

USENIX Security Symposium (USENIX Security '14). USENIX Association, San Diego, California, USA, 37–49. https://www.usenix.org/conference/soups2014/proceedings/presentation/kang

19. Jennifer King. 2012. "How Come I'm Allowing Strangers To Go Through My Phone?": Smartphones and Privacy Expectations. In *Proceedings of the Ninth Symposium on Usable Privacy and Security (SOUPS '12)*. USENIX, Washington, DC, USA. http://papers.ssrn.com/sol3/papers.cfm?abstract_id=2493412

20. Aniket Kittur, Ed H. Chi, and Bongwon Suh. 2008. Crowdsourcing User Studies with Mechanical Turk. In *Proceedings of the SIGCHI Conference on Human Factors in Computing Systems (CHI '08)*. ACM, New York, NY, USA, 453–456. DOI: http://dx.doi.org/10.1145/1357054.1357127

21. Kristopher Micinski, Jonathan Fetter-Degges, Jinseong Jeon, Jeffrey S. Foster, and Michael R. Clarkson. 2015. *Checking Interaction-Based Declassification Policies for Android Using Symbolic Execution*. Springer International Publishing, Vienna, Austria, 520–538. DOI: http://dx.doi.org/10.1007/978-3-319-24177-7_26

22. Helen Nissenbaum. 2004. Privacy as Contextual Integrity. *Washington Law Review* 79 (2004), 119–157.

23. Ashwini Rao, Florian Schaub, Norman Sadeh, Alessandro Acquisti, and Ruogu Kang. 2016. Expecting the Unexpected: Understanding Mismatched Privacy Expectations Online. In *Twelfth Symposium on Usable Privacy and Security (SOUPS 2016)*. USENIX Association, Denver, CO, 77–96. https://www.usenix.org/conference/soups2016/technical-sessions/presentation/rao

24. Android Developers Reference. 2016. Manifest.permission_group. (2016). https://developer.android.com/guide/topics/security/permissions.html (Accessed 9-16-2016).

25. Talia Ringer, Dan Grossman, and Franziska Roesner. 2016. AUDACIOUS: User-Driven Access Control with Unmodified Operating Systems. In *Proceedings of the 23rd ACM Conference on Computer and Communications Security*. ACM, Vienna, Austria. http://tlringer.github.io/pdf/audacious.pdf

26. Franziska Roesner and Tadayoshi Kohno. 2013. Securing Embedded User Interfaces: Android and Beyond. In *Proceedings of the 22nd USENIX Security Symposium (USENIX Security '13)*. USENIX, Washington, D.C., 97–112. https://www.usenix.org/conference/usenixsecurity13/technical-sessions/presentation/roesner

27. Franziska Roesner, Tadayoshi Kohno, Alexander Moshchuk, Bryan Parno, Helen J. Wang, and Crispin Cowan. 2012. User-Driven Access Control: Rethinking Permission Granting in Modern Operating Systems. In *Proceedings of the 2012 IEEE Symposium on Security and Privacy (SP '12)*. IEEE Computer Society, Washington, DC, USA, 224–238. DOI: http://dx.doi.org/10.1109/SP.2012.24

28. Stuart E Schechter, Rachna Dhamija, Andy Ozment, and Ian Fischer. The Emperor's New Security Indicators. In *Proceedings of the 2007 IEEE Symposium on Security and Privacy*.

29. Marc Stiegler, Alan H. Karp, Ka-Ping Yee, Tyler Close, and Mark S. Miller. 2006. Polaris: Virus-safe Computing for Windows XP. *Commun. ACM* 49, 9 (Sept. 2006), 83–88. DOI: http://dx.doi.org/10.1145/1151030.1151033

30. Marc Stiegler and Mark S. Miller. 2002. *A Capability-based Client: The DarpaBrowser*. Technical Report Technical Report, Focused Research Topic 5. Combex Inc, Meadowbrook, PA. http://www.combex.com/papers/darpareport/index.html

31. Joshua Sunshine, Serge Egelman, Hazim Almuhimedi, Neha Atri, and Lorrie Faith Cranor. 2009. Crying Wolf - An Empirical Study of SSL Warning Effectiveness.. In *Proceedings of the 18th USENIX Security Symposium*. {}https://www.usenix.org/legacy/events/sec09/tech/full_papers/sunshine.

32. Michael Toomim, Travis Kriplean, Claus Pörtner, and James Landay. 2011. Utility of Human-computer Interactions: Toward a Science of Preference Measurement. In *Proceedings of the SIGCHI Conference on Human Factors in Computing Systems (CHI '11)*. ACM, New York, NY, USA, 2275–2284. DOI: http://dx.doi.org/10.1145/1978942.1979277

33. Primal Wijesekera, Arjun Baokar, Ashkan Hosseini, Serge Egelman, David Wagner, and Konstantin Beznosov. 2015. Android Permissions Remystified: A Field Study on Contextual Integrity. In *Proceedings of the 24th USENIX Security Symposium (USENIX Security '15)*. USENIX Association, Washington, D.C., 499–514. https://www.usenix.org/conference/usenixsecurity15/technical-sessions/presentation/wijesekera

34. Zhemin Yang, Min Yang, Yuan Zhang, Guofei Gu, Peng Ning, and X. Sean Wang. 2013. AppIntent: analyzing sensitive data transmission in android for privacy leakage detection. In *Proceedings of the 2013 ACM SIGSAC conference on Computer and Communications Security (CCS '13)*. ACM, New York, NY, USA, 1043–1054. DOI: http://dx.doi.org/10.1145/2508859.2516676

Where Usability and Security Go Hand-in-Hand: Robust Gesture-Based Authentication for Mobile Systems

Can Liu, Gradeigh D. Clark, Janne Lindqvist
Rutgers University

ABSTRACT
Gestures have recently gained interest as a secure and usable authentication method for mobile devices. Gesture authentication relies on recognition, wherein raw data is collected from user input and preprocessed into a more manageable form before applying recognition algorithms. Preprocessing is done to improve recognition accuracy, but little work has been done in justifying its effects on authentication. We examined the effects of three variables: location, rotation, and scale, on authentication accuracy. We found that an authentication-optimal combination (location invariant, scale variant, and rotation variant) can reduce the error rate by 45.3% on average compared to the recognition-optimal combination (all invariant). We analyzed 13 gesture recognizers and evaluated them with three criteria: authentication accuracy, and resistance against both brute-force and imitation attacks. Our novel multi-expert method (Garda) achieved the lowest error rate (0.015) in authentication accuracy, the lowest error rate (0.040) under imitation attacks, and resisted all brute-force attacks.

ACM Classification Keywords
H.5.2. Information Interfaces and Presentation (e.g. HCI): Input devices and strategies; I.5.2. Pattern Recognition: Classifier design and evaluation

Author Keywords
security; gesture; authentication; mobile device

INTRODUCTION
The number of threats to personal information stored on mobile devices have begun to increase as these devices are more important in day-to-day life. Current authentication methods present their own set of concerns. Text-based passwords have many problems, ranging from password reuse [28, 23] to weak password selection [8]. Biometric methods have difficulties from revoking the authentication token [47] to misidentification [47] (e.g. fingerprint scanner scanning a scarred finger).

The mobile computing and systems community has recently proposed and studied several variations of gesture authentication systems [44, 13, 53, 24, 7, 25, 45, 18, 43, 55]. In the context of this work, gestures are passwords traced out on the

CHI'17, May 06 - 11, 2017, Denver, CO, USA

ACM 978-1-4503-4655-9/17/05...$15.00
DOI: http://dx.doi.org/10.1145/3025453.3025879

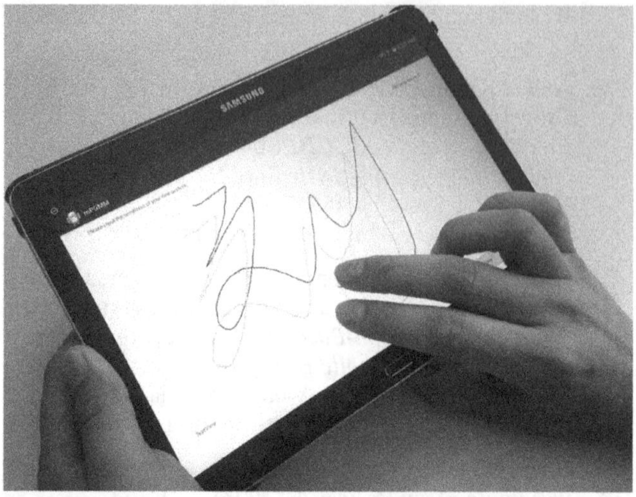

Figure 1. Example of a free-form gesture. The user in the picture has decided to use two fingers, and the corresponding gesture is drawn in different colors for visualization purposes. We note that the actual implementation does not require using visual cues in the generation or recall of the gesture.

surface of a touchscreen using one or more fingers [44] as depicted in Figure 1. Gestures have similarities to graphical password systems, such as the Android 3×3 pattern unlock [50] or the Windows 8 click-based password [54], but have not been shown to suffer from the same weaknesses. They are free from issues of the 3×3 pattern unlock: the limited password space, biased password selection, and low security (less than a 3-digit PIN) [46]. Additionally, gestures have so far not been shown to be weak against attack algorithms, in contrast to, for example, Windows 8 click-based password system [54].

Any gesture-based authentication system will need to have an algorithm to interpret the users' gestures – a gesture recognizer [13]. These recognizers perform preprocessing to the data when computing results. This preprocessing strips information away from a gesture by controlling variables to make it easier to perform the recognition task. For example, a recognizer may need all gestures to be centered at the origin. Information is then lost – the original screen location – at this step. While this makes recognition easier, it is not clear what effects these preprocessing methods have on authentication. Prior work has not justified and analyzed how these preprocessing procedures can affect authentication performance.

Proposed gesture authentication systems have implemented classification methods from Support Vector Machine [7, 25, 24] to Dynamic Time Warping [40, 4, 52, 5]. These systems justify the selection of a particular method with a statement of theoretical advantages over other methods. Based on past

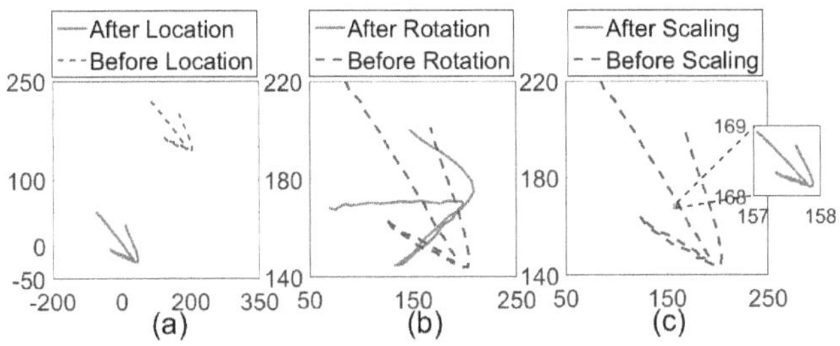

Figure 2. Example gestures before and after separate preprocessing steps. Figure(a) shows location preprocessing; Figure(b) shows rotation preprocessing; Figure(c) shows scale preprocessing.

work, it is hard to judge which recognition method is optimal for authentication.

Previous work on gesture-based authentication can be divided into three thrusts: continuous authentication [24] [7], template-based gesture authentication [25] [45] [18] [13] [43] [55] and user-generated free-form gestures [44, 53]. Continuous authentication is implicit; machine learning models are used to detect whether a user is using the phone a similar way each time. Template-based systems use a reduced space of pre-defined gestures that the users are asked to repeat. Continuous authentication methods are constraining – if the input device's screen size changes, the way the user interacts with the device changes. This is illustrated by the different ways people hold tablets versus smartphones. The two different modalities of interaction make it difficult to recognize the same person on one device with data from another. It is not clear what the usability and security trade-offs are. Free-form user-generated gestures can, in contrast, be used in any environment. In this work, we focus on understanding and implementing a strong novel gesture recognizer for free-form gestures.

Our major contributions are as follows:

We are the first to present the effects of preprocessing invariances on the security and usability of gesture-based authentication systems. We use the Protractor [32] recognizer, a popular algorithm for free-form gesture authentication [44, 53], to analyze the effects of three gesture invariances: scale, rotation, and location. Figure 2 shows examples of three distinct preprocessing steps: scale invariance (gestures are scaled down to a unit area), location invariance (gestures are translated to the same point), and rotation invariance (gestures are rotated to some constant arc). Each one can be turned on or off, leaving eight combinations in total. We examined five gesture datasets and found an authentication-optimal combination (location invariant, scale variant, and rotation variant) that reduces the error rate by 45.3% on average compared to the recognition-optimal combination (all invariant).

We present a comprehensive study of different approaches to implementing gesture-based authentication systems. We designed and implemented two novel Multi-Expert (ME) recognizers: **Garda** and **SVMGarda** recognizers. We also implemented eleven popular recognizer methods:

Sequences matching groups: Protractor, Edit Distance on Real sequence (EDR), Longest Common Subsequences (LCS), Dynamic Time Warping (DTW);

One-class Support Vector Machine (SVM) group: Protractor-, EDR-, LCS-, DTW- kernel based SVM;

Hidden Markov Model (HMM) group: discrete HMM (dHMM), segment HMM (sHMM), continuous HMM (cHMM).

We evaluated the 13 recognizers on three criteria: 1) authentication performance (i.e. equal error rate) with five datasets; 2) imitation attacks with two datasets; 3) brute force attacks. Our result shows that Garda achieved the lowest average error rate (0.015) for authentication performance, the significantly lowest average error rate (0.040) for imitation attacks, and resistance to all brute-force attacks.

RELATED WORK

There are several approaches and analyses related to gesture authentication methods. Sherman et al. [44] introduced a novel information theoretical metric to quantify the security of free-form gestures and demonstrated a way to authenticate multi-touch gestures with Protractor [32]. They do not examine the influence of gesture variants on authentication performance. Clark and Lindqvist [13] gave a systematic rendition of how to evaluate gesture recognition methods. Yang et al. [53] studied free-form gestures and text passwords in the field and showed how gestures outperform text passwords in mobile authentication. De Luca and Lindqvist [33] gave an overview of several usability and security issues with smartphone authentication and different approaches to solve them.

Biometric features of human hands have been leveraged to perform gesture-based authentication [40]. However, this work focuses on the ability of users to perform pre-defined gestures and has high error rates (about 10%) except with user-defined gestures. Similarly, GEAT [43], used biometric features of a user's gesture like finger velocity and stroke time to distinguish different users. 3D gestures have been used for authentication as well. A system using the Microsoft Kinect, called KinWrite [45], has users perform gestures in midair to authenticate themselves. AirAuth [5] also developed a midair gesture recognition method. BoD shapes [18] are 2D gestures collected on the back of a device using two phones connected back to back. XSide [17] is a stroke-based authentication mechanism that uses front or back of smartphones.

Zheng et al. [55] designed an authentication system by recognizing user's tapping password behavior based on a list of features including acceleration, pressure, size and time collected during authentication. De Luca et al. [16] also introduced an authentication scheme based on a user's touch pattern. Burgbacher et al. [9] introduced an authentication scheme based on gesture keyboards. Shirazi et al. [41] introduced a 3D magnetic gesture recognition system. Schaub [42] examined five existing graphical password schemes and found that the design space is expressive enough to capture all aspects of a graphical password. They then give some guidelines for how to design graphical passwords.

Multi-expert systems have been applied to authentication in other context before. For example, Czyz [15] presented a multi-expert system for face authentication with sequential fusion of scores of faces' successive video frames. The final decision is combined by several face authentication schemes. Dimauro et al. [20] presented a multi-expert verification system for processing bank checks. It combines three algorithms: structure-based, component-oriented approach, and a highly-adaptive neural network based method.

Finally, the HCI community has also studied free-form and user-defined gestures from different angles. Oh et al. [36] found that user-defined gestures may be ambiguous so they implemented a mixed-initiative approach to improving gestures quality. Nacenta et al. [35] found that user-defined gestures are easier to remember than pre-designed gestures.

In summary, there has been no prior work on systematically comparing different approaches for implementing gesture recognizers for authentication. Our work contributes by implementing thirteen different approaches, compares them with multiple datasets and under different attack scenarios. Based on this analysis we have presented Garda, a novel multi-expert gesture recognition system for authentication. Our work also shows that Garda is usable on mobile devices. Finally, we present a systematic analysis of how preprocessing steps, a vital part of gesture recognition, affect the performance of gesture-based authentication systems.

ANALYSIS METHODS

Feature Extraction

The gestures in our datasets are collected by mobile devices. Although the sampling rates and dimensions differ, they are consistent across their datasets in that there are multiple measurements for each gesture and that the (x, y) coordinates and timestamps appear in every dataset. These are the only features that were compared.

Recognition Performance Metrics

We use Equal Error Rate (EER) and the Receiver Operating Characteristic (ROC) curve to evaluate the performance of gesture recognizers for authentication. The EER is a point on the ROC curve where the False Acceptance Rate (FAR), the ratio of accepted false attempts to the total number of attempts, is equivalent to the False Reject Rate (FRR), the ratio of rejected true user attempts over the total number of attempts [22]. This represents a usability-security trade-off point: where the number of rejected true attempts equals the number of attackers permitted. The ROC curve and the corresponding FAR and FRR values reflect the behavior of an authentication method with varying thresholds.

We performed two types of attacks to evaluate the security of the recognizers: brute-force and imitation attacks. Resistance to brute-force attacks characterizes a recognizer's resistance to random guessing while resistance to imitation attacks characterizes a recognizer's resistance to shoulder surfing type of attacks. These features correlate with the EER value of the recognizer; the lower the EER is, the stronger the method will be when distinguishing genuine and imitation gestures.

We note that previous works on free-form gestures for authentication such as Sherman et al. [44] and Yang et al. [53] have provided data on the usability and memorability of these type of gestures in the lab and the field. However, our work is focused on recognition performance in an authentication system, thus, other usability evaluations presented in the previous work are beyond our scope and we refer to Sherman et al. [44] and Yang et al. [53] for details.

Invariance Benchmark: Recognition-Optimal Combination

$-family gesture recognition schemes such as $1 [51], Protractor [32], $P [48], and $N [2] implement preprocessing steps for removing a gesture's rotation, scale, and location. This is done to minimize the variations in performance of the same gestures by different people and to correspondingly increase recognition accuracy. We define the choice to make these three gesture variables invariant as the *recognition-optimal* combination.

Previous free-form gesture authentication systems based on Protractor [44, 53] used this recognition-optimal combination in their implementations. They demonstrated the effectiveness of distinguishing gestures from different people and great ability to resist shoulder surfing attacks [44]. However, the past work does not show whether this is optimal for authentication purposes. In our analysis, we use the recognition-optimal combination as a benchmark.

Brute-Force Attack Method

We generated a brute-force attacks with the following steps: 1) Randomly generate two sequences for x and y. 2) Filter the two sequences using a low pass filter with a cutoff frequency at 10 Hz. Remove the first few points that are distorted by the time delay of the filter. 3) Resample the generated gesture by the sampling rate.

The choice for the 10 Hz cutoff is not arbitrary. In our analysis, gestures are resampled to the same length (256). We assume the time to perform a gesture is one second, since we focus on guessing the gesture's shape. By examining the distribution of frequencies for each gesture, we found that the majority of gesture frequencies are concentrated under 10 Hz.

Imitation Attack Method

We used the imitation attack samples from two public datasets: SUSig [30] and MCTY-100 [37]. The attackers were asked to observe legitimate authentication attempts. They were also asked to practice the attacks as many times they wanted. After the attackers were confident of their imitations, they performed the attacks.

RECOGNITION ALGORITHMS

We examined and implemented 13 specific algorithms: Protractor, Edit Distance on Real sequence (EDR), Longest Common Subsequences (LCS), Dynamic Time Warping (DTW); Protractor-, EDR-, LCS-, DTW- kernel based SVM; discrete HMM (dHMM), segment HMM (sHMM), continuous HMM (cHMM); and Gaussian Mixture Models. The knowledge obtained with testing and evaluating these algorithms led us to implement two novel multi-expert approaches: SVM-Garda and Garda. We discuss them later in a separate section.

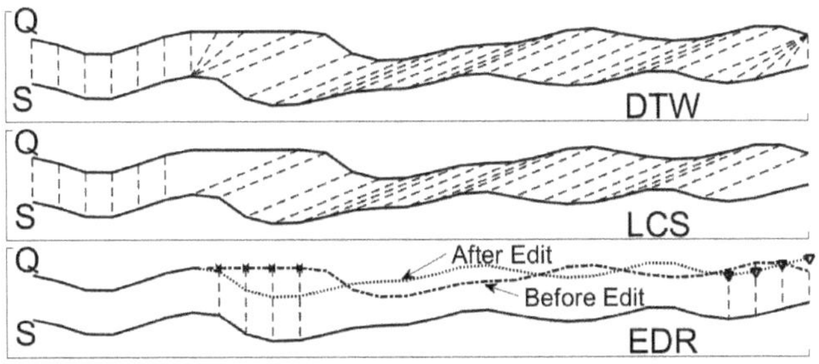

Figure 3. Examples of three alignment methods: DTW, LCS, and EDR. In DTW, all points in the two sequences must be matched with each other; In LCS, only the same subsequences are matched; In EDR, only the difference between two sequences are counted.

Protractor Algorithm

Protractor [32] is a common method used in free-form gesture authentication systems [44, 53]. It is one of the \$-family algorithms [51, 32, 48] that uses geometric similarity between two gesture trials. Recall that there are three types of invariance in a gesture: location, scale and rotation invariance. The procedure of Protractor is: resampling a gesture to fixed points, removing the three variants, and finding the maximum value of cosine distances between recall gesture and template gestures.

Time Series Sequence Matching

Several gesture authentication systems use DTW [40, 4, 18, 52, 5]. LCS [6] and EDR [12] are also similar time series sequence methods. Although LCS and EDR have not been used in published gesture authentication before, they are still alternative methods to DTW and could have higher authentication accuracy. Figure 3 gives examples of these three methods.

Dynamic Time Warping (DTW) is a dynamic programming method for aligning time sequences. Figure 3 shows how DTW seeks the minimum total distance between elements in sequences Q and S by finding the non-decreasing matching pairs of elements. The crucial point is that no elements are discarded through the DTW matching, despite how large the distance between a pair of the elements could be.

Longest Common Subsequences (LCS) [6] is another similarity measurement approach for sequences. The LCS method [6, 34] is used to find the longest common subsequence of two sequences by elastic matching. As shown in the middle of Figure 3, sequence S and Q find the longest subsequence by connecting all small continuous subsequences together. This differs from DTW, which counts the distances of matched sequence points. LCS counts the percentage of matched points in the two sequences – for example, if the length of S and Q is L_S and the number of matched points between the two sequences is L_m, the LCS distance is L_m/L_S.

Edit Distance on Real sequence (EDR) [12] is a method that measures how different two sequences are by counting the number of inserts, delete, and replace operations that are needed to transform one sequence into the other. As shown in the bottom of Figure 3, the EDR distance of the two sequences S and Q is the number of operations that delete the four points with '$\times$' markers and four insert points with '$\bigtriangledown$'. Unlike LCS or DTW, EDR is a method that does not reward matches but rather penalizes gaps and mismatches.

Support Vector Machine

Support Vector Machine (SVM) [14] is another technique used in gesture authentication systems [7, 25, 24]. We used a non-linear SVM classification algorithm with a kernel function to transform the input data into a higher-dimensional feature space. The essential property of Protractor and time series sequence matching algorithms (i.e. LCS, DTW, EDR) also measure the similarity between gestures, meaning we can use them as kernel functions for SVM.

Gaussian Mixture Model

Gaussian Mixture Models (GMM) have been used in voice recognition [10] [11] [38]. It is used to estimate any probability density function. A key feature is that GMM does not consider the order of a sequence. Assume a gesture sequence $X = x_1, ..., x_N$ has D-dimensional feature vectors. The Gaussian Mixture Model of X is a weighted sum of M component Gaussian densities below:

$$p(X|\lambda) = \Sigma_{i=1}^{M} \omega_i p_i(X)$$

where X is a D-dimensional data vector, ω_i, M, refers to the mixture weight, s and $p_i(X)$ corresponds to the component Gaussian densities. The $p_i(X)$ are parameterized by a mean $D \times 1$ vector μ_i, and a $D \times D$ covariance matrix, Σ_i:

$$p_i(X) = \frac{1}{(2\pi)^{D/2}|\Sigma_i|^{1/2}} e^{-\frac{1}{2}(X-\mu_i)'(\Sigma_i)^{-1}(X-\mu_i)}$$

The mixture weights, ω_i satisfy the constraint $\Sigma_{i=1}^{M} \omega_i = 1$. $\lambda = \{\omega_i, \mu_i, \Sigma_i\}, i = 1, ..., M$.

If there is more than one gesture password, the GMM needs to calculate the universal background model (UBM) with the whole users' data and obtain a single λ_{ubm}. We then calculate the similarity score between two gestures by doing:

$$Similarity(X_q) = logp(X_q|\lambda_{tmp}) - logp(X_q|\lambda_{ubm})$$

X_q is the recall sequence, λ_{tmp} is the template gesture model and λ_{ubm} is the UBM model of the dataset.

Hidden Markov Model

Hidden Markov Model (HMM) is a stochastic model used in many types of gesture recognition systems [31, 21, 19]. There are two main directions to build an HMM for gestures.

One way is using the directions between adjacent gesture points as observations of a HMM and train the model [31]. We call this a discrete HMM (dHMM), wherein we divide the directions into 16 equally-spaced arcs. The number of observations for a single gesture part is therefore 16. We found the seven states left-to-right no jump HMM can output the lowest EER out of many other HMM models. The transition matrix is restricted to what is seen in Figure 4.

The other one is segmenting the gesture to identify the critical points as observations of HMM to develop the HMM model [19]. We label this as segmentation HMM (sHMM), where we segment and classify the gestures into basic parts.

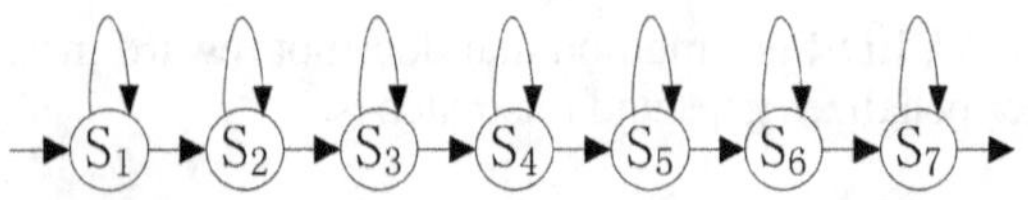

Figure 4. 7 States Left-to-Right No Jump HMM structure. Every state of the HMM has a self transition loop and only can move forward to next neighbour state.

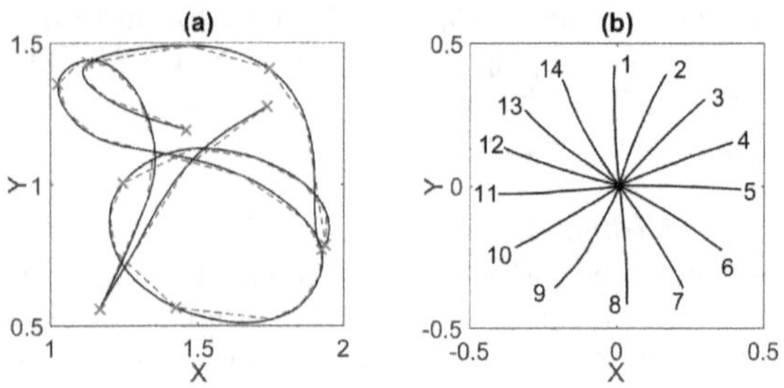

Figure 5. (a) Example of gesture after RDP algorithm and (b) Clustered basic gesture parts. In figure (a), the solid trajectory is the original gesture, the dashed line is the trajectory of the remaining samples after the first round of RDP, the red cross markers ('×') are the samples after the second round of RDP. We find that the gesture samples after the first RDP is still dense and after a second RDP are ready to be used as splitting points. (b) Basic gestures all start from (0,0) to different directions and can be regarded as 14 observations in HMM.

Then, we train the HMM based on those basic gesture parts in each gesture.

There are three steps to build the sHMM. 1) Segmentation; we use the Ramer-Douglas-Peucker (RDP) [26] algorithm for two rounds to reduce the number of points in the gesture. RDP is an approximation method to find a similar curve to the original sequence using fewer points. The dashed line and '×' in Figure 5(a) shows the approximation gesture after the first and second round of RDP, respectively. With the approximation points '×', we segmented the gestures to several basic gesture parts. 2) Clustering. We cluster the segmented gestures into a few basic parts. We first normalize the gesture segments to the same size, then implement K-means as an unsupervised learning method to classify the basic gesture parts into several classes. We found, through observation, that K=14 was the optimal number for basic gesture types. Figure 5(b) shows the 14 basic gesture parts. Thus, the gestures can be represented as combinations of these 14 basic gesture parts. 3) Train HMM. We follow the steps in dHMM to build the HMM for each gesture password from these 14 parts.

In addition to the above, we implemented a continuous HMM (cHMM). Specifically, we divided a gesture evenly into N basic gesture parts. For each basic gesture part, there are several gesture points – we modeled the probability density function of these points with GMMs. Each basic gesture part can be represented by a combination of M Gaussian distributions. By training the HMM with the Baum-Welch algorithm [29] we obtain HMM verifiers for each gesture type. The Baum-Welch algorithm is a special case of the Expectation-Maximization (EM) algorithm [3] and is used to find a locally optimal solution to the HMM training problem.

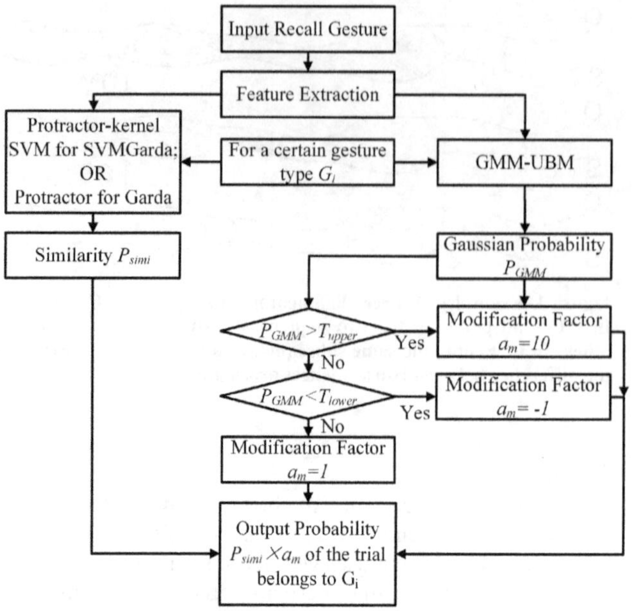

Figure 6. SVMGarda and Garda authentication system. SVMGarda system uses the Protractor kernel SVM method in the top left part of authentication section. Garda system uses the Protractor method. The similarity of Garda between the recall and template gesture is measured by Protractor and GMM-UBM separately. The similarity output of Protractor is P_{simi}. It is modified by different factors based on the comparison result of Gaussian probability of GMM-UBM P_{GMM}, and two thresholds T_{upper} and T_{lower}. If $P_{GMM} > T_{upper}$, it means that GMM-UBM recognizer is confident that two gestures are similar, so the final similarity score of Garda is $10 \times P_{simi}$. If $P_{GMM} < T_{lower}$, it means the GMM-UBM recognizer is confident that two gestures are not similar at all and the final result is $-P_{simi}$. Otherwise, GMM-UBM cannot make a confident judgment, so the final similarity of Garda is the same as P_{simi}.

GARDA AND SVMGARDA AUTHENTICATION SYSTEMS

In this section, we describe our novel gesture authentication system. We developed two different types of multi-expert systems. The first one, called Garda, combines Protractor and GMM-UBM. The other one, called SVMGarda, combines the Protractor kernel SVM and GMM-UBM. Figure 6 gives an overview of our Garda and SVMGarda authentication systems. Unlike other recognizers, which are based on one dimension of recognition, Garda and SVMGarda are better because they recognize gestures in two dimensions: the gesture shape feature (by GMM-UBM) and adjacent points feature (by Protractor or by Protractor kernel SVM).

Multi-expert (ME) classification systems work by combining the results of different classifiers to make the final classification decision [39]. Multi-expert systems can work better than other recognizers since they measure gesture similarities using multiple recognizers. Since the similarity results from the different recognizers are not correlated, the multi-expert system can combine results to achieve a lower EER. We define the similarity score from one recognizer as a single dimension of recognition.

The rationale for selecting Protractor instead of the other time sequence matching method in Garda is that the Protractor has a lower EER compared to LCS, EDR, and DTW. The rationale for combining the GMM-UBM and Protractor is that the

Dataset	Recall Set (Trial #)	Gesture (Types #)	Screen Size (Inches)	Samples
Freeform (Set 1)	11-12	56	10.1	
Freeform (Set 2)	13-17	54	10.1	
$1 Demo	11-30	16	3.8	
Vatavu (Set 1)	11-20	18	6.1	
Vatavu (Set 2)	11-20	20	6.1	
MMG corput	11-30	16	13.3	
HHReco	11-30	13	6.2	
SUSig	11-30	94	3.7	
MCYT -100	11-50	100	6.3	

Table 1. Summary of the seven datasets used in our analysis. The template set of each dataset is always the first ten trials (# 1 to #10) of every type of gesture. The screen size refers to the screen size of device on which the gesture samples were collected for that dataset. SUSig and MCYT-100 datasets also included attacks, which were used in our attack evaluations.

two methods focus on different features of gestures. GMM-UBM does not take the order of gesture points into account, which means it only focuses on the shape of a gesture. Protractor concentrates on the trajectory of a gesture, especially the connections between adjacent gesture points.

There are three steps in both systems. First, the recall gesture is sent to the GMM-UBM authentication verifier. We set two thresholds T_{upper} and T_{lower} for the Gaussian Probability P_{GMM}. If $P_{GMM} > T_{upper}$, we can make the decision that this recall gesture belongs to a certain gesture type G_i. If $P_{GMM} < T_{lower}$, we can decide that this gesture does not belong to gesture type G_i. Otherwise, we cannot decide the gesture's type. Second, the recall gesture is sent to a time-series authentication recognizer. For the Garda system, we use Protractor to measure the similarity. For SVMGarda system, we use the Protractor kernel SVM to measure the similarity P_{simi} that a recall gesture belongs to a certain gesture type G_i. In the last step, we combine the two probabilities together by modifying P_{simi} with a modification factor a_m, which is determined by the GMM-UBM verifier.

DATASETS

Table 1 shows a summary of the datasets we used in our analysis: (i) Freeform gesture dataset [44], (ii) $1 Demo dataset [51], (iii) Vatavu's gesture datasets [49], (iv) MMG corpus dataset [1], (v) HHReco dataset [27], (vi) SUSig [30], and (vii) MCTY-100 [37]. For consistency, we opted to use the first 10 trials from each dataset as Template sets. The remaining trials are called the Recall set. We use the first five datasets to test the authentication accuracy of different recognizers. We use the last two datasets to examine the ability of the recognizers to resist imitation attacks. In total, we used 10872 gestures collected from 328 participants across these seven datasets.

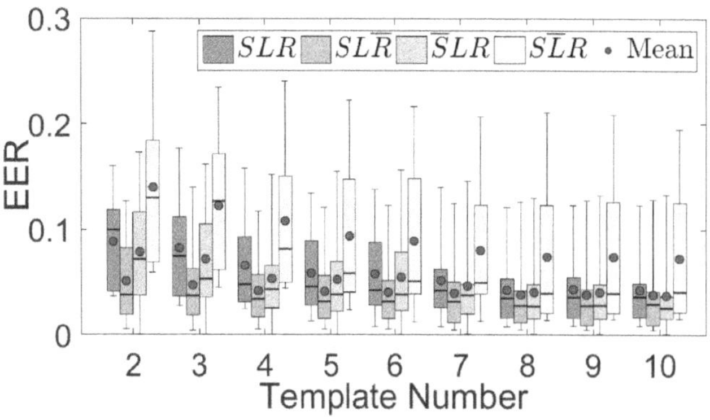

Figure 7. EER values under combinations (SLR), ($SL\bar{R}$), ($\bar{S}LR$), and ($S\bar{L}R$). S, L, and R mean the gesture's scale, location, are rotation are invariants. $\bar{S}$, $\bar{L}$, and $\bar{R}$ mean the these three are variants. The whiskers show the maximum and minimum EER of each group. We can see that rotation alone as variant ($SL\bar{R}$) has obvious positive effect authentication accuracy; scale alone as variant ($\bar{S}LR$) has no obvious effect authentication accuracy; location alone as variant ($S\bar{L}R$) has obvious negative effect on the authentication accuracy.

RESULTS

We first present the results of our analysis of the invariances (rotation, scale, location) and their effect on authentication performance. We follow up with results on the performance of the different recognizers and present results of the brute-force and imitation attacks. Finally, we present the implementation and evaluation of our novel approach Garda operating on a mobile device.

We used two-way ANOVA for testing the statistical significance between the authentication performances of individual gesture invariances and the benchmark since both the invariance combination types and the template numbers can affect the authentication result. We used repeated measures one-way ANOVA to test the statistical significance between the authentication performances of the 13 recognizers on different datasets. We use Bonferroni corrected p-values for the post-hoc test for controlling the familywise error.

Invariances Analysis

Figure 7 shows the individual effects of rotation, location and scaling on authentication performance. In this analysis, we used the EER of the recognition-optimal combination as the benchmark.

A two-way ANOVA test indicated a statistically significant difference between individual gesture invariance authentication performance and the benchmark ($\chi^2(251) = 11.6$, $p < 0.001$), while the interaction effect between the two factors is not statistically significant ($\chi^2(251) = 0.17$, $p = 1$). Thus, we did not consider the interaction effect between the the invariance combination types and the template numbers.

Rotation Invariance

Figure 7 demonstrates that making the gesture rotation as variant can improve the recognition performance (i.e. reduce the EER). The result holds true even with a different number of template gestures across different gesture datasets. This can be explained by a users' drawing habit – people will tend to input their gesture into the tablet the same way every time.

Very rarely, however, do gestures in the same dataset have the same rotation angle as other gestures.

The statistical test between $SL\overline{R}$ and SLR with template number (2 to 10) shows there is no statistically significant difference ($p = 0.373$, $d = 0.42$). The lack of significance stems from the fact that the EER values become relatively close as the number of templates becomes larger (8, 9, 10). A recognizer is more likely to identify a genuine trial when there are more genuine templates to test against. This reduces, overall, the effect of invariance combinations on EER. If we do not consider EERs with large template number (8, 9, 10), then there is statistically significant difference between $SL\overline{R}$ and SLR ($p = 0.013$, $d = 0.56$). As such, allowing for rotation variance can reduce the possibility of accepting false gestures.

Scale Invariance

Figure 7 shows that the scale variable has a slight, positive influence on recognition performance. The primary reason is that Protractor is based on the cosine distance between two gesture sequences. The cosine distance measures the directional difference between two vectors and ignores the Euclidean distance. Thus, the difference among the size of how the gestures are drawn will not affect the relative similarity scores. The statistical test between $\overline{S}LR$ and SLR shows no statistically significant difference ($p = 1$, $d = 0.14$). Taking scale as variant does not have a statistically significant influence on authentication performance.

Location Invariance

Figure 7 shows that taking location as variant has a negative influence on recognition accuracy. The primary reason is that it is hard for people to draw at the same location on the screen when repeating their gestures. The recognition performance is not based on the absolute similarity among trials of the same person; it depends on the relative difference of similarities between genuine trials and imitations. Taking gesture location as variant will reduce the similarity of genuine gestures and increase the similarity of imitation gestures. This makes it more difficult to distinguish the genuine and imitation gestures, and the authentication performance will be worse. The statistical test between $S\overline{L}R$ and SLR shows a statistically significant difference ($p = 9.788 \times 10^{-4}$, $d = 0.61$).

Variants Combinations Effects on Recognition

Figure 8 shows that the combination ($\overline{S}L\overline{R}$) achieves the lowest EER (0.041) on average. It can be explained by the individual effects of the three variables: rotation variant has statistically significant positive effect on EER, location variant has statistically significant negative effect on EER, and scale variant has slightly positive effect on the EER. Compared to the common case of the three combinations (SLR), where the EER = 0.075, the $\overline{S}L\overline{R}$ reduces the EER by 45.3%.

Additionally, the ROC curves of $\overline{S}L\overline{R}$ and $SL\overline{R}$ are very close. It verifies our analysis that the gesture scale variable has no statistically significant effect on EER.

We also can observe that the four combinations that take location as variant ($S\overline{L}R$, $\overline{S}\overline{L}R$, $S\overline{L}\overline{R}$, and $\overline{S}\overline{L}\overline{R}$) are the lowest four ROC curves. This means that, with the same conditions for gesture scale and rotation, taking gesture location as variant will always have a negative effect on authentication accuracy. Generally, the reason is that people cannot keep their gesture's location at a relative fixed place on the touch screen. This means that different gesture locations can distort the similarities among the genuine and fake gestures.

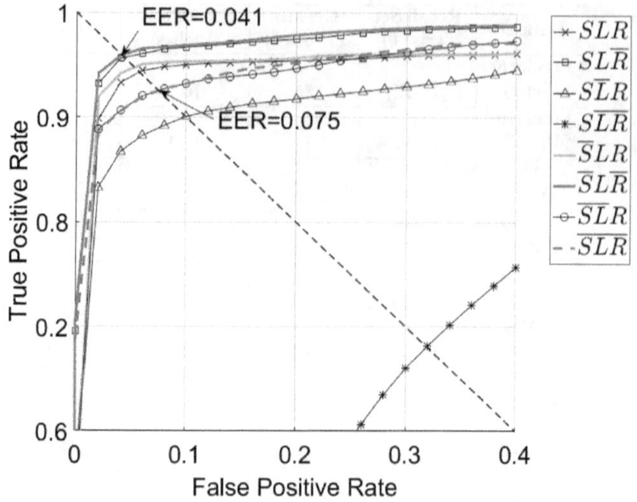

Figure 8. The average ROC curves of the five gesture datasets with two to ten template gestures for the eight combinations of the three variants (Scale, Location, Rotation). ***S*, *L*, and *R* mean the gesture's scale, location, are rotation are invariants.** $\overline{S}$, $\overline{L}$, **and** $\overline{R}$ **mean the these are variant. We can see that the combination (**$\overline{S}L\overline{R}$**) has the lowest EER (=0.041) across the five datasets. While the recognition-optimal case (*SLR*) can only achieve EER=0.075. We conclude that combination (**$\overline{S}L\overline{R}$**) is the optimal authentication selection of three variants.**

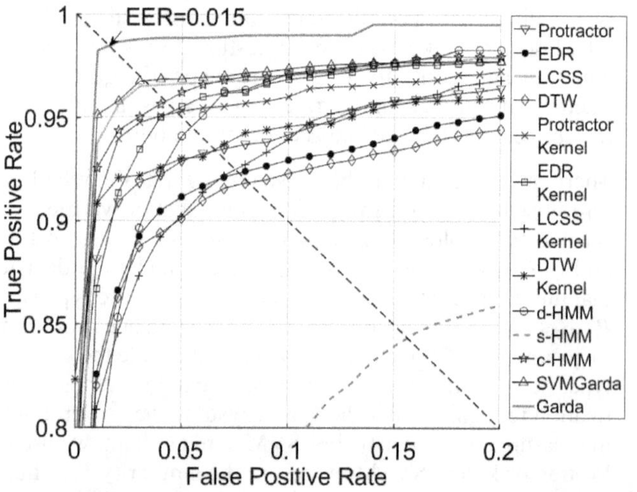

Figure 9. The average ROC curves for the 13 recognition methods over the five gesture datasets. We found that Garda has the lowest EER (0.015). Since the ROC curve of Garda is closest to the up-left corner, it should be the most tolerant of the change of authentication threshold. We conclude that Garda is the best among the 13 methods.

Performance of Different Recognition Methods

To select the optimal recognition method for gestures, we tried 13 different methods in four groups: sequence matching group (Protractor, EDR, LCS, DTW), One-class SVM group (Protractor-, EDR-,LCS-,DTW-kernels), HMM group (dHMM, sHMM, cHMM), and multi-expert group (SVM-

	Freeform (Set 1)		Freeform (Set 2)		MMG		$1 Demo		HHReco		Vatavu (Set 1)		Vatavu (Set 2)	
	EER	t (ms)	EER	t (ms)	EER	t (ms)	EER	t (ms)	EER	t (ms)	EER	t (ms)	EER	t (ms)
Protractor	0.027	0.7	0.105	0.5	0.032	0.6	0.021	0.6	0.015	0.7	0.008	0.8	0.005	0.7
EDR	0.062	27.9	0.137	27.0	0.185	42.8	0.044	42.4	0.032	43.6	0.031	43.1	0.010	41.2
LCS	0.036	22.2	0.121	21.2	0.056	34.1	0.020	33.8	0.013	34.9	0.011	35.1	0.002	34.9
DTW	0.062	3.9	**0.142**	3.5	**0.204**	5.5	0.049	5.5	0.026	5.5	0.011	36.8	0.002	36.5
Protractor Kernel	0.035	5.1	0.141	4.8	0.046	7.2	0.032	5.6	0.047	6.0	0.004	6.7	0.011	4.6
EDR Kernel	0.048	391.1	0.055	419.2	0.119	464.1	0.034	112.7	0.037	128.5	0.009	101.2	0.003	90.4
LCS Kernel	0.036	368.3	0.118	393.9	0.141	489.2	0.058	149.0	0.040	162.6	0.006	141.5	0.006	121.1
DTW Kernel	0.053	471.5	0.113	449.2	0.063	641.1	0.092	314.5	0.028	333.2	0.001	334.1	0.013	339.1
d-HMM	0.036	1.5	.113	1.5	0.065	1.4	0.045	1.4	0.038	1.5	0.023	2.0	0.011	2.1
s-HMM	**0.109**	1.6	0.130	1.2	0.198	1.3	**0.165**	1.3	**0.144**	1.6	**0.140**	1.9	**0.104**	1.8
c-HMM	0.044	3.7	0.104	3.1	0.052	4.9	0.015	4.4	0.034	4.9	0.005	5.7	0	5.7
SVMGarda	0.026	5.3	0.116	5.2	***0.032***	6.3	0.014	5.7	0.012	5.6	0.011	7.1	0	4.7
Garda	***0.019***	1.0	***0.047***	2.4	0.033	2.1	***0.012***	1.7	***0.007***	1.8	***0***	2.2	***0***	2.1

Table 2. EER values against estimated authentication time. Each recognition method is implemented in MATLAB and tested on five gesture datasets in terms of EER and authentication time (t) in milliseconds. Since the authentication time is based on MATLAB computations, it can be only used for a relative comparison among different recognizers. In each dataset, the lowest EER is shown in bold and italic, while the highest EER is only bold. Generally, the ME group always has the lowest EER among different datasets and authentication methods. Between the two ME methods, their EER performances are dependent on the different datasets. However, since Garda has much lower EER than SVMGarda in Freeform (set 2) and the computation cost of Garda is always lower than SVMGarda, we conclude that Garda is the best among the 13 methods.

Garda, Garda). Since our analysis of gesture invariances is based on Protractor, we also used Protractor as the baseline for the comparison of these 13 methods. We evaluated the above methods with EER values, authentication times, brute-force and forgery attacks.

We used 10 gesture trials as the template gesture set to minimize the bias from the template selection. The reason is that the selection of template gestures may effect the recognition performance. The more gesture templates, the less bias that exists in the selected templates.

Figure 9 shows that Garda is the best among the 13 recognizers. We averaged the ROC curves of the five gesture datasets for the 13 recognizers. We found that Garda achieves lowest EER (0.015) in the averaged ROC. The ROC curve of Garda is the closest to the up-left corner, meaning that Garda can recognize the most genuine gestures correctly while rejecting attacks as well as other recognizers.

Table 2 shows that Garda has most of the lowest EERs among the 13 recognition methods through the five datasets. The authentication time for Garda is around 2 ms, which is also among the lowest authentication times. Specifically, both of the two multi-expert methods, Garda and SVMGarda outperform the other recognizers. Garda is also more stable than SVMGarda. For example, in Freeform (Set 2), Garda achieved the lowest EER (0.047), while SVMGarda got a relatively much higher EER (0.116).

Based on repeated measures ANOVA analysis on the 13 recognizers, there is a statistically significant difference between EERs when choosing different recognizers ($\chi^2(90) = 9.71$, $p < 0.001$). From our post-hoc analysis, we found there are no statistically significant differences between Garda and Protractor ($p = 0.121$, $d = 0.52$), Garda and LCS ($p = 0.0749$, $d = 0.68$), Garda and DTW ($p = 0.0545$, $d = 1.17$), Garda and Protractor kernel SVM ($p = 0.0528$, $d = 0.89$), and Garda and SVMGarda ($p = 0.208$, $d = 0.47$). This does not impact our result, since Garda is still the best performing authenticator for the following reasons: First, Protractor cannot prevent brute-force and imitation attacks as well as Garda irrespective of whether its EER is statistically significantly different; Second, Figure 9 also shows that the ROC curve of Garda is much more ideal than the other recognizers.

We found that the authentication times of the one-class SVM group are much longer than the sequence matching group while the EER values are relatively similar. The reason for the longer authentication time is that, with the similarity matrix, SVM methods need an extra step to examine the similarity scores with training gesture trials and converting the similarity to probabilities. Since one-class SVM group distinguishes the gestures based on the sequence matching kernel functions, its ability to distinguish gestures should be the same as sequence matching group methods. Thus, the one-class SVM group has similar EER as sequence matching group methods.

The sHMM method always performs with the worst EER. The reason is that we segment the gesture into several parts based on sharp turns and then classify those parts into 14 observations. We tend to lose a lot of useful information and this makes the gestures more likely to be misclassified.

Performance Under Brute-Force Attacks

Figure 10 shows how the authentication methods resist brute-force attacks. We found that the recognizers' performance are polarized. On the one hand, EDR, LCS, DTW, dHMM, sHMM and Garda resisted all of the brute-force attacks. On the other hand, the brute-force attack cracked most of the gestures of the other recognizers. Specifically, we found that the features of recognizers that can resist attacks are distance based (such as EDR, LCS, and DTW) and time series HMM-based (dHMM, sHMM). SVM was generally weak against these attacks.

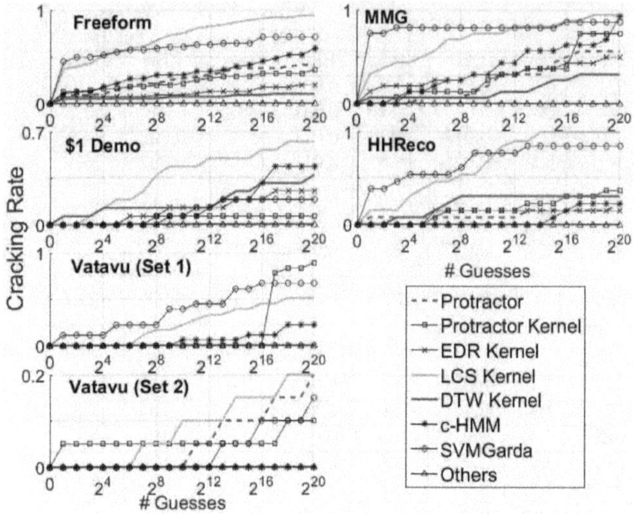

Figure 10. Guessing success rates of brute-force attacks of the 13 authentication systems on different datasets. The "Others" includes Garda, EDR, LCS, DTW, dHMM, and cHMM. From the cracking rates, Garda, EDR, LCS, DTW, dHMM, and cHMM have the best ability on resisting brute force attacks since the success cracking rates of them are 0% through the 6 datasets.

Method	MCYT-100	SUSig
Protractor	0.151	0.350
EDR	0.155	0.366
LCS	0.101	0.420
DTW	0.189	0.371
Protractor Kernel	0.163	0.335
EDR Kernel	0.103	0.402
LCS Kernel	0.084	0.344
DTW Kernel	0.093	0.397
d-HMM	0.233	0.333
s-HMM	0.338	0.445
c-HMM	0.125	0.202
SVMGarda	0.096	0.479
Garda	0.045	0.035

Table 3. The EER of the 13 authentication methods in MCYT-100 and SUSig datasets under skilled forgery attacks. Only Garda has considerable advantages in EER.

Performance Under Imitation Attacks

We used the datasets MCYT-100 and SUSig to examine the 13 methods' performance under imitation attacks. These datasets have samples from both legitimate users and imitation attacks from skilled attackers. We used the first ten legitimate trials for each user as templates and the rest as legitimate authentication attempts. The skilled attackers observed the genuine trials and practiced them until they felt confident with attacks.

Table 3 shows that only Garda outperforms the rest 12 methods on resisting forgery attacks. EER values of Garda are 0.045 and 0.035 in MCYT-100 and SUSig, respectively. In contrast, the lowest EER values for the other methods are 0.084 (LCS Kernel) and 0.202 (c-HMM). In summary, Garda outperforms all of the other approaches against imitation attacks, and none of the other approaches perform well against both of the datasets.

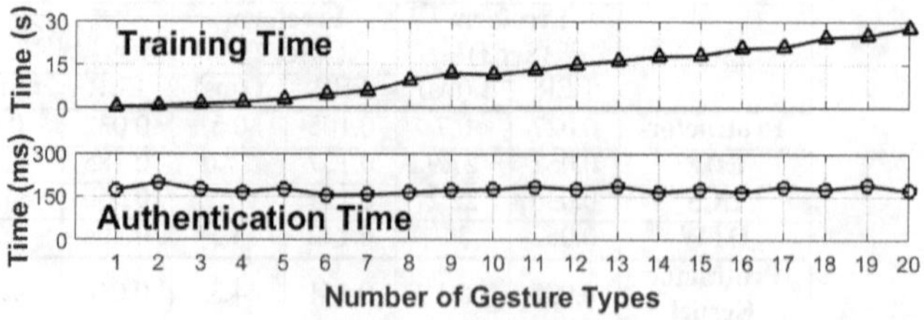

Figure 11. The processing time for training and authentication under different number of gesture passwords. The upper figure shows the time for training, the lower shows the time for authentication. Along with the increasing number of gesture passwords, the training time is gradually increasing while the authentication time stays stable.

Mobile Device Implementation and Evaluation

We implemented Garda, described in Figure 6, on an Android platform. Our test device was a Samsung Galaxy Note 10.1, which had a 1.9 GHz Quad CPU and 3 GB of RAM. For our evaluation, we created 20 new gesture passwords (two templates per gesture) on the mobile device and recorded the processing time for training and authentication with a different number of gesture passwords.

Figure 11 shows our mobile device evaluation results. With the number of gestures (users) increasing, we see that the training time increases while the authentication time stabilizes around 150 ms. The training time increases because Garda uses the Expectation-Maximum algorithm to train the UBM based on all the gesture trials in the dataset and re-train the Gaussian Mixture Model (GMM) for all gesture types based on this new UBM. More gestures lead to more time spent training models. In the authentication phase, we only need one GMM for a given gesture so the authentication time remains stable. However, there are typically not multiple passwords on a mobile device, and the training time even with 20 different gestures is only 30 seconds and could be run in-background over other tasks. All this shows that Garda is an efficient gesture recognizer for a mobile device authentication system.

DISCUSSION

Our evaluation showed that our novel gesture authentication method - Garda - had the best authentication EER (0.015), shortest authentication time, and resisted all of the brute-force attacks and most of the forgery attacks (EER = 0.040). Garda achieves this by combining the individual advantages of the Protractor and GMM-UBM recognition schemes. Protractor identifies the gestures temporally while GMM-UBM identifies the temporal-independent distributions of the coordinate points. Combining these two methods resulted in a more harmonious, effective authentication system.

SVMGarda performed second-best to Garda. The key difference between the two is that SVMGarda uses the cosine similarity from Protractor as a kernel function for the support vector classifier. Protractor uses inverse cosine distance – the least similar gestures are scored at '0' and the most similar gestures (exact match) are scored as infinite. When Protractor is passed through the SVM as a kernel function, the output is changed from a gesture score ranging from [0,inf] to a similarity probability ranging from [0,1]. This has the effect of shrinking the difference between genuine and imitation gestures, making it more likely that SVMGarda will mis-classify.

sHMM performs the worst with an EER of 0.157. Following up gesture segmentation with a classification of the segmented parts removed crucial details from the genuine gestures. This had the side-effect of making them harder to distinguish. Of course, this is a function of the number of gesture segments: if we increase the segments, we can preserve more detail. If we continue to increase segments, sHMM becomes the same as dHMM. This improves the EER from 0.157 to 0.056.

Six recognizers (EDR, LCS, DTW, dHMM, sHMM, and Garda) were capable of resisting all brute-force attacks, but for different reasons. EDR, LCS, and DTW use recognition methods based on the Euclidean distance between genuine and fake gestures. If the gesture points are randomly generated, as they are in the brute-force method, then the matching problem is almost impossible: a randomly generated collection of a hundred-or-so coordinate points need to fall close to a continuous sequence of gesture points clustered very closely together out of thousands of positions on the screen. The result is not surprising when it is viewed this way. For dHMM and sHMM: the randomly generated gesture contains many sudden, random turns that can be used as segmentation points when compared to a user-generated gesture.

There are seven recognizers that were unable to resist brute-force attacks. Authentication thresholds in each scheme are trained to distinguish different users' gestures, and these thresholds are quite loose since they only need to recognize a single genuine gesture from entirely different gestures. There are three reasons for these three groups: Protractor-based methods (Protractor, Protractor-Kernel SVM, SVMGarda), SVM-based methods (Protractor, LCS, DTW, and EDR kernel SVM and SVMGarda), and cHMM. For Protractor-based methods: it depends on cosine distance, which only cares about the directions between two adjacent points. This is easier than matching gestures based on Euclidean distance. For SVM-based methods, it is the same reason as why the EER values are so high: the method transforms a large range of scores [0,inf] to a limited range of probabilities [0,1], increasing the opportunity for mis-classification. cHMM used the distribution of gesture points locations without considering the temporal order, making the brute-force attack more likely to crack cHMM since the attacks are based on randomly generated gestures.

For the imitation attacks, Garda achieved the lowest EER out of all the other methods. The reason that other methods cannot resist imitation attacks is that single time sequence authentication methods are unable to distinguish the variations in genuine gestures and the difference between the genuine and skilled attack gestures.

We can see that the Garda method is robust and practical for mobile authentication. First, the authentication time is short (200 ms) and is also relatively stable as the number of gestures increases. Although we tested 20 gestures (20 different users) in the system to judge its viability, we note that it is unlikely a personal device would have so many different accounts. Even with 20 gestures, 30 seconds is affordable for a one-time training process. The mobile device only needs to store the trials, GMM, and UBM models; therefore, our system can have a short and stable authentication time and still be scalable for large numbers of gestures.

To best of our knowledge, we have presented the first analysis of how the invariances of gesture preprocessing impact the performance of gesture-based authentication systems. We found that an optimal combination (scale variant, location invariant, rotation variant) achieves the lowest EER (0.041) on average. This derives from the combination of individual effects of the three variables: rotation variant has a statistically significant, positive effect on EER; location variant has a statistically significant negative effect on EER; scale variant does not have a statistically significant effect on the EER. The screen sizes on which gestures were collected, 3.75in to 13.3 inches, do not appear to affect our analysis of gesture invariance.

The gesture variable combinations with EERs higher than $\overline{S}L\overline{R}$ can be explained by the individual effects of the three variables. First, since people are unable to draw their gestures at the same place every time, taking gesture's location as variant always has a negative effect on authentication accuracy. Second, these three variables interact with each other. The binary state of one variable can influence other variables, and thus, influence the final recognition accuracy.

CONCLUSIONS

We presented and evaluated a novel multi-expert gesture recognizer design for authentication: Garda. We also implemented and evaluated Garda on a mobile device. All our results show that our implementation can largely improve the performance of gesture-based authentication systems. Garda was the final result of a rigorous evaluation of 13 different methods to implement gesture recognizers. We applied several datasets and two different attacks against the recognizers. Finally, we conducted the first analysis of how tuning the variables of preprocessing methods of gesture recognizers can impact their authentication performance. The presented authentication-optimal combination can reduce up to 45.3% of EER on average compared to recognition-optimal configuration used in previous work. Additional material available at `http://securegestures.org`.

ACKNOWLEDGMENTS

This material is based upon work supported by the National Science Foundation under Grant Number 1228777. Any opinions, findings, and conclusions or recommendations expressed in this material are those of the authors and do not necessarily reflect the views of the National Science Foundation. Gradeigh D. Clark was supported by the Department of Defense (DoD) through the National Defense Science & Engineering Graduate Fellowship (NDSEG) Program.

REFERENCES

1. Lisa Anthony, Radu-Daniel Vatavu, and Jacob O. Wobbrock. 2013. Understanding the Consistency of Users' Pen and Finger Stroke Gesture Articulation. In Proceedings of Graphics Interface 2013 (GI '13). Canadian Information Processing Society, Toronto, Ont.,

Canada, Canada, 87–94. http://dl.acm.org/citation.cfm?id=2532129.2532145

2. Lisa Anthony and Jacob O. Wobbrock. 2010. A Lightweight Multistroke Recognizer for User Interface Prototypes. In Proceedings of Graphics Interface 2010 (GI '10). Canadian Information Processing Society, Toronto, Ont., Canada, Canada, 245–252. http://dl.acm.org/citation.cfm?id=1839214.1839258

3. Donald B. Rubin Arthur P. Dempster, Nan M. Laird. 1977. Maximum Likelihood from Incomplete Data via the EM Algorithm. Journal of the Royal Statistical Society. Series B (Methodological) 39, 1 (1977), 1–38. http://www.jstor.org/stable/2984875

4. Ilhan Aslan, Andreas Uhl, Alexander Meschtscherjakov, and Manfred Tscheligi. 2014. Mid-air Authentication Gestures: An Exploration of Authentication Based on Palm and Finger Motions. In Proceedings of the 16th International Conference on Multimodal Interaction (ICMI '14). ACM, New York, NY, USA, 311–318. DOI: http://dx.doi.org/10.1145/2663204.2663246

5. Md Tanvir Islam Aumi and Sven Kratz. 2014. AirAuth: Evaluating In-air Hand Gestures for Authentication. In Proceedings of the 16th International Conference on Human-computer Interaction with Mobile Devices & Services (MobileHCI '14). ACM, New York, NY, USA, 309–318. DOI: http://dx.doi.org/10.1145/2628363.2628388

6. Lasse Bergroth., Harri Hakonen., and Timo Raita. 2000. A Survey of Longest Common Subsequence Algorithms. In Proceedings of the Seventh International Symposium on String Processing Information Retrieval (SPIRE'00) (SPIRE '00). IEEE Computer Society, Washington, DC, USA. DOI: http://dx.doi.org/10.1109/SPIRE.2000.878178

7. Cheng Bo, Lan Zhang, Xiang-Yang Li, Qiuyuan Huang, and Yu Wang. 2013. SilentSense: Silent User Identification via Touch and Movement Behavioral Biometrics. In Proceedings of the 19th Annual International Conference on Mobile Computing & Networking (MobiCom '13). ACM, New York, NY, USA, 187–190. DOI: http://dx.doi.org/10.1145/2500423.2504572

8. Joseph Bonneau. 2012. The Science of Guessing: Analyzing an Anonymized Corpus of 70 Million Passwords. In 2012 IEEE Symposium on Security and Privacy. 538–552. DOI: http://dx.doi.org/10.1109/SP.2012.49

9. Ulrich Burgbacher and Klaus Hinrichs. 2014. An Implicit Author Verification System for Text Messages Based on Gesture Typing Biometrics. In Proceedings of the SIGCHI Conference on Human Factors in Computing Systems (CHI '14). ACM, New York, NY, USA, 2951–2954. DOI: http://dx.doi.org/10.1145/2556288.2557346

10. William M Campbell, Joseph P Campbell, Douglas A Reynolds, Elliot Singer, and Pedro A Torres-Carrasquillo. 2006a. Support Vector Machines for Speaker and Language Recognition. Computer Speech & Language 20, 2 (2006), 210–229. DOI: http://dx.doi.org/10.1016/j.csl.2005.06.003

11. William M Campbell, Douglas E Sturim, and Douglas A Reynolds. 2006b. Support Vector Machines Using GMM Supervectors for Speaker Verification. Signal Processing Letters, IEEE 13, 5 (2006), 308–311. DOI: http://dx.doi.org/10.1109/LSP.2006.870086

12. Lei Chen, M. Tamer Özsu, and Vincent Oria. 2005. Robust and Fast Similarity Search for Moving Object Trajectories. In Proceedings of the 2005 ACM SIGMOD International Conference on Management of Data (SIGMOD '05). ACM, New York, NY, USA, 491–502. DOI: http://dx.doi.org/10.1145/1066157.1066213

13. Gradeigh D. Clark and Janne Lindqvist. 2015. Engineering Gesture-Based Authentication Systems. Pervasive Computing, IEEE 14, 1 (Jan 2015), 18–25. DOI: http://dx.doi.org/10.1109/MPRV.2015.6

14. Corinna Cortes and Vladimir Vapnik. 1995. Support-vector networks. Machine Learning 20, 3 (1995), 273–297. DOI: http://dx.doi.org/10.1007/BF00994018

15. Jacek Czyz, Mohammad Sadeghi, Josef Kittler, and Luc Vandendorpe. 2004. Decision fusion for face authentication. In Biometric Authentication. Springer, 686–693. DOI: http://dx.doi.org/10.1007/978-3-540-25948-0_93

16. Alexander De Luca, Alina Hang, Frederik Brudy, Christian Lindner, and Heinrich Hussmann. 2012. Touch Me Once and I Know It's You!: Implicit Authentication Based on Touch Screen Patterns. In Proceedings of the SIGCHI Conference on Human Factors in Computing Systems (CHI '12). ACM, New York, NY, USA, 987–996. DOI: http://dx.doi.org/10.1145/2207676.2208544

17. Alexander De Luca, Marian Harbach, Emanuel von Zezschwitz, Max-Emanuel Maurer, Bernhard Ewald Slawik, Heinrich Hussmann, and Matthew Smith. 2014. Now You See Me, Now You Don't: Protecting Smartphone Authentication from Shoulder Surfers. In Proceedings of the SIGCHI Conference on Human Factors in Computing Systems (CHI '14). ACM, New York, NY, USA, 2937–2946. DOI: http://dx.doi.org/10.1145/2556288.2557097

18. Alexander De Luca, Emanuel von Zezschwitz, Ngo Dieu Huong Nguyen, Max-Emanuel Maurer, Elisa Rubegni, Marcello Paolo Scipioni, and Marc Langheinrich. 2013. Back-of-device Authentication on Smartphones. In Proceedings of the SIGCHI Conference on Human Factors in Computing Systems (CHI '13). ACM, New York, NY, USA, 2389–2398. DOI: http://dx.doi.org/10.1145/2470654.2481330

19. Jiang-Wen Deng and Hung tat Tsui. 2000. An HMM-based Approach for Gesture Segmentation and Recognition. In Pattern Recognition, 2000. Proceedings. 15th International Conference on, Vol. 3. 679–682 vol.3. DOI:http://dx.doi.org/10.1109/ICPR.2000.903636

20. Giovanni Dimauro, Sebastiano Impedovo, Giuseppe Pirlo, and A Salzo. 1997. A multi-expert signature verification system for bankcheck processing. International Journal of Pattern Recognition and Artificial Intelligence 11, 05 (1997), 827–844. DOI: http://dx.doi.org/10.1142/S0218001497000378

21. Mahmoud Elmezain, Ayoub Al-Hamadi, and Bernd Michaelis. 2009. Hand Trajectory-based Gesture Spotting and Recognition Using HMM. In 2009 16th IEEE International Conference on Image Processing (ICIP). 3577–3580. DOI: http://dx.doi.org/10.1109/ICIP.2009.5414322

22. Tom Fawcett. 2006. An Introduction to ROC Analysis. Pattern Recogn. Lett. 27, 8 (June 2006), 861–874. DOI: http://dx.doi.org/10.1016/j.patrec.2005.10.010

23. Dinei Florencio and Cormac Herley. 2007. A Large-scale Study of Web Password Habits. In Proceedings of the 16th International Conference on World Wide Web (WWW '07). ACM, New York, NY, USA, 657–666. DOI:http://dx.doi.org/10.1145/1242572.1242661

24. Mario Frank, Ralf Biedert, Eugene Ma, Ivan Martinovic, and Dawn Song. 2013. Touchalytics: On the Applicability of Touchscreen Input As a Behavioral Biometric for Continuous Authentication. Trans. Info. For. Sec. 8, 1 (Jan. 2013), 136–148. DOI: http://dx.doi.org/10.1109/TIFS.2012.2225048

25. Eiji Hayashi, Manuel Maas, and Jason I. Hong. 2014. Wave to Me: User Identification Using Body Lengths and Natural Gestures. In Proceedings of the SIGCHI Conference on Human Factors in Computing Systems (CHI '14). ACM, New York, NY, USA, 3453–3462. DOI:http://dx.doi.org/10.1145/2556288.2557043

26. Paul S Heckbert and Michael Garland. 1997. Survey of Polygonal Surface Simplification Algorithms. Technical Report. DTIC Document. http://oai.dtic.mil/oai/oai?verb=getRecord&metadataPrefix=html&identifier=ADA461098

27. Heloise Hse and A. Richard Newton. 2004. Sketched Symbol Recognition Using Zernike Moments. In Proceedings of the Pattern Recognition, 17th International Conference on (ICPR'04) Volume 1 - Volume 01 (ICPR '04). IEEE Computer Society, Washington, DC, USA, 367–370. DOI: http://dx.doi.org/10.1109/ICPR.2004.838

28. Anil K. Jain, Arun Ross, and Sharath Pankanti. 2006. Biometrics: A Tool for Information Security. Trans. Info. For. Sec. 1, 2 (Nov. 2006), 125–143. DOI: http://dx.doi.org/10.1109/TIFS.2006.873653

29. Frederick Jelinek, Lalit R. Bahl, and Robert L. Mercer. 2006. Design of a Linguistic Statistical Decoder for the Recognition of Continuous Speech. IEEE Trans. Inf. Theor. 21, 3 (Sept. 2006), 250–256. DOI: http://dx.doi.org/10.1109/TIT.1975.1055384

30. Alisher Kholmatov and Berrin Yanikoglu. 2009. SUSIG: An On-line Signature Database, Associated Protocols and Benchmark Results. Pattern Anal. Appl. 12, 3 (Sept. 2009), 227–236. DOI: http://dx.doi.org/10.1007/s10044-008-0118-x

31. Hyeon-Kyu Lee and J. H. Kim. 1999. An HMM-based Threshold Model Approach for Gesture Recognition. IEEE Transactions on Pattern Analysis and Machine Intelligence 21, 10 (Oct 1999), 961–973. DOI: http://dx.doi.org/10.1109/34.799904

32. Yang Li. 2010. Protractor: A Fast and Accurate Gesture Recognizer. In Proceedings of the SIGCHI Conference on Human Factors in Computing Systems (CHI '10). ACM, New York, NY, USA, 2169–2172. DOI: http://dx.doi.org/10.1145/1753326.1753654

33. Alexander De Luca and Janne Lindqvist. 2015. Is secure and usable smartphone authentication asking too much? Computer 48, 5 (May 2015), 64–68. DOI: http://dx.doi.org/10.1109/MC.2015.134

34. Michael D. Morse and Jignesh M. Patel. 2007. An Efficient and Accurate Method for Evaluating Time Series Similarity. In Proceedings of the 2007 ACM SIGMOD International Conference on Management of Data (SIGMOD '07). ACM, New York, NY, USA, 569–580. DOI: http://dx.doi.org/10.1145/1247480.1247544

35. Miguel A. Nacenta, Yemliha Kamber, Yizhou Qiang, and Per Ola Kristensson. 2013. Memorability of Pre-designed and User-defined Gesture Sets. In Proceedings of the SIGCHI Conference on Human Factors in Computing Systems (CHI '13). ACM, New York, NY, USA, 1099–1108. DOI: http://dx.doi.org/10.1145/2470654.2466142

36. Uran Oh and Leah Findlater. 2013. The Challenges and Potential of End-user Gesture Customization. In Proceedings of the SIGCHI Conference on Human Factors in Computing Systems (CHI '13). ACM, New York, NY, USA, 1129–1138. DOI: http://dx.doi.org/10.1145/2470654.2466145

37. Javier Ortega-Garcia, J Fierrez-Aguilar, D Simon, J Gonzalez, M Faundez-Zanuy, V Espinosa, A Satue, I Hernaez, J-J Igarza, C Vivaracho, and others. 2003. MCYT Baseline Corpus: A Bimodal Biometric Database. IEE Proceedings-Vision, Image and Signal Processing 150, 6 (2003), 395–401. DOI: http://dx.doi.org/10.1049/ip-vis:20031078

38. Douglas A. Reynolds, Thomas F. Quatieri, and Robert B. Dunn. 2000. Speaker Verification Using Adapted Gaussian Mixture Models. Digit. Signal Process. 10, 1 (Jan. 2000), 19–41. DOI: http://dx.doi.org/10.1006/dspr.1999.0361

39. Danuta Rutkowska. 2004. Multi-expert Systems. Springer Berlin Heidelberg, Berlin, Heidelberg, 650–658. DOI: http://dx.doi.org/10.1007/978-3-540-24669-5_85

40. Napa Sae-Bae, Kowsar Ahmed, Katherine Isbister, and Nasir Memon. 2012. Biometric-rich Gestures: A Novel Approach to Authentication on Multi-touch Devices. In Proceedings of the SIGCHI Conference on Human Factors in Computing Systems (CHI '12). ACM, New York, NY, USA, 977–986. DOI: http://dx.doi.org/10.1145/2207676.2208543

41. Alireza Sahami Shirazi, Peyman Moghadam, Hamed Ketabdar, and Albrecht Schmidt. 2012. Assessing the Vulnerability of Magnetic Gestural Authentication to Video-based Shoulder Surfing Attacks. In Proceedings of the SIGCHI Conference on Human Factors in Computing Systems (CHI '12). ACM, New York, NY, USA, 2045–2048. DOI: http://dx.doi.org/10.1145/2207676.2208352

42. Florian Schaub, Marcel Walch, Bastian Könings, and Michael Weber. 2013. Exploring the Design Space of Graphical Passwords on Smartphones. In Proceedings of the Ninth Symposium on Usable Privacy and Security (SOUPS '13). ACM, New York, NY, USA, Article 11, 11:1–11:14 pages. DOI: http://dx.doi.org/10.1145/2501604.2501615

43. Muhammad Shahzad, Alex X. Liu, and Arjmand Samuel. 2013. Secure Unlocking of Mobile Touch Screen Devices by Simple Gestures: You Can See It but You Can Not Do It. In Proceedings of the 19th Annual International Conference on Mobile Computing & Networking (MobiCom '13). ACM, New York, NY, USA, 39–50. DOI: http://dx.doi.org/10.1145/2500423.2500434

44. Michael Sherman, Gradeigh Clark, Yulong Yang, Shridatt Sugrim, Arttu Modig, Janne Lindqvist, Antti Oulasvirta, and Teemu Roos. 2014. User-generated Free-form Gestures for Authentication: Security and Memorability. In Proceedings of the 12th Annual International Conference on Mobile Systems, Applications, and Services (MobiSys '14). ACM, New York, NY, USA, 176–189. DOI: http://dx.doi.org/10.1145/2594368.2594375

45. Jing Tian, Chengzhang Qu, Wenyuan Xu, and Song Wang. 2013. KinWrite: Handwriting-Based Authentication Using Kinect. In Proc. of NDSS '13.

46. Sebastian Uellenbeck, Markus Dürmuth, Christopher Wolf, and Thorsten Holz. 2013. Quantifying the Security of Graphical Passwords: The Case of Android Unlock Patterns. In Proceedings of the 2013 ACM SIGSAC Conference on Computer & Communications Security (CCS '13). ACM, New York, NY, USA, 161–172. DOI: http://dx.doi.org/10.1145/2508859.2516700

47. Umut Uludag, Sharath Pankanti, Salil Prabhakar, and Anil K. Jain. 2004. Biometric cryptosystems: issues and challenges. *Proc. IEEE* 92, 6 (June 2004), 948–960. DOI: http://dx.doi.org/10.1109/JPROC.2004.827372

48. Radu-Daniel Vatavu, Lisa Anthony, and Jacob O. Wobbrock. 2012. Gestures As Point Clouds: A $P Recognizer for User Interface Prototypes. In Proceedings of the 14th ACM International Conference on Multimodal Interaction (ICMI '12). ACM, New York, NY, USA, 273–280. DOI: http://dx.doi.org/10.1145/2388676.2388732

49. Radu-Daniel Vatavu, Daniel Vogel, Géry Casiez, and Laurent Grisoni. 2011. Estimating the Perceived Difficulty of Pen Gestures. In Proceedings of the 13th IFIP TC 13 International Conference on Human-computer Interaction - Volume Part II (INTERACT'11). Springer Berlin Heidelberg, Berlin, Heidelberg, 89–106. DOI: http://dx.doi.org/10.1007/978-3-642-23771-3_9

50. Emanuel von Zezschwitz, Paul Dunphy, and Alexander De Luca. 2013. Patterns in the Wild: A Field Study of the Usability of Pattern and Pin-based Authentication on Mobile Devices. In Proceedings of the 15th International Conference on Human-computer Interaction with Mobile Devices and Services (MobileHCI '13). ACM, New York, NY, USA, 261–270. DOI: http://dx.doi.org/10.1145/2493190.2493231

51. Jacob O. Wobbrock, Andrew D. Wilson, and Yang Li. 2007. Gestures Without Libraries, Toolkits or Training: A $1 Recognizer for User Interface Prototypes. In Proceedings of the 20th Annual ACM Symposium on User Interface Software and Technology (UIST '07). ACM, New York, NY, USA, 159–168. DOI: http://dx.doi.org/10.1145/1294211.1294238

52. Junshuang Yang, Yanyan Li, and Mengjun Xie. 2015. MotionAuth: Motion-based authentication for wrist worn smart devices. In Pervasive Computing and Communication Workshops (PerCom Workshops), 2015 IEEE International Conference on. 550–555. DOI: http://dx.doi.org/10.1109/PERCOMW.2015.7134097

53. Yulong Yang, Gradeigh D. Clark, Janne Lindqvist, and Antti Oulasvirta. 2016. Free-Form Gesture Authentication in the Wild. In Proceedings of the SIGCHI Conference on Human Factors in Computing Systems (CHI '16). ACM, New York, NY, USA, 3722–3735. DOI: http://dx.doi.org/10.1145/2858036.2858270

54. Ziming Zhao, Gail-Joon Ahn, Jeong-Jin Seo, and Hongxin Hu. 2013. On the Security of Picture Gesture Authentication. In Presented as part of the 22nd USENIX Security Symposium (USENIX Security 13). USENIX, Washington, D.C., 383–398. https://www.usenix.org/conference/usenixsecurity13/technical-sessions/presentation/zhao

55. Nan Zheng, Kun Bai, Hai Huang, and Haining Wang. 2014. You Are How You Touch: User Verification on Smartphones via Tapping Behaviors. In 2014 IEEE 22nd International Conference on Network Protocols. IEEE, 221–232. DOI: http://dx.doi.org/10.1109/ICNP.2014.43

I'm too Busy to Reset my LinkedIn Password: On the Effectiveness of Password Reset Emails

Jun Ho Huh
Honeywell ACS Labs
junho.huh@honeywell.com

Hyoungshick Kim
Sungkyunkwan University
hyoung@skku.edu

Swathi S.V.P. Rayala
Oregon State University
rayalas@oregonstate.edu

Rakesh B. Bobba
Oregon State University
rakesh.bobba@oregonstate.edu

Konstantin Beznosov
University of British Columbia
beznosov@ece.ubc.ca

ABSTRACT
A common security practice used to deal with a password breach is locking user accounts and sending out an email to tell users that they need to reset their password to unlock their account. This paper evaluates the effectiveness of this security practice based on the password reset email that LinkedIn sent out around May 2016, and through an online survey conducted on 249 LinkedIn users who received that email. Our evaluation shows that only about 46% of the participants reset their passwords. The mean time taken to reset password was 26.3 days, revealing that a significant proportion of the participants reset their password a few weeks, or even months after first receiving the email. Our findings suggest that more effective persuasive measures need to be added to convince users to reset their password in a timely manner, and further reduce the risks associated with delaying password resets.

ACM Classification Keywords
H.5.m. Information Interfaces and Presentation (e.g. HCI): Miscellaneous

Author Keywords
Password reset; password breach; reset email; LinkedIn.

INTRODUCTION
After the LinkedIn's data breach in 2012, it was reported that about 6.5 million user email addresses and passwords were leaked. Those passwords were stored as unsalted SHA-1 hashes, and were vulnerable to offline guessing attacks that use rainbow tables [9]. In May 2016, however, LinkedIn's chief information security officer, Cory Scott, published an official post [10] saying that,

> *".. we became aware of an additional set of data that had just been released that claims to be email and hashed password combinations of more than 100 million LinkedIn members from that same theft in 2012. We are taking immediate steps.. and we will contact those members to reset their passwords."*

LinkedIn sent out a password reset email to potentially affected users, asking them to reset their passwords the next time they sign in. LinkedIn "invalidated" those accounts, meaning that they were locked (unusable) until users reset their passwords. Each of the affected users was asked to visit LinkedIn, sign in with their current password, request a password reset, open a second email that contains a password reset link, and follow that link to create a new password. Dropbox also went through a data breach in 2012, and only recently realized that the breach may have affected 68 million users [7]. They also sent out an email to potentially affected users after locking their accounts. With this account locking practice in place, attackers would also have to compromise the email account of a victim to steal the password reset link, and take control of the account.

Nevertheless, this reliance on the security of an email account (a second channel) has well-known risks [4, 6]: people often use the same password across multiple sites, or make small changes to the current password in order to create a new password. If a user uses the same password for both LinkedIn and their email account, an attacker would be able to obtain the password reset link and reset the password, taking control of the user's account. Similarly, if the password of the user's email account is a small variation of the password used on LinkedIn, an attacker would be able to perform informed guessing of the email account password. Another possible attack involves an attacker signing into LinkedIn with a stolen email and password pair, and requesting a password reset. The attacker then immediately sends a phishing email to the user, requesting the user to copy and paste the password reset link they received on a malicious page (Karlof et. al. [8] showed that such a phishing attack has about 48% success rate). The attacker would then gain access to the password reset link without knowing the user's email password. This attack, however, will not work if the user has already reset his or her password.

To further mitigate such risks of account compromise, it is integral to persuade users to *quickly* reset their passwords. This paper studies the effectiveness of email-based password reset recommendation practices based on the recent real-world LinkedIn case study. We recruited 249 LinkedIn users who received a password reset email from LinkedIn in 2016, and

CHI 2017, May 6-11, 2017, Denver, CO, USA.
Copyright © 2017 ACM ISBN 978-1-4503-4655-9/17/05 ...$15.00.
http://dx.doi.org/10.1145/3025453.3025788

asked them about their experiences with this email. To the best of our knowledge, this is the first empirical analysis of the effectiveness and timeliness of email-based password reset practices used today by many IT companies. Surprisingly, only 46% of the participants reset their password after reading the email. The mean time taken to reset password was 26.3 days (standard deviation of 33.3), with some taking weeks or even months, indicating a significant delay. Only about 32% of those who reset their password (this is about 15% of all participants) did so on the same day they received the email. About 50% of the participants were using the same (LinkedIn) password on at least one other site, increasing the risk of password reset link and account compromise.

METHODOLOGY

We recruited participants on Amazon Mechanical Turk (MTurk) between June and September 2016. We limited MTurk workers to those in the United States, and asked MTurk workers to participate only if (1) they had accounts on LinkedIn, and (2) have received a password reset email from LinkedIn in 2016. Before collecting responses, we conducted an in-person pilot study with 4 LinkedIn users (who received the email) to test our data collection instruments. Up to this point, most of the survey questions were designed as open-ended questions. We then conducted a second pilot study directly on MTurk with 51 participants to collect open-ended responses. Two researchers used *open coding* to code those responses separately, and discussed the identified codes until they reached consensus on all codes. Those codes were then used to create answer options for the final survey questions. The survey consisted of the following parts:

1. **Concerns:** We asked the participants about their concerns with LinkedIn account being hacked, and how many other sites that they use had the same password as their LinkedIn password.
2. **Password reset:** We asked the participants whether they reset their LinkedIn password.
3. **Reasons for (not) resetting password:** We asked the participants why they reset or did not reset their password after reading the password reset email from LinkedIn.
4. **Password reset behavior:** For those who did reset their password, we asked how they created their new password.

To validate whether a participant has received the password reset email, we asked the participants to submit two screenshots: (1) a screenshot of the initial password reset email received from LinkedIn, and (2) a screenshot of the reset confirmation email received after resetting password. The participants were asked to upload the second screenshot only if they reset their password. We paid \$2.00 to all participants except for those who did not submit any screenshot. Hence, there was no reason for the participants to lie about whether they reset their password. We later used those screenshots to validate their eligibility to participate, and extract the *exact date* in which the reset email was first received and the password was reset.

We excluded responses from those who did not provide us with the screenshots, or who did not follow the screenshot instructions (attention checking). To rule out those who reset their password regardless of the content of the email (e.g., someone who tried to sign in without reading the email, and was asked to reset password to unlock their account), we excluded responses from those who answered *"not influential at all"* to the question *"How influential was the password reset email in deciding to reset your password?"* To minimize the effects of the participants habitually choosing options located in certain positions, we randomized option orders in all applicable questions. Our study was approved by a university Institutional Review Board (IRB).

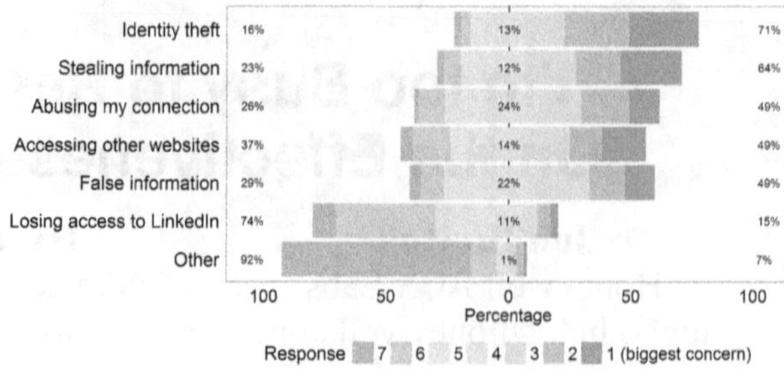

Figure 1. Concerns about LinkedIn account being hacked, sorted based on the overall distribution of the ranks between 1 and 7, where rank 1 is the biggest concern and 7 is the smallest concern.

RESULTS AND RECOMMENDATIONS

Demographics

In total, we recruited 943 LinkedIn users. From the 943 participants, we excluded 685 who failed at least one of the screenshot checks, and 9 who said that the email was "not influential at all." This left 249 (26.41%) responses for data analysis. Most of the participants were whites (72.87%), and the majority were in the age groups of 25–34 (58.63%), 35–44 (22.09%), and 19–24 (11.24%). 54.62% were female. 61.85% had a university degree, 22.89% had master's and doctoral degrees, and 14.06% had a high school diploma. 45 different occupations were reported with computer (15.26%), unemployed (10.44%), and business (9.24%) being the top ones.

Concerns about LinkedIn account being hacked

We asked the participants *"What would concern you the most if your LinkedIn account was hacked? Rank the options below in order of your level of concern, Rank 1 being your biggest concern. If a given option does not concern you at all, leave its ranking as blank. If there is no* `other` *concern, leave its ranking as blank"* We also asked the participants *"If you had* `other` *concern and ranked it, please specify what that reason is."* Figure 1 shows the concerns for LinkedIn account being hacked, sorted based on the overall ranking distributions.

"Someone pretending to be me through identity theft" (`identity theft`) and *"Stealing my personal information from LinkedIn"* (`stealing information`) were the top two concerns. `Identity theft` showed statistically significant difference in the overall ranking distribution against all other reasons (all $p < 0.05$, Bonferroni-corrected Mann-Whitney U test) except for `stealing information`. `Stealing information` showed statistically significant difference against all other reasons (all $p < 0.05$, Bonferroni-corrected MW U test) except for `identity theft` and *"Exploiting and abusing my LinkedIn contacts"* (`abusing my connections`). The participants were least concerned about

Table 1. Percentage of the participants who reset, or did not reset their passwords after receiving the email.

Options	Count
`Yes (I reset)`	114 (45.78%)
`No (I did not reset)`	119 (47.79%)
`I have no idea`	16 (6.43%)

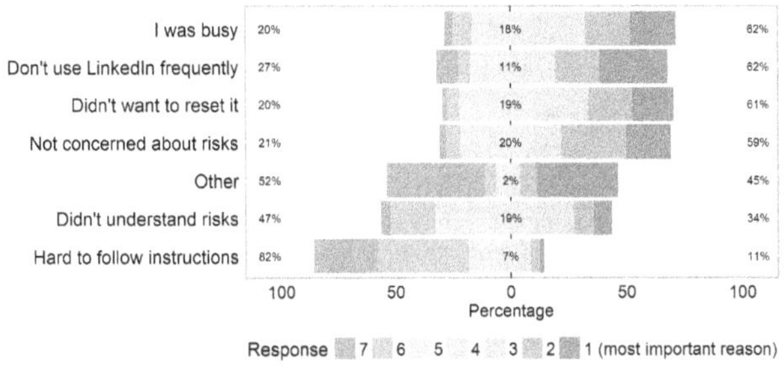

Figure 2. Reasons for *not resetting* password, sorted based on the overall distribution of the ranks between 1 and 7.

"Losing access to my LinkedIn account" (`losing access to LinkedIn`), which showed statistically significant inferiority in ranking distribution against all other reasons (all $p < 0.0001$, Bonferroni-corrected MW U test) except for `other`.

Did you reset your password?

To gauge the number of participants who reset their password, we asked *"In response to receiving the password reset email from LinkedIn, did you reset your password?"* Surprisingly, only 45.78% of the participants reset their passwords as shown in Table 1. 47.79% said they did not reset passwords, implying that their accounts are still at risk of being compromised.

Reasons for not resetting password

To those who did not reset their password, we asked *"If you did not reset your password after reading the email, why did you not reset it? Rank the options below in the order of your level of importance, Rank 1 being the most important reason. If a given reason is not important at all, leave its ranking as blank."* Figure 2 shows the reasons for not resetting password, sorted based on the overall ranking distributions.

Top three reasons for not resetting password were *"I was busy"* (`I was busy`), *"I do not use LinkedIn frequently"* (`don't use LinkedIn frequently`), and *"I did not want to reset my password"* (`didn't want to reset it`), indicating that those who did not reset password tend to be infrequent users, and/or did not feel it was necessary to make time to reset their password. `I was busy` showed statistically significant difference in the overall ranking distribution against *"I did not understand potential security risks to my LinkedIn account"* (`did not understand risks`), *"Instructions for resetting my password were hard to follow"* (`hard to follow instructions`), and `other` (all $p < 0.005$, Bonferroni-corrected MW U test). *"I was not concerned about potential security risks to my LinkedIn account"* (`not concerned about risks`) also ranked high, and did not show any statistically significant inferiority in the ranking distribution against the top three reasons.

These results indicate that the email design needs to be improved to communicate more effectively the importance of resetting password in a timely manner (for instance, using visual design cues such as opinionated design [3]), and clearly convey the `identity theft` and `stealing information` risks associated with delaying password reset.

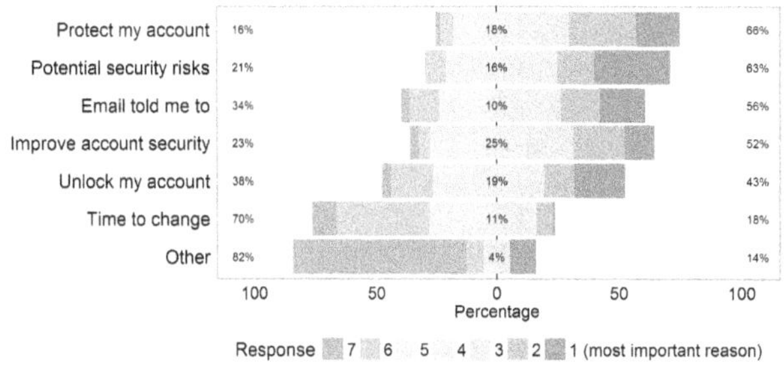

Figure 3. Reasons for *resetting* password.

Reasons for resetting password

To those who did reset their password, we asked *"Why did you reset your password after reading the email?"* We used the same option-ranking format as the previous ("reasons for not resetting") question. Figure 3 shows the reasons for resetting password, sorted based on the overall ranking distributions.

"To protect my LinkedIn account from being accessed by others" (`protect my account`) and *"I became aware of potential security risks associated with my LinkedIn account"* (`potential security risks`) were the top two reasons, showing that security was the top concern. `Protect my account` showed statistically significant superiority in the ranking distribution against *"To unlock my account and continue using LinkedIn"* (`unlock my account`), *"It was about time for me to change my password anyway"* (`time to change`), and `other` (all $p < 0.0005$, Bonferroni-corrected MW U test). `Potential security risks` showed statistically significant difference against `time to change` and `other` (all $p < 0.0001$, Bonferroni-corrected MW U test).

Password reset behaviors

To analyze the time it took for the participants to reset their password, we manually extracted the email received date from the two screenshots that the participants (those who reset password) uploaded. We subtracted the two dates to compute the elapsed time between when a participant first received the password reset email and when they signed into LinkedIn and reset password. Figure 4 shows the elapsed time, and the median and average values, which were 11.5 and 26.3 days (standard deviation of 33.3), respectively. The high variations indicate that some participants reset their passwords quickly – about 32% reset on the same day they received the email (this is only about 15% of all participants though) – whereas some participants took several days, weeks, or even months to reset their passwords. What is concerning is that 50% of those participants took 11.5 (median) or more days to reset their password. This demonstrates the timeliness issues of the password reset email as it has failed to convince those participants to quickly reset their password. To address this gap, we suggest sending another password reset reminder (e.g., after about 11 days) to those who have not yet reset their password.

We also asked *"How many other sites that you use have the same password as your LinkedIn password?"* and *"Among those sites that had the same password as your old LinkedIn*

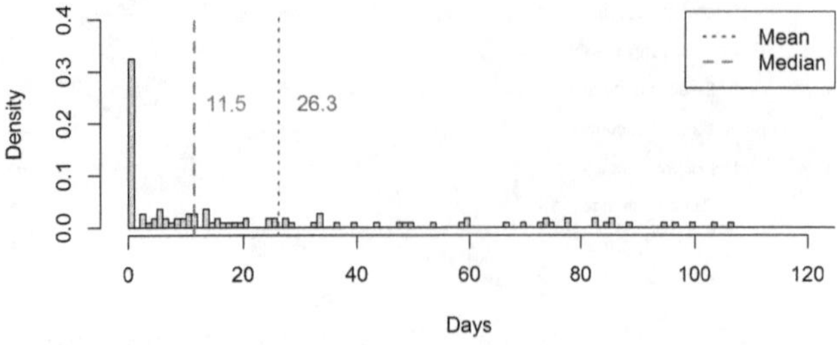

Figure 4. The number of days taken to reset password.

password, how many of those passwords did you also change after receiving the password reset email from LinkedIn?" Overall, about 46% of the participants said they use the same password on other 1-6 sites. About 4% responded that they use the same password on 7 or more sites. Considering that about half of the participants reused the same password, we argue that the risk of account compromise due to an attacker obtaining the password reset link (from a user's inbox) is real, and merely locking user account may not be sufficient. This further emphasizes the importance of persuading affected users to reset their password as soon as they check the email. Among those who reset their LinkedIn password, about 51% said they use the same password on 1-6 sites. But 67% (of that 51%) said they did not change their passwords on any of those 1-6 sites. Since any other account that uses the same password is also at risk (*and its account would not have been locked!*), the password reset email should inform users about such risks, and strongly recommend that users should also change passwords from other sites that use the same password.

We also asked those who reset password about how they created their new password. The proportion of each technique used are shown in Table 2. 46.02% indicated that they used their own method or process for generating new passwords, and 32.74% responded that they followed guidelines for creating strong passwords (e.g., using numbers or uppercase letters). What is worrying is that a significant proportion, 22.12%, indicated that they made small changes to their old, potentially compromised LinkedIn password. Adversaries could easily exploit this behavior, and try permutation guessing attacks based on the old LinkedIn passwords [11]. Another worrying observation is that the 17.70% answered that they simply reused a password from another site. Password reset mechanisms need to be designed to help users avoid making small changes to their old passwords and reusing passwords from other sites.

The results presented in Figure 4 measure the number of days taken to reset password from the date emails were first receieved, and not from the date they were first checked by the participants. Further, all of our MTurk workers were recruited from the United States. Hence, any generalization of the results presented in this paper needs to be performed with caution.

STEALING RESET LINKS WITH PHISHING ATTACKS

Recommending password reset or recovery through an email [6] is a commonly used security practice. Bonneau and Preibusch [1] reported that about 92% of 150 popular websites use an email-based solution, with 44% sending a reset link, 32% sending a new randomly-generated password, and 24% sending the original password. Furnell [5] explored password reset practices used in 10 popular websites (likes of Facebook and Google), and found that unique practice and policy was being used at each website. A user study conducted by Karlof et al. [8] showed that a phishing attack that tricks users into copying and pasting a password reset link has about 48% success rate – implying that the phishing attack we presented in "Introduction" can be highly successful against users who do not reset their passwords in a timely manner. Zhang et al. [11] showed that a changed (new) password can be effectively guessed from knowing the old password. 17% of the 7,700 new passwords were cracked within 5 guesses in an online attack. Chiasson et al. [2] formally quantified security advantages of a password expiration policy that forces users to change password within a fixed interval. Our results were consistent with the findings from [8], showing that the "passive warnings" provided in the reset email from LinkedIn were not sufficiently persuasive.

Table 2. Percentage of the techniques used upon resetting password. We allowed selection of multiple techniques.

Technique	Count
I have my own method	52 (46.02%)
I followed the guidelines for creating strong passwords	37 (32.74%)
I made small changes to my old LinkedIn password	25 (22.12%)
I reused a password from another site	20 (17.70%)
I used a combination of words that are memorable	12 (10.62%)
I used memorable phrases or sentences	11 (9.73%)
I reused one of my old passwords	8 (7.08%)
I used a randomly generated password	8 (7.08%)
I used a password manager to automatically generate a password	6 (5.31%)
Other	1 (0.88%)

CONCLUSIONS AND FUTURE DIRECTIONS

Upon receiving a password reset email from LinkedIn, 47.79% of our study participants did not reset their passwords, indicating that they were simply "too busy." As for those who did reset their passwords, the mean time taken was 26.3 days. A significant proportion of the participants took several weeks or even months to reset their passwords. Those results suggest that the security practice of locking accounts and forcing password reset through emails, in the case of LinkedIn at least, failed to convince users to reset passwords in a timely manner. Password reset emails need to be improved to (i) better explain associated security risks, and (ii) better convey a sense of urgency and persuade users to immediately reset their passwords. We also recommend sending another reset reminder to those who have not yet reset their passwords. While creating a new password, users need to be provided with more security guidance so that they do not just make small changes to their old, potentially compromised passwords.

Acknowledgment

This work was supported by the ITRC (IITP-2016-R0992-16-1006), and the School of EECS at Oregon State University.

REFERENCES

1. Joseph Bonneau and Sören Preibusch. 2010. The Password Thicket: Technical and Market Failures in Human Authentication on the Web. In *Proceedings of the 9th Annual Workshop on the Economics of Information Security*.
2. Sonia Chiasson and P. C. van Oorschot. 2015. Quantifying the security advantage of password expiration policies. *Designs, Codes and Cryptography* 77, 2 (2015), 401–408.
3. Adrienne Porter Felt, Alex Ainslie, Robert W. Reeder, Sunny Consolvo, Somas Thyagaraja, Alan Bettes, Helen Harris, and Jeff Grimes. 2015. Improving SSL Warnings: Comprehension and Adherence. In *Proceedings of the 33rd Conference on Human Factors and Computing Systems*.
4. Dinei Florencio and Cormac Herley. 2007. A Large-scale Study of Web Password Habits. In *Proceedings of the 16th International Conference on World Wide Web*.
5. Steven Furnell. 2007. An assessment of website password practices. *Computers & Security* 26, 7–8 (2007), 445–451.
6. Simson L. Garfinkel. 2003. Email-Based Identification and Authentication: An Alternative to PKI? *IEEE Security and Privacy* 1, 6 (Nov. 2003), 20–26.
7. Patrick Heim. 2016. Resetting passwords to keep your files safe. `https://blogs.dropbox.com/dropbox/2016/08/resetting-passwords-to-keep-your-files-safe/`. (August 2016).
8. Chris Karlof, J. D. Tygar, and David Wagner. 2009. Conditioned-safe Ceremonies and a User Study of an Application to Web Authentication. In *Proceedings of the 16th Network and Distributed System Security Symposium*.
9. Simon Marechal. 2008. Advances in password cracking. *Journal in Computer Virology* 4, 1 (2008), 73–81.
10. Cory Scott. 2016. Protecting Our Members. `https://blog.linkedin.com/2016/05/18/protecting-our-members`. (May 2016).
11. Yinqian Zhang, Fabian Monrose, and Michael K. Reiter. 2010. The Security of Modern Password Expiration: An Algorithmic Framework and Empirical Analysis. In *Proceedings of the 17th ACM Conference on Computer and Communications Security*.

Priming Drivers before Handover in Semi-Autonomous Cars

Remo M.A. van der Heiden
Utrecht University
Utrecht, The Netherlands
r.m.a.vanderheiden@uu.nl

Shamsi T. Iqbal
Microsoft Research
Redmond, USA
shamsi@microsoft.com

Christian P. Janssen
Utrecht University
Utrecht, The Netherlands
c.p.janssen@uu.nl

ABSTRACT
Semi-autonomous vehicles occasionally require control to be handed over to the driver in situations where the vehicle is unable to operate safely. Currently, such handover requests require the driver to take control almost instantaneously. We investigate how auditory pre-alerts that occur well before the handover request impact the success of the handover in a dual task scenario. In a study with a driving simulator, drivers perform tasks on their phone while the car is in an autonomous mode. They receive a repeated burst audio pre-alert or an increasing pulse audio pre-alert preceding the standard warning for immediate handover. Results show that pre-alerts caused people to look more at the road before the handover occurred, and to disengage from the secondary task earlier, compared to when there was no pre-alert. This resulted in safer handover situations. Increasing pulse pre-alerts show particular promise due to their communication of urgency. Our detailed analysis informs the design and evaluation of alerts in safety-critical systems with automation.

Author Keywords
Autonomous cars; multitasking; handover; automation

ACM Classification Keywords
H.1.2 [User/Machine Systems]: Human information processing; H.5.2 [User Interfaces]: Benchmarking; I.2.9 [Robotics]: Autonomous vehicles

INTRODUCTION
With the advent of novel (in-)vehicle technologies, new challenges emerge in managing driver distraction. Research has shown that drivers perform a variety of tasks that may distract from driving including interacting visually and manually with their mobile phones [17,31]. A recent meta-review suggests that distraction is likely to increase even further in 'self-driving' or 'autonomous' vehicles, where cars assume more of the driving responsibilities [16].

CHI 2017, May 06-11, 2017, Denver, CO, USA
© 2017 ACM. ISBN 978-1-4503-4655-9/17/05…$15.00
DOI: http://dx.doi.org/10.1145/3025453.3025507

In such vehicles, gradations of automation can be identified, as defined in various standards [19,39,47]. At the lowest level of automation (e.g., no automation, or level 0 in [47]), the human driver is in full control of the car. In full automation (e.g., level 5 in [47]), the human driver is not involved in any driving task anymore. This is, for example, the vision of the Google autonomous car (e.g., [53])

For the levels in between these extremes (e.g., levels 1-4 in [47]) there is some form of shared responsibilities. For example, even if the car is driving by itself, the driver might need to intervene when the system is uncertain about what action to take. For ease of reference we will use the umbrella term "semi-autonomous vehicle" to describe this wide category. The important characteristics of these systems for our work is that the vehicle can drive relatively independently for some time, but can request the human driver to assist or take over control through an alert.

A natural question that is of relevance to the CHI community is then: what should the specifics of such an alert be? Indeed, various aspects of handover [20] and in-car alerts [44,54] have received attention in the literature. Currently alerts, such as in the Tesla model S, include a brief alert and immediately handover control to the driver. However, given that the driver may not have the proper situational awareness to be able to immediately take the proper action, immediate alerts as such can potentially result in fatal outcomes. Moreover, with higher levels of automation (e.g., level 3 in [47]) such alerts are even more crucial as the car is monitoring the environment for large time intervals and drivers might have disengaged (cf. [16]).

In this research we investigate whether providing a *pre-alert*, an additional alert that commences well before the actual handover request (in our study: 20 s) can help drivers be better prepared to safely navigate the incident for which the handover of control occurs. Designing such a pre-alert for semi-autonomous vehicles presents unique challenges, as drivers distract themselves more with other tasks as automation of the car increases [16]. If they are then asked to take-over, they should not have remnants of their preceding task (e.g., checking e-mail, reading the news) that inhibit their ability to successfully take over (cf. [52]). At the same time, tasks that drivers engage in while in an autonomous vehicle may be more important than the typical secondary task in today's manual cars, making it more challenging to suddenly disengage [22].

In a simulator study, we study the effects of early warnings, or pre-alerts, on handover performance in dual task scenarios. We investigate three research questions: (1) how do pre-alerts affect behavior before take-over including eye-gaze and suspension of the non-driving task, (2) how do drivers perceive the pre-alerts, and (3) how do the pre-alerts affect driving performance. We present two types of pre-alerts: (A) A *repeated burst audio pre-alert*, and (B) an *increasing pulse audio pre-alert*. While the car drives itself, drivers occasionally perform a video transcription or calendar entry task on a mobile phone. Results showed that pre-alerts helped drivers prepare better for taking over control by increasing gaze on the road and earlier suspension of the phone task, followed by quicker reaction to traffic incidents compared to having no pre-alerts.

In the remainder of this paper we first provide more background on multitasking, managing multitasking, and in-car alerts. We then describe our study. Finally, we discuss the results, including their implications for theory and design, limitations, and potential for future work.

RELATED WORK

Driving and Multitasking

Multitasking is a prevalent practice while driving [17,31]. Multiple studies have documented the detrimental effects of cell phone conversations, texting, and interacting with in-vehicle systems while driving [1,9,10,51,46]. Switching from a non-driving task to driving is often challenging. For example, drivers who engage in phone conversations have slower braking reaction time [1,33], degraded steering performance [10], and a higher likelihood of accidents [45] than drivers with no distractions.

In the majority of this preceding work, the driving task has typically been considered the 'primary task' where the driver's focus is expected at all times, with other tasks as 'secondary'. However, as the automation technology matures, human drivers might be required less and less to take-over control of the car. Therefore, they might increasingly engage in other tasks (cf. meta-review in [16]), and those other tasks (e.g., checking e-mails, reading the news, having a conversation, watching a video) might even feel as a primary task with driving as a distraction (cf. [22]).

Managing Multitasking during driving

A known strategy to manage multitasking is to interleave activities, which has been well documented in conceptual frameworks (e.g., [2,6,8,50]). In the domain of driving, multiple studies have looked at how drivers interleave non-driving, secondary tasks with driving. A common strategy is to wait for 'natural breakpoints' in the task to switch attention [11,12,26,27,28,48]; for example, Iqbal et al. showed that drivers chunked a task of providing directions while driving into multiple steps and reoriented to driving at the boundaries between chunks [26]. There are many advantages of interleaving at natural breakpoints: it reduces mental workload [3, 49] as it reduces information that needs to be maintained in memory [7], it frees mental resources such as visual attention for other tasks [50,55], it reduces stress [4], it reduces the time needed for later task resumption (cf. [2]), and it can offer speed-accuracy trade-offs in dynamic environments such as driving [28].

In autonomous vehicles, however, while people are not driving, the non-driving task might capture most of the driver's attention [22]. In a hand-over scenario, people might therefore not want to immediately let go of whatever they were working on. Priming a handover in a timely manner through pre-alerts, as we propose in this paper, has the advantage that it allows drivers to disengage from their 'primary' (non-driving) task at a pace that suits them. Moreover, gradually disengaging from the task and waiting for a natural breakpoint can also benefit the driving task. If interleaving at a more opportune task reduces workload [3,49] and stress [4], then people are in a better mental state to resume driving.

(In-car) Alerts

The idea of using alerts to gain user attention has been explored in many domains. Mediation or alerting has been proposed as one of the four interruption management methods in McFarlane's work [35]. In the driving domain, researchers have explored the effectiveness of systems for aiding driving by providing local danger alerts [14], mediating communications among car passengers [34], or persuading people to drive in a more economical manner [36]. For example, Iqbal et al. explored how alerts can gain user attention while driving and conversing on a cellphone simultaneously, and found that alerts reduced driving errors, while also reducing conversation quality [25].

In the domain of autonomous driving, the idea of using alerts before handover of control has recently gained traction, based on the concern that the current designs of immediate take over may not yield the desired outcome. Most work has focused on the design of the alert, in terms of the timing and modalities so that it conveys the required urgency [20,32,40, 44,54]. For example, Gold et al. [20] showed that alerts happening 7 seconds before the incident resulted in more successful take overs compared to alerts that were presented 5 seconds before. Walch et al. also investigated different timings and modalities [54]. While they found no difference in driving performance, drivers had a preference for the alerts reinforced through both auditory and visual means. There was no significant advantage in driving performance.

Perhaps closest to our work is Politis et al.'s study which tested language based alerts for upcoming incidents [44]. Alerts were delivered via audio, visual, or tactile means. Results showed that drivers quickly transitioned to the driving task for warnings that conveyed urgency, and performance was worst for unimodal visual alerts. Other work has looked at using auditory cues to provide drivers in autonomous vehicles awareness about the environment [5].

This work does not separate the specific scenario of handover where the driver's awareness is put to test by having to react to an incident in very short notice.

Compared to existing work, our research focuses less on the exact timing or ideal conveyance of urgency via the alerts. Rather, we draw upon designs of alerts that have been effective in conveying urgency in a timely manner [18, 21]. Our goal is to understand if a pre-alert (i.e., an early alert well before the final warning) is useful in general, and if so, why and how it supports ease of disengagement from a secondary task. Such a scenario can be crucial in autonomous vehicles.

USER STUDY

In our study of the effects of pre-alerts on preparing for handover, we aim to address three research questions:

RQ1: What do drivers do before handover? We therefore analyze eye-gaze and time on secondary task.

RQ2: How do drivers experience the handover? We therefore look at subjective ratings and physiology.

RQ3: How successful is the handover? We therefore look at the first reaction time, speed reduction, and an analysis of unsafe incidents.

To answers these questions, we conducted a user study using a driving simulator with autonomous capabilities where drivers engage in a non-driving task on a mobile device and are required to take over control in certain driving situations where the car is unable to continue.

Users

Twenty-four drivers (12 M; 12 F) with an average age of 32.5 years (*SD* = 9.6) were selected by quota sampling. Each driver had a valid driver's license and drove on average 5.4 days a week (*SD* = 2.4). All drivers provided informed consent and were compensated with a $50 gift card.

Tasks

Drivers performed two task types: driving (part manual, part autonomous), and a non-driving task on a mobile phone.

Driving task

A simulated driving task was developed in a medium fidelity simulator. Three 47" TVs projected the driving environment. Drivers sat in an adjustable car seat behind a full Ford dashboard. During manual driving, drivers used a steering wheel, gas and brake pedal (transmission was automatic).

Simulation software consisted of the STIsim simulator software. Data was recorded at a rate of 10 data points per second. An eye tracker was mounted on the dashboard to capture eye gazes on the driving scene. A custom scenario was developed, consisting of a drive on a two lane country road with bends and straight road segments without intersections. Oncoming traffic was presented on the opposite lane, not in the driver's lane.

The scenario consisted of manual driving and automated driving trajectories. The car started stationary and drivers had to press the gas pedal to start driving manually. Drivers had to maintain the posted speed limit and remain in lane. Occasional curves were included in each scenario. The curves were subtle enough so braking was not needed but input of drivers was required to stay in their lane safely.

After 1500 feet (25-30 s after the start), an automated voice would state "Automation enabled", and the car assumed driving control. At that point, if desired, drivers could release the steering wheel and the pedals. The car continued to drive itself until it warned drivers when they were needed to take over the driving task. While the car was in auto drive there was no driver initiated way to get back control. In the event of a handover, the car would start by warning the driver and the controls were handed over back to the driver after a voice said: "Automation disabled". Optionally, such a warning could be preceded by a pre-alert, 20 s before handover. The pre-alerts are described in more detail later.

There were four handover scenario varieties, each with two instances – resulting in eight scenarios in total. Examples are shown in Figure 1. The *fog scenarios* had light or heavy fog, and required drivers to slow-down, maintain their lane, and avoid other cars. The *construction works scenario* had cones along the road and required drivers to slow down and steer accurately. One version also included a lane change. The *parked car scenario* had a car that blocked either part of the road, or the full road, requiring the driver to slow down or stop. The *dog scenario* had a dog abruptly crossing the street, requiring the driver to stop in order to avoid hitting the dog.

The scenarios required different types of responses, such as braking and accurate steering. Some scenarios allowed for multiple responses such as braking and steering away from an accident. However, although the simulator allowed for this variety of maneuvers, some were not safe. This is similar to how a driver in real traffic can sometimes respond in different ways, of which only some are safe.

Non-driving tasks

Recent reviews suggest that drivers distract themselves with non-driving tasks more when automation in the car increases, which impacts situational awareness and response times [16]. We therefore also included conditions in which drivers performed non-driving tasks. As the structure of the task can also impact when drivers look at the road [12, 27, 28], we used two tasks. Half the drivers performed a video transcription task while the other half performed a calendar task. These tasks were chosen because they represent tasks that people might prefer to do in an autonomous car – such as watching videos [44] and performing short typing tasks, as reported on a pre-survey. All secondary tasks were conducted on a Nokia Lumia 1520 phone with Windows 8.1.

Video task. A custom developed app (see Figure 2, left) showed a video screen and an input box. Drivers had to play the video (which showed elementary statistics lectures [24])

Figure 1. Four handover scenarios: (a) Fog, (b) Dog crossing, (c) Parked car on the side of the road, (d) Construction works.

and had to transcribe it in the textbox. Controls to play, pause, and forward in the video were embedded in the player. We used the standard keyboard from Windows phone 8.1, with auto-correction and -completion disabled. This allowed for more reliable measurement of writing performance. We logged the timestamp of each keypress.

Calendar task. The alternative task was a calendar task (see Figure 2, right). Drivers were asked to enter event information in a simple calendar interface. The interface had two separate screens, one showed all the upcoming events as a digital flyer, the other showed the input boxes and saved items. We again logged the timestamp of each keypress.

Warning & Pre-alerts

At each hand-over instance, in all conditions, drivers received a voice warning: "automation disabled" 1 s before the handover. Drivers were instructed to take over the driving from the system at this moment. In the *pre-alert* conditions, drivers also received either of two pre-alerts 20 s prior to this final warning. For the pre-alerts we used individual 500 Hz beeps that lasted 150 ms per beep. Beep frequency and length were recommended in the warning literature [38].

Repeated burst audio pre-alert: In this condition, bursts of 3 beeps are played 3 times, with silence in between burst sets. The burst sets started playing at 20, 10, and 1 seconds before the final warning (i.e., in Figure 4: 0, 10, and 19 seconds relative to start of pre-alert phase). Repeated burst alerts are already used in the car context, for example, to notify when a door is not closed firmly or when a car is almost out of fuel.

Increasing pulse audio pre-alert: In this condition, beeps are given throughout the 20 second pre-alert time. However, the interval between consecutive beeps is reduced gradually over time as the driver gets closer to the critical moment. The initial inter-stimulus interval is 1000 ms. The final inter-stimulus interval is 50 ms. An increasing pulse audio alert is already used at other places in the car domain to suggest increased urgency. For example, park assistant alerts decrease the inter-stimulus interval between beeps when a car gets close to another object to suggest urgency to stop. In other studies, increasing pulses (e.g., heartbeats) have also been used to successfully convey urgency [29].

Figure 2. Layout of Video task (left) & Calendar task (right)

No pre-alert: In this baseline condition, no pre-alert is given and drivers are only warned by the final warning voice 1 s before handover of control.

Figure 3 shows a schematic of the different stages in a single run. There are two experimental segments in each run. Each run started with a period of driving by the driver, followed by a period of auto drive during which the driver could engage in a non-driving task (depending on condition). During the auto drive there would be optionally pre-alerts (depending on experimental condition), followed by a final voice warning declaring the handover to the driver. This would be followed by the handover event during which the driver had to start driving. After a while, the second segment started, following the same procedure. The entire run was about 6 minutes long (i.e., roughly 3 minutes per segment).

EXPERIMENTAL DESIGN

We used a 3 x 2 within-subjects design. We manipulated Pre-alert type (*Repeated burst*, *Increasing pulse*, or *No pre-alert*), and number of tasks (*single-task* driving, or *dual-task* driving with secondary task). For each of the six combinations of pre-alerts and number of tasks, we developed one drive/run. Each drive consisted of two hand-over moments that had a critical incident. In sum, each participant had six drives and twelve handover situations.

Ordering of the six conditions was counterbalanced following a Latin Square design, to compensate for learning effects. As we had eight critical events, we randomly assigned these to drivers with the requirement that each run had one incident that might require braking (i.e., dog or parked car) and one incident that required accurate steering (i.e., cones or fog). Finally, we also measured single-task performance as baseline (explained in procedure).

For the secondary task, drivers either performed the video or calendar task (12 drivers per task, randomly assigned).

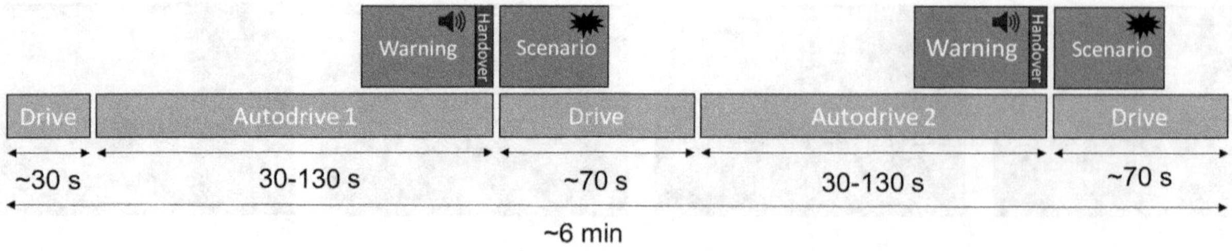

Figure 3. A schematic representation of a run for one condition with two consecutive segments.

PROCEDURE

On arrival, drivers were given an overview of the study and asked to sign an informed consent form as well as to fill out a questionnaire about current driving behavior. They were then asked to make themselves comfortable in the car seat of the simulator, which was adjusted so their foot could reach the pedals and their eyes were visible for the eye tracker.

We then calibrated the eye tracker and set participants up with the Microsoft band2, which was used for measuring heart rate. This was followed by a 2-minute training session on the secondary task (video or calendar, depending on group), followed by training with the driving task. In this single-task practice drive, drivers practiced all 4 types of handover events, and were introduced to the two pre-alerts. The first event was preceded by an increasing pulse pre-alert, the second with a repeated burst pre-alert, the last two had no pre-alert.

The remainder of the experiment consisted of the six experimental drives/runs. In addition, single-task performance with either the video or calendar task (depending on assignment) was performed at a random position in between the experimental drives. After all trials ended the drivers filled out a general questionnaire on their overall experience and preferences about the pre-alerts.

MEASUREMENTS

Below we define our exact measurements, sorted by research question (RQ). Unless otherwise noted, we use a 3 (pre-alert) x 2 (number of tasks) within-subjects analysis of variance (ANOVA) with an alpha-level of .05 for significance. Where needed we use Holm-Bonferroni-corrected post-hoc tests. Error bars in all plots show standardized error of the mean.

Gaze during driving (RQ1) We used an SMI REDn eye tracker which reported tracking status (eyes tracked or not) and X,Y gaze-coordinates at 30 samples/second. The eye tracker was positioned on the dashboard just above the steering wheel. For short drivers an extra cushion was used to make sure their eyes stayed visible during the entire experiment, as tested before the experiment.

For all gaze metrics, the eye-tracker could only track the eyes when the user was looking at the simulator screen (not at the secondary task). We therefore define "looking at the road" as gaze samples where the eye tracker was at least tracking one eye, and "not looking at the road" as moments where no eyes were tracked. Given the large size of the screen and the peripheral location of the phone, this crude metric is a good approximation of actual looking at the road. Based on this information, we calculate what *percentage of drivers* look at the road (e.g., Figure 4) and what *percentage of the time* drivers on average look at the screen. In pilot studies we crosschecked with 2 eye trackers that the eyes were consistently detected when watching the simulator screen.

Disengaging from the secondary task (RQ1). Based on logs of touchscreen keypresses, we determined the interval between the start of the pre-alert phase and the last keypress. Shorter intervals indicate a faster disengagement.

User preferences (RQ2). In a questionnaire, drivers indicated their preferences after the experiment. The questions used a five-point scale ranging from low/poor (1) to high/good (5).

Heart rate (RQ2). A Microsoft Band2 measured the number of beats per minute. One value was logged per second.

Initial reaction time (RQ3). For each handover event we measured the reaction time as the time interval between the moment automation was disabled and the first action of the driver (either a brake press or steering wheel input).

Driver speed reduction (RQ3). For each handover event, we measured at what speed the driver drove, as logged by the simulator at a rate of 10 samples/second.

Unsafe incident analysis (RQ3). For the first 10 seconds after handover, we manually labeled whether observed behavior was unsafe, following conservative but realistic pre-defined rules. In all scenarios, driving more than 10 mph over the posted speed limit, or leaving the highway was labeled unsafe (some drivers drove on the grass). In addition, in one *parked car scenarios* only a full stop avoided a collision; not doing so was labeled unsafe. Also, for one *dog scenario*, some drivers crossed into the lane of incoming traffic, despite that cars might come in. This was also labeled unsafe.

RESULTS

We measured how handover performance changes with the use of pre-alerts and the use of a secondary tasks. We discuss our results in the context of our three research questions.

RQ1: Gaze & phone task engagement before handover

Percentage of drivers looking at the road

Figure 4 shows the percentage of drivers looking at the road in the different stages of handover, relative to the start of the pre-alert (time point 0). In single-task trials (grey lines) we found that at each time point, on average 70 to 80% of the drivers looks at the road. There is a slight increase in the phase before the handover, but this is not different between the various alert conditions.

The pattern is different for the dual-task condition (dark lines). In the phase before the pre-alert (-9 to 0 s), drivers look more at the road when they are in the no pre-alert condition (dashed line) compared to the two pre-alert conditions. This is likely because drivers know that they have no pre-alert to rely on, and want to be prepared for a later handover request.

During the period where the pre-alert is active (0 to 20 s), in both pre-alert conditions (Repeated burst, solid line; increasing pulse, dotted line), drivers look more frequently at the road compared to the no pre-alert condition (dashed line). Moreover, this accumulates over time, as drivers get closer to the handover itself. The two pre-alert conditions are hard to distinguish from one another. Qualitatively, in the repeated burst pre-alert condition drivers start looking at the road after each burst of tones (0, 10, and 19 s). The strongest bump is after the first burst. By contrast, for the increasing pulse pre-alert there is a more gradual increase over time.

In the condition where there is no pre-alert, the percentage drivers looking at the road initially is similar to before the start of the pre-alert. However, 10 seconds before handover the percentage of drivers looking at the road increases, even though they have not yet received an alert. This is because in the simulator parts of the critical event gradually become visible even before the handover request occurs. This is similar to how in real driving visible cues are sometimes available ahead of time (e.g., a traffic jam ahead). Such visual cues make non-distracted drivers look at the scene and prepare. The take-away message from this graph though is that in both pre-alert conditions, drivers look up a lot *earlier* and do *not* rely on input from the road *at the last moment*.

Gaze during auto-drive before the pre-alert period

We quantified the preceding results. First, we looked at the entire auto-drive period before the pre-alert. For each driver, we calculated the percentage of time that they looked at the road. An ANOVA showed that there is a significant effect of number of tasks on the percentage of time drivers spend watching the road $F(1,23) = 344.3$, $p < .001$, $\eta_p^2 = 0.94$. Drivers looked at the road more than ten times as much in single task condition ($M = 71\%$, $SD = 19\%$) compared to dual task condition ($M = 6\%$, $SD = 13\%$). There was also a significant effect of pre-alert, $F(2,46) = 4.441$ $p = .002$, $\eta_p^2 = 0.16$. Post-hoc tests found that gazes at the road during No pre-alert ($M = 9\%$, $SD = 4\%$) was significantly higher than Repeated burst ($M = 4\%$, $SD = 3\%$, $p = .001$) and Increasing pulse ($M = 5\%$, $SD = 4\%$, $p = .016$), as in the no pre-alert condition drivers cannot rely on a signal to warn them, they interleave the tasks more often to check for hazardous situations. The two pre-alerts did not differ from each other ($p > .1$). There was no significant interaction effect ($p > .1$).

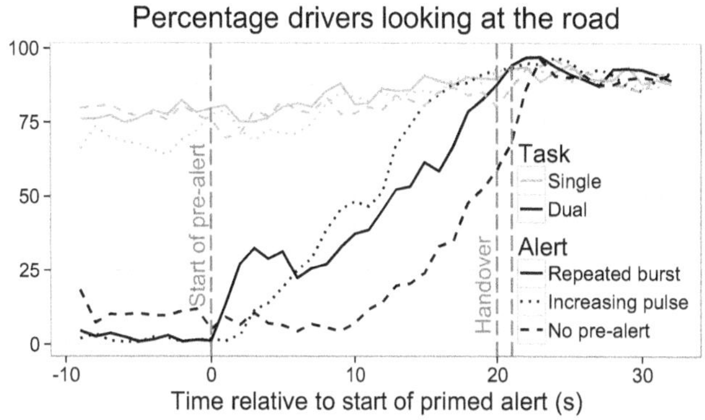

Figure 4. The percentage of drivers looking at the road relative to the start of the primed warning.

Gaze during pre-alert phase

During the pre-alert phase (i.e., 0-20 s in Figure 4), there was again a significant main effect of number of tasks on percentage of time drivers spend watching the road $F(1,23) = 168.7$, $p < .001$, $\eta_p^2 = 0.88$. In general, drivers were looking at the road about twice as much in single task condition ($M = 83\%$, $SD = 18\%$) compared to dual task condition ($M = 42\%$, $SD = 29\%$). There was also a significant main effect of pre-alert, $F(2,46) = 16.28$, $p < .001$, $\eta_p^2 = 0.41$. However, both main effects were affected by a significant interaction effect, $F(2,46) = 15.95$, $p < .001$, $\eta_p^2 = 0.41$. Post-hoc tests revealed that in single-task there was no significant difference between the three pre-alert conditions (all $ps > .1$). However, in dual-task, the percentage gaze at the road was significantly lower in the no pre-alert condition ($M = 23\%$, $SD = 15\%$) compared to repeated burst ($M = 49\%$, $SD = 19\%$) and increasing pulse ($M = 54\%$, $SD = 16\%$) all $ps < .001$. This is expected, as the pre-alerts warn drivers to look at the road and drivers therefore indeed gaze more at the road.

Disengaging from the secondary task

To test whether the alert helped drivers disengage from the secondary phone task, we tested how long they continued after the alert had started using a 3 (Pre-alert type) x 2 (Secondary task type) ANOVA. There was a significant effect of pre-alert on the time drivers continue their phone task after alert onset, $F(2,44) = 30.09$, $p < .001$, $\eta_p^2 = 0.56$. Figure 5 shows the data. Post-hoc tests showed that all three

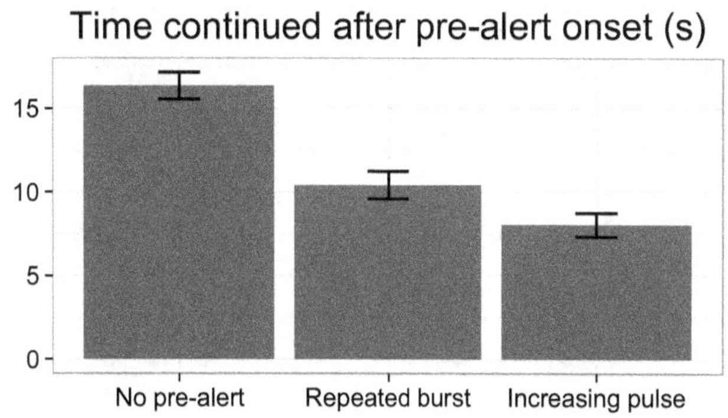

Figure 5. The average time secondary task continued after different alert onsets.

conditions differed significantly from each other (with the difference between increasing pulse and repeated burst with $p = .038$, all other $ps < .001$). As the figure shows, in the increasing pulse condition drivers quit the secondary task twice as fast compared to the no pre-alert condition. The ANOVA also revealed a marginal effect of secondary task, $F(1,22) = 3.81$, $p = .06$, $\eta_p^2 = 0.15$. Disengagement was slightly faster in the calendar task ($M = 10.5$s, $SD = 4.7$s) than the video task ($M = 12.7$s, $SD = 6.0$s). There was no interaction effect, $F(2,44) = 1.5, p > .1$.

RQ2: User experience

User preferences

Subjective feedback revealed overall preference for pre-alerts was divided. Twelve drivers preferred the increasing pulse pre-alert. Feedback included that these drivers liked that they could finish their task and prepare for handover. Twelve other drivers preferred the repeated burst pre-alert, as it felt less disruptive than the increasing pulse.

In the post questionnaire drivers provided various scores for the different pre-alerts on a five-point scale with anchors for low (1) and high (5). In Figure 6 we present the histograms of the score for the metrics (1) annoyance, and (2) disruptiveness of the pre-alert. The responses are again divided, as reflected in the broad distributions. Some trends are that the increasing pulse is reported more frequently as conveying high to too much urgency, and being more frequently considered as highly annoying and disruptive. However, there are also drivers who reported an inverse pattern (e.g., rated annoyance low).

Heart rate

We also tested if the pre-alerts had any effect on drivers' physiology, specifically the average heart rate. Two drivers had to be excluded from this analysis because the measurement stopped during the experiment. The ANOVA found a significant effect of pre-alert on average heart rate $F(2,40) = 4.72, p = .015, \eta_p^2 = 0.18$. Post-hoc tests found that in No pre-alert ($M = 69.8$ bpm, $SD = 6.7$ bpm) the heart rate is significantly higher than in Repeated burst ($M = 68.9$ bpm, $SD = 6.6$ bpm, $p = .034$) and Increasing pulse pre-alert ($M =$ 69.2 bpm, $SD = 6.8$ bpm, $p = .046$). There was no difference between Repeated burst and Increasing pulse ($p > .1$) In addition, heart rate was significantly higher in Dual-task conditions ($M = 69.8$ bpm, $SD = 6.6$ bpm) compared to Single-task ($M = 68.8$ bpm, $SD = 6.8$ bpm), $F(2,40) = 4.719$, $p = .031$, $\eta_p^2 = 0.21$. There was no significant interaction effect ($p > .1$) In summary, heart rates are slightly increased in dual-task conditions, and when there is no pre-alert and the user needs to do the extra task of frequently checking the road. This suggests that extra workload increased heartrate (cf. [37]). Though the effect is small, the trend is consistent with subjective data.

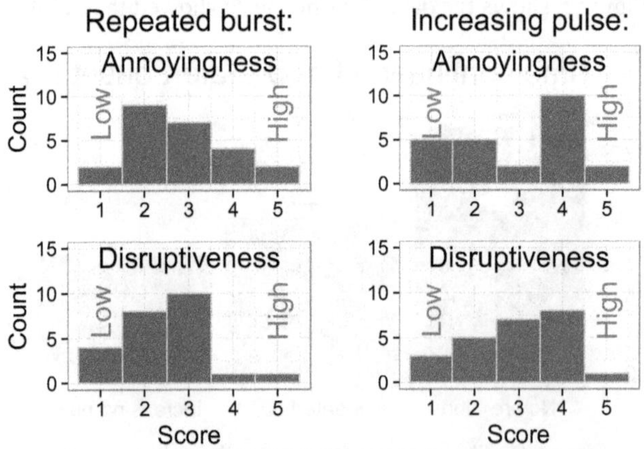

Figure 6. Subjective impression of pre-alerts

RQ3: Success of handover

For the next two measures, we only analyzed the first segment of each driving scenario, as due to a coding error the driving speed was slightly lower on the second segment (60ft/s vs 65ft/s), which affected the time between the end of the pre-alert and the time given to hand-over. In the second segment, there was some delay between the warning that automation was turned off and the time that drivers could actually control the car. This reduces the reliability of the reaction time data on these metrics. This is not the case for the segments that we analyzed.

Initial reaction time

Previous work has mostly analyzed reaction times as a performance metric for handover. Due to the varied nature of our task, reaction to an event can be either braking or steering. We measure reaction time as time until either of these two actions occurs. We combine the data of single- and dual-task trials, resulting in three histograms for each pre-alert condition in Figure 7. Each plot shows data from 48 trials: 24 single, 24 dual. The bars cover 200 ms intervals. In general, most drivers respond within 200 ms (i.e., the first bar is the highest bar in each setting).

However, in driving analyses, we do not only care about the mean and majority of behavior, but also about extremes. This is where conditions differ. In the no pre-alert condition (left), the distribution is more right-tailed (9 trials with response longer than 600 ms, with extremes up to 2.5 s) compared to the repeated burst (5 trials) and increased pulse pre-alert (2 trials). Stated differently: in most cases, most drivers respond timely, but the trend is that more drivers respond timely when a pre-alert is given, with the number of late responses around twice as high in the no pre-alert condition.

Driver speed reduction

We also analyzed driving speed after handover. In critical situations, reducing speed is a smart strategy as this creates more time for an effective response (as less distance is covered per time interval). Figure 8 shows how the average

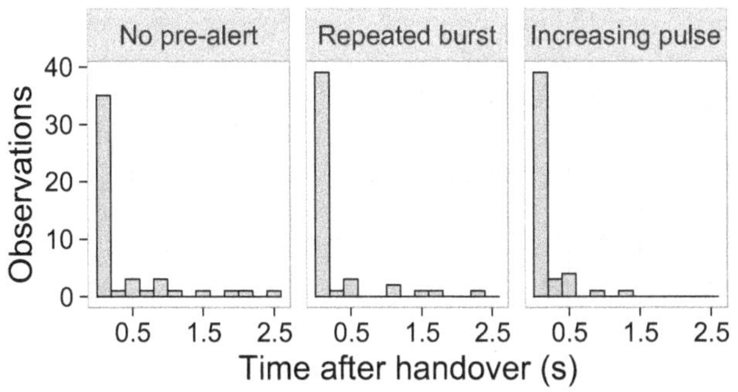

Figure 7. Time until first action after handover.

speed reduces over time in single-task (top figure) and dual-task (bottom figure) for the three pre-alert conditions.

Before the handover (point 0 in the graph), the car drives automatically at a constant speed. Then, at point 0, drivers can take over. In the single-task condition, drivers reduce speed immediately in each condition, with a slight delay in the no pre-alert condition. However, if 95% CI intervals would be drawn, these would overlap between all three conditions, suggesting there is no difference. It shows that without distraction, drivers are prepared to respond.

This is different in the dual-task condition. Here, the brake response in the no pre-alert condition is delayed compared to the two pre-alert conditions. That is, drivers respond later. In fact, if 95% CIs would be drawn around the lines, the confidence intervals between the no pre-alert condition do not overlap with those of the two pre-alert conditions. A standard interpretation of a lack of overlap is that the conditions differ at a 95% confidence level (or with an alpha of .05) [15]. The intervals of the two pre-alert conditions do overlap, indicating there is no significant difference.

Unsafe incident analysis

The final question is: Did the pre-alerts lead to less unsafe behavior? If drivers had more time to look at the road before handover to build situational awareness (RQ1), do they perform better in handling the handover incident?

For this analysis, we looked at all scenario segments (288) and labeled whether unsafe behavior had occurred such as not reducing speed, going into a lane where incoming traffic might occur, or crashing into an object. Of the 288 segments, 34 segments (11.8 %) were marked as unsafe. Given the low numbers, we report the frequency of unsafe behaviors in Table 1, split up by pre-alert type (rows), and single- or dual-task (columns). There is no clear emerging pattern. Specifically, incidents still occur in the two active pre-alert

	Single-task	Dual-task	Total
None	7	6	**13**
Repeated burst	5	8	**13**
Increasing pulse	6	2	**8**
Total	**18**	**16**	**34**

Table 1. Number of segments involving unsafe behavior

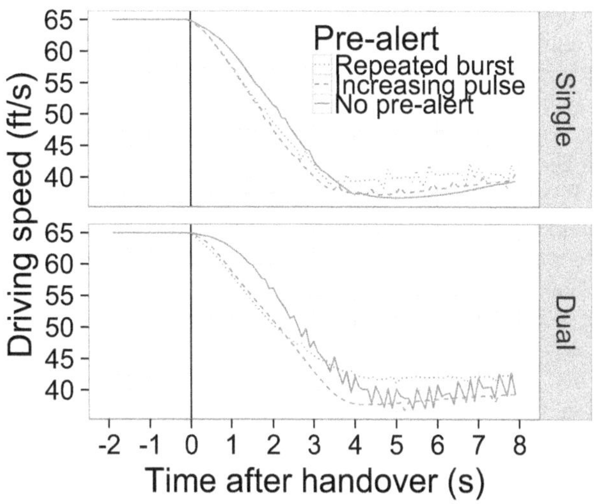

Figure 8. Driving speed after handover.

conditions. Moreover, it is not the case that there are more unsafe behaviors in the dual-task condition compared to single-task condition. If any, the trend in the data is that there were fewer unsafe behaviors in the increasing pulse condition (third row).

Due to this variety of results, we also analyzed whether unsafe behaviors were more frequent for some scenarios compared to others. This could not be done in combination with the type of pre-alert or single-/dual-task, due to the low numbers. In general, unsafe behavior was shown most in scenarios involving braking for a dog (23 segments). This was much higher compared to segments with a parked car (5 segments), construction works (6 segments), or fog (0 segments). Our interpretation of this result is that the dog scenario allowed more freedom to the user of what to do: they could either try to brake, or try to avoid it by driving past it. Moreover, as the object on the road (a dog) was relatively small compared to, for example, a parked car, drivers might not have had extra benefit from the early view of the object due to a pre-alert.

GENERAL DISCUSSION

Summary of results

We investigated how pre-alerts affect the hand-over of control from a semi-autonomous car to a human driver. A recent review showed that drivers distract themselves more with other tasks as automation in the car increases, and that this impacts their situational awareness and ability to respond correctly [16]. Based on theory, we expect that a pre-alert has four benefits (1) it allows a driver the necessary time to disengage from a secondary task [6], (2) this can reduce mental workload [3, 49] and stress [4] and leave drivers in a better state to manage the handover, (3) this allows drivers more time to reorient to the driving task and gain relevant situational awareness, and (4) with sufficient time distracting effects from the non-driving tasks may be reduced (cf. [52]). Our results demonstrate that pre-alerts are indeed beneficial. During the alerting phase (RQ1), drivers disengage from their non-driving tasks earlier when a pre-alert is given (Figure 5), and they look earlier at the road (Figure 4). In their experience (RQ2), drivers were divided in which alert they preferred, though both conveyed some urgency (Figure 6). We also found an effect on heart rate, which was slightly higher in the condition without a pre-alert. This finding needs to be replicated before conclusions can be drawn, but might indicate that a situation with no pre-alert is more stressful, as drivers cannot rely on the pre-alert to notify them. Finally, when looking at driving performance (RQ3), drivers responded faster (by braking or steering) to incidents when they were warned by a pre-alert (Figure 7), and reduced their speed more quickly (Figure 8). In effect this allows them more time to respond to an incident (i.e., at a lower speed it takes longer before an incident location is reached). Finally, there were still unsafe behaviors in all conditions, but these were the lowest with an increasing pulse pre-alert (Table 1).

Between the two pre-alert types, the preferences of drivers were divided. However, the trend in most metrics is that the increasing pulse pre-alert leads to slightly safer performance. For example, in this condition people disengage the earliest from a secondary task (Figure 5), more people experienced it as conveying high urgency (Figure 6), it had the lowest number of slow handovers (Figure 7), and the lowest number of incidents (Table 1).

Given this pattern, a general conclusion is that pre-alerts are useful compared to not getting a pre-alert. However, there is still room for improvement, as unsafe actions still occur.

Implications for theory

Our results confirm the classical result in driver distraction research (e.g., [1,9,10,28,29,33,45,46,51]) that secondary tasks distract from looking at the road (RQ1, Figure 4) and result in longer response times to incidents (RQ3, Figure 7). Our results also suggest that pre-alerts can mitigate some of these problems. This is particularly useful, as driver distraction occurs frequently in regular cars [17,31] and increases with an increase in autonomy of the car [16].

The use of alerts for hand-over situations in semi-autonomous cars is of course not new. However, in contrast to earlier work (e.g., [20]), we focus on alerts that happen ahead of time (*pre*-alerts). Sending an alert too early (e.g., minutes) in advance might not make sense, as there is no situation that the driver can notice and start to anticipate. We focused on a pre-alert of 20 seconds, as previous work has suggested that distraction of secondary tasks can continue up to 27 seconds after the task was finished, with exponential decay [52]. Twenty seconds is therefore an interval that is needed to recover from distractions and to focus on the road.

In our study, drivers still incurred incidents in some of the alert conditions. There are multiple explanations, which require further testing in future studies. First and foremost, there were incidents even in single-task situations, suggesting that some tasks were difficult to handle in general. Second, in the distraction conditions drivers might have persisted too long with the secondary tasks even after the pre-alert and thereby not have taken enough time to react. Finally, similar to [52], even when drivers did finish secondary tasks, drivers might have had remnants of distraction. The balance that needs to be found here is between giving a just-in-time alert such that it is meaningful, while also giving sufficient time to overcome any negative effects of distraction. Further studies are needed to get this balance just right.

Although both pre-alerts that we offered were effective, the increasing pulse performed better on some metrics compared to the repeated burst (e.g., Figure 5,7). Our interpretation is that this is because increasing pulse more clearly conveyed urgency (as also confirmed by the drivers, see Figure 6). This is also in line with theory (e.g., [44]).

As our study takes place in a simulator, there are concerns about how the findings generalize. For example, there are no serious consequences of a crash. However, it also offers many advantages for our setting. First, we can test behaviors in cars that have a level of autonomy beyond those that are currently widely available. Second, we can test extremely dangerous situations such as hand-overs preceding crashes that would be unethical to test on the road. Third, we can measure behavior in-depth with multiple measures including eye-gaze, physiology, preferences, and driving performance. Finally, meta-reviews have demonstrated that situations that are shown to be dangerous in simulator conditions are also dangerous on the road [13, 23]. However, the effect size of the performance decline can differ between the two situations. A specific prediction that our work makes for the regular road is that pre-alerts can be beneficial, but also that even an interval of twenty seconds might not be enough to respond appropriately to an incident in a handover situation. This is particularly the case because everyday traffic is more diverse and perhaps less predictable than our simulator scenarios.

Implications for design

Our findings suggest that pre-alerts can be helpful in managing handover situations. This opens up a large space of future work that explores what the exact nature of pre-alerts can be. Below, we discuss some relevant parameters.

Convey urgency

Our results suggest that pre-alerts should provide a sense of urgency (cf. [29,44]), as in our increasing pulse pre-alert. However, there is still a wide design space to explore regarding exact choices. Relevant parameters include the exact length and timing of the pre-alert, the modality of the pre-alert, and the ability to perhaps also turn a pre-alert off.

Encoding more information in pre-alerts

Our pre-alert only used beeps to indicate that handover had to take place. However, it might be beneficial to also inform the user about why the pre-alert is raised (for example, is a sensor not working, does the car notice traffic), and what concrete actions they are to take (e.g., "Scan your surroundings to see whether you can come to a stop, or can go to another lane"). Preceding work has suggested that such concrete alerts are helpful in the automotive domain [25]. We also used only one modality (audio) for the alert. Exploring multimodal alerts may result in better outcomes [54].

Balance effectiveness with less annoyance

Although the increasing pulse pre-alert trended to be slightly more effective out of the two pre-alerts, many drivers did not like it because it appeared to be annoying. Although the primary function of an alert is to increase safety, a distaste of the pre-alert might disrupt drivers too much. This would also counter two of the benefits of the pre-alert: to allow time to finish a task and to get in a low workload, low stress state. Future work should explore how design can counter this.

Timing of pre-alerts

While we selected a fixed time interval for the pre-alert (20 s before the handover) the timing could also be made dynamic depending on the type of event, level of distraction of the driver, and complexity of the required action. Dynamic timing helps address situations where a pre-alert occurring too early may diminish its urgency, or a pre-alert occurring too late may be deemed useless.

Although our focus has been on the automotive domain, our results can also be applied to other domains in which there is (A) shared control between humans and systems and (B) potential distraction. The implication there is that a pre-alert can benefit the shift of control from system to user. Our results suggest that pre-alerts that convey urgency, such as our increasing pulse pre-alert, are valuable. However, for each domain more tests are needed to determine the timing of these pre-alerts. This should take into account (1) the remnant effects of distraction [52], (2) the time needed to finish any preceding task, and (3) the time that is needed to gain situational awareness in the domain at hand.

Limitations & Future work

We conducted our work in a driving simulator to allow for an in-depth study of human behavior, in an environment where the users cannot incur harm, but that is known from meta-reviews to translate to everyday driving [13, 23]. However, this also has limitations. First, there are no real risks for drivers and they might therefore have acted slightly riskier than in normal life. Second, given the experimental set-up, they might have anticipated some incidents and handovers which lowered response times compared to driving on the road. In everyday life, alerts might be rarer [56], which impacts response time. Third, the study was measured over a relatively short interval (90 minutes per participant) with various incidents, whereas normal driving has incidents less frequently. These limitations do not differ from other valuable driver distraction studies that used simulators, but are to be taken into account nonetheless.

The pre-alerts that we tested were limited in scope. We have discussed relevant parameters to explore. Some specific limitations are the following. First, the use of other modalities and multi-modal pre-alerts (cf. [41,43,44]) needs to be tested. Second, we did not test voice-based commands despite their potential (e.g. [30,42,44]). Finally, our drivers were not able to turn off the pre-alert, whereas this might be a relevant option in real cars, for example, to signal to the car that you noticed the pre-alert.

In our measurements we have tried to give a detailed description of human behavior. However, there is room to go even more detailed. First, our physiological state results were subtle and need to be replicated before solid conclusions can be drawn. Second, our eye-tracking results gave insight in whether and when drivers looked at the road, but more detailed analyses regarding *where* they look would also be beneficial (i.e., to understand what information people gather, what information they might have overlooked).

Finally, in our study we tested technology based on what technology looks like today (e.g., the Tesla model S) and predictions of what future states of shared control are possible (e.g., see [19,47]). However, the history of HCI has shown that interaction between humans and technology can change when disruptive technologies are introduced (e.g., GUIs, touch screens, smartphones). Similarly, currently unanticipated developments in the automotive domain may arise that might fundamentally change the interaction between drivers and cars. This might be particularly the case if fully automated cars without handover are developed (e.g., as in the Google vision). However, until that day we benefit from a basic understanding of human capacity (e.g., when do humans pay attention, how distracting is technology?).

CONCLUSION

Our results show that semi-autonomous cars benefit from pre-alerts that warn for a future handover situation. In particular, pre-alerts that reflect urgency, such as an increasing pulse signal, show high promise.

ACKNOWLEDGEMENTS

We would like to thank Ece Kamar, Eric Horvitz, Michel Pahud and Barbara Grosz for their valuable feedback during this research. RvdH is supported by the Dutch ministry of transportation (Rijkswaterstaat). CPJ is supported by a Marie Skłodowska-Curie fellowship (H2020-MSCA-IF-2015, grant no. 705010, 'Detect and React'). The views or opinions expressed in this paper do not reflect those of the sponsoring organizations.

REFERENCES

1. Hakan Alm and Lena Nilsson. 1995. The effects of a mobile telephone task on driver behavior in a car following situation. *Accident Analysis and Prevention*, 27(5), 707-715. http://doi.org/ 10.1016/0001-4575(95)00026-V

2. Erik M. Altmann and J. Gregory Trafton. 2002. Memory for goals: An activation-based model. *Cognitive Science*, 26(1), 39–83. http://doi.org/10.1016/S0364-0213(01)00058-1

3. Brian P. Bailey and Shamsi T. Iqbal. 2008. Understanding changes in mental workload during execution of goal-directed tasks and its application for interruption management. *ACM Transactions on Computer-Human Interaction* (TOCHI), 14(4), 1-28. http://doi.org/10.1145/1314683.1314689
4. Brian P. Bailey and John Konstan. 2006. On the need for attention-aware systems: Measuring effects of interruption on task performance, error rate, and affective state. *Computers in Human Behavior*, 22(4), 685-708. http://doi.org/10.1016/j.chb.2005.12.009
5. David Beattie, Lynne Baillie, and Martin Halvey. 2015. A comparison of artificial driving sounds for automated vehicles. In *Proceedings of the 2015 ACM International Joint Conference on Pervasive and Ubiquitous Computing* (UbiComp '15). New York, NY: ACM, 451-462. http://doi.org/10.1145/2750858.2807519
6. Deborah A. Boehm-Davis and Roger W. Remington. 2009. Reducing the disruptive effects of interruption: a cognitive framework for analysing the costs and benefits of intervention strategies. *Accident Analysis & Prevention*, 41(5), 1124-1129. http://doi.org/10.1016/j.aap.2009.06.029
7. Jelmer P. Borst, Niels A. Taatgen, Hedderik van Rijn. 2010. The Problem State: A Cognitive Bottleneck in Multitasking. *Journal of Experimental Psychology. Learning, Memory, and Cognition*, 36(2), 363-382. http://doi.org/10.1037/a0018106
8. Jelmer P. Borst, Niels A. Taatgen, Hedderik van Rijn. 2015. What Makes Interruptions Disruptive?: A Process-Model Account of the Effects of the Problem State Bottleneck on Task Interruption and Resumption. In *Proceedings of the ACM Conference on Human Factors in Computing Systems,* New York, NY: ACM, 2971-2980. http://doi.org/10.1145/2702123.2702156
9. Valdimar Briem and Leif R. Hedman. 1995. Behavioral effects of mobile telephone use during simulated driving. *Ergonomics*, 38, 2536-2562. http://doi.org/10.1080/00140139508925285
10. Karel Brookhuis, Gerbrand De Vries, Dick De Waard, 1991. The effects of mobile telephoning on driving performance. *Accident Analysis and Prevention*, 23, 309-316. http://doi.org/10.1016/0001-4575(91)90008-S
11. Duncan P. Brumby, Andrew Howes, Dario D. Salvucci. 2007. A cognitive constraint model of dual-task trade-offs in a highly dynamic driving task. In *Proceedings of the SIGCHI Conference on Human Factors in Computing Systems*, New York, NY: ACM, 233-242. http://doi.org/10.1145/1240624.1240664
12. Duncan P. Brumby, Dario D. Salvucci, Andrew Howes. 2009. Focus on Driving: How Cognitive Constraints Shape the Adaptation of Strategy when Dialing while Driving, In *Proceedings of the SIGCHI conference on Human factors in computing systems*, New York, NY: ACM, 1629-1638. http://doi.org/10.1145/1518701.1518950
13. Jeff K Caird, Chelsea R Willness, Piers Steel, Chip T Scialfa. 2008. A meta-analysis of the effects of cell phones on driver performance. *Accident Analysis & Prevention*, 40(4), 1282-1293. http://doi.org/10.1016/j.aap.2008.01.009
14. Yujia Cao, Sandro Castronovo, Angela Mahr, Christian Müller. 2016. On timing and modality choice with local danger warnings for drivers, In *Proceedings of the 1st International Conference on Automotive User Interfaces and Interactive Vehicular Applications*, Essen, Germany, 75-78. http://doi.org/10.1145/1620509.1620524
15. Geoff Cumming. 2013. *Understanding the new statistics: Effect sizes, confidence intervals, and meta-analysis*. New York, NY: Routledge.
16. Joost de Winter, Riender Happee, Marieke Martens, Neville Stanton. 2014. Effects of adaptive cruise control and highly automated driving on workload and situation awareness: A review of the empirical evidence. *Transportation Research Part F: Traffic Psychology and Behaviour*, 27, 196-217. http://doi.org/10.1016/j.trf.2014.06.016
17. Thomas A. Dingus, Feng Guo, Suzie Lee, Jonathan F. Antin, Miguel Perez, Mindy Buchanan-King, Jonathan Hankey. 2016. Driver crash risk factors and prevalence evaluation using naturalistic driving data. In *Proceedings of the National Academy of Sciences*, 2636-2641. http://doi.org/10.1073/pnas.1513271113
18. Johan Fagerlönn, Stefan Lindberg, and Anna Sirkka. 2012. Graded auditory warnings during in-vehicle use: using sound to guide drivers without additional noise. In *Proceedings of the 4th International Conference on Automotive User Interfaces and Interactive Vehicular Applications* (AutomotiveUI '12). New York, NY: ACM, 85-91. http://doi.org/10.1145/2390256.2390269
19. Tom M. Gasser and Daniel Westhoff. 2012. BASt-study: Definitions of automation and legal issues in Germany. Presented at the Presentation at the Road Vehicle Automation Workshop, Irvine, CA.
20. Christian Gold, Daniel Dambock, Lutz Lorenz and Klaus Bengler. 2013. "Take over!" How long does it take to get the driver back into the loop? *Proceedings of the Human Factors and Ergonomics Society Annual Meeting*, 57(1), 1938-1942. http://doi.org/10.1177/1541931213571433
21. Ellen C. Haas and John G. Casali. 1993. The perceived urgency and detection time of multi-tone and frequency modulated warning signals. In *Proceedings of the human factors and ergonomics society 37th annual meeting,* Santa Monica, CA, USA, 544-548. http://doi.org/10.1080/00140139508925270

22. Peter A. Hancock. 2013. Driven to distraction and back again. In M. A. Regan, J. D. Lee, & T. W. Victor (Eds.), *Driver distraction and inattention advances in research and countermeasures*. Chichester, UK, 9-25.
23. William J. Horrey and Chris D. Wickens. 2006. Examining the impact of cell phone conversations on driving using meta-analytic techniques. *Human Factors,* 48(1), 196-205. http://doi.org/10.1518/001872006776412135
24. Barbara Illowsky and Susan L. Dean. 2008. *Collaborative Statistics*, Connexions.
25. Shamsi T. Iqbal, Eric Horvitz, Yun-Cheng Ju, Ella Mathews. 2011. Hang on a sec!: effects of proactive mediation of phone conversations while driving. In *Proceedings of the SIGCHI Conference on Human Factors in Computing Systems*, New York, NY: ACM, 463-472. http://doi.org/10.1145/1978942.1979008
26. Shamsi T. Iqbal, Yun-Cheng Ju, Eric Horvitz. 2010. Cars, calls, and cognition: investigating driving and divided attention In *Proceedings of the SIGCHI Conference on Human Factors in Computing Systems*, New York, NY: ACM, 1281-1290. http://doi.org/10.1145/1753326.1753518
27. Christian P. Janssen and Duncan P. Brumby. 2010. Strategic Adaptation to Performance Objectives in a Dual-Task Setting. *Cognitive Science*, 34(8), 1548-1560. http://doi.org/10.1111/j.1551-6709.2010.01124.x
28. Christian P. Janssen, Duncan P. Brumby, Rae Garnett. 2012. Natural Break Points The Influence of Priorities and Cognitive and Motor Cues on Dual-Task Interleaving. *Journal of Cognitive Engineering and Decision Making*, 6(1), 5-29. http://doi.org/10.1177/1555343411432339
29. Christian P. Janssen, Shamsi T. Iqbal, Yuncheng Ju. 2014. Sharing a Driver's Context with a Caller via Continuous Audio Cues to Increase Awareness about Driver State. *Journal of Experimental Psychology: Applied*, 20(3), 270. http://doi.org/10.1037/xap0000020
30. Myounghoon Jeon, Thomas M Gable, Benjamin K Davison, Michael A Nees, Jeff Wilson and Bruce N. Walker. 2015. Menu navigation with in-vehicle technologies: Auditory menu cues improve dual task performance, preference, and workload. *International Journal of Human-Computer Interaction*, 31(1), 1-16. http://doi.org/10.1080/10447318.2014.925774
31. Sheila G. Klauer, Feng Guo, Bruce G. Simons-Morton, Marie Claude Ouimet, Suzanne E. Lee and Thomas A. Dingus. 2014. Distracted Driving and Risk of Road Crashes among Novice and Experienced Drivers. *New England Journal of Medicine*, 370(1), 54-59. http://doi.org/10.1056/NEJMsa1204142
32. Jeamin Koo, Jungsuk Kwac, Wendy Ju, Martin Steinert, Larry Leifer and Clifford Nass. 2014. Why did my car just do that? Explaining semiautonomous driving actions to improve driver understanding, trust, and performance. *International Journal on Interactive Design and Manufacturing*, 1-7. http://doi.org/10.1007/s12008-014-0227-2
33. John D Lee, Brent Caven, Steven Haake and Timothy L Brown. 2001. Speech-based Interaction with In-vehicle Computers: The Effect of Speech-based E-mail on Driver's attention to the Roadway. *Human Factors*, 43, 631-640. http://doi.org/10.1518/001872001775870340
34. Angela Mahr, Margarita Pentcheva, Christian Müller. 2009. Towards system-mediated car passenger communication, Proceedings of the *1st International Conference on Automotive User Interfaces and Interactive Vehicular Applications*, Essen, Germany 79-80. http://doi.org/10.1145/1620509.1620525
35. Daniel C. McFarlane. 2002. Comparison of four primary methods for coordinating the interruption of people in human-computer interaction. *Human Computer Interaction*, 17(1), 63-139. http://doi.org/10.1207/S15327051HCI1701_2
36. Alexander Meschtscherjakov, David Wilfinger, Thomas Scherndl, Manfred Tscheligi. 2009. Acceptance of future persuasive in-car interfaces towards a more economic driving behaviour, In *Proceedings of the 1st International Conference on Automotive User Interfaces and Interactive Vehicular Applications*, Essen, Germany, 81-88. http://doi.org/10.1145/1620509.1620526
37. Bruce Mehler, Bryan Reimer and Joseph F Coughlin. 2012. Sensitivity of physiological measures for detecting systematic variations in cognitive demand from a working memory task: an on-road study across three age groups. *Human Factors*, 54(3), 396-412.
38. Todd A. Mondor and G.A. Finley. 2013. The perceived urgency of auditory warning alarms used in the hospital operating room is inappropriate. *Candian Journal of anaesthesia*, 50, 221-228. http://doi.org/10.1007/BF03017788
39. National Highway Traffic Safety Administration. 2013. *Preliminary statement of policy concerning automated vehicles,* Washington, DC.
40. Frederik Naujoks, Christoph Mai and Alexandra Neukum. 2014.The effect of urgency of take-over requests during highly automated driving under distraction conditions. In *Proceedings of the 5th International Conference on Applied Human Factors and Ergonomics AHFE 2014*, 431-438.
41. Ioannis Politis, Stephen Brewster, Frank Pollick. 2014. Evaluating multimodal driver displays under varying situational urgency.

In *Proceedings of the 32nd annual SIGCHI conference on Human Factors in Computing System*, New York, NY: ACM, 2067-4076. http://doi.org/10.1145/2556288.2556988

42. Ioannis Politis, Stephen Brewster, Frank Pollick. 2014. Speech tactons improve speech warnings for drivers. In *Proceedings of the 6th International Conference on Automotive User Interfaces and Interactive Vehicular Applications*, New York, NY: ACM, 1-8. http://doi.org/10.1145/2667317.2667318
43. Ioannis Politis, Stephen Brewster, Frank Pollick. 2013. Evaluating multimodal driver displays of varying urgency. In *Proceedings of the 5th International Conference on Automotive User Interfaces and Interactive Vehicular Aplications,* New York, NY: ACM, 92-99. http://doi.org/10.1145/2516540.2516543
44. Ioannis Politis, Stephen Brewster, Frank Pollick. 2015. Language-based multimodal displays for the handover of control in autonomous cars. In *Proceedings of the 7th International Conference on Automotive User Interfaces and Interactive Vehicular Applications* (AutomotiveUI '15), New York, NY: ACM, 3-10. http://doi.org/10.1145/2799250.2799262
45. Donald A. Redelmeier and Robert J. Tibshirani. 2009. Association between cellular-telephone calls and motor vehicle collisions. *New England Journal of Medicine*, 336(7), 453-458. http://doi.org/10.1056/NEJM199702133360701
46. Nick Reed and R. Robbins. 2008. *The Effect of Text Messaging on Driver Behavior: A Simulator Study Transport Research Lab Report*, PPR 367.
47. SAE International. 2014. *J3016: Taxonomy and Definitions for Terms Related to On-Road Motor Vehicle Automated Driving Systems*. Retrieved from http://standards.sae.org/j3016_201401/.
48. Dario D. Salvucci. 2005. A Multitasking General Executive for Compound Continuous Tasks. *Cognitive Science*, *29*(3), 457–492. http://doi.org/10.1207/s15516709cog0000_19
49. Dario D. Salvucci and Peter Bogunovich. 2010. Multitasking and Monotasking: The Effects of Mental Workload on Deferred Task Interruptions. In *Proceedings of the SIGCHI Conference on Human Factors in Computing Systems,* New York, NY: ACM, 85-88. http://doi.org/ 10.1145/1753326.1753340
50. Dario D. Salvucci and Niels A. Taatgen. 2011. *The Multitasking Mind*. New York, NY: Oxford University Press.
51. Dario D. Salvucci, Daniel Markley, Mark Zuber, Duncan P. Brumby, 2007. iPod distraction: effects of portable music-player use on driver performance. In *Proceedings of the SIGCHI Conference on Human Factors in Computing Systems*, New York, NY: ACM, 243-250. http://doi.org/10.1145/1240624.1240665
52. David L Strayer, Joel M Cooper, Jonna Turrill, James R Coleman and Rachel J Hopman. 2015. *Measuring Cognitive Distraction in the Automobile III: A Comparison of Ten 2015 In-Vehicle Information Systems,* 1-46.
53. Chris Urmson, (2015, May 11). The View from the Front Seat of the Google Self-Driving Car. *Medium.com*. Retrieved from https://medium.com/backchannel/the-view-from-the-front-seat-of-the-google-self-driving-car-46fc9f3e6088
54. Marcel Walch, Kristin Lange, Martin Baumann and Michael Weber. 2015. Autonomous driving: investigating the feasibility of car-driver handover assistance. In *Proceedings of the 7th International Conference on Automotive User Interfaces and Interactive Vehicular Applications*, New York, NY: ACM 11-18. http://doi.org/10.1145/2799250.2799268
55. Chris D. Wickens. 2008. Multiple Resources and Mental Workload. *Human Factors*, 50(3), 449-455. http://doi.org/10.1518/001872008X288394
56. Wolfe M. Jeremy, Todd S. Horowitz, Michael J. Van Wert, Naomi M. Kenner, Skyler S. Place, and Nour Kibbi. 2007. Low target prevalence is a stubborn source of errors in visual search tasks. *Journal of Experimental Psychology: General* 136(4), 623. http://doi.org/10.1037/0096-3445.136.4.623

Toward Measurement of Situation Awareness in Autonomous Vehicles

David Sirkin, Nikolas Martelaro, Mishel Johns, Wendy Ju
Center for Design Research, Stanford University, CA USA
{sirkin, nikmart, mishel, wendyju}@stanford.edu

ABSTRACT
Until vehicles are fully autonomous, safety, legal and ethical obligations require that drivers remain aware of the driving situation. Key decisions about whether a driver can take over when the vehicle is confused, or its capabilities are degraded, depend on understanding whether he or she is responsive and aware of external conditions. The leading techniques for measuring situation awareness in simulated environments are ill-suited to autonomous driving scenarios, and particularly to on-road testing. We have developed a technique, named Daze, to measure situation awareness through real-time, in-situ event alerts. The technique is ecologically valid: it resembles applications people use in actual driving. It is also flexible: it can be used in both simulator and on-road research settings. We performed simulator-based and on-road test deployments to (a) check that Daze could characterize drivers' awareness of their immediate environment and (b) understand practical aspects of the technique's use. Our contributions include the Daze technique, examples of collected data, and ways to analyze such data.

Figure 1. The Daze application, shown during on-road testing.

Author Keywords
Autonomous vehicles; situation awareness; interaction design; measurement

INTRODUCTION
It is tempting to think that someday, when we have fully autonomous vehicles, we will be able to climb into our cars and take a nap on the way to wherever we are headed as the vehicle does the driving. However, such a day is still far off. Even when we are driven by humans, such as taxi drivers, we often feel some need to supervise drivers to make sure that they understand our intentions, that they are competent drivers, and that they are not malingering or adding unnecessary waypoints along the journey. This type of oversight will generally be required in autonomous cars until they gain the capability to perform fully autonomous driving in all possible on-road situations [22]. It is hence necessary to assess the level of situation awareness that people maintain in different autonomous driving scenarios.

Through our experience developing interfaces for autonomous vehicles, we have found a need to measure situation awareness in both simulated and on-road autonomous driving settings. Some of the most commonly used techniques for assessing situation awareness depend on measures of the driver's performance, but these are inappropriate for automated driving. Other techniques [8, 9, 28, 35] require halting a simulation currently in-progress to question drivers about what they notice, but this method does not translate well for measuring situation awareness in vehicles driving on the road. The alternative to these in-situ, halting, measures is to use post-facto interviews and questionnaires, which are affected by people's recall ability and occurrences of subsequent events.

We have developed a system, *Daze*, to enable real-time, in-situ measurement of situation awareness during driving activity [17]. The work contributes a new system and technique to measure situation awareness that works for both manual and automated driving, and in laboratory and on-road testing. It is the only technique that leverages drivers' familiarity with current navigation tools in a naturalistic setting, thus offering high ecological validity, and addressing researchers' need for assessment across contexts.

CHI 2017, May 06-11, 2017, Denver, CO, USA
© 2017 ACM. ISBN 978-1-4503-4655-9/17/05...$15.00
DOI: http://dx.doi.org/10.1145/3025453.3025822

This paper recounts our design process, including the Daze technique's user interaction model and implementation. It therefore emphasizes the contexts we are designing for, the design requirements we identified, the decisions we made, the validation performed, and our subsequent design reflections. In the following sections, we (1) detail the background and motivation for the work, (2) provide an overview of the design of Daze and describe how it works, (3) present an example of data collection and analysis using Daze, and (4) discuss the system in greater depth, to articulate different ways it can be adapted for related automotive studies.

SITUATION AWARENESS

Situation awareness is a critical factor in a driver's ability to make decisions to avoid hazards, plan routes and maintain safe travel. With the advent of automation, many of the current techniques used to assess driver performance [26], workload [13, 37] or behavior [27, 36] become useful only after a transition from autonomous to manual driving has occurred [14]. However, situation awareness is also important to assess prior to transition, given concerns over driver performance [11]. It can also be an indicator of a person's trust in automation [24], and hence will be an increasingly important measure in future automotive studies.

Awareness and Automation

In partially automated vehicles, drivers shift to a more supervisory role, however, they must remain situation aware as they may be called upon to make decisions or retake control of the vehicle if the automated driving system is unable to successfully address a situation [30]. To this point, the National Highway Traffic Safety Administration's (NHTSA) taxonomy of automated vehicles, levels 2 and 3 specify that the driver must be situation aware at all times (level 2), or can become situation aware and able to control the vehicle after some (brief) period (level 3) [21].

Maintaining sufficient alertness may be a challenge in automated vehicles, because with low attentional demand, cognitive resources may throttle back to conserve energy, making sudden rises in cognitive demand exceedingly challenging and potentially dangerous [36]. To quote Hancock's Automation Paradox, *"if you build systems where people are rarely required to respond, they will rarely respond when required"* [12]. Driving research has shown that rapid transitions from a low alertness state to active vehicle control can be quite dangerous [5, 19], as a lack of alertness and a lack of situation awareness can, when combined, lead to poor performance in a safety critical situation.

One of the most widely used models of situation awareness is Endsley's construct, which is comprised of three levels: (1) perception of elements in the environment, (2) comprehension of the situation, and (3) projection of the future state of the ambient environment [9, 10]. These three components are followed by decision and action components. Performance measures based on that action, such as controlling a vehicle, encapsulate the entire situation awareness process.

Techniques for Measuring Awareness

Current techniques for measuring situation awareness in driving settings were originally adapted from aviation testing. These methods include eye-tracking, the simulation freeze technique [9], subjective ratings, question probes (during and post activity), and task performance measures. Of these, measures that can assess awareness independent of driving performance are particularly valuable because they remove the role that driver experience, competence and familiarity with the vehicle play.

Eye-tracking

Eye-tracking can be an effective measure of level 1 situation awareness, providing an objective measure of what drivers see on the road, and thus, what they should perceive [32]. However, laying eyes on an object in the environment does not guarantee perception, as evidenced by the work of Chabris and Simons [6], and Drew et al. [7]. Eye-tracking research is relatively difficult, time consuming and expensive. It requires specialized equipment, and is highly sensitive to ambient conditions. In indoor simulators, eye-tracking systems are challenged to resolve targets located in multiple planes, and in outdoor environments, lighting conditions can interfere with tracking ability.

Physiological Measures

Using attentional resources for situation awareness increases cognitive workload, and the markers of neural activity can be detected using psychophysiological measures [5]. The deeper situation awareness levels of perception and projection are harder to measure: increased mental workload due to attentional processes can be detected by changes in blood flow, as indicated by changes in heart rate and heart rate variability [5]. Direct measures of brain activity can detect which areas of the brain are active, providing finer grained measures of what processes are at work: measuring neuroelectrical activity with an electroencephalogram (EEG) [4] and measurement of blood flow using functional near infrared spectroscopy (fNIRS) [29] have been used for driving research. These measures can be difficult for researchers to implement and interpret [33], especially in ecological settings such as in on-road studies, as they are highly susceptible to noise from muscle activity and from interference from automotive systems.

SAGAT

The freeze frame technique (Situation Awareness Global Assessment Technique, or SAGAT) involves halting a simulation in progress, and querying a person about activity in the environment, such as the position, type and future status of elements within the scene [9]. SAGAT is one of the most well-tested situation awareness measurement techniques for use in simulation environments. It was originally developed for flight interfaces, but has since been applied to driving tasks [16]. However, the freeze frame technique is limited to use within a simulator, and thus is not applicable for on-road driving settings. In addition, its intermittent halts are likely to decrease participants' sense of presence [15] of the simulation, and thus immersion in the situation, threatening a study's ecological validity.

SART
Subjective ranking techniques include ranking by either drivers themselves or by observers. In the area of military aviation, the SART technique involves pilots ranking themselves across 10 dimensions related to situation awareness post flight [35]. Although a well-tested technique, it provides only a subjective measure of driver situation awareness, and must be modified to be sufficiently applicable to non-experts in a driving context. Subjective rankings by observers can provide unobtrusive measures of situation awareness, and have the advantage of being used during live action evaluation or for post-hoc video coding. However, this approach requires many subject matter experts to review participants' behaviors, and results can still be of uncertain accuracy and reliability [28].

Question probes
Question probes can provide objective measures of elements perceived in the environment, and can also address level 2 and level 3 situation awareness. Current best practices for real-time probes are seen in the Situation Present Awareness Method (SPAM) [8]. This method utilizes response accuracy and time measures of situation awareness, although it has yet to be adapted for driving tasks.

Real-time probes are less intrusive than the freeze frame technique, and can also be used in real-world environments. However, they must be carefully designed so as not to draw the driver's attention to elements of the environment, nor should they be too cumbersome to address, as they can distract from drivers' abilities to perform their primary task. Post-driving probes do not interrupt the driving activity, but do rely on drivers' recall abilities for reliable measurement [19].

With automated driving, question probes become a much more useful technique, as the driver can respond to queries while the system controls the vehicle. This ability to respond in-the-moment improves ecological validity for studies in a simulator, as well as safety in an on-road vehicle, such as [2].

THE DAZE PLATFORM
Our intent with the Daze platform is to adapt current best practices in situation awareness assessment, so that they do not require physiological measures or retrospective assessments.

Design Requirements
Through our experience running participants through studies with both simulated and on-road scenarios, we have found that participant behavior often differs between the two. During simulations, drivers are willing to focus more of their attention on interfaces that we are developing than on the virtual environment; alternatively, during on-road studies, drivers focus their attention primarily on the road context, frequently looking away from the interface, due either to the vehicle's motion or concern over approaching danger.

Because simulation is usually used as a proxy for experiments that can be difficult, unsafe or expensive to run on the road, it is important to understand differences in behavior between simulator experiments and on-road experiments. To this end, a measurement technique for situation awareness that is usable in both environments is critical to making translational comparisons. We therefore developed a set of design requirements, where the new system should:

- Function in both simulation and on-road driving scenarios
- Not require halting the simulation or on-road driving
- Capture timing and response data based on driver responses
- Allow the driver to answer queries with a simple and unobtrusive graphical interaction

Regarding driver interaction, measurement techniques such as live question probes are typically verbal exchanges, where representing spatial data can be a challenge. The system should therefore leverage familiar and intuitive pointing gestures and graphical (map) views.

To be consistent with drivers' experiences, and accessible to the research community, the system should also:

- Reflect current (and thus, already familiar) navigation application interaction models
- Require minimal modification to a simulator's operation or a road vehicle's physical interface

With this perspective in mind, we have been developing and testing a driving specific situation awareness assessment technique to complement current evaluation techniques for automotive interfaces and systems.

Design Model
The platform is modeled after the Waze navigation application for mobile devices. A Waze user typically views a map that includes nearby users' locations, and can view, confirm, or post new alerts for the community about ongoing or transient driving conditions or hazards [31]. For example, if there is an accident in a highway exit lane, the application will warn approaching drivers that there is trouble ahead. It will also raise an alert requesting that the user confirm the ongoing existence of the disruption or any traffic that it has caused. If a driver notices that the roadway has cleared, then he or she can update the current state of the environment for the benefit of fellow drivers.

We observed that when drivers create and respond to Waze alerts, they are demonstrating levels 1 and 2 of Endsley's model—perception and comprehension of recent events, and possibly level 3—projection of the environment ahead. By modeling itself after Waze, Daze has a sensible, ecologically valid cover story for asking drivers' inputs about on-road conditions, which can then be used as measures of situation awareness. For example, Daze permits comprehension or projection questions such as *"is the traffic improving or worsening,"* or *"will a police car reach the accident within a minute?"*

Implementation
Since the application runs on a tablet or smartphone, it can be attached to a simulator, fixtured within a moving vehicle or held in someone's hand. During ordinary driving, it displays an overhead map of the environment centered on the car's current location, similar to other navigation tools. The map

Figure 2. Daze ordinarily shows an overhead map centered on the car's location (left). After passing an event, it raises an alert (center). If the user confirms noticing the event, the application shows a closeup map view, asking the user to tap the screen to locate the event (shown with a blue dot), after which the user confirms the location (right).

tracks the car's movement so that the icon for the driver's vehicle is always at its center. Similar to typical navigation maps, it can show route overlays and annotations, and switch between alternate map views (road, satellite).

Maps

From the driver's perspective, the system appears similar in the simulator and on the road, but internally, there are several differences. In the simulator version of Daze, the map(s) shown were drawn using illustration software to represent the virtual environment, and are visually stylized to mimic a blend of Apple Maps[1] and Waze.[2] The simulator servers send current position and alert event messages, which the application reflects as updates to the live map. In the on-road version of Daze, the application builds upon Apple's MapKit framework to update map images as the vehicle moves and to trigger alert messages.

Views

Regarding the type of view to present, according to Taylor et al. [34], an egocentric view (driver's perspective) supports driving through local guidance, which is better for turn-by-turn directions, while an allocentric (overhead) view favors navigation requiring global awareness, including route learning. We chose the latter because Daze's questions ask participants to confirm and locate prior or anticipated events, which requires awareness of the evolving ambient environment.

Alerts

Shortly following events relevant to assessing situation awareness, Daze presents visible and (if needed) audible *alert* messages asking if the driver noticed the event. Alerts are styled after events typically called out in Waze, and that can easily be found on-road and replicated in a simulator, such as traffic, accidents or roadside construction. The alert screen includes *"yes"* and *"no"* buttons. If the driver selects no, the alert disappears; if he or she replies yes, a closeup view of the map, or *callout*, appears and asks the driver to tap the screen to identify the event's location (Fig. 2). These responses are all recorded and time-stamped.

[1] Apple Maps. 2016. http://www.apple.com/ios/maps/
[2] Waze. 2016. http://www.waze.com/

Alerts typically follow their corresponding events by a set time or distance, depending on the study's design, such that drivers cannot view events in side or rearview mirrors to confirm their existence or location. This prevents alerts from making drivers aware of events, and thus contaminating the awareness the technique is designed to assess.

We can use both the driver's error rate in detecting actual or false events, and also the location of the events as measures of situation awareness. Response times to the event queries are another measure of situation awareness, with lower times correlating with higher awareness [3]. Response time could also be a measure of distraction [18], or cognitive load, depending on the study. Additionally, the pop- up nature of alerts is similar to secondary task cognitive load testing techniques [23], and could be employed accordingly.

Both alert and callout screens dismiss themselves after 15 seconds, to avoid one alert cycle running into the next. We assume that a driver's lack of response to an alert or callout screen indicates that the driver has (likely) not noticed the alert.

In the simulator, Daze receives messages about real or false events via UDP messages sent over WiFi from a server. On the road, alerts are triggered by either (a) geofencing, which occurs when the device enters or exits a radius around a preset GPS coordinate, such as a known construction site or school, or (b) receiving UDP messages following the same messaging protocol, sent in-the-moment by an experimenter. Experimenter triggering of alerts while on the road can help researchers assess drivers' awareness of ephemeral events, such as traffic accidents. It can also be used during Wizard of Oz-style experimentation in the simulator or on the road [2, 20].

False alerts represent events which may never have existed, or which may have occurred earlier, but cleared over time. This capability is important both to better represent the way that Daze addresses situation awareness—probing drivers about events which may no longer exist—and to help break the pattern of *event occurs, alert appears,* that drivers might otherwise perceive.

Figure 3. The parking lot where participants first view the test deployment's virtual environment. The child walks forward a few moments after the test begins. Just after, the bicyclist rides from right to left, accompanied by a ringing bell, which pans across the scene.

TEST DEPLOYMENTS

We conducted tests to check the Daze technique's ability to assess situation awareness. The primary goals are to (a) inform the design of the system's interaction model, and (b) provide data to develop an initial set of measures. Their context focuses on drivers' abilities to notice and localize events exterior to the car, and on how visible versus audible cues influence their awareness. These test deployments are the initial stage of a larger project concerning awareness of auditory events in autonomous driving. We present them here to illustrate how Daze can be used, and how the data that it provides can be analyzed, rather than as studies to be assessed on their own. Along the way, we discuss the technique's usability, and include preliminary findings about participants' awareness of audible versus visible events.

Participants

We recruited 12 participants, whose ages ranged from 17 to 58 years (M=28.2, SD=11.5), with 7 men and 5 women. Regarding driving habits, their reported years of driving experience ranged from 1 to 42 years (M=9.9, SD=11.2), with 83.3% having driven within the last two days, and 75.0% typically driving at least once per week. We offered a $25 gift card for participation.

Simulator

We conducted the test deployments in a high presence, whole-chassis, fixed base driving simulator. Participants sat in a late-model Toyota Avalon, and experienced the simulated driving course from the driver's seat. The simulator's visuals feature a 270°wraparound projection screen, rear projection screen (for the rear-view mirror), and two LCD side-view mirrors. The audio system includes two 6-channel speaker rings: one at ground level and another about four meters above the car, and a five-channel in-car audio system, used to enhance exterior sounds. A sub-woofer, attached to the car's body, simulates vibrations from an engine and from road roughness.

Events

A central concern in automation is *out-of-the-loop* experiences, where drivers may be focused on tasks other than driving, yet may need to intervene or resume control if the autonomous system fails to detect or handle potential hazards. To effectively assess situation awareness within this context, it is important that events reflect these potential hazards. We therefore adapt and include events from Bolstad et al.'s *goal-directed task analysis*, specifically, from the goal for avoiding road hazards outlined in [3].

The information requirements for the Bolstad's goal to *avoid road hazards* includes the presence and knowledge of pedestrians, school and construction zones, and road conditions. These potential hazards, in turn, include specific events, such as crosswalks, signs, lane changes, road equipment, speed limit changes, and the behavior of other drivers. These goals, decisions and information requirements were elicited from Bolstad's process, as described in [3].

Test Setting

Within the simulator, participants follow a course through a suburban-urban environment, which includes local, city and highway roads, during a fictional 20-minute autonomous morning drive to work. During a pre-test briefing, we ask participants to *"observe the vehicle's driving, and the environment around them."* These instructions are based on guidance on the driver's expected role, as outlined in the National Highway Safety Administration's recommendations for automation levels 3-4 [3].

The car navigates its way through the course under fully autonomous control, including negotiating its way out of, and into, parking spots at the test's start and completion (Fig. 3). The experience therefore requires no participant interaction with the car's pedals, shift lever or steering wheel. The steering wheel does turn, however, under its own power, in keeping with the car's maneuvers.

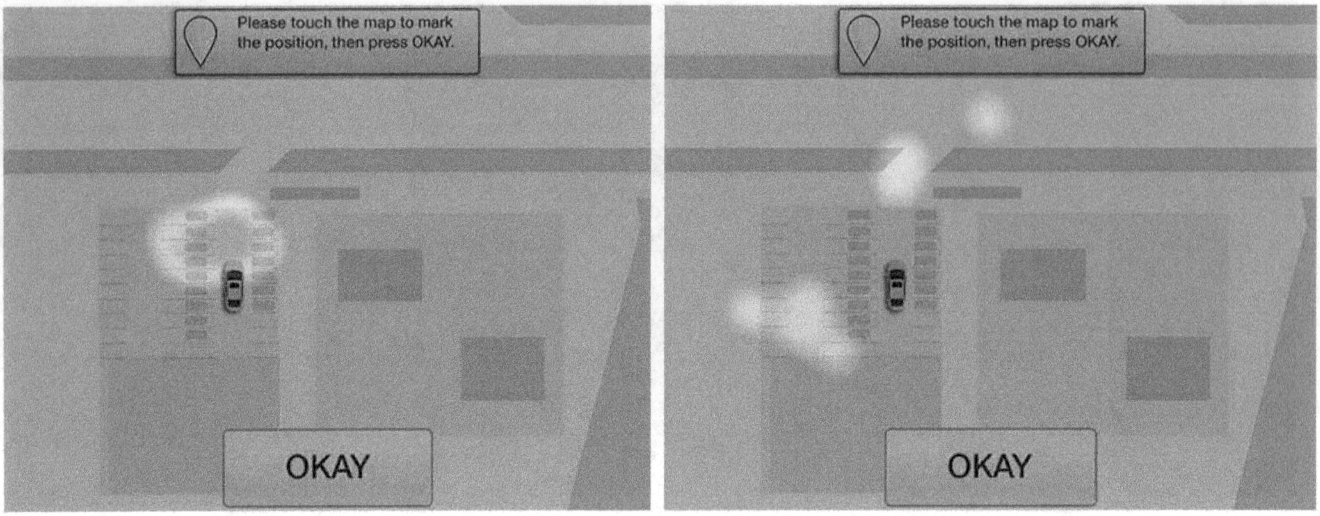

Figure 4. Heat maps showing participant responses to the location of the audible and visible bicyclist (left), and audible but not visible garbage truck (right), which both occur in the parking lot, moments apart, at the start of the drive.

Along the course, 11 events are presented, which are visible, audible, or both visible and audible. Events are based on the goal to avoid road hazards, and include: a child walking nearby, a bicyclist whizzing in front of the car while ringing a bell, a dog barking, an unseen truck unloading, a pedestrian crossing the street with an audible crosswalk signal, a pedestrian crossing another street with no audible signal, an emergency vehicle siren, a helicopter flying overhead, a police car partially concealed behind a highway billboard, a passing train, and a construction site with jack hammers and loaders. (The helicopter is not a road hazard event: we have included it to assess drivers' abilities to project a situation into the future—specifically, a nearby hospital as its destination.)

We attached a tablet computer running Daze to the car's center stack (Fig. 1). The program is set to raise alerts anywhere from 3 to 35 seconds after each event. Alerts are timed so that the event is no longer visible directly or in the mirror. Each Daze alert is accompanied by an audible tone (one of the tablet's built-in chimes). In addition to the alerts that match events in the environment, the tablet also presents three false alerts. These false events ask whether the driver notices a car honking its horn, the presence of a roadside hitchhiker, and a construction site, none of which exist in the simulation.

There are two alternative ways to present alerts that maintain consistency: appearing either a fixed time, or a fixed distance, after passing events. The fixed time approach lowers the interval before questions of recall, but due to variations in vehicle speed and visual obstructions, may allow participants to observe prior events in the surroundings or rearview mirror. We chose the fixed distance approach, as we are concerned with assessing awareness of events that may or may not have occurred, rather than the visibility of those events, which itself would influence situation awareness. For studies that focus on measuring near term comprehension or projection, a brief interval may be preferable.

The Daze application can be set to demonstrate—as the experimenter swipes the tablet's screen—what alerts and callouts look (and sound) like, and how participants may respond. This introductory demonstration is included during the initial pretest briefing, and only occurs once.

Results

Participants correctly identified events that *did* occur 83.3% of the time, and rejected events that *did not* occur 91.7% of the time. Given our test environment, which includes events that are partially obscured visually, as might be the case on real-world roads, participants were most correct in identifying events that were both visible and audible, less so for events that were audible only, and notably less still for events that were visible only (Table 1).

Table 1. Participants' percentage correctness in identifying actual (visible, audible or both) and false events.

Visible Only	*Audible Only*	*Visible + Audible*	*Neither (False)*
58.3%	83.3%	95.8%	91.7%

Participants also identified the *locations* of events with greater precision and accuracy when those events were visible and audible, compared to only visible or only audible. Fig. 4 shows location responses for the bicyclist, who is seen riding across the screen and heard ringing a bell in front of the car, versus the garbage truck, which is heard nearby only moments later, but is not visible at all.

Regarding the time taken between the appearance of an alert and the driver's response, and the appearance of the following location callout and the driver's response, we found that participants were notably quicker for events that were both visible and audible (Table 2).

Table 2. Number of seconds for participants to respond to alerts and callouts for events that are visible, audible or both.

	Visible Only	*Audible Only*	*Visible + Audible*
Alert	4.5	4.2	2.8
Callout	7.9	8.1	5.0

Regarding participants' abilities to project a situation into the future (Endsley's level 3), 73% correctly indicated the (overhead and not visible) helicopter's direction, while 36% correctly identified the nearby hospital as its destination.

Data Analysis

In addition to directly reporting correctly identified events, locations, and response timing, we can derive measures that further inform us about drivers' awareness of events.

Locating Events

We averaged the Euclidean distance of responses for each event e across event types t (visible, audible, both) as a measure of dispersion:

$$d(t) = avg_{e \in t}\sqrt{(x_e - \bar{x}_e)^2 + (y_e - \bar{y}_e)^2} \quad (1)$$

For our test deployments, we recorded dispersion in map units of 1024×768. Knowing the map's scale then allows for translation to simulator or on-road distances. We found that participants were most precise in locating events that were both visible and audible (indicated by lower dispersion), and least precise for events that were audible only (Table 3).

Table 3. Dispersion *d(t)*, and quadrant-level accuracy, of participants' location responses for events that are visible, audible or both.

	Visible Only	*Audible Only*	*Visible + Audible*
Dispersion	53.3	116.3	48.16
Accuracy	85.0%	44.2%	87.8%

Determining response accuracy is challenged by events that are in motion. One approach is to subdivide the map around the car and note the percentage of responses that fall within the regions that contain the event path. The size of these regions then represents the measure's tolerance. For our test deployments, we divided callout views into quadrants centered on the vehicle, and found that accuracy displayed the same pattern as dispersion (Table 3).

Another approach to determine accuracy would apply a similar equation to dispersion, but with distances measured from events' positions or paths, rather than from the mean of participant responses.

Response Timing

We expected that longer response times, as well as larger variation in location estimates, would represent greater uncertainty over event locations, and this is supported by a Pearson correlation coefficient of r=0.82 between the mean of response times across participants for each event, and the dispersion for that event.

Drivers encounter a repeated event in different feature settings through two pedestrian crosswalks, 2.5 minutes apart. The first includes an audible crossing signal and the second does not. All participants correctly identified both events, with slightly faster response times for the second, inaudible event (M=3.0, SD=1.7 vs. M=2.3, SD=1.2). This counters the overall trend of longer response times for inaudible events, and may be due to the proximity (and thus visibility) of the event, combined with learning from repetition of the alert.

Discussion

Our primary objective for these test deployments is to demonstrate, through example, how to analyze the data that Daze collects to draw inferences about situation awareness. The data for these tests suggest that participants are better at *detecting* events around them that are audible, and better at *localizing* events that are visible. This agrees with intuition, and, we expect that audible events prompt drivers to perform a visual search, which, if successful, provides strong support for an event having occurred.

We did not expect strictly audible events to be more correctly identified and located than strictly visible events, although there are several possible explanations. First, audio cues are noticeable even if drivers' visual attention is focused elsewhere in the scene, or car, whereas visual cues can only be identified by direct or peripheral line of sight. Second, most of our events are in motion, relative both to the environment and to the moving car, so correctly identified locations could have been anywhere along those motion paths. This would have affected both visual and audible events, and either one could have been more strongly influenced. A likely outcome is that participants focused greater attention on confirming whether events had occurred at all, rather than locating them precisely.

Participant responses to the tablet, its alerts and location callouts were cautious, yet positive. When asked whether they agreed that the interaction with the application made them more aware of what was happening around them, 58.3% agreed. When asked whether the application interaction broke their sense of immersion in the environment, 66.7% disagreed.

During a semi-structured interview following each simulated drive, participants commented on circumstances where Daze would be most helpful to them: *"If someone's crossing in front of you, like a bicycle or something, I guess I would like it to notify me of events if it's going to affect my experience in the car. Like if the car's going to slam on the brakes."* And regarding awareness while driving: *"I'm not super observant to my environment, so I think that having some type of a cue to alert me to events is useful."* Responses reflect participants' perceptions of Daze as an awareness support technique—likely due to its similarity to familiar navigation applications—rather than an assessment technique, which contributes to ecological validity.

Participants' perceptions of their own abilities to localize audio cues is somewhat lower than the observational data suggests. For example: *"Oftentimes I wasn't exactly sure of what locations things that I was hearing were in. I heard them, and I heard them moving, but when I was asked to identify it, I wasn't about to pick it out."* And similarly: *"I heard more than I saw. There were instances I had to guess where the sound was coming from. I missed a few things too."*

ON-ROAD TESTING

We also tested the on-road version of Daze on public roads. Our goals were to (1) test the reliability of triggering events, (2) evaluate usability while on the road, and (3) gain experience designing a test course.

The first trial explored an automated driving scenario. The test vehicle was based on an on-road simulated autonomous driving platform (in the manner of [2]), and was implemented in a right-hand drive SUV. A passenger in the left front seat (the driver's position in the U.S.) held a tablet computer running the Daze application, while a Driving Wizard operated the vehicle. An Interaction Wizard sat in the rear seat and triggered alerts from a laptop that sent UDP messages over an ad-hoc wireless network to the tablet. The Interaction Wizard had a menu of pre-programmed alerts, including the presence of a road hazard, construction zone, accident, police car and nearby traffic. The Wizard observed the environment around the vehicle and raised event alerts after passing incidents that matched any of those on the menu.

The second trial explored a manual driving scenario. The test vehicle was a standard sedan, with a tablet computer running the Daze application mounted on the center stack (Fig. 1). In this case, the driver operated the vehicle, so there was no Driving Wizard. The Interaction Wizard triggered alerts from a remote location over the cellular data network, similar to the procedure above, only observing the environment through live video from a forward-facing camera on the car's dashboard. We limited use during manual driving due to concern over distraction, but our testing found it acceptable to issue alerts when the vehicle was stopped—as in traffic, at a sign or light, with 30 seconds available for alert and response.

The passenger in the first trial, and driver in the second trial, were both able to view and respond to alerts while the vehicles were en route, and the application collected the same type of response data as in the simulator tests. Since the Interaction Wizard triggered events opportunistically, and distances to events varied, the data were not directly comparable to that collected in the simulator.

We initially raised alerts without an audible cue, and found that the passenger missed several alerts, which timed out without a response. For studies where the response to the alert event is most important, we therefore recommend playing an accompanying audible cue. For studies where driver workload or distraction are the focus, the lack of an audible cue makes noticing the visible-only alert a measure in itself.

Events were not always perceived as we expected. For example, we passed a police station with a number of police vehicles parked outside, but the passenger did not acknowledge them in response to an alert. When asked about this after the drive, the passenger replied that she was expecting queries about police cars to be about those directly on the road, or stopped on the shoulder, not those in a parking lot somewhere to the side of the road, where it would be less relevant to someone driving.

With respect to technical implementation, the wireless connection and messaging worked as expected, with little lag and few dropped messages.

Some of Daze's current features come from discoveries made during this early on-road testing. For instance, we realized that certain landmark events that are always present—such as hospitals or school crossings—could be triggered by geofencing. This reduces the Interaction Wizard's tasks, allowing him or her to better attend to triggering more ephemeral events, such as the presence of pedestrians or bicyclists, emergency vehicles or traffic. We also found that a construction site, which was present during course planning, had cleared before the test drive. We were still able to trigger a construction alert at a subsequent site, highlighting both the inherent variability involved in running tests on real roadways, and also the usefulness of being able to trigger events in an ad-hoc basis.

Overall, on-road testing verified that live event triggering is a feasible approach, and it unearthed several challenges facing on-road usage compared to a simulated environment.

IMPLEMENTATION NOTES

Test Deployments

In our test deployments, we set out to recreate conditions that experimenters might face in simulated and, especially, real-world settings, including circumstances that could pose a challenge to clean data collection, such as fully or partially obscured, or moving, objects of interest. Findings demonstrate that the Daze application, the data it records, and analysis of that data, are able to characterize drivers' awareness of actual versus false event occurrences and their locations. By examining the timing of responses, we can also infer, to some degree, drivers' certainty of their responses, without directly asking.

The test deployments serve primarily as an exploration of the types of data that can be collected, and analysis that can be performed, using the Daze technique to better understand situation awareness. Our findings are influenced by the settings that we created, and questions that we asked about them, and results should be taken as such. For example, halfway through the drive, a pedestrian walks through a crosswalk at the intersection just ahead of the car, and we later ask the participant to locate that pedestrian on a map. Since the pedestrian was seen traveling along a path, anywhere across that path could have been a reasonable response. We therefore focused our analysis on response dispersion, and how that relates to response timing, rather than the exact position or direction implied by particular responses. Another approach might be to clarify the questions posed in alert and callout messages to account for variability in event paths or timing—for example, eliciting more or less specificity in their responses.

On-Road Testing

Insights from the on-road testing include that the platform performed as we had planned, but that field conditions were less predictable than we had expected. As a takeaway, we expect that triggering alerts through geolocation alone may be insufficient, due to the transience of people and places in the physical world, and that the capability to support improvisational action by researchers can be most valuable.

One limitation to this method of on-road situation awareness assessment is that tested events are limited to those that the Interaction Wizard is aware of, or those that have been previously been programmed into a simulator course. This suits the controlled experiments that the technique is designed for, but does not capture the participants' general awareness of all interesting things that might happen in a real environment. It is possible to extend the questions that are asked by incorporating prior information about the course through maps or pre-test scouting drives, or by employing additional experimenters in the field or confederate vehicles that send messages to the Interaction Wizard. Other post-facto analysis techniques, such as interactive video review or post-drive questionnaires, could be used in conjunction with the Daze technique to address such events.

Questioning and Awareness

Daze shares limitations presented by all concurrent situation awareness assessment techniques, including SAGAT and SPAM. For example, in asking people about events, we may bias them towards noticing events that they might otherwise not have noticed. And yet, in their 2013 evaluation of validity and intrusiveness of real-time questioning, Bacon and Strybel *"failed to find evidence supporting the idea that online probing affects subsequent situation awareness"* [1].

We try to limit potential influence by being careful to incorporate *false positive* event questions about things that are not present. Also, we wait several seconds to ask about an event after it has occurred, to make sure that drivers cannot retroactively check behind them for the event in question. In addition, we follow procedures suggested by Endsley [10], such as careful experimenter instruction and randomizing query topic and timing to minimize influence. Endsley reports that *"no intrusion on performance has been repeated in numerous other studies"* using these procedures.

Other limitations need to be addressed through study design. For example, since it is the difference in measurement across conditions rather than the absolute measurement that matters, some bias in events (such as their size, location, apparent motion, or sound profile) can be alright so long as they apply evenly across all conditions. It is also a good idea to include events that induce several senses, including front-rear or side-side movement, high or low frequency vibration, or even scent, so as to assess awareness of conditions and factors that are not exclusively visible or audible.

Questioning and Arousal

Regarding concern over drivers maintaining situation awareness in conditions of low arousal, Pierce et al. find no difference in self perception of workload between real-time and post-study questioning techniques, although they do find that real-time questioning is comparable to other secondary tasks [25]. This suggests that exploring lower levels of situation awareness using Daze may be possible, within the constraints of (any) real-time assessment noted above.

In early testing in the simulator and on-road, we found that participants focus their visual attention on the surroundings, or alternatively, close their eyes to rest, and therefore miss many alerts when they appear. Because we focused on assessing awareness of visible and audible events, and identifying actual versus false events, we set the application to issue a tone with each alert. For research agendas with a stronger emphasis on driver distraction, focus of attention, or awareness of specific events or incoming alerts, the accompanying tone can be disabled through a setting.

Maps and Orientation

The callout screen, which asks participants to locate events on a close-up map, initially included only a map image. We received feedback, during initial testing, that drivers found it challenging to identify their own location, let alone that of another element in the scene, relative to themselves. Thus, we added an overhead image of the car, at a slightly exaggerated scale (similar to Waze), in the center of each map, which improved drivers' responsiveness.

We positioned the image of the car at the location that the car was in the past, when the event occurred; however, it is reasonable to position the car at its location in the present, at the moment when the alert is raised, or to have it reflect the car's continued motion. Indicating which is the case to participants prior to the drive will clarify the procedure, and likely improve responses. We intend to explore these differences during upcoming studies.

REFLECTIONS AND FUTURE WORK

We have shown that Daze collects data useful for the measurement of situation awareness, demonstrated an example analysis using that data, and described many of its design considerations and nuances.

Our test deployments evaluated the platform primarily taking a reflective frame: that is, investigating situation awareness through recall of people, places and events previously observed in the environment. While it is important to understand driver awareness in an automated driving context, the technique can also investigate cuing and information delivery, or provide information about future situations. The test environment included one event that reflects the ability to project future state: the audible, but not visible, helicopter flying toward the hospital, which about one-third of participants inferred as its destination. Daze can thus be used as a means to test the anticipatory abilities of a driver acting in a supervisory role, in addition to other methods, such as driving performance measurement.

We are currently running simulator and on-road studies that employ the technique to explore how alternative interface designs and interaction patterns affect situation awareness. We envision alternative versions, which focus on navigation, text messaging, and even gaming.

Separating the measurement of situation awareness from driving performance, as is necessary in autonomous driving situations, makes the Daze technique useful in other awareness-dependent contexts. We imagine applying a similar approach to personal navigation, augmented reality or wearable computing, to understand how applications or equipment affect users' awareness of the world around them.

The Daze source code and executable are available at `https://github.com/CDR-IxD/Daze`.

ACKNOWLEDGMENTS

The authors thank Sile O'Modhrain for contributing to test deployment procedure and audio and design and Dylan Moore for assistance with data and statistical analyses.

This research was supported by Stanford Center for Design Research's Affiliate Program, and conducted under Stanford University IRB protocols 30016 and 32402.

REFERENCES

1. L. Paige Bacon and Thomas Strybel. 2013. Assessment of the validity and intrusiveness of online-probe questions for situation awareness in a simulated air-traffic-management task with student air-traffic controllers. *Safety Science* 56 (2013), 89–95. http://dx.doi.org/10.1016/j.ssci.2012.06.019
2. Sonia Baltodano, Srinath Sibi, Nikolas Martelaro, Nikhil Gowda, and Wendy Ju. 2015. The RRADS platform: A real road autonomous driving simulation. In *Proc. of the ACM/IEEE Intl. Conf. on Automotive User Interfaces and Interactive Vehicular Interactions*. ACM, 281–288. http://dl.acm.org/citation.cfm?id=2799250.2799288
3. Cheryl A. Bolstad, Haydee M. Cuevas, Jingjing Wang-Costello, Mica R. Endsley, and Linda S. Angell. 2009. Measurement of situation awareness for automobile technologies of the future. In *Performance Metrics for Assessing Driver Distraction*. SAE, 195–213.
4. G. Borghini, G. Vecchiato, J. Toppi, L. Astolfi, A. Maglione, R. Isabella, C. Caltagirone, W. Kong, D. Wei, Z. Zhou, and L. Polidori. 2012. Assessment of mental fatigue during car driving by using high resolution EEG activity and neurophysiologic indices. In *Engineering in Medicine and Biology Society (EMBC), 2012 Annual Intl. Conf. of the IEEE*. IEEE, 6442–6445. http://ieeexplore.ieee.org/xpls/abs_all.jsp?arnumber=6347469
5. Karel A. Brookhuis, Dick De Waard, and Wiel H. Janssen. 2001. Behavioural impacts of advanced driver assistance systems—an overview. *European Journal of Transport and Infrastructure Research* 1, 3 (2001), 245–253. http://www.ejtir.tbm.tudelft.nl/issues/2001_03/pdf/2001_03_02.pdf
6. Christopher Chabris and Daniel Simons. 2011. *The invisible gorilla: And other ways our intuitions deceive us*. Broadway Books. http://dx.doi.org/10.1080/17439760.2012.753466
7. Trafton Drew, Melissa L. H. Võ, and Jeremy M. Wolfe. 2013. The invisible gorilla strikes again: Sustained inattentional blindness in expert observers. *Psychological Science* 24, 9 (2013), 1848–1853. https://doi.org/10.1177/0956797613479386
8. Frank T. Durso, Andrew R. Dattel, S. Banbury, and S. Tremblay. 2004. SPAM: The real-time assessment of SA, S. Banbury and S. Tremblay (Eds.). *A Cognitive Approach to Situation Awareness: Theory and Application* (2004), 137–154.
9. Mica R. Endsley. 1995a. Measurement of situation awareness in dynamic systems. *Human Factors: The Journal of the Human Factors and Ergonomics Society* 37, 1 (1995), 65–84. http://hfs.sagepub.com/content/37/1/65.short
10. Mica R. Endsley. 1995b. Toward a theory of situation awareness in dynamic systems. *Human Factors: The Journal of the Human Factors and Ergonomics Society* 37, 1 (1995), 32–64. http://hfs.sagepub.com/content/37/1/32.short
11. Mica R. Endsley and David B. Kaber. 1999. Level of automation effects on performance, situation awareness and workload in a dynamic control task. *Ergonomics* 42, 3 (1999), 462–492. http://dx.doi.org/10.1080/001401399185595
12. P. A. Hancock. 2014. Automation: How much is too much? *Ergonomics* 57, 3 (2014), 449–454. http://dx.doi.org/10.1080/00140139.2013.816375
13. Sandra G. Hart and Lowell E. Staveland. 1988. Development of NASA-TLX (Task Load Index): Results of empirical and theoretical research. *Advances in psychology* 52 (1988), 139–183. http://dx.doi.org/10.1016/S0166-4115(08)62386-9
14. Key Jung Lee, Yeon Kyoung Joo, and Clifford Nass. 2014. Partially intelligent automobiles and driving experience at the moment of system transition. In *Proc. of the SIGCHI Conf. on Human Factors in Computing Systems*. ACM, 3631–3634. http://dl.acm.org/citation.cfm?id=2557370
15. Kwan Min Lee. 2004. Presence, explicated. *Communication Theory* 14, 1 (2004), 27–50. http://onlinelibrary.wiley.com/doi/10.1111/j.1468-2885.2004.tb00302.x/full
16. R. Ma and David B. Kaber. 2007. Situation awareness and driving performance in a simulated navigation task. *Ergonomics* 50, 8 (2007), 1351–1364. http://dx.doi.org/10.1080/00140130701318913
17. Nikolas Martelaro, David Sirkin, and Wendy Ju. 2015. Daze: A real-time situation awareness measurement tool for driving. In *Proc. of the ACM/IEEE Intl. Conf. on Automotive User Interfaces and Interactive Vehicular Interactions*. ACM, 158–163. http://dl.acm.org/citation.cfm?doid=2809730.2809753
18. M. H. Martens and W. Van Winsum. 2000. Measuring distraction: the peripheral detection task. *TNO Human Factors, Soesterberg, Netherlands* (2000). http://dx.doi.org/10.1016/j.trf.2005.04.009

19. Brian Ka-Jun Mok, Mishel Johns, Key Jung Lee, Hillary Page Ive, David Miller, and Wendy Ju. 2015a. Timing of unstructured transitions of control in automated driving. In *Intelligent Vehicles Symposium*. IEEE, 1167–1172. http://dx.doi.org/10.1109/IVS.2015.7225841

20. Brian Ka-Jun Mok, David Sirkin, Srinath Sibi, David Bryan Miller, and Wendy Ju. 2015b. Understanding driver-automated vehicle interactions through Wizard of Oz design improvisation. In *Proc. Intl. Driving Symposium on Human Factors in Driver Assessment, Training, and Vehicle Design*. 386–392.

21. National Highway Traffic Safety Administration and U.S. Department of Transportation. 2016. *Federal Automated Vehicles Policy: Accelerating the Next Revolution in Roadway Safety*. Washington, DC.

22. National Highway Traffic Safety Administration and others. 2013. *Preliminary Statement of Policy Concerning Automated Vehicles*. Washington, DC.

23. Fred Paas, Juhani E. Tuovinen, Huib Tabbers, and Pascal WM Van Gerven. 2003. Cognitive load measurement as a means to advance cognitive load theory. *Educational Psychologist* 38, 1 (2003), 63–71. http://www.tandfonline.com/doi/abs/10.1207/S15326985EP3801_8

24. Raja Parasuraman, Thomas B. Sheridan, and Christopher D. Wickens. 2008. Situation awareness, mental workload, and trust in automation: Viable, empirically supported cognitive engineering constructs. *Journal of Cognitive Engineering and Decision Making* 2, 2 (2008), 140–160. http://edm.sagepub.com/content/2/2/140.short

25. Russell Pierce, Kim-Phuong L. Vu, Jimmy Nguyen, and Thomas Strybel. 2008. The relationship between SPAM, workload, and task performance on a simulated ATC task. In *Proc. of the Human Factors Ergonomics Society*. 34–38. https://doi.org/10.1177/154193120805200109

26. A. R. Quimby and G. R. Watts. 1981. *Human factors and driving performance*. Technical Report. http://trid.trb.org/view.aspx?id=174634

27. Thomas A. Ranney. 1994. Models of driving behavior: A review of their evolution. *Accident Analysis & Prevention* 26, 6 (1994), 733–750. http://www.sciencedirect.com/science/article/pii/0001457594900515

28. Paul Salmon, Neville Stanton, Guy Walker, and Damian Green. 2006. Situation awareness measurement: A review of applicability for C4i environments. *Applied Ergonomics* 37, 2 (2006), 225–238. http://www.sciencedirect.com/science/article/pii/S0003687005000554

29. Angelo Sassaroli, Feng Zheng, Leanne M. Hirshfield, Audrey Girouard, Erin Treacy Solovey, Robert JK Jacob, and Sergio Fantini. 2008. Discrimination of mental workload levels in human subjects with functional near-infrared spectroscopy. *Journal of Innovative Optical Health Sciences* 1, 02 (2008), 227–237. http://www.worldscientific.com/doi/abs/10.1142/S1793545808000224

30. Thomas B. Sheridan. 2006. Supervisory control. *Handbook of Human Factors and Ergonomics* (2006), 1025–1052. http://onlinelibrary.wiley.com/doi/10.1002/0470048204.ch38/summary

31. Thiago H. Silva, Pedro O.S. Vaz de Melo, Aline Carneiro Viana, Jussara M. Almeida, Juliana Salles, and Antonio AF Loureiro. 2013. Traffic condition is more than colored lines on a map: Characterization of Waze alerts. In *Social Informatics*. Springer, 309–318. http://link.springer.com/chapter/10.1007/978-3-319-03260-3_27

32. M. W. Smolensky. 1993. Toward the physiological measurement of situation awareness: The case for eye movement measurements. In *Proc. of the Human Factors and Ergonomics Society*, Vol. 41.

33. Erin Treacy Solovey, Audrey Girouard, Krysta Chauncey, Leanne M. Hirshfield, Angelo Sassaroli, Feng Zheng, Sergio Fantini, and Robert JK Jacob. 2009. Using fNIRS brain sensing in realistic HCI settings: Experiments and guidelines. In *Proc. ACM Symposium on User Interface Software and Technology*. ACM, 157–166. http://dl.acm.org/citation.cfm?id=1622207

34. Holly A. Taylor, Susan J. Naylor, and Nicholas A. Chechile. 1999. Goal-specific influences on the representation of spatial perspective. *Memory & Cognition* 27, 2 (1999), 309–319. http://link.springer.com/article/10.3758/BF03211414

35. R. M. Taylor. 1990. Situational Awareness Rating Technique (SART): The development of a tool for aircrew systems design. *AGARD, Situational Awareness in Aerospace Operations 17* (1990).

36. Kristie L. Young, Michael A. Regan, and John D. Lee. 2009. *Measuring the effects of driver distraction: Direct driving performance methods and measures*. CRC Press, Boca Raton, FL. http://www.crcnetbase.com/doi/abs/10.1201/9781420007497.ch7

37. Mark S. Young and Neville A. Stanton. 2002. Attention and automation: New perspectives on mental underload and performance. *Theoretical Issues in Ergonomics Science* 3, 2 (2002), 178–194. http://www.tandfonline.com/doi/abs/10.1080/14639220210123789

The Trouble with Autopilots: Assisted and Autonomous Driving on the Social Road

Barry Brown
Mobile Life @ Stockholm University
University of Stockholm, Sweden
Barry@mobilelifecentre.org

Eric Laurier
School of Geosciences
University of Edinburgh, Scotland
Eric.laurier@ed.ac.uk

ABSTRACT
As self-driving cars have grown in sophistication and ability, they have been deployed on the road in both localised tests and as regular private vehicles. In this paper we draw upon publicly available videos of autonomous and assisted driving (specifically the Tesla autopilot and Google self-driving car) to explore how their drivers and the drivers of other cars interact with, and make sense of, the actions of these cars. Our findings provide an early perspective on human interaction with new forms of driving involving assisted-car drivers, autonomous vehicles and other road users. The focus is on social interaction on the road, and how drivers communicate through, and interpret, the movement of cars. We provide suggestions toward increasing the transparency of autopilots' actions for both their driver and other drivers.

Author Keywords
Autonomous cars; self-driving; video analysis; interaction; social road; automobile interfaces; human-robot-interaction

INTRODUCTION
Commercially available cars such as the Tesla Model S and the Volvo XC90 now feature advanced driving assistance and semi-autonomous driving functions, with tens of thousands of these cars being driven on roads worldwide. Along with the controlled tests of fully autonomous cars by organisations like Tesla, Delphi, and Google, we are in the midst of a large scale field-test of an unfamiliar new technology. While fully autonomous test cars have driven several million miles on American roads [28], this is dwarfed by the 140 million miles driven worldwide by Tesla's autopilot [53].

While there is growing commercial activity in this area, there is little published research available on how these new cars are interacting with their own drivers, other road users, and the road environment. In this paper we use interaction analysis to study recordings of self-driving cars, obtained from the YouTube video sharing website. These 'in the wild' videos, made by drivers and passengers, offer a distinctive early perspective on how assisted and autonomous driving is developing on the road and being responded to by other road users. We focus here on recordings of Tesla's 'Autopilot' alongside a smaller set of recordings of Google's self-driving car. The videos offer insights into how they mainly match but also at times disturb driver expectations by manoeuvring rudely or at risk.

CHI 2017, May 06-11, 2017, Denver, CO, USA
 ISBN 978-1-4503-4655-9/17/05...$15.00
DOI: http://dx.doi.org/10.1145/3025453.3025462

We pursue the notion of 'co-driving' where cars take over some functions of driving but rely upon monitoring work done by their human drivers, who intervene should the autopilot, for instance, mis-recognise interpret a road situation. All assisted and autonomous car systems are currently at this level–requiring human intervention in particular road situations. Consequently, we are interested in the interaction between driver and system, but also how these systems interact with *other* drivers. The road is a social space. For human and drivers, each movement of a car is not only functional but communicative [29,39,40,55]. Small changes (or absence of changes) in speed, direction and so on, communicate not only driver intent but also their mood and character (e.g., aggressive, hesitant, unpredictable, selfish).

Recordings made by both drivers of autonomous cars and from the perspective of other road users, pick out what they have identified as "autonomous troubles" [10]. While poorly fashioned movements by self-driving cars make visible the limitations of current driving systems, they also reveal aspects of co-driving that call for specific new design responses. This paper outlines the 'envelope of interaction' in and around self-driving cars: how interactions between cars, drivers and new systems play out, and the opportunities to make those interactions work better. Co-driving presents new challenges and opportunities for design research to shape how cars of the future will be encountered by, drive and be driven by humans.

BACKGROUND
While limited assisted and autonomous driving functions (such as cruise control [6]), have been commercially available in cars since at least the early 1970s, research at Carnegie Mellon in the 1980s pioneered autonomous driving in the form of the Navlab research vehicles [71]–vehicles which could manoeuvre and reason about their environment as they drove around it. In recent years, interest in

autonomous driving has exploded as commercial system capabilities have increased, most notably with advances in computer vision [25], and the success of research prototypes such as the Google self-driving car [26,53]. This has resulted in massive industrial investment into autonomous car research [7].

One clear impetus for industry was the DARPA challenge – a series of DARPA run self-driving car competitions. Fletcher et al [24], dissected a number of "crash" events occurring during that challenge. More recent work has engaged with problems such as challenges in image recognition [23], speed of execution, the role of machine learning in understanding road terrain [72], as well as discussions of the socio-economic impacts and challenges these systems provoke [45]. It is important to note that while there has been impressive progress [44], significant challenges remain on basic tasks–such as using vision to locate a car [11]. Moreover, 'difficult' driving conditions such as police intervention, bad weather conditions, sun glare, even turning left through traffic [43] present significant unsolved problems.

Autonomous vs. assisted driving

The NHTSA classification differentiates different levels of autonomous driving [47])–with levels 1-3 listing different forms of assisted driving (where a human must still monitor the driving and intervene if need be). At Level 4 cars are classified as 'fully autonomous' and can operate unmanned.

Much of the data we examine here involves drivers making use of the Tesla autopilot. There are three main Tesla autopilot functions. First, an adaptive cruise control that relies on distance to the car in front to accelerate and decelerate the car, an auto-steer function that uses road markings and if that fails, uses the car in front, to stay in its lane. In addition, there is an assisted lane-change function, where the driver can use the indicator stalk and, if it is safe, the autopilot will move the car into a parallel lane. The Tesla displays 'what the system has seen' in a display in the centre of the instrument screen, showing vehicles on the road in-front of the car and road markings detected by the camera. These functions sit at level 2 of the NHTSA classification as driver *assistance*. Indeed, the Tesla frequently disengages and gives control back to the driver. In a challenging test of the Tesla, "Car and driver" magazine found that the Tesla required manual intervention 29 times over a 50-mile route in mixed highway, city and rural driving [66] (it should be added that this was far superior to the other cars tested).

The Google Car more squarely fits with NHTSA description of an autonomous car (level 3), in that it is designed to travel and manoeuver autonomously through the environment, making decisions about where to go, and how to navigate with other drivers on the road. The Google Car drives around areas that Google has carefully mapped (some of it using the same Google Car). However, the Google car is still level 3 because human monitoring is required. An indication of the reliability of the software is given by reports by Google to the Californian Department of Motor Vehicles concerning "disengagements" (where either the human takes over or the car itself hands over to the driver). In 2015, the Google Car generated roughly one disengagement per 3,000 miles of autonomous driving. By comparison the human accident rate is around one crash per half a million miles [8]. While very few of these disengagements have led to accidents, a pessimistic reading is that even the Google Car, in a mapped and relatively simple road environment, is not yet equal to a human driver. This suggestion is supported by reports from Google, for example, that there are still challenges in fundamentals, such as detecting traffic lights [23,61].

Human robot interaction

Given the move toward autonomy in movement, one resource for thinking about human interaction with self-driving cars is the human-robot-interaction community [27]. Human responses to the design and movement of different robots has been extensively investigated [33,42,51,62]. For example, Alač's [3] work on children interacting with educational robots, used video analysis to understand how children differentiate between robots, toys and other humans. Alač discusses how robots move from being seen as static objects, to being perceived as 'agents'–objects that have a reactive logic to their movements. Yet there is the potential of robots going further and being perceived as social, engaging in the world of humans, with some limited access to the situation [69, 46].

Transport safety

A second academic field with direct interest in autonomous functioning in transport systems is that of transport safety–a field that has shaped (and perhaps dominated) much of our understanding of the driving task and opportunities for automation (e.g. [2,67]). Drawing on experience with aircraft, autopilot researchers have become increasingly concerned by potential safety shortcomings that increased autonomy and de-skilling of drivers could create [12]. In aircraft, the autopilot has been associated with lowered awareness of the situation, over-dependence on automated features and simple lack of practice in manoeuvring the vehicle [20]. This research highlights that automating certain system functions may not necessarily result in safer vehicles. Within HCI, a number of workshops have discussed [48,49] issues around autonomous cars, alongside research on topics such as the transition between driver and system [41] and the 'ironies of automation' [5] in that automation may lead to less effective systems overall as automatic systems often do not make problems apparent until too late [47].

Mobility

A third body of literature of use in understanding the consequences of assisted and autonomous driving is social scientific work on road mobility [15,65]. The key issue raised by this work is that the road is a setting which is not only socially organised [29] but, is sometimes sociable [35,36], and almost constantly risks becoming an anti-social environment. Jack Katz's [37] study of road rage underlined how most drivers are highly sensitive to the actions of other drivers. Driving together in traffic is, then, a collective practice, particularly susceptible to disruption by actions that appear not to follow, maintain or repair its moral order [16,39,50,52].

METHODS

Online collections of third party video provide a rarely tapped source of data on interaction and technology-use across an array of settings, particularly around the use of new technologies (e.g. unboxing new products, tutorials, trials etc.). YouTube now forms the world's largest repository of third party video, though care should be exercised over how its videos are searched for, organised and re-used [38]. Several researchers in CHI have already used YouTube data [9,32]. In the social sciences, YouTube data fits well with established conventions of using secondary data and connects with recent initiatives in large scale qualitative datasets.

Third party recordings are a rapid method for providing first person perspectives of early adopters and user reports of general issues which can then invoke more detailed experimental or ethnographic work. In some cases, third parties provide access to events which planned data collection would find almost impossible to capture (in our case, certain drop-outs and near-misses on the road). Third party video collected from online sources has been used previously to study policing practices [34], intergenerational communication [30], argumentative communication [60] and mobile device use [9,32]. Using third party data does mean a loss of control compared to methods such as equipping drivers with cameras (e.g. [10]) but does have advantages in terms of scope, access and availability.

For this study, we collected 10.5 hours of video from YouTube. There are 69 clips come from 63 individual up-loaders from UK, USA, Germany, France, Sweden, Hong Kong, Iceland and Canada. The clips are, on average, 9 minutes long, some are very much longer–7 of our clips were over 30 minutes long. The clips were selected for their depiction of uncut footage of driving under the control of an assisted or autonomous driving system. We used a range of search terms to collect videos of the Tesla 'autopilot', the Google Car, and other videos of driving assistance in use. We discarded news reports, or commercially produced material and sought 'naturalistic' videos of cars being driven. These car journeys were recorded by drivers using in-car dash-cams and similar set-ups to those used by professional researchers. In one case an uploader recorded trips using no less than 8 cameras to capture different perspectives in and around his car (Figure 4). In contrast, about one third (26) of the clips were recorded using a single mobile phone. Together these videos contain a mix of commentaries, comic moments (e.g., friends being shocked by the Tesla acceleration), reviews, travelogues and long stretches of silent driving. While the shorter clips are dominated by performances for the camera, this is not the case in the longer clips. The 'performed' driving was itself useful given much of it has equivalences with common data collection procedures used by CHI researchers such as 'think-alouds' and interviewee responses. The majority of the videos contained Tesla self-driving functionality; although we also found two clips of the Volvo XC90, and one of a Honda Civic which both have similar 'pilot assist' functionality. In terms of the Google Car we found a smaller corpus of 11 minutes from 9 clips, along with clips from a Google SXSW presentation of the Google Car, notable for including six video clips of 'interesting incidents' involving the Google Car.

For our analysis, clips were downloaded broken into smaller fragments which were tagged with keywords and transcribed. The fragments were analysed in group data sessions. The analysis focused on looking for examples of other drivers reacting to autonymous functions, on road 'troubles', driver interventions and interactions between the car and other drivers. In further individual and group data analysis sessions we surveyed the clips, editing the video down to 93 short (around one minute) edited clips for focused analysis, of which we then selected 34 clips for detailed analysis. Our analytic approach builds on earlier analyses of how drivers co-ordinate and manage their driving with each other [10,29,40,50] and on Watson's [73] studies of specialized forms of driving.

ETHICS

While nearly all of our clips make use of dash-cameras, around a fifth of the recordings appear to have been made by drivers holding their phone while they drive. While a 'new' technology (like the Tesla) is interesting to many YouTube viewers, the desire to record can encourage drivers to film in less than safe conditions. While we did not gather the data, we have concerns over drivers driving unsafely to produce recordings. A related concern is that the clips that we have analysed often feature driving outside the guidelines issued by Tesla about the use of their function, such as using the Autopilot on non-divided roads. As researchers, however, we would argue that examining and presenting this data alongside 'safe' practice is important in order to understand driving as it is actually occurring [10].

FINDINGS

As mentioned above, our goal in looking at these videos is to begin outlining the new 'envelope of interaction' surrounding self-driving cars, and thereby to understand how the interactions of both drivers and other road users are developing as autonomous cars become more prevalent.

Our results span two aspects of autonomous driving. First we discuss the role that assisted driving plays in reshaping driving practice, and in particular the development of 'co-driving' which is a form of involvement of both driver and autopilot. We examine how drivers adapt their driving to take advantage of the features and limitations of their car's new systems. Second, we look at the relationship between the autopilot and other road users and a selection of the problems that arise through the lack of accountability and understanding that autonomous and assisted cars communicate.

Driving with the autopilot

An initial striking feature of many of the videos is that they show cars being manoeuvred with no hands on the steering wheel. Indeed, some of our drivers start their clips with a slow passing of the hand around the wheel, reminiscent of a magician's 'look no hands' gesture. However, assisted driving is certainly not completely 'hands free'. Drivers monitor their car because they have experienced it making unpredictable and potentially dangerous movements, as well as dropping control in more predictable ways:

''The first time it went through this road it would lurch. I had to grab the steering wheel and it was like, every one, I had to be ready. Eventually I could keep auto-steer on and I would hold the steering wheel. Sometimes it would deactivate because it really wanted to get off and sometimes it wouldn't. [...] I am still ready to take over. Here comes another ''Do I take it no I don't take it''. I'm not sure that the exact voice autopilot thinks in but it's probably close. Ehm. See it learnt [images] Oh there. It was a pretty big lurch. That wasn't me at all. So it lurched over but then it corrected itself, so apparently it doesn't know that one very well''

Figure 1: Lurching (arrow indicates brief shift in direction) (source Tesla EVangelist)

Monitoring 'lurches' and lines on the dashboard display

Figure 1 offers an example of the Tesla autopilot driving on the road. Here a driver is reporting at some length on how the autopilot 'thinks' – describing 'lurches' it makes when it drives past different exit lanes it is unsure about. Since the autopilot has in the past moved toward exiting, the driver is now prepared to intervene, having learnt to detect the autopilot's exit-move at its first initiation, and thus being ready to force the car to stay in the correct lane. This first clip demonstrates how the autopilot requires a level of monitoring about what will happen next. Indeed, in this clip the driver also goes on to discuss the 'higher level' functions of the autopilot where the system 'learns' over time, so as to not take unwanted highway exits. The discussion shows not only that the driver is monitoring his car as it drives, but also that he is understanding it through its movements on the road system. Through those moves he is learning about how it learns, and how it makes some of its decisions in relation to the road's features.

''Oh. it exited me I didn't want to exit. [...] It made a mistake''

Figure 2: Disappearing lane markings & exiting (source tuan)

Part of co-driving with the autopilot is anticipating or noticing situations where it will make mistakes. In Figure 2 the autopilot followed the edge-markings of an exit lane as a continuation of the current lane and the car exits the highway incorrectly. The edge-markings it is following are displayed on the dashboard and disappear when it cannot track them (see figure 2). The driver is left to exclaim that the car 'exited me', and 'I didn't want to exit'. Failing to notice and correct the autopilot's misrecognitionmis-interpretation, visible on the dashboard, then leads to taking the wrong exit, with all the potential navigational troubles this involves.

Drivers learn to co-drive and intervene in order to prevent common autopilot mistakes, e.g. grabbing the steering wheel when the car lurches as in and/or follows a line or vehicle in error (as in fig. 1 and 2). Co-driving with an autopilot thus includes monitoring the movement of the car and watching the dashboard for instances when the autopilot has 'lost its way'

Dealing with 'troubles'

Drivers learn how much monitoring the autopilot needs, and adopt expectations for situations that lead to autopilot error. In our earlier work [10] we discussed how GPS does not make drivers 'docile', instead drivers incorporate new technology into their driving: watching for mistakes and/or trying to decode the 'troubles' that an imperfect technology creates in a real world context. Likewise, drivers of the Tesla adapt their analyses of the road situation. They develop an understanding of how the autopilot is sensing the road, and, correspondingly, the autopilot's capacities and limitations. In the videos, drivers discuss how they have become aware of the features of the road that lead to problems for the autopilot (such as sunshine, blind summits, blind corners). Similar to other forms of specialised driving (e.g. driving in forests, rally driving) autopilot drivers acquire a sensitivity to what features of the road are 'dangerous' in relation to the autopilot, even though they would cause minimal challenges to a typical human driver.

This awareness of autopilot capacities and incapacities produces distinct 'co-driving' practices (cf. [58]) that can also be seen in how drivers use the controls available to the driver while in autopilot. In particular, the autopilot allows drivers to set a 'target speed' which it will attempt to accelerate toward. While it is capped at the speed limit plus 10 mph, we observed drivers changing the target speed according to an assessment of the local road conditions. So, for example in Figure 3 a driver slows down the car as they approach a corner. Drivers also adjusted their speed to control overtaking behaviour such as when approaching hazards (e.g. tunnels & bridges) or tight curves in the road.

''Around this corner I'm going to slow down the cruise control cause it's a blind corner''

Figure 3: adjusting speed on corner (source Mark Jackson)

Figure 4: overtaking manoeuvre delayed until motorcycle passes (source Furious S8)

Drivers monitored the road and traffic to time their overtaking manoeuvres. In the Tesla, the driver can initiate a semi-automatic lane change by selecting the car's indicator lever. In Figure 4, for example, one driver overtakes two trucks and, just as he is about to return to the right lane, a motorcycle appears and overtakes the car on the inside. The driver holds their hand at the indicator, only flicking it, once the motorcycle passed the car. Waiting on the motorbike demonstrates a form of driving that is sensitive to the abilities of the autopilot, as well as remaining engaged with the environment.

Appropriating the autopilot

Co-driving is reminiscent of Suchman's description of 'human machine reconfigurations' [68] where both the driver, and the car jointly produce driving – a joint action that is accentuated rather than eliminated by the autopilot. Drivers discussed different expectations about driving, about what the autopilot can 'learn', and what situations are suitable or not for using the self-driving features. One driver discussed how the car can conduct the stop-go driving required in a slow-moving traffic queue:

''An interesting use for autopilot that I've found is if you're waiting at a long wait for the four-way stop sign […] autopilot will just keep an eye on the car for you and do stop and go until it's your turn. Just remember when you finally approach the stop sign the car will just continue to follow the one behind it. At this current version of software 7.1 the car will not stop or see stop signs […] please, please, exercise caution. […] I will demonstrate. The car in front of me goes, now my car will continue to go, but since there's nobody in front of me, I will take control.''

By selecting the autopilot, he had found that it could undertake part of the repetitive tasks of queuing. Yet, as this user is also aware, the autopilot edges the car forward by piggybacking on the car-in-front's stopping and starting (which, of course, is also piggybacking on the next car-in-front). Consequently, he stresses the need to take over from the autopilot when it reaches the intersection.

Tesla advises drivers to only use autopilot when a car is moving on a highway, with the autopilot maintaining speed. Yet, here, the driver demonstrates how he has discovered another use, deploying it at queued stop-intersections. While the autopilot can "stop and go", the driver makes further sense of the queue with their greater awareness of the situation [68], taking over the car when it becomes necessary, "Since there's nobody in front of me I will take control." Other drivers in our collection remarked upon (and demonstrated) the autopilot queuing at controlled stops (such as traffic lights), by simply following the movements of the car in front. In many cases, then, autopilot can undertake otherwise dull driving tasks–with supervision.

Driving safely

As one of the first cars on the road with advanced autonomous features, the safety of the Tesla has generated considerable media attention. In particular, a dispute between Mobileye (who make image recognition software for assisted driving) and Tesla arose following a fatal accident involving a Tesla that failed to recognise a car with a trailer crossing its path. Tesla claimed that the autopilot was safer than human highway driving, while Mobileye commented on the danger of "consumer and regulatory confusion [resulting in] mistrust that puts in jeopardy technological advances that can save lives[1]." Clearly there is dispute even amongst manufacturers about the appropriate situations for safe autopilot use.

The Tesla car has extra safety features, such as auto-brake, that can engage during ordinary non-autopilot supported driving to prevent accidents. One clip in our corpus involves a Tesla driving at night, where a car drives suddenly across the lane in front of the Tesla, with the car automatically and suddenly braking safely. Yet, these features are by no means perfect. In a contrasting clip, the Tesla creeps along a highway at a slow speed approaching a stationary truck and trailer which are partially positioned on the hard shoulder. The stationary truck is not detected either by the autopilot (which should slow down), or the emergency braking system. The Tesla collides with the trailer, fortunately at a low speed. The problem appears to be one of differentiating between objects in, and not, in the car's path. Trailers seem to cause particular problems for the Tesla's visual system at this point.

Indeed, many of the safety-related videos in our corpus feature 'drop outs' from autopilot control where the car occupants are put in danger. These videos are given dramatic titles; "auto pilot auto steer almost crash", "Tesla Auto Pilot fail!", "Tesla Autopilot tried to kill me!" (Figure 5).

Image 1. *Autopilot on, sun glare on camera*
Image 2. *Autopilot alarm starts*
Image 3. *Car veers suddenly left into lane of approaching car.*
Image 4. *Driver grabs wheel and turns quickly right, ''Whooo-a''*

Figure 5: "Tesla Autopilot tried to kill me!" (source RockTreeStar)

In Figure 5, a Tesla driver documented a near miss with oncoming vehicles when the autopilot drops out due to sun glare. The seriousness of the failures underlines the problem of drivers establishing and understanding the situated dangers of autopilot use and becoming attuned to those settings where the autopilot will struggle. As we have noted earlier in the paper, many drivers are learning how to co-drive with autopilots and which elements of the labour of driving they can delegate to the autopilot.

The autopilot and other drivers on the road

So far, we have examined the relationship between autopilot and the car's driver. In this section we move on to the relationship the autopilot has with *other* drivers. It is here that the 'communicative' aspects of car movement become all the more significant given that the autopilot is analysing the movement of vehicles which communicate the intended-actions of those other drivers, and those other drivers are also analysing the movement of cars controlled by autopilot as communicating their intended-actions.

Offers and rejections

Much of the Tesla's autopilot driving passes without incident, with the car remaining in lane correctly, and with cars moving around it. In our corpus there are nevertheless occasions when the Tesla causes 'troubles' in traffic. One aspect of watching the autopilot make its way through traffic is that, like many AI systems before it, it lacks equal access to other drivers' intended-actions. For example, in Figure 6, the autopilot changes lane causing minor troubles for the car behind. The move is initiated by driver using the indicator lever to issue the command to move to the left lane (which also activates the flashing indicator). The driver's action itself is in response to his noticing a white truck trying to merge onto the highway from a slip-road. The episode, then, starts with a demonstration of what "good" driving is - the graciousness of letting drivers in from a slip road.

In the moments that these first actions take to unfold (and as is typical for heavy traffic) a silver car approaches from behind, in the desired lane to the Tesla's left. The accelerating car, however, on seeing the indicator flashing on the Tesla, stops accelerating – leaving a space on the road and thereby making an 'offer' of a gap to the Tesla (Figure 6, Image 1). From the silver car's perspective, the Tesla appears not to be taking the offer (it makes no change in trajectory). The absence of response leads the silver car to remove its offer by starting to close the gap. At the last minute the Tesla moves across into the lane and 'cuts the car up' (Image 2). In the clip then while the driver has been considerate toward one driver, the autopilot has potentially upset another in the next moment. The action produced by the autopilot's robotic coordination might not 'bother' another autopilot, but is recognisable by a human driver as rude. The driver of the Tesla also notices this, '*well* we pulled in ahead of that guy [...] ', his "well" preface marking the trouble he's about to report.

[1] http://www.mobileye.com/press-room/mobileye-responds-to-false-allegations/

''Well… we pulled in ahead of that guy and from what I saw it wasn't something he was exactly encouraging''

Figure 6: Ignoring the offer (Source: Garth Woodworth)

With its limited access to the traffic situation, the autopilot could not, of course, be expected to recognise the offer as considerate and its delay as marking that it declined an offer and its subsequent abrupt lane shift potentially upsetting the silver car. Our point rather is that the 'rudeness' of the autopilot demonstrates that driving involves norms of mobile conduct with others. Autopilots have been introduced into a social situation, and while at times they can produce safe and reliable driving, they also at times can fail to recognise and display normative features of driving in traffic, e.g. making and accepting offers. This is not to say that human drivers are consistently aware of other drivers but, at their best, they produce movements that are not merely agented–responsive to conditions to satisfy goals–they are *social*, responsive to a background knowledge of what manoeuvres are thoughtless, polite, safe in traffic.

Analysing what just this gap could mean

Related to autopilots not being able to access what fellow members of traffic are up to, they then have limited access to how their own movements on the road are being taken up by other drivers. For an example of failing to understand what a particular spatial arrangement potentially means, we can pass over to the Google Car–and a clip extracted from a talk by the principle engineer of the Google Car (Chris Urmson). In an overview talk he outlines how the car must cope not only with the routine but also the exceptional acts of other drivers on the road.**Error! Reference source not found.**

Figure 7 shows both a representation of the autopilot's model of the situation and the view from the rear of two Google cars travelling together. Another car comes out of an exit on the left, crosses across two lanes and wedges itself orthogonally to the traffic flow, in a space between two self-driving cars. The narrator uses the driver as an example of eccentric driving practices–"people who do, I do not know what". Yet the narrator is forgetting that other drivers do not see two Google cars travelling in a convoy. They see a second car make a noticeably slow approach to the car in front, projecting. Moreover, while approaching slowly, the second car is also leaving a large gap between it and the car in-front. A gap that is straight ahead of the car that is stuck in a yard. It appears to then be potentially offering a way out for the stuck car. In fact, the Google Car does deal with the car's acceptance appropriately, by stopping leaving sufficient space for sideways car.

''And of course we have people who do, I do not know what sometimes on the road. Like this guy [image] pulling out between two self-driving cars. (laughter) You have to ask what are you thinking''

Figure 7: Seeing the gap (source: SXSW)

Gaps between cars (such as that between the two Google Cars) are not just 'safe/unsafe' distances on the road, but are used in displaying attitudes, maintaining norms and so on. Moving quickly to form a minimal gap with a car in front can be seen by other drivers as 'denying' any requests to merge or move through the gap. In this case, by contrast, slowly driving forward and leaving a gap, the second Google Car appears to have been recruited to help the stuck car. While the clip's narrator formulates the other driver's move as obscure and perhaps dangerous, to us the situation is recognisable as the give and take encountered on busy roads. Drivers frequently push into gaps where they can find them, and 'bend' traffic laws (such as turning left and crossing the highway margin). Congested traffic in complex road layouts rely on driver generosity, negotiation, compromises, fiat, bullying and more.

The 'trouble' that the Google Car's deceleration and inter-car vehicle spacing occasionally produces also occurs with Tesla's autopilot, in that it also leaves 'gap' which are not attuned to local social circumstances. In our collection the 'gap' is frequently taken by other drivers, resulting in the autopilot slowing down and pulling back to create the same space, into which other cars then drive. Local judgements are required because while good driving mandates that one leaves a sufficient space in front of one's car (for braking distance), in congested traffic situations drivers typically leave less inter-vehicle space, and, as we have seen, depending on the timing and spacing of its appearance, other drivers make inferences about the gaps as offers, opportunities, refusals or avoidance.

For example, in one clip from our collection, an autopilot approached an entry ramp on the highway, and 'allowed' a car onto the highway in front. Of course, the car was not 'allowing', but simply because of its slower speed it left a 'gap' which was visible to the merging driver as an opportunity. The gap itself was tight and the merging driver hesitated slightly before moving to take it. The merging driver quickly moving into the next lane as soon as it was clear. Maintaining a one car gap with the car in front 'offers' a space to other drivers, but since the gap is not an offer to the autopilot (just a gap to be maintained) the 'offer' is not then adjusted by the autopilot on recognizing it as being 'taken'.

Figure 8: Near miss as two lanes merge (source: Garth Woodworth)

Accountability: Driving as if other people are watching

A concept that we draw on to understand vehicle movement in traffic is *accountability*. In common use accountability is often equated with responsibility, in ethnomethodology accountability is taken to be deeply engrained in interaction: human actions are produced with an orientation toward their observable-reportable character. We assume that each party can witness one another's action as those actions and call them to account for them. Accountable activities become important in road traffic because vehicles use shared mobile methods which make their actions observable to other vehicles, and their accountability is reflexively tied to each emerging traffic situation. Failing to recognise what other drivers are doing can produce not only rude, but also dangerous driving, especially when other drivers expect their movements to be understood [36]. In Figure 8, a Tesla on autopilot approaches two lanes that are about to merge into one. Before the lanes merge a truck quickly overtakes in the 'fast' lane (Image 1) while the autopilot holds its speed at 90 km/h (the speed limit+10km). During the section where the lanes are merging, a second car accelerates up in the fast lane, also attempting to overtake in front of the Tesla (Image 2). Yet, the autopilot maintains its speed–is slower than the overtaking car (allowing it to overtake), but it does not fall back in the rapidly narrowing road (Image 3). The other drivers expect the Tesla, because it is in the lane being merged to defer to the cars continuing lane. The autopilot mechanically maintains the set speed and trajectory, only narrowly avoiding clipping the overtaking car. The Tesla fails to recognise where it ought to decelerate in order to defer. Our point, again, is not the failings of the autopilot as such (the operations are outside of its designed specifications), but that vehicles make local judgements on which car should progress and which should defer. In this case the car is making an accountable dash to go in front of the Tesla before the road narrows to a single lane. Yet the projected action is not taken into account by the autopilot, and moreover, the autopilot cannot grasp that its own failure to close the gap behind the truck is indicating that it is going to 'let the other car in'.

As a driver, one's movements in traffic on the road are *accountable* to others – they are monitored by others. They are treated as first, having a local history, second, in their course and, third, as indications of future intent. They are treated as (mostly) responsive to the ongoing actions of fellow members of traffic. Autopilots do not share the same sense of accountability and that is part of the troubles they raise for other members of traffic.

Hesitation and creeping

Last, let us look at a traffic situation where precise timing and small movements are used by multiple drivers–driving through a four-way stop-intersection. In Figure 9, a driver with a dash-cam (from which they regularly upload to YouTube) spots the Google Car and follows it. The Google Car stops at a four-way junction in a manner which looks appropriate given that cars are approaching from the sides. The Google Car begins to edge forward to take its turn but then brakes suddenly while still at the start of its manoeuvre. The car behind (from which the driver is recording the Google Car) also starts to move, but then also has to brake suddenly, when the Google Car breaks. Accidents at junctions like this are commonplace with novice or beginner drivers, because their hesitation at a junction is not anticipated by drivers behind. In this case, two cars go in front of the 'slot' the Google Car should have taken at the intersection, with the second 'late to junction car' driving onto the intersection after the Google Car is moving, causing it to suddenly brake when it sees that its path forward is blocked.

Figure 9: Google Car hesitates at a four-way junction (Source: The Dashcam Store)

Research on four-way stop-intersections has underlined the importance of 'creeping' into the intersection to reserve a turn [13,14]. The creeping acts to show that a driver is attentive to the situation, and that they are ready to precisely take their 'slot' on the four-way intersection. By *not* creeping the Google Car finds itself 'cut up' by a car that slows but then accelerates to cross the intersection. In this case, it is the *lack* of motion by the Google Car, at just that moment of the other car slowing, that is seen as hesitation, which then leaves the 'slot' to be taken by that other driver. Naturally programmed to drive safely the Google Car frequently appears to other drivers as a hesitant and slow driver. In other clips, we saw similar cut-ups and drivers tailgate the Google Car to 'push' it through junctions (e.g., in Figure 8).

DISCUSSION

Our goal here has not been to review the current generation of autonomous vehicles and driver assistance systems, they are changing rapidly and require careful consideration by researchers with the relevant technical expertise. Rather, taking inspiration from earlier reflections on AI [18,19], we have examined what happens when AI meets the complex social, embodied world of driving in traffic, and hinted at the challenges of designing autonomous vehicles for this world. In our discussion we focus on three issues. The first concern how drivers will have to remain engaged with autopilots, though in new ways that will reconfigure how driving is accomplished. The second engages with the transparency of autopilot actions and designing for the accountability of its activities to drivers inside and outside the car. The third turns to the importance for sense-making of pre-actions and considers the troubles raised by total transparency.

Engaging with assistance

In an earlier paper [10] we documented the troubles raised by GPS navigation systems for drivers. Given that driving assistance systems rely, to greater or lesser degrees, on navigation systems, our earlier arguments have renewed relevance. 'Natural normal troubles' of GPS use arose that needed to be dealt with as part of wayfinding. For the drivers we observed, successful navigation involved 'active driving'–listening and judging the GPS's instructions. Similarly, the co-driving we have described here depended upon the active engagement of a driver. The assisted driving systems often made minor mistakes, suffered drop-outs, or upset other drivers. Successful co-driving requires retained levels of engagement that vary with the situation. Emerging situations thus needed ongoing assessment by the driver as to whether the driver is likely to be called upon to intervene in an executive role.

Debates around the safety of assisted and autonomous driving seem only likely to intensify as the technology becomes both more common and more advanced [75]. Although piloting planes happens within a heavily regulated transport system we can still learn from the longer history of safety in that sector [1,56]. While autopilot use has made plane travel much safer, they heave created new troubles for commercial passenger plane pilots. For instance, when autopilot systems fail there is the danger of the 'startle' effect, where pilots that have not been involved in the situation lose valuable time in their initial panic and absence of understanding of what has led to an alarm. Designing for co-driving will require attention to how to keep drivers engaged, so that they are ready to return to driving when necessary. Designing for situated driver-assistance is far safer than designing for near-autonomy.

For other drivers on the road, the autopilot creates trouble in part because when assumed to be just another driver it behaves unexpectedly, leading to confusion and frustration. As we have described above, troubles in interaction with other drivers, such as unexpected lane changes, hesitations and losing a turn in traffic, emerge not from incompetent or faulty autonomous driving but rather vehicle movements that inadvertently communicate intended courses of action which are then not taken or a different action emerges than expected. While these troubles did not lead to accidents, they do lead to unnecessary disruption to traffic. One simple solution, which the current iteration of the Google Car has adopted by becoming a 'bubble car', is to be visible at-a-glance as a 'self-driving' vehicle. Obvious external markers shift other drivers' expectations of the predictably and meaning of a vehicle's actions.

Transparency and accountability

In discussions of algorithmic systems [21,59] more broadly, there have been calls for systems to be more *transparent* in showing their current state and ongoing processes. Notable here is Pasquale's critique of the lack of 'algorithmic transparency' in AI systems [57]. Recent work has, however, questioned whether systems, such as artificial neural networks, could ever be transparent in a form that humans could easily make sense of or, equally, that attempting to achieve transparency will make unrealistic demands on regulators or users [4]. Transparency is a problem for both the driver within a vehicle and other drivers outside of that vehicle. For the latter, a potential solution to the problem of transparency is to build on how car drivers already make their actions transparent to other drivers. Researchers at Nissan have explored how autopilots could show recognition of the acts of other road users through extensions on the car indicator [14] thereby building on existing signalling system for communicating with other drivers.

From the findings in this paper our suggestion is that for both the driver inside the car and for other cars, the movements of the vehicle made by the autopilot should be designed with an understanding of how those movements will be understood by both the driver and by other vehicles involved in emergent situations. Cars would then make movements not just as a by-product of travelling towards their destination, but as a central part of how they communicate. Small movements can show that they have, noticed another vehicle, are ready to take their slot, or, are denying a slot to another driver.

What would drawing on existing embodied communicative practices by drivers mean in practice? Rather than attempting to offer visualizations of its state, the autopilot would–through its motions and related actions–demonstrate what it is doing to others. So, for example, when merging into traffic an autopilot will turn the car slightly to direct it towards a parallel car in order to indicate the intention to enter in front of that car. This movement is followed by a wait for a response from the other driver, and if one is not forthcoming an autopilot then decelerates to enter behind that car (see figure 8). Developing these movement protocols for autopilots requires an explicit focus, then, on current communicative practices of vehicles in traffic. In other words, building for transparency asks us to look back to early CSCW discussions where the notion of accountability prioritised designing systems which produce accounts that are useful as resources for users from without (driving in traffic) rather than within (AI states & processes) [17].

The social road

Work on multi-agent models for autonomous vehicles has recently engaged with systems that discover features of different drivers [74,54], as well as understanding the effects that drivers' movements have on other road users. As Sadigh *et al* write, *"other drivers do not operate in isolation: an autonomous car's actions will actually have effects on what other drivers will do"[63]*. In this paper we have attempted to move these arguments further – to explore how thinking of the road as inherently social, as well as logistical, should influence the technologies we build. Here, we have only started to outline the ways in which drivers make sense of and make use of the actions of others.

One valuable resource is interactional work which has documented how numerous actions (such as offers, invitations and rejections etc.) are signalled before they are underway with "pre-actions" [64, chapter 4]. For example, when collaboration involves tools, the project-ability of a request is relied upon to support close collaboration [70]. Parties collaborating in a situation need to see in common what others will be doing next, so (for example) picking up a microphone can be seen as a "pre" to using that microphone to make an announcement [31, chapter 4]. In driving in traffic there are many actions that other drivers make that can be seen as 'pre' moves, moves that are available to other drivers. For example, in our discussion above of the Google Car at a stop intersection, 'creeping' acts as 'pre' to crossing the intersection.

An added social complexity, however, is that while driving is often cooperative it can also be competitive and conflictual. Consequently, making a driver's intentions transparent to others, on congested roads, will, at times, act against the interests of a driver. Katz [37] quotes a driver who explained that they never indicated when driving in LA, as that would just be 'giving information away to the enemy'. Accordingly, a completely transparent autopilot might end up being open to exploitation by ruthless and/or harried human drivers. So, for example, a self-driving car that avoids collisions by always slowing down could be safely 'cut up' by a human driver, because they can assume that the autonomous car will always stop. With all safety technologies, there is also the challenge of 'risk compensation' [22], where improved safety is adopted by drivers to then drive faster, or more aggressively. In terms of self-driving cars it may be that this 'risk compensation' will occur not only with those in the car being controlled, but also with other drivers who might take advantage of the cautiousness of the autonomous driving system.

CONCLUSION

In this paper we have documented the challenges that drivers with autopilots experience on real world roads. Outside of test environments autonomous cars are not things of wonder, but are just another car progressing through the social order of traffic. Using videos of autonomous and assisted cars selected from third party recordings we have engaged with both how HCI can help design better autopilots and the dangers that badly designed autopilots might create. Rather than assuming human drivers will disappear with the rise of autonomous vehicles we have shown instead how it is the nature of driving that is reconfigured through allowing the autopilot to undertake simple tasks as a co-pilot, with situated supervision.

REFERENCES

1. Airbus. Flight Operations Briefing Note: Standard Operating Procedures Optimum Use of Automation: FLT_OPS – SOP – SEQ 02 – REV 03 – JUL. 2006.
2. Motoyuki Akamatsu, Paul Green, and Klaus Bengler. 2013. Automotive Technology and Human Factors Research: Past, Present, and Future. *International Journal of Vehicular Technology* 2013: e526180. https://doi.org/10.1155/2013/526180
3. Morana Alač. 2015. Social robots: Things or agents? *AI & SOCIETY*: 31, 4, 519-535. https://doi:10.1007/s00146-015-0631-6
4. Mike Ananny and Kate Crawford. 2016. Seeing without knowing: Limitations of the transparency ideal and its application to algorithmic accountability. *New Media & Society* online first https://doi.org/10.1177/1461444816676645
5. Lisanne Bainbridge. 1983. Ironies of automation. *Automatica* 19, 6: 775–779.
6. K. Bengler, K. Dietmayer, B. Farber, M. Maurer, C. Stiller, and H. Winner. 2014. Three Decades of Driver Assistance Systems: Review and Future Perspectives. *IEEE Intelligent Transportation Systems Magazine* 6, 4: 6–22. https://doi.org/10.1109/MITS.2014.2336271
7. Mark Bergen. 2015. Meet the Companies Building Self-Driving Cars for Google and Tesla (And Maybe Apple). *Recode*. Retrieved September 20, 2016 from http://www.recode.net/2015/10/27/11620026/meet-the-companies-building-self-driving-cars-for-google-and-tesla
8. Kavi Bhalla and Dinesh Mohan. 2016. Understanding the road safety performance of OECD countries. In *Transport planning and traffic safety: making cities, roads, and vehicles safer*, Geetam Tiwari and Dinesh Mohan (eds.) CRC Press, UK, 1–15.
9. Mark Blythe and Paul Cairns. 2009. Critical Methods and User Generated Content: The iPhone on YouTube. In *Proceedings of the SIGCHI Conference on Human Factors in Computing Systems* (CHI '09), 1467–1476. https://doi.org/10.1145/1518701.1518923
10. Barry Brown and Eric Laurier. 2012. The Normal Natural Troubles of Driving with GPS. In *Proceedings of the SIGCHI Conference on Human Factors in Computing Systems* (CHI '12), 1621–1630. https://doi.org/10.1145/2207676.2208285
11. Cesar Cadena, Luca Carlone, Henry Carrillo, Yasir Latif, Davide Scaramuzza, Jose Neira, Ian D. Reid, and John J. Leonard. 2016. Simultaneous Localization And Mapping: Present, Future, and the Robust-Perception Age. *arXiv preprint arXiv:1606.05830*. Retrieved September 20, 2016 from http://arxiv.org/abs/1606.05830
12. Stephen M. Casner, Edwin L. Hutchins, and Don Norman. 2016. The challenges of partially automated driving. *Communications of the ACM* 59, 5: 70–77.
13. Melisa Cefkin and Erik Vinkhuyzen. 2016. Developing Socially Acceptable Autonomous Vehicles. *Ethnographic Praxis in Industry Conference Proceedings*, p. 522–534 https://www.epicpeople.org
14. Melissa Cefkin. 2016. Human-Machine Interactions and the Coming Age of Autonomy | Platypus. *Platypus: the castac blog*. Retrieved September 20, 2016 from http://blog.castac.org/2016/01/age-of-autonomy/
15. Tim Dant. 2004. The driver-car. *Theory, Culture & Society* 21, 4–5: 61–79.
16. Elwys De Stefani. 2015. Formulating instructions. First actions in driving lessons. Retrieved September 20, 2016 from https://lirias.kuleuven.be/handle/123456789/533703
17. Paul Dourish. 1997. Accounting for system behaviour: Representation, reflection and resourceful action. *Computers and Design in Context, MIT Press, Cambridge, MA, USA*: 145–170.
18. Hubert Dreyfus, Stuart E. Dreyfus, and Tom Athanasiou. 2000. *Mind over machine*. Simon and Schuster. Retrieved September 20, 2016 from https://www.google.com/books?hl=en&lr=&id=e9W9m_4q4pYC&oi=fnd&pg=PR9&dq=mind+over+machine&ots=FiOEE8W6O2&sig=LkUriFSZzKIYLpgAn5cqkva2NJs
19. Hubert L. Dreyfus. 1992. *What computers still can't do: a critique of artificial reason*. MIT press. Retrieved September 20, 2016 from http://books.google.com/books?hl=en&lr=&id=7vS2y-mQmpAC&oi=fnd&pg=PR9&dq=info:tDOnc5P0VbAJ:scholar.google.com&ots=1U2dRHuvTz&sig=8YrnhoWEpclD-PdrCp3CzQtIfNY
20. Mica R. Endsley and Esin O. Kiris. 1995. The out-of-the-loop performance problem and level of control in automation. *Human Factors: The Journal of the Human Factors and Ergonomics Society* 37, 2: 381–394.
21. Motahhare Eslami, Aimee Rickman, Kristen Vaccaro, Amirhossein Aleyasen, Andy Vuong, Karrie Karahalios, Kevin Hamilton, and Christian Sandvig. 2015. I always assumed that I wasn't really that close to [her]: Reasoning about Invisible Algorithms in News Feeds. In *Proceedings of the 33rd Annual ACM Conference on Human Factors in Computing Systems*, 153–162. Retrieved December 21, 2016 from http://dl.acm.org/citation.cfm?id=2702556
22. William N. Evans and John D. Graham. 1991. Risk reduction or risk compensation? The case of mandatory safety-belt use laws. *Journal of Risk and Uncertainty* 4, 1: 61–73.
23. Nathaniel Fairfield and Chris Urmson. 2011. Traffic light mapping and detection. In *Robotics and Automation (ICRA), 2011 IEEE International Conference on*, 5421–5426. Retrieved September 20, 2016 from

http://ieeexplore.ieee.org/xpls/abs_all.jsp?arnumber=5980164

24. Luke Fletcher, Seth Teller, Edwin Olson, David Moore, Yoshiaki Kuwata, Jonathan How, John Leonard, Isaac Miller, Mark Campbell, Dan Huttenlocher, and others. 2008. The MIT–Cornell collision and why it happened. *Journal of Field Robotics* 25, 10: 775–807.
25. A. Geiger, P. Lenz, and R. Urtasun. 2012. Are we ready for autonomous driving? The KITTI vision benchmark suite. In *2012 IEEE Conference on Computer Vision and Pattern Recognition (CVPR)*, 3354–3361. https://doi.org/10.1109/CVPR.2012.6248074
26. Lee Gomes. 2014. Google's Self-Driving Cars Still Face Many Obstacles. *MIT Technology Review*. Retrieved September 20, 2016 from https://www.technologyreview.com/s/530276/hidden-obstacles-for-googles-self-driving-cars/
27. Michael A. Goodrich and Alan C. Schultz. 2007. Human-robot interaction: a survey. *Foundations and trends in human-computer interaction* 1, 3: 203–275.
28. Google. 2016. *Google Self-Driving Car Project Monthly Report August 2016*. Retrieved from https://static.googleusercontent.com/media/www.google.com/en//selfdrivingcar/files/reports/report-0816.pdf
29. Pentti Haddington. 2012. Movement in action: Initiating social navigation in cars. Retrieved September 20, 2016 from http://www.degruyter.com/view/j/sem.2012.2012.issue-191/sem-2012-0059/sem-2012-0059.xml
30. Dave Harley and Geraldine Fitzpatrick. 2009. YouTube and intergenerational communication: the case of Geriatric1927. *Universal access in the information society* 8, 1: 5–20.
31. Christian Heath and Paul Luff. 2000. *Technology in Action*. Cambridge University Press
32. Juan Pablo Hourcade, Sarah L. Mascher, David Wu, and Luiza Pantoja. 2015. Look, My Baby Is Using an iPad! An Analysis of YouTube Videos of Infants and Toddlers Using Tablets. In *Proceedings of the 33rd Annual ACM Conference on Human Factors in Computing Systems* (CHI '15), 1915–1924. https://doi.org/10.1145/2702123.2702266
33. Chien-Ming Huang and Bilge Mutlu. 2012. Robot behavior toolkit: generating effective social behaviors for robots. In *Proceedings of the seventh annual ACM/IEEE international conference on Human-Robot Interaction*, 25–32. Retrieved September 20, 2016 from http://dl.acm.org/citation.cfm?id=2157694
34. Nikki Jones and Geoffrey Raymond. 2012. "The Camera Rolls" Using Third-Party Video in Field Research. *The Annals of the American Academy of Political and Social Science* 642, 1: 109–123.
35. Oskar Juhlin. 2001. Traffic behaviour as social interaction - Implications for the design of artificial drivers. In *The Social Production of Technology : On the everyday life of things*, Hans Glimell and Oskar Juhlin (eds.). BAS, Goteburg, Sweden, 19–38.
36. Oskar Juhlin. 2010. *Social Media on the Road*. Springer
37. Jack Katz. 1999. *How Emotions Work*. Chicago University Press.
38. Eric Laurier. 2016. YouTube: fragments of a video-tropic atlas. *Area* 48, 4: 488-495
39. Eric Laurier, Barry Brown, and Hayden Lorimer. 2012. What it means to change lanes: actions, emotions and wayfinding in the family car. *Semiotica* 191, 1: 117-135.
40. Eric Laurier, Hayden Lorimer, Barry Brown, Owen Jones, Oskar Juhlin, Alison Noble, Mark Perry, David Pica, Paul Sormani, and Ignatz Strebel. 2008. Driving and "passengering": notes on the ordinary organization of car travel. *Mobilities* 3, 1: 1–23.
41. Key Jung Lee, Yeon Kyoung Joo, and Clifford Nass. 2014. Partially Intelligent Automobiles and Driving Experience at the Moment of System Transition. In *Proceedings of the SIGCHI Conference on Human Factors in Computing Systems* (CHI '14), 3631–3634. https://doi.org/10.1145/2556288.2557370
42. Iolanda Leite, Carlos Martinho, and Ana Paiva. 2013. Social robots for long-term interaction: a survey. *International Journal of Social Robotics* 5, 2: 291–308.
43. John Leonard. 2015. Mapping, Localization, and Self-Driving Vehicles. Retrieved from http://ilp.mit.edu/images/conferences/2016/ict/presentations/Leonard.2016.ICT.pdf
44. S. Lowry, N. Sünderhauf, P. Newman, J. J. Leonard, D. Cox, P. Corke, and M. J. Milford. 2016. Visual Place Recognition: A Survey. *IEEE Transactions on Robotics* 32, 1: 1–19. https://doi.org/10.1109/TRO.2015.2496823
45. Markus Maurer, J. Christian Gerdes, Barbara Lenz, and Hermann Winner. 2016. Autonomous driving: technical, legal and social aspects. Retrieved September 20, 2016 from http://dl.acm.org/citation.cfm?id=2965082
46. Ross Mead and Maja Mataric. 2016. Robots Have Needs Too: How and Why People Adapt Their Proxemic Behavior to Improve Robot Social Signal Understanding. *Journal of Human-Robot Interaction* 5, 2: 48–68.
47. Alexander Meschtscherjakov, Rod McCall, Nicolas Louveton, Thomas Engel, Manfred Tscheligi, and Vincent Koenig. 2015. MaDSAV: maintaining driving skills in semi-autonomous vehicles. In *Adjunct Proceedings of the 7th International Conference on Automotive User Interfaces and Interactive Vehicular Applications*, 136–139. Retrieved September 20, 2016 from http://dl.acm.org/citation.cfm?id=2809732
48. Alexander Meschtscherjakov, Manfred Tscheligi, Dalila Szostak, Sven Krome, Bastian Pfleging, Rabindra Ratan, Ioannis Politis, Sonia Baltodano, Dave Miller, and Wendy Ju. 2016. HCI and

Autonomous Vehicles: Contextual Experience Informs Design. In *Proceedings of the 2016 CHI Conference Extended Abstracts on Human Factors in Computing Systems* (CHI EA '16), 3542–3549. https://doi.org/10.1145/2851581.2856489

49. Alexander Meschtscherjakov, Manfred Tscheligi, Dalila Szostak, Rabindra Ratan, Roderick McCall, Ioannis Politis, and Sven Krome. 2015. Experiencing Autonomous Vehicles: Crossing the Boundaries Between a Drive and a Ride. In *Proceedings of the 33rd Annual ACM Conference Extended Abstracts on Human Factors in Computing Systems* (CHI EA '15), 2413–2416. https://doi.org/10.1145/2702613.2702661
50. Lorenza Mondada. 2012. Talking and driving: multi-activity in the car. *Semiotica* 2012, 191: 223–256.
51. Bilge Mutlu, Takayuki Kanda, Jodi Forlizzi, Jessica Hodgins, and Hiroshi Ishiguro. 2012. Conversational gaze mechanisms for humanlike robots. *ACM Transactions on Interactive Intelligent Systems (TiiS)* 1, 2: 12.
52. Maurice Nevile. 2012. Interaction as distraction in driving: A body of evidence. *Semiotica*, 191: 169–196.
53. Nick Statt. 2016. Tesla customers have driven 100 million miles with Autopilot active. *The Verge*. Retrieved from http://www.theverge.com/2016/5/24/11761098/tesla-autopilot-self-driving-cars-100-million-miles
54. J. Nilsson, J. Silvlin, M. Brannstrom, E. Coelingh, and J. Fredriksson. 2016. If, When, and How to Perform Lane Change Maneuvers on Highways. *IEEE Intelligent Transportation Systems Magazine* 8, 4: 68–78. https://doi.org/10.1109/MITS.2016.2565718
55. Don Norman. 1992. *Turn Signals Are the Facial Expressions of Automobiles*. Addison Wesley.
56. Raja Parasuraman and Victor Riley. 1997. Humans and automation: Use, misuse, disuse, abuse. *Human Factors: The Journal of the Human Factors and Ergonomics Society* 39, 2: 230–253.
57. Frank Pasquale. 2015. *The black box society: The secret algorithms that control money and information*. Harvard University Press.
58. E. Pollard, P. Morignot, and F. Nashashibi. 2013. An ontology-based model to determine the automation level of an automated vehicle for co-driving. In *2013 16th International Conference on Information Fusion (FUSION)*, 596–603.
59. Gary Pritchard, John Vines, Pam Briggs, Lisa Thomas, and Patrick Olivier. 2014. Digitally driven: how location based services impact the work practices of London bus drivers. *In Proceedings of the SIGCHI Conference on Human Factors in Computing Systems (CHI '14)*. ACM, New York, NY, USA, 3617-3626. http://dx.doi.org/10.1145/2556288.2557156.
60. Edward Reynolds. 2011. Enticing a challengeable in arguments: sequence, epistemics and preference organisation. *Pragmatics* 21, 3: 411–430.
61. Daniel Rosenband. 2016. Are we there yet? Silicon in self-driving cars. Retrieved from http://www.hotchips.org/video-for-keynote-2-are-we-there-yet-silicon-in-self-driving-cars-by-daniel-rosenband-of-google-available-to-all/
62. Selma Sabanovic, Marek P. Michalowski, and Reid Simmons. 2006. Robots in the wild: Observing human-robot social interaction outside the lab. In *9th IEEE International Workshop on Advanced Motion Control, 2006.*, 596–601. Retrieved September 20, 2016 from http://ieeexplore.ieee.org/xpls/abs_all.jsp?arnumber=1631758
63. Dorsa Sadigh, Shankar Sastry, Sanjit A. Seshia, and Anca D. Dragan. 2016. Planning for autonomous cars that leverages effects on human actions. In *Proceedings of the Robotics: Science and Systems Conference (RSS)*. Retrieved December 21, 2016 from https://pdfs.semanticscholar.org/e3e1/a23e0096f8ca51b783812310d44673a3c89a.pdf
64. Emanuel A. Schegloff. 2007. *Sequence organization in interaction: Volume 1: A primer in conversation analysis*. Cambridge University Press.
65. Mimi Sheller. 2007. Bodies, cybercars and the mundane incorporation of automated mobilities. *Social & Cultural Geography* 8, 2: 175–197.
66. Don Sherman. 2016. Semi-Autonomous Cars Compared! Tesla Model S vs. BMW 750i, Infiniti Q50S, and Mercedes-Benz S65 AMG - Feature. *Car and driver*. Retrieved September 20, 2016 from http://www.caranddriver.com/features/semi-autonomous-cars-compared-tesla-vs-bmw-mercedes-and-infiniti-feature
67. Neville A. Stanton and Philip Marsden. 1996. From fly-by-wire to drive-by-wire: Safety implications of automation in vehicles. *Safety Science* 24, 1: 35–49. https://doi.org/10.1016/S0925-7535(96)00067-7
68. Lucille Alice Suchman. 2007. *Human-machine reconfigurations: plans and situated actions*. Cambridge University Press.
69. Lucy Suchman. 1987. *Plans and situated actions: The problem of human-machine communication*. Cambridge University Press.
70. Marcus Sanchez Svensson, Christian Heath, and Paul Luff. 2007. Instrumental action: the timely exchange of implements during surgical operations. In *ECSCW 2007*. Springer, 41–60. Retrieved September 20, 2016 from http://link.springer.com/10.1007/978-1-84800-031-5_3
71. C. Thorpe, M. Herbert, T. Kanade, and S. Shafer. 1991. Toward autonomous driving: the CMU Navlab. I. Perception. *IEEE Expert* 6, 4: 31–42. https://doi.org/10.1109/64.85919
72. Sebastian Thrun, Michael Montemerlo, and Andrei Aron. Probabilistic Terrain Analysis For High-Speed Desert Driving. Retrieved September 20, 2016 from http://robots.stanford.edu/papers/thrun.mapping-Stanley.pdf

73. Rod Watson. 1999. Driving in forests and mountains: A pure and applied ethnography. *Ethnographic studies* 3: 50–60. https://doi.org/10.5449/idslu-001103654
74. Junqing Wei, John M. Dolan, and Bakhtiar Litkouhi. 2013. Autonomous vehicle social behavior for highway entrance ramp management. In *Intelligent Vehicles Symposium (IV), 2013 IEEE*, 201–207. Retrieved December 21, 2016 from http://ieeexplore.ieee.org/xpls/abs_all.jsp?arnumber=6629471
75. Junko Yoshida. 2016. Autopilot: Flying vs. Driving. Can lessons learned from aviation apply to cars? *EE Times*. Retrieved December 10, 2016 from http://www.eetimes.com/document.asp?doc_id=1329271

Understanding the Cost of Driving Trips

Caleb Southern, Yunnuo Cheng, Cheng Zhang, Gregory D. Abowd
College of Computing
Georgia Institute of Technology
Atlanta, GA 30322 USA
{caleb.southern, yunnuo.cheng, chengzhang, abowd}@gatech.edu

ABSTRACT
Driving is the second highest expense for the average American household. Yet few people know the total cost of owning and operating their vehicles, and most cannot estimate accurately how much a common driving trip (like a daily commute) costs. There are an increasing number of viable alternatives for personal transportation, such as car services (e.g. Uber, Lyft), in addition to ridesharing, transit, biking, and walking. Cost is one factor in transportation mode choice, and awareness of the cost of driving is useful in making better informed decisions. To bridge this awareness gap, we built and deployed a system that makes the total cost of each driving trip (including depreciation, maintenance, insurance, and fuel) visible to the user. After this intervention, participants were able to more accurately and confidently estimate costs of their driving commutes, and transfer this knowledge to other trips for which they had not seen a cost.

AUTHOR KEYWORDS
Transportation; driving; mode choice; personal informatics.

ACM Classification Keywords
H.5.2 Information Interfaces and Presentation: User Interfaces

INTRODUCTION
Driving is the dominant mode of personal transportation in the United States. Owning and operating a vehicle is a major household expense. According to the Bureau of Labor Statistics, the average American household in 2015 spent more on driving ($9,503, or 17% of all expenses) than on any other category except housing [1].

Many alternatives to driving alone or owning a private vehicle, including ridesharing (e.g., carpooling), car services (e.g., Uber or taxis), and public transit, are priced on a *per-trip* basis. Cost is one factor people may consider when choosing to change their transportation behavior. In the Transtheoretical Model, the first stage of behavior change is *Precontemplation*, in which people may not be fully aware or informed of the consequences of their actions [11]. Many people do not have a good understanding of the Total Cost of Ownership (TCO) of owning and operating a vehicle, especially on a per-trip basis, because the component expenses (e.g., depreciation, maintenance, insurance, fuel) are incurred on disparate timescales. Furthermore, Thaler and Sunstein argue in *Nudge* that "choice architects" (such as designers of information systems) can make previously invisible information (such as vehicle depreciation per driving trip) *salient*, or visible, in order to inform people's decisions [12]. In this paper, we explore increasing people's knowledge of the TCO of driving trips as a first step toward behavior change in transportation mode choice.

Our contribution is the development and evaluation of a mobile system that estimates the total cost of each driving trip and reports this cost to the driver at the end of that trip. Our model aggregates both fixed and per-trip costs, including ownership (depreciation), fuel, maintenance, insurance, taxes, and fees, and produces a personalized cost estimate for each driving trip, based on the user's specific vehicle and actual fuel use and distance traveled.

Related Work
While a great deal of work in HCI and Personal Informatics focuses on areas such as health, fitness, and diet tracking, relatively little work has looked at transportation [2, 9]. Much of the HCI work on transportation focuses on driving style, rather than mode choice, including areas such as aggressive driving [7] or optimizing fuel economy [13]. HCI researchers have explored how personal transportation mode choice can be influenced by awareness of environmental impact [5] or the convenience and reliability of bus transit [4]. Other decision factors in mode choice include, but are not limited to, travel time and cost.

The transportation literature demonstrates that cost, while not the only factor, can be an effective lever in personal mode choice decisions. Since World War II, transportation planners have explored strategies to encourage people to choose alternatives other than driving alone, as part of Transportation Demand Management (TDM) programs [10]. The goals of TDM include reducing traffic congestion, improving air quality, and reducing the need for parking

CHI 2017, May 06 - 11, 2017, Denver, CO, USA

ACM 978-1-4503-4655-9/17/05…$15.00
DOI: http://dx.doi.org/10.1145/3025453.3025686

[10, 14, 15]. Best practice TDM strategies often include financial incentives for people who make alternative mode choices for their commute to work. For example, a company or government may provide free or discounted transit passes, free or discounted parking for carpool vehicles, or directly pay cash incentives to people who choose alternatives other than driving alone [3, 10].

SYSTEM

In order to estimate and present to the user the total cost of a driving trip, we developed: (1) a per-trip model of the Total Cost of Ownership for a given vehicle; and (2) an implementation of the model on a mobile device for use in a vehicle.

Cost Model

The Total Cost of Ownership for a vehicle includes both fixed costs, which are incurred regardless of how much or little the vehicle is driven, and per-trip costs. Our model accounts for the fixed costs of time-value depreciation, insurance, taxes, and fees, and the per-trip costs of fuel, per-mile depreciation, and maintenance.

The inputs to our model are fuel used and distance traveled for a given trip. The output is the estimated total cost of ownership applied to that driving trip. To determine the coefficients for our model, we collect: the year, make, model, and odometer reading of the vehicle; its insurance cost; an estimate of how many miles per year it is driven; and published local average current fuel prices.

We estimated depreciation using data from Kelley Blue Book (KBB) [8], a commercial database that provides the locally estimated resale value of vehicles the United States. To estimate the per-mile depreciation, we compared the current value of the vehicle to the value of the same vehicle with an odometer reading of 10,000 miles higher. We divided the price difference by 10,000 as a linear estimate of the per-mile depreciation. To estimate the fixed per-year depreciation, independent of how many miles driven, we compared the current value of the vehicle to the same vehicle and odometer reading, but one year older. We estimated fixed taxes and fees based on publisheds rates for the local jurisdiction. These linear calculations are suitable approximations for short periods such as one week, but an exponential model would be required for use over longer time periods.

In order to allocate the fixed costs to each driving trip, we employed a user-provided estimate how many miles per year the vehicle was driven. We then allocated the annual total fixed costs proportionately to each driving trip, based on the trip distance divided by the annual mileage. For example, if a vehicle had $5000 in total annual fixed costs, was driven 10,000 miles per year, then our model would allocate $5.00 of fixed costs for a trip of 10.0 miles.

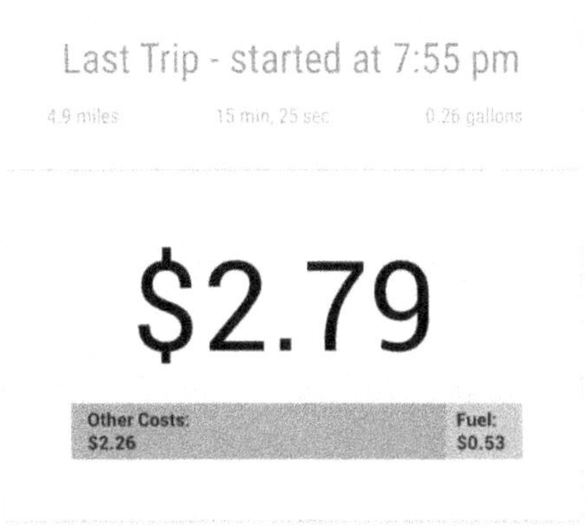

Figure 1: Trip cost meter display.

Implementation

Our system consists of an Android phone and a Bluetooth-enabled On-Board Diagnostics (OBD) interface to the vehicle. The OBD device is used to indirectly determine the fuel usage (from either Mass Air Flow or Manifold Air Pressure data) and to detect the start and stop of each driving trip (from RPM or voltage drop data). We employed a commercial Android application, Torque Pro [6], which offers an API for reading OBD data from the vehicle. We used the GPS sensor on the phone to calculate the driving distance of each trip, based on 1 Hz samples of location data, which offers higher resolution than the 1 km resolution distance data available from the OBD interface.

The phone display is blank before and during driving trips (to avoid distracted driving), and only displays the driving cost immediately after each trip (when the user turns off the ignition). After each trip, the phone audibly alerts the driver, and the driver is then presented with a screen to tap his or her name in order the see the trip cost display. The username screen allows us to track whether the user viewed the cost or ignored the device after each logged trip. The trip cost display (Figure 1) shows the total cost of the driving trip based on our model, breaks out the "Fuel" and "Other Costs" components, and presents the mileage, duration, and fuel usage of the trip.

EVALUATION

We describe an intervention to evaluate the impact of our trip cost meter system on participants' awareness of the total cost of their driving trips.

Participants

We recruited 14 participants who drove gasoline-powered vehicles (including hybrids) frequently each week in Atlanta, GA, a large urban area of the United States. Nine participants (three female), ranging in age from 19 to 39 (median = 24.5) completed the study. Five participants did not complete the study due to technical problems with the trip segmentation or fuel data reported by the OBD device. Three participants who completed the study were not affiliated with our university.

	P1	P2	P3	P4	P7	P11	P12	P13	P14
Commute Trip :: Num Trips Viewed	7	10	3	6	7	3	9	2	2
Modeled Cost (from trip logs)	*$7.19*	*$14.34*	*$5.96*	*$2.60*	*$1.35*	*$4.03*	*$3.29*	*$1.58*	*$1.57*
Estimate : Pre	$2.50	$4.00	$5.00	$10.00	$1.50	$5.00	$1.35	$4.00	$0.20
Estimate : Post	$6.58	$13.50	$5.74	$2.00	$1.50	$4.00	$3.30	$2.17	$1.50
Estimate : Follow-Up				$3.00		$.4.00	$4.00		$2.00
Relative Error : Pre	65.2%	72.1%	16.0%	284.9%	10.9%	24.1%	59.0%	152.8%	87.3%
Relative Error : Post	8.5%	5.8%	3.6%	23.0%	10.9%	0.7%	0.2%	37.2%	4.7%
Relative Error : Follow-Up				15.5%		0.7%	21.4%		27.0%
Confidence : Pre→Post→Follow-Up	2→4	3→4	4→4	1→4→1	3→4	2→3→2	3→4→4	3→4	2→4→3
Second Trip :: Num Trips Viewed	3	-	-	-	-	-	-	-	1
Modeled Cost (post hoc)	*$1.11*	*$1.59*	*$7.82*	*$23.23*	*$10.13*	*$1.62*	*$9.33*	*$0.93*	*$1.49*
Estimate : Pre	$0.10	$0.50	$7.00	$15.00	$3.00	$2.00	$2.10	$2.50	$0.15
Estimate : Post	$1.05	$2.00	$7.00	$10.00	$20.00	$2.00	$6.85	$1.50	$1.00
Estimate : Follow-Up				$6.00		$2.00	$7.00		$1.50
Relative Error : Pre	91.0%	68.6%	10.5%	35.4%	70.4%	23.6%	77.5%	168.6%	89.9%
Relative Error : Post	5.3%	25.6%	10.5%	57.0%	97.4%	23.6%	26.5%	61.2%	32.9%
Relative Error : Follow-Up				74.2%		23.6%	24.9%		0.6%
Confidence : Pre→Post→Follow-Up	2→4	3→3	4→4	1→4→1	2→2	2→3→2	3→4→4	3→3	2→3→2

Table 1: Driving data per participant.

Apparatus

We provided each participant with a dedicated Android phone to keep in his or her vehicle, an OBD adapter, and a 20,000 mAh external battery which allowed the system to run for 5-7 days without requiring recharging or an external power source.

Protocol

Each participant completed an entry survey, an intervention with the above trip cost apparatus, and an exit survey and interview. In the entry and exit survey, we asked each participant to identify and provide street addresses for two common driving trips: (1) their commute from home to work (or school); and (2) another common trip, such as home to the grocery store. We then asked each participant two questions for each specified trip: "Estimate the total cost of this driving trip (one-way)"; and "On a scale from 1 ('I have no idea') to 5 ('My answer is correct'), how confident are you in this cost?"

For the intervention, we deployed the system in each participant's vehicle for 5-7 days (until the battery ran out). During the installation, we entered the model coefficients based on the participant's personal vehicle and calibrated our application settings based on how that specific vehicle's OBD protocol reported fuel usage and RPM or voltage data to determine engine on/off events. Calibrating the OBD data for each vehicle was an unfortunately laborious process that greatly impacted our ability to scale the study. Immediately after each driving trip, the system allowed participants to see the estimated total cost of that trip. Participants could not review the trip costs later, so our evaluation reflected their memories of the reported trip cost meter that appeared each time they turned off their vehicles.

During the exit interview, we asked participants to discuss their overall impression of the system and the presented information, anything that surprised them, anything they might do differently as a result of having this information, and additional thoughts and reflections.

After four months, we invited participants to a follow-up session. We asked them the same driving cost estimate and confidence questions regarding their two designated common trips, and asked them in an interview about their transportation behavior and choices.

RESULTS AND DISCUSSION

Nine participants recorded a total of 145 driving trips (6-21 per participant). Of these, 62 trips were commutes between home and work or school, and participants viewed the trip cost for 49 of these. Each participant logged between 3 and 10 commute trips, and viewed between 2 and 10 commute costs. Four participants (P4, P11, P12, P14) took part in the follow-up four months after the intervention. Participants' cost estimates and confidence levels for the pre-intervention, post-intervention, and follow-up session are presented in Table 1. Because the data are not normally distributed and the sample size is small, we used the Wilcoxon signed-rank test to compare the pre- and post-intervention data for participants' cost estimate accuracy and for their reported confidence.

Accuracy

We calculated the relative error of participants' estimates of their driving costs, as compared to the modeled driving cost, for both the pre and post surveys.

$$Relative\ Error = \frac{|Estimate - Actual|}{Actual} \times 100\%$$

For the modeled cost of the commute trip, we used the average cost over all instances of this trip, in either direction, logged during the study.

A Wilcoxon signed-rank test showed a statistically significant change in the relative error of participants' commuting cost estimates after the intervention ($Z=-2.521$, $p=.012$). The median relative errors of participants' commuting cost estimates as compared to the modeled cost values decreased from 65.2% in the pre-intervention survey to 5.8% in the post-intervention survey. Participants' average cost estimates decreased from 85.8% relative error (SD=86.4%) in the pre survey to 10.5% relative error (SD=12.1%) in the post survey. No participant exhibited a worse relative error in their commute cost estimate after the intervention.

Seven of the nine participants did not drive their second designated common trip during the study period, and thus did not see cost estimates for these trips. Using the driving distance from Google Maps and the average fuel economy from actual logged trips, we calculated a post hoc modeled cost for the second common trip using our trip cost model. Overall, participants' cost estimates for the second trip improved on average from 70.6% relative error (SD=46.8%) in the pre survey to 37.8% relative error (SD=29.1%) in the post survey. Five participants improved their estimates, two estimated the same, and two participants' estimates were worse.

In the follow-up four months later, all four participants were more accurate in their commute cost estimates as compared to the pre-intervention survey, indicating that they retained knowledge of their driving costs despite their decreased confidence. For the second common trip, three participants were at least as accurate as in the pre-survey, while P4 was progressively less accurate for both the post-survey and the follow-up.

Confidence

A Wilcoxon signed-rank test showed a statistically significant change in participants' confidence in their commuting cost estimates after the intervention (Z=-2.588, p=.010). The median values of participants' confidence levels in their commuting cost estimates (on a scale of 1=low to 5=high) increased from 3 in the pre-intervention survey to 4 in the post-intervention survey. Their average confidence increased from 2.6 (SD=0.9) before to 3.9 (SD=0.3) after the intervention. In the post survey, all participants reported a confidence of 4 out of 5, except P11 who reported 3. The confidence increased for all participants except P3, who reported 4 out of 5 in both the pre and post surveys.

Impact on Awareness

In the exit interview, all participants except P3 told us they were surprised by the total cost of their driving trips. P12 initially expected a lower per-trip cost, but "after several days I started to understand you may include the maintenance also . . . . maybe the insurance. . . . And then I realized maybe the cost for each trip is actually higher than expected."

P3 was unique among the participants in describing having previously considered the total cost of ownership of his vehicle, and was also the most accurate and confident in his initial estimates of the two trip costs. "It was in the ballpark of what I was expecting. . . . I realized a lot of my costs are actually payments, insurance, depreciation. . . . It was almost a revalidation that this car costs me more than the fuel [because] you know psychologically we don't see [the other costs]."

Reflecting on Behavior Change

Three of the four participants who took part in follow-up interviews four months after the intervention reported changes in their transportation behavior.

P12 previously drove to school daily. "Every Tuesday I . . . take Lyft instead of driving from my apartment to school" in order to "save some money on gas, and also . . . save some mileage for my car, so I don't have . . . to do the maintenance."

P14, who previously drove to work daily, recently moved. "I live close enough so I can walk and that's one of the benefits I had in mind of moving. So I'm not gonna have to drive that much to save on fuel costs."

After the intervention, P4 stated, "living in such a driving city I think it's still not enough for me to start looking at the public transportation." In the follow-up, P4 reported that he recently moved to a home closer to MARTA, the local subway. "I never thought I would ever take MARTA and I took it now. Now a MARTA believer," because he "didn't want to drive to the airport in rush hour traffic and pay for parking. So instead I paid . . . $5 round trip to do that."

These three participants described cost savings (for fuel, maintenance, and parking) as one of the reasons for their behavior change. Though we cannot directly connect this consideration of cost to our intervention, we are inspired by these results to explore how future studies can better link increased awareness of driving cost (something we clearly established) to transportation choices.

In the exit interviews, P3 and P7 stated that convenience was a more important factor in their transportation decisions than cost, and P13 described convenience as an additional factor. P1, who did not pay for her vehicle, was motivated more by trip time than cost. P1 and P13 were the only participants who expressed environmental impact as a factor in their transportation choices.

Limitations

We acknowledge that the generalizability of our results may be limited by several factors, including but not limited to a potential U.S.-centric bias and the low number and limited diversity of our participants.

CONCLUSION

Prior to using our trip cost meter, most participants exhibited a poor understanding of the total cost of their driving trips. We demonstrated that a simple and short intervention with our trip cost meter increased knowledge of the cost of a common driving trip (e.g., daily commute). Some people were able to transfer this knowledge to other driving trips, for which they had not used the trip cost meter. The three participants who changed their transportation behavior after the intervention each reported cost as one of the factors in their decision.

REFERENCES

1. Bureau of Labor Statistics. 2016. CONSUMER EXPENDITURES – 2015. Retrieved September 21, 2016 from http://www.bls.gov/news.release/pdf/cesan.pdf
2. Daniel A. Epstein, An Ping, James Fogarty, and Sean A. Munson. 2015. A lived informatics model of personal informatics. In *Proceedings of the 2015 ACM International Joint Conference on Pervasive and Ubiquitous Computing* (UbiComp '15), 731-742. http://dx.doi.org/10.1145/2750858.2804250
3. E. Ferguson. 1990. Transportation Demand Management Planning, Development, and Implementation. *Journal of the American Planning Association* 56, 4: 442-456.
4. Brian Ferris, Kari Watkins, and Alan Borning. 2010. OneBusAway: results from providing real-time arrival information for public transit. In *Proceedings of the SIGCHI Conference on Human Factors in Computing Systems* (CHI '10), 1807-1816. http://dx.doi.org/10.1145/1753326.1753597
5. Jon Froehlich, Tawanna Dillahunt, Predrag Klasnja, Jennifer Mankoff, Sunny Consolvo, Beverly Harrison, and James A. Landay. 2009. UbiGreen: investigating a mobile tool for tracking and supporting green transportation habits. In *Proceedings of the SIGCHI Conference on Human Factors in Computing Systems* (CHI '09), 1043-1052. http://dx.doi.org/10.1145/1518701.1518861
6. Ian Hawkins. 2016. Torque – OBD Performance and Diagnostics for your Vehicle. Retrieved September 21, 2016 from https://torque-bhp.com/
7. Jin-Hyuk Hong, Ben Margines, and Anind K. Dey. 2014. A smartphone-based sensing platform to model aggressive driving behaviors. In *Proceedings of the SIGCHI Conference on Human Factors in Computing Systems* (CHI '14), 4047-4056. http://dx.doi.org/10.1145/2556288.2557321
8. Kelley Blue Book Co. 2016. Kelley Blue Book – New and Used Car Price Values, Expert Car Reviews. Retrieved September 21, 2016 from http://www.kbb.com/
9. Ian Li, Anind Dey, and Jodi Forlizzi. 2010. A stage-based model of personal informatics systems. In *Proceedings of the SIGCHI Conference on Human Factors in Computing Systems* (CHI '10), 557-566. http://dx.doi.org/10.1145/1753326.1753409
10. M. D. Meyer. 1999. Demand management as an element of transportation policy: using carrots and sticks to influence travel behavior. *Transportation research. Part A, Policy and practice* 33,7-8: 575 -599.
11. James O. Prochaska and Wayne F. Velicer. 1997. The transtheoretical model of health behavior change. *American journal of health promotion* 12,1: 38-48.
12. Richard H. Thaler and Cass R Sunstein. 2008. *Nudge: Improving Decisions about Health, Wealth, and Happiness.* Yale University Press.
13. Johannes Tulusan, Thorsten Staake, and Elgar Fleisch. 2012. Providing eco-driving feedback to corporate car drivers: what impact does a smartphone application have on their fuel efficiency?. In *Proceedings of the 2012 ACM Conference on Ubiquitous Computing* (UbiComp '12), 212-215. http://dx.doi.org/10.1145/2370216.2370250
14. M. Wachs. 1991. Policy Implications of Recent Behavioral Research in Transportation Demand Management. *Journal of Planning Literature* 5.4: 333-341.
15. P. L. Winters. 2000. Transportation Demand Management. Retrieved September 21, 2016 from http://onlinepubs.trb.org/onlinepubs/millennium/00123.pdf

Making Ritual Machines: The Mobile Phone as a Networked Material for Research Products

David Chatting[1], David S. Kirk[2], Abigail C. Durrant[2],
Chris Elsden[1], Paulina Yurman[3], Jo-Anne Bichard[4]
[1]Open Lab. Newcastle University, Newcastle upon Tyne, UK, {david.chatting; c.r.elsden}@ncl.ac.uk
[2]Northumbria University, Newcastle upon Tyne, UK, {david.kirk; abigail.durrant}@northumbria.ac.uk
[3]Design Department. Goldsmiths University of London, London, UK, p.yurman@gold.ac.uk
[4]The Helen Hamlyn Centre for Design. Royal College of Art, London, UK, jo-anne.bichard@rca.ac.uk

ABSTRACT
Viewing the mobile telephone as a networked material, we demonstrate the ways in which we have used it to make Research Products for the 'Family Rituals 2.0' inquiry of families separated by work. Drawing from a diversity of sources we survey and deconstruct the phone as a material that can be worked to a vast range of technical effects, extended by hardware and configured by software. We demonstrate the transformations of hacking and prototyping practices necessary to construct complex Research Products through the case study of our machines. We offer the Interaction Design community seven specific and actionable techniques for using mobile telephones in Research Products. Finally, we open up a broader discussion for researchers and practitioners using mobile phones as a design material in their work.

Author Keywords
Prototype; Research Product; Mobile Telephone; Tangible

ACM Classification Keywords
H.5.m. Information interfaces and presentation (e.g., HCI): Miscellaneous.

INTRODUCTION
Changing patterns of work-related mobility and domestic arrangements mean that *mobile workers* face socio-technical challenges for supporting and engaging in family life whilst travelling for work. This was the subject of our inquiry in the recent project Family Rituals 2.0.

Through a Research through Design (RtD) approach [20] and a critical technical practice [1], we have developed bespoke Ritual Machines for five real families who experience separation from home due to work, as material explorations of their lives and practices. This incorporated phases of design ethnography [42,2], the use of Cultural Probes [22], prototyping and Technology Probes [26]. Our machines are playful, provocative and perturbing. They are not solutions to any *problem* of absence from home per se, but rather a way of soliciting further reflection providing a situated *ticket to talk* about families' attitudes to home and work, the ritualized activities that constitute *being a family* and the concomitant role of technology [30]. Each family typically lived with a machine for a period of one month.

Our focus on *ritual* [9] as an activity within domestic arrangements brought to the fore a variety of artifacts and the tacit practices around them. Previous work demonstrates the value of tangible objects to the structuration of ritual activities in the home [40] and this, alongside extant work on the communicative value of *phatic technologies* for domestic settings [23,24], led us to develop and deploy *smart networked things*.

Designing for spaces like the home, truly in the wild, and for bespoke artifacts that must interweave with enduring practices of domestic routine, over extended periods of time, behooves the development of Technology Probes with a certain stability and fit with their environment. With this in mind, we have been drawn to the articulation of the *Research Product*, as recently given by Odom et al. [38] which emphasizes the *finish*, *fit* and *independence* of the artifact.

As a small team with limited time and budget, our pragmatic focus was on the resources we could draw upon to produce and deploy a series of highly finished bespoke Research Products. Our Family Rituals' probes and machines are assemblages of found technologies, third-party modules and bespoke electronics, combined in ways most familiar to practices of prototyping and hacking. Across all five of our engagements, the modern mobile phone featured significantly as a design material, inexpensively providing a plethora of diverse technical features to be combined in software in potentially complex ways.

CHI 2017, May 06-11, 2017, Denver, CO, USA
ACM 978-1-4503-4655-9/17/05.
http://dx.doi.org/10.1145/3025453.3025630

In this paper we aim to contribute to the emerging discourse around Research Products, through the provision of a detailed description of our design process in the Family Rituals project. In particular, we share strategies for the *use of mobile phones as a design material* for those engaged in design research projects, especially those working with *smart things* [31]. Detailed accounts of these Family Rituals engagements are published elsewhere [30] and will be forthcoming.

Our paper is split into five sections. First we consider the tensions between hacking, prototyping and Research Products. Second, we analyze the modern mobile phone as a resource and networked material, including a review of ways it can be worked to different technical effects. Third, for our Cultural Probes and each of the five Family Rituals' machines, we show and reflect upon how the phone was transformed to offer the qualities needed in Research Products. Fourth, we offer seven generalizable techniques. Fifth, our closing sections offer reflections on this process for researchers and practitioners.

HACKING, PROTOTYPING AND RESEARCH PRODUCTS

In this section we consider the practices of hacking and prototyping, and how they are integrated with and different from the production of the Research Product [38] in a Research through Design inquiry [20].

The hacking and adaptation of existing hardware and software have long been essential activities in communicating and exploring future propositions through prototypes and in the production of ad hoc solutions.

The rise of the so-called Maker Movement is scaffolded by a set of readily adaptable and affordable tools (such as laser cutting and 3D printing) and modules (notably the Arduino and Raspberry Pi). Frequently these activities are made communal in Hacker and Maker Spaces. These *open* tools and practices continue to permeate academia, start-up and corporate industrial design. Lindtner et al. [33] discuss this in specific reference to innovation in tangible and ubiquitous computing, from hacks to product propositions.

Beyond their instrumental use in Research & Development, *prototypes* are a material output of Research through Design approaches in practice-based research. Arrigoni et al. [7, p.9] remind us that they, *"are becoming relevant not just as a step of development in product manufacturing, but as something endowed with intrinsic value both as an artistic medium and a research process."* Odom et al. [38] offers us a comprehensive discussion of the role and nature of prototyping within HCI research.

Turning to specific techniques for hacking and repurposing found devices, Petrelli et al. [39] introduce three productive ways to create fast Tangible Computing concept prototypes. They identify three modes of hacking: *embedding*, *cracking it open* and *collating*. They emphasize the rapid development of physical prototypes in combination with digital fabrication techniques, where behavior is largely derived from simple adaptations of the found device; for instance a voice recorder. this makes the original selection of the device very important.

We have engaged with Research Products [38] retrospectively. Throughout the development of our machines we struggled to find a vocabulary to describe our necessary concerns in designing and building complex systems working independently in a complex world over a sustained period of time. We felt that our development and use of the machines went beyond a common use of *prototype*, with its connotations of fragility and there being a *moment* of *demonstration*. Odom et al.'s articulation of *Research Products* gave us the vocabulary we were seeking and a framework to productively apply.

We now offer some points of reflection, comparison and critique on the qualities of Research Products (*inquiry driven*, *finish*, *independence* and *fit*) as suggested by Odom et al. [ibid].

With regard to *inquiry driven*, our machines were designed as a critical inquiry of the present, rather than being *"designed to ask particular research questions about potential alternative futures"* [38, p.2551]. We find this future orientation somewhat problematic and at odds with a focus on the artifact's evident reality. Similarly, our designs did not consciously *embody theoretical stances* or an explicit hypothesis. Yet in broader terms they clearly were *inquiry driven* with regards to families experiencing work-related separation.

The *finish* of our machines communicates that they are to all intents and purposes real and consequential, not provisional. It speaks of our effort and commitment. Finish goes beyond a surface level reading; it is present in both the physical materials and the electronic behavior of the artifact. Finish elevates the fragile hack and is not achieved in haste. Finish builds *independence* from our intervention; distinguishing it from the context-defined prototypes and demonstrations. We hoped that these machines would develop rituals over long periods of time, so they had to work more or less independently.

Through our engagements with the families and resulting bespoke machines, we are deliberately attempting to manipulate the *fit* into their lives and their environments, be that familiar or strange. We have previously written about *making technology at home* [30]. However, we do not argue that the fit must be individually bespoke; batch produced multiples, such as the Datacatcher [21], might also be considered as a Research Product. Arguably, levels of both finish and fit should not simply determine whether something is, or is not, a Research Product, when manipulation of those qualities themselves might directly relate to the research questions being addressed.

Our machines are 'one-offs', produced largely in-house within the constraints of limited budgets, time, equipment, skills and labor. The complex technical effects we produced result from assemblages of found technologies, third-party modules and bespoke electronics; configured by techniques drawn from hacking and prototyping, yet exhibiting the properties of Research Products. Significantly, in all our machines, the mobile telephone is exploited as a readily available, complex and configurable material. In contrast to Petrelli et al.'s [39] found function, this flexibility offers a complexity of outcome, necessarily being produced relatively slowly and deliberately.

We acknowledge that for specific telephony functions it is evidently possible to specify and build hardware without hacking an existing device and that this approach offers a level of finish and control that we cannot otherwise expect to meet [21,36]. Additionally, that this is highly suitable for batch manufacture. However, as we shall discuss, the modern mobile phone offers an abundance of technologies that we can reconfigure at little cost in software as part of a small scale exploratory Research through Design project.

Our contribution is to demonstrate transformations of hacking and prototyping practices in the production of Research Products with the required *finish* and consequential *independence*. We offer seven techniques addressing how the mobile phone can be worked as a networked material to this outcome.

THE MOBILE PHONE AS A RESOURCE

The mobile telephone is a modern phenomenon, the product of global supply chains, agreements and infrastructures, incorporating the intellectual and physical work of millions of people. With a global demand, the cost of these extraordinary devices has been driven below any reasonable expectation. We have recently purchased a new Android telephone in Walmart (USA) for $5, complete with touch screen, compass, accelerometer and GPS. Low-end smartphones are now regularly available in the UK for $50 or less. Secondhand, repaired [25] and discarded devices further add to this availability.

We should not approach the availability of the mobile telephone uncritically. These devices exploit human labor and natural resources at a global scale. We must acknowledge our privilege. Initiatives such as Fairphone (fairphone.com) draw our attention to these issues.

An attempt to enumerate the technologies available in the modern mobile telephone would include: microphone, speaker, telephony (to make and answer calls), SMS and MMS messaging, Internet connectivity (mobile data or WiFi), backlight colour graphical display, touch (frequently multi-touch) input, camera (often front and rear facing), fingerprint reader, GPS receiver, magnetometer (compass), accelerometer, gyroscope, altimeter, barometer, thermometer, Bluetooth, NFC (read and write), FM radio, multimedia playback, storage (including SD card), processing, rechargeable battery, vibration motor and a bright light. Significantly all these technologies are configurable by software to complex effect.

The current dominance of the Android and iOS platforms, their associated tools and APIs vastly simplifies the task of deploying software on innumerable devices. By *rooting* these devices we gain deeper access to normally privileged commands; the legal status of this varies internationally.

These inexpensive and highly featured devices are therefore very attractive as a resource for building prototypes and Research Products, where software affords reconfiguration and experimentation at a far lower cost than bespoke hardware. This is an approach we used extensively throughout the Family Rituals project.

THE MOBILE PHONE AS A NETWORKED MATERIAL

We find it productive to consider the mobile phone, a collection of diverse technologies with a small and typically uncomplicated form, as a complex material with properties we can work to many technical effects. Further, we conceptualize it as a networked material that is inherently entangled with the complexity of the world. This is in the tradition of Martinussen and Arnall's [34] analysis of RFID as a material for design. Ingold has a body of work (notably [28]) that argues for the proper consideration of *materials and their properties* over notions of materiality and material culture [37] that draw our attentions towards abstract concepts and philosophy. Materials, Ingold contends, are too often left underexplored in inquiry. Responding to Ingold's provocation, we pull focus herein on the core material features of the mobile phone; these are relatively fixed with certain affordances that must be worked with in the design process.

To support our contention that the mobile phone is a material to be worked, we now give exemplars that exploit the constituent technologies in material ways. We draw these from a set of otherwise diverse sources; significantly many come from the hacking and making communities. It is clearly not an exhaustive survey. We shall later show how some were applied in the Family Rituals project.

Telephony

Telephony has been used in a number of interesting ways, often in combination with an Interactive Voice Response (IVR) service hosted on the telephone network and available by dialing a specific number. Callers can interact with their voice and by pressing numbers on their keypad. This is attractive as it requires no software to be installed on the telephone itself and so can be used with any generation of device. Crivellaro [17] demonstrates this for engaging local communities in aural discourses on change. Here a handset is housed in a suitcase and keypad buttons are labeled appropriately on a fascia, which obscures unused functions. RootIO [18] hosts a radio station as IVR on an Android device for contributors to call into to; it is connected to a transmitter, battery and solar panel.

Audio

Beyond recording and playback there are a number of techniques for appropriating the telephone's audio features.

The 3.5mm jack socket provides a near universal way to attach speakers or headphones. Increasingly now with the introduction of headphones with an on-cord microphone this is a TRRS (Tip-Ring-Ring-Sleeve) jack. While there is no standard, iOS devices and most Android phones share the same wiring. The additional microphone line also allows simple signaling for play/pause and volume. Since iOS 5.0 and Android 4.3, the volume button has been enabled as a convenient physical camera trigger. Combining these innovations leads us to the Selfie Stick! This enables simply implemented external button inputs. However, this is set to change with Apple's recent high profile rejection of the 3.5mm jack in the iPhone 7.

The Square Reader (squareup.com/reader) is a commercial credit card reader that uses an external circuit to read the magnetic stripe in via the microphone input. The Maker community has also developed several ways to encode instructions in audio signals, for instance Terasaki's Smartphone Servo [46] directly controls up to two servo motors from the stereo jack; an external battery is required. Disney's Acoustruments [32] constructs an ultrasonic pathway, a physical pipe, between the speaker and microphone; the audio properties of which are changed during interaction. A variety of path designs allow rotations, pressure and orientation to be sensed.

Display

The typically color backlit display affords several adaptations. Simplest of all, it can be framed, breaking up the given rectangular form. Luckybite's BirdBox alarm clock [13] does this, making a window through which we see the time or footage from a nesting box. The Palm Top Theater [35] uses three parallel half-silvered mirrors held at 45 degrees to the screen, to create a multi-depth display. Google Cardboard [15] constructs a cardboard frame that extends the display with stereo lens and allows it to worn against the face. Randle's Shepherd [43] uses light sensors attached to the display, selectively illuminated by onscreen graphics, to trigger an external circuit.

Multi-touch

The modern multi-touch sensor can be exploited in a number of ways, depending on the underlying technology; typically either capacitive (electrical) or resistive (pressure). Befurt's Auto Tinder Swipper [8] generates a faux swipe gesture on capacitive devices; an electrically grounded stylus is moved across the surface of the screen with a servomotor. Randle's Shepherd [43] makes four faux touches in four fixed positions using a similar technique. In this way an external circuit can manipulate UI elements made available in software.

There are a number of approaches giving objects interactive qualities when placed on screen. Typically for capacitive multi-touch, conductive materials electrically extend the touch from the fingers through the object onto the screen; for instance Aeschlimann's Little Boxes [2]. Disney's AppMATes (appmatestoys.com), uses this with an identifiable configuration of pads in contact with the screen to recognize a specific toy car. In addition, light pipes in the toy channel illumination from the screen to allow the car's headlights to be operated.

Magnetometer

While typically used as a compass for location based applications, the magnetometer has many wider uses detecting changes in the local electromagnetic field. A set of interactions have been shown with passive magnet based approaches. The first version of Google Cardboard [16] used the changing position of a strong neodymium magnet as a button and could be sited on the exterior of the case. A range of familiar controllers (sliders, buttons, knobs, etc.) were enabled in this way by Hwang et al. [27]. Bianchi [12] demonstrated a series of interactions based on a tangible's position and orientation with respect to the phone. Bennett's Resonant Bits [11] show the gestural potential of such tangibles in bespoke physical forms. Active circuits to manipulate the phone's electromagnetic field have also been shown. Desbonnet's Poor Man's NFC [19] actives a small coil to send data, albeit slowly. Finally, Sturgeon and Ray [45] used the magnetometer to sense the electric fields of local appliances.

Computation

Even low-end mobile devices offer considerable computational resources that can be operationalized by other systems. Typically, these might be connected by USB or Bluetooth, using software on the phone to orchestrate behaviour between external sensors and actuators. For Android development boards such as Sparkfun's IOIO are attractive, connected and powered by USB OTG (On the Go) or by Bluetooth Low Energy with an external battery. Apple restricts the development of hardware accessories for iOS and Bluetooth is the most available option. Coupled with software development tools that assume little experience of programming computation becomes a ready resource.

Network

The ability of these devices to react to and initiate action over distant networks is widely exploited. To take one example, the Rainforest Connection project [49] uses the surprising levels of GSM connectivity in the forest to create a network of modified mobile phones running software to detect the characteristic sounds of chainsaws; giving a real-time alert for illegal logging. The units have a weatherproof enclosure and are adapted for solar power.

Camera

Various optical adaptations can be made to the camera. Most apparently there are a range of external lens that can be fitted, some giving a microscopic or fisheye view, others creating novelty filters. Public Lab's fluorescence spectrometry [48] goes beyond this; using an ad hoc prism, made from a CD, to identify a range of environment contaminants in the wake of the 2010 BP oil disaster.

MAKING RITUAL MACHINES WITH MOBILE PHONES

Below we describe the use of mobile phones in the design of our Family Rituals' engagements, both for the Cultural Probes and five Ritual Machines (our Research Products); transforming the exploits we have previously identified.

Cultural Probes - Digital Question Box

Our initial engagements with the families were framed around interviews and Cultural Probe [22] packs. Each pack contained a playful collection of diverse printed and object-based activities that, when completed, would provide us a glimpse of their domestic life and everyday rituals. A detailed description of our packs can be found in [30].

Our Cultural Probes included a Digital Question Box (Figure 1) that asked timely questions on a small screen, for instance *"How did you take a break today?"* The family responded by writing an answer on paper that was posted into a slot in the box, which was used in the next interview as material to structure the conversation. The answers tended to be given spontaneously and quite casually. No other interactions with the device were available.

The design of this Cultural Probe was based on an inexpensive Android mobile telephone with a custom app. Questions were displayed at different times of the day, each for a finite time, typically an hour. We developed a series of laser-cut cardboard phone housings, (after Petrelli [39], *embedding*). We explored birdhouse shapes (inspired in part by the Luckybite BirdBox [13]) and devices that contained a mechanical shutter to reveal a new question; intended to create a moment of occasion.

Written as a replacement lock-screen, the app is always shown. Messages were either delivered in real-time from us by SMS or scheduled from a file. In later versions an SMS microformat specified the duration of display. Using SMS required no on-site configuration to be made on delivery.

The construction of the box framed the screen and gave access to the power button (with a pencil inserted) and to the USB charging port; specific to the embedded phone. Typically they were permanently plugged in and always on.

The mechanical shutter was driven by a servomotor and an Adafruit Trinket microcontroller. It triggered on the appearance of a white dot on screen, read by a LDR sensor (as Randle [43]). For power the Trinket was wired in parallel to the telephone's USB connection.

The embedded phone exploited *the network* and *display*.

Figure 1: Digital Question Box

Machine 1 - Drinking Together Whilst Apart

Drinking Together Whilst Apart (Figure 2) is a machine that pours a glass of wine in synchrony with a beer bottle-opener being used. A Bluetooth-enabled bottle opener connects to an iPhone and a WiFi wine machine. It was designed for participants Craig and Holly to live with. They enjoy a drink together at the end of the day when they've done *"all the serious stuff"* and this machine questions whether this ritual could be meaningfully extended when they are separated. We intended for the wine machine to be installed at home, with the bottle-opener being taken with Craig, the travelling partner. (See [30] for a full description of the design process and associated ethnographic study).

The wine dispenser contains a WiFi connected Arduino Yun controlling a high-torque servomotor that mechanically operates an unmodified wine optic. Sensors detect the glass and LEDs cause it to be illuminated when inserted.

The design of the bottle-opener posed several important challenges. Firstly it operated mechanically to remove bottle-tops. Secondly it was able to sense and communicate this event across the Internet in real-time. Thirdly it presented no problems for Craig in the likely circumstance that it would be taken through airport security, or similar.

A musical bottle-opener was used as donor for the *teeth* of the device, which also provided a convenient sensor - based on the conductance of a metal bottle-top. We opted to use an app on Craig's own iPhone as a means of making the Internet connection (across any available network) and to be a point of interaction. A Bluetooth 4.0 module provided the local communication between the bottle-opener and the telephone. The circuit was powered with a watch battery and had a power switch, described as a flight-mode. The components were fitted on a custom PCB, enclosed in a laser-cut acrylic case, intended to publically convey a professional (perhaps mass-manufactured) finish.

When a glass is placed in the machine a notification is sent to the iPhone using the Apple Push Notification Service [4], stating "Glass Inserted" and optionally opening the app. The app shows the state of the machine at any given moment, whether the bottle installed or the glass is present (and whether it full or empty) and whether the opener is connected.

The phone is primarily used as means of providing *computation* and *networking*.

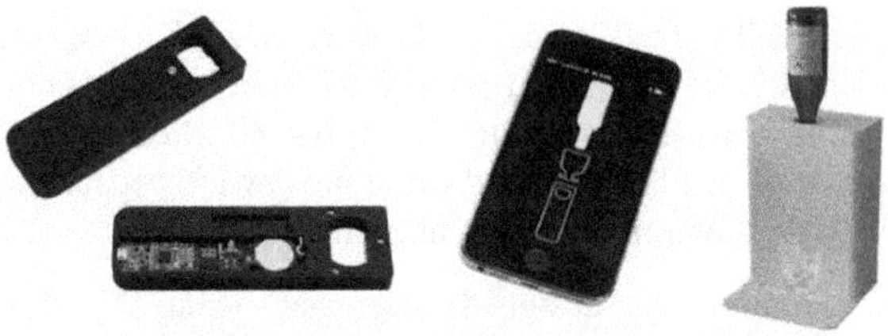

Figure 2: Drinking Together Whilst Apart

Machine 2 - Anticipation of Time Together

Anticipation of Time Together (Figure 3) counts down to a family event; a mechanical flip-dot display shows the passing time through an animation reminiscent of a sand timer. It is designed as a piece of furniture, standing at just under one meter tall. See [30] for a full description of the design process and associated ethnographic study.

This machine was designed for Hywel and Jesper, reflecting their love of travel and frequent separation. Whilst apart they could see the display of the machine through an app we designed for their personal iPhones. In addition, they could communicate touches through the screen that were displayed in real-time. However, to set the time that they were anticipating, they needed to be together in front of the display. Through this interaction, we sought to structure a small ritual and enjoyed the Cold War film language of double locks and secure systems requiring two people to initiate a sequence. Further the interaction spanned the two screens, so that they would be moved together to complete the display.

The display uses two commercially available flip-dot modules under the control of a Raspberry Pi 2, which uses WiFi to connect to the Internet. The proximate interactions with the iPhones are achieved through a Bluetooth 4.0 dongle that advertises an Apple iBeacon [5] around the display and allows each iPhone to report their distance to it.

The two phones are exploited as point of interaction and remote view of the machine, across the *network*. When proximate, there is a local cooperative behaviour using their identical forms, treating it as a continuous display.

Figure 3: Anticipation of Time Together

Machine 3 - Connecting Through Housework

Connecting Through Housework (Figure 4) is a robotic vacuum cleaner that operates at home only when a mobile totem device, carried remotely, moves at speed. The robot's behavior reflects the routines of the distant family member.

This machine was designed for David, Irene and their two teenage children: Rikard and Rebecca. David works away from home for prolonged periods in a different county to his family. During our interviews, the children made the joke that they miss their Dad when he's away, because they have to do more of the chores at home.

The machine was designed such that when David was away, the robot would mirror his routine, moving silently when he was walking, and starting to clean at higher speeds when he was using some form of transportation. Returning to his *work-home* at the end of each day, the vacuum would seek its recharging station. It would expose David's routine movements whilst contributing to housework in his absence.

David's totem contains an Android mobile telephone running a custom app that measures his speed by GPS and communicates this across the Internet to the vacuum. The vacuum is a modified Roomba 650 (irobot.com) controlled by an Arduino Yun connected to the home WiFi network, using the iRobot Serial Interface [29] to control behavior.

Touching the totem display causes the light on the robot to be instantaneously momentarily brighter; giving it a shake causes the robot to make a rotating action. Tapping the robot causes it to stop. This is acknowledged on the mobile device by playing a knock sound vibrating and changing the display. This notification is sent by an Internet/SMS gateway; proving a convenient means to address the phone in real-time.

Both the robot and totem have a similar single light display and a shared color language. This communicates a low battery (red flashing) or the loss of a data connection (blue flashing). Static colors are a representation of David's location calculated from the HSV color wheel, where the compass bearing to home determines the hue; and the distance from home the saturation. In this way different places have recognizably different colors, without revealing a precise location. Additionally, David's totem reflects his speed by animating the light along a Lissajous figure.

The Android phone is enclosed in a wooden case, through a circular window a portion of the display is visible and touch interactions can be made. There is a hole for USB charging and the power button is accessible under an end cap.

This deployment had serious technical problems. We needed to take GPS position throughout the day, from which to determine speed, but we were mindful of the effects this would have on battery life so the sample rate was set at 15-minute intervals. At home and work the device did not get good GPS reception inside. GPS can be supplemented with location derived from WiFi networks, but we had disabled this not wanting to introduce a WiFi configuration step. The consequence of these decisions was that the phone's low-specification GPS receiver infrequently got a good location fix and failed to measure speed reliably.

In this case, we embedded and reconfigured the phone's *display*, *sensors*, *computation* and *networking*.

Figure 4: Connecting Through Housework

Machine 4 - A Message in a Jam

A Message in a Jam (Figure 5) is a machine for a lorry driver who is separated from her family, which allows them to send audio messages to her that are delivered at the point that a traffic jam is encountered. To date it has not yet been deployed.

This Machine was designed for Lisa and Will, who live with their children: Alex (26), Oliver (16), Steve (12), Kevin (11), Billy (9) and Rachel (8). Lisa is a 'tramper', a long distance lorry driver working across the UK. She was away for up to five nights every week, sleeping overnight in her truck cabin. Hold-ups seriously impacted Lisa's day and caused a good deal of stress in meeting tight delivery times. We wondered if we could make a counterpoint to this.

An electronic jam jar at home allowed audio messages to be left for Lisa and the speaker in her cab received these messages - playing them automatically when there was a traffic jam.

At home messages are spoken into the jam jar. Removing the lid starts the recording and the message is sent when the lid is replaced. The glass jar contains custom electronics on a printed circuit board that records audio messages, illuminates the jar to show that a message is contained and connects to WiFi to transfer the recording to the server. In the lorry the speaker contains an Android phone using GPS to determine location and measure speed; in combination with online traffic services it determines if Lisa is currently in a traffic jam and if she is, downloads and replays any new messages from the jam jar.

The speaker contains the Android phone and external amplifier circuit that is powered by an additional LiPo battery; this is charged via a power management module that also charges the phone battery, from a mains adapter. The phone's screen is almost completely obscured by the case, expect for a tiny window that reports status (battery, GPS and data) and allows Lisa to replay recent messages with small touch gestures. Lisa can mute the device using the volume switch on the front that is wired to make a faux touch on the capacitive touchscreen. A power button on the back panel allows her to turn it on and off. This panel can be removed for maintenance and gives access to the phone and its buttons. The phone and electronics are contained within a removable internal frame.

In summary we embedded the phone's *network*, *computation*, *audio* and *multi-touch* technologies.

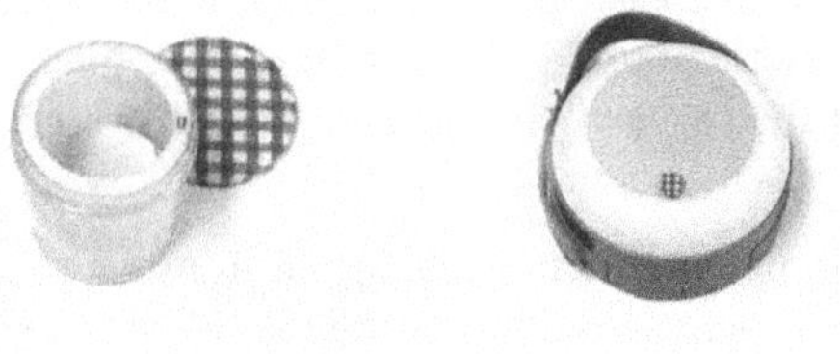

Figure 5: A Message in a Jam

Machine 5 - Where are You?

Where are You? (Figure 6) is a telescope that allows an eight-year-old boy, Joseph, to find his parents, Emmie and Mark, when they are working away. The telescope lived at home with Joseph, the travelling parent took the mobile 'flag' totem.

By pointing the telescope in different directions and by zooming with the focus wheel, Joseph could explore beyond his village, across whole country and beyond. Inside he saw an illustrated world of towns, cities and landmarks. Wherever Mark and Emmie went, when they planted the flag it would appear in the telescope world. Joseph had a paper map so that he could record these places when he found them. We hoped the telescope would begin conversations either on the telephone whilst the parents were away or when together with the map on their return. The design of this machine is discussed further in [15].

The telescope is constructed from laser-cut acrylic and cardboard, held by elastic bands. It is designed using familiar materials and we asked Joseph to build it for himself with our illustrated instructions. The display is driven by an iPhone that runs a bespoke app using the compass (magnetometer), accelerometer and gyroscope to determine the telescope's position. A click wheel allows the viewing distance to be changed in incremental steps; an Incremental Digital Rotary Encoder is wired to make two faux touches on the capacitive touchscreen. The iPhone is held on an internal frame by elastic bands, which mounts the click wheel and gives access to the power button and charging socket. The telescope obtains the location of the flag from our servers, over WiFi.

The flag totem is also constructed from laser-cut acrylic and cardboard; it contains an Android telephone. When the small acrylic flag is pushed into the hole, it triggers the pressure sensitive screen and our app causes the screen to change color; the current location, determined by GPS, is sent by the mobile data service to our servers. This action, essentially a button press, is deliberately elaborated with the physical flag to make a *moment* of ritual. We find Saffer's *microinteractions* a useful lens [44].

The totem does not track location all the time, only when the action is made to mark that place. The flag will stay visible in the telescope world until it is moved.

The telescope exploits the phone's *display*, *multi-touch*, *sensors*, *computation* and *network*. The totem uses the display, *multi-touch*, *location*, *sensors* and *network*.

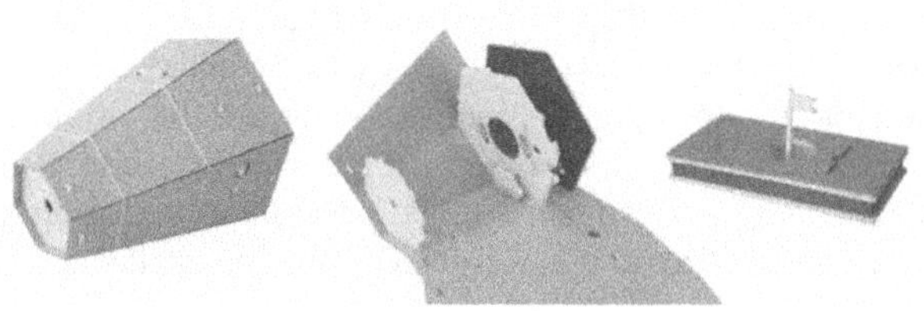

Figure 6: Where Are You?

TECHNIQUES FOR MAKING RESEARCH PRODUCTS

We now identify seven techniques that can be applied by others in making Research Products using the mobile phone as a networked material; illustrated by our Ritual Machines. Each seeks to build the required *finish* and consequential *independence*. In none do we *crack it open*, preferring to build on the integrity (and stability) of the original device.

Making Enclosures

Where we have created a single function device (digital question box, machines 3, 4 & 5) as opposed to an app on a device that continues to function as a *phone* (machines 1 & 2), it has been *embedded* and enclosed. Our intention is to *make it strange* [10], to perturb reading it as *"a mobile phone in a box"*. Our designs manipulate physical affordances to match the new operation of the device. Necessarily, this inherits many of the properties of the enclosed phone; the artifact will always be larger and heavier.

The enclosure does much of our initial work in transforming the device into a Research Product. It frames the initial engagement and is our first opportunity to demonstrate its *finish*. Choice of material and attention to detail demonstrate care and seriousness.

Each of our embedded designs allowed access to the system buttons and the screen for interaction, through their enclosures. For machine 3 the phone could be (and was) simply slid from the case. For the speaker in machine 4, removing the back panel to access the internal frame exposed the three Android system buttons (back, home, overview) - see Figure 7. Our most successful design was the frame for the telescope, giving access to the home button through the fascia and allowing simple removal of the iPhone by removing the elastic bands, allowing complete access – see Figure 8.

Reconfiguring Displays

In all the machines in which the phone is *embedded*, we have reconfigured the display (digital question box, machines 3, 4 & 5) and windowed a portion of it with an unusual circular format. This further defamiliarizes the artifact. For the travelers' totem in machines 3 and 5 we further reduced the graphical capacity of the display to show only simple light patterns. The digital question box and machine 4 predominately shows only white text on a black background. We have deliberately diminished these displays, only the telescope in machine 5 necessarily showed rich color imagery.

As the primary site of interaction for mobile phones reconfiguring the display also reconfigures the interaction, specifically via touch. While this can be managed within the app this does present challenges for configuration and maintenance outside the app where the full-screen and system buttons often need to be accessible; necessitating some means of removing the device from the enclosure.

Extending Interactions - Faux Touch

The Message in Jam (machine 4) speaker has a volume control with an integrated power switch to mute the device; the Where are You? (machine 5) totem device actives when the flag is inserted and the telescope uses has a zoom wheel. In both we extended the multi-touch, making a faux touch on the screen, without additional circuitry or power.

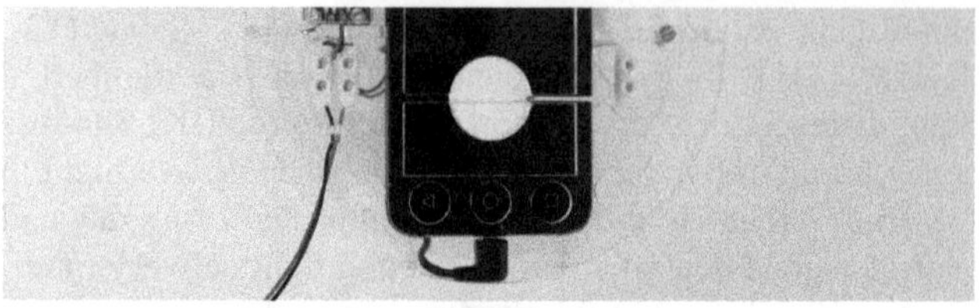

Figure 7: A Message in a Jam – speaker's internal frame access to system buttons and faux touch

The mute switch for machine 4's speaker was our first experimentation with extending a capacitive touch screen, as per Befurt [8]. We used aluminum foil tape, stuck to the internal frame, and held in contact with a region of the screen. This plate is wired through the switch to the device's ground, obtained via the USB charging port – see Figure 7. Ground may also be found through the audio jack or off the case. If the phone has a metal body, this plate needs to be kept out of contact. In this case there is only one input, but there could be multiple. With a UI button component positioned on-screen under the plate, the switch is reliably read and fixed within the frame it is very robust.

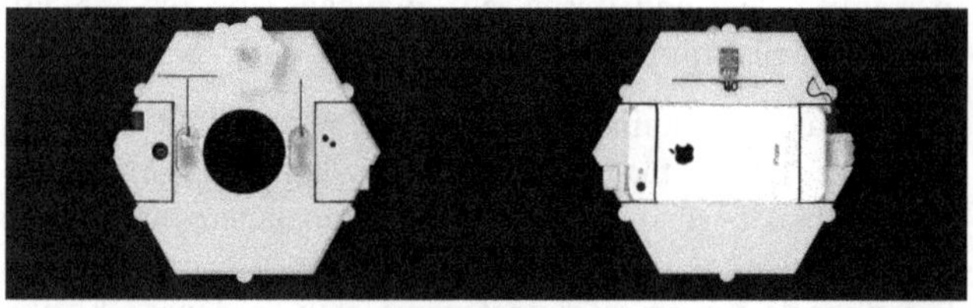

Figure 8: Where are You? – telescope's internal frame

The Where are You? telescope has a wheel that rotates either clockwise to zoom out or anticlockwise to zoom in. We considered using a magnetic effect, as per Bianchi [12], but the telescope already makes use of the magnetometer to obtain a compass bearing. We also considered using the headphone cord volume control buttons, but Apple's SDK does not currently support direct access. Instead we used the capacitive touch technique with an Incremental Digital Rotary Encoder; essentially two switches. After a great deal of experimentation with much smaller foil based plates (including the use of gels and conductive inks between them and the screen) we settled on two relatively large, thumb-sized, copper plates held tight to the screen and read by a *view* supporting multi-touch. The plates are wired through the two switches and to ground, which is obtained from the jack socket. See Figure 8.

Calculating the direction and speed from the rotary encoder relies on precise relative timings of the two switches changing state for each click of the wheel. For a minority of cases direction was decoded in error, typically where the processor had some load. By designing the interaction so that the wheel is rotated by several clicks before the action completed, the direction is reliably resolved with a majority vote.

Surprisingly the Android phone we used for the Where are You? totem device used a resistive sensor. We had assumed it to be capacitive, making prototypes where the flag pushed against a microswitch wired to the screen and conductive ink ran the length of the flag making a circuit between the fingers and the screen. However, it was simply enough that the flag be inserted in the hole, pushed against the screen.

Enabling Networking

There are significant challenges creating the *independence* and transparency of experience we desire with networking, namely: configuration, connection and coverage.

Secure WiFi networks necessitate a configuration step for each location; specifying the SSID and password. Where the device continues to function as the participant's phone (machines 1 & 2), this presents little difficulty; but for *embedded* phones we need to design the configuration carefully - as later described.

Mobile data (GSM) offers a configuration-less location-independent alternative; although the bandwidth can be limited and the data plan usage needs monitoring. Mobile data was used in one way or another by all our machines.

For real-time two-way phatic communication (e.g. machines 1, 2 & 3) a peer-to-peer connection needs to be established. For TCP/IP connections behind a router using Network Address Translation (likely the case with a home network), the IP address of the remote device is insufficient to establish this link. With machines 1, 2 & 3 we used the Yaler (yaler.net) service as a relay, in combination with an intermediary/logging script on our server.

SMS text messaging is useful solution for an incoming connection, in often near real-time. Internet SMS gateways, such as Clockwork (clockworksms.com), allow HTTP requests to initiate an SMS message to be sent. The notification that the robot was paused, for machine 3, was sent in this way. For iOS devices messages can be sent via an HTTP request and the Apple Push Notification Service [4], as we did for the *glass inserted* event in machine 1.

All these wireless network solutions have coverage. All our machines create an alert if the network is unavailable.

Managing Power

As Petrelli et al. [39] suggest power management is a key challenge in repurposing found devices. An attraction of the mobile phone is the integrated battery, charging and power management; including the ability to report the battery level in software. This enables the app to give low power alerts.

In all our embedded designs we have exposed the USB charging point through the machine's case and provided a button mechanically coupled to the soft power button of the embedded device (Figure 9). We could have *cracked it open* and rewired the button, but it was important to keep the integrity of the device for both simplicity and reliability.

Where we necessarily have externally powered circuitry (the Digital Question Box shutter and machine 4's amplifier), we have a single power point. Machine 4's additional battery is charged by the same circuit as the phone, although in this case the charging point its extended to a jack on the back panel.

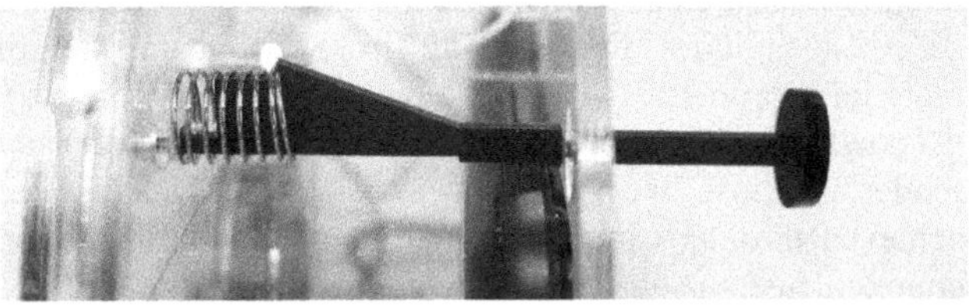

Figure 9: A Message in a Jam – speaker button (side view)

Supporting Configuration

We attempted to reduce the degree of configuration at the point of delivery; if this required the intervention of the family we provided illustrated instructions. For: *embedded* machines 3, 4 & 5 and the Digital Question Box we used mobile data services to give a wide coverage and require no on-site configuration. As noted, this decision had negative consequences for machine 3.

For machine 5, configuration was part of the self-build process, as the family built the iPhone telescope enclosure for themselves. This allowed the WiFi to be configured before the iPhone was attached to the internal frame. Otherwise the faux touch pads obscure vital areas of the screen, preventing configuration. Elastic bands allow easy removal. We continue to seek a good way to configure WiFi from within our apps, or by an externally connected device.

Rewiring Software

Our approach extends the mobile phone with hardware and configures it with software. Given the plethora of technologies inside and the arbitrary connections to be made by networking, the potential of this diversity and complexity is staggering. Being software, its function can be changed at little cost and without physical modification. The software determines the behavior of the machine and further demonstrates *finish* as part of the experience of use.

For the *embedded* machines we need to take over the device. For iOS we used Apple's Guided Access [6] to present our app in a locked kiosk mode, disabling all other access. For Android devices we wrote a lock-screen app that started automatically when the screen becomes locked. By leaving the unlock function unimplemented this runs full screen and reappears whenever the power button is pressed. We necessarily disabled screensavers, key-locks, updates and unnecessary background data.

These techniques can be used on their own, or together, and in a practical way demonstrate how to work with the materiality of the phone at a level of *finish* and *independence* demanded by Research Products.

DISCUSSION

Drawing on our account of the Family Rituals project and the techniques we have developed with this Research through Design process, we now seek to open up a broader discussion for researchers and practitioners using mobile phones as a material in their work – particularly for making tangible Research Products. Essentially we have presented a set of techniques for selecting from an abundance of material properties (technologies and affordances), *purposing* and making them *coherent* and *stable*, and rendering those we disregard invisible. This has been achieved through careful physical augmentation and often complex custom software. There are clear parallels with the approach that Pierce and Paulos' have in rendering their Counterfunctional Things [41]; for example, their Inaccessible Digital Camera.

While our intentions are different, there is a clear point of comparison with Petrelli's encouragement to use found objects and found function for fast prototyping [39]. Our use of the mobile telephone as a material and software, facilitate our Research Products, rather than making our process *fast* per se. Indeed through the case studies and techniques we describe, we show how viewing the mobile phone as a networked material discloses the remarkable affordances of the device. These allow us to produce complex Research Products and experiences with participants that go well beyond the making of prototypes (slow or fast) or hacking found objects.

We have not approached Research Products uncritically. We previously offered some reflections on the properties of *inquiry driven*, *finish*, *independence* and *fit*. Specifically, that we do not see a necessity that the inquiry be future orientated; also that *finish*, *independence* and *fit* may each be manipulated to make the experience strange, to deliberately perturb particular readings – the cardboard construction of the telescope can be seen in this way.

Beyond their status as Research Products, we argue that our Ritual Machines be used for speculation; they are to some degree working artifacts from an alternative present. Our families would not have bought or sought these as products. No such bespoke products would exist were it not for their development for our study. As such there is a degree of fiction, of role-playing, as they negotiate and make meaning with these strange objects within their daily routines. In Wakkary et al.'s [47] terms, interacting with such *counterfactual* artifacts, participants are drawn to *material speculation*. The appropriation of the mobile phone as a networked material might be read in Pierce and Paulos' [41] terms to support the exploration and transformation of counterfunctional devices.

The abundance of technical possibility and the illegibility of behavior from form alone is a powerful tool for material speculation, but raises questions about the way the underlying nature of the technology should be revealed to users; especially over a potentially long deployment. Many of the techniques discussed deal explicitly with this tension – the extent to which the device should be perceived more or less as a phone. How might this support or undermine the speculation? Again this is a point of distinction with technologies developed to a specific brief or a hacked single function device (e.g. a Dictaphone). Participants may be justifiably concerned that the mobile phone within the machine is surreptitiously live-streaming the microphone or logging location, etc.

In Family Rituals, we chose to make the families aware of the nature of the machines. In the printed material we gave them and in our conversations, we were clear that the devices contained mobile phones and made them aware of the information we were (and were not) collecting. In the case of the *Where are You?* telescope, the family configured the iPhone and built it into the device themselves. Hywell and Jesper commented that they enjoyed seeing us engaging in the process of configuring the *Anticipation Machine* as it revealed to them some of the work that had brought it into reality. This all builds trust with the families, on a personal and technical level, contributing to the necessary *independence* of the devices.

Through a long-term deployment there will be inevitable glitches of the hacked device, which expose its phone-ness. These need to be perceived as fleeting and forgettable; moments of 'misfunction', but not long-term malfunction.

CONCLUSION

Our five machines treat the mobile phone as a tangible networked material. In describing seven specific but generalizable techniques, we show how more than a prototype, or hacked device, mobile phones can be reworked to provide the *finish* and *independence* of Research Products. Lastly, we argue that the immense possibilities of a mobile phone as a design material, present opportunities to be used for material speculation.

In this way, we hope to offer the CHI community both practical approaches to exploit the multiple affordances of mobile phones as a networked material, and advance the case for their embedding as tangible and compelling Research Products.

ACKNOWLEDGEMENTS

We thank our participants, and the EPSRC for funding this research (EP/K025678/1). We extend thanks to our anonymous reviewers. Data supporting this publication is not openly available due to ethical considerations. Access may be possible under appropriate agreement. Additional metadata record at 10.17634/122700-2. Please contact Newcastle Research Data Service at rdm@ncl.ac.uk for further information or access requests.

REFERENCES

1. Philip E. Agre. 1997. Computation and Human Experience, Cambridge University Press, New York, NY.
2. Joelle Aeschlimann. 2012. Little Boxes – Music box for the iPad. (July 2012). Retrieved September 20, 2016 from https://vimeo.com/45704273
3. Robert J. Anderson. 1994. Representations and requirements: the value of ethnography in system design. *Human-computer interaction* 9.3: 151-182.
4. Apple. Apple Push Notification Service. Retrieved September 20, 2016 from https://developer.apple.com/library/content/documentation/NetworkingInternet/Conceptual/RemoteNotificationsPG/Chapters/ApplePushService.html
5. Apple. iBeacon for Developers. Retrieved September 20, 2016 from https://developer.apple.com/ibeacon/
6. Apple. Use Guided Access with iPhone, iPad, and iPod touch. 2016. Retrieved September 20, 2016 from https://support.apple.com/en-gb/HT202612
7. Gabriella Arrigoni, Tom Schofield, Teresa Almeida, David Chatting, Ben Freeth, Annika Haas and Diego Trujillo-Pisanty. 2014. Betagrams: Maker Culture and the Aesthetics of Prototyping. *All Makers Now* (July 2014), 9-16.
8. James Befurt. 2014. How an enhgineer uses Tinder. (December 2014). Retrieved September 20, 2016 from https://www.youtube.com/watch?v=Qgnxb-O-CBQ
9. Catherine Bell. 2010. Ritual: Perspectives and Dimensions. Oxford University Press
10. Genevieve Bell, Mark Blythe, and Phoebe Sengers. 2005. Making by making strange: Defamiliarization and the design of domestic technologies. *ACM Trans. Comput.-Hum. Interact.* 12, 2 (June 2005), 149-173. DOI: http://dx.doi.org/10.1145/1067860.1067862
11. Peter Bennett, Jarrod Knibbe, Florent Berthaut, and Kirsten Cater. 2015. Resonant Bits: Controlling Digital Musical Instruments with Resonance and the Ideomotor Effect. In *Proceedings of the international conference on New Interfaces for Musical Expression* (NIME 2015). The School of Music and the Center for Computation and Technology (CCT), Louisiana State University, Baton Rouge, Louisiana, USA, 176-177.
12. Andrea Bianchi and Ian Oakley. 2013. Designing tangible magnetic appcessories. In *Proceedings of the 7th International Conference on Tangible, Embedded and Embodied Interaction* (TEI '13). ACM, New York, NY, USA, 255-258. DOI: http://dx.doi.org/10.1145/2460625.2460667
13. Durrell Bishop and Tom Hulbert. 2009. Luckybite BirdBox (December 2009) Retrieved September 20, 2016 from https://vimeo.com/20639763
14. David Chatting, David S. Kirk, Paulina Yurman, and Jo-Anne Bichard. 2015. Designing for family phatic communication: a design critique approach. In *Proceedings of the 2015 British HCI Conference* (British HCI '15). ACM, New York, NY, USA, 175-183. DOI: http://dx.doi.org/10.1145/2783446.2783566
15. David Chatting, Paulina Yurman, David P. Green, Jo-Anne Bichard and David S. Kirk. 2017. Ritual Machine V: Where are You? Proceedings of the 3rd Biennial Research Through Design Conference. 2017.
16. David Coz and Damien Henry. 2014. Google Cardboard. (June 2014). Retrieved September 20, 2016 from https://www.google.com/get/cardboard/
17. Clara Crivellaro, Alex Taylor, Vasillis Vlachokyriakos, Rob Comber, Bettina Nissen, and Peter Wright. 2016. Re-Making Places: HCI, 'Community Building' and Change. In *Proceedings of the 2016 CHI Conference on Human Factors in Computing Systems* (CHI '16). ACM, New York, NY, USA, 2958-2969. DOI: http://dx.doi.org/10.1145/2858036.2858332
18. Chris Csíkszentmihályi and Jude Mukundane. 2016. RootIO: ICT+ Telephony for Grassroots Radio. *ST-Africa* (May 2016).
19. Joe Desbonnet. 2011. Arduino to Android IO on the cheap (aka Poor Man's NFC). (May 2011) Retrieved September 20, 2016 from http://jdesbonnet.blogspot.co.uk/2011/05/arduino-to-android-io-on-cheap-aka-poor.html
20. William Gaver. 2012. What should we expect from research through design?. In *Proceedings of the SIGCHI Conference on Human Factors in Computing Systems* (CHI '12). ACM, New York, NY, USA, 937-946. DOI: http://dx.doi.org/10.1145/2207676.2208538
21. William Gaver, Andy Boucher, Nadine Jarvis, David Cameron, Mark Hauenstein, Sarah Pennington, John Bowers, James Pike, Robin Beitra, and Liliana Ovalle. 2016. The Datacatcher: Batch Deployment and Documentation of 130 Location-Aware, Mobile Devices That Put Sociopolitically-Relevant Big Data in People's Hands: Polyphonic Interpretation at Scale. In *Proceedings of the 2016 CHI Conference on Human Factors in Computing Systems* (CHI '16). ACM, New York, NY, USA, 1597-1607. DOI: http://dx.doi.org/10.1145/2858036.2858472
22. William Gaver, Tony Dunne, and Elena Pacenti. 1999. Design: Cultural probes. *interactions* 6, 1 (January 1999), 21-29. DOI: http://dx.doi.org/10.1145/291224.291235
23. Martin R. Gibbs, Frank Vetere, Marcus Bunyan, and Steve Howard. 2005. SynchroMate: a phatic technology for mediating intimacy. In *Proceedings of the 2005 conference on Designing for User eXperience* (DUX '05). AIGA: American Institute of Graphic Arts, New York, NY, USA, Article 37 .

24. Marc Hassenzahl, Stephanie Heidecker, Kai Eckoldt, Sarah Diefenbach, and Uwe Hillmann. 2012. All You Need is Love: Current Strategies of Mediating Intimate Relationships through Technology. *ACM Trans. Comput.-Hum. Interact.* 19, 4, Article 30 (December 2012), 19 pages. DOI: http://dx.doi.org/10.1145/2395131.2395137
25. Lara Houston, Steven J. Jackson, Daniela K. Rosner, Syed Ishtiaque Ahmed, Meg Young, and Laewoo Kang. 2016. Values in Repair. In *Proceedings of the 2016 CHI Conference on Human Factors in Computing Systems* (CHI '16). ACM, New York, NY, USA, 1403-1414. DOI: http://dx.doi.org/10.1145/2858036.2858470
26. Hilary Hutchinson, Wendy Mackay, Bo Westerlund, Benjamin B. Bederson, Allison Druin, Catherine Plaisant, Michel Beaudouin-Lafon, Stéphane Conversy, Helen Evans, Heiko Hansen, Nicolas Roussel, and Björn Eiderbäck. 2003. Technology probes: inspiring design for and with families. In *Proceedings of the SIGCHI Conference on Human Factors in Computing Systems* (CHI '03). ACM, New York, NY, USA, 17-24. DOI: http://dx.doi.org/10.1145/642611.642616
27. Sungjae Hwang, Myungwook Ahn, and Kwang-yun Wohn. 2013. MagGetz: customizable passive tangible controllers on and around conventional mobile devices. In *Proceedings of the 26th annual ACM symposium on User interface software and technology* (UIST '13). ACM, New York, NY, USA, 411-416. DOI: http://dx.doi.org/10.1145/2501988.2501991
28. Tim Ingold. 2007. Materials against materiality. *Archaeological dialogues*, *14*(01), 1-16.
29. iRobot. iRobot Create Open Interface http://www.irobot.com/filelibrary/create/Create%20Open%20Interface_v2.pdf
30. David S. Kirk, David Chatting, Paulina Yurman, and Jo-Anne Bichard. 2016. Ritual Machines I & II: Making Technology at Home. In *Proceedings of the 2016 CHI Conference on Human Factors in Computing Systems* (CHI '16). ACM, New York, NY, USA, 2474-2486. DOI: https://doi.org/10.1145/2858036.2858424
31. Mike Kuniavsky, Smart Things: Ubiquitous Computing User Experience Design, Morgan Kaufmann Publishers Inc., San Francisco, CA, 2010
32. Gierad Laput, Eric Brockmeyer, Scott E. Hudson, and Chris Harrison. 2015. Acoustruments: Passive, Acoustically-Driven, Interactive Controls for Handheld Devices. In *Proceedings of the 33rd Annual ACM Conference on Human Factors in Computing Systems* (CHI '15). ACM, New York, NY, USA, 2161-2170. DOI: http://dx.doi.org/10.1145/2702123.2702414
33. Silvia Lindtner, Garnet D. Hertz, and Paul Dourish. 2014. Emerging sites of HCI innovation: hackerspaces, hardware startups & incubators. In *Proceedings of the SIGCHI Conference on Human Factors in Computing Systems* (CHI '14). ACM, New York, NY, USA, 439-448. DOI: http://dx.doi.org/10.1145/2556288.2557132
34. Einar Sneve Martinussen and Timo Arnall. 2009. Designing with RFID. In *Proceedings of the 3rd International Conference on Tangible and Embedded Interaction* (TEI '09). ACM, New York, NY, USA, 343-350. DOI: http://dx.doi.org/10.1145/1517664.1517734
35. Jitsuro Mase. 2010. Palm Top Theater. (November 2010). Retrieved September 20, 2016 from https://www.youtube.com/watch?v=na-R4rZkzH0
36. David A. Mellis and Leah Buechley. 2014. Do-it-yourself cellphones: an investigation into the possibilities and limits of high-tech diy. In *Proceedings of the SIGCHI Conference on Human Factors in Computing Systems* (CHI '14). ACM, New York, NY, USA, 1723-1732. DOI: http://dx.doi.org/10.1145/2556288.2557309
37. Daniel Miller. 1998. Material Culture: Why Some Things Matter.
38. William Odom, Ron Wakkary, Youn-kyung Lim, Audrey Desjardins, Bart Hengeveld, and Richard Banks. 2016. From Research Prototype to Research Product. In *Proceedings of the 2016 CHI Conference on Human Factors in Computing Systems* (CHI '16). ACM, New York, NY, USA, 2549-2561. DOI: http://dx.doi.org/10.1145/2858036.2858447
39. Daniela Petrelli, Nick Dulake, Mark Marshall, Matt Willox, Fabio Caparrelli, and Robin Goldberg. 2014. Prototyping tangibles: exploring form and interaction. In *Proceedings of the 8th International Conference on Tangible, Embedded and Embodied Interaction* (TEI '14). ACM, New York, NY, USA, 41-48. DOI: http://dx.doi.org/10.1145/2540930.2540966
40. Daniela Petrelli and Ann Light. 2014. Family Rituals and the Potential for Interaction Design: A Study of Christmas. *ACM Trans. Comput.-Hum. Interact.* 21, 3, Article 16 (June 2014), 29 pages. DOI: http://dx.doi.org/10.1145/2617571
41. James Pierce and Eric Paulos. 2014. Counterfunctional things: exploring possibilities in designing digital limitations. In Proceedings of the 2014 conference on Designing interactive systems (DIS '14). ACM, New York, NY, USA, 375-384. DOI: http://dx.doi.org/10.1145/2598510.2598522
42. Dave Randall, Richard Harper, and Mark Rouncefield. 2007. *Fieldwork for Design: Theory and Practice (Computer Supported Cooperative Work)*. Springer-Verlag New York, Inc., Secaucus, NJ, USA.

43. Tom Randle. 2014. Shepherd - The leap sheep cheating machine. (February 2014). Retrieved September 20, 2016 from http://tomrandle.github.io/Shepherd/

44. Dan Saffer. 2013. *Microinteractions: Designing with Details*. O'Reilly Media, Inc.

45. Luke Sturgeon and Shamik Ray. 2013. Visualising electromagnetic fields. (May 2013). Retrieved September 20, 2016 from https://vimeo.com/65321968

46. Kazuhisa Terasaki. 2013. Smartphone Servo. (September 2013). Retrieved September 20, 2016 from http://makezine.com/projects/make-34/smartphone-servo/

47. Ron Wakkary, William Odom, Sabrina Hauser, Garnet Hertz, and Henry Lin. 2015. Material speculation: actual artifacts for critical inquiry. In *Proceedings of The Fifth Decennial Aarhus Conference on Critical Alternatives* (AA '15). Aarhus University Press 97-108. DOI: http://dx.doi.org/10.7146/aahcc.v1i1.21299

48. Jeffrey Yoo Warren. 2012. Public Lab DIY Spectrometry Kit. (August 2012). Retrieved September 20, 2016 from https://www.kickstarter.com/projects/jywarren/public-lab-diy-spectrometry-kit/description

49. Topher White. 2014. Rainforest Connection. (September 2014). Retrieved September 20, 2016 from https://www.ted.com/talks/topher_white_what_can_save_the_rainforest_your_used_cell_phone?language=en.

Products as Agents: Metaphors for Designing the Products of the IoT Age

Nazli Cila[1], Iskander Smit[2], Elisa Giaccardi[3], Ben Kröse[1]
[1] Amsterdam University of Applied Sciences, Digital Life Centre, Amsterdam, The Netherlands, n.cila@hva.nl, b.j.a.krose@hva.nl
[2] Info.nl, Amsterdam, The Netherlands, iskander@info.nl
[3] Delft University of Technology, Department of Industrial Design, Delft, The Netherlands, e.giaccardi@tudelft.nl

ABSTRACT
Design-based inquiries into the networked products of the Internet of Things (IoT) lack a coherent understanding of the effect of such products on society. This paper proposes a new taxonomy for networked products, which would allow articulation on their current state and future, and provide insights to designers for creating meaningful and aesthetic products of IoT. Central to this framework is the proposition that our current product-scape should be understood as a distribution of material agencies and best analyzed through the metaphor of "agency". We identify three types of agencies, i.e., the Collector, the Actor, and the Creator, and discuss how this approach could create new design methodologies to create more meaningful networked products that would empower people in their everyday lives.

Author Keywords
Internet of Things; networked products; agency; metaphor; interaction design.

ACM Classification Keywords
H.5.m. Information interfaces and presentation: Miscellaneous.

INTRODUCTION
Products of the 21st century are quite different from their older brothers and sisters. Since information processing has become cheap and widespread, the capability to collect and handle information has become one of the many 'materials' from which products can be made [38]. Through gaining computational power and network connectivity, cars, thermostats, and even light bulbs have begun to communicate with their users, manufacturers, and of course one another. The speed and scale of this "Internet of Things" (IoT) provide new design opportunities to empower people and enrich their everyday life. In order to gain insights on how to create networked products that attain these aims, as design researchers, we are required to better understand not only the technical infrastructure and technological parameters of networked products (as IoT is generally tackled in engineering and computer sciences), but also the social relationships of these products with everyday practices of people [37].

CHI 2017, May 06-11, 2017, Denver, CO, USA
© 2017 ACM. ISBN 978-1-4503-4655-9/17/05…$15.00
DOI: http://dx.doi.org/10.1145/3025453.3025797

For the past couple of decades, there has been a shift in the definition of designers' main task from designing "things", which are objects, to designing Things, namely socio-material assemblies [6,7]. Things have become political gatherings around shared matters of concern with a visible effect in the world. When it comes to the current product-scape of IoT, however, we fail to observe this Thing-ness. This situation is humorously demonstrated at the blog "we put a chip on it" (http://weputachipinit.tumblr.com/). Its tagline "It was just a dumb thing. Then we put a chip in it. Now it's a smart thing" accurately summarizes the current approach towards smart products. Clothespins that notify you when the laundry is dry or socks that keep track of how many times they were washed indicate how shortsightedly IoT could be executed. Being smart, however, has a lot more potential.

Networked products should be a hybrid of technological developments and cultural articulation [37]. They need to be in a form that enables users to invite these products into their lives and makes an impact on people's life quality. Design practice has been trying to invent the new IoT medium by exploring the new affordances and challenges that being connected brings [46]. Design research, therefore, should catch up with the practice by undertaking inquiries into what these products mean for design culture and society and how to create empowering networked products that go beyond simply embedding a chip in something. Coming to grips with the IoT demands new ways of seeing, understanding and asking pertinent questions about the ontological nature of smart and connected products and their impact on users' lives. Frameworks and theories in interaction design help making strategic choices about how to proceed and where to invest energy [36]. In this paper, we propose a framework that is based on the metaphor of "agency" in order to do so.

In our understanding, IoT currently deals with four different types of products: (1) products that connect to its users to inform their status and receive orders, (2) products that connect to its users and learn from these interactions to become more intelligent, (3) products that are connected to other products to exchange status information that is used to steer rule-based behavior, and (4) products that do not connect to the user or other products via Internet, but have an internal architecture that can adapt to the behavior of the user. All these types indicate a capacity to sense and act autonomously. These products can learn and evolve. They can reveal new patterns and change our minds. In other words, they are actants with performative roles in our lives. Seeing them as agents can help us unravel the ecologies between products and users, provide guidance about analyzing and discussing the products of IoT, and eventually offer a new framework for developing methodologies to design them better.

The IoT field is no stranger to metaphors. Kuniavsky, for instance, uses the term "information shadow" to refer to the digital information that tails a product's usage [38]. Rose uses the metaphor of enchantment to describe the pleasant experiences that well-designed smart products provide [49]. As casting a magic spell to an ordinary object, the smart products gain some remarkable ability that make them more useful, engaging and delightful, than their ordinary self. Romero, Pousman and Mateas describe the potential of ubiquitous computer systems to sense and react unpredictably to the behavior of users as an "alien presence" [48]. IoT as a field is susceptible to using descriptive metaphors, because many concepts of the field are rather abstract and the effect of its outcomes are difficult to grasp, which is what metaphors are good at overcoming. Although these metaphors vividly evoke the invisible, yet powerfully present potential of IoT, they do not offer a framework in which we can systematically compare and abstract the use and impact of smart products.

In his seminal work, Schön introduces the term "generative metaphor" in order to broaden the extend of metaphor from being a frame for looking at things to a process by which new perspectives on the world come into existence [52]. We consider that the potential of smart products to change behaviors of users and their capacity to make a visible effect on society call for a generative metaphor. A metaphor of agency can provide such new way of thinking as it accounts for the ways we currently communicate and work with an ecosystem of responsive objects.

In the remainder of this paper, we will first draw selectively from the perspectives on object agency coming from various disciplines. Then, we will present a taxonomy that is based on our understanding of how agency is and will be manifested in smart products. We discuss and reinterpret products that fall under each type of agency in the taxonomy, and point out to specific issues that are raised through their material agency. Finally, we argue for a theoretical approach that follows from an understanding of product agency by discussing the benefits of this metaphor, propose design methodologies that are fitting for creating agents and discuss the design challenges that follow from the form and behavior of such agents.

THE RISE OF AGENCY

Scientific inquiry into the notion of agency is not new to the science and technology studies, humanities, feminist studies and philosophy. Over the past decades, scholarship in these disciplines has started to retire from perspectives that place human beings at its center. This non-anthropocentric understanding prompts considering human as a single knot in a system where many other nonhuman actors are also at play. Each human or nonhuman actor in the system exerts impact on others.

The most prominent account in this regard is Actor-Network Theory (ANT). ANT offers valuable insights into mapping the complex relationships between technologies and humans. Scholars in this tradition revoke the privilege of human actor and discuss the ontological symmetry of humans and nonhumans in networks of relations [40,42]. In other words, human and nonhuman are studied as equal actors in any kind of network, and their agencies can be continuously transformed into one another. This flat ontology is also at focus in materialist philosophies, e.g., [10,13,31]. In particular, "Object-oriented ontology" (OOO) represents the philosophical positions that dissociate philosophy from anthropocentrism and consider objects to live an existence that exceeds the relations with humans. Central to this proposition is considering objects "as entities in their own right without requiring recourse to human use, perception, or meaning making" [19].

As a matter of fact, this is the argument that ANT and OOO stand apart. Although both perspectives ascribe human and nonhuman equal being, in OOO the reality of objects is binary—something is either real or not regardless of the relations it enters into [14]. In ANT, on the other hand, alliances take the center stage and the reality of objects is defined through each object's relation to other actors. The more an object enters into additional alliances and extends the range of its effect on other actants, the more real it becomes [14]. Therefore, there is a constant dynamic transformation of things through coupling.

Another theory from social sciences, activity theory, also supports this claim. According to activity theory, understanding two or more actors (subject and object in activity theory terminology) is only possible through analyzing the relationship/activity between them—an understanding that cannot be achieved by focusing on the subject or object separately [36]. Agency, the ability to act for producing effects, is a fundamental attribute of both subject and object. However, not every entity can be a subject. Subjects have needs that drive them for acting in the world, which turns the agency manifested by the subject into a special character: it is the ability and also the "need" to act. For this reason, only living things can be subjects. Nonhuman have the ability to act but not the need to act, which makes the relationship between the subject and the object asymmetrical. For this reason, activity theory rejects the symmetry granted to humans and nonhumans by ANT and OOO. In these theories nonhuman can delegate action to human, but in activity theory delegation always flows from human to all other kinds of agents (a detailed comparison of agencies between ANT and activity theory can be found in [36]). This theoretical position is also held by Ingold, who considers agency to signify intentionality [33,34]. Agency in his view is not an innate property of things but is something that emerges out of encounters with other things or human beings and actualized in specific situations.

This argument advocates for a relational, emergent form of agency as in ANT. The relational agency provides ANT to align with feminist theorizing in which there is an emphasis on the relational character of our capacities for action. Corresponding with the arguments of ANT and OOO, feminist theorist Barad also sees agency as something that occurs instead of something that one has [4]. In her view, everything is entangled with everything else. Studying any sort of situation where agency is displayed, that is any kind of knowledge practice, requires making an "agential cut" between what is included and what is excluded from the thing being studied. Barad argues that separations are temporarily enacted so one can examine something long enough to gain knowledge about it [4]. Agential cuts are a means for thinking about complex systems and cultures, and a critical framework for discussing what is brought forth or ignored when analyzing such complexities.

Regardless of their different viewpoints over the ontological symmetry between human and nonhuman or the definition of agency, all these theories coming from different disciplines have effectively challenged the traditional perspectives that restrict agency to humans. What these approaches have in common is seeing objects not solely as augmenters of human action, but as peers within a complex network [35]. In this paper, we do not adopt the arguments of any of these approaches directly as our theoretical foundation but rather aim to appropriate their main message that humans and nonhumans are both capable of action and making an impact on each other. This approach of distributed agency corresponds well with design, especially since the products have become smarter and more responsive.

The integration of (largely) autonomous set of interacting objects in everyday life has been explored from the early days of Ubiquitous Computing. In his seminal work, Weiser (1991) envisioned a world in which computing is so pervasive that everyday devices can sense their relationship to us and to each other and coordinate their actions accordingly [56]. Weiser's key objectives were ubiquity, i.e., embedding computation into the many aspects of the physical world, and invisibility, i.e., having these computers to operate autonomously [21]. Carrying the UbiComp principles one step further, the Ambient Intelligence (AmI) paradigm of the late nineties presented a vision on digital systems for the year 2010 and beyond [2]. AmI refers to the environment-embedded electronic systems that are sensitive and responsive to the presence of people, where many products cooperate seamlessly with one another to improve the user experience [1]. The word intelligence in AmI refers to having digital surroundings exhibit specific forms of social interaction, such as recognizing people, personalizing to their preferences, adapting themselves, and possible acting upon users' behalf [1]. Recently, the concept "human-computer integration" has been proposed to replace the traditional human-computer interaction [23]. Integration is defined through a codependent partnership between the user and the product—in which partners construct meaning around each other's activities, negotiate and sometimes compromise—that carries the straightforward command-and-respond way of interacting with products and systems further towards a more symbiotic relationship.

All these perspectives emphasize how products and systems have become more autonomous with the developing technologies. Yet, there are different ways that smart products could display autonomy. Below, this taxonomy will be presented.

PRODUCTS AS AGENTS TAXONOMY

Products of IoT can exhibit different behaviors as agents. We consider that the current trends in IoT point out to three roles: the Collector, the Actor, and the Creator. Each behavior sketches out different aspects of the HCI design space that need further attention and calls for a different mode of inquiry. These roles are not meant as disconnected categories, but rather envisioned as a scale. The degree of product agency increases from the Collector type towards the Creator type. Also within the same category, some products may display more agency than the others. We will be using this taxonomy to compare, abstract, and generalize the current approaches and trends in HCI research, as well as to discuss how to proceed in order to create better networked products.

The Collector

(Also known as: the data reader; Used for: understanding, making invisible patterns visible)

The first type of agency we can elicit from IoT has to do with the Collector products which sense and process information. They have the ability to aggregate data from embedded sensors or social media platforms and feed the data back to its user, to other users, or to other products. These products are sometimes referred to as smart things [38], meta-products [32], everyware [30], or hybrid products [31]. Most of the Collector products have a dual identity—a physical form and a virtual existence that is connected to online services. Well-known self-monitoring devices such as Jawbone or FitBit, for example, allow people to collect and utilize data on everyday activities like sleep patterns or the number of steps walked, and therefore, can be considered as part of this category.

Laurel describes one of the functions of sensors as inviting nature into collaboration [41]. When a sensor gathers information about bird migrations, wind, or processes inside a living being, the invisible patterns of nature are brought into the realm of senses. Lapka personal environment monitor, in a similar vein, render the invisible radiation, electromagnetic fields, and humidity in a room into abstract shapes to be displayed on a cellphone (Figure 1). Having entered our daily lives tremendously, the Collector products are not only able to tap into environmental factors, but also reveal people's patterns of behavior and webs of practices. In this sense, they serve as "co-ethnographers" [28]. They have access to data and patterns that we as humans do not, and thus, help us see what was previously invisible. As an example, the connected baby bottle designed by Bogers and his colleagues reveals the correlations between feeding quality and environmental noise, formula temperature, teat size, and feeding location [9]. During the testing of the product, the parents welcomed these less obvious insights because they made certain patterns in their feeding practice visible, which prompted the parents to make changes in their practice to have a better experience.

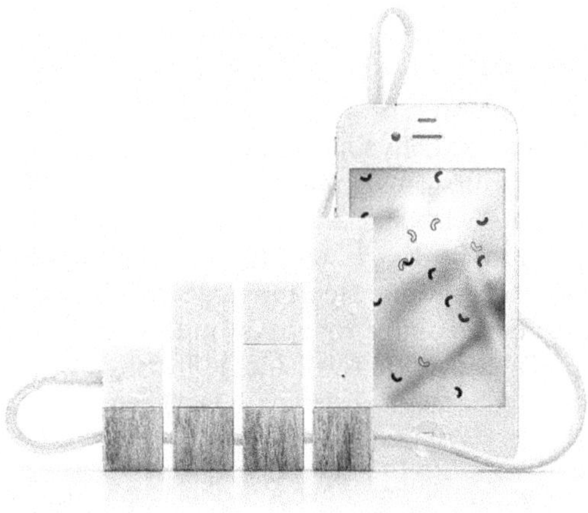

Figure 1. Lapka personal environment monitor.

On a larger scale, in "smart cities" where many products and apps contribute to a pulsing cloud of urban data, the same co-ethnography is also at play. DiSalvo, Jenkins, and Lodato discuss the notion of "computed civics", i.e., the situation in which civic participation emerges from computation [18]. Examples include sensor systems that count car throughput on particular roads or cycling apps that gather data on the quality of cyclists' routes. The data collected by these systems provide detailed knowledge about the city and city life, which is utilized in the design of physical infrastructure, creation of policy, or justification of planning decisions. In such ways these systems create a new kind of civics, where it is not the citizens themselves, but instead their mobile phones or sensors are doing the civic volunteering [18]. This is a fascinating display of agency; the Collector products participate in social and political exchange.

Whether it is on personal, societal, or environmental level, the Collector products measure one or multiple parameters that are invisible to human perception, visualize this data on a screen or on the product itself, and provide handles for insight into everyday life, which has an enormous potential for molding users' behavior and social practices.

The Actor

(Also known as: the interventionist; Used for: creating dialogs)

The second type of agency involves the Actor products, which act autonomously according to the behaviors of users or other products. These products sense and interpret data like the Collector products, but also respond to it. Designers create a potential space for the product behavior. The users navigate in this space and perceive the product's behavior while the product is also engaged in autonomous interpretation of the users' behavior. Perhaps the best-known smart device, Google Nest is an Actor product in our taxonomy as it monitors users' activities throughout the day and learns to adapt itself and the environment according to their behavior patterns.

In the interactions with the Actor products, the user and the product continuously delegate action to each other. Marenko argues that this situation induces animistic responses in users [44]. The more the product seems intelligent and autonomous, the more our experience to deal with it tilts toward animism. As a matter of fact, the animistic behaviors of products can enable fluid and meaningful interactions between users and interactive systems. Van Allen and McVeigh-Schultz deliberately employed animism as a methodological framework in their design case of six interactive objects called Anithings [55]. Each Anithing has different intentions, personality, and inner life. Their exploration shows that these qualities of Actor products have a potential to trigger myth-making tendencies of people and produce pleasant user-product interactions.

A similar pleasurable interaction is also experienced through the use of the Addicted Toaster (Figure 2) [47]. As a behavior that some Actor products are prone to, the toaster exploits online social network services to mimic sentience and gain identity. It nudges its owner to consume more toast by tweeting about it. Sterling names such material objects with immaterial identities that engage in conversations with other actors as "spimes" [53]. Many of the Actor products in fact fall under the spime category.

Figure 2. Addicted Toaster by Simone Rebaudengo and Haque Design+Research (Courtesy of Simone Rebaudengo).

As in Collector products, the reach of the Actor products has started to extend beyond the home environment. With the advancement of the smart city notion, cities have become a playground to experiment with material agency as well. The Hello Lamppost project, for instance, uses pre-existing identifier codes on street furniture to enable people sending text messages to the objects like post boxes or trash bins (http://www.hellolamppost.co.uk/). The objects hold a conversation with the user by passing on the information that other residents had sent before (Figure 3). These conversations are intended as an opportunity to share memories of the city and rediscover local environments. While the Hello Lamppost had a playful aim and interaction, Bambea intends to ascribe sentience to the lampposts in order to improve health of the residents of Amsterdam (http://digitallifecentre.nl/projecten/bambea/). It is a computing system that is composed of beacons and a smartphone app. The beacons are attached onto the lampposts in Oost Park in Amsterdam, which have the lampposts send motivational messages to the smartphones of runners in order to coach their running experience.

Figure 3. Hello Lamppost by PAN Studio, Tom Armitage and Gyorgyi Galik (Courtesy of Playable City).

Regardless of being embedded at home or outside environments, using Actor products requires coordination and negotiation. They sometimes nudge the users subtly to change their behavior, as in Bambea where the lampposts mainly "suggest" a better route, speed, or additional exercises. But sometimes the Actor products make more dramatic interventions. For example, the Addicted Toaster relocates itself to a new home if neglected or the Amazon trashcan of MIT Media Lab scan the barcodes of things thrown away and have them reordered from Amazon automatically [15]. Although the intensity and limits of the intervention could vary, what is common among the Actor products is their intention to make a visible effect on everyday life and practices.

The Creator

(Also known as: the self-aware; Used for: creating futures)

The last type of agency is drawn from near future scenarios, in which the products will become the Creator of futures. Active research is being conducted on robots that can be used in daily lives [12] and a robotic future that merges with everyday products [3]. This indicates that robots and AI are breaking free from their traditional anthropometric looks and entering the daily lives of people. Then why not these everyday robots, or more aptly the everyday products with robotic qualities, start making a tangible difference on their form, the environment they are in, and the way they are used?

The ability to learn and evolve is a continuous concern in the robotics and AI fields. Bongard, Zykov and Lipson have been developing the Starfish, which is the first robot to develop some sort of "self-awareness" [11]. The robot synthesizes a predictive model of its own body through the interaction with its environment and uses this model to develop new behaviors without an internal mathematical model constructed by engineers. Carrying the self-awareness concept one step further, Samuelsen and Glette have been developing a robot system that has a connection with a 3D printer and is able to print new robots or customized robot parts instantly to tackle any situation they face [51].

As the algorithms have become this sophisticated, what kind of a future it will hold when everyday products with robotic qualities become self-aware about their form, environment, and usage? The vision of personal fabricators to expand outside of laboratories into homes has started to become a reality [27]. Connecting the self-aware everyday robots to 3D printers, as in the previous example, could open up an immense playground for displaying product agency. Since a toaster can arrange itself new host families by using the Internet (i.e., the Addicted Toaster), may be in the near future it could also order custom-made 3D printed pieces to be delivered at its owner's home for the toaster to be used more efficiently.

Such not-there-yet but feasible scenarios will not only affect the users' authority at home, but also influence the nature of the design process. Devendorf and Ryokai tackle the new configurations of humans and machines in hybrid making [17]. They invited users to mimic a 3D printer in order to elicit personal reflections on human-machine-product relationship and expose tensions between agency and control. Based on this, another configuration could be the machine taking charge of improving itself or its connected products. When the nonhumans will start to conceive such futures, designers will have to give up some authorial control and come up with concepts and forms that would prompt "free agents" to make choices and take actions that would yield to satisfying outcomes [17]. Through the new forms of product agency, new roles for designers in creation are bound to emerge.

DISCUSSION

Users' tendency for ascribing intelligence or intentionality to products has been a longstanding concern in HCI. What is recent, however, is the realization that a product is contextualized within a network of other products, users, values, and contexts, and that it gains an agency via establishing relationships with the actors in this network. This theoretical position of shared agency and the generative metaphor used for describing the situation open up new investigative opportunities for the design and study of new forms of entanglements with smart products.

First, it brings in a broader perspective to adopt when creating a nonhuman actor, i.e., a smart object, as a component of ecologies involving complex interactions and interrelations. Designing from an agency standpoint requires considering the interdependence of human and nonhuman actors, and crafting meaningful interactions between all the relevant actors in a context. Second, the symmetry between human and nonhuman advocated by this perspective enables exploring new design possibilities that may be overlooked in a typical human-centered design process. DiSalvo and Lukens argue that a non-anthropocentric approach in design, when used as a deliberate exercise, allows designers to break free from the human form, capabilities and affordances, consider the ways nonhuman may figure into action and experience, and eventually see a technology with a fresh eye [19]. Third, through the agency perspective, we can strive toward a new way of discussing and envisioning the use of the smart products. It allows for a better articulation about the impact of these products in society and discussing the ethics of such interactions. In all these means, the agency metaphor extends the theoretical and social agendas of contemporary HCI research.

In what follows we examine the considerations that play a role in the design of agent products. We start by discussing the potential design methods that are suitable for tackling each type of agency. Next, we discuss the social, aesthetic, and ethical implications of delegating control to autonomous agents. Finally, we present considerations that need to be taken into account when giving form to these products and the potential uses of their designed behaviors. We consider that these issues could offer insights into using the full potential of smart products, as opposed to being limited with just sensor embedding.

Designing agents

Interaction and product designers are faced with new forms of material affordances when creating networked products. These products are typically spread across various platforms, technologies, and infrastructures (e.g., Google Nest uses a sensor platform, an application platform, WiFi network, database, and so on). This requires a holistic approach during design, in which each component is designed with and around to produce a coherent product experience [37]. This integratedness needs to be present in addressing the ecosystem that the product is in as well. As argued by ANT and activity theory, studying multiple actors means studying the relationships in between. In the design of smart products, instead of addressing each product "vertically", i.e., being only responsible for its form and behavior, a horizontal approach is needed where the designer is also responsible for considering the multiple overlapping relationships with other products and contexts while giving form and ascribing behavior to a product.

Although a holistic and horizontal approach that works across various platforms and connects various actors applies to the design of all agents, different design methods may fit better to each type of agency. The main issue with the Collector products, for instance, is finding ways to use the collected contextual, experiential and behavioral data as creative design material in the design process—as a step going further than using them solely for optimize and validate design [9]. In the design process of the Collector products, a combination of sensor data and ethnographic methods would work best in revealing the complex architecture of practices and values surrounding the use of these products [16]. Ethnography is well equipped to position data in specific socio-cultural situations and offer in depth insights of the use context and experiences. Together, these analyses could grant the designers the relevant quantitative data coming from the algorithms interpreting the sensor data and the qualitative data that unveil the forms of practice the object partakes in. Such knowledge, when fed back into the iterative design process, help to bridge the gap between sensor data insights and real experiences, and help designers to create products that are well-fitting to the use context.

The design process of the Actor products is a viable arena for experimenting with speculative design. These products have an autonomous character, and hence, a strong potential to make an impact on the user and everyday practices in ways that are currently unknown to us. In order imagine and critically reflect on these futures, the discursive space created by the speculative design would work well [43].

While doing so, a "maker" approach is also needed. Material engagement is an important factor to care for the critical matter at hand. The behavior of the Actor products should be carefully crafted considering various use situations and interactions. Research-through-design methods could allow for exploring not only the material affordances of an Actor product, but also its effects on socio-cultural situations. Knutsen, for example, goes through a "critical making" process of a playful networked product that peaks out according to his friends' activity at Foursquare in order to discover infrastructural landscape of IoT with its material and immaterial relationships [37]. This approach, he argues, enabled him to engage with the critical matter of technologies differently than would have been the case by studying existing products. Similarly, Rozendaal suggests using animated low-fidelity mockups in order to bring autonomous "objects with intent" to life [50]. These mockups are invaluable to understand an object's expressiveness in relation to its purpose and reflect on its possible implications on user activity and behavior. Overall, these RTD experiments, address the possibilities and problems implicit in the design of the Actor products and bring about a range of procedural and conceptual insights to be articulated [25].

When it comes to the Creator type of smart products, the main question to tackle is how designers and design researchers can conceive of a vision when the products start to use the data they collect to make physical interventions on the way they look, move, or behave. A speculative design approach, but this time using "design fiction" as a method, can again be of help here. Design fiction is a prototyping technique that is particularly tailored to facilitate studying near futures and investigate where the ideal situation is located within the range of possible futures [43]. By not allowing the current technical and social mechanisms to influence the discursive space, design fictions can help to imagine how designers, users, and Creator products can work together to create new concepts or improvements in the current products and how this situation will effect the nature of the design process. By doing so, the assumptions about the role of the designer and his/her relationships with smart products are challenged. Employing design fiction methods can open up new questions and unfamiliar opportunities in this regard.

What all these proposed methods have in common is an acknowledgement of the ongoing interaction between human and nonhuman and looking for methods of design research that give both an equal voice. A thing-centered perspective can bring unique insights about the role of objects in human practices, and thus open up design opportunities that we may not be able to see with traditional user-centered design methods [28,29]. This requires a methodological re-orientation towards the concerns of objects in shaping how technologies are imagined, realized, and researched [45]. Ordinary objects should be engaged in the design process as participants to collaboratively elicit new insights. This non-anthropocentric approach does not eliminate the human agency. It is just a shift away from privileging human activities and desires over other agents in order to better understand, describe, and critique a given scenario, which eventually broadens the conditions and issues of design and design research [19].

Delegating control

Our commonsense understanding of reciprocity holds that the way we behave toward others affects the way others behave in return. But how does this human conduct apply to our interactions with smart products that display autonomous behavior? These products should know when to respond and when to delegate in order to provide pleasant experiences. Failing to engage in this proper social conduct can cause a growing tension between human and product agency. Striking examples in this regard are illustrated in the Uninvited Guests video, which is a critical depiction of the tension between an elderly man and his "smart" devices at home and how he deceives the system, as would be expected from anyone whose boundaries and routines are invaded by smart products alike [54].

As the smart products gain more autonomy, it becomes imperative to train these with the art of social grace and diplomacy. Let us take the talking shoe of Adidas and Google collaboration as an example (Figure 4). The sneakers have a microprocessor that translates the pressure sensor and accelerometer readings into audio instructions. This enables the shoes literally speak with the wearer and encourage physical movement by offering pep talk or sometimes trash talk (an Actor product). Compared to FitBit or other Collector type products that track movement and offer encouragement through a screen, the talking shoe is quite vocal and expressive for the same purpose. Although it may be easier to form an emotional bond with the latter one (and possibly, being more encouraged to move), the situation that one is in may not always be appropriate to deal with this shoe. That is why these sneakers will always be in the gadget category, rather than entering everyday lives as everyday products. To develop a meaningful interaction between users and smart products, the context in which the interaction takes place should be investigated well, together with how people in a specific situation may respond to the product.

Such conflicts may not only be between the user and the product but also among products. When each product has its own goals and agendas, who will mediate the emerging conflicts? Bihr and Thorne give the example of different home appliances fighting over the blinds being open or closed on the basis of their respective goals, such as the coffee machine wanting them closed so the milk lasts longer, the plants wants them open, the Nest wants them closed to keep the temperature low, and so on [5]. For now the users are the ones to moderate these conflicts, but when there will be a time when products are able to take on more negotiation among them, new challenges for interaction designers will arise.

The autonomous behaviors also raise ethical challenges to consider how interaction design can be sensitive to the situation in which it intervenes. Fallman challenges the question of what is ethical design in the contexts of material objects enhanced with digital capacities [22]. He emphasizes the ethical and moral responsibility on the part of the designer rather than the user. For example, designers should consider how people might wish to overrule the autonomous actions performed by the smart product in particular contexts. Expecting that a smart product would be able to foresee and respond appropriately to any possible situation is a naïve idea in our current reality. Being teased by your shoe by it asking if you are a statue would be something funny when one is hanging out with friends at home, but it could be slightly embarrassing when waiting for the bus with strangers; and it is most probably difficult for the shoe to make a differentiation between these two situations. Rozendaal gives the responsibility here to the designers [50]. Designers should create some space of freedom for the users, which allows a product to display an autonomous action but this action could always be tempered or overridden by the user depending on the situation they s/he is in.

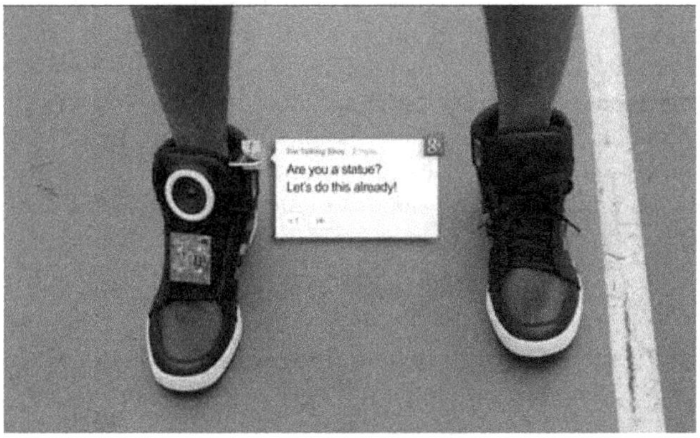

Figure 4. Talking shoe by 72andSunny, Google, and YesYesNo (Courtesy of 72andSunny and YesYesNo).

In the design of the smart products to know when to respond and when to delegate, guiding visions must be developed, which provide the means for analyzing and discussing the social, cultural, ethical, moral, ecological, and political implications of these experiences and how they foster particular relationships between users, designers, artifacts, and contexts [22]. The same ethical considerations surely also apply to the design of the Collector type of products, whose promise of easier and healthier lives, and more efficient and greener cities is hinged on getting hold of more data, or to the Creator type products which will change the relationship between designer and user and the nature of the design process. As in any kind of design process, here the core values of moral epistemic standing, i.e., human welfare, privacy, universal usability, and informed consent, should be followed [24].

Form and behavior of agents

An understandable trap to fall when giving form to agents is to be (unintentionally) affected by the "ultimate agent" of our times—a robot. Currently the form of robots is more commonly influenced by their historical and fictional representations, based on the assumption that it is more natural for humans to interact with humanoid than abstract forms [3]. However, considering that the use context of most smart products is home environment and everyday life, following a normative product design methodology is a better route to shape these products. The "robotification" of products should be by incorporating a clear functional purpose and adapting them to the domestic landscape using established modes of interaction, rather than simulating the human form and capacities [3].

A good and classic example in this regard is the Technological Dreams Series (Figure 5). This project is an exploration of the near future where robots become cohabitants in daily life and the ways they could relate with us [20]. The beauty of these robots, or Actor type products in our taxonomy, comes from the abstraction: their form is adapted to accommodate brand new technologies, but still appearing familiar. A similar approach can also be seen in the aforementioned examples of the smart baby bottle or Amazon trash can: They appear as autonomous everyday products, instead of robots.

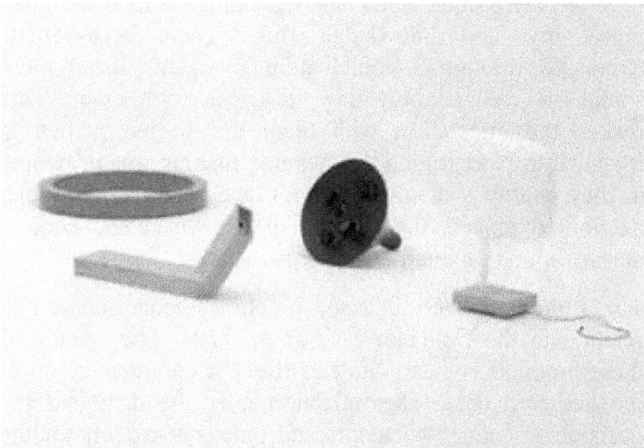

Figure 5. Technological Dreams Series: No. 1, Robots by Dunne & Raby (Courtesy of Fiona Raby).

We judge sentience through actions, intentions, and personality. Smart products display behaviors that evoke the perception of sentience. These kinetic behaviors provoke action from the user. The Caterpillar extension cable, for example, initiates a dialogue with the user about his/her energy consumption by twisting and turning as if in pain when the TV is left on stand-by (Figure 6) [39]. The product could have exhibited other agent behaviors to communicate the same message, such as Tweeting about it or automatically turning off the TV, yet the Caterpillar employs a powerful means—by relying on the user's empathy to act upon the artificial pain s/he causes on the product. Such animistic behaviors are significant for creating an emotive connection between the user and the product.

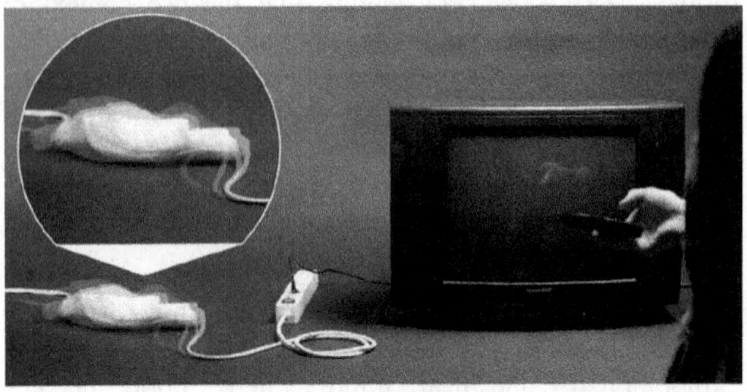

Figure 6. The Never Hungry caterpillar by Matthias Laschke, Marc Hassenzahl and Sarah Diefenbach (Courtesy of Matthias Laschke).

Instead of targeting a specific goal or solving a task, the physical behaviors of the products can also be designed for stimulating thinking and reflection. In the previously mentioned Anithings project, for example, the Actor type products are designed to have a life of their own, where they display unique behaviors depending on their assigned personality and knowledge [55]. Their behavior is expressed through a combination of visual display and sound, as well as how they influence each other. This makes the interaction with them unexpected, which is intended to "foreground the meaning making role of people as they interact with an ecology of heterogeneous, tangible, networked objects that behave in the world and acquire narrative, mythic qualities in people's lives."

The same approach is also sometimes experimented in relation to the Collector type of products. The agency of these products comes to an end after the communication of the gathered data. The reflection over the data and the decision to change behaviors and practices are left for the consideration of the users. HCI field has been exploring with other means of data communication than the aggregated numbers and stats. For example, the home health horoscope of Gaver and his colleagues communicates sensor data through the language and form of daily horoscopes [26]. The system embraces the ambiguity of data interpretation by shifting the responsibility for interpretation from the system to the user. Similarly, Romero, Pousman and Mateas's Tableau Machine is a system that deliberately avoids one-to-one mappings between data and display in order to engage the user in co-interpretation [48]. These examples demonstrate how users and products can work together for making sense of patterns, and the Collector products can be used as provocateurs for reflection.

CONCLUSION

In this paper we have argued that IoT design and research could benefit from a generative metaphor of product agency to describe the new affordances, challenges, and opportunities of smart and networked products. That is, these products are active agents in shaping the network of relationships they are in together with other human and nonhuman actors. They collect data, act on data, and make visible interventions in the contexts they are in based on data, which are all powerful displays of agency. We called out three types of behaviors that smart products exhibit as agents, i.e., the Collector, the Actor, and the Creator, and described some projects that employ that sort of agency in attempt to discuss the current and potential socio-cultural impact of such products.

The notion of agency, we propose, is valuable to come up with new opportunities and experiences of designing for IoT. While agency is a concept that has started to appear in the discussions in HCI to offer a pluralistic approach to meaningful interactions between all the actors involved in a context without merely focusing on human [19, 28, 35, 36, 45], we also need inquiries into the design process of such agents with regard to the relevant design methods to be used, the extent of the negotiation and delegation between the agent and the user, and the forms and behaviors that are suitable for them, which is the discussion this paper intended to start. The agency metaphor and its related taxonomy we offer hope to suggest new theoretical, methodological and practical directions for HCI research.

HCI is considered to be in its "third wave" presently, that is a shift from a narrow task-orientation to a broader concern of improving the quality of everyday experiences [8]. Smart products should have this mission as well. They already influence the rhythms and routines of our lives, which will potentially change our cultures, beliefs and preferences in the near future. An extended discussion of these behaviors and effects would facilitate enrichment and deepening of the current discussion on creating user experiences with smart products, and how to provide empowerment and behavior change through these agents.

ACKNOWLEDGMENTS

We thank Chris Speed for his invaluable insights on the subject which helped shaping some arguments in this paper.

REFERENCES

1. Emile Aarts and Boris de Ruyter. 2009. New research perspectives on ambient intelligence. *Ambient Int and Smart Envi* 1, 1: 5-14.

2. Emile Aarts and Stefano Marzano. 2003. *The new everyday: Visions of ambient intelligence.* 010 Publishing.
3. James Henry Auger. 2014. Living with robots: A speculative design approach. *Journal of Human-Robot Interaction* 3, 1: 20-42.
4. Karen Barad. 2007. *Meeting the universe halfway: Quantum physics and the entanglement of matter and meaning.* Duke University Press.
5. Peter Bihr and Michelle Thorne. 2016. Understanding the connected home: Thoughts on living in tomorrow's connected home. Retrieved Dec 30, 2016 from https://www.gitbook.com/book/connected-home-book/understanding-the-connected-home/details
6. Thomas Binder, Giorgio De Michelis, Pelle Ehn, Giulio Jacucci, Per Linde and Ina Wagner. 2011. *Design things*. MIT Press.
7. Erling Bjögvinsson, Pelle Ehn, and Per-Anders Hillgren. 2012. Design things and design thinking: Contemporary participatory design challenges. *Design Issues* 28, 3: 101-116.
8. Susanne Bødker. 2006. When second wave HCI meets third wave challenges. In *Proceedings of the 4th Nordic conference on Human-computer interaction: changing roles* (NordiCHI '06), Anders Mørch, Konrad Morgan, Tone Bratteteig, Gautam Ghosh, and Dag Svanaes (Eds.). ACM, New York, NY, USA, 1-8. DOI=http://dx.doi.org/10.1145/1182475.1182476
9. Sander Bogers, Joep Frens, Janne van Kollenburg, Eva Deckers, and Caroline Hummels. 2016. Connected Baby Bottle: A Design Case Study Towards a Framework for Data-Enabled Design. In *Proceedings of the 2016 ACM Conference on Designing Interactive Systems* (DIS '16). ACM, New York, NY, USA, 301-311. DOI: http://dx.doi.org/10.1145/2901790.2901855
10. Ian Bogost. 2012. *Alien phenomenology or what it's like to be a thing*. University of Minnesota Press.
11. Josh Bongard, Victor Zykov and Hod Lipson. 2006. Resilient machines through continuous self-modeling. *Science* 314, 5802: 1118-1121.
12. Cynthia Breazeal and Fardad Faridi. 2016. Robot. U.S. Patent D761,895, Filed Nov 24, 2015, issued July 19, 2016.
13. Levi R. Bryant. 2011. *The democracy of objects*. Open Humanities Press.
14. Levi R. Bryant. 2009. Being an Object-Oriented Ontologist and Actor-Network-Theorist is Hard! Retrieved Sep 11, 2016 from https://larvalsubjects.wordpress.com/2009/12/01/being-an-object-oriented-ontologist-and-actor-network-theorist-is-hard/
15. Susannah Cahalan. 2014. The future is now: The 10 gadgets that will change your life. Retrieved Sep 11, 2016 from http://nypost.com/2014/07/12/10-futuristic-gadgets-that-will-change-your-world/
16. Nazli Cila, Elisa Giaccardi, Melissa Caldwell, Fionn Tynan-O'Mahony, Chris Speed, and Neil Rubens. 2015. Listening to an Everyday Kettle: How Can the Data Objects Collect Be Useful for Design Research?. In *Proceedings of the Participatory Innovation Conference*. The Hague, NL, 500-506.
17. Laura Devendorf and Kimiko Ryokai. 2015. Being the Machine: Reconfiguring Agency and Control in Hybrid Fabrication. In *Proceedings of the 33rd Annual ACM Conference on Human Factors in Computing Systems* (CHI '15). ACM, New York, NY, USA, 2477-2486. DOI: http://dx.doi.org/10.1145/2702123.2702547
18. Carl DiSalvo, Tom Jenkins, and Thomas Lodato. 2016. Designing Speculative Civics. In *Proceedings of the 2016 CHI Conference on Human Factors in Computing Systems* (CHI '16). ACM, New York, NY, USA, 4979-4990. DOI: http://dx.doi.org/10.1145/2858036.2858505
19. Carl DiSalvo and Jonathan Lukens. 2011. Non-anthropocentrism and the non-human in design: Possibilities for designing new forms of engagement with and through technology. In *From social butterfly to engaged citizen: urban informatics, social media, ubiquitous computing, and mobile technology to support citizen engagement,* Marcus Foth, Laura Forlano, Christine Satchell and Martin Gibbs (eds.), MIT Press, 421-437.
20. Anthony Dunne and Fiona Raby. 2007. Technological Dreams Series: No.1, Robots. Retrieved Sep 20, 2016 from http://www.dunneandraby.co.uk/content/projects/10/0
21. Deborah Estrin, David Culler, Kris Pister, and Gaurav Sukhatme. 2002. Connecting physical world with pervasive networks. *IEEE Pervasive Computing* 1, 1: 59-69. DOI=10.1109/MPRV.2002.993145
22. Daniel Fallman. 2011. The new good: exploring the potential of philosophy of technology to contribute to human-computer interaction. In *Proceedings of the SIGCHI Conference on Human Factors in Computing Systems* (CHI '11). ACM, New York, NY, USA, 1051-1060. DOI=http://dx.doi.org/10.1145/1978942.1979099
23. Umer Farooq and Jonathan Grudin. 2016. Human-computer integration. *interactions* 23, 6 (October 2016), 26-32. DOI: http://dx.doi.org/10.1145/3001896
24. Batya Friedman and Peter H. Kahn, Jr.. 2002. Human values, ethics, and design. In *The human-computer interaction handbook*, Julie A. Jacko and Andrew Sears (Eds.). L. Erlbaum Associates Inc., Hillsdale, NJ, USA 1177-1201.
25. William Gaver. 2012. What should we expect from research through design?. In *Proceedings of the SIGCHI Conference on Human Factors in Computing Systems* (CHI '12). ACM, New York, NY, USA, 937-946. DOI=http://dx.doi.org/10.1145/2207676.2208538

26. William Gaver, Phoebe Sengers, Tobie Kerridge, Joseph Kaye, and John Bowers. 2007. Enhancing ubiquitous computing with user interpretation: field testing the home health horoscope. In *Proceedings of the SIGCHI Conference on Human Factors in Computing Systems* (CHI '07). ACM, New York, NY, USA, 537-546. DOI=http://dx.doi.org/10.1145/1240624.1240711
27. Neil Gershenfeld. 2008. *Fab: the coming revolution on your desktop--from personal computers to personal fabrication.* Basic Books,
28. Elisa Giaccardi, Chris Speed, Nazli Cila and Melissa L. Caldwell. 2016. Things as co-ethnographers: Implications of a thing perspective for design and anthropology. In Design Anthropological Futures, Rachel C. Smith, Kasper T. Vaskilde, Mette G. Kjaersgaard, Ton Otto, Joachim Halse, Thomas Binder (eds.). Bloomsbury Academic, 235-248.
29. Elisa Giaccardi, Chris Speed, and Neil Rubens. 2014. Things making things: An ethnography of the impossible. Retrieved Sep 11, 2016 from https://kadk.dk/co-design/research-network-design-anthropology/
30. Adam Greenfield. 2006. *Everyware: The dawning age of ubiquiotous computing*. New Riders.
31. Graham Harman. 2011. *The quadruple object.* Zer0 books.
32. Wimer Hazenberg, Menno Huisman and Sara Cordoba Rubino. 2011. *Meta products: Building the internet of things.* BIS Publishers.
33. Tim Ingold. 2013. *Making: Anthropology, archaeology, art and architecture*. Routledge.
34. Tim Ingold. 2011. *Being Alive: Essays on movement, knowledge and description*. Routledge.
35. Tom Jenkins, Christopher A. Le Dantec, Carl DiSalvo, Thomas Lodato, and Mariam Asad. 2016. Object-Oriented Publics. In *Proceedings of the 2016 CHI Conference on Human Factors in Computing Systems* (CHI '16). ACM, New York, NY, USA, 827-839. DOI: http://dx.doi.org/10.1145/2858036.2858565
36. Viktor Kaptelinin and Bonnie A. Nardi. 2006. *Acting with technology: Activity theory and interaction design*. MIT press.
37. Jørn Knutsen. 2014. Uprooting products of the networked city. *Int J of Design* 8, 1: 127-142.
38. Mike Kuniavsky. 2010. *Smart things: Ubiquitous computing user experience design*. Morgan Kaufmann.
39. Matthias Laschke, Sarah Diefenbach, and Marc Hassenzahl. 2011. "Annoying, but in a nice way": An inquiry into the experience of frictional feedback. *Int J of Design* 9, 2: 129-140.
40. Bruno Latour. 2011. Networks, societies, spheres: Reflections of an actor-network theorist. *Int J of Communication* 5, 15: 786-810.
41. Brenda Laurel. 2008. Design animism. In *Re(searching) the digital Bauhaus*, Thomas Binder, Jonas Löwgren and Lone Malmorg (eds.). Springer, London, UK, 251-274.
42. John Law. 2009. Actor network theory and material semiotics. In *The new Blackwell companion to social theory*, Bryan S. Turner (ed.). Wiley-Blackwell, Sussex, UK, 141-158.
43. Joseph Lindley and Robert Potts. 2014. A machine learning: an example of HCI prototyping with design fiction. In *Proceedings of the 8th Nordic Conference on Human-Computer Interaction: Fun, Fast, Foundational* (NordiCHI '14). ACM, New York, NY, USA, 1081-1084. DOI: http://dx.doi.org/10.1145/2639189.2670281
44. Betti Marenko. 2014. Neo-animism and design: A new paradigm in object theory. *Design and Culture* 6, 2: 219-242.
45. Bjorn Nansen, Luke van Ryn, Frank Vetere, Toni Robertson, Margot Brereton, and Paul Dourish. 2014. An internet of social things. In *Proceedings of the 26th Australian Computer-Human Interaction Conference on Designing Futures: the Future of Design* (OzCHI '14). ACM, New York, NY, USA, 87-96. DOI=http://dx.doi.org/10.1145/2686612.2686624
46. Kjetil Nordby. 2010. Conceptual designing and technology: Short-range RFID as design material. *Int J of Design* 4, 1: 29-44.
47. Simone Rebaudengo, Walter Aprile, and Paul Hekkert. 2012. Addicted products, a scenario of future interactions where products are addicted to being used. In *Out of control: Proceedings of the 8th international conference on design and emotion*, London, UK, 1-10.
48. Mario Romero, Zachary Pousman and Michael Mateas. 2007. Alien presence in the home: The design of Tableau machine. *Pers and Ubi Comp* 12, 5: 373-382.
49. David Rose. 2014. *Enchanted objects: Design, human desire, and the Internet of things*. Simon and Schuster.
50. Marco Rozendaal. 2016. Objects with intent: a new paradigm for interaction design. *interactions* 23, 3 (April 2016), 62-65. DOI=http://dx.doi.org/10.1145/2911330
51. Eivind Samuelsen and Kyrre Glette. 2015. Real-World Reproduction of Evolved Robot Morphologies: Automated Categorization and Evaluation. In *European Conference on the Applications of Evolutionary Computation*. Springer International Publishing, 771-782.
52. Donald Schön. 1979. Generative metaphor: A perspective on problem-setting in social policy. In *Metaphor and thought*, Andrew Ortony (ed.). Cambridge University Press, Cambridge, UK, 138–163.

53. Bruce Sterling. 2005. *Shaping things*. MIT Press.

54. Superflux. 2015. Uninvited guests. Video. (20 May 2015.). Retrieved Sep 17, 2016 from https://vimeo.com/128873380

55. Philip van Allen, Joshua McVeigh-Schultz, Brooklyn Brown, Hye Mi Kim, and Daniel Lara. 2013. AniThings: animism and heterogeneous multiplicity. In *CHI '13 Extended Abstracts on Human Factors in Computing Systems* (CHI EA '13). ACM, New York, NY, USA, 2247-2256. DOI: http://dx.doi.org/10.1145/2468356.2468746

56. Mark Weiser. 1991. The computer for the 21st century. *Scientific American* 265, 3: 94-104.

Pause: A Multi-lifespan Design Mechanism

Batya Friedman
University of Washington
Seattle, WA 98195 USA
batya@uw.edu

Daisy Yoo
University of Washington
Seattle, WA 98195 USA
dyoo@uw.edu

** The two authors contributed equally to this work.*

ABSTRACT
At times, inaction may be a wise course of action. This insight lies at the heart of the design mechanism of *pause*. In this note, we explore the construct of pause, its rhythms, and nuances of enacting pause. Throughout, we draw on our experience engaging with pause in the multi-lifespan design of information systems for transitional justice. Five rhythms are identified: periodic hiatus, pending future event, responding to the socio-political climate, (temporary) closure, and laying fallow. In addition, we provide heuristics for managing pause and then restarting the design process. We then explore the scalability of pause from longer (e.g., multi-lifespan design) to shorter timeframes. We conclude with reflections on the potential benefits and open questions about pause as a design mechanism.

Author Keywords
Multi-lifespan design; pause; design mechanism

ACM Classification Keywords
H.5.m. Information interfaces and presentation (e.g., HCI): Miscellaneous

INTRODUCTION
At times, inaction may be a wise course of action. This insight lies at the heart of the multi-lifespan design mechanism of *pause*. Though simple to state, pause is a nuanced and unexpected mechanism, rarely found in most design approaches. Yet, used well, pause can be a game changer in how designers navigate complex socio-technical design challenges and uncertainties, in particular, over the longer term.

Multi-lifespan design [2, 3] differs fundamentally from most modern day design approaches that seek fast solutions to both small and large design problems. In contrast, multi-lifespan design engages problems that by virtue of the problem structure are unlikely to be solved within a single human lifespan – for example, problems tied to limitations of the human psyche to heal from cyclical violence or to slow moving natural processes such as reforestation. Pause fits naturally within this design framing. To be sure, pause requires a certain sort of temporal spaciousness; the long-running processes of multi-lifespan design allow enough room to embrace pause, or even multiple pauses.

CHI 2017, May 06-11, 2017, Denver, CO, USA
© 2017 ACM. ISBN 978-1-4503-4655-9/17/05...$15.00
DOI: http://dx.doi.org/10.1145/3025453.3026031

"Pause," as a design mechanism, shares some sensibilities as well as some important differences with the "implication not to design (technology)" as articulated by Baumer and Silberman [1]. They call attention to design processes that result in the conclusion that the better course of action is not to build a technology. In contrast, this work focuses on identifying places and ways in which pausing (not fully stopping) the design process may be beneficial to a design. Pausing carries with it the possibility of and commitment to restarting the design process at a later time; it stops short of a hard-edged categorical decision to discontinue or to not design a technical solution. Indeed, one of the challenges for pause entails communicating clearly when a lack of action comprises an instance of pause versus an instance of pulling the plug on a design process.

Given the temporal aspect of pause, it is also useful to consider connections to the slow technology and slow design movements; these movements emphasize technology design to support the user's reflection [4, 5, 8, 9]. As Hallnäs and Redstörm [5] write: "slow technology…is *not* supposed to reduce cognitive load or make digital information and computational resources more readily available. Slow technology is not about making technology invisible, but about exposing technology in a way that encourages people to reflect and think about it" (p. 204). Slow design is less about slowing down the user experience per se and more about reconfiguring the nature of the user experience itself. Grosse-Hering and her colleagues [4] write: "This is not from designing interactions that require more time per se, but by stimulating the user to use more time for those parts of the interaction that are meaningful and less for those that are not meaningful" (p. 3431). In contrast to slow technology's and slow design's focus on the user experience, our work on pause pertains to the temporal cadence of the design process itself.

Here we examine one mechanism for slowing down the design process: that of pause. Throughout, we draw on our experience engaging with pause in the multi-lifespan design of information systems for transitional justice. Our focus is the Voices from the Rwanda Tribunal project [10], a historically significant collection of 49 video interviews conducted in 2008 with personnel from the International Criminal Tribunal for Rwanda (ICTR). The collection has been made publically accessible online at www.tribunalvoices.org. Engaging with Rwandans, the international justice community, and global publics, this on-going research explores how information systems and design can support the long-term processes of transitional justice in Rwanda and elsewhere [3, 6, 11, 12].

In this note we explore the construct of pause, its rhythms, and nuances of enacting pause. We provide heuristics for managing pause and then restarting the design process. Then we extend the scalability of pause from longer (e.g., multi-lifespan design) to shorter timeframes. We conclude with reflections on the potential benefits of pause as a strategic design mechanism.

CONCEPTUALIZING *PAUSE*

Pause entails stopping temporarily from an action with a commitment to restart. Looking from the outside in, at the time of stopping it can be difficult to distinguish a temporary stop (pause) from a final one. Yet much is at stake with this distinction. After all, "stopping" a project in progress often carries with it negative connotations. In milder versions, stopping a project midstream can be interpreted as abandonment that carries an assumption of lack of interest. In a stronger version, stopping midstream can be interpreted as a determination of non-viability – that is, failure. Thus, at the point where one institutes a stop there is a moment of labeling which is paramount: Is this pause? Or is this failure?

Our experience indicates numerous circumstances for which pause might be a legitimate design response. The changing state of technical infrastructure and technology penetration is one: if significant improvements or changes are anticipated that would enable a different range of design solutions, then pausing to allow those technological changes to occur may be strategic. Changing socio-political conditions are another: certain design solutions may not be viable in certain socio-political contexts; pausing to allow those socio-political changes to occur may also be strategic. Third, limited financial and other resources may dictate pause, requiring a hiatus in the project work until further resources can be obtained. Lastly, from the individual researcher perspective, pause may be useful to address fatigue or other personal circumstances (e.g., birth of a child, death of a loved one).

RHYTHMS OF PAUSE

Not all pause is alike. When to pause, for how long, and under what conditions to restart take on different cadences – what one might think of as the rhythms of pause. Here we explicate five rhythms of pause that arose in the course of our multi-lifespan design work with the Voices from the Rwanda Tribunal project and illustrate each rhythm with an example from that work. Some of these instances were intentional from the beginning, while others were emergent, arising in situ.

1 Periodic Hiatus. This form of pause refers to an aspect of a project that requires regular but not continuous attention. For example, maintaining the archival copies of the Voices from the Rwanda Tribunal collection fits with this notion of periodic hiatus. Specifically, the archival copies are reviewed every two years and refreshed every five years to ensure on-going data integrity and access. Otherwise, the archival copies remain untouched.

2 Pending Future Event. In this form of pause, an aspect of the project is on hold until a specified amount of time passes or particular conditions are met. For example, two interviews in the Voices from the Rwanda Tribunal collection will be released pending specified future events. In one case, an interview is sealed for a specific duration (i.e., 30 years) and in the other case tied to a specific occurrence (i.e., until all first instance trials have been completed by the ICTR). In the latter case, the specific date initially may not be foreseeable.

3 Tango: Responding to the Socio-political Climate. Another form of pause is entangled with the rhythm of changing socio-political conditions. Here, agile assessments of key stakeholders and political contexts are employed to determine if and when a good time to act has arisen. Until such a determination, the project may pause. For example, with the Voices from the Rwanda Tribunal project, aspects of the on-going interaction design evolved (and continue to evolve) in response to the Rwandan government's evolving legislation that governs speech related to the 1994 genocide (e.g., Genocide Ideology Law). Specifically, we have put on hold development of an un-moderated online discussion forum, so as to ensure compliance with current Rwandan law [6]. We continue to monitor the development of Rwandan law on this topic, with an eye toward new interaction design opportunities.

4 (Temporary) Closure. In some instances, an aspect of the project is halted without clarity concerning whether or not this aspect would be restarted at some future point. In this circumstance, this aspect of the project hovers between pause and closure until a final determination is made. We encountered such an instance with respect to the design of an information portal for transitional justice in Rwanda, that would link various materials tied to transitional justice in Rwanda, including documents from the ICTR, the traditional Rwandan Gacaca courts, interviews from the Voices from the Rwanda Tribunal, and other sources. While initially appealing to a complex set of stakeholders, as the political conditions changed, interest in (and, hence, the viability of) the information portal waned. Until finalized, we consider this form of pause to be temporary closure and note that in some ways it comprises a special case of responding to the socio-political climate (described above).

5 Laying Fallow. This form of pause serves the purpose of refreshing people, resources, or other aspects of the project. Such fallow periods aid with project sustainability and can act as a counterpoint to what might be experienced as relentless project workflow leading to burnout. (i) With respect to research, technical, political, and other partners, this form of pause can provide an opportunity to harmonize the project rhythm with other commitments – to other projects, people, or circumstances – preserving collaborative relationships over the longer term. For example, in the Voices from the Rwanda Tribunal project we have worked with our partner organization Never Again Rwanda [7] on a range of related projects with fallow periods in between: in 2009 (workshop with youth), 2014 (information portal for transitional justice in Rwanda), and 2015 (research method training for Rwandan NGO research staff) in part, in response to that organization's shifting agendas and capacity. (ii) Within the project team, laying fallow can take the form of personal (or personnel) pause. For the kind of longer-term commitments associated with multi-lifespan design, project team members will need periodic opportunities to refresh, akin to the academic practice of sabbatical. As opposed to leaving the project permanently, in some instances team members will rejoin the project after a period of downtime with renewed vigor and insights. As the Voices of the Rwanda Tribunal project enters its ninth year, several team members have practiced this form of pause.

PAUSE IN ACTION: HEURISTICS

During the course of pause, not all activities cease. Rather, certain on-going activities are critical to managing pause and enabling meaningful restart. We highlight heuristics for a pause and restart process, largely in sequential order.

Articulate a Rationale and Rhythm for Pause. When considering the possibility of pause, a helpful early step entails articulating a rationale for pausing the design process. As noted earlier, motivations for pause might include anticipated change in technology, change in socio-political conditions, lack of resources, or researcher circumstances. Once a rationale has been established, then an appropriate rhythm for the pause can be identified accordingly (e.g., periodic hiatus, pending future event, tango, [temporary] closure, or laying fallow), including which aspects of the project need to be paused and potentially for what duration (e.g., scope, timeframe).

Initiating Pause. Based on the identified rhythm, the specific event or circumstances that trigger the enactment of pausing can be identified. When the trigger occurs, pause is initiated.

Documentation. Minimizing a loss of knowledge and experience during the period of pause is key to enabling a smooth transition when restarting the project at some later point. Toward this end, it is important to judiciously collect and document relevant project knowledge, personnel, and processes, not only prior to but also during the period of pause.

Managing Expectations and Maintaining Relationships. Oftentimes, pausing an aspect of a project may also pause engagement with related team members as well as external partners, many of whom will need to be re-engaged when the project restarts. Moreover, some may interpret pause as abandonment and, reciprocally, lose commitment. As such, some effort to manage expectations and maintain relationships is warranted. Particularly, the rhythm of pause and expectation for restarting need to be clearly communicated with appropriate frequency.

Monitoring for Restart Conditions. Depending on the rhythm of a given pause, different information gathering practices will be needed to enable restart conditions. For example, a pending future event requires researchers to attend to a particular timeframe or event as a basis to restart. In contrast, a tango rhythm requires researchers to attend broadly to a social-political climate at reasonable intervals with an eye toward when certain conditions are met to determine when to restart.

Restarting: After Pause. Based on the identified rhythm and monitored conditions, the specific event or circumstances that trigger the action of restarting can be identified. Depending on the conditions, starting after a pause may entail a number of complex activities including re-engaging with partners, refreshing knowledge about the project among team members, reviewing and reassessing project goals, and revisiting project personnel and research partnerships.

Calling the Shots. A person or persons will need to be unambiguously in charge of the pausing process and empowered to make relevant project decisions. Their duties entail ensuring a clear rationale and rhythm for pause, initiating the pause, adequate documentation, management of expectations, maintenance of relationships, and monitoring for restart conditions. They also have the crucial responsibility to determine when to restart the project.

PAUSE IN ACTION: SCALABILITY

To illustrate pause-in-action, we describe an example from our experience with the Voices from the Rwanda Tribunal project, that of periodic hiatus. In addition, to explore the broader applicability of pause beyond multi-lifespan design, we provide a hypothetical scenario of pause within a shorter-term design project, that of a pending future event.

Periodic hiatus. As mentioned above, maintaining the archives of the Voices of the Rwanda Tribunal collection requires periodic attention followed by long periods of quiet. When we began this project, our first goal was to secure the archival copies of the collection. After the collection was safely tucked away ("initiating pause"), we stepped back to consider the long-term ongoing maintenance of the collection. At that point we conducted the necessary research to determine what sort of cycles would be needed for what types of maintenance activities (i.e., a 2-year *review* cycle which examines the replica sets to identify emergent issues, and a 5-year *refresh* cycle which generates new replica sets). That resulted in a detailed archival schedule with accompanying rationale for procedures ("articulate a rationale and rhythm for pause," "documentation"), which was shared among key stakeholders. The documentation was used as a boundary object to help ensure shared expectations for periodic refresh among the research team and the staff at the University of Washington (UW) Libraries Special Collections where the archival copies are stored ("managing expectations and relationships"). Inspection of those documents positioned the research team and the library staff to discuss roles and responsibilities (e.g., who would be responsible for doing what and when; "calling the shots") as well as surfaced questions about long-term resources for maintaining the collection. The regular periodic nature of the maintenance made the restart conditions – a particular month and year – readily visible ("restarting"). We generated new replica sets in 2014 and are poised for the next refresh to occur in 2019. The maintenance documents and shared expectations continue to guide our long-term planning for the project, particularly with resource allocation and seeking future funding for preserving the collection.

Pending future event.  In terms of timescale, pause is not limited to multi-lifespan design, but can be also useful for projects at shorter timeframes. In particular, as design researchers increasingly engage with uncertainty – whether it pertains to their research setting (e.g., shifting online social space, conflict settings) or project resources (e.g., funding, human resources) – pausing a project may be an effective design strategy. Here we describe a hypothetical scenario in which uncertainty arises: designing a new chat room for a small online community of critics on film and television. To understand the context, researchers decide to monitor and collect online conversations for one month in order to conduct social network analyses and content analyses. However, about two weeks into the study a post goes viral on the Internet, drawing public attention to the website. Thousands of new users subscribe to the community including trolls and spammers. Social dynamics change, norms are disrupted. The design team discusses the emergent situation. The team decides to put the data collection on hold for three months ("initiating pause") and restart when the community has re-stabilized ("articulating a rationale and rhythm for pause"). Data collected prior to and immediately following the viral post are annotated and archived ("documentation"). In the interim, each researcher focuses on other projects ("managing expectations"). After three months, the project leader monitors web traffic for signs of stabilization ("monitoring for restart conditions"). If conditions are met, the project restarts ("restarting: after pause").

REFLECTIONS ON PAUSE

This note contributes an argument and associated practice for pause as a strategic design mechanism. Granted, all design projects at some level of granularity have periods of inactivity. That said, as demonstrated here, a meaningful distinction can be made between project inactivity per se and the use of pause as a strategic mechanism in design. One that is particularly suited to multi-lifespan design; though, as illustrated above, can be used effectively with projects at shorter timescales.

The benefits of an explicit design mechanism of pause are at least three-fold. First, the capacity to use pause intentionally and strategically in the design process, as warranted by project goals and changing conditions. Second, the ability to plan for lapses in project activity (e.g., the heuristics above provide useful guidance on how effectively to navigate these lapses). And, third, a language for communicating about project inactivity that is distinct from project failure.

We conclude with some open questions about pause as a design mechanism – questions that point toward considerations for future work and further design reflection. One set of questions concerns how to determine the pause. What markers indicate that pause might be a viable or even preferred mechanism at a given point in the ongoing stream of a design process? How do researchers know when to restart? These questions go beyond simplistic responses such as marking a calendar. While some pause rhythms embed relatively straightforward stop and restart conditions (e.g., periodic hiatus), others rely on nuanced assessments of socio-technical change (and resulting climate) that can defy ready judgment. Relatedly, could pause be determined after the fact, say at the time of restarting? For example, could a post-hoc determination of pause serve as a helpful rhetorical move? Might the language of "pause and restart" (rather than that of "reviving or resuscitating failing projects") ease the reinvigoration of research activities with external partners? Another set of questions concerns assessing the usefulness or lack thereof of any given pause. How does one meaningfully evaluate the impact of a pause in the design process when there are no visible actions? What evidence could be brought to bear?

While powerful, pause is a mechanism to be used judiciously – based on thoughtful rationale with reasonably well-articulated restart conditions. Going forward, we hope others working within different contexts and timeframes will expand the rhythms of pause. Furthermore, we hope this work will inspire a broader conversation about re-imagining the parameters for successful design processes.

ACKNOWLEDGMENTS

We thank all those who have participated in the Voices from the Rwanda Tribunal project over the years. This material is based upon work supported by the National Science Foundation under grant no. IIS-1302709.

REFERENCES

1. Eric P. S. Baumer and M. Six Silberman. 2011. When the implication is not to design (technology). In *Proceedings of the SIGCHI Conference on Human Factors in Computing* Systems (CHI '11), 2271-2274. http://doi.acm.org/ 10.1145/1978942.1979275
2. Batya Friedman and Lisa P. Nathan. 2010. Multi-lifespan information system design: a research initiative for the HCI community. In *Proceedings of the SIGCHI Conference on Human Factors in Computing* Systems (CHI '10), 2242-2246. http://doi.acm.org/10.1145/1753326.1753665
3. Batya Friedman,.Lisa P. Nathan, and Daisy Yoo. 2016. Multi-lifespan information system design in support of transitional justice: evolving situated design principles for the long(er) term. *Interacting with Computers*, iwv045. http://doi.org/10.1093/iwc/iwv045
4. Barbara Grosse-Hering, Jon Mason, Dzmitry Aliakseyeu, Conny Bakker, and Pieter Desmet. 2013. Slow design for meaningful interactions. In *Proceedings of the SIGCHI Conference on Human Factors in Computing Systems* (CHI '13), 3431-3440. http://doi.acm.org/10.1145/2470654.2466472
5. Lars Hallnäs and Johan Redstörm. 2001. Slow technology – designing for reflection. *Personal and Ubiquitous Computing* 5: 201-212.
6. Lisa P. Nathan, Nell Carden Grey, Milli Lake, Trond Nilsen, Elizabeth Utter, Robert F. Utter, Mark Ring, Zoe Kahn, and Batya Friedman. 2011. Multi-lifespan information system design: investigating a new design approach in Rwanda. In *Proceedings of the SIGCHI Conference on Human Factors in Computing Systems* (CHI '11), 591-597. http://doi.acm.org/10.1145/1753326.1753665
7. Never Again Rwanda website. 2016. Retrieved September 19, 2016 from http://neveragainrwanda.org
8. William Odom. 2015. Understanding long-term interactions with a slow technology: an investigation of experiences with FutureMe. In *Proceedings of the SIGCHI Conference on Human Factors in Computing Systems* (CHI '15), 575-584. http://doi.acm.org/10.1145/2702123.2702221
9. Carolyn F. Strause and Alastair Fuad-Luke. 2008. The slow design principles: a new interrogative and reflexive tool for design research and practice. In *Proceedings of Changing the Change* (2008).
10. Voices from the Rwanda Tribunal website. 2016. Retrieved September 19, 2016 from http://www.tribunalvoices.org
11. Daisy Yoo, Milli Lake, Trond Nilsen, Molly E. Utter, Robert Alsdorf, Theoneste Bizimana, Lisa P. Nathan, Mark Ring, Elizabeth J. Utter, Robert F. Utter, and Batya Friedman. 2013. Envisioning Across Generations: A Multi-lifespan Information System for International Justice in Rwanda. In *Proceedings of the SIGCHI Conference on Human Factors in Computing Systems (CHI 2013)*, 2527-2536. http://doi.acm.org/10.1145/2470654.2481349
12. Daisy Yoo, Katie Derthick, K., Shaghayegh Ghassemian, Jean Hakizimana, Brian Gill, and Batya Friedman. 2016. Multi-lifespan design thinking: two methods and a case study with the Rwandan diaspora. In *Proceedings of the SIGCHI Conference on Human Factors in Computing Systems* (CHI '16), 4423-4434. http://doi.acm.org/10.1145/2858036.2858366

Interdependent Wearables (for Play): A Strong Concept for Design

Katherine Isbister
University of California Santa Cruz
Santa Cruz, USA
katherine.isbister@ucsc.edu

Kaho Abe
New York University
New York, USA
kaho@kahoabe.net

Michael Karlesky
New York University
New York, USA
mike@karlesky.net

ABSTRACT
Typically wearable devices are conceived of and constructed as stand-alone, individually based technologies. However, in practice wearables become part of the social context and ecology of overall device use. We present a strong concept for design: *Interdependent Wearables (for play)*: wearables designed to require shared attention and mutual awareness, with interdependent functionality that encourages and rewards collocated interaction. The concept arose through design, development, and public exhibition of *Hotaru*, a collocated social game that uses wearables as game controllers. *Hotaru* has been shown in festivals and also formally playtested with 62 individuals. To more fully articulate the Interdependent Wearables strong concept, we compared this system's design with wearable and embodied systems for play and other purposes, and drew upon relevant HCI theory. The work is of benefit to those in the HCI/UX community focused on the design and development of social wearable technologies, especially those interested in supporting collocated interaction.

Author Keywords
Social wearables; collocated interaction; strong concept; interdependent wearables; embodied interaction.

ACM Classification Keywords
H.5.m. Information interfaces and presentation (e.g., HCI): Miscellaneous.

INTRODUCTION
Wearable technologies have been of interest to HCI researchers for many years (e.g. [20], [7]), and have become a robust commercial category in the last 5-10 years, with the introduction of smart watches and the increasing diversity of fitness tracking devices. The first wave of these devices was focused on quantifying data about the self [36], with some facility for sharing activity data with others. In the last few years, smart watches have begun to support networked social interaction through messaging, calendars, email, and other social coordination and connection tools [28], such as Snapchat Micro [10]. However, wearables have not yet begun to robustly support collocated social interaction—interaction between people in the same place [19]. In fact some commercial wearables have been critiqued for perturbing collocated interaction—some so dramatically as to lead to their ban from public spaces such as bars [18].

CHI 2017, May 06 - 11, 2017, Denver, CO, USA

ACM 978-1-4503-4655-9/17/05 $15.00
DOI: http://dx.doi.org/10.1145/3025453.3025939

Wearables experts in the commercial sector have declared the next phase of development 'the social age of wearable tech,' envisioning "a future where wearing technology isn't just about measuring and monitoring, but instead about enhancing our body's ability to communicate, express, and empathise with others." [4]. Our research team believes that thoughtful and sensitive design can lead to the fruition of such a vision, producing wearable technology that truly augments collocated engagement rather than intruding upon it. We envision wearables that heighten expressiveness and allow additional layers of social signaling, which are artfully crafted so as not to interfere with, but rather to enhance mutual attention, collaboration, and play. To deliver this vision, we believe there is a need to reframe design practice to focus upon the unique opportunities that technology has to augment mutual engagement and attention [13]. In this paper we present a strong design concept [11] that can aid in shaping design practice to support collocated interaction of this kind: *interdependent wearables (for play)*. The concept arose from insights we had during the design, development, and exhibition of a game that uses social wearables [14]. The primary contribution of this paper is the introduction of this strong concept to help shape research and design practice in constructing wearables to support collocated interaction. Though this strong concept arose in the context of play, we believe it can also hold value for social wearable design outside the 'magic circle' [5], [34] of games.

RELATED WORK
Höök and Löwgren [11] introduced the notion of strong concepts as a formulation for sharing generative intermediate-level design knowledge. Strong concepts combine a clear definition of a design idea with both vertical grounding through comparison and contrast with

related systems, and horizontal grounding in relevant theory. We have followed this structure in framing the strong concept contributed in this paper.

HCI researchers have recently pointed out the value in focusing on supporting collocated social interaction with technology (e.g. [19]). Within the games community, a number of scholars have turned their attention toward support of collocated play in recent years [24], [25], [31], [35], with some preliminary work on both wearables and costumes as they relate to social play [14], [33]. HCI practitioners outside games have turned attention to managing ecologies of devices to take into account social dynamics, using frameworks such as proxemics (the study of interpersonal distance) [22] and the spectator experience (understanding how technologies influence those who observe an interaction) [29] . The current paper contributes a strong concept that can be of potential value to these ongoing research streams both within and outside games and play, particularly of use in thinking about social wearables. It is our hope that this strong concept can help spur ideation and prototyping of wearables to better support collocated social interaction.

HOTARU'S INTERDEPENDENT WEARABLES

We begin with a brief description of the system whose design inspired the strong concept. *Hotaru* was created by an accomplished independent game designer, Kaho Abe, with a specialty in movement-based social games. She developed the game working in collaboration with an HCI researcher interested in wearable computing to support and enhance collocated social interaction. The team received funding from an initiative aimed at pairing artists and researchers to investigate the future of computational fashion.

Abe was interested in combining costume and gesture, to create a physical enactment of the gameplay identities players take on when they engage in avatar-based play [13]. She was inspired by a Japanese television show with superheroes who have costumes with powers they unlock by making special gestures. The idea was to combine costume-like wearables and special collaborative gestures to unlock players' powers together, building camaraderie and connection through interdependence and shared mission. *Hotaru* means 'lightning bug' in Japanese. She conceived of a game in which the players seemed like fireflies battling together to keep smog at bay. She designed the wearable elements to be simple and evocative of this theme. (see Figure 1).

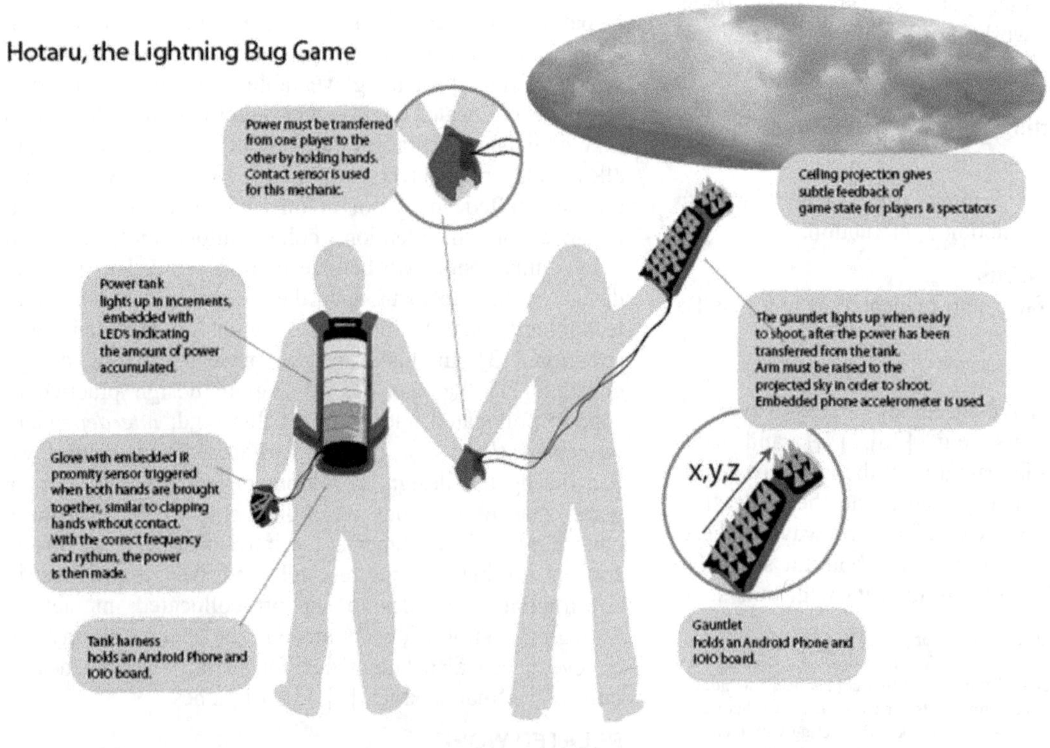

Figure 1. An overview of components of *Hotaru*.

To play *Hotaru*, one player puts on a gauntlet, and the other puts on an energy collection 'tank'. Both wearables illuminate when 'energy' flows through them. The object of the game is to collect energy, then aim it at projected 'smog' to dissipate it. This requires the coordination of both players. The person with the tank moves their hands in an energy collecting gesture to 'fill' their tank. This is indicated by illuminating segments of the tank lighting up.

This player cannot see the tank, so they need the other player to keep an eye on it and tell them when the tank is full. Then the players must hold hands for the energy to 'transfer' between them. The second player waits until their gauntlet fills with energy (indicated by all the spikes on the gauntlet illuminating). Then this player quickly raises their hand in the air to release the energy. This causes the gauntlet to emit a loud 'firing' noise. The end goal is to collaborate to release energy as many times as possible in a limited time window (please also see uploaded video, and a prior paper describing the overall installation [14]).

TOWARDS A STRONG CONCEPT

Hotaru has been a success from the perspective of the independent games world—it has been shown at IndieCade, the premier venue for independent games in the US, as well as a variety of international festivals. We conducted and documented more formal playtests with 62 individuals as well, to explore the effects of the design upon their experience. Insights from festival showings as well as these playtests helped shape the strong concept presented in this paper. Here, we briefly describe the playtest procedure and results, as supportive evidence for the usefulness of the ideas and tactics that were realized in this design, which are at the core of the strong concept. A primary question of interest in the playtests was whether playing the game increased feelings of connectedness, as we had intended would be the case with the design.

Study Participants and Procedure

We conducted three public playtests of the game in March and April of 2015, which were approved for data collection by our human subjects board. There were a total of 62 unique players who participated for a total of 33 rounds of play. We did not collect self-identified gender data, however a visual review of the logs indicated 28 unique male-seeming participants and 34 unique female-seeming participants.

Figure 2. We took snapshots of players before and after play.

We video recorded play, and also asked participants to take a moment to have 'before' and 'after' photos snapped of them standing together (see Figure 2). Afterward, each player completed a paper-based survey. This survey asked players which wearable they chose (to link their answers to videos/photos for later analysis), then asked them to clarify what, if any, prior relationship they had to the person with whom they played. They were asked if they thought playing the game had influence on their trust, liking, or connection to the person they played with, and if they answered yes, prompted to explain how so. They were also asked how it felt to play the game, with room for open-ended response.

Results

We looked at how many participants responded 'yes' to the question of whether they game influenced their trust, liking, and connection to the person with whom they played the game. Of 66 unique answers (4 players completed multiple rounds of the game with different partners), 48 were 'yeses' (73%). The 27% who said 'no' did not report bad experiences with the game, and did not show any pattern of either being strangers or well-known to one another. Of players who did not know each other at all before play (a total of 12), 9 answered 'yes' (75%). Free text responses to the prompt 'If yes, please tell us how so,' elicited several common themes related to connection:

Relying on one another and communication: Thirteen players pointed to the way the game required them to rely on one another as a strategy for encouraging connection. For example, "we had to rely on each other for a common goal," "must rely on the other one to complete the task, can't without them," "there was, for the gauntlet wearer, a reliance on the tank." Several players pointed out that the game encouraged communication in order to accomplish the common goal: "we had to communicate with each other about the game," "we learned how to communicate more," "I had to let her know when she was fully charged."

Physical contact: Five players pointed to the physical contact from hand holding as something that caused an increase in trust, liking and connection. "Holding hands makes trust better ESPECIALLY when you get the high score!" "Hand sweat sharing, physical contact." As one player eloquently put it, "The connected, cooperative energy of playing the game created an isolated moment where working together was the apex of expression. We have now done something together, where holding hands was the only way to connect."

Working together: Sixteen players more generally referenced working together toward a common goal, as the reason for increased trust, liking, and connection. Example statements included: "Working together, I think, created a stronger connection." And "we had a common goal so wanting to achieve the goal brings us together even more."

Figure 3 a,b. Sample post-play images. 3a shows no signs of connection, whereas players in 3b are physically close, lean toward one another, smile, and use similar, energetic poses.

There are various cues of trust, connection, and liking that can be observed from body postures and facial expressions [21], [22]. These include decreased distance between individuals; coordination of gestures and poses; increased smiling and more energetic body poses; and turning and leaning more toward one another. Overall, only 4 out of 33 pairs showed *none* of these signs of increased connection when comparing their before and after photos (see figure 3 for a comparison of an after-play image with no signs of connection and closeness versus one with many signs—see also figure 2). *(Note: We were not able to discern from players' survey responses precisely why these few pairs did not show signs of increased connection).*

Discussion

As we had anticipated, players reported that the game helped them to feel more connected to one another, and this was also visible in the difference between the before and after photos of pairs. Many attributed this to specific aspects of the game's design (hand holding, interdependence, collaboration). Players enjoyed taking on interdependent roles, and working closely together physically. Of course, these playtests and the questions accompanying them were just a start in terms of fully understanding the impact of the system and teasing out the details of why and how players were affected. We intend to further analyze the video record in future toward a more nuanced understanding. And we could certainly refine the survey instruments that we used in these playtests for future iterations.

For the purposes of elucidating the strong concept introduced in this paper, designing, tuning, then observing the results of the game for players in these playtests (and at festival showings) led us to conclude that the designer's intuitions about the potential for and value of creating interdependence through wearables had born fruit, and could perhaps be useful to others in the HCI community. We engaged in a literature review of related theory and systems alongside the design and playtesting of the game, which also helped us to articulate an appropriate strong concept to encapsulate and communicate these design insights.

STRONG CONCEPT ARTICULATION

We propose the strong concept of Interdependent Wearables (at play). By interdependent, we mean wearables intentionally designed to require shared attention and mutual awareness, offering interdependent functionality to users that encourages and rewards collocated interaction. We propose that wearables designed with these characteristics can help build camaraderie and connection in collocated interaction, and that this is a valuable strong concept to influence next steps in wearable design.

Taking *Hotaru* as an example, players need to keep a close eye on one another's wearable to figure out what to do next and to succeed in gameplay. The gauntlet wearer watches the tank to see when enough energy has been collected. Then the tank wearer watches the gauntlet wearer to know when it's time to begin collecting again. Each wearable element depends upon the other for completion of the game task, including the necessity for joining hands to 'transfer' energy. The wearables encourage and reward close collaboration and coordination, eliciting mutual attention, and building connection and camaraderie.

Vertical grounding: Strong concepts should be articulated using other relevant system examples as vertical grounding. There have been other experiments in the indie game world with creating interdependent wearables, though these games have been competitive rather than collaborative in nature. For example, in *Swordfight* [27] players strap Atari 2600 controllers onto their crotch region and attempt to use their joystick to press the other player's button first. In *Hit Me!* [1], players wear hardhats with cameras mounted on them. Each player tries to push the doorbell-style button at the top of the other's helmet to snap a photo and win a point. These games have custom-built wearable elements that require close mutual attention and they do engender a form of collaboration and camaraderie in the service of the competition. Earlier wearable game systems in HCI such as *Wriggle* [16] and *Emroll* [37] encouraged close coordination, but did not require shared attention and mutual awareness in the same ways as the other games mentioned. Both *Emroll* and *Wriggle* require close attention to a large shared screen, taking player attention away from one another's bodies. There are other collocated physical games that use held controllers rather than wearables, such as *Musical Embrace* [12] and *Intangle* [8]. These games also require close coordination and social use of physical controller devices, though the devices are not worn on the body. Finally, there are games that explore the artful crafting of mutual attention through networked physical/digital interaction, such as *Can You See Me Now* [2], a game in which online players were chased by 'runners' who had to sprint through real city streets.

Working from these examples, we believe a strong component of successful interdependent wearables is the thoughtful management of co-present gaze, a notion that can be seen in other writings about the support of collaborative play [31], [32]. It is also worth noting that though our concept focuses on wearables (devices worn on the body), these examples suggest a continuum of devices the concept could apply to, which might include tangibles and body-focused sensor-based interactions. We focused the concept on wearables in particular as an area that can benefit from this articulation the most.

To demonstrate the potential and reach of the concept outside the realm of play, we note that Mitchell [23] points to a number of non-game interactive art and media pieces that make use of touch and wearable elements, many of which elicit mutual attention and interdependence. Löwgren's *Mediated Body* system can also be considered an exemplar [11], as can Schiphorst's exhale [30]. In exhale, for example, participants don flowing silk skirts with linings that 'breathe' (using fans and vibrators) and make subtle sounds in response to the breathing of all of the participants in the exhibition (each person wears a breath sensor around their rib cage). These sensations induce mutual attention upon breathing rhythms by bringing the impact of these rhythms from others closer in to one's own body. Synchrony of breathing is a natural part of engaging in attentive interaction [26] that is thus heightened by this system, enhancing mutual awareness of this social cue. Changes in any one person's breathing affects the movement of everyone's garments, enhancing mutual awareness through interdependence.

Gemio is a recent commercial example of a wearable that starts to approach this strong concept [3]. *Gemio* bracelets are composed of programmable 'gems' that can respond when friends are near (and also to messages sent through Snapchat). Light patterns can project 'secret' signals readily decodable among collocated friends. The bracelets have other sensors that could allow for rich collocated interaction: "An optical colour sensor means users can point the bracelet at what they're wearing and have the device automatically match the hue. There's an accelerometer and also a microphone so that the smart jewellery can light up in time to music." [3]. Contrast these affordances with the typical social features of most current generation wearables such as smart watches, which support text or audio messaging through a small screen not as well suited to engaging and directing shared attention and physical collaboration.

All of these systems demonstrate qualities highlighted in the strong concept that have been percolating in the design research and practice community, and which are just beginning to appear in commercial wearables. We believe articulating and sharing this strong concept will help to scaffold future efforts in this direction.

Horizontal grounding: Strong concepts should also be explicitly related to relevant theoretical constructs. To us, the most closely related concept in the HCI literature is ([21], [22])'s notion of supporting human proxemics within an ecology of devices. These researchers propose that ubiquitous systems should attune to human proxemics (management of interpersonal distance and orientation) to better engage in appropriate and adept human computer interaction. Game researchers have extended this notion of proxemics into choices about designing collocated games supported by technology [25] and have taken a look at interpersonal bodily interactions and how best to facilitate positive social experiences in games that extend all the way to bodily contact [8] . Game researchers have also emphasized the importance of giving players a 'head-up' positioning, putting the focus on other players rather than on individual technologies [31], [32]. We see Interdependent Wearables as a concept that deals with a particular subset of these interrelated proxemics and co-presence concepts—offering guidance and insights about the interplay between devices distributed among people in a given collocated setting.

A related strong concept is the Suppleness use quality proposed by [15], which frames a use quality that depends upon subtle social signals, emergent dynamics, and the privileging of moment-to-moment interaction. Suppleness offers experiential values, but does not articulate specific mechanisms for achieving those values. We see Interdependent Wearables as one particular strategy for achieving Suppleness.

Finally, we situate Interdependent Wearables within the larger turn in HCI toward considerations of embodiment [6]. We see this strong concept as adding considerations of explicitly designing for embodied co-experience in collocated settings—creating devices that provide affordances for encouraging mutual embodied awareness and interdependence.

CONCLUSION

We have introduced a strong concept that arose from design and development of a game played using social wearables. The concept—Interdependent Wearables (for Play)—offers HCI researchers and practitioners a generative lens for designing to support collocated social interaction using wearable technology. We believe this concept can help us to break out of certain hidden assumptions that get designed into wearables unconsciously—that the device should be for a single person's focused attention, that the device's signaling should be attuned to that individual person rather than also communicate gracefully with others, that the device's primary task is to aid the individual in efficiency and networked communication. We developed this strong concept during the creation of wearables designed for play, as part of the *Hotaru* game. While these wearables are fanciful and exaggerated, and thus more suitable for game settings, early commercial prototypes such as the Gemio show the potential of a non-game design space that can be further opened up in part through taking up this strong concept. Whether for work or play, it is our belief that Interdependent Wearables offer the potential to build camaraderie and connection by design, and to improve collocated social atmosphere and co-engagement. We are currently iterating upon the work begun with *Hotaru*, creating further social wearables to investigate the potential in this design space.

ACKNOWLEDGEMENTS

Thanks to Eyebeam Atelier for support of this project through use of a Rockefeller Cultural Innovation Fund grant awarded to them. Thanks to the Game Innovation Lab, and to all those who participated in the creation and playtesting of this game.

REFERENCES

1. Kaho Abe. 2014. Hit Me!. Retrieved September 15, 2016 from http://kahoabe.net/?portfolio=hit-me
2. S. Benford, A. Crabtree, M. Flintham, A. Drozd, R. Anastasi, M. Paxton, N. Tandavanitj, M. Adams, and J. Row-Farr. 2006. Can you see me now? *ACM Trans. Comput.-Hum. Interact.*, vol. 13, no. 1, pp. 100–133, Mar. 2006.
3. S. Charara. 2016. Gemio: Smart Bracelet Light Messages are the New Snapchat, *Wearable: Tech for your Connected Self*, 14-Jan-2016. Retrieved September 15, 2015 from http://www.wareable.com/smart-jewellery/gemio-smart-bracelet-light-messages-new-snapchat
4. A. Cosco. 2016. The social age of wearable tech: From Quantified Self to emotional second skin," *Wareable*. [Online]. Retrieved September 15, 2016 from http://www.wareable.com/wearable-tech/the-social-age-of-wearable-tech-beyond-the-quantified-self
5. B. DeKoven. 2013. *The well-played game: a player's philosophy*. MIT Press.
6. P. Dourish. 2004. *Where the Action Is: The Foundations of Embodied Interaction*. MIT Press.
7. M. Fukumoto and Y. Suenaga. 1994. 'FingeRing': a full-time wearable interface. In *Proceedings of CHI '94*, pp. 81–82. http://doi.acm.org/ 10.1145/259963.260056
8. J. Garner, G. Wood, S. Danilovic, J. Hammer, and F. Mueller. 2014. Intangle: exploring interpersonal bodily interactions through sharing controllers. In *Proceedings of CHI PLAY '14,* pp. 413–414, http://doi.acm.org/_10.1145/2658537.2661306.
9. E. T. Hall. 1968. Proxemics. *Curr. Anthropol.*, vol. 9, no. 2–3, pp. 83–108.
10. B. Heater. 2013. Snapchat Micro will bring disappearing messages to Samsung's Galaxy Gear. *Engadget*. [Online]. Retrieved September 20, 2016 from https://www.engadget.com/2013/09/09/snapchat-galaxy-gear/
11. K. Höök and J. Löwgren. 2012. Strong concepts: Intermediate-level knowledge in interaction design research. *ACM Trans. Comput.-Hum. Interact.*, vol. 19, no. 3, pp. 1–18.
12. A. Huggard, A. De Mel, J. Garner, C. "Chad" Toprak, A. Chatham, and F. "Floyd" Mueller. 2013. Musical Embrace: Exploring Social Awkwardness in Digital Games. In *Proceedings of the 2013 ACM International Joint Conference on Pervasive and Ubiquitous Computing*, New York, NY, USA, pp. 725–728.
13. K. Isbister. 2016. Connecting through play. *Interactions*, vol. 23, no. 4, pp. 26–33.
14. K. Isbister and K. Abe. 2015. Costumes as Game Controllers: An Exploration of Wearables to Suit Social Play. In *Proceedings of the Ninth International Conference on Tangible, Embedded, and Embodied Interaction*, pp. 691–696.
15. K. Isbister and K. Höök. 2009. On Being Supple: In Search of Rigor Without Rigidity in Meeting New Design and Evaluation Challenges for HCI Practitioners. In *Proceedings of the SIGCHI Conference on Human Factors in Computing Systems*, pp. 2233–2242.
16. K. Isbister, U. Schwekendiek, and J. Frye. 2011. Wriggle: An Exploration of Emotional and Social Effects of Movement. In *CHI '11 Extended Abstracts on Human Factors in Computing Systems*, pp. 1885–1890.
17. M. L. Knapp, J. A. Hall, and T. G. Horgan. 2013. *Nonverbal Communication in Human Interaction*, 8 edition. Cengage Learning.
18. K. Levy. 2014. A Surprising Number of Places Have Banned Google Glass in San Francisco. *Business Insider*. Retrieved September 15, 2016 from http://www.businessinsider.com/google-glass-ban-san-francisco-2014-3
19. S. Lundgren, J. E. Fischer, S. Reeves, and O. Torgersson. 2015. Designing Mobile Experiences for Collocated Interaction. In *Proceedings of the 18th ACM Conference on Computer Supported Cooperative Work & Social Computing,* pp. 496–507.
20. S. Mann. 1996. Smart clothing: the shift to wearable computing. *Commun. ACM*, vol. 39, no. 8, pp. 23–24.
21. N. Marquardt, R. Diaz-Marino, S. Boring, and S. Greenberg. 2011. The proximity toolkit: prototyping proxemic interactions in ubiquitous computing ecologies. p. 315.
22. N. Marquardt and S. Greenberg. 2015. *Proxemic interactions: from theory to practice*. Morgan and Claypool.
23. R. Mitchell. 2015. Sensing mine, yours, theirs, and ours: interpersonal ubiquitous interactions. In *Adjunct Proceedings of the 2015 ACM International Joint Conference on Pervasive and Ubiquitous Computing and Proceedings of the 2015 ACM International Symposium on Wearable Computers*, pp. 933–938.
24. F. Mueller and K. Isbister. 2014. Movement-based Game Guidelines. In *Proceedings of the SIGCHI Conference on Human Factors in Computing Systems*, pp. 2191–2200.
25. F. Mueller, S. Stellmach, S. Greenberg, A. Dippon, S. Boll, J. Garner, R. Khot, A. Naseem, and D. Altimira. 2014. Proxemics play: understanding proxemics for designing digital play experiences. In *Proceedings of*

the 2014 conference on Designing interactive systems, pp. 533–542.

26. C. Nagaoka, M. Komori, and S. Yoshikawa. 2005. Synchrony tendency: interactional synchrony and congruence of nonverbal behavior in social interaction, In *Proceedings of the 2005 International Conference on Active Media Technology*, doi: 10.1109/AMT.2005.1505415.
27. R. Nasser. 2012. Swordfight. Retrieved September 15, 2016 from http://nas.sr/swordfight/
28. S. Pizza, B. Brown, D. McMillan, and A. Lampinen. 2016. Smartwatch in vivo. In *Proceedings of the 2016 CHI Conference on Human Factors in Computing Systems*, pp. 5456-5469.
29. S. Reeves. 2011. *Designing Interfaces in Public Settings: Understanding the Role of the Spectator in Human-Computer Interaction*, 2011 edition. Springer.
30. T. Schiphorst. 2005. exhale: (breath between bodies), In *Proceedings of SIGGRAPH '05, article no. 6.* http://doi.acm.org/10.1145/1187297.1187304
31. E. M. Segura and K. Isbister. 2015. Enabling Co-Located Physical Social Play: A Framework for Design and Evaluation. In *Game User Experience Evaluation*, R. Bernhaupt, Ed. Springer International Publishing, pp. 209–238.
32. I. Soute. 2007. HUGs: head-up games. In *Proceedings of the 6th international conference on Interaction design and children*, pp. 205-208.
33. J. Tanenbaum and K. Tanenbaum. 2015. Envisioning the Future of Wearable Play: Conceptual Models for Props and Costumes as Game Controllers. In *Proceedings of Foundations of Digital Games*, Pacific Grove, California, USA.
34. K. S. Tekinbas and E. Zimmerman. 2003. *Rules of Play: Game Design Fundamentals*. MIT Press.
35. A. Waern, M. Montola, and J. Stenros. 2009. The three-sixty illusion: designing for immersion in pervasive games. In *Proceedings of the SIGCHI Conference on Human Factors in Computing Systems*, pp. 1549-1558.
36. G. Wolf. 2011. What is The Quantified Self?. *Quantified Self*, Retrieved September 6, 2016 from http://quantifiedself.com/2011/03/what-is-the-quantified-self/
37. F. Zangouei, M. A. B. Gashti, K. Höök, T. Tijs, G.-J. de Vries, and J. Westerink. 2010. How to stay in the emotional rollercoaster: lessons learnt from designing EmRoll. In *Proceedings of the 6th Nordic Conference on Human-Computer Interaction: Extending Boundaries,* pp. 571-580.

How Methods Make Designers

Seyram Avle
University of Michigan
Ann Arbor, USA
Seyram@umich.edu

Silvia Lindtner
University of Michigan
Ann Arbor, USA
lindtner@umich.edu

Kaiton Williams
Cornell University
Ithaca, USA
kaiton@cs.cornell.edu

ABSTRACT
Through their combination of lifestyle and method, Silicon Valley models for tech production such as design thinking, startup incubators, lean management, etc. are spreading across the globe. These paradigms are positioned by product designers, politicians, investors and corporations alike as replicable routes to individual and national empowerment. They are portrayed as universal templates, portable across national borders and applicable to local needs. We draw from our ethnographic engagements with tech entrepreneurial efforts in Ghana, China, and Jamaica to unpack the stakes involved in their uptake, showing that while local actors produce situated alternatives, their work nevertheless often results in a continued valorization of these seemingly universal methods. We argue that design methods shape not only use practices, but have consequences for the life worlds of professional designers. This includes how they impact personal and national identities, confer legitimacy in transnational innovation circles, and secure access to social and economic resources. Ultimately, we call for an inclusion of these factors in ongoing conversations about design and design methods.

Author Keywords
Design methods; ethnography; China; Ghana; Jamaica; Silicon Valley.

ACM Classification Keywords
H.5.m. Information interfaces and presentation (e.g., HCI): Miscellaneous;

INTRODUCTION
The last ten years have witnessed a standardization of a series of design methods that have come to represent what counts as innovative. We construe methods, here, loosely to refer to approaches such as designer and start-up toolkits, how-to guides, events as well as spaces and organizational approaches including, but not limited to, design thinking, startup weekends, the lean startup, hackathons, pitch contests, incubators and accelerators, co-working spaces, and many more. While not all of these methods have originated from the Silicon Valley region per se, they are positioned by diverse stakeholders, from governments to entrepreneurs and designers themselves, as the essential tools of a contemporary culture of technology production that the valley has come to represent. From new incubator programs in Chinese factories to design thinking workshops in Aarhus, these methods have found fertile ground in diverse regions [20, 28]. They are understood across different interests, cultural norms and regions as representative of "the right way" to do cutting-edge design and contemporary technology innovation. They constitute, in other words, a methodological hegemony: a dominating approach towards design and technology production. And, while they share a proposition that good design and production rests on taking seriously culturally-specific user demands and experiences, they also share a common ideal of how one best arrives at this: a set of pre-packaged toolkits, handbooks, and guides that shape the design process.

In this paper, we provide ethnographic accounts of the ways in which this methodological hegemony and standardization has extended beyond more familiar and established technology hubs like Silicon Valley. In research that spans regions in China, Ghana, Jamaica, and the United States, we have witnessed various endorsements of this "Silicon Valley method" (henceforth referred to as the 'SV method') by cities, regional and national governments, private and public institutions, designers and entrepreneurs alike. Across sites, this has proliferated a call for the cultivation of innovative thinking and entrepreneurship. This has been accompanied by an allocation of resources towards incubators, design thinking programs, the hosting of hackathons, start-up weekends, and pitch contests. Often, and as we will show here, an underlying motivation is to rebrand cities, local regions and whole nations as emergent tech innovation hubs arising from the periphery [8].2, 8]. Silicon Valley's methodological hegemony extends through and across borders, though not without contestation, and is aided by an infrastructure jointly constituted by educational institutions, financial investments, and the people who flow in and out of the San Francisco Bay Area [41, 42, 43].

Prior research in HCI has addressed such processes of Western hegemony at the site of technology production and computing. Dourish & Mainwaring [13], for instance, argue that ubiquitous computing can be linked to a 'colonial intellectual tradition' that uses universalizing discourse to locate innovation in relation to, and as emanating from,

CHI 2017, May 06 - 11, 2017, Denver, CO, USA

ACM 978-1-4503-4655-9/17/05 $15.00
DOI: http://dx.doi.org/10.1145/3025453.3025864

specific sites, predominantly in the West. The logics of this 'colonizing impulse' make certain ideas hegemonic practice. Our goal is to add to this discussion by drawing attention to how specific ideas about design have emerged as seemingly universal approaches applicable to diverse social, cultural, and economic contexts. More specifically, we examine how privileged modes of technology design shape professional identities. Extending from [2, 20, 45], we unpack how a professional identity around design practice emerges from within a center-periphery narrative, how it figures into design concerns, and how the socio-economic realities of the global market shape contemporary design practices. This includes accounting for how designers may not, and sometimes cannot, disentangle the design of products and services from sociopolitical and national aspirations [1, 2].

In doing so we focus particular attention on how the uptake and contestation of the SV method unfolds through desires of global belonging and legitimacy, dreams and hopes for alternate futures, and ultimately the pragmatic realities of making a living. In ethnographic detail, we show how a myriad of actors – including governments, corporations, individual entrepreneurs, and NGOs – jointly proliferate and sustain a universal approach to technology design, often without specifically intending to do so. We show how the seductive draw of the SV method lies exactly in its universal promise of local applicability, individual and collective transformation. When that promise becomes too difficult to realize, we observed contestation of its universal reach and the development of situated alternatives. Yet much of this work is underemphasized, or is located within the universal template in order to align with hegemonic methods whose use confers legitimacy in global tech networks.

In what follows, we briefly cover our methods, and then present prior work that situates the shift in global digital labor towards entrepreneurship and individual self-actualization. We follow that with an overview of the main theme of methodological hegemony, the contours of which we reveal through ethnographic accounts. We trace the social and material infrastructures that support this hegemonic approach in each site, and unpack how it interplays with mechanisms of identity and nation building. We highlight the frictions between the hopes for these methods, and their disappointments. We then reflect on why it is important for design research and practice in and beyond HCI to consider the livelihoods of designers.

METHODS

We draw on ethnographic work in China, Ghana, Jamaica, and the United States. This work covers participant observation and interviews from six years of work/engagement in China (Shenzhen, Beijing, and Shanghai) by the second author, six years of research in Ghana (Accra and Kumasi) by the first author, and three years of research in Jamaica (Kingston) by the third author, and across Silicon Valley. The authors worked, variously in their respective sites, within tech incubators, makerspaces, accelerators, startups, and co-working spaces. We attended multiple events including hackathons, pitching competitions, workshops, coding & startup bootcamps, conducting in depth and informal interviews with founders, designers, manufacturers, government officials, and others. The second and third author were also active as team partners and designer researchers, working side by side with startups, organizing workshops, and conducting trainings, e.g. [26, 28, 47]. Each of us has followed the transnational connections of people and ideas between our sites and regions in North America including the San Francisco Bay Area, New York, and Boston, tracing the paths our interlocutors built. Additional details on our methods, which we cannot do justice in the space allotted here, can be found in [1, 2, 27, 28, 47].

This paper is an outcome of frequent conversations at multiple conferences, including CHI, between the authors on the practices, ideas, and consequences of design and business methods we were independently observing in our sites. We formalized our analysis by working inductively on each of our datasets, noting themes and patterns as they emerged, and tracing them as they cut across and diffracted within our sites. This collective reading of each site through the others was both comparative and multi-sited allowing us to heed commonality and differences that revealed the role of design in each space. Following the method of multi-sited ethnography [32], we attended to the ways in which our interlocutors themselves drew out connections to multiple other places and sites as they situated their own work. What emerged across our sites was that Silicon Valley's methods amounted to strategies both for the production of technology and for living. In all three sites, we found various commitments and practices of directly engaging with Silicon Valley, and with what we call its proxy agents. Proxy agents include, for instance, people who have either worked in some capacity in Silicon Valley or in an adjacent industry such as in venture capital or in an allied institution, often universities (particularly in China) but also international non-governmental organizations in Ghana and Jamaica.

We critically unpack the notion of a Silicon Valley approach as a universal framing that works across diverse sites by focusing on how its narrative of design and innovation played out in unique ways in relation to the political economies and social structures of our three sites. While not a specific focus in this paper, we are guided by a historical perspective that takes into account how the respective colonial, postcolonial, neoliberal and capitalist developments in each region in part shape discourse and practice today. For instance, histories of neoliberal experimentation post-independence, followed by development efforts and NGO infrastructures, cannot be disentangled from how the role of technology design is construed in Ghana and Jamaica today. In China, a confluence of economic reform and opening in the 1980s, contemporary ambitions to reposition it on a global stage of economic and technoscientific prowess, and a history of colonial occupation and humiliation in the 19th century, all shape contemporary technology practice, as well as policy and imaginations of the country's relation to Silicon Valley. These historical and contemporary national and geopolitical processes shape our analysis and discussions across the three sites, and yet within the constraints of this paper, we cannot do justice to their complexity or the myriad of prior work in area studies, postcolonial studies, and history that has tackled them in detail.

Our analysis includes relevant stakeholders whose presence and participation in the spaces we examined helped to maintain Silicon Valley's methodological hegemony. In all three sites, the state exerted different degrees of influence in directing policy towards one method or the other. In China, for instance, the national government has begun taking up the discourse and approaches offered by elite technology entrepreneurs in major cities, leveraging their existing relationships with Silicon Valley even as it tries to remake the nation along what it perceives as an emancipatory path of modernization for its people. We similarly trace the interactions and interventions of a range of actors in Ghana and Jamaica who feature in design and tech entrepreneurial spaces. Foreign funders and other interested parties have emerged out of what is best described as the NGO & aid infrastructure active in Africa, the Caribbean and other parts of the Global South. Together with our interlocutors (who we anonymize in our accounts below), state representatives, and Silicon Valley evangelists, they provide the foundation of a methodological hegemony that shapes professional identities and livelihoods.

GLOBAL LABOR & THE ALLURE OF INDIVIDUALIZED ENTREPRENEURIALISM

The desire to transform regions into knowledge economies and dot them with innovation hubs is not a new impulse. The novelty lies in the global scale and the range of actors involved in implementing these ambitions. Researchers of tech work and labor have long documented how the rise of so-called creative and knowledge economies has been accompanied by an increasing in the precarity of labor and neoliberal modes of governance that stipulate that the future of whole nations rests on citizens becoming self-entrepreneurial and self-actualizing subjects. Neff, for instance, documents how risk-taking came to be seen as a good and necessary skill for people working in the American IT industry [37]. Whether running a startup or working for a large tech corporation like IBM or Microsoft, to work entrepreneurially or participate in what Neff calls "venture labor" became a mandate to be successful in Silicon Valley and beyond. Doing so represents not just new sites of work, but also sites of "self-making" where design practices inform artifact and personal identity. Similar processes have been documented by researchers who have studied the rise and fall of creative industry policies in the UK [10, 29, 33]. Since the 1990s, policies have been implemented that "promise freedom to self-actualize while also subjugating (individuals) to a normalization of risk and uncertainty" [29]. These developments are understood as a shift in work and labor security structures in Post-Fordism societies that have normalized precariousness and further extended a neoliberal mode of governance to those "areas long considered secure" [29]. In other words, with the rise of flexible work and the demand to turn individuals into risk takers [37] it is increasingly difficult to discern between the secure and the precarious.

In her studies of the information industry in the Caribbean and the pursuit of entrepreneurial flexibility more broadly, Freeman finds that what she terms "the entrepreneurial enterprise" is also the central site of "neoliberal self-creation and labor in today's global economy" [14, 15], entangling selfhood and labor in a common project. In our sites, governments and the private sector promoted entrepreneurship as holding promise for individual and national futures in a moment where prior promises of creative work and socio-economic development began to appear hollow. Within these spaces, the self emerges as an entrepreneurial project under constant renovation, much like the digital products common in them. In our sites, the neoliberal undercurrents in visions of self- entrepreneurship have in drastic ways shaped social life and livelihoods, rather vividly for instance through Structural Adjustment Programs implemented by the World Bank and International Monetary Fund (IMF) in Ghana and Jamaica in the 1980s and 1990s.

The trope of individual empowerment and techno-utopianism that emanates from Silicon Valley is a powerful one that often hides the reality of increasing precariousness [26]. What Neff described as the new cool – launch parties, hackathons, coding, etc. – are even more so now part of the global Zeitgeist. We see this across regions and scales: high schoolers dropping out to move to San Francisco [6], the introduction of coding to pre-schoolers [7], hackathons hosted from Rio to Rome, Accra to the Zambezi. Incubators and accelerators dedicated to digital technologies have sprung up across this expanse. Across Africa alone, at time of writing, the count was close to 100 tech hubs in just under five years [49], and in China, makerspaces have sprung up in the thousands seemingly overnight [27].

METHODOLOGICAL HEGEMONY

The professional identity of a tech entrepreneur combines design and engineering with business acumen. Silicon Valley lore propagates online through industry news and blogs, and through global news media via stories of highly visible tech entrepreneurs of some of the world's most highly valued companies (which are increasingly tech companies) [11]. These accounts provide ready models for how a tech entrepreneur should behave, work, and live [18]. Many of our interlocutors could recite the founding stories of Facebook, Uber, and other 'unicorns'. They were familiar with the current signposts towards tech success, and like their peers in SV, are conversant in lean management and design thinking, know of and attended global events like TechCrunch's Disrupt, participated in hackathons and bootcamps, pitched to investors, and sought the shelter and support of incubators.

These templates were never taken wholesale or rejected outright. Certainly, there were those of our interlocutors who were more or less enthusiastic about what it means to 'speak the language of innovation' but even within those shades, it was rarely simply one or the other. We found many complex negotiations of identity and enactments of professional design and production methods. Our underlying goal is to show how our interlocutors were actively reworking universal appeals and approaches through the everyday, making sense of their environment, and adapting what they saw as necessary to succeed as professionals.

In what follows then, we document various scales of how SV methods materialize, unpacking how the making of professional identity was entangled with projects of branding particular regions and nations as innovation hubs. For instance, political aspirations to mark China as a global leader in technological innovation and economic development have motivated policy reforms aimed at cultivating an entrepreneurial spirit and innovation thinking across "the masses". This is in stark contrast to Ghana where the government has largely been laissez-faire about the tech industry with industry actors more focused on building an 'ecosystem' that succeeds in spite of (in their view) the government's lack of commitment. Meanwhile in Jamaica, tech entrepreneurship has become an outlet for youth frustrations, and a fulcrum for effecting the transition to a knowledge economy and securing a position in the global economy that it has been denied since the removal of preferential trade agreements. Both Ghana and Jamaica's involvements with the World Bank, first through Structural Adjustment policies, and today through its underwriting of tech entrepreneurship efforts, reflects how SV's proxy agents fit within larger historical and contemporary efforts in building technological futures. Taken together, all these cases demonstrate not only the hopes and aspirations associated with SV methods but also the tensions and challenges our interlocutors navigated as they incorporate these approaches into their professional work and identity.

Nation-making & the making of professional identity

Making Creative China

In 2014, the Taiwanese contract manufacturer Foxconn turned one of its former Nokia manufacturing facilities in Beijing into the hardware incubator Innoconn. Spanning two floors, the former assembly line of the factory was converted into the kinds of open office space many in Silicon Valley have come to understand as necessary to produce innovative ideas: an assortment of desks behind glass walls, whiteboards distributed throughout the space, colorful chairs and high-ceilings that expose the building's pipes and electronic infrastructure. These transformed the former production site in seemingly authentic ways into what has become a global chic of contemporary innovation culture. One of the first things one can't help but notice when entering the remodeled office spaces is a wall-sized mural made of Apple iPhone covers that together form the immediately recognizable shape of Steve Job's head. Within seconds of a glance, the mural signaled that the factory was now a place where people could turn themselves into the kind of entrepreneurial designer Steve Jobs symbolizes.

The 2014 factory-turned-incubator in Beijing was one of the latest investments by national and foreign entities into China's desire to remake itself from a site that produced for the world into a site that originated its own ideas. Over the last two years, incubator spaces like Innoconn have opened up in the thousands in Chinese factories, IT corporations, schools, universities, and libraries. In a 2015 policy entitled "mass makerspace 众创空间 - mass entrepreneurship 大众创业 – mass innovation 万众创新," the Chinese government officially endorsed experiments like Innoconn as a model for the nation as a whole. The underlying vision of the policy – as articulated in numerous government speeches and texts – was that a "maker" approach was ideally positioned to help China cultivate an attitude of entrepreneurship, which in turn would help transform the nation as a whole into a knowledge economy and a globally renowned hub for innovation. The "mass" in the policy represents the goal of cultivating an entrepreneurial mindset and mobilizing many – if not masses of – people in China to start their own businesses. These new spaces would enable China, as prime minister Li Keqiang 李克强 put it when he introduced the new policy, "nurture an environment for entrepreneurship and innovation as well as to allow people to realize their full potential" [46]. With the new policy, funding was made available to provinces and regions across the country to set up new spaces for people to incubate businesses.

The new policy, however, not only made money available to turn old buildings into new offices. It was, more importantly, an articulation of a particular kind of professional identity. The future of the nation, it posited, rested on the ability of many Chinese, across class and professional background, to turn themselves into entrepreneurial professionals. Government officials positioned this project of cultivating an entrepreneurial ethos among the masses as implementing, at last, the long-held ambition of overcoming foreign imperialism by transforming the nation into a leader in technological and scientific innovation, a project that has occupied China since it lost the Opium Wars in the 1890s [38]. Since China joined the WTO in 2001, government officials have argued that this could be accomplished by turning the nation into a creative society and developing a creative industry [50]. With the help of foreign advisors from the UK and Australia, local policies were implemented that borrowed from creative industry policy texts and approaches in the West to enable China's transition into a globally recognized creative producer. These policies have led to radical transformations of many city neighborhoods, displaced millions of migrants to make room for the practices of a global elite of creatives, and are considered today as a largely failed experiment. Creative and cultural production thus remained a project all too vague and exclusive.

The more recent shift towards entrepreneurship, mass making and incubation positioned these earlier ideas of turning China into a knowledge economy and to fight Western hegemony as suddenly feasible. The setup of incubator spaces, makerspaces, and co-working spaces in a variety of settings, rural and urban, white collar- and blue-collar work environments, should transform, so Chinese politicians envisioned, in concrete ways what work and professional identity mean in China today. Much of this contemporary shift towards entrepreneurship, albeit positioned as establishing China as independent from the West, is enabled by alliances with corporations and individuals who evidence experience in Silicon Valley type start-up and entrepreneurship culture. The irony is that the wish to overcome Western hegemony is implemented by positioning Silicon Valley models as the crux to overcome Western imperialism.

Entrepreneurial visions and a future Ghana

Walking into one of the tech hubs in Accra during fieldwork one day in early 2016, Avle noticed one of the co-founders, Jake, practicing a short speech in the corner. After being told he was prepping for a video application for a fellowship with one of the US's elite universities with a popular design-focused program, Avle watched him fine-tune a few takes before sitting down to chat. Jake was enthusiastic but somewhat nervous about the application. He had achieved a lot – creating a tech focused co-working space that attracted leading figures in Ghana's fledgling tech industry. The "beauty" of the fellowship, for him, was that it was "highly explorative" and that it would help him combine SV start up methods with the financial infrastructure in Ghana. He thought the opportunity to engage with "some of the top minds" from the SV area made this an opportunity too good to miss.

Jake was one of the most outspoken tech entrepreneurs Avle interacted with in Ghana. Like many others, his view of SV methods was that they necessarily had to be adapted to Ghana's business and economic culture, but the underlying ideas were valid and worth pursuing as a way of life. Unlike many others though, he had greater openness to working with government to implement policies that would be more beneficial to the local tech industry, rather than simply keeping them at arm's length. Here, he felt his generation of Ghanaians could apply some of what he described as their 'pragmatism' to work out a way to guide government action towards investing more in the tech sector.

Most interlocutors distanced themselves and their profession in general from state efforts and what was perceived as the government' failures at supporting innovation in Ghana. Many agreed that the state paid lip service to working towards turning Ghana into a knowledge society and hindered rather than enabled innovation. The view was that state incompetence and the myopic view of successive governments have made Ghana an unnecessarily difficult terrain to do business in general and tech business in particular. This difficulty was experienced at the micro level of the day-to-day business environment and on the macro level, the absence of supporting infrastructures towards innovation.

To that end, Jake and others welcomed interest from aid and non-governmental organizations that previously used to deal directly with the Ghanaian government but had recently started instead turning to tech hubs as a way of implementing creative and entrepreneurship policies that came from their parent organizations. For instance, some of the Danish government's funding for 'cultural development' had recently gone towards supporting activities in tech hubs. Other European and American organizations such as Hivos, Stichting Doen, Making All Voices Count, the EU, The World Bank and its InfoDev Group, US Embassies, USAID, DFID, SeedStars, Koltai, & Dahlberg, all work alongside multinational tech companies like Google, IBM, and Microsoft to endorse and fund 'innovation' and tech programs in Ghana. The pragmatism Jake mentioned was about taking 'unconventional' routes such as leveraging resources from such agencies, to build an 'ecosystem' that worked for Ghana's contemporary economic situation. For Jake, moving between unconventional funding sources, working as a government policy ally (even if unpopular), was to be able to answer the key question "what template do you use to grow a tech company in Ghana?"

This question underscores the underlying narrative presented by SV and its proxy agents: that its methods are at the same time both universal and particular. However, the devil was in the details; many tech entrepreneurs agreed that what could be made particular was the crux of the challenge in Ghana. Comparing how many days it took to register his business and get the documents verified in the UK (2.5 hours) to how long it took him to do so in Ghana (17 months, granted he tried to do it from outside the country), one interlocutor, Delali, remarked that "you need a lot more labor to get things done in Ghana". Another, Yaw, described how doing everyday things like visiting prospective clients was a physically laborious process, one that required doing things like queuing, walking under a hot sun, sitting long hours in traffic etc. on top of contending with bureaucratic issues and business culture that made negotiations protracted. Such descriptions of the actual daily work of producing technology portrayed a bodily and viscerally-felt dimension of technology production that is often absent from the Silicon Valley success stories floated around tech spaces. More importantly, they show how tech entrepreneurs locate their professional identities to other forms of work and how they fit into the broad project of building a different, better future for Ghana.

Jake, Delali, Yaw, and most of the tech entrepreneurs interviewed in Ghana ultimately saw Silicon Valley as more of a place of inspiration, motivation, and validation, and as less a reflection of the conditions in which all tech entrepreneurs must work. To Yaw for instance, producing digital technology in Ghana was "not necessarily [about] building another Silicon Valley, but when you hear the stories it motivates you. It's a motivational factor, but for us, it's really being able to solve a problem for clients". When Jake talked about a "growth hacking template", he meant one that combined lessons from successful Ghanaian entrepreneurs outside the tech industry and how their methods can be combined with the SV methods (on starting up, pitching, pivoting, design thinking, etc.) that he and other tech entrepreneurs used. What was stake, as was often articulated to Avle, was Ghana's technological future and the glory of being a part of that future. The ideal outcome for these tech entrepreneurs was to build an 'ecosystem' for tech entrepreneurship and technology production that created a technologically advanced future for Ghana, one that will have its own successful variations of SV methods, suitable for the local context. To do so, they had to position themselves and take from not just Silicon Valley but other forms of entrepreneurial work in Ghana.

Get Up, Start Up, Jamaica

In Jamaica, the focus on tech entrepreneurship has emerged within the context of a nation-making endeavor. The current 25-year plan, Vision 2030, plans to route the country to Developed Nation status. This vision couples the expansion of technical infrastructure with the development of knowledge industries as a transformational path for its citizenry and a new basis for the country's economy. The current production of ICTs as a route to realizing nationalist and personal ideals is anchored within the historical context of slavery, colonialism, and the globalization inherent in the island's place in The New World.

The plan is part of a longstanding attempt to craft national futures through technical possibility. Arguably, much of this began with the laying of submarine fiber for voice transmission in the late 1800s. Then, a public-private partnership of colonial officials and promoters of cable connections crafted a politics and technology of Empire as a universal vision enabled by the network [34]. This continued with the stressing of modernity, cybernetic theory and technical achievement, but this time as way to demonstrate transcendental unity during the independence movement of the mid 1900s. Then, as today, the Jamaican people were to be exemplars of cosmopolitanism, their orderly mind, body, and modernity crucial at the time to helping achieving legitimacy and political autonomy from England [35].

This desire to bind technology use and production to personal and national identity making would manifest again during the establishment of the Informatics and Business Process Outsourcing industries in the 1980s & 90s [36], and now today in the promotion of ICT entrepreneurship. Evident across these efforts is an evolving relationship between technology and identity: first one of order and accuracy, embodied in the computer terminals and orderly cubicles of the Informatics Industry; and now one of disruption and individualization, ushered in with the advent of the smartphone and the influence of Silicon Valley startup methodologies and rhetoric.

Instrumentally, much of the support of this recent style of tech entrepreneurship has been to address chronic youth unemployment, and stem brain drain. In this effort, the government is joined by a wide array of private and public institutions. Various corporate efforts, both local and international take place in parallel with a series of efforts funded and facilitated by the World Bank Group. While the Bank's efforts are aligned with and supportive of the Government-led initiative, their program is spread across the Caribbean, and policy and practical decisions about curriculum, and even the target areas/industries that are "fundable" for startups (for e.g. the "sharing economy"), emanate from Bank staff who circulate between other hub initiatives spread across the globe.

Through EPIC (Entrepreneurship Programme for Innovation in the Caribbean), the Bank has created a pipeline for tech entrepreneurs that is spread across several sites: long-term training sessions and bootcamps for teaching mobile development and "lean" startup methods; pitching competitions where graduates demonstrate both product and startup acumen; and an incubator/accelerator where startups can find material support and further training to mature their products. These sites work together, with participants circulating among them.

Digital Jam (DJ) is one example of the combination of pitching competition, training program, and startup conference, that in 2014 was in its "3.0" iteration. The conference focuses on training mobile app developers and in preparing youth for opportunities in "microwork and e-lancing." In a World Bank publication covering the event, titled "Silicon Valley casts its nets in the Caribbean", Fabio Pittaluga, the "World Bank Innovation Expert" responsible for organizing the event recaps: "Through this effort, Jamaica and other Caribbean countries will join numerous business networks that *stretch out from Silicon Valley to the rest of the world to connect the region's youth with the technology giants* and other employers...This is a worldwide revolution in the making." [emphasis ours] [48]

While it is a judged competition, the facilitators are keen to position it not just as a contest but as a program of progressive education in the values of tech production. The lead up to DJ features extensive mentoring sessions where participants learn not just how to design apps, but how to present both self and idea. Here's Richard Shaw, one of the mentors, as covered in a blog post: "The world is changing… practices that worked well at one time must be regularly revised. The younger generation see the world through a 'different lens'." He positions what's being taught as not just tech methods but "values and core beliefs that are applicable across generations", and once "these values are absorbed and understood, then the younger generation can unleash their talents" [25].

The training program is steeped in the language of SV design & engineering practices. This entails a comfort with publicly embracing failure (against established social norms) and human-centered design focus on the user and the social context of use, seen as missing from local design practices. Teams learn to present themselves within The Pitch as a marriage of technical know-how ("the CTO") and business acumen ("the CEO"), describing their product and its development processes, while displaying entrepreneurial stances. As participants progress through this pipeline, what counts as technology and design is progressively shaped, ideas are narrowed down, and methods sharpened.

Aspirations, hopes & frictions

Upgrading China

In 2012, HAX, one of the world's first hardware accelerators opened its doors in Shenzhen, Guangdong. It was around this time that the city of Shenzhen, a manufacturing hub just North of Hong Kong, rather than the internationally more well-known cities like Shanghai and Beijing, began garnering attention in Western tech entrepreneurship networks. Makers excited to turn their ideas from prototype into end-consumer products from smart home appliances to wearables and robotics began traveling to Shenzhen [27, 28]. "Shenzhen is a place where stuff still gets made. That expertise is concentrated there," Dale Dougherty, founder of Make Media, described this draw of Shenzhen to Lindtner in a 2014 interview. Other maker-turned-entrepreneurs would speak of their partnerships with factories and of an informal economy of manufacturing that was still at work in the wider Guangdong region that permitted them, despite language barriers, quick entry into a previously unfamiliar cultural practice of industrial production.

What started out with individual makers and early incubator projects like HAX soon received attention by foreign investors, high-profile corporations and institutions from the United States and Europe like Intel, the MIT Media Lab, the British Council, Make Media, Arduino, Microsoft, and more. These endorsements by Western entities further legitimized the project of Shenzhen as an ideal laboratory to innovate in hardware. By 2015, both city and national governments had officially endorsed Shenzhen as a model for tech entrepreneurship and innovation for China as a whole. Lindtner has written elsewhere extensively about the remake of Shenzhen into a rising innovation hub, today often referred to as the "Silicon Valley of Hardware" [see for instance, [26, 27, 28, 47]. The focus, here, in particular is on how a portrayal of Shenzhen in line with and following the innovation trajectory of Silicon Valley began rendering invisible exactly the kinds of informal production culture that had attracted entrepreneurs to Shenzhen in the first place.

One of the first destinations of many newcomers to Shenzhen interested in hardware and entrepreneurship has been the electronic market of Huaqiangbei 华强北. Comprising a 15-by-15 city block area, Huaqiangbei is made up of department store buildings, some 20-30 stories high, filled with a tight labyrinth of stalls of vendors selling anything from new and recycled small electronic components all the way to finished products such as mobile phones, tablets, hoverboards, selfie sticks, security cameras, and much more. Huaqiangbei has been featured in numerous blog posts of Western hardware enthusiasts and journalistic accounts to describe Shenzhen's unique approach to entrepreneurial tinkering. In 2015, a couple of months after the official announcement of China's new mass makerspace policy described earlier, Shenzhen hosted its second featured Maker Faire. It was the first time the city government of Shenzhen had officially endorsed and financially backed the event. Hand in hand with the Maker Faire came an urban redesign of the Huaqiangbei electronic market. The market space was transformed into a glossy interface of China's latest industrial products on display. The redesign wasn't only about an aesthetic transformation. The city government's goal was to transform the informal economy of Chinese manufacturing that had enabled the rise of the young city of Shenzhen from a region of agriculture to a metropolis of more than 15 million people and the world's largest hub of electronic manufacturing in only 10 years. What was holding the nation back, many in China agreed, was its history and practice of informal production, symbolized by the Huaqiangbei electronic markets -- a gray market that produced knock-offs alongside new products to niche markets in regions of Africa, India, Latin America. Incubator spaces, makerspaces, and co-working spaces would have to take their place, so the government envisioned, making room for a new generation of entrepreneurs, trained in Silicon Valley methods and globally networked.

The goal was to promote Shenzhen as a partner to regions like Silicon Valley and to retrain those who had worked in industrial design and manufacturing in Shenzhen as entrepreneurial designers recognizable to the language, behaviors, and customs of Silicon Valley. Shenzhen's new maker and incubator spaces, its factories, national and international corporations like Intel and Huawei, and the local city government began hosting pitch contests, hackathons, startup weekends, maker competitions, and many more similar events. At one such event, Lindtner met Wu Xun. Wu Xun had come to Shenzhen about 10 years earlier at the urging of a relative. "Shenzhen was a place where you could still make yourself," Wu reflected. He had worked his way up from engineer to starting his own business, producing and selling tablets to markets in Europe and South America. The new policy on mass entrepreneurship, according to Wu, was a good thing, for now. It enabled him to rebrand his business and get funding for his projects. However, in day-to-day practice, this project of rebranding was not as straightforward as the new policy documents promised.

As Wu was standing on stage, pitching his latest project of an open source PC stick to a mixed audience of Chinese and foreign makers, entrepreneurs, and venture capitalist, people in the audience nervously shifted in their seats and awkwardly gazed around the room. Wu was speaking in a loud voice, far too loud for the closeness of the microphone that somebody had attached to his head, his voice echoing in the auditorium. He could offer services for Western makers, he elaborated in his speech, based on his ten-year experience of mass production in China. Wu was passionate, but in a manner that didn't fit the expected voice and language of tech entrepreneurial enthusiasm that has become so common to pitch contests, TED talks, and Kickstarter videos. In some ways, the glitch, Wu's misfit, made the absurdity of training people to pitch and present themselves over and over and in the same way visible. The audience felt uncomfortable. Halted and embarrassed clapping followed Wu's speech. "I am not sure," he said later when asked how he thought his talk went, "I hope to get to collaborate with lots of foreign makers!"

Ghana: A different grind

The corporeal/ tangible/material aspects of creating software products added color to being a tech entrepreneur in Ghana. As a tech entrepreneur in Accra, you were likely to have access to places connected to the internet, with air conditioning, and in general validated you as a special kind of person. At the same time, you were also trying to beat Accra's traffic, trying to network as much as you can and understand that yours was "a completely different grind". On a daily basis, one had to put on the outfit of a tech entrepreneur and be in the right places, even if one didn't understand what goes on. Peter, a tech entrepreneur articulated this to Avle as follows, "you basically have to fake it till you make it or just keep faking it till you die, which seems to be the thing here now… You just keep winging it for so long that you tell yourself every morning that you are an expert, just to be able to live with it."

While being a tech entrepreneur had its performative aspects, it became a lifestyle for those who were fully committed to it. The majority of those who showed up in the hubs and events Avle attended were either full time employees of banks, insurance companies, telecom service providers and other similar corporate jobs, using their spare time to learn how to be a tech entrepreneur or were engaged in multiple ventures. Some of those part time entrepreneurs were learning to become tech designers, learning the language of tech entrepreneurship, and how to join this global cadre of 'problem solvers'. "The tech scene is a side hustle for a lot of people," noted Peter, something that was necessary in Accra. This notion of technology production as a 'side hustle' was consistent with the story about the Ghanaian economy more broadly, characterized by self-employment, with many having to rely on multiple sources of income to hedge against low wages.

At time of Avle's research, the Accra tech scene was comprised of regular events such as hackathons, talks, workshops, 'meet-ups', etc., most of which took place in two main hubs: Impact Hub and iSpace. At these hubs, part time tech entrepreneurs intermingled with "full timers" who were in start-up mode or has already started a successful business. The latter were often deemed 'resource persons' on hand to speak or provide input as judges for start-up competitions. Ever so often, people from outside the country or with experiences outside Ghana, particularly in Silicon Valley, (including 'returnees' in the tech sector [1]) filled this role, but often it was mostly 'local' folks mingling and working in a shared space. Hubs are where new entrants into tech entrepreneurship are enticed, nurtured, and challenged, depending on one's viewpoint. For instance, across the first class of students at iSpace's "Code to Startup" program, a 12-week training aimed at teaching people how to code in order to ultimately launch a viable product, many had joined because they wanted to learn to code or get better at coding and not that they wanted to build a tech focused business or launch a product. Within a few weeks, many had 'caught the bug' and were thinking beyond 'simply learning to code' and about how they might use technology to 'solve problems in Ghana'.

The hubs also served as venues for organizations to hold their own tech related events. These events, held by what we've referred to as proxy SV agents, such as NGOs, the US embassy, the World Bank, etc., were often styled after SV start-up culture, with similar rules, aesthetics and terms of engagement. For instance, all hackathons followed a particular kind of template: a challenge was issued, followed by a call for competitors, people then signed up (usually in teams), and converged at a dedicated location and work together throughout a specified timeframe, in order to finally pitch their solutions to a jury often made up of a mix of local tech stars and almost always at least one foreigner.

Since 2012, an increasing number of multinational firms (MNCs) in banking and telecommunications have been using hackathons to crowdsource ideas to leverage their APIs, or to generate innovative solutions to an in-house problem or for a new product. As one-time events organized by such proxy agents, hackathons largely served the interests of the organizing entity. Still, participation for the up and coming tech entrepreneur promised exposure and the possibility of funding. Exposure was expressed to Avle as visibility of skills, which promised to be turned into collaborations, sponsorships, new clients, etc. This possibility was, of course, up against the potentially exploitative nature of the power imbalance between an MNC and a young coder hoping to make new contacts. One complaint heard was that one had to do exactly what the organizer wanted or risk being cut off from funds, something that was described as possibly derailing one's projects. At the same time, other interlocutors were fine with that - having different expectations going into such events. Still others were more concerned about the terms and conditions that applied to whatever they created at the hackathon. David, (a designer and coder) described how he had taken issue with the wording of a couple of hackathon contracts with a bank and telecom firm that essentially signs over his design to them and been asked if he was a lawyer.

Navigating in between worlds in Jamaica

Tech production is often presented by government actors and other industry supporters, unproblematically, as an "easy" route to success for youths. In speeches at Digital Jam and several other events in 2014, Julian Robinson, the then Minister of State for Science, Technology, Energy and Mining, frequently used Flappy Birds --- a smartphone game popular at the time --- as an evocative example of a success possible from a globally marginal place. The game's developer was based in Vietnam, and it had become a sudden hit, earning him thousands of dollars a day through in-game advertising.

The success of the game was presented without its details or complications: a message to youth about what hard work and following a proven formula (ad-supported smartphone games) could yield. But there was a dark side that the Minister was either unaware of, or unwilling to mention. While some accounts of the game presented it as an overnight success, it was the most recent in a set of many other games by the developer that had met with little success. The developer, frustrated in part with harassment about the game's legendary difficulty, the relentless press coverage, and accusations of copyright infringement, pulled the game from the app store and disappeared from public life.

Similarly, many of the budding entrepreneurs drawn into these programs by global media coverage of the industry, and rhetoric like the Minister's, struggled with the realities of the workload: the significant amount of new material to learn, the time and work necessary to produce an artifact, and securing funding and users. For many of them, these methods are embraced within a desire to establish oneself as a startup tech entrepreneur different from both earlier local variants of tech entrepreneurship, and entrepreneurship generally.

This entails both a vision of oneself as a global actor (traveling to international tech hubs, often sponsored by aid agencies) and adhering to the "up to the time" methods (which include embracing buzzy terms such Lean, Scrum, Agile, & GitHub, or avoiding 'outmoded' languages like PHP). Reflecting on the work of entrepreneurs, Pablo, a Jamaican entrepreneur visiting Silicon Valley notes the difference between what he has been doing and the work of local entrepreneur or "hustlers" who don't pursue "proper business practices" that reflect a science, and never look beyond the local market. In doing so he channels rhetoric that reinforces the neutral hegemonic position of SV methods: universal, modern, and rational; ready for international markets and scaling. Pablo's pursuit of the startup life is driven from poor experiences working within companies where he felt powerless and without agency. Pursuing a startup is a key part of a creative, self-empowered lifestyle. For others that Williams spoke with, this is compounded by a paucity of opportunities for "good" tech work locally.

While at least 3 well-regarded local universities churn out graduates in Computer Science and related fields, there aren't enough jobs to occupy them all. And where jobs do exist, they're often within slower-moving large institutions (banking, insurance) that often do not allow for the use of methods that are featured in the online tech hubs (e.g. ycombinator & reddit) that dominate local mailing lists and developer meetups. This leads to an exploration in personal time or a search for opportunities that allows for a use of these tools. Often an entrepreneurial effort arises as a site to implement a desired technology & product first, and to address the needs of the market second. This is accelerated by a cultural pattern that embraces entrepreneurialism as well as flexibility and occupational multiplicity [9].

Their heroes are Silicon Valley tech visionaries. They are embraced for their financial success but also for their methods, which offer a stark break from "local" practices through their engineering-orientation or attention to design. It's not just that they want to do as well (financially) as these figures: they want to do it in the same way. For instance, Pablo readily admits to being star struck by successful tech leaders in the past, because of their connection to recognizable brands like Apple or Google. And he is able to name and channel Silicon Valley figures whom Williams has difficulty summoning and recalling despite living in the valley for 13 years, much of it spent working within similar companies. Pablo knows local San Francisco "celebrities" like Karl the Fog, a twitter account detailing local weather patterns. This may seem slight but it's important: SF is a mecca, and many local eyes are turned toward it, no matter how distant. In a casual conversation outside a futurist event at a recently opened co-working space in a newly gentrifying block of SOMA in San Francisco, someone asks Pablo the question Williams has heard so many times addressed to entrepreneurs: "where are you based?" His response, "in between SF & Jamaica" is symbolic of the "in-betweenness" many of these entrepreneurs navigate: at some remove from Jamaican practices, in tune with a SV tech disposition.

DISCUSSION

New life-worlds and professional identities are brought into being when Chinese factories transform their empty assembly lines into incubators, when the World Bank hosts Digital Jam sessions, and when Accra's iSpace trains people in how to code. We have traced how the global appeal of such design methods lies exactly in their promise to upgrade individuals and nations along a trajectory of Western innovation hubs. Yet, none of this happens without contestation, frictions, and awkward misfits. We have shown, for instance, the irony that lies in China's attempts to use Silicon Valley design methods to undermine Western hegemony as well as the tensions that arise when governments try to intervene in spaces tech entrepreneurs have carved for themselves in Ghana and Jamaica. Much is at stake in all these sites; the future of the nation, especially its place in global comparison, is portrayed as hinging on the successful upgrading of individuals into entrepreneurial citizens and on the making of a new kind of professional identity. This identity is of professionals who converse with ease in a globalized culture of "designerly" innovation.

What is HCI's stance? Do we have a say and do we want to have a say in what and whose methods become central to the making of policy, professional life-worlds, whole nations, and geopolitical relations? In some sense, it seems natural that we should. HCI has long been concerned with how methods shape use practices and users. Over the years as HCI has transitioned to a third wave [5], increasing attention has been paid not only to the instrumental aspects of our methodological approaches or the immediate concerns of the desk environment but also to the cultural, political, social, and economic processes of design and use. HCI researchers have also long reflected on their own values and ideals that might be embedded in the systems they design, and as a result have developed a myriad of critical, reflective, speculative, and other novel approaches to design and its evaluation.

However, comparatively little attention has been paid to the relationship between the shifts in methods and the profession of design itself. We contend that this is particularly important in sites that are both physical and cultural distant from the centers of production of those methods (e.g. SV). This paper begins to address this gap by accounting for the mechanisms and infrastructures through which particular design and research methods become dominant across regions, and by attending to how they shape the identity of the professional designer.

We have shown that professional design identities include entrepreneurial actions that are often not considered to be part of design. We have also demonstrated that the uptake of hegemonic methods is not a simple linear process, but subject to circulations, negotiations and frictions as well as individual and collective aspirations of global belonging. We could end our account there but we believe HCI can do more than just witness how certain methods come to dominate over others. Indeed, we strongly believe that the relevance of HCI as a field hinges in part on taking seriously how research and design methods, many of which have origins in HCI, are playing a central role in the hegemony of broader entrepreneurial innovation culture. What then, is there to be done?

We believe that one response lies in bringing into this conversation the rich body of work that has emerged within HCI devising critical alternatives to computing ideals and methods. Feminist HCI [3, 4], research through design [51, 17], speculative design [16, 31], reflective design [44], and many other approaches all share a commitment to envisioning alternatives to what counts as good design, as well as who and what is included in doing so. However, these critical approaches towards computing have only in limited ways been taken up or connected with the body of HCI research that has put forward a critical research agenda towards transnationalism, globalization, postcolonial processes, politics of innovation, and so on, e.g. [2, 13, 19, 20, 29, 45, 47, 21]. We believe that much can be gained by bringing these two fields into more direct conversation.

One possible starting point, we argue, is to locate the designer's lifeworld and professional identity as key elements in uncovering design methods and what counts as design. This entails understanding how the exigencies of eking out a living shape particular practices at the site of design, which are in turn shaped by individual hopes and aspirations. That is, we argue for a context of design that includes the designer herself, where aspects of life and business are prioritized over, or considered as important as technical or designerly aspects, and that HCI acknowledge and interrogate that with the goal of refining how we define design.

Second, we call for a broader lens for surveying the unintended consequences of design methods. In our accounts, we show how the proxy agents that maintain the valley's hegemony might be individual entrepreneurs and venture capitalists, development agencies with or without an explicitly neoliberal agenda, state bodies seeking work for the underemployed, or multinationals looking for new markets. The exact constitution and specific intent of these agents varied across our sites but their work collectively contributed to the narrowing of appropriate design approaches, and the proliferation of increasingly precarious forms of labor. Silicon Valley might not be the genesis of these approaches but it has effectively concentrated them. The Valley's templates and exhortations nudge sites at its periphery toward the standardizations needed for the mobility of capital rather than regional specificities needed to support emergent design practices. These moves are often accomplished through ostensibly optimistic and hopeful projects: grand visions of a technologically powered and globally-aligned future that may not ultimately support the very workforce being asked to change.

What could a critical HCI practice look like that acknowledges its own entanglements with good design, cutting-edge innovation, with what is rendered as the right kind of method, and who is framed as an innovator? How can we devise research and design methods as compelling as design thinking without giving up on our commitment to criticality and reflection? The answers to these questions certainly lie beyond the scope of what can be accomplished in one paper, but we hope we have started a nudge, little it may be, towards a collaborative and cross-disciplinary project within HCI that takes seriously and intervenes in the methodological hegemony of design methods.

ACKNOWLEDGMENTS

We thank all our interlocutors in China, Ghana, Jamaica, and Silicon Valley, as well as the anonymous reviewers for their roles. This work was supported in part by the National

Science Foundation under awards 1513596, 1217685, and 1321065.

REFERENCES

1. Seyram Avle. 2014. Articulating and enacting development: Skilled returnees in Ghana's ICT industry. Information Technologies & International Development 10(4), 1-13.
2. Seyram Avle and Silvia Lindtner. 2016. Design(ing) "here" and "there": Tech Entrepreneurs, Global Markets, and Reflexivity in Design Processes. In Proceedings of SIGCHI Conference on Human Factors in Computing Systems (CHI '16), 2233 - 2245.
3. Shaowen Bardzell. 2010. Feminist HCI: taking stock and outlining an agenda for design. In Proceedings of the SIGCHI Conference on Human Factors in Computing Systems (CHI '10). ACM, New York, NY, USA, 1301-1310. DOI=http://dx.doi.org/10.1145/1753326.1753521
4. Shaowen Bardzell and Jeffrey Bardzell. 2011. Towards a feminist HCI methodology: social science, feminism, and HCI. In Proceedings of the SIGCHI Conference on Human Factors in Computing Systems (CHI '11). ACM, New York, NY, USA, 675-684. DOI=http://dx.doi.org/10.1145/1978942.1979041
5. Susanna Bodker. 2006. When second wave HCI meets third wave challenges. In proceedings of NordiCHI '06.
6. Nellie Bowles. 2015. The real teens of Silicon Valley. The California Sunday Magazine. Retrieved from https://stories.californiasunday.com/2015-06-07/real-teenagers-silicon-valley
7. David Buckingham. 2015. Why children should NOT be taught to code. David Buckingham.net Retrieved from https://davidbuckingham.net/2015/07/13/why-children-should-not-be-taught-to-code/
8. Anita Chan. 2014. Networking Peripheries. Technological Futures and the Myth of Digital Universalism. Cambridge, MA: MIT Press.
9. Michael Costello. 1997. Occupational multiplicity and rural development patterns in the Third World. Philippine Sociological Review.
10. Michael Curtin and Kevin Sanson. 2016. Precarious creativity. University of California Press.
11. Jerry Davis. 2016. The vanishing American corporation: Navigating the hazards of a new economy. Berrett-Koehler.
12. Greig De Peuter. 2011. Creative economy and labor precarity a contested convergence." Journal of communication inquiry 35.4, 417-425.
13. Paul Dourish and Scott D. Mainwaring. 2012. Ubicomp's Colonial Impulse. In *Proceedings. of UbiComp'12*, Springer, 133-142.
14. Carla Freeman. 2014. Entrepreneurial Selves: Neoliberal Respectability and the Making of a Caribbean Middle Class. Duke University Press
15. Carla Freeman. 2000. High Tech and High Heels In the Global Economy: Women, Work, and Pink-collar Identities In the Caribbean. Duke University Press.
16. Forlano, Laura and Anijo Mathew. 2014. "From Design Fiction to Design Friction: Speculative and Participatory Design of Values-Embedded Urban Technology." *Journal of Urban Technology* 21(4):7–24.
17. William Gaver. 2012. What should we expect from research through design?. In Proceedings of the SIGCHI Conference on Human Factors in Computing Systems (CHI '12). ACM, New York, NY, USA, 937-946. DOI: http://dx.doi.org/10.1145/2207676.2208538
18. Matt Haber. "For Some Men, Mark Zuckerberg Is a Lifestyle Guru." 2016. Retrieved September 21 2016 from http://www.nytimes.com/2016/02/28/fashion/mens-style/mark-zuckerberg-lifestyle-guru.html
19. Lilly Irani. 2015. "Hackathons and the Making of Entrepreneurial Citizenship." Science, Technology & Human Values 1–26.
20. Lilly Irani, Paul Dourish, Melissa Mazmanian. 2010. Shopping for sharpies in Seattle. Mundane Infrastructures of Transnational Design. In Proc. of ICIC'10.
21. Lily Irani, Janet Vertesi, Paul Dourish, Kavita Philip, and Rebecca Grinter. 2010. Postcolonial Computing: A Lens on Design and Development. *In Proceedings of the SIGCHI Conference on Human Factors in Computing Systems*, 1311-1320.
22. Sheila Jasanoff. 2004. States of knowledge: the co-production of science and the social order. Routledge.
23. Michael Keane. 2007. Created in China: the Great New Leap Forward, London: Routledge.
24. Lee, M., Nam, T., Lee, Y., Row, Y., Lim, Y., Kim, D., Seok, J., Odom, W., Zimmerman, J., Forlizzi, J., Higuera, A., Marchitto, M., Canas, J., Moore, H. 2013. Bridging Research and Practice in Design: Reflections of the Project on Value Construction with Virtual Possessions. In proceedings of 5th International Congress of International Association of Societies of Design Research. Tokyo, Japan. IASDR '13
25. Emma Lewis. Jammin', Digitally: The Mentor. 2014. Retrieved September 21 2016 from https://petchary.wordpress.com/2014/02/07/jammin-digitally-the-mentor/
26. Silvia Lindtner, Shaowen Bardzell and Jeffrey Bardzell. 2016. Reconstituting the utopian vision of making: HCI after technosolutionism. In Proceedings

of SIGCHI Conference on Human Factors in Computing Systems (CHI '16), CHI '16, 1390 - 1402.

27. Silvia Lindtner. 2014. Hackerspaces and Internet of Things in China: How Makers are reinventing Industrial Production, Innovation & the Self. Journal of China Information, Special Issue on "Political Contestation in Chinese Digital Spaces" (ed. Guobin Yang), Vol. 28, No. 2, pp. 145-167.
28. Silvia Lindtner, Anna Greenspan, David Li. 2015. Designed in Shenzhen: Shanzhai Manufacturers and Maker Entrepreneurs. In Proc. of Aarhus Series of Human Centered Computing, [S.I.}, v.1, n.1, p.12.
29. Lindtner, S., Anderson, K., Dourish, P. 2012. Cultural Appropriation: Information Technologies as Sites of Transnational Imagination. Proc. ACM Conf. Computer-Supported Cooperative Work CSCW 2012 (Seattle, WA), 77-86.
30. Isabell Lorey. 2015. State of Insecurity. Verso, London.
31. Lukens, Jonathan and Carl Disalvo. 2011. "Speculative Design and Technological Fluency." International Journal of Learning and Media 3(4):23–40.
32. George Marcus. 1995. Ethnography in/of the World System: The Emergence of Multi-sited Ethnography. Annu. Rev. Anthropol. 24:95-117.
33. Angela McRobbie. 2016. Be Creative: Making a Living in the New Culture Industries. Polity Press.
34. Bill Maurer. 2001. Recharting the Caribbean. Univ of Michigan Press.
35. Bill Maurer. 2001. Islands in the Net: Rewiring Technological and Financial Circuits in the" Offshore" Caribbean. Comparative Studies in Society and History 43, 3, 467–501.
36. Beverley Mullings. 2004. Globalization and the territorialization of the new Caribbean service economy. *Journal of Economic Geography*, 4(3), 275–298.
37. Gina Neff. 2012. Venture Labor. Work and the Burden of Risk in Innovation Industries. Cambridge, Massachusetts: MIT Press.
38. Justin O'Connor. 2012. Shanghai Modern: Replaying Futures Past. *Culture Unbound: Journal of Current Cultural Research*, Vol 4, 15-34.
39. Odom, W., Zimmerman, J., Forlizzi, J. (2011). Teenagers and Their Virtual Possessions: Design Opportunities and Issues. In proceedings of SIGCHI Conference on Human Factors in Computing Systems. Vancouver, Canada. CHI '11. ACM Press, 1491-1500.
40. Planning Institute of Jamaica. 2009. Vision 2030 Jamaica: National Development Plan. Planning Institute of Jamaica.
41. AnnaLee Saxenian 1996. *Regional advantage*. Harvard University Press.
42. AnnaLee Saxenian. 2005. "From brain drain to brain circulation: Transnational communities and regional upgrading in India and China." *Studies in comparative international development* 40.2 (2005): 35-61.
43. AnnaLee Saxenian. 2007. The new argonauts: Regional advantage in a global economy. Harvard University Press.
44. Phoebe Sengers, Kirsten Boehner, Shay David, and Joseph 'Jofish' Kaye. 2005. Reflective design. In Proceedings of the 4th decennial conference on Critical computing: between sense and sensibility ACM, http://dx.doi.org/10.1145/1094562.1094569
45. Alex Taylor. 2011. Out there. In Proceedings of the ACM SIGCHI Conference on Human Factors in Computing Systems (CHI'11), pp. 685-694.
46. The State Council. The People's Republic of China. 2015. Guideline to boost entrepreneurship and innovation. Source: http://english.gov.cn/policies/latest_releases/2015/03/11/content_281475069667730.htm, last accessed January 2017
47. Amanda Williams, Silvia Lindtner, Ken Anderson, Paul Dourish. 2013. Multi-sited Design: an Analytical Lens for Transnational HCI. Human-Computer Interaction, Vol. 29:1, 78-108.
48. The World Bank. Silicon Valley Casts Its Nets in the Caribbean. 2014. Retrieved September 21 2016 from http://www.worldbank.org/en/news/feature/2014/01/07/silicon-valley-casts-nets-in-caribbean
49. The World Bank. 2015. Tech hubs across Africa: Which will be the legacy-makers? The World Bank IC4D blog. Retrieved from http://blogs.worldbank.org/ic4d/tech-hubs-across-africa-which-will-be-legacy-makers
50. Fan Yang. 2015. Faked in China. Nation Branding, Counterfeit Culture, and Globalization. Indiana University Press.
51. John Zimmerman, Jodi Forlizzi, and Shelley Evenson. 2007. Research through design as a method for interaction design research in HCI. In Proceedings of the SIGCHI Conference on Human Factors in Computing Systems (CHI '07). ACM, New York, NY, USA, 493-502. DOI http://dx.doi.org/10.1145/1240624.1240704

Consumer to Creator: How Households Buy Furniture to Inform Design and Fabrication interfaces

Bokyung Lee **Gyeol Han** **Jundong Park** **Daniel Saakes**

Department of Industrial Design
KAIST, Republic of Korea
{boing222, hgyeols, messinger, saakes}@kaist.ac.kr

ABSTRACT

Emerging technologies for digital design and fabrication let people participate in the making of objects that were previously dominated by professional designers. A growing body of work in HCI provides understanding in the activities of designing and making by novices and in maker communities. However, we know little about how casual users might employ these technologies with the goal of having an object in their home that satisfies a need. We present a long-term qualitative study in which we followed 16 households during a purchasing process of furniture items for their homes. We looked into how families discover what they need, find solutions, realize a solution in their house and put it to use. The results provide insights into their design activities and workflow and we identify two distinct stages: understanding needs and prototyping a solution. Based on the findings, we discuss the social practice of acquiring and appropriating furniture in the home and within families, and identify design opportunities for digital design and fabrication to support people as they create the objects they need, want and desire.

ACM Classification Keywords

H.5.2. Information Interfaces and Presentation (e.g. HCI): Graphical User Interfaces

Author Keywords

fabrication; design; purchase; furniture; qualitative study

INTRODUCTION

People select furniture items through careful considerations. When they buy a chair for their desk, they are concerned with ergonomics and comfort and tend to test the real product in a store. When they buy a new rug to decorate a room, they explore styles to match their interior. Also, as furniture is shared within a family, the purchasing process has multiple stakeholders. To make decisions that satisfy their requirements, people employ various practices to discover what they need, find possible solutions and prototype candidate solutions in their house. Whereas people traditionally relied on information from manufacturers, they are increasingly relying on user generated contents. Although most furniture used to be acquired offline, the current trend is online shopping and requires new ways of understanding the fit of a solution. Users have natural hesitation to purchase a product that they have not yet experienced in person [31], and this is the case with online purchase, customization and perhaps with digital fabrication.

We see the practice of buying durable things as *variant design* [29], and see people as *everyday designers* [46] who want to acquire a product that satisfies their needs. With such a 'design lens', we aim to gain insights in the practice of buying items [47] to inform the practice of customizing items and as a means to reflect on future fabrication interfaces for makers or casual users. We are interested in how people go through such a decision-making processes with an emphasis on how they figure out what they need and how they find or prototype solutions in and for their homes. Although understanding the purchase decision-making process is the core of consumer behavior research [3] and mass customization toolkits [41, 45], they do not look into the prototyping activities users perform in their homes. Current HCI research into fabrication interfaces [14, 33] has a focus on modeling 3D geometry. However, the process that takes place before configuring or modeling the solution has not been fully explored. This gap in the literature is the driving force of this paper.

We build on the rich tradition of studies in people's houses [8, 20, 30, 46, 51] to gain a thorough understanding into the social practice [34, 38] of appropriating new furniture items. We captured the entire furniture purchasing process of 16 households through a diary study complemented with two house visit interviews: before purchase, right after purchase, and a telephone interview two months after the item was put into use. Insights from this study extend the understanding of *design-in-use* [46] with an understanding of the 'design process' regarding introducing new items. Our study indicates that families start with a breadth-first top down mutual exploration of the solution and problem space, followed by a depth-first testing and prototyping stage. Our results contribute to prior studies regarding expertise in design [9].

This paper makes two contributions. First, it provides empirical findings regarding the households' furniture purchasing cycle, and shows the key activities and sources observed in each stage. Next, we documented social practices as high-level insights, and suggest several design opportunities for non-professional fabrication tools derived from real-life needs and behaviors.

CHI 2017, May 06-11, 2017, Denver, CO, USA

 ISBN 978-1-4503-4655-9/17/05...$15.00

DOI: http://dx.doi.org/10.1145/3025453.3025666

RELATED WORK

The availability of low-cost fabrication devices has motivated research into digital design and fabrication technologies for non-professionals. Several studies [14, 22, 33, 48] aim to support users in their creation of 3D CAD models and in the generation of fabrication-ready 3D models based on 2D sketch input or from clay models. Advances in real-time simulation provide users with interactive feedback and suggestions on aspects such as the manufacturability [33] and the structural integrity [42] and allow users to embed professional engineering and aesthetic knowledge into the design tool. Other research projects consider the object within the context of use and let users engage in design with existing objects [14, 23, 49] to make objects that fit other objects or to situate the modeling task within the intended use environment. Another body of work looks into DIY enthusiasts [32] and maker communities that make use of these tools. These studies reveal how people engage in such activities and are motivated by enjoyment, skill building, creativity and a feeling of accomplishment [21]. Online and offline communities of practice [16] are instrumental for information exchange, inspiration and education.

Whereas for these communities the creativity and crafts are the main driver, we are interested in the application of fabrication as an alternative for purchasing readily available objects. Hudson [18] studied the workflow of casual users that use a public 3D printing center with the goal of making objects. Typically, these users are new to designing objects and have trouble relating interdependencies of design decisions with the fabricated objects. A recent study into how casual users prototype by hand in a design session [5] reveals similar barriers attributed to the relationship between sketches (shape) and fabrication challenges (process). Also, this study revealed that people face difficulties explaining sketches and fabrication methods to each-other. These indicate differences between expert amateurs [21] who use digital fabrication as a goal and casual users for whom it is a means, and the result is the goal.

Shewbridge et al. [36] placed an imaginary 3D printer in twelve households. In a longitudinal study, they asked people to document what they would do with it. Most objects that participants wanted to fabricate were duplications: more of the same, sometimes improved; only seldom did they talk about new objects. Those results indicate the mundane customization scenarios that Pahl and Beitz [29] call variant design, a unique product within a known principle solution. Decisions such as choosing a color for a wall [50] are preceded by a design process that begins with a vague notion that considers nearby furniture and perceptual attributes regarding color tones. Several sources are used for inspiration and information such as magazines and display homes. In this paper we are interested in understanding the process of casual users and how they prototype and make decisions in their home.

We build on ethnographic studies of people's homes that indicate differences between design for professionals and for use in households, as domestic life is not characterized by a shared objective but by a diverse range of contrasting interests [8]. Wakkary et al. [46] show how object use evolves over time in conjunction with need satisfaction and call this *design-in-use*. Families test out new systems by concurrently adapting their routines to the system and adapting the system to the daily routine [11]. Likewise, Woo and Lim [51] studied how households program rules for IoT smart home automation and identified several stages in how these devices are put to use. In a *motivation* stage, which precedes a programming stage, participants identify a need. After programming and implementation, stages follows a *use-through-routine* stage in which the rules are tested in daily routines and adapted as insight in their routines grows. These studies reveal the rich and iterative process of how users appropriate objects in their daily lives [12]. The studies also show the roles of family members; for instance, the programmer is not always the user. Given these insights, we expect to find similar rich and informal methods when we follow households as they select new objects in their homes.

From the field of Consumer Behavior, we learn that decision making is shared within families and between spouses [39, 40]. Similar to results found in the ethnographic studies, family members take various roles in the process that leads to a purchase. Roles include those of information gatherers, influencers, decision makers and purchasers [37]. A key theory is the consumer decision-making model of Engel, Kollat and Blackwell (EKB) [3]. This model assumes that people who purchase items go through a fixed sequence of distinct stages consisting of 1) problem recognition, 2) information search, 3) evaluation of alternatives, 4) purchase and 5) post-purchase evaluation. In the three stages leading up to the purchase, *consumers* make use of a variety of information and inspiration sources both external (e.g. visiting shops and searching websites) and internal (e.g. prior experience, advice from friends and relatives). Although it has been criticized taking a utilitarian perspective [3], too rational and linear, the EKB model still mapped well to our pre-purchase stages and the different types of information sources we found in our study.

People have trouble understanding their needs, finding products that suit those needs or configuring a customized product [31]. Therefore, recommender websites provide various means to let people compare alternatives. Likewise, mass customization websites support iterations and guide users through a configuration process. A combination of design parameters results in product performance that matches a user need [41]. Hence, these toolkits try to match the user's skill [10] and repartition the design task to present the user-need parameters to the users [45]. We identify the information needs for buying objects and how people work together. We argue that buying objects provides insight into how people would make objects. It is not about making a creative or innovative design, but coming up with a solution for the home that fulfills a need and is appropriate for the situation.

THE STUDY

The EKB model [3] provides a high-level overview of how people acquire goods from a vendor's perspective. However, it provides little insight into the actual practices that are important for future design and fabrication interfaces, e.g. how people test potential solutions in their houses and how they share inspiration among family members. Hence, we con-

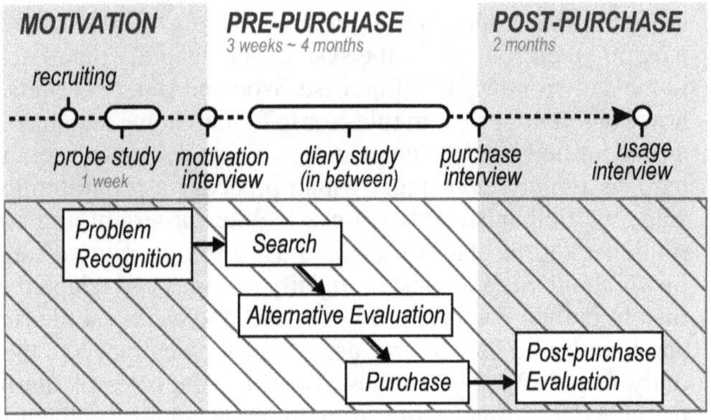

Figure 1. The research process consisted of three phases (corresponding to the EKB model): motivation, pre-purchase, and post-purchase. We started with a probe study and motivation interview, followed by a diary study until the moment of purchase. Directly followed by a purchasing interview, and a post-purchase interview about one-month later.

ducted a long-term qualitative study with 16 households. Two field interviews in the participant's homes enabled them to refer to their furniture and show their routines [4] and a diary study let participants log events related to their furniture decision making. A follow-up interview two months after the purchase was conducted to let participants reflect on their purchases. The entire study was held from February to August in 2016, and on average it took participants 105 days from the first *motivation* interview to the *purchase* interview (Figure 1).

Item Category Selection

We selected furniture as a product category for this study because of three reasons. First, furniture items are durable goods and purchase decisions take considerable effort compared to commodities that are routinely purchased or fast fashion items that are bought in the spur of the moment. Hence, we expect households to engage in an extensive selection process prior to purchase. Second, furniture items have to meet a variety of requirements. They have to match the existing interior, and have to fit within the available space as well as have ergonomic and comfort considerations. Finally, furniture items are typically shared among family members, which means that the purchasing process has multiple stakeholders. For these reasons, we assume that selecting furniture is situated and collaborative and that users go through an elaborate purchasing process. In addition, we see digital fabrication of personalized and customized furniture as a feasible scenario in the near future which encourages further investigation (e.g. Opendesk [28]).

Participants

The sixteen households had 29 members in total, all from a metropolitan area in South Korea. The main criteria for participation was who already had a plan to purchase a furniture item. We recruited participants through flyers posted in apartments, social media, and online communities of housewives. The participants' ages ranged from 19-48 for main household members and 4-18 for their offspring. Their occupations varied, but all were middle class, as shown in Table 1. We selected households of four types: single male, single female, young couples without children and couples with children. The

	Type A. Single Male	
A1	Ph.D student [Industrial Design] (29)	Chair ($80)
A2	Undergraduate student [Biomolecular Engineering] (21)	Wardrobe ($90)
A3	R&D office worker (27)	Side desk ($80)
A4	Undergraduate student [Undeclared Major] (19)	Rug ($15)
	Type B. Single Female	
B1	UX designer (25)	Rug ($15)
B2	Researcher (25)	Rug ($20)
B3	Ph.D student [Chemical Engineering] (25)	Desk ($40), Chair ($45)
B4	Ph.D student [Aerospace Engineering] (27)	Rug ($50)
	Type C. Couples without Children	
C1	H: Post-doc [Biology] (32) / W: Ph.D [Biology] (26)	Side table ($30), Stool ($30)
C2	H: Company Employee (27) / W: Ph.D student [Chemistry] (28)	Table ($155), 2 Chairs ($20)
C3	H: Ph.D student [Computer Science] (26) / W: Researcher (26)	Sofa ($900)
C4	H: Ph.D student [Mechanical Engineering] (27) / W: Housewife (27)	2 Chairs($130), Cabinet ($40)
	Type D. Couples with Children	
D1	H: Company Employee (36) / W: Part-time worker (41) / D (6) / S (4)	Shelves ($20)
D2	H: Salesman (34) / W: Housewive (33) / S (6)	Hanger ($80)
D3	H: Professor (54) / W: Housewive (48) / D1 [Mechanical Equipment Enginnering] (23) / D2 (18)	4 Chairs ($240)
D4	H: Company Employee (41) / W: Housewife (38) / D (16)	2 Stools ($130)

Table 1. The demographic information of the participants (H:husband, W:wife, S:son, D:daughter), and furnitures they bought including cost.

single households, except one, are living in semi-furnished apartments equipped with basic furniture such as a bed, desk and closet. Households in type C are newlyweds, who recently moved into new houses, less than a year ago, and were in the middle of the process of buying new interior items. All the families in type D had been living together for more than 6 years and had fully furnished homes. None of them had professional knowledge of making furniture; only two people out of 29 had some experience as makers (in fabricating wooden furniture) and could be considered as expert amateurs [21].

Research Process

We followed a process similar to that used in related studies [19, 51] and we planned for three stages. The first is problem recognition, which took place prior to the recruitment; the first intake interview was conducted to understand their *motivation* to buy an item. The second stage consisted of the *pre-purchase* and concluded with the moment of purchase and a second interview. Two months after the purchase we conducted a chat-based interview to let the participants evaluate their purchase in the after purchase use-stage (Figure 1).

The goal of the ***motivation*** phase was twofold: to gain a thorough understanding of participants' living situations and their motivation to buy new furniture. We sensitized participants with a probe package [26, 44], especially for the following *motivation* interview. The probe consisted of worksheets, various tools and furniture stickers selected from interior magazines. Worksheets were divided over 4 days, and each day the participants were asked to reflect on their houses, existing furniture and previous experience with those by drawing a floor-plan or making a collage. We visited the participants' homes, when they finished the probe, and conducted the *motivation* interview with all family members. We started the interview by asking for background information, residential situation, house structure and history of other furniture at home to understand the differences between the diverse characteristics of each family member. Then, to gain insight into their process and needs, we continued with questions about the item they planned to buy, their motivations and activities they had already performed for the purchase. The interview took about 40 minutes per household.

The second phase is ***pre-purchasing***. In this phase, participants kept a diary to record their purchase-related activities or considerations until they bought the actual product in a popular social messaging application [27]. We assumed that the impact of the diary study on the process would be minimal, but inevitable, because all participants frequently used a smartphone and this application was deeply rooted in their daily activities from communicating with relatives and friends to ordering food and calling taxis. Because we provided a digital messaging application as a logging tool, the participants were able to easily take and upload photos at any location. In addition, as all household members shared one chat room, we could easily capture the collaborative process among households. As soon as they purchased the product, we scheduled the *purchasing* interview to understand the entire process that participants went through when buying their item. The interview followed a semi-structured format, allowing the interviewer to probe further about each diary entry; also, participants were able to show and tell about their purchase in their houses. The interview took between 20-60 minutes.

The final phase is ***post-purchasing***, in which the users use the furniture item. About two months after the purchase, we conducted a chat-interview to let participants reflect on usage and asked how they used the product, their satisfaction level, the points they missed in the previous purchase and needs for future items.

Data Analysis

The qualitative data was stored and managed using the data management software NVivo. The results from the diary study, and the transcribed narratives from two interviews, were used for the analysis procedure. Our approach consisted of three steps, similar to those in [19]: open coding, axial coding and iterative quantitative analysis. The ***open coding*** was done with results from the nine households that finished first. This coding aimed at identifying the key structure of the purchasing process, without any assumptions. This process was done five times with identical comments for different aspects: activities, requirements, sources, barriers and enablers and roles. Using ***axial coding***, we categorized the initial set of phenomena described by open codes. Open codes were grouped into categories that were subsequently analyzed in terms of similar objectives. This resulted in a set of four stages of the design workflow, and relevant categories for activities, sources, and barriers for each stage. Then, all the quotations from 16 households were classified as being primarily related to one among the categories of the four stages. This process was independently conducted by the first and one additional researcher (Interrater agreement K=.81). Quotes for which no agreement was attained were excluded from the analysis. Finally, a furniture 'design' workflow that can be applied to all participants was discovered, and key activities, key sources and needs were identified accordingly.

DESIGN WORKFLOW

As shown in Table 1, participating households bought various types of furniture. They spent a considerable amount of time understanding their needs and exploring solutions available on the market. In total, it took 14-83 days from starting motivation to settling on a single appropriate item. Then, a second stage followed in which they employed various activities to test fit the item in their houses. All households iterated a few times before making the actual purchase, and this second process took from 1-27 days. After using it for 30-50 days, they indicated several issues with the items in actual daily use, even though they selected the items with careful considerations. We framed these procedures as a product design process [7] with alternating stages of diverging and converging. The workflow consists of four stages: *motivation*, *exploration*, *realization*, and *use*, as shown in Figure 2. These stages were observed in all 16 households, but the details varied based on the purchase motivation, familiarity with the item and household type; and are detailed below.

Motivation

The households displayed a wide variety of *motivations* to understand that they needed a new furniture item in their houses. Some participants were motivated by uncomfortable experiences using their existing furniture. For example, B3 decided to buy a new desk to replace her previous one, which was uncomfortable to use with her computer. Some participants were attached to their furniture and tried to upgrade their existing items instead of replacing them, as in an *appropriation* process [46]. C4 mentioned, *"The sofa we bought at IKEA was originally meant for two purposes: as kid's bed and a small sofa. But was not that comfortable compared to other sofas. So, we decided to buy extra cushions for it."*

Two newly married couples, who recently moved into new apartments, had to buy basic items such as a sofa, bed, dining table and chairs for the first time. Several families (C1, C2, C4), bought *additional furniture* to solve daily functional issues related to their lifestyle. D2 mentioned, *"My husband always leaves his clothes on the bed without arranging them because there is not enough space in our wardrobes. So, we decided to buy one more clothes hangers."* On the other hand, some families were eager to have extra items to decorate their houses for aesthetic purposes. D1 commented, *"I thought the plant named Tillandsia would make the room interior beautiful. I want to put that plant on a new wall shelf to decorate the living room."* All households came up with a certain price range in the *motivation* stage.

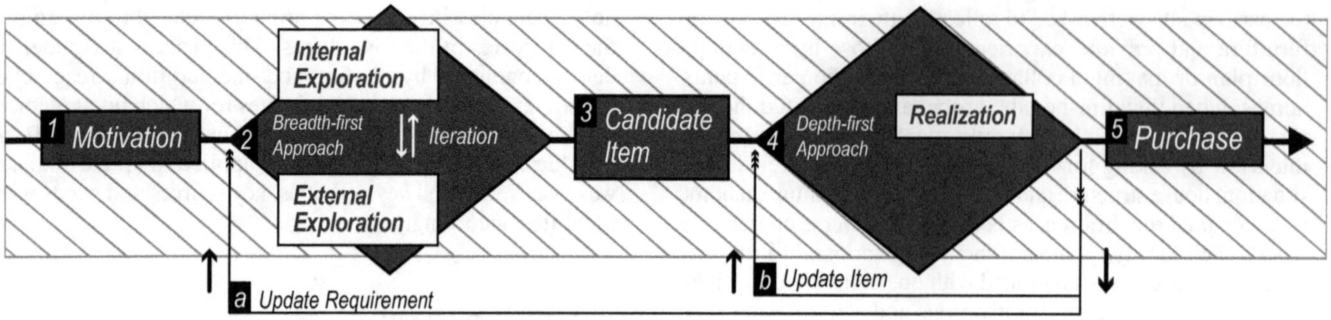

Figure 2. The purchase workflow observed in all households. This diagram corresponds to the double diamond design process.

Exploration

With a clearly identified need for a new furniture item, participants engaged in an analysis stage. They explored the solution space to find trends and products available in the market (external analysis), and the problem space to gain insights into their requirements (internal analysis). These spaces co-evolved [13] during the process. C4, for instance, had the requirement of matching material with their wooden table and used 'wood' as a keyword to search online for chairs. However, when participants couldn't find solutions that satisfied a requirement, they went back to the external sources and got inspirations from experts or other users and updated their requirements. For instance, C2 wife stated in a diary entry that she had difficulty finding a proper size table to fit in her house that was also comfortable to use. So she searched on an online community of housewives and realized that other people had solved this issue with an extendable table.

External Analysis: Understanding the Solution Space

The external analysis consisted of an online search that was mostly focused on the styling of items. Participants visited both online furniture stores as well as blogs with photos made by users. All households except 2 participants used their mobile phones to collect favorite items as images. When they encountered favorite furniture in department stores (C4), restaurants (D2) or friends' houses (D3), they took pictures with their phones to add to their collections. During the interview, D1 wife showed various furniture and interior images with her mobile phone that were downloaded from an online mall and community, *"When I found an image I liked, I downloaded it on the mobile phone. As time goes by, more images piled up in my album."*

Compared to their knowledge of commodities and fashion items, participants had little experience in buying furniture. Therefore, they extensively utilized sources such as online marketplaces and search engines. Through exposure [43], people gained insight into features and styling. In the diary study, D1 wife revealed she had visited an online mall and looked at all the images in the shelf section to learn the various design possibilities. Typically, participants review large quantities of items and, during this process, some develop a personal taste. C1 husband stated, *"The first time, I reviewed as many images as possible, but by excluding images I didn't like, I discovered my taste."* Only two out of 16 households visited offline stores to see various types of furniture.

Acquiring fashionable or popular items was important for 14 households. Some households obtained *trend* data from browsing through curated collections or luxury websites. B2 pointed out in the diary, *"Rather than the normal online marketplace, I visited curated shopping sites in order to check items evaluated by a professional merchandise planner."* Other participants used crowds to obtain a sense for popular items. For example, B4 checked the best seller items in a well-known online mall by using the ranking filter function.

We discovered that user-generated content had a large impact on all the households as they explored how other people deal with similar design requirements and motivations. All households collected user-made photos of the *product-in-use* to see how it was used in real life situations. For example, D2 wife found how other users with similar houses decorated their rooms through pictures in an online community or on blogs, and downloaded all the images to copy their style. Single households mentioned that they were inspired by people in similar residential situations and also had to decorate a semi-furnished room with a small amount of money.

When participants had no experience using a piece of furniture, *online user reviews* also worked as a source of experiential information. Sometimes, newly married couples got information on parents' experiences for basic furniture, such as sofas. C2 mentioned that their parent's experiences were helpful because they had already experienced four different sofa designs. In addition, some participants spent lots of time studying *expert knowledge* of a certain product. When some households had a specific style they liked, such as 'modern', they visited websites of brands selling that style to check how professional designers design matching furniture. B3 and D4, on the other hand, were planning to buy a chair and the ergonomics were their main concern. So they educated themselves with information online to learn about ergonomic posture and height.

Internal Exploration: Understanding the Problem Space

While exploring product aesthetics from various external sources, participants also gained insight in their design requirements. Price was an important requirement but was already determined during the motivation stage. Other requirements were implicitly made and shared, and none of the participants

House	House atmosphere	- Color that represents same feeling as house interior - Matching color with current house wall or floor
	House layout	- Proper item style that harmonizes with current layout - Proper features that emphasizes spatial efficiency - Proper size for spatial efficiency - Proper size that fits in certain space
Nearby Items	Pair-using furniture	- Matching color / material with pair furniture - Similar style / design with pair furniture - Relatively proper size with pair furniture
	Together-use personal items	- Proper features for personal items - Proper sizes that fits to personal items
Users	Ergonomic uses	- Proper features for ergonomic use - Proper sizes for ergonomic use
	Functional uses	- Features from previous usage experience - Features for future usage plan

Table 2. The list of design requirements related to the house, items and users, which are implicitly made in the internal exploration.

made a list. The relative weight of requirements surfaced during the interviews but was also not made explicit. For instance, A3 regarded 'size' that fits his house as a primary requirement for his desk, and A2 considered 'number of shelves' as the most important factor for his wardrobe. Some households attached great importance to aesthetic aspects, for example, A4 stated that 'ethnic style' was essential. For ergonomic products such as chairs, soft constraints such as comfortability or healthiness were crucial for both B3 and C4.

A number of requirements concerned the *layout and interior of their houses*. All participants expressed the desire to find materials that match with their current interior and tended to express ideal color through 'adjectives' that demonstrate the feeling of their current house [50]. For example, C4 stated, *"As our bedroom atmosphere is cozy, as you can see, steel is not a good option. The material should be warm-colored."* For participants who lived in small houses, size and space-saving features were important requirements. B3 mentioned, *"As there is a large window in front of the future desk place, there should be no desk-shelves in the front of the window. Also, I need to access the window easily to open it and to put my plants on the windowsill. So the desk should not cross the window outline."*

Participants defined dimensions through several activities. B1 drew a floor plan and brainstormed the best size by drawing various sizes and positions of the desk on the floor (Figure 3a). Two households did physical prototyping activities by using other objects. C1 husband positioned a side table near the sofa to test and check the appropriate height and color. He re-enacted their activities during the interview, as shown in Figure 3b. Also, people defined the maximum length of the item by measuring the available space and defined the minimum length by measuring the size of the object with a ruler.

Existing *pair-use items* provided several constraints for the planned new items. C1 wanted to match the color of the side table with their sofa, and B3 mentioned that she wanted to match the color tone of the wood between the shelves and the desk. For B2, nearby furniture acted as a size constraint. She stated, *"The size of the rug should not pass the bed nor the cabinet. If it does, it might look like a floor cover."* The dimensions of items such as shelves and tabletop surfaces directly relate to the size of other items. For instance, A3 set the minimum size of the desk with the width of his electronic piano, which is needed for music work. D1 wanted to define a proper space for the shelves so that they could place their tissue boxes on it.

Other requirements originated from *comfort and usage patterns*. Several people indicated the importance of ergonomics. C2 tried to estimate a comfortable height for a new table when used with their existing stool. So, the wife sat on the stool and estimated the proper height by moving her hands up and down. C1 wanted to estimate a proper height for a new side table when sitting on their low-height sofa. They measured the height of the sofa with a flexible ruler and kept that as a reference. In the case of other households, who bought furniture for additional functional purposes, participants tried to find proper features or sizes by imagining future use. For example, C4 wife mentioned, *"We currently put our hair dryer on the floor. But we want to improve this. So we need new shelves to put towels and our hair dryer."* In case they replaced old items with new ones, they obtained requirements from their own experience of previous furniture. For instance, the child of D2 family once got injured because the TV cabinet had sharp corners. Hence, safety and sharp edges were their main considerations for the next purchase.

Realization

When households started to frequently discuss a single item, they started *realizing* a solution in their houses. In this stage, they switched to a depth-first search and evaluated items through various prototyping activities and by getting advice from others. However, if that object did not fully satisfy their requirements, they iterated with a new candidate object (Figure 2b) While they were making iterations, they further detailed their design requirements and tastes.

Finding alternative candidate items (Figure 2a) was performed using keywords they collected in the *exploration* stage. Common keywords include materials (e.g., wooden desk, fabric sofa) or styles (e.g., ethnic rug). A3 and B3 discovered an exceptional way to use 'size' as a keyword during *exploration*, such as '800 desks' for 80cm width desks. This keyword based search was a barrier for several participants as they failed to specify their style [5, 50] and instead used adjectives such as 'warm-tone sofa' or 'cool-feeling rug.'

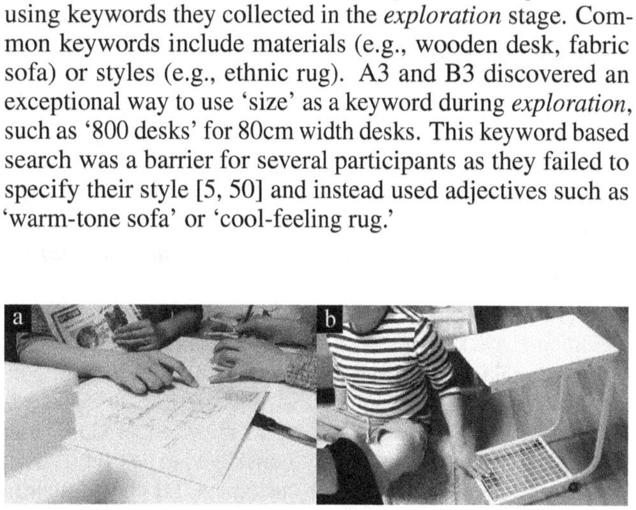

Figure 3. Prototyping activities in the Exploration stage: (a) B1 drawing a floorplan and brainstorming, and (b) C1 husband testing their existing side table to identify requirements.

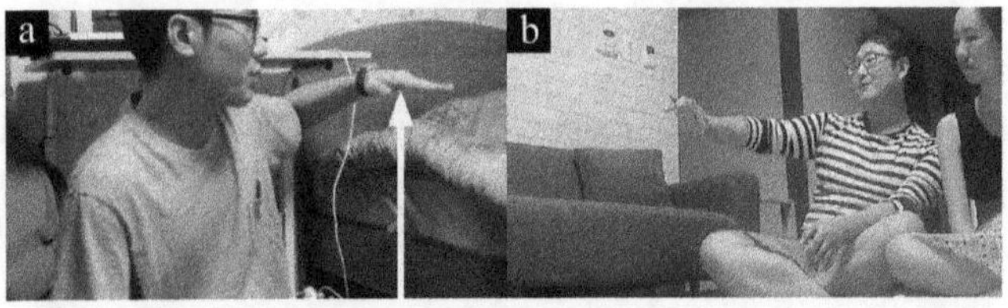

Figure 4. Prototyping activities in the Realization stage: (a) A3 estimating the appropriate height of a side table, and (b) C1 using his mobile phone with a product photo to visualize it in place.

Prototyping with their House

All households had difficulty imagining the product in use in their houses, regardless of whether they found it offline or online. Their primary need was to visualize the item in their home. To this end, C2 brought photos of their interior to the IKEA furniture mall to select a product with a similar material. During the interview, B1 showed photos she found in the online user reviews that had interiors similar to her room. C1 also found a photo of a product decorated with the same cushion as theirs. Such photos assured people that the item would look good in their house. Other participants tried to visualize the candidate item in their home. D3 asked the seller to bring leather samples for their chair, *"By comparing that sample material with our sofa leather, we selected the best one that matched our home."* Many households measured dimensions with measuring tape so that they could easily assess the position of an item. One household, C1, used his phone with a product photo as a low-tech augmented reality display to simulate the product as if it were in the room (Figure 4b).

Every household wanted to check candidate items for comfort. The easiest way to do this was to visit the offline store and test use the item directly. For example, C4, in an offline mall, sat on the chairs one by one to test how comfortable they were. From the interviews, we discovered that people who buy expensive or ergonomic furniture preferably visit offline stores to experience the products before purchase. However, as people using online malls cannot experience the product, they relied on indirect tests. C1 measured the height of the sofa they had with a retractable ruler, and then used the results to calculate the height ratio between the sofa and the target chair. Using this relative height with the pair-use item, C1 estimated the comfort. But several households indicated having trouble estimating dimensions relative to their body. C1 mentioned, *"I tried to check the usability and comfortability of this side table when it is used with this low sofa. But it is hard to figure out how."*

Getting Expert Advice from Others

Before making decisions, participants needed to gain confidence by consulting others. Several participants asked for advice from people who had expert knowledge. C3, D1 and D3 asked salespeople, who they considered to be experts due to their extended experience with customers. D1 shared their history of wallpaper selection, *"At first, we decided to cover our wall with white solid color, but the seller stopped us and told us that it is too boring. She recommended another item with a light stripe pattern, which was a bit more refined."* Some participants asked for opinions from acquaintances who knew their houses or preferences. For example, B2 mentioned during the interview, *"I would rather get an opinion from people who visit my house often, who are frequent visitors, and also the future user of the product. ... She knows my house situation very well, so I expect she can give me a useful opinion."* A2, A4 and B4 asked for feedback from friends who were in similar situations. To gain confidence on item quality, they relied on opinions from the crowd, especially when buying online. Most participants looked at user reviews and checked other users' feedback to learn what to avoid. For instance, B1 mentioned, *"When I buy things online, I always check if anyone has complained about the color of the real product compared to the picture."*

For some participants, it was hard to find furniture that fully satisfied their needs. In this case, D3 decided to upgrade their previous chair, and D4 customized the height of their new stool. Otherwise, they had to compromise among requirements. For example, B3 mentioned, *"I decided to buy a simple table without any extra shelves on it. That was the only option for a pretty desk. Otherwise, I would have had to buy an ugly desk. So I bought one extra wood shelf separately to complement the functionality."*

Usage at Home

After purchasing the items, participants start using them in their homes and routines. Three households, A3, A4 and C4, were satisfied with their purchases and mentioned in the post-purchase interview that they would prefer to buy the same one again. The other 12 households were mostly satisfied with their decisions but indicated minor problems with the item in use. One household, D4, found major problems with their stools' comfort. People who bought a cheap item as a prototype, explained how they had reflected after the first purchase iteration. A4 pointed out that he would choose the size again based on the rug they had already bought. B2 stated that she would choose a thicker one because the current one is not durable.

Most participants realized they had made errors estimating dimensions. C2, for example, believed they could select proper sized items without measuring, and visited offline stores without any numeric information. However, after placing the items in their home, they realized that the table was too big and could not use the extension function, as shown in Figure 5a. Other participants measured the available space or objects with a tape measure; however, they failed to identify the appropriate size for their bodies. D4 wife even considered ergonomic guidelines for chair heights, but her husband did not apply that properly in their design due to his lack of skill. As a result, the stool they ordered was too low for their island table.

Errors in dimensioning were often because participants used dimensions that satisfy one requirement and did not take other important usage requirements into account. These issues surfaced when they started to use the items. For example, B2 approximated the size of her rug based on her house layout. But when her friend visited and they had dinner, she realized that the rug was a bit small for two people and a table. Similarly, D1 only considered body height when installing shelves

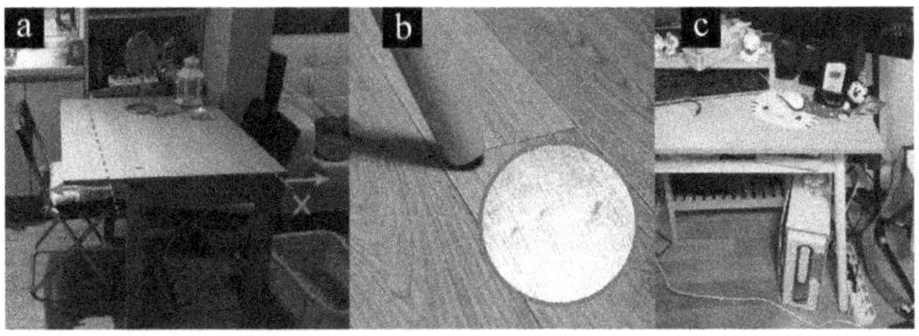

Figure 5. Usage problems found: (a) C2 bought a table too large to use the extension function, (b) C4 bought a chair which made dents and scratches on the floor, (c) B3 could not place the computer efficiently due to slanted table legs.

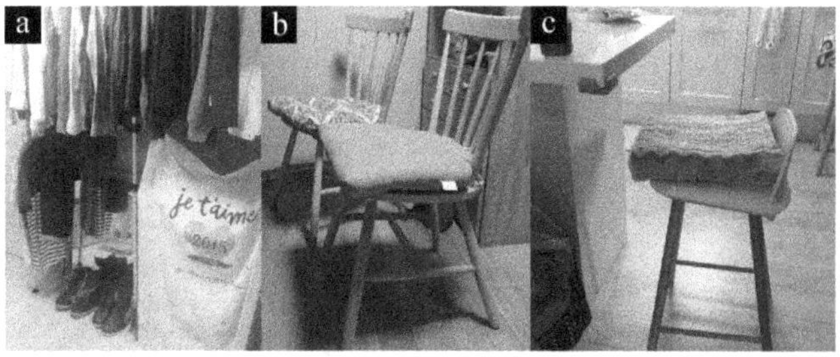

Figure 6. Appropriation of furniture to overcome problems: (a) D2 covered their clothes hanger rack with fabric, (b) C4 decorated a chair with colorful cushions, (c) D4 used a thick cushion to make the chair higher.

on the wall, but forgot that their children frequently stood on the sofa, and as a result, they often hit their heads. In some cases, we discovered that products that participants bought revealed other problems they did not expect. C4 bought their chair after carefully testing it for comfort at offline shops; however, they did not think about the leg details. After using it for a while, they found that their new chair made numerous dents and scratches on the floor, as depicted in Figure 5b.

Some participants selected products on aesthetics and found issues in the product's functionality. For example, B3 liked the design of a desk with slanted legs. However, when in use, she found that her computer didn't fit because of the leg angle, as shown in Figure 5c. In B1's case, she bought a rug to protect the floor from the dents caused by her chair, but as she focused more on the aesthetic requirements, the rug she selected turned out to be too thin, and still made marks on the floor. Some aesthetic dissatisfaction was occasionally shown from households who bought furniture from online malls without seeing the actual product. B1 was unsatisfied with the color of the wood since the color was much lighter than she expected. Also, D2 was not happy with the looks of the steel legs. But, overall, most people didn't mention significant problems with aesthetics.

Active participants tried to overcome problems by appropriation [46]. In the case of D2, she was not happy with the appearance of her choice, so she covered the clothes hanger rack with fabric (Figure 6a). C4 couple bought two wooden chairs because the husband preferred a simple combination. The wife accepted his opinion, but she decorated the chairs with colorful cushions she had bought previously (Figure 6b). D4, on the other hand, found that their chair was too low to sit. So, the wife put a thick cushion on the chair so that their daughters could comfortably eat their breakfast (Figure 6c). Some people found new and unplanned uses for their purchases. A4 did laundry and then hung his rug to dry near the main door. The next day, when he came back from school, he realized that the rug looks very pretty on the wall, and kept using it for wall decoration. Five people changed the position or layout of a product after they had used it for a while.

COLLABORATION AMONG FAMILY MEMBERS

As furniture is a shared item, all family members (in the non-single households) participated during the entire purchasing cycle. Although we conducted a study with a small number of samples, we observed two styles of collaboration during the *exploration* stage. The young couples (type C) discussed and made all decisions together during the entire process. C1 explored online images together while sitting on the sofa side by side and C4 visited offline stores together for better discussion. C4 mentioned, *"Online shopping is usually a lonely activity. However, when we go out to offline store, we discuss why I like certain items. That is one of the reasons I prefer offline exploration."* When non-co-located and direct communication was impossible, they shared the output from their individual *exploration* frequently through social messaging applications. (C2 husband, diary-*"Hey, I found one reference photo for our new dining table. Please take a look. What do you think?"*, C3 wife, diary-*"Hey, please check this website. Here, you can see various types of sofas. If you select style keywords in the right tab, the sofa images filter accordingly . If you tell me which style you like the most, I will refer to that."*) However, they had trouble in communication because it was hard to share their thoughts with words. Therefore, they used product images as a communication tool.

On the other hand, we found that households with experience in buying items, such as type D, took a different approach. A *leading designer* explored the furniture style and occasionally shared results for discussion and input from their spouse. D1 mentioned, *"I did not want to share every photo I found during my personal exploration period. If so, we might discuss too many things, and eventually fight. So I prefer having personal time for exploration, and then discuss with him with the options I come up with."* The *follower*only considered specific details such as installation or size. In our study, the role of *leading designer* was usually taken by the wife. As all four wives were not full-time workers, they had more time compared to their husbands, and more interest in interior items. But, when the primary user of the target item was the husband, he took the role of leading designer. D1 husband mentioned, *"The shelves in the study room were bought by myself, not her. I searched for various options before i finally found this item at the IKEA."*

When making decisions in the *realization* stage, all couples showed a cooperative process. When they had conflicting opinions, they started to persuade each other by describing the merits the product might have in the future. C4 wife persuaded her husband to buy a chair with a square shaped back by highlighting that she can hang her handbag on it. Eventually, all compromised and made decisions together. For

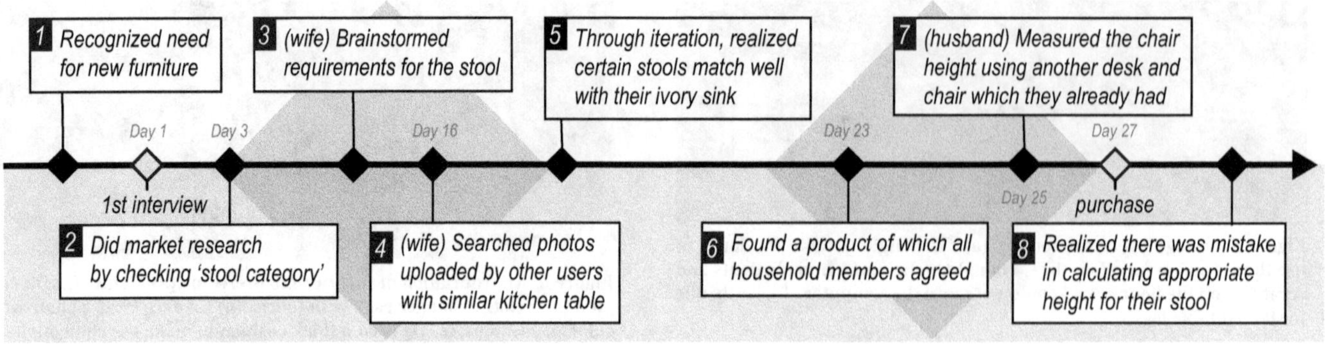

Figure 7. Journey map of family D4. They went through several stages before they purchased their stool.

example, C1 mentioned *"I like having bricks in the living room. Actually, my husband does not like antique style, but he compromised with my opinion by selecting a white brick wall."* Most of the families went through persuasion and compromise steps, except D1, who bought very cheap products to test them out. Children made little contribution to the process, only providing occasional comments on style during the final stage.

DISCUSSION

This study with 16 households provides insight into the journey that casual users make when purchasing furniture for their houses. As illustrated in Figure 7, families engage in a collaborative and iterative [35] process during which they define their requirements and taste, and gain insight into the features and use-scenarios of the items they want. We framed this purchasing journey as a design process [7]. Two distinct stages were found in the workflow: for 'understanding design requirements' and for 'prototyping solutions in their house,' which relate to the *pre-purchase search* and *evaluation of alternatives* in the EKB model [3] in consumer behavior, and the *definition* and *execution* stages in the double diamond model [7]. In this section we highlight five insights we found in the practice of acquiring and appropriating furniture items in the home and within families through the 'lens of design'. Then, we reflected on how these insights encourage the future customization and fabrication interface.

External Information Sources for Casual Users

The participants consulted a wide variety of external information sources during the process. User-generated content such as user reviews [17] or photos shared by users had a greater influence on the decision making than the vendor-supplied information as those are seen as more trustworthy and realistic. In the *exploration* stage, personal blogs and websites [2] with photos of users' real house were found to be instrumental for education and inspiration, similar to the online resources maker communities [21] use for whom the processes is the goal. To address the needs of casual users (for whom the solution is the goal), maker resources could include context-in-use information regarding the DIY object, in addition to fabrication instructions.

In contrast, in the *realization* stage, participants relied on in-depth qualitative information. They required opinions, feedback and suggestions [15] to avoid common pitfalls and usability issues. In this stage, users turned to experts such as friends or parents (for expertise in usage), salespeople and professional designers (for expertise in product features), rather than crowd knowledge. Hence, for this stage, we could think of teleoperation interfaces for experts to give in-depth advice on location.

In the *exploration* stage, the most sought information was related to styling, and participants collected large quantities of related images while developing or refining their taste. Using images proved a convenient way to materialize their ideas because they found it difficult to describe aspects of style. However, when they wanted to match the style of new items with their existing furniture or home, they were forced to verbalize these existing aspects as keywords in search engines. When casual users use fabrication interfaces to customize their items, they are likely to encounter similar issues expressing the style they want. Including images as input for style or providing automatic style suggestions, could decrease the gap between what they want and what they make.

Situated and Experiential Prototyping at Home

In the study, we found that all households use prototyping to gain understanding in their requirements and to test the fit of the furniture in their houses. We identified a wide variety of strategies. In the *exploration* stage, these activities did not include specific items, but mostly focussed on the available space and relationship with existing items. Sketching floor plans and prototyping future items with existing furniture situated in the target space helped let them explore solutions and understand the spatial impact.

However, prototyping in the *realization* stage was mostly for visualizing items in their house. Some visualized the product on a one-to-one scale with tapeline, and one held a phone with a photo to simulate the product in the room. Another participant asked the seller to bring sample materials to their home to check whether the color matches well with the other furniture. Therefore, a system that allows people to design directly in the environment would help the participants in their information need. Fabrication tools should support situated prototyping or direct visualization, such as Protopiper [1], which act as an extension of tapeline, but should also enable rapid design iterations.

We frequently observed participants face difficulties trying to estimate the future product for comfort and use using their body. After having used the item for 8 weeks, most participants indicated unanticipated usability or comfort problems. Except three households, they had bought cheap alternatives (less than $15) to try out the product in-use before making a decision. These prototyping activities show similarities to experience prototyping [6]. Research into situated modeling [22, 24] aims to support casual users to model virtual furniture in the target environment. However, as these models are virtual, providing feedback on the product *in-use* is challenging. To some extend feedback on ergonomics could be embedded in the design application similar to physical [42] or fabrication simulations. However, interactive prototyping that includes physical feedback in-use, is a challenge for the future and might involve low-cost cardboard prototypes, haptics, or shape-changing furniture.

Mobile Media in the Design Process

In contrast to earlier studies into furniture purchase [25], we found that in South Korea, all households exclusively used mobile phones in both stages. Only 3 out of 16 households occasionally used a PC or laptop to organize bookmarks or watch images on a large screen. Images collected during the information gathering were saved in online albums, even if the original, paper version was available for collection. This practice helps sharing and curating ideas or thoughts between families or friends by sending images using social network services (SNS). With consideration to C4's comment that they prefer offline-shopping as they wanted to communicate directly while seeing the same product, the mobile SNS compensates for the pitfall of online-exploration and provide effective non-co-located collaboration among stakeholders. The future fabrication tools should reflect the qualities of SNS, which are non-co-located, non-synchronous and over time.

Another reason for using mobile devices was portability and easy accessibility at any time or place. In the *exploration* stage, mobile devices were used as a medium to connect online and offline sources (e.g, bring inspirational sources from web to the living room, and bring the interior to the offline store). Future mobile fabrication interfaces should consider to situate the design practices not only in the living room, but also everywhere including friends' houses or department stores where they get inspirations.

Collaborative Process among Households

We discovered that spouses participated and collaborated in different ways. Some couples prefer exploring product aesthetics and discussing opinions in a synchronous and co-located situation. However, in other couples, one person took charge. Various factors influence the type of collaboration: whether they are moving into a new house or replacing an existing item, their familiarity with the product and whether they are the primary user or the trust level between spouses (how well they know each other). However, all final decisions were made in their house and made together through in-depth discussion. Unlike professional designers, the family members are both designers as well as users of the items. So, while they make decisions, they reminded their partners on what to consider if the partner forgets something. The single households, however, get help from other friends or parents who know their lifestyle or preferred style for making final decisions.

The type of collaboration also seems different when discussing aspects of styling or functions. As described above, people communicate mostly through images for aesthetics (e.g., expressing color by pointing at a color in a picture). In contrast, functional aspects are discussed through embodied prototyping or with use-scenarios or usage-experiences when non-co-located. When one spouse describes a preferred scenario, both of them brainstorm which product could satisfy their needs.

Although furniture is a shared product, and decision making is shared within the household, current design and fabrication tools for casual users are mostly focused on single user interaction. In order to make fabrication tools suitable for people's daily lives, interfaces should support collaboration and should be able to support process. Also, the tools should think in roles or personas, e.g. user, decision maker, stylist or evaluator. Additionally, in order to support single families, who do not have a partner, to help make good decisions, a collaborative virtual partner could be considered.

Temporality in Design

We observed design conflicts in terms of temporality [12] when designing both for their current reality and their future situation. Families with children expected to use the new purchase for about 9 years, but for other household types this was less than 3 years. Single households lowered the priority of aesthetic aspects and tried to select cheap solutions within the boundary of requirements, as they plan to throw it away when moving out. In contrast, families tend to take into account temporal qualities and also their future home and family situation while selecting furniture. For instance, the family who bought cushions for their uncomfortable sofa actually intended the sofa as a bed for their future offspring in their next apartment. This exemplifies the complexity of the process of purchasing furniture.

LIMITATIONS AND FUTURE WORK

In our study, participants bought various types of items, with various types of motivations. Although a broad understanding of the design workflow was possible from this variety, it is necessary to focus on one type of product or motivation for in-depth analysis. In addition, our study was conducted with only 16 middle-income households living in South Korea. However, in order to avoid cultural issues regarding houses, such as sedentary lifestyle or impact of DIY furniture, the study should also be conducted with people in western cultures. Also, the practices of design might be different for other types of product, such as non-durable, small, wearable items, so further investigation on other item categories should be performed.

ACKNOWLEDGMENTS

This research was supported by Basic Science Research Program through the National Research Foundation of Korea (NRF) funded by the Ministry of Science, ICT & Future Planning (NRF-2015R1C1A1A01051808)

REFERENCES

1. Harshit Agrawal, Udayan Umapathi, Robert Kovacs, Johannes Frohnhofen, Hsiang-Ting Chen, Stefanie Mueller, and Patrick Baudisch. 2015. Protopiper: Physically Sketching Room-Sized Objects at Actual Scale. In *Proceedings of the 28th Annual ACM Symposium on User Interface Software & Technology (UIST '15)*. ACM, New York, NY, USA, 427–436. DOI: http://dx.doi.org/10.1145/2807442.2807505
2. Zeynep Arsel and Jonathan Bean. 2013. Taste Regimes and Market-Mediated Practice. *Journal of Consumer Research* 39, 5 (2013), 899–917.
3. Rachel Ashman, Michael R. Solomon, and Julia Wolny. 2015. An old model for a new age: Consumer decision making in participatory digital culture. *Journal of Customer Behaviour* 14, 2 (2015), 127–146. DOI: http://dx.doi.org/doi:10.1362/147539215X14373846805743
4. Hugh Beyer and Karen Holtzblatt. 1998. *Contextual Design: Defining Customer-centered Systems*. Morgan Kaufmann Publishers Inc., San Francisco, CA, USA.
5. Adrien Bousseau, Theophanis Tsandilas, Lora Oehlberg, and Wendy E. Mackay. 2016. How Novices Sketch and Prototype Hand-Fabricated Objects. In *Proceedings of the 2016 CHI Conference on Human Factors in Computing Systems (CHI '16)*. ACM, New York, NY, USA, 397–408. DOI:http://dx.doi.org/10.1145/2858036.2858159
6. Marion Buchenau and Jane Fulton Suri. 2000. Experience Prototyping. In *Proceedings of the 3rd Conference on Designing Interactive Systems: Processes, Practices, Methods, and Techniques (DIS '00)*. ACM, New York, NY, USA, 424–433. DOI: http://dx.doi.org/10.1145/347642.347802
7. Design Counsil. 2007. A Study of the Design Process. (2007). Retrieved July 3, 2016 from www.designcouncil.org.uk/resources/report/11-lessons-managing-design-global-brands.
8. Andy Crabtree and Tom Rodden. 2004. Domestic Routines and Design for the Home. *Comput. Supported Coop. Work* 13, 2 (April 2004), 191–220. DOI: http://dx.doi.org/10.1023/B:COSU.0000045712.26840.a4
9. Nigel Cross. 2004. Expertise in design: an overview. *Design Studies* 25, 5 (2004), 427 – 441. DOI: http://dx.doi.org/10.1016/j.destud.2004.06.002 Expertise in Design.
10. Darren W. Dahl and C. Page Moreau. 2007. Thinking Inside the Box: Why Consumers Enjoy Constrained Creative Experiences. *Journal of Marketing Research* 44, 3 (2007), 357–369. DOI: http://dx.doi.org/10.1509/jmkr.44.3.357
11. Audrey Desjardins and Ron Wakkary. 2013. Manifestations of Everyday Design: Guiding Goals and Motivations. In *Proceedings of the 9th ACM Conference on Creativity & Cognition (C&C '13)*. ACM, New York, NY, USA, 253–262. DOI: http://dx.doi.org/10.1145/2466627.2466643
12. Audrey Desjardins and Ron Wakkary. 2016. Living In A Prototype: A Reconfigured Space. In *Proceedings of the 2016 CHI Conference on Human Factors in Computing Systems (CHI '16)*. ACM, New York, NY, USA, 5274–5285. DOI: http://dx.doi.org/10.1145/2858036.2858261
13. Kees Dorst and Nigel Cross. 2001. Creativity in the design process: co-evolution of problem–solution. *Design Studies* 22, 5 (2001), 425 – 437. DOI: http://dx.doi.org/10.1016/S0142-694X(01)00009-6
14. Sean Follmer, David Carr, Emily Lovell, and Hiroshi Ishii. 2010. CopyCAD: Remixing Physical Objects with Copy and Paste from the Real World. In *Adjunct Proceedings of the 23Nd Annual ACM Symposium on User Interface Software and Technology (UIST '10)*. ACM, New York, NY, USA, 381–382. DOI: http://dx.doi.org/10.1145/1866218.1866230
15. Nikolaus Franke, Peter Keinz, and Martin Schreier. 2008. Complementing mass customization toolkits with user communities: How peer input improves customer self-design. *Journal of product innovation management* 25, 6 (2008), 546–559.
16. Elizabeth Goodman and Daniela Rosner. 2011. From Garments to Gardens: Negotiating Material Relationships Online and 'by Hand'. In *Proceedings of the SIGCHI Conference on Human Factors in Computing Systems (CHI '11)*. ACM, New York, NY, USA, 2257–2266. DOI: http://dx.doi.org/10.1145/1978942.1979273
17. Steffen Hedegaard and Jakob Grue Simonsen. 2013. Extracting Usability and User Experience Information from Online User Reviews. In *Proceedings of the SIGCHI Conference on Human Factors in Computing Systems (CHI '13)*. ACM, New York, NY, USA, 2089–2098. DOI: http://dx.doi.org/10.1145/2470654.2481286
18. Nathaniel Hudson, Celena Alcock, and Parmit K. Chilana. 2016. Understanding Newcomers to 3D Printing: Motivations, Workflows, and Barriers of Casual Makers *(CHI '16)*. ACM, New York, NY, USA, 384–396. DOI: http://dx.doi.org/10.1145/2858036.2858266
19. Evangelos Karapanos, John Zimmerman, Jodi Forlizzi, and Jean-Bernard Martens. 2009. User Experience over Time: An Initial Framework. In *Proceedings of the SIGCHI Conference on Human Factors in Computing Systems (CHI '09)*. ACM, New York, NY, USA, 729–738. DOI:http://dx.doi.org/10.1145/1518701.1518814
20. Ilpo Koskinen, Kristo Kuusela, Katja Battarbee, Anne Soronen, Frans Mäyrä, Jussi Mikkonen, and Mari Zakrzewski. 2006. Morphome: A Constructive Field Study of Proactive Information Technology in the Home. In *Proceedings of the 6th Conference on Designing Interactive Systems (DIS '06)*. ACM, New York, NY, USA, 179–188. DOI: http://dx.doi.org/10.1145/1142405.1142435

21. Stacey Kuznetsov and Eric Paulos. 2010. Rise of the Expert Amateur: DIY Projects, Communities, and Cultures. In *Proceedings of the 6th Nordic Conference on Human-Computer Interaction: Extending Boundaries (NordiCHI '10)*. ACM, New York, NY, USA, 295–304. DOI:http://dx.doi.org/10.1145/1868914.1868950

22. Manfred Lau, Masaki Hirose, Akira Ohgawara, Jun Mitani, and Takeo Igarashi. 2012. Situated Modeling: A Shape-stamping Interface with Tangible Primitives. In *Proceedings of the Sixth International Conference on Tangible, Embedded and Embodied Interaction (TEI '12)*. ACM, New York, NY, USA, 275–282. DOI: http://dx.doi.org/10.1145/2148131.2148190

23. Manfred Lau, Greg Saul, Jun Mitani, and Takeo Igarashi. 2010. Modeling-in-context: User Design of Complementary Objects with a Single Photo. In *Proceedings of the Seventh Sketch-Based Interfaces and Modeling Symposium (SBIM '10)*. Eurographics Association, Aire-la-Ville, Switzerland, Switzerland, 17–24. http://dl.acm.org/citation.cfm?id=1923363.1923367

24. Bokyung Lee, Minjoo Cho, Joonhee Min, and Daniel Saakes. 2016. Posing and Acting As Input for Personalizing Furniture. In *Proceedings of the 9th Nordic Conference on Human-Computer Interaction (NordiCHI '16)*. ACM, New York, NY, USA, Article 44, 10 pages. DOI:http://dx.doi.org/10.1145/2971485.2971487

25. Torsten Lihra and Raoul Graf. 2007. Multi-channel communication and consumer choice in the household furniture buying process. *Direct Marketing: An International Journal* 1, 3 (2007), 146–160.

26. Tuuli Mattelmäki. 2005. Applying probes : from inspirational notes to collaborative insights. *CoDesign* 1, 2 (2005), 83–102. DOI: http://dx.doi.org/10.1080/15719880500135821

27. Andrea Moed, Elizabeth Goodman, and Mike Kuniavsky. 2012. *Observing the User Experience: A Practitioner's Guide to User Research (Interactive Technologies)*. Elsevier Science.

28. Opendesk. 2016. Opendesk-A different approach to design furniture. (2016). Retrieved Dec25 , 2016 from https://www.opendesk.cc/.

29. Gerhard Pahl, W Beitz, Jörg Feldhusen, and Karl-Heinrich Grote. 2007. *Engineering Design. A Systematic Approach* (3 ed.). Springer-Verlag, London. DOI:http://dx.doi.org/10.1007/978-1-84628-319-2

30. James Pierce and Eric Paulos. 2011. Second-hand Interactions: Investigating Reacquisition and Dispossession Practices Around Domestic Objects. In *Proceedings of the SIGCHI Conference on Human Factors in Computing Systems (CHI '11)*. ACM, New York, NY, USA, 2385–2394. DOI: http://dx.doi.org/10.1145/1978942.1979291

31. Taylor Randall, Christian Terwiesch, and Karl T. Ulrich. 2005. Principles for User Design of Customized Products. *California Management Review* 47, 4 (2005), 68–85. DOI:http://dx.doi.org/10.2307/41166317

32. Daniela Rosner and Jonathan Bean. 2009. Learning from IKEA Hacking: I'M Not One to Decoupage a Tabletop and Call It a Day.. In *Proceedings of the SIGCHI Conference on Human Factors in Computing Systems (CHI '09)*. ACM, New York, NY, USA, 419–422. DOI: http://dx.doi.org/10.1145/1518701.1518768

33. Greg Saul, Manfred Lau, Jun Mitani, and Takeo Igarashi. 2011. SketchChair: An All-in-one Chair Design System for End Users. In *Proceedings of the Fifth International Conference on Tangible, Embedded, and Embodied Interaction (TEI '11)*. ACM, New York, NY, USA, 73–80. DOI:http://dx.doi.org/10.1145/1935701.1935717

34. Theodore R Schatzki. 1996. *Social practices: A Wittgensteinian approach to human activity and the social*. Cambridge Univ Press.

35. Donald A Schön. 1983. *The reflective practitioner: How professionals think in action*. Vol. 5126. Basic books.

36. Rita Shewbridge, Amy Hurst, and Shaun K. Kane. 2014. Everyday Making: Identifying Future Uses for 3D Printing in the Home. In *Proceedings of the 2014 Conference on Designing Interactive Systems (DIS '14)*. ACM, New York, NY, USA, 815–824. DOI: http://dx.doi.org/10.1145/2598510.2598544

37. Leon Shiffman and Leslie Lazar Kanuk. 2004. *Consumer behavior* (8 ed.). Pearson Prentice Hall.

38. Elizabeth Shove, Mika Pantzar, and Matt Watson. 2012. *The dynamics of social practice: Everyday life and how it changes*. Sage Publications.

39. Jeffry A. Simpson, Vladas Griskevicius, and Alexander J. Rothman. 2012. Consumer decisions in relationships. *Journal of Consumer Psychology* 22, 3 (2012), 304 – 314. DOI:http://dx.doi.org/10.1016/j.jcps.2011.09.007

40. G. J. Szybillo and A. Sosanie. 1977. Family decision making: Husband, wife and children. *Advances in Consumer Research* 4 (1977), 46–49.

41. Karl Ulrich and Steven Eppinger. 2004. *Product Design and Development*. McGraw-Hill, New York, NY, USA.

42. Nobuyuki Umentani, Takeo Igarashi, and Niloy J. Mitra. 2015. Guided Exploration of Physically Valid Shapes for Furniture Design. *Commun. ACM* 58, 9 (Aug. 2015), 116–124. DOI:http://dx.doi.org/10.1145/2801945

43. Valentijn Visch, Ed Tan, and Daniel Saakes. 2015. Viewer Knowledge: Application of Exposure-based Layperson Knowledge in Genre-specific Animation Production. *International Journal of Design* 9, 1 (2015).

44. Froukje Sleeswijk Visser, Pieter Jan Stappers, Remko Van der Lugt, and Elizabeth BN Sanders. 2005. Contextmapping: experiences from practice. *CoDesign* 1, 2 (2005), 119–149.

45. Eric von Hippel. 2005. *Democratizing Innovation*. The MIT Press, Cambridge, MA, USA.

46. Ron Wakkary and Leah Maestri. 2007. The Resourcefulness of Everyday Design. In *Proceedings of the 6th ACM SIGCHI Conference on Creativity & Cognition (C&C '07)*. ACM, New York, NY, USA, 163–172. DOI: http://dx.doi.org/10.1145/1254960.1254984

47. Alan Warde. 2005. Consumption and Theories of Practice. *Journal of Consumer Culture* 5, 2 (2005), 131–153. DOI: http://dx.doi.org/10.1177/1469540505053090

48. Christian Weichel, Jason Alexander, Abhijit Karnik, and Hans Gellersen. 2015. SPATA: Spatio-Tangible Tools for Fabrication-Aware Design. In *Proceedings of the Ninth International Conference on Tangible, Embedded, and Embodied Interaction (TEI '15)*. ACM, New York, NY, USA, 189–196. DOI: http://dx.doi.org/10.1145/2677199.2680576

49. Christian Weichel, Manfred Lau, David Kim, Nicolas Villar, and Hans W. Gellersen. 2014. MixFab: A Mixed-reality Environment for Personal Fabrication. In *Proceedings of the 32Nd Annual ACM Conference on Human Factors in Computing Systems (CHI '14)*. ACM, New York, NY, USA, 3855–3864. DOI: http://dx.doi.org/10.1145/2556288.2557090

50. Allen T.W. Whitfield and Lucila R de Destefani. 2011. Mundane aesthetics. *Psychology of Aesthetics, Creativity, and the Arts* 5, 3 (2011), 291–299.

51. Jong-bum Woo and Youn-kyung Lim. 2015. User Experience in Do-it-yourself-style Smart Homes. In *Proceedings of the 2015 ACM International Joint Conference on Pervasive and Ubiquitous Computing (UbiComp '15)*. ACM, New York, NY, USA, 779–790. DOI: http://dx.doi.org/10.1145/2750858.2806063

Stretching the Bounds of 3D Printing with Embedded Textiles

Michael L. Rivera[1], Melissa Moukperian[2], Daniel Ashbrook[3], Jennifer Mankoff[1], Scott E. Hudson[1]

[1]Human-Computer Interaction Institute
Carnegie Mellon University
{mlrivera, jmankoff, scott.hudson}@cs.cmu.edu

[2]College of Imaging Arts and Sciences
[3]Golisano College of Computing and Information Sciences
Rochester Institute of Technology
{daniel.ashbrook, mdmfaa}@rit.edu

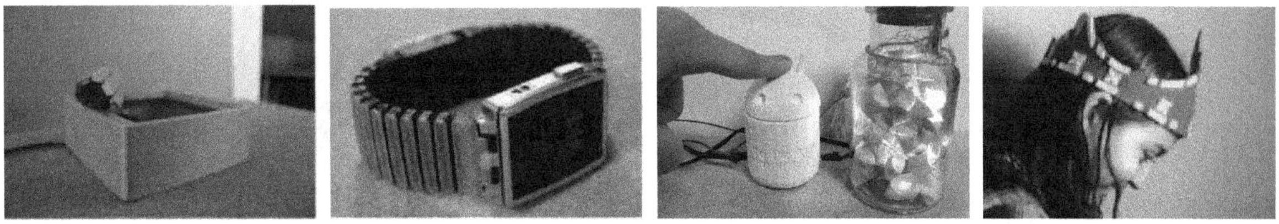

(a) (b) (c) (d)

Figure 1. A range of textile-embedded 3D printed objects fabricated using our techniques – a box with a rolling lid containing a mesh of polyester and strings for actuation (a); a functional watchband printed on a polyester mesh (b); a figure with a pressure-sensitive head that controls an embedded displacement sensor containing a mesh of nylon and spandex fibers (c); a 22 inch (56 cm) crown printed on a single piece of felt larger than the print bed (d).

ABSTRACT

Textiles are an old and well developed technology that have many desirable characteristics. They can be easily folded, twisted, deformed, or cut; some can be stretched; many are soft. Textiles can maintain their shape when placed under tension and can even be engineered with variable stretching ability. Conversely, 3D printing is a relatively new technology that can precisely produce functional, rigid objects with custom geometry. Combining 3D printing and textiles opens up new opportunities for rapidly creating rigid objects with embedded flexibility as well as soft materials imbued with additional functionality. In this paper, we introduce a suite of techniques for integrating 3D printing with textiles during the printing process, opening up a new design space that takes inspiration from both fields. We demonstrate how the malleability, stretchability and aesthetic qualities of textiles can enhance rigid printed objects, and how textiles can be augmented with functional properties enabled by 3D printing.

Author Keywords

Additive manufacturing; 3D printing; soft materials; textiles; interactive devices.

ACM Classification Keywords

H.5.2. [Information Interfaces and Presentation (*e.g.*, HCI)]: User Interfaces.

CHI 2017, May 06-11, 2017, Denver, CO, USA
© 2017 ACM. ISBN 978-1-4503-4655-9/17/05 ...$15.00
DOI: http://dx.doi.org/10.1145/3025453.3025460

INTRODUCTION

Textiles are a very well developed technology: techniques for the construction, manipulation, and modification of textiles have been refined for millennia [5]. Textiles offer many desirable characteristics: they can be easily folded, twisted or deformed; some can maintain shape when placed under tension and preserve functional qualities when cut. These and other properties such as aesthetic appearance, warmth, and versatility have afforded textiles a rich history of practical uses extending from clothing and decoration to more functional objects such as furniture and even as parts of buildings [6].

In contrast, 3D printing is a relatively new technology that offers a means of fabricating items with precise custom geometries. While most 3D printing techniques create rigid objects–typically from plastic and more recently from metal–we believe 3D printed objects can benefit greatly from the flexibility, stretchability, and aesthetic qualities found in many textiles. Similarly, the utility of textiles can be augmented by the use of computer-aided design software and the accuracy and functional properties of 3D printing. As illustrated in Figure 1, the combination of 3D printing and textiles creates a new design space for rigid objects with embedded flexibility and soft materials imbued with functionality. In this paper, we present the following contributions:

- we introduce a series of design primitives enabled by combining 3D printing and textiles;
- we demonstrate a set of techniques for successfully combining 3D printing and textiles, including details on how to successfully adhere plastic to fabric, how to include fabric in a print, and methods for achieving high-quality results;

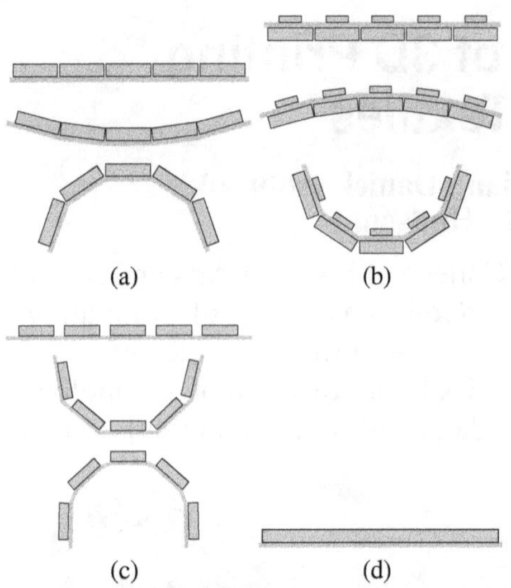

Figure 2. Primitives for stiffening in a single dimension by adding plastic (gray) to fabric (blue). Closely spaced elements printed onto the fabric can prevent it from bending up while allowing it to relax down (a); widely spaced top elements coupled with closely spaced bottom elements enforce the opposite motion (b). Using widely spaced elements allow the fabric to flex in both directions (c), while a solid bar prevents flexing entirely (d).

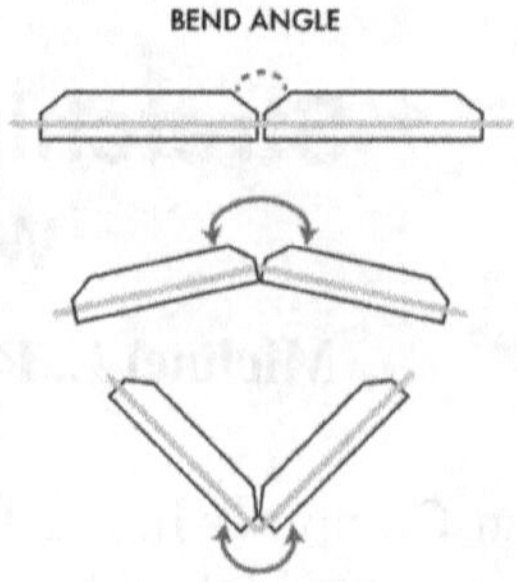

Figure 3. Plastic segments that restrict the bend angles of a textile.

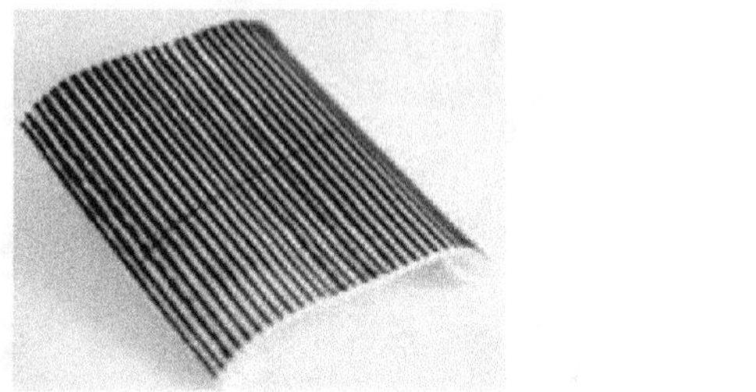

Figure 4. A textile that is only capable of rolling or flexing along the axis parallel to the plastic segments.

- we show how embedding textiles can enable the creation of customized input devices on consumer printers in new ways;
- we illustrate how our techniques enable the rapid creation of objects larger than the print bed.

We show each of these techniques and demonstrate their utility through an array of examples, starting with reusable design primitives and mechanisms which can be combined to create useful objects. For example, Figure 1a shows controlled bending being used in a retractable box lid, demonstrating how the direction, degree, and shape of bends can be controlled by fabricating plastic elements on fabric. We also show the benefits of 3D printing for fabric layers that extend beyond the print bed (Figure 1d), creating arbitrarily shaped reinforced holes (grommets) in fabric, and providing one way of addressing the problem of fast prototyping. We show working examples of input devices such as buttons (Figure 1c), sliders, and knobs that take advantage of the stretchy nature of knit fabric to sense user input. In addition to supporting the implementation of basic sensing mechanisms, fabric conveys other benefits. For example, a mechanical slider can make use of the stretchable properties of spandex to re-center its slider thumb.

RELATED WORK

The properties of textiles have long been explored in the material science and textile manufacturing communities [13, 15, 14, 11]. Their structure of interlocking fibers—either natural or manufactured—gives textiles a breadth of characteristics that are useful beyond their appearance. Some textiles can absorb sound or moisture, and be engineered with specific stretchability [15]. Others may be coated with polymers that block wind and water, or are sensitive to heat [32].

Fabric—the material produced by interlacing fibers through weaving, knitting, crocheting, or bonding—can also be designed to provide further variations in properties such as stretchability and permeability. For example, fabric engineered with large spaces between fibers, or interstices, can facilitate faster diffusion of liquids such as water or hot plastic between the fibers [36]. Shaping and/or stiffening of fabric is accomplished by attaching it to rigid objects, draping it over rigid objects, sewing seams and darts, and layering fabrics. These are all fairly labor-intensive actions that require some skill and knowledge about sewing and textile-working.

Textiles have recently captured the imagination of the 3D printing community, which can benefit from aesthetic and other properties of textiles, while reducing the manual labor needed to create with them. For example, Hudson [17] described a new type of 3D printer that prints in needle-felted yarn, enabling the creation of new soft objects such as teddy bears. Peng *et al.* [27] created a layered fabric printer, which uses textiles as the printing medium, cut with a laser cutter and adhered together using an iron and heat sensitive adhesive. This printer could combine two different textiles, enabling, for example, the embedding of conductive material in a print.

Others have chosen to manipulate the aesthetic properties of 3D printed objects without changing the underlying materials. For example, HapticPrint adds surface textures for primarily aesthetic purposes [35] while Laput *et al.* show that a consumer fused deposition modeling (FDM) printer can create hair-like extrusions without modification to the hardware [19]. Melnikova *et al.* explore a variety of lace-like structures and knit-like structures using combinations of hard and flexible materials laid down using either selective laser sintering (SLS) or FDM machines [20].

There has been limited prior research into combining FDM printing with existing textiles. Pei *et al.* show that it is possible to directly 3D print plastic onto textiles [26], exploring

Figure 5. A shell printed dodecahedron fabricated by printing through a polyester mesh. The faces of the object were printed flat on a single sheet of fabric that was cut post-printing (a). Rubber bands we used to actuate the shell mesh into final 3D for (b).

structures such as a latch and hook, and demonstrating the potential for printing braille or even an articulated part affecting flexibility. They also examine the quality of adhesion acceptability *via* visual and surface inspection, suggesting PLA has strong adhesion with certain fabrics. However, they do not measure the force that can be held by a bond between plastic and fabric nor the extent to which a fabric will stretch before the bond breaks. Mikkonen *et al.* create flexible, 3D printed objects intended to be integrated with cloth [21]. However, they use standard methods for attaching hard objects to textiles, such as printing buttons and sewing them on, or inserting boning into a corset. Sabantina *et al.* demonstrate simple 3D printed forms combined with textile structures and their mechanical and geometric properties [31]. Our work extends theirs by realizing a set of usable design primitives, techniques and exemplars that support combining textiles with 3D printed components, and provides direction and guidance for exploring this design space. Finally, 3D printer manufacturer 3D Systems added fashion-oriented printing-onto-fabric capabilities to its consumer-level Cube printer shortly before discontinuing production of the printer [1].

In the domain of textiles, and particularly fashion design, the ability to add structure and manipulability to fabric has long been of interest, although less of the focus has been on fabrication methods, and more on fabrication outcomes. For example, computer-aided design (CAD) and manufacturing (CAM) have long been an aspect of fashion design. Driven in part by the needs of realism in animation, textiles can now be modeled in great detail [4, 7].

Augmentation of textiles in various ways has also long been a focus of interest, from Spyn's approach to attaching storytelling to knitting [30] to TeeBoard's ability to support easy embedding of electronics in clothing [24]. Combining technology and textiles has become more accessible to end users (*e.g.*, [28, 29]) and is a domain in which innovation takes place as much by hobbyists as by academics [2]. For example, a recent Instructable describes some basic techniques for directly printing onto fabric [18]. Our work expands the set of techniques for successful printing (*e.g.*, discussing how to compensate for issues like tilting and sagging of fabric during printing, selective adherence control, and combinations needed to fabricate devices like a retracting mechanical slider).

Another area of relevance is the shaping and mechanical articulation of 3D objects (see [12] for a survey of this area). Here we may draw from origami [10], marionette design [8], materials engineering [33], mechanism design [9], and shape-changing interfaces [37, 16, 25]. However, our work expands this design space by accommodating a different set of trade-offs due to different materials and fabrication techniques.

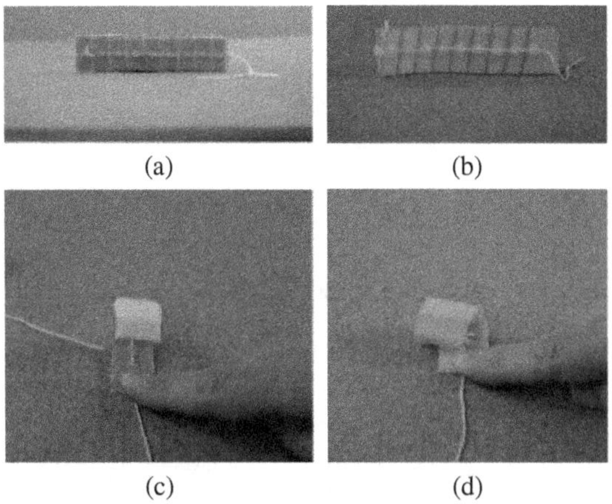

Figure 6. Textile-embedded, string actuated mechanical arms with variable bend angles– (a) and (c) show straight segments of plastic lead to a simple roll that aligns with the axis of the channel; (b) and (d) show angled segments of plastic cause the roll to skew to the left.

DESIGN PRIMITIVES

Our exploration of textile-embedded printing takes place at three different levels: fully working objects (we discuss six examples at the end of the paper); low-level techniques for successfully 3D printing with textiles; and design primitives for accomplishing specific higher level goals. In this section, we introduce these design primitives, showing how the differing properties of textiles and plastic can complement each other. In subsequent sections, we explain techniques for achieving this fusion of materials, and illustrate a number of fully-working examples.

Selective Stiffening

Adding plastic to fabric enables selective stiffening of the fabric, controlling where and how the fabric can bend or stretch. Applying this basic primitive allows us to build up a number of higher-level primitives, including mechanically-actuated devices, interactive, sensor-based objects, and larger scale fabrications using fabric skins.

Printed plastic normally cannot bend unless hinges are included in its design, which often requires a level of precision hard to achieve in consumer grade printers and/or additional assembly steps. In contrast, most common textiles are not normally rigid at all. Many techniques exist for adding stiffness to fabric, such as incorporating additional hard materials (*e.g.*, cardboard or plastic whalebone); however, adding these materials can be labor-intensive and require considerable knowledge of and skill in sewing and textile shaping.

By printing plastic onto fabric, we can *selectively stiffen* different areas of the fabric, controlling how the fabric is able to bend (Figure 4). Figure 2 illustrates the different ways we can control bending in a single dimension. By controlling the spacing of 3D printed elements on top of fabric, we can allow or prevent bending in the direction perpendicular to the fabric.

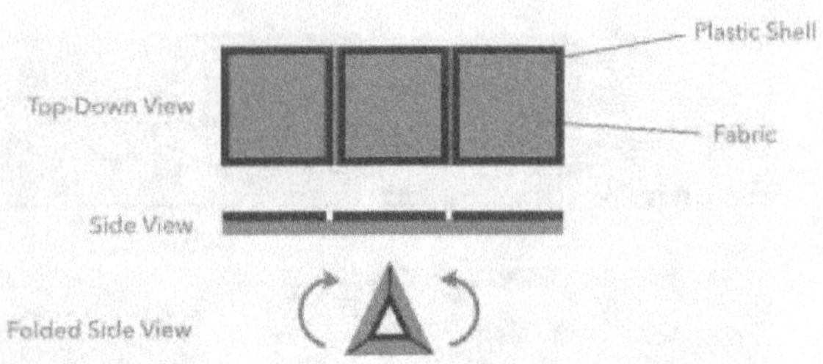

Figure 7. A shell printed triangular prism first printed flat and then folded to its 3D form.

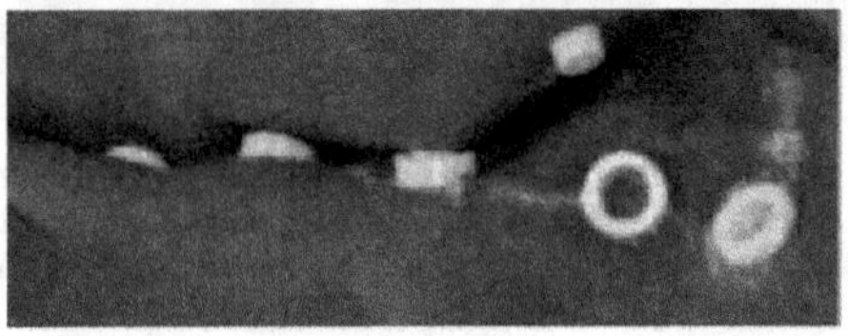

Figure 8. 3D Printed snaps printed onto a fabric.

Incorporating the fabric mid-print allows us to control bending in the opposite direction as well.

In addition to controlling direction of bend, we can also control *degree* of bend by manipulating the amount and shape of added plastic. Specifically, the bend angle can be controlled by using closely spaced stiffeners with angled side cutoffs or explicit side braces. As illustrated in Figure 3, the bend angle will be approximately the sum of the two side angles in the bend direction, and will remain small in the opposite direction (unless additional bending support on the opposite side is provided). Note however, that the exact bend angle may depend on the stretch of the small section of fabric between the stiffeners. Consequently, for fabrics with very high stretch it may be necessary to experiment to obtain an exact angle.

Individual one-dimensional bends can be composed to create more complex shapes and motions. For example, Figure 6 illustrates curling shapes produced using angled and straight stiffening segments. Figure 5 illustrates the creation of a 3D solid shape by folding from a flat object. We achieve the final shape by printing each edge in the polygonal model with a pair of braces that have an bend angle equal to half the dihedral angle for that edge.

Selective Adherence

By selectively adhering plastic to the fabric, we can control the degree of flexing and stretching in the plane of the fabric, in addition to bending out of it. We can further customize behavior by selectively manipulating the areas where plastic adheres to the fabric. We can control adherence by placing painter's tape over areas of the textile where plastic is placed but should not adhere. We are then free to print on and around the tape, which supports the hot plastic while preventing it from bonding with the surface below. After printing is complete, the fabric can shift or stretch while being in contact with, but not adhered to, the plastic. This technique allows us, for example, to create a mechanical slider which is free to move and retract using stretchy fabric (Figure 18b).

Figure 9. Arbitrarily shaped grommets 3D printed onto a polyester mesh. The centers of the grommets were cut out after printing.

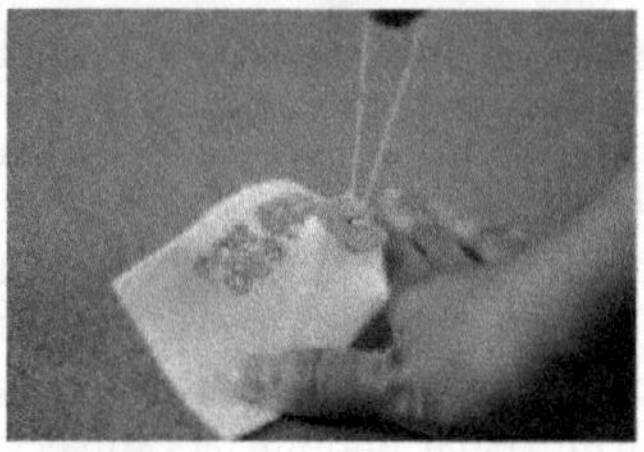

Figure 10. Plastic extruded onto a textile with a fuzzy surface creates very strong adherence. The plastic seen here is difficult to separate from a piece of felt.

Mechanical Action

By building on the stiffening primitives, we can begin to create more complex interactive devices. Constraining the bend of the fabric in specific ways can create simple mechanisms. Figures 6a and 6c illustrate how a string affixed to one end of a strip of stiffening segments can create a rolling mechanism. By varying the angle at which the segments are placed next to each other, the strip can be made to curl as it rolls up (Figures 6b and 6d). Figure 1a illustrates a hybrid textile/printed box with a segmented lid. Controlled by a motor, the box's lid can automatically curl open and uncurl closed.

Fast Production

Current FDM printing is slow, taking many hours to fabricate larger objects. Previous research has explored different methods to speed up the printing process such as printing in lower fidelity [22, 23] or reusing previously printed objects [34]. However, fabricating plastic layer-by-layer is still inherently time-consuming.

One of the key advantages of using textiles with 3D printing is that layers of fabric are pre-fabricated, opening up the possibility of saving print time by selectively replacing some of the printed plastic with fabric. However, to emulate the hard plastic it replaces, the fabric may need to be reinforced so that does not bend. We may stiffen fabric with a small amount of plastic support printed over the surface, similar to use of wireframes for faster printing by Mueller *et al.* [22]. We term the technique for fashioning objects like this "shell printing" because we construct the outer shell of an object using textile panels created with this method (Figure 7).

There are several options for assembling a shell print. The easiest methods are to add structure for fastening shells together such as 3D printed snaps (Figure 8) and clips, glue the panels together at the edges. If desired, the panels can also be sewn.

Large Objects

An advantage of printing on fabric is that it can be larger than the print bed, allowing a print to be "continued" in 2D. This allows us to repeatedly print on the same piece of fabric,

Figure 11. Instron adhesion test setup. Left: attachment of fabric and plastic sample to test column; right: fabric anchor (yellow) with test in progress.

repositioning it on the print bed and moving already printed sections out of the way, resulting in a continuous print larger than the printer itself. The restriction of this approach, similar to other work involving adding to existing fabrication [34], is that to prevent obstructing the extruder's movement, the gaps between each printed section must be larger than the size of the extruder nozzle. Another issue that arises is proper alignment of a textile such that printing can be done where desired. One solution is to use a skirt layer to assist in positioning the textile on the print bed. We have also successfully experimented with using a laser pointer attached to the extruder head to guide alignment of a print each time the textile is moved. Figure 1d illustrates a wearable object longer than the print bed fabricated in this way.

Reconfiguring Textiles

Textiles have many options for post processing. For example, assembly of a shell print can be done through printed snaps (Figure 8) or textile-working techniques like sewing. A textile can be cut to size or shape after printing to remove excess material; it can also be cut to adjust a part if the exact sizing is not known at design time. Reinforcing plastic may be printed around holes—creating grommets—to protect the fabric's raw edges from fraying and provide passage for cords or strings. Figure 9 shows several examples of arbitrary grommet shapes.

We note that augmentations such as snaps and grommets can be readily provided by more conventional means. However, having a way to 3D print these as well allows us to reduce the number of separate manufacturing steps to create an object. In addition, it provides a flexible way to mix these conventional fixed form augmentations with the kinds of highly custom structures which are most readily achieved with 3D printing.

Summary

The addition of fabric in the context of consumer-grade 3D printing enables a set of novel design primitives that printed plastic alone cannot realize. With stiffening constructs, we can control how the fabric flexes; composing these allows for more complex flexing behavior and allows for mechanical properties such as rolling and snapping. Using a material such as painter's tape, we can selectively prevent the plastic from adhering to the fabric, allowing for further movement possibilities.

BASIC TECHNIQUES FOR 3D PRINTING WITH TEXTILES

Strong adherence between textiles and 3D printed plastic is necessary to achieve the properties we describe above. We conducted extensive experiments—both informal and formal—to determine the best methods to achieve a strong bond, as well as techniques for combining our design primitives to create more complex structures.

In our experiments, we used unmodified consumer-grade FDM 3D printers, PLA and ABS filament, and a variety of different textiles. Note that there is inherent variability in measurements related to our process. The temperature for 3D printing a plastic varies based on the calibration of the 3D printer as well as the quality and type of filament used [3]. For example, the ideal print temperature of PLA is typically between 180–230°C. Similarly, coatings and variations in material make-up of fibers may alter how a textile interacts with printed plastic. Information about the presence and types of coatings on textiles is not easily available, particularly if textiles are purchased off the shelf. Thus some degree of experimentation around parameters such as extrusion temperature is required when attempting to print with embedded textiles.

The two main factors we consider for successfully combining fabric and plastic are *adherence* and *stability*. Adherence refers to the ability of the plastic filament to attach to the textile, while stabilizing the fabric with respect to the printer is also necessary to achieve success, particularly when printing tall objects.

Adherence

Because FDM printing lays down print material in layers, it is critical that each layer bonds to the previous one. When incorporating textiles in an FDM print, the textile can be considered a "layer" as well.

Due to variability in factors such as printer temperature and textile coatings, experimentation is required to attain optimal adherence, such that the textile cannot not be easily separated from a print (Figure 10). We found that PLA, for example, often adheres better to fabric when extruded at a slightly higher temperature than typical (210-220°C). The high temperature produces lower viscosity and facilitates a longer settling period for the plastic to cool and solidify, allowing it to partially seep into the fabric for a stronger bond.

For thin fabric, approximately less than 0.4mm thick, the best adherence resulted from simply securing the fabric and proceeding with printing without leaving extra space in the model for the fabric layer: the force and heat of the extruder pressing into the fabric assisted in achieving a good bond between the plastic and textile. For thicker fabric, however, the extruder can catch on the fabric, displacing it during the print process. In this case, it is necessary to raise the height of the next layer of plastic to be printed, leaving space for the fabric.

When a fabric is not used as the first layer of a print but instead sandwiched the fabric between two layers of plastic, it will not

ID	Name	Treatment	Composition	Thread count	Weight
A	Ripstop Nylon	—	100% nylon	196	68
B	Sport Nylon	—	100% nylon	113	91
C	Symphony Broadcloth	—	65% polyester, 35% cotton	208	112
D	Voile	—	65% polyester, 35% cotton	120	53
E	Premium Muslin	Bleached	100% cotton	204	125
F	Sew Essential	Bleached	100% cotton	142	114

Table 1. Test fabric properties. All fabrics tested were plain weave. Thread count is threads per square inch and weight is grams per square meter.

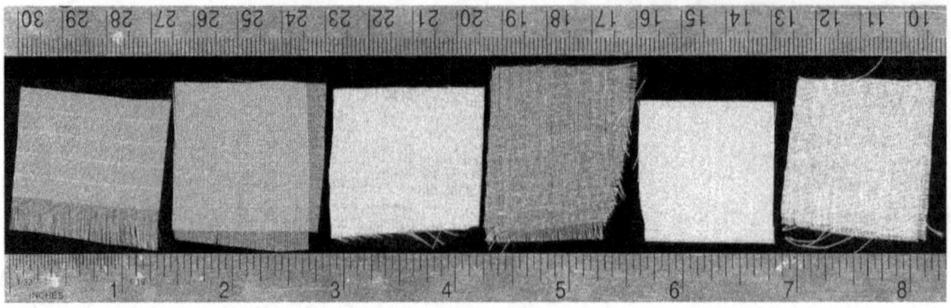

Figure 12. The fabrics used in strain testing; in order of Table 1 (A–F) from left to right. The top ruler is in centimeters; the bottom is in inches.

normally adhere to the layer below it. If it should be adhered, the fabric must have holes, or interstices, for the melted plastic to flow through. These openings may be an intrinsic part of the fabric, in the case of netting or other low-density textiles, or can be artificially created by cutting.

Adhesion Testing

Pei *et al.* examine the quality of adhesion between plastic and fabric through visual and surface inspection [26]. However, they do not provide quantitative insights about the bond strength. We achieved a preliminary characterization of the bonding performance of plastic and fabric using an Instron model 5567 strain tester to measure the force required to separate plastic printed onto different types of fabric. Figure 11 illustrates our testing setup: we printed a 1-in (2.54 cm) diameter "plug" of plastic on a sample of fabric, affixed it to the lower arm of the Instron and attached the upper arm's clamp to the plug. The machine then pulled the two arms apart until the plug separated from the fabric, measuring the amount of force required during the extension.

We measured a baseline of performance using basic materials and default printer configurations. We performed the test using two plastic types, ABS and PLA, both un-colored, from Mitus[1]. Our fabric samples were similarly un-dyed and, as much as we were able to determine, un-coated. We printed the plastic at manufacturer-recommended temperatures (248°C for ABS and 210°C for PLA) on an Ultimaker 3D printer. Figure 13 illustrates the results of our adherence test. Table 1 describes the properties of the six fabrics we tested, and Figure 12 shows images of each fabric.

Our results demonstrate that the adhesion capabilities can vary widely based on the composition of a fabric and the filament used for printing, which is useful in supporting different functionality. For example, the combination of Sew Essential fabric with PLA is capable of sustaining a weight of 50 N (11 pounds of force) which is equivalent to a grocery bag full of food. Similarly, the Voile fabric with PLA can extend about 1 cm in length with a small amount of force (approximately 10 N or 2 pounds of force) without adhesion failing. This property can be used to support mechanical action such as retraction in a slider.

[1]`http://mitusbrand.com`

Stabilization

When 3D printing with plastic alone, as long as the printer is calibrated and the bed is appropriately prepared, the plastic will adhere, providing a stable surface for further layers of printing. Unfortunately, the mechanical advantages of fabrics—their abilities to compress, flex, and stretch—are also potential disadvantages when it comes to the actual print process. For example, the relative motion between the print head and the fabric can cause lateral forces to be exerted on the fabric which can then shift or stretch; fabric placed across gaps can sag; and taller prints can tilt or twist as the fabric flexes. Extra steps that prevent these issues must be taken to provide a stable surface on which to print. We describe solutions below and illustrate them in Figure 14.

Shifting

Unless a piece of fabric is secured to the print bed, it will simply be pushed around by the print head as it moves. As discussed in the Section Adherence, for thicker fabrics we can position the print head such that it does not catch, but this can lessen adherence. Textiles with a low degree of stretch may be fixed in place at the edges with tape or clamps similar to [18]. For fabric with a higher degree of stretch, it may be necessary to secure the underside as well to prevent shifting during the print process. In our experiments, we found that double-sided tape was effective at preventing this unwanted motion.

For fabric that is intended as a middle layer of the print—for example, in our displacement sensor in Figure 15—the same technique of fixing the fabric in place at the edges applies. Alternatively, if it is undesirable to drape the fabric over the edges of the print, another strategy is to use glue. In our experiments, we found that gel-viscosity cyanoacrylate adhesive was highly effective in bonding fabric pieces mid-print.

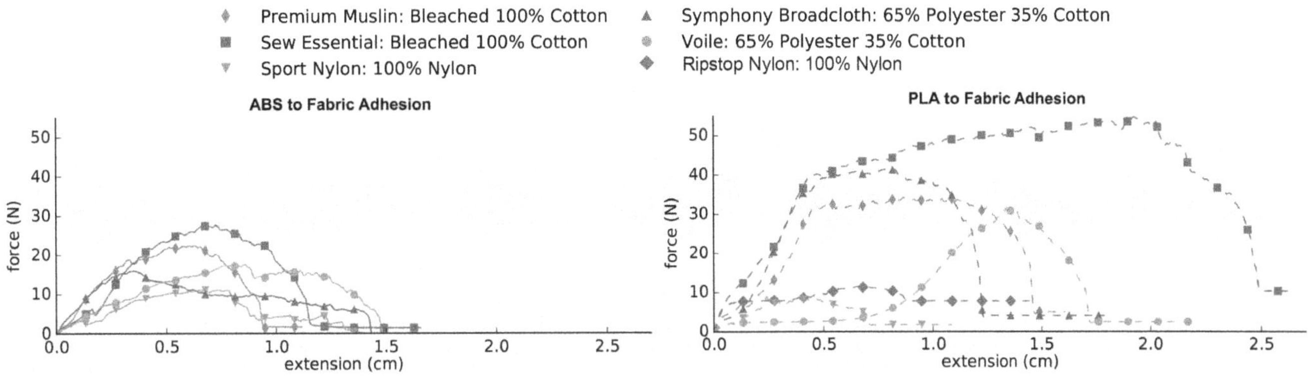

Figure 13. Results of adherence testing showing force exerted for a given extension. Both graphs are on the same scale; the left is for ABS and the right is for PLA.

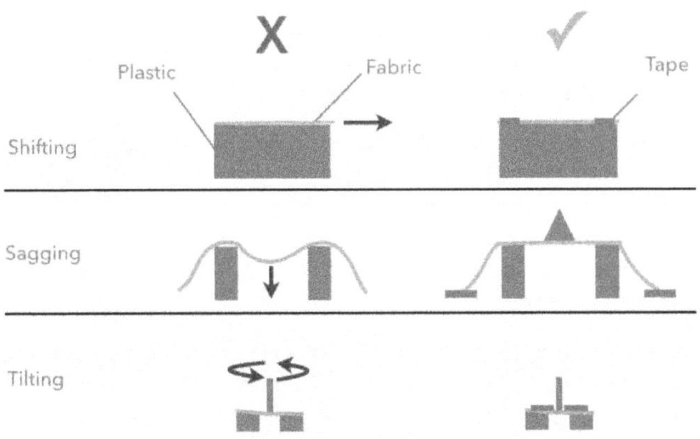

Figure 14. Stabilization problems and solutions.

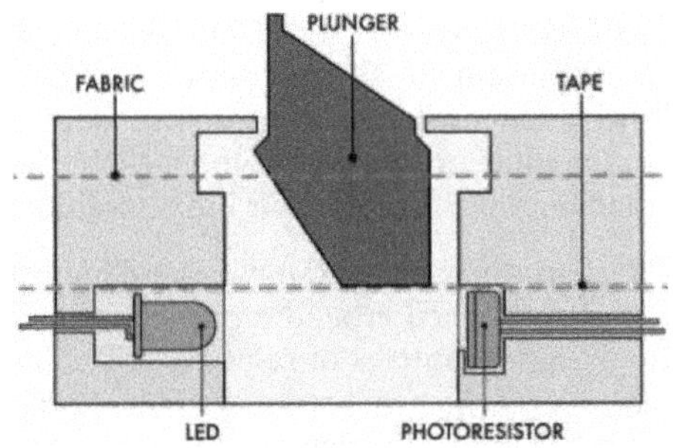

Figure 15. Cross-section of a textile-embedded displacement sensor. The tape is inserted with electrical components during the printing process. The tape acts as temporary support for printing the plunger. It is later removed using an opening on the underside of the object (Figure 16).

Figure 16. The underside of the displacement sensor showing the suspended plunger.

Stretching

The ability of some textiles to stretch adds opportunities to be embedded into 3D prints. For example, stretch can facilitate the creation of resizable objects and even pressure-sensitive input devices (Figure 1c). However, stretch can also create problems by introducing movement that makes objects tilt as more layers added to them. Additionally, textiles made of nylon or spandex fibers may shift or melt due to contact with the extruder. Calibrating the extruder to print just above the surface of the textile and placing painter's tape over it can reduce stretching as demonstrated by [18].

Sagging

An advantage of textiles is their ability to easily bridge large gaps in a print. However, they may sag if not well supported and printing may cause the fabric to dip, leading to improper layer alignment and poor adhesion of plastic. This problem can be reduced by first placing painter's tape over a gap to support the fabric (Figure 17c), or by using one of the shifting-reduction methods to keep the textile taut over the gap.

Tilting

Tilting occurs when the object being printed has a small contact area with a textile and a comparatively large height. As the height rises, it is more likely that the print head will be able to push the object aside causing inaccurate (or even in-air) printing. This effect is worsened by textiles that stretch. We can correct tilting by placing painter's tape directly on a textile near problem spots to reduce stretching, or by adding double-sided tape between the textile and the print bed or underlying printed support material to hold it steady.

Printing Beyond a Single Layer

A fundamental limitation of printing on fabric is that the fabric must lie horizontal to the print plane. Otherwise, it may obstruct the movement of the extruder and prevent hot plastic from being properly laid down. Other research has investigated layering fabric [27], but this technique—in addition to requiring a custom 3D printer and pre-loaded fabric—constrains printing to *only* textile layers and does not incorporate plastic. Our approach does not have these constraints.

Textiles intended to fold may be printed flat and then folded (such as those described in the Section Design Primitives). Fabric may also be folded up and around after some number of plastic layers are printed, by pausing the printing process to

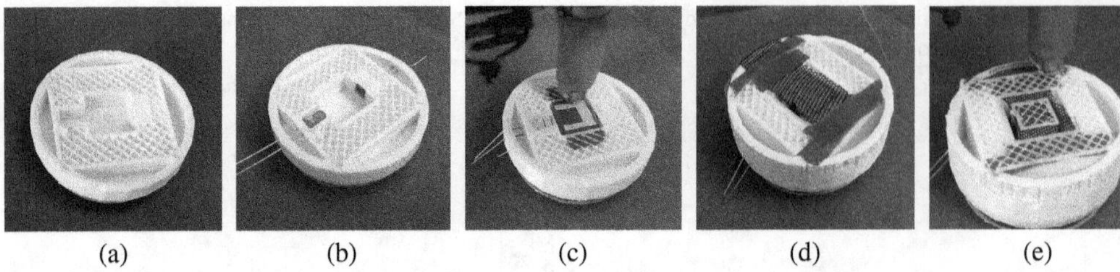

(a) (b) (c) (d) (e)

Figure 17. Process for a fabricated pressure sensitive button. The print is paused when it has enough layers to house the electrical components (a). The electronics are inserted (b). A piece of painter's tape is inserted to bridge the gap between the electronics to support printing the plunger (c). The print is paused again after enough layers have been printed for the plunger so that a stretchable fabric can be laid across the gap and affixed using painter's tape (d). The printing process is resumed and the subsequent layers of plastic adhere to the fabric and the plastic below (e).

place the textile. In many cases, excess fabric is small enough to fit on the print bed, and naturally remains out of the way as layers are added. In other cases, fabric can be folded or rolled and secured out of the way of any moving parts during printing. For our largest print, a felt crown measuring 22 inches (56 cm) in length, we were able to fold the felt such that only one segment of the crown was on the print bed at any given time. The remaining fabric rested to the side in a direction that did not interfere with the extruder or print bed motion.

Summary

Textiles are easy to incorporate into the 3D printing process with unmodified consumer-grade technology. Although any given design requires some experimentation to be successful, such experimentation is common with non-fabric based prints as well. We are confident that others can easily adopt our techniques to incorporate textiles into their 3D prints.

EXAMPLES

In this section, we present a series of ten end-to-end examples that demonstrate applications of our design primitives to create novel printed objects, ranging from interactive devices to wearables and toys.

Input Devices

Our design primitives can be used with stretchable textiles to quickly fabricate customized input devices. We created a reusable displacement sensor whose electrical components are embedded during the printing process, as illustrated in Figure 15. The displacement sensor allows custom actuation mechanisms to be quickly fabricated, snapped on top, and tried out before deciding on a final design.

The principle of operation behind the displacement sensor (Figure 18a) is to sense the movement of a fabric-suspended plunger: when the plunger is moved, it occludes light produced by an LED in proportion to the amount of displacement. We detect this change using a photoresistor placed directly across from the LED inside of the object.

The inside of the displacement sensor is hollow to allow the the plunger to move freely (Figure 15). During the printing process, we temporarily support the plunger with tape (Figure 17c). Once enough layers of the plunger are printed, we pause the print and securely lay down a thin stretch fabric composed of nylon and spandex fibers (Figure 17d). We resume the print to finish fabrication of the object (Figure 17e), embedding the fabric partially inside the plunger. Finally, we remove the support tape through the opening on the underside of the object (Figure 16). This leaves the plunger suspended in mid-air by the stretch fabric.

Once the base of the displacement sensor is constructed, we may snap on additional actuation mechanisms to test. Here we illustrate a slider, knob, button, and a final custom shape.

Slider: The slider thumb is constructed using a stretchable polyester mesh, which causes it to snap back to its position in the middle of the box shown in Figure 18b when released. As shown in Figure 15, the displacement sensor is wedge shaped. This causes its height to vary linearly as the slider thumb moves across it.

Knob: We convert rotation into pressure on the displacement sensor using a 3D printed threaded screw with a knob printed on top (Figure 18c). As the knob is turned, it gradually lowers to displace the plunger. The displacement of the plunger is proportional to the amount of rotation.

Button: The pressure-sensing button applies mechanical force to the top of the plunger (Figure 18d). Tension in the textile under the displacement sensor opposes downward motion while allowing the textile to slowly stretch. Once the pressure applied to the plunger is relieved, the mesh retracts and the plunger (and button) return to their initial positions.

Custom Button: As a final example, we demonstrate a custom 3D shape designed around a pressure sensitive button. Using the design primitives of selective stiffening, selective adherence, and mechanical action, we quickly fabricated the inexpensive, "android" illustrated in Figure 1c. Fabric embedded in the android's body supports sensing while giving its head the aesthetic qualities of a bobble-head figure.

Actuated Box with Interactive Control

Textiles can facilitate the creation of functional objects that have variable stiffness and actuation properties. We created a box with a textile-embedded lid that rolls open upon actuation. The lid was printed with a flexible mesh made of polyester fibers and two strings fixed at one end of the lid for actuation (Figure 19). The button uses the fabric-embedded displacement sensor described in the previous section (Figure 18a).

The lid combines several design primitives. Plastic sections placed along the lid's diagonals demonstrate controlled bending and mechanical action *via* selective stiffening, resulting in restricting the lid to rolling. The strings are placed through channels on top and bottom of the mesh and are fixed to one

Figure 18. Textile-embedded input devices– our displacement sensor (a); a retractable slider (b); a knob (c); and a pressure sensitive button (d).

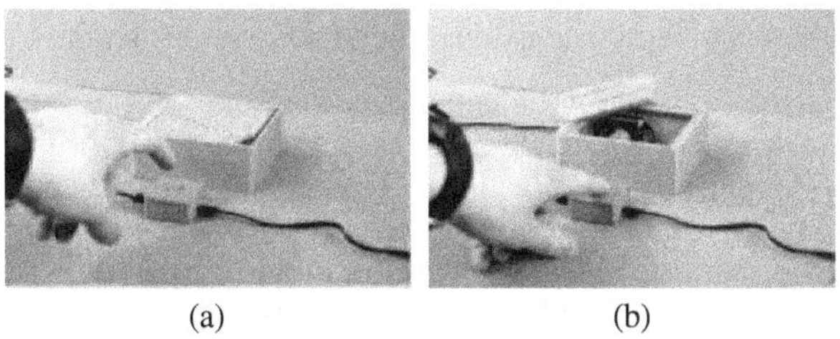

Figure 19. Textile-embedded box fabricated *via* controlled bending. The box lid is composed of a polyester mesh and embedded strings that are printed on to allow the box's lid to roll open and unroll closed.

end of the lid such that pulling one results in rolling and pulling the other results in unrolling.

Six-Panel Fabric Lampshade

Our six-inch (152 mm) cube-shaped lampshade (Figure 20a) was constructed out of five identical panels with a sixth panel modified to accommodate the light bulb (Figure 20b). Each panel was printed separately with short tabs to allow it to be glued to its neighboring panel.

The lampshade demonstrates shell printing. The light bulb mounting point is a type of custom grommet. In addition, the lampshade illustrates reconfiguring *via* trimming and attachment. While we chose to glue the panels together, other options could include a cord through grommets (*e.g.,* Figure 9) or press snaps (*e.g.,* Figure 8) for easy access to the light bulb. Printing each panel took about 30 minutes and overall the lampshade took three hours from start to full assembly. Printing a full 6x6x6 inch plastic cube on our printer, in contrast, would take an order of magnitude longer (12 hours for a cube frame or 29 hours for a closed hollow cube).

Folding Polyhedron

Figure 5 illustrates a dodecahedron designed as a seven-inch (180 mm) flat sheet of pentagonal faces similar to how the shape would be created *via* origami. In its folded form, the shape measures three inches (76 mm) in height. The dodecahedron is secured in its assembled position by small rubber bands wrapped around the pegs visible in Figure 5a.

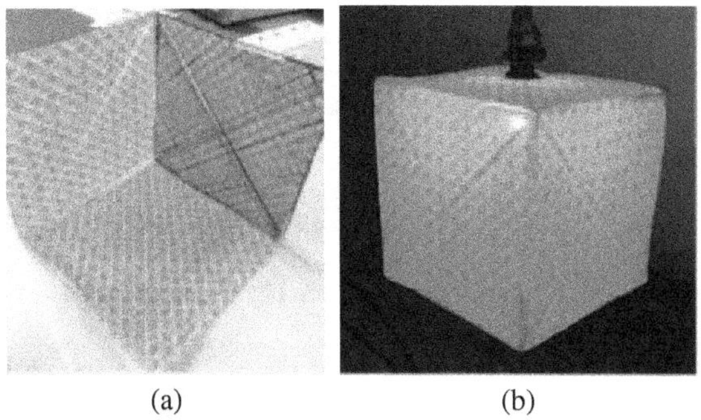

Figure 20. The shell printed lampshade was constructed by gluing together six panels printed onto fabric (a). The top panel was cut to accommodate a light bulb (b).

The dodecahedron demonstrates controlled bending using the technique shown at the bottom of Figure 3. A small gap was left between adjacent sides of the shape to create hinges and plastic was used to limit their bending to be close to the proper dihedral angle for a pentagonal dodecahedron (116.56°).

When fabricating the object, we first printed a layer of plastic for the rigid walls of the dodecahedron. A low-density, flexible nylon fabric was then placed above the surface layer and fixed to the print bed. Printing was resumed and the subsequent layers of plastic printed through the fabric adhering to the plastic beneath.

Crown

We created a wearable, 22 inch (56 cm) crown, shown in Figures 1d and 21. The crown's decorations were printed as series of rectangular sections onto a single large piece of felt that extended beyond print bed.

We preprocessed the 3D model of the crown to separate it into sections. During the printing process, we aligned each section using a laser pointer attached to the print head, completed its printing, and then readjusted the portion of felt on the bed to print the next section. The crown made use of decorative elements, grommets, and a post-processing step of cutting the felt to the outer shape of the plastic.

Flex Watchband

The flexible watchband shown in Figure 22 consists of four types of plastic, two layers of fabric, and a magnetic clasp. It is primarily constructed of layers of NinjaTek SemiFlex filament and two layers of polyester mesh fabric. The fabric is folded up and around at the end of the watchband to strengthen the connection around the metal pin that secures the watchband to the watch.

We constructed the watchband from bars of SemiFlex, with only fabric crossing the gaps between them (leading to controlled bending in the direction around the wrist). The fabric is folded up and around the semi-flex to connect the two layers of fabric and provide extra strength.

The watchband went through several design iterations. Early iterations did not prove mechanically robust and lasted only

Figure 21. A 22 inch crown fabricated on a single sheet of felt by printing in rectangular sections.

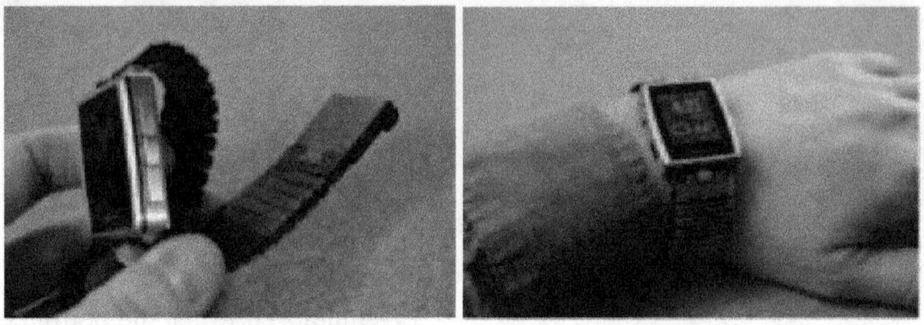

Figure 22. A watchband that supports hinging to a watch face. Stiffeners on the mesh fabric afford flexibility similar to a linked watchband.

a few days before fractures in the brittle material near the attachment pins occurred. We improved robustness where the band connects to the watch—an area with less than 2mm of material between the metal mounting pin and the watch body—by looping fabric around the end of the band, including the metal mounting pins inside the plastic of the band. The fibers of this polyester mesh have higher tensile strength than the printed plastic that they wrap around, and hence substantially strengthen it. The compliant nature of the SemiFlex plastic used for this part of the band eliminates most of the brittleness that would occur with a hard plastic such as PLA.

We used PLA to provide complementary capabilities: this harder material was required for some of the functional parts of the magnetic latch. In addition, we used three separate colors of PLA for aesthetic purposes: translucent to give an overall silver tone to the band, and black and white for a logo on the latch.

After the design improvements outlined above, the band has proven much more robust. It was used daily by one of the authors for about four months (until the watch it was built for began to fail).

LIMITATIONS

Our examples demonstrate the range of possibilities enabled by combining 3D printing and textiles. However this combination also poses some limitations. Some textiles can experience permanent stretching over time. In our custom button, this effect gave the button a "squishier" feel. Our watchband also stretched slightly over the months it had been in use; choosing a different mesh for the interior of future bands may mitigate this issue.

The durability of textiles embedded in 3D printed objects can be limited as well. Towards the end of its testing period, our watchband experienced some fraying of the connecting fabric near non-flexible latch components; an extra reinforcing fabric layer in these problem spots would likely mitigate this issue. Similarly, we discovered durability is an issue for the strings in the actuated box due to them rubbing each time the lid rolls and unrolls. We used braided gel-spun ultra-high molecular weight polyethylene fishing line to address this issue.

Lastly, for printing objects larger than the print bed, a limitation of our approach is the need to leave large (print-head wide) gaps between sections. Without sufficiently sized gaps, printing artifacts may be produced such as those visible in the rightmost side of the crown in Figure 21. Better software support for dividing up an object and printing appropriate fiduciary markers would help with fabrication and reduce printing artifacts.

CONCLUSION

We have demonstrated a capability to control, manipulate and mix fabric with 3D printing. These techniques open a design space that creates new possibilities for rapidly fabricating rigid objects with embedded flexibility and soft materials imbued with functionality.

While we showcase the use of fabric with 3D printing, these techniques are not mutually exclusive with others: different techniques afford different pro and cons. For the watchband, we used a flexible plastic (SemiFlex) because it was soft against the skin and reduced moisture absorption (*e.g.,* from sweat) while fabric could have retained moisture. Similarly, we used fishing line for strings within the actuated box to address durability issues.

Taken as a group, our final examples illustrate the range of new physical objects that are enabled by the use of textiles during 3D printing. Our techniques create objects that can meet a wider range of human needs by encompassing more pleasing materials and larger sizes than typical consumer-grade 3D prints. In addition, the ability to easily enhance arbitrarily shaped physical objects with interactivity opens new avenues for exploration in clothing-based input sensors and the design of compliant mechanisms and other soft functional parts. More broadly, our work allows HCI practitioners to combine the aesthetics and flexibility of textiles with the rigidity and functionality of 3D prints.

ACKNOWLEDGMENTS

We wish to thank Peregrine Hawthorn and Michael Longley at the Rochester Institute of Technology for their valuable fabrication assistance. This work was funded in part by the National Science Foundation under grant NSF IIS-1464377.

This material is based upon work funded and supported by the Department of Defense under Contract No. FA8721-05-C-0003 with Carnegie Mellon University for the operation of the Software Engineering Institute, a federally funded research and development center. [Distribution Statement A] This material has been approved for public release and unlimited distribution. Please see Copyright notice for non-US Government use and distribution. DM-0004343

REFERENCES

1. 3D Systems. 2015. How to create a fabricate 3D tech-style fashion. (2015). https://www.youtube.com/watch?v=qKiHso484vw
2. Lea Albaugh. 2015. Lea, making things: clothes that move: why, and how? (2015). http://www.instamatique.com/blog/clothes-that-move-why-and-how/
3. All3DP. 2016. 27 great 3D printer filament types (a guide). (2016). https://all3dp.com/best-3d-printer-filament-types-pla-abs-pet-exotic-wood-metal/
4. David Baraff and Andrew Witkin. 1998. Large steps in cloth simulation. In *Proceedings of the 25th annual conference on Computer graphics and interactive techniques - SIGGRAPH '98*. ACM Press, New York, New York, USA, 43–54. DOI: http://dx.doi.org/10.1145/280814.280821
5. E.J.W. Barber. 1991. *Prehistoric textiles: The development of cloth in the neolithic and bronze ages with special reference to the aegean.* Princeton University Press. https://books.google.com/books?id=HnSlynSfeEIC
6. Benjamin Bridgens and Matthew Birchall. 2012. Form and function: The significance of material properties in the design of tensile fabric structures. *Engineering Structures* 44 (2012), 1 – 12. DOI: http://dx.doi.org/10.1016/j.engstruct.2012.05.044
7. Robert Bridson, Ronald Fedkiw, and John Anderson. 2002. Robust treatment of collisions, contact and friction for cloth animation. In *Proceedings of the 29th annual conference on Computer graphics and interactive techniques - SIGGRAPH '02*, Vol. 21. ACM Press, New York, New York, USA, 594. DOI: http://dx.doi.org/10.1145/566570.566623
8. I-Ming Chen, Shusong Xing, R. Tay, and Song Huat Yeo. 2005. Many strings attached: from conventional to robotic marionette manipulation. *IEEE Robotics Automation Magazine* 12, 1 (Mar 2005), 59–74. DOI: http://dx.doi.org/10.1109/MRA.2005.1411420
9. Stelian Coros, Bernhard Thomaszewski, Gioacchino Noris, Shinjiro Sueda, Moira Forberg, Robert W. Sumner, Wojciech Matusik, and Bernd Bickel. 2013. Computational Design of Mechanical Characters. *ACM Trans. Graph.* 32, 4, Article 83 (Jul 2013), Article 83, 12 pages. DOI: http://dx.doi.org/10.1145/2461912.2461953
10. Erik D. Demaine and Martin L. Demaine. 2001. Recent results in computational origami. In *Origami^3: Proceedings of the 3rd International Meeting of Origami Science, Math, and Education (OSME 2001).* A K Peters, Monterey, California, 3–16.
11. Stephen Eichhorn, John W.S. Hearle, Mike Jaffe, and Takeshi Kikutani. 2009. *Handbook of textile fibre structure: Natural, regenerated, inorganic and specialist fibres*. Vol. 2. Elsevier.
12. Michael Eisenberg. 2003. Mindstuff educational technology beyond the computer. *Convergence: The International Journal of Research into New Media Technologies* 9, 2 (2003), 29–53.
13. John W.S. Hearle. 1967. The structural mechanics of fibers. In *Journal of Polymer Science Part C: Polymer Symposia*, Vol. 20. Wiley Online Library, 215–251.
14. John W.S. Hearle, Percy Grosberg, and Stanley Backer. 1969. *Structural mechanics of fibers, yarns, and fabrics.* Wiley–Interscience.
15. John W.S. Hearle and William E. Morton. 2008. *Physical properties of textile fibres.* Elsevier.
16. Felix Heibeck, Basheer Tome, Clark Della Silva, and Hiroshi Ishii. 2015. uniMorph: Fabricating thin film composites for shape-changing interfaces. In *Proceedings of the 28th Annual ACM Symposium on User Interface Software & Technology (UIST '15).* ACM, New York, NY, USA, 233–242. DOI: http://dx.doi.org/10.1145/2807442.2807472
17. Scott E. Hudson. 2014. Printing Teddy Bears: A Technique for 3D Printing of Soft Interactive Objects. In *Proceedings of the SIGCHI Conference on Human Factors in Computing Systems (CHI '14).* ACM, New York, NY, USA, 459–468. DOI: http://dx.doi.org/10.1145/2556288.2557338
18. Instructables. 2016. How to 3D print onto fabric. (2016). http://www.instructables.com/id/How-to-3D-Print-Onto-Fabric/
19. Gierad Laput, Xiang 'Anthony' Chen, and Chris Harrison. 2015. 3D printed hair: fused deposition modeling of soft strands, fibers, and bristles. In *Proceedings of the 28th Annual ACM Symposium on User Interface Software & Technology (UIST '15).* ACM, New York, NY, USA, 593–597. DOI: http://dx.doi.org/10.1145/2807442.2807484
20. R. Melnikova, A. Ehrmann, and K. Finsterbusch. 2014. 3D printing of textile-based structures by fused deposition modelling (FDM) with different polymer materials. In *IOP Conference Series: Materials Science and Engineering*, Vol. 62. IOP Publishing, 012018.
21. Jussi Mikkonen, Reetta Myllymäki, Sari Kivioja, Santeri Vanhakartano, and Helena Suonsilta. 2013. Printed material and fabric. *Nordes* 1, 5 (2013).

22. Stefanie Mueller, Sangha Im, Serafima Gurevich, Alexander Teibrich, Lisa Pfisterer, François Guimbretière, and Patrick Baudisch. 2014a. WirePrint: 3D printed previews for fast prototyping. In *Proceedings of the 27th annual ACM Symposium on User Interface Software & Technology (UIST '14)*. ACM, 273–280.

23. Stefanie Mueller, Tobias Mohr, Kerstin Guenther, Johannes Frohnhofen, Kai-Adrian Rollmann, and Patrick Baudisch. 2014b. faBrickation: Fast 3D printing of functional objects by integrating construction kit building blocks. In *CHI '14 Extended Abstracts on Human Factors in Computing Systems (CHI EA '14)*. ACM, New York, NY, USA, 527–530. DOI: http://dx.doi.org/10.1145/2559206.2574779

24. Grace Ngai, Stephen C.F. Chan, Joey C.Y. Cheung, and Winnie W.Y. Lau. 2009. The TeeBoard: An Education-friendly Construction Platform for e-Textiles and Wearable Computing. In *Proceedings of the SIGCHI Conference on Human Factors in Computing Systems (CHI '09)*. ACM, New York, NY, USA, 249–258. DOI: http://dx.doi.org/10.1145/1518701.1518742

25. Simon Olberding, Sergio Soto Ortega, Klaus Hildebrandt, and Jürgen Steimle. 2015. Foldio: Digital fabrication of interactive and shape-changing objects with foldable printed electronics. In *Proceedings of the 28th Annual ACM Symposium on User Interface Software & Technology (UIST '15)*. ACM, New York, NY, USA, 223–232. DOI: http://dx.doi.org/10.1145/2807442.2807494

26. Eujin Pei, Jinsong Shen, and Jennifer Watling. 2015. Direct 3D printing of polymers onto textiles: experimental studies and applications. *Rapid Prototyping Journal* 21, 5 (Aug 2015), 556–571. DOI: http://dx.doi.org/10.1108/RPJ-09-2014-0126

27. Huaishu Peng, Jennifer Mankoff, Scott E. Hudson, and James McCann. 2015. A layered fabric 3D printer for soft interactive objects. In *Proceedings of the 33rd Annual ACM Conference on Human Factors in Computing Systems (CHI '15)*, Vol. 1. ACM Press, New York, New York, USA, 1789–1798. DOI: http://dx.doi.org/10.1145/2702123.2702327

28. Hannah Perner-Wilson, Leah Buechley, and Mika Satomi. 2011. Handcrafting Textile Interfaces from a Kit-of-no-parts. In *Proceedings of the Fifth International Conference on Tangible, Embedded, and Embodied Interaction (TEI '11)*. ACM, New York, NY, USA, 61–68. DOI: http://dx.doi.org/10.1145/1935701.1935715

29. Ivan Poupyrev, Nan-Wei Gong, Shiho Fukuhara, Mustafa Emre Karagozler, Carsten Schwesig, and Karen E. Robinson. 2016. Project Jacquard: Interactive digital textiles at scale. In *Proceedings of the 2016 CHI Conference on Human Factors in Computing Systems (CHI '16)*. ACM, New York, NY, USA, 4216–4227. DOI: http://dx.doi.org/10.1145/2858036.2858176

30. Daniela K. Rosner and Kimiko Ryokai. 2008. Spyn: Augmenting knitting to support storytelling and reflection. In *Proceedings of the 10th International Conference on Ubiquitous Computing (UbiComp '08)*. ACM, New York, NY, USA, 340–349. DOI: http://dx.doi.org/10.1145/1409635.1409682

31. Lilia Sabantina, Franziska Kinzel, Andrea Ehrmann, and Karin Finsterbusch. 2015. Combining 3D printed forms with textile structures-mechanical and geometrical properties of multi-material systems. In *IOP Conference Series: Materials Science and Engineering*, Vol. 87. IOP Publishing, 012005.

32. Ashish Kumar Sen. 2007. *Coated textiles: principles and applications*. Crc Press.

33. Michael J. Sinclair and Kerwin Wang. 2003. Thermal actuator improvements: tapering and folding. In *Proceedings of SPIE - The International Society for Optical Engineering*, Jung-Chih Chiao, Vijay K. Varadan, and Carles CanÂL' (Eds.). 237–251. DOI: http://dx.doi.org/10.1117/12.499129

34. Alexander Teibrich, Stefanie Mueller, François Guimbretière, Robert Kovacs, Stefan Neubert, and Patrick Baudisch. 2015. Patching physical objects. In *Proceedings of the 28th Annual ACM Symposium on User Interface Software & Technology (UIST '15)*. ACM, New York, NY, USA, 83–91. DOI: http://dx.doi.org/10.1145/2807442.2807467

35. Cesar Torres, Tim Campbell, Neil Kumar, and Eric Paulos. 2015. HapticPrint: Designing feel aesthetics for 3D printing. In *Proceedings of the 28th Annual ACM Symposium on User Interface Software & Technology - UIST '15*. ACM Press, New York, New York, USA, 583–591. DOI: http://dx.doi.org/10.1145/2807442.2807492

36. John T. Williams. 2009. *Textiles for cold weather apparel*. Elsevier.

37. Lining Yao, Ryuma Niiyama, Jifei Ou, Sean Follmer, Clark Della Silva, and Hiroshi Ishii. 2013. PneUI: Pneumatically actuated soft composite materials for shape changing interfaces. In *Proceedings of the 26th annual ACM Symposium on User Interface Software & Technology (UIST '13)*. ACM, ACM, 13–22.

WeaveMesh: A Low-Fidelity and Low-Cost Prototyping Approach for 3D Models Created by Flexible Assembly

Ye Tao*, Guanyun Wang*, Caowei Zhang, Nannan Lu, Xiaolian Zhang, Cheng Yao, Fangtian Ying

Zhejiang University, Hangzhou, China

{taoye, guanyun, zhangcw, lunannan, xiaolian, yaoch, yingft}@zju.edu.cn

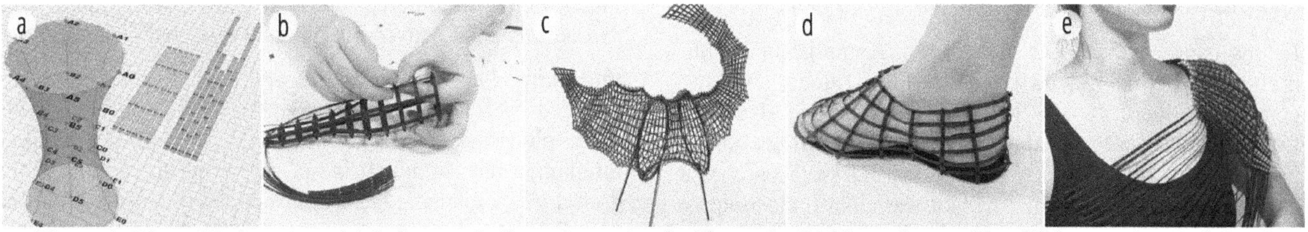

Figure 1. WeaveMesh system. (a) Software platform for customizable mesh; (b) Manual assembly with low-cost material and connectors; (c) Outcome of one test: an abstract sculpture with multiple surfaces; (d) Created a fitted shoe by flexible assembly; (e) Outcome of one test: an interactive cape attached with optical fiber.

ABSTRACT

To meet the increasing requirements of HCI researchers who are prototyping a variety of forms to create novel interfaces under a ubiquitous situation, we present WeaveMesh, a low-fidelity and low-cost rapid prototyping system that produces 3D objects in a mesh structure. Inspired by hand-weaving craft, WeaveMesh supports a highly customizable software platform, which is applicable for simulating and facilitating freeform surface constructions composed of woven lines arranged in a regular grid, which can serve as a guide for easy assembly. In addition, mobilizable connectors are suggested to support flexible assembly, which can be revised, recycled, and reused to facilitate short iterations. Furthermore, compared to common additive and subtractive techniques, WeaveMesh has a better balance between time and material saving. In this paper, we will introduce the system in detail and demonstrate the feasibility of the technique through various 3D models in the area of interactive media, products and architecture.

Author Keywords

Rapid prototyping; low-fidelity fabrication; UV mesh.

ACM Classification Keywords

H.5.2. Information interfaces and presentation (e.g., HCI): User interfaces.

*The first two authors contributed equally to this work.

CHI 2017, May 06 - 11, 2017, Denver, CO, USA

ACM 978-1-4503-4655-9/17/05...$15.00

DOI: http://dx.doi.org/10.1145/3025453.3025699

INTRODUCTION

Common rapid prototyping tools, such as 3D printers and laser cutters, as a way of data-driven production, impel HCI researchers to create digital fabrication methods that are not dependent on machines. A low-fidelity fabrication approach was achieved to speed up all intermediate versions. Unfortunately, the one-off objects fabricated in each version cost actual material waste, and the irreversible process inevitably slowed down design iterations.

We therefore argue that the process of rapid fabrication for quick design iterations is not yet optimal. In other experiences, such as traditional craft, artisans have achieved an efficient method through constant modification during the process of production. In product design, low-fidelity techniques, such as sketching and draft prototyping give designers an easy trial-and-error procedure. This tradeoff is effective in the early design stages, because it encourages designers to try various versions before investing additional resources, thus resulting in superior designs [7]. A similar concept, flexible assembly technology, is applied in industrial production. The reconfigurable assembly method improves adaptability and reduces cost, especially for modern personalized demands [31].

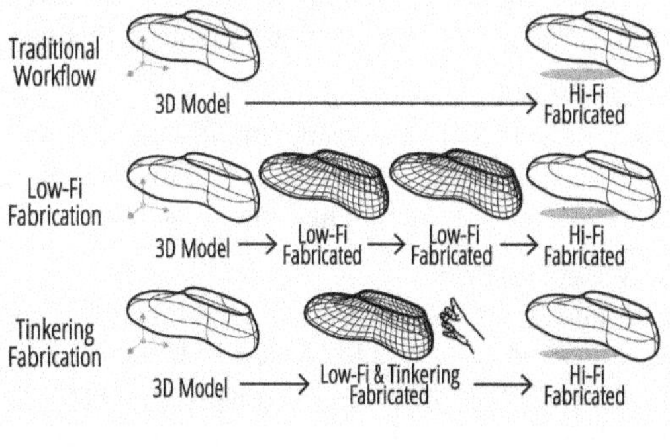

Figure 2. Tinkering fabrication: only one intermedia version is fabricated as fast assembly and manual adjustment.

We argue that the same principle should be applied to rapid prototyping, as concept tinkering can be viewed as a valid and valuable style of engaging with a project [29]. In contrast to the data-driven workflow, in which the 3D model is fabricated followed by data revision in each iteration, manual tinkering gives an intuitive impression to guide users constantly trying out ideas, making adjustments and refinements, and then experimenting with new possibilities until they are ready to fabricate the finished high-fidelity version (Figure 2).

In this paper, we present WeaveMesh (established on our preliminary works [32, 33]) as a novel low-fidelity and low-cost fabrication approach that is not only fast but also fully flexible in terms of assembly in the early stage of the design process. The key idea is to replace the 3D surfaces with a computational UV mesh. The software platform outputs assembly instructions that are marked on widely used materials (e.g., paperboard, pp films, bamboo pieces, etc.) using a cutter machine. Tinkering as a style of making requires manual involvement, such as assembling and modifying, to construct the final prototype. At the same time, mobilizable connectors are suggested to support flexible assembly, which can be revised, recycled, and reused to facilitate short iterations. In short, WeaveMesh system could push different stages of the iteration process:

1) For functional iteration: With low-cost materials, flexible shape attributes, and mesh characteristics, WeaveMesh can be a prototype carrier. For instance, in HCI research, it can be easily combined with other hardware (e.g., in the installation of sensors and actuators, or in combination with optical fiber), so feasibility tests can accelerate the functional iteration process.

2) For concept iteration: The manual assembly provides user behavior and action space, which also leads to the generation of new ideas. For example, users will get feedback from each step when building physical objects through hand working then make decisions, thus increasing their opportunity to propose better design solutions.

3) For digital/accurate iteration: it provides a series of widgets to support the loop from physical to digital for accurate iteration.

We will introduce the system in detail and validate the feasibility through various 3D models later in this paper.

RELATED WORK

The work presented in this paper builds on the notions of personal fabrication, interactive fabrication, rapid fabrication of 3D objects and making objects in meshes.

Personal Fabrication

Personal fabrication devices such as laser cutters and 3D printers allow users to create physical objects rapidly [16]. To lower the entry barrier for nonprofessional users to personal fabrication, a number of HCI researchers have developed new approaches that make the path to prototyping much smoother. For instance, *SketchChair* [30] and *Plushie* [21] allow novice users to customize objects with drawing; Lau et al. [19] presented a furniture-making approach with automatically generating fabricatable parts and connectors from a 3D virtual model. In the study of 3D printing, different approaches have been explored in terms of materials (*xPrint* [35, 36]), modeling methods (*MixFab* [37]), application fields (*ExoSkin* [14]), etc. Generally, researchers have emphasized that personal fabrication is increasingly ubiquitous through the development and availability of new user-friendly and low-cost technologies.

Interactive Fabrication with Craft

Inspired by traditional craft activities which provides real-time physical feedback, Willis et al. [38] proposed interactive fabrication. It is not surprising to see that more digital mediums have been reintroduced to craft and hybrid materials. Amit Zoran's group created a range of projects (*FreeD* [42], *Hybrid Basketry* [41], *The Hybrid Bricolage* [13], etc.) to discuss more about how the new digital techniques contribute to traditional craft during the process of hand-making. In addition, a number of projects demonstrated new ways of combining modern fabrication with material-based craft (e.g., clay [18], wax [26], fabric [11], everyday materials [12]). Like these systems, we draw inspiration from weaving craft to develop WeaveMesh, which allows users to engage in the process of fabrication.

Rapid Fabrication of 3D Objects

In the field of rapid fabrication, several new solutions have been proposed to speed up the process of prototyping based on laser cutters or 3D printers. *faBrickation* [24] uses Lego bricks to replace most of the model volume and only 3D-print regions where high resolution is required. *Platener* [6] follows the same idea by converting the bulk of the volume into laser-cuttable parts while using 3D-printed parts for complex shapes. *LaserOrigami* [23] shows a novel rapid prototyping system that produces 3D objects with a laser cutter by cutting and folding an acrylic sheet. Unlike *Autodesk 123D Make* [2], a rapid prototyping software program that involves simple converting a 3D model into planar slices, *CardBoardiZer* [40] allows users to build foldable and articulable objects using cardboard material in less time. To expand the existing approaches to rapid fabrication for 3D creations, we propose a new molding solution by converting a 3D model into a mesh structure on the surface and further into planar pieces for manual assembly.

Making Objects in Meshes

Previous research has led to a variety of mesh methods for 3D prototyping. *WirePrint* [22] and *On-The-Fly Print* [25] were proposed to print mesh edges directly, saving significant time to give designers a quick preview of 3D models. With the goal of printing 3D wireframes using arbitrary meshes, Wu et al. [39] proposed an algorithm to generate plans for 5DOF printers. For the non-printing fabrication system, Cignoni et al. [8] introduced an innovative method that allows users to produce complex fabricable structures. Instead of converting an existing 3D model to intersecting pieces, *FlatFitFab* [20] enables users to manipulate mesh designs directly from laser-cuttable parts. In addition, *Protopiper* [5] is a handheld fabrication device that allows users to prototype large-scale objects in wireframe mode with plastic tubes. On the commercial side, many design tools have been demonstrated to expand the space of mesh design, such as the handheld 3D printing pen *3Doodler* [1], comprehensive 3D editor *Autodesk 123D Make* [2], and building block toy *Zometool* [4].

On the other hand, objects made from meshes may provide a better aesthetic experience. Many artists, such as Cooper [10] and Taylor [34], consider wire meshes as a popular medium in abstract and figural sculptural art design. Garg et al. [15] developed a computational approach for designing similar wire mesh structures with temporary wooden grids. In our work, we seek a middle ground of making mesh objects efficiently while ensuring they are aesthetically pleasing.

WEAVEMESH SYSTEM

The system is inspired by the traditional hand-weaving molding technique, which is characterized by woven strips that cover the surface instead of filling the entity. Compared to common 3D printing, the method relies on the twisted structure of the mutual restraint force of the woven strips, not the adhesive properties of the material. This implementation is what ensures the structure's flexibility. The weaving characteristic and tinkering with indigenous materials also inspired us to expand the possibilities of weaving mesh structures in modern manufacturing technology.

WeaveMesh contains a software platform developed on top of Rhino and Grasshopper plugins [17] and manual-aided hardware connectors. WeaveMesh is designed with a few goals in mind:

1) The system needs to ensure an easy and accessible technique for non-experts according to the specification.

2) The software platform should provide highly customizable tools that can accommodate different shapes, such as shape segmentation and joints, resolution definitions, strip sizes and mesh assembly specification.

3) The technique should provide conditions for tinkering to take full advantage of the flexibility of mesh structures and to facilitate short iterations.

4) The physical prototype needs to be easily and rapidly made out of low-cost, accessible materials and tools, especially at the early conceptual design stages.

Workflow

In order to achieve the above mentioned design goals, WeaveMesh was created to produce customizable and low-fidelity mesh prototypes directly from digital 3D models. As shown in Figure 3, the workflow unfolds as follows: The user (1) inputs a desired 3D model in rhino software (Figure 3a), (2) customizes the mesh parameters with one surface once, such as quantity, direction, and width (Figure 3b), (3) develops the two-direction strip patterns with reference points ready to be cut (Figure 3c), and then (4) hand assembles (Figure 3d) and tangibly modifies (Figure 4) the prototype simultaneously to complete the iteration before finishing the high-fidelity version.

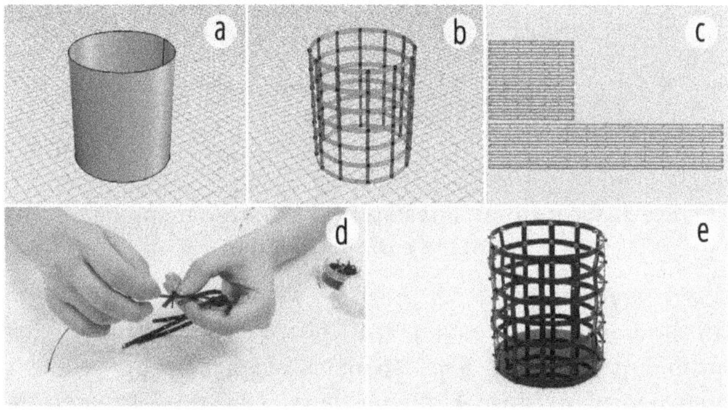

Figure 3. WeaveMesh workflow illustrated by a cup case: (a) creating a model in rhino software, (b) converting it into a mesh structure in Grasshopper, (c) simulating 2D pattern before cutting, (d) assembling, (d) obtaining first-version prototype.

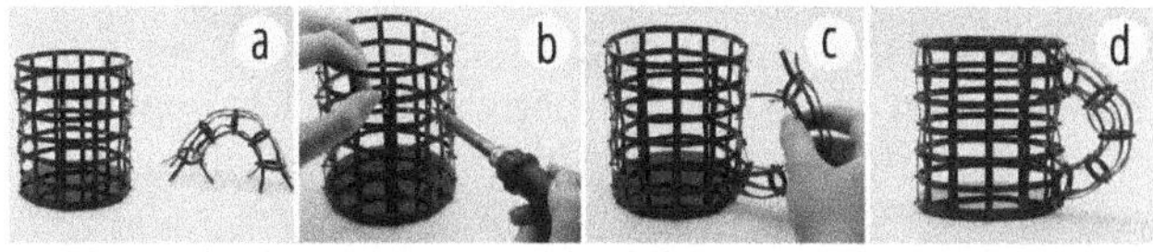

Figure 4. Tinker process: (a) adding one part. (b) making holes, (c) connecting two parts, (d) obtaining second-version prototype.

Customizable Mesh and Software

Here, the implementation of first-edition WeaveMesh software is performed to analyze the UV mesh mapping of a single surface of a 3D model separately.

UV mesh mapping

The UV mapping is operated on Grasshopper in Rhino software. It transfers the surface into two lists of curves, and the curves are the lists of the points. To avoid confusion, we name the two lists of curves M and N respectively. As shown in Figure 5, we do the UV mapping in the cup as an example. The parameters for M and N are 6 and 5. Therefore, we get two curve lists as follows:

M = {	N ={
(A0, B0, C0, D0, E0),	(A0, A1, A2, A3, A4, A0),
(A1, B1, C1, D1, E1),	(B0, B1, B2, B3, B4, B0),
(A2, B2, C2, D2, E2),	(C0, C1, C2, C3, C4, C0),
(A3, B3, C3, D3, E3),	(D0, D1, D2, D3, D4, D0),
(A4, B4, C4, D4, E4),	(E0, E1, E2, E3, E4, E0)}
(A0, B0, C0, D0, E0)}	

Point A0 can be initialized with any point on one of the edges in Figure 5b, and then the other points are initialized after A0.

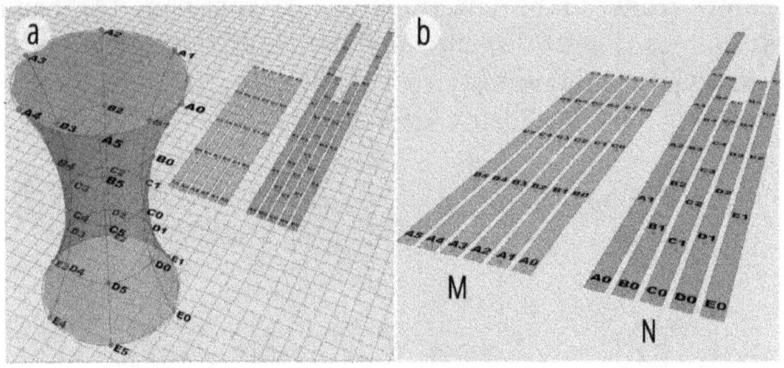

Figure 5. WeaveMesh interface: (a) UV mesh mapping, (b) 2D pattern and specification.

Vertices property

In the traditional weaving craft process, one of the biggest problems faced by non-experts is staggering up or down between two strips. Although there is no need to keep the weaving method in the actual assembly process benefit by connecting components, we retain and extend the "one warp, one weft" [9] characteristic in the software to make it applicable to hand-weaving methods, facilitate manual operation, and reduce the risk of errors in connecting a number of UV strips. Based on UV mapping, we assign each point an upper/lower property and set them opposite to each other. Here is a pseudocode of the varying diamond pattern:

```
Input: the 2-D arrays M and N
Mark the point A0 as UPPER point
Let p be the point A0
for each neighbor point np of p with no mark do
        mark np as the opposite to p
        let p be the point np
        mark the corresponding points in N as the opposite
```

2D pattern and specification

Since the UV strips are separate similar ones that are difficult to pick out in the manual process, we arranged for the order number in 2D pattern generation.

As the UV mesh map shows, the curves were automatically generated in two groups, M and N, and we straightened the curves without changing their lengths. As shown in Figure 5b, we put the lines on the coordinate plane in the order that they follow in M and N respectively. The alphabetical and numerical marks on the points of the curves map to the lines correspondingly. The points that share the same mark connect together, for example the B2 point of M and the B2 of N.

In manual work, users can fix group M first, rotate group N counterclockwise 90 degrees, overlap the M and N at right angles, and finally connect the corresponding vertices of the two groups together (Figure 5b).

Customizable tools

We offer tools to customize the parameters of the strips, such as the quantity and size of the UV strips and points (Figure 6).

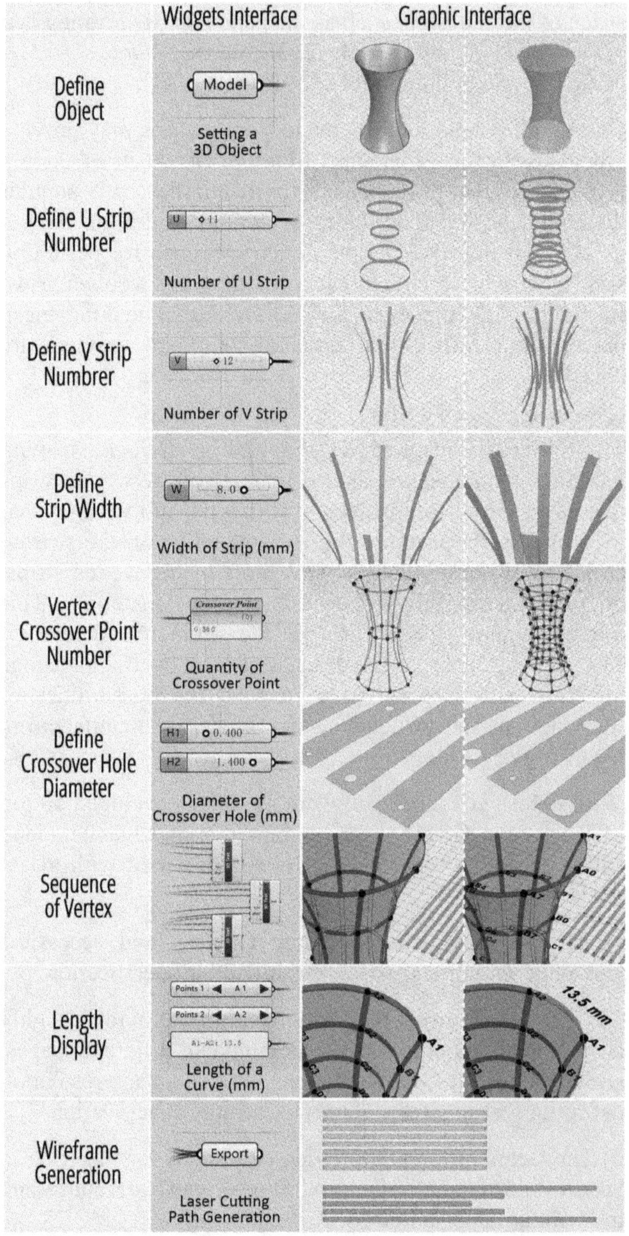

Figure 6. Customizable tools in WeaveMesh software.

Hardware

The hardware system includes a machine tool and connecting components. The machine tool is used to mark the reference points (i.e. apex crossed by UV strips) on the material. In our case, we use a laser cutter that help efficiently convert the digital patterns into flat prototypes. Otherwise, die-cutter, milling cutter, or hand cutter can be used.

Components are connected to fix UV strips at each apex position. As Figure 7a shows, it can across and stuck two strips together by the structure of thin middle and thick on both ends. In our case, we use low-cost earrings ($1 one hundred) or invisible fastenings ($6 one hundred) as the connecting components that can be used repeatedly and easily purchased.

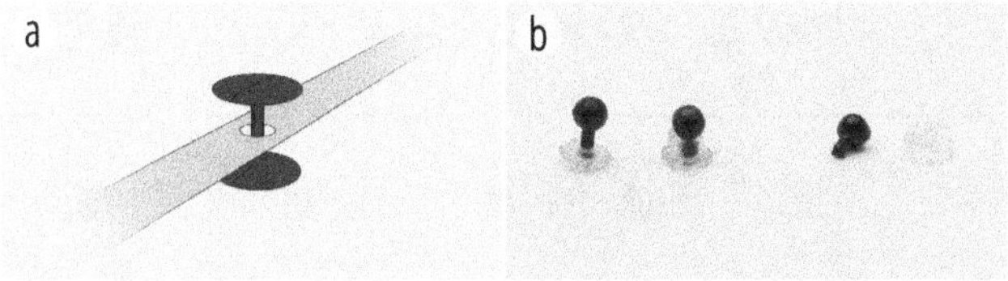

Figure 7. (a) The structure of connecting components; (b) The low-cost earring connectors used in this paper.

EXTENDING SYSTEM

In this section, we present extensions to our basic approach that allow us to handle additional scenarios.

Structure Library

A four-corner mesh structure is more flexible compared to a triangular mesh structure, especially when the vertices can be rotated. In tangible operating practice, we suggest that it can serve as a transformative and moveable model function. Here, we summarize two common structural examples of the activities for quick use.

Scalable structure: This can be applied for distance conversion. As Figure 8 shows, the mesh structure is built on a right circular cylinder composed of the weft rings and vertical warp strips. When the weft rings rotate, the warp strips tilt in the same direction; thus, the spaces between the wefts are reduced to achieve a shrink state. Reverse rotation, similarly, achieve a stretching state.

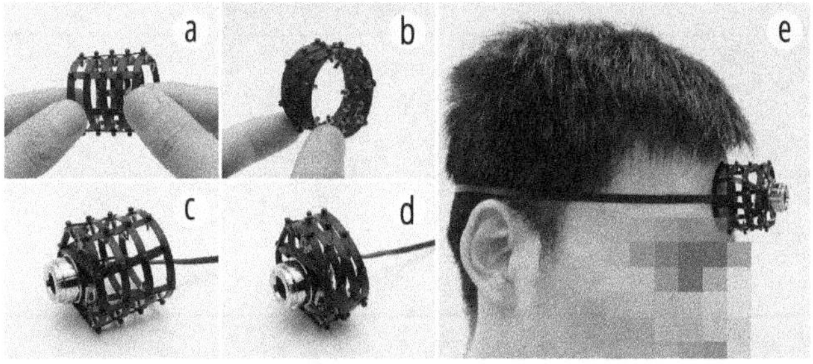

Figure 8. Scalable structure: (a) a stretching state, (b) a shrink state, (c, d and e) an application: a headset camera.

Belt clasp structure: This can be applied for dimensionality conversion, especially for wearable media areas. Like a belt, it is one strip with spaced distribution points, which can achieve one circular ring belts on different scales (Figure 9). Users can quickly choose the data file with the target size in the system.

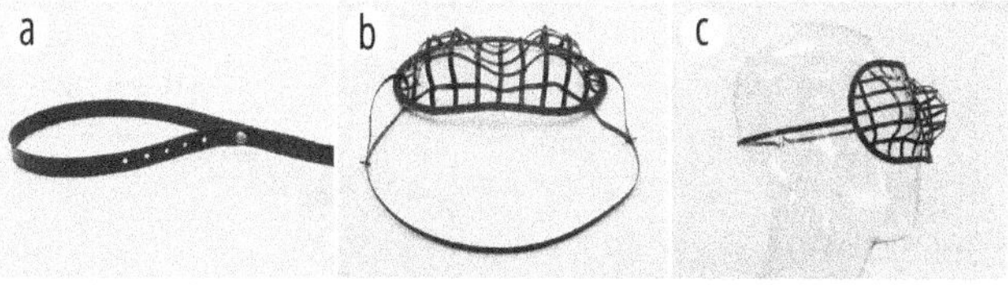

Figure 9. Belt clasp structure: (a) the belt, (b and c) an application: a blinder.

Material Options

This method is suitable for easy-to-cut material with elasticity and toughness properties. The elasticity guarantees curved surfaces in the actual model, because the mesh structure is built on the original model. It also requires a certain toughness that can support three-dimensional shapes. Due to immediate changes in the modeling process, the material should be easy to cut.

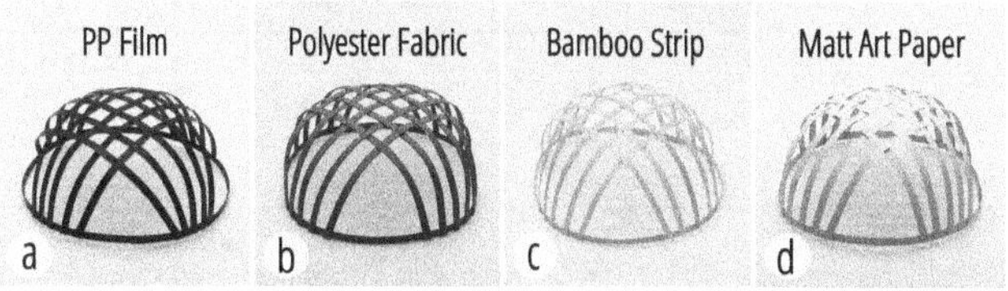

Figure 10. The candidate materials: (a) 0.3mm Thick Polypropylene (PP) Film; (b) 0.4mm Thick Polyester Fabric; (c) 0.25mm Thick Bamboo Strip; (d) 200g Matt Art Paper

The candidate materials include everything from natural materials to synthetic materials, but they should be inexpensive and as thin as paper. Figure 10 highlights the available materials that we have preliminary tested in UV mesh structures. As shown in Figure 10a, PP film, also known as polypropene, is used in a wide variety of applications including packaging and labeling, textiles, and reusable containers of various types. In the experiments, we selected it as the main material, because it has all the relevant properties of candidate materials with high strength, and can be easily and cheaply purchased (less than $3 one square meters).

EXPERIMENT AND RESULTS

The 0.45mm-thick PP film was used as the experimental material, and it is shown in Table 1 (on the next page) after the 2D pattern is generated and cut. For the overall cutting setup, we used a relatively higher speed (1000mm/s) and lower force (57 grams) laser cutter, and almost all the experimental items could be completed in less than 10 min of cutting. Our system requires manual user involvement, such as assembling and modifying to construct the final prototype.

Prototypical Results

Table 1 shows our prototypical results using 9 demonstrated examples. According to the WeaveMesh results on a number of 3D objects, our creative software platform allows more improvements for quick and easy assembly.

Name	Model	Prototype	Resolution (U × V Quantity)	Quantity of Vertex	Time Assembly (mm : ss)	Volume (L × W × H mm)	Pattern Area (L × W mm)	Material Utilization
(a) 2.5D Single Peak		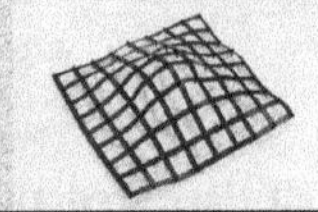	9 × 9	81	15:56	140 × 140 × 38	171 × 90	92 %
(b) 2.5D Twin Peaks	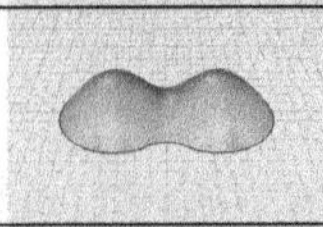	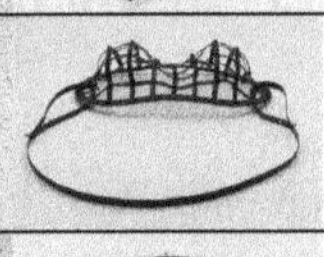	5 × 9	45	10:06	154 × 94 × 28	209 × 56	63 %
(c) Fat Cylinder		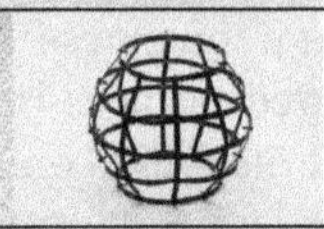	5 × 10	50	12:08	108 × 108 × 80	341 × 60	89 %
(d) Thin Cylinder		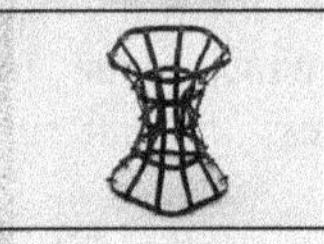	5 × 10	50	12:38	70 × 70 × 80	224 × 60	86 %
(e) Arch Cylinder	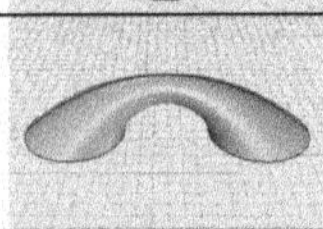	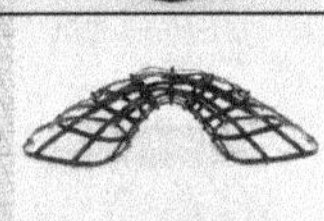	9 × 8	72	15:24	216 × 76 × 46	282 × 72	67 %
(f) Circular Ring	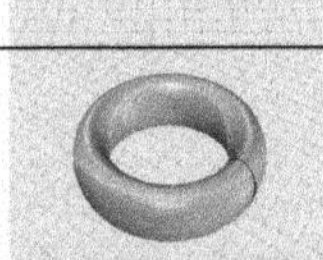	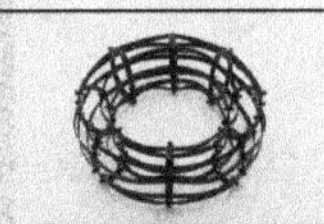	8 × 8	64	20:16	106 × 106 × 36	382 × 60	88 %
(g) Two-Part Cap			Top: 7 × 14 Bottom: 15 × 14	308	78:58	215 × 190 × 230	643 × 116	64 %
(h) Three-Part Pot		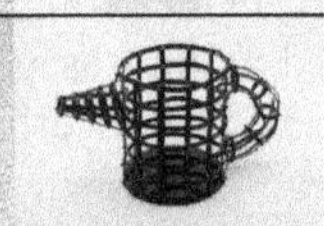	Left: 6 × 5 Middle: 7 × 12 Right: 6 × 5	144	41:22	177 × 90 × 100	287 × 95	88 %
			12 × 13	156	35:02	50 × 50 × 180	192 × 96	83 %
(i) Bottle Cylinder			10 × 8	80	20:24	50 × 50 × 180	192 × 72	84 %
	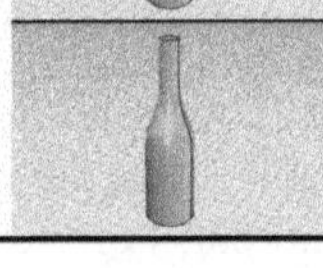	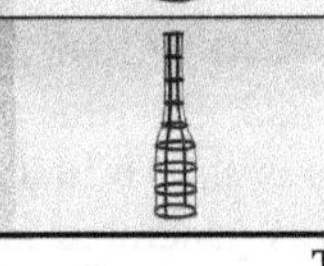	8 × 4	32	08:29	50 × 50 × 180	192 × 48	96 %

Table 1. Experimental case collection.

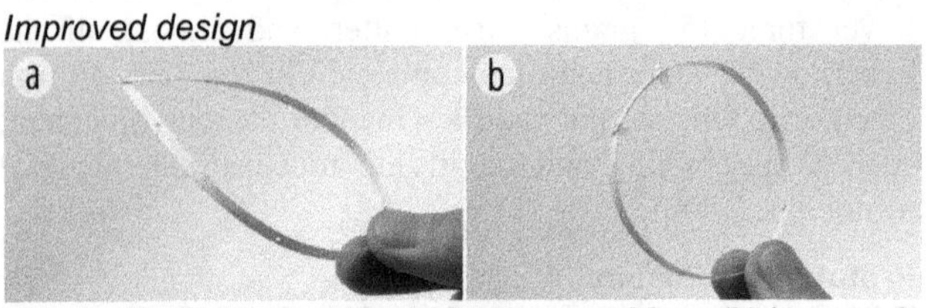

Figure 11. Circle structure: (a) corner problem, (b) improved design with two overlap points.

Circle structure: This is an essential part of the torus, which requires each strip to be connected end to end. In the actual connecting process, we found that corners often appeared when connecting the circle by one point of intersection, as shown in Figure 11. Therefore, we improved the generated 2D pattern by adding a point n+1 to each strip (n represents the last point of the original strip), making the circle structure fixed in a ring.

Figure 12. The improved 2D pattern was cut on the material.

2D pattern arrangement: This relates to the legibility of specification and the material utilization. We improved the arrangement so that the automatic generation pattern was divided into groups, and the groups of strips connected with each other without gaps (Figure 12). The related figure notation is also automatically generated.

Model resolution

In WeaveMesh, the user can intuitively set the resolution, because the software can simulate the UV mapping on the 3D model in real time while setting the quantity of UV strips. Meanwhile, the quantity of UV strips determines the quantity of vertices, the assembly time and material consumed correspondingly. In Table 1i, we tested the bottle model with three different resolution levels, R_l, R_m, and R_h, to provide a reference (R_l represents relatively low fidelity, R_m represents medium fidelity, and R_h represents relatively high fidelity).

Time Evaluation

In order to understand the construction efficiency using our system, we studied the relationship between the quantity of vertices and the speed of assembly of our 10 demonstrated prototypes (for more statistic see Table 1). Our experimental results showed that the assembly time is proportional to the quantity of vertices, which should be set at the optimal quantity of 50 to 360 for an item-sized model and take 12 to 90 minutes in manual assembly. The estimated time would be appeared in the software with the quantity of vertices calculate by 15 seconds for one vertex under comprehensive factors.

Material Evaluation

To speed up the transformation of the reference point from the vector data to the actual material, we selected planar material that can be cut by a laser cutter. All the target shapes were long strips that could be seamlessly arranged, thus significantly increasing material utilization compared to other irregular shapes. Table 1 shows the statistics on volume, material area, and utilization. Our experimental results showed that the material utilization appears in the range of 60% to 96%.

Usability Discussion and Comparison

Using WeaveMesh, the user is able to customize a 3D model through the choice of resolutions, quickly fabricate the pattern using cutters on demand, and complete the model through simple manual assembly and modification with connectors. It is fast and user friendly as users only need to load the digital 3D model and specify the parameters, and then the system generates the 2D patterns ready for cutting and assembly.

The selection of PP film as our building material offers accessibility to novice users. PP film and other similar sheet-like materials are low-cost everyday material that users are familiar with and can be easily accessed by novice users. Compared with other materials, such as acrylic, sheets can be cut by almost all cutting tools to support timely tinkering. The objects can be easily adjusted and enhanced by using scissors, soldering irons and components to cut, make holes and attach other objects or decorative materials (e.g., electronics, LEDs, and optical fibers). Tinkering with objects generated by WeaveMesh and other objects has multiple benefits for both learning and expression [27] as it invites broader participation and deepens the learning outcomes by allowing for a range of new solutions.

In order to better position the approach in practice, we further compared WeaveMesh with two common data-driven methods, additive and subtractive techniques, which have been widely used in the prototyping field of HCI research. We herein carefully compare the workflow, ease of interaction, fabrication statistics, and final prototypical results using the interlocked slices of Autodesk 123D Make (Table 2a) and 3D printer (Table 2b) and our WeaveMesh (Table 2c). The bracelet model was selected for all three methods with identical scales (10cm x 10cm x 4cm) and comparable resolution.

Approach	Prototype	Time of Preparation	Time of Assembly	Material Utilization
(a) Interlocked Slices	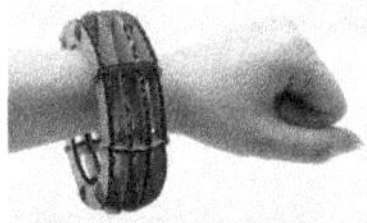	5min (Laser Cutting)	5min	18 %
(b) 3D Printing	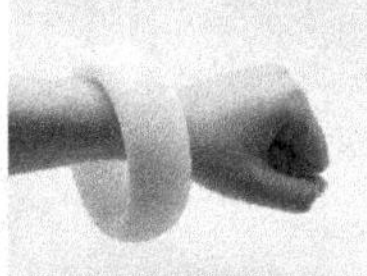	14h 50min (or 1h 45min)	0min	100 %
(c) WeaveMesh	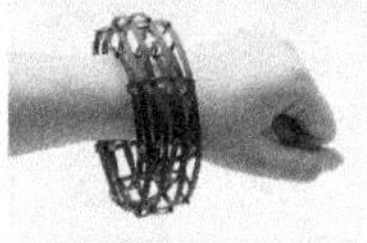	2min (Laser Cutting)	20min	88 %

Table 2. A bracelet case was fabricated respectively by (a) interlocked slices, (b) 3D printing, and (c) WeaveMesh.

In Autodesk 123D Make, the user is allowed to quickly manipulate the total number and orientation of planar sections with slots. We created the bracelet model with the same resolution as WeaveMesh in quantity of U and V, 4 and 8. In the 2D pattern, we found that the Autodesk 123D Make system generated regions with multiple shapes with large spare areas, which led to 82% wasted leftover material. In the 3D printing system, we used a general 3D printer with the Fused Deposition Modelling (FDM) [28] method by heating plastic material. It achieved almost 100% material utilization. However, it took in total 14 hours and 50 min to print the bracelet. As Mueller et al. presented a low-fi fabrication method can be 8.5 times faster [22], a 3D wireframe of the bracelet would take about 1 hour and 45 min. Our method, WeaveMesh required in total 22 min to fabricate with 88% material utilization. WeaveMesh was in the middle in terms of time and material consumption, provided a surface composition without occupied thickness, and exerted a more flexible space in manual modeling. In addition, the users needed dexterity and patience to keep track of the large number of individual parts, their locations and sequence for assembly.

APPLICATION

To demonstrate WeaveMesh, we now present three application examples of custom-fabricated objects. They instantiate diverse dimensions of the design space and demonstrate the potential for applications in interaction design, architectural design, and ergonomics.

Interactive Fashion Design

Technology of interaction has been increasingly integrated into fashion design. For instance, *Caress of the Gaze* [3] was created as a 3D printed garment that detects and responds to the gaze of others. To show how WeaveMesh will contribute to fashion design with interactive technology, we assembled a cape in 1.5 hours (Figure 13a). Furthermore, we weaved optical fibers within holes from the mesh and set up a sensing system with an optic PPG sensor. The pulse data was converted to the LED's color signal shown with optical fibers. Figure 13d and Figure 13e depict the color expression with heartbeat data during relaxation and a deep-breathing exercise.

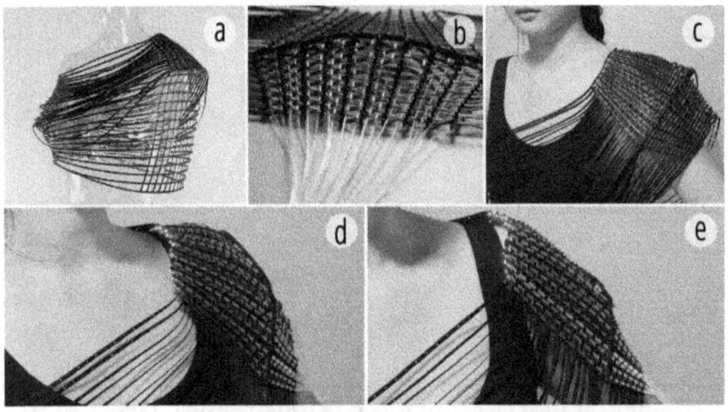

Figure 13. An interactive cape was created using WeaveMesh as a support texture for optical fiber.

Building Models and Art Works

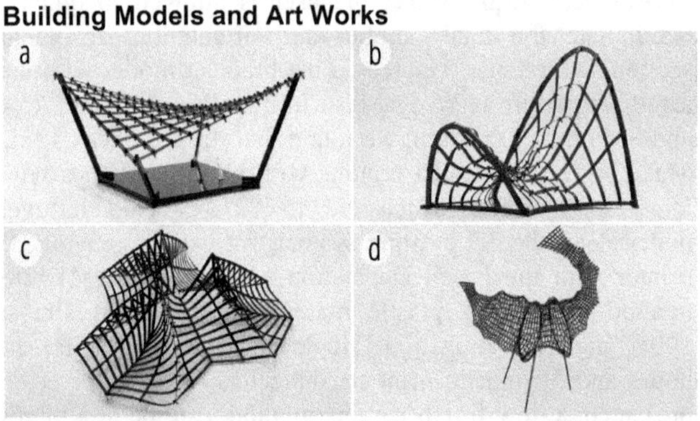

Figure 14. Surface composition in four cases was illustrated in different ways using WeaveMesh: (a, b) single-surface supported by stiff acrylic; (c, d) multiple surfaces connected with each other.

With the property of mesh, WeaveMesh can be used as a new approach with unique aesthetic characteristics to make models for architecture and art. We have prototyped three buildings and one art work with different surface designs. An independent surface was fabricated as the roof, which provided with adaptability and flexibility (Figure 14a, b), while a tent model was composed of multiple surfaces (Figure 14c). A large-scale sculpture was assembled with multiple surfaces (Figure 14d).

Industrial Design

Through this application, we intend to demonstrate that WeaveMesh is a quick method of enabling users to sense the physical size of virtual models during the design process. In addition, it speeds up the iteration process with a fast trial-and-error procedure. We designed a 3D shoe model as shown in Figure 15a and then made the physical object with a mesh upper and cardboard sole in equal proportion (we assembled the shoe's upper in around 17 minutes and the joint upper with sole in 8 minutes) (Figure 15b). It was found that the heel part of this shoe was a little small when a girl tried it on. We disassembled and expanded the strips of the heel part until it fitted well, which took 5 minutes (Figure 15c,d). In the following steps, we measured the length of the expanded stripes between two identified points (Figure 15g), while the 3D model curves were modified to correspond to the physical lengths with length display widget (Figure 6), then generated the final model (Figure 15h).

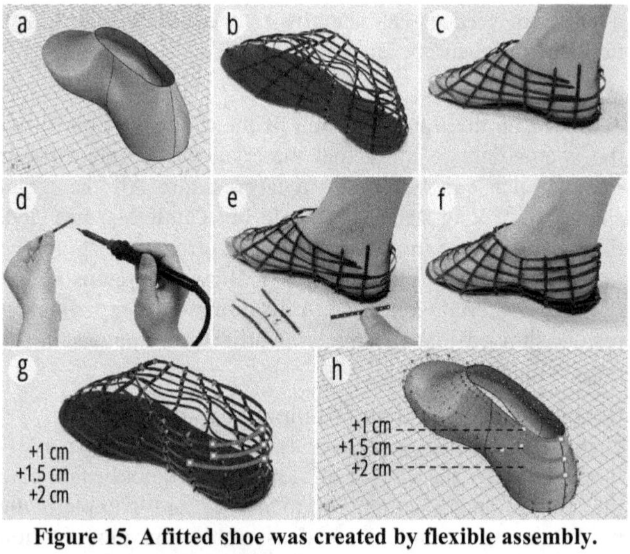

Figure 15. A fitted shoe was created by flexible assembly.

DISCUSSION, BENEFITS, AND LIMITATIONS

In WeaveMesh, the workflow can be operated as 3D-2D-3D (3D modeling in digital software, convert the model to 2D meshes' strips, and assemble the 2D strips to 3D physical model). The goal of WeaveMesh is supportive for early prototyping and iterative design.

To make our approach applicable to a wide range of users, we demonstrated how to create the specifications and shown that users can easily learn how to assemble and tinker with both dynamic and static models. For example, when a HCI researcher is willing to make an interactive cape (Figure 13) to inquire into the deep relationship between light and emotion, WeaveMesh provides a familiar workflow: 3D-2D-3D; if an artist has a higher aesthetic requirement, WeaveMesh achieves a desirable artistic effect with smooth curves or mesh patterns (Figure 14); when an industrial designer intends to design a pair of shoes with suitable size, WeaveMesh speeds up the iteration process with a fast trial-and-error procedure (Figure 15).

Conversely, our approach is not suitable for advanced design stages. For instance, when users need to test their design's physical strength, or objects are required to perform mechanical functions. In addition, WeaveMesh is limited in its ability to recognize the surface normal, that is, some double-sided surfaces rely on manual operation to determine the direction (Figure 16).

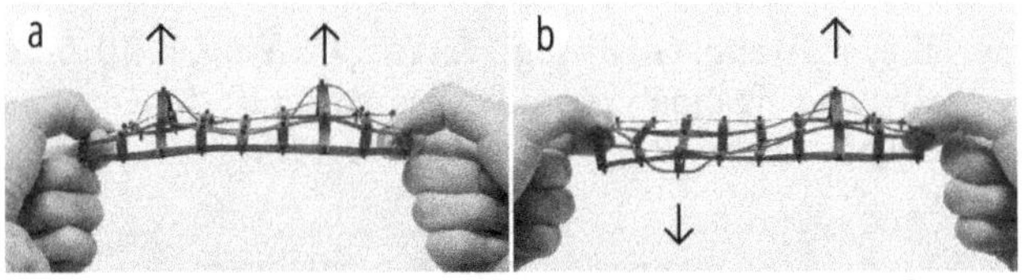

Figure 16. Limitation in recognizing double-sided surfaces.

For the formation of the shape, WeaveMesh can achieve 2.5D surface, cylinder, ring body and their variants. It is limited in large curvature of surface, such as the ring body (Figure 17), the top U strip of the ring cannot stick on the V strips because it will bend V strips at right angles to perpendicular direction. In such cases, it can be formed at the less than 45 degrees angle benefiting from the elasticity of material. However, a bigger angle would cause a bigger error on surface.

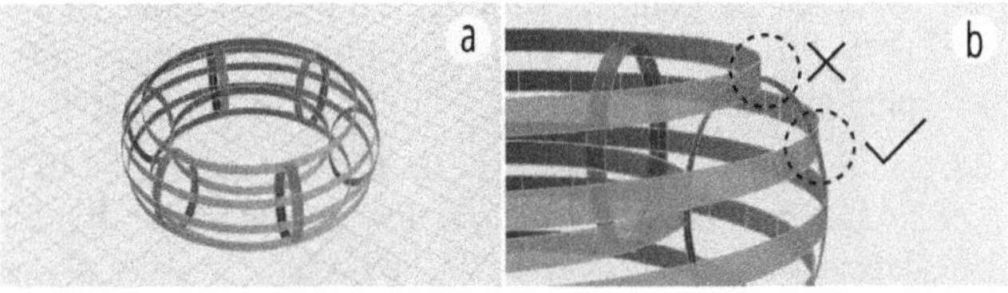

Figure 17. Limitation in prototyping a large curvature of a surface.

CONCLUSION AND FUTURE WORK

In this paper, we proposed a novel approach to low-fidelity 3D prototyping, i.e., covering a filled model and guided with a UV mesh map to enable easy manual assembly. Our experiment and evaluation showed that this approach could be easily operated and has a better balance between time and material saving, which makes it even more affordable for users to tinker and iterate.

Currently, we use a general UV mapping algorithm in which UV mapping is arranged homogeneously, thus limiting the restoration of big complex differences in a surface. For future work, a more advanced algorithm could separate a complex surface into different pieces to generate varied accuracy meshes that will better match the shape of 3D model. In addition, we will discuss more about room-size models and the material requirements for scaling up, such as thick and relatively flexible materials (e.g. bamboo strips in Fig.10) with more width sizes and bamboo weaving architecture as a reference. Certainly, more experiments on material selection, mesh location, connection, etc. are required.

ACKNOWLEDGMENTS

The authors thank all the reviewers for providing valuable insights and suggestions that have helped in substantially improving this paper, as well as all volunteers for general support. This project is supported by the State Key Program of National Natural Science of China (Grant No. 61332017), National Key Technologies R&D Program (Grant No. 2015BAF14B01).

REFERENCES

1. *3Doodler*. Available from: http://the3doodler.com/.
2. *Autodesk 123D Make*. Available from: http://www.123dapp.com/make.
3. *Caress of the gaze*. Available from: http://behnazfarahi.com/caress-of-the-gaze/.
4. *Zometool*. Available from: http://www.zometool.com/.
5. Agrawal, H., Umapathi, U., Kovacs, R., Frohnhofen, J., Chen, H.-T., Mueller, S., Baudisch, P. 2015. Protopiper: Physically Sketching Room-Sized Objects at Actual Scale. *Proc. of UIST 2015*, 427-436.
6. Beyer, D., Gurevich, S., Mueller, S., Chen, H.-T., Baudisch, P. 2015. Platener: Low-fidelity fabrication of 3D Objects by substituting 3D print with laser-cut plates. *Proc. of CHI 2015*, 1799-1806.
7. Buxton, B. 2010. *Sketching user experiences: getting the design right and the right design*. Morgan Kaufmann.
8. Cignoni, P., Pietroni, N., Malomo, L., Scopigno, R. 2014. Field-aligned mesh joinery. *ACM Transactions on Graphics (TOG) 33*, 11.
9. Collier, A.M. 1970. *A handbook of textiles*. Pergamon Press.
10. Cooper, R. *Shadow sculpture*. Available from: http://www.randycooperart.com.
11. Devendorf, L., Lo, J., Howell, N., Lee, J.L., Gong, N.-W., Karagozler, M.E., Fukuhara, S., Poupyrev, I., Paulos, E., Ryokai, K. 2016. I don't Want to Wear a Screen: Probing Perceptions of and Possibilities for Dynamic Displays on Clothing. *Proc. of CHI 2016*, 6028-6039.
12. Devendorf, L., Ryokai, K. 2015. Being the Machine: Reconfiguring Agency and Control in Hybrid Fabrication. *Proc. of CHI 2015*, 2477-2486.
13. Efrat, T.A., Mizrahi, M., Zoran, A. 2016. The Hybrid Bricolage-Bridging Parametric Design with Craft through Algorithmic Modularity. *Proc. of CHI 2016*, 5984-5995.
14. Gannon, M., Grossman, T., Fitzmaurice, G. 2016. ExoSkin: On-Body Fabrication. *Proc. of CHI 2016*, 5996-6007.

15. Garg, A., Sageman-Furnas, A.O., Deng, B., Yue, Y., Grinspun, E., Pauly, M., Wardetzky, M. 2014. Wire Mesh Design. *ACM Transactions on Graphics (TOG) 33*, 66.
16. Gershenfeld, N. 2008. *Fab: the coming revolution on your desktop--from personal computers to personal fabrication*. Basic Books.
17. Grasshopper. Available from: http://www.grasshopper3d.com/.
18. Jones, M.D., Seppi, K., Olsen, D.R. 2016. What you Sculpt is What you Get: Modeling Physical Interactive Devices with Clay and 3D Printed Widgets. *Proc. of CHI 2016*, 876-886.
19. Lau, M., Ohgawara, A., Mitani, J., Igarashi, T. 2011. Converting 3D furniture models to fabricatable parts and connectors. *ACM Transactions on Graphics (TOG) 30*, 85.
20. McCrae, J., Umetani, N., Singh, K. 2014. FlatFitFab: interactive modeling with planar sections. *Proc. of UIST 2014*, 13-22.
21. Mori, Y., Igarashi, T. 2007. Plushie: an interactive design system for plush toys. *Proc. of ACM Transactions on Graphics (TOG)*, 45.
22. Mueller, S., Im, S., Gurevich, S., Teibrich, A., Pfisterer, L., Guimbretière, F., Baudisch, P. 2014. WirePrint: 3D printed previews for fast prototyping. *Proc. of UIST 2014*, 273-280.
23. Mueller, S., Kruck, B., Baudisch, P. 2013. LaserOrigami: laser-cutting 3D objects. *Proc. of CHI 2013*, 2585-2592.
24. Mueller, S., Mohr, T., Guenther, K., Frohnhofen, J., Baudisch, P. 2014. faBrickation: fast 3D printing of functional objects by integrating construction kit building blocks. *Proc. of CHI 2014*, 3827-3834.
25. Peng, H., Wu, R., Marschner, S., Guimbretière, F. 2016. On-The-Fly Print: Incremental Printing While Modelling. *Proc. of CHI 2016*, 887-896.
26. Peng, H., Zoran, A., Guimbretière, F.V. 2015. D-Coil: A Hands-on Approach to Digital 3D Models Design. *Proc. of CHI 2015*, 1807-1815.
27. Peppler, K. 2013. STEAM-Powered Computing Education: Using E-Textiles to Integrate the Arts and STEM. *Computer 46*, 38-43.
28. Prajapati, D., Nandwana, S., Aggarwal, V. Fused Deposition Modelling.
29. Resnick, M., Rosenbaum, E. 2013. Designing for tinkerability. *Design, make, play: Growing the next generation of STEM innovators*, 163-181.
30. Saul, G., Lau, M., Mitani, J., Igarashi, T. 2011. SketchChair: an all-in-one chair design system for end users. *Proc. of TEI 2011*, 73-80.
31. Spinadel, P., Fugger, E. 1989. The technology approach to flexible assembly. *Assembly Automation 9*, 195-199.
32. Tao, Y., Lu, N., Zhang, C., Wang, G., Yao, C., Ying, F. 2016. CompuWoven: A Computer-Aided Fabrication Approach to Hand-Woven Craft. *Proc. of CHI 2016 Extended Abstracts*, 2328-2333.
33. Tao, Y., Wang, G., Zhang, X., Yao, C., Ying, F. 2015. A weaving creation system for bamboo craft-design collaborations. *Proc. of SIGGRAPH Asia 2015 Posters*, 3.
34. Taylor, N. *Wire mesh sculpture*. Available from: http://www.nikkitaylorsculpture.co.uk.
35. Wang, G., Yao, L., Wang, W., Ou, J., Cheng, C.-Y., Ishii, H. 2016. xPrint: A Modularized Liquid Printer for Smart Materials Deposition. *Proc. of CHI 2016*, 5743-5752.
36. Wang, G., Yao, L., Wang, W., Ou, J., Cheng, C.-Y., Ishii, H. 2015. xPrint: from design to fabrication for shape changing interfaces by printing solution materials. *Proc. of SIGGRAPH Asia 2015 Posters*, 7.
37. Weichel, C., Lau, M., Kim, D., Villar, N., Gellersen, H.W. 2014. MixFab: a mixed-reality environment for personal fabrication. *Proc. of CHI 2014*, 3855-3864.
38. Willis, K.D., Xu, C., Wu, K.-J., Levin, G., Gross, M.D. 2011. Interactive fabrication: new interfaces for digital fabrication. *Proc. of TEI 2011*, 69-72.
39. Wu, R., Peng, H., Guimbretière, F., Marschner, S. 2016. Printing arbitrary meshes with a 5DOF wireframe printer. *ACM Transactions on Graphics (TOG) 35*, 101.
40. Zhang, Y., Gao, W., Paredes, L., Ramani, K. 2016. CardBoardiZer: Creatively Customize, Articulate and Fold 3D Mesh Models. *Proc. of CHI 2016*, 897-907.
41. Zoran, A. 2013. Hybrid Basketry: Interweaving Digital Practice within Contemporary Craft. *Leonardo 46*, 324-331.
42. Zoran, A., Paradiso, J.A. 2013. FreeD: a freehand digital sculpting tool. *Proc. of CHI 2013*, 2613-2616.

A Framework for Speechreading Acquisition Tools

Benjamin M. Gorman
University of Dundee
Dundee, Scotland
b.gorman@dundee.ac.uk

David R. Flatla
University of Dundee
Dundee, Scotland
d.flatla@dundee.ac.uk

ABSTRACT
At least 360 million people worldwide have disabling hearing loss that frequently causes difficulties in day-to-day conversations. Traditional technology (e.g., hearing aids) often fails to offer enough value, has low adoption rates, and can result in social stigma. Speechreading can dramatically improve conversational understanding, but speechreading is a skill that can be challenging to learn. To address this, we developed a novel speechreading acquisition framework that can be used to design Speechreading Acquisition Tools (SATs) – a new type of technology to improve speechreading acquisition. We interviewed seven speechreading tutors and used thematic analysis to identify and organise the key elements of our framework. We then evaluated our framework by using it to: 1) categorise every tutor-identified speechreading teaching technique, 2) critically evaluate existing conversational aids, and 3) design three new SATs. Through the use of SATs designed using our framework, the speechreading abilities of people with hearing loss around the world should be enhanced, thereby improving the conversational foundation of their day-to-day lives.

ACM Classification Keywords
K.4.2 Social Issues: Assistive technologies for persons with disabilities

Author Keywords
Speechreading; Lipreading; Hearing Loss; Deafness

INTRODUCTION
More than 11 million people (1 in 6) in the UK have some degree of hearing loss [1] and in the USA, an estimated 30 million people (12.7%) 12 years and older have hearing loss in both ears [10]. On a global scale, the World Health Organisation estimates that 360 million people (~5%) worldwide have disabling hearing loss[1] [53]. Hearing loss prevalence increases with age [10], resulting in an anticipated growth in hearing loss in the future (e.g., 1 in 5 people are expected to have hearing loss by 2035 in the UK [2]).

[1]Hearing loss greater than 40 dB in the better hearing ear in adults and greater than 30 dB in the better hearing ear in children.

CHI 2017, May 06-11, 2017, Denver, CO, USA.
ACM 978-1-4503-4655-9/17/05.
http://dx.doi.org/10.1145/3025453.3025560

Hearing loss results in difficulties understanding what others are saying during conversation [49]. Considering that the quality of our communication, our willingness to engage in conversation, and our level of apprehension about conversations all profoundly affect the quality of our lives [18], conversational difficulties due to hearing loss can result in social isolation [22], career stagnation [39], and a decrease in overall life satisfaction [49]. Hearing aids are intended to help reduce conversational difficulties, but are expensive [11], often counterproductive in noisy environments [25], and have low adoption rates (~14% [1]) due to a lack of comfort [40] and perceived social stigma [30].

People who are deaf or have a hearing loss find that speechreading (commonly called lipreading) can overcome many of the barriers when communicating with others [18]. Speechreading can be described as a special case of audio-visual speech recognition where emphasis is placed on the visible, rather than on the audible, speech information. Speechreading helps to improve conversational confidence (thereby reducing social isolation), enhance employability, and improve educational outcomes [49]. Speechreading also does not rely on the other conversation partner's knowledge of a Signed Language or a technique such as Cued Speech [19]. Speechreading is also partially used by those without hearing loss (albeit subconsciously) [26], so it is already a natural component of conversation, thereby limiting the chances for stigmatisation.

However, speechreading is a skill that takes considerable practice and training to acquire [34]. Publicly-funded speechreading classes are sometimes provided, and have been shown to improve speechreading acquisition [5]. However, classes are only provided in a handful of countries around the world; there is an insufficient number of classes running in areas in which they are provided (e.g., only 50 of an estimated 325 required classes are currently running in Scotland [5]) and classes require mobility to attend.

To help expand speechreading training worldwide, we developed a novel framework that can be used to develop Speechreading Acquisition Tools (SATs) – a new type of technology designed specifically to improve speechreading acquisition. Through the development and release of SATs, people with hearing loss will be able to augment their class-based learning, or learn on their own if no suitable classes are available.

To develop our framework, we conducted in-depth interviews with 7 of the 21 Scottish speechreading tutors [5] to explore their background, approach to teaching, current use of technology, and thoughts on how speechreading can be improved.

Through thematic analysis of our interview transcripts, we identified four main themes relevant to the future development of speechreading acquisition tools: 1) speechreading as a skill, 2) access to speechreading, 3) teaching practices, and 4) attitudes to technology. Using these themes, we developed our framework, which consists of two dimensions (*Type of Skill* and *Amount of Information*), each with three levels (*Analytic/Synthetic/Hybrid* and *Low/Medium/High*, respectively).

To evaluate our framework, we used it to: 1) classify every existing speechreading teaching technique identified by our participants, 2) critically reflect on previously-developed solutions, and 3) design three new SATs for enhancing speechreading acquisition and proficiency.

By employing our framework in this fashion, we show that it: 1) comprehensively reflects existing speechreading teaching practice, 2) can be used to help understand the strengths and weaknesses of previously-developed solutions, and 3) can be used to identify clear opportunities for the development of new SATs to help improve speechreading skill acquisition. Through the dissemination and adoption of our framework into the research community and assistive technology commercial sector, we foresee new technology being developed to help improve speechreading acquisition worldwide. Once in the hands of people with hearing loss, SATs will help enhance their speechreading capabilities, increasing their conversational confidence and reducing their social isolation.

This paper makes five contributions: First, we contribute novel speechreading tutor interview data and thematic analysis of that data. Second, we describe our speechreading acquisition framework for developing new technological tools for improving speechreading acquisition. Third, we evaluate our framework by fitting existing teaching techniques and existing solutions into the framework. Fourth, we define and describe Speechreading Acquisition Technologies (SATs). Fifth, we outline how to use our framework by designing three new SATs to improve speechreading acquisition.

BACKGROUND & RELATED WORK

Speechreading

The atomic unit of spoken language is the *phoneme*. Phonemes are combined to form words. For example, */b/*, */æ/*, and */t/* are the phonemes for "bat". There are 48 commonly-recognised phonemes in the English language [46]. For each phoneme, a speaker's lips, teeth, and tongue produce a visual representation known as a *viseme* [23].

People with hearing loss try to map visemes to phonemes in order to understand what a speaker is saying [9]. Hearing loss causes the audible phoneme to be lost or difficult to perceive, but the viseme is still available. For example, */l/* and */r/* are acoustically similar in English (especially when following another consonant, such as 'grass' vs. 'glass'), but are generated using distinct visemes, so this visual difference can be used to determine if a speaker has said */l/* or */r/*.

Although 'reading' visemes to understand what someone is saying works for many phonemes, there are also phonemes that are represented by similar visemes [36]. For example, */v/* is a voiced phoneme (the vocal cords vibrate), which is audibly distinct from */f/*, which is not voiced. However, the viseme for */v/* is very similar to the viseme for */f/*, making the words *'fan'* and *'van'* difficult to distinguish visually.[2] As a result, novice speechreaders (e.g., someone who has received no formal speechreading training) often find it difficult to fully understand what a speaker is saying, resulting in confusion, frustration, and reduced conversational confidence [18].

Conversation Aids & SATs

We define a *Conversation Aid* as any technique or technology that enables or supports face-to-face conversation. We describe existing conversation aids below in the second evaluation of our framework, however at this stage it is important to recognise that *Conversation Aids* are a superset of *Speechreading Acquisition Tools*, as the latter have been designed specifically to be used by speechreaders.

Speechreading Teaching Methods

Early speechreading training was focussed on skill acquisition as a by-product of learning speech production [24]. The explicit teaching of speechreading in classes with methodologies that were primarily concerned with speech recognition did not occur until the 19th century [32].

Speechreading classes primarily focus on learning how different mouth shapes are produced during speech [34], as well as how to use conversational repair strategies to gain important contextual information to help 'fill in' any gaps in understanding [34]. Classes also include information about hearing aids or other assistive listening devices, and give people a social space to meet with others who have a hearing loss [49]. Classes can also improve an individual's self-confidence [8], and help attendees become more knowledgeable about their hearing loss and how they can make communication easier.

There are two main approaches to teaching speechreading: *synthetic* and *analytic*. Synthetic methods use a 'top-down' approach in which the speechreader is encouraged to focus on the gist of the conversation to help them determine individual words. Synthetic methods are often referred to as 'mind-training' or 'context-training', as they rely on lexical ability to understand the topic of the conversation. Synthetic methods consider the sentence to be the basic unit of speech [49].

Analytic methods use a 'bottom-up' approach in which the speechreader is encouraged to focus on individual speech movements to identify the word, phrase or sentence [49]. Analytic methods are often referred to as 'eye-training' as the speechreader focusses on the visual aspects of a speaker to disambiguate visual speech patterns. Analytic methods hold that the syllable or phoneme is the basic unit of speech [32].

The Nitchie Method [41] was initially developed using an analytic approach, however it shifted towards a synthetic approach in later years. Nitchie is credited with establishing the foundations of modern speechreading training as well as the synthetic approach to speechreading. His method stresses that eye-training materials and those based around association or

[2] We encourage readers to make *'ffffff'* and *'vvvvvv'* sounds to hear the difference, and to make these sounds plus 'fan' and 'van' in front of a mirror to see the lack of visual difference.

ID	Gender	Age	Hearing Loss	Cause	HA/CI Use	Years Signing	Years Teaching
P1	F	78	Profound Hearing Loss	Childhood Illness	Cochlear Implant	32	32
P2	F	68	Severe Hearing Loss	Childhood Illness	One Hearing Aid	None	14
P3	F	61	Typical Hearing	-	None	None	12
P4	F	57	Typical Hearing	-	None	None	18
P5	F	42	Typical Hearing*	-	None	3	6 Months
P6	F	67	Moderate Hearing Loss	Not Specified	One Hearing Aid	None	7
P7	F	66	Severe Hearing Loss	Congenital Hearing Loss	Two Hearing Aids	19	1

Table 1. Summary of participant demographics. HA/CI = Hearing Aid/Cochlear Implant. Years Signing = Number of Years Using Sign Language (BSL). Years Teaching = Number of Years Teaching Speechreading. '*' indicates severe hearing loss for eight months due to viral infection.

context be separated. He also believed that context training was more important than training for visual disambiguation.

The Kinzie Method [35] uses a synthetic approach to speechreading and includes mirror practice (where the student talks before a mirror to learn visual differences between speech movements) and the use of voice. Materials in this method are organised into graded lessons for both children and adults, with sentences forming the basis of instruction [35].

The Mueller-Walle Method [15] is an analytic approach that emphasises eye-training through syllable drills, which are rhythmic drills consisting of contrasting syllables that are restricted to sound combinations found in the English language. Syllable drills are spoken as quickly as possible by the tutor.

The Jena Method [17] is an analytic approach that emphasises syllable drills and stresses kinaesthetic awareness during speech production as well as audition and eye-training. Eye-training is accomplished through syllable drills in a similar manner as the Mueller-Walle and early Nitchie Methods. During the drills, the speaker is expected to speak in unison with the instructor and imitate their lip and jaw movements thereby concentrating on the kinaesthetic sensations experienced.

Although the methods described above give us a theoretical understanding of the approaches to speechreading training, we wanted to base our framework on current practice (which is most likely influenced by these theories). As such, we conducted interviews with practicing speechreading tutors to generate the dataset needed to develop our framework.

METHOD

We conducted individual interviews with seven Scottish speechreading tutors [5] to explore their background, approach to teaching, current use of technology, and thoughts on how speechreading can be improved. With participant's informed consent, we audio recorded each interview, then transcribed and thematically analysed [13] the transcripts.

Aims

We had five main aims (phrased as questions) guiding our interviews: 1) Do speechreading tutors primarily employ analytic or synthetic training approaches? 2) What do speechreading tutors consider to be the basic unit of speechreading? 3) What technology (if any) do speechreading tutors currently use to teach speechreading? 4) Do speechreading tutors feel that speechreading training could be improved with new technology or training techniques? 5) How do speechreading students continue to learn when not in class? Our interview guide is included in the supplementary materials ('InterviewGuide.pdf').

Participants

Scotland is the one of the few countries that provides formal training for speechreading tutors. As such, our participants all reside in Scotland, and offer classes throughout central Scotland. Participants were recruited through direct emails via contact details obtained from the Scottish Course to Train Tutors of Lipreading (SCTTL, http://www.scotlipreading.org.uk/), along with word-of-mouth. Participant details are summarised in Table 1. All participants were female (aged from 42 to 78). The 21 tutors listed on SCTTL were all female, therefore we could not balance genders. The range of teaching experience was from six months to 32 years. Our participants self-reported details about their hearing, which we classified into five levels using the textual descriptions of hearing loss identified by Action On Hearing Loss [3]: Typical Hearing, and Mild, Moderate, Severe, and Profound Hearing Loss. The participants' backgrounds were varied:

P1, 78, has had profound hearing loss from a young age. She has been teaching speechreading for 32 years after being asked to take over a class by a friend. She has no formal teacher or speechreading training. P1 teaches three classes a week.

P2, 68, has severe hearing loss. She has been teaching speechreading for 12 years. She was a high school science teacher who retired early due to her hearing loss. She had attended speechreading classes for around two years before her tutor convinced her to take the SCTTL so that she could teach classes herself. P2 teaches two classes a week.

P3, 61, has typical hearing. She has been teaching speechreading for 12 years. She previously worked as a subtitler for the BBC. Her father had a hearing loss which motivated her to become a speechreading tutor. She undertook the SCTTL at the same time as P2. P3 teaches two classes a week.

P4, 57, has typical hearing. She has been teaching speechreading for 18 years. She also works as a Speech and Language Therapist for the Scottish National Health Service. P4 teaches one class per week and also trains tutors as part of the SCTTL.

P5, 42, has typical hearing, however she experienced severe hearing loss for eight months after a viral infection. She has been teaching speechreading for six months. Her motivation for teaching started after experiencing hearing loss. P5 initially wanted to learn to sign to increase access for deaf individuals at her community centre where she works. However, upon realising that the deaf community in her area instead required a speechreading tutor she undertook the SCTTL. P5 teaches two classes a week.

P6, 67, has moderate hearing loss. She has been teaching speechreading for seven years. She temporarily lost her hearing due to a viral infection 10 years ago, so her daughter encouraged her to learn speechreading to help her cope. After a year within the class, her tutor encouraged her to take the SCTTL. P6 teaches four classes a week.

P7, 66, has severe hearing loss. She has been teaching speechreading for one year. Her motivation for becoming a speechreading tutor was to help individuals who experience hearing loss later in life; she worked in a library and noticed that these individuals seemed prone to isolation. She also took the SCTTL. P7 teaches three classes a week.

Approach

After obtaining ethical approval, we conducted semi-structured one-to-one interviews. Interviews took place in mutually-convenient and quiet locations. The mean interview time was 40 minutes (max 74 minutes, min 28 minutes); some interviews took longer due to participants discussing past students and their experiences interacting with them. The interviews consisted of questions that explored their background, general teaching approach, assessment, current use of technology and their thoughts on where speechreading could be improved in the future. The interview questions were open-ended (for example, "Why did you decide to become a lipreading tutor?" [3]) and we let the participant lead whenever possible [7], encouraging elaboration by asking probing follow-up questions when necessary [7] (e.g., "And do they find that helpful?"). Audio recordings were gathered during the interviews. Transcripts were coded and analysed using thematic analysis [13], grouping similar experiences together in order to identify themes across all participant interviews. The themes were refined through an iterative thematic analysis process to generate a final, distinct set of themes.

Phases Of Analysis

Phase 1: Becoming Familiar With the Data

We manually transcribed the interviews using custom-built software. We strove for a verbatim account of all verbal and nonverbal (e.g., laughs) utterances. We added punctuation where necessary to indicate pauses, full sentences, and questions. We formatted our transcripts using 'Interviewer:' to indicate interview statements and 'Participant1:' to indicate statements by P1. All names and locations were removed to maintain anonymity. Our interview transcripts are included in the 'Transcripts' folder in the supplementary materials.

Phase 2: Generating Initial Codes

We started by reading paper copies of the transcripts and manually highlighting all interesting extracts. We then transferred our highlighted extracts into MAXQDA12 [4], resulting in 502 extracted elements from the original transcripts.

[3]In the UK, 'speechreading' is referred to as 'lipreading', therefore in discussions with participants we used the term 'lipreading'.

[4]A qualitative analysis software package, http://www.maxqda.com/

Using the 'coded segment' feature of MAXQDA12, we then systematically processed our original 502 elements iteratively using a data-driven approach to ensure that our final themes emerged exclusively from our interview data.

During this process, we coded for maximum diversity of potential themes and patterns, and did not discard data unless it was clearly not relevant to the research (e.g., an unrelated anecdote). We also kept enough of the text around each coded segment to retain the segment's context, because a common criticism of coding is that the context is often lost [16].

By giving equal attention to each extract, we further segmented our extracts and coded them using iteratively-shaped codes, resulting in 944 coded segments under 116 unique codes. Our MAXQDA12 data file containing our final coded segments and codes is included in the 'Analysis.mx12' file in the supplementary materials.

As we followed Braun and Clarke's [13] 15-point checklist of criteria for good thematic analysis, we did not conduct inter-rater coding. Inter-rater reliability checks are not always used in thematic analysis since there is scepticism regarding such tests [4, 42, 50]; it can be argued that one researcher merely trains another to think as she or he does when looking at a fragment of text and so the reliability check does not establish that the codes are objective but merely that two people can apply the same subjective perspective to the text [37].

Phase 3: Searching for Themes

In this phase, we created a short definition for each code that described when that code would be used and what it represented across the entire data set. We then printed each code plus its definition on individual strips of paper, and iteratively organised the strips into 'theme-piles' on a whiteboard. Using the resulting 'theme-piles', we produced an initial thematic map. Our initial thematic map is in the 'InitialThematicMap.png' file in the supplementary materials.

Phase 4: Reviewing Themes

Starting with our initial thematic map from Phase 3, we removed themes that did not directly relate to the study aims outlined above. We then reviewed the collection of coded extracts for each remaining theme to ensure that they formed a coherent pattern. Finally, we re-read our original transcripts to check that our revised themes provided suitable coverage.

Phase 5: Defining and Naming Themes

Once our thematic map was finalised (Figure 1), we defined each theme by examining its collection of coded extracts to determine the main aspect of the data captured by the theme. We then revisited the collection of coded extracts for each theme, refining the story told by each theme. Finally, we produced internally-consistent accounts, with an accompanying narrative for each theme.

FINDINGS

Through our thematic analysis, we identified four themes: 1) speechreading as a skill, 2) access to speechreading, 3) teaching practices, and 4) attitudes to technology. We now explore each theme in detail using quotes from participants to scaffold the narrative of each theme.

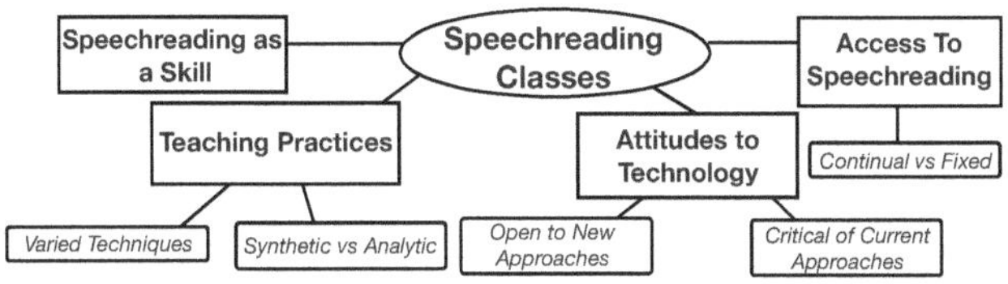

Figure 1. Final thematic map of four main themes and their subthemes.

Speechreading as a Skill

Our participants saw speechreading as a skill, one that requires long periods of concentration and focus to learn. Classes are typically two hours long with a short break, so students focus for around an hour at a time. All seven participants discussed the need for concentration and focus within classes:

> P4: *"For the person themselves they need that confidence, that assertiveness, to do that, they also need to concentrate and pay attention for that length of time."*

> P6: *"...not looking around the room and trying to listen but actually just focusing...the amount of concentration these people give, it's amazing...it's as almost as they are drilling holes in you...it's excellent, it's really good."*

As illustrated by these comments, a student's ability to focus and concentrate is of paramount importance to learning speechreading. A high level of concentration is necessary due to the limitations of speechreading – many aspects of speech (e.g., voicing) are mostly audible instead of visible:

> P2: *"I warn them beforehand, that only 1/3 of speech is lip-readable...they are aware that there is a limitation to what we are doing but it's an added help to everything they do...it's useful but it doesn't solve all your problems."*

In addition to the level of concentration required and the limitations of speechreading, participants also described additional factors that pose difficulties for students, such as particular words or speech movements having little visual difference:

> P6: *"Knowing that...some of these skills are very subtle, you are not going to see huge [differences]. Some speech movements are very clear, [but] when you get to others there are some sounds that are so subtle you can hardly see them...vowel at the beginning of the word, like 'ahead'...it's difficult to spot. Sometimes if you can't lipread, [it] could be that there is a vowel in there that you are not aware of."*

> P1: *"Certain words and sounds they find really difficult. I have to repeat them...I go over things quite a lot."*

Many participants identified how different accents can affect individual speech movements as well:

> P4: *"Sometimes you've got...English [as opposed to Scottish] vowel sounds coming at you and therefore sometimes you look and think 'I don't know what that is'. Because it's got the accent it kind of changes things."*

The challenges of speechreading, plus the level of concentration required, often lead to fatigue during and after class:

> P2: *"And there are times when you get tired and your lipreading is absolutely rubbish."*

> P4: *"As to how tiring it is to sit and watch somebody for...two hours, we build in breaks but it's still a lot of effort and concentration. It's very tiring and I think that's what comes after two or three weeks...somebody will come up to you and say I went home and I was absolutely exhausted. I didn't realise how tiring it was."*

Access to Speechreading

Access to speechreading classes was discussed by all participants. In particular, participants focussed on issues surrounding funding of classes, the length of classes and how students beginning classes (and the general public) have little awareness of what is involved in learning speechreading:

> P4: *"...it's a very difficult one, lipreading is...kinda like a Cinderella Service [ignored or treated as less important]. People don't recognise that actually everybody lipreads to a certain extent. I think what could be improved with lipreading is general awareness of the fact that everybody lipreads, so...more people would be aware of it and more people would therefore come to the classes."*

Participants also highlighted that local governments can view speechreading classes as recreational, causing funding issues:

> P7: *"I would prefer it to come under university rather than sitting under [local governments], because it is a life changing skill...rather than a hobby or a job."*

> P2: *"Some authorities regard it as a recreational thing"*

Continual vs. Fixed

A subtheme within access reflects whether speechreading classes should be continual or fixed length. All tutors agreed that classes should be continual.

> P1: *"I do think that judging by this and my [other] class that it's important for the class to be ongoing unless they for individual reasons want to drop out."*

> P2: *"It's a continual practice thing...you could really do with a little practice every week...for the rest of your life."*

However, many of the tutors teach fixed-length classes. This was generally due to funding issues, with many local governments only offering two years of speechreading classes:

> P6: *"I know, two years is our maximum and then you have to go on to a paid class."*

> P2: *"So I'm paid by [anonymised] city council. They provide two years free lipreading, I am the only tutor in [anonymised] that does it. I did one on the Tuesday, two on a Thursday, but the budget is decreasing every year. We don't know how long this will go on for. I only teach for thirty weeks...that's all the council will pay you for."*

> P5: *"This is a problem for me especially because I have got funding from [anonymised], and they will not perpetually fund something. So I have got funding for one year of lipreading classes, which is a 30 week course."*

In some cases, local governments offer no funding for classes, and students living in these areas pay for classes.

> P3: *"They do pay in the [anonymised] groups. In the other groups no they didn't pay.*

Students also appear to be willing to attend continual classes rather than fixed length classes. This is supported by participants reporting that students only stop attending classes due to becoming ill or passing away.

> Interviewer: *"So why do people stop coming to a class?"* P7: *"I haven't had any experience of that, they have all been very faithful including [over] the holidays."*

> P1: *"Some people do drop away. Usually they either die or [grow] too old. Some people died in this class and they died in my [anonymised] class too. Not many have just dropped out."*

> P6: *"People who come tend to stay. A gentleman stopped coming to this class about a year ago. He is...very old, in his 90's. He lives about 10 miles down the road and has to come by bus and therefore it's very difficult for him."*

Teaching Practices

Teaching practices varied widely, with all tutors using a variety of approaches and techniques to teach speechreading.

Synthetic vs. Analytic

Synthetic and analytic are the two main approaches to teach speechreading. Although the teaching methods described in our Background section typically emphasise one over the other, all of our tutors draw from both approaches as needed:

> P4: *"We tend to have a general topic for the class...if I am doing something on a movement, 'f'...I might choose a topic that begins with that sound...I might talk about 'fireworks' or 'fire'. The whole lesson will not be around that particular speech sound...I would do a follow up story or exercise with that sound appearing it in regularly."*

> P6: *"If you know the context, you can make a really good guess, which is a lot of lipreading anyway. If they are talking about horse racing then there is not going to be anybody talking about ballet dancers, it's unlikely. Knowing that it's very subtle, that some of these skills are very subtle...some speech movements are very clear, when you get to others there are some sounds that are so subtle you can hardly see them."*

Varied Techniques

Tutors did not mention the teaching methods introduced earlier, but discussed techniques that can be linked to these methods. Participant descriptions of techniques were often fragmented throughout an interview, resulting in many relevant quotes. We provide condensed summaries (without using quotes) of these descriptions below and refer readers to our supplementary materials for more details.

Mirror Practice: student speaks into a mirror to see his/her own mouth shapes and the visual differences between speech sounds. Used by all seven tutors. Analytic.

Quick Recognition Exercises (QREs) or *Syllable Drills*: rhythmic drills consisting of contrasting syllables or words spoken as quickly as possible in different orders by tutor. Class members repeat back. Used by all seven tutors. Analytic.

Cue Recognition: encompasses looking for body language, facial emotion, and hand gestures. Used by all seven tutors. Analytic and synthetic – Hybrid.

Speech Movements or *Lip Shapes*: focussed attention on the visual representation of a single speech sound on its own or within a word. Used by all seven tutors. Analytic.

Pair Work: focussed speechreading practice in pairs. Used by all seven tutors. Hybrid.

Stories: tutor speaks a multi-sentence story with known topic to the class. Used by P2, P3, P4, P5, P6 and P7. Synthetic.

Fingerspelling: spelling spoken words using sign language hand movements. Tutors typically sign only the first speech sound of a word. Used by P2, P4, P5 and P7. Analytic.

Scenarios: basing a lesson around pretending you are in a specific place such as the dentist, so all material is based on that scenario. Used by P1, P2, P4 and P5. Synthetic.

Word Quizzes: based around a topic, such as 'animals', and students having to watch for an animal for each letter of the alphabet. Used by P2, P5 and P7. Hybrid.

Framed Sentences: tutor says a topic-based sentence such as *'In my garden I have ____'*, but mouths the blanked word. Used by P2 and P5. Synthetic.

Mystery Object: an unknown object is hidden using paper or cloth. The tutor speaks a number of 'hint' sentences to aid identification. Used by P2 and P3. Synthetic.

Kinaesthetic awareness was the only technique tutors discussed that was not used to teach speechreading. P4 and P7 mentioned that it was useful when teaching students aspects of speech production such as controlling the loudness of their voice, but did not mention its place within speechreading.

Attitudes To Technology

Participants appear to use some non-specialised technology in their classes (e.g., hearing aids, loop systems, videos, PowerPoint) and five tutors reported informing students of Lipreadingpractice.co.uk, a website containing videos of some of the exercises used within classes. It is interesting to note here that recently-trained tutors were more critical of existing practices and were more open to using new technology.

Critical Of Current Approaches

Participants were critical of current approaches to learning speechreading using technology. Subtitles were praised for allowing individuals to enjoy videos, however tutors also reported that subtitles do not improve speechreading as students have to either watch the subtitles or watch the video:

> P4: *"I never advocate watching television to practice lipreading. If you have ever tried...it's horrendous!"*

Lipreadingpractice.co.uk was also criticised for having distracting videos and limited training material:

> P2: *"The trouble with a lipreading site like that is there are only so many stories. Eventually, if...you've got a good memory, you are just gonna know them all."*

Open To New Approaches

Participants were open to new approaches involving technology and several discussed how mobile apps could be developed to help students practice outside of classes:

> Interviewer: *"Do you think that people who are looking into learning lipreading would benefit from additional kinds of new technology to help?"*
> P3: *"I would think so yes. But I don't have the technological ability so I can't tell you what it would be. But I'm sure because there is so much out there, iPhones, iPads and you know tablets and all that. Surely to goodness there must be something that we can do that will help."*

> P5: *"I mean I don't know if there [are] lipreading apps. I think a lipreading app would be good. Just for people to practice...apps are the way forward aren't they? How you would develop it I'm not quite sure...it would just need to be about the shapes and practicing the words and having a bit of context..."*

FRAMEWORK

Our themes highlight how speechreading acquisition can be enhanced through the development of new assistive tools that will help resolve issues regarding the lack of access, and can also be specialised to different speechreading teaching approaches. We call these tools Speechreading Acquisition Tools (SATs) – a new type of technology designed specifically to improve speechreading acquisition. We believe that through the development and release of SATs, people with hearing loss will be able to augment their class-based learning, or learn on their own if they are unable to attend a speechreading classes.

To facilitate the transition of knowledge from our thematic analysis to researchers, Assistive Technology (AT) commercial sector, and AT enthusiasts, we developed a *speechreading acquisition framework*. Our framework can be used to design SATs by individuals who may have a varied amount of knowledge of speechreading, phonetics and hearing loss.

Framework Design

Our thematic analysis identified numerous speechreading teaching techniques with each technique emphasising analytic, synthetic, or hybrid (analytic and synthetic) speechreading skills. Each teaching technique also provides a different amount of information, so that they can be chosen to complement a student's current speechreading ability.

Identifying that 'skill type' and 'information amount' apply to each teaching technique, we used these as the base dimensions for our framework: *Type of Skill* and *Amount of Information*. The dimensions are continuous in nature, but to improve framework accessibility we discretised each into three levels (*Analytic/Hybrid/Synthetic* and *Low/Medium/High*, respectively), resulting in a 3x3 cell-based grid as shown in Figure 2.

We classify a technique as *Analytic* if it focusses on visual disambiguation. A technique that focusses on leveraging the

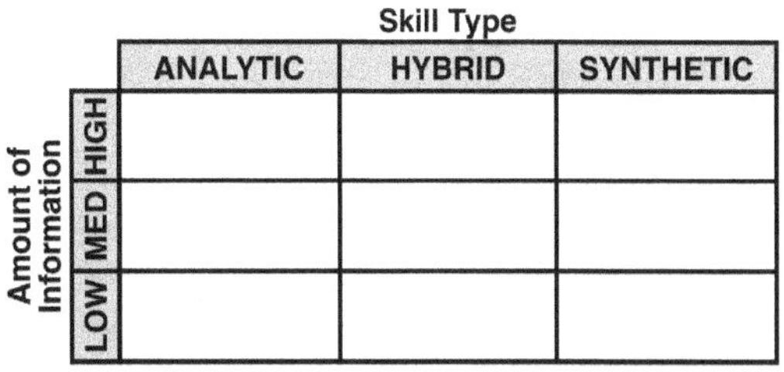

Figure 2. Our speechreading acquisition framework, with two dimensions: *Type of Skill* and *Amount of Information*, each split into three levels (*Analytic/Hybrid/Synthetic* and *Low/Medium/High*, respectively)

context is classified as *Synthetic*. *Hybrid* techniques focus on both analytic and synthetic approaches to speechreading.

As the basic unit of analytic teaching methods is the phoneme, analytic techniques that provide individual phonemes are classified as *Medium*, techniques that provide non-phonemic information (e.g., speech production properties) are *Low*, and techniques that provide more than phonemes (e.g., whole words) are *High*. The basic unit of synthetic teaching methods is the sentence, so synthetic techniques that provide the topic of a specific sentence are classified as *Medium*, techniques that provide less (e.g., the topic of a conversation) are *Low*, and techniques that provide more information (e.g., the topic and context of a sentence) are *High*.

FRAMEWORK EVALUATION

To evaluate our framework, we now use it to 1) classify existing teaching techniques, 2) critically reflect on previously-developed solutions, and 3) identify and describe three new technologies for enhancing speechreading acquisition and proficiency. By employing our framework in this fashion, we show that it 1) comprehensively reflects existing speechreading teaching practice, 2) can be used to help understand the strengths and weaknesses of previously-developed solutions, and 3) can be used to identify clear opportunities for the development of new SATs to improve speechreading acquisition.

Teaching Techniques

To evaluate our framework, we first fit existing teaching techniques within our framework cells. The goal of this evaluation is to assess our framework's coverage; accommodating every teaching technique identified by our interview participants indicates good coverage, any teaching techniques not fitting within our framework indicate framework incompleteness.

Fitting Identified Teaching Techniques

We now describe our classification rationale for each teaching technique described in our Teaching Practices section above. Our classifications can be seen in Figure 3.

Speech Movements and *Lip Shapes*: **analytic** and **low information** as the student is only informed of the target speech-movement(s) and has to identify the rest of the word(s).

Finger Spelling: **analytic** and **medium information** as the first letter is signed but the rest of the word has to be identified.

QREs: **analytic** and **high information** as the student knows the words or syllables spoken, so only has to order them.

Amount of Information	Skill Type: ANALYTIC	HYBRID	SYNTHETIC
HIGH	Mirror Practice, QREs	Word Quizzes (name the animals)	Framed Sentence Exercises
MED	Finger Spelling (initial letter)	Cue Recognition (body language)	Scenarios
LOW	Speech Movements, Lip Shapes	Pair Work	Mystery Object*, Stories

Figure 3. Placement of teaching techniques into our framework. The '*' indicates the starting amount of information provided by this technique (Mystery Object), but this level increases as more clues are given.

Mirror Practice: **analytic** and **high information** as the student knows the words and movements they are speaking.

Pair Work: **hybrid** and **low information** as the student may not be familiar with their partner's facial movements, but may know the conversation topic.

Cue Recognition: **hybrid** and **medium information** as facial expressions and hand gestures provide a substantial amount of context to an utterance.

Word Quizzes: **hybrid** and **high information** as the student is given the first letter of a word within a precise topic.

Stories: **synthetic** and **low information** as only the topic of the story is given.

Mystery Object: **synthetic** and **low information** as the student is only aware of the shape of the object hidden beneath the cover, however information increases as more clues are given.

Scenarios: **synthetic** and **medium information** as a specific context is provided and all material is based on that context.

Framed Sentence Exercises: **synthetic** and **high information** as the student is told the sentence and guesses one word; the sentence provides a high degree of contextual information.

As shown in Figure 3, our framework accommodates all of the identified teaching techniques with no gaps, thereby increasing our confidence in the coverage of our framework.

Existing Conversation Aids & SATs

In the second stage of our evaluation, we fit existing conversation aids and SATs into our framework to get a deeper sense of the coverage of our framework. Through this process we also critically reflect on the design of existing conversation aids and SATs as well as identify where new opportunities lie.

Fitting Existing Conversation Aids & SATs

We now briefly describe existing conversational aids and SATs identified via literature search, and provide our reasoning for where we fit each in our framework (placements in Figure 4).

Signed Languages (e.g., American and British Sign Language) are languages that use hand, arm, and facial gestures to facilitate communication. A signed language provides **high information** and is a **hybrid** approach as it relies on analytic skills to understand unfamiliar names and words (typically communicated using finger spelling) and synthetic skills (e.g., facial expressions) to understand particular aspects of a conversation (e.g., identifying a question). *Cued Speech* [19] is a system of eight hand-shapes placed in four positions around the mouth that aim to clarify lip-patterns during speechreading. As such Cued Speech is **analytic** and provides **high information** as its cues disambiguate all phonemes.

In spite of their benefits and sign language's importance to Deaf culture [44], sign language (cued speech) needs to be known by both conversation parters in order to help; it does not help conversations with people who do not know the language.

The earliest example of technology aiding speechreading can be seen in *Upton's Eyeglasses* [51]. This SAT used a clip-on microphone to detect speech, and processed the signal via high- and low-pass filters to classify spoken phoneme components. An LED matrix was positioned at the side of a pair of modified eyeglasses, and its light output was channeled so that it appeared at the centre of that side's lens, enabling an early augmented reality system (e.g., the bottom LED illuminated when a phoneme was voiced, making it appear as if the speaker's throat was glowing). Due to their focus on speech components, Upton's Eyeglasses are **analytic** and provide **low information**, as the wearer is only provided information about how a sound is produced. Much later, a similar peripheral-display approach was taken by *Ebrahimi* et al. [21].

Similar to Upton's Eyeglasses, *Tactile SATs* provide spoken phoneme information using tactile feedback. One such display of voice fundamental frequency showed a 10% improvement in a speech discrimination task [12], however a later study found positive results in terms of identifying voicing and for consonant identification, but no benefit for speechreading words in sentences [55]. As they are very similar to Upton's SAT, *Tactile SATs* are **analytic** and provide **low information**.

iBaldi [38] is an iOS application that overlays a visualisation of speech components onto an animated talking head. The visualisation shows one of three coloured discs (nasality in red, friction in white, voicing in blue) by iBaldi's mouth when he makes the corresponding sound. *iBaldi* provides similar information as Upton, so it is **analytic** and **low information**.

SATs that focus on helping identify components of speech based on how they are produced (Upton, Ebrahimi, Tactile, iBaldi) contradict typical speechreading approaches by training the speechreader to focus on *auditory* aspects of speech, rather than *visual*. Even though these aids can provide rich information, this information is of limited value to someone whose understanding of speech is primarily visual, not audible.

Spectrograms visualise frequency (Y-axis) over time (X-axis), with intensity mapped to colour. Linguists can use them to identify words, but this requires extensive training [28]. *Watanabe* et al. [52] improved spectrograms by integrating different speech features into a single image, but the evaluation used participants with extensive spectrogram-reading experience, so the technique's generalisability to speechreading is unknown. Both examples of *Spectrograms* are **analytic** aids, and provide **high information** due to the richness of the visualised data.

Lip Assistant [54] is an SAT that generates magnified realistic animations of a speaker's lips that are superimposed on the bottom left of a video. *Lip Assistant* is **analytic** as it focusses exclusively on lip shapes and it provides **low information**.

Amount of Information	Skill Type: ANALYTIC	HYBRID	SYNTHETIC
HIGH	Cued Speech, Spectrograms	Subtitles, Signed Languages	
MED		LipreadingPractice	CME (C)
LOW	Upton, Ebrahimi, TactileSATs, CME(A) Lip Assistant, iBaldi		CME (B) DAVID

Figure 4. Placement of conversation aids/SATs into our framework.

Subtitles (captions) present the speech (analytic) and sound effects (synthetic) of video as on-screen text. As such, they are a **hybrid** approach and provide **high information**, however they also require the viewer to split their attention between reading the subtitles and watching the video content; one eye-tracking study found that participants spent ~84% of their viewing time focussed exclusively on subtitles [33]. The design of Lip Assistant also suggests it is sensitive to split attention.

ConversationMadeEasy [48] is an SAT comprised of three programs, each presenting videos of speakers with or without audio. The programs increase in complexity: Program A is for **analytic** training with **low information**, and program B is for **synthetic** sentence training providing **low information**. Program C is for **synthetic** scenario-based training with commands or questions based on the scenarios given within a closed response set of four pictured options. As such, Program C provides **medium information**.

DAVID [47] is an SAT offering videos of sentences on everyday topics, such as 'going shopping'. The student watches and responds by typing the complete sentence or content words, or via multiple choice. DAVID also provides repair strategies such as repeating the sentence, or presenting words in isolation. DAVID is a **synthetic** SAT providing **low information**.

Lipreadingpractice.co.uk is a website-based SAT offering subtitled videos of consonants, vowels, and passages. The speaker says these with and without voice, shown from the front and from a profile angle, and repeats each a number of times. Words and phrases are provided as written exercises. *Lipreading Practice* is a **hybrid** SAT providing **low information**.

As shown in Figure 4, our framework can accommodate existing conversation aids and SATs, increasing our confidence in its coverage. More importantly, we also located gaps in the previous work. We next use our framework to design three new SATs that address these gaps, but also reflect the knowledge gained via our thematic analysis presented earlier.

Framework-Inspired SAT Examples

To further evaluate our framework we now demonstrate how it can be used to design new SATs. Below, we explain how we used our framework to design and prototype one speechreading acquisition tool, as well as to propose two additional SATs that we plan to build and evaluate as future work.

PhonemeViz

There are currently no **analytic** SATs that provide **medium information** to speechreaders during conversations. In addition, no SATs map to how fingerspelling is used within classes.

PhonemeViz places the character(s) of the most recently spoken initial phoneme just to the side of a speaker's lips. This design should enable a speechreader to focus on the speaker's eyes and lip movements (as in traditional speechreading), while also monitoring changes in PhonemeViz's state using their peripheral vision to help disambiguate confusing visemes. PhonemeViz can be overlaid onto video or displayed on a transparent head mounted display (Figure 5, left) to augment natural speechreading and enhance speechreading acquisition, although for any real-time applications, new automated speech recognition algorithms tuned to intial phonemes are needed.

In our pilot evaluation of a PhonemeViz prototype [27], PhonemeViz enabled all participants to achieve 100% word recognition (showing successful viseme disambiguation), and participants lauded PhonemeViz in subjective and qualitative feedback. Our initial results demonstrate that visualising a **medium** amount of **analytic** information can improve visual-only speechreading in constrained word recognition tasks.

MirrorTrainer

Our interviews revealed that mirror training plays a key role in speechreading training (used by all seven participants) and is used at home by students. However, traditional mirror training does not fully develop **hybrid** skills as students cannot assess themselves (because they have full knowledge of what they are saying), and the technique trains them to read their own speech (instead of other people). Despite its value in classes, mirror training is not reflected in currently available SATs.

Most mobile devices now have front-facing cameras that could be used to provide speechreaders with a '21st century' mirror. Utilising the front facing camera, the *MirrorTrainer* app would allow speechreaders to practice their own speech movements (with or without additional context) similar to how mirror training is currently used. However, MirrorTrainer could also capture and store videos of speech movements in a 'speech movement library'. Coupled with a simple user input-based 'labelling' function, MirrorTrainer would have a repository of videos containing known speech movement content (Figure 5, middle) that could be used to overcome the 'full knowledge' limitation of current mirror practice. Users could then share their speech movement libraries with each other, overcoming the 'self-training' limitation of traditional mirror training. In addition, MirrorTrainer users could gather coded videos of friends and family, allowing them to practice speechreading on those they speak with most. Such a MirrorTraining app would provide a variable (**low** to **high**) amount of information.

ContextCueView

Scenarios are used by four of our participants, who emphasised that scenarios provide a rich context for speechreading training. However, there are currently no tools to help speechreaders during real-life versions of scenarios used in class. In addition, there are no SATs that provide **high synthetic** information.

In certain situations, phrases and topics can be pre-associated with a given location or situation. These associations can be shown using a constellation diagram [34], in which a text label for the situation is placed in the middle while related topics and phrases radiate out from the situation label. Constella-

Figure 5. Left to right: PhonemeViz viewed through Epson Moverio glasses (http://www.epson.com/moverio) for 'bat', MirrorTrainer showing multiple words for the speech movement 'p/b/m' (images from vidTIMIT [45]), ContextCueView showing synthetic conversation cues for a coffee shop interaction using Google Glass (https://developers.google.com/glass/).

tion diagrams help by prompting the speechreader to consider potential phrases and topics in advance of a given situation.

ContextCueView would gather contextual data (e.g., GPS, date/time) to anticipate a user's situation. Using this contextual data, ContextCueView would load a matching previously-generated constellation diagram. ContextCueView constellation diagrams would be stored in a central repository, and collectively curated to rapidly provide constellation diagrams for a variety of situations. ContextCueView could run on a mobile device and operate like a 'contextual phrase book', but it is also well-suited for a glanceable display (Figure 5, right).

DISCUSSION

Summary of Contributions

Through thematic analysis of our interviews with speechreading tutors, we identified four main themes relevant to the future development of speechreading: *speechreading as a skill*, limited *access to speechreading*, a broad range of *teaching practices*, and mixed *attitudes to technology*. Using our themes, we developed a novel framework to help design new Speechreading Acquisition Tools (SATs). In evaluating our framework, we demonstrated that it can accommodate current teaching techniques and existing solutions, as well as be used to design new SATs. We developed a prototype of one new SAT named *PhonemeViz* and proposed two additional SATs that we will build and evaluate as future work.

Limitations

First, we based our framework on data obtained exclusively from Scottish speechreading tutors, many of whom were trained on the same course – it is possible that these tutors use outdated techniques, reducing the value of our framework. However, Scotland is one of the few countries in the world that provides accredited speechreading tutor training – most other countries provide no formal training. As such, it is arguable that Scotland's training course is based on best practices.

Second, fitting a technology into our framework does not guarantee that it will be useful for speechreading acquisition. For example, spectrograms provide a high amount of analytic information (which should make them very helpful), but this information is difficult to utilise without considerable training [28]. Likewise, Upton's Eyeglasses and iBaldi provide a low amount of analytic information, but focus on speech production instead of appearance (one of our tutors – a Speech and Language Therapist – indicated that she *"...[switches] off [her] speech therapy brain because [she] would go with sounds but in lipreading it is very much the shape and presentation on the lips."*). Our framework provides substantial guidance for the design of new SATs, but any resulting SATs still need to be evaluated using speechreaders. We argue that this is a strength of our framework not a limitation, as our framework serves to complement and enhance existing best-practice participatory design approaches, not attempt to replace them.

Third, our framework does not distinguish between SATs focussing on speechreading training versus 'live' speechreading. However, as discussed, PhonemeViz and ContextCueView can be extended to 'live' speechreading, suggesting that some SATs can be adapted for both. Therefore, we leave this flexibility within our framework but will consider future refinements to make this distinction more explicit in the future.

Generalisations & Extensions

Our framework currently focusses on English speechreading acquisition, but can be extended to support speechreading in other languages. French [6], German [14], and Japanese [31] each have their own confusing viseme-phoneme mappings, however their speechreading techniques for distinguishing between mouth-shapes (analytic), and conversational repair strategies (synthetic) are similar to English, so our framework should generalise to developing SATs for other languages.

Our framework can also be extended to help develop technology for other skill-based speech domains. For example, speech therapy uses a variety of approaches [20], and already features a number of speech production aids [29, 43]. Likewise, our approach can be extended to language learning, as understanding a foreign language is analytic (e.g., pronunciation) and synthetic (e.g., using context to distinguish homonyms). In particular, ContextCueView (described above) might easily extend to supporting in-situ foreign language conversations.

CONCLUSION & FUTURE WORK

Many people around the world have conversation-impairing hearing loss. Speechreading can dramatically improve conversational understanding, but is a challenging skill to learn. To help design new Speechreading Acquisition Tools (SATs), we developed a framework based on thematic analysis of interviews with speechreading tutors. We then evaluated our framework by using it to classify identified teaching techniques, critique existing solutions, and we demonstrated how to use our framework to design three new SATs. Our future work is focussed on continuing to develop and evaluate our novel SATs in a participatory process involving speechreaders.

REFERENCES

1. Action On Hearing Loss 2011. Facts and figures on deafness and tinnitus. (2011).
2. Action On Hearing Loss 2015. Hearing Matters. https://www.actiononhearingloss.org.uk/supporting-you/policy-research-and-influencing/research/hearing-matters.aspx. (2015).
3. Action On Hearing Loss 2016. Describing Deafness. https://www.actiononhearingloss.org.uk/your-hearing/about-deafness-and-hearing-loss/deafness/describing-deafness.aspx. (2016).
4. David Armstrong, Ann Gosling, John Weinman, and Theresa Marteau. 1997. The place of inter-rater reliability in qualitative research: an empirical study. *Sociology* 31, 3 (1997), 597–606.
5. L Armstrong. 2015. On everybody's lips. http://www.scotlipreading.org.uk/files/1914/2686/1587/On_everybodys_lips_-_report.pdf. (2015).
6. C. Benoît, M. T. Lallouache, T. Mohamadi, and C. Abry. 1992. A set of French visemes for visual speech synthesis. In *Talking Machines: Theories, Models and Designs*, G. Bailly and C. Benoît (Eds.). Elsevier Science Publishers B. V., North-Holland, Amsterdam, 485–504.
7. H Russell Bernard. 2011. *Research methods in anthropology: Qualitative and quantitative approaches*. Rowman Altamira, Lanham, Maryland.
8. CA Binnie. 1977. Attitude changes following speechreading training. *Scandinavian Audiology* 6, 1 (1977), 13–19.
9. Carl A Binnie, Allen A Montgomery, and Pamela L Jackson. 1974. Auditory and visual contributions to the perception of consonants. *Journal of speech, language, and hearing research* 17, 4 (1974), 619–630.
10. Dan G. Blazer, Sarah Domnitz, and Catharyn T. Liverman (Eds.). 2016. *Hearing Health Care for Adults: Priorities for Improving Access and Affordability*. The National Academies Press, Washington, D.C.
11. Jan Blustein and Barbara E Weinstein. 2016. Opening the Market for Lower Cost Hearing Aids: Regulatory Change Can Improve the Health of Older Americans. *American journal of public health* 106, 6 (2016), 1032–1035.
12. Arthur Boothroyd, Liat Kishon-Rabin, and Robin Waldstein. 1995. Studies of tactile speechreading enhancement in deaf adults. In *Seminars in Hearing*, Vol. 16. Thieme Medical Publishers, Inc., New York, NY, 328–340.
13. Virginia Braun and Victoria Clarke. 2006. Using thematic analysis in psychology. *Qualitative research in psychology* 3, 2 (2006), 77–101.
14. Christoph Bregler and Yochai Konig. 1994. "Eigenlips" for robust speech recognition. In *Acoustics, Speech, and Signal Processing ICASSP-94.*, Vol. 2. IEEE, Piscataway, NJ, II–669.
15. Martha Emma Bruhn. 1949. *The Mueller-Walle Method of Lipreading for The Hard of Hearing*. Volta Bureau, Washington, D.C.
16. Alan Bryman. 2015. *Social research methods*. Oxford University Press, Oxford, United Kingdom.
17. Anna Mae Bunger. 1961. *Speech reading, Jena method: a textbook with lesson plans in full development for hard of hearing adults and discussion of adaptations for hard of hearing and deaf children*. The Interstate, Chicago, IL.
18. Ruth Campbell, Barbara Dodd, and Denis K Burnham. 1998. *Hearing by eye II*. Vol. 2. Psychology Press, Hove, United Kingdom.
19. Richard Orin Cornett. 1967. Cued speech. *Am. Ann. Deaf.* 112, 1 (1967), 3–13.
20. Gary S Dell, Franklin Chang, and Zenzi M Griffin. 1999. Connectionist models of language production: Lexical access and grammatical encoding. *Cognitive Science* 23, 4 (1999), 517–542.
21. D Ebrahimi and H Kunov. 1991. Peripheral vision lipreading aid. *IEEE transactions on biomedical engineering* 38, 10 (1991), 944–952.
22. Melisa Echalier. 2010. In it together: the impact of hearing loss on personal relationships. (2010).
23. Cletus G Fisher. 1968. Confusions among visually perceived consonants. *Journal of Speech, Language, and Hearing Research* 11, 4 (1968), 796–804.
24. Marilyn French-St George and Richard G Stoker. 1988. Speechreading: An historical perspective. *The Volta Review* 90, 5 (1988), 17–21.
25. Stuart Gatehouse, Graham Naylor, and Clous Elberling. 2003. Benefits from hearing aids in relation to the interaction between the user and the environment. *International Journal of Audiology* 42, sup1 (2003), 77–85.
26. E Goldstein. 2013. *Sensation and perception*. Cengage Learning, Independence, KY.
27. Benjamin M Gorman. 2016. Reducing viseme confusion in speech-reading. *ACM SIGACCESS Accessibility and Computing* 114 (2016), 36–43.
28. Beth G Greene, David B Pisoni, and Thomas D Carrell. 1984. Recognition of speech spectrograms. *JASA* 76, 1 (1984), 32–43.
29. Joshua Hailpern, Karrie Karahalios, and James Halle. 2009. Creating a spoken impact: encouraging vocalization through audio visual feedback in children with ASD. In *Proceedings of the SIGCHI conference on human factors in computing systems*. ACM, ACM, New York, NY, 453–462.
30. Louise Hickson, Carly Meyer, Karen Lovelock, Michelle Lampert, and Asad Khan. 2014. Factors associated with success with hearing aids in older adults. *International journal of audiology* 53, sup1 (2014), S18–S27.

31. Shizuo Hiki and Yumiko Fukuda. 1997. Negative Effect of Homophones on Speechreading in Japanese. In *Audio-Visual Speech Processing: Computational & Cognitive Science Approaches*. ISCA, Baxias, France, 9–12.

32. Janet Jeffers and Margaret Barley. 1980. *Speechreading (lipreading)*. Charles C. Thomas Publisher, Springfield, IL.

33. Carl J Jensema, Ramalinga Sarma Danturthi, and Robert Burch. 2000. Time spent viewing captions on television programs. *Am. Ann. Deaf.* 145, 5 (2000), 464–468.

34. Harriet Kaplan, Scott J Bally, and Carol Garretson. 1985. *Speechreading: A way to improve understanding*. Gallaudet University Press, Chicago, IL.

35. C.E Kinzie and R. Kinzie. 1920. The Kinzie method of speech reading. *Volta Review* 22 (1920), 609–19.

36. Patrick Lucey, Terrence Martin, and Sridha Sridharan. 2004. Confusability of phonemes grouped according to their viseme classes in noisy environments. In *Proc. of Australian Int. Conf. on Speech Science & Tech.* Australasian Speech Science and Technology Association (ASSTA), Canberra City, ACT, Australia, 265–270.

37. David F Marks and Lucy Yardley. 2004. *Research methods for clinical and health psychology*. Sage, Thousand Oaks, CA, United States.

38. Dominic W Massaro, Michael M Cohen, Walter Schwartz, Sam Vanderhyden, and Heidi Meyer. 2013. Facilitating Speech Understanding for Hearing-Challenged Perceivers in Face-to-Face Conversation and Spoken Presentations. *ICTHP* (2013).

39. Laura Matthews. 2011. Unlimited potential?: a research report into hearing loss in the workplace. (2011).

40. Abby McCormack and Heather Fortnum. 2013. Why do people fitted with hearing aids not wear them? *International Journal of Audiology* 52, 5 (2013), 360–368.

41. Edward Bartlett Nitchie. 1919. *Lip-reading Principles and Practise: A Hand-book for Teachers and for Self Instruction*. Frederick A. Stokes Company, New York, NY.

42. Catherine Pope, Sue Ziebland, and Nicholas Mays. 2000. Analysing qualitative data. *Bmj* 320, 7227 (2000), 114–116.

43. Zoe Roxburgh, James M Scobbie, and Joanne Cleland. 2015. Articulation therapy for children with cleft palate using visual articulatory models and ultrasound biofeedback. *Proceedings of the 18th ICPhS, Glasgow* 0858 (2015).

44. Oliver Sacks. 2009. *Seeing voices: A journey into the world of the deaf.* Pan Macmillan, London, United Kingdom.

45. Conrad Sanderson and Brian C Lovell. 2009. Multi-region probabilistic histograms for robust and scalable identity inference. In *International Conference on Biometrics*. Springer, New York, NY, 199–208.

46. June E Shoup. 1980. Phonological aspects of speech recognition. In *Trends in speech recognition*. Prentice Hall, Englewood Cliffs, NJ, 125–138.

47. Donald G. Sims, C Dorn, C Clark, L Bryant, and B Mumford. 2002. New developments in computer assisted speechreading and auditory training. *Paper presented at the American Speech-Language Hearing Association convention* (2002).

48. Nancy Tye-Murray. 2002. Conversation made easy: Speechreading and conversation training for individuals who have hearing loss (adults and teenagers). *St. Louis: Central Institute for the Deaf* (2002).

49. Nancy Tye-Murray. 2014. *Foundations of aural rehabilitation: Children, adults, and their family members*. Nelson Education, Scarborough, ON, Canada.

50. University of Auckland, School of Psychology 2016. Why don't we advocate multiple-coders and inter-rater reliability for TA? https://www.psych.auckland.ac.nz/en/about/our-research/research-groups/thematic-analysis/frequently-asked-questions-8.html#c83c77d6d1c625135085e489bd66e765. (2016).

51. Hubert W Upton. 1968. Wearable eyeglass speechreading aid. *American Annals of the Deaf* 113, 2 (1968), 222–229.

52. Akira Watanabe, Shingo Tomishige, and Masahiro Nakatake. 2000. Speech visualization by integrating features for the hearing impaired. *IEEE Trans. Speech Audio Process.* 8, 4 (2000), 454–466.

53. WHO 2015. Deafness and hearing loss, Fact sheet N.300. http://www.who.int/mediacentre/factsheets/fs300/en/. (2015).

54. Lei Xie, Yi Wang, and Zhi-Qiang Liu. 2006. Lip Assistant: Visualize Speech for Hearing Impaired People in Multimedia Services. In *Proc. SMC'06*, Vol. 5. IEEE, Piscataway, NJ, 4331–4336.

55. Hanfeng Yuan, Charlotte M Reed, and Nathaniel I Durlach. 2005. Tactual display of consonant voicing as a supplement to lipreading. *The Journal of the Acoustical society of America* 118, 2 (2005), 1003–1015.

FLight: A Low-Cost Reading and Writing System for Economically Less-Privileged Visually-Impaired People Exploiting Ink-based Braille System

Tusher Chakraborty, Taslim Arefin Khan, and A. B. M. Alim Al Islam
Bangladesh University of Engineering and Technology, Dhaka, Bangladesh.
tusherchakraborty@matholympiad.org.bd,arefin612@gmail.com,alim_razi@cse.buet.ac.bd

ABSTRACT
Reading printed documents and writing on a paper pose a great challenge for visually-impaired people. Existing studies that attempt to solve these challenges are expensive and not feasible in low-income context. Moreover, these studies solve reading and writing problems separately. On the contrary, in this study, we propose *FLight*, a low-cost reading and writing system for economically less-privileged people. *FLight* uses ink-based Braille characters as the medium of textual representation. This helps in keeping a compact spatial representation of texts, yet achieving a low-cost status. Additionally, *FLight* utilizes a low-cost wearable device to enhance ease of reading by visually-impaired people. We conduct a participatory design and iterative evaluation involving five visually-impaired children in Bangladesh for more than 18 months. Our user evaluation reveals that *FLight* is easy-to-use, and exhibits a potential low-cost solution for economically less-privileged visually-impaired people.

Author Keywords
Assistive technology; Wearable device; Braille; Economically less-privileged people

ACM Classification Keywords
K.4.2 Social Issues: Assistive technologies for persons with disabilities

INTRODUCTION
Access to printed text is always a challenge for people having visual impairments. According to WHO, there are approximately 285 million visually-impaired people worldwide, and 90% of them live in low-income settings [6]. While technological advancements have reaped benefits to the sighted peers, challenges involved in reading and writing by visually-impaired people still remain an open problem. Recent development in smart phones and computer vision algorithms have paved paths to new solutions. However, these solutions are expensive which make them unfeasible for economically less-privileged people.

CHI 2017, May 6-11, 2017, Denver, CO, USA.
Copyright © 2017 ACM ISBN 978-1-4503-4655-9/17/05 ...$15.00.
http://dx.doi.org/10.1145/3025453.3025646

The palpable dot based conventional Braille system has been perceived as a difficult and arduous process because of the effort necessary to learn Braille [18]. Consequently, the popularity and literacy rate of Braille generally remains low [3, 17]. The wide market penetration of smart phones and gadgets is one of the reasons behind the fall of Braille's popularity. Ironically, Braille has its influence in the later part of a visually-impaired person's life. Visually-impaired adults having prior Braille literacy exhibit 56% employment rate compared to 23% observed for individuals habituated with plain texts [27, 28]. Moreover, a report from the US Department of Education [22] states that youth with visual impairment are more likely to attend post-secondary school than those with other disabilities. Since this group shows more inclination towards education, a number of research studies have been conducted to solve their reading and writing problems.

There are attempts to ease reading process in both smart phone and wearable form-factor [9, 24, 30]. Computer vision and OCR based algorithms have solved plain text based reading problems. There are applications which offer text writing exploiting speech input or multi-touch gesture input [1, 4, 5]. However, they certainly do not help writing on paper. Braille is often used for writing using embossing kits, so Braille-like smart phone writing applications aim to both help in learning Braille, and rely on existing expertise in writing Braille for faster input [11, 20]. The ease of text based reading and the compactness of Braille based writing have developed two disjoint groups of research studies. Even though smart phones provide alternative solutions to reading and writing problems, it is far from ideal for economically less-privileged people to afford smart phones [21].

Since smart phones and gadgets alone cannot solve this problem, we attempt to investigate whether reviving Braille can help. There are two arguments why Braille is still important. First, Braille has a relationship with employment as discussed before. Second, a study reveals that non-visual free-form handwriting by the visually-impaired is often messy and space inefficient, because, they lack necessary spatial feedback and shape awareness [25]. Since existing solutions also rely on Braille-based writing for faster input, a coherent solution for reading and writing problems is less likely without Braille.

It is now necessary to establish why this coherent solution is important for economically less-privileged people. Developing countries account for 97% of the total world population growth [13]. While it is true that technology penetration is moving fast, people in this region tend to avoid complex functionalities of smart phones [19]. For example, they struggle with navigating through hierarchical organization of information in smart phones. They even struggle with choosing contacts from contact book. They use mobile phones mainly for voice communication [19]. However, the socio-economic infrastructure to support Braille education is also appalling. For example, as a developing country, Bangladesh has only one government run Braille printing press. Palpable Braille printing is expensive. Our investigation in this study reveals that printing Braille book is 65× expensive than printing plain text book (see Table 1). A quick solution to printing problem is utilizing existing normal ink-based printers available in our homes and offices. Two mutually related problems arise here - first, ink-based printing provides no haptic means of reading, second, even if we print using ink-based printers, most state-of-the-art solutions rely on computer vision or OCR techniques, which are unaffordable in low-income settings.

Our study here encompasses solving these two design challenges, plus ensuring a common ground for both reading and writing problems, and yet maintaining a low-cost status. To address these challenges, we take advantage of the reflective characteristics of visible light and employ a novel technique to discern textual patterns. With no camera to capture and analyze the pattern for us, we exploit a simplistic and spatially compact pattern that visually-impaired are already familiar with - Braille. In this study, we undertake a participatory design process involving visually-impaired people, develop a novel low-cost (<$10) wearable device that helps in reading, and a custom-off-the-shelf (COTS) pen that enables writing exploiting ink-based Braille system. Our proposed system exploits finger-held devices, and light plays a cardinal role in reading. As a result, we name our system *FLight.* We also refer the reader to our prior work that presents a simple pen for the visually-impaired to ease reading process [7]. In this paper, our contributions are as follows -

- We design and develop a low-cost (<$10) novel system that helps visually-impaired people in reading and writing ink-based Braille characters. Our solution exploiting ink-based printing reduces cost by more than 80% compared to palpable Braille printing system.
- We undertake a participatory design process involving five visually-impaired children. In a more than 18 months long study, we iteratively design *FLight* from a pen to a wearable form-factor based on their feedback. We also demonstrate culture-specific system design as a use-case study in human-computer interaction design.
- To contrast with our prior work [7] - (a) we make transition in design space - from a commodity pen to a wearable glove, (b) we improve the reading speed from 2 words per minute (wpm) to 13 wpm, (c) we lessen the cognitive stress of identifying Braille dots and recognizing the character, and (d) we introduce Braille writing feature that coherently work with the wearable (reading tool).

RELATED WORK

A number of research studies have been carried out in both academia and industry to solve reading and writing problems of visually-impaired people.

Reading Aid and Technique

Reading devices and techniques vary in the nature of interaction with the users and the modality of their usage. We categorize them here based on the latter.

Mobile Applications: The era of smart phones helped researchers to quickly develop applications that provide audio feedback to the users. Shen and Coughlan [29] describe a prototype smart phone application that reads printed texts. ZoomText [31], SayText [8], etc., are similar examples of text-based readers. Contrary to these applications, VBraille [15] helps in reading by virtually dividing the smart phone screen into six zones corresponding to six dots of a Braille character. It uses vibration when user touches different screen zones to convey presence of a raise dot.

Wearable Solutions: Wearable solutions here are mostly accompanied by a camera to assist in vision, and generates either haptic or audio output, or in some cases both. OrCam [24](price $2,500) is a smart wearable eye glass designed to assist visually-impaired people in reading printed texts. FingerReader [30] is a smart finger-worn device that helps blind users with reading. However, FingerReader may not work under poor lighting condition. HandSight [32] addresses this problem by introducing a self-illuminating finger-worn device.

Braille Based Devices: Conventional Braille reading utilizes haptic senses of the readers. In refreshable Braille displays, the dots of a Braille cell are formed by pins independently controlled by actuators [12]. UbiBraille [23] is a vibration based Braille reading device that actuates the six fingers mapped with six dots of a Braille character.

Writing Aids and Techniques

McSig [25] explores non-visual free-form hand writing by visually-impaired students. No-Look Notes [4] is a pioneering work on the first multi-touch enabled phone screens, which revealed that arranging characters in 8-segment pie menu is less erroneous and more faster than speech based input. Similarly, MTITK [5] is a mobile keyboard where users tap to enter a text, and gesture to edit it. Touchplates [16] is a low-cost acrylic board overlay on a touchscreen providing tactile cues to the soft keyboard displayed underneath. Among the Braille based inputs, BrailleTouch [11] takes Braille input on six virtually divided zones corresponding to six dots on a smart phone. TypeInBraille [20] uses touch-based gestures on smart phones to input one row of a Braille character at a time. In both cases, an audio feedback is provided. Azenkot et al., [2] mapped fingers with Braille dots, and experimented with single hand input versus both hands input. Another work [1] explored speech input by blind people. Their study revealed that participants were satisfied with speech input, however, they spent an average of 80.3% of their time editing the texts.

What is There for the Economically Less-Privileged?

Medhi et al., [21] showed that more than half of the existing mobile phone subscribers live in low-income countries, and most of them are subscribers of low-cost feature phones. Consequently, it is far from ideal for people having low per capita income to afford smart phones. Moreover, apart from

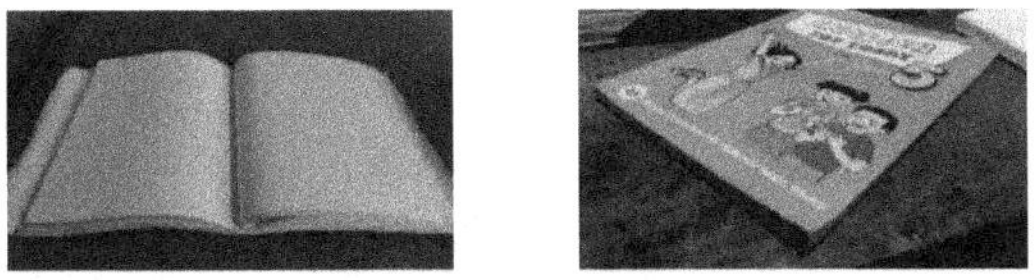

(a) A Braille book (b) Plain print book

Figure 1. English language book for Class 5 in Bangladesh

	Braille print	Plain print
Dimension (l×w×h) cm	27×24×4	25×21×0.7
Number of pages	203	104
Cost (USD)	50	0.76

Table 1. Comparison between Braille and plain text books

standalone devices, some solutions (e.g., FingerReader, HandSight) come with expensive companion computing devices, such as a computer or tablet. We now refer the reader to our first attempt on designing a low-cost reading solution for economically less-privileged people. EyePen [7] is a commodity pen that helps visually-impaired people in reading Braille printed from regular ink-jet printers. The reading process of EyePen is slow. In this paper, we address improvement in reading speed and incorporate writing as a new feature.

RESEARCH CONTEXT

Our more than 18 months long study was conducted at the National Foundation for Betterment of the Disabled at Mirpur, Dhaka. This organization supports basic education and rehabilitation program for different forms of disabilities. As of September 2016, this organization has 30 boys and 18 girls in its school for visually-impaired. We chose this school because of suitable geo-location and it also reflected problems of low-income settings. The monthly tuition fee varies by classes. We report here the average \$3.75 per students. All students reside at the on campus dormitory. The school has ten teachers; five of them have different forms of visual impairment and are quite fluent in Braille. Students of Class 5 are the seniors in this school. After that, they continue high school in other government-run or private schools. The school authority reported that approximately 20% of these students no longer continue education because of various reasons such as poverty, difficulties with Braille, etc.

Books: Braille embossers are expensive [10]. There is only one government run Braille printing press in Bangladesh. Figure 1a shows a Braille printed English book under the national curriculum of Bangladesh. Figure 1b shows the corresponding print for sighted peers. Table 1 demonstrates a comparison between these two books as an example. Here, considering only printing cost, Braille book is 65× costlier than plain print book. Although students in this school receive Braille books free of cost from the government, our primary concern here is the massive cost involvement in printing Braille books. Moreover, the only Braille press struggles to supply academic books in time. Students once spent at least half of their academic year without books [14].

Supporting Tools: The conventional writing system in Braille is complex because it is done from *right to left*. In order to read the same, they flip the paper and read from left to right. Figure 2 shows a supporting tool that assists them

Figure 2. Supporting tool for writing in Braille

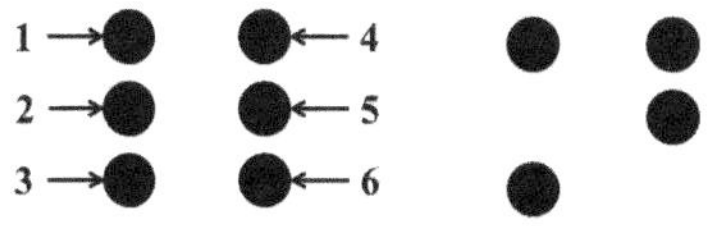

(a) A Braille cell (b) Braille representation of 'N'

Figure 3. Printed form of Braille in our system

Participant	Category	Initial Braille learning period	Age (years)	Writing hand
P1	Blind	1.5 months	8	Left
P2	Blind	4 months	9	Right
P3	Blind	1 months	10	Right
P4	Low vision	5 month	10	Right
P5	Low vision	1.5 months	11	Right

Table 2. Demography of participants

while writing. It has 30 Braille cells per line. Each cell has six small notches for six Braille dots. Visually-impaired people use a small stylus with metallic tip to bore holes at appropriate notches. They use heavy paper such as art paper while writing and are able to utilize only one side of the paper.

Use of Technology: While conducting our study in that school, we found that none of the students were using a smart phone. Some of them used feature mobile phones having physical keyboard. Physical keyboard played an important part because it provided necessary tactile feedback while dialing numbers for voice call. This on-site experience also motivated us to think beyond smart phones.

FLIGHT

FLight evolved through a collaborative evaluation and feedback from a dedicated and strong focus group. Over a period of more than 18 months, this focus group helped us in shaping and outlining *FLight*.

Focus Group and Design Goals

We targeted one primary group and two secondary groups as focus group participants. The primary group consisted of five children from the school. We collaborated directly with the primary focus group to study the usability of our developed system and received feedback for further improvement. The two secondary focus groups consisted of school teachers and two visually-impaired undergraduate students from University of Dhaka (DU). These groups participated in design discussions, idea generation, and also provided feedback. Table 2 shows a demography of primary focus group participants. Following the classification provided by WHO [6], we group moderate and severe visual impairment under 'low vision', and complete vision loss under 'blindness'. Conforming with WHO standard, we refer low vision and blindness together under the umbrella term 'visual impairment'.

Underlying Operational Mechanism

To remind the reader, our endeavor here is to design a system that coherently solves reading and writing problems exploiting

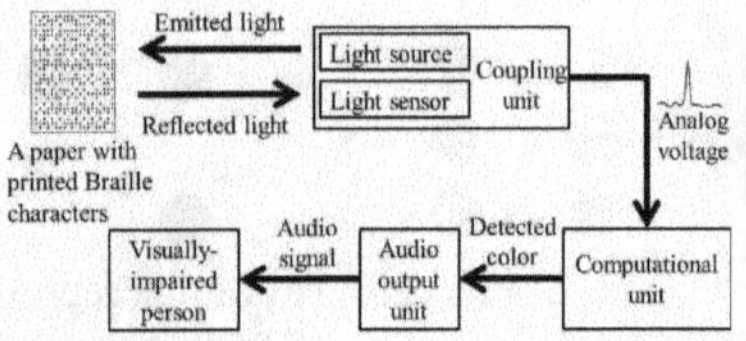

Figure 4. Block diagram of underlying mechanism

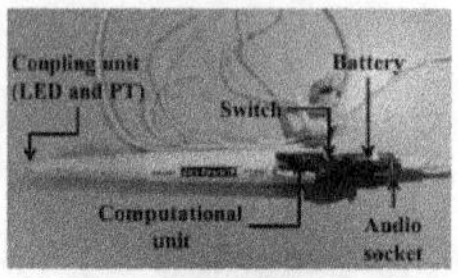

Figure 5. Pen-shaped active sensing body developed in phase 1

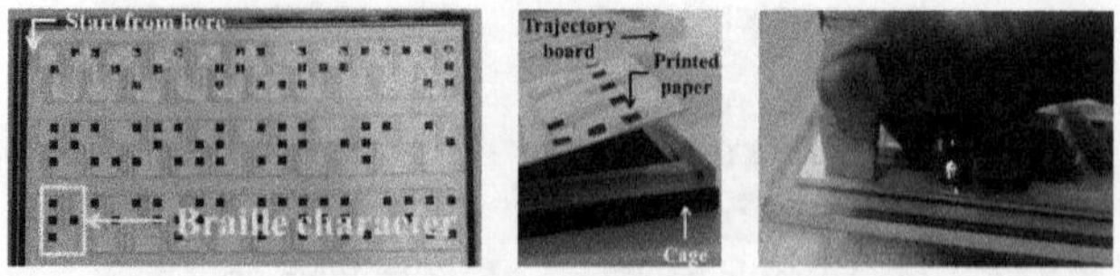

(a) Trajectory board with printed page (b) Closer look (c) Tip fits the drilled hole

Figure 6. Modified printed page and trajectory board used in phase 2

ink-based Braille system. Figure 3a shows an ink-based form of a Braille cell with six filled-circular (or square) dots. Figure 3b shows the character 'N' in Braille format in our system. Using ink-based printers, we wish to print each character in Braille format as shown. With no haptic feedback and no camera to help, how exactly are we going to provide feedback to the user? Here, we present the underlying operational mechanism that works at the core of our system, followed by a simplified operational block diagram.

A black-colored surface absorbs most of the incident light energy, whereas, a white-colored surface reflects most of the incident light energy. As a result, the intensity of light reflected from a white-colored surface is significantly higher than that from a black-colored surface. To corroborate this phenomenon, we conduct a testbed experiment in different ambient lighting conditions. The experimental setup consists of a white paper having printed black colored region on it, and a coupling of LED and phototransistor (PT). Experimental results confirm that there is a significant difference between the voltages generated by PT for two different colored regions [7].

Figure 4 represents a simplified block diagram of the underlying operational mechanism of our system. The system consists of four units: (1) A paper with printed Braille characters, (2) A Coupling unit, (3) A Computational unit, and (4) An audio output unit. In our proposed system, we print Braille characters in black ink over white papers using normal ink-jet printers. Components $2-4$ are used to recognize Braille characters and generate an audio output to visually-impaired people.

Using the underlying system design, we develop our system phase by phase. In each phase, we accumulate user feedback and revise our system accordingly in the next phase.

PRELIMINARY WORK

For simplicity of exposition, we summarize here the first two iterative phases presented in our prior work [7]. Although we summarize here key points in terms of design and user evaluation, we refer the reader to our prior work for details.

Phase 1

The initial design presented in our prior work was mostly intuition driven. We summarize here our first design followed by the user feedback.

Tangible Object Design

Designing for visually-impaired is always challenging. The social model of disability [18] and the demand for portable assistive tools helped us understand the subtlety involved while designing assistive tools for the visually-impaired. Consequently, our design evolved as a pervasive portable pen-shaped body. Figure 5 shows a snapshot of the pen. This pen generates an audible beep when it detects the presence of a black-colored region on the white paper placed beneath the pen tip.

Using this pen, we intended to read Braille characters similar to that presented in Figure 3. To do so, a visually-impaired person needs to perceive the relative positions of Braille characters and their dots. We facilitated this process by designing a predefined trajectory to drag the pen tip on the printed paper. Here, the visually-impaired participants perceived this trajectory through audio-feedback generated by the pen instead of haptic feedback. We would like to refer the reader to our prior work [7] for the details on reading procedure.

Usability Analysis

Analyzing the feedback from the first user evaluation involving our focus group, we pointed out several crucial aspects:

- Following the predefined trajectory exploiting the audio-feedback is strenuous for a visually-impaired person.
- Since the threshold demarcating black and white region depends on ambient lighting condition [7], the pen undergoes an initial calibration to set the threshold value. This calibration process makes the reading procedure cumbersome. Nevertheless, the threshold could also change with the change in ambient lighting condition while reading.

Phase 2

In the second phase, we addressed the problems and integrated the improvement suggestions provided by the focus group after the first deployment. Although we summarize here key points in terms of design consideration and user evaluation, we encourage the reader to our prior work for details [7].

Solving The Alignment and Calibration Issues

The first user evaluation allowed us to contemplate at the way visually-impaired people behave and perceive information. One of the key aspects of conventional Braille reading system is that, it leverages the haptic sense of the reader by tiny palpable bumps or raised dots. However, our preliminary system depended on the correctness in dragging the pen along a predefined trajectory by leveraging the auditory senses only, which was difficult and error-prone. Consequently, we needed to produce a way that could make use of the haptic sense.

We attempted to leverage the haptic sense through using a hard thick board. To do so, we developed a novel board that contained a trajectory drilled along the thickness and guides tip of the pen-shaped body to follow a predefined path (as shown in Figure 6). Besides, the hole on trajectory board and the tip were shaped in such a way that the hole fits the tip (as shown in Figure 6c). To do so, an opaque boundary was

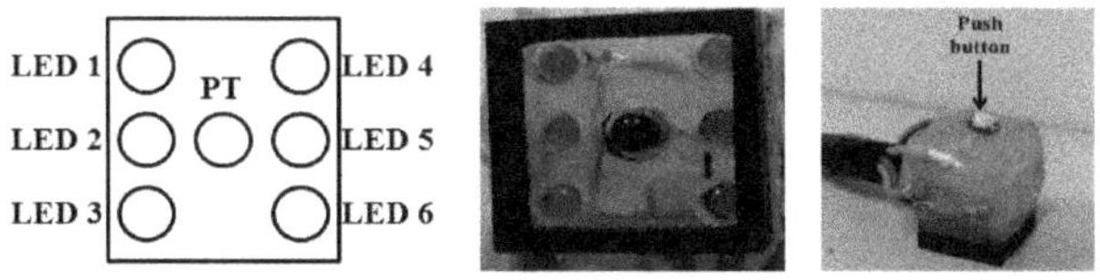

(a) LED, PT placements (b) Front view (c) Entire view

Figure 7. Modified Coupling unit in phase 3

built around the LED and PT. The modified design of the tip implicitly solved the calibration problem, as the opaque wall kept the Coupling unit out of the influence of ambient light.

User Evaluation

We conducted a second user evaluation based on the improvements made in phase 2. Due to space limitations, based on the user feedback, we outline here only two crucial aspects that can drive us towards further improvement.

- **Escalating Reading Process:** Using the current prototype of our system, one can read as much as 2 words per minute. When we asked the participants to comment about our system, P2 and P5 used their imagination and said that, *"It would have been better if this pen could tell me the character, or at least enumerate the dot positions"*.
- **Potential for Aiding in Writing:** Although the temporal disadvantages of our system was a concerning issue, the focus group expressed interest on exploiting the aiding capability of ink-based Braille in writing. P3 opined that our system could be more useful during writing.

PHASE 3

The second deployment turned our focus towards two pivotal aspects: escalating reading process and potential of ink-based writing. In this section, first, we delineate how we develop the wearable solution *FLight* to speed-up the reading process. Second, we delineate our proposed ink-based Braille writing feature that coherently work with this wearable.

Improvements

Up until phase 2, our system could detect only one Braille dot at a time. The previous user evaluation revealed that it required around 5s to recognize a single Braille character, since a visually-impaired person have to scan all the six dot positions of a single Braille character through placing the pen-tip (i.e., the Coupling unit) on six different dot positions in sequence. This extent of time required for recognizing a character is significantly higher than the conventional palpable system. Here, though it merely takes 5ms to detect a dot, the time consuming part in recognizing a character is the manual movement of pen-tip to six different dot positions of a Braille character. An intuitive idea to address this problem is to detect all the six possible dots of a single Braille character without any manual movement, i.e., by keeping the tip of *FLight* fixed at one position. Driven by the same intuition, one might think of incorporating six pairs of LED and PT to detect six different dots at the same time. However, from the pragmatic point of view, there will arise several problems in such a design: (1) integration of five more PTs will demand five more analog to digital converter (ADC) channels of microcontroller and that will give rise to both power consumption and hardware

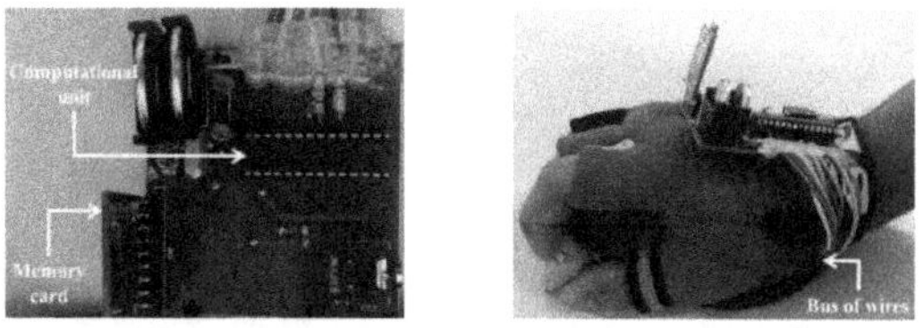

(a) Modified circuit board (b) Wearable glove

Figure 8. Modified *FLight* and its circuit board in phase 3

redundancy, (2) the expensive part of the Coupling unit is PT which costs around 60 times more than the cost of an LED and thus the integration of five more PTs will demand colossal cost, (3) integration of six pairs of LED and PT will increase the size of the Coupling unit, which can result in much lower character density than current implementation, and (4) since power consumption is a crucial issue here, it will not be a wise decision to turn six LEDs on at a time.

Modified Coupling Unit: As a remedy, we modify the Coupling unit in such a way that it escalates the reading procedure and does not give rise to the aforementioned problems. Our new design of the Coupling unit subsumes only one PT and six LEDs, as shown in Figure 7. The six LEDs are positioned in such a way that whenever the Coupling unit is placed over a Braille character, all six LEDs are placed exactly on top of corresponding six dots of the Braille character. Therefore, the six LEDs are arranged in 3×2 matrix as shown in Figure 7a, where the PT is placed in between the two columns. Here, using one PT in a judicious manner, we make six pairs of LED and PT in the temporal domain. To further elaborate, we do not simultaneously keep all the LEDs turned on, rather we turn the LEDs on one by one. Thus, when we turn any one of the six LEDs on, the region beneath the LED is illuminated only, and the light reflected from that region hits the PT. Consequently, the voltage generated by the PT represents color of the region situated directly beneath the LED. Iterating the same process for all the six LEDs, we can get color of the regions beneath the LEDs and thus, the system recognizes the absence/presence of all six dots.

The Wearable: We explore the design space of wearables and employ our changes in a comfortable and lightweight hand glove. Such a wearable form-factor offers portability, ease-of-access, and impacts social interaction positively [33]. Figure 8a shows the new circuit board of *FLight*, which we affix on the glove. Since our intention is to recognize a Braille character and dictate the corresponding audio clip to the user, we also include a memory card (available in local market at price below \$1.5) to store all alphanumeric audio clips. Figure 8b shows the complete wearable glove for reading.

Modified Trajectory Board: The modified trajectory board is much simpler than the previous one. It consists of 130 rectangular shaped holes and each hole covers a Braille character printed on a paper, which is attached beneath the board (as shown in Figure 9a). The hole on trajectory board and the Coupling unit are shaped in such a way that the hole fits the Coupling unit (as shown in Figure 9b).

While reading a Braille character, a visually-impaired person places the Coupling unit in the corresponding rectangular

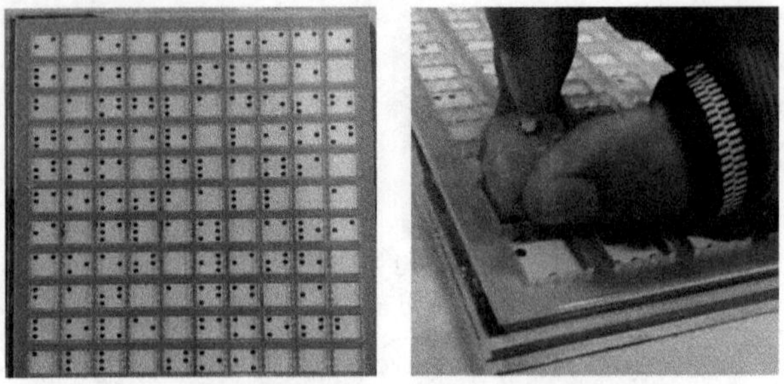

(a) The board with printed paper (b) Coupling unit fits the board

Figure 9. Modified trajectory board used in phase 3

(a) (b) (c) (d)

Figure 10. Writing system design and procedure

drilled hole of the trajectory board (as shown in Figure 9b). Since power consumption is crucial here, we design the system such that the system reads only when the reader wishes to read. This is done by introducing a push switch as shown in Figure 7c. The push button is placed in such a position that when a visually-impaired person holds the Coupling unit, the index finger automatically comes over the push button (as shown in Figure 9b). Upon placing the Coupling unit in a hole, the visually-impaired person presses the button to activate the reading procedure. Next, the Computational unit turns the LED on, which corresponds to the Braille dot '1', on for 5ms and takes reading of voltage generated by the PT. Then, the voltage is compared with a pre-defined threshold, which is set experimentally as discussed earlier, to detect the presence/absence of dot '1'. After that, the Computational unit turns that LED off and turns the next LED on, which corresponds to the Braille dot '2'. In a similar manner, it scans all six dots of the Braille character within only 60ms and recognizes the alphanumeric character represented by that Braille character. Upon recognizing the Braille character, the Computational unit searches the database for corresponding sound and plays it.

Note that, our current prototype allows us to print 130 Braille characters on each side of a page, making it 260 overall per page. Here, for prototyping purpose, we used Dual in-line package(DIP) of LED and PT. Commercial production subsumes Surface Mount Device(SMD) which is 3 to 4 times smaller in dimension than DIP. This can significantly increase char density (∼ 600 characters/page).

Ink-based Braille Writing

Up to this point, we have delineated the evolution of *FLight* as a reading tool for visually-impaired people exploiting ink-based Braille system. Keeping alive our central motivation to design a common ground for reading and writing, we design a low-cost COTS writing aid for visually-impaired people exploiting ink-based Braille system. In our design, we attempt to leverage the haptic sense of a visually-impaired person ensuring a low-cost status. Here, we use a retractable marker available in local market at less than $1. It is important to ensure that visually-impaired writers place dot exactly where they intended. To ensure swift writing movement and alignment, we design a small frame made of acrylic (as shown in Figure 10a), which we attach at the tip of this marker (as shown in Figure 10b). The writing procedure subsumes the existing trajectory board used in phase 3 with a small modification. Note that this modification does not influence the reading procedure described in phase 3. We make 6 mini concave notches on two vertical walls of a single hole on existing trajectory board (as shown in Figure 10c). Each vertical wall contains 3 concave notches keeping same relative positions corresponding to the Braille dot positions. While writing a Braille dot, a visually-impaired person fits one of two convex mountings of the frame with a concave notch which corresponds to that Braille dot (as shown in Figure 10d), utilizing the haptic sense.

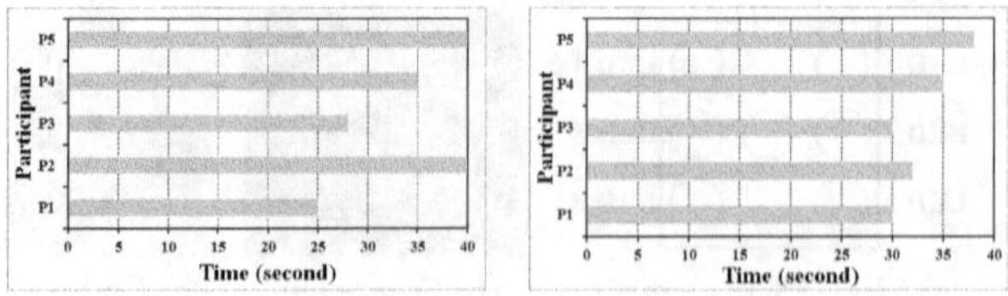

(a) For reading (b) For writing

Figure 11. Training period

SYSTEM EVALUATION

We conducted a series of evaluations to explore whether *FLight* can provide a coherent reading and writing support for visually-impaired people. In this section, we delineate the results of evaluations followed a usability survey.

Reading

The most interesting aspect of working with visually-impaired children was their enthusiasm and intuition towards a new object. In this phase too, we followed these steps while evaluating our system - (1) introduce the system to each participants individually, (2) let the participants touch and feel the system and hear from them what they are touching, (3) a hands-on demonstration to the participants on how to operate the system, and (4) let the participants use the system on their own.

Training Period

We consider steps 3-4 as the training period. We define training period as the time during which the participants were completely able to demonstrate by themselves on how to use *FLight*. Figure 11a shows the training time for reading. Surprisingly, the maximum training time period for any participant was 40 seconds. Two issues accounted for such a small time. First, we found their perception and intuition towards haptic sense very strong during step 2. Second, their prior experience with the previous iterations [7] helped them anticipate the behavior of our system. Note that, we reserved steps 1-2 for informal training time. While sighted peers can use vision to understand the behavior of a system, non-sighted people mostly use their haptic sense to understand a system. Hence, we kept provision for informal discussions during steps 1-2.

Reading with FLight

We organized the reading sessions in gradual improving order - (1) reading (listening) to every audible character using *FLight*,

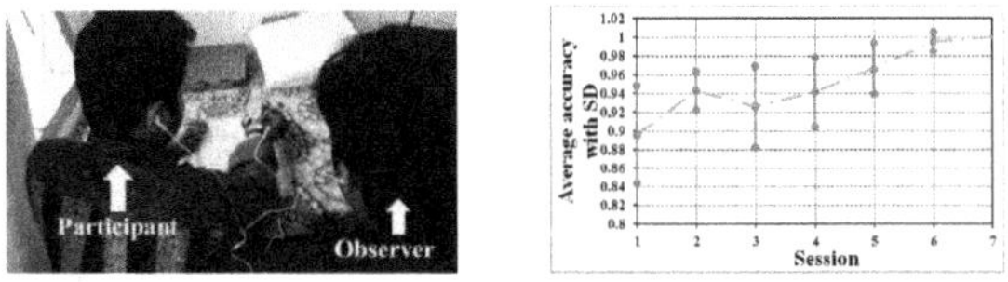

(a) Sharing earphone to observe errors (b) Accuracy of recognizing characters

Figure 12. Experimental process and accuracy of reading characters

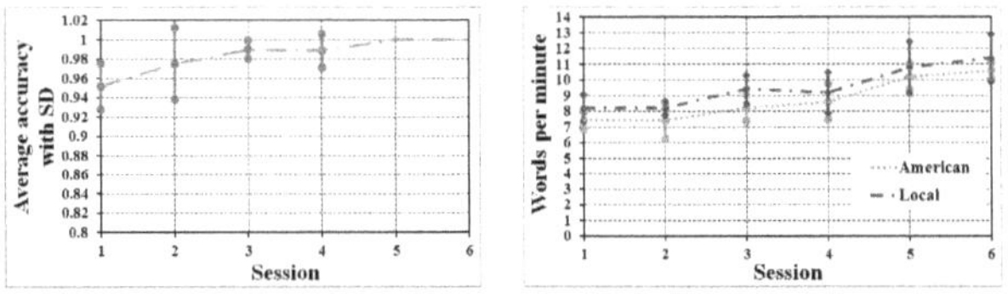

(a) Accuracy of forming word (b) Words formed per minute

Figure 13. Statistics while forming word by recognizing individual character(s)

(2) forming words from just read characters. In doing so, we took note of two important errors - **system error** is an error generated by our system, and **human error** is an error on behalf of the human, for example, the system outputs 'B' when there is an actual 'B', however, the human mistakenly perceives that as 'D'.

Reading (recognizing) Single Character: We asked participants to read aloud characters as they hear them. This is called oral reading. To cross-check for errors while reading, we asked them to put one earphone in their best ear, and used the other for ourself, as shown in Figure 12a. In Figure 12b we report the accuracy of reading simple characters in Braille using *FLight*. In each session, we provided a set of 100 alphanumeric characters that were randomly organized. We continued until Session 7, where all the participants correctly enunciated the characters. It led us to an interesting finding - **accent** played an important while participants struggled to perceive the system dictated character. The default audio clip that we used here dictated characters in American accent. P4 complained, *"It's a bit strange. 'T' and 'P' sounds similar. Why?"* As shown in Figure 12b, in Session 1, the accuracy of recognizing characters was 89% (SD=5). With each session, they became more habituated and adapted themselves with the nuances of this accent. For example, in Session 6, only P2 made mistakes in 3 characters. Here, the **system error** was 0% for all sessions.

Forming Word: We then asked the participants to form word as they read the characters. We conducted this experiment in oral mode. To remind our readers, *FLight* provides audible dictation of the characters to participants, and provides no audible sound when a space was found. We provided printed documents with meaningful words in the form of sentences. We started counting reading time using a stopwatch whenever a participant was ready to read. In six consecutive sessions that lasted for ten minutes each, the accuracy of forming word peaked in the last two sessions, as shown in Figure 13a. It clearly shows that participants adapted to *FLight* with time and practice. During these sessions, P3 and P5 made personal best of 11 wpm. We provided regular and age appropriate dictionary words that had diversity in word-length, such as words so small as 2 characters to words so large as 12 characters.

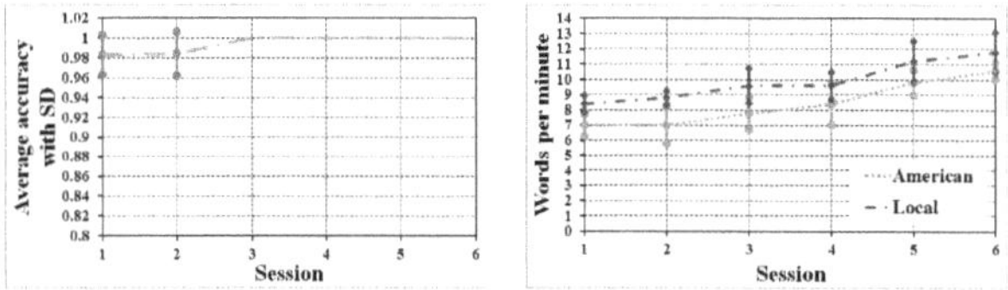

(a) Accuracy of forming word (b) Words formed per minute

Figure 14. Statistics while forming word by recognizing character(s) all together at the space interval

	Standard Braille	Using FLight
Silent reading (wpm)	33 (± 9)	25 (± 4)
Oral reading (wpm)	19 (± 7)	12 (± 1)

Table 3. Standard Braille reading speed vs. reading speed using *FLight*

Preliminary Feedback on Reading: We summarize here the preliminary feedback from the participants on reading.

1. Participants had to memorize just-read characters in order to form words which was cumbersome. All the participants raised this issue upon completing the six sessions.
2. The default audible sound having American accent was troublesome. The participants were habituated with local accent. Consequently, their accuracy of recognizing characters improved slowly (Figure 12b).

Recognizing Characters at Space Interval: We address the preliminary feedback and modify *FLight* for the second time in phase 3. This time *FLight* does not dictate the character immediately after scanning it, rather it provides a smooth audible tone as a feedback and saves the characters in a run-time queue. When a space is scanned *FLight* dictates just-read audible characters from the queue. The visually-impaired person can hear these characters repeatedly by pressing the push button at space. However, when *FLight* starts to scan a new character after scanning a space, it overwrites the queue. The relative advantage of this arrangement is clear from Figure 14a, where accuracy improved than that in Figure 13a. Figure 14b illustrates the advantage over temporal domain.

Our endeavor in this phase was to escalate the reading procedure using *FLight*. Here, we achieved up to 13 wpm while reading, which is 6× more than that of previous phase. Additionally, in Table 3, we show a comparison between standard Braille reading speed and the reading speed using *FLight* in wpm. Pertaining to other studies such as [26] that quantifies reading speed, we also report here silent reading and oral reading. In silent reading, the reader is allowed to read silently with sustained attention, concentration, and comfort. In oral reading, the reader is asked to read aloud. Since our primary goal was to evaluate the accuracy of *FLight*, our sessions were conducted in oral reading mode to measure wpm and the errors while reading. Additionally, we conducted two more informal sessions in silent reading mode to report a quantitative comparison in Table 3.

Writing

The adoption of writing was very quick after a short training session. They intuitively started to use one hand to move the

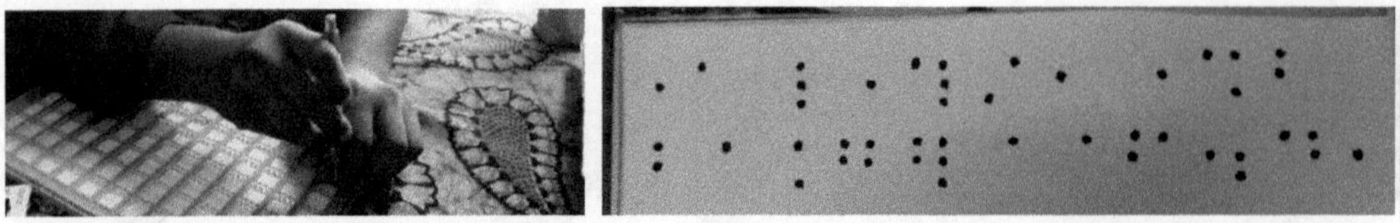

(a) A visually-impaired person while writing (b) Small portion of a paragraph written by P4

Figure 15. Deployment of writing tool involving the focus group

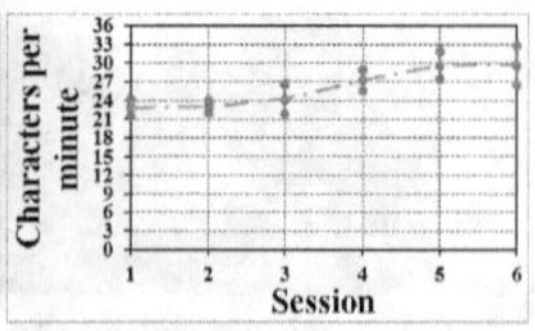

Figure 16. Characters written per minute

marker and another hand to press the push button of marker (as shown in Figure 15a). We noted down the time during which the participants were able to achieve a spatial awareness required for writing using the marker and our trajectory board. We again found their perception towards haptic senses very strong, the results of which were reflected in Figure 11b.

We asked the participants to write a paragraph for ten minutes in each session, topics included but not limited to their country, their favorite hobby, their parents, etc. Figure 15b presents a snapshot showing small portion of a paragraph written by P4. We then shuffled each piece of writing among the participants and let them read what others have written. We report here characters written per minute in Figure 16. This session was lengthy because we cross-checked with the writer what he actually intended to write. Nevertheless, when we asked them to read back the written pieces, we evaluated based on what was written only. Owing to previous practices, the participants were able to read and understand the written characters. This time the accuracy of reading was 100%.

Usability Survey

In addition to performing user evaluation, we perform a usability survey that explores both formal and informal comments and reviews from focus group participants.

Ease of Use: Our iterative design method helped us to gain generous feedback from focus group participants. Our reading technique evolved from an object (pen) [7] to a wearable form-factor, with significant improvement. All of the participants liked our wearable glove. P3 said, *"Well, I like this glove-thing more. It tells me the character, not that irritating beep like before."* We found them happy knowing that they can read printed materials from regular printers. *"Really? You can do that?"*, exclaimed P5 in a surprising tone. P3 explained why his friend was surprised, *"We do not have Braille versions of any non-academic books, so we do not read story books, we listen to radio sometimes."* The audible character feedback generated some concerns. The initial American accent appeared to be difficult for them. They struggled with alphabets having closely related phonetic sounds in American accent. For example, {'B', 'P', 'T'}, {'B', 'D'}, and {'I', 'Y'}. The error rates were discussed in section "Phase 3". We later experimented with a local dialect of English alphabets. They were also curious about writing when we said they can write with a pen too. However, P2 said, *"I would love a shorter pen for writing that fits my fist."* Shorter retractable pen, although available in other countries, were unfortunately absent in the local market of Bangladesh.

Will Grown-ups Accept *FLight*?: We made formal and informal discussions with two visually-impaired undergraduate students at the University of Dhaka (DU). We asked them to try out *FLight*. We found them excited in the beginning, however, we felt that they were reluctant to try out further after two sessions. We then asked them how they manage their daily academic activities. Three important facts evolved here - (1) they do not have Braille books in the university although DU own one Braille embosser which has been out of service for some years, (2) they rely on audio recitations made by their fellow sighted peers, and (3) none of them own a smart phone or gadget, rather they find feature phones easy to use. These facts are important, particularly because other low income countries reflect them as well. Nevertheless, when we asked them how they appear in examinations, they replied, *"We bring a junior as a writer; we dictate, they write."* Consequently, it became clear to us their apparent disinterest to use *FLight*, because they had long deserted reading and writing in Braille, and were more used to with audio based activities. This led us to focus on children as primary participant, because, early adoption of a system always plays a vital role in its future uses.

Statement	P1	P2	P3	P4	P5
The wearable was comfortable	5	5	5	4	4
I prefer gloves over previous pen	5	5	5	4	5
Reading was easy	5	3	5	4	3
Writing was easy	4	3	5	4	4
Writing was intuitive	5	5	5	5	5
I enjoyed *FLight* overall	5	5	5	5	5
I will use *FLight* in future	5	3	3	2	4

Table 4. Results from the questionnaire on 5-point Likert scale

Summary: We summarize the user feedback in Table 4. We let the participants answer or express their opinion based on the 5-point Likert scale. Here, '1' referred to 'strongly disagree', '2' referred to 'disagree', '3' referred to 'undecided', '4' referred to 'agree', and '5' referred to 'strongly agree'.

DISCUSSION

In this section, we discuss the reading speed, Braille proficiency, and the cost effectiveness pertinent to *FLight*.

Reading Speed: From Table 3 we see that wpm count using *FLight* is close to that of the standard Braille reading speed in both cases for the same set of participants. Although wpm count using *FLight* appear as a concerning issue, note that, our participants are students from Class 1 to 5 whose average wpm is less than adults' wpm measure. Moreover, the reported values in Table 3 conform with [26] for the same age group. Besides, one of the teachers at the school also commented about the reading speed, *"The last time a student said your devices could read 2 wpm, right? And now its 13 wpm! This*

	Using Braille	Using FLight
Dimension (l×w×h) cm	27×24×4	29.7×21×4.5
Number of pages	203	542
Printing cost	$52	$8
Paper cost (500 pages)	$31.93	$3.83

Table 5. Comparison between Braille printing and printing for *FLight*

is great improvement. You see, people take a month long to grasp Braille itself, so with practice they can improve with your device as well."

Braille proficiency: While we argue that Braille is important, it might appear to the reader that *FLight* is penalizing Braille proficiency while reading. There are two reasons why *FLight* facilitates such reading process. First, from [7], we know that perceiving the relative positions of six dots and simultaneously recognizing the character was slow and stressful. *FLight* addressed these two issues by automating the character recognition process and providing an audio-feedback based on the recognized character. Second, *FLight* offers a coherent solution to address reading and writing problems. Writing with *FLight* requires as much proficiency in Braille as required in standard Braille. Therefore, *FLight* does not penalize Braille proficiency as a coherent solution. As a low-cost tool with an inclusive design addressing both reading and writing problems, *FLight* encourages Braille proficiency similar to standard Braille.

How Low is Our Low-cost?: In Table 5 we show a comparison between conventional Braille printing and printing for *FLight* for the same text book of Class 5. In terms of only printing cost, our system is 80% more cost-effective than Braille printing. Note that, we have excluded here other variable and fixed cost involved in production, such as labor cost, transport cost, maintenance cost, etc. The press owners were reluctant to share these information with us fearing us to be journalists or other private competitors. We therefore reserve from reporting *unsure* and *approximate* numbers. Moreover, visually-impaired people use art papers while writing by boring holes. While using *FLight*, a visually-impaired person can use normal paper, which is 8× cheaper than art paper. Note that, our current implementation is fashioned by hand-made lab equipments and limited to DIP package only. Character density is influenced by the size of our reading device. This has been discussed in section "Phase 3". Overall, *FLight* is a cost-effective system than state-of-the-art practices.

FUTURE WORK

We summarize here the potential future work in this section.

Continuous Reading: The current difficulty in temporal domain is due to a limitation in tactile representation and feedback. Contrary to existing implementation, a system with continuous scan and read will improve reading time and words per minute count.

Multi-button Retractable Pen: Instead of a single button retractable pen, we wish to explore the use of six-button (corresponding to six dots) retractable pen. The size of the tip will be similar to the size of the current Coupling unit, having six independent nib corresponding to six buttons.

CONCLUSION

In this study, we propose *FLight*, a low-cost system comprising a wearable device for reading, a retractable pen for writing, and a tactile trajectory board for assisting reading and writing. *FLight* uses Braille as the underlying medium of textual representation. In this system, Braille characters are printed using normal ink-based printers available in our homes and offices. We exploit the classical reflection model of light, design a low-cost (<$10) wearable device for recognizing Braille characters, and provide audible feedback. Besides, the retractable pen with COTS frame at the tip serves tactile grip while writing using the trajectory board. The entire design process evolved in a participatory fashion involving focus group members. We evaluated our system with the focus group members consisting five visually-impaired children. Using our system, participants achieved up to 13 words per minute (wpm) in reading and 33 characters per minute (cpm) in writing.

We observed an uncompromising importance of accents in the audible feedback. Participants favored local accent English over American accent. We also observed significant improvement on reading speed (wpm) over successive sessions. The least time period a participant in our focus group took to learn conventional palpable Braille system is 1 month; consequently we believe that with improvements in the device and practice by the participants, reading wpm and writing cpm will improve. On top of everything, *FLight* is cost-effective, as printing Braille characters based on normal ink can reduce printing cost by more than 80%. Such a cost-saving system is very important and significantly impacts the lives of less-privileged visually-impaired people.

ACKNOWLEDGMENT

We sincerely thank our shepherd AC and the reviewers for their insightful comments and feedback.

REFERENCES

1. S. Azenkot and N. B Lee. 2013. Exploring the Use of Speech Input by Blind People on Mobile Devices. In *Proceedings of the 15th International ACM SIGACCESS Conference on Computers and Accessibility*. ACM, 11.
2. S. Azenkot, J. O Wobbrock, S. Prasain, and R. E Ladner. 2012. Input Finger Detection for Nonvisual Touch Screen Text Entry in Perkinput. In *Proceedings of Graphics Interface 2012*. Canadian Information Processing Society, 121–129.
3. American Foundation for the Blind. 2015. School Experience for Children and Youth with Vision Loss. (January 2015). Retrieved February 21, 2016 from `http://goo.gl/1Np4m2`.
4. M. N Bonner, J. T Brudvik, G. D Abowd, and W K. Edwards. 2010. No-look notes: Accessible Eyes-free Multi-touch Text Entry. In *International Conference on Pervasive Computing*. Springer, 409–426.
5. M. C. Buzzi, M. Buzzi, B. Leporini, and A. Trujillo. 2014. Designing a Text Entry Multimodal Keypad for Blind Users of Touchscreen Mobile Phones. In *Proceedings of the 16th international ACM SIGACCESS Conference on Computers & Accessibility*. ACM, 131–136.

6. Media Center. 2014. Visual impairment and blindness. (August 2014). Retrieved February 15, 2016 from http://goo.gl/BG8XTG.
7. T. Chakraborty, T. A. Khan, and ABM Islam. 2016. EyePen: Ease of Reading for Less-Privileged Visually-Impaired People. In *Proceedings of the 7th Annual Symposium on Computing for Development*. ACM, 13.
8. DocScanner. 2010. SayText. (June 2010). Retrieved March 23, 2016 from http://goo.gl/aLvPBS.
9. Be My Eyes. 2016. Be My Eyes | Lend your eyes to the blind. (2016). Retrieved September 15, 2016 from http://goo.gl/wiBP0B.
10. American Foundation for the Blind. 2016. Braille Printers. (2016). Retrieved September 18, 2016 from https://goo.gl/C14WYk.
11. B. Frey, C. Southern, and M. Romero. 2011. Brailletouch: Mobile Texting for the Visually Impaired. In *International Conference on Universal Access in Human-Computer Interaction*. Springer, 19–25.
12. T. Fukuda, H. Morita, F. Arai, H. Ishihara, and H. Matsuura. 1997. Micro Resonator Using Electromagnetic Actuator for Tactile Display. In *Micromechatronics and Human Science, 1997. Proceedings of the 1997 International Symposium on*. IEEE, 143–148.
13. Carl Haub. 2012. Fact Sheet: World Population Trends 2012. (2012). Retrieved September 18, 2016 from https://goo.gl/LvZ2Hr.
14. Mansura Hussain. 2012. Delayed supply of books for visually-impaired. (2012). Retrieved September 15, 2016 from https://goo.gl/4xzrnP.
15. C. Jayant, C. Acuario, W. Johnson, J. Hollier, and R. Ladner. 2010. V-braille: Haptic Braille Perception Using a Touch-screen and Vibration on Mobile Phones. In *Proceedings of the 12th International ACM SIGACCESS Conference on Computers and Accessibility*. ACM, 295–296.
16. S. K Kane, M. R. Morris, and J. O Wobbrock. 2013. Touchplates: Low-cost Tactile Overlays for Visually Impaired Touch Screen Users. In *Proceedings of the 15th International ACM SIGACCESS Conference on Computers and Accessibility*. ACM, 22.
17. R. M. Leonard. 2001. *Statistics on vision impairment: A resource manual* (5th ed.). Lighthouse International.
18. Vincent Lévesque. 2005. Blindness, Technology and Haptics. *Center for Intelligent Machines* (2005), 19–21.
19. I. M. Thies. 2015. User interface design for low-literate and novice users: past, present and future. *Foundations and Trends in Human-Computer Interaction* 8, 1 (2015), 1–72.
20. S. Mascetti, C. Bernareggi, and M. Belotti. 2012. TypeInBraille: Quick Eyes-free Typing on Smartphones. In *International Conference on Computers for Handicapped Persons*. Springer, 615–622.
21. I. Medhi, M. Jain, A. Tewari, M. Bhavsar, M. Matheke-Fischer, and E. Cutrell. 2012. Combating Rural Child Malnutrition Through Inexpensive Mobile Phones. In *Proceedings of the 7th Nordic Conference on Human-Computer Interaction: Making Sense Through Design*. ACM, 635–644.
22. L. Newman, M. Wagner, R. Cameto, A. Knokey, J. A. Buckley, and D. Malouf. 2009. The Post-High School Outcomes of Youth With Disabilities up to 4 Years After High School. (2009). Retrieved September 18, 2016 from https://goo.gl/eL0axg.
23. H. Nicolau, J. Guerreiro, T. Guerreiro, and L. Carriço. 2013. UbiBraille: Designing and Evaluating a Vibrotactile Braille-reading Device. In *Proceedings of the 15th International ACM SIGACCESS Conference on Computers and Accessibility*. ACM, 23.
24. OrCam. 2016. OrCam - See for Yourself. (2016). Retrieved February 20, 2016 from www.orcam.com.
25. B. Plimmer, A. Crossan, S. A Brewster, and R. Blagojevic. 2008. Multimodal Collaborative Handwriting Training for Visually-Impaired People. In *Proceedings of the SIGCHI Conference on Human Factors in Computing Systems*. ACM, 393–402.
26. D. Radojichikj and D. Blagoj. 2015. Students with visual impairments: Braille reading rate. *International Journal of Cognitive Research in Science, Engineering and Education (IJCRSEE)* 3, 1 (2015), 1–5.
27. Ruby Ryles. 1996. The Impact of Braille Reading Skills on Employment, Income, Education, and Reading Habits. *Journal of Visual Impairment and Blindness* 90 (1996), 219–226.
28. Ruby Ryles. 1999. New Research Study: Early Braille Education Vital in Establishing Lifelong Literacy. *Future Reflections* 18, 2 (1999).
29. H. Shen and J. M. Coughlan. 2012. Towards a Real-Time System for Finding and Reading Signs for Visually Impaired Users.. In *ICCHP (2)*, Vol. 7383. Springer, 41–47.
30. R. Shilkrot, J. Huber, W. Meng Ee, P. Maes, and S. Nanayakkara. 2015. FingerReader: A Wearable Device to Explore Printed Text on The Go. In *Proceedings of the 33rd Annual ACM Conference on Human Factors in Computing Systems*. ACM, 2363–2372.
31. Ai Squared. 2016. ZoomText. (2016). Retrieved on March 22, 2016 from http://goo.gl/LFLQSj.
32. L. Stearns, R. Du, U. Oh, C. Jou, L. Findlater, D. A Ross, and J. E. Froehlich. 2016. Evaluating Haptic and Auditory Directional Guidance to Assist Blind People in Reading Printed Text Using Finger-Mounted Cameras. (2016).
33. H. Ye, M. Malu, U. Oh, and L. Findlater. 2014. Current and future mobile and wearable device use by people with visual impairments. In *Proceedings of the SIGCHI Conference on Human Factors in Computing Systems*. ACM, 3123–3132.

Teaching Language and Culture with a Virtual Reality Game

Alan Cheng[1], Lei Yang[2], and Erik Andersen[1]
[1]Department of Computer Science, [2]Department of City and Regional Planning, Cornell University
{ayc48, ly292, ela63}@cornell.edu

ABSTRACT
Many people want to learn a language but find it difficult to stay engaged. Ideally, we would have language learning tools that can make language learning more enjoyable by simulating immersion in a foreign language environment. Therefore, we adapted *Crystallize*, a 3D video game for learning Japanese, so that it can be played in virtual reality with the Oculus Rift. Specifically, we explored whether we could leverage virtual reality technology to teach embodied cultural interaction, such as bowing in Japanese greetings. To evaluate the impact of our virtual reality game designs, we conducted a formative user study with 68 participants. We present results showing that the virtual reality design trained players how and when to bow, and that it increased participants' sense of involvement in Japanese culture. Our results suggest that virtual reality technology provides an opportunity to leverage culturally-relevant physical interaction, which can enhance the design of language learning technology and virtual reality games.

Author Keywords
language learning, video games, virtual reality

ACM Classification Keywords
H.5.0. Information Interfaces and Presentation: General

INTRODUCTION
Learning a second language is a goal shared by many, from children in bilingual environments to adult immigrants seeking employment to people wishing to travel abroad. However, many people find it difficult to stay engaged and also to learn vocabulary and grammar in context. Although many people learn languages through popular online tools like DuoLingo [36] and Rosetta Stone [26], much of the vibrancy of the real-world experiences that can make language learning fun and relevant do not translate to these systems.

On the other end of the spectrum, studying abroad provides ample opportunities to be exposed to a foreign language, assimilate into another culture, and apply language in context. Indeed, many studies have analyzed the positive effects of studying abroad on language acquisition [31, 15]. However, studying abroad is not an option for everyone due to financial cost, lack of opportunity, or insufficient time. Ideally, we would have immersive language tools that simulate the experience of being in a foreign language environment as deeply as possible, so that an aspiring learner can learn both language and culture from observation, as well as harness their potential for motivation.

CHI 2017, May 06 - 11, 2017, Denver, CO, USA

ISBN 978-1-4503-4655-9/17/05...$15.00
DOI: http://dx.doi.org/10.1145/3025453.3025857

The emergence of high-quality, low-cost virtual reality headsets in recent years has sparked a surge in interest in the technology, including for educational purposes [17, 22]. Virtual reality has also been used for virtual tourism [16, 5] to situate people in other places without actually being present.

In this paper, we discuss our experiences in designing a virtual reality game for learning language. Building off of *Crystallize* [9, 10], an existing 3D video game for learning the Japanese language, we created a new version of this game that works with the Oculus Rift, a virtual reality headset system. In particular, we explored whether we could use virtual reality to design game mechanics around culturally-relevant embodied physical interaction, such as bowing in Japanese greetings.

To evaluate the effectiveness of our VR game design process, we conducted a formative user evaluation with 68 participants. Our results provide initial evidence that porting to VR and adding VR-specific game mechanics to *Crystallize* was useful for increasing involvement in Japanese culture and teaching players how to bow. However, players encountered some challenges, including feeling sick while using the virtual reality headset. The impact on learning itself was also inconclusive. Nevertheless, this formative evaluation indicates that we were able to leverage some benefits of VR, which will inform future development of the game. Furthermore, the integration of physical cultural artifacts like bowing has implications for the design of language learning technology and virtual reality games.

RELATED WORK

Virtual reality and education
Virtual reality has great potential for education across a wide spectrum of fields. One such field is surgical education. Currently, aspiring surgeons learn surgical skills in the operating room, and while this provides the most realistic environment, there is much left to be desired from a pedagogical perspective. The focus is on the patient rather than the learner, and steps in the surgery can not be adapted to the student's needs. However, a VR surgical environment would allow students to practice and learn without any danger to an actual patient. The VR environment can cater to students by allowing them to make mistakes, repeat steps, and pause as needed [17]. Furthermore, surgical competence can both be taught and measured automatically with VR software [22].

Construct3D is an augmented reality mathematics and geometry learning tool that allows students to draw and visualize virtual three-dimensional objects in real three-dimensional space. Student participants in a pilot study by Kaufmann et al. were able to learn how to use the VR tool quickly and thought that it created a good environment for experimentation, which suggests that tools like *Construct3D* can be effective supplements to a traditional classroom curriculum [19].

The sense of *presence* is the defining experience of virtual reality [28]. The main factors thought to influence presence are: high-resolution information, environmental consistency, possibility for navigation and interaction with other avatars, and similarity of a virtual avatar to one's own body [34]. Immersion and involvement are both necessary for experiencing presence, and presence leads to increased learning and performance [38]. Therefore, we focused our design of the virtual reality version of *Crystallize* around enabling presence.

Language learning tools

There are many computer-based tools for learning languages. MicroMandarin utilizes the user's real world location to suggest vocabulary words [14]. Tip Tap Tones trains users to recognize tones in Chinese [13]. Dearman et al. used a desktop wallpaper to teach vocabulary [12]. We build on these ideas and make them more engaging by creating a holistic experience in a 3D virtual reality video game.

Rosetta Stone [26] is a highly successful tool that mainly teaches language through a series of pictures. A typical task features a set of four or more pictures that each show a certain situation, such as a boy eating or a girl running, and asks the user to identify the picture that most closely matches a phrase in the target language. Rosetta Stone offers many advantages over traditional curricula: the learner receives immediate feedback, information is presented in a visual context, and meaning is often learned through inference. Our work builds on these ideas but also features an interactive 3D environment that provides a deep, situated, virtual reality context and prioritizes experimentation and completion of tasks and goals in that environment.

DuoLingo [36] is another successful tool that teaches language by asking the learner to translate sentences. DuoLingo also has a highly structured learning progression and has achievements and point systems to motivate users. Although 34 hours of DuoLingo has been shown to be equivalent to a first-semester college course in Spanish, many students stopped using it within 2 hours [35]. Our work also uses game-like elements to incentivize users, but it teaches linguistic concepts in a situated physical context rather than through pure translation.

There are some existing video games that focus on teaching languages. A good summary can be found in [29]. For example, *Sanjigenjiten* uses a 3D environment to teach vocabulary words [18]. This game makes use of visual context to teach vocabulary meanings, but it does not provide a deep learning progression. Zengo Sayu [25] is a virtual environment for learning Japanese in which the player explores a location and hears audio cues of words. However, it is not really a game.

Crystallize is a 3D language learning game that teaches language material in *its physical context*, motivated by the theories of situated cognition [8] and encoding specificity [32]. The game provides opportunities for players to learn words from context and gamifies language learning through a quest system that requires players to solve challenges that involve learning new words and using them to construct target sentences. The conceptual components of this game involve understanding specific vocabulary words and understanding grammatical constructions. Two evaluations of *Crystallize* have been conducted: a preliminary lab study with 42 participants [9] and an "in the wild" study with 186 participants from Reddit [10]. Both studies showed statistically significant learning gains.

Interaction design for virtual reality

Interaction in virtual reality is a major challenge. Early work [33] found that presence is better when users walk around in the real world (corresponding to movement in the virtual world), compared to walking in place or pressing a button to "fly" around. Our work attempts to create a similar sense of presence but with the act of bowing instead of walking.

Other work has focused on enabling high-fidelity interaction with virtual environments. Much of this work has focused on providing haptic feedback [4, 6] for hand motions. In this work, we explore the potential of a different kind of virtual reality input, which is to use head motions of the headset itself to enable culturally relevant physical input for a language learning scenario.

Recently, Tan et al. [30] studied virtual reality games and found that VR can heighten game experiences. They also found that although virtual reality can make players sick, they still had a positive reaction to the experience. In this work, our goal was to leverage some of the benefits of VR while abating negative impacts as much as possible.

CRYSTALLIZE IN VIRTUAL REALITY

Since a major goal of *Crystallize* is to gamify language learning by simulating immersion in a target language environment, ideally it should try to maximize the sense of immersion. Therefore, we extended *Crystallize* by adding virtual reality support using the Oculus Rift (Figure 2). Our porting of *Crystallize* to VR was primarily motivated by the following two-part design question: (1) How can we best leverage VR to improve a language learning game, and (2) Can VR help us "gamify" cultural interaction by introducing physical cultural artifacts (like bowing) into the user interface?

To explore the impact of VR on *Crystallize*, we created a new VR demo that is separate from the existing game. The port itself is fairly simple, with only minor changes. The camera angle was changed from third-person to first-person. The original UI has been mostly preserved, with some adjustments to make viewing it in VR more comfortable.

Creating a sense of presence

Some elements of presence were created from the virtual reality environment itself: the culturally-relevant background and the first-person perspective. Three of the factors described by

Figure 1. Overhead view of the *Crystallize* virtual reality scenario that we set up to test the ability of virtual reality to communicate cultural and language information. Players navigated through a Japanese teahouse and solved language learning questions by interacting with non-player-controlled characters.

Figure 2. Using Unity, we made *Crystallize* work with the Oculus Rift.

Usoh [34] were present: ability to navigate, ability to interact with other virtual avatars, environmental consistency, and high-resolution graphics. However, there was no virtual avatar to represent the player (if the player looked down, he or she would not see a virtual representation of himself or herself).

We also increased the sense of presence through embodying physical actions where possible. Although overall navigation was done with the keyboard (to avoid needing to play the game in a large room where one can walk around freely; besides, the Oculus does not support full-motion VR), we did include some basic gestural information. In Japanese culture, one often bows to other people when meeting them in formal settings. This is called *o-jigi* (お辞儀). Therefore, the VR version of *Crystallize* was designed so that players were expected to bow

Figure 3. An example of an eavesdropping dialogue. The player can listen in on NPC dialogues and collect new words to add to the inventory.

when meeting new people. The head-tracking of the Oculus Rift was set up to detect if the player actually bowed.

The demo itself

The demo takes place in a traditional Japanese teahouse, which presents Japanese featured elements, including sliding shoji doors made from wood and paper, wooden floor passages, a bamboo courtyard, Japanese paintings, and a tatami (bamboo floor mat) room, with NPCs scattered about (Figure 1).

The VR demo is a self-contained experience separate from the main *Crystallize* game, and it uses a subset of the mechanics present in *Crystallize* along with the VR integration. In terms of gameplay, it comprises eight dialogues with NPCs scattered throughout the teahouse. There are two types of dialogues, all conducted solely in Japanese: (1) eavesdropping dialogue, in which two NPCs speak to each other and the player must learn new words from their conversation by dragging those words

Figure 4. An example of a multiple-choice conversation dialogue in VR. The player must select an appropriate response based on what the NPC said.

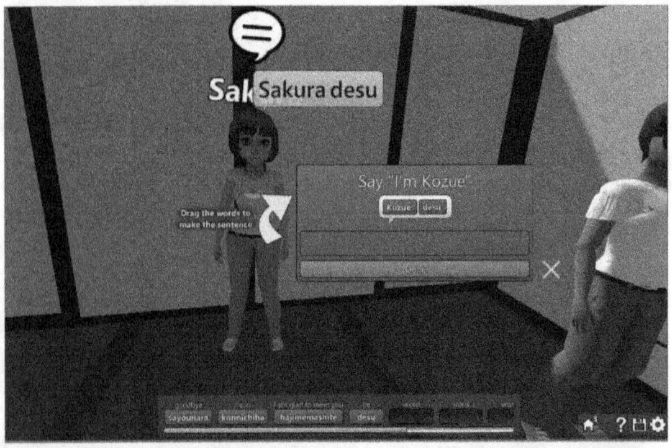

Figure 5. An example of a sentence-construction conversation dialogue in VR. The player must arrange vocabulary words in the correct order in order to respond to the NPC.

into the inventory (Figure 3), and (2) conversation dialogue, in which the player engages a single NPC in conversation. In conversations, the player is prompted to select the appropriate response from multiple choices (Figure 4) and, in some cases, asked to construct a sentence given several vocabulary words (Figure 5). Also, the player is prompted to bow in response to an NPC's bow when engaged in conversation.

Gameplay progresses in a linear fashion. Whenever a conversation with an NPC is available, the conversation must be successfully completed before the player is allowed to move on to the next conversation. Occasionally the player will be lacking a word needed to complete a dialogue; in this case, the player needs to seek out the appropriate eavesdropping NPC group to obtain the vocabulary word. The series of dialogues, along with their categorization and required player actions to complete, is listed in Figure 6.

The vocabulary words selected were chosen to include set greeting phrases like *sayounara* (Goodbye.), as well as some words and grammatical particles that can be arranged to form sentences, such as *namae* (name), used in the sentences *o namae wa?* (Your name?) and *watashi no namae wa [name] desu* (My name is [name]). This mix of vocabulary types allowed us to provide sentence construction challenges to the player in addition to multiple choice prompts, as mentioned previously.

TEACHING PLAYERS TO BOW

In Japanese culture, greetings such as *konnichiwa* (Hello.) and *hajimemashite* (Nice to meet you.) are often accompanied with a small bow, and the other party responds with a similar greeting and bow. Knowing how to bow and, just as important, when to bow is a key part of communication in Japan, so we wanted to teach players by integrating this cultural behavior into *Crystallize*.

Bowing is one example of physical cultural behaviors, and mastering such cultural artifacts is an important aspect of becoming proficient in a foreign language. However, cultural competence has often not received as much attention as linguistic material [11, 37]. Therefore, we explored whether we could use virtual reality to integrate cultural artifacts into the experience. In particular, we tried to leverage the sense of presence that virtual reality can provide to enable a natural mechanism for nonverbal cultural interaction. Physicality plays a significant role in communication [7, 21] and there have been attempts in character animation to emulate it [20].

The simplest way to implement a bowing mechanic would involve the player clicking a button or pressing a key to perform a bow. However, with this control scheme, the player's action (clicking or pressing) does not capture the physicality of the bowing motion. Instead, we realized that the act of bowing could be naturally adapted to virtual reality—because players already know how to bow in real life, we can have players apply that knowledge in the cultural context of a Japanese conversation through our VR simulation.

Using the angle of the head mount, we attempted to detect when the player bowed. If the head was lowered by at least 22.5° and then raised above that threshold again, the motion registered as a successful bow. We experimented with various angles until we found one that minimized both discomfort and the chance of unintentionally triggering a bow. Ideally, we would have emulated the standard Japanese greeting bow (15° from the hip while standing), but since the Oculus can only track the head, a 22.5° bow of the head seems to be a reasonable approximation [27].

In the game demo, we teach the cultural practice of bowing by integrating it into NPC conversations at the appropriate times. Just like in real Japanese conversations, NPCs in the game may bow while saying greeting phrases. When this occurs, the player must bow in return in order to successfully continue the conversation.

Tutorial design

Our tutorial design for teaching bowing was motivated by two principles. First, there is empirical support for the common belief that text tutorials are not necessarily effective, particularly in situations where the player can learn through experimentation instead of reading [2]. Second, work in math education has found positive benefits of gradually fading out tutorials to enable a smooth transition from solely following instructions to performing the task without help [24, 3]. Therefore, the

Number	Type	Content
1	Eavesdropping	Learn *konnichiwa* (Hello.)
2	Eavesdropping	Learn *sayonara* (Goodbye.)
3	Conversation	Reply with "Hello." and learn to bow
4	Eavesdropping	Learn *hajimemashite* (Nice to meet you.)
5	Eavesdropping	Learn *o namae wa?* (Your name?), *[name] desu* (I'm [name].)
6	Conversation	Reply with "Nice to meet you.", bow, reply with "I'm [name].", learn *yoroshiku onegaishimasu* (Please take care of me.), bow
7	Eavesdropping	Learn *watashi no namae wa [name] desu.* (My name is [name])
8	Conversation	Bow*, reply with "Hello.", bow, reply with "My name is [name])
9*	Conversation	Reply with "Nice to meet you.", bow, reply with "Your name?", reply with

Figure 6. The list of in-game dialogues. Items marked with an asterisk (*) were added in a later version of the demo.

Figure 7. Using the Oculus Rift head tracking, we trained players to bow when greeting other characters in Japanese. A few seconds after the NPC bows, the player is given a prompt to bow. The third panel shows the player's field of view mid-bow.

bowing tutorials are minimal in text and gradually fade out over time.

When an NPC bows to the player in the game, a prompt with the words "Please bow." appear on the screen afterward. During the first instance, the prompt appears right away to instruct the player when to bow. From then on, the game lengthens the time between the NPC's bow and the message prompting the player to bow. The second time, the game waits one second before prompting. The third time, two seconds; the fourth and each subsequent time after that, four seconds. If the player completes a bow before the prompt appears, that suggests the player both acknowledged the NPC's bow and knew to execute the correct response by bowing in return, therefore signaling that the player has most likely learned the desired behavior. The sequence of events involved in a bowing exchange is portrayed in Figure 7.

FORMATIVE USER STUDY

We conducted a formative user study in order to gain initial insights on the design of our VR port of *Crystallize*. This study focused on evaluating the following questions: (1) Does the VR version of the game improve language acquisition and stimulate interest in the language's culture more effectively than the non-VR version, and (2) Could players can be taught cultural behaviors, like bowing, through the help of VR?

To test these hypotheses, we conducted a study with a total of 68 participants recruited from the university community through events. The only requirement to participate in the study was a self-reported lack of familiarity with Japanese language and culture. This study took place over two weeks.

To evaluate the impact of the addition of virtual reality and the bowing mechanic on the effectiveness of the game design, we created two versions of the demo. One was played without virtual reality on a regular computer screen. The other was played with the Oculus Rift head-mounted display. The VR and non-VR versions were the same except that the VR version included bowing.

Experimental protocol

Participants were informed that they would be playing a video game for learning Japanese. Participants then completed a pre-game survey in which to provide some demographic information, such as gender and ethnicity, state their level of interest in Japanese culture and language, and take a pretest for Japanese vocabulary proficiency. The pretest involved matching Japanese words (that appear in the demo) to their English definitions.

To evaluate the impact of adding virtual reality (and bowing), we were primarily interested in players' first experience with the game. Therefore, players were randomly assigned to play either the VR or non-VR version. Participants were given basic instructions on how to play the game, such as how to interact with in-game characters by clicking on them. Each play session took approximately 15-20 minutes. Participants then completed a post-game survey in which they completed a vocabulary posttest that was identical to the pretest except for item order. Participants then compared their level of interest in Japanese culture and language to before.

Next, in order to collect additional data on bowing and reactions to the two versions, participants were asked to play the version they did not play first. Then they completed a second post-game survey in which they provided additional feedback on the experience. In addition to the surveys, we recorded bowing data, including how long it took for the player to bow after the NPC bowed, whether the bow was performed before the prompt, and the angle of the bow.

Towards the end of the data collection, we added a ninth dialogue and an extra bow in the eighth dialogue (in VR), as shown in Figure 6. 15 of the 68 participants played these updated VR and non-VR versions. We analyzed all 68 participants in one group because we did not think that this change significantly affected players' reactions to the VR and non-VR versions.

RESULTS

We analyzed (1) whether players learned cultural information through the VR bowing mechanic, (2) how players reacted to the VR and non-VR versions, (3) negative effects of VR, (4) players' overall reactions to the experience, and (5) the impact of the VR demo on learning.

The VR demo trained players how to bow

As mentioned previously, participants were expected to bow in response to an in-game NPC bowing, with a textual prompt appearing on-screen if the participant does not bow within a few seconds. We define a "unprompted bow" as one that is performed before the prompt appears. If the participant performs an unprompted bow, it is likely that he/she recognized, without being explicitly reminded, that the appropriate cultural response to the other party bowing is to bow in return.

Aside from the first time bowing is introduced, where the prompt appears immediately, there are three bowing opportunities in the VR version of the game. We found that 34 out of the 68 participants (50.0%) performed at least one unprompted bow, which suggests that players were able to learn when to bow.

Overall, the average bow angle that players reached was 45.8°. This angle is deeper than the culturally-appropriate standing bow angle of 15° and the game-specific detection angle of 22.5°. This indicates that although the game appears to be training players when to bow, it may be necessary to provide additional angular feedback and refine the bow detection angle so that players learn the most appropriate angle. Furthermore, future work must verify experimentally that the bowing knowledge that players acquire transfers to real conversations in a way that native speakers would find appropriate.

The VR demo led to increased involvement in culture

Although all participants played both the VR and non-VR versions, the surveys given after playing each demo consisted of different questions. Therefore, we analyzed the impact of the demo version in a between-subjects manner because these were not repeated measures. Since the survey questions asked for Likert-style responses, we used the non-parametric Mann-Whitney U-test to analyze the differences between the VR and non-VR versions. These results can been seen in Figure 8.

We found a statistically significant effect for the impact of the VR version on perceived involvement in Japanese culture. We found that players of the VR demo felt more involved in Japanese culture ($M = 3.18$, $SD = 1.03$) than the non-VR players ($M = 2.47$, $SD = 0.86$), $Z = 2.70, p = 0.007$.

VR made people dizzy

The virtual reality experience suffered from some technological and interface defects. According to the user experience feedback, 23.5% (16/68) of the comments expressed negative feelings such as "dizziness" and "sickness", and 27.9% (19/68) of the comments revealed user interface problems such as difficulty reading words in the inventory toward the bottom of the UI plane. These issues influenced the participants' self-evaluations.

In other words, despite our efforts to adapt the original UI of *Crystallize* to work similarly in VR, users still often struggled with reading and interacting with the UI in a VR environment. One participant wrote that "the combination of controlling the UI with the mouse felt disorientating", and another commented, "Having to click and drag a menu at the bottom of the screen wasn't particularly intuitive in the VR version", suggesting that trying to retain the original drag-and-drop UI in the VR version of the game may not have been the ideal approach for a natural VR experience. Our main takeaway here is that VR necessitates more significant changes, primarily to enable movement without sickness and user input without relying on the keyboard and mouse, which are blocked by the headset.

In addition, since the experiment was designed to complete within 30 minutes, no more than two questions were devoted to a particular research question. More questions need to be added and further debriefing is needed in the future.

Participants enjoyed the VR experience

While many participants felt motion sickness and dizziness while playing, a majority of participants reacted positively to the experience: 58.8% (40/68) of participants wrote positive comments towards using VR to interact with cultural context. Not only did 17.6% (12/68) of participants report feeling more immersed when using VR compared to non-VR, but some participants also noted that they felt more involved in the game and its world. One wrote that he/she felt "more involved within the game world, more connected to the people I was speaking to", while another noted, "I felt like at least I was 'looking' at a person at eye-level, and it was fun to 'talk' with them!" This feedback reinforces the idea that, on top of situating the user in a cultural context, VR can also help users connect with that culture and the people within it.

Furthermore, participants found bowing in VR to be a unique and enjoyable experience, with 17.6% (12/68) praising the bowing feature in particular as part of their feedback. However, one participant did express some confusion as to when bowing was supposed to occur ("[...] it seemed to happen at odd

Question	Condition	Size	Mean	SD	Results
Compared to before, how interested are you in the Japanese language now?	VR Non-VR	34 34	3.65 3.35	0.69 0.85	$Z = 1.28$ $p = 0.20$
Compared to before, how much are you interested in Japanese culture now?	VR Non-VR	34 34	3.41 3.09	0.67 0.67	$Z = 1.55$ $p = 0.12$
How interesting was the content presented in the game?	VR Non-VR	34 34	3.29 2.88	0.87 0.81	$Z = 1.87$ $p = 0.06$
How much attention did you pay to the content presented in the game?	VR Non-VR	34 34	3.50 3.18	0.96 0.97	$Z = 1.19$ $p = 0.23$
How much did you feel involved in Japanese culture while playing the game?	VR Non-VR	34 34	3.18 2.47	1.03 0.86	$Z = 2.70$ $p = 0.007$

Figure 8. Analysis of survey questions. Response options used a Likert scale, spanning from 1 (None/not at all) to 5 (Very much/a great deal).

moments between snippets of conversation."), which suggests that there is still room in the game to teach the proper contexts in which to bow in Japanese culture. An interesting way to fill in this gap would be to allow players to initiate bows to NPCs on their own volition and provide feedback through the NPCs as to whether the bows were performed at an appropriate time.

Impact of the VR demo on learning was inconclusive

To measure language acquisition, we computed the difference in score between the pre-test and the post-test as the number of words learned for each participant. Both tests contained the same eight vocabulary words and had the player match each Japanese word to its equivalent, though the ordering of words was different for the two tests.

We used an unpaired t-test to analyze the number of words learned between participants in the VR and non-VR conditions. Though participants had self-reported a lack of familiarity with the Japanese language, eight participants scored a perfect 8 out of 8 on the pre-test. For this analysis, we omit those participants, as well as one participant that scored 3 points lower on the post-test compared to the pre-test.

Data	Condition	Size	Mean	Results
Words learned	VR Non-VR	31 28	4.77 5.39	$t(57) = 0.889$ $p = 0.377$

The number of words learned by participants in the VR condition ($M = 4.77, SD = 2.77$) turned out to be lower than that of those in Non-VR ($M = 5.39, SD = 2.56$), though the difference was not statistically significant. We suspect that the user interaction issues and the cognitive overhead in adapting to the unfamiliar VR interface and mastering the UI may have contributed to less effective learning [23].

Design implications

Our results provide some evidence that players can learn about culture and cultural behaviors, such as bowing, through immersive VR environments that are designed to enable them. They show that virtual reality can provide the basis for game designs that stimulate virtual participation and feelings of involvement in a foreign culture.

Most importantly, they suggest that the sense of immersive presence provided by VR yields a valuable opportunity to open up additional input channels for meaningful physical interaction. This is particularly useful for games and simulations for language learning due to the importance of physical interaction. After viewing an instruction like "please bow," players could figure out what to do fairly naturally because it corresponded to an embodied action. Hopefully, virtual reality technology (such as the HTC Vive hand-held controllers) will become useful for training other kinds of culturally-grounded physical interaction, such as gestures and posture.

Limitations

We acknowledge the presence of multiple confounding factors, such as that bowing existed only in the virtual reality version. Therefore, we analyzed the results of this experiment in order to evaluate the design of the virtual reality game, and not to draw general conclusions about the impact of virtual reality. Furthermore, the study may have conflated players' natural enthusiasm for VR with their responses to the game experience. However, we believe this weakness can also be viewed as a strength: since motivation is an issue in language learning, harnessing natural enthusiasm for VR seems beneficial.

CONCLUSIONS

We adapted *Crystallize*, a 3D language-learning game, to virtual reality by adding integration with the Oculus Rift. In particular, we explored whether we could use virtual reality to design game mechanics around culturally-relevant embodied physical interaction, such as bowing in Japanese greetings.

We conducted a formative user study to evaluate the design of the ported game. Through adding VR and bowing, we observed a statistically significant increase in the participants' sense of cultural involvement. However, there is no obvious evidence that the language learning outcomes improved thus far. As for the usability of the VR game, participants were able to play through the entire demo and enjoy the experience, despite the problems introduced by using VR with the Oculus (motion sickness and inability to see the keyboard). This suggests that our fairly direct port of *Crystallize* was usable.

In future work, we plan to take steps to increase the sense of immersion further, such as exploring speech recognition as a primary input mechanism. Speech input would also have the side effect of reducing dependence on UI, which we expect will decrease player confusion with interacting with the UI in VR. We also hope to release both the VR and non-VR versions of the game online to gather longitudinal data and investigate whether participants would return to the game.

As 3D reconstruction technology [1] improves, this provides additional opportunities to feature *real* locations for language learning exercises. We plan to investigate whether this will increase engagement, as well as develop techniques to "gamify" these locations by adding non-player-controlled characters and interactive situations.

REFERENCES

1. Sameer Agarwal, Noah Snavely, Ian Simon, Steven M Seitz, and Richard Szeliski. 2009. Building rome in a day. In *2009 IEEE 12th international conference on computer vision*. IEEE, 72–79.
2. Erik Andersen, Eleanor O'Rourke, Yun-En Liu, Rich Snider, Jeff Lowdermilk, David Truong, Seth Cooper, and Zoran Popovic. 2012. The impact of tutorials on games of varying complexity. In *Proceedings of the SIGCHI Conference on Human Factors in Computing Systems*. ACM, 59–68.
3. Robert K Atkinson, Alexander Renkl, and Mary Margaret Merrill. 2003. Transitioning From Studying Examples to Solving Problems: Effects of Self-Explanation Prompts and Fading Worked-Out Steps. *Journal of Educational Psychology* 95, 4 (2003), 774.
4. Mahdi Azmandian, Mark Hancock, Hrvoje Benko, Eyal Ofek, and Andrew D Wilson. 2016. Haptic Retargeting: Dynamic Repurposing of Passive Haptics for Enhanced Virtual Reality Experiences. In *Proceedings of the 2016 CHI Conference on Human Factors in Computing Systems*. ACM, 1968–1979.
5. BBC. 2015. British Museum offers virtual reality tour of Bronze Age. `http://www.bbc.com/news/technology-33772694`, *BBC News* (2015).
6. Hrvoje Benko, Christian Holz, Mike Sinclair, and Eyal Ofek. 2016. NormalTouch and TextureTouch: High-fidelity 3D Haptic Shape Rendering on Handheld Virtual Reality Controllers. In *Proceedings of the 29th Annual Symposium on User Interface Software and Technology*. ACM, 717–728.
7. Ray L Birdwhistell. 1952. *Introduction to kinesics*. University of Louisville.
8. John Seely Brown, Allan Collins, and Paul Duguid. 1989. Situated cognition and the culture of learning. *Educational researcher* 18, 1 (1989), 32–42.
9. Gabriel Culbertson, Erik Andersen, Walker White, Daniel Zhang, and Malte Jung. Crystallize: An Immersive, Collaborative Game for Second Language Learning. In *CSCW 2016*.
10. Gabriel Culbertson, Shiyu Wang, Malte Jung, and Erik Andersen. Crystallize: An Immersive, Collaborative Game for Second Language Learning. In *CHI 2016*.
11. Louise Damen. 1987. *Culture learning: The fifth dimension in the language classroom*. Vol. 11478. Addison Wesley Publishing Company.
12. David Dearman and Khai Truong. 2012. Evaluating the implicit acquisition of second language vocabulary using a live wallpaper. In *Proceedings of the SIGCHI Conference on Human Factors in Computing Systems*. ACM, 1391–1400.
13. Darren Edge, Kai-Yin Cheng, Michael Whitney, Yao Qian, Zhijie Yan, and Frank Soong. 2012. Tip tap tones: mobile microtraining of mandarin sounds. In *Proceedings of the 14th international conference on Human-computer interaction with mobile devices and services*. ACM, 427–430.
14. Darren Edge, Elly Searle, Kevin Chiu, Jing Zhao, and James A Landay. 2011. MicroMandarin: mobile language learning in context. In *Proceedings of the SIGCHI Conference on Human Factors in Computing Systems*. ACM, 3169–3178.
15. Barbara F Freed. 1995. *Second language acquisition in a study abroad context*. Vol. 9. John Benjamins Publishing.
16. Daniel A Guttentag. 2010. Virtual reality: Applications and implications for tourism. *Tourism Management* 31, 5 (2010), 637–651.
17. Randy S Haluck and Thomas M Krummel. 2000. Computers and virtual reality for surgical education in the 21st century. *Archives of surgery* 135, 7 (2000), 786–792.
18. Robert Howland, Sachi Urano, and Junichi Hoshino. 2012. SanjigenJiten: computer assisted language learning system within a 3d game environment. In *Advances in Computer Entertainment*. Springer, 262–273.
19. Hannes Kaufmann, Dieter Schmalstieg, and Michael Wagner. 2000. Construct3D: a virtual reality application for mathematics and geometry education. *Education and information technologies* 5, 4 (2000), 263–276.
20. Sergey Levine, Philipp Krähenbühl, Sebastian Thrun, and Vladlen Koltun. 2010. Gesture controllers. In *ACM Transactions on Graphics (TOG)*, Vol. 29. ACM, 124.
21. David McNeill. 1992. *Hand and mind: What gestures reveal about thought*. University of Chicago press.
22. David Ota, Bowen Loftin, Tim Saito, Robert Lea, and James Keller. 1995. Virtual reality in surgical education. *Computers in Biology and Medicine* 25, 2 (1995), 127–137.
23. Joseph Psotka. 1995. Immersive training systems: Virtual reality and education and training. *Instructional science* 23, 5-6 (1995), 405–431.
24. Alexander Renkl, Robert K Atkinson, Uwe H Maier, and Richard Staley. 2002. From example study to problem solving: Smooth transitions help learning. *The Journal of Experimental Education* 70, 4 (2002), 293–315.
25. Howard Rose and Mark Billinghurst. 1995. Zengo Sayu: An immersive educational environment for learning Japanese. *University of Washington, Human Interface Technology Laboratory, Report No. r-95-4* (1995).

26. Rosetta Stone. Rosetta Stone. `http://www.rosettastone.com/`. (????).

27. H Shibata, J Takahashi, and J Gyoba. 2015. [Subjective impressions of bowing actions and their appropriateness in specific social contexts]. *Shinrigaku kenkyu: The Japanese journal of psychology* 85, 6 (2015), 571–578.

28. Jonathan Steuer. 1992. Defining virtual reality: Dimensions determining telepresence. *Journal of communication* 42, 4 (1992), 73–93.

29. Julie E Sykes, Jonathon Reinhardt, Judith E Liskin-Gasparro, and Manel Lacorte. 2012. *Language at play: Digital games in second and foreign language teaching and learning*. Pearson Higher Ed.

30. Chek Tien Tan, Tuck Wah Leong, Songjia Shen, Christopher Dubravs, and Chen Si. 2015. Exploring Gameplay Experiences on the Oculus Rift. In *Proceedings of the 2015 Annual Symposium on Computer-Human Interaction in Play*. ACM, 253–263.

31. Koichi Tanaka and Rod Ellis. 2003. Study abroad, language proficiency, and learner beliefs about language learning. *JALT journal* 25, 1 (2003), 63–85.

32. Endel Tulving and Donald M Thomson. 1973. Encoding specificity and retrieval processes in episodic memory. *Psychological review* 80, 5 (1973), 352.

33. Martin Usoh, Kevin Arthur, Mary C Whitton, Rui Bastos, Anthony Steed, Mel Slater, and Frederick P Brooks Jr. 1999. Walking> walking-in-place> flying, in virtual environments. In *Proceedings of the 26th annual conference on Computer graphics and interactive techniques*. ACM Press/Addison-Wesley Publishing Co., 359–364.

34. Martin Usoh, Ernest Catena, Sima Arman, and Mel Slater. 2000. Using presence questionnaires in reality. *Presence: Teleoperators and Virtual Environments* 9, 5 (2000), 497–503.

35. Roumen Vesselinov and John Grego. 2012. Duolingo effectiveness study. *City University of New York, USA* (2012).

36. Luis von Ahn. 2013. Duolingo: learn a language for free while helping to translate the web. In *Proceedings of the 2013 international conference on Intelligent user interfaces*. ACM, 1–2.

37. Paige D Ware and Claire Kramsch. 2005. Toward an intercultural stance: Teaching German and English through telecollaboration. *The Modern Language Journal* 89, 2 (2005), 190–205.

38. Bob G Witmer and Michael J Singer. 1998. Measuring presence in virtual environments: A presence questionnaire. *Presence: Teleoperators and virtual environments* 7, 3 (1998), 225–240.

Identifying how Visually Impaired People Explore Raised-line Diagrams to Improve the Design of Touch Interfaces

Sandra Bardot[1, 2], Marcos Serrano[1, 2], Bernard Oriola[2,1], Christophe Jouffrais[2,1]

[1] University of Toulouse – IRIT
Toulouse, France
{firstname.lastname}@irit.fr

[2] CNRS - IRIT
Toulouse, France
{firstname.lastname}@irit.fr

ABSTRACT

Raised-line diagrams are widely used by visually impaired (VI) people to read maps, drawings or graphs. While previous work has identified general exploration strategies for raised-line drawings, we have limited knowledge on how this exploration is performed in detail and how it extends to other types of diagrams such as maps or graphs, frequently used in specialized schools. Such information can be crucial for the design of accessible interfaces on touchscreens. We conducted a study in which participants were asked to explore five types of raised-line diagrams (common drawings, perspective drawings, mathematical graphs, neighborhood maps, and geographical maps) while tracking both hands fingers. Relying on a first set of results, we proposed a set of design guidelines for touch interfaces.

Author Keywords

Raised-line diagram; blind; tactile exploration; tactile maps; tactile drawings; bimanual exploration; finger tracking.

ACM Classification Keywords

H.5.2. User Interfaces: User-centered design. Input devices and strategies,

INTRODUCTION

Raised-line diagrams provide visually impaired (VI) people with access to graphs, drawings or maps [16]. Usually, they are hand-made because the content must be adapted and simplified. Moreover, they must be printed beforehand, which can be tedious and expensive in a teaching context. Then, it is pertinent to use digital versions of the diagrams that are accessible through adapted non-visual interactions.

Many approaches have been proposed, and can be summarized into three large categories. The first one consists in using refreshable displays that can dynamically raise up and down small pins providing a perceptible relief for manual exploration [20, 24]. A second category relies on tangible objects that represent important elements of a drawing, and can be linked to each other to render lines and areas [18, 4]. The last category consists in using finger tracking devices (touchscreens, cameras, etc.) to follow finger movement over a digital map, and render the content with auditory or vibrational feedback [2, 6, 5, 10, 25]. However, the process of converting physical content to digital cues is performed empirically. Understanding how VI people explore physical raised-line diagrams, and which elements are of importance, could help to design non-visual tactile interfaces.

In psychology, several studies aimed to assess the capacity to identify raised-line diagrams. In general, these studies compared tactile exploration of sighted, early and late blind people who had to recognize drawings of common objects (car, fruit, tool, etc.). For instance, Heller et al. [1] compared the blind and sighted children exploring raised-line drawings, and showed that they reach the same performance when sighted are guided during exploration. Lebaz et al. [13] showed that the performance depended on the type of common drawing being used in the study ("flat" 2D drawings, or with 3D cues). However, these studies mainly relied on identification rates, and did not inform about the hand movements that were used.

Our goal was to understand the main role: 1) of hands (and fingers) during raised-line diagrams exploration, according to 2) diagram type, and 3) user expertise. We used different raised-line diagrams including drawings, mathematical graphs, and neighborhood or geographical maps. We developed an experimental setup to track the fingers of both hands during tactile exploration. We recruited 6 visually impaired and 6 sighted blindfolded subjects who explored the diagrams. The results were based on accurate tracking of the exploration movements, and highlight different exploration patterns concerning the movement of both hands and the covering of the diagrams. They showed that performance was significantly different according to the diagram types and user profiles.

RELATED WORK

It has been shown that it is difficult to name tactile pictures for naive subjects [7]. It has also been shown that tactile recognition of drawings depends on previous visual experience. However, studies comparing tactile recognition rate of sighted, early and late blind people showed that blind people can either perform better (see e.g. [7]) or worse (see e.g. [14, 17]) than sighted people. In fact, it

CHI 2017, May 06-11, 2017, Denver, CO, USA
© 2017 ACM. ISBN 978-1-4503-4655-9/17/05...$15.00
DOI: http://dx.doi.org/10.1145/3025453.3025582

seems that the difficulty of picture recognition varies with complexity, familiarity, and categorical information [8, 9].

The procedures used to explore real 3D objects have an impact on the type and quality of information available [15], and affect the performance at haptic recognition tasks. Hence exploration procedures, but also the more general strategies combining these procedures, probably depend on the intended goal of the task. For instance, one might want to learn quickly as much as possible about an object, or alternatively test some hypothesis about that object. These general principles probably apply to the tactile exploration of 2D raised-line diagrams too. Recent studies depicted specific hand movements during the exploration of raised-lines diagrams with blindfolded participants [22]. They showed that, most of the time, subjects used their index finger(s), either alone or in combination with other fingers. Although subjects were usually unaware of how they moved their hands, the movements were both purposive and systematic [22]. Another study showed that both hands were used more than 83% of the time, which significantly increased identification of raised line drawings [23]. In fact these patterns of hand movement have been called exploratory procedures [19]. They include lateral motion (moving the fingers back and forth across a texture or feature), contour following (tracing an edge within the image), and whole-hand exploration of global shape [19]. However these different studies did not systematically depict exploratory procedures according to the drawing being explored or the task being performed [12].

Tactile exploration of a digital drawing on a touch-screen display is even more difficult [11]. Guerreiro et al. [6] focused on the observation of bimanual exploration (one finger of each hand) on large touchscreens during four specific tasks (locate, relocate, count, relate). They identified seven features and four strategies that appeared when visually impaired subjects were exploring drawings that resemble geographical maps with a few landmarks only. This work clearly showed that specific strategies appear in relation to the tasks being performed. However, the study relied on one map-like diagram only and did not consider other types of diagrams (e.g. common drawing or mathematical graph).

In the current study, we used a setup made of a touchscreen and a camera which allowed for accurate tracking of hands and fingers movements. Our method extends previous work [3] based on a depth-camera that could not accurately separate the fingers from the surface during tactile exploration. Our setup leverages quantifying the hand movements involved during the tactile exploration of different types of raised-line diagrams.

STUDY: EXPLORATION STRATEGIES

The goal of our study was to understand the role of each hand during the tactile exploration of different types of diagrams (drawings, graphs or maps) by users with different expertise (sighted blind-folded or visually impaired).

Raised-line diagrams

In psychology research, most of the studies concerning tactile exploration relied on common drawings [13, 21, 23]. But common drawings are not the most used diagrams by VI people. Indeed, in specialized schools, students have geography, math, and locomotion lessons, which rely on raised-line charts and maps. Hence, we selected five different types of diagrams (Figure 1). All the diagrams were made with the assistance of a professional tactile document maker. We also performed several iterations with VI users to refine height and width of the raised lines, as well as the legibility of Braille text. We designed three diagrams of each type, except for the Common Drawings (we used 10 of them, see task below). All the diagrams were printed in A3 landscape format on Zytech swell paper.

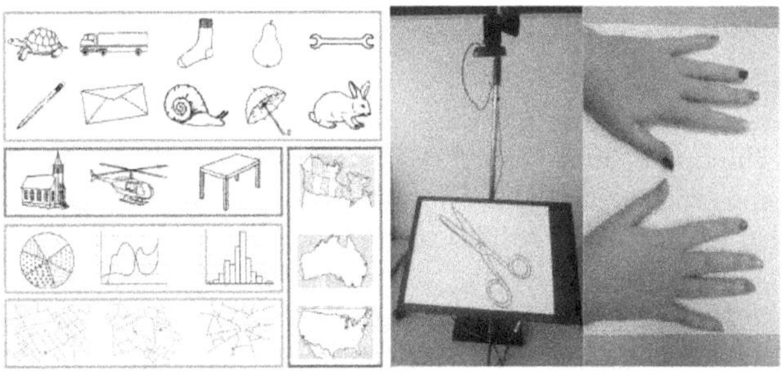

Figure 1. Diagrams used (left) and experimental setup (right): a raised-line drawing is placed over the touchscreen. A camera located above the drawing tracks fingers movements.

Common Drawings (C-Drawings) and Perspective Drawings (P-Drawings): they were issued from the Snodgrass and Vanderwart set of images [21]. Selected C-Drawings were: scissors, envelope, sock, open-end wrench, pencil, umbrella, truck, snail, turtle, rabbit, and pear. P-Drawings represented a couch, church, table, and helicopter. They included perspective cues.

Mathematical graphs (Graphs): We used graphs frequently used in specialized schools, i.e. histograms and plots.

Neighborhood maps (N-Maps): Delimited zone of a city. We added two itinerary points (starting and ending) as well as shops, represented by an empty triangle, a solid triangle, and filled circles, respectively.

Geographical maps (G-Maps): Two types of maps were included, representing a country with either a few main cities or the regions within the country. The cities were represented by solid points, with the first two letters written in Braille. Borders between regions were represented by dotted lines. A few regions included a different texture that emphasized a specific element. Seas and oceans were represented with a specific texture.

Tasks and instructions

During the study, each participant explored 22 diagrams: 10 Common Drawings, and 3 drawings of the four other types.

The study was divided in two steps. The first step consisted in identifying 10 C-Drawings as fast as possible (max time allowed: 90s). The drawing category was mentioned beforehand (e.g. object or animal). We measured the time needed to identify the drawing. The goal was to assess the expertise level of each participant in terms of raised-line diagram exploration. The second step consisted in the exploration of the four other types of diagrams by blocks of 3 trials (total of 12 trials). First, the participants explored a diagram for 30s (*free exploration*). Then, they had another 60s to explore the same diagram in order to answer a question (*driven exploration*). The questions varied according to the type of diagram: for P-Drawings, they had to identify the object among 4 choices. For Graphs, they had to find specific min and max values. For N- Maps, they had to find the number of stores between the starting and ending points. For G-Maps, they had to compare different regions. No instructions were given concerning the use of one or two hands.

Participants
We recruited two groups of participants: 6 sighted subjects who were blind-folded (BF, 3 females), and 6 visually impaired subjects (VI, 5 females). These two groups should show contrasted results because BFs are non-experts of tactile exploration but can rely on previous visual knowledge to identify drawings. In contrast, VIs are experts of tactile exploration but with very few, if any, previous visual knowledge. BFs were 2 university students and 4 staff members aged 27 on average (SD=2). VIs were 5 teachers and 1 radio-program presenter aged 46 on average (SD=14). Among them, 5 were early blind and 1 had very limited residual vision (light perception). She was blindfolded during the study.

Before the experiment, we conducted an interview to assess proficiency in braille reading and raised-line diagrams exploration (on a 5-points Likert scale). All VI participants rated their expertise between 2 and 5 (M=4,5) for Braille reading and between 1 and 4 (M=3) for tactile exploration. They all used their left hand as the main reading hand but differently: 1 read with left hand only, 5 with both hands. The 5 VI teachers explore raised-line diagrams several times per week. BFs had no prior experience with raised-lines diagrams.

Design and procedure
Our study followed a within-participants design, with one factor: Diagram type (C-Drawings, P-Drawings, Graphs, N-Maps, and G-Maps). The order of the last 4 blocks (1 block for each diagram type) was counterbalanced across participants. Within each block, the order of the 3 trials was random. Users were free to take a break between blocks.

Experimental setup
The subject was comfortably sitting in front of the tactile drawing placed over a 22-inch (1680x1050px) multi-touch screen (Fig. 1). We used a Logitech C270 webcam (1280x720 px) located above the touch screen in order to track the ten fingers according to colored markers placed on each nail (Fig. 1). The acquisition rates were 50 Hz for the camera and 100 Hz for the touchscreen.

Collected data
We collected the coordinates of the 10 fingers, as well as the touch status. We also measured the exploration time needed to answer the questions. In addition, subjects had to rate the difficulty for each type of diagram. At the end of the session, we asked them whether they were aware of using any specific exploration strategy. We also collected their subjective feeling about the number of hands and fingers they used, and why for.

RESULTS
We computed a Univariate ANOVA with a Bonferroni Pairwise post-hoc test to compare the results.

Exploration times and accuracy
We found main effects of diagram type ($F_{4,44}$=6.9, p<.001) and user group ($F_{1,11}$=8.1, p=.005) on exploration times. The averaged exploration times were 45.9s for BF participants and 39.4s for VI participants. Post-hoc comparison revealed a significant difference (p<.001) between C-Drawings (M=44.7 s) and P-Drawings (M=27.5 s) exploration times.

Concerning accuracy, we found a main effect of diagram type ($F_{4,44}$=8.7, p<.001) and an interaction between diagram type and user group ($F_{1,11}$=8.7, p=.006). Post-hoc comparison showed a significant difference between C-Drawings and N-Maps (p=.002) and C-Drawings and P-Drawings (p<.001). The accuracy per diagram type was (BF vs. VI participants): C-Drawings (58.6 vs. 41.3%); G-Maps (27.7 vs. 70.5%); Graphs (62.5 vs. 75%); N-Maps (11 vs. 31%); and P-Drawings (93.7 vs. 5%).

Diagram covering
We measured the covering for each type of diagram, i.e. the percentage of diagram that was explored. We found a main effect of diagram type ($F_{4,44}$=4.5, p=.003) and user group ($F_{1,11}$=9.1, p=.003) on covering. Post-hoc comparison showed a significant difference between C-Drawings on one side, and N-Maps (p=.002), G-Maps (p=.002), and Graphs (p=.01) on the other side. The averaged diagram covering was 65.7% for BF and 52.2% for VI participants. The covering per diagram type (BF vs. VI participants) were: C-Drawings (74.2 vs. 59.7%); G-Maps (51.6 vs. 44.1%); Graphs (52.3 vs. 51.1%); N-Maps (55.4 vs. 40.6%); and P-Drawings (75.7 vs. 46.1%).

Exploration distance per diagram and per hand
We measured the total exploration distance for each hand and diagram (Fig. 2 Left). We found an effect of the user group on the distance covered by the right ($F_{1,11}$=61, p<.001) and left hands ($F_{1,11}$=17.5, p<.001). For BF participants, the exploration distances were 460 and 727 cm for the left and right hand respectively. For VI participants, the exploration distances were 769 and 257 cm for the left and right hand respectively.

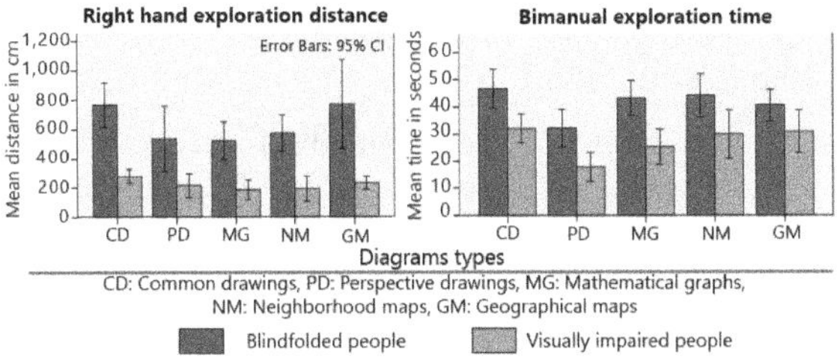

Figure 2. Left: Mean exploration distance for the right hand. Right: Time when both hands moved simultaneously (bimanual exploration).

Bimanual exploration

For each trial, we also computed the time during which both hands were moving simultaneously (bimanual exploration time; see Fig 2). We found an effect of diagram type ($F_{4,44}$=3.8, p=.004) and user group ($F_{1,11}$=27.5, p<.001). The bimanual exploration times were 43s (83.6%) and 28.7s (74.6%) for BF and VI participants respectively.

DISCUSSION

These results showed that VI subjects were faster than BF subjects when considering all the diagram types. They are similar to the results from [7], and probably reflect the greater expertise of VI subjects. However, another result is striking. Although BF and VI subjects reached the same overall identification performance (52%), the percentage of correct responses was significantly different according to the type of drawing. For instance, VI subjects reached 31% of correct responses on N-Maps whereas BF subjects only reached 11% correctness. In fact, VI subjects were better at exploring G-Maps and N-Maps. On the contrary, BF subjects were better at identifying C-Drawings and P-Drawings. This result confirms that exploration of tactile drawing depends on complexity, familiarity, and categorical information [8,9], but also shows that recognition depends on the type of drawing being explored, as well as the expertise of the user. It is probable that VI adults more frequently explore maps and mathematical diagrams than drawings of objects. In addition, drawings rely on visual conventions (occlusions and perspectives) that are less significant to VI people [7].

Our results also highlighted that VI participants covered a smaller exploration distance than BF for all diagram types (52% vs. 66%), although they got equivalent success rates. We observed that VI subjects focused on salient areas of the diagrams (such as the ears on the Rabbit drawing) to identify the diagram type, which made their exploration more efficient. Overall, Drawings required a more extensive exploration than Maps and Graphs.

Exploration distance per hand highlighted that VI and BL subjects had opposite hand behaviors: VI mainly used left hand (769 cm per trial), which is their braille reading dominant hand, while BL subjects used mostly right hand (727 cm). Interestingly, VI subjects covered a limited distance with right hand (257 cm per trial), and BF subjects spent more time performing bimanual exploration. This observation probably reflects that VI subjects appropriately use the second hand as an anchor that helps to understand the drawing, which is a valuable exploratory procedure.

DESIGNING INTERACTIVE ACCESSIBLE DRAWINGS

Our results confirm that VI people are able to explore tactile displays effectively but, depending on their own expertise or the type of diagram being explored, they may benefit from instructions or guidance. According to the format (A3) of the diagrams used in the current study, this preliminary work can provide general design guidelines for tactile displays larger than smartphone or tablet screens.

Touch robustness: Because participants laid their hand on the surface, we frequently observed more than ten simultaneous touch events (16 for BF and 17 for VI), corresponding to additional contacts with the palm. Then, although touch interfaces should enable more than two fingers for tactile exploration, they must prevent unexpected touch events, for instance by combining touch and camera tracking.

Content Simplification: A substantial amount of the raised-lines are not used for completing the different tasks. Then tactile drawings could be further simplified, but in a way that is specific to each type of drawing.

Multimodal Information Sharing: Common drawings require thorough exploration for identification. Then, interfaces may provide both contextual and local feedback (e.g. "rabbit" and "ears"). N-Maps raised exploration issues related to locating specific points. Then, interfaces may provide hand guidance cues (e.g. vibrotactile cues). In general, additional cues (e.g. sound or vibratory pattern) may highlight salient regions of the diagrams to facilitate exploration.

Interaction Menus: VI subjects mainly use their dominant hand for exploration. The non-dominant hand often stays steady, as an anchor. Hence, validation or selection commands could be assigned to the non-dominant hand. These commands should be contextual.

CONCLUSION AND FUTURE WORK

This preliminary study, as well as the general design guidelines that we provide, should be extended. The method can be used in the field of experimental psychology to better understand the role of each finger during tactile exploration. The method can also be used to address specific design questions according to the types of diagrams, tasks, and targeted users.

ACKNOWLEDGMENTS

We thank all the participants, "Cherchons pour Voir" lab, and Lestrade specialized institute (Toulouse, FR). This work was granted by AccessiMap ANR-14-CE17-0018.

REFERENCES

1. D'Angiulli, A., Kennedy, J. M., & Heller, M. A. 1998. Blind children recognizing tactile pictures respond like sighted children given guidance in exploration. *Scand.J.Psychol*, *39*(3), 187–190.
2. Sandra Bardot, Marcos Serrano, and Christophe Jouffrais. 2016. From tactile to virtual: using a smartwatch to improve spatial map exploration for visually impaired users. In *Proceedings of the 18th International Conference on Human-Computer Interaction with Mobile Devices and Services* (MobileHCI '16). ACM, New York, NY, USA, 100-111. DOI: http://dx.doi.org/10.1145/2935334.2935342
3. Anke Brock, Samuel Lebaz, Bernard Oriola, Delphine Picard, Christophe Jouffrais, and Philippe Truillet. 2012. Kin'touch: understanding how visually impaired people explore tactile maps. In *CHI '12 Extended Abstracts on Human Factors in Computing Systems* (CHI EA '12). ACM, New York, NY, USA, 2471-2476. DOI: http://dx.doi.org/10.1145/2212776.2223821
4. Julie Ducasse, Marc J-M Macé, Marcos Serrano, and Christophe Jouffrais. 2016. Tangible Reels: Construction and Exploration of Tangible Maps by Visually Impaired Users. In *Proceedings of the 2016 CHI Conference on Human Factors in Computing Systems* (CHI '16). ACM, New York, NY, USA, 2186-2197. DOI: http://dx.doi.org/10.1145/2858036.2858058
5. Nicholas A. Giudice, Hari Prasath Palani, Eric Brenner, and Kevin M. Kramer. 2012. Learning non-visual graphical information using a touch-based vibro-audio interface. In *Proceedings of the 14th international ACM SIGACCESS conference on Computers and accessibility* (ASSETS '12). ACM, New York, NY, USA, 103-110. DOI=http://dx.doi.org/10.1145/2384916.2384935
6. Tiago Guerreiro, Kyle Montague, João Guerreiro, Rafael Nunes, Hugo Nicolau, and Daniel J.V. Gonçalves. 2015. Blind People Interacting with Large Touch Surfaces: Strategies for One-handed and Two-handed Exploration. In *Proceedings of the 2015 International Conference on Interactive Tabletops & Surfaces* (ITS '15). ACM, New York, NY, USA, 25-34. DOI: http://dx.doi.org/10.1145/2817721.2817743
7. Heller MA. 1989. Picture and pattern perception in the sighted and blind: The advantage of the late blind. *Perception*;18:379.
8. Heller MA, Calcaterra JA, Burson LL, Tyler LA. 1996. Tactual picture identification by blind and sighted people: Effects of providing categorical information. *Percept Psychophys*;58.
9. Heller, M. A. 2002. Tactile picture perception in sighted and blind people. *Behavioural Brain Research*, *135*(1–2), 65–68. Journal Article. http://doi.org/Pm:12356435
10. Shaun K. Kane, Meredith Ringel Morris, Annuska Z. Perkins, Daniel Wigdor, Richard E. Ladner, and Jacob O. Wobbrock. 2011. Access overlays: improving non-visual access to large touch screens for blind users. In *Proceedings of the 24th annual ACM symposium on User interface software and technology* (UIST '11). ACM, New York, NY, USA, 273-282. DOI=http://dx.doi.org/10.1145/2047196.2047232
11. Klatzky, R.L., Giudice, N.A., Bennett, C.R., & Loomis, J.M. 2014.Touch-Screen Technology for the Dynamic Display of 2D Spatial Information without Vision: Promise and progress. *Multisensory Research*. 27(5-6), 359-378.
12. Klatzky R L, Lederman S J. 1987. The Intelligent Hand", *chapter in The Psychology of Learning and Motivation* Ed. G Bower (New York: Academic Press) pp. 121-151
13. Lebaz, S., Jouffrais, C., & Picard, D. 2012. Haptic identification of raised-line drawings: high visuospatial imagers outperform low visuospatial imagers. *Psychological Research*, *76*(5), 667–675. http://doi.org/10.1007/s00426-011-0351-6
14. Lederman SJ, Klatzky RL, Chataway C, Summers CD. 1990. Visual mediation and the haptic recognition of two-dimensional pictures of common objects. *Percept Psychophys*. Jan;47(1):54-64.
15. Lederman, S. J., & Klatzky, R. L. 1993. Extracting object properties through haptic exploration. *Acta Psychol (Amst)*, *84*(1), 29–40.
16. AK Lobben. 2005. Identifying the needs of tactile map makers. *Proceedings of XXII International Cartographic Conference*.
17. Jack M Loomis, Roberta L Klatzky and Susan J Lederman. 1991. Similarity of Tactual and Visual Picture Recognition with Limited Field of View. *In Perception* vol. 20 no. 2 167-177. DOI: 10.1068/p200167
18. David McGookin, Euan Robertson, and Stephen Brewster. 2010. Clutching at straws: using tangible interaction to provide non-visual access to graphs. In *Proceedings of the SIGCHI Conference on Human Factors in Computing Systems* (CHI '10). ACM, New York, NY, USA, 1715-1724. DOI=http://dx.doi.org/10.1145/1753326.1753583
19. O'Modhrain, S., Giudice, N. A., Gardner, J. A., & Legge, G. E. 2015. Designing media for visually-impaired users of refreshable touch displays: Possibilities and pitfalls. *Transactions on Haptics*. 8(3), 248-257.
20. Bernhard Schmitz and Thomas Ertl. 2012. Interactively Displaying Maps on a Tactile Graphics Display.

Spatial Knowledge Acquisition with Limited Information Displays (SKALID 2012), 13–18.

21. Snodgrass J, Vanderwart M, 1980. A standardized set of 260 pictures: Norms for name agreement, image agreement, familiarity, and visual complexity. *Journal of Experimental Psychology: Human Learning and Memory*, 6: 174-215.
22. Symmons M, Richardson B. 2000. Raised line drawings are spontaneously explored with a single finger. *Perception* 29(5):621-626.
23. Wijntjes MW, van Lienen T, Verstijnen IM, Kappers AM. 2008. The influence of picture size on recognition and exploratory behaviour in raised-line drawings. *Perception*.;37(4):602-14.
24. Limin Zeng and Gerhard Weber. 2012. ATMap: Annotated Tactile Maps for the Visually Impaired. *International Training School, Cognitive Behavioural Systems* (COST 2102), LNCS Volume 7403, Springer Berlin Heidelberg, 29.
25. Zhao, H., Plaisant, C., Shneiderman, B., and Lazar, J. 2008. Data Sonification for Users with Visual Impairment. *ACM Transactions on Computer-Human Interaction* 15, 1: 1–28.

Sensing and Handling Engagement Dynamics in Human-Robot Interaction Involving Peripheral Computing Devices

Mingfei Sun
Hong Kong University of Science and Technology
Hong Kong
mingfei.sun@ust.hk

Zhenjie Zhao
Hong Kong University of Science and Technology
Hong Kong
zzhaoao@cse.ust.hk

Xiaojuan Ma
Hong Kong University of Science and Technology
Hong Kong
mxj@cse.ust.hk

ABSTRACT
When human partners attend to peripheral computing devices while interacting with conversational robots, the inability of the robots to determine the actual engagement level of the human partners after gaze shift may cause communication breakdown. In this paper, we propose a real-time perception model for robots to estimate human partners' engagement dynamics, and investigate different robot behavior strategies to handle ambiguities in humans' status and ensure the flow of the conversation. In particular, we define four novel types of engagement status and propose a real-time engagement inference model that weighs humans' social signals dynamically according to the involvement of the computing devices. We further design two robot behavior strategies (*explicit* and *implicit*) to help resolve uncertainties in engagement inference and mitigate the impact of uncoupling, based on an annotated human-human interaction video corpus. We conducted a within-subject experiment to assess the efficacy and usefulness of the proposed engagement inference model and behavior strategies. Results show that robots with our engagement model can deliver better service and smoother conversations as an assistant, and people find the implicit strategy more polite and appropriate.

ACM Classification Keywords
H.5.2 Information Interfaces and Presentation: User Interfaces - interaction styles.: H.1.2 Models and Principles: User/Machine Systems - human factors. I.2.9 Robotics.

Author Keywords
Human-Robot Interaction; Engagement Awareness; Peripheral Computing Devices; Robot Behaviors.

INTRODUCTION
The use of computing devices, e.g., Personal Computers (PC), mobile phones, wearable devices, in peripheral settings during face-to-face communication has become common in our daily life. These peripheral devices can potentially influence the quality of our conversations [27]. For example, when talking with friends, we may occasionally search for information on our phones, or attend to notifications from social media applications. In these scenarios, our partners may notice such attention shift, and react accordingly, e.g., raising their voice, or pausing until our attention comes back, to prevent possible communication breakdowns.

CHI 2017, May 06-11, 2017, Denver, CO, USA
© 2017 ACM. ISBN 978-1-4503-4655-9/17/05...$15.00
DOI: http://dx.doi.org/10.1145/3025453.3025469

Figure 1: One participant is using the laptop while still maintains interaction with the robot

Similar situations could happen in Human-Robot Interaction (HRI) with the presence of peripheral computing devices, as shown in Figure 1. If the robot cannot tell whether people are still engaged and fails to make proper responses, the interaction flow may be interrupted, leading to potential information loss for human participants.

However, perceiving human partners' engagement dynamics and making proper reactions for robots are challenging. First, when human participants suddenly allocate their attention to peripheral computing devices, the intention is unclear to the robots and the consequent engagement status is ambiguous. For example, when people start to type in laptops, they may be taking relevant notes of the conversation, or replying to irrelevant emails. In the former case, the human participants may still listen to the robots and remain engaged in the conversation, while in the latter, they might be completely out of the loop. In other words, different intentions of using computing devices may lead to engagement ambiguities for robots to handle, which is often overlooked in previous research.

Second, for robots, behaving appropriately based on different engagement status of human partners is also a non-trivial task. For instance, the robots can either wait until the humans' attention comes back or actively raise their voices to regain their human partners' attention. Different strategies may result in disparate human perceptions towards their robot partners, which may ultimately have an impact on the quality of the communication. In interpersonal interactions, people have formulated various strategies to make the conversation smoother and more effective [13]. However, whether and how robots can adopt these similar strategies is still under investigated.

In this paper, we consider the computing devices as social beings which can compete for humans' attention with robots. Under this assumption, we define four new types of engagement status based on the human participants' social signals, such as gaze, head pose, and voice. The new types of engagement status offer a fine-grained description of humans' engagement dynamics. We further build a real-time engagement inference model, which captures the inter-state transitions and adjusts the weights on different social signals dynamically according to the involvement of the computing devices. In addition, based on behavioral coding results of a Human-Human Interaction video corpus in a similar configuration with peripheral computing devices present, we design two behavior strategies (*explicit* and *implicit*) for robots to handle the ambiguity problems and ensure successful Human-Robot communication. To evaluate the effectiveness and usefulness of our model and strategy designs, we conduct a within-subject user study of HRI involving a laptop as the peripheral computing device with 27 participants, and analyze their experiences and perceptions through questionnaires and interviews. The participants reflect that the robots with our engagement inference model can perceive their engagement status changes, and are capable of mitigating potential communication breakdowns compared to the one without. In addition, our analysis results reveal that the robots with the *implicit* and *explicit* behavior strategies can handle the information delivery tasks equally well; however, the *implicit* robot is considered to be more polite and appropriate. We also give some implications for behavior designs of engagement-aware robots based on our experimental findings.

RELATED WORK

Peripheral Computing in Interpersonal Communication

The involvement of computing devices in interpersonal communication has been studied for many years. Newman and Smith [28] explored laptop usage in meeting scenarios. They found that laptop users are more likely to drift their attention to less relevant tasks on the laptops, and have difficulty in re-engaging the conversation. In their work, the computing devices, i.e., laptops, are regarded as distractions of the communication. However, the computing devices can also serve as the facilitators for smooth communication. For example, Teevan *et al.* [39] designed a system that allows the effective interaction between presenters and audiences. By building channels to show real-time aggregated feedback of audiences through mobile phones, the presenters are dynamically connected with the audience. And the audiences feel more engaged when they can instantly provide feedback to the presenter. Similarly, Mattias *et al.* [5] studied phone use during meetings and explored its potential influence among attendees. Through experiments in real meetings, they concluded that proper using of smart phones can keep participants' attention on meeting-related tasks and the smart phones can achieve a collaborative presence in meetings. In addition, Hoffman *et al.* [15] showed that peripheral computing devices can also enhance face-to-face interactions as an empathy-evoking supplement. They designed an ambient lamp that can monitor and respond to ongoing conversations on the side. Study showed that participants find the lamp more as a companion than a distraction to the interpersonal communication. Other similar phenomena of using computing devices have also been studied in education and family scenarios [10, 14, 2, 29], where the pros and cons of computing device usage are widely discussed.

Over the years, researchers tried to explore human participants' perceptions and responses to peripheral computing devices in many different application scenarios. Some research on augmented interactive room [17] and ambient displays [42] showed that such systems can act as an additional information channel that may divert users' attention from the focus tasks. Other studies explore the use of ordinary computing devices in peripheral settings. Greatbatch *et al.* [13] considered computing devices in medical consultant scenarios and described how patients coordinate their responses when doctors are using computers. Their research suggests that patients have the impulse to figure out doctor's engagement status, e.g., asking for response, within a certain period. Iqbal *et al.* [16] studied the usage of computing devices, e.g., mobile phones and laptops, in presentations and explored the cost and attitudes about the usage. They reported that audiences worry about missing certain amount of information when using the computing devices. And the presenters are concerned about "whether the device is used in a positive way (e.g., taking notes) or a negative way (e.g., distract by instant messages)". Oduor *et al.* [29] reported people's responses to the usage of mobile devices in home settings. Their results show that people tend to guess what activities the other members are doing when they are using mobile devices. If the activities are relevant to the conversation, e.g., searching locations for family picnics when talking about weekend plans, the usage of these devices is acceptable and beneficial. Otherwise, such usage may lead to frustrations and breakdowns of the conversation. All these studies on computing device usage yields an insight into their influence on participants' engagement status in interpersonal communication. However, little research has explored the effect of computing device usage in HRI. Previous research look mostly into multiparty HRI with a pure face-to-face conversation, in reality, such HRI might involve other computing devices which could complicate the situation. First, the robot in HRI with computing devices situated has no access to the content on these peripheral devices, making it hard to assess their relevance to the on-going conversation. However, the relevance may be inferred from the speeches of human partners in multiparty face-to-face interaction. Second, the robot may have little clue on the start and end time of the attention shift caused by the computing devices, while, in multiparty interactions, such information can be predicted by leveraging turn-taking signals. Furthermore, how the robot should respond to human partner's use of computing devices to avoid potential communication breakdowns still remains under investigated.

Engagement Measurements

In HRI community, engagement is defined as "the process by which interactors start, maintain, and end their perceived connections to each other during an interaction" [35]. Studies of social and service robots, e.g., museum robots [45], bartender robots [12], dialog agents [6], often assume full engagement status from human participants during interaction and allow few distractions from peripheral computing devices. Under this assumption, previous research focused on different periods of "engagement", i.e., "start", "maintain" and "end", and proposed multiple methods to infer engagement status of human partners. Bohus *et al.* [6, 8] built forecasting models to predict people's intents to start or end the conversation in a situated dialog system. Yamazaki and other researchers [45, 38, 41, 24] focused more on determining people's willingness to maintain the interaction in education and entertainment scenarios.

Most of existing engagement inference models take humans' social signals, e.g., gaze, head pose, body orientation, etc., as input. Among all the social signals, gaze is considered to be one of the most efficient indicators [23]. And gaze related features, like eye contact [44], gaze direction [18], gaze pattern [25], are widely adopted to determine the engagement status of human participants. But since the precise gaze estimation requires expensive equipment, researchers have leveraged the head pose as an alternative cue for engagement measurement [31, 1, 3, 21, 41, 26, 34, 20]. Combining multiple cues to get more accurate estimation of engagement is also adopted in [34, 7, 33, 43, 8, 4, 11], and such combination can provide better engagement estimation than the gaze cue alone [33]. Moreover, some models also incorporate other interaction features, e.g., contextual information [11], conversational history [30], to further improve the engagement inference. However, one potential drawback of the cue-combined methods is that the weights of different cues are often fixed. When human partners in HRI are fully engaged in the conversation, gaze and head pose are the strongest indicators of their engagement status. But if they divert their gaze to the peripheral computing devices, the significance of gaze and head pose for engagement may be downplayed by other cues, e.g., head motion (nodding, etc.), voice feedback, and so on. With the fixed weights on multiple cues, the conventional model can hardly tackle this problem. Furthermore, most of the cue-based measurements of engagement for human partners in HRI are binary [43], (engaged or disengaged), or scaled (based on the engagement strength [24]). Such binary or scaled measurements can hardly describe the dynamic process of engagement. Engagement is expected to "wax and wane" over the interaction [24], and this is especially true when human participants are using computing devices while still involved in the interaction. They might repeatedly divert their attention between the devices and other participants, and dynamically modify their behaviors, e.g., nodding. In such situations, the engagement status of human partners is changing, but it is difficult to infer the corresponding binary values or scaled engagement strengths.

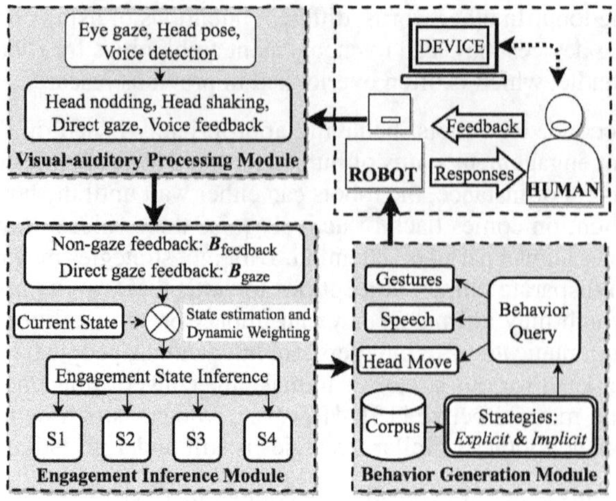

Figure 2: System overview.

Ambiguity Handling Strategy Design

Ambiguity handling have been studied for decades. For example, in spoken dialog system, the conversational agents may encounter various ambiguities caused by understanding errors. These uncertainties have a negative impact on the dialog performance. If the dialog agents fail to respond appropriately, the communication flows are likely to be disrupted. Researchers in this domain have designed and evaluate multiple strategies for the dialog agents. For example, Bohus and Rudnicky [9] experimented 10 strategies, including repeat asking, further inquiring, uncertainty claiming, etc., for the agents to resolve error-induced ambiguity. Their results show that the further inquiring can achieve the best performance. Marsi and Rooden [22] designed audio-visual expressions, e.g., audio with facial expressions, as well as audio-alone expressions for the embodied agent with a talking head to express confusions. The comparison between the two expressions suggests that the ambiguity can be more reliably resolved via audio-visual expressions. Pejsa *et al.* [32] created two sets of strategies, i.e., speaking policy and listening policy, to stress uncertainty information for a situated conversational agent. The virtual agent can choose policy based on the detected uncertainty state. These studies concentrate on the dialog uncertainties and consider more about the misunderstandings rather than the engagement ambiguity. Yet the proposed strategies can be inspiring for our robot strategy design.

MODEL AND SYSTEM DESIGN

In this section, we introduce our engagement inference model and robot behavior generation in detail.

System Overview

Our system [1] consists of three components: *Visual-auditory Processing*, *Engagement Inference*, and *Behavior Generation*,

[1]Downloadable in `https://hcihkust.github.io/EngageDynamics/`

as shown in Figure 2. During the interaction with human partners, the robot keeps capturing and analyzing human participants' social signals, e.g., head pose, voice, etc., in the *Visual-auditory Processing* module. The results are then fed into the *Engagement Inference* module, which infers human engagement states in real time by adjusting the weights of the detected social signals dynamically. These states are further used in the *Behavior Generation* module to guide the robot's behaviors according to our predefined behavior codebook[2]. The detailed descriptions of each module are presented in the following subsections.

Visual-auditory Processing

The *Visual-auditory Processing* module exploits the toolkit provided by Aldebaran[3] to capture basic social signals, including gaze direction, head pose and voice information. We then extract high-level semantic social indicators, such as head nodding $B_{headnod}$, head shaking $B_{headshake}$, direct gaze B_{gaze}, and voice B_{voice}, from the low-level social signals as follows:

Head nodding/shaking. We denote the head pose as $\mathbf{v}_h^{(t)} = [yaw^{(t)}, pitch^{(t)}, roll^{(t)}]$, where $yaw^{(t)}$, $pitch^{(t)}$, $roll^{(t)}$ are yaw, pitch, roll angles in the robot coordinate system at time t, respectively. To detect head nodding indicator $B_{headnod}$ at time t, we calculate the absolute deviation of pitch angles within the past N data points: $\delta_{nod} = \frac{1}{N}\sum_{n=0}^{N-1}|pitch^{(t-n)} - \mu_{nod}|$, where $\mu_{nod} = \frac{1}{N}\sum_{n=0}^{N-1} pitch^{(t-n)}$. In our experiment, we set $N = 50$ with sampling rate 25fps (frame per second) according to the pilot study results. If $\delta_{nod} > 0.4$, we set $B_{headnod} = 1$, otherwise $B_{headnod} = 0$. Similarly, we use the yaw angles to obtain the head shaking indicator and set $B_{headshake} = 1$ if the head shaking is detected, otherwise, $B_{headshake} = 0$.

Direct gaze. We use the gaze indicator directly from Aldebaran gaze analysis toolkit, which computes the gaze direction angles $[yaw^{(t)}, pitch^{(t)}]$ relative to the plane of the participant's face. If the participant is looking at the robot, we set $B_{gaze} = 1$, otherwise, $B_{gaze} = 0$.

Voice. We use a 20ms (millisecond) buffer to store the latest raw sound segment. If the total energy of this buffer exceeds a predefined threshold (obtained from the pilot study results), the voice signal is assumed to be detected, $B_{voice} = 1$, otherwise, $B_{voice} = 0$.

Engagement Inference

To reflect humans' engagement dynamics, we define four engagement states as shown in Figure 3 based on two sets of clues. One is direct gaze, B_{gaze}, and the other is the collective non-gaze clues, $B_{feedback} = B_{headnod} \vee B_{headshaking} \vee B_{voice}$, where $\vee$ is the logical *or* operation. The four states, S1, S2, S3 and S4, are defined as follows. The state S1 denotes that the participants are fully engaged as they are looking at the robot, $B_{gaze} = 1$, e.g., **a** in Figure 3. The state S2 denotes that the human participant shifts gaze away, $B_{gaze} = 0$, but is still engaged as indicated by the non-gaze feedback signals, $B_{feedback} = 1$, e.g., **b** in Figure 3. The state S3 denotes that the participants do not show any feedback signals, i.e., $B_{gaze} = 0$ and $B_{feedback} = 0$, for less than 6s (second), e.g., **c** in Figure 3. The state S4 denotes that the participant is assumed to be disengaged, as no social feedback signals are detected, i.e., $B_{gaze} = 0$ and $B_{feedback} = 0$, for more than 6s, e.g., **d** in Figure 3.

[2]Downloadable in https://hcihkust.github.io/EngageDynamics/
[3]http://doc.aldebaran.com/2-1/naoqi/index.html

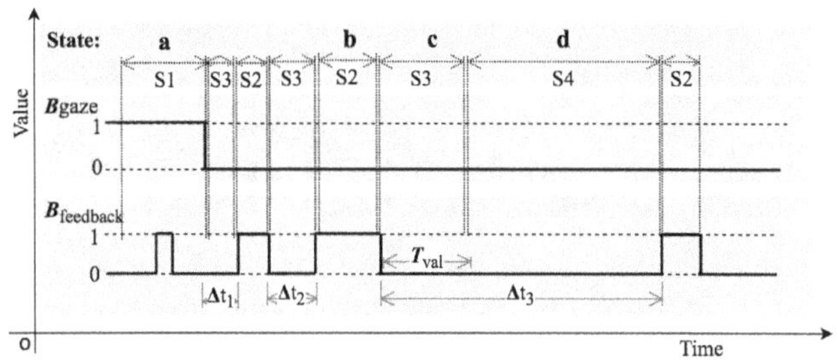

Figure 3: The engagement state S1, S2, S3 and S4. Δt_1, Δt_2 and Δt_3 are time duration of no feedback signals. T_{val} is a predefined threshold (6 seconds) to trigger S3 to transit to S4.

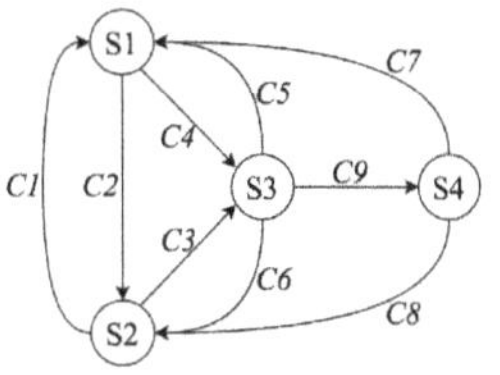

Conditions	Descriptions
C1, C5, C7	$B_{gaze} = 1$
C2, C6, C8	$B_{gaze} = 0, B_{feedback} = 1$
C3, C4	$B_{gaze} = 0, B_{feedback} = 0$
C9	$B_{gaze} = 0, B_{feedback} = 0, \Delta t > 6s$

Figure 4: The transitions of engagement states

We further introduce transitions between these predefined states as illustrated in Figure 4 to explain the underlying principles of the engagement inference. In state S1, the participants' engagement is most certain since they are looking at the robot. From S1 to S2/S3, the gaze has been diverted and the robot has to rely on the non-gaze cues to estimate participants' engagement. Thus, we put more weights on the non-gaze indicator $B_{feedback}$. In other words, the non-gaze cues (head nodding, head shaking, voice) are the only factor to differentiate whether a participant is in S2 or S3. The robot will also assume the participants to be engaged if any non-gaze cues are detected, $B_{feedback} = 1$. Conversely, in state S1, more weights will be put on the gaze indicator B_{gaze}, as the value of $B_{feedback}$ has little impact on this state.

If the participants do not look at the robot and provide no other signals for a short while, i.e., in state S3, there are no clear evidences to determine participants' engagement. Given that the next transition state of S3 could either be engaged, e.g., S1 and S2, or disengaged, e.g., S4, the robot would need additional information to better disambiguate the engagement status in S3. Hence we design a set of handling strategies for the robot, to which the participants' reactions can provide more clues to their actual engagement status, and may ultimately affect the quality of the communication. In the following subsection, we provide detailed descriptions of engagement handling strategy design.

(a) (b) (c)

Figure 5: Snapshots from our video corpus: (a) A raises the hand to regain B's attention. (b) speaker A slows down and waits for B. (c) A turns around to look at B to make sure B is fully engaged.

Cues	Example codes
Gaze	Mutual gaze, gaze sweeping...
Eye Movement	Rapid blinking, looking up...
Head Movement	Nod, shake, toss...
Head Orientation	Turning around, lowering...
Gesture	Pointing, returning to rest position...
Hand Movement	Finger tapping, waving...
Body Orientation	Turning towards, leaning forward...
Body Movement	Stretching, blending...
Posture	Mirroring, standing up...
Speech	Greetings, questions, small talk...
Conjunctions	yeah, OK, well...

Table 1: Cue codes in our codebook

Behavior Generation

The *Behavior Generation* Module is designed to determine what to do and how to do it when different states are detected. Specifically, the robot should exercise state-sensitive behaviors in S1, S2, S3 and S4 to make information delivery smoother and more effective, especially when the engagement status is ambiguous (in S3). To design appropriate behaviors for the robot, we learn from Human-Human Interaction and adapt human strategies in the following three steps.

First, we built a video corpus of multiparty work-related Human-Human Interactions to extract engagement-related actions under different scenes. We shadowed two teams to record their group meetings over a semester. Team A is a course project team with four Master students in Human-Computer Interaction, and Team B is an interest group of three faculties and one Ph.D. student in Design and Human-Computer Interaction. The final corpus, about 850min (minute) in total, contains 17 videos that capture different scenes, such as project planning, presentation rehearsal, design discussion, and meeting arrangement. Some snapshots of the video corpus are shown in Figure 5.

Second, we annotated human behaviors in the video corpus based on a pre-compiled codebook. The codes consist of a variety of essential verbal and non-verbal cues detectable by existing sensors for estimating each conversational participant's engagement status and others' reactions. We construct the initial codebook based on literature review, and further refined it according to sample clips from our video corpus. Table 1 shows examples of cue codes in the codebook. We hired a professional video annotation service to code the participants' engagement status as defined in this paper and their corresponding social signals based on this codebook. The final version of the annotation consists of social signals, the corresponding engagement status, the associated participants, the context, the consequences and the time stamps. Figure 5 shows a few examples: (a) when person A is referring to an important event while his partner B is looking at her laptop, A may infer B is disengaged and thus raise his hand to regain B's attention. (b) The team is discussing their product roadmap when person B suddenly attends to his laptop for a social message, the speaker A therefore slows down and waits. (c) When the speaker A starts an urgent event, he turns around to look at his partner B to imply the importance. These provide essential insights into possible responses the robot should give under the similar circumstances.

Third, by analyzing speakers' behaviors when listeners are possibly disengaged, we find two styles of behavior patterns, perhaps due to different personalities and/or social roles. We denote these two types of strategies as *explicit* and *implicit*, respectively, based on our codebook. The *explicit* strategy expresses views more openly and proactively, such as saying "are your listening?", raising hands to attract attention, etc. The *implicit* strategy will express the speakers' intents in a submissive manner, such as pausing for a moment, saying "I will wait for you", etc. To evaluate the appropriateness and effectiveness of these two strategies for HRI, we conduct a comparative study with a control condition, *unawareness*, which contains no behavior strategies when attention shifts are detected. The detailed behavior manners of the above three strategies are summarized in Table 2.

EXPERIMENT

In order to evaluate the capability of the proposed engagement inference model and different behavior strategy designs, we conduct a within-subject controlled experiment with 27 participants. In this study, we measure the participants' responses and perceptions during dyadic conversations with a robot assistant in work settings where peripheral computing devices may sidetrack humans' attention. More specifically, we use the robot default mode without any behavior strategy as the control condition, denoted as *unawareness*. We design two versions of robot assistants with our engagement inference model but employ different behavior strategies: *explicit* versus *implicit* (see section Model and System Design for more details).

In the experiment, each participant interacts with three versions of robots separately to explore how well the robot can handle engagement dynamics caused by the involvement of peripheral computing devices. To minimize learning and order effects, we counterbalance the order of the three designs of robots as well as their assignments to three different scenarios in a work environment, i.e., *Morning Report*, *Arrange Meetings*, and *Daily Summary*.

Table 3 shows the snippets of the scripts for different scenarios and examples of responses from the three versions of robots

Engagement States	The Robot's Behaviors		
	Explicit	*Implicit*	*Unawareness*
State $S1$: The user is looking at the robot.	The robot talks without pauses	The robot talks without pauses	The robot talks without pauses
State $S2$: The user stops looking at the robot but shows feedback signals.	The robot shifts its attention based on the user's head pose and begin talking slowly.	The robot shifts its attention based on the user's head pose and begin talking slowly.	The robot continues talking as before.
State $S3$: The user attends to the laptop and shows no feedback signals for a short period.	The robot will wait for a while and then directly ask the user's engagement, e.g., "Are you still with me?", "Are you listening?", "Are you following me?", etc. Meanwhile, the robot will also adjust its posture to the partner when asking.	The robot will wait for a while and then pop out filler words, e.g., "Mmm", "Uhm", "Well", "Fine". Meanwhile, the robot will also move its head to follow the user's attention.	The robot continues talking as before.
State $S4$: The user attends to the laptop for quite a long time without any feedback.	The robot will raise the hand to regain attention from the user, e.g., "Hey, listen to me, it's important!", "Hey, you don't want to miss this information!". After that the robot will repeat the last few sentences.	The robot will stop the current conversation and wait for the user to finish the tasks by saying "No problem, I will wait for you.", "OK, I will pause for a moment.", etc.	The robot continues talking as before.

Table 2: The behavior strategies of our three versions of robot assistants under different engagement states.

Scenario	Script Samples
Morning Report	"You have a meeting with Amy at 10am." "You will talk with Amy to decide whether you are going to hike there."
Arrange Meetings	"Davis wants to meet you at twelve o'clock this Tuesday!" "Dr. Wang emailed to confirm next week's meeting arrangement.'
Daily Summary	"Today you have finished your math assignments." "You have to prepare for tomorrow's language course presentation."

Table 3: Script samples in our experiment.

in response to various events. We treat the different robot behavior strategies as our independent variable, and evaluate them in terms of the quality of the service, the perceptions of robots, and user experience.

Hypotheses

Our engagement inference model can detect and disambiguate dynamics in human engagement shifts, based on which robots can respond in different manners. Previous works show that in Human-Human Interaction exercising engagement awareness behaviors can make conversations smoother and more comfortable [32]. Therefore, we hypothesize that:

H1. Robots with our engagement inference model, regardless of their actual styles of behaviors, can better mitigate communication break downs caused by peripheral computing devices. More specifically, human partners will (*H1a*) experience significantly less information loss, (*H1b*) be significantly easier to resume the conversation after using the computing devices, and (*H1c*) feel that the conversation is significantly smoother overall.

H2. Robots with our engagement inference model in general are (*H2a*) perceived to be significantly more competent as an assistant in work settings than those without, and (*H2b*) are significantly more welcomed for future usage.

For manipulation check of our engagement awareness model, we ask people if the robot assistants are aware of their changes of attention on a 7-point Likert scale.

We further hypothesize that different manners of engagement inference robot behaviors can result in different human perceptions of the robots. More specifically:

H3. Compared to those with *explicit* strategy, robots using implicit strategy are perceived to be significantly (*H3a*) less annoying, (*H3b*) less controlling, (*H3c*) less aggressive, (*H3d*) more considerate, (*H3e*) more appropriate, and (*H3f*) more polite.

In our study, we measure these different aspects (derived from [37], [19], [40], [36]) on a 7-point Likert scale.

Experiment Design and Setup

In our experiment, an Aldebaran Nao [4] serves as the robot agent, and we utilize its embedded functions to detect head pose, gaze, and voice. In addition, we use the default implementation as the baseline for the *unawareness* mode. In the other two engagement sensitive modes, the robot captures the social signals from the participant through its visual and audio sensors, and sends the data via WiFi to a back-end laptop (Intel CPU 2.3GHz, 10GB RAM, Ubuntu 14.04) which runs

[4] https://www.ald.softbankrobotics.com/en/cool-robots/nao

our algorithms to estimate the engagement status. Based on the results, the laptop sends command to the robot to adjust its behaviors according to the predefined strategy on the fly.

During the experiment, the participant is asked to sit up straight in a cubic with the Nao robot standing on the table on their right hand side. To the participant's left, a laptop (MacBook Pro with Retina display 13", Intel CPU 2.7GHz, 8GB RAM) serves as the peripheral computing device. As shown in Figure 1. The Nao robot is roughly the same height as the participant in sitting position, and the distance between the robot and its partner is between 0.4m and 1.5m for better social signal detection. Note that the distance may vary as the participant may change the body orientation and/or posture. The Nao robot can rotate, tilt and bend its head and upper body actively, and can also gesture with its hands. However, we do not allow the robot to walk around on the table to avoid unintentional interference with the conversations or tasks due to sudden movements.

The study consists of three sessions, each involving a different version of the robot (*explicit*, *implicit*, and *unawareness*) in one of the three different scenarios (*Morning Report*, *Arrange Meetings*, and *Daily Summary*). In each session, while the participants are interacting with the robot in English, an experimenter sitting in another cubic sends two requests for the participants to complete from the back-end computer to the laptop on the participant side via a social messaging application at random. On the participants' machine, the requests automatically pop up with a notification sound. The requests can be relevant (e.g., "describe the professor as much as possible") or irrelevant (e.g., "what's your favorite app in your mobile phone?') to the conversation at the time.

With participants' consent, we record the whole experiment by a Panasonic video camera.

Participants

We recruit 27 volunteers from a local university (seven females, average age: 24, SD: 1.72) by word-of-mouth and flyers. According to the pre-screening survey, 10 of them report that they have some experiences of interacting with physical or virtual conversational robots, such as Apple Siri [5]. All participants are university students with different education background. They all have TOEFL score above 95 or IELTS score above 7.0, which indicates that they have no problem communicating with the robot in English.

Procedure

After obtaining the consents from participants, we introduce the procedure of the experiment. Each participant takes part in three sessions in a counterbalanced order. In each session, the robot first introduces itself, has some small talks with the participants, and then start the task-related topics. During the conversations, the participant attends to the laptop on the side twice upon the arrival of requests through the messaging application. Each session lasts for less than 10 minutes depending on individual speed of completing the requests. At the end of each session, we ask the participant to fill out a questionnaire

[5] http://www.apple.com/ios/siri/

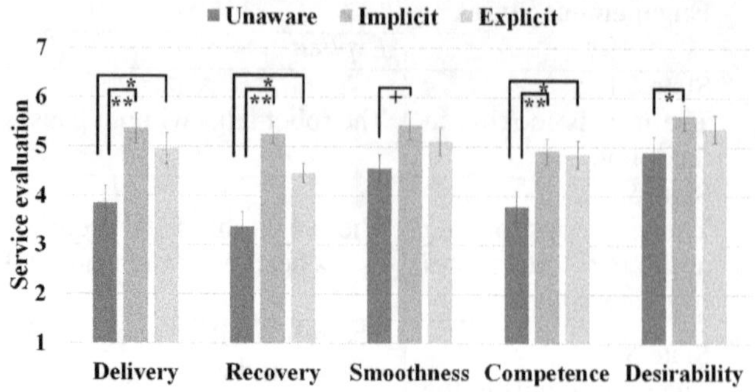

Figure 6: Means and standard errors of the service evaluation of our robot assistants on a 7-point Likert scale (+: $.05 < p < .1$, *: $p < .05$, **: $p < .01$)

to rate the service performance of the robot assistant. Upon the completion of the three sessions, the participant compares and rates the three versions of robots in terms of perceptions and user experience on a 7-point Likert scale, and the participant can review the video recordings if needed. In the end, we conduct an in-depth interview with the participant to find out more about the feelings regarding the robot.

During the pilot study, we detected some transition errors in our model, mostly caused by face/gaze tracking failures. To mitigate this issue, in the experiment, we program the robot to remind the participant to sit up straight or move closer to it, if failed to detect any face or estimate the head pose. In the meantime, we keep monitoring our system log and mark any misbehavior of the robot without interrupting the ongoing experiment. In the post-study interview, we ask additional questions about the user's perceptions and reactions to these incidents to help improve the performance of our system.

ANALYSIS AND RESULTS

We summarize the statistical analyses and interview results, in terms of participants' perceptions of the service and the robot.

Manipulation Check

The manipulation check for engagement awareness conditions shows that the manipulation is effective (repeated measures MANOVA, $F(2,52) = 37.02$, $p < 0.01$, $\eta^2 = .59$). The robots with our engagement model are indeed perceived as being able to detect participants' engagement dynamics (*explicit*: $M = 5.41, SD = 1.65$; *implicit*: $M = 5.67, SD = 1.41$) than the one without ($M = 2.67, SD = 1.52$); Bonferroni post-hoc test $p < 0.05$.

Service Evaluation

Figure 6 shows the robot's ability to avoid communication break downs due to the presence of peripheral computing devices.

The engagement-aware robots are significantly more capable of minimizing information loss when interruptions occur during their conversations with the human partners than the insensitive one (repeated measures MANOVA, $F(2,52) = 8.51$, $p < 0.01$, $\eta^2 = .25$; ***H1a*** accepted). The participants feel that both the *explicit* robot ($M = 4.96, SD = 1.65$) and

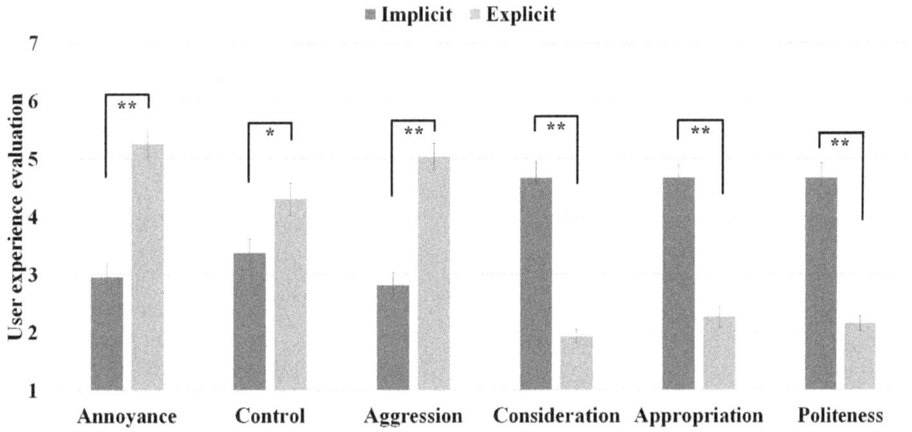

Figure 7: Means and standard errors of the user experience evaluation of our robot assistants on a 7-point Likert scale (+: $.05 < p < .1$, *: $p < .05$, **: $p < .01$)

the *implicit* robot ($M = 5.37, SD = 1.55$) deliver significantly more information than the default *unawareness* one ($M = 3.85, SD = 1.83$); Bonferroni post-hoc test $p < 0.05$. There are no significant differences between the two behavior strategies.

Similarly, participants suggest that they can recover from the interruptions and resume the conversation significantly more easily with the robots running our engagement inference model (repeated measures MANOVA, $F(2, 52) = 13.75$, $p < 0.01$, $\eta^2 = .35$; ***H1b*** accepted). Both the *explicit* ($M = 4.74, SD =$ 1.48) and the *implicit* ($M = 5.26$, $SD = 1.43$) robots can resolve uncoupling significantly better than the baseline robot ($M = 3.37, SD = 1.45$); Bonferroni post-hoc test $p < 0.05$.

Furthermore, the conversations with engagement-aware robots are significantly smoother than that with the ordinary robot ($F(2, 52) = 3.61$, $p < 0.05$, $\eta^2 = .12$; ***H1c*** accepted). Bonferroni post-hoc check shows that handling attention shift using *implicit* strategy ($M = 5.44$, $SD = 1.22$) can lead to marginally smoother conversations than the baseline robot ($M = 4.56$, $SD = 1.63$; $p = 0.07$). But the effect of the explicit strategy ($M = 5.11, SD = 1.01$) is not significant.

In terms of competence and desirability, results show that the participants view the robots with our engagement inference model as more competent than the ones without. (repeated measures MANOVA, $F(2, 52) = 8.01$, $p < 0.01$, $\eta^2 = .24$; ***H2a*** accepted) Bonferroni post-hoc test suggests that while behavior strategies have no significant impact on the perceived competence, participants feel that the robots with our engagement model (*implicit*: $M = 4.93$, $SD = 1.21$; *explicit*: $M = 4.85$, $SD = 1.43$) are significantly better at their jobs than the ones without ($M = 3.78$, $SD = 1.72$; $p < 0.05$).

Similarly, participants prefer working with the engagement-aware robots in the future, significantly more than the baseline one (repeated measures MANOVA, $F(2, 52) = 3.25$, $p <$ 0.05, $\eta^2 = .11$). Bonferroni post-hoc test further reveals that people prefer significantly more the implicit robot ($M = 5.63$, $SD = 1.28$) than the baseline robot ($M = 4.89$, $SD = 1.63$; $p < 0.05$). But the difference between the explicit robot ($M = 5.37$, $SD = 1.45$) and the baseline one is not significant. Therefore, ***H2b*** is only partially accepted.

Robot Evaluation and User Experience

To further explore the underlying rationales of participants' preferences, we ask them to compare the *explicit* and *implicit* robots in terms of *annoyance*, *controlling*, *aggression*, *consideration*, *appropriateness*, and *politeness* on a 7-point Likert scale. The statistical results are shown in Figure 7.

In general, participants find the explicit robot to be ($M = 5.26$, $SD = 1.20$) significantly more annoying than the implicit one ($M = 2.96$, $SD = 1.26$); repeated measures MANOVA, $F(2, 52) = 17.76$, $p < 0.01$, $\eta^2 = .41$; Bonferroni post-hoc test $p < 0.01$ (***H3a*** accepted). This is also confirmed in the post-study interviews:

> *"I like the first one (implicit) the most. It is more patient. The last one (explicit) is too annoying as it kept talking when I was responding to the requests. It is quite noisy. ... I have no special feeling for the second one (unawareness). ... "* – P12 (Male, age: 26)

Participants feel that the explicit robot ($M = 4.30$, $SD =$ 1.46) is significantly more controlling than the implicit one ($M = 3.37$, $SD = 1.25$); repeated measures MANOVA, $F(2, 52) = 3.45$, $p < 0.05$, $\eta^2 = .12$; Bonferroni post-hoc test $p < 0.05$ (***H3b*** accepted). Some participants commented in the interview that:

> *"It (explicit) always said "Are you listening to me?" It persisted until I finally turned back to it. The other robot (implicit) just waited for me."* – P9 (Male, age: 24)

Similarly, the explicit robot ($M = 5.04$, $SD = 1.19$) is more aggressive than the implicit one ($M = 2.81$, $SD = 1.18$); repeated measures MANOVA, $F(2, 52) = 16.40$, $p < 0.01$, $\eta^2 = .39$; Bonferroni post-hoc test $p < 0.05$ (***H3c*** accepted).

Overall, resolving ambiguity and handling disengagement in the implicit manner ($M = 4.67$, $SD = 1.47$) are perceived to be significantly more considerate than that in the explicit manner ($M = 1.93$, $SD = 0.62$); repeated measures MANOVA,

$F(2, 52) = 78.37$, $p < 0.01$, $\eta^2 = .75$; Bonferroni post-hoc test $p < 0.01$ (***H3e*** accepted). One participant mentioned in the interview that:

> *"I really appreciate the robot (implicit) giving me time and space to work on the computer, very thoughtful."* – P20 (Female, age: 23)

Participants thinks the implicit robot ($M = 4.67$, $SD = 1.21$) to be significant more socially appropriate than the explicit one ($M = 2.26$, $SD = 0.94$); repeated measures ANOVA, $F(2, 52) = 56.85$, $p < 0.01$, $\eta^2 = .69$; Bonferroni post-hoc test $p < 0.01$ (***H3e*** accepted). Similar effects are found in the politeness rating. Participants think the the implicit robot ($M = 4.67$, $SD = 1.30$) to be more polite than the explicit one ($M = 2.15$, $SD = 0.66$); repeated measures MANOVA, $F(2, 52) = 58.97$, $p < 0.01$, $\eta^2 = .69$; Bonferroni post-hoc test $p < 0.01$ (***H3f*** accepted).

In the interviews, some participants also mentioned the following points,

> *"I like the last robot (implicit) manner of speaking. It sounds more polite than others, and it handled the interruption quite tactfully ..."* – P21 (Male, age: 24)
>
> *"The last robot (unawareness) simply rushes the conversations. The second robot (implicit) instead takes its time and waits for me, which is respectful. ... "* – P19 (Male, age: 23)

In summary, our engagement inference model is effective in HRI with peripheral computing devices situated. Our model can detect the engagement state transitions of human partners, and adjust the weights of different cues (i.e., head pose, gaze, etc.) to resolve potential ambiguities. This can help the robots conduct smoother and more effective conversations. In addition, although the two versions of our engagement-aware robots of different handling strategies achieve similar service performance and competence ratings, participants have a more positive experience with the *implicit* design. They report the *implicit* robot more considerate and polite, which shows that robot behavior design is critical to successful HRI.

DISCUSSION

In this section, we discuss some insights derived from our study and the limitations of this work.

Implications for Design

Based on data analysis and interview results, we summarize some implications for designing engagement-aware robot behaviors.

Pausing to Acknowledge Computing Devices' Involvement

When robot assistants detect their human partners' attention shift to other devices, regardless of the actual purposes, it is better for the robots to pause for a short moment to acknowledge the event. Then the robots can take subsequent actions according to certain behavior strategies. This gives the participants the sense that the robots are aware of the attention shift, which may result in more effective communication. In addition, most of the participants report that the implicit robots are more "considerate" and "polite" and thus prefer the implicit strategy for HRI.

Robot Behaviors Should Be Context-aware

After a brief pause when the attention shift of human partners is detected, whether robots should continue waiting or should need to urge the human partners to re-enter the conversation could depend on various contextual factors of the HRI, including task-related factors e.g., relevance and urgency, user-related factors e.g., cognitive capacity and emotion, and environment-related factors e.g., existence of other distractions. For example, when the human and robot team is working on an urgent task, it is necessary for the robot to attract its human partner proactively to quickly recover the conversation from interruption. If the task is not as time critical, it might be better for the robot to wait, which could result in smoother and more comfortable communication.

Robot Behaviors Should Be Intent Sensitive

Robots should be sensitive of their human partners' intentions, which might be inferred through the interaction. For example, when robots keep requesting their human partners' attention back to the current interaction while the partners persistently ignore the requests, robots should respect the partners' intents and adjust their behavior strategies.

Consider Potential Negative Experience Caused by Robots

Some participants prefer the unawareness strategy even though they cannot follow up with the conversation. One possible reason may be the "guilty feeling" of the participants. When robots say "are you listening to me?" (*explicit*) or "you are doing other tasks. I will wait for you." (*implicit*), these speeches may make partners feel guilty as if they had caused some troubles. Therefore, we suggest that the potential negative emotional experiences caused by robots' behaviors should be considered when designing engagement-aware robots. In addition, we identify two other types of behaviors that might lead to negative feelings from our participants' feedback.

Repetitive behaviors. Some participants mention that the explicit strategy is quite annoying as the robot keeps saying similar speeches like "are you listening to me?". Although we designed several different statements to regain participants' attention and alternate them randomly during conversation, participants are still likely to experience the repetitive requests if they do not show responses to the robot for a long time. Therefore, having a larger and more expressive vocabulary is needed to avoid the negative experience.

Speaking in constant pace. Some participants say that the *unawareness* robot speaks too fast, and they find it hard to follow the conversation. In fact, all the three versions of robots have same talking speed. However, the explicit and implicit strategies may change the paces based on the interactions, which may make the conversation more comprehensible and engaging.

Limitations

Our work has several limitations. First, our experiment setup contains only one laptop as the peripheral computing device.

However, several participants did use their phones unexpectedly during the experiments. Although our inference model successfully detects these phone use events, we need more systematic study on multi-device situations. Second, our current engagement inference model cannot handle the face occlusion problem. When participants rest their chins on hands, it is difficult for the face detector embedded in the Nao robot to locate their faces and estimate the head poses accurately, hence it is hard to infer the engagement status. Similarly, the face detector in the Nao robot cannot handle large face rotation angles, which can result in unsatisfactory estimation accuracy of our engagement inference model. Third, we do not consider different participants' personalities, and only use fixed robot behaviors for different strategies. If robot assistants can recognize human personality and respond accordingly, smoother and more effective information communication can be expected. Fourth, we do not differentiate active engagement from passive engagement. In this study, there is no specific purpose for the interaction. Hence, the participants listen passively to the robot during interaction for most of the time. However, they may turn into active listeners if asked to complete a quiz based on what the robot has said, and thus are likely to behave rather differently. We will further investigate the effects of these two modes in follow-up studies. Fifth, we restrict the robot's mobility to avoid unintended interference. However, if given more freedom, the robot could try out more expressive engagement handling strategies by incorporating speech, gesture, body languages, and movement in space. Last, in our experiment, the conversational turns between the robot and humans are not balanced, and the dialog system we employ can only handle small talks. The robot is still far from satisfactory to carry out fluent conversations like a real human.

CONCLUSION AND FUTURE WORK

We propose a new real-time engagement inference model by distinguishing engagement level in a find-grained scale. Based on the proposed model, we investigate two different robot behavior strategies. Our experiment results show that our engagement inference model and behavior strategies are useful and effective during Human-Robot Interaction when peripheral computing devices are considered. We also find it meaningful to make robots wait for the participants when their attention is not on the current conversation. Future works could include improving the performance of our engagement inference model in more scenarios and deploying our system in the real HRI.

ACKNOWLEDGMENTS

We thank the WeChat-HKUST Joint Laboratory on Artificial Intelligence Technology (WHAT LAB) grant#1516144-0, and NSF CIFellows grant#1019343, for sponsoring this research.

REFERENCES

1. Jeremy N. Bailenson, Andrew C. Beall, Jack Loomis, Jim Blascovich, and Matthew Turk. 2005. Transformed social interaction, augmented gaze, and social influence in immersive virtual environments. *Human Communication Research* 31, 4 (2005), 511–537. DOI: http://dx.doi.org/10.1093/hcr/31.4.511
2. Louise Barkhuus. 2005. Bring your own laptop unless you want to follow the lecture: Alternative communication in the classroom. *Proceedings of the 2005 international ACM ...* (2005), 140–143. DOI: http://dx.doi.org/10.1145/1099203.1099230
3. Maren Bennewitz, Felix Faber, Dominik Joho, Michael Schreiber, and Sven Behnke. 2005a. Integrating vision and speech for conversations with multiple persons. *2005 IEEE/RSJ International Conference on Intelligent Robots and Systems, IROS* (2005), 1295–1300. DOI: http://dx.doi.org/10.1109/IROS.2005.1545158
4. Maren Bennewitz, Felix Faber, Dominik Joho, Michael Schreiber, and Sven Behnke. 2005b. Towards a humanoid museum guide robot that interacts with multiple persons. *Proceedings of 2005 5th IEEE-RAS International Conference on Humanoid Robots* 2005 (2005), 418–423. DOI:http://dx.doi.org/10.1109/ICHR.2005.1573603
5. Matthias Böhmer, T. Scott Saponas, and Jaime Teevan. 2013. Smartphone use does not have to be rude. *Proceedings of the 15th international conference on Human-computer interaction with mobile devices and services - MobileHCI '13* (2013), 342. DOI: http://dx.doi.org/10.1145/2493190.2493237
6. Dan Bohus and Eric Horvitz. 2009. Dialog in the Open World : Platform and Applications. *Behaviour* (2009), 31–38. DOI:http://dx.doi.org/10.1145/1647314.1647323
7. Dan Bohus and Eric Horvitz. 2010. Facilitating multiparty dialog with gaze, gesture, and speech. *International Conference on Multimodal Interfaces and the Workshop on Machine Learning for Multimodal Interaction on - ICMI-MLMI '10* (2010), 1. DOI: http://dx.doi.org/10.1145/1891903.1891910
8. Dan Bohus and Eric Horvitz. 2014. Managing Human-Robot Engagement with Forecasts and... um... Hesitations. *Proceedings of the 16th International Conference on Multimodal Interaction* (2014), 2–9. DOI: http://dx.doi.org/10.1145/2663204.2663241
9. Dan Bohus and Alexander Rudnicky. 2005. Sorry, I Didn't Catch That! - An Investigation of Non-understanding Errors and Recovery Strategies. *6th SIGdial Workshop on Discourse and Dialogue* (2005). http://www.isca-speech.org/archive
10. Andrea Beth Campbell and Roy P Pargas. 2003. Laptops in the classroom. *ACM SIGCSE Bulletin* 35, 1 (2003), 98. DOI:http://dx.doi.org/10.1145/792548.611942
11. Ginevra Castellano, Andre Pereira, Iolanda Leite, Ana Paiva, and Peter W Mcowan. 2009. Detecting User Engagement with a Robot Companion Using Task and Social Interaction-based Features Interaction scenario. *Proceedings of the 2009 international conference on Multimodal interfaces* (2009), 119–125. DOI: http://dx.doi.org/10.1145/1647314.1647336
12. Mary Ellen Foster, Andre Gaschler, and Manuel Giuliani. 2013. How Can I Help You? Comparing Engagement

Classification Strategies for a Robot Bartender. In *Proceedings of the 15th ACM on International conference on multimodal interaction - ICMI '13*. 255–262. DOI: http://dx.doi.org/10.1145/2522848.2522879

13. David Greatbatch, Paul Luff, Christian Heath, and Peter Campion. 1993. Interpersonal communication and human-computer interaction: an examination of the use of computers in medical consultations. *Interacting with computers* 5, 2 (1993), 193–216.
14. Helene Hembrooke and Geri Gay. 2003. The laptop and the lecture: The effects of multitasking in learning environments. *Journal of Computing in Higher Education* 15, 1 (2003), 46–64. DOI: http://dx.doi.org/10.1007/BF02940852
15. Guy Hoffman, Oren Zuckerman, Gilad Hirschberger, Michal Luria, and Tal Shani-sherman. 2015. Design and Evaluation of a Peripheral Robotic Conversation Companion. *Proceedings of the Tenth Annual ACM/IEEE International Conference on Human-Robot Interaction* (2015), 3–10. DOI: http://dx.doi.org/10.1145/2696454.2696495
16. Shamsi T. Iqbal, Jonathan Grudin, and Eric Horvitz. 2011. Peripheral computing during presentations. *Proceedings of the 2011 annual conference on Human factors in computing systems - CHI '11* (2011), 891. DOI: http://dx.doi.org/10.1145/1978942.1979073
17. Hiroshi Ishii, Craig Wisneski, Scott Brave, Andrew Dahley, Matt Gorbet, Brygg Ullmer, and Paul Yarin. 1998. ambientROOM: Integrating Ambient Media with Architectural Space. In *Proceedings of the Conference on Human Factors in Computing Systems: Making the Impossible Possible (CHI'98)*. 173–174. DOI: http://dx.doi.org/10.1145/286498.286652
18. R Ishii, Yi Nakano, and Toyoaki Nishida. 2013. Gaze awareness in conversational agents: Estimating a user's conversational engagement from eye gaze. *ACM Transactions on Interactive Intelligent Systems* 3, 2 (2013), 1–11. DOI: http://dx.doi.org/10.1145/2499474.2499480
19. Min Kyung Lee, Sara Kiesler, Jodi Forlizzi, Siddhartha Srinivasa, and Paul Rybski. 2010. Gracefully mitigating breakdowns in robotic services. *2010 5th ACM/IEEE International Conference on Human-Robot Interaction (HRI)* (2010), 203–210. DOI: http://dx.doi.org/10.1109/HRI.2010.5453195
20. Severin Lemaignan, Fernando Garcia, Alexis Jacq, and Pierre Dillenbourg. 2016. From real-time attention assessment to "with-me-ness" in human-robot interaction. *2016 11th ACM/IEEE International Conference on Human-Robot Interaction (HRI)* (2016), 157–164. DOI: http://dx.doi.org/10.1109/HRI.2016.7451747
21. Liyuan Li, Xinguo Yu, Jun Li, Gang Wang, Ji-Yu Shi, Yeow-Kee Tan, and Haizhou Li. 2012. Vision-based attention estimation and selection for social robot to perform natural interaction in the open world. *Human-Robot Interaction (HRI), 2012 7th ACM/IEEE International Conference on* 3 (2012), 183–184. DOI: http://dx.doi.org/10.1145/2157689.2157746
22. Erwin Marsi and Ferdi Van Rooden. 2007. Expressing Uncertainty with a Talking Head in a Multimodal Question-Answering System. *Communication And Cognition* (2007). DOI: http://dx.doi.org/citeulike-article-id:2429269
23. AJung Moon, Daniel M. Troniak, Brian Gleeson, Matthew K. X. J. Pan, Minhua Zeng, Benjamin A. Blumer, Karon MacLean, and Elizabeth A. Croft. 2014. Meet me where I'm gazing: how shared attention gaze affects human-robot handover timing. *Human-Robot Interaction* (2014), 334–341. DOI: http://dx.doi.org/10.1145/2559636.2559656
24. Samer Al Moubayed and Jill Fain Lehman. 2015. Toward Better Understanding of Engagement in Multiparty Spoken Interaction with Children. (2015), 211–218. DOI: http://dx.doi.org/10.1145/2818346.2820733
25. Yukiko I. Nakano and Ryo Ishii. 2010. Estimating user's engagement from eye-gaze behaviors in human-agent conversations. *Proceedings of the 15th international conference on Intelligent user interfaces - IUI '10* (2010), 139. DOI:http://dx.doi.org/10.1145/1719970.1719990
26. Yukiko I. Nakano, Takashi Yoshino, Misato Yatsushiro, and Yutaka Takase. 2015. Generating Robot Gaze on the Basis of Participation Roles and Dominance Estimation in Multiparty Interaction. *ACM Transactions on Interactive Intelligent Systems* 5, 4 (2015), 1–23. DOI: http://dx.doi.org/10.1145/2743028
27. William Newman. 2006. Must electronic gadgets disrupt our face-to-face conversations? *Interactions* 13, 6 (2006), 18. DOI:http://dx.doi.org/10.1145/1167948.1167968
28. William Newman and EL Smith. 2006. Disruption of Meetings by Laptop Use: Is There a 10-Second Solution? *CHI'06 Extended Abstracts on Human Factors in ...* (2006), 1145–1150. DOI: http://dx.doi.org/10.1145/1125451.1125667
29. Erick Oduor, Carman Neustaedter, William Odom, Anthony Tang, Niala Moallem, Melanie Tory, and Pourang Irani. 2016. The frustrations and benefits of mobile device usage in the home when co-present with family members. (2016). DOI: http://dx.doi.org/10.1145/2901790.2901809
30. Catharine Oertel, Kenneth A. Funes Mora, Joakim Gustafson, and Jean-Marc Odobez. 2015. Deciphering the Silent Participant. In *Proceedings of the 2015 ACM on International Conference on Multimodal Interaction - ICMI '15*. 107–114. DOI: http://dx.doi.org/10.1145/2818346.2820759
31. Kazuhiro Otsuka, Yoshinao Takemae, and Junji Yamato. 2005. A probabilistic inference of multiparty-conversation structure based on Markov-switching models of gaze patterns, head

directions, and utterances. *Proceedings of the 7th International Conference on Multimodal Interfaces* (2005), 191–198. DOI: http://dx.doi.org/10.1145/1088463.1088497

32. Tomislav Pejsa, Dan Bohus, Michael F. Cohen, Chit W. Saw, James Mahoney, and Eric Horvitz. 2014. Natural Communication about Uncertainties in Situated Interaction. *International Conference on Multimodal Interaction* (2014), 283–290. DOI: http://dx.doi.org/10.1145/2663204.2663249

33. Julia Schwarz, Charles Claudius Marais, Tommer Leyvand, Scott E. Hudson, and Jennifer Mankoff. 2014. Combining body pose, gaze, and gesture to determine intention to interact in vision-based interfaces. *Proceedings of the 32nd annual ACM conference on Human factors in computing systems - CHI '14* (2014), 3443–3452. DOI: http://dx.doi.org/10.1145/2556288.2556989

34. Samira Sheikhi and Jean Marc Odobez. 2015. Combining dynamic head pose-gaze mapping with the robot conversational state for attention recognition in human-robot interactions. *Pattern Recognition Letters* 66 (2015), 81–90. DOI: http://dx.doi.org/10.1016/j.patrec.2014.10.002

35. Candace L. Sidner, Christopher Lee, Cory D. Kidd, Neal Lesh, and Charles Rich. 2005. Explorations in engagement for humans and robots. *Artificial Intelligence* 166, 1-2 (2005), 140–164. DOI: http://dx.doi.org/10.1016/j.artint.2005.03.005

36. Vasant Srinivasan and Leila Takayama. 2016. Help Me Please: Robot Politeness Strategies for Soliciting Help From Humans. *Proceedings of the 2016 CHI Conference on Human Factors in Computing Systems* (2016), 4945–4955. DOI: http://dx.doi.org/10.1145/2858036.2858217

37. Megan Strait, Lara Vujovic, Victoria Floerke, Matthias Scheutz, and Heather Urry. 2015. Too Much Humanness for Human-Robot Interaction: Exposure to Highly Humanlike Robots Elicits Aversive Responding in Observers. *Proceedings of the ACM CHI'15 Conference on Human Factors in Computing Systems* 1 (2015), 3593–3602. DOI: http://dx.doi.org/10.1145/2702123.2702415

38. Daniel Szafir and Bilge Mutlu. 2012. Pay attention! Designing Adaptive Agents that Monitor and Improve User Engagement. *Proceedings of the 2012 ACM annual conference on Human Factors in Computing Systems - CHI '12* (2012), 11. DOI: http://dx.doi.org/10.1145/2207676.2207679

39. Jaime Teevan, Daniel Liebling, Ann Paradiso, Carlos Garcia Jurado Suarez, Curtis von Veh, and Darren Gehring. 2012. Displaying mobile feedback during a presentation. *Proceedings of the 14th international conference on Human-computer interaction with mobile devices and services - MobileHCI '12* (2012), 379. DOI: http://dx.doi.org/10.1145/2371574.2371633

40. Cristen Torrey, Susan R. Fussell, and Sara Kiesler. 2013. How a robot should give advice. *ACM/IEEE International Conference on Human-Robot Interaction* (2013), 275–282. DOI: http://dx.doi.org/10.1109/HRI.2013.6483599

41. Marynel Vázquez, Aaron Steinfeld, Scott E Hudson, and Jodi Forlizzi. 2014. Spatial and Other Social Engagement Cues in a Child-robot Interaction: Effects of a Sidekick. *Proceedings of the 2014 ACM/IEEE International Conference on Human-robot Interaction* (2014), 391–398. DOI:http://dx.doi.org/10.1145/2559636.2559684

42. Daniel Vogel and Ravin Balakrishnan. 2004. Interactive public ambient displays. *Proceedings of the 2004 ACM Symposium on User Interface Software and Technology* (2004), 137. DOI: http://dx.doi.org/10.1145/1029632.1029656

43. Qianli Xu, Liyuan Li, and Gang Wang. 2013. Designing engagement-aware agents for multiparty conversations. *Proceedings of the SIGCHI Conference on Human Factors in Computing Systems - CHI '13* (2013), 2233–2242. DOI: http://dx.doi.org/10.1145/2470654.2481308

44. Tian (Linger) Xu, Hui Zhang, and Chen Yu. 2016. See You See Me: The Role of Eye Contact in Multimodal Human-Robot Interaction. *ACM Transactions on Interactive Intelligent Systems* 6, 1 (2016), 1–22. DOI: http://dx.doi.org/10.1145/2882970

45. Keiichi Yamazaki, Akiko Yamazaki, Mai Okada, Yoshinori Kuno, Yoshinori Kobayashi, Yosuke Hoshi, Karola Pitsch, Paul Luff, Dirk Lehn, and Christian Heath. 2009. Revealing Gauguin:Engaging Visitors in Robot Guide's Explanation in an Art Museum. (2009). DOI: http://dx.doi.org/10.1145/1518701.1518919

Managing Uncertainty in Time Expressions for Virtual Assistants

Xin Rong†*, **Adam Fourney**‡, **Robin N. Brewer**¶*, **Meredith Ringel Morris**‡, **Paul N. Bennett**‡
†University of Michigan, ‡Microsoft Research, ¶Northwestern University
ronxin@umich.edu, adamfo@microsoft.com, rnbrewer@u.northwestern.edu, merrie@microsoft.com, pauben@microsoft.com

ABSTRACT
"Remind me to get milk *later this afternoon.*" In communications and planning, people often express uncertainty about time using imprecise temporal expressions (ITEs). Unfortunately, modern virtual assistants often lack system support to capture the intents behind these expressions. This can result in unnatural interactions and undesirable interruptions (e.g., having a work reminder delivered at 12pm when out at lunch, because the user said "this afternoon"). In this paper we explore existing practices, expectations, and preferences surrounding the use of ITEs. Our mixed methods approach employs surveys, interviews, and an analysis of a large corpus of written communications. We find that people frequently use a diverse set of ITEs in both communication and planning. These uses reflect a variety of motivations, such as conveying uncertainty or task priority. In addition, we find that people have a variety of expectations about time input and management when interacting with virtual assistants. We conclude with design implications for future virtual assistants.

ACM Classification Keywords
H.5.m. Information Interfaces and Presentation (e.g. HCI): Miscellaneous

Author Keywords
Time expressions; virtual assistants; uncertainty management

INTRODUCTION
Virtual assistants (e.g., Apple's Siri, Microsoft's Cortana, Amazon's Alexa, or Google Now) allow people to use natural language to access a device's commands, settings, and integrated services. In many cases, these interactions require that the user communicate a date and/or time. Examples of such scenarios include: creating appointments, setting up reminders, or asking virtual assistants about weather, news, sports, etc. Whether issuing commands or retrieving information, users are encouraged, by convention and instruction [18, 37], to structure their utterances as if they were talking with a real person. However, as we show, these types of interpersonal communications often give rise to temporal expressions that are imprecise, nuanced, and ambiguous. To adopt this style in a virtual assistant is to inherit the challenges of recognizing and managing temporal uncertainty.

*Work done while at Microsoft Research.

CHI 2017, May 6-11, 2017, Denver, CO, USA.

http://dx.doi.org/10.1145/3025453.3025674

Type	Expression
Imprecise	a little more than a week later tomorrow evening this weekend
Precise Date	21 September 2016 tomorrow this Thanksgiving
Precise Time	21 September 2016, 8:00pm EDT 8:00 a.m. tomorrow in 15 minutes

Table 1. Examples of imprecise and precise time expressions: a precise date resolves to the entirety of a specific calendar day when taken *in conjunction with a reference time* (e.g., the time the expression was uttered). A precise time resolves to a date and time down to the minute.

In contrast, modern virtual assistants often insist that dates and times be specified precisely, or will rigidly map a limited set of temporal expressions to predetermined wall-clock times (e.g., mapping "morning" to 7:00am). While early resolution of these expressions may be the easiest solution for system designers and implementers, this strategy can lead to breakdowns in the user experience. First, we show that people are often strategic in their use of temporal expressions so as to convey their own uncertainty, commitment, or task priority. In these scenarios, insisting that people input specific times or dates may increase the burden of using the system. Likewise, overly literal interpretations of temporal expressions may result in reminders or notifications being delivered at inappropriate times (e.g., a user specifying "this afternoon" may not want or expect a reminder to be delivered at precisely 12:00pm).

In this paper we investigate these and related issues pertaining to imprecise temporal expressions (ITEs) in interactions with virtual assistants. For the purpose of this work, we define an ITE as a temporal expression that neither resolves to a *precise date* (i.e., the entirety of a calendar day), nor a *precise time* (i.e., a time with both hour and minute specified), as outlined in Table 1. Our research on ITEs is structured around answering the following research questions (see Figure 1):

- **Motivations**: When do people prefer to use imprecise time expressions? What motivations underlie these choices?
- **Manifestations**: How are temporal expressions manifest in interpersonal communications? What can these occurrences

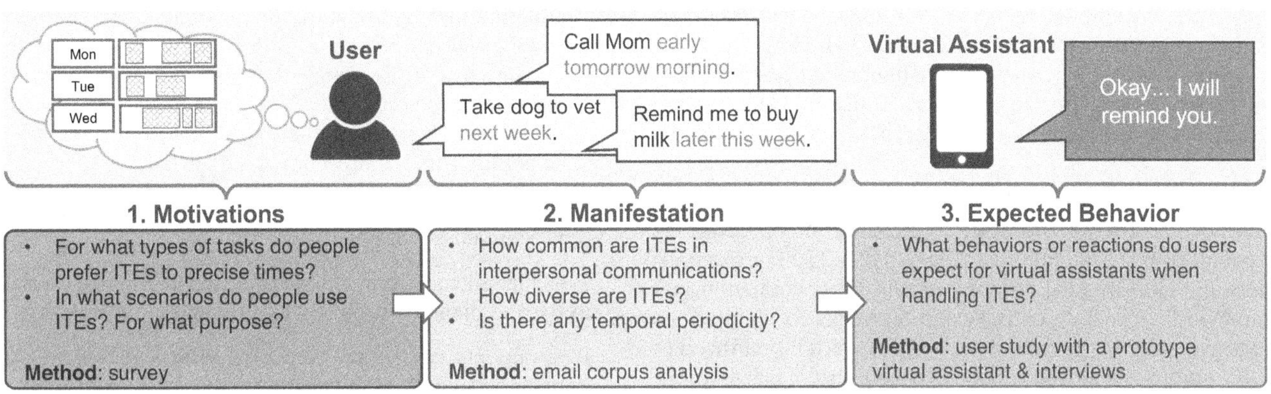

Figure 1. Three aspects of ITE management: user motivations, ITE manifestation, and the expectations for virtual assistants.

tell us about the prevalence and variety of expressions a virtual assistant might encounter in the wild?

- **Expectations**: What are people's expectations when using temporal expressions with virtual assistants?

Given the varied nature of these research questions, our investigations employ a mix of methods. We begin by reporting the results of a survey that broadly characterizes people's motivations for using precise or imprecise temporal expressions when interacting with virtual assistants. Next, given that interactions with modern virtual assistants are styled around natural conversations, we report how temporal expressions are manifested in a large corpus of interpersonal email communications. Finally, we describe a prototype virtual assistant/productivity application we developed to serve as a design probe for this research. This assistant provides support for the broad set of expressions and interpretations obtained from our survey and email studies. We describe the themes that emerged from interviews with 14 participants who used this interface. These in-person interviews were designed to gather a deeper, and more nuanced view of peoples' expectations when using temporal expressions in this context.

Taken together, results from these studies generate insights about the sources of uncertainty that arise with temporal expressions, and describe why management of these temporal uncertainties is important for the development of virtual assistants. In the remainder of this paper we review related work, then introduce the three studies outlined above. We present a set of design implications, then more broadly discuss the implications and limitations of this research.

RELATED WORK

We review related work that handles detection and reasoning about imprecise time expressions (ITEs), as well as research on how virtual assistants manage prospective tasks and handle uncertainties in user input.

Extracting and Reasoning About Time Expressions

Existing work has recognized that ITEs occur in a variety of contexts (e.g. news corpora, electronic health records) [3, 9, 31, 36]. Multiple strategies and solutions have been proposed to both detect and reason about these entities. For detecting temporal expressions, rule-based systems have been shown to perform well, including GUTime [19], HeidelTime [33], SUTime [6], and HINX [36], which can annotate the extracted time phrases as standard markups, such as TIDEs [10] or TimeML [26]. Probabilistic frameworks are an alternative, and have the advantage of leveraging contextual information, such as verb tenses in the sentence, to determine proper temporal interpretation [1, 16]. Tissot [36] combines fuzzy set theory and crowdsourcing to obtain normalization for time phrases that are grounded by human judges. We do not focus on improving the extraction of imprecise time expressions – we mainly rely on existing systems (SUTime) to do such work, but also show how ITEs can be expanded using an existing corpus. Instead, our primary focus is on studying the user intent behind embedding uncertainty in time expressions.

For reasoning about ITEs, solutions have been proposed to place events in temporal sequences to help answer queries related to historical events [9, 29], or to solve constraint-based scheduling problems such as taxi dispatching [34]. These works leverage fuzzy set theory [40, 41] and the fuzzy temporal interval relational models [30] to handle the impreciseness of time representations. However, existing work has not explored the original motivations for people's use of imprecise times, nor has it explored their use in interactive settings.

Time Management by Virtual Assistants

Past work has also explored how virtual assistants can manage time schedules in personal or team settings [7, 8, 14, 15, 28]. In particular, past work has explored triggering reminders based on contextual signals, such as location [17, 32], activities [7], and time [12]. Studies have also identified strong patterns in people's time selections when using reminder apps to manage routine activities [12, 32]. For example, a large-scale log analysis of a commercial virtual assistant has shown that a reminder's creation time and its content are predictive of the user-specified notification time [12].

To automate people's routine activity management, intelligent assistants have been built to execute routine tasks, including handling emails [11], scheduling meetings [39], and managing calendars [2, 4, 22, 28]. The framework of such systems can be built with a Belief-Desire-Intention (BDI) model [27, 35, 38].

User preference modeling, online learning, and constraint reasoning constitute important components [4]. However, these past works have relied on people using precise times. In this paper, we have a special focus on the use of ITEs and we reveal that strong patterns and preferences exist here as well.

Uncertainty Management by Virtual Assistants

Another set of work addresses uncertainty in conversations between humans and intelligent agents [24, 25]. For example, Paek and Horvitz [24] propose a multi-layer computational framework consisting of Bayesian networks for guiding actions given conversational inputs with uncertainty. Pineau et al. [25] propose a mobile robotic assistant system that employs a Partially Observable Markov Decision Process to handle uncertainty in observations. Our work can help to motivate and ground such efforts in data obtained from multiple sources reflecting users' actual usage, preferences, and opinions about time scheduling with uncertainty.

Closest to our work is research done by Martin and Holtzman [20], who propose Kairoscope, a time management approach that is based on relative event sequences instead of precise times. It allows the user to specify imprecise times such as "tomorrow" or "later this week" and uses peer-to-peer agent communication to negotiate and dynamically reschedule event times. Our work compliments their research by greatly expanding the set of expressions to consider, and by exploring the reasons and motivations for using ITEs in the first place.

In summary, our contributions beyond the existing work include: (1) new data analysis that reveals the motivation behind the usage of ITEs; (2) characterizing the prevalence of ITEs in computer-mediated conversations by measuring the frequency, variety, and periodicity of a large set of ITEs; (3) understanding people's expectations of the behaviors of virtual assistants in situations where ITEs are used; and (4) design implications specific to managing uncertainties for modern virtual assistant systems based on the gathered data and observations.

MOTIVATIONS FOR USING IMPRECISE TIME

In this section, we address the first research question by reporting the results of a large survey. The survey sought to characterize the factors that underlie people's choices of temporal expressions in interactions with virtual assistants.

Procedure

The survey consisted of two sections, and was emailed to a random set of 6,000 employees within a large IT corporation. Demographic information was collected at the end of the questionnaire. We describe the survey's components below.

Levels of temporal precision and certainty

The first section presented respondents with concrete situations that required them to consider how they would specify times and dates to a virtual assistant. This section served the dual role of grounding the main content questions of the survey, while also gathering data about the types of scenarios most likely to evoke temporal expressions at varying levels of precision. The following prompt was presented:

> Imagine that, at this particular moment, you are about to use a virtual assistant to create a to-do list. Further suppose that, upon adding each item to the list, the virtual assistant asks you to specify a date and/or time. For each to-do item, please complete the following sentence by selecting from the drop-down menus below:
>
> "I am most comfortable answering with a date / time that is accurate to within..."

Possible sentence completions are listed in Figure 2 (horizontal axis), and range from as low as a minute to as high as a year.

Respondents were then presented with a list of five to-do items, and five blank spaces in which they could input their own items. Respondents were asked to input at least two of their own items. Pre-populated items were randomly selected from the five most common reminder categories identified by Graus et al. in [12]. The tasks (and their categories) were: pick up laundry (run errand), pay phone bill (chores), call mom (communicate), start cooking (manage process), and take medicine (eat/consume).

When and why ITEs are preferred

The second section of the survey was designed to more generally explore the situations that might trigger people to use imprecise temporal expressions. Respondents were asked to more generally reflect on the situations where they might use imprecise temporal expressions over giving precise times. The following prompt was presented:

> Modern virtual assistants can help you manage your to-do lists by associating precise times with each item. Like an alarm clock, these precise times specify both hour and minute (e.g., 8:05am). Mirroring human assistants, virtual assistants can also increasingly cope with imprecise time expressions (e.g., "in a few hours", "this evening", "later this week", "on the weekend", etc.)
>
> Rate your agreement to each of the following statements.
>
> "I prefer to use imprecise time expressions (e.g., 'in a few hours', 'this evening', etc.) when ..."

We then asked the respondents to respond to 11 sentence completions (abbreviated in Figure 4). Two additional options served as catch-all categories: *"for most tasks/todo-items"* or *"in few, or almost no, situations."* All items were scored on a 5-point Likert scale (strongly disagree = 1, strongly agree = 5).

Results

338 respondents completed the entire survey, while an additional 182 participants provided partial responses (response rate: 8.0%, completion rate: 65.0%). In our analysis, we only consider those 338 who completed the survey in its entirety.

73.7% (n = 249) of the respondents were male, and 83.4% (n = 282) reported having a bachelor's or advanced academic degree. Respondents reported occupying a diverse set of roles within the company: 24.6% (n = 83) were software developers, 21.6% (n = 73) worked in sales or marketing, and 16.9% (n = 57) worked in managerial positions. The remaining 37.0% of respondents (n = 125) worked in a number of specific roles,

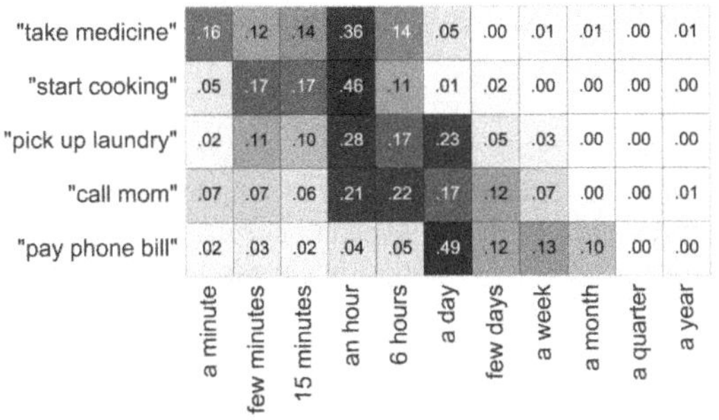

Figure 2. Respondent preference for various levels of temporal precision over the five sample to-do items provided in the questionnaire.

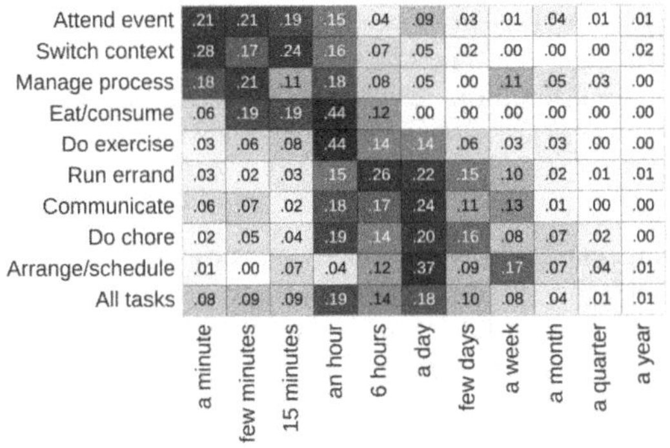

Figure 3. Respondent preference for various levels of temporal precision over the 865 respondent-provided to-do items. Items are organized into nine task categories, adapted from [12].

including: technical writers, supply chain engineers, security consultants, legal advisers, etc.

Regarding prior experience with virtual assistants, 17.8% (n = 60) of respondents indicated that they interacted with a virtual assistant (any one of Siri, Google Now, Cortana, and Echo/Alexa) earlier the same day; 30.8% (n = 104) earlier in the week; 15.1% (n = 51) earlier in the month; 22.5% (n = 76) more than a month ago; and 13.9% (n = 47) never. Overall a majority of the respondents (63.5%) had interacted with a virtual assistant within the past month.

Levels of temporal precision and certainty

Figure 2 summarizes responses for the pre-populated to-do items. Figure 3 summarizes responses for the 865 user-provided items, manually classified into nine task categories adapted from [12].[1] Together, these figures express the two main findings from this portion of the questionnaire: (1) temporal uncertainty varies considerably by task type, and (2) respondents were rarely comfortable expressing minute-level precisions (occurring in only 2% to 16% of responses for the pre-populated items listed in Figure 2, and in 9% of the user-provided items in Figure 3). Recognizing the possibility that some respondents may have conflated minute-level responses with hour-level responses (e.g., for items like "8:00am"), we further report that hour and minute-level precisions combine to account for at most 52% of responses.

[1] The open-ended survey data were manually labeled by one of the authors.

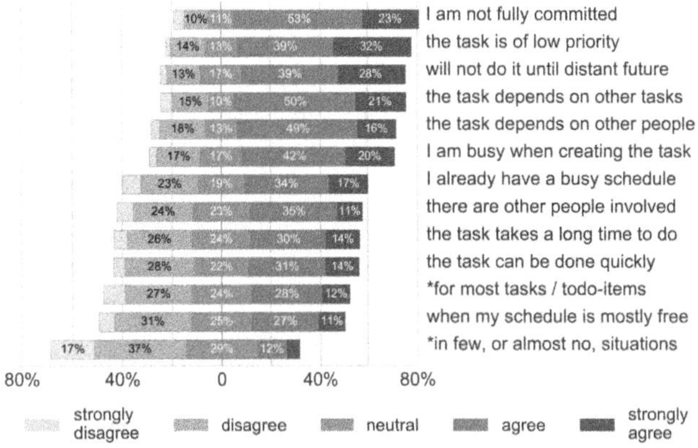

Figure 4. List of situations where people prefer to use imprecise time expressions over precise time expressions. Items are scored on a 5-point Likert scale ranging from 1 (strongly disagree) to 5 (strongly agree). Starred (*) items are two catch-all categories.

Further analysis of user-provided tasks reveals additional nuance. For example, respondents were more comfortable with higher levels of precision for tasks involving the attendance of an event (e.g., "meet at restaurant") than when scheduling or arranging events (e.g., "make reservations for dinner"). This difference is highly statistically significant (Mann–Whitney U = 8618.5, two-tailed $p < 0.001$). Likewise, we find that respondents preferred to be less precise when referring to chores (e.g., "*organize clothes*") or running errands (e.g., "*go to the post office*"). These findings appeal to our intuitions about *external dependencies* (scheduling), and *task priority* (chores and errands), which we explore further in the next section.

When and why ITEs are preferred

Notably, we find that 40.2% (n = 136) of respondents reported that "*(they) prefer to use imprecise temporal expressions for most tasks / to-do items.*" This is significantly more than the 16.9% (n = 57) of respondents who reported that "*(they) prefer to use imprecise temporal expressions in few, or almost no, situations*" (Mann–Whitney U=67656.0, $p < 0.001$).

Further investigation reveals that the leading situation where people prefer to use imprecise time is when they are not fully committed to the task (Figure 4). Five other situations closely follow: "*when the task is low priority*", "*when the task will not be executed until the distant future*", "*when the task depends on other tasks*", "*when the task depends on other people*", and "*when I am busy at the time of creating the task*".

Finally, we studied the responses of the 57 respondents who felt that imprecise temporal expressions were preferred in "*almost no situations*." Even within this group, respondents were more likely to prefer imprecise temporal expressions when: "*(they) have not fully committed to the task*" (75% agreement), "*when the task will not be executed until the distant future*" (74% agreement), and "*when the task is low priority*" (65% agreement). In each of these three cases, a Binomial test finds these preferences to be statistically significant at the 0.05 level ($p < 0.001$, $p < 0.001$, and $p = 0.033$, respectively).

Discussion

From the results of the survey's first section, we conclude that when managing common tasks, people are only occasionally comfortable with minute-level precision. At present, however, minute-level precision is required by contemporary virtual assistants when scheduling notifications or reminders [12].

Responses to the second section of the survey mirrored those from the first section, reinforcing the need for virtual assistants to consider task priority and external dependencies when interpreting ITEs. To this end, we note that the situation "*when there are other people involved*" is similar to "*when the task depends on other people*", but lacks the language suggesting a dependency. Accordingly, we find that the former expression has much lower preference for imprecise temporal expressions than the latter (p<0.001, by Mann–Whitney U). Additionally, the tendency to prefer imprecision "when busy" at task creation time suggests that cognitive load may also be a factor.

In summary, we find that there are many common scenarios in which people are likely to prefer imprecise time expressions when interacting with virtual assistants. Imprecision was found to be most appropriate for tasks of low commitment or priority or when tasks involved external dependencies. Next, we characterize how these ITEs are likely to manifest.

MANIFESTATION OF IMPRECISE TIME

To answer our next research question, we analyzed a large email corpus consisting of interpersonal communications. By extracting and analyzing the characteristics of temporal expressions found in this corpus, we can devise a set of ITEs to consider in the later stage of the research and also draw design implications for virtual assistants.

Data

Our analysis used the publicly available Avocado dataset, a corpus of emails exchanged between 279 correspondents "of a defunct information technology company" [23]. Although the language used in email conversations may differ from that with virtual assistants, the Avocado corpus exhibits a number of desirable properties. In particular, as mentioned above, because the email exchanges occurred between human correspondents, the corpus affords an opportunity to observe how temporal expressions occur without user expectations of the limitations of existing virtual assistants. Moreover, since the email conversations contain temporal metadata (i.e., sent time stamps), we are able to analyze the temporal patterns of the occurrences of any given expression.

Procedure

Preprocessing

The dataset required several cleaning and normalization steps prior to linguistic processing. First, we extracted the text in the email body of each email, discarding the subject, senders, recipients, and other header fields. We then removed quoted content from email replies (or forwarded messages) so that each original message was analyzed only once. This resulted in 379,332 valid emails. We then also removed 74,053 messages that appeared to be spam or machine-generated. 305,279 emails remained after all the filtering steps. Finally, all text content was transformed to lower case and then tokenized for further analyses.

Extracting temporal expressions

Our analyses required that we extract a broad range of temporal expressions from the Avocado corpus. To this end we used SUTime, a rule-based temporal expression tagger [6] capable of detecting both precise dates or times (e.g., "October 3rd"), and a limited set of ITEs (e.g., "Saturday morning").

To expand the coverage to a broader set of temporal expressions, we performed an additional amplification procedure. First, we identified common keywords, prefixes, and suffixes occurring in the temporal expressions already identified by SUTime. We then computed the cross product over these three sets, thus generating additional candidate expressions. Finally, we again filtered the results on the Avocado corpus, keeping only those expressions occurring at least once.

Categorizing temporal expressions

Having extracted temporal expressions from the Avocado dataset, the second step of the procedure was to classify each expression as either cleanly resolving to a precise date/time, or as an expression that was unresolvable (i.e., an ITE). A rule-based classifier was developed for this purpose, and operated as follows – temporal expressions were classified as precise if they met *all* of the following conditions: (1) identified by SUTime; (2) did not occur near approximation keywords (e.g., "around", or "in about"); and (3) were not ascribed any special annotation by SUTime. For example, SUTime outputs special annotations such as "2017-SU" when parsing the phrase "next summer", and "2016-09-21EV" when parsing the phrase "tomorrow evening". Temporal expressions failing any of these checks were labeled as ITEs. In the remainder of this section, we are primarily concerned about ITEs.

Human interpretation of temporal expressions

Finally, while the Avocado corpus contains a record of when imprecise temporal expressions were invoked (email *sent* time), it lacks information about how those expressions may have been intended or interpreted. To gather these mappings, we tasked crowd workers with labeling a small set of 53 extracted expressions. A sample labeling task reads: "*assuming that today is Monday Jan 11th, what does 'later this week' mean to you?*" Workers were then asked to choose a date range by selecting a start date and an end date from a calendar widget. For each expression considered, a human intelligence task (HIT) was prepared for all seven days of the week. For each question, 50 judgments were collected. In total, 308 workers contributed to judgments. All workers resided in English-speaking countries, and were recruited from the Clickworker.com crowd-sourcing platform.

Results

ITEs are common

Chief among our findings is the observation that 36.2% of all temporal expressions in the email corpus could not be automatically resolved to specific dates or times.

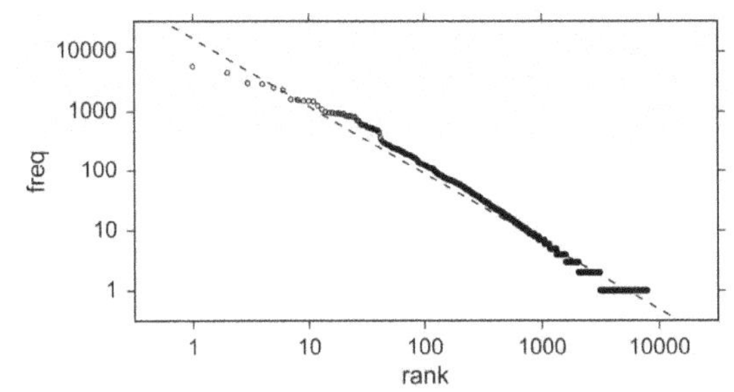

Figure 5. Occurrence frequencies of imprecise time expressions in the Avocado email dataset follow Zipf's law.

Expression	Count
next week	5653
this week	4436
last week	2979
lunch	2881
this morning	2501
a little more than a week later	1
no later than tomorrow noon	1
around the end of this week or early next week	1
morning Friday, or at latest, very early next week	1
lunch tomorrow, or later in the day	1

Table 2. Examples of imprecise temporal expressions. Top: most frequent expressions. Bottom: selected complex expressions.

ITEs follow a power law distribution

In addition to reporting aggregate frequencies (above), we also investigated the occurrence rates of individual temporal expressions. Our analysis reveals that the frequencies of ITEs follow a power-law distribution, with the most common expressions occurring exponentially more often than the least common expressions (Figure 5). Importantly, 79.7% of all expressions are observed 3 or fewer times, and 60.4% of all expressions are observed only once. Most expressions occur with low frequency, and many are complex (Table 2).

ITEs exhibit temporal periodicity

Finally, our analysis reveals that a number of expressions present periodicity in their use. To illustrate this pattern, for a given time expression, we look at the sent time of each email containing the time expression. We then count the occurrences of selected popular expressions, binning over the days of week (Figure 6), or over three-hour slots each day (Figure 7). We normalize the counts based on the total number of emails sent on each day, or time block, respectively. For example, Figure 6(a) indicates that the mentions of "later this week" occur most often on Mondays and Tuesdays, and mentions of "early next week" occur most often on Fridays.

Figure 6(b) provides a sanity check – the peak use of a given day of the week (e.g., "Thursday") does not occur on that particular day, or even adjacent days. Note that, on a given Thursday, the word "today" becomes available for some intended uses. Likewise, on Wednesday, the word "tomorrow" becomes available. This explains why the mentions of "Thursday" peak on Tuesday, and the mentions of the other days of week share a similar trend. Figure 6(c) illustrates the distribution of mentions for a set of ambiguous terms. The mentions

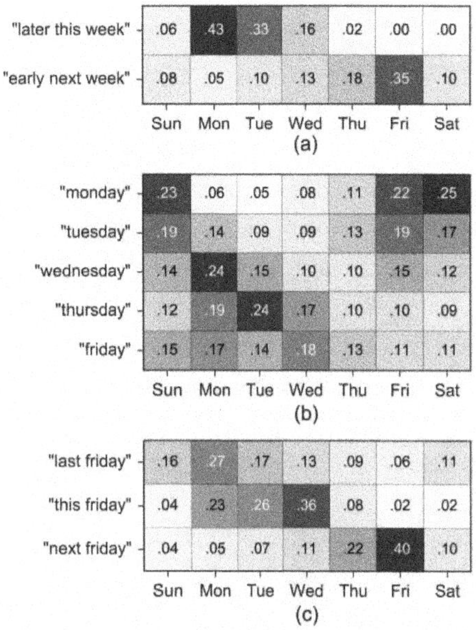

Figure 6. Normalized usage frequency of imprecise time expressions per day-of-week in the Avocado data set.

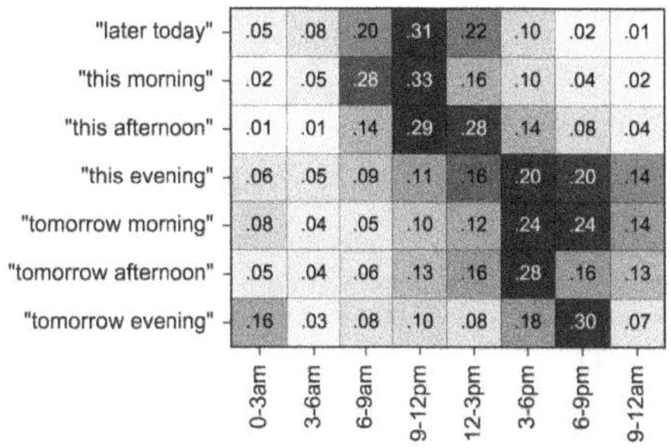

Figure 7. Normalized usage frequency of ITEs per 3-hour slot of a day in the Avocado data set.

of "last Friday" occur most often on Mondays, mentions of "this Friday" occur most often on Wednesdays, and mentions of "next Friday" occur most often on Fridays.

Within the scope of a day, some expressions also exhibit periodicity (Figure 7). For example, the mentions of "later today" occur most often in the morning between 9am–12pm. So do the mentions of "this morning." In comparison, mentions of the parts of day for the next day most often occur in the evenings.

Given the observed periodicities in ITE occurrences, we hypothesized that temporal context may also play a role in people's interpretations of ITEs. To examine this hypothesis, we examined the times ascribed to ITEs by crowd workers. We observed that the interpretation of ITEs varies depending on the time in which it is considered. For example, when the given reference time is early in the work week, the interpretations of the phrase "next weekend" are characterized by a bimodal distribution (Figure 8). Here, some judges interpret the phrase to mean the closest upcoming weekend, while others interpret the phrase to mean the weekend that concludes the following week. However, by Wednesday, much of the ambiguity is gone.

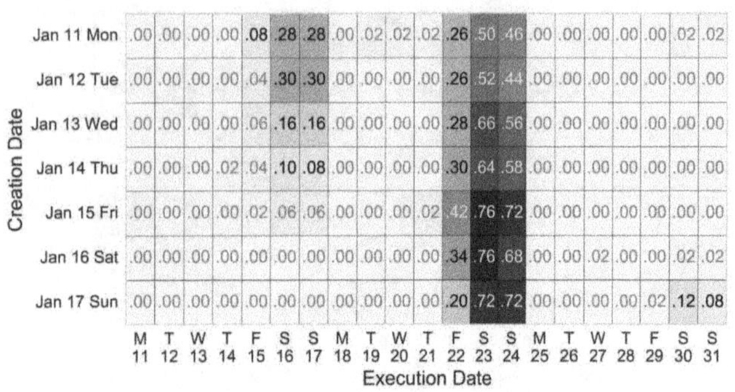

Figure 8. Interpretation of "next weekend" on different days of the week based on the crowdsourced results. The numbers shown are the proportion of workers that include the particular execution date in their range of interpretation.

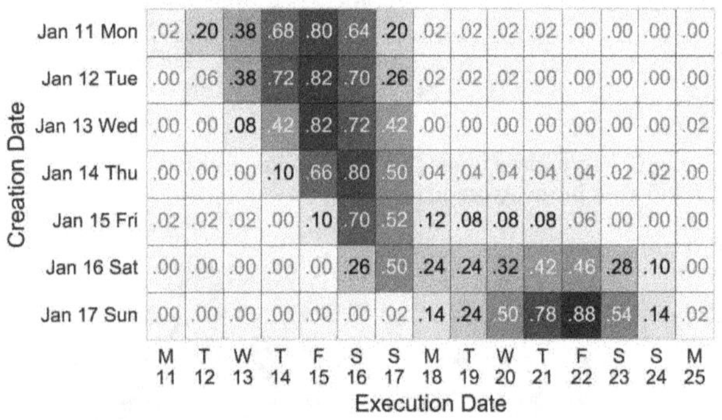

Figure 9. Interpretation of "later this week" on different days of the week based on the crowdsourced results. The numbers shown are the proportion of workers that include the particular execution date in their range of interpretation.

Likewise, Figure 9 summarizes the result we obtained for the interpretation of "later this week." Agreeing with intuition, "later this week" is most often interpreted to mean the remainder of the work week (ending Friday). However, an interesting discrepancy arises on Thursdays. Specifically, from Monday to Wednesday, the interpreted distribution peaks on Friday. However, beginning on Thursday the peak in interpreted times shifts to Saturday. We hypothesize that the crowd workers shifted their estimates because, beginning Thursday, the Friday is most naturally referred to simply as "tomorrow".

Discussion

So far we have presented three main findings from the email corpus analysis. We now discuss the implications of these results.

First, ITEs being very common implies that if virtual assistants are unable to interpret these expressions, they may be missing a third or more of all temporal expressions occurring in the natural communications they seek to understand and emulate.

Second, ITEs being very diverse implies that virtual assistants must be effective in resolving *long-tail* temporal expressions. While heuristics can be developed to resolve the most common ITEs, such as "next week," "this morning," "this afternoon," "this weekend," and "tomorrow morning," inspection of long-tail expressions reveals more complex temporal expressions (Table 2) that may create difficulties not only for extraction, but also for downstream interpretation and action (e.g., triggering reminders).

Third, ITEs exhibiting periodic regularities implies that date and time are a crucial context for correctly interpreting these expressions. Designers of virtual assistant are advised to consider these issues when developing interactions. For example, when the user says "later this week" on a Friday, which is a rare event according to its past occurrence frequencies, the system may verify with the user by asking what she really means. Similarly, if the user says "next weekend" on a Monday, which is very ambiguous according to the interpretation model, the system may also actively verify with the user.

In summary, and in response to our second research question, we find that ITEs represent a large class of temporal expressions occurring in computer-mediated communications, both in terms of frequency and in diversity. Moreover, we find that both the past occurrences and present interpretations of ITEs are themselves governed by temporal processes. These findings have immediate implications for the design of virtual assistants, which we have outlined above, and later revisit.

EXPECTATIONS FROM VIRTUAL ASSISTANTS

To answer our final research question, we conducted an in-person interview study with 14 participants. The study was designed to gather a more nuanced view of peoples' expectations of virtual assistants in scenarios where interactions involve temporal expressions.

Design Probe Apparatus

A prototype virtual assistant system was developed to serve as a design probe, with the goal of grounding the interviews, and guiding participants to speak in concrete terms about their expectations around ITEs. It is the dialog with participants, and not the system itself, which forms a primary contribution of this paper. To this end, the virtual assistant's functionality was limited: the system allowed the user to create and manage a list of memos and reminders; it recognized ITEs using the same method as in the email corpus study; and, it used heuristic rules to map ITEs to actual time intervals (Figure 11); however, it could not deliver reminders as notifications.

Nevertheless, one feature of the prototype distinguishes it from existing virtual assistants. Namely, the prototype prominently displayed a curated list of items deemed relevant to the current moment. This region of the display was referred to as the *Corkboard* (Figure 10), and it allowed multiple items with imprecise and overlapping time periods to be displayed together without evoking the sense of conflict that arises in calendaring applications when two entries overlap. When creating a memo or a to-do item (Figure 11), the user could schedule the time period in which the given item would be displayed in this region by either: (1) including temporal expressions in the text content of the item (Figure 11, e.g., "get coffee after work"); or (2) manually selecting from a list of common expressions (e.g., "today", "tomorrow", etc.); or (3) picking a precise date or time from a calendar or time picker widget.

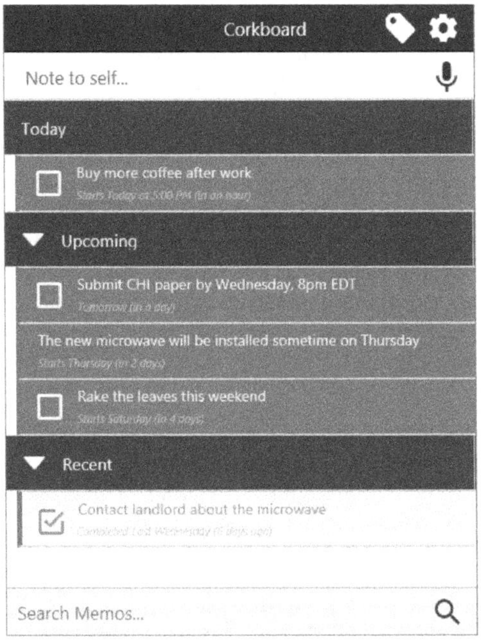

Figure 10. Our virtual assistant's *Corkboard* screen displays a short list of items relevant to a given moment in time.

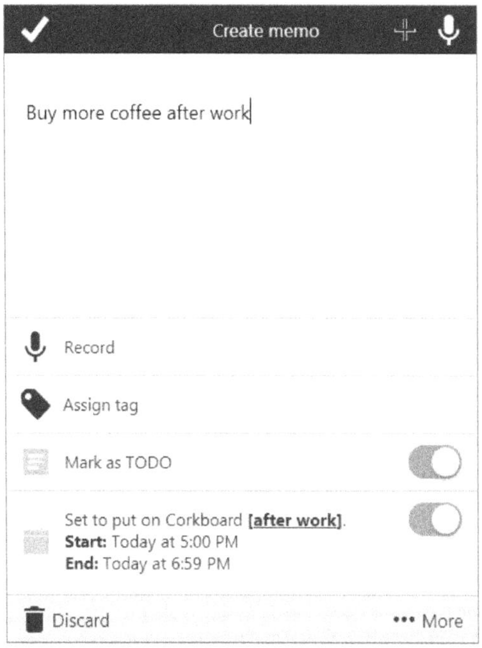

Figure 11. Participants can include temporal expressions in the text of their memos, or can click on the scheduling panel (bottom) to pick times or dates from a list of suggestions or from a calendar.

Procedure

Participants were recruited by email, within the same large IT organization as the earlier survey. Participants were screened for past experience with Android smart phones, ensuring that they were familiar with the UI conventions of the device used in the study. In total, 14 participants were interviewed (5 female, mean age = 31 years), and each received a $5 food voucher as remuneration.

Upon arriving to the interview, participants were presented a brief video tutorial demonstrating the features of the probe system. Participants were then tasked with inputting four of their own personal to-do items they wished to remember. After participants entered the four notes, the interviewer (an author on this paper) revisited each item in turn, and asked participants to comment on the appropriateness of the system's interpretations. The interviewer also asked participants if they would like to receive additional notifications or reminders for each item. These discussions were recorded and transcribed. Iterative open-coding techniques were applied to identify the common themes.

At the end of the interview, participants completed a questionnaire which included both open-ended questions about the usability of the system and a balanced subset[2] of Likert items from the System Usability Scale (SUS) [5]. Individual Likert items were scored on a 5-point scale (strongly disagree = 1, strongly agree = 5). Given our research focus, and the limited implementation of the design probe, this exit questionnaire served as a check to ensure that the system was of sufficient quality and completeness to effectively ground the discussions – we did not want the interviewees dwelling on software bugs or missing features.

[2]We used four positively-worded and four negatively-worded items.

Results and Discussion

General impressions

All 14 participants successfully accomplished their input tasks. Of the 56 items generated in total, 23 items contained an in-line temporal expression, 9 items were assigned times from the list of suggestions, and 6 items were assigned times via the calendar or time-picker widgets. The remaining 18 items lacked any explicit temporal cues, and defaulted to "today" (i.e., the item was scheduled to remain displayed for the rest of the day). In-line temporal expressions ranged from simple (e.g., "*Freshman orientation September 25th*", P4), to complex (e.g., "*Set up Tokyo meeting with (a business) early next week for an evening meeting*", P8).

The virtual assistant also received high scores on specific SUS usability items: 12 participants agreed that the system was easy to use (M=3.4, SD=0.82), 10 participants agreed that they felt confident using the system (M=3.2, SD=0.77), and all 14 participants agreed that most people would learn the system quickly (M=3.4, SD=0.82). Conversely, 9 participants *disagreed* with the statement asserting that the system was cumbersome (M=1.9, SD=0.88), and all 14 participants disagreed with the statement asserting that they would require technical support to use the system (M=1.3, SD=0.47).

Finally, we report participants' favorite and least favorite features. 7 of the 14 participants listed the ability to dictate memos and to-dos as their favorite feature (e.g., "*simple and easy voice input*"), while 6 participants listed the system's ability to detect in-line temporal expressions as their favorite feature (e.g., "*it was smart about figuring out the time starts and ends*"). Conversely, the list of least favorite features was varied, and many concerns pertained to specifics of the UI (e.g., "*I was expecting a save button rather than a back button*")

Themes

Common themes that emerged from the participants' comments on the system are summarized and discussed below.

Implied flexibility. A prevalent theme that emerged from the interviews was that many items carried an implied flexibility in scheduling. For example, after inputting the item "*Buy Christmas presents*", participant 1 (P1) noted that the system should display the item "*somewhere in December*," and that "*(he) doesn't care if that's the first, second, third, tenth, twentieth (of December), but it should be before the 24th.*" Likewise, after inputting the note "*revisit will in 5 years*," P14 was surprised by the system's literal interpretation of August 26, 2021 – exactly five years from the day the entry was created. The participant noted that the item did not require a specific date, and that the appropriate granularity was at the level of months. These sentiments were best summarized by P1, who noted:

> "*I want the reminder to be as imprecise as my time instruction. If I say 11am and 3 minutes and 10 seconds, I expect a very precise reminder that notifies me maybe a minute before that, but if I say 'next month', then I expect it to remind me a few days ahead, even a few weeks ahead of it.*"

Implied constraints. While the former items carried implicit flexibility, others required that the system consider unstated constraints. For example, when P4 input the to-do item "*Remember to pack presents tomorrow*," the assistant responded by offering to display the item on the Corkboard from 12:00am to 11:59pm on the day following the interview. When asked if this response was appropriate, P4 responded "*So probably what I should have put in here was 'tomorrow night' since that's exactly what I meant, or what would have been more useful to me.*" Likewise, after inputting the to-do "*do corporate training tomorrow*", P2 noted that "*business hours would have made more sense.*" In these particular cases, participants expected the system to understand the natural constraints of the tasks: packing is done at home and on-the-job training is done at work.

In several instances, implied constraints co-occurred with implied flexibility. For example, after entering "*Go to grocery store on Sunday*," P5 responded:

> "*Ideally it should look at my calendar and figure out when is a good time to go. Or, actually, several different time slots. It's kind of a vague thing, right.*"

In this latter situation, the participant wanted the system to recognize both that the task was flexible, and that it required about two hours of free time to complete.

Implied task preparation time. In other cases, system interpretations were problematic because they failed to capture preparation times. For example, upon inputting the phrase "*Make pumpkin pie for thanksgiving*," P5 noted that "*I would need ingredients so I would probably want (a reminder) a few days before.*" Likewise, when P6 input the item "*Pack bags for Sunday*," she noted that her flight departed Sunday morning, and that her bags would have to be packed well in advance.

These two examples illustrate a common trend: prefix words like "by" or "for" often indicate a planning activity, and thus could prove to be useful signals that the system should consider preparation time.

However, there were also cases where the need for preparation was implicit. Upon inputting the note "*Remember Mom's birthday June 25*," P3 noted he wanted the information to appear at least a week before so that he would have time to find a present. Likewise, P4 noted that, for any item occurring in the early morning, she would like a reminder "*sometime before bed, saying 'hey you've got things early tomorrow'.*" This evening notification would serve to "*remind (her) to set the alarm a little earlier.*"

Complex expressions. Several situations arose in which the language was complex or ambiguous. For example, P13 recorded the memo "*Follow up with (a friend) about dinner plans either Saturday or Sunday.*" Upon seeing the item was scheduled for display on the following Saturday, P13 remarked that the interpretation was incorrect, then explained: "*It's not like I was telling it to mark it for Saturday or Sunday, I was telling it I need to follow up with her about Saturday or Sunday.*" Likewise, upon inputting "*Buy tickets for the concert next month*," P9 was disappointed the system misinterpreted "next month" as the time when tickets should be purchased, rather than the time at which the concert was occurring.

In summary, we found that participants often expected our virtual assistant to recognize implicit flexibilities, constraints, and preparation activities. Consequently, even when items contained precise temporal expressions (e.g., specific dates), they often exhibited characteristics similar to ITEs. As such, it is especially important that virtual assistants be designed to handle temporal uncertainty. To this end, we present design implications in the next section.

DESIGN IMPLICATIONS

Throughout the discussions in the previous sections, there are several recurring themes that are indicative of how virtual assistants should behave when addressing ITEs. These expected behaviors are summarized below.

Respect uncertainty. Both our survey and interview studies indicate that ITEs can serve various communicative purposes, such as to convey task unimportance and schedule flexibility (Figure 4). Therefore, virtual assistants should avoid early resolution of uncertainty, unless absolutely necessary. Consider, for example, a scenario in which a person marks a task or memo for "*later this week.*" At the moment of this interaction the person may lack the information (or the time) required to more precisely schedule the item. If, in this instant, the assistant prompts the user to input a precise time, then it is likely to appear tone-deaf to this reality.

Recognize uncertainty. Our analysis of the Avocado email corpus reveals that ITEs are frequent and diverse – 36.2% of observed time expressions were imprecise, and nearly 80% were observed 3 or fewer times (Figure 5 and Table 2). Complex, "long-tail" expressions were also observed to occur in the interview study. This is notable because, in contrast to the

Avocado email corpus, interviewees formed their utterances with the expectation that they would be interpreted by a virtual assistant. If virtual assistants are to be designed to respect ITEs, they must be able to generalize such that they recognize expressions rarely seen in pre-existing corpora.

Embrace flexibility. Designing virtual assistants to delay the resolution of uncertainty, as above, raises an obvious question: When should temporal uncertainty be resolved? A reasonable strategy is to have virtual assistants embrace any inherent flexibility, and they should do so opportunistically. Continuing the previous "later this week" example, unless "this week" is drawing to an end, there is likely plenty of time for the virtual assistant to seek additional clarification as part of some later maintenance task. For instance, the assistant might ask for scheduling guidance the next time the user opens their calendar, or as part of daily briefings delivered at convenient downtimes (e.g., at the start or end of the day). These low-urgency situations may even lend themselves well to crowd-sourcing scenarios, where crowd-workers can leverage common knowledge to identify implicit details and constraints.

Notify intelligently. In situations where uncertainty is high and urgency is low, virtual assistants should strive to deliver information using non-intrusive methods. For example, the lock screen of a phone or the watch face of a wearable device could provide convenient ambient displays for this type of information – especially given their associations with timekeeping. Such a mechanism can be supported by proactive behavior models proposed in existing literature [4, 38].

Leverage implicit knowledge. Our interview study indicates that users expect virtual assistants to possess more real-world knowledge than they currently do. Overall, we advocate making advances in the following three areas: (1) recognizing cultural or personal milestones, such as holidays and birthdays; (2) identifying natural constraints (e.g., packing a suitcase is likely done at home; baking a pie likely takes a few hours, etc.); and, (3) learning individual users' behavior patterns, such as commute schedule or sleep patterns.

DISCUSSION AND LIMITATIONS

In this paper, we explored existing practices, expectations, and preferences surrounding the use of temporal expressions in interactions with virtual assistants. Our analyses employed multiple complementary methodologies, and considered data contributed by 631 individuals.[3] Whenever possible, our reporting highlighted themes common to two or more methods or data sets to detail the opinions of the specified demographic.

That being said, we caution readers against overly generalizing these findings. Our survey respondents and interview participants, together with the individuals represented by the Avocado email corpus, were employees of U.S.-based technology companies at the time of data collection. While our data sets cover a variety of job roles, it remains to be shown how well these findings apply to a more general U.S. population, and, especially, to a more general global population. We are particularly interested in learning how cultural milestones (e.g., holidays), attitudes (e.g., on punctuality) and norms (e.g., the time meals are consumed) may impact the issues considered in this paper. We leave these investigations to future research.

[3]Includes 338 survey respondents, 279 email account holders in the Avocado data set, and 14 interview participants.

It is also worth noting that the situations presented in the survey and interviews focus on task management scenarios (i.e., to-dos and memos). These scenarios are common: Graus et al. reported that 576,080 time-based reminders were created between January and February 2015, in a subsample of 92,264 US-resident users of Cortana-enabled mobile devices [12]. However, these calendaring/reminder scenarios are by no means the only tasks performed with virtual assistants. In 2014, Jiang et al. reported that such interactions accounted for 18.2% of Cortana's primary operations (i.e., all operations excluding chit-chats and generic Web searches) [13]. In the future, it will be important to consider how temporal expressions are manifest in other scenarios involving virtual assistants.

Finally, it is worth considering how legacy bias [21] – one's past experience with virtual assistants – may influence participant responses. The specific concern is that virtual assistants differ in syntax and features. Our demographic collection was not sufficiently fine-grained to allow us to compare the user populations of specific virtual assistants. However, our survey did ask if participants had *any* past experience with virtual assistants. Our subsequent analysis failed to find any significant differences between respondents who reported previous experience with virtual assistants, and those who did not (Mann–Whitney U, $\alpha = 0.05$, with, and without, Bonferroni correction). Differences between the user populations of competing virtual assistants would be interesting, if found; but, we leave this to future work.

CONCLUSION

We have investigated the motivation, manifestation, and expectation surrounding the use of imprecise temporal expressions in people's communication with virtual assistants. We have found that the primary motivations of using imprecise time expressions involve low level of commitment, low task priority, or external dependencies of the tasks in question. We also use text corpus analysis to find that imprecise temporal expressions have high variability and many exhibit temporal dependencies. Additionally, our interviews reveal that people expect the virtual assistants to be able to handle the implied flexibility, implied constraints, and task preparation activities from people's imprecise temporal expressions. Finally, we draw design implications for future virtual assistants; they should: (1) respect uncertainty by delaying early resolution unless absolutely necessary; (2) recognize uncertainty by supporting the long-tail of imprecise temporal expressions; (3) embrace flexibility by considering engaging with the user during down-times or alternative metaphors (such as our Corkboard) that enable uncertainty to be resolved at a later time; (4) adopt alternative strategies to deliver reminder notifications appropriate to the uncertainty of a time expression; and (5) leverage implicit personal information or world knowledge through sources such as calendars, external event knowledge (e.g., traffic), and predicted or user-entered preferences.

REFERENCES

1. Gabor Angeli, Christopher D. Manning, and Daniel Jurafsky. 2012. Parsing Time: Learning to Interpret Time Expressions. In *Proc. NAACL HLT '12*. ACL, 446–455.
2. Jacob Bank, Zachary Cain, Yoav Shoham, Caroline Suen, and Dan Ariely. 2012. Turning personal calendars into scheduling assistants. In *Proc. CHI '12*. ACM, 2667–2672.
3. Frank Bentley, David A Shamma Joseph 'Jofish' Kaye, and John Alexis Guerra-Gomez. 2016. The 32 Days Of Christmas: Understanding Temporal Intent in Image Search Queries. In *Proc. CHI '16*. ACM, 5710–5714.
4. Pauline M. Berry, Melinda Gervasio, Bart Peintner, and Neil Yorke-Smith. 2011. PTIME: Personalized Assistance for Calendaring. *ACM TIST* (2011), 40:1–40:22.
5. John Brooke and others. 1996. SUS-A quick and dirty usability scale. *Usability Evaluation in Industry* 189, 194 (1996), 4–7.
6. Angel X Chang and Christopher D Manning. 2012. SUTime: A library for recognizing and normalizing time expressions. In *Proc. LREC '12*. 3735–3740.
7. Richard W DeVaul, Brian Clarkson, and others. 2000. The memory glasses: towards a wearable, context aware, situation-appropriate reminder system. In *CHI 2000 Workshop on Situated Interaction in Ubiquitous Computing*. ACM.
8. Anind K Dey and Gregory D Abowd. 2000. CybreMinder: A context-aware system for supporting reminders. In *International Symposium on Handheld and Ubiquitous Computing*. Springer, 172–186.
9. Didier Dubois and Henri Prade. 1989. Processing fuzzy temporal knowledge. *IEEE Transactions on Systems, Man, and Cybernetics* 19, 4 (1989), 729–744.
10. Lisa Ferro, Laurie Gerber, Inderjeet Mani, Beth Sundheim, and George Wilson. 2005. TIDES 2005 standard for the annotation of temporal expressions. (2005).
11. Michael Freed, Jaime G Carbonell, Geoffrey J Gordon, Jordan Hayes, Brad A Myers, Daniel P Siewiorek, Stephen F Smith, Aaron Steinfeld, and Anthony Tomasic. 2008. RADAR: A Personal Assistant that Learns to Reduce Email Overload. In *Proc. AAAI '08*. 1287–1293.
12. David Graus, Paul N. Bennett, Ryen W. White, and Eric Horvitz. 2016. Analyzing and Predicting Task Reminders. (2016), 7–15.
13. Jiepu Jiang, Ahmed Hassan Awadallah, Rosie Jones, Umut Ozertem, Imed Zitouni, Ranjitha Gurunath Kulkarni, and Omar Zia Khan. 2015. Automatic Online Evaluation of Intelligent Assistants. In *Proc. WWW '15*. ACM, 506–516.
14. Ece Kamar and Eric Horvitz. 2011. Jogger: models for context-sensitive reminding. In *Proc. AAMAS '11*. IFAAMAS, 1089–1090.
15. Mik Lamming and Mike Flynn. 1994. Forget-me-not: Intimate computing in support of human memory. In *Proc. FRIEND21, '94 Int. Symp. on Next Generation Human Interface*. 4.
16. Kenton Lee, Yoav Artzi, Jesse Dodge, and Luke Zettlemoyer. 2014. Context-dependent Semantic Parsing for Time Expressions. In *ACL*. 1437–1447.
17. Pamela J Ludford, Dan Frankowski, Ken Reily, Kurt Wilms, and Loren Terveen. 2006. Because I carry my cell phone anyway: functional location-based reminder applications. In *Proc. CHI '06*. ACM, 889–898.
18. Ewa Luger and Abigail Sellen. 2016. Like Having a Really Bad PA: The Gulf between User Expectation and Experience of Conversational Agents. In *Proc. CHI '16*. ACM, 5286–5297.
19. Inderjeet Mani and George Wilson. 2000. Robust temporal processing of news. In *Proc. ACL 2000*. ACL, 69–76.
20. Reed Martin and Henry Holtzman. 2011. Kairoscope: managing time perception and scheduling through social event coordination. In *Proc. CHI '11*. ACM, 1969–1978.
21. Meredith Ringel Morris, Andreea Danielescu, Steven Drucker, Danyel Fisher, Bongshin Lee, m. c. schraefel, and Jacob O. Wobbrock. 2014. Reducing Legacy Bias in Gesture Elicitation Studies. *Interactions* 21, 3 (2014), 40–45.
22. Karen Myers, Pauline Berry, Jim Blythe, Ken Conley, Melinda Gervasio, Deborah L McGuinness, David Morley, Avi Pfeffer, Martha Pollack, and Milind Tambe. 2007. An intelligent personal assistant for task and time management. *AI Magazine* 28, 2 (2007), 47.
23. Douglas Oard, William Webber, David Kirsch, and Sergey Golitsynskiy. 2015. Avocado Research Email Collection. LDC2015T03. DVD. Philadelphia: Linguistic Data Consortium. (2015).
24. Tim Paek and Eric Horvitz. 1999. Uncertainty, utility, and misunderstanding: A decision-theoretic perspective on grounding in conversational systems. In *AAAI Fall Symposium on Psychological Models of Communication in Collaborative Systems, Cape Cod, MA*.
25. Joelle Pineau, Michael Montemerlo, Martha Pollack, Nicholas Roy, and Sebastian Thrun. 2003. Towards robotic assistants in nursing homes: Challenges and results. *Robotics and autonomous systems* 42, 3 (2003), 271–281.
26. James Pustejovsky, Patrick Hanks, Roser Sauri, Andrew See, Robert Gaizauskas, Andrea Setzer, Dragomir Radev, Beth Sundheim, David Day, Lisa Ferro, and others. 2003. The timebank corpus. In *Corpus linguistics*, Vol. 2003. 40.
27. Anand S Rao and Michael P Georgeff. 1992. An abstract architecture for rational agents. *KR* 92 (1992), 439–449.

28. Ioannis Refanidis and Neil Yorke-Smith. 2010. A constraint-based approach to scheduling an individual's activities. *ACM Transactions on Intelligent Systems and Technology (TIST)* 1, 2 (2010), 12.
29. Frank Schilder and Christopher Habel. 2003. Temporal Information Extraction for Temporal Question Answering. In *New Directions in Question Answering*. 35–44.
30. Steven Schockaert and Martine De Cock. 2008. Temporal reasoning about fuzzy intervals. *Artificial Intelligence* 172, 8 (2008), 1158–1193.
31. Steven Schockaert, Martine De Cock, and Etienne E Kerre. 2007. Qualitative Temporal Reasoning about Vague Events. In *IJCAI*. 569–574.
32. Timothy Sohn, Kevin A Li, Gunny Lee, Ian Smith, James Scott, and William G Griswold. 2005. Place-its: A study of location-based reminders on mobile phones. In *Proc. UbiComp '05*. ACM, 232–250.
33. Jannik Strötgen and Michael Gertz. 2010. HeidelTime: High quality rule-based extraction and normalization of temporal expressions. In *Proc. International Workshop on Semantic Evaluation*. ACL, 321–324.
34. Éric Taillard, Philippe Badeau, Michel Gendreau, François Guertin, and Jean-Yves Potvin. 1997. A tabu search heuristic for the vehicle routing problem with soft time windows. *Transportation science* 31, 2 (1997), 170–186.
35. John Thangarajah, James Harland, David Morley, and Neil Yorke-Smith. 2008. Suspending and resuming tasks in BDI agents. In *Proc. AAMAS '08*. IFAAMAS, 405–412.
36. Hegler Correa Tissot. 2016. *Normalisation of imprecise temporal expressions extracted from text*. Ph.D. Dissertation. University of Paraná.
37. Giorgio Vassallo, Giovanni Pilato, Agnese Augello, and Salvatore Gaglio. 2010. *Phase Coherence in Conceptual Spaces for Conversational Agents*. New York, NY, USA: Wiley, IEEE Press.
38. Neil Yorke-Smith, Shahin Saadati, Karen L Myers, and David N Morley. 2012. The design of a proactive personal agent for task management. *International Journal on Artificial Intelligence Tools* 21, 01 (2012), 1250004.
39. Luis Zabala, Cristina Perfecto, J Unzilla, and A Ferro. 2001. Integrating automatic task scheduling and Web-based agenda in a virtual campus environment. In *Proc. ITHET '01*.
40. Lotfi A Zadeh. 1994. Soft computing and fuzzy logic. *IEEE software* 11, 6 (1994), 48.
41. H-J Zimmermann. 2010. Fuzzy set theory. *Wiley Interdisciplinary Reviews: Computational Statistics* 2, 3 (2010), 317–332.

Comparing Social Robot, Screen and Voice Interfaces for Smart-Home Control

Michal Luria
Media Innovation Lab
Interdisciplinary Center
Herzliya
Herzliya, Israel
michal.luria@idc.ac.il

Guy Hoffman
Sibley School of Mechanical
and Aerospace Engineering
Cornell University
Ithaca, NY
hoffman@cornell.edu

Oren Zuckerman
Media Innovation Lab
Interdisciplinary Center
Herzliya
Herzliya, Israel
orenz@idc.ac.il

ABSTRACT
With domestic technology on the rise, the quantity and complexity of smart-home devices are becoming an important interaction design challenge. We present a novel design for a home control interface in the form of a social robot, commanded via tangible icons and giving feedback through expressive gestures. We experimentally compare the robot to three common smart-home interfaces: a voice-control loudspeaker; a wall-mounted touch-screen; and a mobile application. Our findings suggest that interfaces that rate higher on flow rate lower on usability, and vice versa. Participants' sense of control is highest using familiar interfaces, and lowest using voice control. Situation awareness is highest using the robot, and also lowest using voice control. These findings raise questions about voice control as a smart-home interface, and suggest that embodied social robots could provide for an engaging interface with high situation awareness, but also that their usability remains a considerable design challenge.

ACM Classification Keywords
H.5.2 Information Interfaces and Presentation (e.g. HCI): User Interfaces

Author Keywords
social robots; embodied interaction; human-robot interaction; interface modalities; smart-home control; domestic technology; home automation

INTRODUCTION
Two new categories of interactive technology are increasingly entering the domestic space: Home appliances with new sensing and control capabilities, collectively called *Smart-Home* or *Internet of Things* (IoT) devices [1], and expressive interactive robotic companions, also called *Social Robots* [5].

Researchers have been divided over the desired user experience in domestic spaces, ranging from high system autonomy and invisibility [55, 51, 56], to promoting the user's sense of control and engagement [29, 48]. Additionally, a wide range of interaction modalities for the home have been designed and researched, including GUI [8], voice control [58, 39], gesture input [35], and augmented reality interfaces [53].

In contrast to the above-mentioned interfaces, social robots provide for an alternative mode of interaction. Interacting with a robot is an embodied experience: Robots express their internal state and other information using gestures and nonverbal behavior (NVB) [6, 38]. Furthermore, by sharing physical space and objects with their users, they encourage interaction schemas that involve physical action on the part of the human [49, 59]. The literature suggests that embodied interaction could provide advantages over screen-based, virtual, or augmented reality interfaces. These include thinking-through-doing and higher performance [33], better learning and memory [14, 45], and higher engagement [62]. Thus, social robots are a promising new model for smart-home control, balancing autonomy and engagement, and providing the benefits of embodied interaction.

Although social robots for smart-home control are already appearing on the consumer market, the research on the topic is sparse. In the past, comparisons have been made between other non-robotic modalities for smart-home control [8, 34], while social robots and tangible interfaces were compared to screen interfaces in other contexts of the domestic space, e.g., game play [57], education [62], and weight-loss coaching [32]. However, we do not know of a comparison between a social robot and traditional interfaces in the context of smart-home control.

In this paper we present such a comparison. Using a within-subject experimental design, we compare the use of an embodied robot interface with three common interfaces for smart-home control: a voice-controlled speaker device, a wall-mounted touch screen, and a mobile application (Figure 2).

We gave participants a list of home control chores while tasking them with a cognitive-load activity. In each round they used one of the four interfaces. We measured quantitative and qualitative indicators including usability, flow, enjoyment, control, distraction, and situation awareness.

Our analysis finds the following: (1) A trade-off between perceived *usability*, and perceived *flow*. For interfaces which

CHI 2017, May 06-11, 2017, Denver, CO, USA
©2017 ACM. ISBN 978-1-4503-4655-9/17/05...$15.00
DOI: http://dx.doi.org/10.1145/3025453.3025786

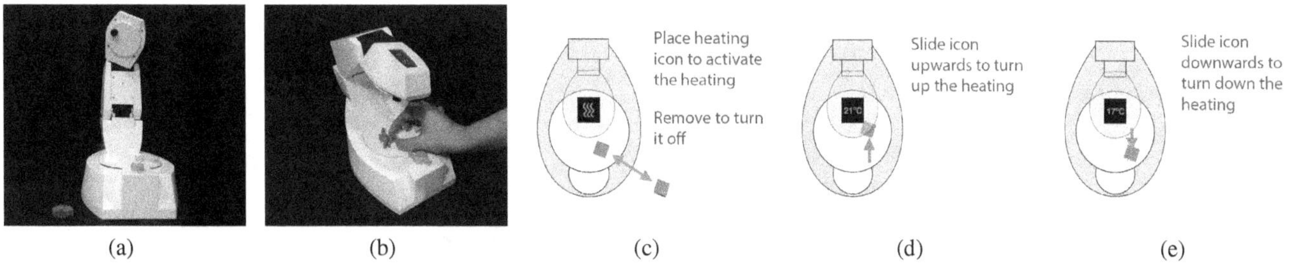

Figure 1. Vyo, the embodied social robot interface for smart-home control we designed and used in this experiment. The robot is inspired by a microscope metaphor allowing the user insight into the state of smart-home devices, each represented by a tangible icon. Vyo doubles as a social agent when it rises to express face-to-face gestures (a) and becomes an examination tool when it is facing down (b). The robot is commanded by placing the device icons onto its turntable (c) and moving them as physical sliders to adjust settings (d-e).

rated high on perceived *flow*, the rated *usability* was low, and vice versa; (2) the robot was rated with the highest *situation awareness*, and voice control was rated lowest; (3) participants' *sense of control* was rated highest using familiar interfaces (wall-mounted screen and mobile application). However, voice control was perceived with particularly low sense of control in the interaction; (4) although unfamiliar interfaces were said to be somewhat *distracting*, the most familiar one, the mobile application, was described as a highly distracting interface.

These results raise questions about voice control and mobile application interfaces for domestic environments. They also suggest that social robots are good candidates for embodied interfaces in automated homes, promising to be highly engaging, visible, and encouraging thinking-through-doing. Nevertheless, when designing robots as home interfaces there is a need to overcome outstanding issues concerning usability.

RELATED WORK

Smart-Home Interfaces: Invisible or Engaging?

Researchers are divided if domestic technology should blend into the background or engage users. Striving to support Weiser's original vision of calm computing [55], automated, transparent, and seamlessly integrated smart-home technologies have been developed [13, 60, 47]. The downside in this approach is that home automation could become unpredictable—users lack feedback on events in their domestic environment and therefore lose sense of control over the state of their home [34, 44].

This led others to argue that technology should empower users by allowing them to make decisions for themselves, rather than having the home make decisions for them [29]. Home technology should therefore be designed for involvement and engagement [48], and with affordances for the status of their homes [19]. This could help restore users' sense of control [29] and allow for flexibility [17].

Embodied Interaction

Research on embodied interaction focuses on interfaces that incorporate a growing range of human capacities, in contrast to textual and graphical interfaces [18]. The literature points out the advantages embodiment brings to interaction design: It promises an opportunity to bring social and human values back in balance and to create meaning in interaction [28]. It also allows expert users to maximize interaction efficiency through motor memory and simultaneous action [33]. The visibility and persistence of embodied interfaces serve as reminders [61], and can help coordinate between co-workers and house members. Finally, gesturing can promote users' thinking and communication skills, play a role in lightening cognitive load [22] and communicating complex thoughts [2]. Thus, embodied interaction using gestures encourages "thinking-through-doing" [33].

Robots constitute an embodied interface in two ways. They communicate their intentions using gestures and other nonverbal behavior, and they encourage users to physically engage in interaction with them by sharing the same physical space and physical objects.

Smart-Homes and Social Robots

In fact, embodied social robots have been suggested as candidates for an increasing number of applications integrated in our daily lives, including service providers [31], delivery robots [36], therapeutic assistants [54] and tour guides [9]. Furthermore, robots are intended for deployment in homes for a variety of purposes, such as assistants for the elderly [4, 43], security robots [10], entertainment devices [23], and personal companions [25, 46].

Research suggests that social robots are perceived and interacted with differently that other forms of technology. Intentions are attributed to abstract robots that use simple 2D-movement [50], and owners of robotic vacuum cleaners define their robots' personality traits and the social relationships with them [20, 52]. This suggests that social robots could have unique interaction potential and novel effects when used as interfaces to technology in people's homes.

OVERVIEW

In order to study the benefits and drawbacks of social robotics in the context of domestic interaction, we designed an expressive social robot, Vyo, as an embodied interface for smart-home control [37]. In this study, we evaluate Vyo's design by comparing it to other common smart-home interfaces: a voice-controlled speaker device, a wall-mounted touch-screen, and a mobile device application (Figure 2).

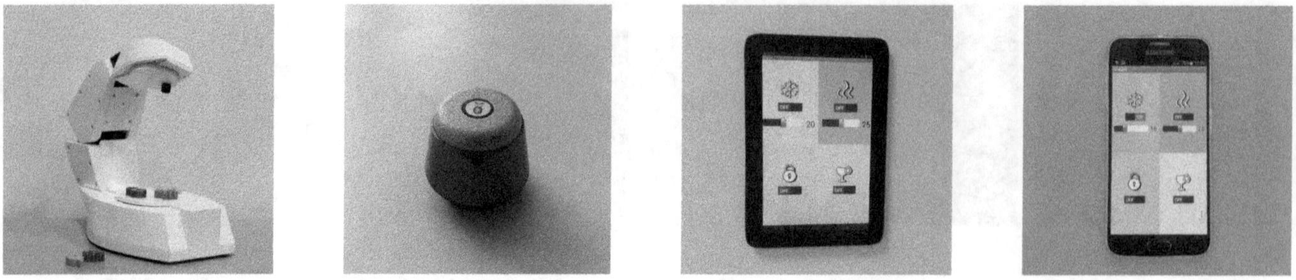

(a) Embodied Social Robot (b) Voice-Controlled Speaker (c) Wall-Mounted Screen (d) Mobile Application

Figure 2. The four smart-home control interfaces compared in this study.

Embodied Robot Interface

Vyo is a social robot that serves as a central interface for smart-home control [37] (Figure 1). Building on the notions of ubiquitous computing [55] and engaging interfaces [48], we designed Vyo as a new interaction paradigm that combines expressive robotics and tangible user interfaces. The robot uses tangible icons as a means of user input, and a combination of physical gestures and low-fidelity screen icons for output. This design suggests an alternative to the commonly used interaction modalities of most social robots, which highlight bidirectional speech, touch screens, and high-resolution informational displays.

The design process is provided in detail in [37] and summarized below. It was driven by five design goals: engaging, unobtrusive, device-like, respectful and reassuring:

Engaging — A smart-home interface should promote the user's sense of control and raise their awareness to the status of their home. One of the ways to do so is to evoke engagement and bring back "excitement of interaction" by designing a tangible interface [48].

Unobtrusive — Domestic technology should be at least partially automated and strive not to disturb house members [56]. We therefore aimed to design a robot that would stay in the periphery of attention, and would come to the foreground only when necessary [27].

Device-like — Based on the notion of designing non-anthropomorphic robots [26] and supported by [16]'s finding that people prefer their home robot to be device-like or butler-like, our third goal was for the robot to resemble a device rather than a human or a pet.

Respectful — As also described in [16], users expect their robots to be polite and show awareness of social situations. We therefore defined 'Respectful' as one of our design goals.

Reassuring — According to previously conducted interviews [37], home technology should be reliable and trustworthy. The robot should therefore express reliability and reassure the user throughout the interaction using gestures and nonverbal behavior.

After setting these goals, the design process was along two interleaved paths in the spirit of [26]. One was the design of the robot's morphology, including its scale, shape and materials. The other was the design of the robot's nonverbal behavior (NVB). 3D character animations were used to explore movement patterns for the robot; improvisation studies with professional actors were conducted to inspire NVB; and puppet designers assisted in developing the robot's gestures. These two paths ultimately shaped an interaction schema that was then evaluated in an early-stage user study, together with the robot's size and NVB. The findings helped us make design decisions that shaped the robot's final size, gestures, and interaction schemas.

The robot uses embodied and physical interaction modalities for both input and output, and is inspired by a microscope metaphor. Supporting the design goal of *engaging* and *reassuring*, physical icons are used as an input communication channel with the robot. Each icon is designed to represent a smart-home device, controlled by placing it on the robot's turntable (Figure 1c). When an icon is placed, the robot responds with expressive physical gestures and a screen icon, indicating it has turned on the device. By sliding an icon the user can adjust control parameters (Figure 1d–e). For example, sliding the heating icon upwards will increase the home temperature. When the icon is removed from the turntable, the robot turns off the device and acknowledges this action with an expressive gesture. This interaction design choice supports both the visibility and the thinking-through-doing principles of embodied interaction.

The microscope metaphor suggests a mental model of "examining" devices in the home and supports the *device-like* and *engaging* design goals. While one could argue that a microscope is more of a scientific tool than a domestic device, it also relates to the excitement and sense of discovery of educational microscopes. Importantly, it is a familiar device capable of supporting a predictable mental model.

The robot, however, is not just a passive tool, but straddles the boundary between device and social agent. For example, it rises to face the user in a conversational front-facing pose (Figure 1a), and a rotating lens-like feature on the robot's face enables minimalistic, but also surprisingly expressive, facial gestures. When the robot detects problems in the smart-home environment, it uses peripheral gestures indicating nervousness instead of sound or LED notifications. This supports the *unobtrusive* design goal.

The integrated low-fidelity screen on the back of the robot's head measures 1.8 inches in the diagonal, and is exposed when the robot performs a bowing gesture. The gesture moves Vyo back from its conversational stance as a social agent to that of an examination device (Figure 1b). This bowing gesture is aligned with the design goal of *respectful*, while the action of hiding the screen when in conversation also relates to the design goal of being *unobtrusive*.

The robot's hardware and software are built on a Raspberry Pi 2 PC-on-board system, running a combination of Python and Java code. The robot moves using 5 Robotis Dynamixel motors, and integrates a TFT display and a loudspeaker. Its internal frame is laser-cut from 6-mm acrylic and its shell is made out of sanded and painted 3D-printed acrylonitrile butadiene styrene (ABS).

In our experiment, the robot was introduced to participants as "a robot interface for smart-home management, controlled by placing physical icons on its turntable", making sure not to expose participants to descriptions that might influence their perception of the robot. During the experiment it was controlled using a Wizard-of-Oz (WoZ) desktop application [24].

Voice-Control Speaker

The voice control interface is a small speaker with an LED indicating when it is on (Figure 2b). The interface was designed to highlight and support advantages of voice-controlled interfaces: intuitive, by using spoken language as its input, ubiquitous, in that it can be activated from anywhere in the room, and "hand free, eyes free" [11].

To dismiss potential technical problems in speech analysis and to ensure full comprehension of the participants' spoken language, we also used a WoZ method for feedback. This allowed us to focus on the user experience of a voice interface regardless of technical issues.

We designed the feedback of the system according to the design guidelines of [30]. The system would give auditory feedback to user input using slightly altered wording to indicate the correct recognition has taken place. The main disadvantage of auditory feedback is in the disruption of other auditory information held in the memory of an individual [30]. However, since vocal feedback is prominent in existing commercial voice control interfaces, we implemented this feedback in our system as well.

In this study participants would be instructed to say "Smart-Home" to activate the interface before giving it a command. We prerecorded audio clip sentences for feedback, manually voiced by a commercially available voice-control device (Amazon Echo), for example: "The heating is set to 29 degrees". We also recorded several responses for scenarios in which participants might say something unclear or unrelated to their task, such as: "Sorry, I did not understand the question I heard. Could you repeat that?". The prerecorded audio clips would be manually played in real time according to participants' actions and a WoZ script written in advance.

Wall-Mounted Touch Screen

We designed a smart-home control application optimized for an Android tablet device (Figure 2c). The tablet would be fixed to a wall for the experiment, representing common wall-mounted touch screen interfaces in smart-homes today. The user interface of the application was designed based on existing smart-home control applications by commercial companies. The interface is divided into four sections, one for each device. We also added a representative icon and background color for each section according to the physical icons used by the robot in form and color to eliminate confounding differences between the designed systems.

For each device, the interface had an on/off toggle button that could be changed by either touching or swiping it, with immediate visual feedback. For temperature control (heating, cooling) we placed a slider with a number representing the current temperature to its right. When a user would move the slider, the temperature would immediately adjust. The interface was designed based on interaction design guidelines, considering affordances, signifiers and feedback [41], but also according to contemporary user interface (UI) conventions (toggle buttons, sliders). In addition, we made sure the UI elements would be large enough for easy control using an average-sized finger [12]. During the experiment the screen would always stay on.

Mobile Application

The mobile device application interface was the same interface as the wall-mounted one, but adapted for a Samsung Galaxy J5 personal mobile device running Android (Figure 2d). It was adapted by scaling the interface down to fit the mobile device properly, and the buttons were repositioned accordingly. The button size, however, was maintained in order to enable easy touch interaction. Throughout the experiment participants would be asked to lock the mobile device screen between interactions and hold onto it or place it in their pocket, to better simulate the way we interact with mobile devices in casual day-to-day operation.

STUDY

We conducted an exploratory controlled experimental study comparing the four interfaces described above and investigating the following research questions:

- Whether and how the choice of interface affects users' **perceived flow** of using the interface.
- Whether and how the choice of interface affects users' **perceived usability** of the interface.
- Whether and how the choice of interface affects users' **distraction** and **cognitive load**.
- Which interface users **prefer**, find the most **comfortable**, most **enjoyable**, and most **natural**.
- Which interface gives users the best **situation awareness** of the state of the home.

Participants

We recruited 42 undergraduate students who received extra credit for their participation (25 female, age $M = 22.07, SD = 2.58$). The students were recruited from the university's international school. This allowed us to include participants from 19 different countries and to examine multicultural perspectives (USA = 9, France = 9, Israel = 4, Germany = 2, Canada = 2, Panama = 2, Other = 14). We ran the experiment in English, and while English was not the native language for most participants, their lectures and homework all require college-level English. Nevertheless, we used simple vocabulary in the experiment materials, questionnaires, and interviews, and have no reason to believe that any English language barrier played a major confounding role.

Method

The experiment was conducted within-subjects, with one independent variable—the interface used to perform a series of smart-home control tasks. This variable included four conditions: embodied robot (ROB), voice control (VOC), wall-mounted touch screen (WAL), and mobile application (APP).

In the experiment, participants were asked to simulate a situation where they control several devices in a smart-home environment while being loaded with a cognitive task to simulate the distractions in the home (the "Copying Task" described below). The experiment included four rounds for each participant. In each round participants were asked to use a different interface for the smart-home control tasks (four conditions), counterbalanced for order.

The Copying Task

Throughout the experiment participants had a cognitive load task of copying words from a list to a whiteboard in the room (Figure 3). The task of short-term memorizing random words was found to require high concentration, and was previously used to evaluate external disruptions—when participants were disrupted, more time was required to recall words [21]. Thus, counting the number of words participants manage to copy for each round would serve as a measure of disruption and cognitive load for each interface. We also wanted to keep participants physically busy to simulate the occasionally demanding home environment. For this reason we placed the list of words on one wall, and the whiteboard on another.

Procedure

Each round of the experiment started with participants doing the main copying task. In each round the task was interrupted five times by a knock on the door. With every interruption, participants were instructed to stop the copying task, approach the smart-home control task list in the room and execute the next task on the list. The tasks were control tasks for four devices in the home (e.g. "Turn on the dishwasher", "Change the heating temperature to 29 degrees"). All tasks were to be executed using the interface introduced at the beginning of the round. The interfaces and smart-home control tasks were counterbalanced for order. Furthermore, the experimenter interrupted the copying task at fixed time points in each condition, ensuring the number of words copied in each round would be a valid quantitative measure.

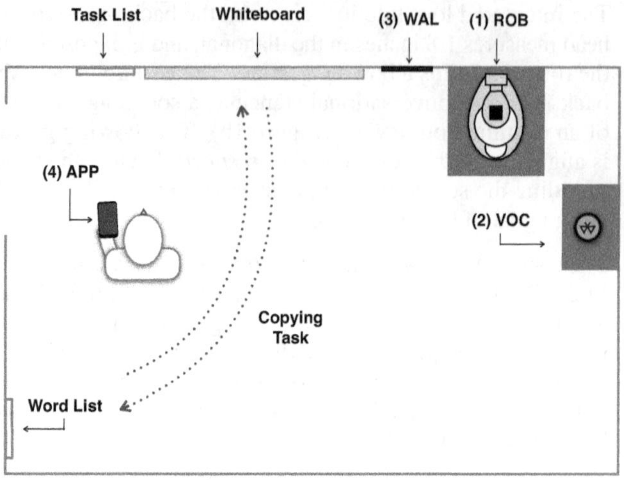

Figure 3. Diagram of the experimental setup. Participants were asked to copy words from the word list to the whiteboard. When interrupted by a knock on the door, they performed the next task on the Task List using one of four interfaces (1)–(4).

After each round, participants answered a short questionnaire regarding their experience. They were also asked what devices were on and what the home temperature was. We did not intend to measure if their answers were accurate, but to trigger their ability to recall the home status after using a specific interface. At the end of all four rounds, the participants were interviewed using a semi-structured interview script written in advance.

Measures

We used quantitative and qualitative measures. We collected data from written questionnaires and verbally asked categorical questions for subjective quantitative measures. As an objective measure, we counted the number of words participants were able to copy with each interface. Finally, we conducted qualitative semi-structured interviews.

Questionnaires

The questionnaires evaluated each interface according to two scales. In the first scale participants rated the *flow* they had experienced using an interface on an 8 item scale. The notion of *flow*, frequently used in the field of HCI, expresses focus, deep involvement and enjoyment one experiences when performing an activity [15]. The scale was adapted from [62], removing 3 items that were irrelevant to our interfaces. The second scale in the questionnaire measured *usability*, taken in its full form from [7] (SUS). All measures were on a scale of 1–7.

Quantified User Preferences

The post-experimental interview included asking participants to choose their top interface in different categories: which interface they liked most, which they liked least, which was most comfortable, most natural, most enjoyable, and using what interfaces was it easiest and hardest to recall the status of the home at the end of the round. We then counted the answers that expressed a preference for a particular interface in each category.

Table 1. Quantitative measures from questionnaires and word transfer count. Each cell shows mean±std. Bold indicates conditions with means significantly higher ($p < 0.05$) than one or more other conditions in corrected pairwise comparisons.

Measure	ROB	VOC	WAL	APP
Flow	**5.40±0.67**	4.95±1.05	4.82±0.96	4.65±1.13
Usability	5.30±1.21	5.69±0.88	**6.22±0.60**	**6.23±0.59**
Word Count	28.36 ±7.46	29.93±9.24	**33.02±8.84**	29.45±9.37

Word Count in the Copying Task

At the end of each round the experimenter counted and noted the number of words participants were able to copy, before erasing the words from the whiteboard for the next round.

Interviews

Semi-structured interviews were conducted at the end of the study. Participants were asked to elaborate on their experience with each interface, including what they liked, disliked, what difficulties they encountered and so on. The interview transcriptions were read and analyzed separately by two research assistants. The analysis was driven by key aspects and research questions defined in advance, but allowed space for discovery of additional patterns if indicated by both research assistants. If a disagreement regarding a specific aspect or pattern emerged, it was resolved by discussion with reference to the transcripts.

FINDINGS

We first present the main findings along two main themes: (a) Flow and Enjoyment, and (b) Comfort and Usability, using quantitative and qualitative measures. We analyze the questionnaires using a one-way repeated measures ANOVA with pairwise comparison post-hoc t-tests. For effect size, we report the generalized η^2 measure, which is recommended for repeated measures analysis [42, 3]. We then report on the objective word count measure, and add notable insights we recognized when analyzing the qualitative interviews.

Flow and Enjoyment

Questionnaires

Self reported questionnaires that measure perceived *flow* were administered after each round. A one-way repeated measures ANOVA shows that the interface modality has a significant effect on reported flow, $F(3,123) = 6.42, p < 0.001, \eta^2 = 0.08$ (Figure 4(a)). Pairwise comparisons using repeated measures t-tests with a Bonferroni correction show that ROB is significantly higher on perceived flow than WAL ($p < 0.05$) and APP ($p < 0.01$), with no other comparisons resulting in significant differences. Table 1 shows full descriptive statistics for all questionnaire scales.

Interviews

Interviews supported these quantitative results by pointing out that when participants interacted with the robot, they felt intrigued and excited to continue the interaction:

> "It [ROB] gives you more associations... it develops such amazing imagination"

> "I wanted to try it [ROB] more. You can play with it, which creates this excitement. You just want to use it again"

Table 2. Quantified User Preferences: Participants chose which interface they liked most and least, which was most comfortable, natural and enjoyable, and with which interface was it easiest and hardest to recall. *Negative preference.

Measure	ROB	VOC	WAL	APP
Most Enjoyable	**68%**	25%	3.5%	3.5%
Liked Best	**38%**	**34%**	16%	12%
Liked Least*	**33%**	**33%**	17%	17%
Most Comfortable	0%	17%	24%	**59%**
Most Natural	0%	21%	15%	**64%**
Easy to Recall State	**61%**	21%	9%	9%
Hard to Recall State*	4.5%	**61%**	9.5%	19%

In contrast, the screen-based interfaces (WAL, APP) were described as mundane, common, and automatic:

> "It [APP] did not urge me to explore it more... just doing what I do every day."

> "It [WAL] is good. But it's not interesting. It didn't develop curiosity."

Quantified User Preferences

Table 2 shows the quantified user preferences. When participants were asked what interface was most enjoyable, a majority (67.8%) chose ROB. Participants were also asked what interface they liked most and least, taking all of the interface qualities into consideration. 37.5% liked ROB most, and 34.3% preferred VOC. However, when participants were asked to select their least favorite interface, the results were surprisingly similar: 33.3% selected ROB, and 33.3% selected VOC. The full results are presented in Table 2.

Usability and Comfort

Questionnaires

We measured the perceived *usability* of each interface using the 10-item SUS scale [7]. A one-way repeated measures ANOVA shows that the interface modality has a significant effect on reported usability, $F(3,123) = 15.67, p < 0.001, \eta^2 = 0.17$ (Figure 4(b)). Pairwise comparisons using repeated measures t-tests with a Bonferroni correction show that both the WAL and APP conditions are significantly higher on perceived usability than ROB ($p < 0.001$) and VOC ($p < 0.01$), with no other comparisons resulting in significant differences. Table 1 shows full descriptive statistics for all questionnaire scales.

Quantified Findings

Participants were asked which interface they perceived as most *comfortable* and most *natural.* In line with the above findings, 58.6% of participants indicated APP was most *comfortable.* APP was also selected as the most *natural* interface, with a 63.6% selection rate. Table 2 shows the complete quantified data.

Interviews

During the interviews, WAL and APP were also described as interfaces participants generally felt very comfortable and familiar with:

> "It [APP] is very easy to use. People carry it in their backpacks, go to school, go to work. People have it

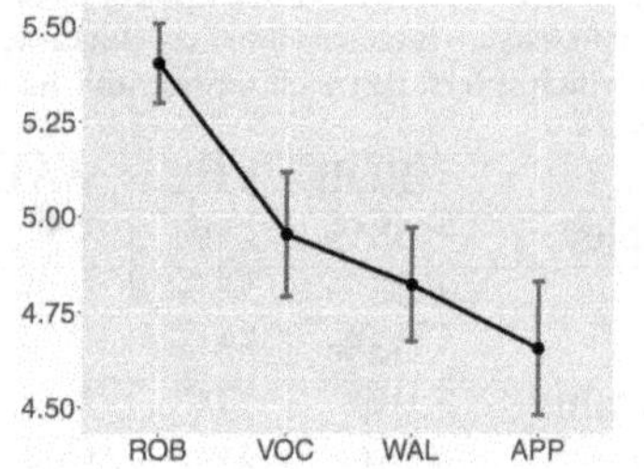

(a) Flow by Condition

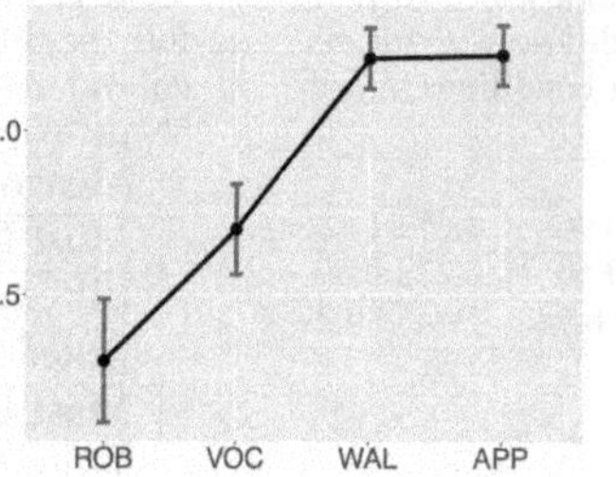

(b) Usability by Condition

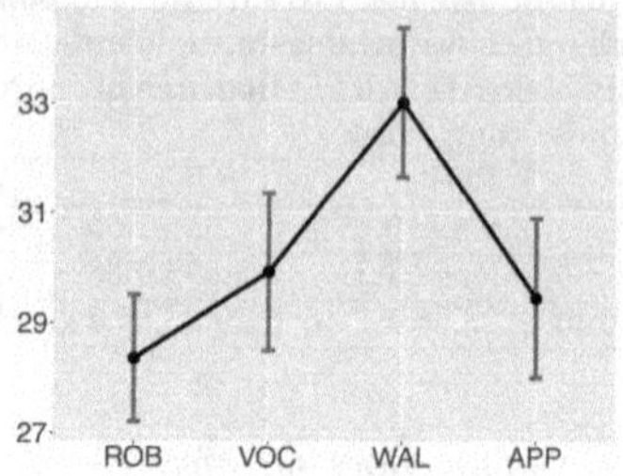

(c) Word Count by Condition

Figure 4. Quantitative measures: Self-reported mean *flow* (left) and *usability* (center), and the mean number of copied words per interface (right). Error bars indicate standard error of mean ($n = 42$)

> wherever they are going, next to their bed. It is very convenient"

> "The tablet [WAL] is the most safe and secure thing to have for me... I feel it is reliable...it is there always, it is always going to work."

ROB, however, was described as an interface difficult to use:

> "I would not want to use it [ROB] all the time because it takes more time.... If you are in your house you want it to be quick... I do not want to wait for it. The robot takes more time"

> "I guess specifically for me, if [you are] not technologically inclined, that [ROB] was the most difficult to use"

With regards to VOC, participants generally liked being able to give a vocal command. It allowed them to do it from anywhere in the room and without the use of hands. However, at times they perceived the interaction as confusing:

> "I really liked the voice [interface]. I really liked the option to be anywhere in the room and still be able to talk and that it recognized it."

> "[Using] the voice [interface] you had to stop, you had to think what you need to say"

Word Count in Copying Task

We measured the number of words participants were able to copy with each interface in their main copying task. A one-way repeated measures ANOVA shows that the interface modality has a significant effect on the word count, $F(3,123) = 5.53, p < 0.01, \eta^2 = 0.04$ (Figure 4(c)) Pairwise comparisons using repeated measures t-tests with a Bonferroni correction show that WAL condition had significantly more words copied than ROB ($p < 0.01$) condition, with no other comparisons resulting in significant differences. Table 1 shows full descriptive statistics for all questionnaire scales.

Insights from Qualitative Interviews

In addition to our main findings, we identified three notable themes in our qualitative interviews: Sense of Control, Situation Awareness and Distraction.

Sense of Control

When using familiar interfaces (WAL, APP), participants expressed feeling very confident and in control:

> "[What interface felt most comfortable?]" — "Tablet [WAL]. Because you feel fully in control with it. You are ultimately the one touching the screen and deciding what to do"

> "It [APP] is part of us, like a third hand"

We expected the interaction using physical icons with ROB to also encourage participants' perceived sense of control, but this was not found to be true:

> "This [ROB] is kind of scary: it is smart, it is intelligent. I would not like having it in my house controlling the most important things"

> "In the end you don't have much control over what it does, it can do its own thing"

Participants felt even more strongly about VOC—not only did they mention lack of control over the interface, they also felt substantial discomfort:

> "I didn't like it [VOC] because I feel like it was always listening to me, and I have to be very careful [about] how I speak to him"

> "[Using VOC] it kind of feels like you are deciding, but someone else is also deciding for you. On that one [WAL] it feels like you have full control, but here [VOC] it is like you are waiting for them to accept what you are saying... The disadvantage is that you do not feel 100% in control like with other interfaces. It feels like you are requesting something from your home and then you have to wait for it to be approved"

> "I don't like it [VOC]. I don't like talking to myself in a room with myself, it feels very awkward and weird... I don't know it's weird having a voice talk back to you. It is a little bit creepy."

Some expressed a more ambivalent relationship with the voice interface, that evoked both positive and negative emotions simultaneously:

> "It [VOC] seems to be really cool. You can talk to your home. I don't know - I can't really explain why but I

> didn't feel comfortable with it. Because it's a machine and it was answering me. I just felt uncomfortable"

> "It [VOC] would become kind of your friend after a while, like the voice. You would feel very comfortable with it, almost like you were not alone? Maybe that is a little bit scary".

In conclusion, the touch-screen interfaces elicited a sense that users were in control, were alone in the room and in charge, and using the interfaces as tools. In contrast, both ROB and VOC elicited a sense of an additional "presence" that might make decision on its own. In the case of VOC, there was an added sentiment of discomfort talking to a machine.

Situation Awareness

In our study, participants were asked to recall what smart-home devices are turned on, and what is the current home temperature at the end of each round. They were later asked using which interfaces was this information easiest and hardest to recall. 61% of participants claimed it was easiest to recall using ROB. 67% claimed the hardest to recall was using VOC (See Table 2).

One way in which this insight was explained in the interviews was because of the *visibility* of the robot's physical icons, as opposed to the VOC, where there was no visible indication regarding the home status, only immediate voice feedback:

> "Here [ROB] when you are out of your house and you leave the A/C on you can see that it's on, you go out and you see the icon there. Here [VOC] you see nothing."

> "At the end I didn't know anything [with VOC]. It was so easy to do the commands, but at the end you didn't know what was going on."

WAL was also described as an interface with high visibility:

> "It's kind of like a computer board where you can see everything that is going on in your house. Very simple, very straightforward, you can see a clear display of what is working and what is not"

Other participants attributed their ability to recall the status of the home, as well as their inability do to so, to the existence or lack of *physical interaction*:

> "With the robot I was holding the tangible icons, so it registered"

> "I think that the robot is easy [to remember what is on], because you are moving [phicons], you are actually thinking of what you are doing"

> "[With] the voice [VOC] it was harder for me to remember. You are just speaking, you do not have to look or do a physical action, you just have to speak. For me it is harder to remember when you are just talking."

In conclusion, while ROB was recognized for both giving visual feedback and enabling participants to think-through-doing, VOC was described as an interface that lacks these qualities. WAL, although described with high visibility, was not perceived as an interface that encourages thinking-through-doing. Neither of these qualities were attributed to APP.

Distraction

One of the qualities we seek in a home control system is for it to disturb the user only when it is necessary, preferably in a non-disruptive way. This was our motivation for the copying task—we wanted to evaluate how disruptive each one of the interfaces was.

Using unfamiliar interfaces (VOC, ROB), participants felt completing the home control tasks was distracting:

> "The robot [ROB], the disadvantage is that it moves around and it reacts to whatever you are doing so it throws you off a little bit. Same with the speaker [VOC]"

> "It [VOC] is kind of like when you are in a middle of a task and someone interrupts you... Every time I had to say something I quickly forgot what I was doing."

> "The minute you speak you immediately forget what you are doing"

This could be due to the novelty of the interfaces. However, several participants thought ROB suggests a unique, "silent" interaction:

> "I liked the robot most"—"Why?"—"Because you are taking something and you are putting [it]. There is no noise, it is silent."

Surprisingly, the unfamiliar interfaces were not the only ones perceived as distracting. The most familiar interface, APP, was described as a highly disruptive one:

> "Not everything has to be in one device. Sometimes it is distracting. It is kind of like when you have a bedroom where you sleep, sometimes you can not study there, because you rest there... Or [the] kitchen, you can not study in the kitchen, because you think about food... The same with the phone... immediately someone sends me an email or someone calls you, it is distracting."

> "I didn't like that because it reminds me a lot of driving and texting at the same time... That experience for me reminds me of trying to get too many things done at once."

WAL was not mentioned as a distracting interface during the interviews. Moreover, the quantitative finding of the number of copied words in the copying task supports that WAL was the least distracting interface in the experiment (see Figure 4(c) and Table 1).

DISCUSSION

The interfaces we compared represent different levels of familiarity for users. The mobile application is the most familiar interface, as most people use it on a daily basis. Wall-mounted screens, voice-controlled speaker devices, and social robots are less familiar, in this order.

Our findings align with this gradation; they show that the more familiar an interface was, the more usable, comfortable, and natural participants felt using it. A notable exception is that VOC was rated slightly more natural than WAL. On the other hand, participants perceived interactions with familiar interfaces as mundane and predicable. This is reflected by lower perception of flow, lower situation awareness and less attention when using familiar interfaces. Our strongest finding is thus a trade-off between flow and usability, following the gradient of familiarity.

Embodied Robot vs Voice Control

The two most unfamiliar interfaces are VOC and ROB; at time of writing, most users would have little experience using them. But while they are similar in familiarity, they present two contrasting interaction paradigms: out-loud voice control on the one hand (VOC), and peripheral, tangible, and silent interaction through physical icons and expressive gestures on the other (ROB).

According to our qualitative findings, the main perceived advantage of the voice interface lies in the user's ability to control the home from any location in the room, and free of using their hands.

However, VOC seemed to have evoked more negative feelings: Participants described the interaction as intimidating and as one that causes unease.

In addition, ROB was perceived with significantly better flow than WAL and APP. whereas the interaction with VOC, also novel, did not show similar results. ROB was also by far the popular pick for most enjoyable interface, chosen almost three times more often than VOC.

Familiarity, Situation Awareness, and Sense of Control

Another interesting findings is in the relationship between familiarity, flow, and sense of control. The most familiar (and thus low-flow) interfaces (WAL and APP) gave participants a better sense of control than less familiar, high-flow ones (VOC and ROB). However, the inverse relation between flow and sense of control was not fully inverse—participants described feeling more in control with ROB than with VOC, although ROB's flow was also rated higher. This speaks in support of the design choice of a tangible embodied interface, suggesting it might maintain both a high perceived sense of control and high perceived flow.

Situation awareness could partially explain ROB's higher sense of control. Participants had the highest situation awareness using ROB, and the lowest of all four interfaces using VOC, i.e—it was easiest to recall the status of the home using ROB, and hardest using VOC. The interviews explained these results in two ways.

One explanation was the visibility of ROB's physical icons, whereas VOC had no visual feedback. According to Nielsen [40], visual indication on the interface's current state is critical and should be given to the user at all times. The second explanation to the high situation awareness using ROB can be attributed to the physical action required to control it. Participants were thinking-through-doing, while VOC is controlled using solely vocal commands. Previous work [33] discusses the importance of physical interaction using interactive systems, and claims it encourages thinking and learning. Although WAL was also described with high visibility, participants did not mention it as an interface in which they were thinking-through-doing. APP evoked neither of these traits.

A final surprising finding relates to distraction. APP, arguably the most familiar interface to participants, was perceived as the most distracting interface, while WAL seems to be the least distracting one, as reflected in the high word-copying rates using it.

Tying our findings to the interface's differences in familiarity, visibility, and embodiment is clearly only one possible interpretation. We did not directly test these hypotheses or measure our participants' familiarity or sense of visibility and embodiment with each of the interfaces. This experimental evaluation is left for future work.

LIMITATIONS

An important limitation of our study is the possibility of a "novelty effect" when interacting with interfaces unfamiliar to participants. The novelty effect could explain the high perceived flow and enjoyment using ROB and VOC. However, given the differences between ROB and VOC, both novel interfaces, the novelty effect can explain these results only to a certain extent. In addition, some of the results cannot be explained by the novelty effect at all, for example the high situation awareness for ROB, low situation awareness and negative perception of VOC, the low distraction for WAL, but high distraction for APP. To fully address the "novelty effect" issue, future long-term studies deploying these technologies in peoples' homes are required.

An additional limitation of the study is that we could not isolate the differences that are inherent in the nature of each interface (for example the range of locations from which one can use the device and the response time of visual vs. auditory feedback). These trade-offs should be kept in mind when designing for a specific interaction modality.

Furthermore, the robot combines two separate interaction modalities which differentiate it from the other interfaces in this experiment: physical input (tangible icons) and physical output (gestures). Our experiment did not tease apart these two variables. In this work, our goal was to evaluate the new robot design as a whole. Studying its various interaction aspects in isolation is left for future work.

Finally, there is a clear difference between a device that is designed specifically for the purpose of smart-home control (ROB, WAL) and devices designed for more than one purpose (VOC, APP). Single-purpose devices take away the added complication of selecting the particular application a user wants to use. There is also a consideration that some technologies reuse devices that people might already own and toward which they have a personal long-term relation. This is most obvious with respect to the mobile application.

CONCLUSION

As the popularity of smart-home and IoT devices grows, an increasing number of technologies are entering our domestic spaces. To control these devices, diverse interfaces and interaction modalities are introduced to users, including voice control, screen-based interfaces, embodied interactions, and most recently, social robots.

We suggest a unique design approach to the social robot paradigm. The interaction with Vyo, the robot used in this experiment, differs from the common wisdom of how users wish to interact with most domestic social robots today. Vyo suggests a quiet, peripheral, and tangible interaction through physical icons, gestures unaccompanied by notification sounds, and only intermittent use of a low-fidelity display. This is in contrast to the almost ubiquitous social robot design approach which includes high-resolution information-rich displays, bidirectional human-robot voice interaction, and touch-screen input.

In this paper we compared this social robot to common home control interfaces in an experimental exploratory study. Our findings from the comparison between robot, voice controlled, wall-mounted and mobile application interfaces show clear advantages and disadvantages for each interface.

The advantages of the embodied robot were flow, engagement, enjoyment, and high situation awareness regarding the state of the home. Its disadvantages were low perceived usability and low perceived sense of control. Further research should be conducted to better understand the low perceived usability finding. Usability is linked to familiarity with an interface, and a certain learning curve is expected to form new interaction habits. We recommend evaluating how long-term interaction with such an embodied interface would evolve over time and how it might influence perceived usability. In addition, usability issues may be addressed by improving performance using sensing and providing feedback with better accuracy and clarity.

The hands-free and ubiquitous control offered by the voice interface were its clear advantage. However, our findings shed light on critical disadvantages of this interface that raise questions on the appropriateness of such an interface for smart-home management. Participants felt out of control, showed low situation awareness, and expressed discomfort and aversion towards the voice interface. We recommend that designers of voice interfaces address these issues by providing better vocal feedback, and perhaps by adding visual indication for information that is critical to the user's sense of control.

The main advantage of the wall-mounted screen interface was its usability: It was perceived as efficient, comfortable and straightforward. It was also found to be the least distracting interface. The disadvantages were low perceived flow, and low enjoyment. There are interesting differences between this interface and the second screen-based interface, the mobile application. Further research is required to better understand the qualities that make the wall-mounted interface less disruptive, a highly desirable aspect in the design of smart-home interfaces.

The obvious advantages of the mobile application—the fact that everyone already has one—is also a major disadvantage. Participants felt highly distracted using the mobile device, although it was not their own personal device but one given to them for the experiment. None of the participants received incoming messages, calls, or other notifications. This suggests that even though mobile devices are a simple and usable solution for remote control of automated homes, they might not be the ideal interface for control inside one's domestic space.

In sum, despite the usability shortcomings of the social robot interface, we conclude that it holds promise as a new interaction paradigm for smart-home control, where engagement, enjoyment, and situation awareness are critical aspects for a successful user experience.

ACKNOWLEDGMENTS

We would like to thank SK Telecom for supporting this research project. This study was also partially supported by The European Commission FP7 Program (Grant #CIG-293733), The I-CORE Program of the Planning and Budgeting Committee (Grant #1716/12), The Israel Science Foundation (Grant #1716/12), and The Israel Ministry of Science, Technology and Space (Grant #54178). We would also like to thanks Lucy Anderson, Rob Aimi, Benny Megidish, Ziv Geurts and Shar Leyb for their assistance and contribution to the project.

REFERENCES

1. Muhammad Raisul Alam, Mamun Bin Ibne Reaz, and Mohd Alauddin Mohd Ali. 2012. A review of smart homes—past, present, and future. *Systems, Man, and Cybernetics, Part C: Applications and Reviews, IEEE Transactions on* 42, 6 (2012), 1190–1203.

2. Martha W Alibali, Sotaro Kita, and Amanda J Young. 2000. Gesture and the process of speech production: We think, therefore we gesture. *Language and cognitive processes* 15, 6 (2000), 593–613.

3. Roger Bakeman. 2005. Recommended effect size statistics for repeated measures designs. *Behavior research methods* 37, 3 (2005), 379–384.

4. Gregory Baltus, Dieter Fox, Francine Gemperle, Jennifer Goetz, Tad Hirsch, Dimitris Magaritis, Mike Montemerlo, Joelle Pineau, Nicholas Roy, Jamie Schulte, and others. 2000. Towards personal service robots for the elderly. In *Proc. of the Workshop on Interactive Robotics and Entertainment (WIRE-2000)*.

5. Cynthia Breazeal, Kerstin Dautenhahn, and Takayuki Kanda. 2016. Social Robotics. In *Springer Handbook of Robotics*. Springer, 1935–1972.

6. Cynthia Breazeal and Paul Fitzpatrick. 2000. That certain look: Social amplification of animate vision. In *Proceedings of the AAAI fall symposium on society of intelligence agents?the human in the loop*.

7. John Brooke and others. 1996. SUS-A quick and dirty usability scale. *Usability evaluation in industry* 189, 194 (1996), 4–7.

8. Barry Brumitt and Jonathan J Cadiz. 2001. Let there be light" examining interfaces for homes of the future. In *Human Computer Interaction. INTERACT'01. IFIP TC. 13 International Conference on Human Computer Interaction. IOS Press, Amsterdam, Netherlands; 2001; xxvii+ 897 pp.* 375–82.
9. Wolfram Burgard, Armin B Cremers, Dieter Fox, Dirk Hähnel, Gerhard Lakemeyer, Dirk Schulz, Walter Steiner, and Sebastian Thrun. 1999. Experiences with an interactive museum tour-guide robot. *Artificial intelligence* 114, 1 (1999), 3–55.
10. Chia-Wei Chang, Kuan-Ting Chen, Hsiu-Li Lin, Chih-Kai Wang, and Jong-Hann Jean. 2007. Development of a patrol robot for home security with network assisted interactions. In *SICE, 2007 Annual Conference*. IEEE, 924–928.
11. Michael Harris Cohen, James P Giangola, and Jennifer Balogh. 2004. *Voice user interface design*. Addison-Wesley Professional.
12. Herbert A Colle and Keith J Hiszem. 2004. Standing at a kiosk: Effects of key size and spacing on touch screen numeric keypad performance and user preference. *Ergonomics* 47, 13 (2004), 1406–1423.
13. Diane J Cook, G Michael Youngblood, Edwin O Heierman III, Karthik Gopalratnam, Sira Rao, Andrey Litvin, and Farhan Khawaja. 2003. MavHome: An Agent-Based Smart Home.. In *PerCom*, Vol. 3. 521–524.
14. Susan Wagner Cook, Zachary Mitchell, and Susan Goldin-Meadow. 2008. Gesturing makes learning last. *Cognition* 106, 2 (2008), 1047–1058.
15. Mihaly Csikszentmihalyi. 2000. *Beyond boredom and anxiety.* Jossey-Bass.
16. Kerstin Dautenhahn, Sarah Woods, Christina Kaouri, Michael L Walters, Kheng Lee Koay, and Iain Werry. 2005. What is a robot companion-friend, assistant or butler?. In *Intelligent Robots and Systems, 2005.(IROS 2005). 2005 IEEE/RSJ International Conference on.* IEEE, 1192–1197.
17. Scott Davidoff, Min Kyung Lee, Charles Yiu, John Zimmerman, and Anind K Dey. 2006. Principles of smart home control. In *UbiComp 2006: Ubiquitous Computing*. Springer, 19–34.
18. Paul Dourish. 2004. *Where the action is: the foundations of embodied interaction.* MIT press.
19. W Keith Edwards and Rebecca E Grinter. 2001. At home with ubiquitous computing: Seven challenges. In *International Conference on Ubiquitous Computing*. Springer, 256–272.
20. Jodi Forlizzi and Carl DiSalvo. 2006. Service robots in the domestic environment: a study of the roomba vacuum in the home. In *Proceedings of the 1st ACM SIGCHI/SIGART conference on Human-robot interaction.* ACM, 258–265.
21. Tony Gillie and Donald Broadbent. 1989. What makes interruptions disruptive? A study of length, similarity, and complexity. *Psychological research* 50, 4 (1989), 243–250.
22. Susan Goldin-Meadow, Howard Nusbaum, Spencer D Kelly, and Susan Wagner. 2001. Explaining math: Gesturing lightens the load. *Psychological Science* 12, 6 (2001), 516–522.
23. Guy Hoffman. 2012. Dumb robots, smart phones: A case study of music listening companionship. In *RO-MAN*. IEEE, 358–363.
24. Guy Hoffman. 2016. OpenWoZ: A Runtime-Configurable Wizard-of-Oz Framework for Human-Robot Interaction. In *2016 AAAI Spring Symposium Series*.
25. Guy Hoffman, Gurit E Birnbaum, Keinan Vanunu, Omri Sass, and Harry T Reis. 2014. Robot responsiveness to human disclosure affects social impression and appeal. In *Proceedings of the 2014 ACM/IEEE international conference on Human-robot interaction.* ACM, 1–8.
26. Guy Hoffman and Wendy Ju. 2014. Designing Robots With Movement in Mind. *Journal of Human-Robot Interaction* 3, 1 (2014), 89–122.
27. Guy Hoffman, Oren Zuckerman, Gilad Hirschberger, Michal Luria, and Tal Shani-Sherman. 2015. Design and Evaluation of a Peripheral Robotic Conversation Companion. In *Proc. of the Tenth Annual ACM/IEEE Int'l Conf. on HRI.* ACM, 3–10.
28. Caroline Hummels, Kees CJ Overbeeke, and Sietske Klooster. 2007. Move to get moved: a search for methods, tools and knowledge to design for expressive and rich movement-based interaction. *Personal and Ubiquitous Computing* 11, 8 (2007), 677–690.
29. Stephen S Intille. 2002. Designing a home of the future. *IEEE pervasive computing* 1, 2 (2002), 76–82.
30. D Jones, K Hapeshi, and C Frankish. 1989. Design guidelines for speech recognition interfaces. *Applied Ergonomics* 20, 1 (1989), 47–52.
31. Takayuki Kanda, Dylan F Glas, Masahiro Shiomi, Hiroshi Ishiguro, and Norihiro Hagita. 2008. Who will be the customer?: a social robot that anticipates people's behavior from their trajectories. In *Proceedings of the 10th international conference on Ubiquitous computing*. ACM, 380–389.
32. Cory D Kidd and Cynthia Breazeal. 2008. Robots at home: Understanding long-term human-robot interaction. In *2008 IEEE/RSJ International Conference on Intelligent Robots and Systems*. IEEE, 3230–3235.
33. Scott R Klemmer, Björn Hartmann, and Leila Takayama. 2006. How bodies matter: five themes for interaction design. In *Proceedings of the 6th conference on Designing Interactive systems*. ACM, 140–149.

34. Tiiu Koskela and Kaisa Väänänen-Vainio-Mattila. 2004. Evolution towards smart home environments: empirical evaluation of three user interfaces. *Personal and Ubiquitous Computing* 8, 3-4 (2004), 234–240.

35. Christine Kühnel, Tilo Westermann, Fabian Hemmert, Sven Kratz, Alexander Müller, and Sebastian Möller. 2011. I'm home: Defining and evaluating a gesture set for smart-home control. *International Journal of Human-Computer Studies* 69, 11 (2011), 693–704.

36. Min Kyung Lee, Jodi Forlizzi, Paul E Rybski, Frederick Crabbe, Wayne Chung, Josh Finkle, Eric Glaser, and Sara Kiesler. 2009. The snackbot: documenting the design of a robot for long-term human-robot interaction. In *HRI, 2009 4th ACM/IEEE Int'l Conf. on HRI*. IEEE, 7–14.

37. Michal Luria, Guy Hoffman, Benny Megidish, Oren Zuckerman, and Sung Park. 2016. Designing Vyo, a robotic Smart Home assistant: Bridging the gap between device and social agent. In *Robot and Human Interactive Communication (RO-MAN), 2016 25th IEEE International Symposium on*. IEEE, 1019–1025.

38. Hiroshi Mizoguchi, Tomomasa Sato, Katsuyuki Takagi, Masayuki Nakao, and Yotaro Hatamura. 1997. Realization of expressive mobile robot. In *Robotics and Automation, 1997. Proceedings., 1997 IEEE International Conference on*, Vol. 1. IEEE, 581–586.

39. Sebastian Möller, Jan Krebber, Alexander Raake, Paula Smeele, Martin Rajman, Mirek Melichar, Vincenzo Pallotta, Gianna Tsakou, Basilis Kladis, Anestis Vovos, and others. 2004. INSPIRE: Evaluation of a smart-home system for infotainment management and device control. *arXiv preprint cs/0410063* (2004).

40. Jakob Nielsen. 1994. Enhancing the explanatory power of usability heuristics. In *Proceedings of the SIGCHI conference on Human Factors in Computing Systems*. ACM, 152–158.

41. Donald A Norman. 2013. *The design of everyday things: Revised and expanded edition*. Basic books.

42. Stephen Olejnik and James Algina. 2003. Generalized eta and omega squared statistics: measures of effect size for some common research designs. *Psychological methods* 8, 4 (2003), 434.

43. Kwang-Hyun Park, Hyong-Euk Lee, Youngmin Kim, and Z Zenn Bien. 2008. A steward robot for human-friendly human-machine interaction in a smart house environment. *Automation Science and Engineering, IEEE Transactions on* 5, 1 (2008), 21–25.

44. Erika Shehan Poole, Marshini Chetty, Rebecca E Grinter, and W Keith Edwards. 2008. More than meets the eye: transforming the user experience of home network management. In *Proceedings of the 7th ACM conference on Designing interactive systems*. ACM, 455–464.

45. Sara Price, Yvonne Rogers, Michael Scaife, Danae Stanton, and Helen Neale. 2003. Using 'tangibles' to promote novel forms of playful learning. *Interacting with computers* 15, 2 (2003), 169–185.

46. Pranav Rane, Varun Mhatre, and Lakshmi Kurup. 2014. Study of a home robot: Jibo. In *International Journal of Engineering Research and Technology*, Vol. 3. ESRSA Publications.

47. Parisa Rashidi and Diane J Cook. 2009. Keeping the resident in the loop: adapting the smart home to the user. *IEEE Transactions on systems, man, and cybernetics-part A: systems and humans* 39, 5 (2009), 949–959.

48. Yvonne Rogers. 2006. Moving on from weiser's vision of calm computing: Engaging ubicomp experiences. In *UbiComp 2006: Ubiquitous Computing*. Springer, 404–421.

49. Takanori Shibata, Toshihiro Tashima, and Kazuo Tanie. 1999. Emergence of emotional behavior through physical interaction between human and robot. In *Robotics and Automation, 1999. Proceedings. 1999 IEEE International Conference on*, Vol. 4. IEEE, 2868–2873.

50. David Sirkin, Brian Mok, Stephen Yang, and Wendy Ju. 2015. Mechanical ottoman: how robotic furniture offers and withdraws support. In *Proceedings of the Tenth Annual ACM/IEEE International Conference on Human-Robot Interaction*. ACM, 11–18.

51. Norbert Streitz and Paddy Nixon. 2005. The disappearing computer. *Commun. ACM* 48, 3 (2005), 32–35.

52. Ja-Young Sung, Lan Guo, Rebecca E Grinter, and Henrik I Christensen. 2007. *"My Roomba Is Rambo": Intimate Home Appliances*. Springer.

53. Ahmed Mohmmad Ullah, Md Rashedul Islam, Sayeda Farzana Aktar, and SK Alamgir Hossain. 2012. Remote-touch: Augmented reality based marker tracking for smart home control. In *Computer and Information Technology (ICCIT), 2012 15th International Conference on*. IEEE, 473–477.

54. Kazuyoshi Wada, Takanori Shibata, Tomoko Saito, Kayoko Sakamoto, and Kazuo Tanie. 2005. Psychological and social effects of one year robot assisted activity on elderly people at a health service facility for the aged. In *Proceedings of the 2005 IEEE international conference on robotics and automation*. IEEE, 2785–2790.

55. Mark Weiser. 1991. The computer for the 21st century. *Scientific american* 265, 3 (1991), 94–104.

56. Allison Woodruff, Sally Augustin, and Brooke Foucault. 2007. Sabbath day home automation: it's like mixing technology and religion. In *Proceedings of the SIGCHI conference on Human factors in computing systems*. ACM, 527–536.

57. Lesley Xie, Alissa N Antle, and Nima Motamedi. 2008. Are tangibles more fun?: comparing children's enjoyment and engagement using physical, graphical and tangible user interfaces. In *Proceedings of the 2nd international conference on Tangible and embedded interaction*. ACM, 191–198.

58. Alexander Yates, Oren Etzioni, and Daniel Weld. 2003. A reliable natural language interface to household appliances. In *Proceedings of the 8th international conference on Intelligent user interfaces*. ACM, 189–196.

59. Steve Yohanan, Mavis Chan, Jeremy Hopkins, Haibo Sun, and Karon MacLean. 2005. Hapticat: exploration of affective touch. In *Proceedings of the 7th international conference on Multimodal interfaces*. ACM, 222–229.

60. Baris Yuksekkaya, A Alper Kayalar, M Bilgehan Tosun, M Kaan Ozcan, and Ali Ziya Alkar. 2006. A GSM, internet and speech controlled wireless interactive home automation system. *IEEE Transactions on Consumer Electronics* 52, 3 (2006), 837–843.

61. Oren Zuckerman. 2015. Objects for change: A case study of a tangible user interface for behavior change. In *Proceedings of the Ninth International Conference on Tangible, Embedded, and Embodied Interaction*. ACM, 649–654.

62. Oren Zuckerman and Ayelet Gal-Oz. 2013. To TUI or not to TUI: Evaluating performance and preference in tangible vs. graphical user interfaces. *Int'l Journal of Human-Computer Studies* 71, 7 (2013), 803–820.

Author Index

NOTES

NOTES

NOTES

NOTES

NOTES

NOTES

NOTES

NOTES

NOTES

NOTES

NOTES

NOTES

NOTES

NOTES

NOTES

NOTES

NOTES

NOTES

NOTES

NOTES

NOTES

NOTES

www.ingramcontent.com/pod-product-compliance
Lightning Source LLC
LaVergne TN
LVHW082006200926
848481LV00010B/2815
* 9 7 8 1 4 5 0 3 5 4 6 0 8 *